Julius Adler

Memory, Attention, and Decision-Making

Memory, Attention, and Decision-Making

A Unifying Computational Neuroscience Approach

Edmund T. Rolls

University of Oxford
Department of Experimental Psychology
Oxford
England

OXFORD

UNIVERSITY PRESS

OXFORD

UNIVERSITY PRESS

Great Clarendon Street, Oxford ox2 6dp

Oxford University Press is a department of the University of Oxford.
It furthers the University's objective of excellence in research, scholarship,
and education by publishing worldwide in

Oxford New York

Auckland Cape Town Dar es Salaam Hong Kong Karachi
Kuala Lumpur Madrid Melbourne Mexico City Nairobi
New Delhi Shanghai Taipei Toronto

With offices in

Argentina Austria Brazil Chile Czech Republic France Greece
Guatemala Hungary Italy Japan Poland Portugal Singapore
South Korea Switzerland Thailand Turkey Ukraine Vietnam

Oxford is a registered trade mark of Oxford University Press
in the UK and in certain other countries

Published in the United States
by Oxford University Press Inc., New York

British Library Cataloguing in Publication Data

Data available

Library of Congress Cataloging in Publication Data

Data available

Typeset by the author and Cepha Imaging Pvt. Ltd., India
Printed in Great Britain
on acid-free paper by
Biddles Ltd., King's Lynn

ISBN 978–0–19–923270–3
1 3 5 7 9 10 8 6 4 2

Preface

The overall aim of this book is to provide insight into how memory systems in the brain work; how the operation of these systems is fundamental to understanding many aspects of brain function including perception, decision-making, and action selection; and how interactions between these systems provide an account of many cognitive phenomena including attention and emotion. It is shown that to do this, a neurocomputational approach is needed. The book provides Appendices that describe many of the building blocks of the neurocomputational approach, and that are designed to be useful for teaching.

To understand how the brain works, including how it functions in memory, attention, and decision-making, it is necessary to combine different approaches, including neural computation. Neurophysiology at the single neuron level is needed because this is the level at which information is exchanged between the computing elements of the brain. Evidence from the effects of brain damage, including that available from neuropsychology, is needed to help understand what different parts of the system do, and indeed what each part is necessary for. Neuroimaging is useful to indicate where in the human brain different processes take place, and to show which functions can be dissociated from each other. Knowledge of the biophysical and synaptic properties of neurons is essential to understand how the computing elements of the brain work, and therefore what the building blocks of biologically realistic computational models should be. Knowledge of the anatomical and functional architecture of the cortex is needed to show what types of neuronal network actually perform the computation. And finally the approach of neural computation is needed, as this is required to link together all the empirical evidence to produce an understanding of how the system actually works. This book utilizes evidence from all these disciplines to develop an understanding of how different types of memory, perception, attention, and decision-making are implemented by processing in the brain.

I emphasize that to understand memory, perception, attention, and decision-making in the brain, we are dealing with large-scale computational systems with interactions between the parts, and that this understanding requires analysis at the computational and global level of the operation of many neurons to perform together a useful function. Understanding at the molecular level is important for helping to understand how these large-scale computational processes are implemented in the brain, but will not by itself give any account of what computations are performed to implement these cognitive functions. Instead, understanding cognitive functions such as object recognition, memory recall, attention, and decision-making requires single neuron data to be closely linked to computational models of how the interactions between large numbers of neurons and many networks of neurons allow these cognitive problems to be solved. The single neuron level is important in this approach, for the single neurons can be thought of as the computational units of the system, and is the level at which the information is exchanged by the spiking activity between the computational elements of the brain. The single neuron level is therefore, because it is the level at which information is communicated between the computing elements of the brain, the fundamental level of information processing, and the level at which the information can be read out (by recording the spiking activity) in order to understand what information is being represented and processed in each brain area.

With its focus on how the brain works at the computational neuroscience level, this book is distinct from the many excellent books on neuroscience that describe much evidence about brain structure and function, but do not aim to provide an understanding of how the brain works at the computational level. This book aims to forge an understanding of how some key brain systems may operate at the computational level, so that we can understand how the brain actually performs some of its complex and necessarily computational functions in memory, perception, attention, and decision-making.

A test of whether one's understanding is correct is to simulate the processing on a computer, and to show whether the simulation can perform the tasks of memory systems in the brain, and whether the simulation has similar properties to the real brain. The approach of neural computation leads to a precise definition of how the computation is performed, and to precise and quantitative tests of the theories produced. How memory systems in the brain work is a paradigm example of this approach, because memory-like operations which involve altered functionality as a result of synaptic modification are at the heart of how all computations in the brain are performed. It happens that attention and decision-making can be understood in terms of interactions between and fundamental operations in memory systems in the brain, and therefore it is natural to treat these areas of cognitive neuroscience as well as memory in this book. The same fundamental concepts based on the operation of neuronal circuitry can be applied to all these functions, as is shown in this book.

One of the distinctive properties of this book is that it links the neural computation approach not only firmly to neuronal neurophysiology, which provides much of the primary data about how the brain operates, but also to psychophysical studies (for example of attention); to neuropsychological studies of patients with brain damage; and to functional magnetic resonance imaging (fMRI) (and other neuroimaging) approaches. The empirical evidence that is brought to bear is largely from non-human primates and from humans, because of the considerable similarity of their memory and related systems, and the overall aims to understand how memory and related functions are implemented in the human brain, and the disorders that arise after brain damage.

The overall aims of the book are developed further, and the plan of the book is described, in Chapter 1, Section 1.1.

Part of the material described in the book reflects work performed in collaboration with many colleagues, whose tremendous contributions are warmly appreciated. The contributions of many will be evident from the references cited in the text. Especial appreciation is due to Gustavo Deco, Simon M. Stringer, and Alessandro Treves who have contributed greatly in an always interesting and fruitful research collaboration on computational aspects of brain function, and to many neurophysiology and functional neuroimaging colleagues who have contributed to the empirical discoveries that provide the foundation to which the computational neuroscience must always be closely linked, and whose names are cited throughout the text. Much of the work described would not have been possible without financial support from a number of sources, particularly the Medical Research Council of the UK, the Human Frontier Science Program, the Wellcome Trust, and the James S. McDonnell Foundation. The book was typeset by the author using LaTeX and WinEdt.

The cover shows part of the picture Psyche Opening the Golden Box painted in 1903 by J. W. Waterhouse. The metaphor is to look inside the system of the mind and the brain, in order to understand how the brain functions, and thereby better to understand and treat its disorders. Updates to the publications cited in this book are available at http://www.cns.ox.ac.uk.

I dedicate this work to the overlapping group: my family, friends, and colleagues – in salutem praesentium, in memoriam absentium.

Contents

1   Introduction

1.1   Introduction and overview

To understand how the brain works, including how it functions in memory, it is necessary to combine different approaches, including neural computation. Neurophysiology at the single neuron level is needed because this is the level at which information is exchanged between the computing elements of the brain. Evidence from the effects of brain damage, including that available from neuropsychology, is needed to help understand what different parts of the system do, and indeed what each part is necessary for. Neuroimaging is useful to indicate where in the human brain different processes take place, and to show which functions can be dissociated from each other. Knowledge of the biophysical and synaptic properties of neurons is essential to understand how the computing elements of the brain work, and therefore what the building blocks of biologically realistic computational models should be. Knowledge of the anatomical and functional architecture of the cortex is needed to show what types of neuronal network actually perform the computation. And finally the approach of neural computation is needed, as this is required to link together all the empirical evidence to produce an understanding of how the system actually works. This book utilizes evidence from all these disciplines to develop an understanding of how different types of memory, attention, and decision-making are implemented by processing in the brain.

A test of whether one's understanding is correct is to simulate the processing on a computer, and to show whether the simulation can perform the tasks of memory systems in the brain, and whether the simulation has similar properties to the real brain. The approach of neural computation leads to a precise definition of how the computation is performed, and to precise and quantitative tests of the theories produced. How memory systems in the brain work is a paradigm example of this approach, because memory-like operations which involve altered functionality as a result of synaptic modification are at the heart of how all computations in the brain are performed. It happens that attention and decision-making can be understood in terms of interactions between and fundamental operations in memory systems in the brain, and therefore it is natural to treat these areas of cognitive neuroscience as well as memory in this book. The same fundamental concepts based on the operation of neuronal circuitry can be applied to all these functions, as is shown in this book.

One of the distinctive properties of this book is that it links the neural computation approach not only firmly to neuronal neurophysiology, which provides much of the primary data about how the brain operates, but also to psychophysical studies (for example of attention); to neuropsychological studies of patients with brain damage; and to functional magnetic resonance imaging (fMRI) (and other neuroimaging) approaches. The empirical evidence that is brought to bear is largely from non-human primates and from humans, because of the considerable similarity of their memory and related systems, and the overall aims to understand how memory and related functions are implemented in the human brain, and the disorders that arise after brain damage.

The overall plan of the book is as follows.

Chapter 1 provides an introduction to information processing in neural systems in the brain.

Chapter 2 describes a major memory system in the brain, the hippocampo-cortical system.

Chapter 3 describes the brain systems in which rewards and punishers come to be represented, and the many types of learning about rewards and punishers. Understanding these systems is fundamental, as emotions can be considered as states elicited by reinforcers (rewards and punishers), and motivations can be considered as states in which we will work to obtain reinforcers. Moreover, these systems are fundamental for understanding brain design in a Darwinian context, as the specification of which stimuli are reinforcers and therefore goals for action is a key concept in understanding fitness in an evolutionary context.

Chapter 4 considers how perceptual representations, of for example objects, can be understood by self-organizing learning in visual cortical areas. The learning of representations of objects that are invariant with respect to size, position on the retina, and even view is fundamental for the operation of memory systems that receive these perceptual representations, for only then can generalization of the memory of the object with its location in the environment, reward value, etc. occur correctly to other views etc. of the same object. It transpires that the enormous computational problem of learning invariant representations of objects, faces etc. is solved by cortical mechanisms that perform interesting types of self-organizing learning, as described in Chapter 4.

Chapter 5 describes how short-term memory can be implemented in cortical circuitry, and key systems in the brain for different types of short-term memory. Short-term memory mechanisms are important in many of the types of cognitive processing described in the following chapters.

Chapter 6 develops an understanding of attentional mechanisms that involves the subject of attention being held in a short-term memory, and the activity in this short-term memory acting as the source of a bias to influence the competition between representations in perceptual and memory areas of the brain. Interactions between the short-term memory and perceptual networks are key in understanding the dynamical, temporal processing involved in attention. The concepts are applied to understanding many attentional disorders.

Chapter 7 shows how probabilistic decision-making can be understood in terms of the way in which an attractor network settles from spontaneous activity into a state that represents a decision in a way that depends on the probabilistic spiking of finite numbers of neurons in the network.

Chapter 8 shows how action and strategy selection can be influenced in networks in the prefrontal cortex by a top-down rule-based process that operates in a similar way to a top-down attentional network. In this framework, action selection can be understood by hierarchically organized networks which map from stimulus to action, and in which the selection can be understood by the rule-biasing effect on intermediate networks in the hierarchy.

Chapter 9 shows how the short-term memory network that holds the current rule for stimulus-to-action mapping, for stimulus-to-reward mapping, and for attention, can be reset to a different state as a result of feedback received from the environment.

Many of the processes described in the book, such as reward- and punishment-based learning, attention, decision-making networks, and systems for selecting actions and strategies, are all involved more generally in decision-making, and processes involved in decision-making in the brain are brought together in Chapter 10.

Overall, the book thus considers how memory systems actually work in the brain, and how the operation of what are effectively different types of memory and learning systems is fundamental to understanding many cognitive processes beyond memory, including object recognition, attention, and decision-making. Indeed, because the brain operates effectively by altering the connections between neurons in neuronal circuits, and then allowing different networks to operate both hierarchically and interactively, much of brain function can be understood in terms of the types of processing described in this book.

Because many of the processes involved in memory, perception, attention, and decision-making in the brain can be understood in terms of the operation of different types of memory networks, and interactions between these networks, their operation is described in Appendix B, with some of the basic mathematical concepts covered in Appendix A. Appendix B provides quite a self-contained overview of neural networks, in the sense that those not already familiar with neural computation can find many of the fundamentals and foundations here.

I emphasize that to understand memory, perception, attention, and decision-making in the brain, we are dealing with large-scale computational systems with interactions between the parts, and that this understanding requires analysis at the computational and global level of the operation of many neurons to perform together a useful function. Understanding at the molecular level is important for helping to understand how these large-scale computational processes are implemented in the brain, but will not by itself give any account of what computations are performed to implement these cognitive functions. Instead, understanding cognitive functions such as object recognition, memory recall, attention, and decision-making requires single neuron data to be closely linked to computational models of how the interactions between large numbers of neurons and many networks of neurons allow these cognitive problems to be solved. The single neuron level is important in this approach, for the single neurons can be thought of as the computational units of the system, and is the level at which the information is exchanged by the spiking activity between the computational elements of the brain. The single neuron level is therefore, because it is the level at which information is communicated between the computing elements of the brain, the fundamental level of information processing, and the level at which the information can be read out (by recording the spiking activity) in order to understand what information is being represented and processed in each brain area.

Because of this importance of being able to analyze the activity of single neurons and populations of neurons in order to understand brain function, Appendix C describes rigorous approaches to understanding the information represented by neurons, and summarizes evidence on how the information is actually represented. In that the information encoded by different neurons is shown to be different, this confirms that what is being represented, and how it is represented, requires the level of analysis to encompass the single neuron level. Understanding how neurons represent information is fundamental for understanding how neurons and networks of neurons read the code from other neurons, and the actual nature of the computation that could be performed in a memory network. The networks described in this book are consistent in their operation with the evidence presented in Appendix C on cortical neuronal information encoding. The neurocomputational approach taken in this book enables the single neuron level of analysis to be linked to the level of large-scale neuronal networks and the interactions between them, so that large-scale processes such as memory retrieval, object recognition, attention, and decision-making can be understood.

In the rest of this Chapter, I introduce some of the background for understanding brain computation, such as how single neurons operate, how some of the essential features of this can be captured by simple formalisms, and some of the biological background to what it can be taken happens in the nervous system, such as synaptic modification based on information available locally at each synapse.

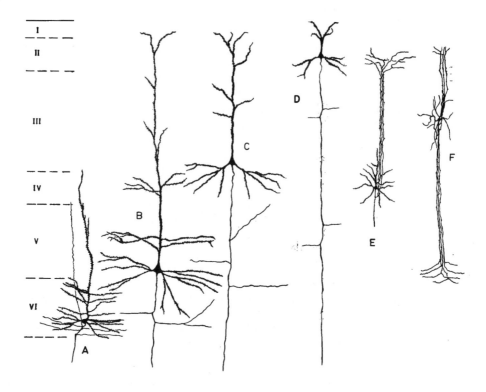

Fig. 1.1 Examples of neurons found in the brain. Cell types in the cerebral neocortex are shown. The different laminae of the cortex are designated I–VI, with I at the surface. Cells A–D are pyramidal cells in the different layers. Cell E is a spiny stellate cell, and F is a double bouquet cell. (After Jones 1981; see Jones and Peters 1984, p. 7.)

1.2 Neurons in the brain, and their representation in neuronal networks

Neurons in the vertebrate brain typically have, extending from the cell body, large dendrites which receive inputs from other neurons through connections called synapses. The synapses operate by chemical transmission. When a synaptic terminal receives an all-or-nothing action potential from the neuron of which it is a terminal, it releases a transmitter that crosses the synaptic cleft and produces either depolarization or hyperpolarization in the postsynaptic neuron, by opening particular ionic channels. (A textbook such as Kandel, Schwartz and Jessel (2000) gives further information on this process.) Summation of a number of such depolarizations or excitatory inputs within the time constant of the receiving neuron, which is typically 15–25 ms, produces sufficient depolarization that the neuron fires an action potential. There are often 5,000–20,000 inputs per neuron. Examples of cortical neurons are shown in Fig. 1.1, and further examples are shown in Shepherd (2004) and Rolls and Treves (1998). Once firing is initiated in the cell body (or axon initial segment of the cell body), the action potential is conducted in an all-or-nothing way to reach the synaptic terminals of the neuron, whence it may affect other neurons. Any inputs the neuron receives that cause it to become hyperpolarized make it less likely to fire (because the membrane potential is moved away from the critical threshold at which an action potential is initiated), and are described as inhibitory. The neuron can thus be thought of in a simple way as a computational element that sums its inputs within its time constant and, whenever this sum, minus any inhibitory effects, exceeds

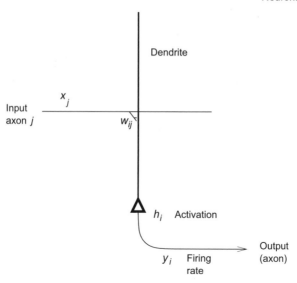

Fig. 1.2 Notation used to describe an individual neuron in a network model. By convention, we generally represent the dendrite as thick, and vertically oriented (as this is the normal way that neuroscientists view cortical pyramidal cells under the microscope); and the axon as thin. The cell body or soma is indicated between them. The firing rate we also call the activity of the neuron.

a threshold, produces an action potential that propagates to all of its outputs. This simple idea is incorporated in many neuronal network models using a formalism of a type described in the next section.

1.3 A formalism for approaching the operation of single neurons in a network

Let us consider a neuron i as shown in Fig. 1.2, which receives inputs from axons that we label j through synapses of strength w_{ij}. The first subscript (i) refers to the receiving neuron, and the second subscript (j) to the particular input. j counts from 1 to C, where C is the number of synapses or connections received. The firing rate of the ith neuron is denoted as y_i, and that of the jth input to the neuron as x_j. To express the idea that the neuron makes a simple linear summation of the inputs it receives, we can write the activation of neuron i, denoted h_i, as

$$h_i = \sum_j x_j w_{ij} \tag{1.1}$$

where $\sum_j$ indicates that the sum is over the C input axons (or connections) indexed by j to each neuron. The multiplicative form here indicates that activation should be produced by an axon only if it is firing, and depending on the strength of the synapse w_{ij} from input axon j onto the dendrite of the receiving neuron i. Equation 1.1 indicates that the strength of the activation reflects how fast the axon j is firing (that is x_j), and how strong the synapse w_{ij} is. The sum of all such activations expresses the idea that summation (of synaptic currents in real neurons) occurs along the length of the dendrite, to produce activation at the cell body, where the activation h_i is converted into firing y_i. This conversion can be expressed as

$$y_i = \mathrm{f}(h_i) \tag{1.2}$$

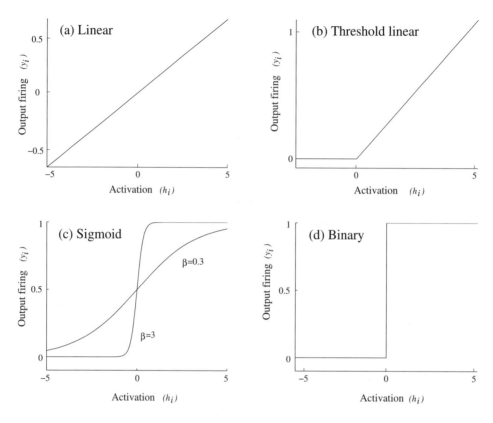

Fig. 1.3 Different types of activation function. The activation function relates the output activity (or firing rate), y_i, of the neuron (i) to its activation, h_i. (a) Linear. (b) Threshold linear. (c) Sigmoid. [One mathematical exemplar of this class of activation function is $y_i = 1/(1 + \exp(-2\beta h_i))$.] The output of this function, also sometimes known as the logistic function, is 0 for an input of $-\infty$, 0.5 for 0, and 1 for $+\infty$. The function incorporates a threshold at the lower end, followed by a linear portion, and then an asymptotic approach to the maximum value at the top end of the function. The parameter β controls the steepness of the almost linear part of the function round $h_i = 0$. If β is small, the output goes smoothly and slowly from 0 to 1 as h_i goes from $-\infty$ to $+\infty$. If β is large, the curve is very steep, and approximates a binary threshold activation function. (d) Binary threshold.

which indicates that the firing rate is a function (f) of the postsynaptic activation. The function is called the activation function in this case. The function at its simplest could be linear, so that the firing rate would be proportional to the activation (see Fig. 1.3). Real neurons have thresholds, with firing occurring only if the activation is above the threshold. A threshold linear activation function is shown in Fig. 1.3. This has been useful in formal analysis of the properties of neural networks. Neurons also have firing rates that become saturated at a maximum rate, and we could express this as the sigmoid activation function shown in Fig. 1.3c. Another simple activation function, used in some models of neural networks, is the binary threshold function (Fig. 1.3d), which indicates that if the activation is below threshold, there is no firing, and that if the activation is above threshold, the neuron fires maximally. Some non-linearity in the activation function is an advantage, for it enables many useful computations to be performed in neuronal networks, including removing interfering effects of similar memories, and enabling neurons to perform logical operations, such as firing only if several inputs are present simultaneously.

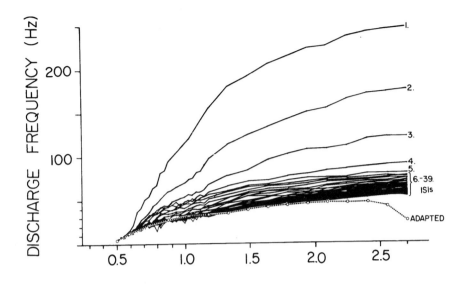

Fig. 1.4 Frequency – current plot (the closest experimental analogue of the activation function) for a CA1 pyramidal cell. The firing frequency (in Hz) in response to the injection of 1.5 s long, rectangular depolarizing current pulses has been plotted against the strength of the current pulses (in nA) (abscissa). The first 39 interspike intervals (ISIs) are plotted as instantaneous frequency (1 / ISI), together with the average frequency of the adapted firing during the last part of the current injection (circles and broken line). The plot indicates a current threshold at approximately 0.5 nA, a linear range with a tendency to saturate, for the initial instantaneous rate, above approximately 200 Hz, and the phenomenon of adaptation, which is not reproduced in simple non-dynamical models (see further Appendix A5 of Rolls and Treves 1998). (Reprinted with permission from Lanthorn, Storm and Andersen 1984.)

A property implied by equation 1.1 is that the postsynaptic membrane is electrically short, and so summates its inputs irrespective of where on the dendrite the input is received. In real neurons, the transduction of current into firing frequency (the analogue of the transfer function of equation 1.2) is generally studied not with synaptic inputs but by applying a steady current through an electrode into the soma. Examples of the resulting curves, which illustrate the additional phenomenon of firing rate adaptation, are shown in Fig. 1.4.

1.4 Synaptic modification

For a neuronal network to perform useful computation, that is to produce a given output when it receives a particular input, the synaptic weights must be set up appropriately. This is often performed by synaptic modification occurring during learning.

A simple learning rule that was originally presaged by Donald Hebb (1949) proposes that synapses increase in strength when there is conjunctive presynaptic and postsynaptic activity. The Hebb rule can be expressed more formally as follows

$$\delta w_{ij} = \alpha y_i x_j \tag{1.3}$$

where δw_{ij} is the change of the synaptic weight w_{ij} which results from the simultaneous (or conjunctive) presence of presynaptic firing x_j and postsynaptic firing y_i (or strong depolarization), and α is a learning rate constant that specifies how much the synapses alter on any one pairing. The presynaptic and postsynaptic activity must be present approximately simultaneously (to within perhaps 100–500 ms in the real brain).

The Hebb rule is expressed in this multiplicative form to reflect the idea that both presynaptic and postsynaptic activity must be present for the synapses to increase in strength. The multiplicative form also reflects the idea that strong pre- and postsynaptic firing will produce a larger change of synaptic weight than smaller firing rates. The Hebb rule thus captures what is typically found in studies of associative Long-Term Potentiation (LTP) in the brain, described in Section 1.5.

One useful property of large neurons in the brain, such as cortical pyramidal cells, is that with their short electrical length, the postsynaptic term, y_i, is available on much of the dendrite of a cell. The implication of this is that once sufficient postsynaptic activation has been produced, any active presynaptic terminal on the neuron will show synaptic strengthening. This enables associations between coactive inputs, or correlated activity in input axons, to be learned by neurons using this simple associative learning rule.

If, in contrast, a group of coactive axons made synapses close together on a small dendrite, then the local depolarization might be intense, and only these synapses would modify onto the dendrite. (A single distant active synapse might not modify in this type of neuron, because of the long electrotonic length of the dendrite.) The computation in this case is described as Sigma-Pi ($\Sigma\Pi$), to indicate that there is a local product computed during learning; this allows a particular set of locally active synapses to modify together, and then the output of the neuron can reflect the sum of such local multiplications (see Rumelhart and McClelland (1986), Koch (1999)). Sigma-Pi neurons are not used in most of the networks described in this book. There has been some work on how such neurons, if present in the brain, might utilize this functionality in the computation of invariant representations (Mel, Ruderman and Archie 1998, Mel and Fiser 2000) (see Section 4.6).

1.5 Long-term potentiation and long-term depression as models of synaptic modification

Long-term potentiation (LTP) and long-term depression (LTD) provide useful models of some of the synaptic modifications that occur in the brain. The synaptic changes found appear to be synapse-specific, and to depend on information available locally at the synapse. LTP and LTD may thus provide a good model of the biological synaptic modifications involved in real neuronal network operations in the brain. Some of the properties of LTP and LTD are described next, together with evidence that implicates them in learning in at least some brain systems. Even if they turn out not to be the basis for the synaptic modifications that occur during learning, they have many of the properties that would be needed by some of the synaptic modification systems used by the brain.

Long-term potentiation is a use-dependent and sustained increase in synaptic strength that can be induced by brief periods of synaptic stimulation. It is usually measured as a sustained increase in the amplitude of electrically evoked responses in specific neural pathways following brief trains of high-frequency stimulation (see Fig. 1.5b). For example, high frequency stimulation of the Schaffer collateral inputs to the hippocampal CA1 cells results in a larger response recorded from the CA1 cells to single test pulse stimulation of the pathway. LTP is long-lasting, in that its effect can be measured for hours in hippocampal slices, and in chronic in vivo experiments in some cases it may last for months. LTP becomes evident rapidly, typically in less than 1 minute. LTP is in some brain systems associative. This is illustrated in Fig. 1.5c, in which a weak input to a group of cells (e.g. the commissural input to CA1) does not show LTP unless it is given at the same time as (i.e. associatively with) another input (which

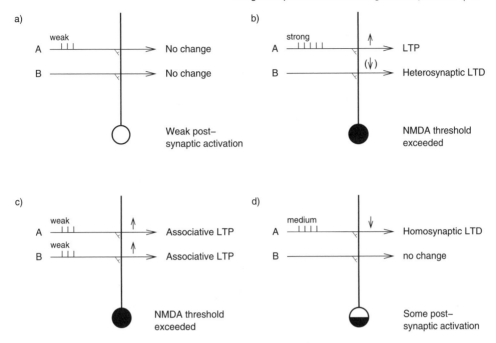

Fig. 1.5 Schematic illustration of synaptic modification rules as revealed by long-term potentiation (LTP) and long-term depression (LTD). The activation of the postsynaptic neuron is indicated by the extent to which its soma is black. There are two sets of inputs to the neuron: A and B. (a) A weak input (indicated by three spikes) on the set A of input axons produces little postsynaptic activation, and there is no change in synaptic strength. (b) A strong input (indicated by five spikes) on the set A of input axons produces strong postsynaptic activation, and the active synapses increase in strength. This is LTP. It is homosynaptic in that the synapses that increase in strength are the same as those through which the neuron is activated. LTP is synapse-specific, in that the inactive axons, B, do not show LTP. They either do not change in strength, or they may weaken. The weakening is called heterosynaptic LTD, because the synapses that weaken are other than those through which the neuron is activated (hetero- is Greek for other). (c) Two weak inputs present simultaneously on A and B summate to produce strong postsynaptic activation, and both sets of active synapses show LTP. (d) Intermediate strength firing on A produces some activation, but not strong activation, of the postsynaptic neuron. The active synapses become weaker. This is homosynaptic LTD, in that the synapses that weaken are the same as those through which the neuron is activated (homo- is Greek for same).

could be weak or strong) to the cells. The associativity arises because it is only when sufficient activation of the postsynaptic neuron to exceed the threshold of NMDA receptors (see below) is produced that any learning can occur. The two weak inputs summate to produce sufficient depolarization to exceed the threshold. This associative property is shown very clearly in experiments in which LTP of an input to a single cell only occurs if the cell membrane is depolarized by passing current through it at the same time as the input arrives at the cell. The depolarization alone or the input alone is not sufficient to produce the LTP, and the LTP is thus associative. Moreover, in that the presynaptic input and the postsynaptic depolarization must occur at about the same time (within approximately 500 ms), the LTP requires temporal contiguity. LTP is also synapse-specific, in that, for example, an inactive input to a cell does not show LTP even if the cell is strongly activated by other inputs (Fig. 1.5b, input B).

These spatiotemporal properties of long term potentiation can be understood in terms of actions of the inputs on the postsynaptic cell, which in the hippocampus has two classes of receptor, NMDA (N-methyl-D-aspartate) and AMPA (alpha-amino-3-hydroxy-5-methyl-

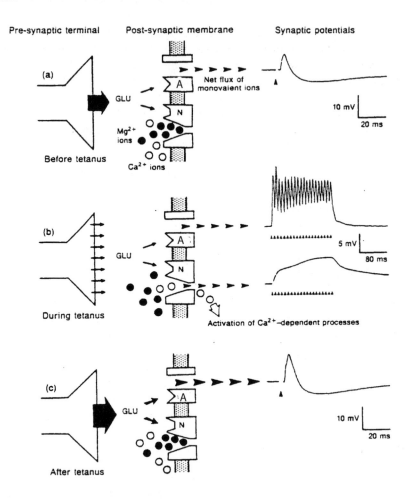

Fig. 1.6 The mechanism of induction of LTP in the CA1 region of the hippocampus. (a) Neurotransmitter (e.g. L-glutamate, GLU) is released and acts upon both AMPA (A) and NMDA (N) receptors. The NMDA receptors are blocked by magnesium and the excitatory synaptic response (EPSP) is therefore mediated primarily by ion flow through the channels associated with AMPA receptors. (b) During high-frequency activation ('tetanus'), the magnesium block of the ion channels associated with NMDA receptors is released by depolarization. Activation of the NMDA receptor by transmitter now results in ions moving through the channel. In this way, calcium enters the postsynaptic region to trigger various intracellular mechanisms which eventually result in an alteration of synaptic efficacy. (c) Subsequent low-frequency stimulation results in a greater EPSP. See text for further details. (After Collingridge and Bliss 1987.)

isoxasole-4-propionic acid), activated by the glutamate released by the presynaptic terminals. The NMDA receptor channels are normally blocked by Mg^{2+}, but when the cell is strongly depolarized by strong tetanic stimulation of the type necessary to induce LTP, the Mg^{2+} block is removed, and Ca^{2+} entering via the NMDA receptor channels triggers events that lead to the potentiated synaptic transmission (see Fig. 1.6). Part of the evidence for this is that NMDA antagonists such as AP5 (D-2-amino-5-phosphonopentanoate) block LTP. Further, if the postsynaptic membrane is voltage clamped to prevent depolarization by a strong input, then LTP does not occur. The voltage-dependence of the NMDA receptor channels introduces a threshold and thus a non-linearity that contributes to a number of the phenomena of some types of LTP, such as cooperativity (many small inputs together produce sufficient depolarization to allow the NMDA receptors to operate); associativity (a weak input alone will not produce sufficient depolarization of the postsynaptic cell to enable the NMDA receptors to be activated, but the depolarization will be sufficient if there is also a strong input); and temporal contiguity between the different inputs that show LTP (in that if inputs occur non-conjunctively, the depolarization shows insufficient summation to reach the required level, or some of the inputs may arrive when the depolarization has decayed). Once the LTP has become established (which can be within one minute of the strong input to the cell), the LTP is expressed through the AMPA receptors, in that AP5 blocks only the establishment of LTP, and not its subsequent expression (Bliss and Collingridge 1993, Nicoll and Malenka 1995, Fazeli and Collingridge 1996, Lynch 2004, Collingridge and Bliss 1987).

There are a number of possibilities about what change is triggered by the entry of Ca^{2+} to the postsynaptic cell to mediate LTP. One possibility is that somehow a messenger reaches the presynaptic terminals from the postsynaptic membrane and, if the terminals are active, causes them to release more transmitter in future whenever they are activated by an action potential. Consistent with this possibility is the observation that, after LTP has been induced, more transmitter appears to be released from the presynaptic endings. Another possibility is that the postsynaptic membrane changes just where Ca^{2+} has entered, so that AMPA receptors become more responsive to glutamate released in future. Consistent with this possibility is the observation that after LTP, the postsynaptic cell may respond more to locally applied glutamate (using a microiontophoretic technique).

The rule that underlies associative LTP is thus that synapses connecting two neurons become stronger if there is conjunctive presynaptic and (strong) postsynaptic activity. This learning rule for synaptic modification is sometimes called the Hebb rule, after Donald Hebb of McGill University who drew attention to this possibility, and its potential importance in learning, in 1949.

In that LTP is long-lasting, develops rapidly, is synapse-specific, and is in some cases associative, it is of interest as a potential synaptic mechanism underlying some forms of memory. Evidence linking it directly to some forms of learning comes from experiments in which it has been shown that the drug AP5 infused so that it reaches the hippocampus to block NMDA receptors blocks spatial learning mediated by the hippocampus (see Morris (1989), Martin, Grimwood and Morris (2000)). The task learned by the rats was to find the location relative to cues in a room of a platform submerged in an opaque liquid (milk). Interestingly, if the rats had already learned where the platform was, then the NMDA infusion did not block performance of the task. This is a close parallel to LTP, in that the learning, but not the subsequent expression of what had been learned, was blocked by the NMDA antagonist AP5. Although there is still some uncertainty about the experimental evidence that links LTP to learning (see for example Martin, Grimwood and Morris (2000) and Lynch (2004)), there is a need for a synapse-specific modifiability of synaptic strengths on neurons if neuronal networks are to learn. If LTP is not always an exact model of the synaptic modification that occurs during learning, then something with many of the properties of LTP is nevertheless needed, and is likely to be present in the brain given the functions known to be implemented in many brain regions (see Rolls and Treves (1998)).

In another model of the role of LTP in memory, Davis (2000) has studied the role of the amygdala in learning associations to fear-inducing stimuli. He has shown that blockade of NMDA synapses in the amygdala interferes with this type of learning, consistent with the idea that LTP also provides a useful model of this type of learning (see further Chapter 3).

Long-Term Depression (LTD) can also occur. It can in principle be associative or non-associative. In associative LTD, the alteration of synaptic strength depends on the pre- and post-synaptic activities. There are two types. Heterosynaptic LTD occurs when the postsynaptic neuron is strongly activated, and there is low presynaptic activity (see Fig. 1.5b input B, and Table B.1 on page 556). Heterosynaptic LTD is so-called because the synapse that weakens is other than (hetero-) the one through which the postsynaptic neuron is activated. Heterosynaptic LTD is important in associative neuronal networks, and in competitive neuronal networks (see Appendix B). In competitive neural networks it would be helpful if the degree of heterosynaptic LTD depended on the existing strength of the synapse, and there is some evidence that this may be the case (see Appendix B). Homosynaptic LTD occurs when the presynaptic neuron is strongly active, and the postsynaptic neuron has some, but low, activity (see Fig. 1.5d and Table B.1). Homosynaptic LTD is so-called because the synapse that weakens is the same as (homo-) the one that is active. Heterosynaptic and homosynaptic LTD are found in the neocortex (Artola and Singer 1993, Singer 1995, Frégnac 1996) and hippocampus (Christie 1996), and in many cases are dependent on activation of NMDA receptors (see also Fazeli and Collingridge (1996)). LTD in the cerebellum is evident as weakening of active parallel fibre to Purkinje cell synapses when the climbing fibre connecting to a Purkinje cell is active (Ito 1984, Ito 1989, Ito 1993b, Ito 1993a).

An interesting time-dependence of LTP and LTD has been observed, with LTP occurring especially when the presynaptic spikes precede by a few ms the post-synaptic activation, and LTD occurring when the pre-synaptic spikes follow the post-synaptic activation by a few milliseconds (ms) (Markram, Lübke, Frotscher and Sakmann 1997, Bi and Poo 1998, Bi and Poo 2001, Senn, Markram and Tsodyks 2001, Dan and Poo 2004, Dan and Poo 2006). This is referred to as spike timing-dependent plasticity, STDP. This type of temporally asymmetric Hebbian learning rule, demonstrated in the hippocampus and neocortex, can induce associations over time, and not just between simultaneous events. Networks of neurons with such synapses can learn sequences (Minai and Levy 1993), enabling them to predict the future state of the postsynaptic neuron based on past experience (Abbott and Blum 1996) (see further Koch (1999), Markram, Pikus, Gupta and Tsodyks (1998) and Abbott and Nelson (2000)). This mechanism, because of its apparent time-specificity for periods in the range of ms or tens of ms, could also encourage neurons to learn to respond to temporally synchronous pre-synaptic firing (Gerstner, Kreiter, Markram and Herz 1997, Gutig and Sompolinsky 2006), and indeed to decrease the synaptic strengths from neurons that fire at random times with respect to the synchronized group. This mechanism might also play a role in the normalization of the strength of synaptic connection strengths onto a neuron. Further, there is accumulating evidence (Sjöström, Turrigiano and Nelson 2001) that a more realistic description of the protocols for inducing LTP and LTD probably requires a combination of dependence on spike timing – to take into account the effects of the backpropagating action potential – and dependence on the sub-threshold depolarization of the postsynaptic neuron. However these spike timing dependent synaptic modifications may be evident primarily at low firing rates rather than those that often occur in the brain (Sjöström, Turrigiano and Nelson 2001), and may not be especially reproducible in the cerebral neocortex (see further Section 8.3). Under the somewhat steady-state conditions of the firing of neurons in the higher parts of the ventral visual system on the 10 ms timescale that are observed not only when single stimuli are presented for 500 ms (see Fig. 4.13), but also when macaques have found a search target and are looking at it (in the experiments described in Sections 4.2.3 and 4.5.9.1), the average of the pre-synaptic and postsynaptic rates are likely to be the important determinants of synaptic modification. Part of the reason for this is that correlations between the firing of simultaneously recorded inferior temporal cortex neurons are not common, and if present are not very strong or typically restricted to a short time window in the order of 10 ms (see Section C.3.7). This point is also made in the context that each neuron has thousands of inputs, several tens of which are normally likely to be active when a cell is firing above its spontaneous firing rate and is strongly depolarized. This may make it unlikely statistically that there will be a strong correlation between a particular presynaptic spike and postsynaptic firing, and thus that this is likely to be a main determinant of synaptic strength under these natural conditions.

1.6   Distributed representations

When considering the operation of many neuronal networks in the brain, it is found that many useful properties arise if each input to the network (arriving on the axons as **x**) is encoded in the activity of an ensemble or population of the axons or input lines (distributed encoding), and is not signalled by the activity of a single input, which is called local encoding. We start off with some definitions, and then highlight some of the differences, and summarize some evidence that shows the type of encoding used in some brain regions. Then in Appendix B (e.g. Table B.2), I show how many of the useful properties of the neuronal networks described depend on distributed encoding. In Appendix C, I review evidence on the encoding actually found in visual cortical areas.

1.6.1   Definitions

A *local representation* is one in which all the information that a particular stimulus or event occurred is provided by the activity of one of the neurons. In a famous example, a single neuron might be active only if one's grandmother was being seen. An implication is that most neurons in the brain regions where objects or events are represented would fire only very rarely. A problem with this type of encoding is that a new neuron would be needed for every object or event that has to be represented. There are many other disadvantages of this type of encoding, many of which will become apparent in this book. Moreover, there is evidence that objects are represented in the brain by a different type of encoding.

A *fully distributed representation* is one in which all the information that a particular stimulus or event occurred is provided by the activity of the full set of neurons. If the neurons are binary (e.g. either active or not), the most distributed encoding is when half the neurons are active for any one stimulus or event.

A *sparse distributed representation* is a distributed representation in which a small proportion of the neurons is active at any one time. In a sparse representation with binary neurons, less than half of the neurons are active for any one stimulus or event. For binary neurons, we can use as a measure of the sparseness the proportion of neurons in the active state. For neurons with real, continuously variable, values of firing rates, the sparseness a^{p} of the representation provided by the population can be measured, by extending the binary notion of the proportion of neurons that are firing, as

$$a^{\mathrm{p}} = \frac{(\sum\limits_{i=1}^{N} y_i/N)^2}{\sum\limits_{i=1}^{N} y_i^2/N} \tag{1.4}$$

where y_i is the firing rate of the ith neuron in the set of N neurons (Treves and Rolls 1991). This is referred to as the population sparseness, and measures of sparseness are considered in detail in Section C.3.1. A low value of the sparseness a^{p} indicates that few neurons are firing for any one stimulus.

Coarse coding utilizes overlaps of receptive fields, and can compute positions in the input space using differences between the firing levels of coactive cells (e.g. colour-tuned cones in the retina). The representation implied is very distributed. Fine coding (in which, for example, a neuron may be 'tuned' to the exact orientation and position of a stimulus) implies more local coding.

1.6.2 Advantages of different types of coding

One advantage of distributed encoding is that the similarity between two representations can be reflected by the correlation between the two patterns of activity that represent the different stimuli. We have already introduced the idea that the input to a neuron is represented by the activity of its set of input axons x_j, where j indexes the axons, numbered from $j = 1, C$ (see Fig. 1.2 and equation 1.1). Now the set of activities of the input axons is a vector (a vector is an ordered set of numbers; Appendix A provides a summary of some of the concepts involved). We can denote as $\mathbf{x}^1$ the vector of axonal activity that represents stimulus 1, and $\mathbf{x}^2$ the vector that represents stimulus 2. Then the similarity between the two vectors, and thus the two stimuli, is reflected by the correlation between the two vectors. The correlation will be high if the activity of each axon in the two representations is similar; and will become more and more different as the activity of more and more of the axons differs in the two representations. Thus the similarity of two inputs can be represented in a graded or continuous way if (this type of) distributed encoding is used. This enables generalization to similar stimuli, or to incomplete versions of a stimulus (if it is, for example, partly seen or partly remembered), to occur. With a local representation, either one stimulus or another is represented, each by its own neuron firing, and similarities between different stimuli are not encoded.

Another advantage of distributed encoding is that the number of different stimuli that can be represented by a set of C components (e.g. the activity of C axons) can be very large. A simple example is provided by the binary encoding of an 8-element vector. One component can code for which of two stimuli has been seen, 2 components (or bits in a computer byte) for 4 stimuli, 3 components for 8 stimuli, 8 components for 256 stimuli, etc. That is, the number of stimuli increases exponentially with the number of components (or, in this case, axons) in the representation. (In this simple binary illustrative case, the number of stimuli that can be encoded is 2^C.) Put the other way round, even if a neuron has only a limited number of inputs (e.g. a few thousand), it can nevertheless receive a great deal of information about which stimulus was present. This ability of a neuron with a limited number of inputs to receive information about which of potentially very many input events is present is probably one factor that makes computation by the brain possible. With local encoding, the number of stimuli that can be encoded increases only linearly with the number C of axons or components (because a different component is needed to represent each new stimulus). (In our example, only 8 stimuli could be represented by 8 axons.)

In the real brain, there is now good evidence that in a number of brain systems, including the high-order visual and olfactory cortices, and the hippocampus, distributed encoding with the above two properties, of representing similarity, and of exponentially increasing encoding capacity as the number of neurons in the representation increases, is found (Rolls and Tovee 1995b, Abbott, Rolls and Tovee 1996, Rolls, Treves and Tovee 1997b, Rolls, Treves, Robertson, Georges-François and Panzeri 1998, Rolls, Franco, Aggelopoulos and Reece 2003b, Rolls, Aggelopoulos, Franco and Treves 2004, Franco, Rolls, Aggelopoulos and Treves 2004, Aggelopoulos, Franco and Rolls 2005, Rolls, Franco, Aggelopoulos and Jerez 2006b) (see Appendix C). For example, in the primate inferior temporal visual cortex, the number of faces or objects that can be represented increases approximately exponentially with the number of neurons in the population (see Appendix C). If we consider instead the information about which stimulus is seen, we see that this rises approximately linearly with the number of neurons in the representation (see Appendix C). This corresponds to an exponential rise in the number of stimuli encoded, because information is a log measure (see

Appendix C). A similar result has been found for the encoding of position in space by the primate hippocampus (Rolls, Treves, Robertson, Georges-François and Panzeri 1998).

It is particularly important that the information can be read from the ensemble of neurons using a simple measure of the similarity of vectors, the correlation (or dot product, see Appendix A) between two vectors. The importance of this is that it is essentially vector similarity operations that characterize the operation of many neuronal networks (see Appendix B). The neurophysiological results show that both the ability to reflect similarity by vector correlation, and the utilization of exponential coding capacity, are properties of real neuronal networks found in the brain.

To emphasize one of the points being made here, although the binary encoding used in the 8-bit vector described above has optimal capacity for binary encoding, it is not optimal for vector similarity operations. For example, the two very similar numbers 127 and 128 are represented by 01111111 and 10000000 with binary encoding, yet the correlation or bit overlap of these vectors is 0. The brain, in contrast, uses a code that has the attractive property of exponentially increasing capacity with the number of neurons in the representation, though it is different from the simple binary encoding of numbers used in computers; and at the same time the brain codes stimuli in such a way that the code can be read off with simple dot product or correlation-related decoding, which is what is specified for the elementary neuronal network operation shown in equation 1.2 (see Section 1.6).

1.7   Neuronal network approaches versus connectionism

The approach taken in this book is to introduce how real neuronal networks in the brain may compute, and thus to achieve a fundamental and realistic basis for understanding brain function. This may be contrasted with connectionism, which aims to understand cognitive function by analysing processing in neuron-like computing systems. Connectionist systems are neuron-like in that they analyze computation in systems with large numbers of computing elements in which the information which governs how the network computes is stored in the connection strengths between the nodes (or "neurons") in the network. However, in many connectionist models the individual units or nodes are not intended to model individual neurons, and the variables that are used in the simulations are not intended to correspond to quantities that can be measured in the real brain. Moreover, connectionist approaches use learning rules in which the synaptic modification (the strength of the connections between the nodes) is determined by algorithms that require information that is not local to the synapse, that is, evident in the pre- and post-synaptic firing rates (see further Appendix B). Instead, in many connectionist systems, information about how to modify synaptic strengths is propagated backwards from the output of the network to affect neurons hidden deep within the network (see Section B.12). Because it is not clear that this is biologically plausible, we have instead in this text concentrated on introducing neuronal network architectures which are more biologically plausible, and which use a local learning rule. Connectionist approaches (see for example McClelland and Rumelhart (1986), McLeod, Plunkett and Rolls (1998)) are very valuable, for they show what can be achieved computationally with networks in which the connection strength determines the computation that the network achieves with quite simple computing elements. However, as models of brain function, many connectionist networks achieve almost too much, by solving problems with a carefully limited number of "neurons" or nodes, which contributes to the ability of such networks to generalize successfully over the problem space. Connectionist schemes thus make an important start to understanding how complex computations (such as language) could be implemented in brain-like systems. In doing this, connectionist models often use simplified representations of the inputs and

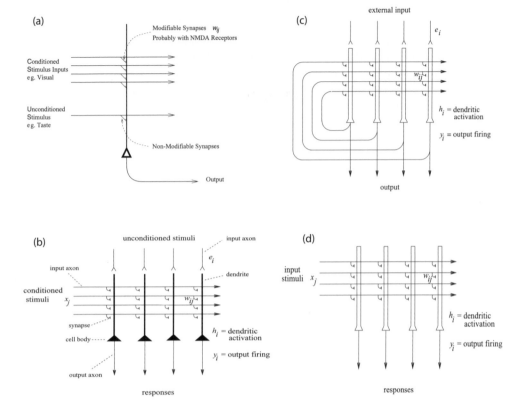

Fig. 1.7 Three network architectures that use local learning rules: (a) pattern association introduced with a single output neuron; (b) pattern association network; (c) autoassociation network; (d) competitive network.

outputs, which are often crucial to the way in which the problem is solved. In addition, they may use learning algorithms that are really too powerful for the brain to perform, and therefore they can be taken only as a guide to how cognitive functions might be implemented by neuronal networks in the brain. In this book, we focus on more biologically plausible neuronal networks.

1.8 Introduction to three neuronal network architectures

With neurons of the type outlined in Section 1.3, and an associative learning rule of the type described in Section 1.4, three neuronal network architectures arise that appear to be used in many different brain regions. The three architectures will be described in Appendix B, and a brief introduction is provided here.

In the first architecture (see Fig. 1.7a and b), pattern associations can be learned. The output neurons are driven by an unconditioned stimulus. A conditioned stimulus reaches the output neurons by associatively modifiable synapses w_{ij}. If the conditioned stimulus is paired during learning with activation of the output neurons produced by the unconditioned stimulus, then later, after learning, due to the associative synaptic modification, the conditioned stimulus alone will produce the same output as the conditioned stimulus. Pattern associators are described in Appendix B.

In the second architecture, the output neurons have recurrent associatively modifiable synaptic connections w_{ij} to other neurons in the network (see Fig. 1.7c). When an external input causes the output neurons to fire, then associative links are formed through the modifiable synapses that connect the set of neurons that is active. Later, if only a fraction of the original input pattern is presented, then the associative synaptic connections or weights allow the whole of the memory to be retrieved. This is called completion. Because the components of the pattern are associated with each other as a result of the associatively modifiable recurrent connections, this is called an autoassociative memory. It is believed to be used in the brain for many purposes, including short-term memory; episodic memory, in which the parts of a memory of an episode are associated together; and helping to define the response properties of cortical neurons, which have collaterals between themselves within a limited region.

In the third architecture, the main input to the output neurons is received through associatively modifiable synapses w_{ij} (see Fig. 1.7d). Because of the initial values of the synaptic strengths, or because every axon does not contact every output neuron, different patterns tend to activate different output neurons. When one pattern is being presented, the most strongly activated neurons tend via lateral inhibition to inhibit the other neurons. For this reason the network is called competitive. During the presentation of that pattern, associative modification of the active axons onto the active postsynaptic neuron takes place. Later, that or similar patterns will have a greater chance of activating that neuron or set of neurons. Other neurons learn to respond to other input patterns. In this way, a network is built that can categorize patterns, placing similar patterns into the same category. This is useful as a preprocessor for sensory information, self-organizes to produce feature analyzers, and finds uses in many other parts of the brain too.

All three architectures require inhibitory interneurons, which receive inputs from the principal neurons in the network (usually the pyramidal cells shown in Fig. 1.7) and implement feedback inhibition by connections to the pyramidal cells. The inhibition is usually implemented by GABA neurons, and maintains a small proportion of the pyramidal cells active.

These are three fundamental building blocks for neural architectures in the brain. They are often used in combination with each other. Because they are some of the building blocks of some of the architectures found in the brain, they are described in Appendix B.

1.9   Systems-level analysis of brain function

To understand the neuronal network operations of any one brain region, it is useful to have an idea of the systems-level organization of the brain, in order to understand how the networks in each region provide a particular computational function as part of an overall computational scheme. In the context of vision, it is very useful to appreciate the different processing streams, and some of the outputs that each has. Some of the processing streams are shown in Fig. 1.8. Some of these regions are shown in the drawings of the primate brain in the next few Figures. Each of these routes is described in turn. The description is based primarily on studies in non-human primates, for they have well-developed cortical areas that in many cases correspond to those found in humans, and it has been possible to analyze their connectivity and their functions by recording the activity of neurons in them.

Information in the *'ventral or what'* visual cortical processing stream projects after the primary visual cortex, area V1, to the secondary visual cortex (V2), and then via area V4 to the posterior and then to the anterior inferior temporal visual cortex (see Figs. 1.8, 1.9, and 1.10).

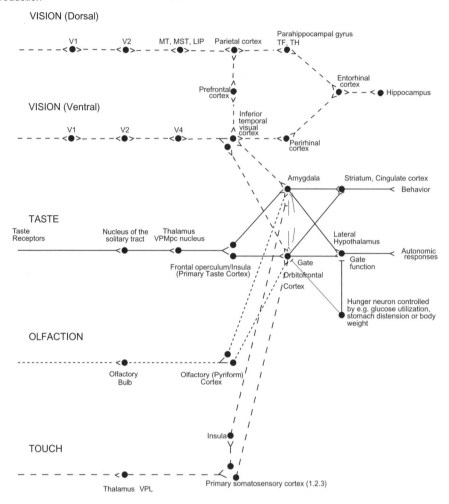

Fig. 1.8 The pathways involved in some different memory systems described in the text. Forward connections start from early cortical areas on the left. To emphasise that backprojections are important in many memory systems, they are made explicit in the synaptic terminals drawn in the upper part of the diagram, but are a property of most of the connections shown. The top pathway, also shown in Fig. 1.11, shows the connections in the 'dorsal or where visual pathway' from V1 to V2, MT, MST, 7a etc, with some connections reaching the dorsolateral prefrontal cortex and frontal eye fields. The second pathway, also shown in Fig. 1.9, shows the connections in the 'ventral or what visual pathway' from V1 to V2, V4, the inferior temporal visual cortex, etc., with some connections reaching the amygdala and orbitofrontal cortex. The two systems project via the parahippocampal gyrus and perirhinal cortex respectively to the hippocampus, and both systems have projections to the dorsolateral prefrontal cortex. The taste pathways project after the primary taste cortex to the orbitofrontal cortex and amygdala. The olfactory pathways project from the primary olfactory, pyriform, cortex to the orbitofrontal cortex and amygdala. The bottom pathway shows the connections from the primary somatosensory cortex, areas 1, 2 and 3, to the mid-insula, orbitofrontal cortex, and amygdala. Somatosensory areas 1, 2 and 3 also project via area 5 in the parietal cortex, to area 7b.

Information processing along this stream is primarily unimodal, as shown by the fact that inputs from other modalities (such as taste or smell) do not anatomically have significant inputs to these regions, and by the fact that neurons in these areas respond primarily to visual stimuli, and not to taste or olfactory stimuli, etc. (Rolls 2000a, Baylis, Rolls and

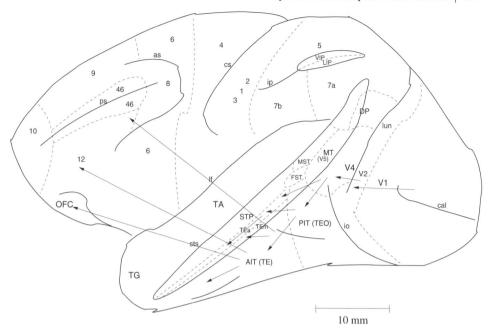

Fig. 1.9 Lateral view of the macaque brain showing the connections in the 'ventral or what visual pathway' from V1 to V2, V4, the inferior temporal visual cortex, etc., with some connections reaching the amygdala and orbitofrontal cortex. as, arcuate sulcus; cal, calcarine sulcus; cs, central sulcus; lf, lateral (or Sylvian) fissure; lun, lunate sulcus; ps, principal sulcus; io, inferior occipital sulcus; ip, intraparietal sulcus (which has been opened to reveal some of the areas it contains); sts, superior temporal sulcus (which has been opened to reveal some of the areas it contains). AIT, anterior inferior temporal cortex; FST, visual motion processing area; LIP, lateral intraparietal area; MST, visual motion processing area; MT, visual motion processing area (also called V5); OFC, orbitofrontal cortex; PIT, posterior inferior temporal cortex; STP, superior temporal plane; TA, architectonic area including auditory association cortex; TE, architectonic area including high order visual association cortex, and some of its subareas TEa and TEm; TG, architectonic area in the temporal pole; V1–V4, visual areas 1–4; VIP, ventral intraparietal area; TEO, architectonic area including posterior visual association cortex. The numbers refer to architectonic areas, and have the following approximate functional equivalence: 1, 2, 3, somatosensory cortex (posterior to the central sulcus); 4, motor cortex; 5, superior parietal lobule; 7a, inferior parietal lobule, visual part; 7b, inferior parietal lobule, somatosensory part; 6, lateral premotor cortex; 8, frontal eye field; 12, inferior convexity prefrontal cortex; 46, dorsolateral prefrontal cortex.

Leonard 1987, Ungerleider 1995, Rolls and Deco 2002). The representation built along this pathway is mainly about what object is being viewed, independently of exactly where it is on the retina, of its size, and even of the angle with which it is viewed (see Chapter 4 and Rolls and Deco (2002)), and for this reason it is frequently referred to as the 'what' visual pathway. The representation is also independent of whether the object is associated with reward or punishment, that is the representation is about objects per se (Rolls, Judge and Sanghera 1977). The computation that must be performed along this stream is thus primarily to build a representation of objects that shows invariance. After this processing, the visual representation is interfaced to other sensory systems in areas in which simple associations must be learned between stimuli in different modalities (see Chapters 2 and 3). The representation must thus be in a form in which the simple generalization properties of associative networks can be useful. Given that the association is about what object is present (and not where it is on the retina), the representation computed in sensory systems must be in a form that allows the simple correlations computed by associative networks to reflect

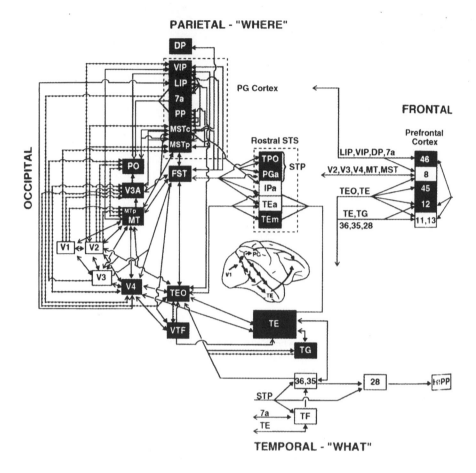

Fig. 1.10 Visual processing pathways in monkeys. Solid lines indicate connections arising from both central and peripheral visual field representations; dotted lines indicate connections restricted to peripheral visual field representations. Shaded boxes in the 'ventral (lower) or what' stream indicate visual areas related primarily to object vision; shaded boxes in the 'dorsal or where' stream indicate areas related primarily to spatial vision; and white boxes indicate areas not clearly allied with only one stream. Abbreviations: DP, dorsal prelunate area; FST, fundus of the superior temporal area; HIPP, hippocampus; LIP, lateral intraparietal area; MSTc, medial superior temporal area, central visual field representation; MSTp, medial superior temporal area, peripheral visual field representation; MT, middle temporal area; MTp, middle temporal area, peripheral visual field representation; PO, parieto-occipital area; PP, posterior parietal sulcal zone; STP, superior temporal polysensory area; V1, primary visual cortex; V2, visual area 2; V3, visual area 3; V3A, visual area 3, part A; V4, visual area 4; and VIP, ventral intraparietal area. Inferior parietal area 7a; prefrontal areas 8, 11 to 13, 45 and 46 are from Brodmann (1925). Inferior temporal areas TE and TEO, parahippocampal area TF, temporal pole area TG, and inferior parietal area PG are from Von Bonin and Bailey (1947). Rostral superior temporal sulcal (STS) areas are from Seltzer and Pandya (1978) and VTF is the visually responsive portion of area TF (Boussaoud, Desimone and Ungerleider 1991). (Reprinted with permission from Ungerleider 1995.)

similarities between objects, and not between their positions on the retina. The way in which such invariant sensory representations could be built in the brain is the subject of Chapter 4.

The ventral visual stream converges with other mainly unimodal information processing streams for taste, olfaction, touch, and hearing in a number of areas, particularly the amygdala

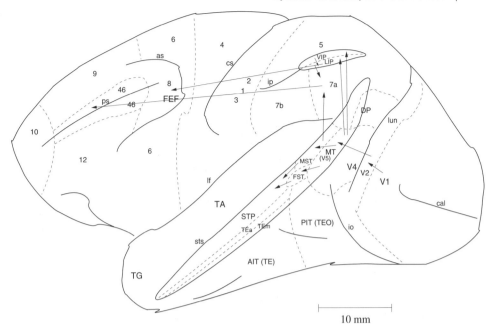

Fig. 1.11 Lateral view of the macaque brain showing the connections in the 'dorsal or where visual pathway' from V1 to V2, MST, LIP, VIP, and parietal cortex area 7a, with some connections then reaching the dorsolateral prefrontal cortex. Abbreviations as in Fig. 1.9. FEF - frontal eye field.

and orbitofrontal cortex (see Figs. 1.8, 1.9, and 1.10). These areas appear to be necessary for learning to associate sensory stimuli with other reinforcing (rewarding or punishing) stimuli. For example, the amygdala is involved in learning associations between the sight of food and its taste. (The taste is a primary or innate reinforcer.) The orbitofrontal cortex is especially involved in rapidly relearning these associations, when environmental contingencies change (see Rolls (2005) and Rolls (2000e)). They thus are brain regions in which the computation at least includes simple pattern association (e.g. between the sight of an object and its taste). In the orbitofrontal cortex, this association learning is also used to produce a representation of flavour, in that neurons are found in the orbitofrontal cortex that are activated by both olfactory and taste stimuli (Rolls and Baylis 1994), and in that the neuronal responses in this region reflect in some cases olfactory to taste association learning (Rolls, Critchley, Mason and Wakeman 1996b, Critchley and Rolls 1996b). In these regions too, the representation is concerned not only with what sensory stimulus is present, but for some neurons, with its hedonic or reward-related properties, which are often computed by association with stimuli in other modalities. For example, many of the visual neurons in the orbitofrontal cortex respond to the sight of food only when hunger is present. This probably occurs because the visual inputs here have been associated with a taste input, which itself in this region only occurs to a food if hunger is present, that is when the taste is rewarding (see Chapter 3, Rolls (2005), and Rolls (2000e)). The outputs from these associative memory systems, the amygdala and orbitofrontal cortex, project onwards to structures such as the hypothalamus, through which they control autonomic and endocrine responses such as salivation and insulin release to the sight of food; and to the striatum, including the ventral striatum, through which behaviour to learned reinforcing stimuli is produced.

The *'dorsal or where' visual processing stream* shown in Figs. 1.8, 1.11, and 1.10 is that from V1 to MT, MST and thus to the parietal cortex (see Ungerleider (1995); Ungerleider and Haxby (1994); and Rolls and Deco (2002)). This 'where' pathway for primate vision is involved in representing where stimuli are relative to the animal (i.e. in egocentric space), and the motion of these stimuli. Neurons here respond, for example, to stimuli in visual space around the animal, including the distance from the observer, and also respond to optic flow or to moving stimuli. Outputs of this system control eye movements to visual stimuli (both slow pursuit and saccadic eye movements). These outputs proceed partly via the frontal eye fields, which then project to the striatum, and then via the substantia nigra reach the superior colliculus (Goldberg 2000). Other outputs of these regions are to the dorsolateral prefrontal cortex, area 46, which is important as a short-term memory for where fixation should occur next, as shown by the effects of lesions to the prefrontal cortex on saccades to remembered targets, and by neuronal activity in this region (Goldman-Rakic 1996). The dorsolateral prefrontal cortex short-term memory systems in area 46 with spatial information received from the parietal cortex play an important role in attention, by holding on-line the target being attended to, as described in Chapters 6, 8 and 9.

The hippocampus receives inputs from both the 'what' and the 'where' visual systems (Chapter 2). By rapidly learning associations between conjunctive inputs in these systems, it is able to form memories of particular events occurring in particular places at particular times. To do this, it needs to store whatever is being represented in each of many cortical areas at a given time, and later to recall the whole memory from a part of it. The types of network it contains that are involved in this simple memory function are described in Chapter 2.

1.10 Introduction to the fine structure of the cerebral neocortex

An important part of the approach to understanding how the cerebral cortex could implement the computational processes that underlie visual perception is to take into account as much as possible its fine structure and connectivity, as these provide important indicators of and constraints on how it computes.

1.10.1 The fine structure and connectivity of the neocortex

The neocortex consists of many areas that can be distinguished by the appearance of the cells (cytoarchitecture) and fibres or axons (myeloarchitecture), but nevertheless, the basic organization of the different neocortical areas has many similarities, and it is this basic organization that is considered here. Useful sources for more detailed descriptions of neocortical structure and function are the book 'Cerebral Cortex' edited by Jones and Peters (Jones and Peters (1984) and Peters and Jones (1984)); and Douglas, Markram and Martin (2004). Approaches to quantitative aspects of the connectivity are provided by Braitenberg and Schuz (1991) and by Abeles (1991). Some of the connections described in Sections 1.10.2 and 1.10.3 are shown schematically in Fig. 1.13.

1.10.2 Excitatory cells and connections

Some of the cell types found in the neocortex are shown in Fig. 1.1. Cells A–D are pyramidal cells. The dendrites (shown thick in Fig. 1.1) are covered in spines, which receive the excitatory synaptic inputs to the cell. Pyramidal cells with cell bodies in different laminae of the cortex (shown in Fig. 1.1 as I–VI) not only have different distributions of their dendrites, but also different distributions of their axons (shown thin in Fig. 1.1), which connect both within that cortical area and to other brain regions outside that cortical area (see labelling at the bottom of Fig. 1.13).

The main information-bearing afferents to a cortical area have many terminals in layer 4. (By these afferents, we mean primarily those from the thalamus or from the preceding cortical area. We do not mean the cortico-cortical backprojections, nor the subcortical cholinergic, noradrenergic, dopaminergic, and serotonergic inputs, which are numerically minor, although they are important in setting cortical cell thresholds, excitability, and adaptation, see for example Douglas, Markram and Martin (2004).) In primary sensory cortical areas only there are spiny stellate cells in a rather expanded layer 4, and the thalamic terminals synapse onto these cells (Lund 1984, Martin 1984, Douglas and Martin 1990, Douglas, Markram and Martin 2004, Levitt, Lund and Yoshioka 1996). (Primary sensory cortical areas receive their inputs from the primary sensory thalamic nucleus for a sensory modality. An example is the primate striate cortex which receives inputs from the lateral geniculate nucleus, which in turn receives inputs from the retinal ganglion cells. Spiny stellate cells are so-called because they have radially arranged, star-like, dendrites. Their axons usually terminate within the cortical area in which they are located.) Each thalamic axon makes 1,000–10,000 synapses, not more than several (or at most 10) of which are onto any one spiny stellate cell. In addition to these afferent terminals, there are some terminals of the thalamic afferents onto pyramidal cells with cell bodies in layers 6 and 3 (Martin 1984) (and terminals onto inhibitory interneurons such as basket cells, which thus provide for a feedforward inhibition) (see Fig. 1.12). Even in layer 4, the thalamic axons provide less than 20% of the synapses. The spiny stellate neurons in layer 4 have axons which terminate in layers 3 and 2, at least partly on dendrites of pyramidal cells with cell bodies in layers 3 and 2. (These synapses are of Type I, that is are asymmetrical and are on spines, so that they are probably excitatory. Their transmitter is probably glutamate.) These layer 3 and 2 pyramidal cells provide the onward cortico-cortical projection with axons which project into layer 4 of the next cortical area. For example, layer 3 and 2 pyramidal cells in the primary visual (striate) cortex of the macaque monkey project into the second visual area (V2), layer 4.

In non-primary sensory areas, important information-bearing afferents from a preceding cortical area terminate in layer 4, but there are no or few spiny stellate cells in this layer (Lund 1984, Levitt, Lund and Yoshioka 1996). Layer 4 still looks 'granular' (due to the presence of many small cells), but these cells are typically small pyramidal cells (Lund 1984). (It may be noted here that spiny stellate cells and small pyramidal cells are similar in many ways, with a few main differences including the absence of a major apical dendrite in a spiny stellate which accounts for its non-pyramidal, star-shaped, appearance; and for many spiny stellate cells, the absence of an axon that projects outside its cortical area.) The terminals presumably make synapses with these small pyramidal cells, and also presumably with the dendrites of cells from other layers, including the basal dendrites of deep layer 3 pyramidal cells (see Fig. 1.13).

The axons of the *superficial (layer 2 and 3) pyramidal cells* have collaterals and terminals in layer 5 (see Fig. 1.13), and synapses are made with the dendrites of the layer 5 pyramidal cells (Martin 1984). The axons also typically project out of that cortical area, and on to the next cortical area in sequence, where they terminate in layer 4, forming the forward cortico-cortical projection. It is also from these pyramidal cells that projections to the amygdala arise in some sensory areas that are high in the hierarchy (Amaral, Price, Pitkanen and Carmichael 1992).

The axons of the *layer 5 pyramidal cells* have many collaterals in layer 6 (see Fig. 1.1), where synapses could be made with the layer 6 pyramidal cells (based on indirect evidence, see Fig. 13 of Martin (1984)), and axons of these cells typically leave the cortex to project to subcortical sites (such as the striatum), or back to the preceding cortical area to terminate in layer 1. It is remarkable that there are as many of these backprojections as there are forward connections between two sequential cortical areas. The possible computational significance of this connectivity is considered below in Section 1.11 and in Chapter 2.

The *layer 6 pyramidal cells* have prolific dendritic arborizations in layer 4 (see Fig. 1.1), and receive synapses from thalamic afferents (Martin 1984), and also presumably from pyramidal cells in other cortical layers. The axons of these cells form backprojections to the thalamic nucleus which projects into that cortical area, and also axons of cells in layer 6 contribute to the backprojections to layer 1 of the preceding cortical area (see Jones and Peters (1984) and Peters and Jones (1984); see Figs. 1.1 and 1.13).

Although the pyramidal and spiny stellate cells form the great majority of neocortical neurons with excitatory outputs, there are in addition several further cell types (see Peters and Jones (1984), Chapter 4). Bipolar cells are found in layers 3 and 5, and are characterized by having two dendritic systems, one ascending and the other descending, which, together with the axon distribution, are confined to a narrow vertical column often less than 50 μm in diameter (Peters 1984a). Bipolar cells form asymmetrical (presumed excitatory) synapses with pyramidal cells, and may serve to emphasize activity within a narrow vertical column.

1.10.3   Inhibitory cells and connections

There are a number of types of neocortical inhibitory neurons. All are described as smooth in that they have no spines, and use GABA (gamma-amino-butyric acid) as a transmitter. (In older terminology they were called Type II.) A number of types of inhibitory neuron can be distinguished, best by their axonal distributions (Szentagothai 1978, Peters and Regidor 1981, Douglas, Markram and Martin 2004). One type is the *basket cell*, present in layers 3–6, which has few spines on its dendrites so that it is described as smooth, and has an axon that participates in the formation of weaves of preterminal axons which surround the cell bodies of pyramidal cells and form synapses directly onto the cell body, but also onto the dendritic spines (Somogyi, Kisvarday, Martin and Whitteridge 1983) (Fig. 1.12). Basket cells comprise 5–7% of the total cortical cell population, compared with approximately 72% for pyramidal cells (Sloper and Powell 1979b, Sloper and Powell 1979a). Basket cells receive synapses from the main extrinsic afferents to the neocortex, including thalamic afferents (Fig. 1.12), so that they must contribute to a feedforward type of inhibition of pyramidal cells. The inhibition is feedforward in that the input signal activates the basket cells and the pyramidal cells by independent routes, so that the basket cells can produce inhibition of pyramidal cells that does not depend on whether the pyramidal cells have already fired. Feedforward inhibition of this type not only enhances stability of the system by damping the responsiveness of the pyramidal cell simultaneously with a large new input, but can also be conceived of as a mechanism which normalizes the magnitude of the input vector received by each small region of neocortex (see further Appendix B). In fact, the feedforward mechanism allows the pyramidal cells to be set at the appropriate sensitivity for the input they are about to receive. Basket cells can also be polysynaptically activated by an afferent volley in the thalamo-cortical projection (Martin 1984), so that they may receive inputs from pyramidal cells, and thus participate in feedback inhibition of pyramidal cells.

The transmitter used by the basket cells is gamma-amino-butyric acid (GABA), which opens chloride channels in the postsynaptic membrane. Because the reversal potential for Cl^- is approximately -10 mV relative to rest, opening the Cl^- channels does produce an inhibitory postsynaptic potential (IPSP), which results in some hyperpolarization, especially in the dendrites. This is a subtractive effect, hence it is a linear type of inhibition (Douglas and Martin 1990). However, a major effect of the opening of the Cl^- channels in the cell body is that this decreases the membrane resistance, thus producing a shunting effect. The importance of shunting is that it decreases the magnitude of excitatory postsynaptic potentials (EPSPs) (cf.

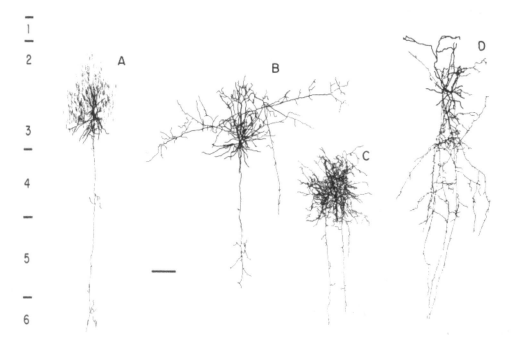

Fig. 1.12 Smooth cells from cat visual cortex. (A) Chandelier or axoaxonic cell. (B) Large basket cell of layer 3. Basket cells, present in layers 3–6, have few spines on their dendrites so that they are described as smooth, and have an axon which participates in the formation of weaves of preterminal axons which surround the cell bodies of pyramidal cells and form synapses directly onto the cell body. (C) Small basket or clutch cell of layer 3. The major portion of the axonal arbor is confined to layer 4. (D) Double bouquet cell. The axon collaterals run vertically. The cortical layers are as indicated. Bar = 100 μm. (Reproduced with permission from Douglas and Martin 1990, Fig. 12.4.)

Andersen, Dingledine, Gjerstad, Langmoen and Laursen (1980) for hippocampal pyramidal cells), so that the effect of shunting is to produce division (i.e. a multiplicative reduction) of the excitatory inputs received by the cell, and not just to act by subtraction (see further Bloomfield (1974), Martin (1984), Douglas and Martin (1990)). Thus, when modelling the normalization of the activity of cortical pyramidal cells, it is common to include division in the normalization function (cf. Appendix B). It is notable that the dendrites of basket cells can extend laterally 0.5 mm or more (primarily within the layer in which the cell body is located), and that the axons can also extend laterally from the cell body 0.5–1.5 mm. Thus the basket cells produce a form of lateral inhibition which is quite spatially extensive. There is some evidence that each basket cell may make 4–5 synapses with a given pyramidal cell, that each pyramidal cell may receive from 10–30 basket cells, and that each basket cell may inhibit approximately 300 pyramidal cells (Martin 1984, Douglas and Martin 1990, Douglas, Markram and Martin 2004). The basket cells are sometimes called clutch cells.

A second type of GABA-containing inhibitory interneuron is the *axoaxonic (or 'chandelier') cell*, named because it synapses onto the initial segment of the axon of pyramidal cells. The pyramidal cells receiving this type of inhibition are almost all in layers 2 and 3, and much less in the deep cortical layers. One effect that axoaxonic cells probably produce is thus prevention of outputs from layer 2 and 3 pyramidal cells reaching the pyramidal cells in the deep layers, or from reaching the next cortical area. Up to five axoaxonic cells converge onto a pyramidal cell, and each axoaxonic cell may project to several hundred pyramidal cells scattered in a region that may be several hundred microns in length (Martin 1984, Peters 1984b).

This implies that axoaxonic cells provide a rather simple device for preventing runaway over-activity of pyramidal cells, but little is known yet about the afferents to axoaxonic cells, so that the functions of these neurons are very incompletely understood.

A third type of (usually smooth and inhibitory) cell is the *double bouquet cell*, which has primarily vertically organized axons. These cells have their cell bodies in layer 2 or 3, and have an axon traversing layers 2–5, usually in a tight bundle consisting of varicose, radially oriented collaterals often confined to a narrow vertical column 50 μm in diameter (Somogyi and Cowey 1984). Double bouquet cells receive symmetrical, type II (presumed inhibitory) synapses, and also make type II synapses, perhaps onto the apical dendrites of pyramidal cells, so that these neurons may serve, by this double inhibitory effect, to emphasize activity within a narrow vertical column.

Another type of GABA-containing inhibitory interneuron is the smooth and sparsely spinous non-pyramidal (multipolar) neuron with local axonal plexuses (Peters and Saint Marie 1984). In addition to extrinsic afferents, these neurons receive many type I (presumed excitatory) terminals from pyramidal cells, and have inhibitory terminals on pyramidal cells, so that they may provide for the very important function of feedback or recurrent lateral inhibition (see Appendix B).

1.10.4   Quantitative aspects of cortical architecture

Some quantitative aspects of cortical architecture are described, because, although only preliminary data are available, they are crucial for developing an understanding of how the neocortex could work. Further evidence is provided by Braitenberg and Schuz (1991), and by Abeles (1991). Typical values, many of them after Abeles (1991), are shown in Table 1.1. The figures given are for a rather generalized case, and indicate the order of magnitude. The number of synapses per neuron (20,000) is an estimate for monkeys; those for humans may be closer to 40,000, and for the mouse, closer to 8,000. The number of 18,000 excitatory synapses made by a pyramidal cell is set to match the number of excitatory synapses received by pyramidal cells, for the great majority of cortical excitatory synapses are made from axons of cortical, principally pyramidal, cells.

Microanatomical studies show that pyramidal cells rarely make more than one connection with any other pyramidal cell, even when they are adjacent in the same area of the cerebral cortex. An interesting calculation takes the number of local connections made by a pyramidal cell within the approximately 1 mm of its local axonal arborization (say 9,000), and the number of pyramidal cells with dendrites in the same region, and suggests that the probability that a pyramidal cell makes a synapse with its neighbour is low, approximately 0.1 (Braitenberg and Schuz 1991, Abeles 1991). This fits with the estimate from simultaneous recording of nearby pyramidal cells using spike-triggered averaging to monitor time-locked EPSPs (Abeles 1991, Thomson and Deuchars 1994).

Now the implication of the pyramidal cell to pyramidal cell connectivity just described is that within a cortical area of perhaps 1 mm^2, the region within which typical pyramidal cells have dendritic trees and their local axonal arborization, there is a probability of excitatory-to-excitatory cell connection of 0.1. Moreover, this population of mutually interconnected neurons is served by 'its own' population of inhibitory interneurons (which have a spatial receiving and sending zone in the order of 1 mm^2), enabling local threshold setting and optimization of the set of neurons with 'high' (0.1) connection probability in that region. Such an architecture is effectively recurrent or re-entrant. It may be expected to show some of the properties of recurrent networks, including the fast dynamics described in Appendix B. Such fast dynamics may be facilitated by the fact that cortical neurons in the awake behaving monkey generally have a low spontaneous rate of firing (personal observations; see

Table 1.1 Typical quantitative estimates for neocortex (partly after Abeles (1991) and reflecting estimates in macaques)

Neuronal density	20,000–40,000/mm^3
Neuronal composition:	
Pyramidal	75%
Spiny stellate	10%
Inhibitory neurons, for example smooth stellate, chandelier	15%
Synaptic density	8 x 10^8/mm^3
Numbers of synapses on pyramidal cells:	
Excitatory synapses from remote sources onto each neuron	9,000
Excitatory synapses from local sources onto each neuron	9,000
Inhibitory synapses onto each neuron	2,000
Pyramidal cell dendritic length	10 mm
Number of synapses made by axons of pyramidal cells	18,000
Number of synapses on inhibitory neurons	2,000
Number of synapses made by inhibitory neurons	300
Dendritic length density	400 m/mm^3
Axonal length density	3,200 m/mm^3
Typical cortical thickness	2 mm
Cortical area	
human (assuming 3 mm for cortical thickness)	300,000 mm^2
macaque (assuming 2 mm for cortical thickness)	30,000 mm^2
rat (assuming 2 mm for cortical thickness)	300 mm^2

for example Rolls and Tovee (1995b), Rolls, Treves, Tovee and Panzeri (1997d), and Franco, Rolls, Aggelopoulos and Jerez (2007)), which means that even any small additional input may produce some spikes sooner than would otherwise have occurred, because some of the neurons may be very close to a threshold for firing. It might also show some of the autoassociative retrieval of information typical of autoassociation networks, if the synapses between the nearby pyramidal cells have the appropriate (Hebbian) modifiability. In this context, the value of 0.1 for the probability of a connection between nearby neocortical pyramidal cells is of interest, for the connection probability between hippocampal CA3 pyramidal is approximately 0.02–0.04, and this is thought to be sufficient to sustain associative retrieval (see Appendix B and Rolls and Treves (1998)).

In the neocortex, each 1 mm^2 region within which there is a relatively high density of recurrent collateral connections between pyramidal cells probably overlaps somewhat continuously with the next. This raises the issue of modules in the cortex, described by many authors as regions of the order of 1 mm^2 (with different authors giving different sizes), in which there are vertically oriented columns of neurons that may share some property (for example, responding to the same orientation of a visual stimulus), and that may be anatomically marked (for example Powell (1981), Mountcastle (1984), see Douglas, Mahowald and Martin (1996)). The anatomy just described, with the local connections between nearby (1 mm) pyramidal cells, and the local inhibitory neurons, may provide a network basis for starting to understand the columnar architecture of the neocortex, for it implies that local recurrent connectivity on this scale implementing local re-entrancy is a feature of cortical computation. We can note that the neocortex could not be a single, global, autoassociation network, because the number of memories that could be stored in an autoassociation network, rather than increasing with the number of neurons in the network, is limited by the number of recurrent connections per neuron, which is in the order of 10,000 (see Table 1.1), or less, depending on the species, as pointed out by O'Kane and Treves (1992). This would be an impossibly small capacity for the whole cortex. It is suggested that instead a principle of cortical design is that it does have in part local connectivity, so that each part can have its own processing and storage, which may be triggered by other modules, but is a distinct operation from that which occurs simultaneously in other modules.

An interesting parallel between the hippocampus and any small patch of neocortex is the allocation of a set of many small excitatory (usually non-pyramidal, spiny stellate or granular) cells at the input side. In the neocortex this is layer 4, in the hippocampus the dentate gyrus. In both cases, these cells receive the feedforward inputs and relay them to a population of pyramidal cells (in layers 2–3 of the neocortex and in the CA3 field of the hippocampus) which have extensive recurrent collateral connections. In both cases, the pyramidal cells receive inputs both as relayed by the preprocessing array and directly. Such analogies might indicate that the functional roles of neocortical layer 4 cells and of dentate granule cells could be partially the same (see Rolls and Treves (1998)).

The short-range high density of connectivity may also contribute to the formation of cortical topographic maps, as described in Appendix B. This may help to ensure that different parameters of the input space are represented in a nearly continuous fashion across the cortex, to the extent that the reduction in dimensionality allows it; or when preserving strict continuity is not possible, to produce the clustering of cells with similar response properties, as illustrated for example by colour 'blobs' in striate cortex, or by the local clustering of face cells in the temporal cortical visual areas (Rolls 2007i, Rolls 2008a).

1.10.5 Functional pathways through the cortical layers

Because of the complexity of the circuitry of the cerebral cortex, some of which is summarized in Fig. 1.13, there are only preliminary indications available now of how information is processed by the cortex. In primary sensory cortical areas, the main extrinsic 'forward' input is from the thalamus, and ends in layer 4, where synapses are formed onto spiny stellate cells. These in turn project heavily onto pyramidal cells in layers 3 and 2, which in turn send projections forward to the next cortical area. The situation is made more complex than this by the fact that the thalamic afferents also synapse onto the basal dendrites in or close to the layer 2 pyramidal cells, as well as onto layer 6 pyramidal cells and inhibitory interneurons. Given that the functional implications of this particular architecture are not fully clear, it would be of interest to examine the strength of the functional links between thalamic afferents and different classes of cortical cell using cross-correlation techniques, to determine which neurons are strongly activated by thalamic afferents with monosynaptic or polysynaptic delays. Given that this is technically difficult, an alternative approach has been to use electrical stimulation of the thalamic afferents to classify cortical neurons as mono- or poly-synaptically driven, then to examine the response properties of the neuron to physiological (visual) inputs, and finally to fill the cell with horseradish peroxidase so that its full structure can be studied (see for example Martin (1984)). Using these techniques, it has been shown in the cat visual cortex that spiny stellate cells can indeed be driven monosynaptically by thalamic afferents to the cortex. Further, many of these neurons have S-type receptive fields, that is they have distinct on and off regions of the receptive field, and respond with orientation tuning to elongated visual stimuli (Martin 1984) (see Rolls and Deco (2002)). Further, consistent with the anatomy just described, pyramidal cells in the deep part of layer 3, and in layer 6, could also be monosynaptically activated by thalamic afferents, and had S-type receptive fields (Martin 1984). Also consistent with the anatomy just described, pyramidal cells in layer 2

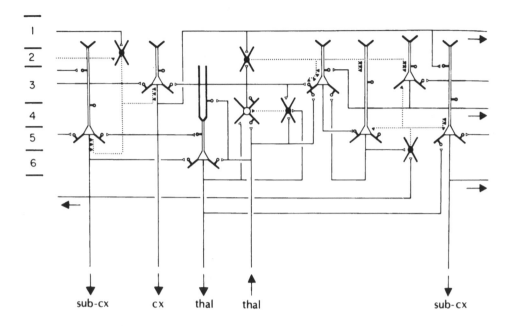

Fig. 1.13 Basic circuit for visual cortex. Excitatory neurons, which are spiny and use glutamate as a transmitter, and include the pyramidal and spiny stellate cells, are indicated by open somata; their axons are indicated by solid lines, and their synaptic boutons by open symbols. Inhibitory (smooth, GABAergic) neurons are indicated by black (filled) somata; their axons are indicated by dotted lines, and their synaptic boutons by solid symbols. thal, thalamus; cx, cortex; sub-cx, subcortex. Cortical layers 1–6 are as indicated. (Reproduced with permission from Douglas and Martin 1990, Fig. 12.7.)

were di- (or poly-) synaptically activated by stimulation of the afferents from the thalamus, but also had S-type receptive fields.

Inputs could reach the layer 5 pyramidal cells from the pyramidal cells in layers 2 and 3, the axons of which ramify extensively in layer 5, in which the layer 5 pyramidal cells have widespread basal dendrites (see Fig. 1.1), and also perhaps from thalamic afferents. Many layer 5 pyramidal cells are di- or trisynaptically activated by stimulation of the thalamic afferents, consistent with them receiving inputs from monosynaptically activated deep layer 3 pyramidal cells, or from disynaptically activated pyramidal cells in layer 2 and upper layer 3 (Martin 1984). Interestingly, many of the layer 5 pyramidal cells had C-type receptive fields, that is they did not have distinct on and off regions, but did respond with orientation tuning to elongated visual stimuli (Martin 1984) (see Rolls and Deco (2002)).

Studies on the function of inhibitory pathways in the cortex are also beginning. The fact that basket cells often receive strong thalamic inputs, and that they terminate on pyramidal cell bodies where part of their action is to shunt the membrane, suggests that they act in part as a feedforward inhibitory system that normalizes the thalamic influence on pyramidal cells by dividing their response in proportion to the average of the thalamic input received (see Appendix B). The smaller and numerous smooth (or sparsely spiny) non-pyramidal cells that are inhibitory may receive inputs from pyramidal cells as well as inhibit them, so that these neurons could perform the very important function of recurrent or feedback inhibition (see Appendix B). It is only feedback inhibition that can take into account not only the inputs received by an area of cortex, but also the effects that these inputs have, once multiplied by the synaptic weight vector on each neuron, so that recurrent inhibition is necessary for competition and contrast enhancement (see Appendix B).

Another way in which the role of inhibition in the cortex can be analyzed is by applying a drug such as bicuculline using iontophoresis (which blocks GABA receptors to a single neuron), while examining the response properties of the neuron (see Sillito (1984)). With this technique, it has been shown that in the visual cortex of the cat, layer 4 simple cells lose their orientation and directional selectivity. Similar effects are observed in some complex cells, but the selectivity of other complex cells may be less affected by blocking the effect of endogenously released GABA in this way (Sillito 1984). One possible reason for this is that the inputs to complex cells must often synapse onto the dendrites far from the cell body, and distant synapses will probably be unaffected by the GABA receptor blocker released near the cell body. The experiments reveal that inhibition is very important for the normal selectivity of many visual cortex neurons for orientation and the direction of movement. Many of the cells displayed almost no orientation selectivity without inhibition. This implies that not only is the inhibition important for maintaining the neuron on an appropriate part of its activation function, but also that lateral inhibition between neurons is important because it allows the responses of a single neuron (which need not be markedly biased by its excitatory input) to have its responsiveness set by the activity of neighbouring neurons (see Appendix B).

1.10.6 The scale of lateral excitatory and inhibitory effects, and the concept of modules

The forward cortico-cortical afferents to a cortical area sometimes have a columnar pattern to their distribution, with the column width 200–300 μm in diameter (see Eccles (1984)). Similarly, individual thalamo-cortical axons often end in patches in layer 4 which are 200–300 μm in diameter (Martin 1984). The dendrites of spiny stellate cells are in the region of 500 μm in diameter, and their axons can distribute in patches 200–300 μm across, separated by distances of up to 1 mm (Martin 1984). The dendrites of layer 2 and 3 pyramidal cells can be approximately 300 μm in diameter, but after this the relatively narrow column appears to become less important, for the axons of the superficial pyramidal cells can distribute over 1 mm or more, both in layers 2 and 3, and in layer 5 (Martin 1984). Other neurons that may contribute to the maintenance of processing in relatively narrow columns are the double bouquet cells, which because they receive inhibitory inputs, and themselves produce inhibition, all within a column perhaps 50 μm across (see above), would tend to enhance local excitation. The bipolar cells, which form excitatory synapses with pyramidal cells, may also serve to emphasize activity within a narrow vertical column approximately 50 μm across. These two mechanisms for enhancing local excitation operate against a much broader-ranging set of lateral inhibitory processes, and could it is suggested have the effect of increasing contrast between the firing rates of pyramidal cells 50 μm apart, and thus be very important in competitive interactions between pyramidal cells. Indeed, the lateral inhibitory effects are broader than the excitatory effects described so far, in that for example the axons of basket cells spread laterally 500 μm or more (see above) (although those of the small, smooth non-pyramidal cells are closer to 300 μm – see Peters and Saint Marie (1984)). Such short-range local excitatory interactions with longer range inhibition not only provide for contrast enhancement and for competitive interactions, but also can result in the formation of maps in which neurons with similar responses are grouped together and neurons with dissimilar response are more widely separated (see Appendix B). Thus these local interactions are consistent with the possibilities that cortical pyramidal cells form a competitive network (see Appendix B and below), and that cortical maps are formed at least partly as a result of local

found, for example, that quite posterior visual areas are activated during recall of visual (but not auditory) scenes (Kosslyn 1994). The backprojections are probably in this situation acting as pattern associators.

The quantitative analysis of the recall that could be implemented through the hippocampal backprojection synapses to the neocortex, and then via multiple stages of cortico-cortical backprojections, makes it clear that the most important quantitative factor influencing the number of memories that can be recalled is the number of backprojecting synapses onto each cortical neuron in the backprojecting pathways (see Section 2.3.7, Fig. 2.1, Treves and Rolls (1994), and Treves and Rolls (1991)). This provides an interpretation of why there are in general as many backprojecting synapses between two adjacent cortical areas as forward connections. The number of synapses on each neuron devoted to the backprojections needs to be large to recall as many memories as possible, but need not be larger than the number of forward inputs to each neuron, which influences the number of possible classifications that the neuron can perform with its forward inputs (see Section 2.3.7).

An implication of these ideas is that if the backprojections are used for recall, as seems likely as just discussed, then this would place severe constraints on their use for functions such as error backpropagation (see Appendix B). It would be difficult to use the backprojections in cortical architecture to convey an appropriate error signal from the output layer back to the earlier, hidden, layers if the backprojection synapses are also to be set up associatively to implement recall.

1.11.4 Semantic priming

A third property of this backprojection architecture is that it could implement semantic priming, by using the backprojecting neurons to provide a small activation of just those neurons that are appropriate for responding to that semantic category of input stimulus.

1.11.5 Attention

In the same way, attention could operate from higher to lower levels, to selectively facilitate only certain pyramidal cells by using the backprojections. Indeed, the backprojections described could produce many of the 'top-down' influences that are common in perception (cf. Fig. B.19 and Chapters 6, 8 and 9).

1.11.6 Autoassociative storage, and constraint satisfaction

If the forward connections from one cortical area to the next, and the return backprojections, are both associatively modifiable, then the coupled networks could be regarded as, effectively, an autoassociative network. (Autoassociation networks are described in Section B.3). A pattern of activity in one cortical area would be associated with a pattern in the next that occurred regularly with it. This could enable higher cortical areas to influence the state of earlier cortical areas, and could be especially influential in the type of situation shown in Fig. B.19 in which some convergence occurs at the higher area. For example, if one of the earlier stages (for example the olfactory stage in Fig. B.19) had a noisy input on a particular occasion, its representation could be cleaned up if a taste input normally associated with it was present. The higher cortical area would be forced into the correct pattern of firing by the taste input, and this would feed back as a constraint to affect the state into which the olfactory area settled. This could be a useful general effect in the cerebral cortex, in that constraints arising only after information has converged from different sources at a higher level could feed back to influence the representations that earlier parts of the network settle into. This is a way in which top-down processing could be implemented, and is analyzed in Section B.9.

The autoassociative effect between two forward and backward connected cortical areas could also be used in short-term memory functions (see Section 5.1), to implement the types of short-term memory effect described in Appendix B and Chapter 5. Such connections could also be used to implement a trace learning rule as described in Chapter 4.

With this overview, it is now time to consider memory, object recognition, attention, and decision-making systems in the brain.

2 The hippocampus and memory

2.1 Introduction

In this Chapter a computational neuroscience approach to hippocampal function in memory is described. Then tests of the theory based especially on subregion analysis of the hippocampal system are described, followed by an evaluation of the theoretical proposals, and a comparison with other theories.

The theory was originally developed as described next, and was preceded by work of Marr (1971) who developed a mathematical model, which although not applied to particular networks within the hippocampus and dealing with binary neurons and binary synapses which utilised heavily the properties of the binomial distribution, was important in utilizing computational concepts. The model was assessed by Willshaw and Buckingham (1990)[1]. Early work of Gardner-Medwin (1976) showed how progressive recall could operate in a network of binary neurons with binary synapses.

Rolls (1987) produced a theory of the hippocampus in which the CA3 neurons operated as an autoassociation memory to store episodic memories including object and place memories, and the dentate granule cells operated as a preprocessing stage for this by performing pattern separation so that the mossy fibres could act to set up different representations for each memory to be stored in the CA3 cells[2]. He suggested that the CA1 cells operate as a recoder for the information recalled from the CA3 cells to a partial memory cue, so that the recalled information would be represented more efficiently to enable recall, via the backprojection synapses, of activity in the neocortical areas similar to that which had been present during the original episode. This theory was developed further (Rolls 1989a, Rolls 1989b, Rolls 1989e, Rolls 1989f, Rolls 1990b, Rolls 1990c), including further details about how the backprojections could operate (Rolls 1989b, Rolls 1989e), and how the dentate granule cells could operate as a competitive network (Rolls 1989a). Quantitative aspects of the theory were then developed with A. Treves, who brought the expertise of theoretical physics applied previously mainly to understand the properties of fully connected attractor networks with binary neurons (Amit 1989, Hopfield 1982) to bear on the much more diluted connectivity of the recurrent collateral connections found in real biological networks (e.g. 2% between CA3

---

[1] Marr (1971) showed how a network with recurrent collaterals could complete a memory using a partial retrieval cue, and how sparse representations could increase the number of memories stored. The analysis of these auto-association or attractor networks was developed by Kohonen (1977) and Hopfield (1982), and the value of sparse representations was quantified by Treves and Rolls (1991). Marr (1971) did not specify the functions of the dentate granule cells vs the CA3 cells vs the CA1 cells (which were addressed in the Rolls (1989) papers and by Treves and Rolls (1992) and Treves and Rolls (1994)), nor how retrieval to the neocortex of hippocampal memories could be produced, for which a quantitative theory was developed by Treves and Rolls (1994). In addition, Treves and Rolls (1994) and Rolls and Treves (1998) have argued that approaches to neurocomputation which base their calculations on what would happen in the tail of an exponential, Poisson, or binomial distribution are very fragile.

[2] McNaughton and Morris (1987) at about the same time suggested that the CA3 network might be an autoassociation network, and that the mossy fibre to CA3 connections might implement 'detonator' synapses. However, the concepts that the diluted mossy fibre connectivity might implement selection of a new random set of CA3 cells for each new memory, and that a direct perforant path input to CA3 was needed to initiate retrieval, were introduced by Treves and Rolls (1992). Contributions by Levy (1989); McNaughton (1991); Hasselmo, Schnell and Barkai (1995); McClelland, McNaughton and O'Reilly (1995); and many others, are described below.

pyramidal cells in the rat), in networks of neurons with graded (continuously variable) firing rates, graded synaptic strengths, and sparse representations in which only a small proportion of the neurons is active at any one time, as is found in the hippocampus (Treves 1990, Treves and Rolls 1991). These developments in understanding quantitatively the operation of more biologically relevant recurrent networks with modifiable synapses were applied quantitatively to the CA3 region (Treves and Rolls 1991), and to the issue of why there are separate mossy fibre and perforant path inputs to the CA3 cells of the hippocampus (Treves and Rolls 1992). This whole model of the hippocampus was described in more detail, and a quantitative treatment of the theory of recall by backprojection pathways in the brain was provided by Treves and Rolls (1994).

The speed of operation of the CA3 system, and of the cortico-cortical recall backprojections, was addressed in a number of new developments (Battaglia and Treves 1998b, Panzeri, Rolls, Battaglia and Lavis 2001, Simmen, Rolls and Treves 1996a, Treves 1993). Rolls (1995c) produced a simulation of the operation of the major parts of the hippocampus from the entorhinal cortex through the dentate, CA3, and CA1 cells back to the hippocampus, which established the quantitative feasibility of the whole theory, and raised a number of important issues considered below, including the role of topography within parts of the hippocampal internal connectivity. The simulation also emphasized some of the advantages, for a system that must store many different memories, of a binary representation, in which for any one memory the neurons were either firing or not, as opposed to having continuously graded firing rates. The simulation by Rolls (1995c) also showed how recall, if not perfect at the stage of the CA3 cells, was improved by associative synapses at subsequent stages, including the connections of the CA3 cells to the CA1 cells, and the connections of the CA1 cells to the entorhinal cortex cells. Further developments of the theory, and new developments introduced here, are described below.

Tests of the theory including analysis of the functions of different subregions of the hippocampus are described in Section 2.4.

2.2   Systems-level functions of the hippocampus

Any theory of the hippocampus must state at the systems level what is computed by the hippocampus. Some of the relevant evidence comes from the systems-level connections of the hippocampus (Section 2.2.1), from the effects of damage to the hippocampus (Section 2.2.2), and from the responses of neurons in the hippocampus during behaviour (Section 2.2.4).

2.2.1   Systems-level anatomy

Fig. 2.1 shows that the primate hippocampus receives major inputs via the entorhinal cortex (area 28). These come from the highly developed parahippocampal gyrus (areas TF and TH) as well as the perirhinal cortex, and thereby from the ends of many processing streams of the cerebral association cortex, including the visual and auditory temporal lobe association cortical areas, the prefrontal cortex, and the parietal cortex (Amaral et al. 1992, Amaral 1987, Suzuki and Amaral 1994a, Van Hoesen 1982, Witter, Wouterlood, Naber and Van Haeften 2000b, Lavenex, Suzuki and Amaral 2004, Johnston and Amaral 2004). The hippocampus is thus by its connections potentially able to associate together object representations (from the temporal lobe visual and auditory areas) and spatial representations. In addition, the entorhinal cortex receives inputs from the amygdala, and the orbitofrontal cortex, which could provide reward-related information to the hippocampus (Carmichael and Price 1995b, Suzuki and Amaral 1994a, Pitkanen, Kelly and Amaral 2002, Stefanacci, Suzuki and Amaral 1996). The

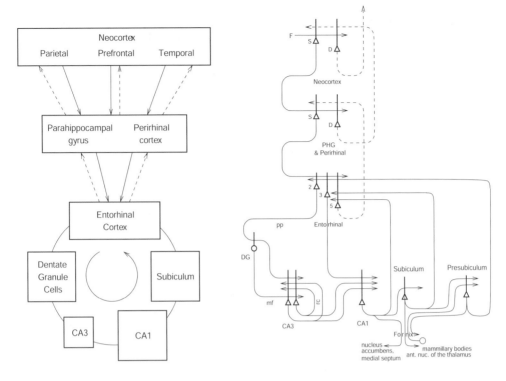

Fig. 2.1 Forward connections (solid lines) from areas of cerebral association neocortex via the parahip-pocampal gyrus and perirhinal cortex, and entorhinal cortex, to the hippocampus; and backprojections (dashed lines) via the hippocampal CA1 pyramidal cells, subiculum, and parahippocampal gyrus to the neocortex. There is great convergence in the forward connections down to the single network implemented in the CA3 pyramidal cells; and great divergence again in the backprojections. Left: block diagram. Right: more detailed representation of some of the principal excitatory neurons in the pathways. Abbreviations: D, deep pyramidal cells; DG, dentate granule cells; F, forward inputs to areas of the association cortex from preceding cortical areas in the hierarchy. mf: mossy fibres; PHG, parahippocampal gyrus and perirhinal cortex; pp, perforant path; rc, recurrent collaterals of the CA3 hippocampal pyramidal cells; S, superficial pyramidal cells; 2, pyramidal cells in layer 2 of the entorhinal cortex; 3, pyramidal cells in layer 3 of the entorhinal cortex; 5, 6, pyramidal cells in the deep layers of the entorhinal cortex. The thick lines above the cell bodies represent the dendrites.

connections are analogous in the rat, although areas such as the temporal lobe visual cortical areas are not well developed in rodents, and the parahippocampal gyrus may be represented by the dorsal perirhinal cortex (Burwell, Witter and Amaral 1995).

Given that some topographic segregation is maintained in the afferents to the hippocampus in the perirhinal and parahippocampal cortices (Amaral and Witter 1989), it may be that these areas are able to subserve memory within one of these topographically separated areas, of for example visual object, or spatial, or olfactory information. In contrast, the final convergence afforded by the hippocampus into one network in CA3 (see Fig. 2.1) may be especially appropriate for an episodic memory typically involving arbitrary associations between any of the inputs to the hippocampus, e.g. spatial, vestibular related to self-motion, visual object, olfactory, and auditory (see below). There are also direct subcortical inputs from for example the amygdala and septum (Amaral 1986).

The primary output from the hippocampus to neocortex originates in CA1 and projects to subiculum, entorhinal cortex, and parahippocampal structures (areas TF-TH) as well as

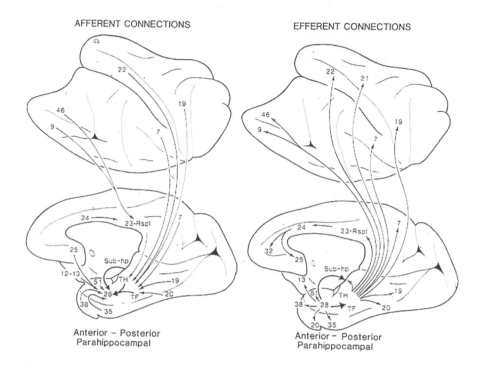

Fig. 2.2 Connections of the primate hippocampus with the neocortex (after Van Hoesen 1982). A medial view of the macaque brain is shown below, and a lateral view is shown inverted above. The hippocampus receives its inputs via the parahippocampal gyrus (areas TF and TH), and the perirhinal cortex (areas 35 and 36), which in turn project to the entorhinal cortex (area 28). The return projections to the neocortex (shown on the right) pass through the same areas. Cortical areas 19, 20, and 21 are visual association areas, 22 is auditory association cortex, 7 is parietal association cortex, and 9, 46, 12, and 13 are areas of frontal association cortex in the prefrontal cortex.

prefrontal cortex (Delatour and Witter 2002, Van Hoesen 1982, Witter 1993, van Haeften, Baks-te Bulte, Goede, Wouterlood and Witter 2003). CA1 and subiculum also project via the fimbria/fornix to subcortical areas such as the mammillary bodies and anterior thalamic nuclei (see Fig. 2.1). In addition to the projections originating in CA1, projections out of Ammon's horn also originate in CA3. Many researchers have reported that CA3 projects to the lateral and medial septal nuclei (Amaral and Witter 1995, Risold and Swanson 1997, Gaykema, van der Kuil, Hersh and Luiten 1991). The lateral septum also has projections to the medial septum (Jakab and Leranth 1995), which in turn projects to subiculum and eventually entorhinal cortex (Amaral and Witter 1995, Jakab and Leranth 1995).

2.2.2 Evidence from the effects of damage to the hippocampus

Damage to the hippocampus or to some of its connections such as the fornix in monkeys produces deficits in learning about the places of objects and about the places where responses should be made (Buckley and Gaffan 2000). For example, macaques and humans with damage to the hippocampal system or fornix are impaired in object–place memory tasks in which not only the objects seen, but where they were seen, must be remembered (Burgess, Maguire and O'Keefe 2002, Crane and Milner 2005, Gaffan 1994, Gaffan and Saunders 1985, Parkinson, Murray and Mishkin 1988, Smith and Milner 1981). Posterior parahippocampal lesions in macaques impair even a simple type of object–place learning in which the memory load is just one pair of trial-unique stimuli (Malkova and Mishkin 2003). Further, neurotoxic lesions that selectively damage the primate hippocampus impair spatial scene memory (Murray, Baxter and Gaffan 1998). Also, fornix lesions impair conditional left–right discrimination learning, in which the visual appearance of an object specifies whether a response is to be made to the left or the right (Rupniak and Gaffan 1987). A comparable deficit is found in humans (Petrides 1985). Fornix sectioned monkeys are also impaired in learning on the basis of a spatial cue which object to choose (e.g. if two objects are on the left, choose object A, but if the two objects are on the right, choose object B) (Gaffan and Harrison 1989a). Monkeys with fornix damage are also impaired in using information about their place in an environment. For example, Gaffan and Harrison (1989b) found learning impairments when which of two or more objects the monkey had to choose depended on the position of the monkey in the room. Rats with hippocampal lesions are impaired in using environmental spatial cues to remember particular places (Cassaday and Rawlins 1997, Martin et al. 2000, O'Keefe and Nadel 1978, Jarrard 1993, Kesner, Lee and Gilbert 2004), to utilize spatial cues or bridge delays (Kesner 1998, Kesner and Rolls 2001, Rawlins 1985, Kesner et al. 2004), or it has been argued to perform relational operations on remembered material (Eichenbaum 1997).

One way of relating the impairment of spatial processing to other aspects of hippocampal function is to note that this spatial processing involves a snapshot type of memory, in which one whole scene must be remembered. This memory may then be a special case of episodic memory, which involves an arbitrary association of a particular set of events which describe a past episode (Rolls 2008b). Further, the non-spatial tasks impaired by damage to the hippocampal system may be impaired because they are tasks in which a memory of a particular episode or context rather than of a general rule is involved (Gaffan, Saunders, Gaffan, Harrison, Shields and Owen 1984). Further, the deficit in paired associate learning in humans may be especially evident when this involves arbitrary associations between words, for example window – lake. Consistent with this, single neurons in the human hippocampus may respond not only to the sight or name of a film star, but also to objects associated with them, such as a bicycle (Quiroga, Reddy, Kreiman, Koch and Fried 2005). The right (spatial) vs left (word) specialization of function in the human hippocampus (Crane and Milner 2005, Burgess et al. 2002), associated in humans with a less well developed hippocampal commissural system, could be related to the fact that arbitrary associations between words and places are not required.

It is suggested that the reason why the hippocampus is used for the spatial and non-spatial types of memory described above, and the reason that makes these two types of memory so analogous, is that the hippocampus contains one stage, the CA3 stage, which acts as an autoassociation memory. It is suggested that an autoassociation memory implemented by the CA3 neurons equally enables whole (spatial) scene or episodic memories to be formed, with a snapshot quality that depends on the arbitrary associations that can be made and the short temporal window which characterises the synaptic modifiability in this system (Rolls 1990b, Rolls 1990c, Rolls 1987, Rolls 1989b, Rolls 1989e). The hypothesis is that the autoassociation memory enables arbitrary sets of concurrent neuronal firings, representing for example the spatial context where an episode occurred, the people present during the episode, and what was seen during the episode, to be associated together and stored as one event. (The associations are arbitrary in the sense that any representation within CA3 may be associated with any other representation in CA3.) The issue of the types of item, e.g. spatial, for which this type of associativity is hippocampus-dependent is considered below. Later recall of that episode from the hippocampus in response to a partial cue can then lead to reinstatement of the activity in the neocortex that was originally present during the episode. The theory described here shows how the episodic memory could be stored in the hippocampus, and later retrieved from the hippocampus and thereby to the neocortex using backprojections.

It is now evident that recognition memory (tested for example in primates by the ability to recognise a sample visual stimulus in a delayed match to sample task) is not impaired by hippocampal damage, produced for example by neurotoxic lesions (Murray et al. 1998, Baxter and Murray 2001b, Baxter and Murray 2001a). As shown below in Section 2.2.6, perirhinal cortex lesions do impair visual recognition memory in this type of task.

The extensive literature on the effects of hippocampal damage in rats is considered in Section 2.4, in particular the parts of it that involve selective lesions to different subregions of the hippocampus and allow the theory described here to be tested. The theory described here is intended to be as relevant to rodents as to primates including humans, the main difference being that the spatial representation used in the hippocampus of rats is about the place where the rat is, whereas the spatial representation in primates includes a representation of space "out there", as represented by spatial view cells (see Section 2.2.4).

2.2.3 The necessity to recall information from the hippocampus

The information about episodic events recalled from the hippocampus could be used to help form semantic memories (Rolls 1990b, Rolls 1989b, Rolls 1989e, Rolls 1989f, Treves and Rolls 1994). For example, remembering many particular journeys could help to build a geographic cognitive map in the neocortex. The hippocampus and neocortex would thus be complementary memory systems, with the hippocampus being used for rapid, 'on the fly', unstructured storage of information involving activity potentially arriving from many areas of the neocortex; while the neocortex would gradually build and adjust, on the basis of much accumulating information, the semantic representation (Rolls 1989b, Treves and Rolls 1994, McClelland et al. 1995). A view close to this in which a hippocampal episodic memory trace helps to build a neocortical semantic memory has also been developed by Moscovitch, Rosenbaum, Gilboa, Addis, Westmacott, Grady, McAndrews, Levine, Black, Winocur and Nadel (2005). The quantitative evidence considered below (Section 2.3.2.1) and by Treves and Rolls (1994) on the storage capacity of the CA3 system indicates that episodic memories could be stored in the hippocampus for at least a considerable period.

This raises the issue of the possible gradient of retrograde amnesia following hippocampal damage, and of whether information originally hippocampus-dependent for acquisition gradually becomes 'consolidated' in the neocortex and thereby becomes independent of the hippocampus over time (McGaugh 2000, Debiec, LeDoux and Nader 2002). The issue of whether memories stored some time before hippocampal damage are less impaired than more recent memories, and whether the time course is minutes, hours, days, weeks or years is a debated issue (Gaffan 1993, Squire 1992). (In humans, there is evidence for a gradient of retrograde amnesia; in rats and monkeys, hippocampal damage in many studies appears to impair previously learned hippocampal-type memories, suggesting that in these animals, at least with the rather limited numbers of different memories that need to be stored in the tasks used, the information remains in the hippocampus for long periods.) If there is a gradient of retrograde amnesia related to hippocampal damage, then this suggests that information may be retrieved from the hippocampus if it is needed, allowing the possibility of incorporating the retrieved information into neocortical memory stores. If on the other hand there is no gradient of retrograde amnesia related to hippocampal damage, but old as well as recent memories of the hippocampal type are stored in the hippocampus, and lost if it is damaged, then again this implies the necessity of a mechanism to retrieve information stored in the hippocampus, and to use this retrieved information to affect neural circuits elsewhere (for if this were not the case, information stored in the hippocampus could never be used for anything). The current perspective is thus that whichever view of the gradient of retrograde amnesia is correct, information stored in the hippocampus will need to be retrieved and affect other parts of the brain in order to be used. The present theory shows how information could be retrieved within the hippocampus, and how this retrieved information could enable the activity in neocortical areas that was present during the original storage of the episodic event to be reinstated, thus implementing recall. The backprojections from the hippocampus to the neocortex are one of the two major outputs of the hippocampus (see Fig. 2.1). The backprojections are most likely to be involved in what is described by humans as recall, and in enabling information about an episode captured on the fly to be incorporated into long-term, possibly semantic, neocortical stores with a rich associative structure (McClelland et al. 1995). As a result of such neocortical recall, action may be initiated.

The other major set of outputs from the hippocampus projects via the fimbria/fornix system to the anterior nucleus of the thalamus (both directly and via the mammillary bodies), which in turn projects to the cingulate cortex. This may provide an output for more action-directed use of information stored in the hippocampus, for example in the initiation of conditional spatial responses in a visual conditional spatial response task (Rupniak and Gaffan 1987, Miyashita, Rolls, Cahusac, Niki and Feigenbaum 1989). In such a task, a rapid mapping must be learned between a visual stimulus and a spatial response, and a new mapping must be learned each day. The hippocampus is involved in this rapid visual to spatial response mapping (Rupniak and Gaffan 1987), and the way in which hippocampal circuitry may be appropriate for this is that the CA3 region enables signals originating from very different parts of the cerebral cortex to be associated rapidly together (see below).

2.2.4   Systems-level neurophysiology of the primate hippocampus

The systems-level neurophysiology of the hippocampus shows what information could be stored or processed by the hippocampus. To understand how the hippocampus works it is not sufficient to state just that it can store information – one needs to know what information. The systems-level neurophysiology of the primate hippocampus has been reviewed recently by Rolls and Xiang (2006), and a summary is provided here because it provides a perspective relevant to understanding the function of the human hippocampus that is somewhat different from that provided by the properties of place cells in rodents, which have been reviewed elsewhere (McNaughton, Barnes and O'Keefe 1983, Muller, Kubie, Bostock, Taube and Quirk 1991, Jeffery and Hayman 2004, O'Keefe 1984, Jeffery, Anderson, Hayman and Chakraborty 2004).

The primate hippocampus contains spatial cells that respond when the monkey looks at a certain part of space, for example at one quadrant of a video monitor while the monkey is performing an object–place memory task in which he must remember where on the monitor he has seen particular images (Rolls, Miyashita, Cahusac, Kesner, Niki, Feigenbaum and Bach 1989b). Approximately 9% of the hippocampal neurons have such spatial view fields, and about 2.4% combine information about the position in space with information about the object that is in that position in space (Rolls et al. 1989b). The latter point shows that information from very different parts of the cerebral cortex (parietal for spatial information, and inferior temporal for visual information about objects) is brought together onto single neurons in the primate hippocampus. The representation of space is for the majority of hippocampal neurons in allocentric not egocentric coordinates (Feigenbaum and Rolls 1991).

In rats, place cells are found, which respond depending on the place where the rat is in a spatial environment (McNaughton et al. 1983, Muller et al. 1991, O'Keefe 1984). To analyse whether such cells might be present in the primate hippocampus, Rolls and O'Mara (1993) and Rolls and O'Mara (1995) recorded the responses of hippocampal cells when macaques were moved in a small chair or robot on wheels in a cue-controlled testing environment.

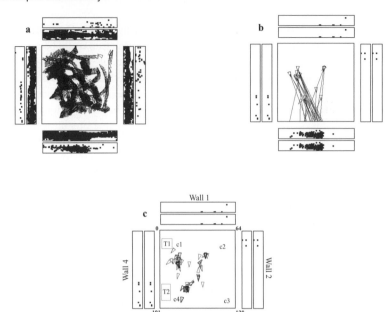

Fig. 2.3 Examples of the firing of a hippocampal spatial view cell when the monkey was walking around the laboratory. (a) The firing of the cell is indicated by the spots in the outer set of 4 rectangles, each of which represents one of the walls of the room. There is one spot on the outer rectangle for each action potential. The base of the wall is towards the centre of each rectangle. The positions on the walls fixated during the recording sessions are indicated by points in the inner set of 4 rectangles, each of which also represents a wall of the room. The central square is a plan view of the room, with a triangle printed every 250 ms to indicate the position of the monkey, thus showing that many different places were visited during the recording sessions. (b) A similar representation of the same 3 recording sessions as in (a), but modified to indicate some of the range of monkey positions and horizontal gaze directions when the cell fired at more than 12 spikes/s. (c) A similar representation of the same 3 recording sessions as in (b), but modified to indicate more fully the range of places when the cell fired. The triangle indicates the current position of the monkey, and the line projected from it shows which part of the wall is being viewed at any one time while the monkey is walking. One spot is shown for each action potential. (After Georges-François, Rolls and Robertson 1999.)

The most common type of cell responded to the part of space at which the monkeys were looking, independently of the place where the monkey was. Ono, Nakamura, Nishijo and Eifuku (1993) performed studies on the representation of space in the primate hippocampus while the monkey was moved in a cab to different places in a room. They found that 13.4% of hippocampal formation neurons fired more when the monkey was at some but not other places in the test area, but it was not clear whether the responses of these neurons occurred to the place where the monkey was independently of spatial view, or whether the responses of place-like cells were view dependent.

Place cells fire best during active locomotion by the rat (Foster, Castro and McNaughton 1989). To investigate whether place cells might be present in monkeys if active locomotion was being performed, we (Georges-François, Rolls and Robertson 1999, Robertson, Rolls and Georges-François 1998, Rolls, Robertson and Georges-François 1997a, Rolls, Treves, Robertson, Georges-François and Panzeri 1998) recorded from single hippocampal neurons while monkeys moved themselves round the test environment by walking (or running) on

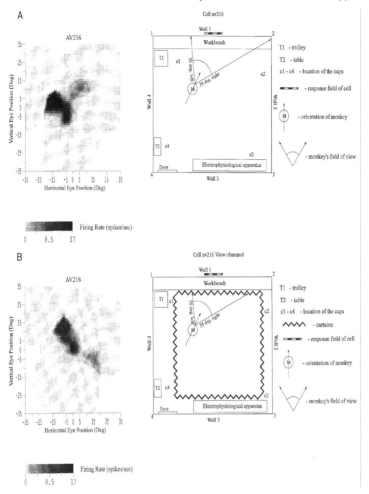

Fig. 2.4 Idiothetic update of the firing of a hippocampal spatial view cell. This cell fired when the macaque looked towards the effective spatial view even when it was obscured. The firing is shown with the monkey stationary with his head facing in the direction indicated by the arrow when the curtains were drawn open (A) or were drawn closed (B). Left: firing rate of the cell in spikes/s is indicated by the blackness (a calibration bar in spikes/s is shown below) projected onto the monkey's field of view. The two-dimensional firing rate profile of the cell was smoothed for clarity using a 2-dimensional Gaussian spatial filter. The space adequately sampled by the eye movements of the monkey is indicated by shading. Right: a plan view of the room to indicate the monkey's view of the wall is shown. M, position of the monkey. (After Robertson, Rolls and Georges-François 1998.)

all fours. We found that these hippocampal "spatial view neurons" responded significantly differently for different allocentric spatial views and had information about spatial view in their firing rate, but did not respond differently just on the basis of eye position, head direction, or place. If the view details are obscured by curtains and darkness, then some spatial view neurons (especially those in CA1 and less those in CA3) continue to respond when the monkey looks towards the spatial view field (see example in Fig. 2.4). This experiment (Robertson et al. 1998, Rolls et al. 1997a) shows that primate hippocampal spatial view neurons can be updated for at least short periods by idiothetic (self-motion) cues including eye position and head direction signals. Consistent with this, a small drift is sometimes evident after a delay when the view details are obscured, consistent with inaccuracies in the temporal path integration of these signals, which is then corrected by showing the visual scene again.

It is essential to measure the firing rate of a primate hippocampal cell with different head directions so that different spatial views can be compared, as testing with just one head direction (Matsumura, Nishijo, Tamura, Eifuku, Endo and Ono 1999) cannot provide evidence that will distinguish a place cell from a spatial view cell. These points will need to be borne in mind in future studies of hippocampal neuronal activity in primates including humans (Ekstrom, Kahana, Caplan, Fields, Isham, Newman and Fried 2003, Fried, MacDonald and Wilson 1997, Kreiman, Koch and Freid 2000), and simultaneous recording of head position, head direction, and eye position, as described by Rolls and colleagues (Georges-François et al. 1999, Robertson et al. 1998, Rolls et al. 1997a, Rolls et al. 1998) will be needed. To distinguish spatial view from place cells it will be important to test neurons while the primate or human is in one place with all the different spatial views visible from that place; and also to test the same neuron when the organism is in a different place, but at least some of the same spatial views are visible, as has been done in our primate recording.

A fundamental question about the function of the primate including human hippocampus is whether object as well as allocentric spatial information is represented. To investigate this, Rolls, Xiang and Franco (2005c) made recordings from single hippocampal formation neurons while macaques performed an object–place memory task which required the monkeys to learn associations between objects and where they were shown in a room. Some neurons (10%) responded differently to different objects independently of location; other neurons (13%) responded to the spatial view independently of which object was present at the location; and some neurons (12%) responded to a combination of a particular object and the place where it was shown in the room. An example of a neuron responding to a particular object–place combination is shown in Fig. 2.5. These results show that there are separate as well as combined representations of objects and their locations in space in the primate hippocampus. This is a property required in an episodic memory system, for which association between objects and the places where they are seen, is prototypical. The results thus show that requirements for a human episodic memory system, separate and combined neuronal representations of objects and where they are seen "out there" in the environment, are present in the primate hippocampus (Rolls, Xiang and Franco 2005c).

Primate hippocampal neuronal activity has also been shown to be related to the recall of memories. In a one-trial object–place recall task, images of an object in one position on a screen, and of a second object in a different position on the screen, were shown successively. Then one of the objects was shown at the top of the screen, and the monkey had to recall the position in which it had been shown earlier in the trial, and to touch that location (Rolls and Xiang 2006). In addition to neurons that responded to the objects or places, a new type of neuronal response was found in which 5% of hippocampal neurons had place-related responses when a place was being recalled by an object cue.

The primate anterior hippocampus (which corresponds to the rodent ventral hippocampus) receives inputs from brain regions involved in reward processing such as the amygdala and orbitofrontal cortex (Carmichael and Price 1995b, Suzuki and Amaral 1994a, Pitkanen et al. 2002, Stefanacci et al. 1996). To investigate how this affective input may be incorporated into primate hippocampal function, Rolls and Xiang (2005) recorded neuronal activity while macaques performed a reward-place association task in which each spatial scene shown on a video monitor had one location which if touched yielded a preferred fruit juice reward, and a second location which yielded a less preferred juice reward. Each scene had different locations for the different rewards. Of 312 hippocampal neurons analyzed, 18% responded more to the location of the preferred reward in different scenes, and 5% to the location of the less preferred reward (Rolls and Xiang 2005). An example of one of these neurons, responding to the place

Object AND Place-related activity

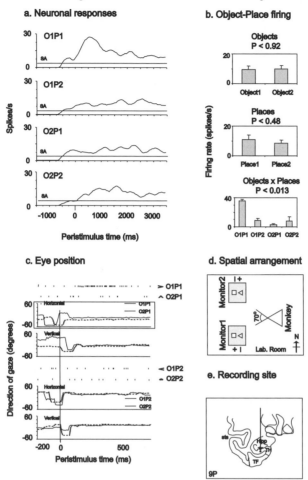

Fig. 2.5 A hippocampal neuron (BL003c8a) with firing occurring to a particular combination of an object and place (Object 1–Place 1, O1P1). (a) Peristimulus time histograms showing the response of the neuron to each object–place combination. (b) The firing rate response of the neuron on different trials sorted according to the object that was shown on the trial, the place where the object was shown, and the combination of which object was shown with the place where it was shown. In the object*position bar histograms, O1P1 = Object 1 in Place 1, etc. The mean responses ± sem are shown. (c) Trials to show the eye positions on 4 different trials. (d) Schematic diagram showing the spatial arrangement used in the Go–NoGo object–place combination task in this experiment. + indicates that a Go (lick) response to that object–place combination will be rewarded, and a minus that it will be punished. Only one object was shown on the screen at a time. The room was approximately 4 m x 4 m, and the distance of the monkey from the monitors was typically 1.5–2 m in the different experiments. The triangle labelled monkey shows the position of the monkey, and the angle shows the approximate angle subtended by the video display monitors. (e) The recording site of the neuron. Hipp, hippocampus; Prh, perirhinal cortex; rhs, rhinal sulcus; sts, superior temporal sulcus; TE, inferior temporal visual cortex. 9P = 9 mm Posterior to the sphenoid reference. (After Rolls, Xiang and Franco 2005c.)

in each scene of a preferred reward, is shown in Fig. 2.6. When the locations of the preferred rewards in the scenes were reversed, 60% of 44 neurons tested reversed the location to which they responded, showing that the reward-place associations could be altered by new learning

a. Neuronal responses to rewards at locations in 3 scenes

c. Spatial arrangement

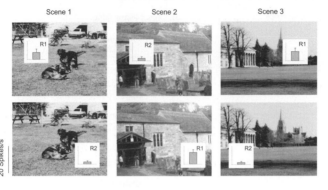

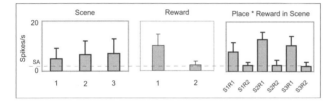

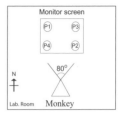

b. Place-Reward firing

d. Recording site

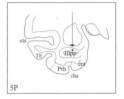

Fig. 2.6 A hippocampal neuron that encoded the particular rewards available at different locations in different scenes. On each trial the monkey could touch a circled location in the scene, and, depending on the location, received either a preferred juice reward or a less preferred juice reward. (a) Firing rate inserts to show the firing in 3 different scenes (S1–S3) of the locations associated with reward 1 (R1, preferred) and reward 2 (R2). The mean responses ± sem are shown. SA, spontaneous firing rate. (b) The firing rates sorted by scene, by reward (1 vs 2), and by scene-reward combinations (e.g. scene 1 reward 1 = S1R1). (c) The spatial arrangement on the screen of the 4 spatial locations (P1–P4). (d) The recording site of the neuron. ent, entorhinal cortex; Hipp, hippocampal pyramidal cell field CA3/CA1 and dentate gyrus; Prh, perirhinal cortex; rhs, rhinal sulcus; sts, superior temporal sulcus; TE, inferior temporal visual cortex. (After Rolls and Xiang 2005.)

in a few trials. The majority (82%) of these 44 hippocampal reward-place neurons tested did not respond to object-reward associations in a visual discrimination object-reward association task. Thus the primate hippocampus contains a representation of the reward associations of places "out there" being viewed, and this is a way in which affective information can be stored as part of an episodic memory, and how the current mood state may influence the retrieval of episodic memories (Rolls and Xiang 2005). There is consistent recent evidence that rewards available in a spatial environment can influence the responsiveness of rodent place neurons (Hölscher, Jacob and Mallot 2003a, Tabuchi, Mulder and Wiener 2003).

In another type of task for which the primate hippocampus is needed, conditional spatial response learning, in which the monkeys had to learn which spatial response to make to different stimuli, that is, to acquire associations between visual stimuli and spatial responses, 14% of hippocampal neurons responded to particular combinations of visual stimuli and spatial responses (Miyashita, Rolls, Cahusac, Niki and Feigenbaum 1989). The firing of these neurons could not be accounted for by the motor requirements of the task, nor wholly by the stimulus aspects of the task, as demonstrated by testing their firing in related visual discrimination tasks. These results showed that single hippocampal neurons respond to combinations of the visual stimuli and the spatial responses with which they must become associated in conditional response tasks, and are consistent with the computational theory described above according to which part of the mechanism of this learning involves associations between visual stimuli and spatial responses learned by single hippocampal neurons. In a following study by Cahusac, Rolls, Miyashita and Niki (1993), it was found that during such conditional spatial response learning, 22% of this type of neuron analysed in the hippocampus and parahippocampal gyrus altered their responses so that their activity, which was initially equal to the two new stimuli, became progressively differential to the two stimuli when the monkey learned to make different responses to the two stimuli (Cahusac, Rolls, Miyashita and Niki 1993). These changes occurred for different neurons just before, at, or just after the time when the monkey learned the correct response to make to the stimuli, and are consistent with the hypothesis that when new associations between objects and places (in this case the places for responses) are learned, some hippocampal neurons learn to respond to the new associations that are required to solve the task. Similar findings have been described by Wirth, Yanike, Frank, Smith, Brown and Suzuki (2003).

Another type of neuron found in the primate hippocampus responds to whole body motion (O'Mara, Rolls, Berthoz and Kesner 1994). Some of these neurons respond to linear motion, and others to axial whole body rotation (which can be produced by sitting the macaque on a moving robot). Some of these neurons respond when the visual field is obscured, and thus respond on the basis of vestibular or proprioceptive inputs. Other neurons respond to rotation of the visual environment round the macaque, and thus encode motion by visual optic flow cues. Some neurons respond to both these types of input (O'Mara, Rolls, Berthoz and Kesner 1994). The significance of these neurons is that they could be part of the way in which self-motion, i.e. idiothetic, cues are used to update the representation in the hippocampal formation of the current head direction, or the current position, and of the current spatial view, as described further below. These whole body motion neurons could also be useful in episodic memory, by encoding the movements that were taking place on a particular occasion.

Further properties of primate hippocampal neurons are reviewed by Rolls and Xiang (2006).

2.2.5   Head direction cells in the presubiculum

Head direction cells found in rats (Ranck 1985, Taube, Muller and Ranck 1990a, Taube, Goodridge, Golob, Dudchenko and Stackman 1996, Muller, Ranck and Taube 1996, Wiener and Taube 2005) and in primates (Robertson, Rolls, Georges-François and Panzeri 1999) respond maximally when the animal's head is facing in a particular preferred direction. An example of a primate head direction cell recorded in the presubiculum of the monkey is shown in Fig. 2.7. Similar cells are found in the rat pre-/post-subiculum, but also in a number of connected structures including the anterior thalamic nuclei (Taube et al. 1996, Wiener and Taube 2005). The firing rate of these cells is a function of the head direction of the monkey, with a response that is typically 10–100 times larger to the optimal as compared to the opposite head direction. The mean half-amplitude width of the tuning of the cells was 76 degrees. The response of head direction cells in the presubiculum was not influenced by the place where the monkey was, there being the same tuning to head direction at different places in a room, and even outside the room. The response of these cells was also independent of the 'spatial view' observed by the monkey, and also the position of the eyes in the head. The cells maintain their tuning for periods of at least several minutes when the view details are obscured or the room is darkened (Robertson, Rolls, Georges-François and Panzeri 1999).

This representation of head direction could be useful together with the hippocampal spatial view cells and whole body motion cells found in primates in a number of spatial and memory functions. One is path integration for head direction, the process by which in the absence of visual input one's head direction is updated based on idiothetic, that is self-motion,

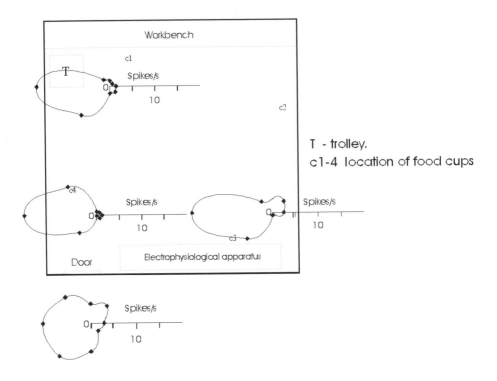

Fig. 2.7 The responses of a primate head direction cell. Polar response plots of the firing rate (in spikes/s) when the monkey was stationary at different positions (shown at the 0 on the firing rate scale) in (and one outside) the room are shown. The monkey was rotated to face in each direction. The mean response of the cell from at least 4 different firing rate measurements in each head direction in pseudorandom sequence are shown. c1–c3: cups to which the monkey could walk on all fours to obtain food. Polar firing rate response plots are superimposed on an overhead view of the square room to show where the firing for each plot was recorded. The plot at the lower left was taken outside the room, in the corridor, where the same head direction firing was maintained. (After Robertson, Rolls, Georges-Francois and Panzeri 1999.)

signals reflecting recent movements or movement 'paths'. The memory mechanism required is an integration over time of self-motion signals produced by for example vestibular inputs or motor commands. Network computational mechanisms by which this memory function may be performed are described in Section B.5.5. Another memory function for which head direction cells may be important is in episodic memory. An episodic memory might include for example the fact that one had turned right by 90 degrees in the dark, and was therefore facing towards a particular spatial view, which one could later recall. Another spatial / memory function in which head direction cells are implicated is in updating using path integration one's representation of the place where one is located. Indeed, place cells in rats may be updated in the dark through an effect of head direction cells in rotating the place map, and normally the place cell and head direction maps are kept in alignment (Leutgeb, Leutgeb, Treves, Meyer, Barnes, McNaughton, Moser and Moser 2005, Wiener and Taube 2005, Yoganarasimha, Yu and Knierim 2006).

Self-organizing continuous attractor neural networks that can perform path integration from velocity signals are described in Section B.5.5 and include head direction from head

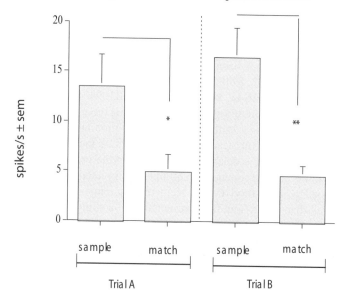

Fig. 2.8 'Resetting' of perirhinal cortex neuronal responses between trials in a short-term memory task (delayed match to sample). Neuronal responses are larger to the sample than the match presentation of a particular image within a trial, and are large to the sample on the next trial ('Trial B') even if it is the same image that has just been shown a few seconds earlier as the match image on the preceding trial. * = p<0.01 and **= p<0.005 in a Wilcoxon post-hoc test. The mean and sem of the responses across neurons are shown. (After Holscher and Rolls 2002.)

velocity (Stringer, Trappenberg, Rolls and De Araujo 2002b, Stringer and Rolls 2006); place from whole body motion (Stringer, Trappenberg, Rolls and De Araujo 2002b, Stringer, Rolls, Trappenberg and De Araujo 2002a), and spatial view from eye and whole body motion (Stringer, Rolls and Trappenberg 2004, Stringer, Rolls and Trappenberg 2005, Rolls and Stringer 2005). Path integration of head direction is reflected in the firing of neurons in the presubiculum, and mechanisms outside the hippocampus, perhaps in the dorsal tegmental nucleus (Taube, Muller and Ranck 1990b, Sharp 1996, Bassett and Taube 2005), probably implement path integration for head direction.

2.2.6 Perirhinal cortex, recognition memory, and long-term familiarity memory

The functions of the perirhinal cortex are different to those of the hippocampus, and are reviewed here partly because it provides afferents to the hippocampus via the entorhinal cortex, and partly to show that the computations performed in it are different to hippocampal computations. The location of the perirhinal cortex is shown in Fig. 2.10.

The perirhinal cortex is involved in recognition memory in that damage to the perirhinal cortex produces impairments in recognition memory tasks in which several items intervene between the sample presentation of a stimulus and its presentation again as a match stimulus (Malkova, Bachevalier, Mishkin and Saunders 2001, Zola-Morgan, Squire, Amaral and Suzuki 1989, Zola-Morgan, Squire and Ramus 1994). In macaques, damage to the perirhinal cortex rather than to the hippocampus produces deficits in recognition memory measured in a delayed match to sample task with intervening stimuli (Murray, Baxter and Gaffan 1998, Baxter and Murray 2001b, Baxter and Murray 2001a, Buckley and Gaffan 2006). Further, damage to the perirhinal cortex rather than to the hippocampus is believed to underlie the impairment in recognition memory found in amnesia in humans associated with medial temporal lobe damage (Buckley and Gaffan 2000, Buckley and Gaffan 2006).

Neurophysiologically, it has been shown that many inferior temporal cortex (area TE) neurons (Rolls and Deco 2002, Rolls 2000a), which provide visual inputs to the perirhinal cortex (Suzuki and Amaral 1994a, Suzuki and Amaral 1994b), respond more to the first, than to the second, presentation of a stimulus in a running recognition task with trial-unique stimuli (Baylis and Rolls 1987). In this running recognition task (originally developed for neurophysiology by Rolls, Perrett, Caan and Wilson (1982)), there is typically a presentation of a novel stimulus, and after a delay which may be in the order of minutes or more and in which other stimuli may be shown, the stimulus is presented again as 'familiar', and the monkey can respond to obtain food reward. Many inferior temporal cortex neurons responded more to the 'novel' than to the 'familiar' presentation of a stimulus, where 'familiar' in this task reflects a change produced by seeing the stimulus typically once (or a few times) before. (A small proportion of neurons respond more to the familiar (second) than to the novel (first) presentation of each visual stimulus.) In the inferior temporal cortex this memory spanned up to 1–2 intervening stimuli between the first (novel) and second (familiar) presentations of a given stimulus (Baylis and Rolls 1987), and when recordings are made more ventrally, towards and within the perirhinal cortex, the memory span increases to several or more intervening stimuli (Wilson, Riches and Brown 1990, Brown and Xiang 1998, Xiang and Brown 1998). The implication is that the inferior temporal visual cortex can implement a very simple form of recognition memory in which neurons respond more to the first compared to a second presentation of a stimulus with 1–2 intervening stimuli, and that the same rather simple type of recognition process can extend over more intervening stimuli as one moves towards the perirhinal cortex. The underlying mechanism could be a type of habituation or adaptation which is partly stimulus-specific because neurons in these regions can have different responses to different stimuli. For comparison, very few primate hippocampal neurons have activity related to recognition memory (Rolls, Cahusac, Feigenbaum and Miyashita 1993).

The perirhinal cortex is directly or closely connected with a number of other brain regions involved in the long-term recognition memory for visual stimuli. Relatively far forward in the orbitofrontal cortex, in area 11, neurons are activated by novel visual stimuli (Rolls, Browning, Inoue and Hernadi 2005a), and activations in humans are produced by novel visual stimuli (Frey and Petrides 2002). The responses of these neurons decrease over on average 5 presentations of a novel stimulus, and may be related to long-term memory in that the responses do not occur to a stimulus that was shown as novel 24 h earlier (Rolls, Browning, Inoue and Hernadi 2005a). Using the running recognition memory task, Rolls, Perrett, Caan and Wilson (1982) discovered a population of neurons that responded to familiar visual stimuli and were related to long-term memory at the anterior border of the thalamus, in a region that is at the border of the ventral anterior thalamic nucleus (VA) and the reticular nucleus of the thalamus (see also Wilson and Rolls (1990c)). Neurons that were also activated in a running recognition memory task by familiar stimuli and that may be related to these thalamic neurons were described by Xiang and Brown (2004) in a ventromedial prefrontal region that they termed PFCvm, and a ventrolateral prefrontal region that they termed PFCo. Wilson and Rolls (1993) showed that the activity of some neurons in the amygdala was related to stimulus novelty (with memory spans of 2–10 intervening other stimuli) and of others to familiarity in monkeys performing recognition memory tasks. Wilson and Rolls (1990c) described neuronal responses related to novel visual stimuli in the substantia innominata and diagonal band of Broca. These neurons, also activated in other memory tasks (Wilson and Rolls 1990b, Wilson and Rolls 1990a), may be the cholinergic neurons that project to the cerebral cortex and that may, by providing acetylcholine to the cerebral cortex, help in the consolidation of memories by the release of acetylcholine at the time that a memory is being formed in the neocortex. Consistent with this, cholinergic basal forebrain lesions produce severe learning impairments in learning visual scenes and in object-reward associations (Easton, Ridley, Baker and Gaffan 2002), and damage to the cholinergic basal forebrain neurons is implicated in Alzheimer's disease (Whitehouse, Price, Struble, Clarke, Coyle and Delong 1982, Bierer, Haroutunian, Gabriel, Knott, Carlin, Purohit, Perl, Schmeidler, Kanof and Davis 1995). The neurophysiological evidence of Wilson and Rolls (1990c), Wilson and Rolls (1990b) and Wilson and Rolls (1990a) indicates that these basal forebrain neurons do change their firing rate during different types of association memory and recognition tasks, and thus the phasic release of acetyl choline to the cortex at the time of memory formation may be important to consolidation, by facilitating LTP (Bear and Singer 1986).

This interconnected perirhinal cortex / orbitofrontal cortex system may thus be involved in setting up neurons that respond differently to novel and familiar stimuli and thereby implement recognition memory, and may also influence the operation of other memory systems by influences on the basal forebrain cholinergic neurons which have widespread connections to the cerebral cortex.

A second type of memory in which the perirhinal cortex is involved is the short-term memory for visual stimuli. In a task typically performed with non-trial-unique stimuli, a delayed matching-to-sample task with up to several intervening stimuli, some perirhinal cortex neurons respond more to the match stimulus than to the sample stimulus (Miller, Li and Desimone 1993b). Many other neurons in this task respond more to the sample ('novel') than to the match ('familiar') presentations of the stimuli. There is active engagement of the perirhinal cortex in this delayed matching-to-sample task, in that the response of these neurons is always larger to the sample than to the match stimulus, even if the stimulus shown as the sample has been seen just seconds ago on a previous trial (Hölscher and Rolls 2002), as shown in Fig. 2.8. Thus this short-term memory in the perirhinal cortex is actively reset at the start of the next trial (Hölscher and Rolls 2002).

A third type of memory in which the perirhinal cortex is implicated is paired associate learning (a model of semantic long-term memory), which is represented by a population of neurons in a restricted part of area 36 where the neuronal responses may occur to both members of a pair of pictures used in the paired association task (Miyashita, Kameyama, Hasegawa and Fukushima 1998, Miyashita, Okuno, Tokuyama, Ihara and Nakajima 1996). Another very plausible function for these associations across time is not semantic memory but instead view invariant learning, which can be helped by associations across time, as described in Chapter 4, and which may be impaired by perirhinal cortex lesions (Buckley, Booth, Rolls and Gaffan 2001).

Evidence that the perirhinal cortex is involved in a fourth type of memory, long-term familiarity memory, comes from a neuronal recording study in which it was shown that perirhinal cortex neuronal responses in the rhesus macaque gradually increase in magnitude to a set of stimuli as that set is repeated for 400 presentations each 1.3 s long (Hölscher, Rolls and Xiang 2003b). The single neurons were recorded in the perirhinal cortex in monkeys performing a delayed matching-to-sample task with up to 3 intervening stimuli, using a set of very familiar visual stimuli used for several weeks. When a novel set of stimuli was introduced, the neuronal responses were on average only 47% of the magnitude of the responses to the familiar set of stimuli. It was shown in eight different replications in three monkeys that the responses of the perirhinal cortex neurons gradually increased over hundreds of presentations of the new set of (initially novel) stimuli to become as large as to the already familiar stimuli. Examples of three replications are shown in Fig. 2.9, and the recording sites were in the

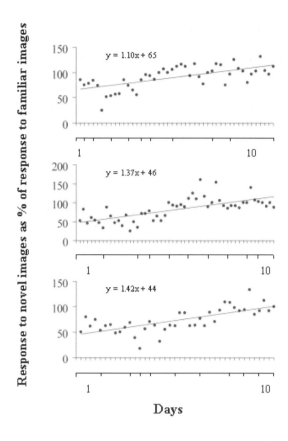

Fig. 2.9 Perirhinal cortex neurons reflect the long-term familiarity of visual stimuli. The average response of each neuron (shown by a full circle) to a set of 15 novel stimuli introduced on day 1 is shown as a proportion of the neuron's response to a very familiar set of stimuli. In each experiment on a neuron, each visual stimulus was shown for approximately 13 1-s periods. Several neurons were analyzed on some days. Thus in the order of 500 exposures to each stimulus in the novel set were required before the response to the initially novel set of stimuli was as large as to the already very familiar set of stimuli. Each stimulus was an image of an object presented on a video monitor. The 3 separate graphs are for 3 separate replications of the whole experiment. (After Hölscher and Rolls 2001, and Hölscher, Rolls and Xiang 2003b.)

perirhinal cortex as indicated in Fig. 2.10 (see Hölscher, Rolls and Xiang (2003b)). The mean number of 1.3 s presentations to induce this effect was 400 occurring over 7–13 days. These results show that perirhinal cortex neurons represent the very long-term familiarity of visual stimuli (Hölscher, Rolls and Xiang 2003b). A representation of the long-term familiarity of visual stimuli may be important for many aspects of social and other behaviour, and part of the impairment in temporal lobe amnesia may be related to the difficulty of building representations of the degree of familiarity of stimuli. It has been shown that long-term familiarity memory can be modelled by neurons with synapses with a small amount of long-term potentiation which occurs at every presentation of a given stimulus, but which also incorporate hetero-synaptic long-term depression to make the learning self-limiting (Rolls, Franco and Stringer 2005b).

A fifth type of memory in which the perirhinal cortex is implicated is in tasks in which the stimuli to be discriminated are made up of a small number of features that are combined in

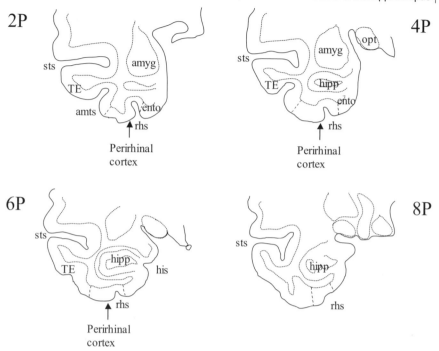

Fig. 2.10 The locations of the perirhinal cortex (areas 35 and 36 in and near the banks of the rhinal sulcus), the entorhinal cortex, and the hippocampus in macaques. The coronal (transverse) sections are at different distances behind (P, posterior to) an anatomical marker, the sphenoid bone, which is approximately at the anterior–posterior position of the optic chiasm and anterior commissure. amts, anterior middle temporal sulcus; amyg, amygdala; ento, entorhinal cortex; hipp, hippocampus; his, hippocampal sulcus; opt, optic tract; rhs, rhinal sulcus; sts, superior temporal sulcus; TE, inferior temporal visual cortex.

different combinations. The features in each stimulus are thus highly overlapping, and the task requires setting up different representations of the different but highly overlapping feature conjunctions in a low-dimensional feature space. This is very different to object representations as they typically occur in the world, in which each object is a particular combination of features from a very high-dimensional feature space, so that the representations of different objects in general have much less overlap in feature space, and the inferior temporal visual cortex can form object representations by forming neurons that respond to different combinations of features from a high-dimensional feature space. In any case, it is argued that perirhinal cortex lesions impair the discrimination between stimuli according to how ambiguous they are in terms of their degree of overlap of a few features (Bussey and Saksida 2005, Buckley and Gaffan 2006, Bussey, Saksida and Murray 2002, Bussey, Saksida and Murray 2003, Bussey, Saksida and Murray 2005). (However, a more mnemonic than perceptual case is made by Hampton (2005) based on the evidence for delay-dependent deficits produced by perirhinal cortex lesions in recognition memory tasks, and reversal-learning impairments which reflect a more associative than perceptual role for the perirhinal cortex.) In the extreme case, such a stimulus set might require A+, B+, but AB- (where A+ means that A is rewarded), which requires a non-linear discrimination. One way to solve such memory problems is to add a further layer to an existing object representation network, where further combinations of what is represented at earlier layers can be formed. This is equivalent to adding a fifth layer to the VisNet architecture described in Chapter 4, and adding such an additional layer, which

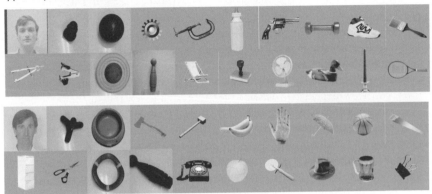

Fig. 2.11 Some examples of the objects and faces encoded by anterior inferior temporal cortex neurons (see text, and further examples in Fig. C.7).

might correspond to adding a perirhinal cortex layer to an inferior temporal cortex layer, does, as expected, help a network to solve the class of problem where the stimuli consist of different highly overlapping combinations of a small number of features (Cowell, Bussey and Saksida 2006).

It then becomes a somewhat semantic issue about whether one considers that the perirhinal cortex is involved in object perception as well as in memory (Bussey and Saksida 2005, Buckley and Gaffan 2006). My own view is that the perirhinal cortex can be thought of as involved in the memory for and discrimination between stimuli when the stimuli are composed of a small number of features with different combinations of features for different stimuli, so that in this way, and perhaps in other ways, the stimuli, which could be objects, are ambiguous. The perirhinal cortex may thus contribute in these special cases. These special cases should be distinguished from object perception that occurs with normal objects in the world, in which each object is composed of a combination of features drawn from a high-dimensional feature space. Object representation in this sense is implemented in the anterior inferior temporal visual cortex, as shown by evidence described in Chapter 4 and Appendix C. The evidence includes the findings that the object that has been presented on a single trial can be read off (decoded) from the firing of anterior inferior temporal cortex neurons with position, size, view, spatial frequency, and lighting invariance. Each neuron is tuned to a subset of the objects with a firing rate probability distribution that is frequently close to exponential, indicating that each neuron has high responses to a few objects, to which it is 'tuned', with smaller responses to a few objects, and very little response to most objects. Moreover, the coding for objects is very efficient, in that the response profiles of different neurons to a set of objects are uncorrelated, and this contributes to the information provided by different neurons being independent, so that the number of objects encoded by a population of neurons increases exponentially with the number neurons. These properties are found for objects drawn from the real world, including fruits, bottles, and a multitude of small toys, with some examples illustrated in Figs. 2.11, C.7, 4.4, 4.62, C.24, 4.67, and elsewhere (Booth and Rolls 1998, Rolls and Tovee 1995b). (The objects are shown as greyscale images so that colour can not be used as a defining feature.) These properties are also found for faces, which are certainly not just 'features', but are complex combinations of features where the features must be presented in the correct spatial arrangement for many of the neurons to respond, and where even the spacing of the features is important (Perrett, Rolls and Caan 1982, Rolls, Tovee, Purcell, Stewart and Azzopardi 1994b). The variety of the tuning of anterior inferior temporal cortex neurons is enormously wide, as befits a system that is involved in object representation, with some neurons responding to quite simple features such as low spatial frequency gratings, or the texture of the material from which objects are made, through to more complex features such as eyes or nose or mouth, through to neurons that only respond to combinations of these if they are in the correct spatial arrangement, through to neurons with view-dependent responses, and through to neurons with view-independent responses that can be finely tuned to objects or faces (Perrett, Rolls and Caan 1982, Rolls, Tovee, Purcell, Stewart and Azzopardi 1994b, Tanaka 1996, Booth and Rolls 1998, Franco, Rolls, Aggelopoulos and Jerez 2007, Rolls and Deco 2002), with many further sources cited in Chapter 4 and Appendix C. Neurons responding to one or several features are more likely to be found in the posterior inferior temporal cortex (Tanaka 1996) (see Fig. 1.9), whereas neurons responding to objects or faces and often requiring a complex combination of features to be present are found in the anterior inferior temporal cortex (see Fig. 1.9) in which we have recorded (Baylis, Rolls and Leonard 1987, Rolls, Tovee, Purcell, Stewart and Azzopardi 1994b, Booth and Rolls 1998, Rolls and Tovee 1995b, Rolls 2007i, Franco, Rolls, Aggelopoulos and Jerez 2007, Rolls 2007f). The anterior inferior temporal cortex neurons even maintain their object selectivity when the objects are presented in complex natural backgrounds (Rolls, Aggelopoulos and Zheng 2003a, Aggelopoulos, Franco and Rolls 2005) or are surrounded by other objects (Aggelopoulos and Rolls 2005). With this range of the type of tuning of inferior temporal cortex neurons, it is sometimes possible to reduce the feature set within an object and obtain a response, while in other cases most of the components need to be present, and in the correct spatial configuration with respect to each other, before the object-encoding or face-encoding neuron will respond (Perrett, Rolls and Caan 1982, Rolls, Tovee, Purcell, Stewart and Azzopardi 1994b, Tanaka 1996).

The perirhinal cortex, by receiving from the inferior temporal visual cortex, and perhaps by performing further conjunction learning to that already implemented by the anterior inferior temporal visual cortex (see Chapter 4), thus has visual representations of objects, and some at least of the perirhinal cortex neurons have view-invariant representations. Another factor that distinguishes the perirhinal cortex is that the perirhinal cortex receives forward inputs from other modalities, including auditory, olfactory and somatosensory (Suzuki and Amaral 1994a, Suzuki and Amaral 1994b). This may enable the perirhinal cortex by combining these multimodal inputs to build representations that reflect the convergence of more than visual inputs. The perirhinal cortex, via its projections to the lateral entorhinal cortex and via the lateral perforant path, could thus introduce object information into the hippocampus for object–place associations. The parahippocampal gyrus, in which cells with spatial information are present in macaques (Rolls, Xiang and Franco 2005c, Rolls and Xiang 2006), could via connections to the medial entorhinal cortex introduce spatial information into the hippocampus, and there is evidence consistent with this in rodents (Hargreaves, Rao, Lee and Knierim 2005). In contrast to the perirhinal cortex, the final convergence afforded by the hippocampus into one network in CA3 (see Fig. 2.1) may enable the hippocampus proper to implement an event or episodic memory typically involving arbitrary associations between any of the inputs to the hippocampus, e.g. spatial, visual object, olfactory, and auditory (see below).

2.3   A theory of the operation of hippocampal circuitry as a memory system

Given the systems-level hypothesis about what the hippocampus performs, and the neurophysiological evidence about what is represented in the primate hippocampus, the next step is to consider how using its internal connectivity and synaptic modifiability the hippocampus could store and retrieve many memories, and how retrieval within the hippocampus could lead to retrieval of the activity in the neocortex that was present during the original learning of the episode. To develop understanding of how this is achieved, we have developed a computational theory of the operation of the hippocampus (Rolls 1989a, Rolls 1989b, Rolls 1989e, Rolls 1989f, Rolls 1987, Treves and Rolls 1994, Rolls 1990b, Rolls 1990c, Treves and Rolls 1991, Treves and Rolls 1992, Rolls 1996c, Rolls and Treves 1998, Rolls, Stringer and Trappenberg 2002, Stringer, Rolls and Trappenberg 2005, Rolls and Stringer 2005, Rolls and Kesner 2006, Rolls, Stringer and Elliot 2006c). This theory, and new developments of it, are outlined next.

2.3.1 Hippocampal circuitry

Fig. 2.1 shows a diagram of hippocampal circuitry that is described next, with useful additional sources including Amaral, Ishizuka and Claiborne (1990), Storm-Mathiesen, Zimmer and Ottersen (1990), Amaral and Witter (1989), Amaral (1993), Naber, Lopes da Silva and Witter (2001), Lavenex, Suzuki and Amaral (2004), Witter et al. (2000b) and Johnston and Amaral (2004).

Projections from the entorhinal cortex layer 2 reach the granule cells (of which there are 10^6 in the rat) in the dentate gyrus (DG), via the perforant path (pp) (Witter 1993). In the dentate gyrus there is a set inhibitory interneurons that provide recurrent inhibition between the granule cells. (In addition, there are some excitatory interneurons in the hilus that interconnect granule cells.) The granule cells project to CA3 cells via the mossy fibres (mf), which provide a sparse but possibly powerful connection to the 3×10^5 CA3 pyramidal cells in the rat. Each CA3 cell receives approximately 50 mossy fibre inputs, so that the sparseness of this connectivity is thus 0.005%. By contrast, there are many more – probably weaker – direct perforant path inputs also from layer 2 of the entorhinal cortex onto each CA3 cell, in the rat in the order of 4×10^3. The largest number of synapses (about 1.2×10^4 in the rat) on the dendrites of CA3 pyramidal cells is, however, provided by the (recurrent) axon collaterals of CA3 cells themselves (rc) (see Fig. 2.14). It is remarkable that the recurrent collaterals are distributed to other CA3 cells throughout the hippocampus (Amaral and Witter 1989, Amaral and Witter 1995, Amaral, Ishizuka and Claiborne 1990, Ishizuka, Weber and Amaral 1990), so that effectively the CA3 system provides a single network, with a connectivity of approximately 2% between the different CA3 neurons given that the connections are bilateral. The neurons that comprise CA3, in turn, project to CA1 neurons via the Schaffer collaterals. In addition, projections that terminate in the CA1 region originate in layer 3 of the entorhinal cortex (see Fig. 2.1).

2.3.2 CA3 as an autoassociation memory

2.3.2.1 Arbitrary associations, and pattern completion in recall

Many of the synapses in the hippocampus show associative modification as shown by long-term potentiation, and this synaptic modification appears to be involved in learning (Lynch 2004, Morris 2003, Morris 1989, Morris, Moser, Riedel, Martin, Sandin, Day and O'Carroll 2003). On the basis of the evidence summarized above, Rolls has proposed that the CA3 stage acts as an autoassociation memory which enables episodic memories to be formed and stored in the CA3 network, and that subsequently the extensive recurrent collateral connectivity allows for the retrieval of a whole representation to be initiated by the activation of some small part of the same representation (the cue) (Rolls 1987, Rolls 1989a, Rolls 1989b, Rolls 1989f, Rolls 1990b, Rolls 1990c). The crucial synaptic modification for this is in the recurrent collateral synapses. (A description of the operation of autoassociative networks is provided in Section B.3 and by Hertz, Krogh and Palmer (1991), Rolls and Treves (1998), and Rolls and Deco

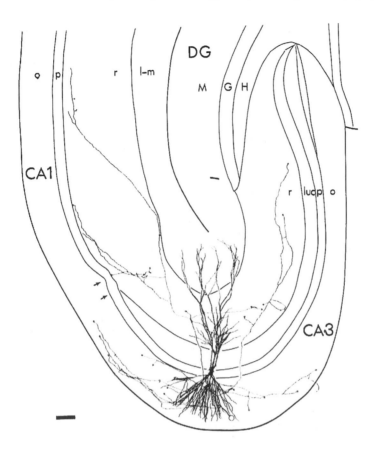

Fig. 2.12 An example of a CA3 neuron from the hippocampus. The thick extensions from the cell body or soma are the dendrites, which form an extensive dendritic tree receiving in this case approximately 12,000 synapses. The axon is the thin connection leaving the cell. It divides into a number of collateral branches. Two axonal branches can be seen in the plane of the section to travel to each end of the population of CA3 cells. One branch (on the left) continues to connect to the next group of cells, the CA1 cells. The junction between the CA3 and CA1 cells is shown by the two arrows. The diagram shows a camera lucida drawing of a single CA3 pyramidal cell intracellularly labelled with horseradish peroxidase. DG, dentate gyrus. The small letters refer to the different strata of the hippocampus. (Reprinted with permission from Ishizuka, Weber and Amaral 1990.)

(2002). The architecture of an autoassociation network is shown in Fig. 2.15.) The hypothesis is that because the CA3 operates effectively as a single network, it can allow arbitrary associations between inputs originating from very different parts of the cerebral cortex to be formed. These might involve associations between information originating in the temporal visual cortex about the presence of an object, and information originating in the parietal cortex about where it is. We have therefore performed quantitative analyses of the storage and retrieval processes in the CA3 network (Treves and Rolls 1991, Treves and Rolls 1992). We have extended previous formal models of autoassociative memory (Amit 1989) by analyzing a network with graded response units, so as to represent more realistically the continuously variable rates at which neurons fire, and with incomplete connectivity (Treves 1990, Treves and Rolls 1991). We have found that in general the maximum number p_{max} of firing patterns that can be (individually) retrieved is proportional to the number C^{RC} of (associatively)

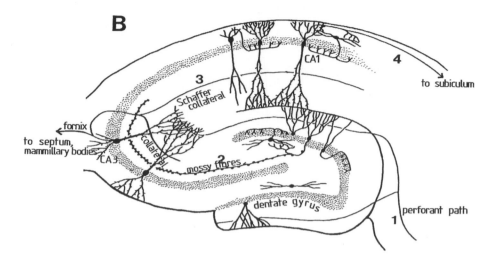

Fig. 2.13 Representation of connections within the hippocampus. Inputs reach the hippocampus through the perforant path (1) which makes synapses with the dendrites of the dentate granule cells and also with the apical dendrites of the CA3 pyramidal cells. The dentate granule cells project via the mossy fibres (2) to the CA3 pyramidal cells. The well-developed recurrent collateral system of the CA3 cells is indicated. The CA3 pyramidal cells project via the Schaffer collaterals (3) to the CA1 pyramidal cells, which in turn have connections (4) to the subiculum.

modifiable recurrent collateral synapses per cell, by a factor that increases roughly with the inverse of the population sparseness a^p of the neuronal representation. The sparseness a^p of the representation can be measured, by extending the binary notion of the proportion of neurons that are firing, as

$$a^\mathrm{p} = \frac{(\sum\limits_{i=1}^{N} y_i/N)^2}{\sum\limits_{i=1}^{N} y_i^2/N} \tag{2.1}$$

where y_i is the firing rate of the ith neuron in the set of N neurons (Treves and Rolls 1991, Rolls and Treves 1998, Rolls and Deco 2002, Franco, Rolls, Aggelopoulos and Jerez 2007). More precisely, Treves and Rolls (1991) and Rolls, Treves, Foster and Perez-Vicente (1997c) have shown that such a network with graded patterns does operate efficiently as an autoassociative network, and can store (and recall correctly) a number of different patterns p as follows

$$p \approx \frac{C^\mathrm{RC}}{a^\mathrm{p} \ln(\frac{1}{a^\mathrm{p}})} k \tag{2.2}$$

where C^RC is the number of synapses on the dendrites of each neuron devoted to the recurrent collaterals from other neurons in the network, and k is a factor that depends weakly on the detailed structure of the rate distribution, on the connectivity pattern, etc., but is roughly in the order of 0.2–0.3. For example, for $C^\mathrm{RC} = 12,000$ and $a^\mathrm{p} = 0.02$ (realistic estimates for the rat), p_max is calculated to be approximately 36,000. This analysis emphasizes the utility of having a sparse representation in the hippocampus, for this enables many different memories to be stored. Third, in order for most associative networks to store information efficiently, heterosynaptic long term depression (as well as LTP) is required (Fazeli and Collingridge

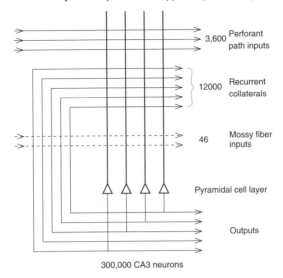

Fig. 2.14 The numbers of connections onto each CA3 cell from three different sources in the rat. (After Treves and Rolls 1992, and Rolls and Treves 1998.)

1996, Rolls and Treves 1990, Treves and Rolls 1991) (see Section B.3). Simulations that are fully consistent with the analytic theory are provided by Simmen, Treves and Rolls (1996b) and Rolls, Treves, Foster and Perez-Vicente (1997c).

We have also indicated how to estimate I, the total amount of information (in bits per synapse) that can be retrieved from the network. I is defined with respect to the information i_p (in bits per cell) contained in each stored firing pattern, by subtracting the amount i_l lost in retrieval and multiplying by p/C^{RC}:

$$I \approx \frac{p}{C^{RC}}(i_p - i_l) \tag{2.3}$$

The maximal value I_{max} of this quantity was found (Treves and Rolls 1991) to be in several interesting cases around 0.2–0.3 bits per synapse, with only a mild dependency on parameters such as the sparseness of coding a^p.

We may then estimate (Treves and Rolls 1992) how much information has to be stored in each pattern for the network to efficiently exploit its information retrieval capacity I_{max}. The estimate is expressed as a requirement on i_p:

$$i_p > a^p \ln\left(\frac{1}{a^p}\right) \tag{2.4}$$

As the information content i_p of each stored pattern depends on the storage process, we see how the retrieval capacity analysis, coupled with the notion that the system is organized so as to be an efficient memory device in a quantitative sense, leads to a constraint on the storage process.

A fundamental property of the autoassociation model of the CA3 recurrent collateral network is that the recall can be symmetric, that is, the whole of the memory can be retrieved from any part. For example, in an object–place autoassociation memory, an object could be recalled from a place retrieval cue, and vice versa. This is not the case with a pattern association network. If for example the CA3 activity represented a place / spatial view, and perforant path inputs with associative synapses to CA3 neurons carried object information

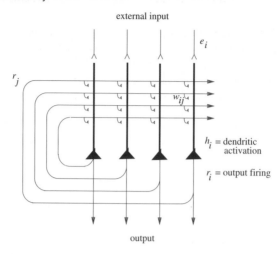

external input

e_i

r_j

w_{ij}

h_i = dendritic activation

r_i = output firing

output

Fig. 2.15 The architecture of an attractor or autoassociation neural network. The architecture of a discrete attractor neural network used for storing discrete patterns is the same as that of a continuous attractor neural network (CANN) used for storing continuous, e.g. spatial, patterns (see further Sections B.3 and B.5).

(consistent with evidence that the lateral perforant path (LPP) may reflect inputs from the perirhinal cortex connecting via the lateral entorhinal cortex (Hargreaves et al. 2005)), then an object could recall a place, but a place could not recall an object.

Another fundamental property is that the recall can be complete even from a small fragment. Thus, it is a prediction that when an incomplete retrieval cue is given, CA3 may be especially important in the retrieval process. Tests of this prediction are described in Section 2.4.

Another fundamental property of the autoassociation model of the CA3 recurrent collateral network is that it can implement a short-term memory by maintaining the firing of neurons using the excitatory recurrent collateral connections. A stable attractor can maintain one memory active in this way for a considerable period, until a new input pushes the attractor to represent a new location or memory (see Section B.3). For example, if one place were being held in a CA3 place short-term memory, then if the rat moved to a new place, the CA3 representation would move to represent the new place, and the short-term memory held in the CA3 network would be lost. It is thus predicted that when the hippocampus is used as a short-term memory with ongoing neuronal activity used to represent the short-term memory, then maintenance of the memory will be very dependent on what happens in the delay period. If the animal is relatively isolated from its environment and does not move around in a well-defined spatial environment (as can be achieved by placing a vertical cylinder / bucket around a rat in the delay period), then the memory may be maintained for a considerable period in the CA3 (and even updated by idiothetic, self-motion, inputs as described below). However, the CA3 short-term memory will be very sensitive to disruption / interference, so that if the rat is allowed to move in the spatial environment during the delay period, then it is predicted that CA3 will not be able to maintain correctly the spatial short-term memory. In the circumstances where a representation must be kept active while the hippocampus (or inferior temporal visual cortex or parietal cortex) must be updating its representation to reflect the new changing perceptual inputs, which must be represented in these brain areas for the ongoing events to have high-level representations, the prefrontal cortex is thought computationally to provide an off-line buffer store, see Section 5.1 and pp 406–412 of Rolls and Deco (2002). The predictions are thus that if there is no task in a delay period (and no need for an off-line buffer store), the hippocampus may be sufficient to perform the short-term memory function (such as remembering a previous location), provided that there is little distraction in the delay period. On the other hand, short-term memory deficits are predicted to be produced by prefrontal cortex lesions if there are intervening stimuli in the delay period.

I note that although there is some spatial gradient in the CA3 recurrent connections, so that the connectivity is not fully uniform (Ishizuka et al. 1990), nevertheless the network will still have the properties of a single interconnected autoassociation network allowing associations between arbitrary neurons to be formed, given the presence of many long-range connections which overlap from different CA3 cells.

A number of points deserve comment. First, if it is stated that a certain number of memories is the upper limit of what could be stored in a given network, then the question is sometimes asked, what constitutes a memory? The answer is precise. Any one memory is represented by the firing rates of the population of neurons that are stored by the associative synaptic modification, and can be correctly recalled later. The firing rates in the primate hippocampus might be constant for a period of for example 1 s in which the monkey was looking at an object in one position in space; synaptic modification would occur in this time period (cf. the time course of LTP, which is sufficiently rapid for this); and the memory of the event would have been stored. The quantitative analysis shows how many such random patterns of rates of the neuronal population can be stored and later recalled correctly. If the rates were constant for 5 s while the rat was at one place or monkey was looking at an object at one position in space, then the memory would be for the pattern of firing of the neurons in this 5-s period. (The pattern of firing of the population refers to the rate at which each neuron in the population of CA3 neurons is firing.)

Second, the question sometimes arises of whether the CA3 neurons operate as an attractor network. An attractor network is one in which a stable pattern of firing is maintained once it has been started. Autoassociation networks trained with modified Hebb rules can store the number of different memories, each one expressed as a stable attractor, indicated in Equation B.15. However, the hippocampal CA3 cells do not necessarily have to operate as a stable attractor: instead, it would be sufficient for the present theory if they can retrieve stored information in response to a partial cue initiating retrieval. The partial cue would remain on during recall, so that the attractor network would be operating in the clamped condition (Rolls and Treves 1998) (see Section B.3). The completion of the partial pattern would then provide more information than entered the hippocampus, and the extra information retrieved would help the next stage to operate. Demonstrations of this by simulations that are fully consistent with the analytic theory are provided by Rolls (1995c), Simmen, Treves and Rolls (1996b), and Rolls, Treves, Foster and Perez-Vicente (1997c).

Third, in order for most associative networks to store information efficiently, hetero-synaptic long term depression (as well as LTP) is required (Rolls and Treves 1990, Treves and Rolls 1991, Rolls 1996b). Without heterosynaptic LTD, there would otherwise always be a correlation between any set of positively firing inputs acting as the input pattern vector to a neuron. LTD effectively enables the average firing of each input axon to be subtracted from its input at any one time, reducing the average correlation between different pattern vectors to be stored to a low value (Rolls 1996b) (see Section B.3).

Given that the memory capacity of the hippocampal CA3 system is limited, it is necessary to have some form of forgetting in this store, or another mechanism, to ensure that its capacity is not exceeded. (Exceeding the capacity can lead to a loss of much of the information retrievable from the network.) Heterosynaptic LTD could help this forgetting, by enabling new memories to overwrite old memories (Rolls 1996b) (see Section B.16). The limited capacity of the CA3 system does also provide one of the arguments that some transfer of information from the hippocampus to neocortical memory stores may be useful (see Treves and Rolls (1994)). Given its limited capacity, the hippocampus might be a useful store for only a limited period, which might be in the order of days, weeks, or months. This period may well depend on the acquisition rate of new episodic memories. If the animal were in a constant and limited environment, then as new information is not being added to the hippocampus, the representations in the hippocampus would remain stable and persistent. These hypotheses have clear experimental implications, both for recordings from single neurons and for the gradient of retrograde amnesia, both of which might be expected to depend on whether the environment is stable or frequently changing. They show that the conditions under which a gradient of retrograde amnesia might be demonstrable would be when large numbers of new memories are being acquired, not when only a few memories (few in the case of the hippocampus being less than a few hundred) are being learned.

The potential link to the gradient of retrograde amnesia is that the retrograde memories lost in amnesia are those not yet consolidated in longer term storage (in the neocortex). As they are still held in the hippocampus, their number has to be less than the storage capacity of the (presumed) CA3 autoassociative memory. Therefore the time gradient of the amnesia provides not only a measure of a characteristic time for consolidation, but also an upper bound on the rate of storage of new memories in CA3. For example, if one were to take as a measure of the time gradient in the monkey, say, 5 weeks (about 50,000 min) (Squire 1992) and as a reasonable estimate of the capacity of CA3 in the monkey e.g $p = 50,000$, then one would conclude that there is an upper bound on the rate of storage in CA3 of not more than one new memory per minute, on average. (This might be an average over many weeks; the fastest rate might be closer to 1 per s, see Treves and Rolls (1994).) These quantitative considerations are consistent with the concept described in Section 2.2.3 that retrieval of episodic memories from the hippocampus for a considerable time after they have been stored would be useful in helping the neocortex to build a semantic memory (Rolls 1990b, Rolls 1989f, Rolls 1989b, Rolls 1990b, Treves and Rolls 1994, Moscovitch et al. 2005, McClelland et al. 1995).

2.3.2.2 Continuous, spatial, patterns and CA3 representations

The fact that spatial patterns, which imply continuous representations of space, are represented in the hippocampus has led to the application of continuous attractor models to help understand hippocampal function. Such models have been developed by Samsonovich and McNaughton (1997), Battaglia and Treves (1998b), Rolls, Stringer and Trappenberg (2002), Stringer, Trappenberg, Rolls and De Araujo (2002b), Stringer, Rolls, Trappenberg and De Araujo (2002a), Stringer and Rolls (2002), Stringer, Rolls and Trappenberg (2004), Stringer, Rolls and Trappenberg (2005), and Stringer and Rolls (2006) (see Section B.5).

A class of network that can maintain the firing of its neurons to represent any location along a continuous physical dimension such as spatial position, head direction, etc. is a 'continuous attractor' neural network (CANN). It uses excitatory recurrent collateral connections between the neurons (as are present in CA3) to reflect the distance between the neurons in the state space of the animal (e.g. place or head direction). These networks can maintain the bubble of neural activity constant for long periods wherever it is started to represent the current state (head direction, position, etc) of the animal, and are likely to be involved in many aspects of spatial processing and memory, including spatial vision. Global inhibition is used to keep the number of neurons in a bubble or packet of actively firing neurons relatively constant, and to help to ensure that there is only one activity packet. Continuous attractor networks can be thought of as very similar to autoassociation or discrete attractor networks (see Rolls and Deco (2002)), and have the same architecture, as illustrated in Fig. 2.15. The main difference is that the patterns stored in a CANN are continuous patterns, with each

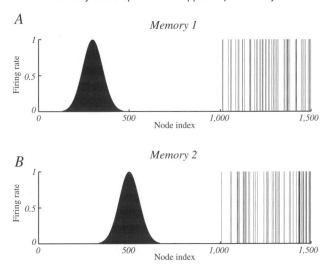

Fig. 2.16 The types of firing patterns stored in continuous attractor networks are illustrated for the patterns present on neurons 1–1,000 for Memory 1 (when the firing is that produced when the spatial state represented is that for location 300), and for Memory 2 (when the firing is that produced when the spatial state represented is that for location 500). The continuous nature of the spatial representation results from the fact that each neuron has a Gaussian firing rate that peaks at its optimal location. This particular mixed network also contains discrete representations that consist of discrete subsets of active binary firing rate neurons in the range 1,001–1,500. The firing of these latter neurons can be thought of as representing the discrete events that occur at the location. Continuous attractor networks by definition contain only continuous representations, but this particular network can store mixed continuous and discrete representations, and is illustrated to show the difference of the firing patterns normally stored in separate continuous attractor and discrete attractor networks. For this particular mixed network, during learning, Memory 1 is stored in the synaptic weights, then Memory 2, etc, and each memory contains a part that is continuously distributed to represent physical space, and a part that represents a discrete event or object.

neuron having broadly tuned firing which decreases with for example a Gaussian function as the distance from the optimal firing location of the cell is varied, and with different neurons having tuning that overlaps throughout the space. Such tuning is illustrated in Fig. 2.16. For comparison, autoassociation networks normally have discrete (separate) patterns (each pattern implemented by the firing of a particular subset of the neurons), with no continuous distribution of the patterns throughout the space (see Fig. 2.16). A consequent difference is that the CANN can maintain its firing at any location in the trained continuous space, whereas a discrete attractor or autoassociation network moves its population of active neurons towards one of the previously learned attractor states, and thus implements the recall of a particular previously learned pattern from an incomplete or noisy (distorted) version of one of the previously learned patterns. The energy landscape of a discrete attractor network (see Section B.3, Hopfield (1982) and Rolls and Deco (2002)) has separate energy minima, each one of which corresponds to a learned pattern, whereas the energy landscape of a continuous attractor network is flat, so that the activity packet remains stable with continuous firing wherever it is started in the state space. (The state space refers to the set of possible spatial states of the animal in its environment, e.g. the set of possible places in a room.) Continuous attractor networks and their application to memory systems in the hippocampus are reviewed next with details in Section B.5, as they are very likely to apply to the operation of systems with spatial representations and recurrent connections, such as the CA3 neurons. Continuous attractor networks have been studied by for example Amari (1977), Zhang (1996), Taylor (1999), and Stringer, Trappenberg, Rolls and De Araujo (2002b).

One key issue in such continuous attractor neural networks is how the synaptic strengths between the neurons in the continuous attractor network could be learned in biological systems, and it has been shown that associative synaptic modification while navigating the environment can implement this, because the spatial representations of nearby locations overlap and therefore become associatively linked (see Section B.5.3 and Stringer, Trappenberg, Rolls and De Araujo (2002b)).

A second key issue in such continuous attractor neural networks is how the bubble of neuronal firing representing one location in the continuous state space should be updated based on non-visual cues to represent a new location in state space (Section B.5.5). This is essentially the problem of path integration: how a system that represents a memory of where the agent is in physical space could be updated based on idiothetic (self-motion) cues such as vestibular cues (which might represent a head velocity signal), or proprioceptive cues (which might update a representation of place based on movements being made in the space, during for example walking in the dark). Examples of classes of neurons that can be updated idiothetically include head direction cells in rats (Muller et al. 1996, Ranck 1985, Taube et al. 1996, Taube et al. 1990a, Bassett and Taube 2005) and primates (Robertson, Rolls, Georges-François and Panzeri 1999), which respond maximally when the animal's head is facing in a preferred direction and can be updated by head rotation in the dark; place cells in rats (O'Keefe 1984, Markus, Qin, Leonard, Skaggs, McNaughton and Barnes 1995, O'Keefe and Dostrovsky 1971, McNaughton et al. 1983, Muller et al. 1991, Jeffery and Hayman 2004, Jeffery et al. 2004) that fire maximally when the animal is in a particular location and can be updated by running in a particular direction in the dark; and spatial view cells in primates that respond when the monkey is looking towards a particular location in space (Georges-François, Rolls and Robertson 1999, Robertson, Rolls and Georges-François 1998, Rolls, Robertson and Georges-François 1997a, Rolls, Treves, Robertson, Georges-François and Panzeri 1998) and can be updated by eye movements in the dark (Robertson, Rolls and Georges-François 1998).

Path integration is described in Section B.5.5, using as an example the update of a head direction representation by a head velocity signal. For example, a proposal about how the synaptic connections from idiothetic inputs to a continuous attractor network can be learned with some biological plausibility, in that the network can be trained by a self-organizing process, was introduced by Stringer, Trappenberg, Rolls and De Araujo (2002b). The mechanism associates a short-term memory trace of the firing of the neurons in the attractor network reflecting recent movements in the state space (e.g. of places), with an idiothetic velocity of movement input (see Fig. B.27). This has been applied to head direction cells (Stringer, Trappenberg, Rolls and De Araujo 2002b, Stringer and Rolls 2006), rat place cells (Stringer, Trappenberg, Rolls and De Araujo 2002b, Stringer, Rolls, Trappenberg and De Araujo 2002a), and primate spatial view cells (Stringer, Rolls and Trappenberg 2004, Stringer, Rolls and Trappenberg 2005, Rolls and Stringer 2005). These attractor networks provide a basis for understanding cognitive maps, and how they are updated by learning and by self-motion. The implication is that to the extent that path integration of place or spatial view representations is performed within the hippocampus itself, then the CA3 system is the most likely part of the hippocampus to be involved in this, because it has the appropriate recurrent collateral connections. Consistent with this, Whishaw and colleagues (Wallace and Whishaw 2003, Maaswinkel, Jarrard and Whishaw 1999, Whishaw, Hines and Wallace 2001) have shown that path integration is impaired by hippocampal lesions.

Part of the neural mechanism for the updating of place by path integration may be in the entorhinal cortex (McNaughton, Battaglia, Jensen, Moser and Moser 2006). Head direction cells are present in the entorhinal cortex, where grid cells (see Section 2.3.3) are also present, and indeed where some cells respond to combinations of grid and head direction (Leutgeb, Leutgeb, Treves, Meyer, Barnes, McNaughton, Moser and Moser 2005, Sargolini, Fyhn, Hafting, McNaughton, Witter, Moser and Moser 2006). Such combination cells in the entorhinal cortex may be part of the mechanism by which the place map is kept in register with the head direction map. The medial entorhinal cortex grid cells are a strong candidate for path integration over distance and direction travelled, for the repeating nature of the grid (see Section 2.3.3 for details and Fig. 2.19) is likely to be a reflection of a continuous attractor cycling once round its ring for every peak observed. The simplification this offers is that the path integration need be learned only once, as it is just an integration over self-movement, and can be used then in any environment. Consistent with this, grid cells are relatively little influenced by the details of the visual cues in the environment in which the rat is tested, apart from the rotation of the whole grid by the head direction cells, which can be set by the environment (Hafting, Fyhn, Molden, Moser and Moser 2005, Fyhn, Molden, Witter, Moser and Moser 2004, Sargolini, Fyhn, Hafting, McNaughton, Witter, Moser and Moser 2006).

If path integration is performed by grid cells in the entorhinal cortex, this leaves open the question of how the distance travelled is incorporated into the spatial or cognitive map of an environment, which will incorporate all the visual landmarks. As these visual cues are not apparently strongly represented in the entorhinal grid cells themselves, the implication is that the distance and direction travelled that is a result of the grid cell path integration needs to be linked into the spatial map of a particular environment, and this is represented as shown by the properties of rat place cells and primate spatial view cells in the hippocampus proper, in CA3 and CA1. The implication is that with an idiothetically defined place computed from the grid cell representation and reflected in the firing of CA3 cells, it then becomes an associative task for the CA3 cells to link associatively that idiothetic representation of place with the visual and other world-based cues, as well as with the objects, odours etc. at those places.

The summary of path integration in the context of grid cells provided by McNaughton et al. (2006) was not self-organizing, that is, the appropriate synaptic strengths for the model to perform the path integration did not become specified as a result of movements in the environment. Self-organizing continuous attractor neural networks that can perform path integration from velocity signals are described in Section B.5.5 and include head direction from head velocity (Stringer, Trappenberg, Rolls and De Araujo 2002b, Stringer and Rolls 2006); place from whole body motion (Stringer, Trappenberg, Rolls and De Araujo 2002b, Stringer, Rolls, Trappenberg and De Araujo 2002a); and spatial view from eye and whole body motion (Stringer, Rolls and Trappenberg 2004, Stringer, Rolls and Trappenberg 2005, Rolls and Stringer 2005). It will be useful to develop a model of grid cell path integration further so that it becomes fully self-organizing.

A third key issue is how stability in the bubble of activity representing the current location can be maintained without much drift in darkness, when it is operating as a memory system. A solution is described in Section B.5.6 (Stringer et al. 2002b).

A fourth key issue is considered in Section B.5.8 in which networks are described that store both continuous patterns and discrete patterns (see Fig. 2.16). These networks can be used to store for example the location in (continuous, physical) space where an object (an item with a discrete representation) is present (Rolls, Stringer and Trappenberg 2002).

2.3.2.3 The dynamics of the recurrent network

The analysis described above of the capacity of a recurrent network such as the CA3 considered steady-state conditions of the firing rates of the neurons. The question arises of how quickly the recurrent network would settle into its final state. With reference to the CA3 network, how long does it take before a pattern of activity, originally evoked in CA3 by afferent inputs, becomes influenced by the activation of recurrent collaterals? In a more general context, recurrent collaterals between the pyramidal cells are an important feature of the connectivity of the cerebral neocortex. How long would it take these collaterals to contribute fully to the activity of cortical cells? If these settling processes took in the order of hundreds of ms, they would be much too slow to contribute usefully to cortical activity, whether in the hippocampus or in the neocortex (Rolls and Deco 2002, Panzeri, Rolls, Battaglia and Lavis 2001, Rolls 1992a, Rolls 2003).

It has been shown that if the neurons are treated not as McCulloch-Pitts neurons that are simply 'updated' at each iteration, or cycle of time steps (and assume the active state if the threshold is exceeded), but instead are analyzed and modelled as 'integrate-and-fire' neurons in real continuous time, then the network can effectively 'relax' into its recall state very rapidly, in one or two time constants of the synapses (Treves 1993, Rolls and Treves 1998, Battaglia and Treves 1998b, Panzeri et al. 2001, Rolls and Deco 2002). This corresponds to perhaps 20 ms in the brain. One factor in this rapid dynamics of autoassociative networks with brain-like 'integrate-and-fire' membrane and synaptic properties is that with some spontaneous activity, some of the neurons in the network are close to threshold already before the recall cue is applied, and hence some of the neurons are very quickly pushed by the recall cue into firing, so that information starts to be exchanged very rapidly (within 1–2 ms of brain time) through the modified synapses by the neurons in the network. The progressive exchange of information starting early on within what would otherwise be thought of as an iteration period (of perhaps 20 ms, corresponding to a neuronal firing rate of 50 spikes/s), is the mechanism accounting for rapid recall in an autoassociative neuronal network made biologically realistic in this way. Further analysis of the fast dynamics of these networks if they are implemented in a biologically plausible way with 'integrate-and-fire' neurons is provided in Section B.6.5, in Appendix A5 of Rolls and Treves (1998), by Treves (1993), by Battaglia and Treves (1998b), and by Panzeri, Rolls, Battaglia and Lavis (2001).

2.3.2.4 Memory for sequences

One of the first extensions of the standard autoassociator paradigm that has been explored in the literature is the capability to store and retrieve not just individual patterns, but whole sequences of patterns. Hopfield (1982) suggested that this could be achieved by adding to the standard connection weights, which associate a pattern with itself, a new, asymmetric component, that associates a pattern with the next one in the sequence. In practice this scheme does not work very well, unless the new component is made to operate on a slower time scale than the purely autoassociative component (Kleinfeld 1986, Sompolinsky and Kanter 1986). With two different time scales, the autoassociative component can stabilize a pattern for a while, before the heteroassociative component moves the network, as it were, into the next pattern. The heteroassociative retrieval cue for the next pattern in the sequence is just the previous pattern in the sequence. A particular type of 'slower' operation occurs if the asymmetric component acts after a delay τ. In this case, the network sweeps through the sequence, staying for a time of order τ in each pattern.

One can see how the necessary ingredient for the storage of sequences is only a minor departure from purely Hebbian learning: in fact, the (symmetric) autoassociative component of the weights can be taken to reflect the Hebbian learning of strictly simultaneous conjunctions of pre- and post-synaptic activity, whereas the (asymmetric) heteroassociative component can be implemented by Hebbian learning of each conjunction of postsynaptic activity with presynaptic activity shifted a time τ in the past. Both components can then be seen as resulting from a generalized Hebbian rule, which increases the weight whenever postsynaptic activity is paired with presynaptic activity occurring within a given time range, which may extend from a few hundred milliseconds in the past up to include strictly simultaneous activity. This is similar to a trace rule (see Chapter 4, and Chapter 8 of Rolls and Deco (2002)), which itself matches very well the observed conditions for induction of long-term potentiation, and appears entirely plausible. The learning rule necessary for learning sequences, though, is more complex than a simple trace rule in that the time-shifted conjunctions of activity that are encoded in the weights must in retrieval produce activations that are time-shifted as well (otherwise one falls back into the Hopfield (1982) proposal, which does not quite work). The synaptic weights should therefore keep separate 'traces' of what was simultaneous and what was time-shifted during the original experience, and this is not very plausible. Levy and colleagues (Levy, Wu and Baxter 1995, Wu, Baxter and Levy 1996) have investigated these issues further, and the temporal asymmetry that may be present in LTP has been suggested as a mechanism that might provide some of the temporal properties that are necessary for the brain to store and recall sequences (Abbott and Blum 1996, Abbott and Nelson 2000, Minai and Levy 1993, Markram et al. 1998). A problem with this suggestion is that, given that the temporal dynamics of attractor networks are inherently very fast when the networks have continuous dynamics, and that the temporal asymmetry in LTP may be in the order of only milliseconds to a few tens of milliseconds, the recall of the sequences would be very fast, perhaps 10–20 ms per step of the sequence, with every step of a 10-step sequence effectively retrieved and gone in a quick-fire session of 100–200 ms.

Rolls and Stringer (see Rolls and Kesner (2006)) have suggested that the over-rapid replay of a sequence of memories stored in an autoassociation network such as CA3 if it included asymmetric synaptic weights to encode a sequence could be controlled by the physical inputs from the environment. If a sequence of places 1, 2, and 3 had been learned by the use of an asymmetric trace learning rule implemented in the CA3 network, then the firing initiated by place 1 would reflect (by the learned association) a small component of place 2 (which might be used to guide navigation to place 2, and which might be separated out from place 1 better by the competitive network action in CA1), but would not move fully away from representing place 1 until the animal moved away from place 1, because of the clamping effect on the CA3 firing of the external input representing place 1 to the recurrent network. In this way, the physical constraints of movements between the different places in the environment would control the speed of readout from the sequence memory. A simulation to illustrate this is shown in Figs. 2.17 and 2.18.

The CA1 neurons might make a useful contribution to this sequential recall by acting as a competitive network that would separate out the patterns represented in CA3 for the current and the next place, and this has been tested in the simulation by Rolls and Stringer (see Rolls and Kesner (2006)). What has been found is that if the representation is set to be less sparse in the CA1 than the CA3, and the CA1 neurons operate on the upper part of a sigmoid activation function, then the next step in the sequence can be represented by a population of neurons in the CA1 better than it can in CA3. (This allows the CA3 representation to be kept sparse, which helps to maximize the number of memories that can be stored.) The CA1 neurons representing the next place in the sequence would be the basis for the animal navigating to that next place. There could be heteroassociative firing of the third item in a sequence, but this would be much weaker. This functionality however could help the disambiguation of long sequences with overlapping parts (Jensen and Lisman 1996).

In the network of Rolls and Stringer (see Rolls and Kesner (2006)), CA3 might, by the continuing firing implemented by autoassociation, allow one item to be held in short-term memory until the next item arrives for heteroassociation. This would enable long time gaps within the sequence during training to be bridged. This has also been confirmed in the simulation (see Fig. 2.17).

The heteroassocative (asymmetric) long term potentiation (LTP) could work as follows: if the effect of input 1 remains at every synapse activated by input 1 for e.g. 100 ms (e.g. as a result of the NMDA receptor glutamate unbinding time constant), then when input 2 drives

Correlations between CA3 firing patterns.

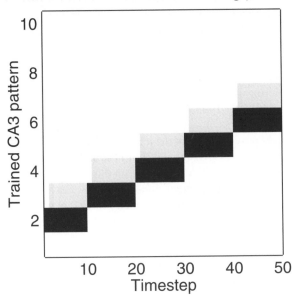

Fig. 2.17 Simulation of sequence learning in an attractor network such as CA3. The 100 neuron network was trained on a sequence of orthogonal patterns, each represented by 10 active binary neurons. The 100 neurons are arranged on the ordinate. In the first 10 timesteps the agent was at place 2, and the firing of the network was correlated mainly with place 2, but also place 3 was being recalled to some extent. (The darkness of the shading represents the correlation with each of the patterns as indicated on the ordinate.) The network did not move fully to place 3 during timesteps 2–10, because the external place cue for place 2 was still present, providing a weak clamping input effected by scaling down the external input corresponding to place 2. At timestep 10 the agent was allowed to reach position 3 by moving the clamping input to position 3. The network then maintained its firing for position 3 due to the autoassociation in the network and the weak clamping input, but also now recalled in part the pattern of firing for step 4 in the sequence, as shown by the grey level of the correlation with pattern 4. Thus use of a weak clamping input representing the current position, which can only change gradually as the agent moves from place to place in the environment, illustrates how autoassociation in the network can help to maintain activity representing the current place, but can also recall weakly the next step in the sequence, which could help the agent to navigate to the next place. The synapses in the network were updated by the normal Hebb rule to implement the autoassociation, and by the temporally asymmetric associative learning rule $\delta w_j = k r_i{}^\tau r_j^{\tau-1}$ when the successive steps in the sequence were being pairwise associated, where τ is the current timestep.

firing of any neuron with these activated synapses, these input 1-related activated synapses will show LTP. This provides a mechanism for presynaptic firing which precedes postsynaptic firing to be effective in implementing LTP. The mechanism is effectively a short-term memory trace in the presynaptic term, and this presynaptic trace will occur for any synapse from a strongly firing neuron independently of whether the synapse is on a postsynaptic neuron that is firing. This occurs because it is the unbinding time constant of the glutamate from the NMDA receptor that implements the presynaptic trace term, and this unbinding time constant (which is long – in the order of 100 ms or more) may not be affected by whether the postsynaptic neuron is firing or not (Lester and Jahr 1995, Erreger, Chen, Wyllie and Traynelis 2004, Lester, Clements, Westbrook and Jahr 1990). Then during recall, a presentation of stimulus 1 will make the neurons activated by stimulus 2 fire, and thus stimulus 1 will lead to the neurons representing stimulus 2 firing, recalling the sequence correctly.

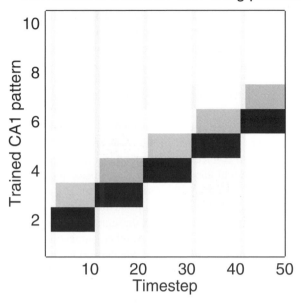

Fig. 2.18 Sequence learning: the corresponding activity in the CA1 network, which operated as a competitive network with an activation function that emphasized low firing rates relative to high firing rates, as can be achieved by a sigmoid activation function. (A square root function was used in the simulations to convert the activations into the firing rates.) The results show that CA1 could represent the next step in the sequence more explicitly than CA3, as shown by the fact that the correlation with the representation of the next step in the sequence is higher than in CA3, as shown by the increased darkness for the next step. Thus, neurons in CA1 could be more useful than CA3 neurons in leading the agent to the next step in the sequence. CA3 neurons, cannot, in these simulations, represent the next step too strongly relative to the current step, as otherwise the network cycles very rapidly through all steps in the sequence.

We note that if an episodic memory is thought to consist of a temporally linked sequence of event memories, then the mechanism for sequence memory just described could implement this type of multiple sequential item episodic memory.

Lisman and colleagues (Jensen and Lisman 1996, Jensen and Lisman 2005, Lisman and Idiart 1995, Jensen, Idiart and Lisman 1996, Lisman, Talamini and Raffone 2005) have suggested that sequences might be encoded by utilizing the neuronal after-depolarization which follows a spike from a neuron by approximately 200 ms to tend to make neurons fire again after they are activated. Interaction with theta oscillations (5–8 Hz) and gamma oscillations (30–80 Hz) in the model would make a set of neurons coding for one item tend to fire first in a new theta cycle. Neurons encoding a second item in a sequence would tend to fire in the next gamma cycle 20 ms later. Neurons encoding a third item in a sequence would tend to fire in the next gamma cycle 20 ms later. To keep the neurons representing one item synchronized, LTP associated with NMDA receptors with a short time constant of e.g. 12 ms is needed. Every theta cycle, the whole sequence is replayed by the model with 20 ms between items. In one version of their model (Jensen and Lisman 2005) this mechanism is suggested to be implemented in the neocortex. To form associations between successive items in a sequence, LTP associated with NMDA receptors with a long time constant of e.g. 150 ms is needed, and this it is suggested might be implemented in the hippocampus (Jensen and Lisman 2005, Lisman et al. 2005). It is a difficulty of the model that every theta cycle, the whole sequence is replayed by the model with 20 ms between items, for if the next item in a sequence is needed (e.g. the third), then the model just replays at this high speed all the following items in a sequence, so a special decoding system would be needed to know which the next item is. The model is also very susceptible to noise. The model also only works if there is great regularity in the spike trains of the neurons, which should repeat at very regular intervals locked to theta, and this is inconsistent with the almost Poisson nature of the spike trains of single neurons found in most brain areas. Further, no experimental evidence has been found that successive items in a remembered sequence are replayed at gamma frequency every theta cycle.

Another way in which a delay could be inserted in a recurrent collateral path in the brain is by inserting another cortical area in the recurrent path. This could fit in with the cortico-cortical backprojection connections described in Fig. 2.1 with return projections to the entorhinal cortex, which might then send information back into the hippocampus, which would introduce some conduction delay (Panzeri, Rolls, Battaglia and Lavis 2001). Another possibility is that the connections between the deep and the superficial layers of the entorhinal cortex help to close a loop from entorhinal cortex through hippocampal circuitry and back to the entorhinal cortex (van Haeften et al. 2003). Another suggestion is that the CA3 system holds by continuing firing a memory for event 1, which can then be associated with event 2 at the CA3 to CA1 synapses if event 2 activates CA1 neurons by the direct entorhinal input (Levy 1989).

Another proposal is that sequence memory can be implemented by using synaptic adaptation to effectively encode the order of the items in a sequence (Deco and Rolls 2005c) (see Section B.10). Whenever the attractor system is quenched into inactivity, the next member of the sequence emerges out of the spontaneous activity, because the least recently activated member of the sequence has the least synaptic or neuronal adaptation. This could be implemented in recurrent networks such as the CA3 or the prefrontal cortex.

For recency short-term memory, the sequence type of memory would be possible, but difficult because once a sequence has been recalled, a system has to "manipulate" the items, picking out which is later (or earlier) in the sequence. A simpler possibility is to use a short term form of long term potentiation (LTP) which decays, and, then the latest of two items can be picked out because when it is seen again, the neuronal response is larger than to the earlier items (Rolls and Deco 2002, Renart, Moreno, Rocha, Parga and Rolls 2001). This type of memory does not explicitly encode sequences, but instead reflects just how recently an item occurred. This could be implemented at any synapses in the system (e.g. in CA3 or CA1), and does not require recurrent collateral connectivity.

2.3.2.5 Mossy fibre inputs to the CA3 cells

We hypothesize that the mossy fibre inputs force efficient information storage by virtue of their strong and sparse influence on the CA3 cell firing rates (Rolls 1987, Rolls 1989b, Rolls 1989f, Treves and Rolls 1992). (The strong effects likely to be mediated by the mossy fibres were also emphasized by McNaughton and Morris (1987) and McNaughton and Nadel (1990).) We hypothesize that the mossy fibre input appears to be particularly appropriate in several ways. First of all, the fact that mossy fibre synapses are large and located very close to the soma makes them relatively powerful in activating the postsynaptic cell. (This should not be taken to imply that a CA3 cell can be fired by a single mossy fibre EPSP.)

Second, the firing activity of dentate granule cells appears to be very sparse (Jung and McNaughton 1993) and this, together with the small number of connections on each CA3 cell, produces a sparse signal, which can then be transformed into an even sparser firing activity in CA3 by a threshold effect[3].

Third, non-associative plasticity of mossy fibres (Brown, Ganong, Kairiss, Keenan and Kelso 1989, Brown, Kairiss and Keenan 1990b) might have a useful effect in enhancing the signal-to-noise ratio, in that a consistently firing mossy fibre would produce non-linearly amplified currents in the postsynaptic cell, which would not happen with an occasionally firing fibre (Treves and Rolls 1992). This plasticity, and also learning in the dentate, would also have the effect that similar fragments of each episode (e.g. the same environmental location) recurring on subsequent occasions would be more likely to activate the same population of CA3 cells, which would have potential advantages in terms of economy of use of the CA3 cells in different memories, and in making some link between different episodic memories with a common feature, such as the same location in space.

Fourth, with only a few, and powerful, active mossy fibre inputs to each CA3 cell, setting a given sparseness of the representation provided by CA3 cells would be simplified, for the EPSPs produced by the mossy fibres would be Poisson distributed with large membrane potential differences for each active mossy fibre. Setting the average firing rate of the dentate granule cells would effectively set the sparseness of the CA3 representation, without great precision being required in the threshold setting of the CA3 cells (Rolls, Treves, Foster and Perez-Vicente 1997c). Part of what is achieved by the mossy fibre input may be setting the sparseness of the CA3 cells correctly, which, as shown above and in Section B.3, is very important in an autoassociative memory store.

Fifth, the non-associative and sparse connectivity properties of the mossy fibre connections to CA3 cells may be appropriate for an episodic memory system that can learn very fast, in one trial. The hypothesis is that the sparse connectivity would help arbitrary relatively uncorrelated sets of CA3 neurons to be activated for even somewhat similar input patterns without the need for any learning of how best to separate the patterns, which in a self-organizing competitive network would take several repetitions (at least) of the set of patterns. The mossy fibre solution may thus be adaptive in a system that must learn in one trial, and for which the CA3 recurrent collateral learning requires uncorrelated sets of CA3 cells to be allocated for each (one-trial) episodic memory. The hypothesis is that the mossy fibre sparse connectivity solution performs the appropriate function without the mossy fibre system having to learn by repeated presentations how best to separate a set of training patterns (see further Section 2.4).

The argument based on information suggests, then, that an input system with the characteristics of the mossy fibres is essential during learning, in that it may act as a sort of (unsupervised) teacher that effectively strongly influences which CA3 neurons fire based on the pattern of granule cell activity. This establishes an information-rich neuronal representation of the episode in the CA3 network (see further Treves and Rolls (1992)). The perforant path input would, the quantitative analysis shows, not produce a pattern of firing in CA3 that contains sufficient information for learning (Treves and Rolls 1992).

On the basis of these points, we predict that the mossy fibres may be necessary for new learning in the hippocampus, but may not be necessary for recall of existing memories from the hippocampus. Experimental evidence consistent with this prediction about the role of the

---

[3]For example, if only 1 granule cell in 100 were active in the dentate gyrus, and each CA3 cell received a connection from 50 randomly placed granule cells, then the number of active mossy fibre inputs received by CA3 cells would follow a Poisson distribution of average $50/100 = 1/2$, i.e. 60% of the cells would not receive any active input, 30% would receive only one, 7.5% two, little more than 1% would receive three, and so on. (It is easy to show from the properties of the Poisson distribution and our definition of sparseness, that the sparseness of the mossy fibre signal as seen by a CA3 cell would be $x/(1 + x)$, with $x = C^{MF} a_{DG}$, assuming equal strengths for all mossy fibre synapses. C^{MF} is the number of mossy fibre connections to a CA3 neuron, and a_{DG} is the sparseness of the representation in the dentate granule cells.) If three mossy fibre inputs were required to fire a CA3 cell and these were the only inputs available, we see that the activity in CA3 would be roughly as sparse, in the example, as in the dentate gyrus.

mossy fibres in learning has been found in rats with disruption of the dentate granule cells (Lassalle, Bataille and Halley 2000) (see Section 2.4).

If acetylcholine does turn down the efficacy of the recurrent collateral synapses between CA3 neurons (Hasselmo et al. 1995), then cholinergic activation also might help to allow external inputs rather than the internal recurrent collateral inputs to dominate the firing of the CA3 neurons during learning, as the current theory proposes. If cholinergic activation at the same time facilitated LTP in the recurrent collaterals (as it appears to in the neocortex), then cholinergic activation could have a useful double role in facilitating new learning at times of behavioural activation, when presumably it may be particularly relevant to allocate some of the limited memory capacity to new memories.

2.3.2.6 Perforant path inputs to CA3 cells

By calculating the amount of information that would end up being carried by a CA3 firing pattern produced solely by the perforant path input and by the effect of the recurrent connections, we have been able to show (Treves and Rolls 1992) that an input of the perforant path type, alone, is unable to direct efficient information storage. Such an input is too weak, it turns out, to drive the firing of the cells, as the 'dynamics' of the network is dominated by the randomizing effect of the recurrent collaterals. This is the manifestation, in the CA3 network, of a general problem affecting storage (i.e. learning) in all autoassociative memories. The problem arises when the system is considered to be activated by a set of input axons making synaptic connections that have to compete with the recurrent connections, rather than having the firing rates of the neurons artificially clamped into a prescribed pattern.

An autoassociative memory network needs afferent inputs also in the other mode of operation, i.e. when it retrieves a previously stored pattern of activity. We have shown (Treves and Rolls 1992) that the requirements on the organization of the afferents are in this case very different, implying the necessity of a second, separate, input system, which we have identified with the perforant path input to CA3. In brief, the argument is based on the notion that the cue available to initiate retrieval might be rather small, i.e. the distribution of activity on the afferent axons might carry a small correlation, $q \ll 1$, with the activity distribution present during learning. In order not to lose this small correlation altogether, but rather transform it into an input current in the CA3 cells that carries a sizable signal – which can then initiate the retrieval of the full pattern by the recurrent collaterals – one needs a large number of associatively modifiable synapses. This is expressed by the following formulas that give the specific signal S produced by sets of associatively modifiable synapses, or by non-associatively modifiable synapses: if C'^{AFF} is the number of afferents per cell,

$$S_{\text{ASS}} \approx \frac{\sqrt{C'^{\text{AFF}}}}{\sqrt{p}} q \qquad (2.5)$$

$$S_{\text{NONASS}} \approx \frac{1}{\sqrt{C'^{\text{AFF}}}} q \qquad (2.6)$$

Associatively modifiable synapses are therefore needed, and are needed in a number C'^{AFF} of the same order as the number of concurrently stored patterns p, so that small cues can be effective; whereas non-associatively modifiable synapses – or even more so, non-modifiable ones – produce very small signals, which decrease in size the larger the number of synapses. In contrast with the storage process, the average strength of these synapses does not now play a crucial role. This suggests that the perforant path system is the one involved in relaying the cues that initiate retrieval.

Before leaving the CA3 cells, it is suggested that separate scaling of the three major classes of excitatory input to the CA3 cells (recurrent collateral, mossy fibre, and perforant path, see Fig. 2.1) could be independently scaled, by virtue of the different classes of inhibitory interneuron which receive their own set of inputs, and end on different parts of the dendrite of the CA3 cells (cf. for CA1 Buhl, Halasy and Somogyi (1994) and Gulyas, Miles, Hajos and Freund (1993)). This possibility is made simpler by having these major classes of input terminate on different segments of the dendrites. Each of these inputs, and the negative feedback produced through inhibitory interneurons when the CA3 cells fire, should for optimal functioning be separately regulated (Rolls 1995c), and the anatomical arrangement of the different types of inhibitory interneuron might be appropriate for achieving this.

2.3.3 Dentate granule cells

The theory is that the dentate granule cell stage of hippocampal processing which precedes the CA3 stage acts in a number of ways to produce during learning the sparse yet efficient (i.e. non-redundant) representation in CA3 neurons that is required for the autoassociation to perform well. Parts of the theory were developed elsewhere (Rolls 1989a, Rolls 1989b, Rolls 1989f, Treves and Rolls 1992), and further developments are described here.

The first way is that the perforant path – dentate granule cell system with its Hebb-like modifiability is suggested to act as a competitive learning network to remove redundancy from the inputs producing a more orthogonal, sparse, and categorised set of outputs (Rolls 1987, Rolls 1989a, Rolls 1989b, Rolls 1989f, Rolls 1990b, Rolls 1990c). Competitive networks are described in Section B.4. The non-linearity in the NMDA receptors may help the operation of such a competitive net, for it ensures that only the most active neurons left after the competitive feedback inhibition have synapses that become modified and thus learn to respond to that input (Rolls 1989a) (see Section B.4.9.3). If the synaptic modification produced in the dentate granule cells lasts for a period of more than the duration of learning the episodic memory, then it could reflect the formation of codes for regularly occurring combinations of active inputs that might need to participate in different episodic memories. Because of the non-linearity in the NMDA receptors, the non-linearity of the competitive interactions between the neurons (produced by feedback inhibition and non-linearity in the activation function of the neurons) need not be so great (Rolls 1989a) (see Section B.4). Because of the feedback inhibition, the competitive process may result in a relatively constant number of strongly active dentate neurons relatively independently of the number of active perforant path inputs to the dentate cells. The operation of the dentate granule cell system as a competitive network may also be facilitated by a Hebb rule of the form:

$$\delta w_{ij} = \alpha y_i (x_j - w_{ij}) \tag{2.7}$$

where δw_{ij} is the change of the synaptic weight w_{ij} that results from the simultaneous (or conjunctive) presence of presynaptic firing x_j and postsynaptic firing or activation y_i, and α is a learning rate constant that specifies how much the synapses alter on any one pairing (see Rolls (1989a) and Appendix B). Incorporation of a rule such as this which implies heterosynaptic long-term depression as well as long-term potentiation (Levy and Desmond 1985, Levy, Colbert and Desmond 1990) makes the sum of the synaptic weights on each neuron remain roughly constant during learning (Oja 1982, Rolls and Deco 2002, Rolls and Treves 1998, Rolls 1989a) (see Section B.4).

This functionality could be used to help build hippocampal place cells in rats from the grid cells present in the medial entorhinal cortex (Hafting et al. 2005). Each grid cell responds to a set of places in a spatial environment, with the places to which a cell responds set out in a regular grid. Different grid cells have different phases (positional offsets) and grid spacings or frequencies (Hafting et al. 2005). We have simulated the dentate granule cells as a system that receives as inputs the activity of a population of grid cells as the animal traverses a spatial

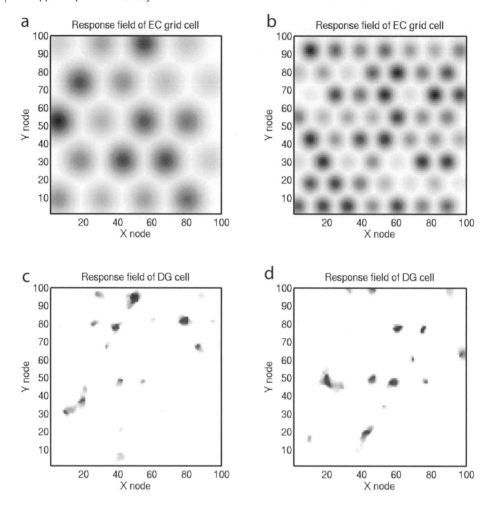

Fig. 2.19 Simulation of competitive learning in the dentate gyrus to produce place cells from the entorhinal cortex grid cell inputs. (a and b) Firing rate profiles of two entorhinal cortex (EC) grid cells with frequencies of 4 and 7 cycles. (c and d) Firing rate profiles of two dentate gyrus (DG) cells with no training. (After Rolls, Stringer and Elliot 2006.) (See colour plates, Appendix E starting on page 789.)

environment, and have shown that the competitive net builds dentate-like place cells from such entorhinal grid cell inputs (Rolls et al. 2006c). This occurs because entorhinal cells with coactive inputs when the animal is in one place become associated together by the action of the competitive net, yet each dentate cell represents primarily one place because the dentate representation is kept sparse, thus helping to implement symmetry-breaking. Simulations to demonstrate this are shown next.

Fig. 2.19a and b show examples of two 2D entorhinal cortex (EC) grid cells (with frequencies of 4 and 7 cycles along the X axis). As in the neurophysiological recordings (Hafting et al. 2005), the firing peaks occur at the vertices of a grid of equilateral triangles. Fig. 2.19c and d show the firing rate profiles of two dentate gyrus (DG) cells without training. Multiple peaks in the response profiles are evident, and this shows that the contrast enhancement and the competitive interactions in the DG layer were not sufficient without training and thereby synaptic modification to produce place-like fields in DG.

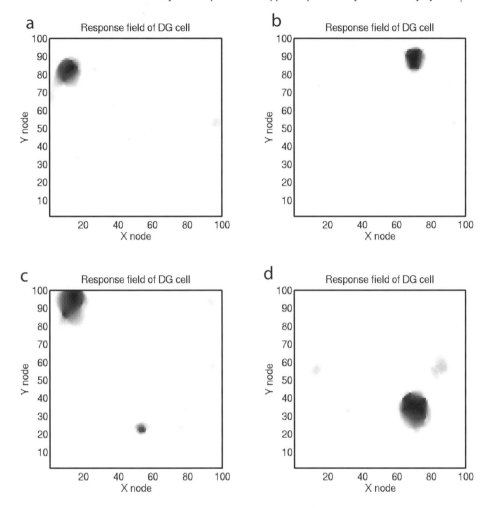

Fig. 2.20 Simulation of competitive learning in the dentate gyrus to produce place cells from the entorhinal cortex grid cell inputs. (a and b) Firing rate profiles of two DG cells after training with the Hebb rule. (c and d) Firing rate profiles of two DG cells after training with the trace rule with $\eta = 0.8$. (After Rolls, Stringer and Elliot 2006.) (See colour plates Appendix E.)

Fig. 2.20a and b show the firing rate profiles of two DG cells after training with the Hebb rule. This type of relatively small 2D place field was frequently found in the simulations. This result shows that competitive learning was sufficient to produce place-like fields in DG. Fig. 2.20c and d show the firing rate profiles of two DG cells after training with the trace rule, which is a modified form of equation B.22 on page 589 that has a short-term memory trace of previous neuronal activity as specified in equation 4.3 on page 300. The use of the trace rule is intended to test the concept that by keeping neurons in a modifiable state for a short time after strong activation (using for example the long time constant of NMDA receptors) the inputs from places near to a recently visited place where the activity of the neuron was high will tend to become associated onto the same postsynaptic neuron, thereby enlarging the place field. In the simulations, the place fields tended to be larger with the trace than with the purely associative Hebb rule shown in equation 2.7.

Although the DG cells illustrated had one main place field, some remaining grid-like firing was sometimes evident in the place fields with both Hebb and trace rule training, and indeed is evident in Fig. 2.20c and d. These are also characteristics of dentate granule cells recorded under the same conditions as the EC grid cell experiments (E. Moser, personal communication). These results were found only with training, with untrained networks showing repeating peaks of firing in large parts of the space as illustrated in Fig. 2.19c and d. These results show that competitive learning can account for the mapping of 2D grid cells in the entorhinal cortex to 2D place cells in the dentate gyrus / CA regions (Rolls, Stringer and Elliot 2006c).

The importance of transforming from a grid cell representation in the entorhinal cortex to a place cell representation (or in primates a spatial view cell representation) in the hippocampus is considered quantitatively next. At least one important function this allows is the formation of memories, formed for example between an object and a place, which is proposed to be a prototypical function of the hippocampus that is fundamental to episodic memory (Rolls 1996c, Rolls and Treves 1998, Rolls and Kesner 2006, Rolls and Xiang 2006). For the formation of such object–place memories in an associative network (in particular, an auto-associative network in the CA3 region of the hippocampus), the place must be made explicit in the representation, and moreover, for high capacity, that is the ability to store and retrieve many memories, the representation must be sparse. By made explicit, I mean that information can be read off easily from the firing rates of the neurons, with different places producing very different sets of neurons firing, so that different representations are relatively orthogonal. The entorhinal cortex representations are not only not sparse (in the simulations of Rolls, Stringer and Elliot (2006c), the sparseness a^p was 0.54), but in addition the typical overlap between the sets of firing of the neuronal populations representing two different places was high (with a mean cosine of the angle or normalized dot product of 0.540). In contrast, the sparseness of the representations formed in the dentate granule cells with Hebb rule training was 0.024, and a typical cosine of the angle was 0.000. (Low values of this measure of sparseness, a^p, defined in equation B.14, indicate sparse representations. The cosine of the angle between two vectors takes the value 1 if they point in the same direction, and the value 0 if they are orthogonal, as described in Appendix A.) These sparse and orthogonal representations are what is required for high capacity storage of object and place, object and reward, and of in general episodic, memories, and this is the function, I propose, of the mapping from entorhinal cortex to hippocampal cells for which Rolls, Stringer and Elliot (2006c) produced a computational model. This concept maps well onto utility in an environment, for it is the place where we are located or at which we are looking in the world with which we wish to associate objects or rewards, and this is made explicit in the dentate granule cell / hippocampal representation (Rolls 1999c, Rolls et al. 2005c, Rolls and Xiang 2005, Rolls and Kesner 2006, Rolls and Xiang 2006). In contrast, the entorhinal cortex may represent self-motion space in a way that is suitable for idiothetic path integration in *any* environment.

The second way in which the dentate granule cell stage acts to produce during learning the sparse yet efficient (i.e. non-redundant) representation in CA3 neurons is also a result of the competitive learning hypothesized to be implemented by the dentate granule cells (Rolls 1987, Rolls 1989a, Rolls 1989b, Rolls 1989f, Rolls 1990b, Rolls 1990c, Rolls 1994b). It is proposed that this allows overlapping (or very similar) inputs to the hippocampus to be separated, in the following way (see also Rolls (1996c)). Consider three patterns B, W, and BW, where BW is a linear combination of B and W. (To make the example very concrete, we could consider binary patterns where B=10, W=01 and BW=11.) Then the memory system is required to associate B with reward, W with reward, but BW with punishment. Without the hippocampus, rats might have more difficulty in solving such problems, particularly when they are spatial, for the dentate / CA3 system in rodents is characterized by being implicated in spatial memory. However, it is a property of competitive neuronal networks that they can separate such overlapping patterns, as has been shown elsewhere (Rolls and

Treves 1998, Rolls 1989a) (see Section B.4); normalization of synaptic weight vectors is required for this property. It is thus an important part of hippocampal neuronal network architecture that there is a competitive network that precedes the CA3 autoassociation system. Without the dentate gyrus, if a conventional autoassociation network were presented with the mixture BW having learned B and W separately, then the autoassociation network would produce a mixed output state, and would therefore be incapable of storing separate memories for B, W and BW. It is suggested therefore that competition in the dentate gyrus is one of the powerful computational features of the hippocampus, and that could enable it to help solve spatial pattern separation tasks. Consistent with this, rats with dentate gyrus lesions are impaired at a metric spatial pattern separation task (Gilbert, Kesner and Lee 2001, Goodrich-Hunsaker, Hunsaker and Kesner 2005) (see Section 2.4). The recoding of grid cells in the entorhinal cortex (Hafting et al. 2005) into small place field cells in the dentate granule cells that was modelled by Rolls, Stringer and Elliot (2006c) can also be considered to be a case where overlapping inputs must be recoded so that different spatial components can be treated differently.

It is noted that Sutherland and Rudy's configural learning hypothesis was similar, but was not tested with spatial pattern separation. Instead, when tested with for example tone and light combinations, it was not consistently found that the hippocampus was important (O'Reilly and Rudy 2001, Sutherland and Rudy 1991). I suggest that application of the configural concept, but applied to spatial pattern separation, may capture part of what the dentate gyrus acting as a competitive network could perform, particularly when a large number of such overlapping spatial memories must be stored and retrieved.

The third way in which the dentate gyrus is hypothesized to contribute to the sparse and relatively orthogonal representations in CA3 arises because of the very low contact probability in the mossy fibre–CA3 connections, and has been explained above in Section 2.3.2.5 and by Treves and Rolls (1992).

A fourth way is that as suggested and explained above in Section 2.3.2.5, the dentate granule cell–mossy fibre input to the CA3 cells may be powerful and its use particularly during learning would be efficient in forcing a new pattern of firing onto the CA3 cells during learning.

2.3.4 The learning of spatial view and place cell representations from visual inputs

In the ways just described, the dentate granule cells could be particularly important in helping to build and prepare spatial representations for the CA3 network. The actual representation of space in the primate hippocampus includes a representation of spatial view, whereas in the rat hippocampus it is of the place where the rat is. The representation in the rat may be related to the fact that with a much less developed visual system than the primate, the rat's representation of space may be defined more by the olfactory and tactile as well as distant visual cues present, and may thus tend to reflect the place where the rat is. However, the spatial representations in the rat and primate could arise from essentially the same computational process as follows (Rolls 1999c, De Araujo, Rolls and Stringer 2001).

The starting assumption is that in both the rat and the primate, the dentate granule cells (and the CA3 and CA1 pyramidal cells) respond to combinations of the inputs received. In the case of the primate, a combination of visual features in the environment will, because of the fovea providing high spatial resolution over a typical viewing angle of perhaps 10–20 degrees, result in the formation of a spatial view cell, the effective trigger for which will thus be a combination of visual features within a relatively small part of space. In contrast, in the rat, given the very extensive visual field subtended by the rodent retina, which may extend over

(a)   (b)

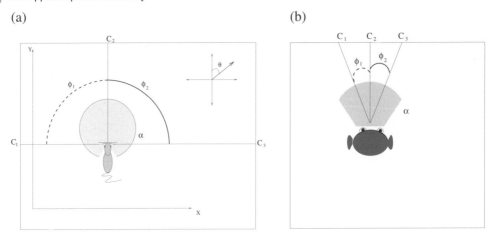

Fig. 2.21 Rat place cells (a) vs primate spatial view cells (b). Sketch of the square containment area in which the agent is situated. The containment area contains a grid of 200×200 possible positions x, y which the agent visits during the simulations, and at each position the agent rotates its head direction θ through 360 degrees in increments of 5 degrees. In addition, the containment area has a number of visual cues distributed evenly around the perimeter. As the agent explores its environment, individual hippocampal cells are stimulated by specific visual cues currently within the field of view of the agent α. On the left is shown the case for a rat with a 270° field of view, while on the right is shown the case for a primate with a 30° field of view, where the shaded areas correspond to the sizes of the fields of view of the agents. In the model, the firing rates of the hippocampal cells are dependent on the angles ϕ subtended by the visual cues (e.g. objects such as buildings in fixed positions in space) currently within the field of view of the agent. (After DeAraujo, Rolls and Stringer 2001.)

180–270 degrees, a combination of visual features formed over such a wide visual angle would effectively define a position in space that is a place (see Fig. 2.21). The actual processes by which the hippocampal formation cells would come to respond to feature combinations could be similar in rats and monkeys, involving for example competitive learning in the dentate granule cells, as utilized in the simulations of De Araujo, Rolls and Stringer (2001) which produced neurons with place-like and spatial view-like tuning. This competitive learning has the required properties, of associating together co-occurrent features, and of ensuring by the competition that each feature combination (representing a place or spatial view) is very different from that of other places or spatial views (pattern separation, and orthogonalizing effect), and is also a sparse representation. Consistent with this, dentate place fields in rats are small (Jung and McNaughton 1993). Although this computation could be performed to some extent also by autoassociation learning in CA3 pyramidal cells, and competitive learning in CA1 pyramidal cells (Rolls and Treves 1998, Treves and Rolls 1994), the combined effect of the dentate competitive learning and the mossy fibre low probability but strong synapses to CA3 cells would enable this part of the hippocampal circuitry to be especially important in separating spatial representations, which as noted above are inherently continuous. The prediction thus is that during the learning of spatial tasks in which the spatial discrimination is difficult (for example because the places are close together), then the dentate system should be especially important. Tests of this prediction are described in Section 2.4.

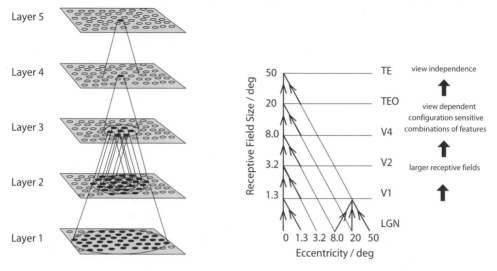

Fig. 2.22 Adding a fifth layer, corresponding to the parahippocampal gyrus / hippocampal system, after the inferior temporal visual cortex (corresponding to layer 4) may lead to the self-organization of spatial view / place cells in layer 5 when whole scenes are presented (see text). Convergence in the visual system is shown in the earlier layers (see Chapter 4). Right – as it occurs in the brain. V1, visual cortex area V1; TEO, posterior inferior temporal cortex; TE, inferior temporal cortex (IT). Left – as implemented in VisNet (layers 1–4). Convergence through the network is designed to provide fourth layer neurons with information from across the entire input retina.

2.3.5 Linking the inferior temporal visual cortex to spatial view and place cell representations

It is now possible to propose a unifying hypothesis of the relation between the ventral visual system, and hippocampal spatial representations. Let us consider a computational architecture in which a fifth layer is added to the VisNet architecture described in Chapter 4, as illustrated in Fig. 2.22. In the anterior inferior temporal visual cortex, which corresponds to the fourth layer of VisNet, neurons respond to objects, but several objects close to the fovea (within approximately 10°) can be represented because many object-tuned neurons have asymmetric receptive fields with respect to the fovea (Aggelopoulos and Rolls 2005) (see Section 4.5.10). If the fifth layer of VisNet performs the same operation as previous layers, it will form neurons that respond to combinations of objects in the scene with the positions of the objects relative spatially to each other incorporated into the representation (as described in Section 4.5.5). The result will be, as described in the preceding paragraph and as simulated by De Araujo, Rolls and Stringer (2001), spatial view neurons in the case of primates when the visual field of the primate has a narrow focus (due to the high resolution fovea), and place cells when as in the rat the visual field is very wide. The trace learning rule is layer 5 should help the spatial view or place fields that develop to be large and single, because of the temporal continuity that is inherent when the agent moves from one part of the view or place space to another, in the same way as has already been shown for the entorhinal grid cell to hippocampal place cell mapping (see Section 2.3.3, Fig. 2.20 and Rolls, Stringer and Elliot (2006c)).

The dentate granule cells form a network expected to be important in this competitive learning of spatial view or place representations based on visual inputs. As the animal navigates through the environment, different spatial view cells would be formed. Because of the overlapping fields of adjacent spatial view neurons, and hence their coactivity as the animal navigates, recurrent collateral associative connections at the next stage of the system, CA3, could form a continuous attractor representation of the environment (see Sections 2.3.2.2 and B.5). We thus have a hypothesis for how the spatial representations are formed as a natural extension of the hierarchically organised competitive networks in the ventral visual system. The expression of such spatial representations in CA3 may be particularly useful for associating those spatial representations with other inputs, such as objects or rewards (see Sections 2.2.4 and 2.3.2).

It will be interesting to perform a simulation to test the details of this hypothesis with VisNet simulations with a fifth layer added and appropriate fixed object combinations in the training set to represent spatial views, which would change as the agent moved through the environment. However, the indications are good, in that in a more artificial network trained by gradient ascent with a goal function that included forming relatively time invariant representations and decorrelating the responses of neurons within each layer of the 5-layer network, place-like cells were formed at the end of the network when the system was trained with a real or simulated robot moving through spatial environments (Wyss, Konig and Verschure 2006). It will be interesting to test whether spatial view cells develop in a VisNet fifth layer if trained with foveate views of the environment, or place cells if trained with wide angle views of the environment, and the utility of testing this with a VisNet-like architecture is that it is embodies a biologically plausible implementation based on neuronally plausible competitive learning and a short-term memory trace learning rule (as described in Chapter 4).

It is an interesting part of the hypothesis just described that because spatial views and places are defined by the relative spatial positions of fixed landmarks (such a buildings), slow learning of such representations over a number of trials might be useful, so that the neurons come to represent spatial views or places, and do not learn to represent a random collection of moveable objects seen once in conjunction. In this context, an alternative brain region to the dentate gyrus for this next layer of VisNet-like processing might be the parahippocampal areas that receive from the inferior temporal visual cortex. Spatial view cells are present in the parahippocampal areas (Georges-François, Rolls and Robertson 1999, Robertson, Rolls and Georges-François 1998, Rolls, Robertson and Georges-François 1997a, Rolls, Treves, Robertson, Georges-François and Panzeri 1998, Rolls, Xiang and Franco 2005c), and neurons with place-like fields (though in some cases as a grid, Hafting et al. (2005)) are found in the medial entorhinal cortex (Moser 2004, Moser and Moser 1998, Brun, Otnass, Molden, Steffenach, Witter, Moser and Moser 2002, Fyhn et al. 2004). These spatial view and place-like representations could be formed in these regions as, effectively, an added layer to VisNet. Moreover, these cortical regions have recurrent collateral connections that could implement a continuous attractor representation. Alternatively, it is possible that these parahippocampal spatial representations reflect the effects of backprojections from the hippocampus to the entorhinal cortex and thus to parahippocampal areas. In either case, it is an interesting and unifying hypothesis that an effect of adding an additional layer to VisNet-like ventral stream visual processing might with training in a natural environment lead to the self-organization, using the same principles as in the ventral visual stream, of spatial view or place representations in parahippocampal or hippocampal areas.

2.3.6 CA1 cells

The amount of information about each episode retrievable from CA3 has to be balanced off against the number of episodes that can be held concurrently in storage. The balance is regulated by the sparseness of the coding. Whatever the amount of information per episode in CA3, one may hypothesize that the organization of the structures that follow CA3 (i.e. CA1, the various subicular fields, and the return projections to neocortex shown in Fig. 2.1) should be optimized so as to preserve and use this information content in its entirety. This would

hundred milliseconds (Rolls 1992a, Rolls and Deco 2002, Rolls 2003); and hippocampal pyramidal cells are activated in visual object-and-place and conditional spatial response tasks with latencies of 120–180 ms (Miyashita, Rolls, Cahusac, Niki and Feigenbaum 1989, Rolls, Miyashita, Cahusac, Kesner, Niki, Feigenbaum and Bach 1989b). Thus, backprojected activity from the hippocampus might be expected to reach association cortical areas such as the inferior temporal visual cortex within 60 – 100 ms of the onset of their firing, and there would be a several hundred millisecond period in which there would be conjunctive feedforward activation present with simultaneous backprojected signals in the association cortex.

During recall, the backprojection connections onto the distal synapses of cortical pyramidal cells would be helped in their efficiency in activating the pyramidal cells by virtue of two factors. The first is that with no forward input to the neocortical pyramidal cells, there would be little shunting of the effects received at the distal dendrites by the more proximal effects on the dendrite normally produced by the forward synapses. Further, without strong forward activation of the pyramidal cells, there would not be very strong feedback and feedforward inhibition via GABA cells, so that there would not be a further major loss of signal due to (shunting) inhibition on the cell body and (subtractive) inhibition on the dendrite. (The converse of this is that when forward inputs are present, as during normal processing of the environment rather than during recall, the forward inputs would, appropriately, dominate the activity of the pyramidal cells, which would be only influenced, not determined, by the backprojecting inputs (Rolls 1989b, Rolls 1989e, Deco and Rolls 2005b).)

The synapses receiving the backprojections would have to be Hebb-modifiable, as suggested by Rolls (1989b) and Rolls (1989e). This would solve the de-addressing problem, which is the problem of how the hippocampus is able to bring into activity during recall just those cortical pyramidal cells that were active when the memory was originally being stored. The solution hypothesized (Rolls 1989b, Rolls 1989e) arises because modification occurs during learning of the synapses from active backprojecting neurons from the hippocampal system onto the dendrites of only those neocortical pyramidal cells active at the time of learning. Without this modifiability of cortical backprojections during learning at some cortical stages at least, it is difficult to see how exactly the correct cortical pyramidal cells active during the original learning experience would be activated during recall. Consistent with this hypothesis (Rolls 1989b, Rolls 1989e), there are NMDA receptors present especially in superficial layers of the cerebral cortex (Monaghan and Cotman 1985), implying Hebb-like learning just where the backprojecting axons make synapses with the apical dendrites of cortical pyramidal cells.

If the backprojection synapses are associatively modifiable, we may consider the duration of the period for which their synaptic modification should persist. What follows from the operation of the system described above is that there would be no point, indeed it would be disadvantageous, if the synaptic modifications lasted for longer than the memory remained in the hippocampal buffer store. What would be optimal would be to arrange for the associative modification of the backprojecting synapses to remain for as long as the memory persists in the hippocampus. This suggests that a similar mechanism for the associative modification within the hippocampus and for that of at least one stage of the backprojecting synapses would be appropriate. It is suggested that the presence of high concentrations of NMDA synapses in the distal parts of the dendrites of neocortical pyramidal cells and within the hippocampus may reflect the similarity of the synaptic modification processes in these two regions (Kirkwood, Dudek, Gold, Aizenman and Bear 1993). It is noted that it would be appropriate to have this similarity of time course (i.e. rapid learning within 1–2 s, and slow decay over perhaps weeks) for at least one stage in the series of backprojecting stages from the CA3 region to the neocortex. Such stages might include the CA1 region, subiculum, entorhinal cortex, and perhaps the parahippocampal gyrus / perirhinal cortex. However from multimodal cortex (e.g. the parahippocampal gyrus) back to earlier cortical stages, it might be desirable for the backprojecting synapses to persist for a long period, so that some types of recall and top-down processing (Rolls and Deco 2002, Rolls 1989b, Rolls 1989e) mediated by the operation of neocortico-neocortical backprojecting synapses could be stable, and might not require modification during the learning of a new episodic memory (see Section 2.5).

An alternative hypothesis to that above is that rapid modifiability of backprojection synapses would be required only at the beginning of the backprojecting stream. Relatively fixed associations from higher to earlier neocortical stages would serve to activate the correct neurons at earlier cortical stages during recall. For example, there might be rapid modifiability from CA3 to CA1 neurons, but relatively fixed connections from there back (McClelland et al. 1995). For such a scheme to work, one would need to produce a theory not only of the formation of semantic memories in the neocortex, but also of how the operations performed according to that theory would lead to recall by setting up appropriately the backprojecting synapses.

We have noted elsewhere that backprojections, which included cortico-cortical backprojections, and backprojections originating from structures such as the hippocampus and amygdala, may have a number of different functions (Rolls and Deco 2002, Rolls 2005, Rolls 1990b, Rolls 1989b, Rolls 1989e, Rolls 1990c, Rolls 1989a, Rolls 1992a). The particular function with which we have been concerned here is how memories stored in the hippocampus might be recalled in regions of the cerebral neocortex.

2.3.8 Backprojections to the neocortex – quantitative aspects

How many backprojecting fibres does one need to synapse on any given neocortical pyramidal cell, in order to implement the mechanism outlined above? Clearly, if neural network theory were to produce a definite constraint of that sort, quantitative anatomical data could be used for verification or falsification.

Attempts to come up with an estimate of the number of synapses required have sometimes followed the simple line of reasoning presented next, which is shown to be unsatisfactory. [The type of argument to be described has been applied to analyse the capacity of pattern association and autoassociation memories (see for example Marr (1971) and Willshaw and Buckingham (1990)), and to show that there are limitations in this type of approach, this approach is considered in this paragraph.] Consider first the assumption that hippocampo-cortical connections are monosynaptic and not modifiable, and that all existing synapses have the same efficacy. Consider further the assumption that a hippocampal representation across N cells of an event consists of $a_h N$ cells firing at the same elevated rate (where a_h is the sparseness of the hippocampal representation), while the remaining $(1 - a_h)N$ cells are silent. If each pyramidal cell in the association areas of neocortex receives synapses from an average C^{HBP} hippocampal axons, there will be an average probability $y = C^{HBP}/N$ of finding a synapse from any given hippocampal cell to any given neocortical one. Across neocortical cells, the number A of synapses of hippocampal origin activated by the retrieval of a particular episodic memory will follow a Poisson distribution of average $y a_h N = a_h C^{HBP}$

$$P(A) = (a_h C^{HBP})^A \exp(-a_h C^{HBP})/A! \tag{2.8}$$

The neocortical cells activated as a result will be those, in the tail of the distribution, receiving at least T active input lines, where T is a given threshold for activation. Requiring that $P(A > T)$ be at least equal to a_{nc}, the fraction of neocortical cells involved in the neocortical representation of the episode, results in a constraint on C^{HBP}. This simple type of calculation can be extended to the case in which hippocampo-cortical projections are taken to be polysynaptic, and mediated by modifiable synapses. In any case, the procedure does not appear to produce a very meaningful constraint for at least three reasons. First, the resulting minimum value of C^{HBP}, being extracted by looking at the tail of an exponential distribution, varies dramatically with any variation in the assumed values of the parameters a_h, a_{nc}, and T. Second, those parameters are ill-defined in principle: a_h and a_{nc} are used having in mind the unrealistic assumption of binary distributions of activity in both the hippocampus and neocortex (although the sparseness of a representation can be defined in general, as shown above, it is the particular definition pertaining to the binary case that is invoked here); while the definition of T is based on unrealistic assumptions about neuronal dynamics (how coincident does one require the various inputs to be in time, in order to generate a single spike, or a train of spikes of given frequency, in the postsynaptic cell?). Third, the calculation assumes that neocortical cells receive no other inputs, excitatory or inhibitory. Relaxing this assumption, to include for example non-specific activation by subcortical afferents, makes the calculation extremely fragile. This argument applies in general to approaches to neurocomputation which base their calculations on what would happen in the tail of an exponential, Poisson, or binomial distribution. Such calculations must be interpreted with great care for the above reasons.

An alternative way to estimate a constraint on C^{HBP}, still based on very simple assumptions, but which is more robust with respect to relaxing those assumptions, is the following.

Consider a polysynaptic sequence of backprojecting stages, from hippocampus to neocortex, as a string of simple (hetero-)associative memories in which, at each stage, the input lines are those coming from the previous stage (closer to the hippocampus) (Treves and Rolls 1994). Implicit in this framework is the assumption that the synapses at each stage are modifiable and have been indeed modified at the time of first experiencing each episode, according to some Hebbian associative plasticity rule. A plausible requirement for a successful hippocampo-directed recall operation is that the signal generated from the hippocampally retrieved pattern of activity, and carried backwards towards neocortex, remains undegraded when compared to the noise due, at each stage, to the interference effects caused by the concurrent storage of other patterns of activity on the same backprojecting synaptic systems. That requirement is equivalent to that used in deriving the storage capacity of such a series of heteroassociative memories, and it was shown in Treves and Rolls (1991) that the maximum number of independently generated activity patterns that can be retrieved is given, essentially, by the same formula as equation 2.2 above

$$p \approx \frac{C}{a \ln(\frac{1}{a})} k' \tag{2.9}$$

where, however, a is now the sparseness of the representation at any given backprojection stage, and C is the average number of (back-)projections each cell of that stage receives from cells of the previous one[4]. (k' is a similar slowly varying factor to that introduced above.) If p is equal to the number of memories held in the hippocampal memory, it is limited by the retrieval capacity of the CA3 network, $p_{\max}$. Putting together the formula for the latter with that shown here, one concludes that, roughly, the requirement implies that the number of afferents of (indirect) hippocampal origin to a given neocortical stage (C^{HBP}) must be $C^{\text{HBP}} = C^{\text{RC}} a_{nc}/a_{\text{CA3}}$, where C^{RC} is the number of recurrent collaterals to any given cell in CA3, the average sparseness of a neocortical representation is a_{nc}, and a_{CA3} is the sparseness of memory representations in CA3.

---

[4]The interesting and important insight here is that multiple iterations through a recurrent autoassociative network can be treated as being formally similar to a whole series of feedforward associative networks, with each new feedforward network equivalent to another iteration in the recurrent network (Treves and Rolls 1991). This formal similarity enables the quantitative analysis developed in general for autoassociation nets (see Treves and Rolls (1991)) to be applied directly to the series of backprojection networks (Treves and Rolls 1994).

The above requirement is very strong: even if representations were to remain as sparse as they are in CA3, which is unlikely, to avoid degrading the signal, C^{HBP} should be as large as C^{RC}, i.e. 12,000 in the rat. Moreover, other sources of noise not considered in the present calculation would add to the severity of the constraint, and partially compensate for the relaxation in the constraint that would result from requiring that only a fraction of the p episodes would involve any given cortical area. If then C^{HBP} has to be of the same order as C^{RC}, one is led to a very definite conclusion: a mechanism of the type envisaged here could not possibly rely on a set of monosynaptic CA3-to-neocortex backprojections. This would imply that, to make a sufficient number of synapses on each of the vast number of neocortical cells, each cell in CA3 has to generate a disproportionate number of synapses (i.e. C^{HBP} times the ratio between the number of neocortical and that of CA3 cells). The required divergence can be kept within reasonable limits only by assuming that the backprojecting system is polysynaptic, provided that the number of cells involved grows gradually at each stage, from CA3 back to neocortical association areas (Treves and Rolls 1994) (cf. Fig. 2.1).

Although backprojections between any two adjacent areas in the cerebral cortex are approximately as numerous as forward projections, and much of the distal parts of the dendrites of cortical pyramidal cells are devoted to backprojections, the actual number of such connections onto each pyramidal cell may be on average only in the order of thousands. Further, not all might reflect backprojection signals originating from the hippocampus, for there are backprojections which might be considered to originate in the amygdala (Amaral et al. 1992) or in multimodal cortical areas (allowing for example for recall of a visual image by an auditory stimulus with which it has been regularly associated). In this situation, one may consider whether the backprojections from any one of these systems would be sufficiently numerous to produce recall. One factor which may help here is that when recall is being produced by the backprojections, it may be assisted by the local recurrent collaterals between nearby ($\approx$1 mm) pyramidal cells which are a feature of neocortical connectivity. These would tend to complete a partial neocortical representation being recalled by the backprojections into a complete recalled pattern. (Note that this completion would be only over the local information present within a cortical area about e.g. visual input or spatial input; it provides a local 'clean-up' mechanism, and could not replace the global autoassociation performed effectively over the activity of very many cortical areas which the CA3 could perform by virtue of its widespread recurrent collateral connectivity.) There are two alternative possibilities about how this would operate. First, if the recurrent collaterals showed slow and long-lasting synaptic modification, then they would be useful in completing the whole of long-term (e.g. semantic) memories. Second, if the neocortical recurrent collaterals showed rapid changes in synaptic modifiability with the same time course as that of hippocampal synaptic modification, then they would be useful in filling in parts of the information forming episodic memories which could be made available locally within an area of the cerebral neocortex.

2.3.9 Simulations of hippocampal operation

In order to test the operation of the whole system for individual parts of which an analytic theory is available (Rolls and Treves 1998, Treves and Rolls 1994, Treves and Rolls 1992, Schultz and Rolls 1999), Rolls (1995c) simulated a scaled down version of the part of the architecture shown in Fig. 2.1 from the entorhinal cortex to the hippocampus and back to the entorhinal cortex. The analytic approaches to the storage capacity of the CA3 network, the role of the mossy fibres and of the perforant path, the functions of CA1, and the operation of the backprojections in recall, were all shown to be computationally plausible in the computer simulations. In the simulation, during recall, partial keys are presented to the entorhinal cortex, completion is produced by the CA3 autoassociation network, and recall is produced in the entorhinal cortex of the original learned vector. The network, which has 1,000 neurons at each stage, can recall large numbers, which approach the calculated storage capacity, of different sparse random vectors. One of the points highlighted by the simulation is that the network operated much better if the CA3 cells operated in binary mode (either firing or not), rather than having continuously graded firing rates (Rolls 1995c). The reason for this is that given that the total amount of information that can be stored in a recurrent network such as the CA3 network is approximately constant independently of how graded the firing rates are in each pattern (Treves 1990), then if much information is used to store the graded firing rates in the firing of CA3 cells, fewer patterns can be stored. The implication of this is that in order to store many memories in the hippocampus, and to be able to recall them at later stages of the system in for example the entorhinal cortex and beyond, it may be advantageous to utilize relatively binary firing rates in the CA3 part at least of the hippocampus.

This finding has been confirmed and clarified by simulation of the CA3 autoassociative system alone, and it has been suggested that the advantage of operation with binary firing rates may be related to the low firing rates characteristic of hippocampal neurons (Rolls, Treves, Foster and Perez-Vicente 1997c).

Another aspect of the theory emphasized by the results of the simulation was the importance of having effectively a single network provided in the hippocampus by the CA3 recurrent collateral network, for only if this operated as a single network (given the constraint of some topography present at earlier stages) could the whole of a memory be completed from any of its parts.

Another aspect of the theory illustrated by these simulations was the information retrieval that can occur at the CA3–CA1 (Schaeffer collateral) synapses if they are associatively modifiable (Schultz and Rolls 1999).

2.4   Tests of the theory

Empirical evidence that tests the theory comes from a wide range of investigation methods, including the effects of selective lesions to different subregions of the hippocampal system, the activity of single neurons in different subregions of the hippocampal system, pharmacological and genetic manipulations of different parts of the system, the detailed neuroanatomy of the system, and functional neuroimaging studies and clinical neuropsychological studies in humans.

Because the theory makes predictions about the functions of different parts of the hippocampal system (e.g. dentate, CA3, and CA1), evidence from subregion analysis is very relevant to testing the theory, and such evidence is included in the following assessment, which starts from the dentate gyrus, and works through to CA1. The evidence comes from the effects of selective lesions to different subregions of the hippocampal system, the activity of single neurons in different subregions, together with pharmacological and genetic manipulations of different parts of the system (Rolls and Kesner 2006).

2.4.1   Dentate gyrus (DG) subregion of the hippocampus

Based on the anatomy of the DG, its input and output pathways, and the development of a computational model, it has been suggested (see Section 2.3, Rolls (1989b), and Rolls (1996c)) that the DG can act as a competitive learning network with Hebb-like modifiability to remove redundancy from the inputs producing a more orthogonal, sparse, and categorized set of outputs. One example of this in the theory is that to the extent that some entorhinal cortex neurons represent space as a grid (Hafting et al. 2005), the correlations in this type of encoding are removed by competitive learning to produce a representation of place, with each place encoded differently from other places (Rolls, Stringer and Elliot 2006c)[5]. To the extent then that DG acts to produce separate representations of different places, it is predicted that the DG will be especially important when memories must be formed about similar places. To form spatial representations, learned conjunctions of sensory inputs including vestibular, olfactory, visual, auditory, and somatosensory may be involved. DG may help to form orthogonal representations based on all these inputs, and could thus help to form orthogonal non-spatial as well as orthogonal spatial representations for use in CA3. In any case, the model predicts that for spatial information, the DG should play an important role in hippocampal memory functions when the spatial information is very similar, for example, when the places are close together.

2.4.1.1 Spatial pattern separation

To examine the contribution of the DG to spatial pattern separation, Gilbert, Kesner and Lee (2001) tested rats with DG lesions using a paradigm that measured one-trial short term memory for spatial location information as a function of spatial similarity between two spatial locations (Gilbert, Kesner and DeCoteau 1998). Rats were trained to displace an object that was randomly positioned to cover a baited food well in 1 of 15 locations along a row of food wells. Following a short delay, the rats were required to choose between two objects identical to the sample phase object. One object was in the same location as the sample phase object and the second object was in a different location along the row of food wells. A rat was rewarded for displacing the object in the same position as the sample phase object (correct choice) but received no reward for displacing the foil object (incorrect choice). Five spatial separations, from 15 cm to 105 cm, were used to separate the correct object from the foil object on the choice phase. The results showed that rats with DG lesions were significantly impaired at short spatial separations; however, the performance of the DG lesioned rats increased as a function of increased spatial separation between the correct object and the foil on the choice phases. The performance of rats with DG lesions matched controls at the largest spatial separation. The graded nature of the impairment and the significant linear increase in performance as a function of increased separation illustrate the deficit in pattern separation produced by DG lesions (see Fig. 2.23). Based on these results, it can be concluded that lesions of the DG decrease efficiency in spatial pattern separation, which resulted in impairments on trials with increased spatial proximity and hence increased spatial similarity among working memory representations (Gilbert, Kesner and Lee 2001). In the same study it was found that CA1 lesions do not produce a deficit in this task.

Additional evidence comes from a study (Goodrich-Hunsaker, Hunsaker and Kesner 2005) using a modified version of an exploratory paradigm developed by Poucet (1989), in which rats with DG lesions and controls were tested on tasks involving a metric spatial manipulation. In this task, a rat was allowed to explore two different visual objects that were separated by a specific distance on a cheese-board maze. On the initial presentation of the objects, the rat explored each object. However, across subsequent presentations of the objects in their respective locations, the rat habituated and eventually spent less time exploring the objects. Once the rat had habituated to the objects and their locations, the metric spatial distance between the two objects was manipulated so the two objects were either closer together or further apart. The time the rat spent exploring each object was recorded. The results showed that DG lesions impaired detection of the metric distance change in that rats with DG lesions

---

[5] Indeed, it was a prediction of the theory that the mapping from entorhinal cortex grid cells to dentate / CA place cells could be achieved by competitive learning, and this prediction was verified by simulation (Rolls, Stringer and Elliot 2006c).

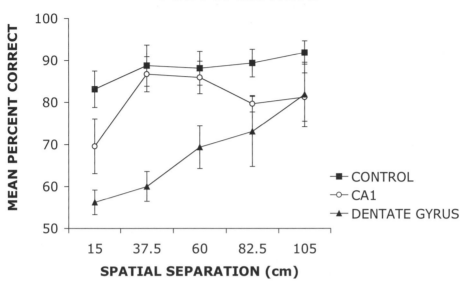

Fig. 2.23 Spatial pattern separation impairment produced by dentate gyrus lesions. Mean percent correct performance as a function of spatial separation of control group, CA1 lesion group, and dentate gyrus lesion group on postoperative trials. A graded impairment was found as a function of the distance between the places only following dentate gyrus lesions. (After Gilbert, Kesner and Lee, 2001.)

spent significantly less time exploring the two objects that were displaced.

The results of both experiments provide empirical validation of the role of DG in spatial pattern separation, and support the prediction from the computational model presented in this chapter.

There are neurophysiological results that are also consistent, in that McNaughton, Barnes, Meltzer and Sutherland (1989) found that following colchicine-induced lesions of the DG, there is a significant decrease in the reliability of CA3 place-related firing. Therefore, if CA3 cells display less reliability following DG lesions, the cells may not form accurate representations of space due to decreased efficiency in pattern separation. Also consistent are the findings that the place fields of DG cells and specifically dentate granular cells (Jung and McNaughton 1993) are small and highly reliable, and this may reflect the role of DG in pattern separation.

These studies thus indicate that the DG plays an important role in spatial pattern separation in spatial memory tasks. Building and utilizing separate representations for other classes of stimuli engage other brain areas, including for objects the inferior temporal visual cortex (Rolls and Deco 2002, Rolls 2000a), for reward value the orbitofrontal cortex (Rolls 2005) and amygdala (Gilbert and Kesner 2002), and for motor responses the caudate nucleus (Kesner and Gilbert 2006).

2.4.1.2 Encoding versus retrieval

The theory postulates that the dentate / mossy fibre system is necessary for setting up the appropriate conditions for optimal storage of new information in the CA3 system (which could be called encoding); and that (especially when an incomplete cue is provided) the retrieval of information from CA3 is optimally cued by the direct entorhinal to CA3 connections.

In strong support of the role of the DG in encoding, a study conducted in mice showed that the mossy fibre projections to CA3 are essential for the encoding of spatial information in a water maze reference memory task, but are not necessary for retrieval (Lassalle, Bataille and Halley 2000).

Another type of evidence comes from a study in which rats had 10 learning trials per day in a Hebb–Williams maze. Lee and Kesner (2004b) found that based on a within-day analysis DG lesions (but not lesions of the perforant path input to CA3) impaired the acquisition of this task, consistent with an encoding or learning impairment. However, when tested using a between-days analysis, retrieval of what had been learned previously was not impaired by DG lesions, but was impaired by lesions of the perforant path input to CA3. This double dissociation is consistent with the hypothesis that the DG is important for optimal encoding, and the entorhinal to CA3 connections for optimal retrieval.

Further evidence for a DG mediation of spatial encoding comes from the observation that rats with DG lesions are impaired in learning the Morris water maze task when the start location varied on each trial (Nanry, Mundy and Tilson 1989, Sutherland, Whishaw and Kolb 1983, Xavier, Oliveira-Filho and Santos 1999). Under these conditions, spatial pattern separation may be at a premium, for different, partially overlapping, subsets of spatial cues are likely to be visible from the different starting locations.

Further evidence consistent with the hypothesis that the DG is important in spatial learning (acquisition) is that rats with DG lesions are impaired on acquisition of spatial contextual fear conditioning (Lee and Kesner 2004a).

However, we note that in the studies described in this section (encoding vs retrieval), during acquisition of these tasks over a number of trials both the storage and the retrieval processes are likely to influence the rate of behavioural learning. Thus, even though in behavioural tasks the deficit can be described as an encoding deficit because it is apparent during initial learning, it is not easy to separate the actual underlying processes by which the DG may be important for setting up the representations for new learning in the CA3 system, and the perforant path to CA3 connections for initiating retrieval especially with a partial cue from CA3.

2.4.2   CA3 subregion of the hippocampus

In the model the CA3 system acts as an autoassociation system. This enables arbitrary (especially spatial in animals and probably language for humans as well) associations to be formed between whatever is represented in the hippocampus, in that for example any place could be associated with any object, and in that the object could be recalled with a spatial recall cue, or the place with an object recall cue. The same system must be capable of fast (one-trial) learning if it is to contribute to forming new episodic memories, though it could also play an important role in the encoding of new information requiring multiple trials. The same system is also predicted to be important in retrieval of hippocampus-dependent information when there is an incomplete retrieval cue. The same system has the property that it can maintain firing activity because of the associative recurrent collateral connections, and for this reason is likely to be important in hippocampus-dependent delay / short-term memory tasks. The CA3 recurrent collateral system could also make a contribution to the learning of sequences if it has some temporal asymmetry in its associative synapses, as described in Section 2.3.2.4. The CA3 system might also contribute to spatial path integration, though this could be performed outside the hippocampus. Tests of these proposed functions are described next.

2.4.2.1   Rapid encoding of new information

The theory proposes that associative learning in the CA3 recurrent collateral connections can occur rapidly, in as little as one trial, so that it can contribute to episodic memory. Evidence for

predicts that the direct perforant path input to CA3 is important in initiating retrieval from the CA3 autoassociation network, especially with an incomplete retrieval cue (see Section 2.3.2.6).

Support for this hypothesis comes from the findings of Lee and Kesner (2004b) and Jerman, Kesner and Hunsaker (2006) that lesions of the DG or CA3 (or a crossed lesion) disrupt within-day learning on the Hebb–Williams maze, but that retrieval of information at the start of the following day is not impaired. In contrast, lesions of the perforant path input to CA3 from entorhinal cortex disrupt retrieval (i.e. initial performance on the following day), but not learning within a day (Lee and Kesner 2004b).

The perforant path can be divided into a medial and lateral component. It has been suggested that the medial component processes spatial information and that the lateral component processes non-spatial (e.g objects, odours) information (Hargreaves et al. 2005, Witter, Groenewegen, Lopes da Silva and Lohman 1989a). In one study, Ferbinteanu, Holsinger and McDonald (1999) showed that lesions of the medial perforant path (MPP) disrupted water maze learning, whereas lateral perforant path (LPP) lesions had no effect. As predicted by the theory, there is associative LTP between the medial or lateral perforant path and the intrinsic commissural/associationalCA3 synapses) (Martinez, Do, Martinez and Derrick 2002). Either place or object recall cues could thus be introduced by the associative MPP and LPP connections to CA3 cells.

In addition, Martinez et al. (2002) demonstrated associative (cooperative) LTP between the medial and lateral perforant path inputs to the CA3 neurons. This could provide a mechanism for object (LPP) – place (MPP) associative learning, with either the object or the place during recall activating a CA3 neuron. However, this LPP to MPP cooperative LTP onto a CA3 neuron would be a low capacity memory system, in that there are only 3,300 PP inputs to a CA3 cell, compared to 12,000 recurrent collaterals in the CA3–CA3 connections, and these numbers are the leading term in the memory capacity of pattern association and autoassociation memory systems (Rolls and Deco 2002, Rolls and Treves 1998) (see Appendix B).

We note that disruption of DG and mossy fibre input into CA3 does not produce a disruption in the acquisition of the object–place paired associate task unless the stimuli are close together, implying that the DG contribution is important particularly when pattern separation is needed (Gilbert and Kesner 2003). The implication is that sufficient input for object–place learning can be introduced into the CA3 system (which is required for this object–place learning) by the perforant path inputs provided that spatial pattern separation is not at a premium (or perhaps the storage of large numbers of different object–place associations is not at a premium, as this is the other condition for which the computational theory indicates that the DG is needed to help produce sparse and orthogonal representations in the CA3 system).

2.4.2.7 Orthogonal representations in CA3

The CA3 subregion may have more distinct representations of different environments than CA1. This may be consistent with the computational point that if CA3 is an autoassociator, the pattern representations in it should be as orthogonal as possible to maximize memory capacity and minimize interference. The actual pattern separation may be performed, the theory holds, as a result of the operation of the dentate granule cells as a competitive net, and the nature of the mossy fibre connections to CA3 cells. Some of the empirical evidence is as follows.

Tanila (1999) showed that CA3 place cells were able to maintain distinct representations of two visually identical environments, and selectively reactivate either one of the representation patterns depending on the experience of the rat. Also, Leutgeb, Leutgeb, Treves, Moser and Moser (2004) recently showed that when rats experienced a completely different environment, CA3 place cells developed orthogonal representations of those different environments by changing their firing rates between the two environments, whereas CA1 place cells maintained similar responses. In a different study Vazdarjanova and Guzowski (2004) placed rats in two different environments separated by $\approx$ 30 min. The two environments differed greatly in that different objects were located in each room. The authors were able to monitor the time course of activations of ensembles of neurons in both CA3 and CA1, using a new immediate-early gene-based brain-imaging method (Arc/H1a catFISH). When the two environments were significantly different, CA3 neurons exhibited lower overlap in their activity between the two environments compared to CA1 neurons. Thus CA3 may represent different environments relatively orthogonally.

In the computational account, each environment would be a separate chart, and the number of charts that could be stored in CA3 would be high if the representations in each chart are relatively orthogonal to those in other charts (see Section B.5.4 and Battaglia and Treves (1998b)), and further, the charts could operate independently (Stringer, Rolls and Trappenberg 2004). Any one chart of one spatial environment can be understood as a continuous attractor network, with place cells with Gaussian shaped place fields, which overlap continuously with each other. In different charts (different spatial environments) the neurons may represent very different parts of space, and neurons representing close places in one environment may represent distant places in another environment (chart).

2.4.2.8 Short-term memory, path integration, and CA3

The CA3 recurrent collateral associative connections suggest that the CA3 system can operate as an attractor network which can be useful in some types of working memory. Support for this idea comes from a variety of studies analysed by Kesner and Rolls (2001), including a study where in the short-term (30 s delay) memory for spatial location task to measure spatial pattern separation, it was shown that CA3 lesioned rats were impaired for all pattern separations, consistent with the hypothesis that the rats could not remember the correct spatial location (Gilbert and Kesner 2006). Furthermore, in the short-term memory-based delayed non-matching to sample place task mentioned above (Lee and Kesner 2003b), lesions of CA3 impaired the acquisition of this task with 10 s delays. Also single neuron activity has been recorded in CA3 during the delay period in rats in a spatial position short-term memory task (Hampson, Hedberg and Deadwyler 2000) and in monkeys in an object–place and a location–scene association short-term memory task (Cahusac, Miyashita and Rolls 1989). The finding that neuronal representations in the hippocampus switch abruptly from representing a square vs a circular environment on which rats have been trained when the environment changes incrementally between the two has also been suggested as evidence that the hippocampus implements attractor dynamics (Wills, Lever, Cacucci, Burgess and O'Keefe 2005).

In a task in which rats were required to remember multiple places, CA3 and CA1 lesions produced a deficit. In the task, during the study phase rats were presented with four different places within sections that were sequentially visited on a newly devised maze (i.e. Tulum maze). Each place was cued by a unique object that was specifically associated with each location within the section during the study phase. Following a 15-s delay and during the test phase in the absence of the cued object, rats were required to recall and revisit the place within one section of the maze that had been previously visited. Both CA1 and CA3 lesions disrupted accurate relocation of a previously visited place (Lee, Jerman and Kesner 2005). Thus, short-term memory for multiple places in a one-trial multiple place task depends on both CA3 and CA1. As an attractor network can in general hold only one item active in a delay period by maintained firing, this type of multiple item short-term memory is computationally predicted to require synaptic modification to store each item, and both CA3 and CA1 appear to contribute to this.

As described in Section 2.3.2.2, to the extent that path integration of place or spatial view representations is performed within the hippocampus itself, then the CA3 system is the most likely subregion of the hippocampus to be involved in this, because it has the appropriate recurrent collateral connections. Consistent with this, Whishaw and colleagues (Wallace and Whishaw 2003, Maaswinkel et al. 1999, Whishaw et al. 2001) and Save, Guazzelli and Poucet (2001) have shown that path integration is impaired by hippocampal lesions. Path integration of head direction is reflected in the firing of neurons in the presubiculum, and mechanisms outside the hippocampus probably implement path integration for head direction (Sharp 2002). Place cells are also updated idiothetically in the dark (Mizumori, Ragozzino, Cooper and Leutgeb 1999), as are CA3 and CA1 primate spatial view cells (Robertson, Rolls and Georges-François 1998).

2.4.3　CA1 subregion of the hippocampus

The CA1 subregion of the hippocampus receives inputs from two major sources: the Schaffer collateral inputs from CA3, and the perforant path inputs from the entorhinal cortex (see Fig. 2.1). CA1 outputs are directed towards the subiculum, entorhinal cortex, prefrontal cortex and many other neural regions including the lateral septum, anterior thalamus, and the mammillary bodies (Amaral and Witter 1995). The anatomical and physiological characteristics suggest that the CA1 can operate as a competitive network and have triggered the development of computational models of CA1 in which for example the CA1 system is involved in the recall process by which backprojections to the cerebral neocortex allow neuronal activity during recall to reflect that present during the original learning (see Section 2.3.7). In this terminology, cortico-cortical backprojections originate from deep (layer 5) pyramidal cells, and terminate on the apical dendrites of pyramidal cells in layer 1 of the preceding cortical area (see Fig. 2.1). In contrast, cortico-cortical forward projections originate from superficial (layers 2 and 3) pyramidal cells, and terminate in the deep layers of the hierarchically next cortical area (see Fig. 2.1) (Rolls and Treves 1998, Rolls and Deco 2002). Within this context, the projections from the entorhinal cortex to DG, CA3 and CA1 can be thought of as forward projections; and from CA1 to entorhinal cortex, subiculum etc. as the start of the backprojection system (see Fig. 2.1).

The evidence reviewed next of the effects of selective damage to CA1 indicates that it makes a special contribution to temporal aspects of memory including associations over a delay period, and sequence memory. There is also evidence relating it to intermediate memory as well as consolidation (see for more detail Rolls and Kesner (2006)). The effects of damage to the CA1 may not be identical to the effects of damage to CA3, because CA1 has some inputs that bypass CA3 (e.g. the direct entorhinal / perforant path input); and CA3 has some outputs that bypass CA1. In particular, the CA3 output through the fimbria projects directly to the lateral septum and then to the medial septum or directly to the medial septum (Amaral and Witter 1995, Risold and Swanson 1997). The medial septum, in turn, provides cholinergic and GABAergic inputs to the hippocampus (Amaral and Witter 1995).

2.4.3.1　Sequence memory and CA1

In Section 2.3.2.4 we described how a sequence memory could be implemented in a recurrent collateral network such as CA3 with some temporal asymmetry in the associative synaptic modification learning rule. One behavioural test in which this type of memory may be needed is in complex maze learning, which is impaired by hippocampal including dorsal hippocampal and CA3 lesions (Jerman et al. 2006). Maze learning could be implemented by pairwise associations between spatial views, or between responses if the task has become habit-based. However, it could also be implemented by associations between views and body responses (e.g. turns), and there might not be an explicitly sequential association involved in this case, as each body action would lead to the next view. Further, in the cases where complex maze learning is impaired by hippocampal lesions, it would remain to be shown that the deficit is due to sequence learning impairments rather than only to spatial learning deficits.

In another paradigm in which a fixed sequence is learned over multiple trials, it appears that pairwise sequential learning and not just temporal decay is required to account for the findings. In a sequential spatial location list learning paradigm, rats are trained by correction to visit the arms of an 8-arm maze in a particular sequence, with food obtained in each arm if a correct choice (made by orienting) is made. Even though lesions of the hippocampus impair the acquisition of this task (learned by control rats in 40 trials), there are no deficits when hippocampus lesions are made after reaching 90–100% correct performance (DeCoteau and Kesner 2000). Thus the hippocampus may be necessary for learning new spatial sequences, but once learned, it appears that other brain systems can implement the behaviour, perhaps using other egocentric or habit strategies.

The implications of these empirical results for the computations underlying sequence learning, and the contributions of the hippocampus to this, are now considered. The hypothesis that temporally asymmetric associations between the successive pairs of items in a sequence are implemented in CA3 by some temporally asymmetric synaptic modifiability (see Section 2.3.2.4) is consistent with the evidence that the learning of the fixed spatial sequence task is impaired by hippocampal lesions (DeCoteau and Kesner 2000). The CA1 network in this situation could help to separate out the representation of the next item in the list from the currently processed item, as illustrated in Fig. 2.18, but in any case as shown by the subregion lesion analysis, is on the output route from CA3. The CA3 attractor network could enable a preceding item in the sequence to be kept active until the next item arrives, and this is incorporated into the simulation illustrated in Fig. 2.17.

2.4.3.2 Associations across time, and CA1

There is evidence implicating the hippocampus in mediating associations across time (Rawlins 1985, Kesner 1998). The subregion analyses described next show that CA1 lesions impair this. Computationally, a strong hypothesis would be that the CA3 system could provide the working memory necessary for hippocampus-dependent associations across time, and that the CA3 then influences the CA1 for this function to be implemented. The actual learning could involve holding one item active in CA3 but continuing firing in an attractor state until the next item in the sequence arrives, when it could be associated with the preceding item by temporally asymmetric synaptic associativity, as described in the model of Rolls and Stringer illustrated in Figs. 2.17 and 2.18. The computational suggestion thus is that associations across time could be implemented in the hippocampus by using the same functionality that may be used for sequence memory.

The CA1 subregion of the hippocampus may play a role in influencing the formation of associations whenever a time component (requiring a memory trace) is introduced between any two stimuli that need to be associated. Support for this idea comes from studies based on a classical conditioning paradigm. Lesions of the hippocampus in rabbits or rats disrupt the acquisition of eye-blink trace conditioning. In trace conditioning a short delay intervenes between the conditioned stimulus (CS) and the unconditioned stimulus (UCS). When, however, a UCS and CS overlap in time (delay conditioning), rabbits with hippocampal damage typically perform as well as normals (Moyer, Deyo and Disterhoft 1990, Weiss, Bouwmeester, Power and Disterhoft 1999). Based on a subregional analysis, it has now been shown that ventral, but not dorsal, CA1 lesions impair at least the retention (tested after 48 h) of trace fear conditioning (Rogers, Hunsaker and Kesner 2006). Similar learning deficits in trace fear conditioning (but not in conditioning without a delay between the CS and UCS), were observed for mice that lacked NMDA receptors in both dorsal and ventral CA1 subregions of the hippocampus (Huerta, Sun, Wilson and Tonegawa 2000). In an interesting study, McEchron,

Tseng and Disterhoft (2003) recorded from single cells in the CA1 region of the hippocampus during and after trace heart rate (fear) conditioning using either a 10 s or 20 s trace interval. They reported that a significant number of cells showed maximal firing on CS-alone retention trials timed to the 10 s or 20 s trace after CS offset. This could reflect the transition from an attractor state implemented in CA3 with its recurrent collaterals that represents the CS to an attractor state that represents the conditioned response (CR) (Deco and Rolls 2003, Deco and Rolls 2005a, Rolls and Deco 2002).

2.4.3.3 Order memory, and CA1

There are also data on order memory, which does not necessarily imply that a particular sequence has been learned, and could be recalled. Estes (1986) summarized data demonstrating that in human memory there are fewer errors for distinguishing items (by specifying the order in which they occurred) that are far apart in a sequence than those that are temporally adjacent. Other studies have also shown that order judgements improve as the number of items in a sequence between the test items increases (Banks 1978, Chiba, Kesner and Reynolds 1994, Madsen and Kesner 1995). This phenomenon is referred to as a temporal distance effect (sometimes referred to as a temporal pattern separation effect). It is assumed to occur because there is more interference for temporally proximal events than temporally distant events.

Based on these findings, Gilbert, Kesner and Lee (2001) tested memory for the temporal order of items in a one-trial sequence learning paradigm. In the task, each rat was given one daily trial consisting of a sample phase followed by a choice phase. During the sample phase, the animal visited each arm of an 8-arm radial maze once in a randomly predetermined order and was given a reward at the end of each arm. The choice phase began immediately following the presentation of the final arm in the sequence. In the choice phase, two arms were opened simultaneously and the animal was allowed to choose between the two arms. To obtain a food reward, the animal had to enter the arm that occurred earliest in the sequence that it had just followed. Temporal separations of 0, 2, 4, and 6 were randomly selected for each choice phase. These values represented the number of arms in the sample phase that intervened between the two arms that were to be used in the test phase. After reaching criterion rats received CA1 lesions. Following surgery, control rats matched their preoperative performance across all temporal separations. In contrast, rats with CA1 lesions performed at chance across 0, 2, or 4 temporal separations and a little better than chance in the case of a 6 separation. The results suggest that the CA1 subregion is involved in memory for spatial location as a function of temporal separation of spatial locations and that lesions of the CA1 decrease efficiency in temporal pattern separation. CA1 lesioned rats cannot separate events across time, perhaps due to an inability to inhibit interference that may be associated with sequentially occurring events. The increase in temporal interference impairs the rat's ability to remember the order of specific events.

Even though CA1 lesions produced a deficit in temporal pattern separation, some computational models (Levy 1996, Lisman and Idiart 1999, Wallenstein and Hasselmo 1997) and the model described above in Section 2.3 have suggested that the CA3 region is an appropriate part of the hippocampus to form a sequence memory, for example by utilising synaptic associativity in the CA3–CA3 recurrent collaterals that has a temporally asymmetric component (Section 2.3.2.4). It was thus of interest to use the temporal order task to determine whether the CA3 region plays an important role in sequence memory. The CA3 lesions impaired the same sequence learning task described above that was also impaired by lesions of the CA1 region (Gilbert and Kesner 2006).

The hippocampus is known to process spatial and temporal information independently (O'Keefe and Nadel 1978, Kesner 1998). In the previous experiments sequence learning and temporal pattern separation were assessed using spatial cues. Therefore, one possibility is that the CA1 and CA3 deficits were due to the processing of spatial rather than non-spatial temporal information. To determine if the hippocampus is critical for processing all domains of temporal information, it is necessary to use a task that does not depend on spatial information. Since the hippocampus does not mediate short-term (delayed match to sample) memory for odours (Dudchenko, Wood and Eichenbaum 2000, Otto and Eichenbaum 1992), it is possible to test whether the hippocampus plays a role in memory for the temporal sequence of odours (i.e. temporal separation effect). Memory for the temporal order for a sequence of odours was assessed in rats based on a varied sequence of five odours, using a similar paradigm described for sequences of spatial locations. Rats with hippocampal lesions were impaired relative to control animals for memory for all temporal distances for the odours, yet the rats were able to discriminate between the odours (Kesner, Gilbert and Barua 2002). In a further subregional analysis, rats with dorsal CA1 lesions show a mild impairment, but rats with ventral CA1 lesions show a severe impairment in memory for the temporal distance for odours (Kesner 2007). Thus, the CA1 appears to be involved in separating events in time for spatial and non-spatial information, so that one event can be remembered distinct from another event, but the dorsal CA1 might play a more important role than the ventral CA1 for spatial information (Chiba, Johnson and Kesner 1992), and conversely ventral CA1 might play a more important role than the dorsal CA1 for odour information.

In a more recent experiment using a paradigm described by Hannesson, Howland and Phillips (2004), it can be shown that temporal order information for visual objects is impaired only by CA1, but not CA3 lesions (Hoge and Kesner 2006). Thus, with respect to sequence learning or memory for order information one hypothesis that would be consistent with the data is that the CA1 is the critical substrate for sequence learning and temporal order or temporal pattern separation. This would be consistent with CA1 deficits in sequence completion of a spatial task and CA1 deficits in temporal order for spatial locations, odour, and visual objects. Dorsal CA3 contributes to this temporal order or sequence process whenever spatial location is also important. When visual objects are used the CA3 region does not play a role. It is not known yet whether for odours the ventral CA3 plays an important role.

In these order tasks the animals are not required to recall the sequence (for example by retracing their steps). Instead, the animals are asked which of two items occurred earlier in the list. To implement this type of memory, some temporally decaying memory trace might provide a model (Marshuetz 2005), and in such a model, temporally adjacent items would have memory traces of more similar strength and would be harder to discriminate than the strengths of the memory traces of more temporally distant items. (We assume that the animal could learn the rule of responding to the stronger or weaker trace.) This temporal decay memory depends on both the CA3 and CA1 (Gilbert, Kesner and Lee 2001).

2.4.3.4 Intermediate memory, and CA1

There is some evidence that the CA1 region is especially involved in an intermediate term memory. For example, rats with CA3, but not CA1 lesions were impaired in the acquisition of a delayed non-match to place task (in an 8-arm maze) with a 10 s delay. Also, when transferred to a new maze in a different room and using a 10 s delay, there was a deficit for CA3, but not CA1 lesioned rats. Deficits for CA1 emerged when rats were transferred to a 5 min delay. Comparable deficits at a 5 min delay were also found for CA3 lesioned rats. It should be noted that similar results as described for the lesion data were obtained following AP5 injections, which impaired transfer to the new environment when made into CA3 but not CA1. At 5 min delays AP5 injections into CA1 produced a sustained deficit in performance, whereas AP5 injections to CA3 did not produce a sustained deficit (Lee and Kesner 2002, Lee and Kesner 2003a).

Although the CA3 system is involved even at short delays in acquiring this spatial short-term memory task, it is not apparently involved in the task once it has been acquired (Lee and Kesner 2003a). The implication is that (after acquisition) the CA3 system is not required to operate as a short-term attractor working memory to hold on line in the 10 s delay the place that has just been shown, although it could contribute to acquisition by operating in this way. The CA3 could also help in acquisition by providing a good spatial representation for the task, and in particular would enable the spatial cues in the environment to be learned. The suggestion therefore is that at the 5 min delay, the system must operate by associative connections from entorhinal cortex to CA1, which enable the sample place in the 8-arm maze to be remembered until the non-match part of the trial 5 min later, and the AP5 impairment after injection into CA1 is consistent with this.

Further evidence for some dissociation of an intermediate-term from a short-term memory in the hippocampus is described by Rolls and Kesner (2006).

How could memories become hippocampal-independent after long time delays? One possibility is that there is active recall to the neocortex which can then use episodic information to build new semantic memories, as described in Section 2.2.3 (Rolls 1989b, Rolls 1989e, Rolls 1990b, Treves and Rolls 1994, McClelland et al. 1995). In this case, the hippocampus could be said to play a role in the consolidation of memories in the neocortex. We note that in another sense a consolidation process is required in the neocortex during the original learning of the episodic memory, in that we hypothesize that associative connections between hippocampal backprojections and neocortical neurons activated by forward inputs are formed (and presumably consolidated) during the original learning, so that later a hippocampal signal can recall neocortical representations. Another possibility is that there are more passive effects of what has been learned in the hippocampus on the neocortex, occurring for example during sleep (Wilson 2002, Wilson and McNaughton 1994). Indeed, given that the hippocampus is massively connected to the neocortex by backprojections as described above, it is very likely that any alteration of the functional connectivity within the hippocampus, for example the coactivity of place neurons representing nearby places in an environment which has just been learned, will have an influence on the correlations found between neocortical neurons also representing the places of events (Wilson 2002, Wilson and McNaughton 1994). In this case, there could be synaptic modification in the neocortex between newly correlated neuronal activity, and this would effectively produce a form of new learning ('consolidation') in the neocortex. Another sense in which consolidation might be used is to refer to the findings considered in this section that there is a time-dependency of the learning in CA1 that seems special, enabling CA1 to contribute to the formation of memories ('consolidation') with long time delays, and also, perhaps with a different time course, to their subsequent forgetting or reconsolidation. The term 'consolidation' could thus be used to refer to many different types of computational process, which should be distinguished.

2.5   Evaluation of the theory of hippocampal function

2.5.1   Quantitative aspects of the model

The computational neuroscience approach to hippocampal function in memory described in this chapter is quantitative, and supported by both formal analyses and quantitative simulations. Many of the points made, such as on the number of memories that can be stored in autoassociative networks, the utility of sparse representations, and the dynamics of the operation of networks with recurrent connections, are quite general, and will apply to networks in a number of different brain areas. With respect to the hippocampus, the theory specifies the maximum number of memories that could be stored in it, and this has implications for how it could be used biologically. It indicates that if this number is approached, it will be useful to have a mechanism for recalling information from the hippocampus for incorporation into memories elsewhere. With respect to recall, the theory provides a quantitative account for why there are as many backprojections as forward projections in the cerebral cortex. Overall, the theory provides an explanation for how this part of the brain could work, and even if this theory needs to be revised, it is suggested that a fully quantitative theory along the lines proposed which is based on the evidence available from a wide range of techniques will be essential before we can say that we understand how a part of the brain operates.

2.5.2 Tests of the theory by hippocampal system subregion analyses

2.5.2.1 Dentate gyrus/mossy fibre system

The studies showing that the dentate/mossy fibre system is especially involved in hippocampal learning and is not necessary for retrieval (Lassalle et al. 2000, Lee and Kesner 2004b) provide strong support for the hypothesis that the DG system sets up the appropriate representations in CA3 for efficient learning, by helping to ensure that the different memory patterns to be stored in CA3 are relatively orthogonal; and that a separate system (the perforant path input to the CA3 network in the theory) initiates retrieval from the CA3 recurrent collateral network (Treves and Rolls 1992). The evidence that spatial metrically close place memory is especially dependent on the dentate gyrus (Gilbert, Kesner and Lee 2001, Goodrich-Hunsaker, Hunsaker and Kesner 2005) is consistent with the hypothesis that the dentate granule cells help CA3 function by setting up relatively uncorrelated representations of spatial information so that the CA3 recurrent collateral system can form distinct memories (Rolls 1989b, Treves and Rolls 1992, Treves and Rolls 1994). An important part of the theory is that the dentate / mossy fibre system by helping to set up relatively orthogonal representations in CA3 for different memories helps to increase the number of memories that can be stored in the CA3 system (which is calculated to be tens of thousands) (Treves and Rolls 1994).

It is useful to note that the non-associative mossy fibre to CA3 synapses are appropriate for a system that performs one-trial (episodic) learning, for it helps to set up orthogonal representations in CA3 even on one trial, without learning. (The CA3 to CA3 synapses would then learn that unique pattern of firing that would be produced on that trial by the mossy fibre pattern separation effect on CA3 firing.) Simulations of hippocampal evolution with genetic algorithms (Rolls and Stringer 2000) show (Rolls and Stringer, in preparation) that if the dentate to CA3 synapses were associative and helped them to operate as a competitive network input system to the CA3 dendrite, this could improve performance. However this competitive effect on CA3 dendrites would only be useful if each memory item to be remembered is presented repeatedly to allow self-organization of these synapses. As repeated presentation of a single item is not a property of episodic memory, it is suggested that the non-associative mossy fibre input system to CA3 is more appropriate than a set of dentate to CA3 synapses that would self-organize competitively over repeated trials.

2.5.2.2 CA3 system

The hypothesis that CA3 operates as an autoassociation or attractor network, and can thereby contribute to pattern completion, short-term memory, recall, rapid (one-trial) encoding, path integration, and sequence memory, for certain types of information, receives considerable support from the subregion analyses. The evidence that pattern completion when an incomplete retrieval cue is presented depends on the CA3 recurrent collateral system (Gold and Kesner 2005, Nakazawa et al. 2002) is consistent with a major prediction of the theory. The evidence that some types of short-term memory depend on the CA3 system (see Sections 2.4.2.8 and

2.4.3.2) is consistent with the hypothesis that it can operate as an attractor network, which has the property that it can keep a memory active by continuing firing of CA3 neurons. A property of this type of memory is that it can be interrupted by new processing or distraction, and it is of interest that in the CA3-dependent short-term memory tasks, the environment is often partially hidden by a bucket, which would tend to help keep the attractor memory from being interrupted by a distractor. It is predicted that these memory tasks will be susceptible to distractors presented in the delay period. The predictions are thus that if there is no task in a delay period (and no need for an off-line buffer store), the hippocampus may be sufficient to perform the short-term memory function (such as remembering a previous location), provided that there is little distraction in the delay period. On the other hand, if there are intervening stimuli in the delay period, then the prefrontal cortex is predicted computationally to be involved. Thus, lesions of the prefrontal cortex are predicted to impair spatial short-term memory tasks particularly when there are intervening items, or much distraction or processing of other stimuli, in the delay period (see Section 2.3.2.1).

The evidence that primate CA3 and CA1 neurons can combine information about objects and places in an object–place memory task (and that other neurons encode just the places or just the objects (Rolls, Xiang and Franco 2005c)), and about rewards and places in a reward–place memory task (Rolls and Xiang 2005); and that CA3 lesions disrupt object–place and odour–place learning in rats (Gilbert and Kesner 2003) is important evidence that the types of information required for these arbitrary types of association are present in the primate and rat hippocampus, and that continuous and discrete representations can be represented in the same network (Rolls, Stringer and Trappenberg 2002) (see Fig. 2.16). Subregion analyses show that place information requires especially the CA3 subregion, and that some types of temporal information (including odour and spatial location order tasks and trace conditioning) may require a combination of CA3 and CA1. The evidence that some hippocampal pyramidal neurons reflect the place to be recalled in an object–place one-trial recall task (Rolls and Xiang 2006) also indicates that the system is useful in episodic (rapid, one-trial) memories. In these cases, the crucial site for the associativity would be the CA3 recurrent collateral system. Subregion analysis in the rat shows that the CA3 subregion is required for one-trial object–place recall (Warthen and Kesner 2007). Subregion analyses provide additional evidence that the CA3 system is important in rapid (one trial) encoding, in for example a one-trial non matching to place task (Lee and Kesner 2002, Lee and Kesner 2003a), in the one-trial object–place recall task with many objects and many places just cited, and in one-trial learning for spatial location in the water maze (Nakazawa, Sun, Quirk, Rondi-Reig, Wilson and Tonegawa 2003).

A theory of how attractor networks could self-organize (that is, could learn the correct synaptic weights) to perform path integration when provided with a movement signal of direction and velocity has been described in Sections 2.3.2.2 and B.5.5. The theory has been developed for head direction cells, place cells, and spatial view cells. If implemented within the hippocampus, it is predicted that this would be in the CA3 system, as it has the recurrent collateral connections that would naturally support the attractor. It has been shown that the hippocampus is necessary for some types of path integration, e.g. for place (Maaswinkel et al. 1999, Save et al. 2001, Wallace and Whishaw 2003, Whishaw et al. 2001), but subregion analyses have not been performed. The path integration over distance and direction travelled may be performed by the entorhinal cortex grid cells, and the prediction is that synaptic modification in the CA3 system would be necessary to link the path integration to a particular environment, but not for performance once an environment has been learned. It is predicted that DG might only be essential if metric accuracy during learning was at a premium (e.g. with obstacles that are close together), as it provides the pattern separation that helps to form place cells from entorhinal cortex grid cells. However, path integration for head direction appears to be performed outside the hippocampus proper (the presubiculum and dorsal tegmental nuclei are possible sites for this), and for place may be performed outside the hippocampus, in that entorhinal cortex grid cells may be updated idiothetically (Hafting, Fyhn, Molden, Moser and Moser 2005, McNaughton, Battaglia, Jensen, Moser and Moser 2006). In this context, it is notable that head direction information could be introduced into the hippocampal system via the presubiculum to entorhinal cortex connections – see Fig. 2.1. Nevertheless, the evidence in primates and rats is that the hippocampus proper does make a contribution to path integration, in that there is some idiothetic update in the dark of spatial view cells in CA3 (which could be implemented by the CA3 recurrent collateral system), but more idiothetic update of CA1 cells (which could be based on information retrieval at the CA3 to CA1 associative synapses based on the CA3 firing) (Robertson, Rolls and Georges-François 1998, Schultz and Rolls 1999).

Sequence memory could be implemented by temporally asymmetric synaptic modifiability in the CA3 system. As noted above in Section 2.4.3.1, this type of memory may be needed in complex maze learning, which is impaired by hippocampal including dorsal hippocampal and CA3 lesions. However, in the cases where complex maze learning is impaired by hippocampal lesions, it would remain to be shown that the deficit is due to sequence learning impairments rather than only to spatial learning deficits. The empirical tests of sequence memory only show this type of memory with training over repeated trials, when it tends to become automatic, and indeed may become habit-based.

The judgement for which item came earlier in a sequence is computationally simpler, for a temporally decaying synaptic trace could implement this. However, a true sequence memory (in which the order of adjacent pairs in the sequence was learned) would tend to recall the next item in a sequence when one item is presented, and this would tend to make items close in the sequence difficult to discriminate, but items far apart in the sequence would be more discriminable. As described in Section 2.3.2.4, computationally the CA1 network might recode the CA3 output to form conjunctive representations by competitive learning. This could make successive items in a sequence more discriminable in CA1 by promoting temporal pattern separation, than they would be in the componential encoding that may be more appropriate for CA3 as an autoassociation network. This interpretation is consistent with the evidence described in Section 2.4.3.3 that CA1 lesions disrupt memory of the temporal order of spatial or odour items (Fortin, Agster and Eichenbaum 2002, Gilbert et al. 2001, Kesner et al. 2002).

The implications of these results for the computations underlying sequence learning, and the contributions of the hippocampus to this, are now considered. The hypothesis that temporally asymmetric associations between the successive pairs of items in a sequence implemented in CA3 by some temporally asymmetric synaptic modifiability (see Section 2.3.2.4) is consistent with the evidence that the learning of the fixed spatial sequence task is impaired by hippocampal lesions (DeCoteau and Kesner 2000). The CA1 network in this situation could help to separate out the representation of the next item in the list from the currently processed item, as illustrated in Fig. 2.18, but in any case as shown by the subregion lesion analysis, CA1 is on the output route from CA3. On the other hand, the one-trial list presentation tasks in which the recency of items in the list is what must be discriminated could be performed by a temporal decay memory, which is CA3 and CA1 dependent (Gilbert et al. 2001).

2.5.2.3 CA1 system

As just noted, CA1 subregion lesions disrupt memory of the temporal order of spatial or odour items. They also impair trace conditioning, and starting in early positions when performing a fixed sequence spatial task that has been learned previously. They also impair learning with long (e.g. 5 min) delays in a non-matching to sample place task (intermediate memory); and in the Hebb–Williams maze impair performance on the first trials on the following day when retrieval is at a premium. All these tasks are also impaired by disruption of direct entorhinal to CA1 connections. As noted in Section 2.4.3.4 on intermediate memory, a hypothesis that may help to unify these findings is that the time course of synaptic changes in CA1 has a different, and longer, time course to that in for example CA3, which allows it to play a particular role in learning these time delay types of memory task.

Computationally, it is noted that the direct entorhinal to CA1 connections could be used in recall, in a way that is analogous to the entorhinal to CA3 projections. Further, the tasks impaired by CA1 but not by CA3 lesions tend to involve non-spatial information, and temporal delays. However, as elaborated below, a main prediction of the computational theory with respect to CA1 is that CA1, and the CA3 to CA1 connections, will be especially important when recall of information is required back to the neocortex using backprojections, in for example place–object recall, and this has not yet been tested by subregion analysis.

A further analysis of the interactions and dissociations between CA3 and CA1 is provided by Rolls and Kesner (2006).

2.5.3 Comparison with other theories of hippocampal function

Hypotheses have been described in this chapter about how a number of different parts of hippocampal and related circuitry might operate. Although these hypotheses are consistent with a theory of how the hippocampus operates, some of these hypotheses could be incorporated into other views or theories. In order to highlight the differences between alternative theories, and in order to lead to constructive analyses that can test them, the theory described above is compared with other theories of hippocampal function in this section. Although the differences between the theories are highlighted in this section, the overall view described here is close in different respects to those of a number of other investigators (Brown and Zador 1990, Eichenbaum, Otto and Cohen 1992, Gaffan 1992, Marr 1971, McNaughton and Nadel 1990, Squire 1992, Moscovitch, Rosenbaum, Gilboa, Addis, Westmacott, Grady, McAndrews, Levine, Black, Winocur and Nadel 2005) and of course priority is not claimed on all the propositions put forward here.

Some theories postulate that the hippocampus performs spatial computation. The theory of O'Keefe and Nadel (1978) that the hippocampus implements a cognitive map, placed great emphasis on spatial function. It supposed that the hippocampus at least holds information about allocentric space in a form which enables rats to find their way in an environment even when novel trajectories are necessary, that is it permits an animal to "go from one place to another independent of particular inputs (cues) or outputs (responses), and to link together conceptually parts of the environment which have never been experienced at the same time". O'Keefe (1990) extended this analysis and produced a computational theory of the hippocampus as a cognitive map, in which the hippocampus performs geometric spatial computations. Key aspects of the theory are that the hippocampus stores the centroid and slope of the distribution of landmarks in an environment, and stores the relationships between the centroid and the individual landmarks. The hippocampus then receives as inputs information about where the rat currently is, and where the rat's target location is, and computes geometrically the body turns and movements necessary to reach the target location. In this sense, the hippocampus is taken to be a spatial computer, which produces an output which is very different from its inputs. This is in contrast to the present theory, in which the hippocampus is a memory device, which is able to recall what was stored in it, using as input a partial cue. The theory of O'Keefe postulates that the hippocampus actually performs a spatial computation. A later theory (Burgess, Jackson, Hartley and O'Keefe 2000, Burgess, Recce and O'Keefe 1994) also makes the same postulate, but now the firing of place cells is determined by the distance and approximate bearing to landmarks, and the navigation is performed by increasing the strength of connections from place cells to "goal cells", and then performing gradient-ascent style search for the goal using the network.

McNaughton, Chen and Markus (1991) have also proposed that the hippocampus is involved in spatial computation. They propose a "compass" solution to the problem of spatial navigation along novel trajectories in known environments, postulating that distances and bearings (i.e. vector quantities) from landmarks are stored, and that computation of a new trajectory involves vector subtraction by the hippocampus. They postulate that a linear associative mapping is performed, using as inputs a "cross-feature" (combination) representation of (head) angular velocity and (its time integral) head direction, to produce as output the future value of the integral (head direction) after some specified time interval. The system can be reset by learned associations between local views of the environment and head direction, so that when later a local view is seen, it can lead to an output from the network which is a (corrected) head direction. They suggest that some of the key signals in the computational system can be identified with the firing of hippocampal cells (e.g. local view cells) and subicular cells (head direction cells). It should be noted that this theory requires a (linear) associative mapping with an output (head direction) different in form from the inputs (head angular velocity over a time period, or local view). This is pattern association (with the conditioned stimulus local view, and the unconditioned stimulus head direction), not autoassociation, and it has been postulated that this pattern association can be performed by the hippocampus (cf. McNaughton and Morris (1987)). This theory is again in contrast to the present theory, in which the hippocampus operates as a memory to store events that occur at the same time, and can recall the whole memory from any part of what was stored. (A pattern associator uses a conditioned stimulus to map an input to a pattern of firing in an output set of neurons which is like that produced in the output neurons by the unconditioned stimulus. A description of pattern associators and autoassociators in a neurobiological context is provided in Appendix B. The present theory is fully consistent with the presence of "spatial view" cells and whole body motion cells in the primate hippocampus (Rolls and Xiang 2006, Rolls 1999c, Rolls and O'Mara 1993) (or place or local view cells in the rat hippocampus, and head direction cells in the presubiculum), for it is often important to store and later recall where one has been (views of the environment, body turns made, etc), and indeed such (episodic) memories are required for navigation by "dead reckoning" in small environments.

The present theory thus holds that the hippocampus is used for the formation of episodic memories using autoassociation. This function is often necessary for successful spatial computation, but is not itself spatial computation. Instead, we believe that spatial computation is more likely to be performed in the neocortex (utilising information if necessary recalled from the hippocampus). Consistent with this view, hippocampal damage impairs the ability to learn new environments but not to perform spatial computations such as finding one's way to a place in a familiar environment, whereas damage to the parietal cortex and parahippocampal cortex can lead to problems such as topographical and other spatial agnosias, in humans (Grusser and Landis 1991, Kolb and Whishaw 2003). This is consistent with spatial computations normally being performed in the neocortex. (In monkeys, there is evidence for a role of the parietal cortex in allocentric spatial computation. For example, monkeys with parietal cortex lesions are impaired at performing a landmark task, in which the object to be chosen is signified by the proximity to it of a "landmark" (another object) (Ungerleider and Mishkin 1982).)

A theory closely related to the present theory of how the hippocampus operates has been developed by McClelland, McNaughton and O'Reilly (1995). It is very similar to the theory we have developed (Rolls 1989a, Rolls 1989b, Rolls 1989f, Rolls 1987, Treves and Rolls 1992, Treves and Rolls 1994, Rolls 1996c, Rolls and Treves 1998, Rolls and Kesner 2006) at the systems level, except that it takes a stronger position on the gradient of retrograde amnesia, emphasises that recall from the hippocampus of episodic information is used to help build semantic representations in the neocortex, and holds that the last set of synapses that are modified rapidly during the learning of each episode are those between the CA3 and the CA1 pyramidal cells (see Fig. 2.1). In the formulation by McClelland, McNaughton and O'Reilly (1995), the entorhinal cortex connections via the perforant path onto the CA1 cells are non-modifiable (in the short term), and allow a representation of neocortical long-term memories to activate the CA1 cells. The new information learned in an episode by the CA3 system is then linked to existing long-term memories by the CA3 to CA1 rapidly modifiable synapses. All the connections from the CA1 back via the subiculum, entorhinal cortex, parahippocampal cortex etc. to the association neocortex are held to be unmodifiable in the short term, during the formation of an episodic memory. The formal argument that leads us to suggest that the backprojecting synapses are associatively modifiable during the learning of an episodic memory is similar to that which we have used to show that for efficient recall, the synapses which initiate recall in the CA3 system (identified above with the perforant path projection to CA3) must be associatively modifiable if recall is to operate efficiently (Treves and Rolls 1992). The present theory holds that it is possible that for several stages back into neocortical processing, the backprojecting synapses should be associatively modifiable, with a similar time course to the time it takes to learn a new episodic memory. It may well be that at earlier stages of cortical processing, for example from inferior temporal visual cortex to V4, and from V4 to V2, the backprojections are relatively more fixed, being formed (still associatively) during early developmental plasticity or during the formation of new long-term semantic memory structures. Having such relatively fixed synaptic strengths in these earlier cortical backprojection systems could ensure that whatever is recalled in higher cortical areas, such as objects, will in turn recall relatively fixed and stable representations of parts of objects or features. Given that the functions of backprojections may include many top-down processing operations, including attention (Deco and Rolls 2005a) and priming, it may be useful to ensure that there is consistency in how higher cortical areas affect activity in earlier "front-end" or preprocessing cortical areas. Indeed, the current theory shows that at least one backprojection stage, the hippocampo-cortical connections must be associatively modifiable during the learning of an episodic memory, but does not require the associative backprojection learning to occur at all backprojection stages during the learning of the episodic memory. Crucial stages might include CA1 to subiculum or to entorhinal cortex (see Fig. 2.1), or entorhinal cortex to parahippocampal gyrus and perirhinal cortex. It would be interesting to test this using local inactivation of NMDA receptors at different stages of the backprojection system to determine where this impairs the learning of for example place–object recall, i.e. a task that is likely to utilize the hippocampo-cortical backprojection pathways.

If a model of the hippocampal / neocortical memory system could store only a small number of patterns, it would not be a good model of the real hippocampal / neocortical memory system in the brain. Indeed, this appears to be a major limitation of another model presented by Alvarez and Squire (1994). The model specifies that the hippocampus helps the operation of a neocortical multimodal memory system in which all memories are stored by associative recurrent collaterals between the neocortical neurons. Although the idea worked in the model with twenty neurons and two patterns to be learned (Alvarez and Squire 1994), the whole idea is computationally not feasible, because the number of memories that can be stored in a single autoassociative network of the type described is limited by the number of inputs per neuron from other neurons, not by the number of neurons in the network (Treves and Rolls 1991, Treves and Rolls 1994). This would render the capacity of the whole neocortical multimodal (or amodal) memory store very low (in the order of the number of inputs per neuron from the other neurons, that is in the order of 5,000–10,000) (O'Kane and Treves 1992). This example makes it clear that it is important to take into account analytic and quantitative approaches when investigating memory systems. The current work is an attempt to do this.

The theory of Lisman et al. (2005) of the memory for sequences has been described and evaluated in Section 2.3.2.4. This theory of sequential recall within the hippocampus is inextricably linked to the internal timing within the hippocampus imposed he believes by the theta and gamma oscillations, and this makes it difficult to recall each item in the sequence as it is needed. It is not specified how one would read out the sequence information, given that the items are only 12 ms apart. The Jensen and Lisman (1996) model requires short time constant NMDA channels, and is therefore unlikely to be implemented in the hippocampus. Hasselmo and Eichenbaum (2005) have taken up some of these sequence ideas and incorporated them into their model, which has its origins in the Rolls and Treves model (Rolls 1989b, Treves and Rolls 1992, Treves and Rolls 1994, Rolls and Treves 1998). The proposal that acetylcholine could be important during encoding by facilitating CA3–CA3 LTP, and should be lower during retrieval (Hasselmo, Schnell and Barkai 1995), is a useful concept.

Another type of sequence memory uses synaptic adaptation to effectively encode the order of the items in a sequence (Deco and Rolls 2005c). This could be implemented in recurrent networks such as the CA3 or the prefrontal cortex.

The aim of this comparison of the present theory with other theories has been to highlight differences between the theories, to assist in the future assessment of the utility and the further development of each of the theories.

Overall, the approach taken in this chapter shows how it is now possible to understand quantitatively how the circuitry in a major brain system could actually operate to store and later recall memories. The principles uncovered illustrate important foundations of many types of brain computation, including forming new representations (in this case of spatial view or place) as a result of hierarchical processing, the functions of attractor networks in the brain, the importance of the sparseness of the representation, the recall of information from a memory system, and the functions of backprojections between cortical areas.

3 Reward- and punishment-related learning; emotion and motivation

3.1 Introduction

Rewards and punishers are important in instrumental learning. Many of the unconditioned stimuli used in classical conditioning have reinforcing properties. Emotions can be considered as states elicited by reinforcing stimuli, that is, by rewards and punishers (Rolls 1999a, Rolls 2005). Understanding the brain mechanisms that underlie learning about reinforcers, i.e. rewards and punishers, is thus very important. We need to understand which stimuli are primary, i.e. unlearned, reinforcers; and we need to understand the associative processes that enable other previously neutral stimuli to become associated with these primary reinforcers by learning. In order to be clear, I start with some definitions, and then with an analysis of the different types of learning that can occur with rewards and punishers (Section 3.2). Then I consider where primary reinforcers are represented (Section 3.4), where and how potential secondary (learned) reinforcers are represented (Section 3.5 and Chapter 4), and then the brain regions that implement stimulus–reinforcer, i.e. emotional, learning, considering the orbitofrontal cortex (Section 3.6), amygdala (Section 3.7), and cingulate cortex (Section 3.8). Then I consider output systems for the effects of rewards and punishers, and for emotion (Section 3.10).

Rolls (2005, 1999a, 1990d, 1986a) has developed the theory not only that emotions can be considered as states elicited by reinforcers, but also that primary reinforcers specified by genes provide an important thoroughly Darwinian solution to how some genes can increase their success by specifying rewards that will increase the fitness of an animal. This is an elegant solution to the problem of how genes can most efficiently influence behaviour. By specifying the reinforcing stimuli that are the goals for action, i.e. rewards and punishers, rather than actions or responses themselves, there is a great simplification in what needs to be specified in the genome (see Rolls (2005) Section 3.5). It would be very difficult for genes to specify an action such as recognising an apple, climbing a tree, reaching for the apple, and then eating it. There are only some cases in which genes specify fixed action patterns, though one well-known example is the herring gull chick's pecking response elicited as a fixed action pattern by the innate releasing stimulus of a red spot on its parent's bill (Tinbergen 1951, Tinbergen 1963). However, by specifying goals, genes leave it open to when the animal is alive for it to learn the best instrumental behaviour to obtain the reward, and this provides great flexibility in behaviour.

A great advantage of this way for genes to guide behaviour is that it is relatively efficient in terms of the number of genes required, in that primary reinforcers such as sweet taste should be rewarding when hungry, and water in the mouth should be rewarding when thirsty, and specifying that a limited number of stimuli should be reinforcers is much simpler that specifying how to perform particular actions, each of which might be quite complex, to particular stimuli (Rolls 2005). To provide an indication of the types of primary reinforcer

Table 3.1 Some primary reinforcers, and the dimensions of the environment to which they are tuned

Taste

Salt taste	reward in salt deficiency
Sweet	reward in energy deficiency
Bitter	punisher, indicator of possible poison
Sour	punisher
Umami	reward, indicator of protein;
	produced by monosodium glutamate and inosine monophosphate
Tannic acid	punisher; it prevents absorption of protein; found in old leaves;
	probably somatosensory rather than strictly gustatory

Odour

Putrefying odour	punisher; hazard to health
Pheromones	reward (depending on hormonal state)

Somatosensory

Pain	punisher
Touch	reward
Grooming	reward; to give grooming may also be a primary reinforcer
Washing	reward
Temperature	reward if helps maintain normal body temperature; otherwise punisher

Visual

Snakes, etc.	punisher for, e.g. primates
Youthfulness	reward, associated with mate choice
Beauty, e.g. symmetry	reward
Secondary sexual characteristics	rewards
Face expression	reward (e.g. smile) or punisher (e.g. threat)
Blue sky, cover, open space	reward, indicator of safety
Flowers	reward (indicator of fruit later in the season?)

Auditory

Warning call	punisher
Aggressive vocalization	punisher
Soothing vocalization	reward (part of the evolutionary history of music,
	which at least in its origins taps into the channels
	used for the communication of emotions)

that may be specified by genes, a partial list is provided in Table 3.1[6].

[6]It may be remarked that of course some goals are defined within a culture, for example writing a novel like one by Tolstoy vs one by Virginia Woolf. But it is argued that it is primary reinforcers specified by genes that make us

Table 3.1 continued **Some primary reinforcers, and the dimensions of the environment to which they are tuned**

Reproduction

Courtship	reward
Sexual behaviour	reward (different reinforcers, including a low waist-to-hip ratio, and attractiveness influenced by symmetry and being found attractive by members of the other sex are discussed by Rolls, 2005)
Mate guarding	reward for a male to protect his parental investment; jealousy results if his mate is courted by another male, because this may ruin his parental investment
Nest building	reward (when expecting young)
Parental attachment	reward
Infant attachment to parents	reward
Crying of infant	punisher to parents; produced to promote successful development

Other

Novel stimuli	rewards (encourage animals to investigate the full possibilities of the multidimensional space in which their genes are operating)
Sleep	reward; minimizes nutritional requirements and protects from danger
Altruism to genetically related individuals	reward (kin altruism)
Altruism to other individuals	reward while the altruism is reciprocated in a 'tit-for-tat' reciprocation (reciprocal altruism) Forgiveness, honesty, and altruistic punishment are associated heuristics (May provide underpinning for some aspects of what is felt to be moral.)
Altruism to other individuals	punisher when the altruism is not reciprocated.
Group acceptance, reputation	reward (social greeting might indicate this) These goals can account for some culturally specified goals
Control over actions	reward
Play	reward
Danger, stimulation, excitement	reward if not too extreme (adaptive because of practice?)
Exercise	reward (keeps the body fit for action)
Mind reading	reward; practice in reading others' minds, which might be adaptive
Solving an intellectual problem	reward (practice in which might be adaptive)
Storing, collecting	reward (e.g. food)
Habitat preference, home, territory	reward
Some responses	reward (e.g. pecking in chickens, pigeons; adaptive because it is a simple way in which eating grain can be programmed for a fixed type of environmental stimulus)
Breathing	reward

Another way in which the genetic specification required can be kept low is that stimulus–reinforcer association learning can then be used to enable quite arbitrary stimuli occurring in

want to be recognised in society because of the advantages this can bring, solve difficult problems, etc, and therefore to perform actions such as writing novels (see further Rolls (2005), Ridley (2003) Chapter 8, Ridley (1993a) pp. 310 ff, Laland and Brown (2002) pp. 271 ff, and Dawkins (1982)).

the lifetime of an animal to become associated with primary reinforcers by stimulus–reinforcer association learning, and thus to lead to actions.

Thus the ways in which primary reinforcers are made explicit in neural representations, stimulus–reinforcer association learning, and the learning of instrumental actions to obtain reinforcers are fundamental to much of brain design for adaptive behaviour (including emotion and motivation), and this chapter considers how these processes are implemented in the brain. Motivation can be defined as a state in which the animal will work to obtain a goal (Rolls 2005). Motivation is usually taken to include the fact that an arbitrary operation action will be performed to obtain the goal, whereas drive does not necessarily imply that an instrumental action is being performed (Rolls 2005).

3.2 Associative processes involved in reward- and punishment-related learning

When a conditioned stimulus (CS) (such as a tone) is paired with a primary reinforcer or unconditioned stimulus (US) (such as a painful stimulus), then there are opportunities for a number of types of association to be formed.

Some of these involve 'classical conditioning' or 'Pavlovian conditioning', in which no action is performed that affects the contingency between the conditioned stimulus and the unconditioned stimulus. Typically an unconditioned response (UR), for example an alteration of heart rate, is produced by the US, and will come to be elicited by the CS as a conditioned response (CR). These responses are typically autonomic (such as the heart beating faster), or endocrine (for example the release of adrenaline (epinephrine in American usage) by the adrenal gland).

In addition, the organism may learn to perform an instrumental action with the skeletal muscles in order to alter the probability that the primary reinforcer will be obtained. In our example, the experimenter might alter the contingencies so that when the tone sounded, if the organism performed an action such as pressing a lever, then the painful stimulus could be avoided. This is confirmed to be instrumental learning if the response that is learned is arbitrary, for example learning to perform the opposite response, such as raising the lever, to avoid the painful stimulus.

In the instrumental learning situation there are still opportunities for many classically conditioned responses including emotional states such as fear to occur, and, as different neural subsystems appear to contribute differently to these different types of learning that occur in emotional situations produced by reinforcers, I will next separate out some of the different associative processes that can occur, to provide a basis for understanding the roles of different neural subsystems in the different emotion-related responses and states, following the general approach reviewed by Cardinal, Parkinson, Hall and Everitt (2002).

3.2.1 Pavlovian or classical conditioning

As shown in Fig. 3.1, Pavlovian conditioning has the potential to create multiple associative representations in the brain, as described next (Cardinal et al. 2002, Mackintosh 1983, Gewirtz and Davis 1998, Dickinson 1980, Cardinal and Everitt 2004).

3.2.1.1 Stimulus–Response association

First, the CS may become directly associated with the UR, a simple stimulus–response association that carries no information about the identity of the US (Kandel 2000) (pathway 1 in Fig. 3.1). Such US-elicited responses include preparatory responses which are not specific to

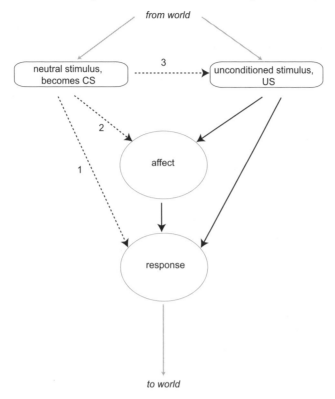

Fig. 3.1 Pavlovian conditioning has the potential to create associations between a conditioned stimulus (CS) and representations of the unconditioned stimulus (US), central affective or emotional states such as fear, and unconditioned responses. The dashed lines labelled 1, 2 and 3 represent associatively learned links described in the text. Several different types of response may be involved, including preparatory responses which are not specific to the type of US involved (e.g. orienting to a stimulus, or increased arousal), and 'consummatory' responses which are specific to the US such as salivation to food, or blinking to an air puff applied to the eye. (After Cardinal, Parkinson, Hall and Everitt 2002.)

the type of US involved (e.g. orienting to a stimulus, or increased arousal), and 'consummatory' responses which are specific to the US such as salivation to food, or blinking to an air puff applied to the eye, or approach to a food. A single US may elicit both preparatory and consummatory responses, and thus the CS may enter into simple S–R associations with several types of response. The nature of the CS can influence which response is evoked; for example if a poorly localized CS such as a tone is paired with food, it may not elicit conditioned approach, while a localized light does. It is notable in this last example that the approach response is skeletal, so that we are going beyond the concept that Pavlovian conditioning applies only to autonomic responses.

3.2.1.2 A representation of affect, i.e. an emotional state

Second, the CS can evoke a representation of affect, i.e. an emotional state, such as fear or the expectation of reward (pathway 2 in Fig. 3.1). It is demonstrated operationally by the phenomenon of transreinforcer blocking. Blocking is a feature of Pavlovian conditioning in which an animal does not learn about one CS in the presence of another CS that already predicts the same US (Dickinson 1980). In *transreinforcer blocking*, the presence of a CS previously paired with shock can block or prevent conditioning to a CS paired with the absence of otherwise expected food reward (Dickinson and Dearing 1979). These two reinforcers share no common properties other than their aversiveness, and therefore the blocking effect must depend on an association between the CS and affect. Affective states, it is argued (Dickinson and Dearing 1979, Konorski 1967, Cardinal et al. 2002), can therefore be independent of the specific reinforcer and response – they are pure 'value' states. However, I note that, at least in humans, affective states normally have content, that is they are about particular reinforcers (such as feeling happy because I am seeing a friend, or feeling happy because I am receiving a gift), and these states are better described by the third type of association, described next.

3.2.1.3 Conditioned-stimulus (CS) – unconditioned stimulus (US) associations

Third, the CS can become associated with the specific sensory properties of the US including its visual appearance, sound, and smell, and its 'consummatory' (primary reinforcing) properties such as its taste, nutritive value, and feel (pathway 3 in Fig. 3.1). An operational demonstration of this type of representation is sensory preconditioning, in which two neutral stimuli are first associated; one neutral stimulus is then paired with a primary reinforcer, and the other stimulus can subsequently evoke a CR (Dickinson 1980). Further evidence for the US specificity of Pavlovian associations comes from the effect of post-conditioning changes in the value of the US. If a CS is paired with a rewarding food, and the food is subsequently devalued by pairing it with a lithium chloride (LiCl) injection to induce nausea, not only does the animal reject the food US, but its reaction to the CS changes (Mackintosh 1983, Holland and Straub 1979). Therefore the CS could not have been associated just with an abstract affective representation, as it was able to retrieve, by association, the new value of the US. As the LiCl pairing does not affect the reaction to a second CS predicting a different food, each CS must have been associated with some specific aspect of its US.

We will see later that different pathways in the brain are involved in the Pavlovian learned autonomic and skeletal responses to a CS, and in the affective representation or state (e.g. fear), which may itself enter into associations and influence choice.

3.2.2 Instrumental learning

In instrumental learning, there is a contingency between the behavioural action and the reinforcing outcome. A number of different learning processes may operate during this procedure (Cardinal et al. 2002, Dickinson 1994, Dickinson and Balleine 1994). These learning processes are summarized next as they help to understand some of the different brain mechanisms that become engaged and affect behaviour when emotion-provoking stimuli are delivered. These learning processes are closely related to emotion, for as argued by Rolls (2005), emotions are states elicited by instrumental reinforcers. Moreover, as argued by Rolls (2005), an important part of the evolutionary adaptive value of emotions is that genes can influence our behaviour efficiently by specifying the goals for our actions, and then instrumental learning in life leads us to learn appropriate behaviours to obtain those gene-specified goals. This of course leads to selection of the genes that specify the goals (rewards and punishers), and thereby promote their own survival into the next generation. Part of the adaptive value of emotional states, as argued by Rolls (2005), is that they persist for some time after the reinforcer has gone, and this continuation enables the reinforcers to influence our behaviour (by unconditioned, classically conditioned, and instrumentally learned, processes) for often a considerable time. These arguments, and the relationship between reinforcers and emotion, are developed much more comprehensively by Rolls (2005).

An example of a goal-directed behaviour is when an organism presses a lever for food because it knows that lever-pressing produces food and that it wants the food. More formally,

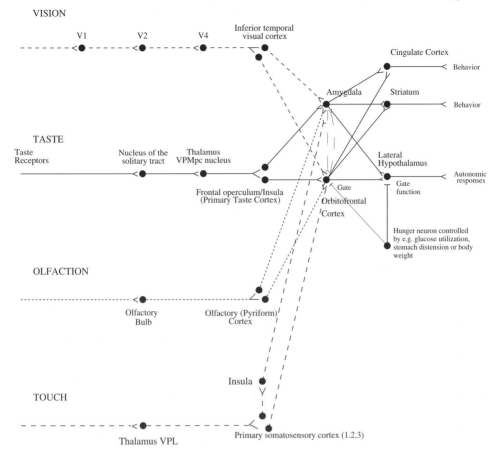

Fig. 3.3 Schematic diagram showing some of the connections of the taste, olfactory, somatosensory, and visual pathways in the brain. V1, primary visual (striate) cortex; V2 and V4, further cortical visual areas. VPL, ventro-postero-lateral nucleus of the thalamus, which conveys somatosensory information to the primary somatosensory cortex (areas 1, 2 and 3).

pain), and to some extent smell, and perhaps certain visual stimuli, such as face expression. There is evidence that there is a representation of the primary reinforcers taste and positive touch in the orbitofrontal cortex. In the terminology of neuroeconomics (see Section 10.6), primary reinforcers often represent the *reward outcome*.

2. Some brain regions are concerned with learning associations between previously neutral stimuli, such as the sight of objects or of individuals' faces, with primary reinforcers. These brain regions include the amygdala and orbitofrontal cortex. For the processing of primary reinforcers, and especially for secondary reinforcers, the brain is organized to process the stimulus first to the object level (so that if the input is visual, the object can be recognized independently of its position on the retina, or size, or view), and then to determine whether the stimulus is rewarding or punishing. Once the relevant brain regions have determined whether the input is reinforcing, whether primary or secondary, the signal is passed directly to output regions of the brain, with no need to produce peripheral body or autonomic responses. In the terminology of neuroeconomics (see Section 10.6), secondary reinforcers often represent the *expected value*.

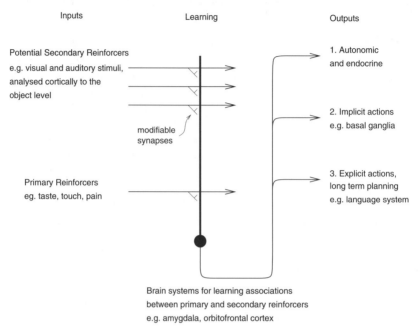

Brain Mechanisms of Emotion

Fig. 3.4 Schematic diagram showing the organization of some of the brain mechanisms underlying emotion, including those involved in learning the reinforcement associations of visual stimuli.

3. The brain regions in which the reinforcing, and hence emotional, value of stimuli are represented interface to three main types of output system:

The first is the autonomic and endocrine system, for producing such changes as increased heart rate and release of adrenaline, which prepare the body for action.

The second type of output is to brain systems concerned with performing actions unconsciously or implicitly, in order to obtain rewards or avoid punishers. These brain systems include the basal ganglia.

The third type of output is to a system capable of planning many steps ahead, and for example deferring short-term rewards in order to execute a long-term plan. This system may use syntactic processing to perform the planning, and is therefore part of a linguistic system which performs explicit (conscious) processing, as described more fully elsewhere (Rolls 2005, Rolls 2004c, Rolls 2003, Rolls 2007a).

3.4 Representations of primary reinforcers

Emotions can be produced by primary reinforcers. (Primary reinforcers are unlearned reinforcers, that is they are innately reinforcing.) Other, previously neutral, stimuli, such as the sight of an object, can by association learning with a primary reinforcer come to be a secondary (or learned) reinforcer, which can also produce an emotional response. For these reasons, in order to understand the neural basis of emotion it is necessary to know where in the processing systems in the brain a sensory input comes to be decoded[7] and treated by the rest of the brain

---

[7] By decoding, I mean what is made explicit in the representation. If the firing of neurons (in for example the inferior temporal visual cortex) reflects which object has been seen invariantly with respect to size, position, reward

(which may try to maximize or minimize its activity) as a primary reinforcer (Rolls 2005).

3.4.1 Taste

In primates, the representation of taste in the taste pathways is independent of its rewarding properties as far as the primary taste cortex, in that neuronal responses in the primary taste cortex in the anterior insula and adjoining frontal operculum are not decreased by feeding to satiety (Rolls, Scott, Sienkiewicz and Yaxley 1988, Yaxley, Rolls and Sienkiewicz 1988, Yaxley, Rolls, Sienkiewicz and Scott 1985, Rolls 2005). In the secondary taste cortex, which is part of the orbitofrontal cortex, the representation is of the food reward value of the taste, in that the taste responses of neurons are modulated by hunger, and decrease to zero when the animal is satiated, and the taste is no longer rewarding (Rolls, Sienkiewicz and Yaxley 1989c) (see Fig. 3.13, Section 3.6.5.1, and Rolls (2005)). Thus taste reward, and also sensory-specific satiety, is represented in the orbitofrontal cortex. There may be some though a less complete modulation by hunger of neuronal taste responses in the amygdala (see Section 3.7), and in this sense taste reward may be less well represented in the amygdala than the orbitofrontal cortex. The orbitofrontal cortex connects to the lateral hypothalamus, and there also it is the reward value of taste that is represented (Burton, Rolls and Mora 1976, Rolls 1981a, Rolls, Murzi, Yaxley, Thorpe and Simpson 1986, Rolls 2005). Section 3.6.5 describes more of the evidence on the representation of the reward value of taste in the orbitofrontal cortex, and Fig. 3.50 shows some of these taste areas in humans.

3.4.2 Smell

For olfaction, it is known that some orbitofrontal cortex olfactory neurons respond to the smell of food only when a monkey has an appetite for that food (Critchley and Rolls 1996a), and consistent results have been found in humans with functional neuroimaging (O'Doherty, Rolls, Francis, Bowtell, McGlone, Kobal, Renner and Ahne 2000). The responses of these neurons thus reflect the reward value of these food-related olfactory stimuli.

It is not yet known in primates whether this modulation of olfactory neuronal responses occurs at earlier processing stages. However, there is evidence in humans that the primary olfactory cortical areas (including the pyriform cortex and cortico-medial amygdala region) represent the identity and intensity of olfactory stimuli, in that in a functional magnetic resonance imaging (fMRI) investigation, activation of these regions was correlated with the subjective intensity ratings but not the subjective pleasantness ratings of six odours (Rolls, Kringelbach and De Araujo 2003c). In contrast, the reward value of odours is represented in the human medial orbitofrontal cortex, in that activation here was correlated with the pleasantness but not intensity ratings of six odours (Rolls et al. 2003c) (cf. Anderson, Christoff, Stappen, Panitz, Ghahremani, Glover, Gabrieli and Sobel (2003)). (In rats, there is some evidence that signals about hunger can influence olfactory processing as far peripherally as the olfactory bulb (Pager, Giachetti, Holley and LeMagnen 1972, Pager 1974).)

---

association, etc., then it can be said that representations of objects have been decoded from the sensory information reaching the retina. Although information about which object has been seen is of course present in the retinal neuronal firing, it is not made explicit at this stage of processing. Instead, local contrast over small regions of the retina is made explicit at the retinal level, in that retinal neurons have small concentric receptive fields responsive to small spots of light. If the firing of neurons in, for example, the orbitofrontal cortex reflects whether an object is currently associated with reward, then we can say that the reward value of objects has been decoded by this stage of processing. The most common way for information to be made explicit in the firing is by altering the firing rate of neurons, though it has been hypothesized that some additional information might be available in the relative time of firing of different neurons. This issue of the representation of information by populations of neurons is considered more comprehensively in Appendix C, by Rolls and Treves (1998), Rolls and Deco (2002), Franco, Rolls, Aggelopoulos and Treves (2004), and Aggelopoulos, Franco and Rolls (2005).

Although some of these primate orbitofrontal cortex olfactory neurons may respond because odours are secondary reinforcers as a result of olfactory-to-taste association learning (Rolls, Critchley, Mason and Wakeman 1996b), it is known that other olfactory neurons in the orbitofrontal cortex do not alter their responses during olfactory-to-taste association learning (Critchley and Rolls 1996b). The responses of these other olfactory neurons could thus reflect information about whether the odour is a primary reinforcer. However, the neurons could also simply be representing the identity of the odour. This issue has not yet been settled.

In humans there is some evidence that pheromone-like odours can influence behaviour (Jacob, McClintock, Zelano and Ober 2002), though probably not through the vomero-nasal olfactory system, which appears to be vestigial in humans (Dulac and Torello 2003, Meredith 2001). In rodents and many mammals (but not humans and Old World monkeys), signals in an accessory olfactory system which includes the vomeronasal organ and the accessory olfactory bulb could act as primary reinforcers which affect attractiveness and aggression, and act as primary reinforcers (Dulac and Torello 2003, Meredith 2001, Rolls 2005).

3.4.3 Pleasant and painful touch

Experiments have been performed to investigate where in the human touch-processing system (see Figs. 3.2 and 3.3) tactile stimuli are decoded and represented in terms of their rewarding value or the pleasure they produce. In order to investigate this, Rolls, O'Doherty, Kringelbach, Francis, Bowtell and McGlone (2003d) performed functional magnetic resonance imaging (fMRI) of humans who were receiving pleasant, neutral, and painful tactile stimuli. They found that a weak but very pleasant touch of the hand with velvet produced much stronger activation of the orbitofrontal cortex than a more intense but affectively neutral touch of the hand with wood. In contrast, the pleasant stimuli produced much less activation of the primary somatosensory cortex S1 than the neutral stimuli (see Fig. 3.5). It was concluded that part of the orbitofrontal cortex is concerned with representing the positively affective aspects of somatosensory stimuli. Nearby, but separate, parts of the human orbitofrontal cortex were shown in the same series of experiments to be activated by taste and olfactory stimuli. Thus the pleasantness of tactile stimuli, which can be powerful primary reinforcers (Taira and Rolls 1996), is correlated with the activity of a part of the orbitofrontal cortex. This part of the orbitofrontal cortex probably receives its somatosensory inputs via the somatosensory cortex both via direct projections and via the insula (Mesulam and Mufson 1982a, Mesulam and Mufson 1982b, Rolls 2005, Rolls 2006c). In contrast, the pleasantness of a tactile stimulus does not appear to be represented explicitly in the somatosensory cortex. The indication thus is that only certain parts of the somatosensory input, which reflect its pleasantness, are passed on (perhaps after appropriate processing) to the orbitofrontal cortex by the somatosensory cortical areas. It was also notable that the pleasant touch activated the most anterior (pregenual) part of the anterior cingulate cortex (see Fig. 3.5).

To investigate how the affective aspects of touch may be modulated by cognitive factors using the principles described in Chapter 6, in an fMRI investigation participants were shown word labels ('rich moisturizing cream' or 'basic cream') while cream was being applied to the forearm, or was seen being applied to a forearm (McCabe, Rolls, Bilderbeck and McGlone 2007, Rolls 2007d). The subjective pleasantness and richness were modulated by the word labels, and so were the fMRI activations to touch in parietal cortex area 7, the insular somatosensory cortex, and the ventral striatum. The cognitive labels influenced the activations to the sight of touch and also the correlations with pleasantness in the pregenual cingulate / orbitofrontal cortex and ventral striatum.

Comparison of the sight of an arm being rubbed with cream to a visual control with no contact revealed effects in the inferior frontal gyrus (a mirror neuron area, in which

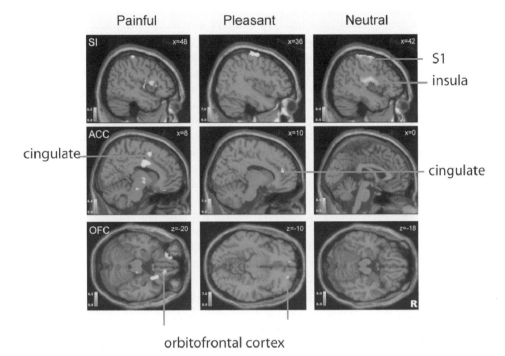

Fig. 3.5 Brain activation to painful, pleasant, and neutral touch of the human brain. The top row shows strongest activation of the somatosensory cortex S1/insula by the neutral touch, on sagittal sections (parallel to the midline). The middle row shows activation of the most anterior part of the anterior cingulate cortex by the pleasant touch, and of a more posterior part by the painful touch, on sagittal sections. The bottom row shows activation of the orbitofrontal cortex by the pleasant and by the painful touch, on axial sections (in the horizontal plane). The activations were thresholded at $p<0.0001$ to show the extent of the activations. (After Rolls, O'Doherty et al. 2003d.) (See colour plates Appendix E.)

neurons respond to motor actions and to the sight of the action being performed (Rizzolatti and Craighero 2004)), area 7, and even S1, implicating these regions in the imagined or intentional aspects of touch. In brain areas receiving visual inputs but also having touch or movement-related firing, associative Hebbian synaptic modification could account for touch or movement-related neurons also being activated by the sight of the touch or movement (Keysers and Perrett 2004).

Touch to the forearm (which has unmyelinated C fibre touch (CT) afferents sensitive to light touch) compared with touch to the glabrous skin of the hand (which does not) (Olausson, Lamarre, Backlund, Morin, Wallin, Starck, Ekholm, Strigo, Worsley, Vallbo and Bushnell 2002) revealed activation in the mid-orbitofrontal cortex, providing an indication that the orbitofrontal cortex may be involved in processing the effects of CT afferents, and thus potentially in any positively hedonic effects mediated through CT fibres (McCabe, Rolls, Bilderbeck and McGlone 2007, Rolls 2007d).

The issue of where the reinforcing properties of activation of the pain pathways is decoded is complex (Melzack and Wall 1996, Perl and Kruger 1996). There are clearly specialized peripheral nerves (including C fibres, with some activated via VR1 or capsaicin receptors) that convey painful stimulation to the central nervous system, and perhaps two main brain systems (Hunt and Mantyh 2001, Julius and Basbaum 2001). One is a spino-parabrachial pathway which originates from the superficial dorsal horn in the spinal cord and may have preferential access to brain areas involved in affect such as the amygdala, and the second is the spinothalamic pathway which distributes nociceptive information to parts of the brain involved in both discrimination and affect (Hunt and Mantyh 2001). At the spinal cord level, there are reflexes that enable a limb to be withdrawn from painful stimulation. But the essence of a reinforcer is that it should enable the probability of an arbitrary (that is any) instrumental response or action to be altered. For this learning to occur, it is probably necessary that the activity should proceed past the central grey in the brainstem, which is an important region for pain processing, to at least the diencephalic (hypothalamus/thalamus) level. This level may be sufficient for at least simple operant responses, such as lifting the tail, to be learned to avoid footshock (Huston and Borbely 1973). For more complex operant responses, it is likely that the basal ganglia must be intact (see Section 3.10.2 and Rolls (2005)).

There appears to be a focus for pain inputs in part of area 3 of the primary somatosensory cortex, as shown by loss of pain sensation after a lesion to this region (Marshall 1951), and by activation measured in PET studies of regions in the primary and the secondary somatosensory cortex (Coghill, Talbot, Evans, Meyer, Gjedde, Bushnell and Duncan 1994), although a more recent PET study from the same Centre implicates the cingulate cortex rather than the somatosensory cortex in the affective aspects of pain (Rainville, Duncan, Price, Carrier and Bushnell 1997). However, there is evidence that structures as recently developed as the orbitofrontal cortex of primates are important in the subjective aspects of pain, for patients with lesions or disconnection of the orbitofrontal cortex may say that they can identify the input as painful, but that it does not produce the same affective feeling as previously (Freeman and Watts 1950, Melzack and Wall 1996). In the fMRI study of Rolls, O'Doherty, Kringelbach, Francis, Bowtell and McGlone (2003d) painful inputs (produced by a stylus) were also applied to the hand, and we found that the orbitofrontal cortex was more strongly activated by the painful touch than by the neutral touch, whereas the somatosensory cortex was relatively more activated by the physically heavier neutral touch (see Fig. 3.5). This provides evidence that negative (see also Petrovich, Petersson, Ghatan, Ston-Elander and Ingvar (2000)) as well as positive aspects of affective touch are especially represented in the orbitofrontal cortex. In this study, as in many studies (Vogt and Sikes 2000, Vogt 2007), a part of the anterior cingulate cortex in or near to the cingulate motor area was also activated by pain (see example in Fig. 3.5 and Section 3.8).

3.4.4 Visual stimuli

Although most visual stimuli are not primary reinforcers, but may become secondary reinforcers as a result of stimulus–reinforcer association learning, it is possible that some visual stimuli, such as the sight of a smiling face or of an angry face, could be primary reinforcers. It has been shown that there is a population of neurons in the cortex in the anterior part of the macaque superior temporal sulcus that categorize face stimuli based on the expression on the face, not based on the identity of the face (Hasselmo, Rolls and Baylis 1989a) (see Section 4.2.9). Thus it is possible that the reinforcing value of face expression could be being decoded by this stage of cortical processing (which is at the same stage approximately as the inferior temporal visual cortex; see Rolls and Deco (2002), and Baylis, Rolls and Leonard (1987)). This cortical region projects into the amygdala, in which face-selective neurons are also found (Leonard, Rolls, Wilson and Baylis 1985). Although it is not yet known whether amygdala face-selective neurons can code for expression or reward as well as identity (Leonard, Rolls, Wilson and Baylis 1985), this does seem likely given that these amygdala neurons receive some of their inputs from the neurons in the cortex in the superior temporal sulcus.

Another population of face-selective neurons is also found in the orbitofrontal cortex (Rolls, Critchley, Browning and Inoue 2006a) (see Section 3.6.5.6), and some of these neurons by being tuned to face expression could represent the primary reinforcing value of a face. Consistent with this, orbitofrontal and cingulate cortex lesions can impair humans' ability to identify the emotional expression on a face (Hornak, Rolls and Wade 1996, Rolls 1999b, Hornak, Bramham, Rolls, Morris, O'Doherty, Bullock and Polkey 2003) (see Section 3.6.6). However, it seems likely that, in addition, at least some of the face-selective neurons in the amygdala and orbitofrontal cortex reflect the secondary reinforcing value of a face, given the role these brain regions play in stimulus–reinforcer association learning (see Sections 3.6 and 3.7).

In humans, it has been found that activation of the orbitofrontal cortex is correlated with the attractiveness of the face being viewed (O'Doherty, Winston, Critchley, Perrett, Burt and Dolan 2003b). This may be an example of a visual primary reinforcer being represented in the orbitofrontal cortex.

It is possible that some auditory stimuli can be primary reinforcers. Where the reinforcement value may be decoded is not yet known, though auditory neurons that respond to vocalization have been found in the orbitofrontal cortex (Rolls, Critchley, Browning and Inoue 2006a) and amygdala (personal observations), and may also be present in the cingulate cortex (Jurgens 2002, West and Larson 1995); and orbitofrontal and cingulate cortex lesions can impair humans' ability to identify the emotional expression in a voice (Hornak, Rolls and Wade 1996, Hornak, Bramham, Rolls, Morris, O'Doherty, Bullock and Polkey 2003) (see Section 3.6.6).

As discussed in Section 3.7.4, novel stimuli are somewhat rewarding and in this sense act as primary reinforcers. The value of this type of reinforcer is that it encourages animals to explore new environments in which their genes might produce a fitness advantage. Neurons that respond to visual stimuli that are associated with rewards, and to novel stimuli, have been discovered in the primate amygdala, and this evidence suggests that these neurons are involved in the primary reinforcing properties of novel stimuli (Wilson and Rolls 1993, Wilson and Rolls 2005).

Further examples of visual and other putative primary reinforcers are given by Rolls (2005) and in Table 3.1.

3.5   Representing potential secondary reinforcers

Many stimuli, such as the sight of an object, have no intrinsic emotional effect. They are not primary reinforcers. Yet they can come as a result of learning to have emotional significance. This type of learning is called stimulus–reinforcer association, and the association is between the sight of the neutral visual stimulus (the potential secondary reinforcer) and the primary reward or punisher (the taste of food, or a painful stimulus). In that both the potential secondary reinforcer and the primary reinforcer are stimuli, stimulus–reinforcer association learning is a type of stimulus–stimulus association learning.

How are the representations of objects built in the brain, and what is the form of the representation appropriate for it to provide the input stimulus in stimulus–reinforcer association learning? These issues are addressed in detail by Rolls and Deco (2002) and in Chapter 4, but some of the relevant issues in the present context of how stimuli should be represented if they are to be appropriate for subsequent evaluation by stimulus–reinforcer association learning brain mechanisms are described in this Section (3.5). The description of the functions of brain mechanisms that play a fundamental role in utilizing these representations for emotional learning and processing starts in Section 3.6.

3.5.1 The requirements of the representation

From an abstract, formal point of view we would want the representation of the to-be-associated stimulus, neutral before stimulus–reinforcer association learning, to have some of the following properties. Evidence that inferior temporal visual cortex neurons do have these properties is described in Chapter 4.

3.5.1.1 Invariance

The representation of the object should be invariant with respect to physical transforms of the object such as size (which varies with distance), position on the retina (translation invariance), and view. The reason that invariance is such an important property is that if we learned, for example, an association between one view of an object and a reward or punisher, it would be extremely unadaptive if when we saw the object again from a different view we did not have the same emotional response to it, or recognize it as a food with a good taste. We need to learn about the reward and punisher associations of objects, not of particular images with a fixed size and position on the retina. This is the fundamental reason why perceptual processing in sensory systems should proceed to the level at which objects are represented invariantly before the representation is used for emotional and motivation-related learning by stimulus–reinforcer association, or by any other memory system.

There are only exceptional circumstances in which we wish to learn, or it would be adaptive to learn, associations to stimuli represented early on in sensory processing streams, before invariant representations are computed. There are exceptional cases though, such as it being appropriate to learn an emotional response to a loud sound represented only as tones, as has been studied by LeDoux (1994) in his model system. We should realise that such cases are exceptions, and that the fundamental design principle is very different, with representations normally being at the object level before there is an interface to emotion learning systems, as described in the work considered below and elsewhere (e.g. Rolls (1986c), Rolls (1986a), Rolls (1990d), Rolls (1999a) and Rolls (2005)).

While the example taken has been from vision, the same is true for other modalities. For example, in audition, we would want to make the same emotional decoding to the word 'Fire' independently of whether we hear it spoken (with very different pitches) by a child, by a woman, or by a man. This could not be decoded without high-level cortical processing, emphasizing the point that normally we need to have emotional responses to stimuli decoded correctly to the level where an object has been made explicit in the representation.

The capacity for view-invariant representation of objects may be especially well developed in primates, as implied for example by the great development in primates of the parts of the temporal lobe concerned with vision (the inferior temporal visual cortex, and the cortex in the superior temporal sulcus, etc., see Chapter 4).

The issue then arises of the organization of vision in non-primates, and whether view-invariant representations are formed when there is a much less well-developed temporal lobe. It may be that for many objects, a sufficiently good representation of objects that is effectively view-invariant can be formed without explicitly computing a view-invariant representation. Take for example the representation of a small fruit such as a raspberry. The nature of this object is that it can be recognized from almost any viewing angle based on the presence of three simple features, (two-dimensional) shape, surface texture, and colour. [Moreover, once one has been identified by, for example, taste, there are likely to be others present locally, and serial feeding (concentrating on one type of food, then switching to another) may take advantage of this.] Thus much behaviour towards objects may take place based on the presence of a simple list of identifying features, rather than by computing true view-invariant representations of objects that look different from different angles (see also Rolls and Deco

(2002), Section 8.2.1). The sophisticated mechanism present in the primate temporal lobe for computing invariant representations of objects may be associated with the evolution of hands, tool use, and stereoscopic vision, and the necessity to recognize and manipulate objects from different angles to make artefacts.

It is certainly of interest that apparently quite complex behaviour, including food selection in birds and insects, may be based on quite simple computational processes, such as in this case object identification based on a list of simple features. We should always be cautious about inferring more complex substrates for behaviour than is really necessary given the capacities. Part of the value of neurophysiological investigation of the primate temporal cortex is that it shows that view-invariant representations are actually computed, even for objects that look very different from different viewing angles (see Section 3.5.3 and Rolls and Deco (2002)).

3.5.1.2 Generalization

If we learn an emotional response to an object, we usually want to generalize the emotional response to other similar objects. An example might be the sight of a pin, which, after stimulus–reinforcer association learning, would generalize to the shape of other similar sharp-pointed objects such as a pencil, a pen, etc. Generalization occurs most easily if each object is represented by a population of neurons firing, each perhaps reflecting different properties of the object. Then if the object alters a little, in that some of its features change, there will still be sufficient similarity of the representation for it to be reasonably correlated with the original representation.

The way in which generalization occurs in the types of neuronal network found in the brain, and the nature of the representation needed, are described by Rolls and Treves (1998) and Rolls and Deco (2002), and in Appendix B. A synopsis of some of the key ideas as they apply most directly to pattern associators, which are types of network involved in learning about which environmental stimuli are associated with reward or with punishment, is provided in Appendix B. The approach is introduced in Fig. 3.6. The unconditioned or primary reinforcer activates the neuron shown (one of many) by unmodifiable synaptic connections (only one of which is drawn in Fig. 3.6). The to-be-conditioned stimulus activates the neuron through a population of modifiable synapses. The association is learned by strengthening those synapses from active conditioned stimulus input axons when the postsynaptic neuron is activated by the primary reinforcer. This is known as the Hebb learning rule (after D. O. Hebb, who in 1949 envisaged a synaptic learning rule of this general form). Later, when only the conditioned stimulus is presented, it activates the postsynaptic neuron through the modified synapses, producing the same firing as that originally produced by the unconditioned stimulus. If the conditioned stimulus is represented by the firing of a set of axons, then we can think of this as a vector. In the same way, we can think of the synaptic weights as another vector. If the input vector matches the weight vector, then the maximal activation of the neuron is produced. If the input vector uses distributed encoding (with perhaps each axon reflecting the presence of one or several features of the object), then a similar vector of firing will represent a similar object. Because many of the strengthened synapses activated by the original stimulus will also be activated by the similar stimulus, the similar stimulus will produce activation of the neuron that is similar to that produced by the original conditioned stimulus. The neuron can thus be thought of as computing the similarity of input patterns of firing, and it is this that results in good generalization (see Appendix B).

This consideration leads to the suggestion that in order to enable good generalization to occur, the to-be-conditioned stimulus, i.e. the potential secondary reinforcer, should be represented with a distributed representation. If, in contrast to a distributed representation, there was a local representation (in which a single neuron would be so specifically tuned that it carried all the information about which stimulus was present), then generalization would be

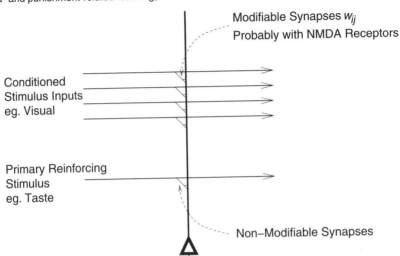

Fig. 3.6 Pattern association between a primary reinforcer, such as the taste of food, which activates neurons through non-modifiable synapses, and a potential secondary reinforcer, such as the sight of food, which has modifiable synapses on to the same neurons. Such a mechanism appears to be implemented in the amygdala and orbitofrontal cortex. (Homosynaptic) long-term depression (see Section 1.5) in a pattern associator in the amygdala could account for the habituating responses to novel visual stimuli which are not associated with primary reinforcers.

much more difficult. If one learned an association to a single neuron firing that represented the object (a grandmother cell), then any small alteration of the stimulus would lead to another neuron firing (so that small perceptual differences between stimuli could be represented), and there would be no generalization.

3.5.1.3 Graceful degradation

If there is minor damage to the nervous system, for example if some neurons die or some synapses are lost, there is no catastrophic change in performance. Instead, as the damage becomes more and more major, there is generally a gradual decline in the performance of the function affected. This is known as graceful degradation (and is a form of fault tolerance). Graceful degradation is a simple property of neural networks that use distributed representations. It arises in a very similar way to generalization. Because each object is represented by an ensemble (or vector) of neuronal activity, if a few of the input axons or the synapses are damaged, then the remainder of the input axons and synapses can still produce activation of the neuron that approximates the correct activation. [As explained in Appendix A and by Rolls and Treves (1998) and Rolls and Deco (2002), the operation performed by a neuron may be thought of as computing the inner or dot product of the input firing rate vector of neuronal activity and the synaptic weight vector. The result is a scalar value, the activation of the neuron. The dot product effectively measures the similarity of the input firing-rate vector and the stored synaptic-weight vector. Provided that the two vectors use distributed representations, then graceful degradation will occur.] Given that the output of the network is produced in practice not by a single neuron but by a population of neurons, loss of a few output neurons (which of course provide the input to the next stage) does not produce catastrophic degradation either (see further Rolls and Treves (1998), Rolls and Deco (2002), and Appendices A and B).

3.5.2 High capacity

We would like the object representation to convey much information, that is to be capable of representing separately (discriminating between) many different objects. At the same time, we would like this high capacity representation to be readable by a pattern associator of the type just described, which reads out the information from the representation using a dot product operation. It turns out that this can be achieved by a distributed representation of the type found in the brain (Rolls and Deco 2002, Franco, Rolls, Aggelopoulos and Treves 2004, Franco, Rolls, Aggelopoulos and Jerez 2007) (see Appendix C).

One property of the representation is that each neuron should convey essentially independent information. The implication of this is that the number of stimuli that can be represented increases exponentially with the number of neurons in the population (because information is a log measure). Another property of the representation is that it should be readable by a simple operation such as a dot product, with each input neuron conveying an approximately similar amount of information. (This is described further in Appendices A–C. The point is that a binary code would be too compact for the properties required.) It turns out that exactly the type of representation required is built for objects in the visual system, and is found elsewhere in the brain too (see Rolls and Treves (1998); Rolls and Deco (2002); Franco, Rolls, Aggelopoulos and Treves (2004); and Aggelopoulos, Franco and Rolls (2005); and Appendix C). Another advantage of this type of representation is that a great deal of information about which object was shown can be read by taking the activity of any reasonably large subset of the population. This means that neurons in the brain do not need to have an input connection from every neuron in the sending population; and this makes the whole issue of brain wiring during development tractable (see Rolls and Treves (1998); Rolls and Deco (2002); and Rolls and Stringer (2000)).

It turns out that not only does the inferior temporal visual cortex have a representation of both faces and non-face objects with the properties described above (see also Sections 4.2 and 2.2.6, and Appendix C), but also it transpires that the inferior temporal visual cortex does not contaminate its representation of objects (which must be used for many different functions in the brain) by having reward representations associated on to the neurons there (see Section 3.5.3). Instead, because its outputs are used for many functions, the reward value of objects is not what determines the response of inferior temporal cortex neurons. (If it did, then we might go blind to objects if they changed from being rewarding to being neutral. Exactly this change of reward value does occur if we eat a food to satiety, yet we can still see the food.) This issue, that the inferior temporal visual cortex is the stage in the object processing stream at which objects become represented, and from which there are major inputs to other parts of the brain which do learn reward and punishment associations of objects, the orbitofrontal cortex and amygdala, is considered next. The reasons for this architectural design are also considered.

3.5.3 Objects, and not their reward and punishment associations, are represented in the inferior temporal visual cortex

We now consider whether associations between visual stimuli and reinforcement are learned, and stored, in the visual cortical areas that proceed from the primary visual cortex, V1, through V2, V4, and the inferior temporal visual cortex (see Figs. 3.2 and 3.3). Is the emotional or motivational valence of visual stimuli represented in these regions? A schematic diagram summarizing some of the conclusions that will be reached is shown in Fig. 3.4.

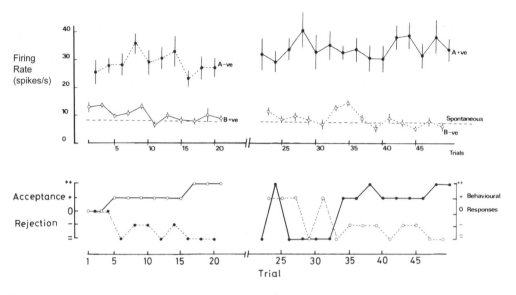

Fig. 3.7 Examples of the responses of a neuron in the inferior temporal visual cortex, showing that its responses (firing rate in spikes/s, upper panel) do not reverse when the reward association of the visual stimuli reverses. For the first 21 trials of the visual discrimination task, visual stimulus A was aversive (−ve, because if the monkey licked he obtained saline), and visual stimulus B was associated with reward (+ve, because if the monkey licked when he saw this stimulus, he obtained fruit juice). The neuron responded more to stimulus A than to stimulus B. After trial 21, the contingencies reversed (so that A was now +ve, and B −ve). The monkey learned the reversal correctly by about trial 35 (lower panel). However, the inferior temporal cortex neuron did not reverse when the reinforcement contingency reversed – it continued to respond to stimulus A after the reversal, even though the stimulus was now +ve. Thus this, and other inferior temporal cortex neurons, respond to the physical aspects of visual stimuli, and not to the stimuli based on their reinforcement association or the reinforcement contingency. (From Rolls, Judge and Sanghera 1977.)

One way to answer the issue just raised is to test monkeys in a learning paradigm in which one visual stimulus is associated with reward (for example glucose taste, or fruit juice taste), and another visual stimulus is associated with an aversive taste, such as a taste of salt. Rolls, Judge and Sanghera (1977) performed just such an experiment and found that single neurons in the inferior temporal visual cortex did not respond differently to objects based on their reward association. To test whether a neuron might be influenced by the reward association, the monkey performed a visual discrimination task in which the reinforcement contingency could be reversed during the experiment. (That is, the visual stimulus, for example a triangle, to which the monkey had to lick to obtain a taste of fruit juice, was after the reversal associated with saline – if the monkey licked to the triangle after the reversal, he obtained a drop of a mildly aversive salt solution.) An example of such an experiment is shown in Fig. 3.7. The neuron responded more to the triangle, both before reversal when it was associated with fruit juice, and after reversal, when the triangle was associated with saline. Thus the reinforcement association of the visual stimuli did not alter the response to the visual stimuli, which was based on the physical properties of the stimuli (for example their shape, colour, or texture). The same was true for the other neurons recorded in this study.

This conclusion, that the responses of inferior temporal neurons during visual discriminations do not code for whether a visual stimulus is associated with reward or punishment, is also consistent with further findings (Ridley, Hester and Ettlinger 1977, Jarvis and

Mishkin 1977, Gross, Bender and Gerstein 1979, Sato, Kawamura and Iwai 1980), including an investigation in which macaques search for food-related stimuli in complex visual scenes (Rolls, Aggelopoulos and Zheng 2003a). In the visual food reward search task the monkeys searched a complex natural visual scene to find and touch one of two objects in order to obtain fruit juice reward. If the wrong object was touched, the monkeys obtained a taste of mildly aversive saline. The neurons responded to one of the selected stimuli in this experiment, and when the reward/punisher was reversed between the stimuli, the neuron continued to respond independently of whether the stimulus was associated with reward or with the punisher (Rolls, Aggelopoulos and Zheng 2003a). This independence from reward association seems to be characteristic of neurons right through the temporal visual cortical areas, and must be true in earlier cortical areas too, in that they provide the inputs to the inferior temporal visual cortex (Rolls and Deco 2002).

3.5.4 Why reward and punishment associations of stimuli are not represented early in information processing in the primate brain

The processing stream that has just been considered is that concerned with objects, that is with what is being looked at. Two fundamental points about pattern association networks for stimulus–reinforcer association learning can be made from what we have considered. The first point is that sensory processing in the primate brain proceeds as far as the invariant representation of objects (invariant with respect to, for example, size, position on the retina, and even view), independently of reward vs punisher association. Why should this be, in terms of systems-level brain organization? The suggestion that is made is that the visual properties of the world about which reward associations must be learned are generally objects (for example the sight of a banana, or of an orange), and are not just raw pixels or edges, with no invariant properties, which is what is represented in the retina and the primary visual cortex (V1). The implication is that the sensory processing must proceed to the stage of the invariant representation of objects before it is appropriate to learn reinforcer associations. The invariance aspect is important too, for if we had different representations for an object at different places in our visual field, then if we learned when an object was at one point on the retina that it was rewarding, we would not generalize correctly to it when presented at another position on the retina. If it had previously been punishing at that retinal position, we might find the same object rewarding when at one point on the retina, and punishing when at another. This is inappropriate given the world in which we live, and in which our brain evolved, in that the most appropriate assumption is that objects have the same reinforcer association wherever they are on the retina.

The same systems-level principle of brain organization is also likely to be true in other sensory systems, such as those for touch and hearing. For example, we do not generally want to learn that a particular pure tone is associated with a reward or punisher. Instead, it might be a particular complex pattern of sounds such as a vocalization that carries a reinforcement signal, and this may be independent of the exact pitch at which it is uttered. Thus, cases in which some modulation of neuronal responses to pure tones in parts of the brain such as the medial geniculate (the thalamic relay for hearing) (LeDoux 1994), where tonotopic tuning is found, may be rather special model systems (that is simplified systems on which to perform experiments), and not reflect the way in which auditory-to-reinforcer pattern associations are normally learned. The same may be true for touch in so far as one considers associations between objects identified by somatosensory input, and primary reinforcers. An example might be selecting a food object from a whole collection of objects in the dark.

The second point, which complements the first, is that the visual system is not provided with the appropriate primary reinforcers for such pattern-association learning, in that visual

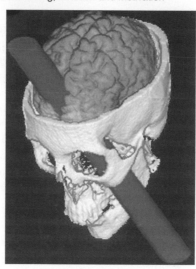

Fig. 3.8 Reconstruction of the possible entry and exit points of the tamping iron that went through Phineas Gage's frontal lobes by Damasio, Grabowski, Frank, Galaburda and Damasio (1994).

processing in the primate brain is mainly unimodal to and through the inferior temporal visual cortex (see Fig. 3.3). It is only after the inferior temporal visual cortex, when it projects to structures such as the amygdala and orbitofrontal cortex, that the appropriate convergence between visual processing pathways and pathways conveying information about primary reinforcers such as taste and touch/pain occurs (Fig. 3.3). We will later, therefore, turn our attention to the amygdala and orbitofrontal cortex, to consider whether they might be the brain regions that contain the neuronal networks for pattern associations involving primary reinforcers. We note at this stage that in order to make the results as relevant as possible to brain function and its disorders in humans, the system being described is that present in primates such as monkeys. In rats, although the organization of the amygdala may be similar, the areas that may correspond to the primate inferior temporal visual cortex and orbitofrontal cortex are less developed.

Evidence that inferior temporal visual cortex neurons do have the properties described in this Section (3.5), including position, size and view invariance, and distributed representations, is provided in Chapter 4.

3.6 The orbitofrontal cortex

3.6.1 Historical background

The prefrontal cortex has for long been implicated in emotion, though it is only relatively recently that there has been a firm scientific foundation for understanding how it functions, by decoding and representing primary reinforcers (unlearned rewards and punishers), and by rapidly learning and reversing stimulus–reinforcer associations. The orbitofrontal cortex thus plays a key role in reward (and punishment) processing in primates including humans. Let us look first at some of the background.

3.6.1.1 Phineas Gage

One of the first indications that the prefrontal cortex is involved in emotion came from the remarkable case of Phineas Gage, who was working as a foreman for a railway development in

Vermont in the USA (Harlow 1848). In 1848, he was tamping down explosives with a tamping iron when unexpectedly the tamping detonated the explosive. The tamping iron, a long bar like a crow bar approximately 3 ft 7 inches long, shot into the air and passed upwards through the front of Phineas Gage's brain (see Fig. 3.8) (Damasio, Grabowski, Frank, Galaburda and Damasio 1994). Gage survived but from that time on became a changed person. Formerly he had held responsibility as a foreman, but after the operation he became less reliable, and did not appear to be so concerned about the consequences of his actions. Moreover, in his personal life, he was described as being a changed person ("No longer Gage", short-tempered, capricious, and profane). However, these personality and emotional changes took place without other general changes in Phineas Gage's intellectual abilities and intelligence. Hannah and Antonio Damasio and colleagues have reconstructed the site of the brain damage from the fractures found in the skull, and have shown that there would have been considerable damage to the lower (or ventral) part of the frontal cortex, which is where the orbitofrontal cortex is located (Damasio et al. 1994, Damasio 1994)). (It is so-called because it is just above the orbit of the eye.) The case of Phineas Gage suggested that the prefrontal cortex is involved in some way in emotion and personality, and that these functions are dissociable in the brain from many other types of brain function.

3.6.1.2 Prefrontal leucotomy

Another historical line of evidence implicates the frontal lobes in emotion. During an investigation of the effects of frontal lobe lesions in non-human primates on a short-term spatial memory task, Jacobsen (1936) noted that after the operation one of his animals became calmer and showed less frustration when reward was not given. Hearing of this emotional change, Moniz, a Portuguese neurosurgeon, argued that anxiety, irrational fears, and emotional hyperexcitability in humans might be treated by damage to the frontal lobes. He operated on twenty patients and published an enthusiastic report of his findings (Moniz 1936) (see Fulton (1951)). This rapidly led to the widespread use of this surgical procedure, and more than 20,000 patients were subjected to prefrontal 'lobotomies' (in which a part of the frontal lobe was removed) or 'leucotomies' (in which some of the white matter connections of the frontal lobe were cut) of varying extent during the next 15 years. Although irrational anxiety or emotional outbursts were sometimes controlled, it was not clear that the surgery treated effectively the symptoms for which it was intended, side-effects were often apparent, and the effects were irreversible (Rylander 1948, Valenstein 1974). For these reasons these operations have been essentially discontinued. A lesson is that very careful and full assessment and follow-up of patients should be performed when a new neurosurgical (or any medical) procedure is being developed, before it is ever considered for widespread use. In relation to pain, patients who underwent a frontal lobotomy sometimes reported that after the operation they still had pain but that it no longer bothered them affectively (Freeman and Watts 1950, Melzack and Wall 1996).

3.6.2 Topology

Given this historical background, we now turn to a more systematic and fundamental consideration of how some parts of the frontal lobes are involved in emotion. The prefrontal cortex is the region of cortex that receives projections from the mediodorsal nucleus of the thalamus and is situated in front of the motor and premotor cortices (areas 4 and 6) in the frontal lobe (see Fig. 3.2). Based on the divisions of the mediodorsal nucleus, the prefrontal cortex may be divided into three main regions (Fuster 1997). First, the magnocellular, medial (meaning towards the midline), part of the mediodorsal nucleus projects to the orbital (ventral) surface of the prefrontal cortex (which includes areas 13 and 12) (see Fig. 3.9). It is called

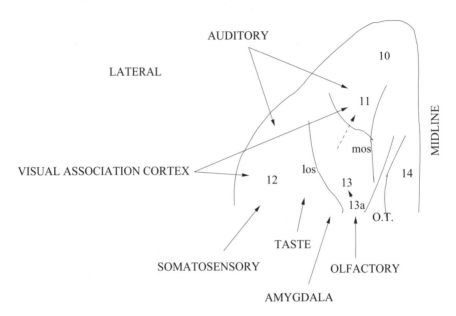

Fig. 3.9 Ventral view of the macaque orbitofrontal cortex. The midline is on the right of the diagram, and the inferior convexity is laterally, on the left. Subdivisions (after Barbas and Pandya 1989), and some afferents to the orbitofrontal cortex, are shown. mos, medial orbital sulcus; los, lateral orbital sulcus.

the orbitofrontal cortex, and is the part of the primate prefrontal cortex that appears to be primarily involved in emotion. The orbitofrontal cortex receives information from the part of the visual system concerned with forming representations of objects (the inferior temporal visual cortex), and taste, olfactory, and touch (somatosensory, body sensory) inputs (see Figs. 3.2 and 3.3). Second, the parvocellular, lateral, part of the mediodorsal nucleus projects to the dorsolateral prefrontal cortex. This part of the prefrontal cortex receives inputs from the parietal cortex, and is involved in tasks such as spatial short-term memory tasks, attention, and, in humans, functions such as planning (see Fuster (1997); Shallice and Burgess (1996); Rolls and Deco (2002); Deco and Rolls (2003)). Third, the pars paralamellaris (most lateral) part of the mediodorsal nucleus projects to the frontal eye fields (area 8) in the anterior bank of the arcuate sulcus.

The orbitofrontal cortex is considered in the rest of this Section. The cortex on the orbital surface of the frontal lobe includes area 13 caudally, area 11 anteriorly, and area 14 medially, and the cortex on the inferior convexity includes area 12 (see Fig. 3.9, and Carmichael and Price (1994); Petrides and Pandya (1994); Ongur and Price (2000); Ongur, Ferry and Price (2003); and Kringelbach and Rolls (2004)). This brain region is poorly developed in rodents, but well developed in primates including humans. To understand the function of this brain region in humans, the majority of the studies described have therefore been performed with macaque monkeys or with humans. There is some variability in the sulcal patterns in the human orbitofrontal cortex (Chiavaras and Petrides 2001), and it is useful to take this into account in imaging studies (Kringelbach and Rolls 2004).

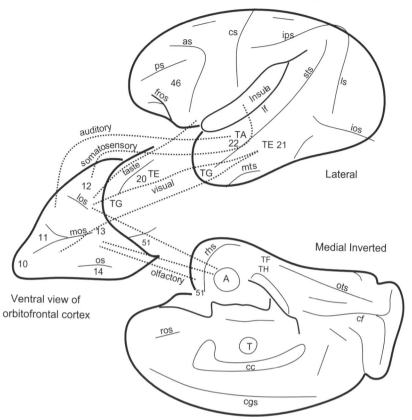

Fig. 3.10 Schematic diagram showing some of the gustatory, olfactory, and visual pathways to the orbito-frontal cortex, and some of the outputs of the orbitofrontal cortex. The secondary taste cortex and the secondary olfactory cortex are within the orbitofrontal cortex. V1, primary visual cortex. V4, visual cort-ical area V4. Abbreviations: as, arcuate sulcus; cc, corpus callosum; cf., calcarine fissure; cgs, cingulate sulcus; cs, central sulcus; ls, lunate sulcus; ios, inferior occipital sulcus; mos, medial orbital sulcus; os, orbital sulcus; ots, occipito-temporal sulcus; ps, principal sulcus; rhs, rhinal sulcus; sts, superior temporal sulcus; lf, lateral (or Sylvian) fissure (which has been opened to reveal the insula); A, amygdala; INS, in-sula; T, thalamus; TE (21), inferior temporal visual cortex; TA (22), superior temporal auditory association cortex; TF and TH, parahippocampal cortex; TG, temporal pole cortex; 12, 13, 11, orbitofrontal cortex; 35, perirhinal cortex; 51, olfactory (prepyriform and periamygdaloid) cortex.

3.6.3 Connections

Some of the connections of the orbitofrontal cortex are shown schematically in Figs. 3.10, 3.2, 3.3 and 3.9.

Rolls, Yaxley and Sienkiewicz (1990) discovered a taste area in the lateral part of the primate orbitofrontal cortex by showing that neurons in it respond to taste placed into the mouth, and showed that this was the secondary taste cortex in that it receives a major projection from the primary taste cortex (Baylis, Rolls and Baylis 1994). More medially, there is an olfactory area (Rolls and Baylis 1994). Anatomically, there are direct connections from the primary olfactory cortex, pyriform cortex, to area 13a of the posterior orbitofrontal cortex, which in turn has onward projections to a middle part of the orbitofrontal cortex (area 11) (Price, Carmichael, Carnes, Clugnet and Kuroda 1991, Morecraft, Geula and Mesulam 1992, Barbas 1993, Carmichael, Clugnet and Price 1994) (see Figs. 3.9 and 3.10). Visceral inputs may reach the posteromedial and lateral areas from the ventral part of the parvicellular division of the ventroposteromedial nucleus of the thalamus (VPMpc) (Carmichael and Price 1995c). Visual inputs reach the orbitofrontal cortex directly from the inferior temporal visual cortex, the cortex in the superior temporal sulcus, and the temporal pole (Jones and Powell 1970, Barbas 1988, Barbas 1993, Barbas 1995, Petrides and Pandya 1988, Barbas and Pandya 1989, Seltzer and Pandya 1989, Morecraft et al. 1992, Carmichael and Price 1995c). There are corresponding auditory inputs (Barbas 1988, Barbas 1993), and somatosensory inputs from somatosensory cortical areas 1, 2 and S2 in the frontal and pericentral operculum, and from the insula (Barbas 1988, Preuss and Goldman-Rakic 1989, Carmichael and Price 1995c). The caudal orbitofrontal cortex has strong reciprocal connections with the amygdala (Price et al. 1991, Carmichael and Price 1995a). The orbitofrontal cortex also receives inputs via the mediodorsal nucleus of the thalamus, pars magnocellularis, which itself receives afferents from temporal lobe structures such as the prepyriform (olfactory) cortex, amygdala, and inferior temporal cortex (Nauta 1972, Krettek and Price 1974, Krettek and Price 1977). The medial orbital areas, and parts of lateral orbital area 12, receive connections from and project to the anterior cingulate cortex (Carmichael and Price 1995a). The medial orbitofrontal cortex receives connections from the subiculum (Carmichael and Price 1995a), which itself receives connections from the hippocampus (see Rolls and Treves (1998)).

The orbitofrontal cortex projects back to temporal lobe areas such as the inferior temporal visual cortex, and, in addition, to the entorhinal cortex (or 'gateway to the hippocampus') and cingulate cortex (Nauta 1964, Insausti, Amaral and Cowan 1987). The orbitofrontal cortex also projects to the preoptic region, lateral hypothalamus and brainstem autonomic areas such as the dorsal motor nucleus of the vagus and the nucleus of the solitary tract, to the ventral tegmental area (Nauta 1964, Johnson, Rosvold and Mishkin 1968, Van der Kooy, Koda, McGinty, Gerfen and Bloom 1984), and to the head of the caudate nucleus (Kemp and Powell 1970). Reviews of the cytoarchitecture and connections of the orbitofrontal cortex are provided by Petrides and Pandya (1994), Pandya (1996), Carmichael and Price (1994), Carmichael and Price (1995a), Carmichael and Price (1995c), Barbas (1995), Ongur and Price (2000), Ongur, Ferry and Price (2003), and Kringelbach and Rolls (2004).

3.6.4 Effects of damage to the orbitofrontal cortex

Damage to the caudal orbitofrontal cortex in the monkey produces emotional changes. These include reduced aggression to humans and to stimuli such as a snake and a doll, a reduced tendency to reject foods such as meat (Butter, Snyder and McDonald 1970, Butter and Snyder 1972, Butter, McDonald and Snyder 1969), and a failure to display the normal preference ranking for different foods (Baylis and Gaffan 1991). In the human, euphoria, irresponsibility, lack of affect, and impulsiveness can follow frontal lobe damage (Kolb and Whishaw 2003, Damasio 1994, Eslinger and Damasio 1985), particularly orbitofrontal cortex damage (Rolls, Hornak, Wade and McGrath 1994a, Hornak, Bramham, Rolls, Morris, O'Doherty, Bullock and Polkey 2003, Berlin, Rolls and Kischka 2004, Berlin, Rolls and Iversen 2005).

These changes that follow frontal lobe damage may be related to a failure to react normally to and learn from non-reward in a number of different situations. This failure is evident as a tendency to respond when responses are inappropriate, e.g. no longer rewarded. In particular, macaques with lesions of the orbitofrontal cortex are impaired at tasks that involve learning about which stimuli are rewarding and which are not, and especially in altering behaviour when reinforcement contingencies change. The monkeys may respond when responses are inappropriate, e.g. no longer rewarded, or may respond to a non-rewarded stimulus. For example, monkeys with orbitofrontal cortex damage are impaired on Go/NoGo task performance, in that they Go on the NoGo trials (Iversen and Mishkin 1970)[8], and in an object-reversal task in that they respond to the object that was formerly rewarded with food, and in extinction in that they continue to respond to an object that is no longer rewarded (Butter 1969, Jones and Mishkin 1972, Meunier, Bachevalier and Mishkin 1997)[9]. There is some evidence for dissociation of function within the orbitofrontal cortex, in that lesions to the inferior convexity produce Go/NoGo and object reversal deficits, whereas damage to the caudal orbitofrontal cortex, area 13, produces the extinction deficit (Rosenkilde 1979). The visual discrimination learning deficit shown by monkeys with orbitofrontal cortex damage (Jones and Mishkin 1972, Baylis and Gaffan 1991) may be due to the tendency of these monkeys not to withhold responses to non-rewarded stimuli (Jones and Mishkin 1972), including foods that are not normally accepted (Butter et al. 1969, Baylis and Gaffan 1991).

Lesions more laterally, in for example the inferior convexity which receives from the inferior temporal visual cortex, can influence tasks in which objects must be remembered for short periods, e.g. delayed matching to sample and delayed matching to non-sample tasks (Passingham 1975, Mishkin and Manning 1978, Kowalska, Bachevalier and Mishkin 1991), and neurons in this region may help to implement this visual object short-term memory by holding the representation active during the delay period (Rosenkilde, Bauer and Fuster 1981, Wilson, O'Sclaidhe and Goldman-Rakic 1993). Whether this inferior convexity area is specifically involved in a short-term object memory is not yet clear, and a medial part of the frontal cortex may also contribute to this function (Kowalska et al. 1991). It should be noted that this short-term memory system for objects (which receives inputs from the temporal lobe visual cortical areas in which objects are represented) is different from the short-term memory system in the dorsolateral part of the prefrontal cortex, which is concerned with spatial short-term memories, consistent with its inputs from the parietal cortex (see, e.g., Williams, Rolls, Leonard and Stern (1993) but see also Deco and Rolls (2003) and Deco, Rolls and Horwitz (2004)). In any case, it is worth noting that this part of the prefrontal cortex could be involved in a function related to short-term memory for objects. This does not exclude this part of the prefrontal cortex from, in addition, being part of the more orbitofrontal system involved in visual to reinforcer association learning and reversal.

The effects of damage to the orbitofrontal cortex in humans are described in Section 3.6.6.

---

[8]In a Go/NoGo task, on a Go trial one visual stimulus is shown, and a response such as licking a tube can be made to obtain a food reward; and on a NoGo trial, a different visual stimulus is shown, and no response must be made otherwise a punishment, of for example a taste of aversive saline, is obtained (Thorpe, Rolls and Maddison 1983, Rolls, Critchley, Mason and Wakeman 1996b). The task tests for stimulus–reward associations, in that one visual stimulus is associated with food reward, and the other with saline punishment if a response is made. There is a different version of a Go/NoGo task on which on NoGo trials no response must be made in order to obtain reward, and this version of the task with symmetrical reinforcement tests for whether one visual stimulus can be mapped to one behaviour, a response, and another visual stimulus to another behaviour, not responding, in order to obtain reward. Unless otherwise specified, it is the first version of the task that uses asymmetrical reinforcement and that tests for stimulus–reinforcer associations that is referred to in this book.

[9]In a visual discrimination reversal task as run in neurophysiological experiments (Thorpe, Rolls and Maddison 1983, Rolls, Critchley, Mason and Wakeman 1996b), on a trial on which one visual stimulus is shown, the S+ or positive discriminative stimulus S^D, a response such as licking a tube can be made to obtain a food reward; and on a trial on which the other visual stimulus is shown, the S– or negative discriminative stimulus S^Δ, no response must be made otherwise a punisher, of for example a taste of aversive saline, is obtained (Thorpe, Rolls and Maddison 1983, Rolls, Critchley, Mason and Wakeman 1996b). After good performance is obtained, the reward association is reversed, so that the visual stimulus that was formerly an S+ becomes an S–, and vice versa. Behaviour typically reverses over a number of trials, so that the new S+ become the stimulus that is worked for. The task tests for the ability to reverse stimulus–reward associations, and if reversal occurs, shows for example that the neuron being recorded encodes the reinforcement association of the visual stimuli, and not the physical identity of visual stimuli. The improvement in reversal learning performance so that after a number of reversals a reversal can take place in as little as one trial (Thorpe, Rolls and Maddison 1983) is referred to as reversal learning set (Deco and Rolls 2005d).

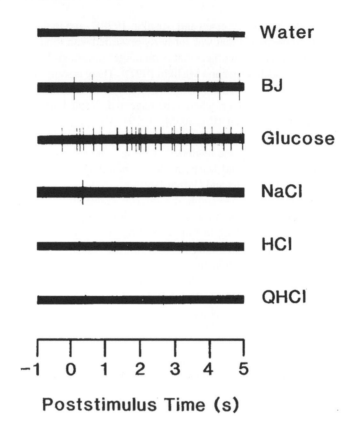

Fig. 3.11 Examples of the responses recorded from one caudolateral orbitofrontal taste cortex neuron to the six taste stimuli, water, 20% blackcurrant juice (BJ), 1 M glucose, 1 M NaCl, 0.01 M HCl, and 0.001 M quinine HCl (QHCl). The stimuli were placed in the mouth at time 0. (From Rolls, Yaxley and Sienkiewicz 1990.)

3.6.5 Neurophysiology and functional neuroimaging of the orbitofrontal cortex

The hypothesis that the orbitofrontal cortex is involved in correcting behavioural responses made to stimuli previously associated with reinforcement has been investigated by making recordings from single neurons in the orbitofrontal cortex while monkeys performed these tasks known to be impaired by damage to the orbitofrontal cortex. It has been shown that some neurons respond to primary reinforcers such as taste and touch; that others respond to learned secondary reinforcers, such as the sight of a rewarded visual stimulus, and thus predict or estimate a reward value; and that the rapid learning of associations between previously neutral visual stimuli and primary reinforcers is reflected in the responses of orbitofrontal cortex neurons in primates (Rolls 2004b, Rolls 2004a, Rolls 2004e, Rolls 2006c). These types of neuron are described next.

3.6.5.1 Taste

One of the discoveries that has helped us to understand the functions of the orbitofrontal cortex in behaviour is that it contains a major cortical representation of taste (Rolls 1989b, Rolls 1995d, Rolls 1997d, Rolls 1999a, Rolls and Scott 2003, Kadohisa, Rolls and Verhagen

OFC

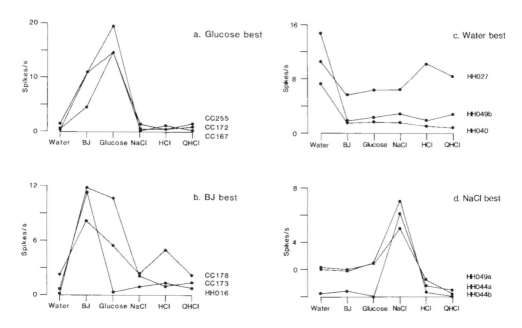

Fig. 3.12 Typical response profiles to different tastes of different orbitofrontal cortex taste neurons. Some responded best to the taste of 1 M glucose (a), to blackcurrant fruit juice (BJ) (b), to water (c), and to 0.1 M sodium chloride (NaCl) (d). HCl, 0.01 M HCl, sour; QHCl, 0.001 M quinine hydrochloride (bitter). (From Rolls, Yaxley and Sienkiewicz 1990.)

2005a, Rolls 2007c, Rolls, Verhagen, Gabbott and Kadohisa 2007c) (cf. Fig. 3.3 and Rolls (2005)). Given that taste can act as a primary reinforcer, that is without learning as a reward or punisher, we now have the start for a fundamental understanding of the functions of the orbitofrontal cortex in stimulus–reinforcer association learning. We now know how one class of primary reinforcer reaches and is represented in the orbitofrontal cortex. A representation of primary reinforcers is essential for a system that is involved in learning associations between previously neutral stimuli and primary reinforcers, e.g. between the sight of an object, and its taste.

The most direct and precise evidence that taste is represented in the primate orbitofrontal cortex comes from recording the activity of single neurons in the macaque monkey orbitofrontal cortex. It has been shown that different single neurons respond differently to the prototypical tastes sweet, salt, bitter, and sour (Rolls, Yaxley and Sienkiewicz 1990), to the 'taste' of water (Rolls, Yaxley and Sienkiewicz 1990), and to the taste of protein or umami (Rolls 2001a) as exemplified by monosodium glutamate (Baylis and Rolls 1991) and inosine monophosphate (Rolls, Critchley, Wakeman and Mason 1996c). Each neuron typically responds to more than one taste, as shown in Figs. 3.11 and 3.12, but each taste can be clearly identified by considering the activity of a population of taste cells (Rolls, Critchley, Verhagen and Kadohisa 2007a). This is called population encoding, and it has many very useful properties that are described in Appendix B and Section 4.2.8, and by Rolls and Treves (1998) and Rolls and Deco (2002). In addition, other neurons are tuned to respond best to astringency (which is a flavour characteristic of tea) as exemplified by tannic acid (Critchley and Rolls 1996c). The input in this case comes through the somatosensory (touch) rather than taste pathways, so astringency is a tactile contribution to flavour. The mouth feel of fat (which contributes to the pleasantness of many foods including chocolate and ice cream) also activates a different population of primate orbitofrontal cortex neurons (see Rolls, Critchley, Browning, Hernadi and Lenard (1999a), and Verhagen, Rolls and Kadohisa (2003)).

The caudolateral part of the orbitofrontal cortex has been shown anatomically to be the secondary taste cortex, in that it receives connections from the primary taste cortex just behind it in the anterior insular/frontal opercular cortex (see Fig. 3.2) (Baylis, Rolls and Baylis 1994). This caudolateral orbitofrontal cortex region then projects on to other regions in the orbitofrontal cortex (Baylis et al. 1994), and neurons with taste responses (in what can be considered as a tertiary gustatory cortical area) can be found in many regions of the orbitofrontal cortex (see Rolls, Yaxley and Sienkiewicz (1990); Rolls and Baylis (1994); Rolls, Critchley, Wakeman and Mason (1996c); Critchley and Rolls (1996c); Rolls, Verhagen and Kadohisa (2003e); and Rolls and Scott (2003)).

There is also evidence from functional neuroimaging that taste can activate the human orbitofrontal cortex. For example, Francis, Rolls, Bowtell, McGlone, O'Doherty, Browning, Clare and Smith (1999) showed that the taste of glucose can activate the human orbitofrontal cortex, and O'Doherty, Rolls, Francis, Bowtell and McGlone (2001b) showed that the taste of glucose and salt activate nearby but separate parts of the human orbitofrontal cortex. De Araujo, Kringelbach, Rolls and Hobden (2003a) showed that umami taste (the taste of protein) as exemplified by monosodium glutamate is represented in the human orbitofrontal cortex as well as in the primary taste cortex as shown by functional magnetic resonance imaging (fMRI). The taste effect of monosodium glutamate (present in e.g. tomato, green vegetables, fish, and human breast milk) was enhanced in an anterior part of the orbitofrontal cortex in particular by combining it with the nucleotide inosine monophosphate (present in e.g. meat and some fish including tuna), and this provides evidence that the activations found in the orbitofrontal cortex are closely related to subjective taste effects. Small, Zald, Jones-Gotman, Zatorre, Petrides and Evans (1999) also found activation of the orbitofrontal cortex by taste.

The nature of the representation of taste in the orbitofrontal cortex is that the reward value of the taste is represented. The evidence for this is that the responses of orbitofrontal taste neurons are modulated by hunger in just the same way as is the reward value or palatability of a taste. In particular, it has been shown that orbitofrontal cortex taste neurons stop responding to the taste of a food with which the monkey is fed to satiety, and that this parallels the decline in the acceptability of the food (see Fig. 3.13) (Rolls, Sienkiewicz and Yaxley 1989c). In contrast, the representation of taste in the primary taste cortex (Scott, Yaxley, Sienkiewicz and Rolls 1986, Yaxley, Rolls and Sienkiewicz 1990) is not modulated by hunger (Rolls, Scott, Sienkiewicz and Yaxley 1988, Yaxley, Rolls and Sienkiewicz 1988). Thus in the primary taste cortex of primates (and at earlier stages of taste processing), the reward value of taste is not represented, and instead the identity of the taste is represented (see further Scott, Yan and Rolls (1995) and Rolls and Scott (2003)).

Additional evidence that the reward value of food is represented in the orbitofrontal cortex is that monkeys work for electrical stimulation of the orbitofrontal cortex if they are hungry, but not if they are satiated (Mora, Avrith, Phillips and Rolls 1979). Thus the electrical stimulation of this brain region produces reward that is equivalent to food for a hungry animal. Further evidence implicating the firing of neurons in the orbitofrontal cortex in reward is that neurons in the orbitofrontal cortex are activated from many brain-stimulation reward sites (Rolls, Burton and Mora 1980, Mora, Avrith and Rolls 1980).

In humans, there is evidence that the reward value, and, what can be directly reported in humans, the subjective pleasantness, of food is represented in the orbitofrontal cortex. The evidence comes from an fMRI study in which humans rated the pleasantness of the flavour of

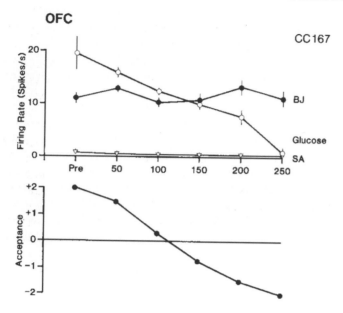

Fig. 3.13 The effect of feeding to satiety with glucose solution on the responses (rate ± sem) of a neuron in the secondary taste cortex to the taste of glucose and of blackcurrant juice (BJ). The spontaneous firing rate is also indicated (SA). Below the neuronal response data, the behavioural measure of the acceptance or rejection of the solution on a scale from +2 (strong acceptance) to −2 (strong rejection) is shown. The solution used to feed to satiety was 20% glucose. The monkey was fed 50 ml of the solution at each stage of the experiment as indicated along the abscissa, until he was satiated as shown by whether he accepted or rejected the solution. Pre is the firing rate of the neuron before the satiety experiment started. (From Rolls, Sienkiewicz and Yaxley 1989b.)

chocolate milk and tomato juice, and then ate one of these foods to satiety. It was found that the pleasantness of the flavour of the food eaten to satiety decreased, and that this decrease in pleasantness was reflected in decreased activation in the orbitofrontal cortex (Kringelbach, O'Doherty, Rolls and Andrews 2003) (see Fig. 3.14). Further evidence that the pleasantness of flavour is represented here is that the flavour of the food not eaten to satiety showed very little decrease, and correspondingly the activation of the orbitofrontal cortex to this food not eaten in the meal showed little decrease. The phenomenon itself is called sensory-specific satiety, is an important property of reward systems, and is described in more detail by Rolls (2005). The experiment of Kringelbach, O'Doherty, Rolls and Andrews (2003) was with a whole food, but further evidence that the pleasantness of taste, or at least a stimulus very closely related to a taste, is represented in the human orbitofrontal cortex is that the orbitofrontal cortex is activated by water in the mouth when thirsty but not when satiated (De Araujo, Kringelbach, Rolls and McGlone 2003b). Thus, the neuroimaging findings with a whole food, and with water when thirsty, provide evidence that the activation to taste *per se* in the human orbitofrontal cortex is related to the subjective pleasantness or affective value of the taste.

Consistent with these anatomical and neurophysiological findings, damage to the caudal orbitofrontal cortex in the monkey produces altered preferences for foods, including a reduced tendency to reject foods such as meat (Butter et al. 1970, Butter and Snyder 1972, Butter et al. 1969), and a failure to display the normal preference ranking for different foods (Baylis and Gaffan 1991). In humans there are few published descriptions of changes of affective

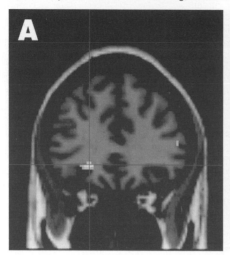
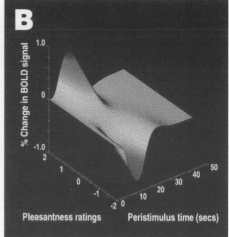

Fig. 3.14 Areas of the human orbitofrontal cortex with activations correlating with pleasantness ratings for food in the mouth. (A) Coronal section through the region of the orbitofrontal cortex from the random effects group analysis showing the peak in the left orbitofrontal cortex (Talairach co-ordinates X,Y,Z=−22,34,−8, z-score=4.06), in which the BOLD signal in the voxels shown in yellow was significantly correlated with the subjects' subjective pleasantness ratings of the foods throughout an experiment in which the subjects were hungry and found the food pleasant, and were then fed to satiety with the food, after which the pleasantness of the food decreased to neutral or slightly unpleasant. The design was a sensory-specific satiety design, and the pleasantness of the food not eaten in the meal, and the BOLD activation in the orbitofrontal cortex, were not altered by eating the other food to satiety. The two foods were tomato juice and chocolate milk. (B) Plot of the magnitude of the fitted haemodynamic response from a representative single subject against the subjective pleasantness ratings (on a scale from −2 to +2) and peristimulus time in seconds. (After Kringelbach, O'Doherty, Rolls and Andrews 2003.) (See colour plates Appendix E.)

reactions to foods after damage to the orbitofrontal cortex (when damage to the olfactory tract which runs just under the orbitofrontal cortex is excluded). However, of the patients in the groups with damage in the orbitofrontal cortex that we have studied (Rolls, Hornak, Wade and McGrath 1994a, Hornak, Rolls and Wade 1996, Hornak, Bramham, Rolls, Morris, O'Doherty, Bullock and Polkey 2003, Hornak, O'Doherty, Bramham, Rolls, Morris, Bullock and Polkey 2004) and in similar patients, the most common complaint they make to the physician is about the quality of their taste and smell sensations. There are large changes in their emotional behaviour which will be described below (Section 3.6.6), but these patients do not usually actually complain about the emotional changes that others observe.

In conclusion, the evidence indicates that the reward value of taste is represented in the primate orbitofrontal cortex. There is also evidence that the corresponding subjective evaluation of taste, how pleasant it is, is related to activation of the orbitofrontal cortex. Thus studies of taste provide evidence that an aspect of affect is represented in the orbitofrontal cortex, and that this is not just general affect, but conveys a rich sensory representation of taste and its reward value, and is able to implement even the variation in the pleasantness of individual tastes as they vary during a meal. Consistent with this, many neurons in the primate orbitofrontal cortex encode the reward value of particular tastes (as shown for example by neurons that respond to the reward value of a sweet taste and others to the reward value of a water taste (Rolls et al. 1989c, Critchley and Rolls 1996a)), and in addition some neurons encode the value of the food that is chosen, where value reflects the quality and quantity of the food available (Padoa-Schioppa and Assad 2006).

Thus there is clear evidence that it is the reward value of taste that is represented in the orbitofrontal cortex (Rolls 2005). Because the orbitofrontal cortex represents the reward value of food whether produced by taste or by olfactory, visual, or mouth texture inputs, in a way that depends on hunger, it is one of the brain regions important in the control of appetite in humans. Understanding the factors that influence the reward value of food is important not only for understanding the control of normal body weight, but also in understanding some of the factors that can contribute to obesity (Rolls 2005, Rolls 2006a, Rolls 2007j, Rolls 2007k).

3.6.5.2 An olfactory representation in the orbitofrontal cortex

Takagi, Tanabe and colleagues (see Takagi (1991)) described single neurons in the macaque orbitofrontal cortex that were activated by odours. A ventral frontal region has been implicated in olfactory processing in humans in PET[10] and fMRI studies (Jones-Gotman and Zatorre 1988, Zatorre and Jones-Gotman 1991, Zatorre, Jones-Gotman, Evans and Meyer 1992, Rolls, Kringelbach and De Araujo 2003c).

Rolls and colleagues have analysed the rules by which orbitofrontal olfactory representations are formed and operate in primates (Rolls 2001b). For 65% of neurons in the orbitofrontal olfactory areas, Critchley and Rolls (1996b) showed that the representation of the olfactory stimulus was independent of its association with taste reward (analysed in an olfactory discrimination task with taste reward, as some orbitofrontal cortex olfactory neurons are bimodal, with responses also to taste stimuli (Rolls and Baylis 1994)). For the remaining 35% of the neurons, the odours to which a neuron responded were influenced by the taste (glucose or saline) with which the odour was associated (Critchley and Rolls 1996b). Thus the odour representation for 35% of orbitofrontal neurons appeared to be built by olfactory-to-taste association learning.

This possibility that the odour representation of some primate orbitofrontal cortex olfactory neurons is built by olfactory-to-taste association learning was confirmed by reversing the taste with which an odour was associated in the reversal of an olfactory discrimination task. It was found that 73% of the sample of neurons analysed altered the way in which they responded to odour when the taste reinforcer association of the odour was reversed (Rolls, Critchley, Mason and Wakeman 1996b). Reversal was shown by 25% of the neurons (see, for example, Fig. 3.15), and 48% altered their activity in that they no longer discriminated after the reversal. These latter neurons thus respond to a particular odour only if it is associated with a taste reward, and not when it is associated with the taste of salt, a punisher. They do not respond to the other odour in the task when it is associated with reward. Thus they respond to a particular combination of an odour, and its being associated with taste reward and not a taste punisher. They may be described as *conditional olfactory-reward neurons*, and may be important in the mechanism by which stimulus–reinforcer (in this case olfactory-to-taste) reversal learning occurs (Deco and Rolls 2005d), as described in Section 3.6.7 and Chapter 9.

The olfactory to taste reversal was quite slow, both neurophysiologically and behaviourally, often requiring 20–80 trials, consistent with the need for some stability of flavour (i.e. olfactory and taste combination) representations. The relatively high proportion of olfactory neurons with modification of responsiveness by taste association in the set of neurons in this experiment was probably related to the fact that the neurons were preselected to show differential responses to the odours associated with different tastes in the olfactory discrimination task. Thus the rule according to which the orbitofrontal olfactory representation was formed was for some neurons by association learning with taste.

We do not yet know whether this is the first stage of processing at which olfactory neuronal responses are determined in some cases by the (taste) reward with which the odour is

---

[10]Positron emission tomography is a method of functional neuroimaging that uses radioactively labelled compounds to measure for example altered blood flow in an area to provide a measure of changing activity.

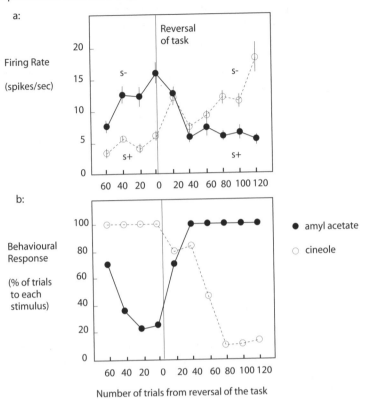

Fig. 3.15 Orbitofrontal cortex: olfactory to taste association reversal. (a) The activity of a single orbitofrontal olfactory neuron during the performance of a two-odour olfactory discrimination task and its reversal is shown. Each point represents the mean poststimulus activity of the neuron in a 500-ms period on approximately 10 trials of the different odourants. The standard errors of these responses are shown. The odourants were amyl acetate (closed circle) (initially S−) and cineole (o) (initially S+). After 80 trials of the task the reward associations of the stimuli were reversed. This neuron reversed its responses to the odourants following the task reversal. (b) The behavioural responses of the monkey during the performance of the olfactory discrimination task. The number of lick responses to each odourant is plotted as a percentage of the number of trials to that odourant in a block of 20 trials of the task. (After Rolls, Critchley, Mason and Wakeman 1996.)

associated, though this is a real possibility in that in an fMRI study in humans described below the pleasantness vs unpleasantness of odours did not affect activations in primary olfactory cortical areas (Rolls, Kringelbach and De Araujo 2003c). (In rodents the encoding may be different, in that an influence of reward-association learning on olfactory neuronal responses in the pyriform cortex (a primary olfactory cortical area) has been reported (Schoenbaum and Eichenbaum 1995).)

The olfactory neurons that do not reverse in the reversal of the olfactory–taste reversal task may be carrying information that is in some cases independent of the reinforcer association (i.e. is about olfactory identity). In other cases, the olfactory representation in the orbitofrontal cortex may reflect associations of odours with other primary reinforcers (for example whether sickness has occurred in association with some smells), or may reflect primary reinforcer value provided by some olfactory stimuli. (For example, the smell of flowers may be innately pleasant and attractive and some other odours may be innately unpleasant – see Table 3.1.) In this situation, the olfactory input to some orbitofrontal cortex neurons may represent an

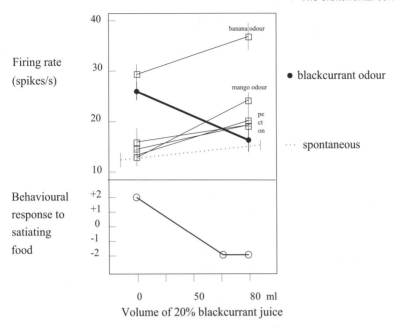

Fig. 3.16 The effect of feeding to satiety on the responses of an olfactory neuron in the orbitofrontal cortex. The monkey was fed to satiety with blackcurrant juice, and the neuronal response to the odour of blackcurrant juice, but not to other odours, decreased as the monkey was being fed to satiety. The neuronal responses reflected the monkey's preference for the blackcurrant juice, as shown in the lower graph. (From Critchley and Rolls 1996a.)

unconditioned stimulus input with which other (for example visual) inputs may become associated.

To analyse the nature of the olfactory representation in the orbitofrontal cortex, Critchley and Rolls (1996a) measured the responses of olfactory neurons that responded to food while they fed the monkey to satiety. They found that the majority of orbitofrontal olfactory neurons reduced their responses to the odour of the food with which the monkey was fed to satiety (see Fig. 3.16). Thus for these neurons, the reward value of the odour is what is represented in the orbitofrontal cortex. We do not yet know whether this is the first stage of processing at which the reward value as influenced by an internal homeostatic need state such as hunger[11] is represented in the primate olfactory system. (In rodents, there is some evidence that hunger can influence olfactory responses even in the olfactory bulb, but the fact that humans can still report accurately the intensity of an odour even when its reward value and pleasantness as influenced by feeding to satiety is decreased to zero suggests that this is not a general property of olfactory processing implemented at early stages in primates including humans, as described by Rolls (2005).)

Consistent with this finding at the neuronal level in non-human primates, activation of a part of the human orbitofrontal cortex is related to the pleasantness of food odour, in that the activation measured with fMRI produced by one food odour, banana, decreased after banana was eaten for lunch to satiety, but remained strong to another food odour, vanilla, not eaten in the meal (O'Doherty, Rolls, Francis, Bowtell, McGlone, Kobal, Renner and Ahne 2000).

Further evidence that pleasant odours are represented in the orbitofrontal cortex is that

---

[11] Homeostasis is the regulation of the internal milieu, and the controls of food and water intake described by Rolls (2005) are examples of behaviours that maintain homeostasis.

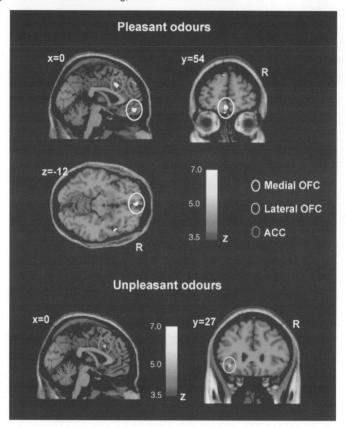

Fig. 3.17 The representation of pleasant and unpleasant odours in the human brain. Top: group con-junction results for the 3 pleasant odours. Sagittal, horizontal and coronal views are shown at the levels indicated, all including the same activation in the medial orbitofrontal cortex, OFC (X,Y,Z = 0,54,–12; z=5.23). Also shown is activation for the 3 pleasant odours in the anterior cingulate cortex, ACC (X,Y,Z= 2,20,32; z=5.44). These activations were significant at p<0.05 fully corrected for multiple comparisons. Bottom: group conjunction results for the 3 unpleasant odours. The sagittal view (left) shows an activated region of the anterior cingulate cortex (X,Y,Z= 0,18,36; z=4.42, p<0.05, SVC). The coronal view (right) shows an activated region of the lateral orbitofrontal cortex (–36,27,–8; z=4.23, p<0.05 SVC). All the activations were thresholded at p<0.00001 to show the extent of the activations. (After Rolls, Kringelbach and de Araujo 2003c.) (See colour plates Appendix E.)

3 pleasant odours (linalyl acetate [floral, sweet], geranyl acetate [floral], and alpha-ionone [woody, slightly food-related]) had overlapping activations in the medial orbitofrontal cortex in a region not activated by three unpleasant odours (hexanoic acid, octanol, and isovaleric acid) (Rolls, Kringelbach and De Araujo 2003c) (see Fig. 3.17). Moreover, activation of the medial orbitofrontal cortex was correlated with the subjective pleasantness ratings of the odours, and activation of the lateral orbitofrontal cortex with the subjective unpleasantness ratings of the odours (see Fig. 3.18). Other studies have also shown activation of the human orbitofrontal cortex by odour (Zatorre et al. 1992, Zatorre, Jones-Gotman and Rouby 2000, Royet, Zald, Versace, Costes, Lavenne, Koenig, Gervais, Routtenberg, Gardner and Huang 2000, Anderson et al. 2003).

Although individual neurons do not encode large amounts of information about which of 7–9 odours has been presented, we have shown that the information does increase linearly with the number of neurons in the sample (Rolls, Critchley and Treves 1996a, Rolls and

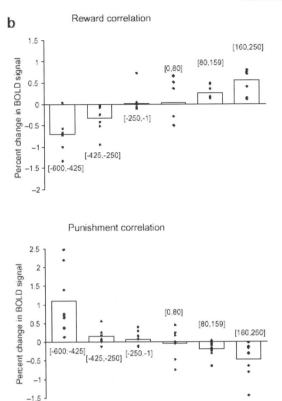

Fig. 3.26 Correlation of brain activations with the amount of money won or lost in a visual discrimination reversal task with probabilistic monetary reward and loss. The mean percent change in BOLD signal from baseline across subjects for 6 different category ranges of monetary gain or loss (plotted along the abscissa). The signal was averaged across a category range within each subject and then the average signal change from each category was averaged across subjects. This is plotted for voxels in the medial OFC that significantly correlated with reward and for voxels in the lateral OFC that significantly correlated with punishment. The ranges of monetary reward and punishment in each category are shown on the chart and were determined by their relative frequencies, which follow from the experimental design. (After O'Doherty, Kringelbach, Rolls, Hornak and Andrews 2001a.)

Redoute 2007b).

Another way in which it has been shown that the visual neurons in the orbitofrontal cortex reflect the expected reward value predicted by visual stimuli is by reducing the reward value by feeding to satiety. With this sensory-specific satiety (or reward devaluation) paradigm, it has been shown that the visual (as well as the olfactory and taste) responses of orbitofrontal cortex neurons in the macaque decrease to zero as the monkey is fed to satiety with one food, but remain unchanged to another food not eaten in the meal (Critchley and Rolls 1996a) (see example in Fig. 3.27). In that these neurons parallel the changing preference of the monkey for the food being eaten to satiety vs the food not being eaten to satiety, they reflect the relative preference for different visual stimuli (Thorpe, Rolls and Maddison 1983, Rolls, Critchley, Mason and Wakeman 1996b) (as found also by Tremblay and Schultz (1999) and Wallis and Miller (2003)). Wallis and Miller (2003) also showed that although some neurons in the dorsolateral prefrontal cortex also reflect the preferences of macaques for visual stimuli, the neurons in the orbitofrontal cortex responded earlier, and, as we found (Thorpe, Rolls and Maddison 1983, Rolls, Critchley, Mason and Wakeman 1996b, Critchley

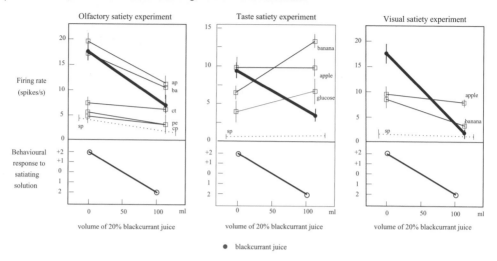

Fig. 3.27 Orbitofrontal cortex neuron with visual, olfactory, and taste responses, showing the responses before and after feeding to satiety with blackcurrant juice. The solid circles show the responses to black-currant juice. The olfactory stimuli included apple (ap), banana (ba), citral (ct), phenylethanol (pe), and caprylic acid (cp). The spontaneous firing rate of the neuron is shown (sp). (After Critchley and Rolls 1996a.)

and Rolls 1996a, Rolls and Baylis 1994), did not reflect the motor responses being made by the macaques. These findings are consistent with the hypothesis that expected reward value is represented in the orbitofrontal cortex, reflects stimulus–reinforcer (sensory–sensory) association learning, and that this information is projected to the dorsolateral prefrontal cortex, where it can be used in tasks requiring planning, for example where rewarding stimuli must be linked to particular responses, and where delays may be involved, in ways that have been modelled by Deco and Rolls (2003) and Deco and Rolls (2005d). Evidence that outcome expectancies encoded by macaque orbitofrontal cortex visual reward, visual punishment, olfactory reward, and olfactory punishment, neurons may also be encoded in a region of the rat brain homologous to the primate orbitofrontal cortex has been described (Schoenbaum, Roesch and Stalnaker 2006).

3.6.5.5 Error neurons in the orbitofrontal cortex, and visual stimulus–reinforcer association learning and reversal

In addition to the neurons that encode the reward association of visual stimuli, other neurons (3.5%) in the orbitofrontal cortex detect different types of non-reward (Thorpe, Rolls and Maddison 1983). For example, some neurons responded in extinction, immediately after a lick had been made to a visual stimulus that had previously been associated with fruit juice reward, and other neurons responded in a reversal task, immediately after the monkey had responded to the previously rewarded visual stimulus, but had obtained the punisher of salt taste rather than reward (see example in Fig. 3.28). These neurons thus respond to a negative reward prediction error (i.e. that less reward is obtained than was expected) (see Sections 10.6.3, B.15.2 and B.15.3).

Different populations of such neurons respond to other types of non-reward, including the removal of a formerly approaching taste reward, and the termination of a taste reward (Thorpe, Rolls and Maddison 1983) (see Table 3.3). The fact that different non-reward neurons respond to different types of non-reward (e.g. some to the noise of a switch that indicated that extinction of free licking for fruit juice had occurred, and others to the first presentation of a

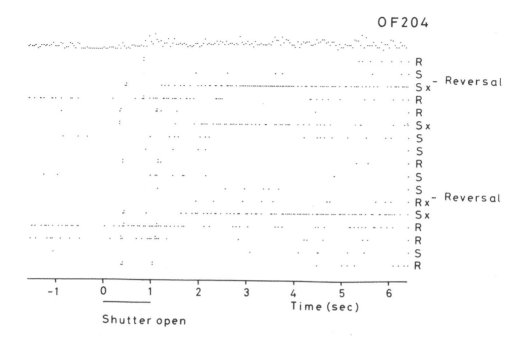

Fig. 3.28 Error neuron: responses of an orbitofrontal cortex neuron that responded only when the monkey licked to a visual stimulus during reversal, expecting to obtain fruit juice reward, but actually obtaining the taste of aversive saline because it was the first trial of reversal. Each single dot represents an action potential; each vertically arranged double dot represents a lick response. The visual stimulus was shown at time 0 for 1 s. The neuron did not respond on most reward (R) or saline (S) trials, but did respond on the trials marked x, which were the first trials after a reversal of the visual discrimination on which the monkey licked to obtain reward, but actually obtained saline because the task had been reversed. It is notable that after an expected reward was not obtained due to a reversal contingency being applied, on the very next trial the macaque selected the previously non-rewarded stimulus. This shows that rapid reversal can be performed by a non-associative process, and must be rule-based. A model for this is the subject of Section 3.6.7 and Chapter 9. (After Thorpe, Rolls and Maddison 1983.)

visual stimulus that was not followed by reward in a visual discrimination task) potentially enables context-specific extinction or reversal to occur. (For example, the fact that fruit juice is no longer available from a lick tube does not necessarily mean that a visual discrimination task will be operating without reward.) Thus the error neurons can be specific to different tasks, and this could provide a mechanism for reversal in one task to be implemented, while at the same time not reversing behaviour in another task. Also, it provides additional evidence to that in Table 3.3 that these neurons did not respond simply as a function of arousal, or just in relation to a general frustrative non-reward/error signal, or to a general reward prediction error (cf. Sections B.15.2, B.15.3 and 3.10.2.5).

The presence of these neurons is fully consistent with the hypothesis that they are part of the mechanism by which the orbitofrontal cortex enables very rapid reversal of behaviour by stimulus–reinforcer association relearning when the association of stimuli with reinforcers is altered or reversed (Rolls 1986c, Rolls 1986a, Rolls 1990d, Rolls 1999a, Rolls 2005). This information appears to be necessary for primates to rapidly alter behavioural responses when reinforcement contingencies are changed, as shown by the effects of damage to the orbitofrontal cortex described above. To the extent that the firing of some dopamine neurons

Table 3.3 Numbers of orbitofrontal cortex neurons responding in different types of extinction or reversal (after Thorpe, Rolls and Maddison 1983). The table shows the tasks (rows) in which individual orbitofrontal neurons responded (1), did not respond (0), or were not tested (blank).

Neuron number	1	2	3	4	5	6	7	8	9	10	11	12	13	14	15	16	17	18
Visual discrim: Reversal	1	0	1	0	0	1	1	0						0				
Visual discrim: Extinction	1																	
Ad lib licking: Reversal	1	1		0	0	0			0	1								
Ad lib licking: Extinction	0	0		0	0	0			0	1								
Taste of saline	0		0	0	0	0	0	0	1	0	0	0	0	0	0	0	0	0
Removal of reward	0		1	1	1	0	1	0	1	1	1	1	1	1	1	1	1	1
Visual arousal	1		1	0	0	0	0	0	1	0	0	0	0	0	1	0	0	0

Table 3.4 Proportion of different types of neuron recorded in the macaque orbitofrontal cortex during sensory testing and visual discrimination reversal and related tasks. (After Thorpe, Rolls and Maddison 1983.)

Sensory testing:

Visual, non-selective	10.7%
Visual, selective (i.e. responding to some objects or images)	13.2%
Visual, food-selective	5.3%
Visual, aversive objects	3.2%
Taste	7.3%
Visual and taste	2.6%
Removal of a food reward	6.3%
Extinction of ad lib licking for juice reward	7.5%

Visual discrimination reversal task:

Visual, reversing in the visual discrimination task	5.3%
Visual, conditional discrimination in the visual discrimination task	2.5%
Visual, stimulus-related (not reversing) in the visual discrimination task	0.8%
Non-reward in the visual discrimination task	0.9%
Auditory tone cue signalling the start of a trial of the visual discrimination task	15.1%

The number of neurons analysed was 463.

may reflect error signals (Waelti, Dickinson and Schultz 2001) (see Section 3.10.2), one might ask where the error information comes from, given that the dopamine neurons themselves may not receive information about expected rewards (e.g. a visual stimulus associated with the sight of food), obtained rewards (e.g. taste), and would have to compute an error from these signals. On the other hand, the orbitofrontal cortex does have all three types of neuron and the required neuroanatomically defined inputs, and this is an important site in the brain for computing *reward prediction error* signals (cf. Sections B.15.2, B.15.3 and 3.10.2.5).

It is interesting to note the proportions of different types of neuron recorded in the orbitofrontal cortex in relation to what might or might not be seen in a human brain imaging study. The proportions of different types of neuron in the study by Thorpe, Rolls and Maddison (1983) are shown in Table 3.4. It is seen that only a relatively small percentage convey information about, for example, which of two visual stimuli is currently reward-associated in a visual discrimination task. An even smaller proportion (3.5%) responds in relation to non-reward, and in any particular non-reward task, the proportion is very small, that is, just a fraction of the 3.5%. The implication is that an imaging study might not reveal really what is happening in a brain structure such as the orbitofrontal cortex where quite small proportions of neurons respond to any particular condition; and, especially, one would need to be very careful not to place much weight on a failure to find activation in a particular task, as the proportion of neurons responding may be small, and the time period for which they respond

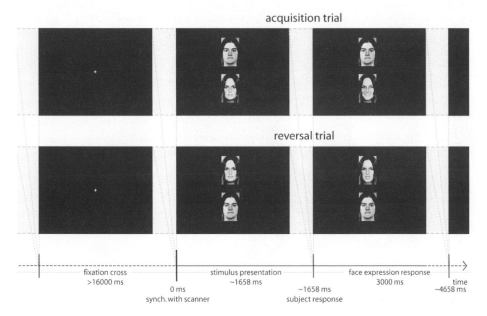

Fig. 3.29 Social reversal task: the trial starts synchronised with the scanner and two people with neutral face expressions are presented to the subject. The subject has to select one of the people by pressing the corresponding button, and the person will then either smile or show an angry face expression for 3,000 ms depending on the current mood of the person. The task for the subject is to keep track of the mood of each person and choose the 'happy' person as much as possible (upper row). Over time (after between 4 and 8 correct trials) this will change so that the 'happy' person becomes 'angry' and vice versa, and the subject has to learn to adapt her choices accordingly (bottom row). Randomly intermixed trials with either two men, or two women, were used to control for possible gender and identification effects, and a fixation cross was presented between trials for at least 16,000 ms. (After Kringelbach and Rolls 2003.)

may be small too. For example, non-reward neurons typically respond for 2–8 s on the first two non-reward trials of extinction or reversal (Thorpe, Rolls and Maddison 1983).

In that most neurons in the macaque orbitofrontal cortex respond to reinforcers and punishers, or to stimuli associated with rewards and punishers, and do not respond in relation to responses, the orbitofrontal cortex is closely related to stimulus processing, including the stimuli that give rise to affective states. When it computes errors, it computes mismatches between stimuli that are expected, and stimuli that are obtained, and in this sense the errors are closely related to those required to correct affective states. This type of error representation may thus be different from that represented in the cingulate cortex, in which behavioural responses are represented, where the errors may be more closely related to errors that arise when action–outcome expectations are not met, and where action–outcome rather than stimulus–reinforcer representations need to be corrected (see Section 3.8).

We have also been able to obtain evidence that non-reward used as a signal to reverse behavioural choice is represented in the human orbitofrontal cortex. Kringelbach and Rolls (2003) used the faces of two different people, and if one face was selected then that face smiled, and if the other was selected, the face showed an angry expression. After good performance was acquired, there were repeated reversals of the visual discrimination task (see Fig. 3.29). Kringelbach and Rolls (2003) found that activation of a lateral part of the orbitofrontal cortex in the fMRI study was produced on the error trials, that is when the human

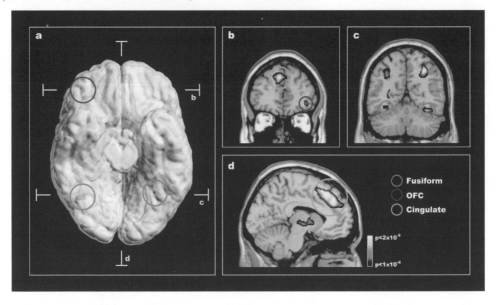

Fig. 3.30 Social reversal: composite figure showing that changing behaviour based on face expression is correlated with increased brain activity in the human orbitofrontal cortex. (a) The figure is based on two different group statistical contrasts from the neuroimaging data which are superimposed on a ventral view of the human brain with the cerebellum removed, and with indication of the location of the two coronal slices (b,c) and the transverse slice (d). The red activations in the orbitofrontal cortex (denoted OFC, maximal activation: z=4.94: 42,42,−8; and z=5.51; X,Y,Z=−46,30,−8) shown on the rendered brain arise from a comparison of reversal events with stable acquisition events, while the blue activations in the fusiform gyrus (denoted Fusiform, maximal activation: z>8; 36,−60,−20 and z=7.80; −30,−56,−16) arise from the main effects of face expression. (b) The coronal slice through the frontal part of the brain shows the cluster in the right orbitofrontal cortex across all nine subjects when comparing reversal events with stable acquisition events. Significant activity was also seen in an extended area of the anterior cingulate/paracingulate cortex (denoted Cingulate, maximal activation: z=6.88; −8,22,52; green circle). (c) The coronal slice through the posterior part of the brain shows the brain response to the main effects of face expression with significant activation in the fusiform gyrus and the cortex in the intraparietal sulcus (maximal activation: z>8; 32,−60, 46; and z>8: −32,−60,44). (d) The transverse slice shows the extent of the activation in the anterior cingulate/paracingulate cortex when comparing reversal events with stable acquisition events. Group statistical results are superimposed on a ventral view of the human brain with the cerebellum removed, and on coronal and transverse slices of the same template brain (activations are thresholded at p=0.0001 for purposes of illustration to show their extent). (After Kringelbach and Rolls 2003.) (See colour plates Appendix E.)

chose a face, and did not obtain the expected reward (see Fig. 3.30). Control tasks showed that the response was related to the error, and the mismatch between what was expected and what was obtained, in that just showing an angry face expression did not selectively activate this part of the lateral orbitofrontal cortex. An interesting aspect of this study that makes it relevant to human social behaviour is that the conditioned stimuli were faces of particular individuals, and the unconditioned stimuli were face expressions. Moreover, the study reveals that the human orbitofrontal cortex is very sensitive to social feedback when it must be used to change behaviour (Kringelbach and Rolls 2003, Kringelbach and Rolls 2004).

3.6.5.6 A representation of faces in the orbitofrontal cortex

Another type of information represented in the orbitofrontal cortex is information about faces. There is a population of orbitofrontal cortex face-selective neurons that respond in many ways

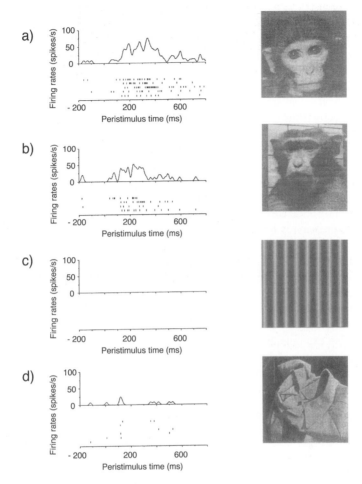

Fig. 3.31 Orbitofrontal cortex face-selective neuron as found in macaques. Peristimulus rastergrams and time histograms are shown. Each trial is a row in the rastergram. Several trials for each stimulus are shown. The ordinate is in spikes/s. The neuron responded best to face (a), also responded, though less to face (b), had different responses to other faces (not shown), and did not respond to non-face stimuli (e.g. (c) and (d)). The stimulus appeared at time 0 on a video monitor. (From Rolls, Critchley, Browning, and Inoue 2006a.)

similarly to those in the temporal cortical visual areas (see Rolls (1984b), Rolls (1992a), Rolls (2000a), Rolls and Deco (2002) and Rolls (2007i) for a description of their properties). The orbitofrontal face-responsive neurons, first observed by Thorpe, Rolls and Maddison (1983), then by Rolls, Critchley, Browning and Inoue (2006a), tend to respond with longer latencies than temporal lobe neurons (130–220 ms typically, compared with 80–100 ms); they also convey information about which face is being seen, that is, about face identity, by having different responses to different faces (see Fig. 3.31). Some of the face identity neurons have similar responses to different views of a face, which is a useful property of neurons responding to face identity. Other neurons have view-dependent responses, and some respond to moving but not still heads. Other neurons are tuned to face expression (Rolls, Critchley, Browning and Inoue 2006a). The neurons with face expression, face movement, or face view-dependent responses would all be useful as part of a system decoding and representing signals important in social interactions. The representation of face identity is also important in social interactions, for it provides some of the information needed in order to make different responses to different individuals. In addition, some orbitofrontal cortex neurons were shown to be tuned to auditory stimuli, including for some neurons the sound of vocalizations. The findings are consistent with the likelihood that these neurons are activated via the inputs from the temporal cortical visual areas in which face-selective neurons are found (see Fig. 3.3), and which project directly to the orbitofrontal cortex. The significance of the neurons is likely to be related to the fact that faces convey information that is important in social reinforcement, both by conveying face expression (cf. Hasselmo, Rolls and Baylis (1989a), which can indicate reinforcement, and by encoding information about which individual is present, also important in evaluating and utilizing reinforcing inputs in social situations (Rolls 2005).

Consistent with these findings in macaques, and as described above, in humans, activation of the lateral orbitofrontal cortex occurs when a rewarding smile expression is expected, but an angry face expression is obtained, in a visual discrimination reversal task (Kringelbach and Rolls 2003). This is an example of the operation of a social reinforcer, and, consistent with these results, Farrow, Zheng, Wilkinson, Spence, Deakin, Tarrier, Griffiths and Woodruff (2001) have found that activation of the orbitofrontal cortex is found when humans are making social judgements. In addition, activation of the medial orbitofrontal cortex is correlated with face attractiveness (O'Doherty et al. 2003b).

Auditory stimuli may have similar representations in the orbitofrontal cortex related to their affective value. For example, Blood, Zatorre, Bermudez and Evans (1999) found a correlation between subjective ratings of dissonance and consonance of musical chords and the activations produced in the orbitofrontal cortex (see also Blood and Zatorre (2001)). Further evidence on activation by auditory stimuli was found by Frey, Kostopoulos and Petrides (2000).

3.6.5.7   Cognitive influences on the orbitofrontal cortex

Affective states, moods, can influence cognitive processing, including perception and memory (see Section 3.11). But cognition can also influence emotional states. This is not only in the sense that cognitively processed events, if decoded as being rewarding or punishing, can produce emotional states (see Rolls (2005)), but also in the sense described here that a cognitive input can bias emotional states in different directions. The modulation is rather like the top-down biased competition effects of attention on perception, not only phenomenologically, but also probably computationally (Rolls and Deco 2002, Deco and Rolls 2003, Deco and Rolls 2005b) (see Chapter 6).

An example of such cognitive influences on the reward/aversive states that are elicited by stimuli was revealed in a study of olfaction described by De Araujo, Rolls, Velazco, Margot and Cayeux (2005). In this investigation, a standard test odour, isovaleric acid (with a small amount of cheddar cheese flavour added to make it more pleasant), was used as the test olfactory stimulus delivered with an olfactometer during functional neuroimaging with fMRI (De Araujo et al. 2005). This odour is somewhat ambiguous, and might be interpreted as the odour emitted by a cheese-like odour (rather like brie), or might be interpreted as a rather pungent and unpleasant body odour. A word was shown during the 8 s odour delivery. On some trials, the test odour was accompanied by the visually presented word 'Cheddar cheese'. On other trials, the test odour was accompanied by the visually presented word 'Body odour'. A word label was used rather than a picture label to make the modulating input very abstract and cognitive. First, it was found (consistent with psychophysical results of Herz and von Clef (2001)) that the word labels influenced the pleasantness ratings of the test odour, as shown in Fig. 3.32.

However, very interestingly, it was found that the word label modulated the activation to the odour in brain regions activated by odours such as the orbitofrontal cortex (secondary

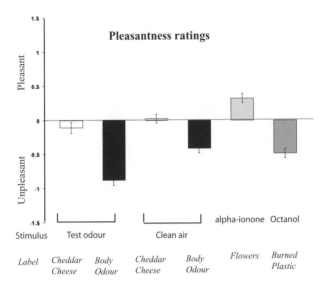

Fig. 3.32 Cognition and emotion. Subjective pleasantness ratings (mean ± sem across subjects) to odours labelled with words. The corresponding stimulus and label to each bar are listed in the lower part of the figure. The test odour (isovaleric acid) and clean air were paired in different trials with a label of either 'Cheddar cheese' or 'Body odour'. (After DeAraujo, Rolls, Velazco, Margot and Cayeux 2005.)

olfactory cortex), cingulate cortex, and amygdala. For example, in the medial orbitofrontal cortex the word label 'Cheddar cheese' caused a larger activation to be produced to the test odour than when the word label 'Body odour' was being presented. In these medial orbitofrontal cortex regions and the amygdala, and even possibly in some parts of the primary olfactory cortical areas, the activations were correlated with the pleasantness ratings, as shown in Fig. 3.33. This is consistent with the finding that the pleasantness of odours is represented in the medial orbitofrontal cortex (Rolls, Kringelbach and De Araujo 2003c).

The effects of the word were smaller when clean air was the stimulus, as shown in Figs. 3.34 and 3.35, indicating that the effects being imaged were not just effects of a word to influence representations by a top-down recall process, but were instead cognitive top-down effects on states elicited by odours. This type of modulation is typical of a top-down modulatory process such as has been analysed quantitatively in the case of attention (Deco and Rolls 2005b) where the interaction between the top-down and bottom-up inputs appears to be multiplicative, and indeed no significant effect of the word when paired with clean air was found in the amygdala and earlier olfactory cortical areas (see Figs. 3.34 and 3.35). A further implication is that the activations in the human amygdala and primary olfactory cortical areas are more closely bound to the eliciting stimulus and are less influenced by cognition than are activations in the orbitofrontal and cingulate cortices.

These findings show that cognition can influence and indeed modulate reward-related (affective) processing as far down the human olfactory system as the secondary olfactory cortex (in the orbitofrontal cortex), and in the amygdala. This emphasizes the importance of cognitive influences on emotion, and shows how, in situations that might range from enjoying food to a romantic evening, the cognitive top-down influences can play an important role in influencing affective representations in the brain. Indeed, these findings lend support to the

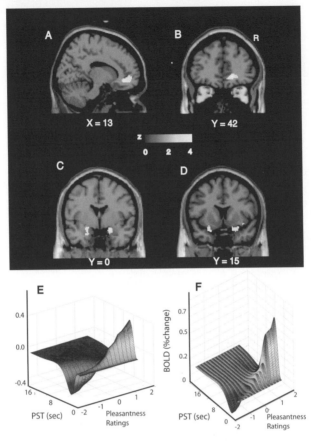

Fig. 3.33 Cognition and emotion. Group (random) effects analysis showing the brain regions where the BOLD signal was correlated with pleasantness ratings given to the test odour. The pleasantness ratings were being modulated by the word labels. (A) Activations in the rostral anterior cingulate cortex, in the region adjoining the medial OFC, shown in a sagittal slice. (B) The same activation shown coronally. (C) Bilateral activations in the amygdala. (D) These activations extended anteriorly to the primary olfactory cortex. The image was thresholded at p<0.0001 uncorrected in order to show the extent of the activation. (E) Parametric plots of the data averaged across all subjects showing that the percentage BOLD change (fitted) correlates with the pleasantness ratings in the region shown in A and B. The parametric plots were very similar for the primary olfactory region shown in D. PST, Post-stimulus time (s). F) Parametric plots for the amygdala region shown in C. (After DeAraujo, Rolls, Velazco, Margot and Cayeux 2005.) (See colour plates Appendix E.)

hypothesis that an interesting role for cognitive systems in emotion is to help set up the optimal conditions in terms of the reinforcers available and contextual surroundings for reinforcers to produce affective states, as treated further in the dual route, implicit vs explicit, hypothesis of actions outlined in Chapter 10 and described by Rolls (2005).

Another dramatic example of what could be a similar phenomenon is that colour can have a strong influence on olfactory judgements. This was demonstrated when a white wine was artificially coloured red with an odourless dye, and it was found that participants (undergraduates at the Faculty of Oenology of the University of Bordeaux) described the wine using the descriptors normally used for red wine (Morrot, Brochet and Dubourdieu 2001). In this case it is possible that cognitive states elicited by the sight of what was believed to be red wine modulated the olfactory representation. Another possibility is that in a multimodal region

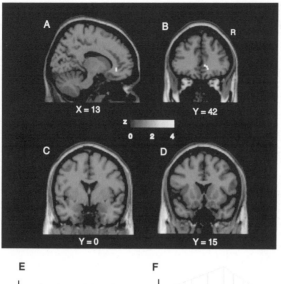

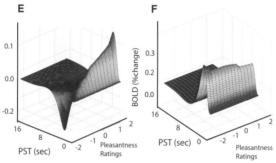

Fig. 3.34 Cognition and emotion. Group (random) effects analysis showing the brain regions where the BOLD signal was correlated with pleasantness ratings given to the clean air. The pleasantness ratings were being modulated by the word labels. (A) Activations in the rostral anterior cingulate cortex, in the region adjoining the medial OFC, shown in a sagittal slice. (B) The same activation shown coronally. No significant correlations were found with clean air in the amygdala (C) or primary olfactory cortex (D). The image was thresholded at $p<0.0001$ uncorrected in order to show the extent of the activation. (E) Parametric plots of the data averaged across all subjects showing that the percentage BOLD change (fitted) correlates with the pleasantness ratings in the region shown in A and B. PST, Post-stimulus time (s). (F) Parametric plots showing activation related to stimulus presentation but not related to the pleasantness ratings for the amygdala region shown in C. (After DeAraujo, Rolls, Velazco, Margot and Cayeux 2005.) (See colour plates Appendix E.)

such as the orbitofrontal cortex where the sight, smell, taste, and texture are brought together onto individual neurons (see Section 3.6.5), the visual input makes a strong contribution to the convergence, and the resulting representation then is available to cognition for verbal description. The mechanism in this case would be feed-forward convergence, rather than the more dramatic top-down biasing of activations to odours in the orbitofrontal cortex produced by word labels described by De Araujo, Rolls, Velazco, Margot and Cayeux (2005).

Cognitive influences produced even at the word level can influence the pleasantness of tactile stimuli. For example, the pleasantness ratings for touch to the arm produced by a moisturizing cream were higher if the word label was 'Rich moisturising cream' vs 'Basic cream', and there was evidence for this modulation in the lateral orbitofrontal cortex for the unpleasantness ratings and in the medial orbitofrontal cortex for the pleasantness ratings (McCabe, Rolls, Bilderbeck and McGlone 2007). Similar cognitive modulations of taste and

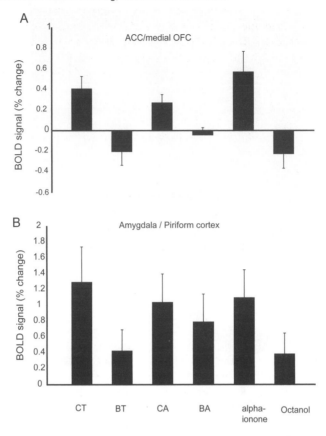

Fig. 3.35 Cognition and emotion. The BOLD signal (% change from control ± sem) in different brain regions when word labels were presented simultaneously with the test odour (T) or clean air (A). C= 'cheddar cheese' label; B= 'body odour' label. The responses to a reference pleasant odour (alpha-ionone) and unpleasant odour (octanol) are also shown. (After DeAraujo, Rolls, Velazco, Margot and Cayeux 2005.)

flavor representations in the orbitofrontal and pregenual cingulate cortices have been found (Grabenhorst, Rolls and Bilderbeck 2008), may play an important role in the selection of food and the amount of food eaten, and are thus relevant to appetite control and obesity. This research shows that top-down language-level cognitive effects reach far down into the earliest cortical areas that represent the appetitive value of taste and flavor.

The mechanisms by which cognitive states have top-down effects on emotion are probably similar to the biased competition mechanisms that subserve top-down attentional effects (Rolls and Deco 2002, Deco and Rolls 2003, Deco and Rolls 2005b, Rolls and Stringer 2001b, Deco and Rolls 2005a) (see Chapter 6 and also Section 3.11). In such systems, it is important that the top-down influence does not determine the activity in the system, otherwise stimuli and events would be imagined, and would not represent what was happening in the world. But by having a weak influence, facilitated by the fact that the top-down backprojection connections are relatively weak (Rolls 1989b, Rolls and Treves 1998, Renart, Parga and Rolls 1999b, Renart, Parga and Rolls 1999a, Renart, Moreno, Rocha, Parga and Rolls 2001, Rolls and Stringer 2001b, Rolls and Deco 2002, Deco and Rolls 2005b, Deco and Rolls 2005a), cognition and attention can have beneficial effects in directing sensory and emotional processing towards stimuli and events that the cognitive system has determined are relevant.

Part of the interest and importance of the studies by De Araujo, Rolls, Velazco, Margot and Cayeux (2005), McCabe, Rolls, Bilderbeck and McGlone (2007), and Grabenhorst, Rolls and Bilderbeck (2008) is that they show that cognitive influences, originating from as high in processing as linguistic representations, can reach down into the first part of the brain in which emotion, affective, hedonic or reward value is made explicit in the representation, the orbitofrontal cortex, to modulate the responses there to affective stimuli. The experiments thus show that linguistic representations can influence how emotional states are represented and thus experienced. It is in this very direct way that cognition can have a powerful effect on emotional states, emotional behaviour, and emotional experience, because the emotional and appetitive representations are altered.

3.6.5.8 The topology of the functional neuroimaging activations in the orbitofrontal cortex

Kringelbach and Rolls (2004) have reviewed evidence that the activations found in functional neuroimaging studies by many types of reward appear to involve relatively medial parts of the human orbitofrontal cortex, and unpleasant stimuli or non-reward more lateral parts of the human orbitofrontal cortex. For example, we have obtained evidence from an experiment using pleasant, painful, and neutral somatosensory stimulation that there is some spatial segregation of the representation of rewards and punishers, where the effects of pleasant somatosensory stimulation are spatially dissociable from the effects of painful stimulation in the human orbitofrontal cortex (Rolls, O'Doherty, Kringelbach, Francis, Bowtell and McGlone 2003d). Further, pleasant odours activate medial, and unpleasant odours lateral, regions of the human orbitofrontal cortex (Rolls, Kringelbach and De Araujo 2003c). Another example comes from the finding that the administration of amphetamine to naive human subjects activated the medial prefrontal cortex (Voellm, De Araujo, Cowen, Rolls, Kringelbach, Smith, Jezzard, Heal and Matthews 2004). An indication that a rewarding effect is being produced by the amphetamine in part because of an action in the orbitofrontal cortex is that macaques will self-administer amphetamine to the orbitofrontal cortex (Phillips, Mora and Rolls 1981). A clear indication of a differentiation in function between medial versus lateral areas of the human orbitofrontal cortex was found in our study investigating visual discrimination reversal learning, which showed a clear dissociation between the medial orbitofrontal areas correlating with monetary gain, and the lateral areas correlating with monetary loss (O'Doherty, Kringelbach, Rolls, Hornak and Andrews 2001a). This result, and some of the other studies included in the meta-analysis (Kringelbach and Rolls 2004), can be interpreted as evidence for a difference between medial orbitofrontal cortex areas involved in decoding and monitoring the reward value of reinforcers, and lateral areas involved in evaluating punishers that when detected may lead to a change in current behaviour. A good example of a study showing the latter involved a visual discrimination reversal task in which face identity was associated with a face expression (Kringelbach and Rolls 2003). When the face expression associated with one of the faces reversed and the face expression was being interpreted as a punisher and indicated that behaviour should change, then lateral parts of the orbitofrontal cortex became activated.

Although our study on abstract reward found that monetary reward and punishment are correlated with activations in different regions of the orbitofrontal cortex (O'Doherty, Kringelbach, Rolls, Hornak and Andrews 2001a), even this evidence does not show that rewards and punishers have totally separate representations in the human brain. In particular, the medial regions of the orbitofrontal cortex that had activations correlating with the magnitude of monetary reward (area 11) also reflected monetary punishers in the sense that the activations in these medial regions correlated positively with the magnitude of monetary wins and negatively with losses (see Fig. 3.25). Similarly, the more lateral regions (area 10) had activations that correlated negatively with the magnitudes of monetary wins and gains, and positively with monetary loss/punishment. This means that in this experiment the medial and lateral regions were apparently coding for both monetary reward and punishment (albeit in opposite ways). The evidence from this experiment would therefore suggest that the segregation between rewards and punishers is not purely spatial but rather encoded in the neuronal responses, which the studies in macaques described above show can be exquisitely tuned differently not only to reinforcers in different sensory modalities (taste, smell, touch etc), but also to combinations of these, and even within any one modality (e.g. with neurons tuned to different tastes). The functional imaging thus provides a very blurred picture of what is really happening at the neuronal and information representation level in the orbitofrontal cortex. Although it is true that similar neurons may tend to cluster together as a result of a self-organizing competitive network with short range excitatory connections (see Section B.4.6), and this may lead to somewhat localized blobs of activity in the cortex, the presence of such blobs should not be taken as more than a gross reflection of the underlying neuronal representations and computations. Integrating over all this heterogeneous neuronal activity is what leads to an fMRI signal (see Section B.6.4).

What account might we give for why so many different types of reward are represented in the human medial orbitofrontal cortex? The types of reward include, as described above and by Rolls (2005), food reward as shown in sensory-specific satiety experiments (Kringelbach, O'Doherty, Rolls and Andrews 2003), pleasant odours (Rolls, Kringelbach and De Araujo 2003c), pleasant touch (Rolls, O'Doherty, Kringelbach, Francis, Bowtell and McGlone 2003d), face attractiveness (O'Doherty et al. 2003b), monetary reward (O'Doherty, Kringelbach, Rolls, Hornak and Andrews 2001a), conditioned stimuli associated with drug self-administration in addicts (Childress, Mozley, McElgin, Fitzgerald, Reivich and O'Brien 1999), and also the administration of amphetamine to drug-naive human subjects (Voellm, De Araujo, Cowen, Rolls, Kringelbach, Smith, Jezzard, Heal and Matthews 2004). The neuronal recording studies described above in macaques show clearly that there is an exquisite representation of the detailed properties of these different stimuli, with different neurons by virtue of their different tuning to each of these properties and to combinations of these properties providing information about all the individual properties of each particular stimulus. For example, as a population, different orbitofrontal cortex neurons in macaques have different responses to the following properties of oral stimuli, with some neurons encoding each property independently, and others responding to different combinations of them: taste, fat texture, viscosity, astringency, grittiness, capsaicin content, odour, and sight (see above and Chapter 5 of Rolls (2005)).

So why are so many of the reward-related properties of stimuli represented in the same medial part of the orbitofrontal cortex? I suggest that part of the functional utility of this is that there can be comparison of the magnitudes of what may be quite different types of reward, implemented by the local lateral inhibition mediated via the inhibitory interneurons.

The architecture required for the implementation is that which is standard for the cerebral cortex: the excitatory pyramidal cells, which are the neurons with the types of often quite selective response just described, connect to inhibitory neurons, which are relatively fewer in number (perhaps 15% of the number of excitatory neurons). The inhibitory neurons receive from random sets of neurons in the vicinity, and project back their summed effects as inhibition to random collections of pyramidal cells. This lateral inhibition system has the effect of controlling the activity of the excitatory neurons, and importantly, the effect of ensuring that the most strongly activated excitatory neurons reduce the activity of less strongly activated excitatory neurons. Contrast enhancement may occur between the competing inputs, and also local scaling of the overall activity of the neurons so that they operate within their working range to reflect in their output firing the inputs being received, in processes that are quantitatively understood and are used in competitive networks (Grossberg 1988, Rolls and Treves 1998, Rolls and Deco 2002, Deco and Rolls 2005b) (see Section B.4). The result of the mutual inhibition is that the relative magnitude of the different rewards available can be compared, and the most strongly firing neurons after the competition reflect the strongest reward.

This type of comparison would be difficult to implement if each type of reward was represented in a different location in the brain, and may be a useful computational outcome of the fact that different types of reward are represented (by different neurons of course) in the same general brain region, the medial orbitofrontal cortex. This computation would provide scaling of different rewards, both relative to each other when presented simultaneously as in a choice situation, and relative to a fixed maximum if only one reward is present. This would thus implement relative reward preference encoding (Rolls, Sienkiewicz and Yaxley 1989c, Tremblay and Schultz 1999).

It may be useful to note that the human medial orbitofrontal cortex region activated by many types of reward may have shifted medially somewhat with respect to its location in macaques. Spurred by the human neuroimaging studies just described, Rolls, Verhagen, Gabbott and Kadohisa (2007c) have made recordings in the topologically most medial part of the macaque orbitofrontal cortex, to determine whether there is a previously undescribed set of reward / taste / olfactory / visual / somatosensory representations in this region. We found only very few such neurons in the part of the macaque orbitofrontal cortex that is less than 3–4 mm from the midline (i.e. areas 14 and 10, and subgenual cingulate cortex area 25). We did find that neurons that respond to the taste, odour, texture, and sight of food start at approximately this laterality, and then extend out laterally from this paramedial orbitofrontal cortex region, through areas 13 and 12 in the mid to the far lateral orbitofrontal cortex, at sites that have been illustrated in a number of papers (e.g. Rolls and Baylis (1994), Critchley and Rolls (1996c), and Rolls, Critchley, Wakeman and Mason (1996c)). Indeed, some of these more medial sites in which taste neurons are common are illustrated in Fig. 3.19 on page 152 from Rolls and Baylis (1994). It is quite clear from a retrograde neuronal tracing study with horseradish peroxidase administered to a region containing taste neurons in the macaque lateral orbitofrontal cortex that the lateral part of the orbitofrontal cortex receives direct inputs from the primary taste cortex in the insula (see Fig. 3.36 and Baylis, Rolls and Baylis (1994)). (The location of the macaque primary taste cortex was described by Pritchard, Hamilton, Morse and Norgren (1986).) More medial orbitofrontal cortex areas (in medial area 13, see Rolls, Verhagen, Gabbott and Kadohisa (2007c)) may also receive inputs directly from the insular and frontal opercular primary taste cortical areas, for, as illustrated in Fig. 3.19, taste neurons are also common in this more medial part of the orbitofrontal cortex (see further Rolls and Baylis (1994) and Critchley and Rolls (1996c)). The more middle / medial part of the orbitofrontal cortex (close to the region indicated in Fig. 3.19) also has neurons that decrease their taste responses in relation to sensory-specific satiety, and a few that do not (Critchley and Rolls 1996a). Thus the macaque posterior orbitofrontal cortex contains taste, and also olfactory and visual, neurons throughout its mediolateral extent, apart from the most medial 3–4 mm. In contrast, the taste and olfactory reward areas in humans appear to reach to the midline, and probably do not extend as far lateral as in non-human primates (see e.g. Figs. 3.17, 3.18, 3.21 and 3.33).

I suggest that as the frontal lobes have developed from macaques to humans, more cortex has been added to the dorsolateral prefrontal cortex areas so important in working memory and hence in attention and executive function (Rolls and Deco 2002, Deco and Rolls 2003) (see Chapters 5 and 6), thus displacing the inferior convexity prefrontal cortex more medially in humans, and displacing the main orbitofrontal cortex areas of macaques more medially in humans, so that they reach as far as the midline. This would be the same trend that occurs in the

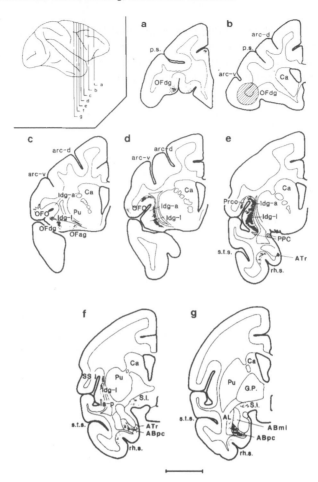

Fig. 3.36 Projections from the primary taste cortex in the upper part of the dysgranular insula and frontal operculum to the orbitofrontal cortex. The horseradish peroxidase injection site into the lateral orbitofrontal cortex where taste neurons were recorded is shown shaded in (b). Filled neurons are shown in e.g.(e) as black circles in the primary taste cortex in the upper part of areas Idg-a (Insula dysgranular area, anterior part: the insular primary taste cortex) and the area labelled Prco in (e) the frontal opercular taste cortex. Abbreviations: AB, basal nucleus of the amygdala with mc magnocellular and pc parvocellular parts; AL, lateral nucleus of the amygdala; arc-d: dorsal limb of the arcuate sulcus; arc-v, ventral limb of the arcuate sulcus; Ca, caudate nucleus; GP, globus pallidus; Idg-l, liminal part of the dysgranular field of the insula; OF, orbitofrontal cortex (with ag agranular and dg dysgranular fields); OFO, orbitofrontal opercular area; PPC, prepyriform cortex (olfactory); Prco, precentral operculum; ps, principal sulcus; Pu, putamen; rh s, rhinal sulcus; SI, substantia innominata; SS 1, primary somatosensory cortex; sts, superior temporal sulcus. (After Baylis, Rolls and Baylis 1994.)

temporal lobes of macaques vs humans, in which the enormous development of language areas in the left hemisphere (and corresponding high order processing areas in the right hemisphere) appears to have displaced at least parts of the inferior temporal visual cortex to be much more ventrally and medially represented in for example the human fusiform face and related areas (Rolls and Deco 2002, Baylis, Rolls and Leonard 1987, Dolan, Fink, Rolls, Booth, Holmes, Frackowiak and Friston 1997, Tovee, Rolls and Ramachandran 1996, Kanwisher, McDermott and Chun 1997, Ishai, Ungerleider, Martin and Haxby 2000).

Another possible topological trend in the human orbitofrontal cortex appears to be present in the posterior to anterior direction, with the possibility of some hierarchy (Kringelbach and Rolls 2004). Very abstract reinforcers such as loss of money appear to be represented further anterior towards the frontal pole (e.g. O'Doherty, Kringelbach, Rolls, Hornak and Andrews (2001a)) than in posterior areas representing simple reinforcers such as taste (e.g. De Araujo, Kringelbach, Rolls and Hobden (2003a); De Araujo, Kringelbach, Rolls and Mc-Glone (2003b)) or thermal intensity (Craig, Chen, Bandy and Reiman 2000, Guest, Grabenhorst, Essick, Chen, Young, McGlone, de Araujo and Rolls 2007). This posterior–anterior trend is clearly demonstrated in the statistical results from the meta-analysis and is likely to reflect some kind of hierarchical processing in the orbitofrontal cortex (Kringelbach and Rolls 2004). Relatively far forward in the orbitofrontal cortex, in area 11, another, memory-related, rather than emotion-related, type of representation is present, for here neurons are activated by novel visual stimuli (Rolls, Browning, Inoue and Hernadi 2005a), and activations in humans are produced by novel visual stimuli (Frey and Petrides 2002). The responses of these neurons decrease over on average 5 presentations of a novel stimulus, and may be related to long-term memory in that the responses do not occur to a stimulus that was novel 24 h earlier (Rolls, Browning, Inoue and Hernadi 2005a).

Another trend is that the main or simple effects in neuroimaging studies of primary reinforcers such as odour and taste tend to be located in relatively more posterior areas of the orbitofrontal cortex, whereas correlations with subjective pleasantness and unpleasantness ratings for frequently the same stimuli tend to be more anterior (Blood, Zatorre, Bermudez and Evans 1999, Blood and Zatorre 2001, De Araujo, Kringelbach, Rolls and Hobden 2003a, De Araujo, Kringelbach, Rolls and McGlone 2003b, Kringelbach, O'Doherty, Rolls and Andrews 2003, O'Doherty, Kringelbach, Rolls, Hornak and Andrews 2001a, O'Doherty, Winston, Critchley, Perrett, Burt and Dolan 2003b, Rolls, Kringelbach and De Araujo 2003c, Voellm, De Araujo, Cowen, Rolls, Kringelbach, Smith, Jezzard, Heal and Matthews 2004, McCabe and Rolls 2007). This is consistent with higher level processing more anteriorly which is on a route to parts of the brain involved in making processing available to conscious experience (Rolls 2005).

Another finding is that areas that have supralinear responses to combinations of sensory inputs, for example taste and smell (De Araujo, Rolls, Kringelbach, McGlone and Phillips 2003c, McCabe and Rolls 2007), or the umami taste stimuli monosodium glutamate (MSG) and inosine 5′-monophosphate (De Araujo, Kringelbach, Rolls and Hobden 2003a), tend to be more anterior than the areas where the components of the combinations are represented in the orbitofrontal cortex. This could easily reflect hierarchy in the system, with convergence tending to increase from more posterior to more anterior orbitofrontal cortex areas, and thus effects of combinations of inputs becoming more evident anteriorly.

3.6.6 The human orbitofrontal cortex

In Section 3.6.5 we have considered evidence from neurophysiology and functional neuro-imaging on the functions of the human orbitofrontal cortex in reward, emotion, and motivation. In this Section we consider complementary evidence from the effects of damage to the human orbitofrontal cortex.

It is of interest that a number of the symptoms of frontal lobe damage in humans appear to be related to the functions described above of representing primary reinforcers, and of altering behaviour when stimulus–reinforcement associations alter, as described next. Thus, humans with frontal lobe damage can show impairments in a number of tasks in which an alteration of behavioural strategy is required in response to a change in environmental reinforcement contingencies (Goodglass and Kaplan 1979, Jouandet and Gazzaniga 1979,

Kolb and Whishaw 2003, Zald and Rauch 2006). For example, Milner (1963) showed that in the Wisconsin card sorting task (in which cards are to be sorted according to the colour, shape, or number of items on each card depending on whether the examiner says 'right' or 'wrong' to each placement), frontal patients had either difficulty in determining the first sorting principle, or in shifting to a second principle when the contingencies change. Also, in stylus mazes frontal patients have difficulty in changing direction when a sound indicates that the correct path has been left (Milner 1982). It is of interest that, in both types of test, frontal patients may be able to verbalize the correct rules yet may be unable to correct their behavioural sets or strategies appropriately.

Some of the personality changes that can follow frontal lobe damage may be related to a similar type of dysfunction. For example, the euphoria, irresponsibility, lack of affect, and lack of concern for the present or future that can follow frontal lobe damage (see Zald and Rauch (2006) and Section 3.6.1 on page 136) may also be related to a dysfunction in altering behaviour appropriately in response to a change in reinforcement contingencies. Indeed, in so far as the orbitofrontal cortex is involved in the disconnection of stimulus–reinforcer associations, and such associations are important in learned emotional responses (see above), then it follows that the orbitofrontal cortex is involved in emotional responses by correcting stimulus–reinforcer associations when they become inappropriate (see below).

The hypotheses about the role of the orbitofrontal cortex in the rapid alteration of stimulus–reinforcer associations, and the functions more generally of the orbitofrontal cortex in human behaviour, have been investigated in recent studies in humans with damage to the ventral parts of the frontal lobe. (The description ventral is given to indicate that there was pathology in the orbitofrontal or related parts of the frontal lobe, and not in the more dorso-lateral parts of the frontal lobe.) A task that was directed at assessing the rapid alteration of stimulus–reinforcer associations was used, because the findings above indicate that the orbitofrontal cortex is involved in this type of learning. This was used instead of the Wisconsin card sorting task, which requires patients to shift from category (or dimension) to category, e.g. from colour to shape. The task used was visual discrimination reversal, in which patients could learn to obtain points by touching one stimulus when it appeared on a video monitor, but had to withhold a response when a different visual stimulus appeared, otherwise a point was lost. After the subjects had acquired the visual discrimination, the reinforcement contingencies unexpectedly reversed. The patients with ventral frontal lesions made more errors in the reversal (or in a similar extinction) task, and completed fewer reversals, than control patients with damage elsewhere in the frontal lobes or in other brain regions (Rolls, Hornak, Wade and McGrath 1994a) (see Fig. 3.37). A reversal deficit in a similar task in patients with ventromedial frontal cortex damage was also reported by Fellows and Farah (2003).

An important aspect of the findings of Rolls, Hornak, Wade and McGrath (1994a) was that the reversal learning impairment correlated highly with the socially inappropriate or disinhibited behaviour of the patients, and also with their subjective evaluation of the changes in their emotional state since the brain damage. The patients were not impaired at other types of memory task, such as paired associate learning. It is of interest that the patients can often verbalize the correct response, yet commit the incorrect action. This is consistent with the hypothesis that the orbitofrontal cortex is normally involved in executing behaviour when the behaviour is performed by implicitly evaluating the reinforcement associations of environmental stimuli (see below). The orbitofrontal cortex seems to be involved in this in both humans and non-human primates, when the learning must be performed rapidly, in, for example, acquisition, and during reversal.

To seek positive confirmation that effects on stimulus–reinforcer association learning and reversal were related to orbitofrontal cortex damage rather than to any other associated pathology, a new reversal-learning task was used with a group of patients with discrete,

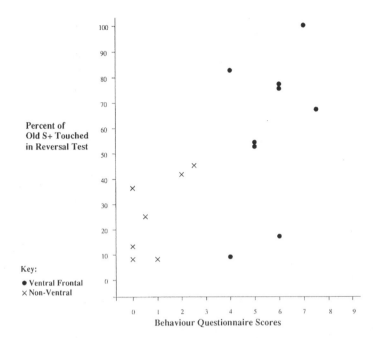

Fig. 3.37 Visual discrimination reversal performance in humans with damage to the ventral part of the frontal lobe. The task was to touch the screen when one image, the S+, was shown in order to obtain a point; and to refrain from touching the screen when a different visual stimulus, the S–, was shown in order to obtain a point. The scattergraph shows that during the reversal the group with ventral damage were more likely to touch the previously rewarded stimulus (Old S+), and that this was related to the score on a Behaviour Questionnaire. Each point represents one patient in the ventral frontal group or in a control group. The Behaviour Questionnaire rating reflected high ratings on at least some of the following: disinhibited or socially inappropriate behaviour; misinterpretation of other people's moods; impulsiveness; unconcern about or underestimation of the seriousness of his condition; and lack of initiative. (From Rolls, Hornak, Rolls and McGrath 1994a.)

surgically produced, lesions of the orbitofrontal cortex. In the new visual discrimination task (the same as that used in our monetary reward functional neuroimaging task, O'Doherty, Kringelbach, Rolls, Hornak and Andrews (2001a)), two stimuli are always present on the video monitor and the patient obtains 'monetary' reward by touching the correct stimulus, and loses 'money' by touching the incorrect stimulus. This design controls for an effect of the lesion in simply increasing the probability that any response will be made (cf. Aron, Fletcher, Bullmore, Sahakian and Robbins (2003) and Clark, Cools and Robbins (2004)). The new task also uses probabilistic amounts of reward and punishment on each trial, to make it harder to use a verbal strategy with an explicit rule. The task also had the advantage that it was the same as that used in our human functional neuroimaging study that had showed activation of the orbitofrontal cortex by monetary gain or loss (O'Doherty et al. 2001a). It was found that a group of patients with bilateral orbitofrontal cortex lesions were severely impaired at the reversal task, in that they accumulated less money (Hornak, O'Doherty, Bramham, Rolls, Morris, Bullock and Polkey 2004) (see Fig. 3.38). These patients often failed to switch their choice of stimulus after a large loss; and often did switch their choice even though they had just received a reward, and this has been quantified in a more recent study (Berlin, Rolls and Kischka 2004). The investigation showed that the impairment was only obtained with bilateral orbitofrontal cortex damage, in that patients with unilateral orbitofrontal cortex (or medial

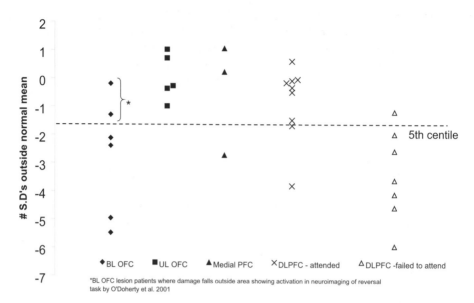

Fig. 3.38 Visual discrimination reversal performance on the probabilistic reversal task in humans with damage to different parts of the ventral part of the frontal lobe. Lesion groups: BL OFC, Bilateral Orbito-frontal cortex; UL OFC, Unilateral Orbitofrontal cortex; Medial PFC, Medial prefrontal cortex; DLPFC, Dorsolateral prefrontal cortex. The patients with bilateral damage to the orbitofrontal cortex performed poorly at the task. Patients with lesions of the dorsolateral prefrontal cortex performed poorly only if they had an attention deficit and failed to pay attention to the part of the display that informed them whether they had won on the current trial of the task. (attended/failed to attend: the patient attended/failed to attend to the crucial feedback during the reversal test, namely the amount won or lost on each trial.) (After Hornak, O'Doherty, Bramham, Rolls et al. 2004.)

prefrontal cortex) lesions were not impaired in the reversal task (see Fig. 3.38).

It is of interest that the patients with bilateral orbitofrontal cortex damage who were impaired at the visual discrimination reversal task had high scores on parts of a Social Behaviour Questionnaire in which the patients were rated on behaviours such as emotion recognition in others (e.g. their sad, angry, or disgusted mood); in interpersonal relationships (such as not caring what others think, and not being close to the family); emotional empathy (e.g. when others are happy, is not happy for them); interpersonal relationships (e.g. does not care what others think, and is not close to his family); public behaviour (is uncooperative); antisocial behaviour (is critical of and impatient with others); impulsivity (does things without thinking); and sociability (is not sociable, and has difficulty making or maintaining close relationships) (Hornak, Bramham, Rolls, Morris, O'Doherty, Bullock and Polkey 2003), all of which could reflect less behavioural sensitivity to different types of punishment and reward. Further, in a Subjective Emotional Change Questionnaire in which the patients reported on any changes in the intensity and/or frequency of their own experience of emotions, the bilateral orbitofrontal cortex lesion patients with deficits in the visual discrimination reversal task reported a number of changes, including changes in sadness, anger, fear and happiness (Hornak, Bramham, Rolls, Morris, O'Doherty, Bullock and Polkey 2003).

As described above, these results are complemented by neuroimaging results with fMRI in normal subjects, which showed that in the same task, activation of the medial orbitofrontal cortex was correlated with how much money was won on single trials, and activation of the lateral orbitofrontal cortex was correlated with how much money was lost on single trials

(O'Doherty, Kringelbach, Rolls, Hornak and Andrews 2001a). Together, these results on the effects of brain damage to the orbitofrontal cortex, and these and other complementary neuroimaging results described later, provide evidence that at least part of the function of the orbitofrontal cortex in emotion, social behaviour, and decision-making is related to representing reinforcers, detecting changes in the reinforcers being received, using these changes to rapidly reset stimulus–reinforcer associations, and rapidly changing behaviour as a result.

An idea of how such stimulus–reinforcer learning may play an important role in normal human behaviour, and may be related to the behavioural changes seen clinically in the patients of Rolls, Hornak, Wade and McGrath (1994a) with ventral frontal lobe damage, can be provided by summarizing the behavioural ratings given by the carers of these patients (Rolls et al. 1994a). The patients were rated high on at least some of the following: disinhibition or socially inappropriate behaviour; violence, verbal abusiveness; lack of initiative; misinterpretation of other people's behaviour; anger or irritability; and lack of concern for their own condition. Such behavioural changes correlated with the stimulus–reinforcer reversal and extinction learning impairment (Rolls et al. 1994a). The suggestion thus is that the insensitivity to reinforcement changes in the learning task may be at least part of what produces the changes in behaviour found in these patients with ventral frontal lobe damage.

The more general impact on the behaviour of these patients is that their irresponsibility tended to affect their everyday lives. For example, if such patients had received their brain damage in a road traffic accident, and compensation had been awarded, the patients often tended to spend their money without appropriate concern for the future, sometimes, for example, buying a very expensive car. Such patients often find it difficult to invest in relationships too, and are sometimes described by their family as having changed personalities, in that they care less about a wide range of factors than before the brain damage. The suggestion that follows from this is that the orbitofrontal cortex may normally be involved in much social behaviour, and the ability to respond rapidly and appropriately to social reinforcers is, of course, an important aspect of primate social behaviour. When Goleman (1995) writes about emotional intelligence, the functions being performed may be those that we are now discussing, and also those concerned with face-expression decoding that are described in this chapter (see further Rolls (2007h)).

Bechara and colleagues also have findings that are consistent with those described above in patients with frontal lobe damage when they perform a gambling task (Bechara, Damasio, Damasio and Anderson 1994, Bechara, Tranel, Damasio and Damasio 1996, Bechara, Damasio, Tranel and Damasio 1997, Damasio 1994, Bechara, Damasio, Tranel and Damasio 2005). In the Iowa gambling task subjects were asked to select cards from four decks of cards and maximize their winnings. During the task, electrodermal activity (skin conductance responses, SCR) of the subject was measured as an index of somatic activation. After each selection of a card, facsimile money is lost or won. Two of the four decks produce large payouts with larger penalties (and can thus be considered high-risk), while the other two decks produce small payouts but smaller penalties (low-risk). The most profitable strategy is therefore to consistently select cards from the two low-risk decks, which is the strategy adopted by normal control subjects. Patients with damage to the ventromedial part of the orbitofrontal cortex, but not the dorsolateral prefrontal cortex, would persistently draw cards from the high-risk packs, and lack anticipatory SCRs while they pondered risky choices. The task was designed to mimic aspects of real-life decision-making that patients with orbitofrontal cortex lesions find difficult. Such decisions typically involve choices between actions associated with differing magnitudes of reward and punishment where the underlying contingencies relating actions to relevant outcomes remain hidden.

Bechara, Damasio, Tranel and Anderson (1998) have since reported a dissociation between subjects with different frontal lobe lesions. All subjects with orbitofrontal cortex lesions were impaired on the gambling task, while only those with the most anteriorly placed lesions were normal on working memory tasks. Other subjects with right dorsolateral/high mesial lesions were impaired on working memory tasks but not on the gambling task. Bechara, Damasio, Damasio and Lee (1999) went on to compare subjects with bilateral amygdala but not orbitofrontal cortex lesions, and subjects with orbitofrontal cortex but not amygdala lesions, and found that all subjects were impaired in the gambling task and all failed to develop anticipatory SCRs. However, while subjects with orbitofrontal cortex lesions still, in general, produced SCRs when receiving a monetary reward or punishment, the subjects with bilateral amygdala lesions failed to do so. Fellows and Farah (2005) found that patients with ventromedial prefrontal or with dorsolateral frontal lobe damage were impaired on the Iowa gambling task, yet only the ventromedial frontal damage group had a reversal deficit. (This reversal deficit can be produced in patients with small bilateral lesions of the orbitofrontal cortex, as shown by Hornak, O'Doherty, Bramham, Rolls, Morris, Bullock and Polkey (2004).) Moreover the deficit on the gambling task of the ventromedial prefrontal patients was related to the fact that in the Iowa gambling task the first few choices of a high-risk deck are rewarded, and that later, when a large loss is received from a high-risk deck, an implicit reversal is required. Thus the deficit of patients with orbitofrontal cortex / ventromedial prefrontal cortex damage in the task may be related at least in part to their failure to perform stimulus–reinforcer association reversal learning, rather than for other reasons.

Most known cases of human orbitofrontal damage have occurred in adulthood, but two cases of damage acquired in early life have been reported (Anderson, Bechara, Damasio, Tranel and Damasio 1999). The two patients showed lifelong behavioural problems, which were resistant to corrective influences. But more importantly, the patients appeared completely to lack knowledge about moral and societal conventions. Interestingly, other patients with late acquired orbitofrontal lesions have retained knowledge of such matters, even if they do not always act in accordance with this explicit knowledge. The lack of this moral knowledge and subsequent reckless behaviour in the two patients with early life damage to the orbitofrontal cortex is consistent with the hypothesis that the orbitofrontal cortex is crucial for stimulus–reinforcer association learning (Rolls 1990d, Rolls 2005). The implication would seem to be that the orbitofrontal cortex is necessary for the development of personal moral-based knowledge based on the processing of rewards and punishers (Dolan 1999).

To investigate the possible significance of face-related inputs to orbitofrontal visual neurons described above, and given that face expression is a reinforcer, we also tested the responses of these patients to faces. We included tests of face (and also voice) expression decoding, because these are ways in which the reinforcing quality of individuals is often indicated. Impairments in the identification of facial and vocal emotional expression were demonstrated in a group of patients with ventral frontal lobe damage who had socially inappropriate behaviour (Hornak, Rolls and Wade 1996, Rolls 1999b) (see Fig. 3.39). The expression identification impairments could occur independently of perceptual impairments in facial recognition, voice discrimination, or environmental sound recognition. The face and voice expression problems did not necessarily occur together in the same patients, providing an indication of separate processing. Poor performance on both expression tests was correlated with the degree of alteration of emotional experience reported by the patients. There was also a strong positive correlation between the degree of altered emotional experience and the severity of the behavioural problems (e.g. disinhibition) found in these patients. A comparison group of patients with brain damage outside the ventral frontal lobe region, without these behavioural problems, was unimpaired on the face expression identification test, was significantly less impaired at vocal expression identification, and reported little subjective emotional change (Hornak, Rolls and Wade 1996, Rolls 1999b).

These findings have been extended, and it has been found that patients with face expression

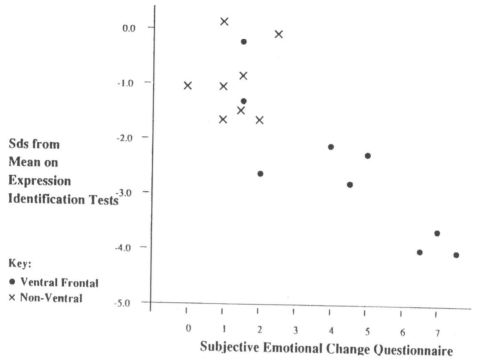

Fig. 3.39 Face expression identification deficit in humans with damage to the ventral part of the frontal lobe, and its relation to the patient's own rating of Subjective Emotional Change since the brain damage, based on sadness (or regret), anger (or frustration), fear (or anxiety), disgust, and excitement or enjoyment. (From Hornak, Rolls and Wade 1996.)

decoding problems do not necessarily have impairments at visual discrimination reversal, and vice versa (Hornak, Bramham, Rolls, Morris, O'Doherty, Bullock and Polkey 2003, Hornak, O'Doherty, Bramham, Rolls, Morris, Bullock and Polkey 2004). This is consistent with some topography in the orbitofrontal cortex (see Section 3.6.5.8 and Rolls and Baylis (1994)).

To obtain clear evidence that the changes in face and voice expression identification, emotional behaviour, and subjective emotional state were related to orbitofrontal cortex damage itself, and not to damage to surrounding areas which is present in many closed head injury patients, we performed these assessments in patients with circumscribed lesions made surgically in the course of treatment (Hornak, Bramham, Rolls, Morris, O'Doherty, Bullock and Polkey 2003). This study also enabled us to determine whether there was functional specialization within the orbitofrontal cortex, and whether damage to nearby and connected areas (such as the anterior cingulate cortex) in which some of the patients had lesions could produce similar effects. We found that some patients with bilateral lesions of the orbitofrontal cortex had deficits in voice and face expression identification, and the group had impairments in social behaviour, and significant changes in their subjective emotional state (Hornak et al. 2003). The same group of patients had deficits on the probabilistic monetary reward task (Hornak et al. 2004). Some patients with unilateral damage restricted to the orbitofrontal cortex also had deficits in voice expression identification, and the group did not have significant changes in social behaviour, or in their subjective emotional state. Patients with unilateral lesions of the antero-ventral part of the anterior cingulate cortex and/or medial prefrontal cortex area BA9 were in some cases impaired on voice and face expression identification, had some change in social behaviour, and had significant changes in their subjective emotional state. Patients with dorsolateral prefrontal cortex lesions or with medial lesions outside the anterior cingulate cortex and medial prefrontal BA9 areas were unimpaired on any of these measures of emotion. In all cases in which voice expression identification was impaired, there were no deficits in control tests of the discrimination of unfamiliar voices and the recognition of environmental sounds.

Overall, these results (Hornak, Bramham, Rolls, Morris, O'Doherty, Bullock and Polkey 2003) thus confirm that damage restricted to the orbitofrontal cortex (produced by surgical lesions) can produce impairments in face and voice expression identification, which may be primary reinforcers. The system is sensitive, in that even patients with unilateral orbitofrontal cortex lesions may be impaired. The impairment is not a generic impairment of the ability to recognize any emotions in others, in that frequently voice but not face expression identification was impaired, and vice versa. This implies some functional specialization for visual vs auditory emotion-related processing in the human orbitofrontal cortex. The results also show that the changes in social behaviour (quantified in the Social Behaviour Questionnaire as described above) can be produced by damage restricted to the orbitofrontal cortex. The results also show that changes in subjective emotional state (frequently including sadness, anger and happiness) can be produced by damage restricted to the orbitofrontal cortex (Hornak et al. 2003). In addition, the patients with bilateral orbitofrontal cortex lesions were impaired on the probabilistic reversal learning task (Hornak et al. 2004). The findings overall thus make clear the types of deficit found in humans with orbitofrontal cortex damage, and can be easily related to underlying fundamental processes in which the orbitofrontal cortex is involved as described throughout Section 3.6, including decoding and representing primary reinforcers, being sensitive to changes in reinforcers, and rapidly readjusting behaviour to stimuli when the reinforcers available change.

The results (Hornak et al. 2003) also extend these investigations to the anterior cingulate cortex (including some of medial prefrontal cortex area BA9) by showing that lesions in these regions can produce voice and/or face expression identification deficits, and marked changes in subjective emotional state (see Section 3.8).

It is also becoming possible to relate the functions of the orbitofrontal cortex to some psychiatric symptoms that may reflect changes in behavioural responses to reinforcers. Berlin, Rolls and Kischka (2004), Berlin and Rolls (2004) and Berlin, Rolls and Iversen (2005) compared the symptoms of patients with a personality disorder syndrome, Borderline Personality Disorder (BPD), with those of patients with lesions of the orbitofrontal cortex. The symptoms of the self-harming Borderline Personality Disorder patients include high impulsivity, affective instability, and emotionality; and low extroversion. It was found that orbitofrontal cortex and Borderline Personality Disorder patients performed similarly in that they were more impulsive, reported more inappropriate behaviours in the Frontal Behaviour Questionnaire, and had more Borderline Personality Disorder characteristics, and anger, and less happiness, than control groups (either normals, or patients with lesions outside the orbitofrontal cortex).

One of the measures of impulsiveness was the Matching Familiar Figures Test. In this standard cognitive behavioural measure of impulsivity, created by Kagan (1966), a participant selects (points to), from a set of highly similar pictures, the one that is exactly the same as the standard reference picture. High impulsiveness is reflected in short latencies to make a choice (which are typically 55 s in control subjects), and errors in the choices made. The other measure of impulsiveness was the Barratt Impulsiveness Scale (Patton, Stanford and Barratt 1995) which is a 30-item questionnaire that assesses non-planning impulsivity (attention to details), motor impulsivity (acting without thinking), and cognitive impulsivity (future oriented thinking and coping stability). Both the orbitofrontal and BPD groups were impaired at both measures of impulsiveness. (A consistent finding is that orbitofrontal cortex lesions affected how long rats decided to wait for rewards (Rudebeck, Walton, Smyth, Bannerman

according to which all areas of the cerebral cortex gain access to the striatum, and compete within the striatum and the rest of the basal ganglia system for behavioural output depending on how strongly each part of the cerebral cortex is calling for output. The striatum then maps (as a result of slow previous habit or stimulus–response learning) each particular type of input to the striatum to the appropriate behavioural output (implemented via the return basal ganglia connections to premotor/prefrontal parts of the cerebral cortex). This is one of the ways in which reinforcing stimuli can exert their influence relatively directly on behavioural output. The importance of this route is attested to by the fact that restricted striatal lesions impair functions implemented by the part of the cortex that projects to the lesioned part of the striatum (Rolls 1984a, Rolls 1994c, Rolls and Johnstone 1992, Rolls and Treves 1998, Rolls 2005) (see Section 3.10.2).

Another set of outputs from the orbitofrontal cortex enables it to influence autonomic function. The fact that ventral prefrontal lesions block autonomic responses to learned reinforcers (Damasio 1994) (actually known since at least the 1950s, e.g. Elithorn, Piercy and Crosskey (1955) in humans; Grueninger, Kimble, Grueninger and Levine (1965) in macaques), is of course consistent with the hypothesis that learned reinforcers elicit autonomic responses via the orbitofrontal cortex and amygdala (see, e.g., Rolls (1986c), Rolls (1986a), Rolls (1990d), and Rolls (2005)). It is worth emphasizing here that this does not prove the hypothesis that behavioural responses elicited by conditioned reinforcers are mediated via peripheral changes, themselves used as 'somatic markers' to determine which response to make. The question of whether there is any returning information from the periphery which is necessary for emotion, as the somatic marker hypothesis postulates, has been considered by Rolls (2005). The present hypothesis is, in contrast, that somatic markers are not part of the route by which emotions are felt or emotional decisions are taken, but that instead the much more direct neural route from the orbitofrontal cortex and amygdala to the basal ganglia provides a pathway that is much more efficient, and is directly implicated in producing, the behavioural responses to learned incentives (Divac, Rosvold and Szwarcbart 1967, Everitt and Robbins 1992, Williams et al. 1993, Rolls 1994c, Rolls 2005). Another potentially important output route from the orbitofrontal cortex is to the cingulate cortex (see Section 3.8). Another route is to explicit verbal outputs, for reported subjective emotional states are influenced by damage to the orbitofrontal cortex (Rolls et al. 1994a, Hornak et al. 2003, Rolls 2005).

3.7   The amygdala

Bilateral damage to the amygdala produces a deficit in learning to associate visual and other stimuli with a primary (i.e. unlearned) reward or punisher. For example, monkeys with damage to the amygdala when shown foods and non-foods pick up both and place them in their mouths. When such visual or auditory discrimination learning and learned emotional responses to stimuli are tested more formally, it is found that animals have difficulty in associating the sight or sound of a stimulus with whether it produces a reward, or is noxious and should be avoided (see Rolls (1990d), Rolls (1992b), Rolls (2000d), and Aggleton (2000)). Similar changes in behaviour have been seen in humans with extensive damage to the temporal lobe. The primate amygdala also contains a population of neurons specialized to respond to faces, and damage to the human amygdala can alter the ability to discriminate between different facial expressions.

The amygdala is implicated in some but not other learning processes involved in emotion, and Section 3.2 provides a description of some of the different associative processes involved in emotion-related learning, as part of the background for considering the functions of the amygdala in emotion, and more generally, for understanding the types of learning that influence decision processes involved in emotional behaviours (see further Chapter 10).

3.7.1 Connections of the amygdala

The amygdala is a subcortical region in the anterior part of the temporal lobe. It receives massive projections in the primate from the overlying temporal lobe cortex (see Amaral, Price, Pitkanen and Carmichael (1992); Van Hoesen (1981)) (see Fig. 3.40). These come in the monkey to overlapping but partly separate regions of the lateral and basal amygdala from the inferior temporal visual cortex, the superior temporal auditory cortex, the cortex of the temporal pole, and the cortex in the superior temporal sulcus. These inputs thus come from the higher stages of sensory processing in the visual and auditory modalities, and not from early cortical processing areas. Via these inputs, the amygdala receives inputs about objects that could become secondary reinforcers, as a result of pattern association in the amygdala with primary reinforcers. The amygdala also receives inputs that are potentially about primary reinforcers, e.g. taste inputs (from the secondary taste cortex, via connections from the orbitofrontal cortex to the amygdala), and somatosensory inputs, potentially about the rewarding or painful aspects of touch (from the somatosensory cortex via the insula) (Mesulam and Mufson 1982a, Mesulam and Mufson 1982b, Friedman, Murray, O'Neill and Mishkin 1986). The amygdala also receives projections from the posterior orbitofrontal cortex (Carmichael and Price 1995a) (see Fig. 3.40, areas 12 and 13).

Subcortical inputs to the amygdala include projections from the midline thalamic nuclei, the subiculum, and CA1 parts of the hippocampal formation, the hypothalamus and substantia innominata, the nucleus of the solitary tract (which receives gustatory and visceral inputs), and from olfactory structures (Amaral et al. 1992, Pitkanen 2000). Although there are some inputs from early on in some sensory pathways, for example auditory inputs from the medial geniculate nucleus (LeDoux 1987, LeDoux 1992), this route is unlikely to be involved in most emotions, for which cortical analysis of the stimulus is likely to be required. Emotions are usually elicited to environmental stimuli analysed to the object level (including other organisms), and not to retinal arrays of spots or the frequency (tone) of a sound as represented in the cochlea. Consistent with this view (that neural systems involved in emotion in primates generally receive from sensory systems where analysis of the identity of the stimulus as an object is performed), neurons in the inferior temporal visual cortex do not have responses related to the association with reinforcement of visual stimuli (Rolls, Judge and Sanghera 1977); whereas such neurons are found in the amygdala and orbitofrontal cortex (see below; cf. Fig. 3.3). Similarly, processing in the taste system of primates up to and including the primary taste cortex reflects the identity of the tastant, whereas its hedonic value as influenced by hunger is reflected in the responses of neurons in the secondary taste cortex (Rolls 1989d, Rolls 1995a, Rolls and Scott 2003, Rolls 2005) (see Fig. 3.3).

The outputs of the amygdala (Amaral et al. 1992) include the well-known projections to the hypothalamus, from the lateral amygdala via the ventral amygdalofugal pathway to the lateral hypothalamus; and from the medial amygdala, which is relatively small in the primate, via the stria terminalis to the medial hypothalamus. The ventral amygdalofugal pathway includes some long descending fibres that project to the autonomic centres in the medulla oblongata, and provides a route for cortically processed signals to reach the brainstem. A further interesting output of the amygdala is to the ventral striatum (Heimer, Switzer and Van Hoesen 1982) including the nucleus accumbens, for via this route information processed in the amygdala could gain access to the basal ganglia and thus influence motor output. (The output of the amygdala also reaches more dorsal parts of the striatum such as the head of the caudate nucleus.) The amygdala also projects to the medial part of the

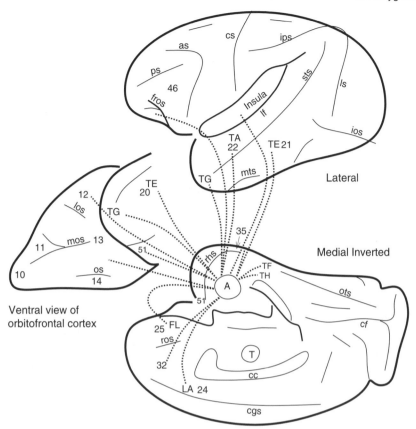

Fig. 3.40 Connections of the amygdala shown on lateral, ventral, and medial inverted views of the monkey brain (after Van Hoesen 1981). Abbreviations: as, arcuate sulcus; cc, corpus callosum; cf, calcarine fissure; cgs, cingulate sulcus; cs, central sulcus; ls, lunate sulcus; ios, inferior occipital sulcus; mos, medial orbital sulcus; os, orbital sulcus; ots, occipito-temporal sulcus; ps, principal sulcus; rhs, rhinal sulcus; sts, superior temporal sulcus; lf, lateral (or Sylvian) fissure (which has been opened to reveal the insula); A, amygdala; INS, insula; T, thalamus; TE (21), inferior temporal visual cortex; TA (22), superior temporal auditory association cortex; TF and TH, parahippocampal cortex; TG, temporal pole cortex; 12, 13, 11, orbitofrontal cortex; 24, part of the cingulate cortex; 35, perirhinal cortex; 51, olfactory (prepyriform and periamygdaloid) cortex. The cortical connections shown provide afferents to the amygdala, but are reciprocated.

mediodorsal nucleus of the thalamus, which projects to the orbitofrontal cortex, providing another output pathway for the amygdala. In addition, the amygdala has direct projections back to many areas of the temporal, orbitofrontal, and insular cortices from which it receives inputs (Amaral et al. 1992) (see Fig. 3.64). It is suggested elsewhere (see Section 1.11 and Chapter 2) (Rolls 1989d, Rolls 1989b, Treves and Rolls 1994, Rolls 1996c, Rolls and Treves 1998, Rolls 2000b, Rolls and Deco 2002) that the functions of these backprojections include the guidance of information representation and storage in the neocortex, and recall (when this is related to reinforcing stimuli). Another interesting set of output pathways of the amygdala are the projections to the entorhinal cortex, which provides the major input to the hippocampus and dentate gyrus, and to the ventral subiculum, which provides a major output of the hippocampus (Amaral et al. 1992). Via these pathways, reward influences may be introduced into the hippocampal memory system, and provide for associations to be formed between viewed places 'out there' and the rewards at those places (Rolls and Xiang 2005) (see Sections 2.2.4 and 3.11).

These anatomical connections of the amygdala indicate that it is strategically placed to receive highly processed information from the cortex and to influence motor systems, autonomic systems, some of the cortical areas from which it receives inputs, and other limbic areas. The functions mediated through these connections will now be considered, using information available from the effects of damage to the amygdala and from the activity of neurons in the amygdala.

3.7.2 Effects of amygdala lesions

Bilateral removal of the amygdala in monkeys produces striking behavioural changes which include tameness, a lack of emotional responsiveness, excessive examination of objects, often with the mouth, and eating of previously rejected items such as meat (Weiskrantz 1956). These behavioural changes comprise much of the Kluver–Bucy syndrome which is produced in monkeys by bilateral anterior temporal lobectomy (Kluver and Bucy 1939). In analyses of the bases of these behavioural changes, it has been observed that there are deficits in some types of learning. For example, Weiskrantz (1956) found that bilateral ablation of the amygdala in the monkey produced a deficit on learning an active avoidance task. The monkeys failed to learn to make a response when a light signalled that shock would follow unless the response was made. He was perhaps the first to suggest that these monkeys had difficulty with forming associations between stimuli and reinforcers, when he suggested that "the effect of amygdalectomy is to make it difficult for reinforcing stimuli, whether positive or negative, to become established or to be recognized as such" (Weiskrantz 1956). In this avoidance task, associations between a stimulus and punishers were impaired.

Evidence soon became available that associations between stimuli and positive reinforcers (reward) were also impaired in, for example, serial reversals of a visual discrimination made to obtain food (Jones and Mishkin 1972, Spiegler and Mishkin 1981). In this task the monkey must learn that food is under one of two objects, and after he has learned this, he must then relearn (reverse) the association as the food is then placed under the other object. Jones and Mishkin (1972) showed that the stages of this task that are particularly affected by damage to this region are those when the monkeys are responding at chance to the two visual stimuli or are starting to respond more to the currently rewarded stimuli, rather than the stage when the monkeys are continuing to make perseverative responses to the previously rewarded visual stimulus. They thus argued that the difficulty produced by this anterior temporal lobe damage is in learning to associate stimuli with reinforcers, in this case with food reward.

There is evidence from lesion studies in monkeys that the amygdala is involved in learning associations between visual stimuli and rewards (Gaffan 1992, Gaffan and Harrison 1987, Gaffan, Gaffan and Harrison 1988, Gaffan, Gaffan and Harrison 1989, Baylis and Gaffan 1991). However, lesion studies are subject to the criticism that the effects of a lesion could be due to inadvertent damage to other brain structures or pathways close to the intended lesion site. For this reason, many of the older lesion studies are being repeated and extended with lesions in which instead of an ablation (removal) or electrolytic lesion (which can damage axons passing through a brain region), a neurotoxin is used to damage neurons in a localized region, but to leave intact fibres of passage.

Using such lesions (made with ibotenic acid) in monkeys, Malkova, Gaffan and Murray (1997) showed that amygdala lesions did not impair visual discrimination learning when the reinforcer was an auditory secondary reinforcer learned as being positively reinforcing preoperatively. This was in contrast to an earlier study by Gaffan and Harrison (1987) (see also Gaffan (1992)). In the study by Malkova et al. (1997) the animals with amygdala lesions were somewhat slower to learn a visual discrimination task for food reward, and made more errors, but with the small numbers of animals (the numbers in the groups were 3 and 4), the difference did not reach statistical significance. It would be interesting to test such animals when the association was directly between a visual stimulus and a primary reinforcer such as taste. (In most such studies, the reward being given is usually solid food, which is seen before it is tasted, and for which the food delivery mechanism makes a noise. These factors mean that the reward for which the animal is working includes secondary reinforcing components, the sight and sound.) However, in the study by Malkova et al. (1997) it was shown that amygdala lesions made with ibotenic acid did impair the processing of reward-related stimuli, in that when the reward value of one set of foods was devalued by feeding it to satiety (i.e. sensory-specific satiety, a reward devaluation procedure, see also Section 3.2.2), the monkeys still chose the visual stimuli associated with the foods with which they had been satiated (Malkova et al. 1997, Baxter and Murray 2000). Further evidence that neurotoxic lesions of the amygdala in primates affect behaviour to stimuli learned as being reward-related as well as punishment-related is that monkeys with neurotoxic lesions of the amygdala showed abnormal patterns of food choice, picking up and eating foods not normally eaten such as meat, and picking up and placing in their mouths inedible objects (Murray, Gaffan and Flint 1996, Baxter and Murray 2000, Baxter and Murray 2002). These symptoms produced by selective amygdala lesions are classical Kluver–Bucy symptoms.

Thus in primates, there is evidence that selective amygdala lesions impair some types of behaviour to learned reward-related stimuli as well as to learned punisher-related stimuli. However, we should not conclude that this is the only brain structure involved in this type of learning, for especially when rapid stimulus–reinforcer association learning is performed in primates, the orbitofrontal cortex is involved, as shown in Section 3.6. Further, studies in macaques with neurotoxic (ibotenic acid) lesions of the amygdala reveal relatively mild deficits in social behaviour (Amaral 2003, Amaral, Bauman, Capitanio, Lavenex, Mason, Mauldin-Jourdain and Mendoza 2003, Bauman, Lavenex, Mason, Capitanio and Amaral 2004), and this is consistent with the trend for the orbitofrontal cortex to become relatively more important in emotion and social behaviour in primates including humans. This is shown for example by the findings that damage to the human orbitofrontal cortex does produce large changes in social and emotional behaviour (see Section 3.6.6).

Another type of evidence linking the amygdala to reinforcement mechanisms is that monkeys will work in order to obtain electrical stimulation of the amygdala, and that single neurons in the amygdala are activated by brain-stimulation reward of a number of different sites (Rolls 1975, Rolls, Burton and Mora 1980).

The symptoms of the Kluver–Bucy syndrome, including the emotional changes, could be a result of this type of deficit in learning stimulus–reinforcer associations (Jones and Mishkin 1972, Mishkin and Aggleton 1981, Rolls 1986c, Rolls 1986a, Rolls 1990d, Rolls 1992b, Rolls 2000d, Rolls 2005). For example, the tameness, the hypoemotionality, the increased orality, and the altered responses to food would arise because of damage to the normal mechanism by which stimuli become associated with a reward or punisher. Other evidence is also consistent with the hypothesis that there is a close relationship between the learning deficit and the emotion-related and other symptoms of the Kluver–Bucy syndrome. For example, in a study of subtotal lesions of the amygdala, Aggleton and Passingham (1981) found that in only those monkeys in which the lesions produced a serial reversal learning deficit was hypoemotionality present.

In rats, there is also evidence that the amygdala is involved in behaviour to stimuli learned as being associated with reward as well as with punishers. In studies to investigate the role of the amygdala in reward-related learning in the rat, Cador, Robbins and Everitt (1989) obtained evidence consistent with the hypothesis that the learned incentive (conditioned reinforcing) effects of previously neutral stimuli paired with rewards are mediated by the amygdala acting through the ventral striatum, in that amphetamine injections into the ventral striatum enhanced the effects of a conditioned reinforcing stimulus only if the amygdala was intact (see further Everitt and Robbins (1992); Robbins, Cador, Taylor and Everitt (1989); Everitt, Cardinal, Hall, Parkinson and Robbins (2000)). In another study, Everitt, Cador and Robbins (1989) showed that excitotoxic lesions of the basolateral amygdala disrupted appetitive sexual responses maintained by a visual conditioned reinforcer, but not the behaviour to the primary reinforcer for the male rats, copulation with a female rat in heat (see further Everitt and Robbins (1992)). (The details of the study were that the learned reinforcer or conditioned stimulus was a light for which the male rats worked on a Fixed Ratio 10 schedule (i.e. 10 responses made to obtain a presentation of the light), with access to the female being allowed for the first FR10 completed after a fixed period of 15 min. This is a second order schedule of reinforcement. For comparison, medial preoptic area lesions eliminated the copulatory behaviour of mounting, intromission, and ejaculation to the primary reinforcer, the female rat, but did not affect the learned appetitive responding for the conditioned or secondary reinforcing stimulus, the light.) In another study demonstrating the role of the amygdala in responses to learned positive reinforcers in rats, Everitt, Morris, O'Brien and Robbins (1991) showed that a conditioned place preference to a place where rats were given 10% sucrose was abolished by bilateral excitotoxic lesions of the basolateral amygdala. Moreover, the output of the amygdala for this learned reinforcement effect on behaviour appears to be via the ventral striatum, for a unilateral lesion of the amygdala and a contralateral lesion of the nucleus accumbens also impaired the conditioned place preference for the place where sucrose was made available (Everitt et al. 1991, Everitt and Robbins 1992). In another study showing the importance of the basolateral amygdala for effects of learned rewards on behaviour, Whitelaw, Markou, Robbins and Everitt (1996) showed that excitotoxic lesions of the basolateral amygdala in rats impaired behavioural responses to a light associated with intravenous administration of cocaine, but not to the primary reinforcer of the cocaine itself. (A second order schedule comparable to that described above was used to show the impairment of drug-seeking behaviour, that is responses made to obtain the light associated with delivery of the drug. Self-administration of the drug in a continuous reinforcement schedule was not impaired, showing that the amygdala is not necessary for the primary reinforcing effects of cocaine.)

It has long been known that rats with lesions of the amygdala display altered fear responses. For example, Rolls and Rolls (1973) showed that rats with amygdala lesions showed less neophobia to new foods. In a model of fear conditioning in the rat, LeDoux and colleagues (see LeDoux (1994), LeDoux (1995), LeDoux (1996); Quirk, Armony, Repa, Li and LeDoux (1996); LeDoux (2000); and Pare, Quirk and LeDoux (2004)) have shown that lesions of the amygdala attenuate fear responses learned when pure tones are associated with footshock. The learned responses include typical classically conditioned responses such as heart-rate changes and freezing to fear-inducing stimuli (see, e.g., LeDoux (1994)), and also operant responses (see, e.g., Gallagher and Holland (1994)). The deficits typically involve particularly the learned (emotional) responses, e.g. fear to the conditioned stimuli, rather than changes in behavioural responses to the unconditioned stimuli such as altered responses to pain per se (but see Hebert, Ardid, Henrie, Tamashiro, Blanchard and Blanchard (1999)). In another type of paradigm, it has been shown that amygdala lesions impair the devaluing effect of pairing a food reward with (aversive) lithium chloride, in that amygdala lesions reduced the classically conditioned responses of the rats to a light previously paired with the food (Hatfield, Han, Conley, Gallagher and Holland 1996).

In a different model of fear-conditioning in the rat, Davis and colleagues (Davis 1992, Davis 1994, Davis, Campeau, Kim and Falls 1995, Davis 2000), have used the fear-potentiated startle test, in which the amplitude of the acoustic startle reflex is increased when elicited in the presence of a stimulus previously paired with shock. The conditioned stimulus can be

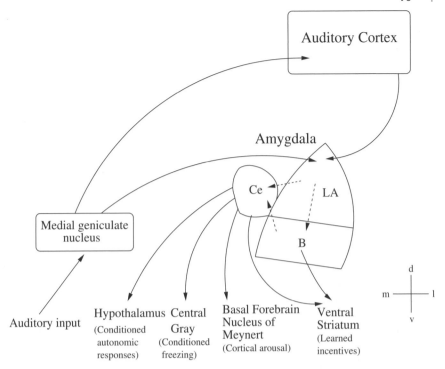

Fig. 3.41 The pathways for fear-conditioning to pure-tone auditory stimuli associated with footshock in the rat (after Quirk, Armony, Repa, Li and LeDoux 1996). The lateral amygdala (LA) receives auditory information directly from the medial part of the medial geniculate nucleus (the auditory thalamic nucleus), and from the auditory cortex. Intra-amygdala projections (directly and via the basal and basal accessory nuclei, B) end in the central nucleus (Ce) of the amygdala. Different output pathways from the central nucleus and the basal nucleus mediate different conditioned fear-related effects. d, dorsal; v, ventral; m, medial; l, lateral.

visual or a low-frequency auditory stimulus. Chemical or electrolytic lesions of either the central nucleus or the lateral and basolateral nuclei of the amygdala block the expression of fear-potentiated startle. These latter amygdala nuclei may be the site of plasticity for fear conditioning, because local infusion of the NMDA (N-methyl-D-aspartate) receptor antagonist AP5 (which blocks long-term potentiation, an index of synaptic plasticity) blocks the acquisition but not the maintenance of fear-potentiated startle (Davis 1992, Davis 1994, Davis et al. 1995, Davis 2000).

There are separate output pathways for the amygdala for different fear-related responses (see Fig. 3.41). Lesions of the lateral hypothalamus (which receives from the central nucleus of the amygdala) blocked conditioned heart rate (autonomic) responses. Lesions of the central grey of the midbrain (which also receives from the central nucleus of the amygdala) blocked the conditioned freezing but not the conditioned autonomic response (LeDoux, Iwata, Cicchetti and Reis 1988), and lesions of the stria terminalis blocked the neuroendocrine responses (Gray, Piechowski, Yracheta, Rittenhouse, Betha and Van der Kar 1993). In addition, cortical arousal may be produced by the conditioned stimuli via the central nucleus of the amygdala outputs to the cholinergic basal forebrain magnocellular nuclei of Meynert (see Section 3.10.5; Kapp, Whalen, Supple and Pascoe (1992); Wilson and Rolls (1990c), Wilson and Rolls (1990b), Wilson and Rolls (1990a); and Rolls and Treves (1998) Section 7.1.5).

The different output routes for different effects mediated by the amygdala are complemented by separate roles of different nuclei within the amygdala in conditioned fear responses (see Cardinal et al. (2002)). In a study by Killcross, Robbins and Everitt (1997), rats with lesions of the central nucleus exhibited a reduction in the suppression of behaviour (i.e. a reduction in freezing) elicited by a conditioned fear stimulus, but were simultaneously able to direct their actions to avoid further presentations of this aversive stimulus. In contrast, animals with lesions of the basolateral amygdala were unable to avoid the conditioned aversive stimulus by their choice behaviour, but exhibited normal conditioned suppression to this stimulus. This double dissociation indicates separable contributions of different amygdaloid nuclei to different types of conditioned fear behaviour, with the central nuclei especially involved in Pavlovian processes such as conditioned suppression of behaviour, and the basolateral amygdala more involved in instrumental, action–outcome, learning (Cardinal et al. 2002).

Different nuclei of the amygdala correspondingly have different functions in reward-related (or appetitive) learning in rats (Cardinal et al. 2002, Everitt, Cardinal, Parkinson and Robbins 2003, Holland and Gallagher 2003, Holland and Gallagher 2004, Everitt et al. 2000, Gallagher 2000). For example, the basolateral amygdala (BLA) nuclei are involved in some motivational aspects of the classically or Pavlovian conditioned effects of rewards (also known as appetitive reinforcers), in that BLA lesions impair the ability of conditioned stimuli (such as a tone) paired with food in associative learning to influence instrumental behaviour (such as bar pressing to earn food) (Holland and Gallagher 2003), perhaps reflecting impaired outputs to feeding systems in the lateral hypothalamus (see Fig. 3.41). (The BLA lesions also impair the learning of second-order associative conditioning, in that the lesioned rats cannot learn an association of an auditory stimulus with a previously conditioned visual stimulus (Setlow, Gallagher and Holland 2002).) In monkeys (Malkova et al. 1997) as well as rats (Cardinal et al. 2002), BLA lesions also impair reinforcer devaluation effects on actions. *The implication is that BLA lesioned animals cannot use a CS to gain access to the current value of its specific US, and in turn use this US representation as a goal for instrumental action, for freezing, or for fear-potentiated startle.* In this sense, BLA lesions may impair the elicitation of learned affective states used to influence these three types of behaviour. The fact that amygdala lesions do not affect food preferences per se (Rolls and Rolls 1973, Murray et al. 1996) suggests that affective states elicited by primary reinforcers are not impaired. In contrast, lesions of the central nucleus of the amygdala impaired the ability of conditioned stimuli (such as a tone) paired with food in associative learning to influence food consumption (Holland and Gallagher 2003), which could reflect a reduction in Pavlovian conditioned arousal produced by output pathways from the central nuclei (see Fig. 3.41 and also Everitt, Cardinal, Parkinson and Robbins (2003)).

We may summarize these investigations performed primarily in the rat by stating that the central nuclei of the amygdala encode or express Pavlovian S–R (stimulus–response, CS–UR) associations (including conditioned suppression, conditioned orienting, conditioned autonomic and endocrine responses, and Pavlovian–instrumental transfer); and modulate perhaps by arousal the associability of representations stored elsewhere in the brain (Gallagher and Holland 1994, Gallagher and Holland 1992, Holland and Gallagher 1999). In contrast, the basolateral amygdala (BLA) encodes or retrieves the affective value of the predicted US, and can use this to influence action–outcome learning via pathways to brain regions such as the nucleus accumbens and prefrontal cortex including the orbitofrontal cortex (Cardinal et al. 2002). We shall see below that the nucleus accumbens is not involved in action–outcome learning itself, but does allow the affective states retrieved by the BLA to conditioned stimuli to influence instrumental behaviour by for example Pavlovian–instrumental transfer, and facilitating locomotor approach to food which appears to be in rats a Pavlovian process (Cardinal et al. 2002, Cardinal and Everitt 2004). This leaves parts of the prefrontal and cingulate cortices as strong candidates for action–outcome learning.

This may be an appropriate place to consider the issue of 'wanting' vs 'liking' discussed by Berridge and Robinson (1998). 'Wanting' or conditioned 'incentive salience' effects are used to describe classically conditioned approach behaviours to rewards (Berridge and Robinson 1998, Berridge and Robinson 2003), and this learning is implemented via the amygdala and ventral striatum, is under control of dopamine (Cardinal et al. 2002), and contributes to addiction (Robinson and Berridge 2003). Conditioned 'incentive salience' effects can influence instrumental responses, made for example to obtain food. Berridge and Robinson (1998) suggest that 'liking' can be measured by orofacial reflexes such as ingesting sweet solutions or rejecting bitter solutions. There is evidence that brain opioid systems are involved in influencing the palatability of and hedonic reactions to foods, in that humans report a reduction in the pleasantness of sucrose solution following administration of naltrexone which blocks opiate receptors, but can still discriminate between sucrose solutions (Bertino, Beauchamp and Engelman 1991, Levine and Billington 2004). One problem here is that orofacial reflexes may reflect brainstem mechanisms that are not at all closely related to the reward value of food as reflected in instrumental actions performed to obtain food. Some of the evidence for this is that these responses occur after decerebration, in which the brainstem is all that remains to control behaviour (Grill and Norgren 1978) (with consistent evidence from anencephalic humans, Steiner et al. (2001)) (see further Section 3.2.2 on page 119). A second point is that normally the rated reward value or pleasantness given in humans to food is closely related to instrumental actions performed to obtain food, as shown by the close relation between pleasantness ratings ('liking') by humans given to a food in a sensory-specific satiety experiment, and whether that food is subsequently eaten in a meal ('wanting') (Rolls, Rowe, Rolls, Kingston, Megson and Gunary 1981b). Third, a confusion may arise when a stimulus–response habit is formed by overlearning, and persists even when the reward is devalued by for example feeding to satiety. This persistence of stimulus–response habits after reward devaluation should not necessarily be interpreted as 'wanting' when not 'liking', for it may just reflect the operation of a stimulus–response habit system that produces responses after overlearning without any guidance from reward, pleasantness, and liking (see further Section 10.7, Rolls (2005), and Cardinal et al. (2002)). I believe that normally liking, defined by pleasantness ratings of stimuli, is very closely related to wanting, that is being willing to perform behaviours (instrumental actions) to obtain a reward of the pleasant stimulus. Thus motivational behaviour is normally controlled by reward stimuli or goals (unless the behaviour is overlearned, see Section 3.2.2), and motivational state (e.g. hunger) modulates the reward value of unconditioned and conditioned stimuli such as the taste and sight of food, as described in Chapter 5 of Rolls (2005). Thus normally, liking a goal object and wanting it are different aspects of how reward systems control instrumental behaviour. Nevertheless, it is possible to dissociate the brain mechanisms involved in 'wanting' and 'liking' experimentally, with the classically conditioned 'incentive salience' stimuli that influence approach and instrumental actions and which influence 'appetitive' (or 'wanting') behaviour implemented in part separately from the reward systems that are activated by a primary reinforcer such as the taste of food during 'consummatory' (or 'liking') behaviour. In a sense, the 'incentive salience' effects require learning to predict primary rewards and punishers, and then to influence behaviours, and thus require additional brain mechanisms to those involved in representing primary rewards and punishers.

One output system of the amygdala is the nucleus accumbens, a part of the striatum (see Section 3.10.2). The core part of the nucleus accumbens is part of the pathway for approach responses to conditioned stimuli ('autoshaping'), and for Pavlovian–instrumental transfer, but not for the learning of new goal-directed instrumental actions (action–outcome learning) (Cardinal et al. 2002, Cardinal and Everitt 2004). Consistently, dopamine release in the core part of the nucleus accumbens is increased by conditioned emotional stimuli, both appetitive and aversive (Cardinal et al. 2002), and this part of the accumbens may be involved in preparatory aspects of rewarded behaviour, including behaviour when there is a reward delay period (Cardinal, Pennicott, Sugathapala, Robbins and Everitt 2001). In contrast, the release of dopamine in the shell part of the nucleus accumbens is produced by primary (i.e. unconditioned) rewards and punishers such as food, and this part of the accumbens may be involved in consummatory behaviour such as eating (Kelley 1999, Cardinal et al. 2002) (see further Section 3.10.2). Psychostimulant drugs such as amphetamine may operate in part by sensitizing the process by which non-contingent Pavlovian conditioned stimuli increase the probability of instrumental behaviour and Pavlovian conditioned approach to rewards (Cardinal et al. 2002), an effect related to 'conditioned salience' or 'wanting' (Berridge and Robinson 1998, Robinson and Berridge 1993).

In summary, there is thus much evidence from the effects of lesions that the amygdala is involved in responses made to stimuli that are associated by learning with primary reinforcers, including rewards as well as punishers. The evidence is consistent with the hypothesis that the amygdala is a brain region for stimulus–reinforcer association learning, and has partly dissociable systems for Pavlovian effects implemented via the central nucleus, and for effects of affective representations implemented via the basolateral amygdala. There is also evidence that it may be involved in whether novel stimuli are approached, for monkeys with amygdala lesions place novel foods and non-food objects in their mouths, and rats with amygdala lesions have decreased neophobia, in that they more quickly accept new foods (Rolls and Rolls 1973) (see also Dunn and Everitt (1988); Rolls (1992b); Rolls (2000d); Wilson and Rolls (1993)).

3.7.3 Neuronal activity in the primate amygdala to reinforcing stimuli

There is now clear evidence that some neurons in the primate amygdala respond to stimuli that are potentially primary reinforcers. For example, Sanghera, Rolls and Roper-Hall (1979) found some amygdala neurons with taste responses, and these were investigated by Scott, Karadi, Oomura, Nishino, Plata-Salaman, Lenard, Giza and Aou (1993). In an extensive study of 1,416 macaque amygdala neurons, Kadohisa, Rolls and Verhagen (2005b) showed that a very rich and detailed representation of the stimulus (such as food) that is in the mouth is provided by neurons that respond to oral stimuli. An example of a macaque amygdala orally responsive neuron is shown in Fig. 3.42. The neuron had different responses to different tastes, different temperatures of what was in the mouth, and different viscosities, but had no response to the texture of fatty oils. Other amygdala neurons were selective for only one modality, responding for example only to the oral texture of fat (Kadohisa, Rolls and Verhagen 2005b). 3.1% of the recorded amygdala neurons responded to oral stimuli. Of the orally responsive neurons, some (39%) represent the viscosity of oral stimuli, tested using carboxymethyl-cellulose in the range 1–10,000 centiPoise. Other neurons (5%) responded to fat in the mouth by encoding its texture (shown by the responses of these neurons to a range of fats, and also to non-fat oils such as silicone oil ($Si(CH_3)_2O)_n$ and mineral oil (pure hydrocarbon), but no or small responses to the cellulose viscosity series or to the fatty acids linoleic acid and lauric acid). Some neurons (7%) responded to gritty texture (produced by microspheres suspended in carboxymethyl cellulose). Some neurons (41%) responded to the temperature of the liquid in the mouth. Some amygdala neurons responded to capsaicin, and some to fatty acids (but not to fats in the mouth). Some amygdala neurons respond to taste, texture and temperature unimodally, but others combine these inputs. 66% (29/44) had taste responses. An interesting difference is that in terms of best responses to different tastes, 57% of the orbitofrontal cortex taste neurons had their best responses to glucose, whereas 21% of the amygdala neurons had their best response to glucose ($\chi^2=12.5$, df=5, P<0.03) (Kadohisa,

bo217

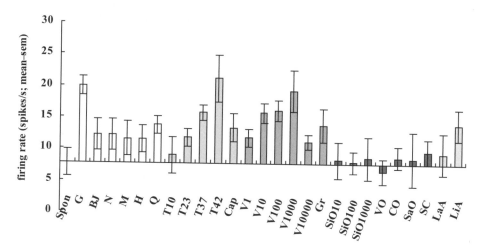

Fig. 3.42 The responses of an amygdala neuron (bo217) with differential responses to taste, temperature, and viscosity. The neuron did not respond to fat texture. The mean ($\pm$ the standard error of the mean, sem) firing rate responses to each stimulus calculated in a 1 s period over 4–6 trials are shown. The spontaneous (Spon) firing rate is shown. G, N, M, H and Q are the taste stimuli. T10–T42 are the temperature stimuli. V1–V10,000 are the CMC viscosity series with the viscosity in cP. The fat texture stimuli were SiO10, SiO100, SiO1000 (silicone oil with the viscosity indicated), vegetable oil (VO), coconut oil (CO) and safflower oil (SaO). BJ is fruit juice; Cap is 10 μM capsaicin; LaA is 0.1 mM lauric acid; LiA is 0.1 mM linoleic acid; Gr is the gritty stimulus. (After Kadohisa, Rolls and Verhagen 2005b.)

Rolls and Verhagen 2005a). (More amygdala neurons had their best responses to sour (HCl) (18%) and monosodium glutamate (14%) (Kadohisa, Rolls and Verhagen 2005a).)

These results show that a very detailed representation of substances in the mouth, which are likely to be primary reinforcers, is present in the primate amygdala (Kadohisa, Rolls and Verhagen 2005b). Less is known though about whether it is the reinforcer value of the stimuli that is represented. It has previously been shown that satiety produces a rather modest (on average 58%) reduction in the responses of amygdala neurons to taste (Yan and Scott 1996, Rolls and Scott 2003), in comparison to the essentially complete reduction of responsiveness found in orbitofrontal cortex taste neurons (Rolls, Sienkiewicz and Yaxley 1989c). Further, the representation in the amygdala of these oral stimuli does not appear to be on any simple hedonic basis, in that no direction in the multidimensional taste space in Fig. 7 of Kadohisa, Rolls and Verhagen (2005b) reflected the measured preference of the monkeys for the stimuli, nor were the response profiles of the neurons to the set of stimuli closely related to the preferences of the macaques for the stimuli (Kadohisa, Rolls and Verhagen 2005b). The failure to find very strong effects of satiety on the responsiveness of amygdala taste neurons mirrors the earlier finding of Sanghera, Rolls and Roper-Hall (1979) of inconsistent effects of feeding to satiety on the responses of amygdala visual neurons responding to the sight of food.

Recordings from single neurons in the amygdala of the monkey have shown that some neurons do respond to visual stimuli, consistent with the inputs from the temporal lobe visual cortex (Sanghera, Rolls and Roper-Hall 1979). Other neurons responded to auditory, gustatory, olfactory, or somatosensory stimuli, or in relation to movements. In tests of whether the

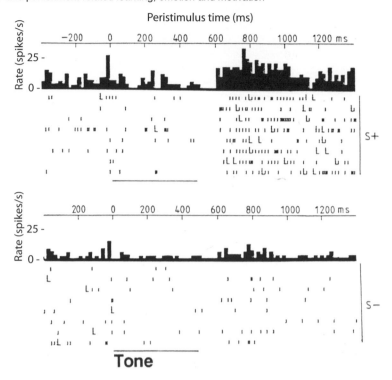

Fig. 3.43 Responses of a primate amygdala neuron in a visual discrimination task. Each tic represents the occurrence of an action potential; each row of tics represents the firing of the neuron on a single trial to the presentation of the S+ visual stimulus (which indicated that a lick could be made to obtain a taste of fruit juice) or of the S− visual stimulus (which indicated that a lick should not be made or (aversive) saline would be delivered. Presentations of the S+ and S− occurred in pseudorandom order but are grouped for clarity. The L indicates the occurrence of the lick response. Bin width = 10 ms. (After Rolls 2000d, and Wilson and Rolls 2005.)

neurons responded on the basis of the association of stimuli with reinforcers, it was found that approximately 20% of the neurons with visual responses had responses that occurred primarily to stimuli associated with reinforcers, for example to food and to a range of stimuli which the monkey had learned signified food in a visual discrimination task (Sanghera, Rolls and Roper-Hall 1979, Rolls 1981c, Wilson and Rolls 1993, Wilson and Rolls 2005, Rolls 2000d) (see example in Fig. 3.43). Many of these neurons responded more to the positive discriminative stimulus (S+) than to the negative visual discriminative stimulus (S−) in the Go/NoGo visual discrimination task, as shown in Fig. 3.44 (Rolls 2000d, Wilson and Rolls 2005). However, none of these neurons (in contrast to some neurons in the hypothalamus and orbitofrontal cortex) responded exclusively to rewarded stimuli, in that all responded at least partly to one or more neutral, novel, or aversive stimuli (see example in Fig. 3.46). Neurons with responses that are probably similar to these have also been described by Ono, Nishino, Sasaki, Fukuda and Muramoto (1980), and by Nishijo, Ono and Nishino (1988) (see Ono and Nishijo (1992)).

The degree to which the visual responses of these amygdala neurons are associated with reinforcers has been assessed in learning tasks. When the association between a visual stimulus and a reinforcer was altered by reversal (so that the visual stimulus formerly associated with juice reward became associated with aversive saline and vice versa), it was found that 10 of 11 neurons did not reverse their responses (and for the other neuron the evidence was not clear)

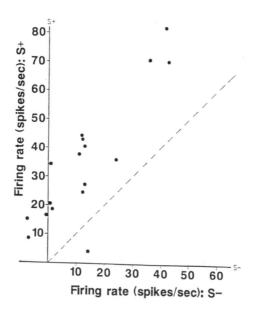

Fig. 3.44 Responses of amygdala neurons that responded more in a visual discrimination task to the reward-related visual stimulus (S+) than to the saline-related visual stimulus (S–). In the task, the macaque monkeys made lick responses to obtain fruit juice when the S+ was the discriminandum, and had to withhold lick responses when the S– was the discriminandum in order to avoid the taste of saline. Each point shows the responses of one neuron to the S+ and to the S– measured in a 0.5 s period starting 100 msec after the visual stimulus was shown. The responses are shown as the change from the spontaneous firing rate. Most of the points lie above the dashed line drawn at 45 degrees, showing that most of these neurons responded more to the S+ than to the S–. (After Rolls 2000d, and Wilson and Rolls 2005.)

(Sanghera, Rolls and Roper-Hall 1979, Rolls 1992b, Rolls 2000d). On the other hand, in a rather simpler relearning situation in which salt was added to a piece of food such as a water melon (but it was difficult to be sure that the monkey looked at the stimulus as much after it was salted), the responses of four amygdala neurons to the sight of the water melon diminished (Nishijo et al. 1988). To obtain further evidence on this issue, Wilson and Rolls (2005) tested visual discrimination reversal learning further using a similar procedure to that of Sanghera, Rolls and Roper-Hall (1979) in which two stimuli, one rewarded, and the other associated with punishment, were shown in random order and using an electronic shutter, so that it could be confirmed that the monkey performed a visual discrimination on every trial. The results are illustrated in Fig. 3.45, which shows that the neuron did not reverse its responses when the reinforcement contingency was reversed in the visual discrimination task. This experiment was repeated for two neurons, with identical results (Wilson and Rolls 2005, Rolls 2005). The fact that if primate amygdala neurons reverse they do so slowly was confirmed in a trace conditioning procedure [in which there is a delay between the end of the conditioned stimulus (a visual image) and the unconditioned stimulus (an air-puff to the eye, or a liquid)] in which if neurons reversed it took 30–60 trials (Paton, Belova, Morrison and Salzman 2006). The evidence now available thus indicates that primate amygdala neurons do not alter their activity as flexibly and rapidly in visual–reinforcer reversal learning as do orbitofrontal cortex neurons (see further Rolls (1992b), Rolls (2000d), and Rolls (2005)). As described above and in Chapter 9, orbitofrontal cortex neurons do show very rapid reversal of their responses in

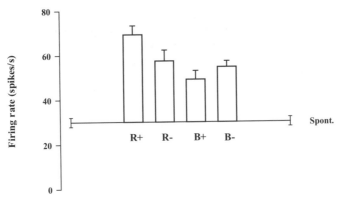

Fig. 3.45 The responses of a macaque amygdala neuron with more activity to a standard rewarded visual stimulus (S+) than to a standard punished visual stimulus (S–) in a Go/NoGo visual discrimination task. The neuron was then tested in a discrimination reversal task with a new pair of stimuli, which were Red and Blue. When the Red stimulus was associated with taste reward (R+), and the blue stimulus was associated with aversive saline if the monkey licked (B–), the neuron did not respond significantly differently to these two stimuli, even though the monkey performed the task correctly. Thus the neuron did not learn the discrimination with the new pair of stimuli. The contingencies were then reversed, and the monkey learned that the Red stimulus was now associated with saline (R–), and the Blue stimulus was associated with taste reward (B+). The neuron did not alter its activity after the reversal. The means and sem of the neuronal responses based on 4–8 trials for each condition are shown. The spontaneous firing rate of the neuron is also shown (Spont.) (After Wilson and Rolls 2005, and Rolls 2005.)

visual discrimination reversal, indeed so fast, in one trial, that it must be rule-based. It therefore seems likely that the orbitofrontal cortex is especially involved when repeated relearning and re-assessment of stimulus–reinforcer associations are required, as described above, rather than initial learning, in which the amygdala may be involved.

LeDoux and colleagues (see LeDoux (1995); LeDoux (1996); Quirk et al. (1996); LeDoux (2000); and Pare et al. (2004)) have made interesting contributions to understanding the role of the amygdala and related systems in fear-conditioning in the rat. They have shown that for some classes of stimulus, such as pure tones, the association between the tone and an aversive unconditioned stimulus (a footshock) is reflected in the responses of neurons in the amygdala. Some of the circuitry involved is shown in Fig. 3.41. The auditory inputs reach the amygdala both from the subcortical, thalamic, auditory nucleus, the medial geniculate (medial part), and from the auditory cortex. These auditory inputs project to the lateral nucleus of the amygdala (LA), which in turn projects to the central nucleus of the amygdala (Ce) both directly and via the basal (B) and accessory basal nuclei of the amygdala. LeDoux has emphasized the role of the subcortical inputs to the amygdala in this type of conditioning, based on the observations that the conditioning to pure tones can take place without the cortex, and that the shortest latencies of the auditory responses in the amygdala are too short to be mediated via the auditory cortex. (Although some conditioning of auditory responses has been found even in the medial geniculate to these pure tones, this conditioning is not of short latency, and LeDoux suggests that it reflects backprojections from the cortex (in which conditioning is also found) to the thalamus.)

The amygdala is well placed anatomically for learning associations between objects and primary reinforcers, for it receives inputs from the higher parts of the visual system, and from systems processing primary reinforcers such as taste, smell, and touch (see Fig. 3.3). The association learning in the amygdala may be implemented by Hebb-modifiable synapses from visual and auditory neurons on to neurons receiving inputs from taste, olfactory, or somatosensory primary reinforcers (see Figs. 3.4 and 3.6; Rolls (1986c); Rolls (1986a); Rolls (1990d); Rolls (1999a)). Consistent with this, Davis and colleagues (Davis 1992, Davis 1994, Davis et al. 1995, Davis 2000) have shown that the stimulus–reinforcer association learning involved in fear-potentiated startle (see Section 3.7.2) is blocked by local application to the lateral amygdala of the NMDA-receptor blocking agent AP5, which blocks long-term potentiation. The hypothesis (see Figs. 3.4 and 3.6, and Appendix B) thus is that synaptic modification takes place between potential secondary reinforcers and primary reinforcers which project on to the same neurons in the amygdala. One index of synaptic modification is long-term potentiation (see Appendix B), and consistent with this hypothesis, the potential evoked in the rat amygdala by a pure tone increased (suggesting long-term potentiation) after the tone was paired with footshock as the unconditioned stimulus (Rogan, Staubli and LeDoux 1997). Further, presentation of a tone paired with application of glutamate iontophoretically to activate a single amygdala neuron produced an increased response later to the tone alone, providing evidence that the site of the synaptic modification was on that neuron in the amygdala (Blair, Schafe, Bauer, Rodrigues and LeDoux 2001, LeDoux 2000, Blair, Tinkelman, Moita and LeDoux 2003).

LeDoux (LeDoux 1992, LeDoux 1995, LeDoux 1996) has described a theory of the neural basis of emotion which is conceptually similar to that of Rolls (Rolls 1975, Rolls 1986c, Rolls 1986a, Rolls 1990d, Rolls 1995d, Rolls 1999a, Rolls 2000f, Rolls 2005), except that he focuses mostly on the role of the amygdala in emotion (and not on other brain regions such as the orbitofrontal cortex, which are poorly developed in the rat); except that he focuses mainly on fear (based on his studies of the role of the amygdala and related structures in fear conditioning in the rat); and except that he suggests from his neurophysiological findings that an important route for conditioned emotional stimuli to influence behaviour is via the subcortical inputs (especially auditory from the medial part of the medial geniculate nucleus of the thalamus) to the amygdala.

This latter issue, of the normal routes for sensory information about potential secondary reinforcers to reach the amygdala via subcortical pathways will now be addressed, because it raises important issues about the stimuli that normally cause emotion, and about brain design. For simple stimuli such as pure tones, there is evidence of subcortical inputs for the conditioned stimuli to the amygdala, and even of the conditioned stimulus–unconditioned stimulus association being learned prior to involvement of the amygdala (see LeDoux (1995); LeDoux (1996); Quirk et al. (1996)). However, as described above in Section 3.5.4 entitled 'Why reward and punishment associations of stimuli are not represented early in information processing in the primate brain', we humans and other animals do not generally want to learn that a particular pure tone is associated with reward or punishment. Instead, it might be a particular complex pattern of sounds such as a vocalization (or, for example, in vision, a face expression) that carries a reinforcement signal, and this may be independent of the exact pitch at which it is uttered. Thus cases in which some modulation of neuronal responses to pure tones in parts of the brain such as the medial geniculate (the thalamic relay for hearing) where tonotopic tuning is found (LeDoux 1994) may be rather special model systems (i.e. simplified systems on which to perform experiments), and not reflect the way in which auditory-to-reinforcer pattern associations are normally learned. (For discrimination of more complex sounds, such as frequency-modulated tone sweeps, the auditory cortex is required.) The same is true for vision, in that we do not normally want to associate particular blobs of light at given positions on our retinae (which is what could be represented at the thalamic level in the lateral geniculate nucleus) with a primary reinforcer, but instead we may want to associate an invariant representation of an object, or of a person's face, or of a facial expression, with a primary reinforcer. Such analysis requires cortical processing, and it is in high-order temporal lobe cortical areas (which provide major afferents to the primate amygdala) that invariant representations of these types of stimulus are found (Rolls 1994a, Wallis and Rolls 1997, Rolls 2000a, Rolls and Deco 2002). Moreover, it is crucial that the representation is invariant (with respect to, for example, position on the retina, size, and, for identity, even viewing angle), so that if an association is learned to the object when in one position on the retina, it can generalize correctly to the same object in different positions on the retina, in different sizes, and even with different viewing angles. For this to occur, the invariant representation must be formed before the object–reinforcer association is learned, otherwise generalization to the same object seen on different occasions would not occur, and different inconsistent associations might even be learned to the same object when seen in slightly different positions on the retina, in slightly different sizes, etc. (see Appendix B and Rolls and Deco (2002)). Rolls and Deco (2002) (see also Chapter 4 and Appendix B) also show that it is not a simple property of neuronal networks that they generalize correctly across variations of position and size; special mechanisms, which happen to take a great deal of cortical visual processing, are required to perform such computations. Similar points may also be made for touch in so far as one considers associations between objects identified by somatosensory input, and primary reinforcers. An example might be selecting a food object by either hand from a whole collection of objects in the dark. These points make it unlikely that the subcortical route for conditioned stimuli to reach the amygdala, suggested by LeDoux (1992), LeDoux (1995), and LeDoux (1996), is generally relevant to the learning of emotional responses to stimuli.

3.7.4 Responses of these amygdala neurons to reinforcing and novel stimuli

As described above, some of the amygdala neurons that responded to rewarding visual stimuli also responded to some other stimuli that were not associated with reward. Wilson and Rolls (2005) (see Rolls (2000d)) discovered a possible reason for this. They showed that these neurons with reward-related responses also responded to relatively novel visual stimuli. This was shown in a serial recognition memory task, in which it was found that these neurons responded the first and the second times that visual stimuli were shown in this task (see Fig. 3.46). On the two presentations of each stimulus used in this task, the stimuli were thus either novel or still relatively novel. When the monkeys are given such relatively novel stimuli outside the task, they will reach out for and explore the objects, and in this respect the novel stimuli are rewarding. Repeated presentation of the stimuli results in habituation of the neuronal response and of behavioural approach, if the stimuli are not associated with a primary reinforcer. It is thus suggested that the amygdala neurons described operate as filters that provide an output if a stimulus is associated with a positive reinforcer, or is positively reinforcing because of relative unfamiliarity, and that provide no output if a stimulus is familiar and has not been associated with a positive primary reinforcer or is associated with a punisher. The functions of this output may be to influence the interest shown in a stimulus, whether it is approached or avoided, whether an affective response occurs to it, and whether a representation of the stimulus is made or maintained via an action mediated through either the basal forebrain nucleus of Meynert or the backprojections to the cerebral cortex (Rolls 1987, Rolls 1989b, Rolls 1990c, Rolls and Treves 1998, Rolls 2000b, Rolls 2005). It is an important adaptation to the environment to explore relatively novel objects or situations, for in this way advantage due to gene inheritance can become expressed and selected for. This function appears to be implemented in the amygdala in this way. Lesions of the amygdala impair the operation of this mechanism, in that objects are approached and explored indiscriminately, relatively independently of whether they are associated with reinforcers (including punishers), or are novel or familiar.

An interesting observation on the neurons that respond to rewarding and to relatively novel visual stimuli was made in the recognition memory task used by Wilson and Rolls (2005)

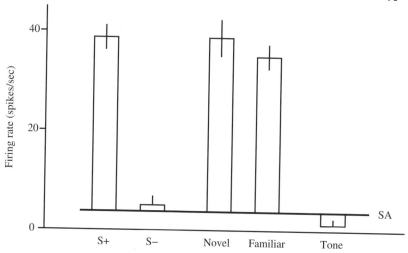

Fig. 3.46 This macaque amygdala neuron responded to the sight of a stimulus associated with food reward (S+), but not to a visual stimulus associated with aversive saline (S−) in a visual discrimination task. The same neuron responded to visual stimuli while they were relatively novel, including here on the first (Novel) and second (Familiar) presentations of new stimuli. The neuron did not respond to the tone that indicated the start of a trial. The visual stimulus appeared when the tone ended, at time=500 ms. SA, spontaneous firing rate of the neuron. The mean responses and the sem to the different stimuli are shown. (After Rolls 2000d, and Wilson and Rolls 2005.)

(see also Rolls (2000d)). It was found that the neurons responded the first time a stimulus was shown, when the monkey had to use the rule 'Do not make a lick response to a stimulus the first time a stimulus is shown, otherwise aversive saline will be obtained', as well as the second time the stimulus was shown when the monkey had to apply the rule 'If a stimulus has been seen before today, lick to it to obtain glucose reward'. Thus these amygdala neurons do not code for reward value when this is based on a rule (e.g. first presentation aversive; second presentation reward), but instead code for reward value when it is decoded on the basis of previous stimulus–reinforcer associations, or when relatively novel stimuli are shown that are treated as rewarding and to be explored.

The details of the neuronal mechanisms that implement the process by which relatively novel stimuli are treated as rewarding in the amygdala are not currently known, but could be as follows. Cortical visual signals which do not show major habituation with repeated visual stimuli, as shown by recordings in the temporal cortical visual areas (see Rolls, Judge and Sanghera (1977), Rolls and Treves (1998) and Rolls and Deco (2002)) reach the amygdala. In the amygdala, neurons respond to these at first, and have the property that they gradually habituate unless the pattern-association mechanism in the amygdala detects co-occurrence of these stimuli with a primary reinforcer, in which case it strengthens the active synapses for that object, so that it continues to produce an output from amygdala neurons that respond to either rewarding or punishing visual stimuli. Neurophysiologically, the habituation condition would correspond in a pattern associator to long-term depression (LTD) of synapses with high presynaptic activity but low postsynaptic activity, that is to homosynaptic LTD (see Fig. 1.5, Rolls and Treves (1998) and Rolls and Deco (2002)).

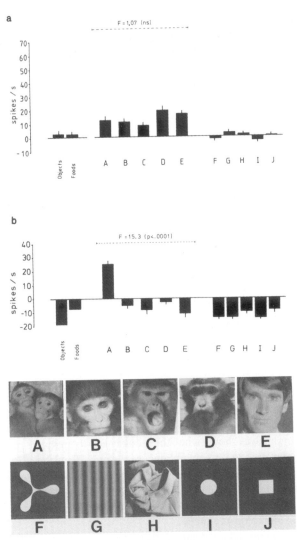

Fig. 3.47 The responses of two neurons (a, b) in the amygdala to a variety of monkey and human face stimuli (A–E), and to non-face stimuli (F–J, objects, and foods). Each bar represents the mean response above baseline with the standard error calculated over 4 to 10 presentations. The F ratio for an analysis of variance calculated over the face sets indicates that the neurons shown range from very selective between faces (neuron b, Y0809) to relatively non-selective (neuron a, Z0264). Some stimuli produced inhibition below the spontaneous firing rate. (After Leonard, Rolls, Wilson and Baylis 1985.)

3.7.5 Neuronal responses in the amygdala to faces

Another interesting group of neurons in the amygdala responds primarily to faces (Rolls 1981c, Leonard, Rolls, Wilson and Baylis 1985). Each of these neurons responds to some but not all of a set of faces, and thus across an ensemble could convey information about the identity of the face (see Fig. 3.47). This representation could be important in stimulus–reinforcer association learning where the stimulus is a face or person. These neurons are found especially in the basal accessory nucleus of the amygdala (see Fig. 3.48; Leonard, Rolls, Wilson and Baylis (1985)), a part of the amygdala that develops markedly in primates (Amaral et al. 1992). It will be of interest to investigate whether some of these amygdala face neurons respond on the basis of facial expression, and could thus represent reinforcers. Some neurons in the amygdala do respond during social interactions (Brothers and Ring 1993).

It is probable that the amygdala neurons responsive to faces receive their inputs from a group of neurons in the cortex in the superior temporal sulcus that respond to faces, often on the basis of features present, such as eyes, hair, or mouth (Perrett, Rolls and Caan 1982, Rolls 2007i) (see Section 4.2), and consistent with this, the response latencies of the amygdala neurons tend to be longer than those of neurons in the cortex in the superior temporal sulcus (Leonard, Rolls, Wilson and Baylis 1985, Rolls 1984b). It has been suggested that this is part of a system that has evolved for the rapid and reliable identification of individuals from their faces, because of the importance of this in primate social behaviour (Rolls 1981c, Rolls 1984b, Rolls 1992b, Rolls 1992a, Rolls 1992c, Leonard, Rolls, Wilson and Baylis 1985, Perrett and Rolls 1983, Leonard, Rolls, Wilson and Baylis 1985, Rolls 2005, Rolls 2007i). The part of this system in the amygdala may be particularly involved in emotional and social responses to faces. According to one possibility, such emotional and social responses would be 'looked up' (in a pattern associator, see Appendix B) by a 'key' stimulus, which consisted of the face of a particular individual (Rolls 1984b, Rolls 1987, Rolls 1990d, Rolls 1992b, Rolls 1992a, Rolls 1992c, Rolls and Treves 1998, Rolls 1999a). Indeed, it is suggested that the tameness of the Kluver–Bucy syndrome, and the changes in amygdalectomized monkeys in their interactions in a social group (Kling and Steklis 1976, Kling and Brothers 1992) (though these are more subtle after selective amygdala lesions, Amaral (2003)), arise because of damage to this system specialized for processing faces (Rolls 1981b, Rolls 1981c, Rolls 1984b, Rolls 1990d, Rolls 1992b, Rolls 1992a, Rolls 1992c, Rolls 2000a, Rolls and Deco 2002). The amygdala may allow neurons that reflect the social significance of faces to be formed using face representations received from the temporal cortical areas, and information about primary reinforcers received from, for example, the somatosensory system (via the insula (Mesulam and Mufson 1982a, Mesulam and Mufson 1982b)), and the gustatory system (via, for example, the orbitofrontal cortex) (see Fig. 3.3).

3.7.6 Evidence from humans

The theory described above about the role of the amygdala in emotion, based largely on research in non-human primates, has been followed up by studies in humans which are producing generally consistent results. One type of evidence comes from the effects of brain damage, which though rarely restricted just to the amygdala, and almost never bilateral, does provide some consistent evidence (Aggleton 1992). For example, in some patients alterations in feeding behaviour and emotion might occur after damage to the amygdala (see Aggleton (1992); Halgren (1992)). In relation to neurons in the macaque amygdala with responses selective for faces and social interactions (Leonard, Rolls, Wilson and Baylis 1985, Brothers and Ring 1993), a patient D.R. has been described who has bilateral damage to or disconnection of the amygdala, and has an impairment of face-expression matching and identification, but not of matching face identity or in discrimination (Young, Aggleton, Hellawell, Johnson, Broks and Hanley 1995, Young, Hellawell, Van de Wal and Johnson 1996). This patient is also impaired at detecting whether someone is gazing at the patient, another important social signal (Perrett, Smith, Potter, Mistlin, Head, Milner and Jeeves 1985b). The same patient is also impaired at the auditory recognition of fear and anger (Scott, Young, Calder, Hellawell, Aggleton and Johnson 1997).

Adolphs, Tranel, Damasio and Damasio (1994) also found face expression but not face identity impairments in a patient (S.M.) with bilateral damage to the amygdala, and extended this to other patients (Adolphs, Tranel and Baron-Cohen 2002, Adolphs, Tranel, Hamann, Young, Calder, Phelps, Anderson, Lee and Damasio 1999) (see also Calder, Young, Rowland,

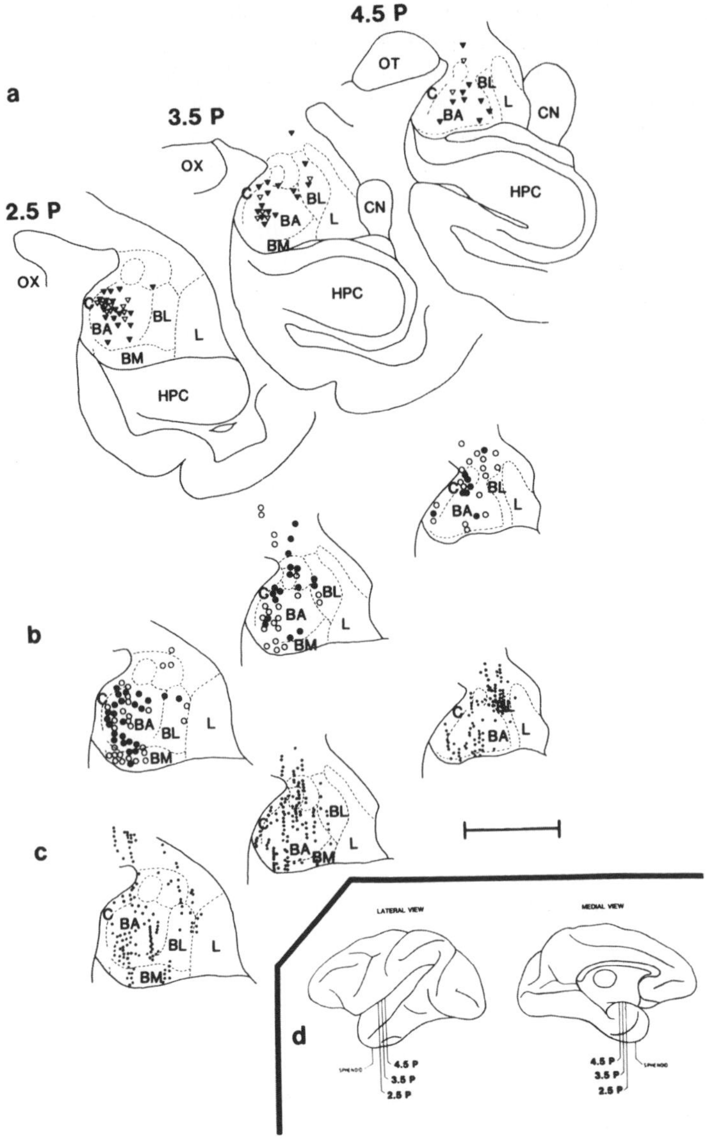

Fig. 3.48 (a) The distribution of neurons responsive to faces in the amygdala of four monkeys. The cells are plotted on three coronal sections at different distances (in mm) posterior (P) to the sphenoid (see inset). Filled triangles, cells selective for faces; open triangles, cells responding to face and hands. (b) Other responsive neurons. Closed circles, cells with other visual responses; open circles, cells responding to cues, movement, or arousal. (c) The locations of non-responsive cells. Abbreviations: BA, basal accessory nucleus of the amygdala; BL, basolateral nucleus of the amygdala; BM, basomedial nucleus of the amygdala; C, cortical nucleus of the amygdala; CN, tail of the caudate nucleus; HPC, hippocampus; L, lateral nucleus of the amygdala; OF, optic tract; OX, optic chiasm. (From Leonard, Rolls, Wilson and Baylis 1985.)

Perrett, Hodges and Etcoff (1996)). A similar impairment was not found in patients with unilateral amygdala damage (Adolphs, Tranel, Damasio and Damasio 1995). The bilateral amygdala patient S.M. was especially impaired at recognizing the face expression of fear, and also rated expressions of fear, anger, and surprise as less intense than control subjects. It has been shown that S.M.'s impairment stems from an inability to make normal use of information from the eye region of faces when judging emotions, which in turn is related to a lack of spontaneous fixations on the eyes during free viewing of faces (Adolphs, Gosselin, Buchanan, Tranel, Schyns and Damasio 2005). Although S.M. fails to look normally at the eye region in all facial expressions, her selective impairment in recognizing fear is explained by the fact that the eyes are the most important feature for identifying this emotion. Indeed, S.M.'s recognition of fearful faces became entirely normal when she was instructed explicitly to look at the eyes. This finding provides a mechanism to explain the amygdala's role in fear recognition, and points to new approaches for the possible rehabilitation of patients with defective emotion perception.

The backprojections to the neocortex from the amygdala may produce larger activations in these cortical areas to visual stimuli which either are fear face expressions, or which occur in association with fear face expressions, for these larger activations are not found in patients with amygdala damage (Phelps 2004, Anderson and Phelps 2001). Patients with amygdala lesions are also impaired at learning conditioned skin conductance responses when a blue square is associated with a shock, and are also impaired in acquiring the same autonomic response to fear by verbally instructed learning or by observational learning (Phelps 2004, Phelps, O'Connor, Gatenby, Gore, Grillon and Davis 2001).

The possibility has been discussed (Blair 2003) that there may be a subcortical pathway to the amygdala which bypasses the temporal cortical visual areas, based partly on evidence that a 'blindsight' patient with a right-sided hemianopia after occipital lobe damage showed some ability to discriminate when guessing between different facial expressions in the blind hemifield (De Gelder, Vroomen, Pourtois and Weiskrantz 1999). Further evidence was that in the same patient activations occurred in the amygdala to fearful vs happy face expressions when these were presented to the blind and seeing hemifields, but only in the fusiform cortex (face) area when the stimuli were presented to the seeing hemifield (Morris, De Gelder, Weiskrantz and Dolan 2001). However, a more relevant cortical area to examine would be the cortex in the anterior part of the superior temporal sulcus, which in macaques as shown by neuronal recording studies (Hasselmo, Rolls and Baylis 1989a) and in human neuroimaging (Haxby, Hoffman and Gobbini 2002) is especially involved in face expression analysis. The evidence from the latency of neuronal responses to faces does not suggest that there is a rapid subcortical pathway for processing faces, for in macaques the latencies of activation of face-selective neurons in the temporal cortex visual areas are typically 80–120 ms (Rolls 1984b, Leonard et al. 1985), in the amygdala are typically 110–180 ms (Leonard, Rolls, Wilson and Baylis 1985), and in the orbitofrontal cortex are typically 130–280 ms (Rolls, Critchley, Browning and Inoue 2006a). These latencies are consistent with cortical processing in the temporal cortical visual areas before neurons become activated by faces in the amygdala and orbitofrontal cortex, both of which receive direct inputs from the temporal cortical visual areas as described above.

Deficits produced by amygdala damage may extend beyond face expression recognition deficits, in that bilateral amygdala patients are impaired at 'theory of mind' attributions not only when these are based on eye gaze, but also when they are related to an inability to recognise 'faux pas' situations in narratives (Stone, Baron-Cohen, Calder, Keane and Young 2003). With respect to autism, in which a 'theory of mind' deficit is a major component (Frith 2001), children with autism have usually been found to be unimpaired in facial affect recognition when the groups are matched on mental age (Baron-Cohen, Wheelwright and Joliffe 1997, Blair 2003). However, some evidence linking the amygdala and autism is that patients with autism or Asperger's syndrome did not activate the amygdala when making mentalistic inferences from the eyes (Baron-Cohen, Ring, Bullmore, Wheelwright, Ashwin and Williams 2000).

There is some evidence that another face expression, disgust, involves special processing by the insula. Not only is there some evidence that the insula can be differentially activated by the face expression of disgust (Phillips 2004, Phillips, Williams, Heining, Herba, Russell, Andrew, Bullmore, Brammer, Williams, Morgan, Young and Gray 2004), but also patient N.K. with an insular lesion is impaired on disgust face and voice expression identification, and on self-experience of disgust (Calder, Keane, Manes, Antoun and Young 2000). It could be that the involvement of the insula is related to the contribution of part of it to visceral/autonomic responses, and indeed Krolak-Salmon, Henaff, Isnard, Tallon-Baudry, Guenot, Vighetto, Bertrand and Mauguiere (2003) found that electrical stimulation in the antero-ventral insula produced feelings related to disgust, including viscero-autonomic feelings.

In another system with some apparent specificity, there is some evidence that patients with lesions in the ventral putamen (which does receive inputs from the inferior temporal visual cortex and contains visually responsive neurons (Caan, Perrett and Rolls 1984)) may have impaired anger face recognition (Calder, Keane, Lawrence and Manes 2004), and this was related to evidence that the D2 dopamine receptor blocker sulpiride decreases the identification of angry face expressions (Lawrence, Calder, McGowan and Grasby 2002). Insofar as activation of the ventral putamen may be larger to angry face expressions and of the insula to disgust face expressions, we might note that skeletomotor responses (likely to be involved in anger) are functions of much of the putamen, and that visceral responses (likely to occur in disgust) may be produced in part via the anteroventral insula. Thus the activations of both regions by faces may be related to the responses normally produced by different face expressions.

For comparison, in a much more extensive series of patients it has been shown that damage to the orbitofrontal cortex can produce face expression deficits in the absence of face identification deficits, and that some patients with orbitofrontal cortex damage are impaired at the auditory identification of emotional sounds (Hornak, Rolls and Wade 1996, Hornak, Bramham, Rolls, Morris, O'Doherty, Bullock and Polkey 2003, Rolls 1999b) (see Section 3.6.6). Interestingly, the visual face expression and auditory vocal expression impairments are partly dissociable in these orbitofrontal patients, indicating partially separate processing systems in the orbitofrontal cortex, and indicating that a general emotional impairment produced by these lesions is not the simple explanation of the alterations in face and voice expression processing after damage to the orbitofrontal cortex. I note that the most consistent change after orbitofrontal cortex damage in our series of patients (Rolls, Hornak, Wade and McGrath 1994a, Hornak, Rolls and Wade 1996, Hornak, Bramham, Rolls, Morris, O'Doherty, Bullock and Polkey 2003, Rolls 1999b, Hornak, O'Doherty, Bramham, Rolls, Morris, Bullock and Polkey 2004) is an alteration in voice and face expression decoding, and that the amygdala is strongly connected to the orbitofrontal cortex.

Functional brain imaging studies have also shown activation of the amygdala by face expression. For example, Morris, Frith, Perrett, Rowland, Young, Calder and Dolan (1996b) found more activation of the left amygdala by face expressions of fear than of happiness in a PET study. They also reported that the activation increased as the intensity of the fear expression increased, and decreased as the intensity of the happy expression increased.

However, although in studies of the effects of amygdala damage in humans greater impairments have been reported to face expressions of fear than to some other expressions (Adolphs et al. 1994, Scott et al. 1997), and in functional brain imaging studies greater activation may be found to certain classes of emotion-provoking stimuli, e.g. to stimuli that provoke fear compared with those that produce happiness (Morris et al. 1996b), it is most unlikely that the amygdala is specialized for the decoding of only certain classes of emotional stimulus, such as fear. This emphasis on fear may be related to the research in rats on the role of the amygdala in fear conditioning (LeDoux 1992, LeDoux 1994, LeDoux 1996, Pare et al. 2004). It is quite clear from single-neuron neurophysiological studies in non-human primates that different amygdala neurons are activated by different classes of both rewarding and punishing stimuli (Sanghera, Rolls and Roper-Hall 1979, Rolls 1992b, Ono and Nishijo 1992, Wilson and Rolls 1993, Wilson and Rolls 2005) and by a wide range of different face stimuli (Leonard, Rolls, Wilson and Baylis 1985). Also, lesions of the macaque amygdala impair the learning of both stimulus–reward and stimulus–punisher associations (see Section 3.7.2). Amygdala lesions with ibotenic acid impair the processing of reward-related stimuli, in that when the reward value of a set of foods was reduced by feeding it to satiety (i.e. sensory-specific satiety), the monkeys still chose the visual stimuli associated with the foods with which they had been satiated (Malkova et al. 1997). Further, electrical stimulation of the macaque and human amygdala at some sites is rewarding, and humans report pleasure from stimulation at such sites (Rolls 1975, Rolls et al. 1980, Sem-Jacobsen 1968, Sem-Jacobsen 1976, Halgren 1992). Further, in a functional neuroimaging study, O'Doherty, Rolls, Francis, Bowtell and McGlone (2001b) showed that activation of the human amygdala was larger and more reliably produced by the pleasant taste of glucose than by the unpleasant taste of salt, both of which are primary reinforcers. Thus any differences in the magnitude of effects between different classes of emotional stimuli that appear in human functional brain imaging studies (Morris et al. 1996b) or even after amygdala damage (Adolphs et al. 1994, Scott et al. 1997) should not be taken as showing that the human amygdala is involved in only some emotions, but instead may reflect differences in the efficacy of the stimuli in leading to strong emotional reactions, or differences in the magnitude per se of different emotions, making some effects more apparent for some emotions than others. Consistent with this view, LaBar, Gitelman, Parrish, Kim, Nobre and Mesulam (2001) showed that both pleasant and unpleasant stimuli produced more activation of the human amygdala than neutral stimuli.

A very interesting clarification is provided by the finding that personality interacts with whether particular stimuli activate the human amygdala. For example, happy face expressions are more likely to activate the human amygdala in extroverts than in introverts (Canli, Sivers, Whitfield, Gotlib and Gabrieli 2002). In addition, positively affective pictures interact with extroversion to produce activation of the amygdala (Canli, Zhao, Desmond, Kang, Gross and Gabrieli 2001). This supports the conceptually important point that part of the basis of personality may be differential sensitivity to different rewards and punishers, and omission and termination of rewards and punishers (see Gray (1970), Matthews and Gilliland (1999) and Rolls (2005)). The observations just described are consistent with the hypothesis that part of the basis of extroversion is increased reactivity to positively affective (as compared to negatively affective) face expressions and other positively affective stimuli including pictures. The exact mechanisms involved may be revealed in the future by genetic studies, and these might potentially address for example whether genes control responses to positively affective stimuli; or whether some more general personality trait by altering perhaps mood produces differential top-down biasing of face expression decoding systems in the way outlined in Section 3.11. It has additionally been found that negative pictures interact with neuroticism in producing differential activation of the human amygdala (Canli et al. 2001).

Additional factors are that some expressions are much more identifiable than others. For example, we (Hornak, Rolls and Wade 1996, Rolls 1999b) found that happy faces were easier to identify than other face expressions in the Ekman set, and that the orbitofrontal patients we studied were not impaired at identifying the (easy) happy face expression, but showed deficits primarily on the more difficult set of other expressions (fear, surprise, anger, sadness, etc.). Another factor in imaging studies in which the human subjects may be slightly apprehensive is that happy expressions may produce some relaxation in the situation, whereas expressions of fear may do the opposite, and this could contribute to the results found. Thus I suggest caution in interpreting human studies as showing that the amygdala (or orbitofrontal cortex) is involved only in certain emotions. It is much more likely that both are involved in emotions produced to rewarding stimuli as well as to punishers.

3.7.7 Amygdala summary

The evidence described in Section 3.7 implicates the amygdala in the processing of a number of stimuli that are primary reinforcers, including the sight, smell, and taste of food, touch, and pain.

The amygdala also receives information about potential secondary reinforcers, such as visual stimuli, including faces. Many of the deficits produced by amygdala damage are related to impairments in learning associations between stimuli and primary reinforcers, e.g. between visual or auditory stimuli and pain.

The amygdala is not concerned only with aversive reinforcers, in that it receives information about food, and in that amygdala lesions impair the altered behaviour that normally occurs to foods when their reward value is reduced by feeding to satiety.

The associative stimulus–reinforcer learning or conditioning in the amygdala may require NMDA receptor activation for the learning, which appears to occur by a process such as long-term potentiation.

We know that autonomic responses learned to conditioned stimuli can depend on outputs from the amygdala to the hypothalamus, and that the effects that learned incentives have on behaviour may involve outputs from the amygdala to the ventral striatum. We also know that there are similar neurons in the ventral striatum to some of those described in the amygdala (Williams, Rolls, Leonard and Stern 1993).

All this evidence is consistent with the hypothesis that there are neuronal networks in the amygdala that perform the required pattern association. Interestingly, there is somewhat of a gap in our knowledge here, for the microcircuitry of the amygdala has been remarkably little studied. It is known from Golgi studies (performed in young rats in which sufficiently few amygdala cells are stained that it is possible to see them individually) that there are pyramidal cells in the amygdala with large dendrites and many synapses (Millhouse and DeOlmos 1983, McDonald 1992, Millhouse 1986). What has not yet been defined is whether visual and taste inputs converge anatomically on to some cells, and whether (as might be predicted) the taste inputs are likely to be strong (e.g. large synapses close to the cell body), whereas the visual inputs are more numerous, and on a part of the dendrite with NMDA receptors. Clearly to bring our understanding fully to the network level, such evidence is required, together with further neurophysiological evidence showing the appropriate convergence at the single neuron level, and evidence that the appropriate synapses on to these single neurons are modifiable by a Hebb-like rule (such as might be implemented using the NMDA receptors, see Appendix B), in a network of the type shown in Fig. 3.6.

At least part of the importance of the amygdala in emotion appears to be that it is involved in this type of emotional learning. However, the amygdala does not appear to provide such rapid relearning of reward-related emotional responses to stimuli as does the orbitofrontal cortex, as described in Section 3.6. Further, the amygdala does not appear in non-human primates and humans to play such an important role in emotional and social behaviour as the orbitofrontal cortex (see Section 3.6).

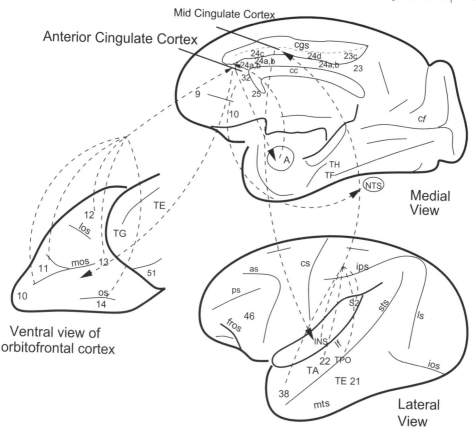

Fig. 3.49 Connections of the anterior (or perigenual) and midcingulate cortical areas. The cingulate sulcus (cgs) has been opened to reveal the cortex in the sulcus, with the dashed line indicating the depths (fundus) of the sulcus. The cingulate cortex is in the lower bank of this sulcus, and in the cingulate gyrus which hooks above the corpus callosum and around the corpus callosum at the front and the back. The anterior (or perigenual) cingulate cortex includes cingulate areas 32 (pregenual cingulate cortex), area 25 (subgenual cingulate cortex), and parts of areas 24a and 24b. (The cortex is called subgenual because it is below the genu (knee) formed by the anterior end of the corpus callosum, cc.) The perigenual cingulate cortex tends to have connections with the amygdala and orbitofrontal cortex, whereas area 24c tends to have connections with the somatosensory insula (INS), the auditory association cortex (22, TA), and with the temporal pole cortex (38). The midcingulate areas include area 24d, which is part of the cingulate motor area. Abbreviations: as, arcuate sulcus; cc, corpus callosum; cf, calcarine fissure; cgs, cingulate sulcus; cs, central sulcus; ls, lunate sulcus; ios, inferior occipital sulcus; mos, medial orbital sulcus; os, orbital sulcus; ps, principal sulcus; sts, superior temporal sulcus; lf, lateral (or Sylvian) fissure (which has been opened to reveal the insula); A, amygdala; INS, insula; NTS, autonomic areas in the medulla, including the nucleus of the solitary tract and the dorsal motor nucleus of the vagus; TE (21), inferior temporal visual cortex; TA (22), superior temporal auditory association cortex; TF and TH, parahippocampal cortex; TPO, multimodal cortical area in the superior temporal sulcus; 38, TG, temporal pole cortex; 12, 13, 11, orbitofrontal cortex; 51, olfactory (prepyriform and periamygdaloid) cortex.

3.8   The cingulate cortex

The anterior or perigenual cingulate cortex area (ACC) occupying approximately the anterior one-third of the cingulate cortex (see Fig. 3.49, area 32 the pregenual cingulate cortex, area 25 the subgenual cingulate cortex, and part of area 24) is implicated in emotion (Rolls 2005, Rolls 2007b). It may be distinguished from a mid-cingulate cortex (MCC) area (occupying approximately the middle third of the cingulate cortex) which has been termed the cingulate motor area (Vogt, Derbyshire and Jones 1996, Vogt 2007) and may be involved in response selection (Rushworth, Walton, Kennerley and Bannerman 2004). In what follows, I will distinguish the anterior or perigenual cingulate cortex (see Section 3.8.1) from the midcingulate cortex (Section 3.8.2). (Perigenual means literally 'around the genu', with the genu being the knee formed by the anterior end of the corpus callosum.)

Vogt et al. (1996) showed that pain produced an increase in regional cerebral blood flow (rCBF, measured with positron emission tomography, PET) in an area of perigenual cingulate cortex which included parts of areas 25, 32, 24a, 24b and/or 24c. Vogt et al. suggested that activation of the anterior part of the cingulate area is related to the affective aspect of pain. There are direct projections to the cingulate cortex from medial thalamic areas that relay pain inputs, including the parafascicular nucleus. In terms of other connections (see Van Hoesen, Morecraft and Vogt (1993); Vogt, Pandya and Rosene (1987); and Vogt and Pandya (1987)), the anterior cingulate cortex is connected to the medial orbitofrontal areas, parts of lateral orbitofrontal area 12 (Carmichael and Price 1995a), the amygdala (which projects strongly to cingulate subgenual area 25) and the temporal pole cortex, and also receives somatosensory inputs from the insula and other somatosensory cortical areas (see Fig. 3.49). The anterior cingulate cortex has output projections to the periaqueductal grey in the midbrain (which is implicated in pain processing), to the nucleus of the solitary tract and dorsal motor nucleus of the vagus (through which autonomic effects can be elicited), and to the ventral striatum and caudate nucleus (through which behavioural responses could be produced).

Consistent with the anterior cingulate region being involved in affect, it includes the area activated by the induction of a sad mood in the study described by Mayberg (1997) and Mayberg, Liotti, Brannan, McGinnis, Mahurin, Jerabek, Silva, Tekell, Martin, Lancaster and Fox (1999). Also consistent with this region being involved in affect, Lane, Fink, Chau and Dolan (1997a) found increased regional blood flow in a PET study in a far anterior part of the cingulate cortex where it adjoins prefrontal cortex when humans paid attention to the affective aspects of pictures they were being shown which contained pleasant images (e.g. flowers) and unpleasant pictures (e.g. a mangled face and a snake). What we will now call the perigenual or anterior cingulate cortex, approximately the anterior one-third of the cingulate cortex and including the pregenual cingulate cortex area 32, the subgenual cingulate cortex area 25, and parts of area 24, is thus related to affect, and will be considered next in Section 3.8.1. The functions of the mid-cingulate area will be considered in Section 3.8.2.

3.8.1 Anterior or perigenual cingulate cortex, reward, and affect

The anterior or perigenual cingulate cortex may be part of an executive, output, response selection system for some emotional states, where the responses can include autonomic responses. Part of the basis for this suggestion is its inputs from somatosensory cortical areas including the insula, and the orbitofrontal cortex and amygdala (see Fig. 3.49), and its outputs to brainstem areas such as the periaqueductal (or central) grey in the midbrain (which is implicated in pain, see Melzack and Wall (1996) and Rolls (2005)), the ventral striatum, and the autonomic brainstem nuclei (see Van Hoesen et al. (1993)). Devinsky, Morrell and Vogt (1995) and Cardinal et al. (2002) review evidence that anterior cingulate lesions in humans produce apathy, autonomic dysregulation, and emotional instability. We ourselves have shown that patients with circumscribed, even unilateral, surgical lesions of the anterior/perigenual cingulate cortex may be impaired at voice and face expression identification, have impaired subjective emotional states, and some changes in social behaviour including being less likely to notice when other people were angry, not being close to his or her family, and doing things without thinking (Hornak, Bramham, Rolls, Morris, O'Doherty, Bullock and Polkey 2003).

In macaques, anterior cingulate cortex lesions can produce a type of social apathy, including diminished social vocalisation, and also emotional and social changes (Hadland, Rushworth, Gaffan and Passingham 2003). Although the exact homology of what is called in rodents anterior cingulate cortex (ACC) is not clear, it is of interest that ACC lesions in rodents impair stimulus–reinforcer association learning, in tasks in which subjects must learn which stimulus to select in each of eight pairs in order to obtain reward (Bussey, Muir, Everitt and Robbins 1997). ACC lesions also impair the Pavlovian associative stimulus–reward learning involved in autoshaping in rodents, but seem to have their effects only when multiple conditioned stimuli must be distinguished, and perhaps when there is some conflict (Cardinal et al. 2002).

Functional neuroimaging studies are now showing that there appear to be separate representations of aversive and positively affective stimuli in the anterior/perigenual cingulate cortex (Rolls 2005, Rolls 2007b), with the results of one series of studies on somatosensory stimuli summarized in Fig. 3.51. The area activated by pain is typically 10–30 mm behind and above the most anterior (i.e. pre- or peri-genual) part of the anterior cingulate cortex (see e.g. Rolls, O'Doherty, Kringelbach, Francis, Bowtell and McGlone (2003d), Fig. 3.5, and Vogt and Sikes (2000)). Pleasant touch was found to activate the most anterior part of the anterior cingulate cortex, just in front of the (genu or knee of the) corpus callosum (i.e. pregenual cingulate cortex) (Rolls, O'Doherty, Kringelbach, Francis, Bowtell and McGlone 2003d) (Fig. 3.5). Oral somatosensory stimuli such as viscosity and fat texture also activate this most anterior part of the anterior cingulate cortex (De Araujo and Rolls 2004).

More than just somatosensory stimuli are represented, however, in that (pleasant) sweet taste also activates the most anterior part of the anterior cingulate cortex (De Araujo and Rolls 2004, De Araujo, Kringelbach, Rolls and Hobden 2003a) (Fig. 3.50). There is now direct neuronal evidence that primary reinforcers are represented in the macaque pregenual cingulate cortex, area 32, in that a small proportion, 1.6%, of neurons have taste responses, with most tuned to sweet taste (Rolls, Verhagen, Gabbott and Kadohisa 2007c). Pleasant odours also activate the pregenual cingulate cortex (Rolls, Kringelbach and De Araujo 2003c) (Figs. 3.17 and 3.18), and cognitive inputs that influence the pleasantness of odours also influence activations to olfactory stimuli in this area (De Araujo et al. 2005) (Figs. 3.33 and 3.34). Unpleasant odours activate further back in the anterior cingulate cortex (Rolls, Kringelbach and De Araujo 2003c) (Fig. 3.17). Activations in the anterior/perigenual cingulate cortex are also produced by the taste of water when it is rewarding because of thirst (De Araujo, Kringelbach, Rolls and McGlone 2003b), and by the flavour of food, made evident by a combination of strawberry odour and sweet taste (Kringelbach, O'Doherty, Rolls and Andrews 2003). The richness and pleasantness of the flavour of a savoury food is also represented in the pregenual cingulate cortex, in that a glutamate taste and savory odour combination produced much greater activation of the medial orbitofrontal cortex and pregenual cingulate cortex than the sum of the activations by the taste and olfactory components presented separately. Further, activations in these brain regions were correlated with the pleasantness and fullness of the umami flavour, and with the consonance of the taste and olfactory components (McCabe and Rolls 2007). Activations in the pregenual cingulate cortex are interestingly related to individual differences in reward, in that there are significantly larger correlations with the subjective pleasantness of the flavour of chocolate in chocolate cravers than in chocolate non-cravers (Rolls and McCabe 2007). The pregenual cingulate cortex is also activated by abstract reward, that is by monetary reward (O'Doherty, Kringelbach, Rolls, Hornak and Andrews 2001a) (Fig. 3.25). The locations of some of these activations are shown in Fig. 3.51, from which it is clear that many positively affective stimuli are represented in the most anterior part of the perigenual cingulate cortex, with some less positively affective or negatively affective stimuli activating a region of the cingulate cortex which is just posterior

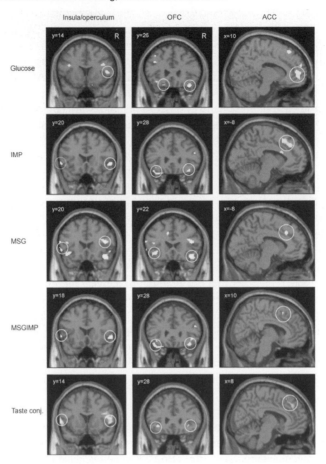

Fig. 3.50 Activation of the human primary taste cortex in the insula/frontal operculum; the orbitofrontal cortex (OFC); and the anterior cingulate cortex (ACC) by taste. The stimuli used included glucose, two umami taste stimuli (monosodium glutamate (MSG) and inosine monophosphate (IMP)), and a mixture of the two umami stimuli. Taste conj. refers to a conjunction analysis over all the taste stimuli. The taste of glucose activated the pregenual cingulate cortex, and the other tastes produced activation further back in the cingulate cortex (right column). (After DeAraujo, Kringelbach, Rolls and Hobden 2003.) (See colour plates Appendix E.)

to this above the corpus callosum.

In addition to the pregenual cingulate sites that are activated in many of our studies of affective stimuli, it is also frequently found that a region at the intersection of the medial prefrontal cortex, the subgenual cingulate cortex, and the orbitofrontal cortex is activated by positively affective stimuli. The region is illustrated in Figs. 3.17 on page 150 and 3.18 (lower region) where activations were correlated with the pleasantness of olfactory stimuli (Rolls, Kringelbach and De Araujo 2003c), in Fig. 3.33A and B where cognitive inputs increased activations that were related to the pleasantness of olfactory stimuli (De Araujo, Rolls, Velazco, Margot and Cayeux 2005), in Fig. 1 of De Araujo, Kringelbach, Rolls and Hobden (2003a) where glucose taste produced activations, and in a similar region in which intraoral fat and sucrose both produced activations (De Araujo and Rolls 2004). This region is also activated by monetary reward (O'Doherty, Kringelbach, Rolls, Hornak and Andrews 2001a). The region is probably part of area 10, and is part of a medial prefrontal network of connected regions

for these situations that the anterior cingulate cortex is especially important. Much affective computation, including the elicitation of affective states, may thus not computationally require the anterior cingulate cortex; but if to obtain the goal particular responses must be selected, then in those affective situations the anterior cingulate cortex may be especially computationally important. We return to the different types of decision-making in Chapter 10.

3.9 Human brain imaging investigations of mood and depression

Mood states can continue for long periods after reinforcing stimuli have been delivered. Some type of memory system is required to keep these mood states active. One possible mechanism is an attractor-based autoassociation system (see Section B.3). Another possible mechanism is a biochemical change in transmitter release or sensitivity. If the system that normally keeps these mood states active for a period becomes dysregulated, then mood states (such as depression) may be present without any apparent reinforcer having been delivered. Brain regions involved in mood and in depression (which has biological and cognitive aspects, Clark and Beck (1999)) have been investigated by mood induction in normal subjects; and by measuring the changes in activity associated with depression, and its treatment by antidepressant drugs (see Mayberg (1997); Mayberg et al. (1999); Mayberg (2003); Drevets and Raichle (1992); Dolan, Bench, Brown, Scott, Friston and Frackowiak (1992); George, Ketter, Parekh, Herscovitch and Post (1996); Dolan (1997); Phillips et al. (2003)).

In one example of this approach, Drevets, Price, Simpson, Todd, Reich, Vannier and Raichle (1997) showed that positron emission tomography (PET) measures of regional blood flow and glucose metabolism and magnetic resonance imaging (MRI)-based measures of grey matter volume are abnormally reduced in the 'subgenual prefrontal cortex' in depressed subjects with familial major depressive disorder ('unipolar depression') and bipolar disorder ('manic-depressive illness') (Ongur, Drevets and Price 1998, Torrey, Webster, Knable, Johnson and Yolken 2000). This cortex is situated on the anterior cingulate gyrus lying ventral to the genu of the corpus callosum and may also be described as the subgenual or subcallosal anterior cingulate cortex (see Fig. 3.49).

In other PET imaging studies, which implicate a similar area although apparently in the opposite direction, treatment-resistant depression is associated with metabolic overactivity in the subgenual cingulate cortex; the recovery of depression associated with fluoxetine treatment is associated with a decrease of glucose metabolism (as indicated by fluorodeoxyglucose PET) in the ventral (subgenual) cingulate area 25; and the induction of a mood of sadness in normal subjects increases glucose metabolism in the same area (Mayberg 1997, Mayberg, Brannan, Mahurin, Jerabek, Brickman, Tekell, Silva, McGinnis, Glass, Martin and Fox 1997, Mayberg et al. 1999, Mayberg 2003, Mayberg et al. 2005) (see Fig. 3.52). At the same time, the induced sadness was associated with reduced glucose metabolism in more dorsal areas such as the dorsal prefrontal cortex (labelled F9 in Fig. 3.52), the inferior parietal cortex, and the mid-cingulate and the posterior cingulate cortex (Mayberg 1997). These mid-cingulate areas are involved in processing sensory and spatial stimuli, in spatial attention, and in sensori-motor responses (see Section 3.8.2 and Koski and Paus (2000)), and the reduced metabolism in these mid-cingulate areas during sadness might reflect less interaction with the environment and less activity which normally accompanies such a change of mood. In contrast, the changes in the more ventral areas such as the ventral (i.e. subgenual) cingulate cortex may be more closely related to the changes in mood per se. Further evidence that the subgenual cingulate cortex is a brain area with activity related to depression is that chronic electrical stimulation

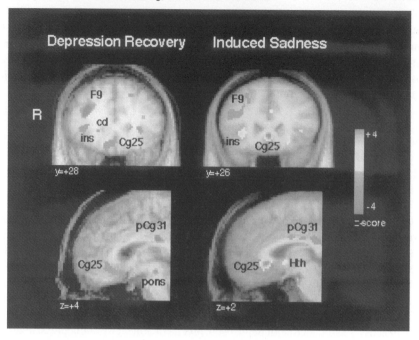

Fig. 3.52 Changes in the subgenual cingulate area (Cg25) associated with the recovery from depression (left), and with the induction of a mood state of sadness (right). Left images: Z-score maps demonstrating changes in regional glucose metabolism (fluorodeoxyglucose PET) in depressed patients following 6 weeks of treatment with the antidepressant fluoxetine. Upper, coronal view; lower, sagittal view. Green indicates that the change is a decrease, and red or yellow an increase (see calibration bar on far right). Right images: changes in regional cerebral blood flow (oxygen-15 water PET) in healthy volunteers 10 min after induction of acute sadness. The recovery from depression and the induction of sadness produce opposite changes in Cg25. Reciprocal changes were seen in a dorsal part of the prefrontal cortex, labelled F9. F, frontal; cd, caudate nucleus; ins, anterior insula; Cg25, subgenual cingulate; Hth, hypothalamus; pCG31, posterior cingulate; R, right. (After Mayberg et al. 1999.) (See colour plates Appendix E.)

in this region has been found to relieve symptoms of treatment-resistant depression in some patients (Mayberg et al. 2005).

Further, anatomical abnormalities of the orbitofrontal cortex are found in patients with depression (Bremner, Vythilingam, Vermetten, Nazeer, Adil, Khan, Staib and Charney 2002, Rajkowska 2000), in whom anhedonia is a key feature, and the orbitofrontal cortex provides inputs to the anterior and subgenual cingulate cortex.

Pharmacological investigations of depression and the effects these have on different brain systems are reviewed by Rolls (2005).

3.10 Output pathways for reward- and punisher-guided behaviour, including emotional responses

3.10.1 The autonomic and endocrine systems

The first output system introduced above in Section 3.3 is the autonomic and endocrine system. Through it changes such as increased heart rate and the release of adrenaline, which prepare the body for action, are produced by emotional stimuli. There are brainstem routes through which peripheral stimuli can produce reflex autonomic responses. In addition, there are outputs from the hypothalamus to the autonomic brainstem centres (Schwaber, Kapp, Higgins and Rapp 1982).

Structures such as the amygdala and orbitofrontal cortex can produce autonomic responses to secondary reinforcing (or classically conditioned) stimuli both directly, for example by direct connections from the amygdala to the dorsal motor nucleus of the vagus (Schwaber et al. 1982), and via the lateral hypothalamus. For example, LeDoux et al. (1988) showed that lesions of the lateral hypothalamus (which receives from the central nucleus of the amygdala) blocked conditioned heart rate (autonomic) responses (see also Kapp et al. (1992)). The outputs of the orbitofrontal cortex are also involved in learned autonomic responses, in that ventral prefrontal lesions block autonomic responses to learned reinforcers (Elithorn, Piercy and Crosskey (1955) and Damasio (1994) in humans; Grueninger, Kimble, Grueninger and Levine (1965) in macaques).

Further, activation of the anterior cingulate cortex in humans is correlated with autonomic states (Nagai, Critchley, Featherstone, Trimble and Dolan 2004), and the subgenual cingulate cortex has strong projections to brainstem structures that control autonomic activity (Gabbott et al. 2003).

3.10.2 Motor systems for implicit responses, including the basal ganglia, reinforcement learning, and dopamine

The second type of output is to brain systems concerned with performing instrumental actions (often unconsciously or implicitly), in order to obtain rewards or avoid punishers. One system involved in instrumental learning, and particularly in action–outcome learning, is the cingulate cortex, described in Section 3.8.

Another brain system involved in instrumental learning, though probably more in stimulus-response habit learning, is the basal ganglia. The basal ganglia, and the dopamine pathways, are considered in this Section. A fuller account is provided by Rolls (2005).

3.10.2.1 Systems-level architecture of the basal ganglia

The point-to-point connectivity of the basal ganglia as shown by experimental anterograde and retrograde neuroanatomical path tracing techniques in the primate is indicated in Figs. 3.53 and 3.54. The general connectivity is for cortical or limbic inputs to reach the striatum, which then projects to the globus pallidus and substantia nigra pars reticulata, which in turn project via the thalamus back to the cerebral cortex. (A review is provided by Gurney, Prescott and Redgrave (2001a).) Within this overall scheme, there is a set of at least partially segregated parallel processing streams, as illustrated in Figs. 3.53 and 3.54 (DeLong, Georgopoulos, Crutcher, Mitchell, Richardson and Alexander 1984, Alexander, Crutcher and DeLong 1990, Rolls and Johnstone 1992, Strick, Dum and Picard 1995, Middleton and Strick 1996b, Middleton and Strick 1996a, Middleton and Strick 2000, Kelly and Strick 2004).

First, the motor cortex (area 4) and somatosensory cortex (areas 3, 1, and 2) project somatotopically to the putamen, which has connections through the globus pallidus and substantia nigra to the ventral anterior thalamic nuclei and thus to the supplementary motor cortex. Experiments with a virus transneuronal pathway tracing technique have shown that there might be at least partial segregation within this stream, with different parts of the globus pallidus projecting via different parts of the ventrolateral (VL) thalamic nuclei to the supplementary motor area, the primary motor cortex (area 4), and to the ventral premotor area on the lateral surface of the hemisphere (Middleton and Strick 1996a).

Second, there is an oculomotor circuit (see Fig. 3.53).

Third, the dorsolateral prefrontal and the parietal cortices project to the head and body of the caudate nucleus, which has connections through parts of the globus pallidus and substantia

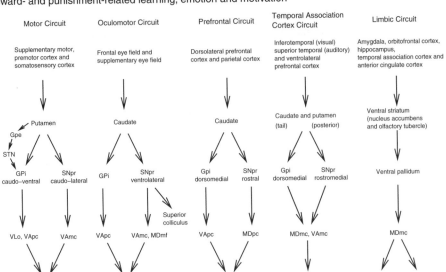

Fig. 3.53 A synthesis of some of the anatomical studies (see text) of the connections of the basal ganglia. GPe, Globus Pallidus, external segment; GPi, Globus Pallidus, internal segment; MD, nucleus medialis dorsalis; SNpr, Substantia Nigra, pars reticulata; VAmc, n. ventralis anterior pars magnocellularis of the thalamus; VApc, n. ventralis anterior pars compacta; VLo, n. ventralis lateralis pars oralis; VLm, n. ventralis pars medialis. An indirect pathway from the striatum via the external segment of the globus pallidus and the subthalamic nucleus (STN) to the internal segment of the globus pallidus is present for the first four circuits (left to right in the Figure) of the basal ganglia.

nigra to the ventral anterior group of thalamic nuclei and thus to the dorsolateral prefrontal cortex (Middleton and Strick 2000, Kelly and Strick 2004).

Fourth, the inferior temporal visual cortex and the ventrolateral (inferior convexity) prefrontal cortex to which it is connected project to the posterior and ventral parts of the putamen and the tail of the caudate nucleus (Kemp and Powell 1970, Saint-Cyr, Ungerleider and Desimone 1990, Graybiel and Kimura 1995). Moreover, part of the globus pallidus, perhaps the part influenced by the temporal lobe visual cortex, area TE, may project back (via the thalamus) to area TE (Middleton and Strick 1996b).

Fifth, and of especial interest in the context of reward mechanisms in the brain, limbic and related structures such as the amygdala, orbitofrontal cortex, and hippocampus project to the ventral striatum (which includes the nucleus accumbens), which has connections through the ventral pallidum to the mediodorsal nucleus of the thalamus and thus to the prefrontal and cingulate cortices (Strick et al. 1995). It is notable that the projections from the amygdala and orbitofrontal cortex are not restricted to the nucleus accumbens, but also occur to the adjacent ventral part of the head of the caudate nucleus (Amaral and Price 1984, Seleman and Goldman-Rakic 1985). These same regions may also project to the striosomes or patches (in for example the head of the caudate nucleus), which are set in the matrix formed by the other cortico-striatal systems (Graybiel and Kimura 1995).

3.10.2.2 Systems-level analysis of the basal ganglia: effects of striatal lesions

Ventral striatum including nucleus accumbens

There is evidence linking the ventral striatum and its dopamine input to reward, for manipulations of this system alter the incentive effects that learned rewarding stimuli have on

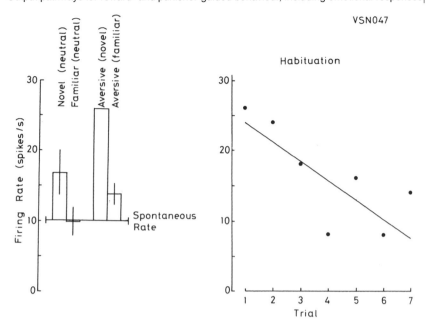

Fig. 3.56 Responses of a ventral striatal neuron to novel visual stimuli. On the right it is shown that the response to novel stimuli, an increase in firing rate to 25 spikes/s from the spontaneous rate of 10 spikes/s, habituated over repeated presentations of the stimulus. The lack of response shown in the left panel to the familiar stimulus was thus only achieved after habituation produced by 4–7 presentations of the stimulus. It is also shown that the neuron responded to aversive stimuli when they had not been seen for more than one day (Aversive (novel)), but did not respond to aversive visual stimuli (such as the sight of a syringe from which the monkey was fed saline, Aversive (familiar)), even though the latter produced arousal. (From Williams, Rolls, Leonard and Stern 1993.)

and novel visual stimuli to influence behaviour. It was notable that although some neurons responded to visual stimuli associated with reward (see Table 3.5), 1.4% responded to visual stimuli associated with punishment, and 12% responded to arousing visual stimuli or non-specifically to visual stimuli (see Table 3.5). It was also notable that these neurons were not restricted to the nucleus accumbens, but were found also in the adjacent ventral part of the head of the caudate nucleus (Rolls and Williams 1987a, Williams, Rolls, Leonard and Stern 1993, Rolls, Thorpe and Maddison 1983b), which also receives projections from both the amygdala (Amaral and Price 1984) and orbitofrontal cortex (Seleman and Goldman-Rakic 1985).

In human fMRI studies, activations in the ventral striatum have been found to conditioned incentive stimuli such as the sight of chocolate, and interestingly the activations were larger in chocolate cravers than in non-cravers (Rolls and McCabe 2007). Activations have also been described that reflect whether monetary rewards can be obtained, and indeed more activation is found for the larger rewards (Knutson, Adams, Fong and Hommer 2001). Interestingly, one of the strongest activations that is found in the ventral striatum is produced by temporal difference reward/punishment prediction errors in Pavlovian (i.e. classical conditioning) tasks (O'Doherty, Dayan, Friston, Critchley and Dolan 2003a, McClure, Berns and Montague 2003, Seymour, O'Doherty, Dayan, Koltzenburg, Jones, Dolan, Friston and Frackowiak 2004). For example, in a classical conditioning task, a first visual stimulus probabilistically predicted high vs low pain, and a second visual stimulus perfectly predicted whether the pain would be high or low on that trial. Activation of the ventral striatum and a part of the insula was related to the temporal difference error, which arose for example at the transition between the first and second visual stimulus if the first visual stimulus had predicted low pain, but the second informed the subject that the pain would be high (Seymour et al. 2004).

The ventral striatum activations may reflect the operation of a 'critic' in reinforcement learning, in that activations in it are related to temporal difference errors in Pavlovian conditions in which actions are not made (O'Doherty, Dayan, Schultz, Deichmann, Friston and Dolan 2004). In contrast, activation in the dorsal striatum may be closely related to temporal difference prediction errors used to correct an actor, as these activations occurred during an instrumental version of the task in which the subjects had to choose between two stimuli associated with a high probability or low probability of obtaining juice reward (O'Doherty et al. 2004). (The distinction between a 'critic' and an 'actor' in reinforcement learning is described in Section B.15.3.)

Activations in the ventral striatum related to temporal difference reward/punishment prediction errors in a probabilistic monetary reward *decision* task are exemplified in a study by Rolls, McCabe and Redoute (2007b). The subjects could choose either on the right to obtain a large reward with a magnitude of 30 pence, or on the left to obtain a smaller reward with a magnitude of 10 pence with a probability of 0.9. On the right, in different trial blocks, the probability of the large reward was 0.9 (making the expected value defined as probability × reward magnitude = 27 pence); or the probability was 0.33 making the expected value 10 pence; or the probability was 0.16 making the expected value 5 pence. (On the trials on which a reward was not obtained, 0 pence was the reward magnitude.) (The concepts of reward magnitude, expected value and expected utility are described in Section 10.6). The participants learned in the blocks of 30 trials with the different expected values on the right whether to press on the right or the left to maximize their winnings. They took typically less than 10 trials to adjust to the unsignalled change in expected value every 30 trials, and analysis was performed for the last 20 trials of each block when the expected value had been learned.

The design of the task meant that sometimes the participants were expecting a low probability of a high reward of 30 pence, and unexpectedly obtained a high reward magnitude of 30 pence. On these trials, the temporal difference prediction error from the expected value part of the trial to the later reward magnitude part of the same trial when subjects were informed whether they would obtain the large reward was positive. On other trials when the expected value was high but probabilistically no reward was obtained, the temporal difference prediction error from the expected value part of the trial to the reward magnitude part of the trial was negative. (Temporal difference (TD) errors are described in Section B.15.3.) It was found that the fMRI BOLD signal in the nucleus accumbens reflected this temporal difference error signal, calculated at the part of the trial when the reward prediction changed from the expected value for that trial block to the actual reward available on that trial, as shown in Fig. 3.57.

Further analyses showed that the activation in the ventral striatum was positively correlated with the reward magnitude actually obtained on that trial but not with the expected value (Fig. 3.57b). Thus the TD error correlation arose in the nucleus accumbens because at the time that the expected value period ended and the subject was informed about how much reward had been obtained on that trial, the BOLD signal changed to a higher value for large rewards, and to a lower value for low or no reward, from a value that was not a function of the expected value on that trial. A TD error correlation was also found in the left inferior frontal gyrus (in or near cortical area 44, Broca's area, as shown in Fig. 3.57), but here the TD correlation arose because the activation became low when the subject was informed that no reward was obtained on a trial, and it appeared that the area was activated especially when the decision was difficult, between two approximately equal values of the expected value. In a part of the midbrain at [14 −20 −16], there was also a correlation with the TD error, but here this was

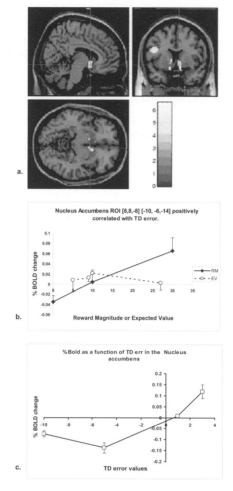

Fig. 3.57 Temporal Difference (TD) error signal in the ventral striatum in a probabilistic monetary decision-making task. (a) A positive correlation between the BOLD signal and the Temporal Difference error was found in the ventral striatum at MNI coordinates [8 8 -8] (p<0.048 fully corrected) and [-10 6 -14] (p<0.01 svc). (b) The percent change in the BOLD signal for the three Reward Magnitudes (RMs of 30 pence, 10 pence, or 0 pence) for the regions of interest defined by the correlation analysis. The means and standard errors are shown. The percent change in the BOLD signal for the four Expected Values (EVs) of 27 pence, 10 pence, 9 pence, and 5 pence) for the same region of interest are also shown. (c) The percent change in the BOLD signal as a function of the TD error in the nucleus accumbens (means ± sem). (After Rolls, McCabe and Redoute 2007.) (See colour plates Appendix E.)

related to a negative correlation between the BOLD signal in the expected value period of each trial and the expected value. (The TD error was thus positive for example whatever reward became available if it was a low expected value trial block, and the TD error was negative if it was a high expected value trial block.) This shows that TD error regressions with functional neuroimaging can arise for a number of different reasons.

In this investigation, the reward magnitude and expected value on a trial were both correlated with the activation in parts of the orbitofrontal cortex, as shown by a conjunction analysis, suggesting that this is a site where the probability of obtaining a reward as well as the reward magnitude are taken into account in representing the expected value. The expected value was negatively correlated with activations in the anterior insula [−38 24 16] in a region that has been implicated in disgust, and interestingly, the activations here were also correlated with the uncertainty of the magnitude of the reward that would be obtained (Rolls, McCabe and Redoute 2007b). These cortical areas may be the origins of some of the signals found in other brain areas, including the midbrain.

These findings do exemplify the fact that activation of the ventral striatum does reflect the changing expectations of reward (see Section B.15.3) during the trials of a task, and indeed this is what is illustrated at the neuronal level in Fig. 3.55, where the neuron altered its firing rate within 170 ms of the monkey being shown a visual stimulus that indicated whether reward or saline was available on that trial. Given that ventral striatal neurons of the type illustrated in Fig. 3.55 alter their activity when the visual stimulus is shown informing the macaque about whether reward is available on that trial, it is in fact not surprising that the fMRI correlation analyses do pick up signals during trials that can be interpreted as temporal difference error signals. Whether these fMRI correlations with a temporal difference error reflect more than the activity of neurons that respond as shown in Fig. 3.55 to the predicted or expected reward value ($\hat{v}$ of Section B.15.3) rather that the phasic temporal difference error (Δ) will be interesting to examine in the future.

Tail of the caudate nucleus, and posteroventral putamen

The projections from the inferior temporal cortex and the prestriate cortex to the striatum arrive mainly, although not exclusively, in the tail (and genu) of the caudate nucleus and in the postero-ventral portions of the putamen (Kemp and Powell 1970, Saint-Cyr et al. 1990). The activity of single neurons was analysed in the tail of the caudate nucleus and adjoining part of the ventral putamen by Caan, Perrett and Rolls (1984). Of 195 neurons analysed in two macaque monkeys, 109 (56%) responded to visual stimuli, with latencies of 90–150 ms for the majority of the neurons. The neurons responded to a limited range of complex visual stimuli, and in some cases responded to simpler stimuli such as bars and edges. Typically (for 75% of neurons tested) the neurons habituated rapidly, within 1–8 exposures, to each visual stimulus, but remained responsive to other visual stimuli with a different pattern. This habituation was orientation-specific, in that the neurons responded to the same pattern shown at an orthogonal orientation. The habituation was also relatively short term, in that at least partial dishabituation to one stimulus could be produced by a single intervening presentation of a different visual stimulus. These neurons were relatively unresponsive in a visual discrimination task, having habituated to the discriminative stimuli that had been presented in the task on many previous trials. Consistent findings were obtained by Brown, Desimone and Mishkin (1995).

Given these responses, it may be suggested that these neurons are involved in short-term pattern-specific habituation to visual stimuli. This system would be distinguishable from other habituation systems (involved, for example, in habituation to spots of light) in that it is specialized for patterned visual stimuli that have been highly processed through visual cortical analysis mechanisms, as shown not only by the nature of the neuronal responses, but also by the fact that this system receives inputs from the inferior temporal visual cortex. It may also be suggested that this sensitivity to visual pattern change may have a role in alerting the monkey's attention to new stimuli. This suggestion is consistent with the changes in attention and orientation to stimuli produced by damage to the striatum.

In view of these neurophysiological findings, and the finding that in a visual discrimination task neurons that reflected the reinforcement contingencies of the stimuli were not found, Caan, Perrett and Rolls (1984) suggested that the tail of the caudate nucleus is not directly involved in the development and maintenance of reward or punishment associations to stimuli (and therefore is not closely involved in emotion-related processing), but may aid visual discrimination performance by its sensitivity to change in visual stimuli. Neurons in some other parts of the striatum may, however, be involved in connecting visual stimuli to appropriate motor responses. For example, in the putamen some neurons have early movement-related firing during the performance of a visual discrimination task (Rolls, Thorpe, Boytim, Szabo and Perrett 1984); and some neurons in the head of the caudate nucleus respond to environmental cues that signal that reward may be obtained (Rolls, Thorpe and Maddison 1983b).

Postero-ventral putamen

Following these investigations on the caudal striatum which implicated it in visual functions related to a short-term habituation or memory process, a further study was performed to investigate the role of the posterior putamen in visual short-term memory tasks (Johnstone and Rolls 1990, Rolls and Johnstone 1992). Both the inferior temporal visual cortex and the prefrontal cortex project to the posterior ventral parts of the putamen (Goldman and Nauta 1977, Van Hoesen, Yeterian and Lavizzo-Mourey 1981) and these cortical areas are known to subserve a variety of complex functions, including functions related to memory. For example, cells in both areas respond in a variety of short-term memory tasks (Fuster 1973, Fuster 1997, Fuster and Jervey 1982, Baylis and Rolls 1987, Miyashita and Chang 1988).

Two main groups of neurons with memory-related activity were found in the postero-ventral putamen in a delayed match-to-sample (DMS) task. In the task, the monkey was shown a sample stimulus, and had to remember it during a 2–5 s delay period, after which if a matching stimulus was shown he could make one response, but if a non-matching stimulus was shown he had to make no response (Johnstone and Rolls 1990, Rolls and Johnstone 1992).

First, 11% of the 621 neurons studied responded to the test stimulus which followed the sample stimulus, but did not respond to the sample stimulus. Of these neurons, 43% responded only on non-match trials (test different from sample), 16% only on match trials (test same as the sample), and 41% to the test stimulus irrespective of whether it was the same or different from the sample. These neuronal responses were not related to the licking motor responses since (i) the neurons did not respond in other tasks in which a lick response was required (for example, in an auditory delayed match-to-sample task which was identical to the visual delayed match-to-sample task except that auditory short-term memory rather than visual short-term memory was required; in a serial recognition memory task; or in a visual discrimination task), and (ii) a periresponse time spike-density function indicated that the stimulus onset better predicted neuronal activity.

Second, 9.5% of the neurons responded in the delay period after the sample stimulus, during which the sample was being remembered. These neurons did not respond in the auditory version of the task, indicating that the responses were visual modality-specific (as were the responses of all other neurons in this part of the putamen with activity related to the delayed match-to-sample task). Given that the visual and auditory tasks were very similar apart from the modality of the input stimuli, this suggests that the activity of the neurons was not related to movements, or to rewards or punishers obtained in the tasks (and is thus not closely linked to emotion-related processing), but instead to modality-specific short-term memory-related processing. The delay-related activity of these neurons probably reflects activity in the cortical area projecting into this part of the striatum.

In recordings made from pallidal neurons it was found that some responded in both visual and auditory versions of the task (Johnstone and Rolls 1990, Rolls and Johnstone 1992). Of 37 neurons responsive in the visual DMS task that were also tested in the auditory version, seven (19%) responded also in the auditory DMS task. The finding that some of the pallidal neurons active in the DMS task were not modality-specific, whereas only visual modality-specific DMS units were located in the postero-ventral part of the striatum, provides evidence that the pallidum may represent a further stage in information processing in which information from

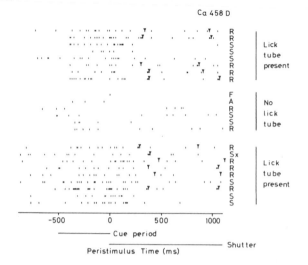

Fig. 3.58 Responses of a cue-related neuron in the head of the caudate nucleus in a Go/NoGo visual discrimination task in which the visual stimulus was presented at time 0. Each trial is a single row of the rastergram, each action potential is represented by a single dot, and a lick made to obtain fruit juice is represented by an inverted triangle. R, Reward trials on which fruit juice was obtained. S, Salt trials on which if a lick was made, a small drop of saline was obtained. Tone and light emitting diode cues were provided starting 500 ms before the visual stimulus was shown. Top set of trials: normal performance of the task with the lick tube close to the mouth. Middle set of trials: the lick tube was removed out of reach, but the tone/LED cue, and discriminative visual stimuli, were still provided. Bottom set of trials: normal performance of the task with the lick tube close to the mouth. F, food reward was shown. A, an aversive visual stimulus was shown. (After Rolls, Thorpe and Maddison 1983.)

different parts of the striatum can converge.

Head of the caudate nucleus

The activity of 394 neurons in the head of the caudate nucleus and most anterior part of the putamen was analysed in three behaving rhesus monkeys (Rolls, Thorpe and Maddison 1983b). Of these neurons, 64.2% had responses related to environmental stimuli, movements, the performance of a visual discrimination task, or eating. However, only relatively small proportions of these neurons had responses that were unconditionally related to visual (9.6%), auditory (3.5%), or gustatory (0.5%) stimuli, or to movements (4.1%). Instead, the majority of the neurons had responses that occurred conditionally in relation to stimuli or movements, in that the responses occurred in only some test situations, *and were often dependent on the performance of a task by the monkeys*. Thus, it was found that in a visual discrimination task 14.5% of the neurons responded during a 0.5 s tone/light cue that signalled the start of each trial (cue-related neurons); 31.1% responded in the period in which the discriminative visual stimuli were shown, with 24.3% of these responding more either to the visual stimulus that predicted food reward or to that that predicted punishment (by a taste of saline) (reward prediction neurons); and 6.2% responded in relation to lick responses.

An example of a *cue-related* neuron in the head of the caudate nucleus that started responding as soon as a tone/light-emitting diode (LED) cue was presented indicating that a trial was about to start is shown in Fig. 3.58. At time 0 a discriminative visual stimulus was shown, which indicated if for example it was a triangle that reward could be obtained, or if it was a square that saline would be obtained if a lick was made. The reward trials (R) on which a lick could be made to obtain fruit juice, and saline (S) trials on which a lick should not be made

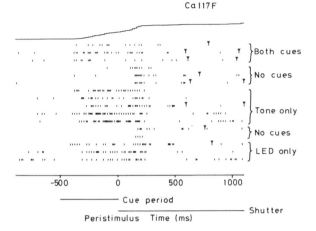

Fig. 3.59 Responses of a cue-related neuron in the head of the caudate nucleus in a Go/NoGo visual discrimination task in which the visual stimulus was presented at time 0, when a mechanical shutter opened to reveal the discriminative stimulus. Each trial is a single row of the rastergram, each action potential is represented by a single dot, and a lick made to obtain fruit juice on Reward trials only is represented by an inverted triangle. Tone and/or light-emitting diode (LED) cues were provided starting 500 ms before the visual stimulus was shown. If no 500 ms warning cue was given for the start of a trial, the neuron responded to the first indication that a trial was beginning, the sound of the shutter opening at time 0. The neuron did not predict whether reward would or would not be obtained, in that there was no differential neuronal response on Reward trials (on which licks were made), compared to non-reward trials (on which licks were correctly not made). The line at the top shows the cusum (cumulative sum) statistic. (After Rolls, Thorpe and Maddison 1983.)

otherwise a drop of aversive saline was obtained, each occurred with probability 0.5. This cue-related neuron stopped responding soon after the visual stimulus appeared, and did not discriminate between reward (R) and punishment (S) trials. It was thus a cue neuron and not a reward-predicting neuron. It could be described as encoding *salience* but not valence. Further evidence that the neuron was not reward or punishment related is that it did not respond on trials on which a food reward was shown (F), or an aversive visual stimulus was shown (A).

If the lick tube was moved away from the lips by a few millimetres so that juice reward could not be obtained (but the tone/LED still sounded, and was followed by a discriminative visual stimulus), the neuron stopped responding to the tone/LED cue, providing evidence that it was only when the tone/LED cue predicted the start of a trial in the visual discrimination task that the head of caudate neuron responded to the cue. This is shown by the middle set of trials in Fig. 3.58. Approximately half of the cue-related neurons tested showed this learning whereby they only responded to a warning cue normally used to start a trial if it actually did signal the start a trial. It typically took just a few trials for this trial-predicting effect of a tone/LED cue to be learned and unlearned by these neurons.

Most of these cue-related neurons learned to respond to whichever cue, either a 500 Hz tone, or a light-emitting diode, signalled the start of a trial (see example in Fig. 3.59).

An example of a *reward-predicting* neuron in the head of the caudate nucleus that started responding as soon as a cue was available that a trial was about to start, and which continued firing after a visual stimulus was shown which indicated that a lick response could be made to obtain juice reward (R), but which stopped firing after a visual stimulus was shown that indicated that if a lick response was made, aversive saline (S) would be obtained, is shown in Fig. 3.60. The reward (R) and saline (S) trials each occurred with probability 0.5. This type of neuron, common in the head of the primate caudate nucleus, thus increased its

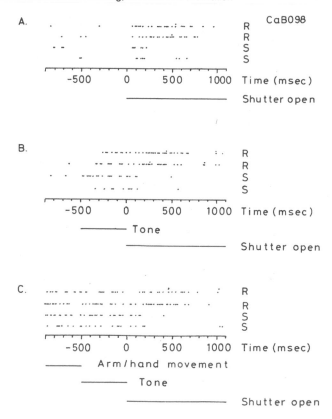

Fig. 3.60 Responses of a reward-predicting neuron in the head of the caudate nucleus in a Go/NoGo visual discrimination task in which the visual stimulus was presented at time 0. Each trial is a single row of the rastergram, each action potential is represented by a single dot, and a lick made to obtain fruit juice is represented by a vertical pair of dots. R, Reward trials on which fruit juice was obtained. S, Salt trials on which if a lick was made, a small drop of saline was obtained. (A) The neuron started to respond approximately 80 ms after the start of the trial when a shutter opened to reveal the discriminative stimulus, continued to respond on reward trials until after the fruit juice was obtained, and stopped responding at approximately 160 ms on trials on which the punisher-related stimulus (S) was shown. (B) The neuron started responding soon after a cue tone sounded indicating the start of a trial. (C) The neuron started responding at the earliest indication that the trial would start, an arm movement made by the macaque to press a button to start the trial. (After Rolls, Thorpe and Maddison 1983.)

firing as soon as the probability of reward increased at the start of a trial to 0.5, learned to respond to the first cue that signalled the start of a trial, and stopped responding as soon as the probability of reward decreased to 0 on punishment (S) trials. These neurons typically did not respond in relation to the cue stimuli, to the visual stimuli, or to movements, when these occurred independently of the task or performance of the task was prevented, for example by withdrawing the lick tube from which fruit juice could be obtained (Rolls, Thorpe and Maddison 1983b) (as illustrated for a cue-related neuron in Fig. 3.58). That is, the responses of these neurons reflected whether reward would be obtained, and more generally, reflect how much reward will be obtained (Cromwell and Schultz 2003). Similar neurons in the head of the caudate nucleus responded to punishment-predicting stimuli, and indeed approximately as many neurons responded to the saline punishment-associated visual stimulus in the Go/NoGo visual discrimination task as to the juice reward-predicting stimulus (Rolls, Thorpe and Maddison 1983b, Rolls, Thorpe, Maddison, Roper-Hall, Puerto and Perrett 1979b, Rolls 1984b). Thus some neurons in the head of the caudate nucleus encode the *valence* of visual stimuli. Consistently, Watanabe, Lauwereyns and Hikosaka (2003) have found that one population of neurons in the primate caudate nucleus responds to rewarded eye movements, and a separate population to unrewarded eye movements.

Similar types of response were found when the neurons were tested outside the visual discrimination task, during feeding. Of the neurons tested during feeding, 25.8% responded when the food was seen by the monkey, 6.2% when he tasted it, and 22.4% during a cue given by the experimenter that a food or non-food object was about to be presented. Further evidence on the nature of these neuronal responses was that many of the neurons with cue-related responses only responded to the tone/light cue stimuli when they were cues for the performance of the task or the presentation of food as described above, and some responded to the different cues used in the task (tone/LED) and feeding test (an arm movement made by the experimenter to reach behind a screen to obtain a food or non-food object) situations (Rolls, Thorpe and Maddison 1983b).

The finding that such neurons may respond to environmental stimuli only when they are significant in predicting for example the onset of a trial (a cue neuron) or the delivery of reward (a reward-predicting neuron) (Rolls, Thorpe, Maddison, Roper-Hall, Puerto and Perrett 1979b, Rolls, Thorpe and Maddison 1983b) was confirmed by Evarts and his colleagues. They showed that some neurons in the putamen only responded to the click of a solenoid when it indicated that a fruit juice reward could be obtained (Evarts and Wise 1984). The findings have also been confirmed by Tremblay and Schultz (1998) (see also Schultz, Tremblay and Hollerman (2003)), who reported that macaque caudate neurons come to respond during learning to cues related to the preparation of movement or expectation of reward, and do not respond to cues that do not predict such events.

We have found that this decoding of the significance of environmental events that are signals for the preparation for or initiation of a behavioural response is represented in the firing of a population of neurons in the dorsolateral prefrontal cortex, which projects into the head of the caudate nucleus (E. T. Rolls and G. C. Baylis, unpublished observations 1984). These neurons respond to the tone cue only if it signals the start of a trial of the visual discrimination task, just as do the corresponding population of neurons in the head of the caudate nucleus. The indication that the decoding of significance is performed by the prefrontal cortex, and that the striatum receives only the results of the cortical computation, is considered below and elsewhere (Rolls and Williams 1987b).

These findings indicate that the head of the caudate nucleus and most anterior part of the putamen contain populations of neurons that respond to predictive sensory cues that enable preparation for the performance of tasks such as feeding and tasks in which movements must be initiated, and others that respond during the performance of such tasks in relation to sensory cue that predict reward, and that the majority of these neurons have no unconditional sensory or motor responses. It has therefore been suggested (Rolls, Thorpe, Maddison, Roper-Hall, Puerto and Perrett 1979b, Rolls, Thorpe and Maddison 1983b) that the anterior neostriatum contains neurons that are important for the utilization of environmental cues for the preparation for behavioural responses, and for particular behavioural responses made in particular situations to particular environmental stimuli, that is in stimulus–motor response habit formation. Different neurons in the cue-related group often respond to different subsets of environmentally significant events, and thus convey some information that would be useful in switching behaviour, in preparing to make responses, and in connecting inputs to particular responses (Rolls, Thorpe, Maddison, Roper-Hall, Puerto and Perrett 1979b, Rolls, Thorpe and Maddison 1983b, Rolls 1984b). Striatal neurons with similar types of response have also been recorded by Wolfram Schultz and colleagues (Schultz, Apicella, Romo and

Scarnati 1995a, Tremblay and Schultz 1998, Cromwell and Schultz 2003, Schultz et al. 2003). Striatal tonically active interneurons (TANs) which have high spontaneous firing rates and respond by decreasing their firing rates may respond to similar cue-predicting and reward-predicting events (Graybiel and Kimura 1995), presumably by receiving inhibitory inputs from the principal striatal neurons described above, the medium spiny neurons.

In human fMRI studies, activations have been described in the striatum that reflect whether monetary rewards can be obtained (Delgado, Nystrom, Fissell, Noll and Fiez 2000, Knutson et al. 2001). They presumably reflect the activity of the reward-predicting neurons (Rolls, Thorpe, Maddison, Roper-Hall, Puerto and Perrett 1979b, Rolls, Thorpe and Maddison 1983b, Rolls 1984b). Activations to monetary reward only if it is being worked for instrumentally (Zink, Pagnoni, Martin-Skurski, Chappelow and Berns 2004) may reflect the type of task dependence illustrated for a cue-related neuron in Fig. 3.58. Human striatal fMRI activations to non-rewarding but salient stimuli (Zink, Pagnoni, Martin, Dhamala and Berns 2003) may reflect the types of trial-predicting (i.e. cue-related) neurons shown in Figs. 3.58 and 3.59 but not reward-predicting neurons of the type shown in Fig. 3.60.

One would expect human striatal activations also to be demonstrable to punishment-predicting stimuli, given that approximately half of the reward/punishment-predicting neurons respond to punishment-predicting stimuli (Rolls, Thorpe, Maddison, Roper-Hall, Puerto and Perrett 1979b, Rolls, Thorpe and Maddison 1983b, Rolls 1984b), and there is some human fMRI evidence for this (Seymour et al. 2004). It is a difficulty for the dopamine reward prediction error hypothesis described below (Schultz, Romo, Ljunberg, Mirenowicz, Hollerman and Dickinson 1995b, Schultz, Dayan and Montague 1997, Waelti et al. 2001, Schultz 2004) that it cannot account for the formation of striatal neurons that fire to predict punishment. [In particular, if dopamine neurons decrease their firing rate if an expected reward is not received or a punishment is received (Mirenowicz and Schultz 1996, Waelti, Dickinson and Schultz 2001, Tobler, Dickinson and Schultz 2003), then this would not promote learning in the striatum whereby striatal neurons might respond more to the stimulus (e.g. a discriminative stimulus in a visual discrimination task) that predicted punishment.] However, such reward and punisher predicting information is reflected in the firing of orbitofrontal cortex neurons, some of which predict reward, and others of which predict punishment (see Section 3.6), and it is presumably by this orbitofrontal cortex route that punishment-predicting neurons in the head of the caudate nucleus receive this information (rather than being reinforced into this type of firing by a dopamine reward error prediction signal).

It is very interesting that the type of neuron shown in Fig. 3.60 has certain similarities to the midbrain dopamine neurons described by Schultz and colleagues (Schultz et al. 1995b, Mirenowicz and Schultz 1996, Waelti et al. 2001), except that the dopamine neurons respond to the transitions in reward probabilities, rather than the reward probabilities themselves which is what appears to be encoded by the type of head of caudate neuron shown in Fig. 3.60. Thus an alternative to the hypothesis that the dopamine neurons provide a reward-prediction error teaching signal (see Section 3.10.2.5) is that the firing of the dopamine neurons may reflect feedback connections from these striatal regions as well as from the hypothalamus in which similar neurons are found (see Sections 3.10.4, 3.10.5, and Rolls (2005)) to the dopamine neurons in the substantia nigra, pars compacta, and ventral tegmental area. These feedback connections would then influence the dopamine neurons for short periods primarily when the firing of the striatal neurons changed, implemented by a high-pass filtering effect. This would leave much more open what the functions of the dopamine neurons are (see Section 3.10.2.5), in that a simple feedback effect might be being implemented (from striatum to the dopamine neurons and back), perhaps to dynamically reset thresholds or gains in the striatum.

Anterior putamen

It is clear that the activity of many neurons in the putamen is related to movements (Anderson 1978, Crutcher and DeLong 1984a, Crutcher and DeLong 1984b, DeLong et al. 1984). There is a somatotopic organization of neurons in the putamen, with separate areas containing neurons responding to arm, leg, or orofacial movements. Some of these neurons respond only to active movements, and others to active and to passive movements. Some of these neurons respond to somatosensory stimulation, with multiple clusters of neurons responding, for example, to the movement of each joint. Some neurons in the putamen have been shown in experiments in which the arm has been given assisting and opposing loads to respond in relation to the direction of an intended movement, rather than in relation to the muscle forces required to execute the movement (Crutcher and DeLong 1984b). Also, the firing rate of neurons in the putamen tends to be linearly related to the amplitude of movements (Crutcher and DeLong 1984b), and this is of potential clinical relevance, since patients with basal ganglia disease frequently have difficulty in controlling the amplitude of their limb movements.

In order to obtain further evidence on specialization of function within the striatum, the activity of neurons in the putamen has been compared with the activity of neurons recorded in different parts of the striatum in the same tasks (Rolls, Thorpe, Boytim, Szabo and Perrett 1984). Of 234 neurons recorded in the putamen of two macaque monkeys during the performance of a visual discrimination task and the other tests in which other striatal neurons have been shown to respond (Rolls, Thorpe and Maddison 1983b, Caan, Perrett and Rolls 1984), 68 (29%) had activity that was phasically related to movements (Rolls, Thorpe, Boytim, Szabo and Perrett 1984). Many of these responded in relation to mouth movements such as licking. Similar neurons were found in the substantia nigra, pars reticulata, to which the putamen projects (Mora, Mogenson and Rolls 1977). The neurons did not have activity related to taste, in that they responded, for example, during tongue protrusion made to a food or non-food object. Some of these neurons responded in relation to the licking mouth movements made in the visual discrimination task, and always also responded when mouth movements were made during clinical testing when a food or non-food object was brought close to the mouth. Their responses were thus unconditionally related to movements, in that they responded in whichever testing situation was used, and were therefore different from the responses of neurons in the head of the caudate nucleus (Rolls, Thorpe and Maddison 1983b).

Of the 68 neurons in the putamen with movement-related activity in these tests, 61 had activity related to mouth movements, and seven had activity related to movements of the body. Of the remaining neurons, 24 (10%) had activity that was task-related in that some change of firing rate associated with the presentation of the tone cue or the opening of the shutter occurred on each trial (Rolls, Thorpe, Boytim, Szabo and Perrett 1984), four had auditory responses, one responded to environmental stimuli (Rolls, Thorpe and Maddison 1983b), and 137 were not responsive in these test situations.

These findings (Rolls, Thorpe, Boytim, Szabo and Perrett 1984) provide further evidence that differences between neuronal activity in different regions of the striatum are found even in the same testing situations, and also that the inputs that activate these neurons are derived functionally from the cortex which projects into a particular region of the striatum (in this case sensori-motor cortex, areas 3, 1, 2, 4, and 6).

3.10.2.4   What computations are performed by the basal ganglia?

The neurophysiological investigations described in Section 3.10.2.3 indicate that reinforcement-related signals do affect neuronal activity in some parts of the striatum, particularly in the ventral striatum. Does the ventral striatum process the inputs in any way before passing them on? Can the ventral striatum be considered as one part of a larger computational system that includes all parts of the basal ganglia, and that operates as a single system with inputs from all parts of the cerebral cortex, allowing selection by competition between all the inputs as well as convergence between them to produce a single behavioural output stream? How do the outputs of the basal ganglia lead to or influence action?

The evidence described above shows that different parts of the basal ganglia have different types of neuronal activity that reflect the input each receives from its cortical areas. Evidence reviewed by Rolls (2005) also shows that the neuronal activity in the striatum does not contain all the information in the cortical areas, but instead appears to reflect computations that have been performed by those cortical areas.

The hypothesis arises from these findings that some parts of the striatum, particularly the caudate nucleus, ventral striatum, and posterior putamen, receive the output of these cortical memory-related and cognitive computations, but do not themselves perform them. Instead, on receiving the cortical and limbic outputs, the striatum may be involved in switching behaviour as appropriate, as determined by the different, sometimes conflicting, information received from these cortical and limbic areas. On this view, the striatum would be particularly involved in the selection of behavioural responses, and in producing one coherent stream of behavioural output, with the possibility to switch if a higher priority input was received. This process may be achieved by a laterally spreading competitive interaction between striatal or pallidal neurons, which might be implemented by the direct inhibitory connections between nearby neurons in the striatum and globus pallidus. In addition, the inhibitory interneurons within the striatum, the dendrites of which in the striatum may cross the boundary between the matrix and striosomes, may play a part in this interaction between striatal processing streams (Groves 1983, Graybiel and Kimura 1995, Groves, Garcia-Munoz, Linder, Manley, Martone and Young 1995).

Dopamine could play an important role in setting the sensitivity of this response selection function, as suggested by direct iontophoresis of dopamine on to single striatal neurons, which produces a similar decrease in the response of the neuron and in its spontaneous activity in the behaving macaque (Rolls, Thorpe, Boytim, Szabo and Perrett 1984, Rolls and Williams 1987b).

In addition to this response selection function by competition, the basal ganglia may, by the convergence discussed, enable signals originating from non-motor parts of the cerebral cortex to be mapped into motor signals to produce behavioural output. The ways in which these computations might be performed are considered next.

Given the anatomy of the basal ganglia, interactions between signals reaching the basal ganglia could happen in a number of different ways. One would be for each part of the striatum to receive at least some input from a number of different cortical regions. As discussed above, there is evidence for patches of input from different sources to be brought adjacent to each other in the striatum (Van Hoesen et al. 1981, Seleman and Goldman-Rakic 1985, Graybiel and Kimura 1995). For example, in the caudate nucleus, different regions of association cortex project to adjacent longitudinal strips (Seleman and Goldman-Rakic 1985). Now, the dendrites of striatal neurons have the shape of large plates which lie at right angles to the incoming cortico-striatal fibres (Percheron, Yelnik and François 1984b, Percheron, Yelnik and François 1984a, Percheron, Yelnik, François, Fenelon and Talbi 1994) (see Figs. 3.61 and 3.62). Thus one way in which interaction may start in the basal ganglia is by virtue of the same striatal neuron receiving inputs on its dendrites from more than just a limited area of the cerebral cortex. This convergence may provide a first level of integration over limited sets of cortico-striatal fibres. The large number of cortical inputs received by each striatal neuron, in the order of 10,000 (Wilson 1995), is consistent with the hypothesis that convergence of inputs carrying different signals is an important aspect of the function of the basal ganglia. The computation that could be performed by this architecture is discussed below for the inputs

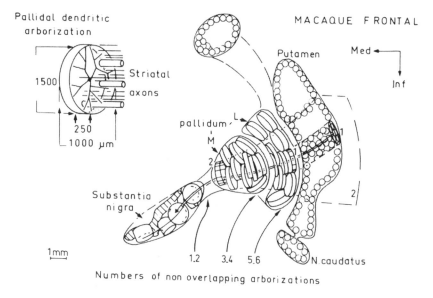

Pallidal dendritic arborization

MACAQUE FRONTAL

Putamen

Med

Inf

Striatal axons

1500

250

1000 µm

pallidum

L

M

Substantia nigra

1mm

1.2 3.4 5.6

N.caudatus

Numbers of non overlapping arborizations

Fig. 3.61 Semi-schematic spatial diagram of the striato-pallido-nigral system (see text). The numbers represent the numbers of non-overlapping arborizations of dendrites in the plane shown. L, lateral or external segment of the globus pallidus; M, medial or internal segment of the globus pallidus. The inserted diagram in the upper left shows the geometry of the dendrites of a typical pallidal neuron, and how the flat dendritic arborization is pierced at right angles by the striatal axons, which make occasional synapses en passage. (Reprinted with permission from Percheron, Yelnik and François 1984b.)

to the globus pallidus, where the connectivity pattern is comparable.

Interaction between neurons and selection of output

The regional segregation of neuronal response types in the striatum described above is consistent with mainly local integration over limited, adjacent sets of cortico-striatal inputs, as suggested by this anatomy. Short-range integration or interactions within the striatum may also be produced by the short length (for example 0.5 mm) of the intra-striatal axons of striatal neurons. These could produce a more widespread influence if the effect of a strong input to one part of the striatum spread like a lateral competition signal (cf. Groves (1983); Groves et al. (1995)). Such a mechanism could contribute to behavioural response selection in the face of different competing input signals to the striatum. The lateral inhibition could operate, for example, between the striatal principal (that is medium spiny) neurons by direct connections (they receive excitatory connections from the cortex, respond by increasing their firing rates, and could inhibit each other by their local axonal arborizations, which spread in an area as large as their dendritic trees, and which utilize GABA as their inhibitory transmitter). Further lateral inhibition could operate in the pallidum and substantia nigra (see Fig. 3.62). Here again there are local axon collaterals, as widespread as the very large pallidal and nigral dendritic fields. The lateral competition could again operate by direct connections between the neurons.

[Note that pallidal and nigral cells have high spontaneous firing rates (often 25–50 spikes/s), and respond (to their inhibitory striatal inputs) by reducing their firing rates below this high spontaneous rate. Such a decrease in the firing rate of one neuron would release inhibition on nearby neurons, causing them to increase their firing rates, equivalent to responding less. It is very interesting that direct inhibitory connections between the neurons can implement selection, even though at the striatal level the neurons have low spontaneous

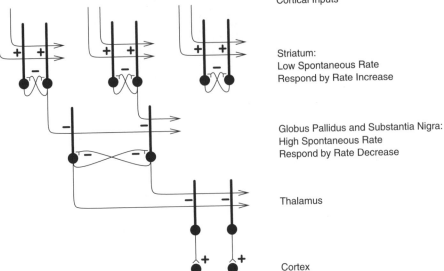

Fig. 3.62 Simple hypothesis of basal ganglia network architecture. A key aspect is that in both the striatum, and in the globus pallidus and substantia nigra pars reticulata, there are direct inhibitory connections (−) between the principal neurons, as shown. These synapses use GABA as a transmitter. Excitatory inputs to the striatum are shown as +. (After Rolls and Treves 1998, and Rolls 1999a.)

firing rates and respond by increasing their firing rates, whereas in the globus pallidus and substantia nigra pars reticulata the neurons have a high spontaneous firing rate, and respond by decreasing their firing rate.]

A selection function of this type between processing streams in the basal ganglia, even without any convergence anatomically between the processing streams implemented by feed-forward inputs, might provide an important computational raison d'être for the basal ganglia. The direct inhibitory local connectivity between the principal neurons within the striatum and globus pallidus would seem to provide a simple, and perhaps evolutionarily old, way in which to implement competition between neurons and processing streams. This might even be a primitive design principle that characterizes the basal ganglia. A system such as the basal ganglia with direct inhibitory recurrent collaterals may have evolved easily because it is easier to make stable than architectures such as the cerebral cortex with recurrent excitatory connections. The basal ganglia architecture may have been especially appropriate in motor systems in which instability could produce movement and co-ordination difficulties (Rolls and Treves 1998, Rolls 1999a). Equations that describe the way in which this mutual inhibition between the principal neurons can result in contrast enhancement of neuronal activity in the different competing neurons, and thus selection, are provided by Grossberg (1988), Gurney et al. (2001a), and Gurney, Prescott and Redgrave (2001b).

This hypothesis of lateral competition between the neurons of the basal ganglia can be sketched simply (see also Fig. 3.62 and Rolls and Treves (1998) Chapter 9, where a more detailed neuronal network theory of the operation of the basal ganglia is presented). The inputs from the cortex to the striatum are excitatory, and competition between striatal neurons is implemented by the use of an inhibitory transmitter (GABA), and direct connections between striatal neurons, within an area which is approximately co-extensive with the dendritic arborization. Given that the lateral connections between the striatal neurons are collaterals of the output axons, the output must be inhibitory on to pallidal and nigral neurons. This means that to transmit signals usefully, and in contrast to striatal neurons, the neurons in the globus pallidus and substantia nigra (pars reticulata) must have high spontaneous firing rates, and respond by reducing their firing rates. These pallidal and nigral neurons then repeat the simple scheme for lateral competition between output neurons by having direct lateral inhibitory connections to the other pallidal and nigral neurons. When nigral and pallidal neurons respond by reducing their firing rates, the reduced inhibition through the recurrent collaterals allows the connected pallidal and nigral neurons that are not part of the most strongly selected route to fire faster, and also at the same time the selected output of the pallidal and nigral neurons with its low firing allows the thalamic neurons to fire faster (as they are released from inhibition). The thalamic neurons then have the standard excitatory influence on their cortical targets.

The simple, and perhaps evolutionarily early, aspect of this basal ganglia architecture is that the striatal, pallidal, and nigral neurons implement competition (for selection) by direct inhibitory recurrent lateral connections of the main output neurons on to other output neurons, with the inputs to each stage of processing (e.g. striatum, globus pallidus) synapsing directly on to the output neurons that inhibit each other (see Fig. 3.62). As noted in Section 10.7, as long as the inhibitory connections between the principal (GABA) neurons do not show associative modifiability, this implements a liner diffusion process to make the selection by competition.

Further levels for integration within the basal ganglia are provided by the striato-pallidal and striato-nigral projections (Percheron, Yelnik and François 1984b, Percheron, Yelnik and François 1984a, Percheron, Yelnik, François, Fenelon and Talbi 1994). The afferent fibres from the striatum again cross at right angles a flat plate or disc formed by the dendrites of the pallidal or nigral neurons (see Fig. 3.61). The discs are approximately 1.5 mm in diameter, and are stacked up one upon the next at right angles to the incoming striatal fibres. The dendritic discs are so large that in the monkey there is room for only perhaps 50 such discs not to overlap in the external pallidal segment, for 10 non-overlapping discs in the medial pallidal segment, and for one overlapping disc in the most medial part of the medial segment of the globus pallidus and in the substantia nigra.

One result of this convergence achieved by this stage of the medial pallidum/substantia nigra is that even if inputs from different cortical regions were kept segregated by specific wiring rules on to different neurons, there might nevertheless well be the possibility for mutual competition between different pallidal neurons, implemented by their mutual inhibitory connections. Given the relatively small number of neurons into which the cortical signals had now been compressed, it would be feasible to have competition (the same effect as lateral inhibition implemented by inhibitory neurons would achieve elsewhere) implemented between the relatively small population of neurons, now all collected into a relatively restricted space, so that the competition could spread widely within these nuclei. This could allow selection by competition between these pathways, that is effectively between information processing in different cortical areas. This could be important in allowing each cortical area to control output when appropriate (depending on the task being performed). Even if full segregation were maintained in the return paths to the cerebral cortex, the return paths could influence each cortical area, allowing it to continue processing if it had the strongest 'call'. Each cortical area on a fully segregated hypothesis might thus have its own non-basal ganglia output routes, but might according to the current suggestion utilize the basal ganglia as a system to select a cortical area or set of areas, depending on how strongly each cortical area is calling for output. The thalamic outputs from the basal ganglia (areas VA and VLo of the thalamus) might according to this hypothesis have to some extent an activity or gain-controlling function on a cortical area (such as might be mediated by diffuse terminals in superficial cortical layers), rather than the strong and selective inputs implemented by a specific thalamic nucleus such as the lateral geniculate.

Convergent mapping within the basal ganglia

In addition to this selection function, it is also attractive to at least consider the further hypothesis that there is some convergent mapping achieved by the basal ganglia. This hypothesis is now considered in more detail. The anatomical arrangement just described does provide a possibility for some convergence on to single striatal neurons of cortical input, and on to single pallidal and nigral (pars reticulata) neurons of signals from relatively different parts of the striatum. For what computation might such anatomy provide a structural basis? Within the pallidum, each dendritic disc is flat, is orthogonal to the input fibres that pierce it, but is not filled with dendritic arborizations. Instead, each dendrite typically consists of 4–5 branches that are spread out to occupy only a small part of the surface area of the dendritic disc (see Fig. 3.61). There are thousands of such sparsely populated plates stacked on top of one another. Each pallidal neuron is contacted by a number of the mass of fibres from the striatum that pass it, and given the relatively small collecting area of each pallidal or nigral neuron (4 or 5 dendritic branches in a plane), each such neuron is thus likely to receive a random combination of inputs from different striatal neurons within its collection field. The thinness of the dendritic sheet may help to ensure that each axon does not make more than a few synapses with each dendrite, and that the combinations of inputs received by each dendrite are approximately random. This architecture thus appears to be appropriate for bringing together at random on to single pallidal and nigral neurons, inputs that originate from quite diverse parts of the cerebral cortex. (This is a two-stage process, cortex to striatum, and striatum to pallidum and substantia nigra.) By the stage of the medial pallidum and substantia nigra, there is the opportunity for the input field of a single neuron to effectively become very wide, although whether in practice this covers very different cortical areas, or is instead limited to a rather segregated cortex–basal ganglia–cortex loop, remains to be confirmed.

Given then that this architecture could allow individual pallidal and nigral neurons to receive random combinations of inputs from different striatal neurons, the following functional implications arise. Simple associative (Hebbian) learning in the striatum would enable strongly firing striatal neurons to increase the strength of the synapses from the active cortical inputs in what would operate as a competitive network. (Descriptions of competitive networks are provided in Appendix B, and by Rolls and Deco (2002), Rolls and Treves (1998), and Hertz, Krogh and Palmer (1991).). In a proposal of Nakahara, Amari and Hikosaka (2002), dopamine can influence the firing rates of the striatal neurons, and thus can indirectly affect the Hebbian learning. In the pallidum, such conjunctive learning of coactive inputs would be more complex, requiring, for example, a strongly inhibited pallidal neuron to show synaptic strengthening from strongly firing but inhibitory inputs from the striatum. Then, if a particular pallidal or nigral neuron received inputs by chance from striatal neurons that responded to an environmental cue signal that something significant was about to happen, and from striatal neurons that fired because the monkey was making a postural adjustment, this conjunction of events might make that pallidal or nigral neuron become inhibited by (that is respond to) either input alone. Then, in the future, the occurrence of only one of the inputs, for example only the environmental cue, would result in a decrease of firing of that pallidal or nigral neuron, and thus in the appropriate postural adjustment being made by virtue of the output connections of that pallidal or nigral neuron.

This is a proposal that the basal ganglia are able to detect combinations of conjunctively active inputs from quite widespread regions of the cerebral cortex using their combinatorial architecture and a property of synaptic modifiability. In this way it would be possible to trigger any complex pattern of behavioural responses by any complex pattern of environmental inputs, using what is effectively an associative network (operating as a competitive network or pattern

error.) This hypothesis has been built into models of learning in which the error signal is used to train synaptic connections in dopamine pathway recipient regions (such as presumably the striatum and orbitofrontal cortex) (Waelti et al. 2001, Dayan and Abbott 2001) (see Section B.15.3).

In a further investigation of the function of dopamine neurons, Fiorillo, Tobler and Schultz (2003) found not only the effects just described (including only small reductions in the firing of dopamine neurons for negative reward prediction errors), but also that the firing rate of the neurons increased steadily during the 2 s period in which another conditioned stimulus was being shown that predicted that reward would be obtained with a probability P of 0.5 (see Fig. 3.63). However, when $P = 0.25$ or $P = 0.75$, the gradually increasing and sustained firing during the conditioned stimulus (CS) was less than when $P = 0.5$. This pattern of results indicates that the tonic, sustained, firing of the dopamine neurons in the delay period reflects reward uncertainty, and not the expected reward, nor the magnitude of the prediction error. Nor could the sustained, tonic, firing indicate expected reward (or expected value, where expected value = probability multiplied by reward value, see Glimcher (2003), Glimcher (2004), and Section 10.6), for this would be highest in the order $P=1.0$, $P=0.75$, $P=0.5$, $P=0.25$, $P=0.0$. Both the phasic and the tonic components were higher for higher reward values (more drops of juice reward). These results are difficult to reconcile with the previously hypothesized (Waelti, Dickinson and Schultz 2001, Dayan and Abbott 2001) 'prediction error' training signal function of the firing of dopamine neurons, for it is difficult to understand how any brain system receiving the phasic ('prediction error') and tonic ('uncertainty of reward') dopamine signals by the same set of neurons could disentangle them and use them for different functions (Shizgal and Arvanitogiannis 2003). Niv, Duff and Dayan (2005), noting the problems of the asymmetry of the hypothesized reward prediction error signals carried by dopamine neurons, have postulated that the ramping activity before the outcome is known may not be related to uncertainty, but could reflect an average across trials of a reward prediction signal moving backwards from the outcome time to the time of the stimulus, and the effects of asymmetry in the error signal related to the low firing rate of the dopamine neurons.

Another problem with the 'reward prediction error' hypothesis for dopamine neurons is the fact that for reward to predict an error, it is necessary to have a correct prediction or expectancy of reward (e.g. neurons that fire to a visual stimulus that precedes a reward), and other neurons that indicate whether reward (e.g. the taste of fruit juice) has been obtained, and both types of neuron (as well as error neurons) are present in the primate orbitofrontal cortex (see Section 3.6), but not in the vicinity of the dopamine neuron cell bodies in the midbrain. (Consistent with this, the anterior cingulate cortex, which receives from the orbitofrontal cortex, contains neurons in humans that respond when expected rewards are not obtained (Williams, Bush, Rauch, Cosgrove and Eskandar 2004).) Indeed, to do this type of error computation, a representation of a very wide range of possible expected rewards [built by object–reward association learning based on inputs from the object representation system, the inferior temporal visual cortex (Rolls and Deco 2002)], and a very wide range of actual rewards [including detailed representations of for example oral taste, texture, temperature, and odour, and even monetary reward value], is needed, and this is exactly what is present in the primate orbitofrontal cortex. The error computation itself thus appears to be performed by brain systems other than dopamine neurons. It would then be a complex and seemingly not adaptive and simple design to send the error signal from the orbitofrontal cortex to the midbrain dopamine neurons, from which it might just be projected back to the orbitofrontal cortex, and to other regions with which the orbitofrontal cortex connects such as the striatum (see Section 3.10.2). It is also noteworthy that rapid reversal cannot in any case easily be computed by a reward prediction error mechanism, as shown in Chapter 9, in which a mechanism that could perform rapid reversal is described.

However, the findings described above on the effects of aversive and salient stimuli on dopaminergic activity suggest an alternative possibility for the functions of dopaminergic activity, that instead it appears to convey information that would be better suited to a preparation or behavioural 'Go' (i.e. prepare to initiate action) role for dopamine release in the striatum. Consistent with this, high levels of dopamine acting via D1 receptors can facilitate the excitability of striatal neurons (Reynolds and Wickens 2002). Evidence that is needed on whether dopaminergic activity is related to preparation or behavioural 'Go' (i.e. prepare to initiate action) functions is whether dopamine neurons respond when the animal has to initiate behaviour actively to escape from or avoid aversive (e.g. painful) stimuli. Although Mirenowicz and Schultz (1996) did record from presumed dopamine neurons when an aversive stimulus such as a puff of air was delivered, and found little activation of dopamine neurons, the monkeys were performing passive avoidance, that is shutting down action. If the neurons do respond when the monkey must initiate action, for example by making several operant responses to escape from or avoid an aversive stimulus, then this would be evidence that the firing of dopamine neurons is related to 'Go' rather than to reward. Overall, many of the findings are more consistent with the hypothesis that instead of acting as the reinforce or error signal in a reinforcement learning system (Houk et al. 1995, Schultz et al. 1995b, Schultz et al. 1997, Tobler et al. 2003, Schultz 2004, Schultz 2006), the dopamine projection to the striatum may act as a 'Go' or 'preparation' signal to set the thresholds of neurons in the striatum, and/or as a general modulatory signal that could help to strengthen synapses of conjunctively active pre- and postsynaptic neurons. In such a system, what is learned would be dependent on the presynaptic and postsynaptic terms of striatal neurons, and would not be explicitly guided by a reinforce/reward signal that would provide feedback after each trial on the degree of success of each trial as in the reinforcement learning algorithm (see Section B.15). The striatum could thus learn associations useful for setting up habit representations, as described in Section 3.10.2.4. On this hypothesis, the crucial aspects of what is learned would depend on conjunctive pre- and postsynaptic activity in the striatum. In this scenario, the dopamine might just reflect activity in the striatum and be used to set thresholds appropriately (based on general behavioural salience) rather than being explicitly forced into a reward prediction error state of firing by unknown inputs. On this hypothesis, a large increase in dopamine release would facilitate Hebbian learning in the corticostriatal system (Reynolds and Wickens 2002) when salient stimuli occurred, and the salience might be produced by for example unexpected or strong rewarding or punishing events, or by novel events, or by events with uncertainty (Seamans and Yang 2004, Shizgal and Arvanitogiannis 2003).

3.10.3 Output systems for explicit responses to emotional stimuli

The third type of output of reward and punishment systems is to a system capable of planning many steps ahead and, for example, deferring short-term rewards in order to execute a long-term plan. This system may use syntactic processing in order to perform the planning, and is therefore part of a linguistic system that performs explicit processing. This system, discussed in Chapter 10 of Rolls (2005), is the one in which explicit, declarative, processing occurs. Processing in this system is frequently associated with reason and rationality, in that many of the consequences of possible actions can be taken into account. The actual computation of how rewarding a particular stimulus or situation is, or will be, probably still depends on activity in the orbitofrontal cortex and amygdala, in that the reward value of stimuli is computed and represented in these regions, and in that it is found that verbalized expressions of the reward (or punishment) value of stimuli are dampened by damage to these systems. (For example, damage to the orbitofrontal cortex renders painful input still identifiable as pain, but without the strong affective, 'unpleasant', reaction to it.)

3.10.4 Basal forebrain and hypothalamus

It was suggested above that the hypothalamus and basal forebrain may provide one output system for the amygdala and orbitofrontal cortex for autonomic and other responses to emotional stimuli. Consistent with this, there are neurons in the lateral hypothalamus and basal forebrain of monkeys that respond to visual stimuli associated with rewards such as food (Rolls 1975, Rolls 1981b, Rolls 1981a, Rolls 1982, Rolls 1986c, Rolls 1986a, Rolls 1986b, Rolls 1990d, Rolls 1993, Rolls 1999a, Rolls, Burton and Mora 1976, Burton, Rolls and Mora 1976, Mora, Rolls and Burton 1976a, Wilson and Rolls 1990b, Wilson and Rolls 1990a). These neurons show rapid reversal of their responses during the reversal of stimulus–reinforcer associations. Other neurons in the hypothalamus responded only to stimuli associated with punishment, that is to aversive visual stimuli (Rolls, Sanghera and Roper-Hall 1979a). The responses of these neurons with reinforcement-related activity would be appropriate for producing autonomic responses to emotional stimuli, via pathways that descend from the hypothalamus towards the brainstem autonomic motor nuclei (Saper, Loewy, Swanson and Cowan 1976, Schwaber et al. 1982). It is also possible that these outputs could influence emotional behaviour, through, for example, the connections from the hypothalamus to the amygdala (Aggleton, Burton and Passingham 1980), to the substantia nigra (Nauta and Domesick 1978), or even by the connections to the neocortex (Divac 1975, Kievit and Kuypers 1975). Indeed, it is suggested that the latter projection, by releasing acetylcholine in the cerebral cortex when emotional stimuli (including reinforcing and novel stimuli) are seen, provides one way in which emotion can influence the storage of memories in the cerebral cortex (Rolls 1987, Wilson and Rolls 1990c, Wilson and Rolls 1990b, Wilson and Rolls 1990a). In this case, the basal forebrain magnocellular neurons may act as a 'cortical strobe' which facilitates memory storage and processing when the neurons are firing fast.

3.10.5 Basal forebrain cholinergic neurons

Before leaving the learning systems in the amygdala and orbitofrontal cortex, it is useful to consider the role in memory of one of the systems to which they project, the basal forebrain magnocellular nuclei of Meynert. The cells in these nuclei lie just lateral to the lateral hypothalamus in the substantia innominata, and extend forward through the preoptic area into the diagonal band of Broca (Mesulam 1990). These cells, many of which are cholinergic, project directly to the cerebral cortex (Divac 1975, Kievit and Kuypers 1975, Mesulam 1990). These cells provide the major cholinergic input to the cerebral cortex, in that if they are lesioned the cortex is depleted of acetylcholine (Mesulam 1990). Loss of these cells does occur in Alzheimer's disease, and there is consequently a reduction in cortical acetylcholine in this disease (Mesulam 1990). This loss of cortical acetylcholine may contribute to the memory loss in Alzheimer's disease, although it may well not be the primary factor in the aetiology.

In order to investigate the role of the basal forebrain nuclei in memory, Aigner, Mitchell, Aggleton, DeLong, Struble, Price, Wenk, Pettigrew and Mishkin (1991) made neurotoxic lesions of them in monkeys. Some impairments on a simple test of recognition memory, delayed non-match-to-sample, were found. Analysis of the effects of similar lesions in rats showed that performance on memory tasks was impaired, perhaps because of failure to attend properly (Muir, Everitt and Robbins 1994). Damage to the cholinergic neurons in this region in monkeys with a selective neurotoxin was also shown to impair memory (Easton and Gaffan 2000, Easton et al. 2002).

There are quite limited numbers of these basal forebrain neurons (in the order of thousands). Given that there are relatively few of these neurons, it is not likely that they carry the information to be stored in cortical memory circuits, for the number of different patterns that could be represented and stored is so small. (The number of different patterns that could be stored is dependent in a leading way on the number of input connections on to each neuron in a pattern associator, see Appendix B.) With these few neurons distributed throughout the cerebral cortex, the memory capacity of the whole system would be impractically small. This argument alone indicates that they are unlikely to carry the information to be stored in cortical memory systems. Instead, they could modulate storage in the cortex of information derived from what provides the numerically major input to cortical neurons, the glutamatergic terminals of other cortical neurons. This modulation may operate by setting thresholds for cortical cells to the appropriate value, or by more directly influencing the cascade of processes involved in long-term potentiation (see Appendix B). There is indeed evidence that acetylcholine is necessary for cortical synaptic modifiability, as shown by studies in which depletion of acetylcholine and noradrenaline impaired cortical LTP/synaptic modifiability (Bear and Singer 1986). However, non-specific effects of damage to the basal forebrain cholinergic neurons are also likely, with cortical neurons becoming much more sluggish in their responses, and showing much more adaptation, in the absence of cholinergic inputs (Markram and Tsodyks 1996, Abbott, Varela, Sen and Nelson 1997) (see below).

The question then arises of whether the basal forebrain cholinergic neurons tonically release acetylcholine, or whether they release it particularly in response to some external influence. To examine this, recordings have been made from basal forebrain neurons, at least some of which project to the cortex (see Rolls (2005)) and will have been the cholinergic neurons just described. It has been found that some of these neurons respond to visual stimuli associated with rewards such as food (Rolls 1975, Rolls 1981b, Rolls 1981a, Rolls 1982, Rolls 1986c, Rolls 1986a, Rolls 1986b, Rolls 1990d, Rolls 1993, Rolls 1999a, Rolls, Burton and Mora 1976, Burton, Rolls and Mora 1976, Mora, Rolls and Burton 1976a, Wilson and Rolls 1990b, Wilson and Rolls 1990a), or with punishment (Rolls, Sanghera and Roper-Hall 1979a), that others respond to novel visual stimuli (Wilson and Rolls 1990c), and that others respond to a range of visual stimuli. For example, in one set of recordings, one group of these neurons (1.5%) responded to novel visual stimuli while monkeys performed recognition or visual discrimination tasks (Wilson and Rolls 1990c). A complementary group of neurons more anteriorly responded to familiar visual stimuli in the same tasks (Rolls, Perrett, Caan and Wilson 1982, Wilson and Rolls 1990c). A third group of neurons (5.7%) responded to positively reinforcing visual stimuli in visual discrimination and in recognition memory tasks (Wilson and Rolls 1990b, Wilson and Rolls 1990a). In addition, a considerable proportion of these neurons (21.8%) responded to any visual stimuli shown in the tasks, and some (13.1%) responded to the tone cue that preceded the presentation of the visual stimuli in the task, and was provided to enable the monkey to alert to the visual stimuli (Wilson and Rolls 1990c). These neurons did not respond to touch to the leg which induced arousal, so their responses did not simply reflect arousal. Neurons in this region receive inputs from the amygdala (see Mesulam (1990); Amaral et al. (1992); Russchen, Amaral and Price (1985)) and orbitofrontal cortex, and it is probably via the amygdala (and orbitofrontal cortex) that the information described here reaches the basal forebrain neurons, for neurons with similar response properties have been found in the amygdala, and the amygdala appears to be involved in decoding visual stimuli that are associated with reinforcers, or are novel (Rolls 1990d, Rolls 1992b, Rolls 2000d, Wilson and Rolls 1993, Wilson and Rolls 2005, Rolls 2005) (see Section 3.7).

It is therefore suggested that the normal physiological function of these basal forebrain neurons is to send a general activation signal to the cortex when certain classes of environmental stimulus occur. These stimuli are often stimuli to which behavioural activation is appropriate or required, such as positively or negatively reinforcing visual stimuli, or novel visual stimuli. The effect of the firing of these neurons on the cortex is excitatory, and in this

3.12   Laterality effects in human reward and emotional processing

In humans, there is some lateralization of function of emotional processing, with the right hemisphere frequently being implicated in processing face expressions. Some of the evidence for this is reviewed next.

A first type of evidence comes from the effects of brain damage in humans. Damage to the left hemisphere (in right-handed people) is more likely to affect language, and to the right hemisphere is more likely to affect emotional processing. This may be evident, for example, in the greater probability of impairments in recognizing facial expressions after right rather than left hemisphere damage (see Etcoff (1989)). Further, patients are more likely to be depressed by a stroke if it is to the left than to the right hemisphere (see Starkstein and Robinson (1991)). This may indicate that to feel depressed, the right hemisphere is normally involved.

A second type of evidence comes from split brain patients (with the corpus callosum sectioned to prevent epilepsy on one side affecting the other side of the brain). These patients may respond behaviourally to an emotion-provoking stimulus which reaches the right hemisphere, even though they cannot specify verbally (with the left hemisphere) what they saw (Gazzaniga 1988). This is clear evidence for separate processing of implicit information about emotion in humans that can be dissociated from explicit, language-based, systems (see Rolls (2005)).

Third, when faces are flashed rapidly on a screen, there may be better performance in identifying the expression on the face when the stimulus is projected to the right than to the left hemisphere (Strauss and Moscowitsch 1981). These effects on face expression identification are not produced just because face-processing modules are lateralized to the right hemisphere: face identification deficits are not necessarily associated with face expression identification impairments.

Fourth, emotions may be more clearly expressed on the left side than the right side of the face, suggesting some specialization of the right hemisphere in controlling face expression (Nicholls, Ellis, Clement and Yoshino 2004). There may further be a weak specialization of the right hemisphere for negative emotions, as there is a trend for left-sided face expression to occur more for negative than positive emotions. Further, a left-sided view of the face was judged as being sadder and a right-sided view was rated as being happier (Nicholls et al. 2004). Consistent with a valence effect whereby the right hemisphere may be more related to negative (e.g. sad) emotions, Davidson, Ekman, Saron, Senulis and Friesen (1990) and Davidson (1992) have some evidence from EEG recording that for negative emotional episodes there is more activation of the right side of the brain; and for positive episodes there is more activation of the left side of the brain. However, there may be individual differences in the activation of prefrontal areas that are related to the affective reactivity of the individual (Davidson 2003).

Why should there be some lateralization of emotional processing in humans? One argument is that whenever a function does not need to be represented bilaterally due to the topology of the body (e.g. we have left and right hands, and separate representations of each hand are needed), then it is more efficient to place the group of neurons concerned with that processing close together. One advantage of placing neurons concerned with similar processing close together is that the length of the connections between the neurons will be minimized. This is important for minimizing brain size and weight, which is a significant factor in evolution. If half the neurons concerned with a particular function were on one side of the brain, and the other half were on the contralateral side, then the total length of the connections between the neurons would be large (see Section B.4.6).

Neurons concerned with the same function are frequently interconnected for a number of reasons. One is that there are recurrent collateral axons between nearby cortical neurons concerned with the same function. One of the functions performed by these excitatory recurrent collaterals is to enable the network to act as a local attractor or autoassociation memory, so that the output of the module can take into account not only the activation produced in any one neuron, but also the activations received by the other connected neurons (see Section B.3). Another way in which this is performed is by using feedback inhibitory interneurons, which are activated by many of the cortical pyramidal cells in a region. This not only helps autoassociation (and pattern association) networks to remain stable, but also is important for competitive networks, in which categorization of stimuli occurs, by effectively allowing the neurons in a population with the strongest activation by a particular stimulus to remain active (see Section B.4).

A second advantage of placing neurons concerned with the same function close together is that this may simplify the wiring rules between neurons which must be implemented genetically (see Section B.4.6). Given that there are in the order of 35,000 genes in the human genome, and more than 10^{14} synapses, it is clearly impossible for genes to specify all the connections between every neuron. Instead, the genetic rules may specify, for example, that neurons of type y receive approximately 12,000 excitatory synapses with associative long-term potentiation and heterosynaptic long-term depression from other neurons of type y in the surrounding 2 mm (this forms a recurrent collateral pathway); make approximately 12,000 excitatory synapses with associative long-term potentiation and heterosynaptic long-term depression with neurons of type z up to 4 mm away (which might be the next cortical area); receive approximately 500 synapses from neurons of type I within 2 mm (which might be GABA-containing inhibitory feedback neurons); and receive approximately 6,000 inputs from neurons of type x up to 4 mm away (which might be the pyramidal cells in the preceding cortical area). This type of specification would build many of the networks found in different brain regions (see Rolls and Stringer (2000) and Rolls and Treves (1998)).

An advantage of this type of genetic specification of connectivity between neuron types, and of keeping neurons concerned with the same computation close together, is that this minimizes the problems of guidance of axons towards their targets. If neurons concerned with the same function were randomly distributed in the brain, then finding the distant correct neurons with which to connect would be an impossible guidance problem. (As it is, some distant parts of the brain that are connected in adults are connected because the connections can be made early in development, before the different brain regions have migrated to become possibly distant.)

All these constraints imply that wherever possible neurons performing the same computation should be close together. Where there is no body-symmetry reason to have separate representations for each side of the body, then the representation would optimally be lateralized. This appears to be the case for certain aspects of emotional processing.

However, it is of interest that this lateralization of function may itself give rise to lateralization of performance. It may be because the brain mechanisms concerned with face expression identification are better represented in the right hemisphere that expression identification is better for the left half of the visual field (which might correspond to the left half of a centrally fixated face). Another possible reason for partial lateralization of human emotion may be that language is predominantly in the left hemisphere (for right-handed people). The result of this may be that although explicit (conscious, verbal) processing related to emotion may take place in the left hemisphere, the implicit type of processing may take place preferentially where there is room in the brain, that is with a bias for the right hemisphere. The suggestion that there are these two types of output route for emotional behaviour is made in Section 3.10, Chapter 10, and by Rolls (2005). The fact that they are to some extent separate types of output processing may account for the fact that they can be placed in different modules,

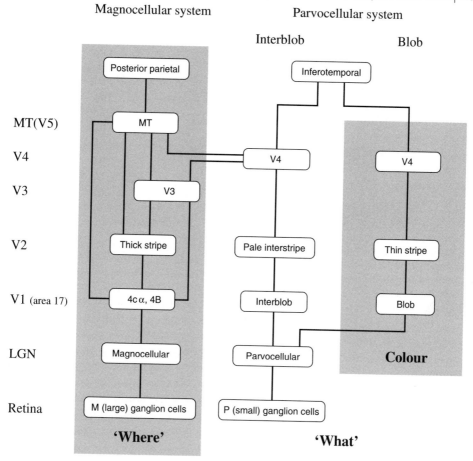

Fig. 4.1 A schematic diagram of the visual pathways from the retina to visual cortical areas. LGN, lateral geniculate nucleus; V1, primary visual cortex; V2, V3, V4, and MT, other visual cortical areas; M, magnocellular; P, parvocellular.

4.2.1 Processing to the inferior temporal cortex in the primate visual system

A schematic diagram to indicate some aspects of the processing involved in object identification from the primary visual cortex, V1, through V2 and V4 to the posterior inferior temporal cortex (TEO) and the anterior inferior temporal cortex (TE) is shown in Fig. 4.2. The approximate location of these visual cortical areas on the brain of a macaque monkey is shown in Figs. 4.3 and 1.9, which also show that TE has a number of different subdivisions. The different TE areas all contain visually responsive neurons, as do many of the areas within the cortex in the superior temporal sulcus (Baylis, Rolls and Leonard 1987). For the purposes of this summary, these areas will be grouped together as the anterior inferior temporal cortex (IT), except where otherwise stated. A description of some of the specializations within this region, and a hypothesis about why there is specialization, is provided in Section 4.2.10. Some of the information processing that takes place through these pathways that must be addressed by computational models is described in the following subsections. A fuller account is provided by Rolls (2000a), Rolls and Deco (2002), Rolls (2007i), Rolls (2007f), and Rolls (2008a).

Many of the studies on neurons in the anterior inferior temporal cortex and cortex in the

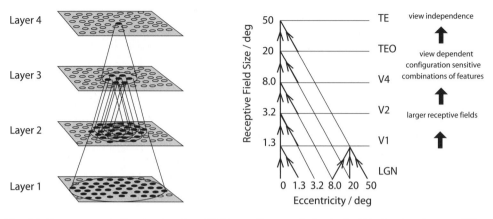

Fig. 4.2 Convergence in the visual system. Right – as it occurs in the brain. V1, visual cortex area V1; TEO, posterior inferior temporal cortex; TE, inferior temporal cortex (IT). Left – as implemented in VisNet. Convergence through the network is designed to provide fourth layer neurons with information from across the entire input retina.

superior temporal sulcus have been performed with neurons that respond particularly to faces, because such neurons can be found regularly in recordings in this region, and therefore provide a good population for systematic studies (Rolls 2000a, Rolls and Deco 2002, Rolls 2007i, Rolls and Deco 2006). The face-selective neurons described in this book are found mainly between 7 mm and 3 mm posterior to the sphenoid reference, which in a 3–4 kg macaque corresponds to approximately 11 to 15 mm anterior to the interaural plane (Baylis, Rolls and Leonard 1987, Rolls 2007i, Rolls 2007f). The 'middle face patch' of Tsao, Freiwald, Tootell and Livingstone (2006) was at A6, which is probably part of the posterior inferior temporal cortex. In the anterior inferior temporal cortex areas we have investigated, there are separate regions specialized for face identity in areas TEa and TEm on the ventral lip of the superior temporal sulcus and the adjacent gyrus, and for face expression and movement in the cortex deep in the superior temporal sulcus (Hasselmo, Rolls and Baylis 1989a, Baylis, Rolls and Leonard 1987, Rolls 2007i) (see Sections 4.2.9 and 4.2.10).

Examples of some of the objects encoded by anterior inferior temporal cortex neurons as described in this book (for example in this Chapter, in Sections 2.2.6 and 3.5, and in Appendix C) are shown in Figs. 2.11 and C.7.

4.2.2 Translation invariance and receptive field size

There is convergence from each small part of a region to the succeeding region (or layer in the hierarchy) in such a way that the receptive field sizes of neurons (for example 1 degree near the fovea in V1) become larger by a factor of approximately 2.5 with each succeeding stage. [The typical parafoveal receptive field sizes found would not be inconsistent with the calculated approximations of, for example, 8 degrees in V4, 20 degrees in TEO, and 50 degrees in inferior temporal cortex (Boussaoud, Desimone and Ungerleider 1991) (see Fig. 4.2).] Such zones of convergence would overlap continuously with each other (see Fig. 4.2). This connectivity provides part of the basis for the fact that many neurons in the temporal cortical visual areas respond to a stimulus relatively independently of where it is in their receptive field, and moreover maintain their stimulus selectivity when the stimulus appears in different parts of the visual field (Gross, Desimone, Albright and Schwartz 1985, Tovee, Rolls

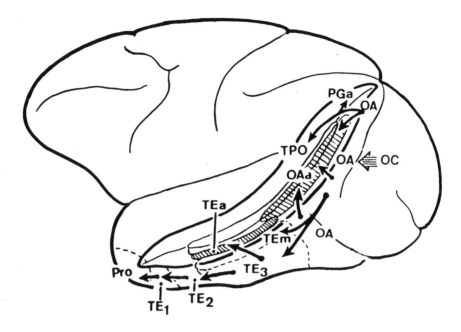

Fig. 4.3 Lateral view of the macaque brain (left hemisphere) showing the different architectonic areas (e.g. TEm, TEa) in and bordering the anterior part of the superior temporal sulcus (STS) of the macaque (see text). The STS has been drawn opened to reveal to reveal the cortical areas inside it, and is circumscribed by a thick line.

and Azzopardi 1994, Rolls, Aggelopoulos and Zheng 2003a). This is called translation or shift invariance. In addition to having topologically appropriate connections, it is necessary for the connections to have the appropriate synaptic weights to perform the mapping of each set of features, or object, to the same set of neurons in IT. How this could be achieved is addressed in the computational neuroscience models described later in this Chapter and by Wallis and Rolls (1997), Rolls and Deco (2002), Rolls and Stringer (2006), and Stringer, Perry, Rolls and Proske (2006).

4.2.3 Reduced translation invariance in natural scenes, and the selection of a rewarded object

Until recently, research on translation invariance considered the case in which there is only one object in the visual field. What happens in a cluttered, natural, environment? Do all objects that can activate an inferior temporal neuron do so whenever they are anywhere within the large receptive fields of inferior temporal neurons (cf. Sato (1989))? If so, the output of the visual system might be confusing for structures that receive inputs from the temporal cortical visual areas. If one of the objects in the visual field was associated with reward, and another with punishment, would the output of the inferior temporal visual cortex to emotion-related brain systems be an amalgam of both stimuli? If so, how would we be able to choose between the stimuli, and have an emotional response to one but not perhaps the other, and select one for action and not the other (see Fig. 4.4)?

In an investigation of this, it was found that the mean firing rate across all cells to a fixated effective face with a non-effective face in the parafovea (centred 8.5 degrees from the fovea)

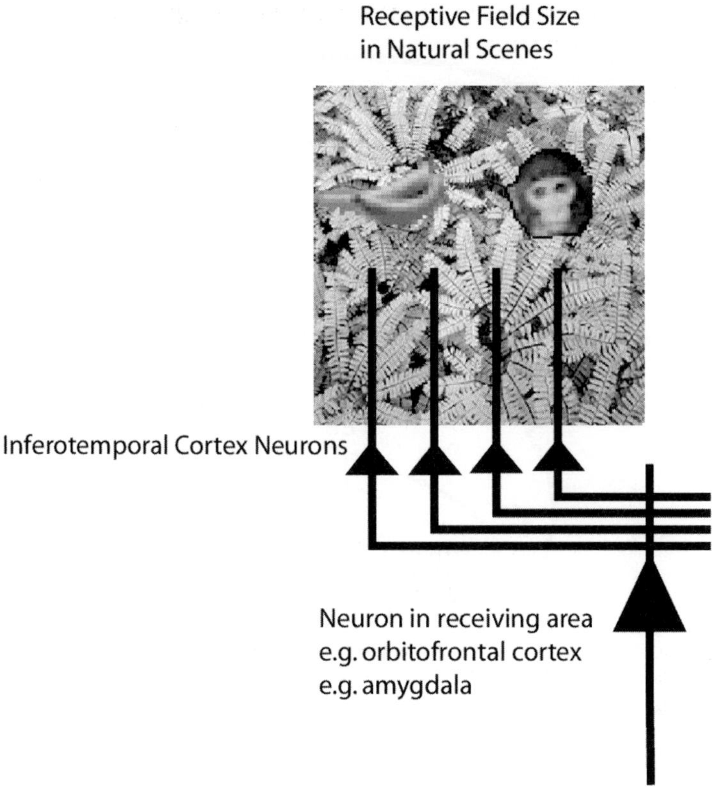

Fig. 4.4 Objects shown in a natural scene, in which the task was to search for and touch one of the stimuli. The objects in the task as run were smaller. The diagram shows that if the receptive fields of inferior temporal cortex neurons are large in natural scenes with multiple objects (in this scene, bananas and a face), then any receiving neuron in structures such as the orbitofrontal cortex and amygdala would receive information from many stimuli in the field of view, and would not be able to provide evidence about each of the stimuli separately.

was 34 spikes/s. On the other hand, the average response to a fixated non-effective face with an effective face in the periphery was 22 spikes/s (Rolls and Tovee 1995a). Thus these cells gave a reliable output about which stimulus is actually present at the fovea, in that their response was larger to a fixated effective face than to a fixated non-effective face, even when there were other parafoveal stimuli effective for the neuron. Thus the neurons provide information biased towards what is present at the fovea, and not equally about what is present anywhere in the visual field. This makes the interface to action simpler, in that what is at the fovea can be interpreted (e.g. by an associative memory) partly independently of the surroundings, and choices and actions can be directed if appropriate to what is at the fovea (cf. Ballard (1993)). These findings are a step towards understanding how the visual system functions in a normal environment (see also Gallant, Connor and Van-Essen (1998), Stringer and Rolls (2000), and Rolls and Deco (2006)).

To investigate further how information is passed from the inferior temporal cortex (IT) to other brain regions to enable stimuli to be selected from natural scenes for action, Rolls, Aggelopoulos and Zheng (2003a) analysed the responses of single and simultaneously recorded IT neurons to stimuli presented in complex natural backgrounds. In one situation, a visual fixation task was performed in which the monkey fixated at different distances from the

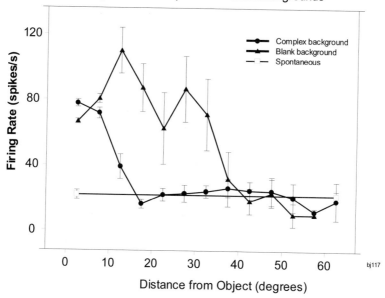

Firing Rate in Complex and Blank Backgrounds

Fig. 4.5 Firing of a temporal cortex cell to an effective stimulus presented either in a blank background or in a natural scene, as a function of the angle in degrees at which the monkey was fixating away from the effective stimulus. The task was to search for and touch the stimulus. (After Rolls, Aggelopoulos and Zheng 2003.)

effective stimulus. In another situation the monkey had to search for two objects on a screen, and a touch of one object was rewarded with juice, and of another object was punished with saline (see Fig. 4.4 for a schematic overview, and Fig. 4.62 on page 354 for the actual display). In both situations neuronal responses to the effective stimuli for the neurons were compared when the objects were presented in the natural scene or on a plain background. It was found that the overall response of the neuron to objects was sometimes somewhat reduced when they were presented in natural scenes, though the selectivity of the neurons remained. However, the main finding was that the magnitudes of the responses of the neurons typically became much less in the real scene the further the monkey fixated in the scene away from the object (see Figs. 4.5 and 4.63, and Section 4.5.9.1). It is proposed that this reduced translation invariance in natural scenes helps an unambiguous representation of an object which may be the target for action to be passed to the brain regions that receive from the primate inferior temporal visual cortex. It helps with the binding problem, by reducing in natural scenes the effective receptive field of inferior temporal cortex neurons to approximately the size of an object in the scene. The computational utility and basis for this is considered in Section 4.5.9 and by Rolls and Deco (2002), Trappenberg, Rolls and Stringer (2002), Deco and Rolls (2004), Aggelopoulos and Rolls (2005), and Rolls and Deco (2006), and includes an advantage for what is at the fovea because of the large cortical magnification of the fovea, and shunting interactions between representations weighted by how far they are from the fovea.

These findings suggest that the principle of providing strong weight to whatever is close to the fovea is an important principle governing the operation of the inferior temporal visual cortex, and in general of the output of the ventral visual system in natural environments. This principle of operation is very important in interfacing the visual system to action systems, because the effective stimulus in making inferior temporal cortex neurons fire is in natural

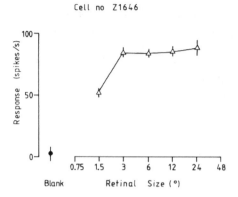

Cell no Z1646

Fig. 4.6 Typical response of an inferior temporal cortex face-selective neuron to faces of different sizes. The size subtended at the retina in degrees is shown. (From Rolls and Baylis 1986.)

scenes usually on or close to the fovea. This means that the spatial coordinates of where the object is in the scene do not have to be represented in the inferior temporal visual cortex, nor passed from it to the action selection system, as the latter can assume that the object making IT neurons fire is close to the fovea in natural scenes. Thus the position in visual space being fixated provides part of the interface between sensory representations of objects and their coordinates as targets for actions in the world. The small receptive fields of IT neurons in natural scenes make this possible. After this, local, egocentric, processing implemented in the dorsal visual processing stream using e.g. stereodisparity may be used to guide action towards objects being fixated (Rolls and Deco 2002).

The reduced receptive field size in complex natural scenes also enables emotions to be selective to just what is being fixated, because this is the information that is transmitted by the firing of IT neurons to structures such as the orbitofrontal cortex and amygdala.

Interestingly, although the size of the receptive fields of inferior temporal cortex neurons become reduced in natural scenes so that neurons in IT respond primarily to the object being fixated, there is nevertheless frequently some asymmetry in the receptive fields (see Section 4.5.10 and Fig. 4.67). This provides a partial solution to how multiple objects and their position in a scene can be captured with a single glance (Aggelopoulos and Rolls 2005).

4.2.4   Size and spatial frequency invariance

Some neurons in the inferior temporal visual cortex and cortex in the anterior part of the superior temporal sulcus (IT/STS) respond relatively independently of the size of an effective face stimulus, with a mean size invariance (to a half maximal response) of 12 times (3.5 octaves) (Rolls and Baylis 1986). An example of the responses of an inferior temporal cortex face-selective neuron to faces of different sizes is shown in Fig. 4.6. This is not a property of a simple single-layer network (see Fig. 4.18), nor of neurons in V1, which respond best to small stimuli, with a typical size-invariance of 1.5 octaves. Also, the neurons typically responded to a face when the information in it had been reduced from 3D to a 2D representation in grey on a monitor, with a response that was on average 0.5 of that to a real face.

Another transform over which recognition is relatively invariant is spatial frequency. For example, a face can be identified when it is blurred (when it contains only low spatial frequencies), and when it is high-pass spatial frequency filtered (when it looks like a line drawing). If the face images to which these neurons respond are low-pass filtered in the spatial frequency domain (so that they are blurred), then many of the neurons still respond when the images contain frequencies only up to 8 cycles per face. Similarly, the neurons still respond to high-pass filtered images (with only high spatial frequency edge information) when frequencies down to only 8 cycles per face are included (Rolls, Baylis and Leonard 1985). Face recognition shows similar invariance with respect to spatial frequency (see Rolls, Baylis and Leonard (1985)). Further analysis of these neurons with narrow (octave) bandpass spatial frequency filtered face stimuli shows that the responses of these neurons to an unfiltered face can not be predicted from a linear combination of their responses to the narrow band stimuli (Rolls, Baylis and Hasselmo 1987). This lack of linearity of these neurons, and their responsiveness to a wide range of spatial frequencies (see also their broad critical band masking (Rolls 2008a)), indicate that in at least this part of the primate visual system recognition does not occur using Fourier analysis of the spatial frequency components of images.

The utility of this representation for memory systems in the brain is that the output of the visual system will represent an object invariantly with respect to position on the retina, size, etc, and this simplifies the functionality required of the (multiple) memory systems, which need then simply associate the object representation with reward (orbitofrontal cortex and amygdala), associate it with position in the environment (hippocampus), recognise it as familiar (perirhinal cortex), associate it with a motor response in a habit memory (basal ganglia), etc. (Rolls 2007g). The associations can be relatively simple, involving for example Hebbian associativity (see chapters throughout this book, and Appendix B).

Some neurons in the temporal cortical visual areas actually represent the absolute size of objects such as faces independently of viewing distance (Rolls and Baylis 1986). This could be called neurophysiological size constancy. The utility of this representation by a small population of neurons is that the absolute size of an object is a useful feature to use as an input to neurons that perform object recognition. Faces only come in certain sizes.

4.2.5 Combinations of features in the correct spatial configuration

Many neurons in this processing stream respond to combinations of features (including objects), but not to single features presented alone, and the features must have the correct spatial arrangement. This has been shown, for example, with faces, for which it has been shown by masking out or presenting parts of the face (for example eyes, mouth, or hair) in isolation, or by jumbling the features in faces, that some cells in the cortex in IT/STS respond only if two or more features are present, and are in the correct spatial arrangement (Perrett, Rolls and Caan 1982, Rolls, Tovee, Purcell, Stewart and Azzopardi 1994b). Fig. 4.7 shows examples of four neurons, the top one of which responds only if all the features are present, and the others of which respond not only to the full face, but also to one or more features. Corresponding evidence has been found for non-face cells. For example, Tanaka, Saito, Fukada and Moriya (1990) showed that some posterior inferior temporal cortex neurons might only respond to the combination of an edge and a small circle if they were in the correct spatial relationship to each other.

Evidence consistent with the suggestion that neurons are responding to combinations of a few variables represented at the preceding stage of cortical processing is that some neurons in V2 and V4 respond to end-stopped lines, to tongues flanked by inhibitory subregions, to combinations of lines, or to combinations of colours (see Rolls and Deco (2002), Hegde and Van Essen (2000) and Ito and Komatsu (2004)). Neurons that respond to combinations of features but not to single features indicate that the system is non-linear (Elliffe, Rolls and Stringer 2002).

The fact that some temporal cortex neurons respond only to objects or faces consisting of a set of features only if the whole combination of features is present and they are in the

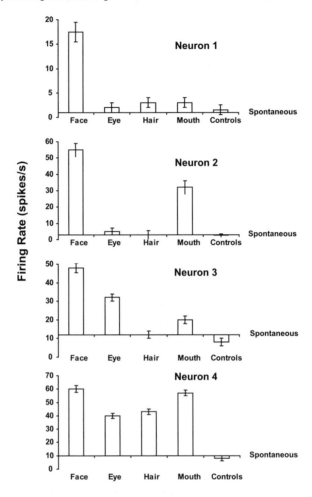

Fig. 4.7 Responses of four temporal cortex neurons to whole faces and to parts of faces. The mean firing rate ± sem are shown. The responses are shown as changes from the spontaneous firing rate of each neuron. Some neurons respond to one or several parts of faces presented alone. Other neurons (of which the top one is an example) respond only to the combination of the parts (and only if they are in the correct spatial configuration with respect to each other as shown by Rolls et al 1994b). The control stimuli were non-face objects. (After Perrett, Rolls and Caan 1982.)

correct spatial arrangement with respect to each other (not jumbled) is part of the evidence that some inferior temporal cortex neurons are tuned to respond to objects or faces.

If a task requires in addition to the normal representation of objects by the inferior temporal cortex, the ability to discriminate between stimuli composed of highly overlapping feature conjunctions in a low-dimensional feature space, then the perirhinal cortex may contribute to this type of discrimination, as described in Section 2.2.6.

4.2.6 A view-invariant representation

For recognizing and learning about objects (including faces), it is important that an output of the visual system should be not only translation- and size-invariant, but also relatively view-invariant. In an investigation of whether there are such neurons, we found that some

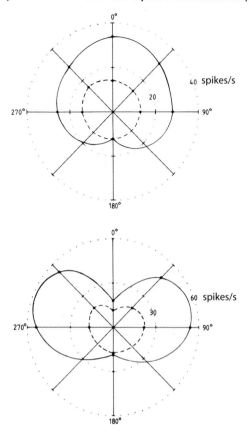

Fig. 4.8 Upper: View invariant response of an inferior temporal cortex neuron to two faces. In the polar response plot, $0°$ is the front of the face, and $90°$ the right profile. The firing rate in spikes/s is shown by the distance from the centre of the plot. The responses to two different faces are shown by the solid and dashed lines. The neuron discriminated between the faces, apart from the view of the back of the head. Lower: View dependent response of an inferior temporal cortex neuron to two faces. The neuron responded best to the left and right profiles. Some neurons respond to only one of the profiles, and this neuron had a small preference for the left profile. (After Hasselmo, Rolls, Baylis and Nalwa 1989b.)

temporal cortical neurons reliably responded differently to the faces of two different individuals independently of viewing angle (Hasselmo, Rolls, Baylis and Nalwa 1989b) (see example in Fig. 4.8 upper), although in most cases (16/18 neurons) the response was not perfectly view-independent. Mixed together in the same cortical regions there are neurons with view-dependent responses (for example Hasselmo, Rolls, Baylis and Nalwa (1989b) and Rolls and Tovee (1995b) (see example in Fig. 4.8 lower)). Such neurons might respond, for example, to a view of a profile of a monkey but not to a full-face view of the same monkey (Perrett et al. 1985b, Hasselmo et al. 1989b).

These findings of view-dependent, partially view-independent, and view-independent representations in the same cortical regions are consistent with the hypothesis discussed below that view-independent representations are being built in these regions by associating together the outputs of neurons that have different view-dependent responses to the same individual. These findings also provide evidence that one output of the visual system includes representations of what is being seen, in a view-independent way that would be useful for object recognition and for learning associations about objects; and that another output is a

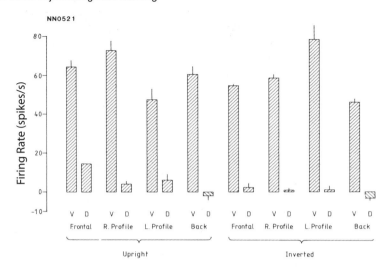

Fig. 4.9 Object-centred encoding: Neuron responding to ventral flexion (V) of the head independently of view even when the head was inverted. Ventral flexion is tilting the head from the full frontal view forwards to face down at 45 degrees. Dorsal flexion is tilting the head until it is looking 45 degrees up. The response is shown as a change in firing rate in spikes/s $\pm$ sem from the spontaneous firing rate. (After Hasselmo, Rolls, Baylis and Nalwa 1989b.)

view-based representation that would be useful in social interactions to determine whether another individual is looking at one, and for selecting details of motor responses, for which the orientation of the object with respect to the viewer is required (Rolls and Deco 2002).

Further evidence that some neurons in the temporal cortical visual areas have object-based rather than view-based responses comes from a study of a population of neurons that responds to moving faces (Hasselmo, Rolls, Baylis and Nalwa 1989b). For example, four neurons responded vigorously to a head undergoing ventral flexion, irrespective of whether the view of the head was full face, of either profile, or even of the back of the head. These different views could only be specified as equivalent in object-based coordinates. Further, the movement specificity was maintained across inversion, with neurons responding for example to ventral flexion of the head irrespective of whether the head was upright or inverted (see example in Fig. 4.9). In this procedure, retinally encoded or viewer-centered movement vectors are reversed, but the object-based description remains the same.

Also consistent with object-based encoding is the finding of a small number of neurons that respond to images of faces of a given absolute size, irrespective of the retinal image size or distance (Rolls and Baylis 1986).

Neurons with view invariant responses to objects seen naturally by macaques have also been described (Booth and Rolls 1998). The stimuli were presented for 0.5 s on a colour video monitor while the monkey performed a visual fixation task. The stimuli were images of 10 real plastic objects that had been in the monkey's cage for several weeks, to enable him to build view invariant representations of the objects. Control stimuli were views of objects that had never been seen as real objects. The neurons analyzed were in the TE cortex in and close to the ventral lip of the anterior part of the superior temporal sulcus. Many neurons were found that responded to some views of some objects. However, for a smaller number of neurons, the responses occurred only to a subset of the objects (using ensemble encoding), irrespective of the viewing angle. Moreover, the firing of a neuron on any one trial, taken at random and irrespective of the particular view of any one object, provided information about

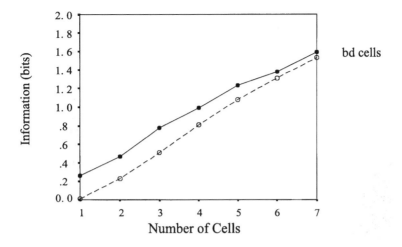

Fig. 4.10 View-independent object encoding: information in a population of different numbers of inferior temporal cortex cells available from a single trial in which one view was shown about which of 10 objects each with 4 different views in the stimulus set had been seen. The solid symbols show the information decoded with a Bayesian probability estimator algorithm, and the open symbols with dot product decoding. (After Booth and Rolls 1998.)

which object had been seen, and this information increased approximately linearly with the number of neurons in the sample (see Fig. 4.10). This is strong quantitative evidence that some neurons in the inferior temporal cortex provide an invariant representation of objects. Moreover, the results of Booth and Rolls (1998) show that the information is available in the firing rates, and has all the desirable properties of distributed representations described above, including exponentially high coding capacity, and rapid speed of readout of the information.

Further evidence consistent with these findings is that some studies have shown that the responses of some visual neurons in the inferior temporal cortex do not depend on the presence or absence of critical features for maximal activation (Perrett, Rolls and Caan 1982, Tanaka 1993, Tanaka 1996). For example, the responses of neuron 4 in Fig. 4.7 responded to several of the features in a face when these features were presented alone (Perrett, Rolls and Caan 1982). In another example, Mikami, Nakamura and Kubota (1994) showed that some TE cells respond to partial views of the same laboratory instrument(s), even when these partial views contain different features. Such functionality is important for object recognition when part of an object is occluded, by for example another object. In a different approach, Logothetis, Pauls, Bulthoff and Poggio (1994) have reported that in monkeys extensively trained (over thousands of trials) to treat different views of computer generated wire-frame 'objects' as the same, a small population of neurons in the inferior temporal cortex did respond to different views of the same wire-frame object (see also Logothetis and Sheinberg (1996)). However, extensive training is not necessary for invariant representations to be formed, and indeed no explicit training in invariant object recognition was given in the experiment by Booth and Rolls (1998), as Rolls' hypothesis (1992a) is that view invariant representations can be learned by associating together the different views of objects as they are moved and inspected naturally in a period that may be in the order of a few seconds. Evidence for this is described in Section 4.2.7.

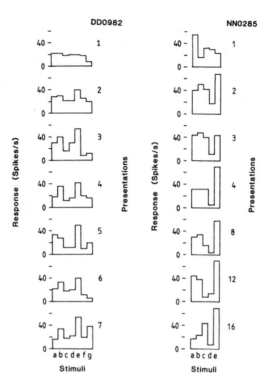

Fig. 4.11 Learning in the responses of inferior temporal cortex neurons. Results for two face-selective neurons are shown. On presentation 1 a set of 7 completely novel faces was shown when recording from neuron DD0982. The firing rates elicited on 1-sec presentations of each stimulus (a-g) are shown. After the first presentation, the set of stimuli was repeated in random sequence for a total of 7 iterations. After the first two presentations, the relative responses of the neuron to the different stimuli settled down to a fairly reliable response profile to the set of stimuli (as shown by statistical analysis). NN0285 – data from a similar experiment with another neuron, and another completely new set of face stimuli. (After Rolls, Baylis, Hasselmo and Nalwa 1989a.)

4.2.7 Learning of new representations in the temporal cortical visual areas

To investigate the idea that visual experience might guide the formation of the responsiveness of neurons so that they provide an economical and ensemble-encoded representation of items actually present in the environment, the responses of inferior temporal cortex face-selective neurons have been analyzed while a set of new faces were shown. Some of the neurons studied in this way altered the relative degree to which they responded to the different members of the set of novel faces over the first few (1–2) presentations of the set (Rolls, Baylis, Hasselmo and Nalwa 1989a) (see examples in Fig. 4.11). If in a different experiment a single novel face was introduced when the responses of a neuron to a set of familiar faces were being recorded, the responses to the set of familiar faces were not disrupted, while the responses to the novel face became stable within a few presentations. Alteration of the tuning of individual neurons in this way may result in a good discrimination over the population as a whole of the faces known to the monkey. This evidence is consistent with the categorization being performed by self-organizing competitive neuronal networks, as described in Section B.4 and elsewhere (Rolls and Treves 1998).

Objects

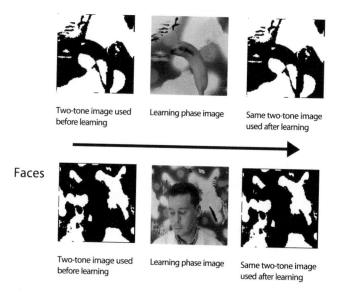

Faces

Fig. 4.12 Images of the type used to investigate rapid learning in the neurophysiological experiments of Tovee, Rolls and Ramachandran (1996) and the PET imaging study of Dolan, Fink, Rolls et al. (1997). When the black and white (two-tone) images at the left are shown, the objects or faces are not generally recognized. After the full grey scale images (middle) have been shown for a few seconds, humans and inferior temporal cortex neurons respond to the faces or objects in the black and white images (right).

Further evidence that these neurons can learn new representations very rapidly comes from an experiment in which binarized black and white (two-tone) images of faces that blended with the background were used (see Fig. 4.12, left). These did not activate face-selective neurons. Full grey-scale images of the same photographs were then shown for ten 0.5 s presentations (Fig. 4.12, middle). In a number of cases, if the neuron happened to be responsive to that face, when the binarized version of the same face was shown next (Fig. 4.12, right), the neurons responded to it (Tovee, Rolls and Ramachandran 1996). This is a direct parallel to the same phenomenon that is observed psychophysically, and provides dramatic evidence that these neurons are influenced by only a very few seconds (in this case 5 s) of experience with a visual stimulus. We have shown a neural correlate of this effect using similar stimuli and a similar paradigm in a PET (positron emission tomography) neuroimaging study in humans, with a region showing an effect of the learning found for faces in the right temporal lobe, and for objects in the left temporal lobe (Dolan, Fink, Rolls, Booth, Holmes, Frackowiak and Friston 1997).

Such rapid learning of representations of new objects appears to be a major type of learning in which the temporal cortical areas are involved. Ways in which this learning could occur are considered later in this Chapter. In addition, some of these neurons may be involved in a short term memory for whether a particular familiar visual stimulus (such as a face) has been seen recently. The evidence for this is that some of these neurons respond differently to recently seen stimuli in short term visual memory tasks (Baylis and Rolls 1987, Miller and Desimone 1994, Xiang and Brown 1998). In the inferior temporal visual cortex proper, neurons respond more to novel than to familiar stimuli, but treat the stimuli as novel if more than one other stimuli intervene between the first (novel) and second (familiar) presentations of a particular stimulus (Baylis and Rolls 1987). More ventrally, in what is in or close to the perirhinal cortex, these memory spans may hold for several intervening stimuli in the same task (Xiang and Brown 1998) (see Section 2.2.6). Some neurons in these areas respond more when a sample stimulus reappears in a delayed match to sample task with intervening stimuli (Miller and Desimone 1994), and the basis for this using a short term memory implemented in the prefrontal cortex is described in Chapter 5. Neurons in the more ventral (perirhinal) cortical area respond during the delay in a match to sample task with a delay between the sample stimulus and the to-be-matched stimulus (Miyashita 1993, Renart, Parga and Rolls 2000) (see Section 2.2.6).

4.2.8 Distributed encoding

An important question for understanding brain function is whether a particular object (or face) is represented in the brain by the firing of one or a few gnostic (or 'grandmother') cells (Barlow 1972), or whether instead the firing of a group or ensemble of cells each with somewhat different responsiveness provides the representation. Advantages of distributed codes (see Section 1.6, Appendix B, Appendix C, Rolls and Treves (1998), and Rolls and Deco (2002)) include generalization and graceful degradation (fault tolerance), and a potentially very high capacity in the number of stimuli that can be represented (that is exponential growth of capacity with the number of neurons in the representation). If the ensemble encoding is sparse, this provides a good input to an associative memory, for then large numbers of stimuli can be stored (see Appendix B of this book, Chapters 2 and 3 of Rolls and Treves (1998), and Chapter 7 of Rolls and Deco (2002)). We have shown that in the inferior temporal visual cortex and cortex in the anterior part of the superior temporal sulcus (IT/STS), responses of a group of neurons, but not of a single neuron, provide evidence on which face was shown. We showed, for example, that these neurons typically respond with a graded set of firing to different faces, with firing rates from 120 spikes/s to the most effective face, to no response at all to a number of the least effective faces (Baylis, Rolls and Leonard 1985, Rolls and Tovee 1995b, Rolls and Deco 2002). In fact, the firing rate probability distribution of a single neuron to a set of stimuli is approximately exponential (Rolls and Tovee 1995b, Treves, Panzeri, Rolls, Booth and Wakeman 1999, Rolls and Deco 2002, Baddeley, Abbott, Booth, Sengpiel, Freeman, Wakeman and Rolls 1997, Franco, Rolls, Aggelopoulos and Jerez 2007). To provide examples, Fig. 4.13 shows typical firing rate changes of a single neuron on different trials to each of several different faces. This makes it clear that from the firing rate on any one trial, information is available about which stimulus was shown, and that the firing rate is graded, with a different firing rate response of the neuron to each stimulus.

The distributed nature of the encoding typical for neurons in the inferior temporal visual cortex is illustrated in Fig. 4.14, which shows that temporal cortical neurons typically responded to several members of a set of five faces, with each neuron having a different profile of responses to each face (Baylis, Rolls and Leonard 1985). It would be difficult for most of these single cells to tell which of even five faces, let alone which of hundreds of faces, had been seen. Yet across a population of such neurons, much information about the particular face that has been seen is provided, as shown below.

The single neuron selectivity or sparseness a^s of the activity of inferior temporal cortex neurons was 0.65 over a set of 68 stimuli including 23 faces and 45 non-face natural scenes, and a measure called the response sparseness a_r^s of the representation, in which the spontaneous rate was subtracted from the firing rate to each stimulus so that the responses of the neuron were being assessed, was 0.38 across the same set of stimuli (Rolls and Tovee 1995b). [For the definition of sparseness see Section C.3.1. For binary neurons (firing for example either at a high rate or not at all), the single neuron sparseness is the proportion of stimuli that a single neuron responds to. These definitions, and what is found in cortical neuronal representations,

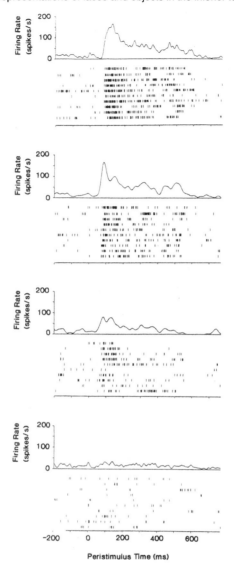

Fig. 4.13 Peristimulus time histograms and rastergrams showing the responses on different trials (originally in random order) of a face-selective neuron in the inferior temporal visual cortex to four different faces. (In the rastergrams each vertical line represents one spike from the neuron, and each row is a separate trial. Each block of the Figure is for a different face.) (From Tovee, Rolls, Treves and Bellis 1993.)

are described further in Sections 1.6, C.3.1 and C.3.2, by Rolls and Deco (2002), and by Franco, Rolls, Aggelopoulos and Jerez (2007).]

It has been possible to apply information theory to show that each neuron conveys on average approximately 0.4 bits of information about which face in a set of 20 faces has been seen (Tovee and Rolls 1995, Tovee, Rolls, Treves and Bellis 1993, Rolls, Treves, Tovee and Panzeri 1997d). If a neuron responded to only one of the faces in the set of 20, then it could convey (if noiseless) 4.6 bits of information about one of the faces (when that face was shown). If, at the other extreme, it responded to half the faces in the set, it would convey 1 bit of information about which face had been seen on any one trial. In fact, the average

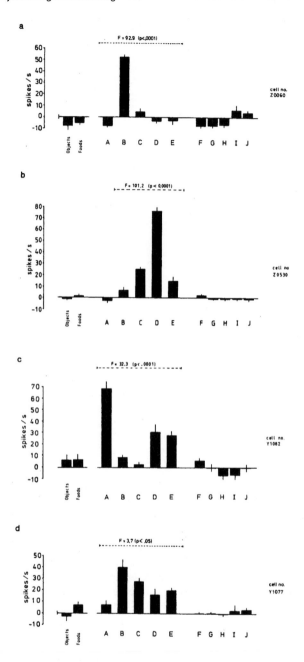

Fig. 4.14 Responses of four different temporal cortex visual neurons to a set of five faces (A–E), and, for comparison, to a wide range of non-face objects and foods. F–J are non-face stimuli. The means and standard errors of the responses computed over 8–10 trials are shown. (From Baylis, Rolls and Leonard 1985.)

maximum information about the best stimulus was 1.8 bits of information. This provides good evidence not only that the representation is distributed, but also that it is a sufficiently reliable

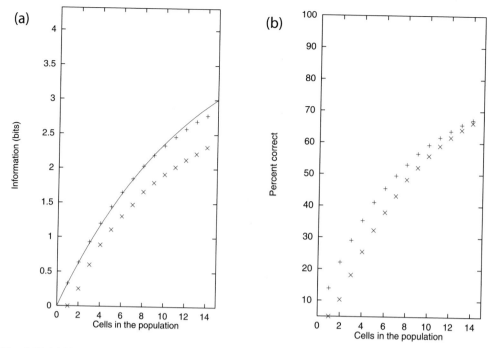

Fig. 4.15 (a) The values for the average information available in the responses of different numbers of these neurons on each trial, about which of a set of 20 face stimuli has been shown. The decoding method was Dot Product (DP, ×) or Probability Estimation (PE, +). The full line indicates the amount of information expected from populations of increasing size, when assuming random correlations within the constraint given by the ceiling (the information in the stimulus set, I = 4.32 bits). (b) The percent correct for the corresponding data to those shown in (a). The measurement period was 500 ms. (After Rolls, Treves and Tovee 1997b.)

representation that useful information can be obtained from it (see Section C.3.2).

An important result is that when the information available from a population of neurons about which of 20 faces has been seen is considered, the information increases approximately linearly as the number of cells in the population increases from 1 to 14 (Rolls, Treves and Tovee 1997b, Abbott, Rolls and Tovee 1996) (see Fig. 4.15 and Section C.3.5). Remembering that the information in bits is a logarithmic measure, this shows that the representational capacity of this population of cells increases exponentially (see Fig. 4.16). This is the case both when an optimal, probability estimation, form of decoding of the activity of the neuronal population is used, and also when the neurally plausible dot product type of decoding is used (Fig. 4.15). (The dot product decoding assumes that what reads out the information from the population activity vector is a neuron or a set of neurons that operates just by forming the dot product of the input population vector and its synaptic weight vector – see Rolls, Treves and Tovee (1997b), and Appendix B.) By simulation of further neurons and further stimuli, we have shown that the capacity grows very impressively, approximately as shown in Fig. 4.16 (Abbott, Rolls and Tovee 1996). The result has been replicated with simultaneously recorded neurons (Rolls, Franco, Aggelopoulos and Reece 2003b, Rolls, Aggelopoulos, Franco and Treves 2004) (see further Section C.3.5). This result is exactly what would be hoped for from a distributed representation. This result is not what would be expected for local encoding, for which the number of stimuli that could be encoded would increase linearly with the number of cells. (Even if the grandmother cells were noisy, adding more replicates to increase reliability

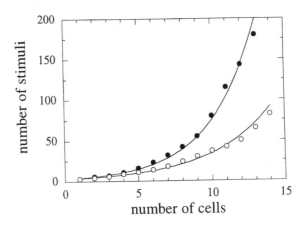

Fig. 4.16 The number of stimuli (in this case from a set of 20 faces) that are encoded in the responses of different numbers of neurons in the temporal lobe visual cortex, based on the results shown in Fig. 4.15. (After Rolls, Treves and Tovee 1997; and Abbott, Rolls and Tovee 1996.)

would not lead to more than a linear increase in the number of stimuli that can be encoded as a function of the number of cells.) Moreover, the encoding in the inferior temporal visual cortex about objects remains based on the spike count from each neuron, and not on the relative time of firing of each neuron or stimulus-dependent synchronization, when analysed with simultaneous single neuron recording (Rolls, Franco, Aggelopoulos and Reece 2003b, Rolls, Aggelopoulos, Franco and Treves 2004, Franco, Rolls, Aggelopoulos and Treves 2004) even in natural scenes when an attentional task is being performed (Aggelopoulos, Franco and Rolls 2005). Further, much of the information is available in short times of e.g. 20 or 50 ms (Tovee and Rolls 1995, Rolls, Franco, Aggelopoulos and Jerez 2006b), so that the receiving neuron does not need to integrate over a long time period to estimate a firing rate.

These findings provide very firm evidence that the encoding built at the end of the visual system is distributed, and that part of the power of this representation is that by receiving inputs from relatively small numbers of such neurons, neurons at the next stage of processing (for example in memory structures such as the hippocampus, amygdala, and orbitofrontal cortex) would obtain information about which of a very great number of objects or faces had been shown.

In this sense, the inferior temporal visual cortex provides a representation of objects and faces, in which information about which object or face is shown is made explicit in the firing of the neurons in such a way that the information can be read off very simply by memory systems such as the orbitofrontal cortex, amygdala, and perirhinal cortex / hippocampal systems. The information can be read off using dot product decoding, that is by using a synaptically weighted sum of inputs from inferior temporal cortex neurons (see further Appendix C and Section 2.2.6). Examples of some of the types of objects and faces that are encoded in this way by anterior inferior temporal cortex neurons are shown in Figs. 2.11 and C.7.

This representational capacity of neuronal populations has fundamental implications for the connectivity of the brain, for it shows that neurons need not have hundreds of thousands or millions of inputs to have available to them information about what is represented in another population of cells, but that instead the real numbers of perhaps 8,000–10,000 synapses per neuron would be adequate for them to receive considerable information from the several different sources between which this set of synapses is allocated.

It may be noted that it is unlikely that there are further processing areas beyond those described where ensemble coding changes into grandmother cell encoding. Anatomically, there does not appear to be a whole further set of visual processing areas present in the brain; and outputs from the temporal lobe visual areas such as those described are taken directly to limbic and related regions such as the amygdala and orbitofrontal cortex, and via the perirhinal and entorhinal cortex to the hippocampus (see Chapter 2, Rolls (2000a), Rolls and Deco (2002), and Rolls and Stringer (2005)). Indeed, tracing this pathway onwards, we have found a population of neurons with face-selective responses in the amygdala, and in the majority of these neurons, different responses occur to different faces, with ensemble (not local) coding still being present (Leonard, Rolls, Wilson and Baylis 1985). The amygdala, in turn, projects to another structure that may be important in other behavioural responses to faces, the ventral striatum, and comparable neurons have also been found in the ventral striatum (Williams, Rolls, Leonard and Stern 1993). We have also recorded from face-responding neurons in the part of the orbitofrontal cortex that receives from the IT/STS cortex, and have found that the encoding there is also not local but is distributed (Rolls, Critchley, Browning and Inoue 2006a).

4.2.9 Face expression, gesture, and view represented in a population of neurons in the cortex in the superior temporal sulcus

In addition to the population of neurons that code for face identity, which tend to have object-based representations and are in areas TEa and TEm on the ventral bank of the superior temporal sulcus, there is a separate population in the cortex in the superior temporal sulcus (e.g. area TPO) that conveys information about facial expression (Hasselmo, Rolls and Baylis 1989a) (see e.g. Fig. 4.17). Some of the neurons in this region tend to have view-based representations (so that information is conveyed for example about whether the face is looking at one, or is looking away), and might respond to moving faces, and to facial gesture (Hasselmo, Rolls, Baylis and Nalwa 1989b).

Thus information in cortical areas that project to the amygdala and orbitofrontal cortex is about face identity, and about face expression and gesture. Both types of information are important in social and emotional responses to other primates (including humans), which must be based on who the individual is as well as on the face expression or gesture being made. One output from the amygdala for this information is probably via the ventral striatum, for a small population of neurons has been found in the ventral striatum with responses selective for faces (Rolls and Williams 1987a, Williams, Rolls, Leonard and Stern 1993).

4.2.10 Specialized regions in the temporal cortical visual areas

As we have just seen, some neurons respond to face identity, and others to face expression (Hasselmo, Rolls and Baylis 1989a). The neurons responsive to expression were found primarily in the cortex in the superior temporal sulcus, while the neurons responsive to identity were found in the inferior temporal gyrus.

A further way in which some of these neurons in the cortex in the superior temporal sulcus may be involved in social interactions is that some of them respond to gestures, for example to a face undergoing ventral flexion (Perrett, Smith, Potter, Mistlin, Head, Milner and Jeeves 1985b, Hasselmo, Rolls, Baylis and Nalwa 1989b). The interpretation of these neurons as being useful for social interactions is that in some cases these neurons respond not only to ventral head flexion, but also to the eyes lowering and the eyelids closing (Hasselmo, Rolls, Baylis and Nalwa 1989b). These movements (turning the head away, breaking eye contact, and eyelid lowering) often occur together when a monkey is breaking social contact with another, and neurons that respond to these components could be built by associative synaptic

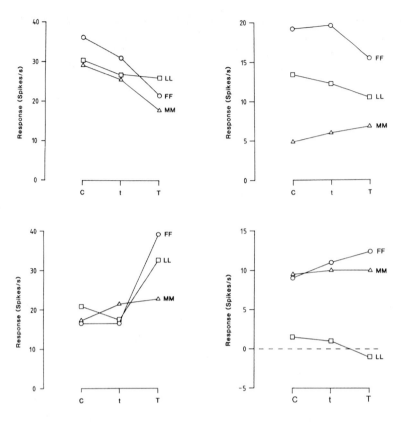

Fig. 4.17 There is a population of neurons in the cortex in the superior temporal sulcus with responses tuned to respond differently to different face expressions. The cells in the two left panels did not discriminate between individuals (faces MM, FF, and MM), but did discriminate between different expressions on the faces of those individuals (C, calm expression; t, mild threat; T, strong threat). In contrast, the cells in the right two panels responded differently to different individuals, and did not discriminate between different expressions. The neurons that discriminated between expressions were found mainly in the cortex in the fundus of the superior temporal sulcus; the neurons that discriminated between identity were in contrast found mainly in the cortex in the lateral part of the ventral lip of the superior temporal sulcus (areas TEa and TEm). (From Hasselmo, Rolls and Baylis 1989a.)

modification. It is also important when decoding facial expression to retain some information about the direction of the head relative to the observer, for this is very important in determining whether a threat is being made in your direction. The presence of view–dependent, head and body gesture (Hasselmo, Rolls, Baylis and Nalwa 1989b), and eye gaze (Perrett, Smith, Potter, Mistlin, Head, Milner and Jeeves 1985b), representations in some of these cortical regions where face expression is represented is consistent with this requirement. In contrast, the TE areas (more ventral, mainly in the macaque inferior temporal gyrus), in which neurons tuned to face identity (Hasselmo, Rolls and Baylis 1989a) and with view–independent responses (Hasselmo, Rolls, Baylis and Nalwa 1989b) are more likely to be found, may be more related to an object–based representation of identity. Of course, for appropriate social and emotional responses, both types of subsystem would be important, for it is necessary to know both the direction of a social gesture, and the identity of the individual, in order to make the correct social or emotional response.

Further evidence for specialization of function in the different architectonically defined areas of the temporal cortex (Seltzer and Pandya 1978) (see Fig. 4.3) was found by Baylis, Rolls and Leonard (1987). Areas TPO, PGa and IPa are multimodal, with neurons that respond to visual, auditory and/or somatosensory inputs. The more ventral areas in the inferior temporal gyrus (areas TE3, TE2, TE1, TEa and TEm) are primarily unimodal visual areas. Areas in the cortex in the anterior and dorsal part of the superior temporal sulcus (e.g. TPO, IPa and IPg) have neurons specialized for the analysis of moving visual stimuli. Neurons responsive primarily to faces are found more frequently in areas TPO, TEa and TEm, where they comprise approximately 20% of the visual neurons responsive to stationary stimuli, in contrast to the other temporal cortical areas in which they comprise 4–10%. The stimuli that activate other cells in these TE regions include simple visual patterns such as gratings, and combinations of simple stimulus features (Gross, Desimone, Albright and Schwartz 1985, Baylis, Rolls and Leonard 1987, Tanaka, Saito, Fukada and Moriya 1990). If patches are identified by fMRI, the proportion of neurons tuned to for example faces may be high (Tsao et al. 2006). Due to the fact that face-selective neurons have a wide distribution (Baylis, Rolls and Leonard 1987), and also occur in different patches (Tsao et al. 2006), it might be expected that only large lesions, or lesions that interrupt outputs of these visual areas, would produce readily apparent face-processing deficits.

Another specialization is that areas TEa and TEm, which receive inter alia from the cortex in the intraparietal sulcus, have neurons that are tuned to binocular disparity, so that information derived from stereopsis about the 3D structure of objects is represented in the inferior temporal cortical visual areas (Janssen, Vogels and Orban 1999, Janssen, Vogels and Orban 2000). Interestingly, these neurons respond only when the black and white regions in the two eyes are correlated (that is, when a white patch in one eye corresponds to a white patch in the other eye) (Janssen, Vogels, Liu and Orban 2003). This corresponds to what we see perceptually and consciously. In contrast, in V1, MT and MST, depth-tuned neurons can respond to anticorrelated depth images, that is where white in one eye corresponds to black in the other (Parker, Cumming and Dodd 2000, DeAngelis, Cumming and Newsome 2000, Parker 2007), and this may be suitable for eye movement control, but much less for shape and object discrimination and identification. It may be expected that other depth cues, such as perspective, surface shading, and occlusion, affect the response properties of some neurons in inferior temporal cortex visual areas. Binocular disparity, and information from these other depth cues, may be used to compute the absolute size of objects, which is represented independently of the distance of the object for a small proportion of inferior temporal cortex neurons (Rolls and Baylis 1986). Knowing the absolute size of an object is useful evidence to include in the identification of an object. Although cues from binocular disparity can thus drive some temporal cortex visual neurons, and there is a small proportion of inferior temporal neurons that respond better to real faces and objects than to 2D representations on a monitor, it is found that the majority of TE neurons respond as well or almost as well to 2D images on a video monitor as to real faces or objects (Perrett, Rolls and Caan 1982). Moreover, the tuning of inferior temporal cortex neurons to images of faces or objects on a video monitor is similar to that to real objects (personal observations of E. T. Rolls).

Neuroimaging data, while not being able to address the details of what is encoded in a brain area or of how it is encoded, does provide evidence consistent with the neurophysiology that there are different face processing systems in the human brain, and different processing subsystems for objects, moving objects, and scenes (Spiridon, Fischl and Kanwisher 2006, Grill-Spector and Malach 2004, Epstein and Kanwisher 1998). For example, Kanwisher, McDermott and Chun (1997) and Ishai, Ungerleider, Martin, Schouten and Haxby (1999) have shown activation by faces of an area in the fusiform gyrus; Hoffman and Haxby (2000) have shown that distinct areas are activated by eye gaze and face identity; Dolan, Fink,

Rolls, Booth, Holmes, Frackowiak and Friston (1997) have shown that a fusiform gyrus area becomes activated after humans learn to identify faces in complex scenes; and the amygdala (Morris, Fritch, Perrett, Rowland, Young, Calder and Dolan 1996a) and orbitofrontal cortex (Blair, Morris, Frith, Perrett and Dolan 1999) may become activated particularly by certain face expressions. Consistent with the neurophysiology described below and by Baylis, Rolls and Leonard (1987), human fMRI studies are now able to detect small patches of non-face and other types of responsiveness in areas that appeared to respond primarily to one category such as faces (Grill-Spector, Sayres and Ress 2006, Haxby 2006).

Different inferior temporal cortex neurons in macaques not only provide different types of information about different aspects of faces, as just described, but also respond differently to different *categories* of visual stimuli, with for example some neurons conveying information primarily about faces, and others about objects (Rolls and Tovee 1995b, Rolls, Treves, Tovee and Panzeri 1997d, Booth and Rolls 1998) (see Appendix C). In fact, when recording in the inferior temporal cortex, one finds small clustered groups of neurons, with neurons within a cluster responding to somewhat similar attributes of stimuli, and different clusters responding to different categories or types of visual stimuli. For example, within the set of neurons responding to moving faces, there are some neuronal clusters that respond to for example ventral and dorsal flexion of the head on the body; others that respond to axial rotation of the head; others that respond to the sight of mouth movements; and others that respond to the gaze direction in a face being viewed (Hasselmo, Rolls, Baylis and Nalwa 1989b, Perrett, Smith, Potter, Mistlin, Head, Milner and Jeeves 1985b). Within the domain of objects, some neuronal clusters respond based on the shapes of the object (e.g. responding to elongated and not round objects), others respond based on the texture of the object being viewed, and others are sensitive to what the object is doing (Hasselmo, Rolls, Baylis and Nalwa 1989b, Perrett, Smith, Mistlin, Chitty, Head, Potter, Broennimann, Milner and Jeeves 1985a). Within a cluster, each neuron is tuned differently, and may combine at least partly with information predominant in other clusters, so that at least some of the neurons in a cluster can become quite selective between different objects, with the preference for individual objects showing the usual exponential firing rate distribution (see Figs. C.4 and C.6). Using optical imaging, Tanaka and colleagues (Tanaka 1996) have seen comparable evidence for different localized clusters of neuronal activation produced by different types or categories of stimuli.

The principle that Rolls proposes underlies this local clustering is the representation of the high dimensional space of objects and their features into a two-dimensional cortical sheet using the local self-organizing mapping principles described in Section B.4.6. In this situation, these principles produce maps that have many fractures, but nevertheless include local clusters of similar neurons. Exactly this clustering can be produced in the model of visual object recognition, VisNet, described in Section 4.5 by replacing the lateral inhibition filter shown in Fig. 4.21 with a difference of Gaussians filter of the type illustrated in Fig. B.20. Such a difference of Gaussians filter would reflect the effects of short range excitatory (recurrent collateral) connections between cortical pyramidal cells, and longer range inhibition produced through inhibitory interneurons. These local clusters minimize the wiring length between neurons, if the computations involve exchange of information within neurons of a similar general type, as will usually be the case (see Section B.4.6). Minimizing wiring length is crucial in keeping brain size relatively low (see Section B.4.6). Another useful property of such self-organizing maps is that they encourage distributed representations in which semi-continuous similarity functions are mapped. This is potentially useful in building representations that then generalize usefully when new stimuli are shown between representations that are already set up continuously in the map.

Another fundamental contribution and key aspect of neocortical design facilitated by the short-range recurrent excitatory connections is that the attractors that are formed are local.

This is fundamentally important, for if the neocortex had long-range connectivity, it would tend to be able to form only as many attractor states as there are connections per neocortical neuron, which would be a severe limit on cortical memory capacity (O'Kane and Treves 1992) (see Sections 1.10.4 and B.9).

It is consistent with this general conceptual background that Krieman, Koch and Fried (2000) have described some neurons in the human temporal lobe that seem to respond to categories of object. This is consistent with the principles just described, although in humans backprojections from language or other cognitive areas concerned for example with tool use might also influence the categories represented in high order cortical areas, as described in Sections B.4.5 and 1.11, and by Farah, Meyer and McMullen (1996) and Farah (2000).

4.3 Approaches to invariant object recognition

A goal of this book is to provide some of the foundations for understanding memory systems in the brain, and how they could function at the computational and neuronal network level. This in turn is fundamental to understanding very many aspects of brain function, for the brain performs many of its functions by what are memory-related operations that involve synaptic modification (see Appendix B). Some of the ways in which the visual system may produce the distributed invariant representations of objects needed for inputs to the emotion-learning systems and other memory systems described in this book are described at the computational level in the rest of this Chapter and by Rolls and Deco (2002) and Rolls and Stringer (2006), and include a hierarchical feed-forward series of competitive networks using convergence from stage to stage; and the use of a modified Hebb synaptic learning rule that incorporates a short-term memory trace of previous neuronal activity to help learn the invariant properties of objects from the temporo-spatial statistics produced by the normal viewing of objects (Rolls and Deco 2002, Wallis and Rolls 1997, Rolls and Milward 2000, Stringer and Rolls 2000, Rolls and Stringer 2001a, Elliffe, Rolls and Stringer 2002, Stringer and Rolls 2002, Deco and Rolls 2004, Rolls and Stringer 2006).

We start by emphasizing that generalization to different positions, sizes, views etc. of an object is not a simple property of one-layer neural networks. Although neural networks do generalize well, the type of generalization they show naturally is to vectors which have a high dot product or correlation with what they have already learned. To make this clear, Fig. 4.18 is a reminder that the activation h_i of each neuron is computed as

$$h_i = \sum_j x_j w_{ij} \qquad (4.1)$$

where the sum is over the C input axons, indexed by j. Now consider translation (or shift) of the input pattern vector by one position. The dot product will now drop to a low level, and the neuron will not respond, even though it is the same pattern, just shifted by one location. This makes the point that special processes are needed to compute invariant representations. Network approaches to such invariant pattern recognition are described in this chapter, and the nature of the problem to be solved is described further in Section B.4.7 and Fig. B.23 on page 587. Once an invariant representation has been computed by a sensory system, it is in a form that is suitable for presentation to a pattern association or autoassociation neural network (see Appendix B).

A number of different computational approaches that have been taken both in artificial vision systems and as suggestions for how the brain performs invariant object recognition are described in this section. This places in context the approach that appears to be taken in the brain and that forms the basis for VisNet described in Section 4.5.

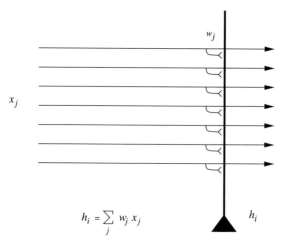

Fig. 4.18 A neuron that computes a dot product of the input pattern with its synaptic weight vector generalizes well to other patterns based on their similarity measured in terms of dot product or correlation, but shows no translation (or size, etc.) invariance.

4.3.1 Feature spaces

One very simple possibility for performing object classification is based on feature spaces, which amount to lists of (the extent to which) different features are present in a particular object. The features might consist of textures, colours, areas, ratios of length to width, etc. The spatial arrangement of the features is not taken into account. If n different properties are used to characterize an object, each viewed object is represented by a set of n real numbers. It then becomes possible to represent an object by a point R^n in an n-dimensional space (where R is the resolution of the real numbers used). Such schemes have been investigated (Tou and Gonzalez 1974, Gibson 1950, Gibson 1979, Bolles and Cain 1982, Mundy and Zisserman 1992, Selfridge 1959, Mel 1997), but, because the relative positions of the different parts are not implemented in the object recognition scheme, are not sensitive to spatial jumbling of the features. For example, if the features consisted of nose, mouth, and eyes, such a system would respond to faces with jumbled arrangements of the eyes, nose, and mouth, which does not match human vision, nor the responses of macaque inferior temporal cortex neurons, which are sensitive to the spatial arrangement of the features in a face (Rolls, Tovee, Purcell, Stewart and Azzopardi 1994b). Similarly, such an object recognition system might not distinguish a normal car from a car with the back wheels removed and placed on the roof. Such systems do not therefore perform shape recognition (where shape implies something about the spatial arrangement of features within an object, see further Ullman (1996)), and something more is needed, and is implemented in the primate visual system. However, I note that the features that are present in objects, e.g. a furry texture, are useful to incorporate in object recognition systems, and the brain may well use, and the model VisNet in principle can use, evidence from which features are present in an object as part of the evidence for identification of a particular object. I note that the features might consist also of for example the pattern of movement that is characteristic of a particular object (such as a buzzing fly), and might use this as part of the input to final object identification.

The capacity to use shape in invariant object recognition is fundamental to primate vision, but may not be used or fully implemented on the visual systems of some other animals with less developed visual systems. For example, pigeons may correctly identify pictures containing people, a particular person, trees, pigeons etc, but may fail to distinguish a figure from a

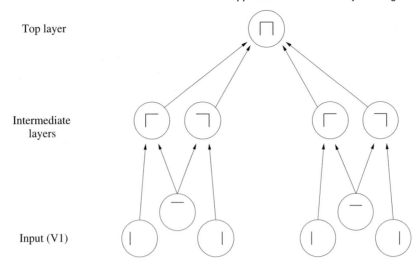

Top layer

Intermediate
layers

Input (V1)

Fig. 4.20 The feature hierarchy approach to object recognition. The inputs may be neurons tuned to oriented straight line segments. In early intermediate layers neurons respond to a combination of these inputs in the correct spatial position with respect to each other. In further intermediate layers, of which there may be several, neurons respond with some invariance to the feature combinations represented early, and form higher order feature combinations. Finally, in the top layer, neurons respond to combinations of what is represented in the preceding intermediate layer, and thus provide evidence about objects in a position (and scale and even view) invariant way. Convergence through the network is designed to provide top layer neurons with information from across the entire input retina, as part of the solution to translation invariance, and other types of invariance are treated similarly.

the responses of primary visual cortex (V1) neurons, and then builds in repeated hierarchical layers features based on what is represented in previous layers. A feature may thus be defined as a combination of what is represented in the previous layer. For example, after V1, features might consist of combinations of straight lines, which might represent longer curved lines (Zucker, Dobbins and Iverson 1989), or terminated lines (in fact represented in V1 as end-stopped cells), corners, 'T' junctions which are characteristic of obscuring edges, and (at least in humans) the arrow and 'Y' vertices which are characteristic properties of man-made environments. Evidence that such feature combination neurons are present in V2 is that some neurons respond to combinations of line elements that join at different angles (Hegde and Van Essen 2000, Ito and Komatsu 2004). (An example of this might be a neuron responding to a 'V' shape at a particular orientation.) As one ascends the hierarchy, neurons might respond to more complex trigger features (such as two parts of a complex figure in the correct spatial arrangement with respect to each other, as shown by Tanaka (1996) for V4 and posterior inferior temporal cortex neurons). Further on, neurons might respond to combinations of several such intermediate-level feature combination neurons, and thus come to respond systematically differently to different objects, and thus to convey information about which object is present. This approach received neurophysiological support early on from the results of Hubel and Wiesel (1962) and Hubel and Wiesel (1968) in the cat and monkey, and much of the data described in Chapter 5 of Rolls and Deco (2002) are consistent with this scheme.

A number of problems need to be solved for such feature hierarchy visual systems to provide a useful model of object recognition in the primate visual system.

First, some way needs to be found to keep the number of feature combination neurons realistic at each stage, without undergoing a combinatorial explosion. If a separate feature combination neuron was needed to code for every possible combination of n types of feature each with a resolution of 2 levels (binary encoding) in the preceding stage, then 2^n neurons would be needed. The suggestion that is made in Section 4.4 is that by forming neurons that respond to low-order combinations of features (neurons that respond to just say 2–4 features from the preceding stage), the number of actual feature analysing neurons can be kept within reasonable numbers. By reasonable we mean the number of neurons actually found at any one stage of the visual system, which, for V4 might be in the order of 60×10^6 neurons (assuming a volume for macaque V4 of approximately 2,000 mm^3, and a cell density of 20,000–40,000 neurons per mm^3, see Table 1.1). This is certainly a large number; but the fact that a large number of neurons is present at each stage of the primate visual system is in fact consistent with the hypothesis that feature combination neurons are part of the way in which the brain solves object recognition. A factor which also helps to keep the number of neurons under control is the statistics of the visual world, which contain great redundancies. The world is not random, and indeed the statistics of natural images are such that many regularities are present (Field 1994), and not every possible combination of pixels on the retina needs to be separately encoded. A third factor which helps to keep the number of connections required onto each neuron under control is that in a multilayer hierarchy each neuron can be set up to receive connections from only a small region of the preceding layer. Thus an individual neuron does not need to have connections from all the neurons in the preceding layer. Over multiple layers, the required convergence can be produced so that the same neurons in the top layer can be activated by an image of an effective object anywhere on the retina (see Fig. 4.2).

A second problem of feature hierarchy approaches is how to map all the different possible images of an individual object through to the same set of neurons in the top layer by modifying the synaptic connections (see Fig. 4.2). The solution discussed in Sections 4.4, 4.5.1.1 and 4.5.4 is the use of a synaptic modification rule with a short-term memory trace of the previous activity of the neuron, to enable it to learn to respond to the now transformed version of what was seen very recently, which, given the statistics of looking at the visual world, will probably be an input from the same object.

A third problem of feature hierarchy approaches is how they can learn in just a few seconds of inspection of an object to recognize it in different transforms, for example in different positions on the retina in which it may never have been presented during training. A solution to this problem is provided in Section 4.5.5, in which it is shown that this can be a natural property of feature hierarchy object recognition systems, if they are trained first for all locations on the intermediate level feature combinations of which new objects will simply be a new combination, and therefore requiring learning only in the upper layers of the hierarchy.

A fourth potential problem of feature hierarchy systems is that when solving translation invariance they need to respond to the same local spatial arrangement of features (which are needed to specify the object), but to ignore the global position of the whole object. It is shown in Section 4.5.5 that feature hierarchy systems can solve this problem by forming feature combination neurons at an early stage of processing (e.g. V1 or V2 in the brain) that respond with high spatial precision to the local arrangement of features. Such neurons would respond differently for example to L, +, and T if they receive inputs from two line-responding neurons. It is shown in Section 4.5.5 that at later layers of the hierarchy, where some of the intermediate level feature combination neurons are starting to show translation invariance, then correct object recognition may still occur because only one object contains just those sets of intermediate level neurons in which the spatial representation of the features is inherent in the encoding.

The type of representation developed in a hierarchical object recognition system, in the brain, and by VisNet as described in the rest of this chapter would be suitable for recognition of an object, and for linking associative memories to objects, but would be less good for making actions in 3D space to particular parts of, or inside, objects, as the 3D coordinates of each part of the object would not be explicitly available. It is therefore proposed that visual fixation is used to locate in foveal vision part of an object to which movements must be made, and that local disparity and other measurements of depth (made explicit in the dorsal visual system) then provide sufficient information for the motor system to make actions relative to the small part of space in which a local, view-dependent, representation of depth would be provided (cf. Ballard (1990)).

One advantage of feature hierarchy systems is that they can operate fast (see Sections B.4 and B.6.6).

A second advantage is that the feature analyzers can be built out of the rather simple competitive networks described in Section B.4 which use a local learning rule, and have no external teacher, so that they are rather biologically plausible. Another advantage is that, once trained on subset features common to most objects, the system can then learn new objects quickly.

A related third advantage is that, if implemented with competitive nets as in the case of VisNet (see Section 4.5), then neurons are allocated by self-organization to represent just the features present in the natural statistics of real images (cf. Field (1994)), and not every possible feature that could be constructed by random combinations of pixels on the retina.

A related fourth advantage of feature hierarchy networks is that because they can utilize competitive networks, they can still produce the best guess at what is in the image under non-ideal conditions, when only parts of objects are visible because for example of occlusion by other objects, etc. The reasons for this are that competitive networks assess the evidence for the presence of certain 'features' to which they are tuned using a dot product operation on their inputs, so that they are inherently tolerant of missing input evidence; and reach a state that reflects the best hypothesis or hypotheses (with soft competition) given the whole set of inputs, because there are competitive interactions between the different neurons (see Section B.4).

A fifth advantage of a feature hierarchy system is that, as shown in Section 4.5.6, the system does not need to perform segmentation into objects as part of pre-processing, nor does it need to be able to identify parts of an object, and can also operate in cluttered scenes in which the object may be partially obscured. The reason for this is that once trained on objects, the system then operates somewhat like an associative memory, mapping the image properties forward onto whatever it has learned about before, and then by competition selecting just the most likely output to be activated. Indeed, the feature hierarchy approach provides a mechanism by which processing at the object recognition level could feed back using backprojections to early cortical areas to provide top-down guidance to assist segmentation. Although backprojections are not built into VisNet2 (Rolls and Milward 2000), they have been added when attentional top-down processing must be incorporated (Deco and Rolls 2004), are present in the brain, and are incorporated into the models described in Chapter 6.

A sixth advantage of feature hierarchy systems is that they can naturally utilize features in the images of objects which are not strictly part of a shape description scheme, such as the fact that different objects have different textures, colours etc. Feature hierarchy systems, because they utilize whatever is represented at earlier stages in forming feature combination neurons at the next stage, naturally incorporate such 'feature list' evidence into their analysis, and have the advantages of that approach (see Section 4.3.1 and also Mel (1997)). Indeed, the feature space approach can utilize a hybrid representation, some of whose dimensions may be discrete and defined in structural terms, while other dimensions may be continuous and defined in terms of metric details, and others may be concerned with non-shape properties such as texture and colour (cf. Edelman (1999)).

A seventh advantage of feature hierarchy systems is that they do not need to utilize 'on the fly' or run-time arbitrary binding of features. Instead, the spatial syntax is effectively hardwired into the system when it is trained, in that the feature combination neurons have learned to respond to their set of features when they are in a given spatial arrangement on the retina.

An eighth advantage of feature hierarchy systems is that they can self-organize (given the right functional architecture, trace synaptic learning rule, and the temporal statistics of the normal visual input from the world), with no need for an external teacher to specify that the neurons must learn to respond to objects. The correct, object, representation self-organizes itself given rather economically specified genetic rules for building the network (cf. Rolls and Stringer (2000)).

Ninth, it is also noted that hierarchical visual systems may recognize 3D objects based on a limited set of 2D views of objects, and that the same architectural rules just stated and implemented in VisNet will correctly associate together the different views of an object. It is part of the concept (see below), and consistent with neurophysiological data (Tanaka 1996), that the neurons in the upper layers will generalize correctly within a view (see Section 4.5.7).

After the immediately following description of early models of a feature hierarchy approach implemented in the Cognitron and Neocognitron, we turn for the remainder of this chapter to analyses of how a feature hierarchy approach to invariant visual object recognition might be implemented in the brain, and how key computational issues could be solved by such a system. The analyses are developed and tested with a model, VisNet, which will shortly be described. Much of the data we have on the operation of the high order visual cortical areas (see Section 4.2, Rolls and Deco (2002) and Rolls (2007i)) suggest that they implement a feature hierarchy approach to visual object recognition, as is made evident in the remainder of this chapter.

4.3.5.1 The Cognitron and Neocognitron

An early computational model of a hierarchical feature-based approach to object recognition, joining other early discussions of this approach (Selfridge 1959, Sutherland 1968, Barlow 1972, Milner 1974), was proposed by Fukushima (1975, 1980, 1989, 1989, 1991). His model used two types of cell within each layer to approach the problem of invariant representations. In each layer, a set of 'simple cells', with defined position, orientation, etc. sensitivity for the stimuli to which they responded, was followed by a set of 'complex cells', which generalized a little over position, orientation, etc. This simple cell – complex cell pairing within each layer provided some invariance. When a neuron in the network using competitive learning with its stimulus set, which was typically letters on a 16×16 pixel array, learned that a particular feature combination had occurred, that type of feature analyzer was replicated in a non-local manner throughout the layer, to provide further translation invariance. Invariant representations were thus learned in a different way from VisNet. Up to eight layers were used. The network could learn to differentiate letters, even with some translation, scaling, or distortion. Although internally it is organized and learns very differently to VisNet, it is an independent example of the fact that useful invariant pattern recognition can be performed by multilayer hierarchical networks. A major biological implausibility of the system is that once one neuron within a layer learned, other similar neurons were set up throughout the layer by a non-local process. A second biological limitation was that no learning rule or self-organizing process was specified as to how the complex cells can provide translation invariant representations of simple cell responses – this was simply handwired. Solutions to both these issues are provided by VisNet.

4.4 Hypotheses about the computational mechanisms in the visual cortex for object recognition

The neurophysiological findings described in Section 4.2, and wider considerations on the possible computational properties of the cerebral cortex (Rolls 1989b, Rolls 1989f, Rolls 1992a, Rolls 1994a, Rolls 1995b, Rolls 1997c, Rolls 2000a, Rolls and Treves 1998, Rolls and Deco 2002), lead to the following outline working hypotheses on object recognition by visual cortical mechanisms (see Rolls (1992a)). The principles underlying the processing of faces and other objects may be similar, but more neurons may become allocated to represent different aspects of faces because of the need to recognize the faces of many different individuals, that is to identify many individuals within the category faces.

Cortical visual processing for object recognition is considered to be organized as a set of hierarchically connected cortical regions consisting at least of V1, V2, V4, posterior inferior temporal cortex (TEO), inferior temporal cortex (e.g. TE3, TEa and TEm), and anterior temporal cortical areas (e.g. TE2 and TE1). (This stream of processing has many connections with a set of cortical areas in the anterior part of the superior temporal sulcus, including area TPO.) There is convergence from each small part of a region to the succeeding region (or layer in the hierarchy) in such a way that the receptive field sizes of neurons (e.g. 1 degree near the fovea in V1) become larger by a factor of approximately 2.5 with each succeeding stage (and the typical parafoveal receptive field sizes found would not be inconsistent with the calculated approximations of e.g. 8 degrees in V4, 20 degrees in TEO, and 50 degrees in the inferior temporal cortex (Boussaoud, Desimone and Ungerleider 1991)) (see Fig. 4.2 on page 264). Such zones of convergence would overlap continuously with each other (see Fig. 4.2). This connectivity would be part of the architecture by which translation invariant representations are computed.

Each layer is considered to act partly as a set of local self-organizing competitive neuronal networks with overlapping inputs. (The region within which competition would be implemented would depend on the spatial properties of inhibitory interneurons, and might operate over distances of 1–2 mm in the cortex.) These competitive nets operate by a single set of forward inputs leading to (typically non-linear, e.g. sigmoid) activation of output neurons; of competition between the output neurons mediated by a set of feedback inhibitory interneurons which receive from many of the principal (in the cortex, pyramidal) cells in the net and project back (via inhibitory interneurons) to many of the principal cells and serve to decrease the firing rates of the less active neurons relative to the rates of the more active neurons; and then of synaptic modification by a modified Hebb rule, such that synapses to strongly activated output neurons from active input axons strengthen, and from inactive input axons weaken (see Section B.4). A biologically plausible form of this learning rule that operates well in such networks is

$$\delta w_{ij} = \alpha y_i (x_j - w_{ij}) \tag{4.2}$$

where α is a learning rate constant, and x_j and w_{ij} are in appropriate units (see Section B.4). Such competitive networks operate to detect correlations between the activity of the input neurons, and to allocate output neurons to respond to each cluster of such correlated inputs. These networks thus act as categorizers. In relation to visual information processing, they would remove redundancy from the input representation, and would develop low entropy representations of the information (cf. Barlow (1985), Barlow, Kaushal and Mitchison (1989)). Such competitive nets are biologically plausible, in that they utilize Hebb-modifiable forward excitatory connections, with competitive inhibition mediated by cortical inhibitory neurons. The competitive scheme I suggest would not result in the formation of 'winner-take-all' or 'grandmother' cells, but would instead result in a small ensemble of active neurons representing each input (Rolls 1989b, Rolls 1989f, Rolls and Treves 1998) (see Section B.4). The scheme has the advantages that the output neurons learn better to distribute themselves between the input patterns (cf. Bennett (1990)), and that the sparse representations formed have utility in maximizing the number of memories that can be stored when, towards the end of the visual system, the visual representation of objects is interfaced to associative memory (Rolls 1989b, Rolls 1989f, Rolls and Treves 1998)[12].

Translation invariance would be computed in such a system by utilizing competitive learning to detect regularities in inputs when real objects are translated in the physical world. The hypothesis is that because objects have continuous properties in space and time in the world, an object at one place on the retina might activate feature analyzers at the next stage of cortical processing, and when the object was translated to a nearby position, because this would occur in a short period (e.g. 0.5 s), the membrane of the postsynaptic neuron would still be in its 'Hebb-modifiable' state (caused for example by calcium entry as a result of the voltage-dependent activation of NMDA receptors), and the presynaptic afferents activated with the object in its new position would thus become strengthened on the still-activated postsynaptic neuron. It is suggested that the short temporal window (e.g. 0.5 s) of Hebb-modifiability helps neurons to learn the statistics of objects moving in the physical world, and at the same time to form different representations of different feature combinations or objects, as these are physically discontinuous and present less regular correlations to the visual system. Földiák (1991) has proposed computing an average activation of the postsynaptic neuron to assist with the same problem. One idea here is that the temporal properties of the biologically implemented learning mechanism are such that it is well suited to detecting the relevant continuities in the world of real objects. Another suggestion is that a memory trace for what has been seen in the last 300 ms appears to be implemented by a mechanism as simple as continued firing of inferior temporal neurons after the stimulus has disappeared, as has been found in masking experiments (Rolls and Tovee 1994, Rolls, Tovee, Purcell, Stewart and Azzopardi 1994b, Rolls, Tovee and Panzeri 1999b, Rolls 2003).

I also suggest that other invariances, for example size, spatial frequency, and rotation invariance, could be learned by a comparable process. (Early processing in V1 which enables different neurons to represent inputs at different spatial scales would allow combinations of the outputs of such neurons to be formed at later stages. Scale invariance would then result from detecting at a later stage which neurons are almost conjunctively active as the size of an object alters.) It is suggested that this process takes place at each stage of the multiple-layer cortical processing hierarchy, so that invariances are learned first over small regions of space, and then over successively larger regions. This limits the size of the connection space within which correlations must be sought.

Increasing complexity of representations could also be built in such a multiple layer hierarchy by similar mechanisms. At each stage or layer the self-organizing competitive nets would result in combinations of inputs becoming the effective stimuli for neurons. In order to avoid the combinatorial explosion, it is proposed, following Feldman (1985), that low-order

---

[12] In that each neuron has graded responses centred about an optimal input, the proposal has some of the advantages with respect to hypersurface reconstruction described by Poggio and Girosi (1990a). However, the system I propose learns differently, in that instead of using perhaps non-biologically plausible algorithms to optimally locate the centres of the receptive fields of the neurons, the neurons use graded competition to spread themselves throughout the input space, depending on the statistics of the inputs received, and perhaps with some guidance from backprojections (see below). In addition, the competitive nets I propose use as a distance function the dot product between the input vector to a neuron and its synaptic weight vector, whereas radial basis function networks use a Gaussian measure of distance (see Section B.4.8). Both systems benefit from the finite width of the response region of each neuron which tapers from a maximum, and is important for enabling the system to generalize smoothly from the examples with which it has learned (cf. Poggio and Girosi (1990b), Poggio and Girosi (1990a)), to help the system to respond for example with the correct invariances as described below.

combinations of inputs would be what is learned by each neuron. (Each input would not be represented by activity in a single input axon, but instead by activity in a set of active input axons.) Evidence consistent with this suggestion that neurons are responding to combinations of a few variables represented at the preceding stage of cortical processing is that some neurons in V1 respond to combinations of bars or edges (see Section 2.5 of Rolls and Deco (2002); Sillito, Grieve, Jones, Cudeiro and Davis (1995); and Shevelev, Novikova, Lazareva, Tikhomirov and Sharaev (1995)); V2 and V4 respond to end-stopped lines, to angles formed by a combination of lines, to tongues flanked by inhibitory subregions, or to combinations of colours (see Hegde and Van Essen (2000), Ito and Komatsu (2004) and Chapter 3 of Rolls and Deco (2002)); in posterior inferior temporal cortex to stimuli which may require two or more simple features to be present (Tanaka, Saito, Fukada and Moriya 1990); and in the temporal cortical face processing areas to images that require the presence of several features in a face (such as eyes, hair, and mouth) in order to respond (Perrett, Rolls and Caan 1982, Yamane, Kaji and Kawano 1988) (see Chapter 5 of Rolls and Deco (2002), Rolls (2007i), and Fig. 4.7). (Precursor cells to face-responsive neurons might, it is suggested, respond to combinations of the outputs of the neurons in V1 that are activated by faces, and might be found in areas such as V4.) It is an important part of this suggestion that some local spatial information would be inherent in the features which were being combined. For example, cells might not respond to the combination of an edge and a small circle unless they were in the correct spatial relation to each other. (This is in fact consistent with the data of Tanaka, Saito, Fukada and Moriya (1990), and with our data on face neurons, in that some faces neurons require the face features to be in the correct spatial configuration, and not jumbled, Rolls, Tovee, Purcell, Stewart and Azzopardi (1994b).) The local spatial information in the features being combined would ensure that the representation at the next level would contain some information about the (local) arrangement of features. Further low-order combinations of such neurons at the next stage would include sufficient local spatial information so that an arbitrary spatial arrangement of the same features would not activate the same neuron, and this is the proposed, and limited, solution which this mechanism would provide for the feature binding problem (Elliffe, Rolls and Stringer 2002) (cf. Malsburg (1990)). By this stage of processing a view-dependent representation of objects suitable for view-dependent processes such as behavioural responses to face expression and gesture would be available.

It is suggested that view-independent representations could be formed by the same type of computation, operating to combine a limited set of views of objects. The plausibility of providing view-independent recognition of objects by combining a set of different views of objects has been proposed by a number of investigators (Koenderink and Van Doorn 1979, Poggio and Edelman 1990, Logothetis, Pauls, Bulthoff and Poggio 1994, Ullman 1996). Consistent with the suggestion that the view-independent representations are formed by combining view-dependent representations in the primate visual system, is the fact that in the temporal cortical areas, neurons with view-independent representations of faces are present in the same cortical areas as neurons with view-dependent representations (from which the view-independent neurons could receive inputs) (Hasselmo, Rolls, Baylis and Nalwa 1989b, Perrett, Smith, Potter, Mistlin, Head, Milner and Jeeves 1985b, Booth and Rolls 1998). This solution to 'object-based' representations is very different from that traditionally proposed for artificial vision systems, in which the coordinates in 3D space of objects are stored in a database, and general-purpose algorithms operate on these to perform transforms such as translation, rotation, and scale change in 3D space (e.g. Marr (1982)). In the present, much more limited but more biologically plausible scheme, the representation would be suitable for recognition of an object, and for linking associative memories to objects, but would be less good for making actions in 3D space to particular parts of, or inside, objects, as the 3D coordinates of each part of the object would not be explicitly available. It is therefore proposed that visual fixation is used to locate in foveal vision part of an object to which movements must be made, and that local disparity and other measurements of depth then provide sufficient information for the motor system to make actions relative to the small part of space in which a local, view-dependent, representation of depth would be provided (cf. Ballard (1990)).

The computational processes proposed above operate by an unsupervised learning mechanism, which utilizes statistical regularities in the physical environment to enable representations to be built. In some cases it may be advantageous to utilize some form of mild teaching input to the visual system, to enable it to learn for example that rather similar visual inputs have very different consequences in the world, so that different representations of them should be built. In other cases, it might be helpful to bring representations together, if they have identical consequences, in order to use storage capacity efficiently. It is proposed elsewhere (Rolls 1989b, Rolls 1989f, Rolls and Treves 1998) (see Section 1.11) that the backprojections from each adjacent cortical region in the hierarchy (and from the amygdala and hippocampus to higher regions of the visual system) play such a role by providing guidance to the competitive networks suggested above to be important in each cortical area. This guidance, and also the capability for recall, are it is suggested implemented by Hebb-modifiable connections from the backprojecting neurons to the principal (pyramidal) neurons of the competitive networks in the preceding stages (Rolls 1989b, Rolls 1989f, Rolls and Treves 1998) (see Section B.4).

The computational processes outlined above use sparse distributed coding with relatively finely tuned neurons with a graded response region centred about an optimal response achieved when the input stimulus matches the synaptic weight vector on a neuron. The distributed nature of the coding but with fine tuning would help to limit the combinatorial explosion, to keep the number of neurons within the biological range. The graded response region would be crucial in enabling the system to generalize correctly to solve for example the invariances. However, such a system would need many neurons, each with considerable learning capacity, to solve visual perception in this way. This is fully consistent with the large number of neurons in the visual system, and with the large number of, probably modifiable, synapses on each neuron (e.g. 5,000). Further, the fact that many neurons are tuned in different ways to faces is consistent with the fact that in such a computational system, many neurons would need to be sensitive (in different ways) to faces, in order to allow recognition of many individual faces when all share a number of common properties.

4.5 The feature hierarchy approach to invariant object recognition: computational issues

The feature hierarchy approach to invariant object recognition was introduced in Section 4.3.5, and advantages and disadvantages of it were discussed. Hypotheses about how object recognition could be implemented in the brain which are consistent with much of the neurophysiology discussed in Section 4.2 and by Rolls and Deco (2002) and Rolls (2007i) were set out in Section 4.4. These hypotheses effectively incorporate a feature hierarchy system while encompassing much of the neurophysiological evidence. In this Section (4.5), we consider the computational issues that arise in such feature hierarchy systems, and in the brain systems that implement visual object recognition. The issues are considered with the help of a particular model, VisNet, which requires precise specification of the hypotheses, and at the same time enables them to be explored and tested numerically and quantitatively. However, we emphasize that the issues to be covered in Section 4.5 are key and major computational issues for architectures of this feature hierarchical type (Rolls and Stringer 2006), and are very relevant to understanding how invariant object recognition is implemented in the brain.

VisNet is a model of invariant object recognition based on Rolls' (1992a) hypotheses. It is a computer simulation that allows hypotheses to be tested and developed about how multilayer hierarchical networks of the type believed to be implemented in the visual cortical pathways operate. The architecture captures a number of aspects of the architecture of the visual cortical pathways, and is described next. The model of course, as with all models, requires precise specification of what is to be implemented, and at the same time involves specified simplifications of the real architecture, as investigations of the fundamental aspects of the information processing being performed are more tractable in a simplified and at the same time quantitatively specified model. First the architecture of the model is described, and this is followed by descriptions of key issues in such multilayer feature hierarchical models, such as the issue of feature binding, the optimal form of training rule for the whole system to self-organize, the operation of the network in natural environments and when objects are partly occluded, how outputs about individual objects can be read out from the network, and the capacity of the system.

4.5.1   The architecture of VisNet

Fundamental elements of Rolls' (1992a) theory for how cortical networks might implement invariant object recognition are described in Section 4.4. They provide the basis for the design of VisNet, and can be summarized as:

- A series of competitive networks, organized in hierarchical layers, exhibiting mutual inhibition over a short range within each layer. These networks allow combinations of features or inputs occurring in a given spatial arrangement to be learned by neurons, ensuring that higher order spatial properties of the input stimuli are represented in the network.
- A convergent series of connections from a localized population of cells in preceding layers to each cell of the following layer, thus allowing the receptive field size of cells to increase through the visual processing areas or layers.
- A modified Hebb-like learning rule incorporating a temporal trace of each cell's previous activity, which, it is suggested, will enable the neurons to learn transform invariances.

The first two elements of Rolls' theory are used to constrain the general architecture of a network model, VisNet, of the processes just described that is intended to learn invariant representations of objects. The simulation results described in this chapter using VisNet show that invariant representations can be learned by the architecture. It is moreover shown that successful learning depends crucially on the use of the modified Hebb rule. The general architecture simulated in VisNet, and the way in which it allows natural images to be used as stimuli, has been chosen to enable some comparisons of neuronal responses in the network and in the brain to similar stimuli to be made.

4.5.1.1   The trace rule

The learning rule implemented in the VisNet simulations utilizes the spatio-temporal constraints placed upon the behaviour of 'real-world' objects to learn about natural object transformations. By presenting consistent sequences of transforming objects the cells in the network can learn to respond to the same object through all of its naturally transformed states, as described by Földiák (1991), Rolls (1992a), Wallis, Rolls and Foldiak (1993), and Wallis and Rolls (1997). The learning rule incorporates a decaying trace of previous cell activity and is henceforth referred to simply as the 'trace' learning rule. The learning paradigm we describe here is intended in principle to enable learning of any of the transforms tolerated by inferior temporal cortex neurons, including position, size, view, lighting, and spatial frequency (Rolls 1992a, Rolls 1994a, Rolls 1995b, Rolls 1997c, Rolls 2000a, Rolls and Deco 2002, Rolls 2007i, Rolls 2007f, Rolls 2008a).

To clarify the reasoning behind this point, consider the situation in which a single neuron is strongly activated by a stimulus forming part of a real world object. The trace of this neuron's activation will then gradually decay over a time period in the order of 0.5 s. If, during this limited time window, the net is presented with a transformed version of the original stimulus then not only will the initially active afferent synapses modify onto the neuron, but so also will the synapses activated by the transformed version of this stimulus. In this way the cell will learn to respond to either appearance of the original stimulus. Making such associations works in practice because it is very likely that within short time periods different aspects of the same object will be being inspected. The cell will not, however, tend to make spurious links across stimuli that are part of different objects because of the unlikelihood in the real world of one object consistently following another.

Various biological bases for this temporal trace have been advanced[13]:

- The persistent firing of neurons for as long as 100–400 ms observed after presentations of stimuli for 16 ms (Rolls and Tovee 1994) could provide a time window within which to associate subsequent images. Maintained activity may potentially be implemented by recurrent connections between as well as within cortical areas (Rolls and Treves 1998, Rolls and Deco 2002) (see Chapter 5)[14].

- The binding period of glutamate in the NMDA channels, which may last for 100 ms or more, may implement a trace rule by producing a narrow time window over which the *average* activity at each presynaptic site affects learning (Rolls 1992a, Rhodes 1992, Földiák 1992, Spruston, Jonas and Sakmann 1995, Hestrin, Sah and Nicoll 1990).

- Chemicals such as nitric oxide may be released during high neural activity and gradually decay in concentration over a short time window during which learning could be enhanced (Földiák 1992, Montague, Gally and Edelman 1991).

The trace update rule used in the baseline simulations of VisNet (Wallis and Rolls 1997) is equivalent to both Földiák's used in the context of translation invariance and to the earlier rule of Sutton and Barto (1981) explored in the context of modelling the temporal properties of classical conditioning, and can be summarized as follows:

$$\delta w_j = \alpha \overline{y}^\tau x_j \tag{4.3}$$

where

$$\overline{y}^\tau = (1 - \eta)y^\tau + \eta \overline{y}^{\tau - 1} \tag{4.4}$$

and

---

[13]The precise mechanisms involved may alter the precise form of the trace rule which should be used. Földiák (1992) describes an alternative trace rule which models individual NMDA channels. Equally, a trace implemented by extended cell firing should be reflected in representing the trace as an external firing rate, rather than an internal signal.

[14]The prolonged firing of inferior temporal cortex neurons during memory delay periods of several seconds, and associative links reported to develop between stimuli presented several seconds apart (Miyashita 1988) are on too long a time scale to be immediately relevant to the present theory. In fact, associations between visual events occurring several seconds apart would, under *normal* environmental conditions, be detrimental to the operation of a network of the type described here, because they would probably arise from different objects. In contrast, the system described benefits from associations between visual events which occur close in time (typically within 1 s), as they are likely to be from the same object.

x_j: j^{th} input to the neuron.

$\overline{y}^\tau$:   Trace value of the output of the neuron at time step τ.

w_j: Synaptic weight between j^{th} input and the neuron.

y: Output from the neuron.

α: Learning rate. Annealed between unity and zero.

η: Trace value. The optimal value varies with presentation sequence length.

To bound the growth of each neuron's synaptic weight vector, $\mathbf{w}_i$ for the ith neuron, its length is explicitly normalized (a method similarly employed by von der Malsburg (1973) which is commonly used in competitive networks, see Section B.4). An alternative, more biologically relevant implementation, using a local weight bounding operation which utilizes a form of heterosynaptic long-term depression (see Section 1.5), has in part been explored using a version of the Oja (1982) rule (see Wallis and Rolls (1997)).

4.5.1.2 The network implemented in VisNet

The network itself is designed as a series of hierarchical, convergent, competitive networks, in accordance with the hypotheses advanced above. The actual network consists of a series of four layers, constructed such that the convergence of information from the most disparate parts of the network's input layer can potentially influence firing in a single neuron in the final layer – see Fig. 4.2. This corresponds to the scheme described by many researchers (Van Essen, Anderson and Felleman 1992, Rolls 1992a, for example) as present in the primate visual system – see Fig. 4.2. The forward connections to a cell in one layer are derived from a topologically related and confined region of the preceding layer. The choice of whether a connection between neurons in adjacent layers exists or not is based upon a Gaussian distribution of connection probabilities which roll off radially from the focal point of connections for each neuron. (A minor extra constraint precludes the repeated connection of any pair of cells.) In particular, the forward connections to a cell in one layer come from a small region of the preceding layer defined by the radius in Table 4.1 which will contain approximately 67% of the connections from the preceding layer. Figure 4.2 shows the general

Table 4.1 VisNet dimensions

	Dimensions	# Connections	Radius
Layer 4	32x32	100	12
Layer 3	32x32	100	9
Layer 2	32x32	100	6
Layer 1	32x32	272	6
Input layer	128x128x32	–	–

convergent network architecture used. Localization and limitation of connectivity in the network is intended to mimic cortical connectivity, partially because of the clear retention of retinal topology through regions of visual cortex. This architecture also encourages the gradual combination of features from layer to layer which has relevance to the binding problem, as described in Section 4.5.5[15].

---

[15] Modelling topological constraints in connectivity leads to an issue concerning neurons at the edges of the network layers. In principle these neurons may either receive no input from beyond the edge of the preceding layer, or have their connections repeatedly sample neurons at the edge of the previous layer. In practice either solution is liable to introduce artificial weighting on the few active inputs at the edge and hence cause the edge to have unwanted influence over the development of the network as a whole. In the real brain such edge-effects would be naturally smoothed by the transition of the locus of cellular input from the fovea to the lower acuity periphery of the visual field. However, it poses a problem here because we are in effect only simulating the small high acuity foveal portion of the visual field in our simulations. As an alternative to the former solutions Wallis and Rolls (1997) elected to

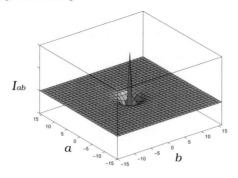

Fig. 4.21 Contrast-enhancing filter, which has the effect of local lateral inhibition. The parameters δ and σ are variables used in equation 4.5 to modify the amount and extent of inhibition respectively.

4.5.1.3 Competition and lateral inhibition

In order to act as a competitive network some form of mutual inhibition is required within each layer, which should help to ensure that all stimuli presented are evenly represented by the neurons in each layer. This is implemented in VisNet by a form of lateral inhibition. The idea behind the lateral inhibition, apart from this being a property of cortical architecture in the brain, was to prevent too many neurons that received inputs from a similar part of the preceding layer responding to the same activity patterns. The purpose of the lateral inhibition was to ensure that different receiving neurons coded for different inputs. This is important in reducing redundancy (see Section B.4). The lateral inhibition is conceived as operating within a radius that was similar to that of the region within which a neuron received converging inputs from the preceding layer (because activity in one zone of topologically organized processing within a layer should not inhibit processing in another zone in the same layer, concerned perhaps with another part of the image)[16].

The lateral inhibition and contrast enhancement just described is actually implemented in VisNet2 (Rolls and Milward 2000) in two stages, to produce filtering of the type illustrated in Fig. 4.21. This lateral inhibition is implemented by convolving the activation of the neurons in a layer with a spatial filter, I, where δ controls the contrast and σ controls the width, and a and b index the distance away from the centre of the filter

$$I_{a,b} = \begin{cases} -\delta e^{-\frac{a^2+b^2}{\sigma^2}} & \text{if } a \neq 0 \text{ or } b \neq 0, \\ 1 - \sum_{a\neq 0,b\neq 0} I_{a,b} & \text{if } a = 0 \text{ and } b = 0. \end{cases} \tag{4.5}$$

form the connections into a toroid, such that connections wrap back onto the network from opposite sides. This wrapping happens at all four layers of the network, and in the way an image on the 'retina' is mapped to the input filters. This solution has the advantage of making all of the boundaries effectively invisible to the network. Further, this procedure does not itself introduce problems into evaluation of the network for the problems set, as many of the critical comparisons in VisNet involve comparisons between a network with the same architecture trained with the trace rule, or with the Hebb rule, or not trained at all. In practice, it is shown below that only the network trained with the trace rule solves the problem of forming invariant representations.

[16] Although the extent of the lateral inhibition actually investigated by Wallis and Rolls (1997) in VisNet operated over adjacent pixels, the lateral inhibition introduced by Rolls and Milward (2000) in what they named VisNet2 and which has been used in subsequent simulations operates over a larger region, set within a layer to approximately half of the radius of convergence from the preceding layer. Indeed, Rolls and Milward (2000) showed in a problem in which invariant representations over 49 locations were being used with a 17 face test set, that the best performance was with intermediate range lateral inhibition, using the parameters for σ shown in Table 4.3. These values of σ set the lateral inhibition radius within a layer to be approximately half that of the spread of the excitatory connections from the preceding layer.

Table 4.2 Sigmoid parameters for the runs with 25 locations by Rolls and Milward (2000)

Layer	1	2	3	4
Percentile	99.2	98	88	91
Slope β	190	40	75	26

Table 4.3 Lateral inhibition parameters for the 25-location runs

Layer	1	2	3	4
Radius, σ	1.38	2.7	4.0	6.0
Contrast, δ	1.5	1.5	1.6	1.4

This is a filter that leaves the average activity unchanged. A modified version of this filter designed as a difference of Gaussians with the same inhibition but shorter range local excitation is being tested to investigate whether the self-organizing maps that this promotes (Section B.4.6) helps the system to provide some continuity in the representations formed. The concept is that this may help the system to code efficiently for large numbers of untrained stimuli that fall between trained stimuli in similarity space.

The second stage involves contrast enhancement. In VisNet (Wallis and Rolls 1997), this was implemented by raising the neuronal activations to a fixed power and normalizing the resulting firing within a layer to have an average firing rate equal to 1.0. In VisNet2 (Rolls and Milward 2000) and in subsequent simulations a more biologically plausible form of the activation function, a sigmoid, was used:

$$y = f^{\text{sigmoid}}(r) = \frac{1}{1 + e^{-2\beta(r-\alpha)}} \tag{4.6}$$

where r is the activation (or firing rate) of the neuron after the lateral inhibition, y is the firing rate after the contrast enhancement produced by the activation function, and β is the slope or gain and α is the threshold or bias of the activation function. The sigmoid bounds the firing rate between 0 and 1 so global normalization is not required. The slope and threshold are held constant within each layer. The slope is constant throughout training, whereas the threshold is used to control the sparseness of firing rates within each layer. The (population) sparseness of the firing within a layer is defined (Rolls and Treves 1998) as:

$$a = \frac{(\sum_i y_i/n)^2}{\sum_i y_i^2/n} \tag{4.7}$$

where n is the number of neurons in the layer. To set the sparseness to a given value, e.g. 5%, the threshold is set to the value of the 95th percentile point of the activations within the layer. (Unless otherwise stated here, the neurons used the sigmoid activation function as just described.)

In most simulations with VisNet2 and later, the sigmoid activation function was used with parameters (selected after a number of optimization runs) as shown in Table 4.2.

In addition, the lateral inhibition parameters normally used in VisNet2 simulations are as shown in Table 4.3[17].

---

[17] Where a power activation function was used in the simulations of Wallis and Rolls (1997), the power for layer 1 was 6, and for the other layers was 2.

4.5.1.4 The input to VisNet

VisNet is provided with a set of input filters which can be applied to an image to produce inputs to the network which correspond to those provided by simple cells in visual cortical area 1 (V1). The purpose of this is to enable within VisNet the more complicated response properties of cells between V1 and the inferior temporal cortex (IT) to be investigated, using as inputs natural stimuli such as those that could be applied to the retina of the real visual system. This is to facilitate comparisons between the activity of neurons in VisNet and those in the real visual system, to the same stimuli. In VisNet no attempt is made to train the response properties of simple cells, but instead we start with a defined series of filters to perform fixed feature extraction to a level equivalent to that of simple cells in V1, as have other researchers in the field (Hummel and Biederman 1992, Buhmann, Lange, von der Malsburg, Vorbrüggen and Würtz 1991, Fukushima 1980), because we wish to simulate the more complicated response properties of cells between V1 and the inferior temporal cortex (IT). The elongated orientation-tuned input filters used accord with the general tuning profiles of simple cells in V1 (Hawken and Parker 1987) and are computed by weighting the difference of two Gaussians by a third orthogonal Gaussian as described by Wallis, Rolls and Foldiak (1993) and Wallis and Rolls (1997). Each individual filter is tuned to spatial frequency (0.0625 to 0.5 cycles / pixel over four octaves); orientation ($0°$ to $135°$ in steps of $45°$); and sign (± 1). Of the 272 layer 1 connections, the number to each group is as shown in Table 4.4. In the VisNet2 (Rolls and Milward 2000) (used for most VisNet simulations) only even symmetric – 'bar detecting' – filter shapes are used, which take the form of a Gaussian shape along the axis of orientation tuning for the filter, and a difference of Gaussians along the perpendicular axis.

This filter is referred to as an oriented difference of Gaussians, or DOG filter[18]. It was chosen for VisNet in preference to the often used Gabor filter on the grounds of its better fit to available neurophysiological data including its zero D.C. response (Hawken and Parker 1987, Wallis, Rolls and Foldiak 1993). Any zero D.C. filter can of course produce a negative as well as positive output, which would mean that this simulation of a simple cell would permit negative as well as positive firing. In contrast to some other models the response of each filter is zero thresholded and the negative results used to form a separate anti-phase input to the network. The filter outputs are also normalized across scales to compensate for the low frequency bias in the images of natural objects. However, Gabor filters have also been tested, and also produce good results with VisNet (Deco and Rolls 2004) (see Section 6.13).

Cells of layer 1 receive a topologically consistent, localized, random selection of the filter responses in the input layer, under the constraint that each cell samples every filter spatial frequency and receives a constant number of inputs. Figure 4.22 shows pictorially the general filter sampling paradigm, and Fig. 4.23 the typical connectivity to a layer 1 cell from the filters of the input layer. The blank squares indicate that no connection exists between the layer 1 cell chosen and the filters of that particular orientation, sign, and spatial frequency.

4.5.1.5 Measures for network performance

A neuron can be said to have learnt an invariant representation if it discriminates one set of stimuli from another set, across all transformations. For example, a neuron's response is translation invariant if its response to one set of stimuli irrespective of presentation is

---

[18] Professor R. Watt, of Stirling University, is thanked for assistance with the implementation of this filter scheme.

Table 4.4 VisNet layer 1 connectivity. The frequency is in cycles per pixel

Frequency	0.5	0.25	0.125	0.0625
# Connections	201	50	13	8

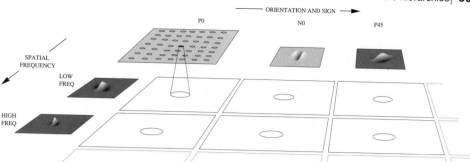

Fig. 4.22 The filter sampling paradigm. Here each square represents the retinal image presented to the network after being filtered by a difference of gaussian filter of the appropriate orientation sign and frequency. The circles represent the consistent retinotopic coordinates used to provide input to a layer 1 cell. The filters double in spatial frequency towards the reader. Left to right the orientation tuning increases from 0° in steps of 45°, with segregated pairs of positive (P) and negative (N) filter responses.

consistently higher than for all other stimuli irrespective of presentation location. Note that we state 'set of stimuli' since neurons in the inferior temporal cortex are not generally selective for a single stimulus but rather a subpopulation of stimuli (Baylis, Rolls and Leonard 1985, Abbott, Rolls and Tovee 1996, Rolls, Treves and Tovee 1997b, Rolls and Treves 1998, Rolls and Deco 2002, Rolls 2007i, Franco, Rolls, Aggelopoulos and Jerez 2007) (see Appendix C). The measure of network performance used in VisNet1 (Wallis and Rolls 1997), the 'Fisher metric' (referred to in some figure labels as the Discrimination Factor), reflects how well a neuron discriminates between stimuli, compared to how well it discriminates between different locations (or more generally the images used rather than the objects, each of which is represented by a set of images, over which invariant stimulus or object representations must be learned). The Fisher measure is very similar to taking the ratio of the two F values in a two-way ANOVA, where one factor is the stimulus shown, and the other factor is the position in which a stimulus is shown. The measure takes a value greater than 1.0 if a neuron has more different responses to the stimuli than to the locations. That is, values greater than 1 indicate invariant representations when this measure is used in the following figures. Further details of how the measure is calculated are given by Wallis and Rolls (1997).

Measures of network performance based on information theory and similar to those used in the analysis of the firing of real neurons in the brain (see Appendix C) were introduced by Rolls and Milward (2000) for VisNet2, and are used in later papers. A single cell information measure was introduced which is the maximum amount of information the cell has about any one stimulus / object independently of which transform (e.g. position on the retina) is shown. Because the competitive algorithm used in VisNet tends to produce local representations (in which single cells become tuned to one stimulus or object), this information measure can approach $\log_2 N_S$ bits, where N_S is the number of different stimuli. Indeed, it is an advantage of this measure that it has a defined maximal value, which enables how well the network is performing to be quantified. Rolls and Milward (2000) showed that the Fisher and single cell information measures were highly correlated, and given the advantage just noted of the information measure, it was adopted in Rolls and Milward (2000) and subsequent papers. Rolls and Milward (2000) also introduced a multiple cell information measure, which has the advantage that it provides a measure of whether all stimuli are encoded by different neurons in the network. Again, a high value of this measure indicates good performance.

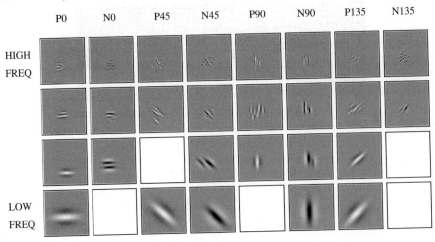

Fig. 4.23 Typical connectivity before training between a single cell in the first layer of the network and the input layer, represented by plotting the receptive fields of every input layer cell connected to the particular layer 1 cell. Separate input layer cells have activity that represents a positive (P) or negative (N) output from the bank of filters which have different orientations in degrees (the columns) and different spatial frequencies (the rows). Here the overall receptive field of the layer 1 cell is centred just below the centre-point of the retina. The connection scheme allows for relatively fewer connections to lower frequency cells than to high frequency cells in order to cover a similar region of the input at each frequency. A blank square indicates that there is no connection to the layer 1 neuron from an input neuron with that particular filter type.

For completeness, we provide further specification of the two information theoretic measures, which are described in detail by Rolls and Milward (2000) (see Appendix C for introduction of the concepts). The measures assess the extent to which either a single cell, or a population of cells, responds to the same stimulus invariantly with respect to its location, yet responds differently to different stimuli. The measures effectively show what one learns about which stimulus was presented from a single presentation of the stimulus at any randomly chosen location. Results for top (4th) layer cells are shown. High information measures thus show that cells fire similarly to the different transforms of a given stimulus (object), and differently to the other stimuli. The single cell stimulus-specific information, $I(s, R)$, is the amount of information the set of responses, R, has about a specific stimulus, s (see Rolls, Treves, Tovee and Panzeri (1997d) and Rolls and Milward (2000)). $I(s, R)$ is given by

$$I(s, R) = \sum_{r \in R} P(r|s) \log_2 \frac{P(r|s)}{P(r)} \tag{4.8}$$

where r is an individual response from the set of responses R of the neuron. For each cell the performance measure used was the maximum amount of information a cell conveyed about any one stimulus. This (rather than the mutual information, $I(S, R)$ where S is the whole set of stimuli s), is appropriate for a competitive network in which the cells tend to become tuned to one stimulus[19].

If all the output cells of VisNet learned to respond to the same stimulus, then the information about the set of stimuli S would be very poor, and would not reach its maximal value of $\log_2$ of the number of stimuli (in bits). The second measure that is used here is the information

---

[19] $I(s, R)$ has more recently been called the stimulus-specific surprise, see DeWeese and Meister (1999). Its average across stimuli is the mutual information $I(S, R)$.

Fig. 4.24 The three stimuli used in the first two experiments.

provided by a set of cells about the stimulus set, using the procedures described by Rolls, Treves and Tovee (1997b) and Rolls and Milward (2000). The multiple cell information is the mutual information between the whole set of stimuli S and of responses R calculated using a decoding procedure in which the stimulus s' that gave rise to the particular firing rate response vector on each trial is estimated. (The decoding step is needed because the high dimensionality of the response space would lead to an inaccurate estimate of the information if the responses were used directly, as described by Rolls, Treves and Tovee (1997b) and Rolls and Treves (1998).) A probability table is then constructed of the real stimuli s and the decoded stimuli s'. From this probability table, the mutual information between the set of actual stimuli S and the decoded estimates S' is calculated as

$$I(S, S') = \sum_{s, s'} P(s, s') \log_2 \frac{P(s, s')}{P(s)P(s')} \tag{4.9}$$

This was calculated for the subset of cells which had as single cells the most information about which stimulus was shown. In particular, in Rolls and Milward (2000) and subsequent papers, the multiple cell information was calculated from the first five cells for each stimulus that had maximal single cell information about that stimulus, that is from a population of 35 cells if there were seven stimuli (each of which might have been shown in for example 9 or 25 positions on the retina).

4.5.2   Initial experiments with VisNet

Having established a network model Wallis and Rolls (1997) (following a first report by Wallis, Rolls and Foldiak (1993)) described four experiments in which the theory of how invariant representations could be formed was tested using a variety of stimuli undergoing a number of natural transformations. In each case the network produced neurons in the final layer whose responses were largely invariant across a transformation and highly discriminating between stimuli or sets of stimuli.

4.5.2.1   'T','L' and '+' as stimuli: learning translation invariance

One of the classical properties of inferior temporal cortex face cells is their invariant response to face stimuli translated across the visual field (Tovee, Rolls and Azzopardi 1994). In this first experiment, the learning of translation invariant representations by VisNet was investigated.

  In order to test the network a set of three stimuli, based upon probable 3D edge cues – consisting of a 'T', 'L' and '+' shape – was constructed[20]. The actual stimuli used are shown in Fig. 4.24. These stimuli were chosen partly because of their significance as form cues, but on a more practical note because they each contain the same fundamental features – namely a horizontal bar conjoined with a vertical bar. In practice this means that the oriented

---

[20]Chakravarty (1979) describes the application of these shapes as cues for the 3D interpretation of edge junctions, and Tanaka et al. (1991) have demonstrated the existence of cells responsive to such stimuli in IT.

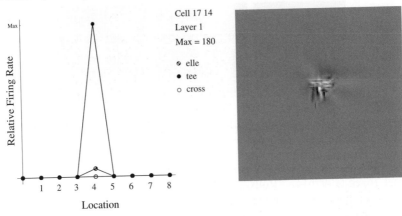

Cell 17 14
Layer 1
Max = 180

○ elle
● tee
○ cross

Relative Firing Rate

Location

Fig. 4.25 The left graph shows the response of a layer 1 neuron to the three training stimuli for the nine training locations. Alongside this are the results of summating all the filter inputs to the neuron. The discrimination factor for this cell was 1.04.

simple cell filters of the input layer cannot distinguish these stimuli on the basis of which features are present. As a consequence of this, the representation of the stimuli received by the network is non-orthogonal and hence considerably more difficult to classify than was the case in earlier experiments involving the trace rule described by Földiák (1991). The expectation is that layer 1 neurons would learn to respond to spatially selective combinations of the basic features thereby helping to distinguish these non-orthogonal stimuli. The trajectory followed by each stimulus consisted of sweeping left to right horizontally across three locations in the top row, and then sweeping back, right to left across the middle row, before returning to the right hand side across the bottom row – tracing out a 'Z' shape path across the retina. Unless stated otherwise this pattern of nine presentation locations was adopted in all image translation experiments described by Wallis and Rolls (1997).

Training was carried out by permutatively presenting all stimuli in each location a total of 800 times. The sequence described above was followed for each stimulus, with the sequence start point and direction of sweep being chosen at random for each of the 800 training trials.

Figures 4.25 and 4.26 show the response after training of a first layer neuron selective for the 'T' stimulus. The weighted sum of all filter inputs reveals the combination of horizontally and vertically tuned filters in identifying the stimulus. In this case many connections to the lower frequency filters have been reduced to zero by the learning process, except at the relevant orientations. This contrasts strongly with the random wiring present before training, as seen previously in Fig. 4.23. It is important that neurons at early stages of feature hierarchy networks respond to combinations of features in defined relative spatial positions, before invariance is built into the system, as this is part of the way that the binding problem is solved, as described in more detail in Section 4.5.5 and by Elliffe, Rolls and Stringer (2002). The feature combination tuning is illustrated by the VisNet layer 1 neuron shown in Figs. 4.25 and 4.26.

Likewise, Fig. 4.27 depicts two neural responses, but now from the two intermediate layers of the network, taken from the top 30 most highly invariant cells, not merely the top two or three. The gradual increase in the discrimination indicates that the tolerance to shifts of the preferred stimulus gradually builds up through the layers.

The results for layer 4 neurons are illustrated in Fig. 4.28. By this stage translation-invariant, stimulus-identifying, cells have emerged. The response profiles confirm the high level of neural selectivity for a particular stimulus irrespective of location.

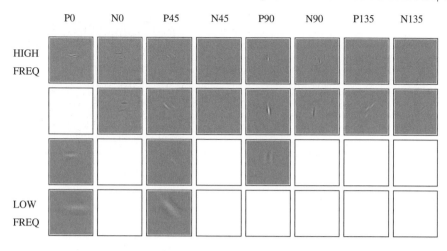

Fig. 4.26 The same cell as in the previous figure and the same input reconstruction results but separated into four rows of differing spatial frequency, and eight columns representing the four filter tuning orientations in positive and negative complementary pairs.

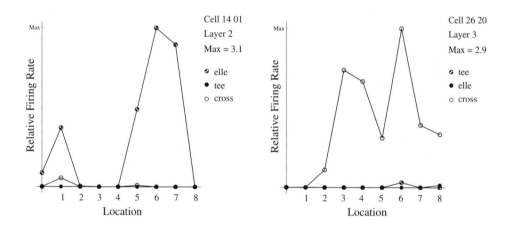

Fig. 4.27 Response profiles for two intermediate layer neurons – discrimination factors 1.34 and 1.64 – in the L, T, and + experiment.

Figure 4.29 contrasts the measure of invariance, or discrimination factor, achieved by cells in the four layers, averaged over five separate runs of the network. Translation invariance clearly increases through the layers, with a considerable increase in translation invariance between layers 3 and 4. This sudden increase may well be a result of the geometry of the network, which enables cells in layer 4 to receive inputs from any part of the input layer.

Having established that invariant cells have emerged in the final layer, we now consider the role of the trace rule, by assessing the network tested under two new conditions. Firstly, the performance of the network was measured before learning occurs, that is with its initially random connection weights. Secondly, the network was trained with η in the trace rule set to 0, which causes learning to proceed in a traceless, standard Hebbian, fashion. (Hebbian learning is purely associative, as shown for example in equation B.19.)

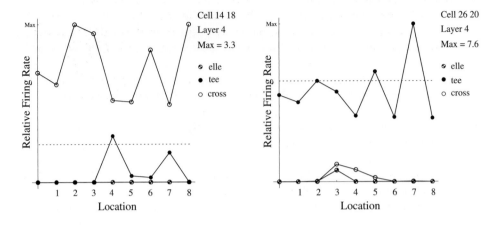

Fig. 4.28 Response profiles for two fourth layer neurons – discrimination factors 4.07 and 3.62 – in the L, T, and + experiment.

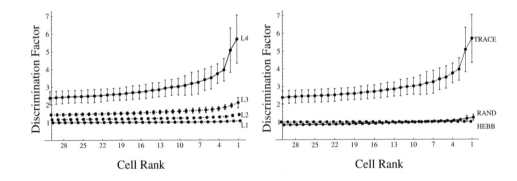

Fig. 4.29 Variation in neural discrimination factors as a measure of performance for the top 30 most highly discriminating cells through the four layers of the network, averaged over five runs of the network in the L, T, and + experiment.

Fig. 4.30 Variation in neural discrimination factors as a measure of performance for the top 30 most highly discriminating cells in the fourth layer for the three training regimes, averaged over five runs of the network.

Figure 4.30 shows the results under the three training conditions. The results show that the trace rule is the decisive factor in establishing the invariant responses in the layer 4 neurons. It is interesting to note that the Hebbian learning results are actually *worse* than those achieved by chance in the untrained net. In general, with Hebbian learning, the most highly discriminating cells barely rate higher than 1. This value of discrimination corresponds to the case in which a cell responds to only one stimulus and in only one location. The poor performance with the Hebb rule comes as a direct consequence of the presentation paradigm being employed. If we consider an image as representing a vector in multidimensional space, a particular image in the top left-hand corner of the input retina will tend to look more like any other image in that same location than the same image presented elsewhere. A simple competitive network using just Hebbian learning will thus tend to categorize images by *where* they are rather than what they are – the exact opposite of what the net was intended to learn. This comparison thus indicates that a small memory trace acting in the standard Hebbian learning paradigm can radically alter the normal vector averaging, image classification, performed by a Hebbian-based competitive network.

One question that emerges about the representation in the final layer of the network relates to how evenly the network divides up its resources to represent the learnt stimuli. It is conceivable that one stimulus stands out among the set of stimuli by containing very distinctive features which would make it easier to categorize. This may produce an unrepresentative number of neurons with high discrimination factors which are in fact all responding to the same stimulus. It is important that at least some cells code for (or provide information about) each of the stimuli. As a simple check on this, the preferred stimulus of each cell was found and the associated measure of discrimination added to a total for each stimulus. This measure in practice never varied by more than a factor of 1.3:1 for all stimuli. The multiple cell information measure used in some later figures addresses the same issue, with similar results.

4.5.2.2 'T','L', and '+' as stimuli: Optimal network parameters

The second series of investigations described by Wallis and Rolls (1997) using the 'T','L' and '+' stimuli, centred upon finding optimal parameters for elements of the network, such as the optimal trace time constant η, which controls the relative effect of previous activities on current learning as described above. The network performance was gauged using a single 800 epoch training run of the network with the median discrimination factor (with the upper and lower quartile values) for the top sixteen cells of the fourth layer being displayed at each parameter value.

Figure 4.31 displays the effect of varying the value of η for the nine standard presentation locations. The optimal value of η might conceivably change with the alteration of the number of training locations, and indeed one might predict that it would be smaller if the number of presentation locations was reduced. To confirm this, network performance was also measured for presentation sweeps over only five locations. Figure 4.32 shows the results of this experiment, which confirm the expected shift in the general profile of the curve towards shorter time constant values. Of course, the optimal value of η derived is in effect a compromise between optimal values for the three layers in which the trace operates. Since neurons in each layer have different effective receptive field sizes, one would expect each layer's neurons to be exposed to different portions of the full sweep of a particular stimulus. This would in turn suggest that the optimal value of η will grow through the layers.

4.5.2.3 Faces as stimuli: translation invariance

The aim of the next set of experiments described by Wallis and Rolls (1997) was to start to address the issues of how the network operates when invariant representations must be learned for a larger number of stimuli, and whether the network can learn when much more complicated, real biological stimuli (faces) are used. The set of face images used appears in Fig. 4.33. In practice, to equalize luminance the D.C. component of the images was removed. In addition, so as to minimize the effect of cast shadows, an oval Hamming window was applied to the face image which also served to remove any hard edges of the image relative to the plain background upon which they were set.

The results of training in the translation invariance paradigm with 7 faces each in 9 locations are shown in Figs. 4.34, 4.35 and 4.36. The network produces neurons with high discrimination factors, and this only occurs if it is trained with the trace rule. Some layer 4 neurons showed a somewhat distributed representation, as illustrated in the examples of layer 4 neurons shown in Fig. 4.34.

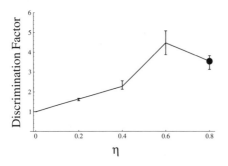

Fig. 4.31 Variation in network performance as a function of the trace rule parameter η in neurons of layers 2 to 4 – over nine locations in the L, T and + experiment.

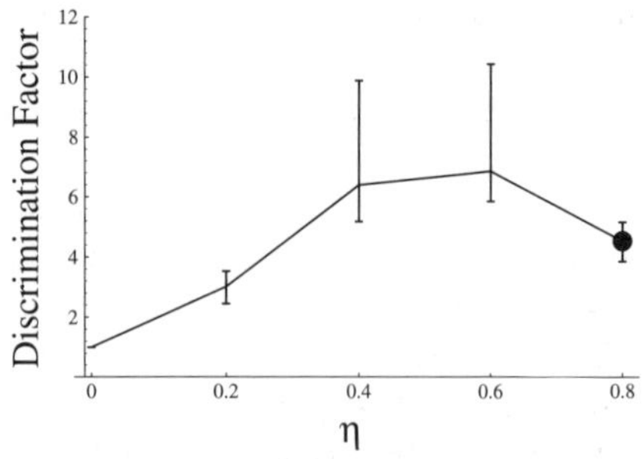

Fig. 4.32 Variation in network performance as a function of the trace rule parameter η in neurons of layers 2 to 4 – over five presentation locations in the L, T and + experiment.

Fig. 4.33 Seven faces used as stimuli in the face translation experiment.

In order to check that there was an invariant representation in layer 4 of VisNet that could be read by a receiving population of neurons, a fifth layer was added to the net which fully sampled the fourth layer cells. This layer was in turn trained in a supervised manner using gradient descent or with a Hebbian associative learning rule. Wallis and Rolls (1997) showed that the object classification performed by the layer 5 network was better if the network had been trained with the trace rule than when it was untrained or was trained with a Hebb rule.

4.5.2.4 Faces as stimuli: view invariance

Given that the network had been shown to be able to operate usefully with a more difficult translation invariance problem, we next addressed the question of whether the network can solve other types of transform invariance, as we had intended. The next experiment addressed this question, by training the network on the problem of 3D stimulus rotation, which produces non-isomorphic transforms, to determine whether the network can build a view-invariant categorization of the stimuli (Wallis and Rolls 1997). The trace rule learning paradigm should, in conjunction with the architecture described here, prove capable of learning any of the transforms tolerated by IT neurons, so long as each stimulus is presented in short sequences during which the transformation occurs and can be learned. This experiment continued with the use of faces but now presented them centrally in the retina in a sequence of different views of a face. The images used are shown in Fig. 4.37. The faces were again smoothed at the

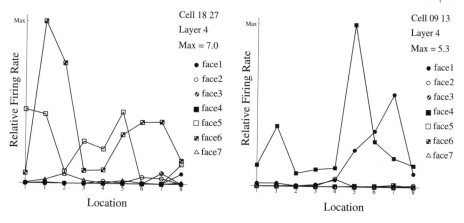

Fig. 4.34 Response profiles for two neurons in the fourth layer – discrimination factors 2.64 and 2.10. The net was trained on 7 faces each in 9 locations.

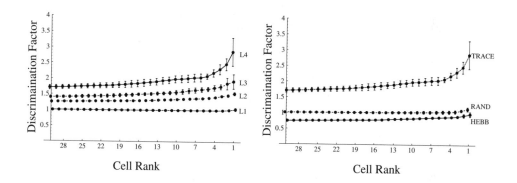

Fig. 4.35 Variation in network performance for the top 30 most highly discriminating cells through the four layers of the network, averaged over five runs of the network. The net was trained on 7 faces each in 9 locations.

Fig. 4.36 Variation in network performance for the top 30 most highly discriminating cells in the fourth layer for the three training regimes, averaged over five runs of the network. The net was trained on 7 faces each in 9 locations.

edges to erase the harsh image boundaries, and the D.C. term was removed. During the 800 epochs of learning, each stimulus was chosen at random, and a sequence of preset views of it was shown, rotating the face either to the left or to the right.

Although the actual number of images being presented is smaller, some 21 views in all, there is good reason to think that this problem may be harder to solve than the previous translation experiments. This is simply due to the fact that all 21 views exactly overlap with one another. The net was indeed able to solve the invariance problem, with examples of invariant layer 4 neuron response profiles appearing in Fig. 4.38.

Figure 4.39 confirms the improvement in invariant stimulus representation found through the layers, and that layer 4 provides a considerable improvement in performance over the previous layers. Figure 4.40 shows the Hebb trained and untrained nets performing equally poorly, whilst the trace trained net shows good invariance across the entire 30 cells selected.

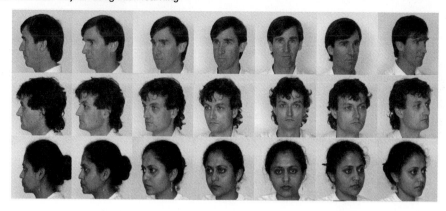

Fig. 4.37 Three faces in seven different views used as stimuli in an experiment by Wallis and Rolls (1997).

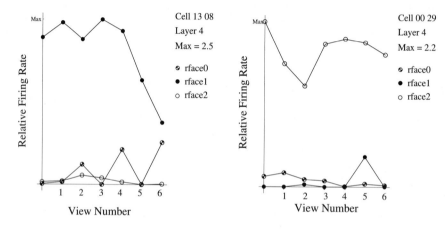

Fig. 4.38 Response profiles for cells in the last two layers of the network – discrimination factors 11.12 and 12.40 – in the experiment with seven different views of each of three faces.

4.5.3 The optimal parameters for the temporal trace used in the learning rule

The trace used in VisNet enables successive features that, based on the natural statistics of the visual input, are likely to be from the same object or feature complex to be associated together. For good performance, the temporal trace needs to be sufficiently long that it covers the period in which features seen by a particular neuron in the hierarchy are likely to come from the same object. On the other hand, the trace should not be so long that it produces associations between features that are parts of different objects, seen when for example the eyes move to another object. One possibility is to reset the trace during saccades between different objects. If explicit trace resetting is not implemented, then the trace should, to optimize the compromise implied by the above, lead to strong associations between temporally close stimuli, and increasingly weaker associations between temporally more distant stimuli. In fact, the trace implemented in VisNet has an exponential decay, and it has been shown that this form is optimal in the situation where the exact duration over which the same object is being viewed varies, and where the natural statistics of the visual input happen also to show a decreasing probability that the same object is being viewed as the time period in question increases (Wallis and

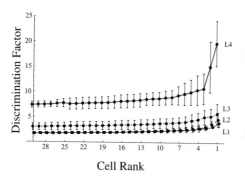 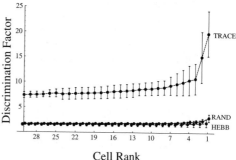

Fig. 4.39 Variation in network performance for the top 30 most highly discriminating cells through the four layers of the network, averaged over five runs of the network in the experiment with seven different views of each of three faces.

Fig. 4.40 Variation in network performance for the top 30 most highly discriminating cells in the fourth layer for the three training regimes, averaged over five runs of the network in the experiment with seven different views of each of three faces.

Baddeley 1997). Moreover, as is made evident in Figs. 4.32 and 4.31, performance can be enhanced if the duration of the trace does at the same time approximately match the period over which the input stimuli are likely to come from the same object or feature complex. Nevertheless, good performance can be obtained in conditions under which the trace rule allows associations to be formed only between successive items in the visual stream (Rolls and Milward 2000, Rolls and Stringer 2001a).

It is also the case that the optimal value of η in the trace rule is likely to be different for different layers of VisNet, and for cortical processing in the 'what' visual stream. For early layers of the system, small movements of the eyes might lead to different feature combinations providing the input to cells (which at early stages have small receptive fields), and a short duration of the trace would be optimal. However, these small eye movements might be around the same object, and later layers of the architecture would benefit from being able to associate together their inputs over longer times, in order to learn about the larger scale properties that characterize individual objects, including for example different views of objects observed as an object turns or is turned. Thus the suggestion is made that the temporal trace could be effectively longer at later stages (e.g. inferior temporal visual cortex) compared to early stages (e.g. V2 and V4) of processing in the visual system. In addition, as will be shown in Section 4.5.5, it is important to form feature combinations with high spatial precision before invariance learning supported by a temporal trace starts, in order that the feature combinations and not the individual features have invariant representations. This leads to the suggestion that the trace rule should either not operate, or be short, at early stages of cortical visual processing such as V1. This is reflected in the operation of VisNet2, which does not use a temporal trace in layer 1 (Rolls and Milward 2000).

4.5.4 Different forms of the trace learning rule, and their relation to error correction and temporal difference learning

The original trace learning rule used in the simulations of Wallis and Rolls (1997) took the form

$$\delta w_j = \alpha \bar{y}^\tau x_j^\tau \tag{4.10}$$

where the trace $\bar{y}^\tau$ is updated according to

$$\bar{y}^\tau = (1 - \eta)y^\tau + \eta\bar{y}^{\tau-1}. \tag{4.11}$$

The parameter $\eta \in [0, 1]$ controls the relative contributions to the trace $\bar{y}^\tau$ from the instantaneous firing rate y^τ and the trace at the previous time step $\bar{y}^{\tau-1}$, where for $\eta = 0$ we have $\bar{y}^\tau = y^\tau$ and equation 4.10 becomes the standard Hebb rule

$$\delta w_j = \alpha y^\tau x_j^\tau. \tag{4.12}$$

At the start of a series of investigations of different forms of the trace learning rule, Rolls and Milward (2000) demonstrated that VisNet's performance could be greatly enhanced with a modified Hebbian learning rule that incorporated a trace of activity from the preceding time steps, with no contribution from the activity being produced by the stimulus at the current time step. This rule took the form

$$\delta w_j = \alpha\bar{y}^{\tau-1}x_j^\tau. \tag{4.13}$$

The trace shown in equation 4.13 is in the postsynaptic term, and similar effects were found if the trace was in the presynaptic term, or in both the pre- and the postsynaptic terms. The crucial difference from the earlier rule (see equation 4.10) was that the trace should be calculated up to only the preceding timestep, with no contribution to the trace from the firing on the current trial to the current stimulus. How might this be understood?

One way to understand this is to note that the trace rule is trying to set up the synaptic weight on trial τ based on whether the neuron, based on its previous history, is responding to that stimulus (in other transforms, e.g. position). Use of the trace rule at $\tau - 1$ does this, that is it takes into account the firing of the neuron on previous trials, with no contribution from the firing being produced by the stimulus on the current trial. On the other hand, use of the trace at time τ in the update takes into account the current firing of the neuron to the stimulus in that particular position, which is not a good estimate of whether that neuron should be allocated to invariantly represent that stimulus. Effectively, using the trace at time τ introduces a Hebbian element into the update, which tends to build position-encoded analyzers, rather than stimulus-encoded analyzers. (The argument has been phrased for a system learning translation invariance, but applies to the learning of all types of invariance.) A particular advantage of using the trace at $\tau - 1$ is that the trace will then on different occasions (due to the randomness in the location sequences used) reflect previous histories with different sets of positions, enabling the learning of the neuron to be based on evidence from the stimulus present in many different positions. Using a term from the current firing in the trace (i.e. the trace calculated at time τ) results in this desirable effect always having an undesirable element from the current firing of the neuron to the stimulus in its current position.

4.5.4.1 The modified Hebbian trace rule and its relation to error correction

The rule of equation 4.13 corrects the weights using a postsynaptic trace obtained from the previous firing (produced by other transforms of the same stimulus), with no contribution to the trace from the current postsynaptic firing (produced by the current transform of the stimulus). Indeed, insofar as the current firing y^τ is not the same as $\bar{y}^{\tau-1}$, this difference can be thought of as an error. This leads to a conceptualization of using the difference between the current firing and the preceding trace as an error correction term, as noted in the context of modelling the temporal properties of classical conditioning by Sutton and Barto (1981), and developed next in the context of invariance learning (see Rolls and Stringer (2001a)).

First, we re-express the rule of equation 4.13 in an alternative form as follows. Suppose we are at timestep τ and have just calculated a neuronal firing rate y^τ and the corresponding trace

$\overline{y}^\tau$ from the trace update equation 4.11. If we assume $\eta \in (0,1)$, then rearranging equation 4.11 gives

$$\overline{y}^{\tau-1} = \frac{1}{\eta}(\overline{y}^\tau - (1-\eta)y^\tau),$$ (4.14)

and substituting equation 4.14 into equation 4.13 gives

$$\begin{aligned}
\delta w_j &= \alpha\frac{1}{\eta}(\overline{y}^\tau - (1-\eta)y^\tau)x_j^\tau \\
&= \alpha\frac{1-\eta}{\eta}(\frac{1}{1-\eta}\overline{y}^\tau - y^\tau)x_j^\tau \\
&= \hat{\alpha}(\hat{\beta}\overline{y}^\tau - y^\tau)x_j^\tau
\end{aligned}$$ (4.15)

where $\hat{\alpha} = \alpha\frac{1-\eta}{\eta}$ and $\hat{\beta} = \frac{1}{1-\eta}$. The modified Hebbian trace learning rule (4.13) is thus equivalent to equation 4.15 which is in the general form of an error correction rule (Hertz, Krogh and Palmer 1991). That is, rule (4.15) involves the subtraction of the current firing rate y^τ from a target value, in this case $\hat{\beta}\overline{y}^\tau$.

Although above we have referred to rule (4.13) as a modified Hebbian rule, we note that it is only associative in the sense of associating *previous* cell firing with the current cell inputs. In the next section we continue to explore the error correction paradigm, examining five alternative examples of this sort of learning rule.

4.5.4.2 Five forms of error correction learning rule

Error correction learning rules are derived from gradient descent minimization (Hertz, Krogh and Palmer 1991), and continually compare the current neuronal output to a target value t and adjust the synaptic weights according to the following equation at a particular timestep τ

$$\delta w_j = \alpha(t - y^\tau)x_j^\tau.$$ (4.16)

In this usual form of gradient descent by error correction, the target t is fixed. However, in keeping with our aim of encouraging neurons to respond similarly to images that occur close together in time it seems reasonable to set the target at a particular timestep, t^τ, to be some function of cell activity occurring close in time, because encouraging neurons to respond to temporal classes will tend to make them respond to the different variants of a given stimulus (Földiák 1991, Rolls 1992a, Wallis and Rolls 1997). For this reason, Rolls and Stringer (2001a) explored a range of error correction rules where the targets t^τ are based on the trace of neuronal activity calculated according to equation 4.11. We note that although the target is not a fixed value as in standard error correction learning, nevertheless the new learning rules perform gradient descent on each timestep, as elaborated below. Although the target may be varying early on in learning, as learning proceeds the target is expected to become more and more constant, as neurons settle to respond invariantly to particular stimuli. The first set of five error correction rules we discuss are as follows.

$$\delta w_j = \alpha(\beta\overline{y}^{\tau-1} - y^\tau)x_j^\tau,$$ (4.17)

$$\delta w_j = \alpha(\beta y^{\tau-1} - y^\tau)x_j^\tau,$$ (4.18)

$$\delta w_j = \alpha(\beta\overline{y}^\tau - y^\tau)x_j^\tau,$$ (4.19)

$$\delta w_j = \alpha(\beta\overline{y}^{\tau+1} - y^\tau)x_j^\tau,$$ (4.20)

$$\delta w_j = \alpha(\beta y^{\tau+1} - y^\tau)x_j^\tau,$$ (4.21)

where updates (4.17), (4.18) and (4.19) are performed at timestep τ, and updates (4.20) and (4.21) are performed at timestep $\tau + 1$. (The reason for adopting this convention is that the

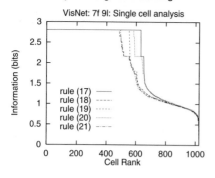
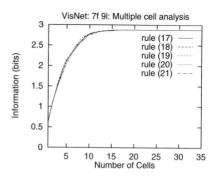

Fig. 4.41 Numerical results with the five error correction rules (4.17), (4.18), (4.19), (4.20), (4.21) (with positive clipping of synaptic weights) trained on 7 faces in 9 locations. On the left are single cell information measures, and on the right are multiple cell information measures. (After Rolls and Stringer 2001a.)

basic form of the error correction rule (4.16) is kept, with the five different rules simply replacing the term t.) It may be readily seen that equations (4.18) and (4.21) are special cases of equations (4.17) and (4.20) respectively, with $\eta = 0$.

These rules are all similar except for their targets t^τ, which are all functions of a temporally nearby value of cell activity. In particular, rule (4.19) is directly related to rule (4.15), but is more general in that the parameter $\hat{\beta} = \frac{1}{1-\eta}$ is replaced by an unconstrained parameter β. In addition, we also note that rule (4.17) is closely related to a rule developed in Peng, Sha, Gan and Wei (1998) for view invariance learning. The above five error correction rules are biologically plausible in that the targets t^τ are all local cell variables (see Appendix B and Rolls and Treves (1998)). In particular, rule (4.19) uses the trace $\bar{y}^\tau$ from the current time level τ, and rules (4.18) and (4.21) do not need exponential trace values $\bar{y}$, instead relying only on the instantaneous firing rates at the current and immediately preceding timesteps. However, all five error correction rules involve decrementing of synaptic weights according to an error which is calculated by subtracting the current activity from a target.

Numerical results with the error correction rules trained on 7 faces in 9 locations are presented in Fig. 4.41. For all the results shown the synaptic weights were clipped to be positive during the simulation, because it is important to test that decrementing synaptic weights purely within the positive interval $w \in [0, \infty)$ will provide significantly enhanced performance. That is, it is important to show that error correction rules do not necessarily require possibly biologically implausible modifiable negative weights. For each of the rules (4.17), (4.18), (4.19), (4.20), (4.21), the parameter β has been individually optimized to the following respective values: 4.9, 2.2, 2.2, 3.8, 2.2. On the left and right are results with the single and multiple cell information measures, respectively. Comparing Fig. 4.41 with Fig. 4.42 shows that all five error correction rules offer considerably improved performance over both the standard trace rule (4.10) and rule (4.13). From the left-hand side of Fig. 4.41 it can be seen that rule (4.17) performs best, and this is probably due to two reasons. Firstly, rule (4.17) incorporates an exponential trace $\bar{y}^{\tau-1}$ in its target t^τ, and we would expect this to help neurons to learn more quickly to respond invariantly to a class of inputs that occur close together in time. Hence, setting $\eta = 0$ as in rule (4.18) results in reduced performance. Secondly, unlike rules (4.19) and (4.20), rule (4.17) does not contain any component of y^τ in its target. If we examine rules (4.19), (4.20), we see that their respective targets $\beta \bar{y}^\tau$, $\beta \bar{y}^{\tau+1}$ contain significant components of y^τ.

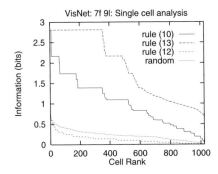

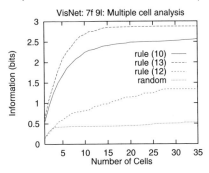

Fig. 4.42 Numerical results with the standard trace rule (4.10), learning rule (4.13), the Hebb rule (4.12), and random weights, trained on 7 faces in 9 locations: single cell information measure (left), multiple cell information measure (right). (After Rolls and Stringer 2001a.)

4.5.4.3 Relationship to temporal difference learning

Rolls and Stringer (2001a) not only considered the relationship of rule (4.13) to error correction, but also considered how the error correction rules shown in equations (4.17), (4.18), (4.19), (4.20) and (4.21) are related to temporal difference learning (Sutton 1988, Sutton and Barto 1998). Sutton (1988) described temporal difference methods in the context of prediction learning. These methods are a class of incremental learning techniques that can learn to predict final outcomes through comparison of successive predictions from the preceding time steps. This is in contrast to traditional supervised learning, which involves the comparison of predictions only with the final outcome. Consider a series of multistep prediction problems in which for each problem there is a sequence of observation vectors, $\mathbf{x}^1$, $\mathbf{x}^2$, ..., $\mathbf{x}^m$, at successive timesteps, followed by a final scalar outcome z. For each sequence of observations temporal difference methods form a sequence of predictions y^1, y^2, ..., y^m, each of which is a prediction of z. These predictions are based on the observation vectors $\mathbf{x}^\tau$ and a vector of modifiable weights $\mathbf{w}$; i.e. the prediction at time step τ is given by $y^\tau(\mathbf{x}^\tau, \mathbf{w})$, and for a linear dependency the prediction is given by $y^\tau = \mathbf{w}^T\mathbf{x}^\tau$. (Note here that $\mathbf{w}^T$ is the transpose of the weight vector $\mathbf{w}$.) The problem of prediction is to calculate the weight vector $\mathbf{w}$ such that the predictions y^τ are good estimates of the outcome z.

The supervised learning approach to the prediction problem is to form pairs of observation vectors $\mathbf{x}^\tau$ and outcome z for all time steps, and compute an update to the weights according to the gradient descent equation

$$\delta\mathbf{w} = \alpha(z - y^\tau)\nabla_\mathbf{w} y^\tau \tag{4.22}$$

where α is a learning rate parameter and $\nabla_\mathbf{w}$ indicates the gradient with respect to the weight vector $\mathbf{w}$. However, this learning procedure requires all calculation to be done at the end of the sequence, once z is known. To remedy this, it is possible to replace method (4.22) with a temporal difference algorithm that is mathematically equivalent but allows the computational workload to be spread out over the entire sequence of observations. Temporal difference methods are a particular approach to updating the weights based on the values of successive predictions, y^τ, $y^{\tau+1}$. Sutton (1988) showed that the following temporal difference algorithm is equivalent to method (4.22)

$$\delta\mathbf{w} = \alpha(y^{\tau+1} - y^\tau)\sum_{k=1}^{\tau}\nabla_\mathbf{w} y^k, \tag{4.23}$$

where $y^{m+1} \equiv z$. However, unlike method (4.22) this can be computed incrementally at each successive time step since each update depends only on $y^{\tau+1}$, y^{τ} and the sum of $\nabla_{\mathbf{w}} y^{k}$ over previous time steps k. The next step taken in Sutton (1988) is to generalize equation (4.23) to the following final form of temporal difference algorithm, known as 'TD(λ)'

$$\delta \mathbf{w} = \alpha(y^{\tau+1} - y^{\tau}) \sum_{k=1}^{\tau} \lambda^{\tau-k} \nabla_{\mathbf{w}} y^{k} \tag{4.24}$$

where $\lambda \in [0, 1]$ is an adjustable parameter that controls the weighting on the vectors $\nabla_{\mathbf{w}} y^{k}$. Equation (4.24) represents a much broader class of learning rules than the more usual gradient descent-based rule (4.23), which is in fact the special case TD(1).

A further special case of equation (4.24) is for $\lambda = 0$, i.e. TD(0), as follows

$$\delta \mathbf{w} = \alpha(y^{\tau+1} - y^{\tau}) \nabla_{\mathbf{w}} y^{\tau}. \tag{4.25}$$

But for problems where y^{τ} is a linear function of $\mathbf{x}^{\tau}$ and $\mathbf{w}$, we have $\nabla_{\mathbf{w}} y^{\tau} = \mathbf{x}^{\tau}$, and so equation (4.25) becomes

$$\delta \mathbf{w} = \alpha(y^{\tau+1} - y^{\tau}) \mathbf{x}^{\tau}. \tag{4.26}$$

If we assume the prediction process is being performed by a neuron with a vector of inputs $\mathbf{x}^{\tau}$, synaptic weight vector $\mathbf{w}$, and output $y^{\tau} = \mathbf{w}^{T} \mathbf{x}^{\tau}$, then we see that the TD(0) algorithm (4.26) is identical to the error correction rule (4.21) with $\beta = 1$. In understanding this comparison with temporal difference learning, it may be useful to note that the firing at the end of a sequence of the transformed exemplars of a stimulus is effectively the temporal difference target z. This establishes a link to temporal difference learning (described further in Section B.15.3). Further, we note that from learning epoch to learning epoch, the target z for a given neuron will gradually settle down to be more and more fixed as learning proceeds.

We now explore in more detail the relation between the error correction rules described above and temporal difference learning. For each sequence of observations with a single outcome the temporal difference method (4.26), when viewed as an error correction rule, is attempting to adapt the weights such that $y^{\tau+1} = y^{\tau}$ for all successive pairs of time steps – the same general idea underlying the error correction rules (4.17), (4.18), (4.19), (4.20), (4.21). Furthermore, in Sutton and Barto (1998), where temporal difference methods are applied to reinforcement learning, the TD(λ) approach is again further generalized by replacing the target $y^{\tau+1}$ by any weighted average of predictions y from arbitrary future timesteps, e.g. $t^{\tau} = \frac{1}{2} y^{\tau+3} + \frac{1}{2} y^{\tau+7}$, including an exponentially weighted average extending forward in time. So a more general form of the temporal difference algorithm has the form

$$\delta \mathbf{w} = \alpha(t^{\tau} - y^{\tau}) \mathbf{x}^{\tau}, \tag{4.27}$$

where here the target t^{τ} is an arbitrary weighted average of the predictions y over future timesteps. Of course, with standard temporal difference methods the target t^{τ} is always an average over *future* timesteps $k = \tau + 1, \tau + 2$, etc. But in the five error correction rules this is only true for the last exemplar (4.21). This is because with the problem of prediction, for example, the ultimate target of the predictions $y^{1},...,y^{m}$ is a final outcome $y^{m+1} \equiv z$. However, this restriction does not apply to our particular application of neurons trained to respond to temporal classes of inputs within VisNet. Here we only wish to set the firing rates $y^{1},...,y^{m}$ to the same value, not some final given value z. However, the more general error correction rules clearly have a close relationship to standard temporal difference algorithms. For example, it can be seen that equation (4.18) with $\beta = 1$ is in some sense a temporal mirror image of equation (4.26), particularly if the updates δw_{j} are added to the weights w_{j}

only at the end of a sequence. That is, rule (4.18) will attempt to set $y^1,...,y^m$ to an *initial* value $y^0 \equiv z$. This relationship to temporal difference algorithms allows us to begin to exploit established temporal difference analyses to investigate the convergence properties of the error correction methods (Rolls and Stringer 2001a).

Although the main aim of Rolls and Stringer (2001a) in relating error correction rules to temporal difference learning was to begin to exploit established temporal difference analyses, they observed that the most general form of temporal difference learning, TD(λ), in fact suggests an interesting generalization to the existing error correction learning rules for which we currently have $\lambda = 0$. Assuming $y^\tau = \mathbf{w}^T\mathbf{x}^\tau$ and $\nabla_{\mathbf{w}}y^\tau = \mathbf{x}^\tau$, the general equation (4.24) for TD(λ) becomes

$$\delta\mathbf{w} = \alpha(y^{\tau+1} - y^\tau)\sum_{k=1}^{\tau}\lambda^{\tau-k}\mathbf{x}^k \qquad (4.28)$$

where the term $\sum_{k=1}^{\tau}\lambda^{\tau-k}\mathbf{x}^k$ is a weighted sum of the vectors $\mathbf{x}^k$. This suggests generalizing the original five error correction rules (4.17), (4.18), (4.19), (4.20), (4.21) by replacing the term x_j^τ by a weighted sum $\hat{x}_j^\tau = \sum_{k=1}^{\tau}\lambda^{\tau-k}x_j^k$ with $\lambda \in [0,1]$. In Sutton (1988) $\hat{x}_j^\tau$ is calculated according to

$$\hat{x}_j^\tau = x_j^\tau + \lambda\hat{x}_j^{\tau-1} \qquad (4.29)$$

with $\hat{x}_j^0 \equiv 0$. This gives the following five temporal difference-inspired error correction rules

$$\delta w_j = \alpha(\beta\overline{y}^{\tau-1} - y^\tau)\hat{x}_j^\tau, \qquad (4.30)$$

$$\delta w_j = \alpha(\beta y^{\tau-1} - y^\tau)\hat{x}_j^\tau, \qquad (4.31)$$

$$\delta w_j = \alpha(\beta\overline{y}^\tau - y^\tau)\hat{x}_j^\tau, \qquad (4.32)$$

$$\delta w_j = \alpha(\beta\overline{y}^{\tau+1} - y^\tau)\hat{x}_j^\tau, \qquad (4.33)$$

$$\delta w_j = \alpha(\beta y^{\tau+1} - y^\tau)\hat{x}_j^\tau, \qquad (4.34)$$

where it may be readily seen that equations (4.31) and (4.34) are special cases of equations (4.30) and (4.33) respectively, with $\eta = 0$. As with the trace $\overline{y}^\tau$, the term $\hat{x}_j^\tau$ is reset to zero when a new stimulus is presented. These five rules can be related to the more general TD(λ) algorithm, but continue to be biologically plausible using only local cell variables. Setting $\lambda = 0$ in rules (4.30), (4.31), (4.32), (4.33), (4.34), gives us back the original error correction rules (4.17), (4.18), (4.19), (4.20), (4.21) which may now be related to TD(0).

Numerical results with error correction rules (4.30), (4.31), (4.32), (4.33), (4.34), and $\hat{x}_j^\tau$ calculated according to equation (4.29) with $\lambda = 1$, with positive clipping of weights, trained on 7 faces in 9 locations are presented in Fig. 4.43. For each of the rules (4.30), (4.31), (4.32), (4.33), (4.34), the parameter β has been individually optimized to the following respective values: 1.7, 1.8, 1.5, 1.6, 1.8. On the left and right are results with the single and multiple cell information measures, respectively. Comparing these five temporal difference-inspired rules it can be seen that the best performance is obtained with rule (4.34) where many more cells reach the maximum level of performance possible with respect to the single cell information measure. In fact, this rule offered the best such results. This may well be due to the fact that this rule may be directly compared to the standard TD(1) learning rule, which itself may be related to classical supervised learning for which there are well known optimality results, as discussed further by Rolls and Stringer (2001a).

From the simulations described by Rolls and Stringer (2001a) it appears that the form of optimization described above associated with TD(1) rather than TD(0) leads to better performance within VisNet. Comparing Figs. 4.41 and 4.43 shows that the TD(1)-like rule (4.34)

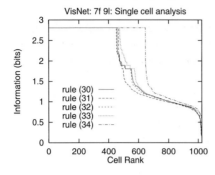
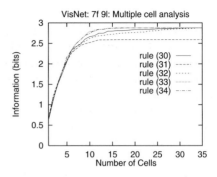

Fig. 4.43 Numerical results with the five temporal difference-inspired error correction rules (4.30), (4.31), (4.32), (4.33), (4.34), and $\hat{x}_j^\tau$ calculated according to equation (4.29) (with positive clipping of synaptic weights) trained on 7 faces in 9 locations. On the left are single cell information measures, and on the right are multiple cell information measures. (After Rolls and Stringer 2001a.)

with $\lambda = 1.0$ and $\beta = 1.8$ gives considerably superior results to the TD(0)-like rule (4.21) with $\beta = 2.2$. In fact, the former of these two rules provided the best single cell information results in these studies. We hypothesize that these results are related to the fact that only a finite set of image sequences is presented to VisNet, and so the type of optimization performed by TD(1) for repeated presentations of a finite data set is more appropriate for this problem than the form of optimization performed by TD(0).

4.5.4.4 Discussion of the different training rules

In terms of biological plausibility, we note the following. First, all the learning rules investigated by Rolls and Stringer (2001a) are local learning rules, and in this sense are biologically plausible (see Appendix B and Rolls and Treves (1998)). (The rules are local in that the terms used to modify the synaptic weights are potentially available in the pre- and post-synaptic elements.)

Second we note that all the rules do require some evidence of the activity on one or more previous stimulus presentations to be available when the synaptic weights are updated. Some of the rules, e.g. learning rule (4.19), use the trace $\overline{y}^\tau$ from the current time level, while rules (4.18) and (4.21) do not need to use an exponential trace of the neuronal firing rate, but only the instantaneous firing rates y at two successive time steps. It is known that synaptic plasticity does involve a combination of separate processes each with potentially differing time courses (Koch 1999), and these different processes could contribute to trace rule learning. Another mechanism suggested for implementing a trace of previous neuronal activity is the continuing firing for often 300 ms produced by a short (16 ms) presentation of a visual stimulus (Rolls and Tovee 1994) which is suggested to be implemented by local cortical recurrent attractor networks (Rolls and Treves 1998).

Third, we note that in utilizing the trace in the targets t^τ, the error correction (or temporal difference inspired) rules perform a comparison of the instantaneous firing y^τ with a temporally nearby value of the activity, and this comparison involves a subtraction. The subtraction provides an error, which is then used to increase or decrease the synaptic weights. This is a somewhat different operation from long-term depression (LTD) as well as long term potentiation (LTP), which are *associative* changes which depend on the pre- and post-synaptic activity. However, it is interesting to note that an error correction rule which appears to involve a subtraction of current firing from a target might be implemented by a combination of an associative process operating with the trace, and an anti-Hebbian process operating to remove the effects of the current firing. For example, the synaptic updates $\delta w_j = \alpha(t^\tau - y^\tau)x_j^\tau$ can be decomposed into two separate associative processes $\alpha t^\tau x_j^\tau$ and $-\alpha y^\tau x_j^\tau$, that may occur independently. (The target, t^τ, could in this case be just the trace of previous neural activity from the preceding trials, excluding any contribution from the current firing.) Another way to implement an error correction rule using associative synaptic modification would be to force the post-synaptic neuron to respond to the error term. Although this has been postulated to be an effect which could be implemented by the climbing fibre system in the cerebellum (Ito 1989, Ito 1984, Rolls and Treves 1998), there is no similar system known for the neocortex, and it is not clear how this particular implementation of error correction might operate in the neocortex.

In Section 4.5.4.2 we describe five learning rules as error correction rules. We now discuss an interesting difference of these error correction rules from error correction rules as conventionally applied. It is usual to derive the general form of error correction learning rule from gradient descent minimization in the following way (Hertz, Krogh and Palmer 1991). Consider the idealized situation of a single neuron with a number of inputs x_j and output $y = \sum_j w_j x_j$, where w_j are the synaptic weights. We assume that there are a number of input patterns and that for the kth input pattern, $\mathbf{x}^k = [x_1^k, x_2^k, ...]^T$, the output y^k has a target value t^k. Hence an error measure or cost function can be defined as

$$e(\mathbf{w}) = \frac{1}{2}\sum_k (t^k - y^k)^2 = \frac{1}{2}\sum_k (t^k - \sum_j w_j x_j^k)^2. \qquad (4.35)$$

This cost function is a function of the input patterns $\mathbf{x}^k$ and the synaptic weight vector $\mathbf{w} = [w_1, w_2, ...]^T$. With a fixed set of input patterns, we can reduce the error measure by employing a gradient descent algorithm to calculate an improved set of synaptic weights. Gradient descent achieves this by moving downhill on the error surface defined in $\mathbf{w}$ space using the update

$$\delta w_j = -\alpha \frac{\partial e}{\partial w_j} = \alpha \sum_k (t^k - y^k) x_j^k. \qquad (4.36)$$

If we update the weights after each pattern k, then the update takes the form of an error correction rule

$$\delta w_j = \alpha(t^k - y^k) x_j^k, \qquad (4.37)$$

which is also commonly referred to as the delta rule or Widrow–Hoff rule (see Widrow and Hoff (1960) and Widrow and Stearns (1985)). Error correction rules continually compare the neuronal output with its pre-specified target value and adjust the synaptic weights accordingly. In contrast, the way Rolls and Stringer (2001a) introduced of utilizing error correction is to specify the target as the activity trace based on the firing rate at nearby timesteps. Now the actual firing at those nearby time steps is not a pre-determined fixed target, but instead depends on how the network has actually evolved. This effectively means the cost function $e(\mathbf{w})$ that is being minimized changes from timestep to timestep. Nevertheless, the concept of calculating an error, and using the magnitude and direction of the error to update the synaptic weights, is the similarity Rolls and Stringer (2001a) made to gradient descent learning.

To conclude this discussion, the error correction and temporal difference rules explored by Rolls and Stringer (2001a) provide interesting approaches to help understand invariant pattern recognition learning. Although we do not know whether the full power of these rules is expressed in the brain, we provided suggestions about how they might be implemented. At the same time, we note that the original trace rule used by Földiák (1991), Rolls (1992a), and Wallis and Rolls (1997) is a simple associative rule, is therefore biologically very plausible, and, while not as powerful as many of the other rules introduced by Rolls and Stringer (2001a), can nevertheless solve the same class of problem. Rolls and Stringer (2001a) also emphasized that although they demonstrated how a number of new error correction and temporal difference rules might play a role in the context of view invariant object recognition, they may also operate elsewhere where it is important for neurons to learn to respond similarly to temporal classes of inputs that tend to occur close together in time.

4.5.5 The issue of feature binding, and a solution

In this section we investigate two key issues that arise in hierarchical layered network architectures, such as VisNet, other examples of which have been described and analyzed by Fukushima (1980), Ackley, Hinton and Sejnowski (1985), Rosenblatt (1961), and Riesenhuber and Poggio (1999b). One issue is whether the network can discriminate between stimuli that are composed of the same basic alphabet of features. The second issue is whether such network architectures can find solutions to the spatial binding problem. These issues are addressed next and by Elliffe, Rolls and Stringer (2002).

The first issue investigated is whether a hierarchical layered network architecture of the type exemplified by VisNet can discriminate stimuli that are composed of a limited set of features and where the different stimuli include cases where the feature sets are subsets and supersets of those in the other stimuli. An issue is that if the network has learned representations of both the parts and the wholes, will the network identify that the whole is present when it is shown, and not just that one or more parts is present. (In many investigations with VisNet, complex stimuli (such as faces) were used where each stimulus might contain unique features not present in the other stimuli.) To address this issue, Elliffe, Rolls and Stringer (2002) used stimuli that are composed from a set of four features which are designed so that each feature is spatially separate from the other features, and no unique combination of firing caused for example by overlap of horizontal and vertical filter outputs in the input representation distinguishes any one stimulus from the others. The results described in Section 4.5.5.4 show that VisNet can indeed learn correct invariant representations of stimuli which do consist of feature sets where individual features do not overlap spatially with each other and where the stimuli can be composed of sets of features which are supersets or subsets of those in other stimuli. Fukushima and Miyake (1982) did not address this crucial issue where different stimuli might be composed of subsets or supersets of the same set of features, although they did show that stimuli with partly overlapping features could be discriminated by the Neocognitron.

In Section 4.5.5.5 we address the spatial binding problem in architectures such as VisNet. This computational problem that needs to be addressed in hierarchical networks such as the primate visual system and VisNet is how representations of features can be (e.g. translation) invariant, yet can specify stimuli or objects in which the features must be specified in the correct spatial arrangement. This is the feature binding problem, discussed for example by von der Malsburg (1990), and arising in the context of hierarchical layered systems (Ackley, Hinton and Sejnowski 1985, Fukushima 1980, Rosenblatt 1961). The issue is whether or not features are bound into the correct combinations in the correct relative spatial positions, or if alternative combinations of known features or the same features in different relative spatial positions would elicit the same responses. All this has to be achieved while at the same time producing position invariant recognition of the whole combination of features, that is, the object. This is a major computational issue that needs to be solved for memory systems in the brain to operate correctly. This can be achieved by what is effectively a learning process that builds into the system a set of neurons in the hierarchical network that enables the recognition process to operate correctly with the appropriate position, size, view etc. invariances.

4.5.5.1 Syntactic binding of separate neuronal ensembles by synchronization

The problem of syntactic binding of neuronal representations, in which some features must be bound together to form one object, and other simultaneously active features must be bound together to represent another object, has been addressed by von der Malsburg (see von der Malsburg (1990)). He has proposed that this could be performed by temporal synchronization of those neurons that were temporarily part of one representation in a different time slot from other neurons that were temporarily part of another representation. The idea is attractive in allowing arbitrary relinking of features in different combinations. Singer, Engel, Konig, and colleagues (Singer, Gray, Engel, Konig, Artola and Brocher 1990, Engel, Konig, Kreiter, Schillen and Singer 1992, Singer and Gray 1995, Singer 1999), and others (Abeles 1991) have obtained some evidence that when features must be bound, synchronization of neuronal populations can occur (but see Shadlen and Movshon (1999)), and this has been modelled (Hummel and Biederman 1992).

Synchronization to implement syntactic binding has a number of disadvantages and limitations (see also Rolls and Treves (1998), Riesenhuber and Poggio (1999a) and Rolls and Deco (2002)). The greatest computational problem is that synchronization does not by itself define the spatial relations between the features being bound, so is not just as a binding mechanism adequate for shape recognition. For example, temporal binding might enable features 1, 2 and 3, which might define one stimulus to be bound together and kept separate from for example another stimulus consisting of features 2, 3 and 4, but would require a further temporal binding (leading in the end potentially to a combinatorial explosion) to indicate the relative spatial positions of the 1, 2 and 3 in the 123 stimulus, so that it can be discriminated from e.g. 312.

A second problem with the synchronization approach to the spatial binding of features is that, when stimulus-dependent temporal synchronization has been rigorously tested with information theoretic approaches, it has so far been found that most of the information available is in the number of spikes, with rather little, less than 5% of the total information, in stimulus-dependent synchronization (Aggelopoulos, Franco and Rolls 2005, Franco, Rolls, Aggelopoulos and Treves 2004, Rolls, Aggelopoulos, Franco and Treves 2004) (see Section C.3.7). For example, Aggelopoulos, Franco and Rolls (2005) showed that when macaques used object-based attention to search for one of two objects to touch in a complex natural scene, between 99% and 94% of the information was present in the firing rates of inferior temporal cortex neurons, and less that 5% in any stimulus-dependent synchrony that was present between the simultaneously recorded inferior temporal cortex neurons. The implication of these results is that any stimulus-dependent synchrony that is present is not quantitatively important as measured by information theoretic analyses under natural scene conditions when feature binding, segmentation of objects from the background, and attention are required. This has been found for the inferior temporal cortex, a brain region where features are put together to form representations of objects (Rolls and Deco 2002), and where attention has strong effects, at least in scenes with blank backgrounds (Rolls, Aggelopoulos and Zheng 2003a). It would of course also be of interest to test the same hypothesis in earlier visual areas, such as V4, with quantitative, information theoretic, techniques. In connection with rate codes, it should be noted that a rate code implies using the number of spikes that arrive in a given time, and that this time can be very short, as little as 20–50 ms, for very useful amounts of information to be made available from a population of neurons (Tovee, Rolls, Treves and Bellis 1993, Rolls and Tovee 1994, Rolls, Tovee, Purcell, Stewart and Azzopardi 1994b, Tovee and Rolls 1995, Rolls, Tovee and Panzeri 1999b, Rolls 2003, Rolls, Franco, Aggelopoulos and Jerez 2006b) (see Section C.3.4).

In the context of VisNet, and how the real visual system may operate to implement object recognition, the use of synchronization does not appear to match the way in which the visual system is organized. For example, von der Malsburg's argument would indicate that, using only a two-layer network, synchronization could provide the necessary feature linking to perform object recognition with relatively few neurons, because they can be reused again and again, linked differently for different objects. In contrast, the primate uses a considerable part of its cortex, perhaps 50% in monkeys, for visual processing, with therefore what could be in the order of 6×10^8 neurons and 6×10^{12} synapses involved (estimating from the values given in Table 1.1), so that the solution adopted by the real visual system may be one which relies on many neurons with simpler processing than arbitrary syntax implemented by synchronous firing of separate assemblies suggests. On the other hand, a solution such as that investigated by VisNet, which forms low-order combinations of what is represented in previous layers, is very demanding in terms of the number of neurons required, and this matches what is found in the primate visual system. It will be fascinating to see how research on these different approaches to processing in the primate visual system develops. For the development of both approaches, the use of well-defined neuronal network models is proving to be very helpful.

4.5.5.2 Sigma-Pi neurons

Another approach to a binding mechanism is to group spatial features based on local mechanisms that might operate for closely adjacent synapses on a dendrite (in what is a Sigma-Pi type of neuron, see Sections 4.6 and A.2.3) (Finkel and Edelman 1987, Mel, Ruderman and Archie 1998). A problem for such architectures is how to force one particular neuron to respond to the same feature combination invariantly with respect to all the ways in which that feature combination might occur in a scene.

4.5.5.3 Binding of features and their relative spatial position by feature combination neurons

The approach to the spatial binding problem that is proposed for VisNet is that individual neurons at an early stage of processing are set up (by learning) to respond to low order combinations of input features occurring in a given relative spatial arrangement and position on the retina (Rolls 1992a, Rolls 1994a, Rolls 1995b, Wallis and Rolls 1997, Rolls and Treves 1998, Elliffe, Rolls and Stringer 2002, Rolls and Deco 2002) (cf. Feldman (1985)). (By low order combinations of input features we mean combinations of a few input features. By forming neurons that respond to combinations of a few features in the correct spatial arrangement the advantages of the scheme for syntactic binding are obtained, yet without the combinatorial explosion that would result if the feature combination neurons responded to combinations of many input features so producing potentially very specifically tuned neurons which very rarely responded.) Then invariant representations are developed in the next layer from these feature combination neurons which already contain evidence on the local spatial arrangement of features. Finally, in later layers, only one stimulus would be specified by the particular set of low order feature combination neurons present, even though each feature combination neuron would itself be somewhat invariant. The overall design of the scheme is shown in Fig. 4.20. Evidence that many neurons in V1 respond to combinations of spatial features with the correct spatial configuration is now starting to appear (see Section 4.4), and neurons that respond to feature combinations (such as two lines with a defined angle between them, and overall orientation) are found in V2 (Hegde and Van Essen 2000, Ito and Komatsu 2004). The tuning of a VisNet layer 1 neuron to a combination of features in the correct relative spatial position is illustrated in Figs. 4.25 and 4.26.

4.5.5.4 Discrimination between stimuli with super- and sub-set feature combinations

Some investigations with VisNet (Wallis and Rolls 1997) have involved groups of stimuli that might be identified by some unique feature common to all transformations of a particular stimulus. This might allow VisNet to solve the problem of transform invariance by simply learning to respond to a unique feature present in each stimulus. For example, even in the case where VisNet was trained on invariant discrimination of T, L, and +, the representation of the T stimulus at the spatial filter level inputs to VisNet might contain unique patterns of filter outputs where the horizontal and vertical parts of the T join. The unique filter outputs thus formed might distinguish the T from for example the L.

Elliffe, Rolls and Stringer (2002) tested whether VisNet is able to form transform invariant cells with stimuli that are specially composed from a common alphabet of features, with no stimulus containing any firing in the spatial filter inputs to VisNet not present in at least one of the other stimuli. The limited alphabet enables the set of stimuli to consist of feature sets which are subsets or supersets of those in the other stimuli.

For these experiments the common pool of stimulus features chosen was a set of two horizontal and two vertical 8×1 bars, each aligned with the sides of a 32×32 square. The stimuli can be constructed by arbitrary combination of these base level features. We note that effectively the stimulus set consists of four features, a top bar (T), a bottom bar (B), a left bar (L), and a right bar (R). Figure 4.44 shows the complete set used, containing every possible image feature combination. (Note that the two double-feature combinations where the features are parallel to each other are not included, in the interests of retaining symmetry and equal inter-object overlap within each feature-combination level.) Subsequent discussion will group these objects by the number of features each contains: single-; double-; triple-; and quadruple-feature objects correspond to the respective rows of Fig. 4.44. Stimuli are referred to by the list of features they contain; e.g. 'LBR' contains the left, bottom, and right features, while 'TL' contains top and left only. Further details of how the stimuli were prepared are provided by Elliffe, Rolls and Stringer (2002).

To train the network a stimulus was presented in a randomized sequence of nine locations in a square grid across the 128×128 input retina. The central location of the square grid was in the centre of the 'retina', and the eight other locations were offset 8 pixels horizontally and/or vertically from this. Two different learning rules were used, 'Hebbian' (4.12), and 'trace' (4.13), and also an untrained condition with random weights. As in earlier work (Wallis and Rolls 1997, Rolls and Milward 2000) only the trace rule led to any cells with invariant responses, and the results shown here are for networks trained with the trace rule.

The results with VisNet trained on the set of stimuli shown in Fig. 4.44 with the trace rule are as follows. Firstly, it was found that single neurons in the top layer learned to differentiate between the stimuli in that the responses of individual neurons were maximal for one of the stimuli and had no response to any of the other stimuli invariantly with respect to location. Secondly, to assess how well every stimulus was encoded for in this way, Fig. 4.45 shows the information available about each of the stimuli consisting of feature singles, feature pairs, feature triples, and the quadruple-feature stimulus 'TLBR'. The single cell information available from the 26–85 cells with best tuning to each of the stimuli is shown. The cells in general conveyed translation invariant information about the stimulus to which they responded, with indeed cells which perfectly discriminated one of the stimuli from all others over every testing position (for all stimuli except 'RTL' and 'TLBR').

The results presented show clearly that the VisNet paradigm can accommodate networks that can perform invariant discrimination of objects which have a subset–superset relationship. The result has important consequences for feature binding and for discriminating stimuli for

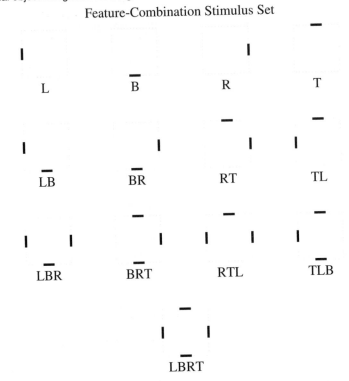

Fig. 4.44 Merged feature objects. All members of the full object set are shown, using a dotted line to represent the central 32×32 square on which the individual features are positioned, with the features themselves shown as dark line segments. Nomenclature is by acronym of the features present. (After Elliffe, Rolls and Stringer 2002.)

other stimuli which may be supersets of the first stimulus. For example, a VisNet cell which responds invariantly to feature combination TL can genuinely signal the presence of exactly that combination, and will not necessarily be activated by T alone, or by TLB. The basis for this separation by competitive networks of stimuli which are subsets and supersets of each other is described in Section B.4, and by Rolls and Treves (1998, Section 4.3.6).

4.5.5.5 Feature binding in a hierarchical network with invariant representations of local feature combinations

In this section we consider the ability of output layer neurons to learn new stimuli if the lower layers are trained solely through exposure to simpler feature combinations from which the new stimuli are composed. A key question we address is how invariant representations of low order feature combinations in the early layers of the visual system are able to uniquely specify the correct spatial arrangement of features in the overall stimulus and contribute to preventing false recognition errors in the output layer.

The problem, and its proposed solution, can be treated as follows. Consider an object 1234 made from the features 1, 2, 3 and 4. The invariant low order feature combinations might represent 12, 23, and 34. Then if neurons at the next layer respond to combinations of the activity of these neurons, the only neurons in the next layer that would respond would be those tuned to 1234, not to for example 3412, which is distinguished from 1234 by the input of a pair neuron responding to 41 rather than to 23. The argument (Rolls 1992a) is that low-order spatial feature combination neurons in the early stage contain sufficient spatial information

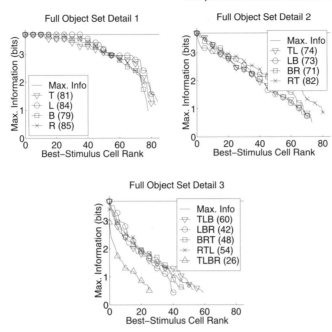

Fig. 4.45 Performance of VisNet2 on the full set of stimuli shown in Fig. 4.44. Separate graphs showing the information available about the stimulus for cells tuned to respond best to each of the stimuli are shown. The number of cells responding best to each of the stimuli is indicated in parentheses. The information values are shown for the different cells ranked according to how much information about that stimulus they encode. Separate graphs are shown for cells tuned to stimuli consisting of single features, pairs of features, and triples of features as well as the quadruple feature stimulus TLBR. (After Elliffe, Rolls and Stringer 2002.)

so that a particular combination of those low-order feature combination neurons specifies a unique object, even if the relative positions of the low-order feature combination neurons are not known, because they are somewhat invariant.

The architecture of VisNet is intended to solve this problem partly by allowing high spatial precision combinations of input features to be formed in layer 1. The actual input features in VisNet are, as described above, the output of oriented spatial-frequency tuned filters, and the combinations of these formed in layer 1 might thus be thought of in a simple way as for example a T or an L or for that matter a Y. Then in layer 2, application of the trace rule might enable neurons to respond to a T with limited spatial invariance (limited to the size of the region of layer 1 from which layer 2 cells receive their input). Then an 'object' such as H might be formed at a higher layer because of a conjunction of two Ts in the same small region.

To show that VisNet can actually solve this problem, Elliffe, Rolls and Stringer (2002) performed the experiments described next. They trained the first two layers of VisNet with feature pair combinations, forming representations of feature pairs with some translation invariance in layer 2. Then they used feature triples as input stimuli, allowed no more learning in layers 1 and 2, and then investigated whether layers 3 and 4 could be trained to produce invariant representations of the triples where the triples could only be distinguished if the local spatial arrangement of the features within the triple had effectively to be encoded in order to distinguish the different triples. For this experiment, they needed stimuli that could be specified in terms of a set of different features (they chose vertical (1), diagonal (2), and horizontal (3) bars) each capable of being shown at a set of different relative spatial positions

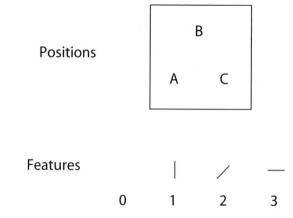

Fig. 4.46 Feature combinations for experiments of Section 4.5.5.5: there are 3 features denoted by 1, 2 and 3 (including a blank space 0) that can be placed in any of 3 positions A, B, and C. Individual stimuli are denoted by three consecutive numbers which refer to the individual features present in positions A, B and C respectively. In the experiments in Section 4.5.5.5, layers 1 and 2 were trained on stimuli consisting of pairs of the features, and layers 3 and 4 were trained on stimuli consisting of triples. Then the network was tested to show whether layer 4 neurons would distinguish between triples, even though the first two layers had only been trained on pairs. In addition, the network was tested to show whether individual cells in layer 4 could distinguish between triples even in locations where the triples were not presented during training. (After Elliffe, Rolls and Stringer 2002.)

(designated A, B and C), as shown in Fig. 4.46. The stimuli are thus defined in terms of what features are present and their precise spatial arrangement with respect to each other. The length of the horizontal and vertical feature bars shown in Fig. 4.46 is 8 pixels. To train the network a stimulus (that is a pair or triple feature combination) is presented in a randomized sequence of nine locations in a square grid across the 128×128 input retina. The central location of the square grid is in the centre of the 'retina', and the eight other locations are offset 8 pixels horizontally and/or vertically from this. We refer to the two and three feature stimuli as 'pairs' and 'triples', respectively. Individual stimuli are denoted by three numbers which refer to the individual features present in positions A, B and C, respectively. For example, a stimulus with positions A and C containing a vertical and diagonal bar, respectively, would be referred to as stimulus 102, where the 0 denotes no feature present in position B. In total there are 18 pairs (120, 130, 210, 230, 310, 320, 012, 013, 021, 023, 031, 032, 102, 103, 201, 203, 301, 302) and 6 triples (123, 132, 213, 231, 312, 321). This nomenclature not only defines which features are present within objects, but also the spatial relationships of their component features. Then the computational problem can be illustrated by considering the triple 123. If invariant representations are formed of single features, then there would be no way that neurons higher in the hierarchy could distinguish the object 123 from 213 or any other arrangement of the three features. An approach to this problem (see e.g. Rolls (1992a)) is to form early on in the processing neurons that respond to overlapping combinations of features in the correct spatial arrangement, and then to develop invariant representations in the next layer from these neurons which already contain evidence on the local spatial arrangement of features. An example might be that with the object 123, the invariant feature pairs would represent 120, 023, and 103. Then if neurons at the next layer correspond to combinations of these neurons, the only next layer neurons that would respond would be those tuned to 123, not to for example 213. The argument is that the low-order spatial feature combination neurons in the early stage contain sufficient spatial information so that a particular combination of those low-order feature combination neurons specifies a unique object, even if the relative

Table 4.5 The different training regimes used in VisNet experiments 1–4 of Section 4.5.5.5. In the no training condition the synaptic weights were left in their initial untrained random values.

	Layers 1, 2	Layers 3, 4
Experiment 1	trained on pairs	trained on triples
Experiment 2	no training	no training
Experiment 3	no training	trained on triples
Experiment 4	trained on triples	trained on triples

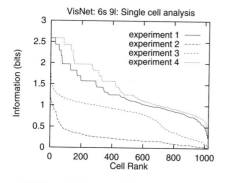
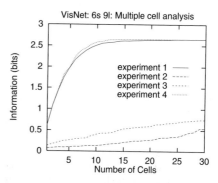

Fig. 4.47 Numerical results for experiments 1–4 as described in Table 4.5, with the trace learning rule (4.13). On the left are single cell information measures, and on the right are multiple cell information measures. (After Elliffe, Rolls and Stringer 2002.)

positions of the low-order feature combination neurons are not known because these neurons are somewhat translation invariant (cf. also Fukushima (1988)).

The stimuli used in the experiments of Elliffe, Rolls and Stringer (2002) were constructed from pre-processed component features as discussed in Section 4.5.5.4. That is, base stimuli containing a single feature were constructed and filtered, and then the pairs and triples were constructed by merging these pre-processed single feature images. In the first experiment layers 1 and 2 of VisNet were trained with the 18 feature pairs, each stimulus being presented in sequences of 9 locations across the input. This led to the formation of neurons that responded to the feature pairs with some translation invariance in layer 2. Then they trained layers 3 and 4 on the 6 feature triples in the same 9 locations, while allowing no more learning in layers 1 and 2, and examined whether the output layer of VisNet had developed transform invariant neurons to the 6 triples. The idea was to test whether layers 3 and 4 could be trained to produce invariant representations of the triples where the triples could only be distinguished if the local spatial arrangement of the features within the triple had effectively to be encoded in order to distinguish the different triples. The results from this experiment were compared and contrasted with results from three other experiments which involved different training regimes for layers 1,2 and layers 3,4. All four experiments are summarized in Table 4.5. Experiment 2 involved no training in layers 1,2 and 3,4, with the synaptic weights left unchanged from their initial random values. These results are included as a baseline performance with which to compare results from the other experiments 1, 3 and 4. The model parameters used in these experiments were as described by Rolls and Milward (2000) and Rolls and Stringer (2001a).

In Fig. 4.47 we present numerical results for the four experiments listed in Table 4.5. On the left are the single cell information measures for all top (4th) layer neurons ranked in order of their invariance to the triples, while on the right are multiple cell information measures. To help to interpret these results we can compute the maximum single cell information measure according to

$$\text{Maximum single cell information} = \log_2(\text{Number of triples}), \qquad (4.38)$$

where the number of triples is 6. This gives a maximum single cell information measure of 2.6 bits for these test cases. First, comparing the results for experiment 1 with the baseline performance of experiment 2 (no training) demonstrates that even with the first two layers trained to form invariant responses to the pairs, and then only layers 3 and 4 trained on feature triples, layer 4 is indeed capable of developing translation invariant neurons that can discriminate effectively between the 6 different feature triples. Indeed, from the single cell information measures it can be seen that a number of cells have reached the maximum level of performance in experiment 1. In addition, the multiple cell information analysis presented in Fig. 4.47 shows that all the stimuli could be discriminated from each other by the firing of a number of cells. Analysis of the response profiles of individual cells showed that a fourth layer cell could respond to one of the triple feature stimuli and have no response to any other of the triple feature stimuli invariantly with respect to location.

A comparison of the results from experiment 1 with those from experiment 3 (see Table 4.5 and Fig. 4.47) reveals that training the first two layers to develop neurons that respond invariantly to the pairs (performed in experiment 1) actually leads to improved invariance of 4th layer neurons to the triples, as compared with when the first two layers are left untrained (experiment 3).

Two conclusions follow from these results (Elliffe, Rolls and Stringer 2002). First, a hierarchical network that seeks to produce invariant representations in the way used by VisNet can solve the feature binding problem. In particular, when feature pairs in layer 2 with some translation invariance are used as the input to later layers, these later layers can nevertheless build invariant representations of objects where all the individual features in the stimulus must occur in the correct spatial position relative to each other. This is possible because the feature combination neurons formed in the first layer (which could be trained just with a Hebb rule) do respond to combinations of input features in the correct spatial configuration, partly because of the limited size of their receptive fields (see e.g. Fig. 4.23). The second conclusion is that even though early layers can in this case only respond to small feature subsets, these provide, with no further training of layers 1 and 2, an adequate basis for learning to discriminate in layers 3 and 4 stimuli consisting of combinations of larger numbers of features. Indeed, comparing results from experiment 1 with experiment 4 (in which all layers were trained on triples, see Table 4.5) demonstrates that training the lower layer neurons to develop invariant responses to the pairs offers almost as good performance as training all layers on the triples (see Fig. 4.47).

4.5.5.6 Stimulus generalization to new locations

Another important aspect of the architecture of VisNet is that it need not be trained with every stimulus in every possible location. Indeed, part of the hypothesis (Rolls 1992a) is that training early layers (e.g. 1–3) with a wide range of visual stimuli will set up feature analyzers in these early layers which are appropriate later on with no further training of early layers for new objects. For example, presentation of a new object might result in large numbers of low order feature combination neurons in early layers of VisNet being active, but the particular set of feature combination neurons active would be different for the new object. The later layers of the network (in VisNet, layer 4) would then learn this new set of active layer 3 neurons as encoding the new object. However, if the new object was then shown in a new location, the same set of layer 3 neurons would be active because they respond with spatial invariance to feature combinations, and given that the layer 3 to 4 connections had already been set up by

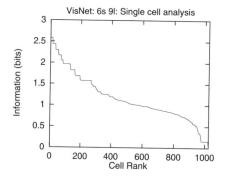 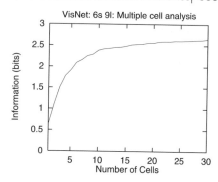

Fig. 4.48 Generalization to new locations: numerical results for a repeat of experiment 1 of Section 4.5.5.5 with the triples presented at only 7 of the original 9 locations during training, and with the trace learning rule (4.13). On the left are single cell information measures, and on the right are multiple cell information measures.

the new object, the correct layer 4 neurons would be activated by the new object in its new untrained location, and without any further training.

To test this hypothesis, Elliffe, Rolls and Stringer (2002) repeated the general procedure of experiment 1 of Section 4.5.5.5, training layers 1 and 2 with feature pairs, but then instead trained layers 3 and 4 on the triples in only 7 of the original 9 locations. The crucial test was to determine whether VisNet could form top layer neurons that responded invariantly to the 6 triples when presented over all nine locations, not just the seven locations at which the triples had been presented during training. The results are presented in Fig. 4.48, with single cell information measures on the left and multiple cell information measures on the right. VisNet is still able to develop some fourth layer neurons with perfect invariance, that is which have invariant responses over all nine location, as shown by the single cell information analysis. The response profiles of individual fourth layer cells showed that they can continue to discriminate between the triples even in the two locations where the triples were not presented during training. In addition, the multiple cell analysis shown in Fig. 4.48 demonstrates that a small population of cells was able to discriminate between all of the stimuli irrespective of location, even though for two of the test locations the triples had not been trained at those particular locations during the training of layers 3 and 4.

4.5.5.7 Discussion of feature binding in hierarchical layered networks

Elliffe, Rolls and Stringer (2002) thus first showed (see Section 4.5.5.4) that hierarchical feature detecting neural networks can learn to respond differently to stimuli that consist of unique combinations of non-unique input features, and that this extends to stimuli that are direct subsets or supersets of the features present in other stimuli.

Second, Elliffe, Rolls and Stringer (2002) investigated (see Section 4.5.5.5) the hypothesis that hierarchical layered networks can produce identification of unique stimuli even when the feature combination neurons used to define the stimuli are themselves partly translation invariant. The stimulus identification should work correctly because feature combination neurons in which the spatial features are bound together with high spatial precision are formed in the first layer. Then at later layers when neurons with some translation invariance are formed, the neurons nevertheless contain information about the relative spatial position of the original features. There is only then one object which will be consistent with the set of active neurons at earlier layers, which though somewhat translation invariant as combination neurons, reflect in the activity of each neuron information about the original spatial position of the features. We note that the trace rule training used in early layers (1 and 2) in Experiments

1 and 4 would set up partly invariant feature combination neurons, and yet the late layers (3 and 4) were able to produce during training neurons in layer 4 that responded to stimuli that consisted of unique spatial arrangements of lower order feature combinations. Moreover, and very interestingly, Elliffe, Rolls and Stringer (2002) were able to demonstrate that VisNet layer 4 neurons would respond correctly to visual stimuli at untrained locations, provided that the feature subsets had been trained in early layers of the network at all locations, and that the whole stimulus had been trained at some locations in the later layers of the network.

The results described by Elliffe, Rolls and Stringer (2002) thus provide one solution to the feature binding problem. The solution which has been shown to work in the model is that in a multilayer competitive network, feature combination neurons which encode the spatial arrangement of the bound features are formed at intermediate layers of the network. Then neurons at later layers of the network which respond to combinations of active intermediate layer neurons do contain sufficient evidence about the local spatial arrangement of the features to identify stimuli because the local spatial arrangement is encoded by the intermediate layer neurons. The information required to solve the visual feature binding problem thus becomes encoded by self-organization into what become hard-wired properties of the network. In this sense, feature binding is not solved at run time by the necessity to instantaneously set up arbitrary syntactic links between sets of co-active neurons. The computational solution proposed to the superset/subset aspect of the binding problem will apply in principle to other multilayer competitive networks, although the issues considered here have not been explicitly addressed in architectures such as the Neocognitron (Fukushima and Miyake 1982).

Consistent with these hypotheses about how VisNet operates to achieve, by layer 4, position-invariant responses to stimuli defined by combinations of features in the correct spatial arrangement, investigations of the effective stimuli for neurons in intermediate layers of VisNet showed as follows. In layer 1, cells responded to the presence of individual features, or to low order combinations of features (e.g. a pair of features) in the correct spatial arrangement at a small number of nearby locations. In layers 2 and 3, neurons responded to single features or to higher order combinations of features (e.g. stimuli composed of feature triples) in more locations. These findings provide direct evidence that VisNet does operate as described above to solve the feature binding problem.

A further issue with hierarchical multilayer architectures such as VisNet is that false binding errors might occur in the following way (Mozer 1991, Mel and Fiser 2000). Consider the output of one layer in such a network in which there is information only about which pairs are present. How then could a neuron in the next layer discriminate between the whole stimulus (such as the triple 123 in the above experiment) and what could be considered a more distributed stimulus or multiple different stimuli composed of the separated subparts of that stimulus (e.g. the pairs 120, 023, 103 occurring in 3 of the 9 training locations in the above experiment)? The problem here is to distinguish a single object from multiple other objects containing the same component combinations (e.g. pairs). We propose that part of the solution to this general problem in real visual systems is implemented through lateral inhibition between neurons in individual layers, and that this mechanism, implemented in VisNet, acts to reduce the possibility of false recognition errors in the following two ways.

First, consider the situation in which neurons in layer N have learned to represent low order feature combinations with location invariance, and where a neuron n in layer $N + 1$ has learned to respond to a particular set Ω of these feature combinations. The problem is that neuron n receives the same input from layer N as long as the same set Ω of feature combinations is present, and cannot distinguish between different spatial arrangements of these feature combinations. The question is how can neuron n respond only to a particular favoured spatial arrangement Ψ of the feature combinations contained within the set Ω. We suggest that as the favoured spatial arrangement Ψ is altered by rearranging the spatial relationships of the component feature combinations, the new feature combinations that are formed in new locations will stimulate additional neurons nearby in layer $N + 1$, and these will tend to inhibit the firing of neuron n. Thus, lateral inhibition within a layer will have the effect of making neurons more selective, ensuring neuron n responds only to a single spatial arrangement Ψ from the set of feature combinations Ω, and hence reducing the possibility of false recognition.

The second way in which lateral inhibition may help to reduce binding errors is through limiting the sparseness of neuronal firing rates within layers. In our discussion above the spurious stimuli we suggested that might lead to false recognition of triples were obtained from splitting up the component feature combinations (pairs) so that they occurred in separate training locations. However, this would lead to an increase in the number of features present in the complete stimulus; triples contain 3 features while their spurious counterparts would contain 6 features (resulting from 3 separate pairs). For this trivial example, the increase in the number of features is not dramatic, but if we consider, say, stimuli composed of 4 features where the component feature combinations represented by lower layers might be triples, then to form spurious stimuli we need to use 12 features (resulting from 4 triples occurring in separate locations). But if the lower layers also represented all possible pairs then the number of features required in the spurious stimuli would increase further. In fact, as the size of the stimulus increases in terms of the number of features, and as the size of the component feature combinations represented by the lower layers increases, there is a combinatorial explosion in terms of the number of features required as we attempt to construct spurious stimuli to trigger false recognition. And the construction of such spurious stimuli will then be prevented through setting a limit on the sparseness of firing rates within layers, which will in turn set a limit on the number of features that can be represented. Lateral inhibition is likely to contribute in both these ways to the performance of VisNet when the stimuli consist of subsets and supersets of each other, as described in Section 4.5.5.4.

Another way is which the problem of multiple objects is addressed is by limiting the size of the receptive fields of inferior temporal cortex neurons so that neurons in IT respond primarily to the object being fixated, but with nevertheless some asymmetry in the receptive fields (see Section 4.5.10). Multiple objects are then 'seen' by virtue of being added to a visuo-spatial scratchpad, as addressed in Section 4.7.

A related issue that arises in this class of network is whether forming neurons that respond to feature combinations in the way described here leads to a combinatorial explosion in the number of neurons required. The solution to this issue that is proposed is to form only low-order combinations of features at any one stage of the network (Rolls (1992a); cf. Feldman (1985)). Using low-order combinations limits the number of neurons required, yet enables the type of computation that relies on feature combination neurons that is analyzed here to still be performed. The actual number of neurons required depends also on the redundancies present in the statistics of real-world images. Even given these factors, it is likely that a large number of neurons would be required if the ventral visual system performs the computation of invariant representations in the manner captured by the hypotheses implemented in VisNet. Consistent with this, a considerable part of the non-human primate brain is devoted to visual information processing. The fact that large numbers of neurons and a multilayer organization are present in the primate ventral visual system is actually thus consistent with the type of model of visual information processing described here.

4.5.6 Operation in a cluttered environment

In this section we consider how hierarchical layered networks of the type exemplified by VisNet operate in cluttered environments. Although there has been much work involving

Fig. 4.49 Cluttered backgrounds used in VisNet simulations: backgrounds 1 and 2 are on the left and right respectively.

object recognition in cluttered environments with artificial vision systems, many such systems typically rely on some form of explicit segmentation followed by search and template matching procedure (see Ullman (1996) for a general review). In natural environments, objects may not only appear against cluttered (natural) backgrounds, but also the object may be partially occluded. Biological nervous systems operate in quite a different manner to those artificial vision systems that rely on search and template matching, and the way in which biological systems cope with cluttered environments and partial occlusion is likely to be quite different also.

One of the factors that will influence the performance of the type of architecture considered here, hierarchically organized series of competitive networks, which form one class of approaches to biologically relevant networks for invariant object recognition (Fukushima 1980, Rolls 1992a, Wallis and Rolls 1997, Poggio and Edelman 1990, Rolls and Treves 1998), is how lateral inhibition and competition are managed within a layer. Even if an object is not obscured, the effect of a cluttered background will be to fire additional neurons, which will in turn to some extent compete with and inhibit those neurons that are specifically tuned to respond to the desired object. Moreover, where the clutter is adjacent to part of the object, the feature analysing neurons activated against a blank background might be different from those activated against a cluttered background, if there is no explicit segmentation process. We consider these issues next, following investigations of Stringer and Rolls (2000).

4.5.6.1 VisNet simulations with stimuli in cluttered backgrounds

In this section we show that recognition of objects learned previously against a blank background is hardly affected by the presence of a natural cluttered background. We go on to consider what happens when VisNet is set the task of learning new stimuli presented against cluttered backgrounds.

The images used for training and testing VisNet in the simulations described next performed by Stringer and Rolls (2000) were specially constructed. There were 7 face stimuli approximately 64 pixels in height constructed without backgrounds from those shown in Fig. 4.33. In addition there were 3 possible backgrounds: a blank background (greyscale 127, where the range is 0–255), and two cluttered backgrounds as shown in Fig. 4.49 which are 128×128 pixels in size. Each image presented to VisNet's 128×128 input retina was composed of a single face stimulus positioned at one of 9 locations on either a blank or cluttered

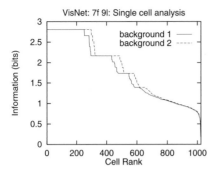

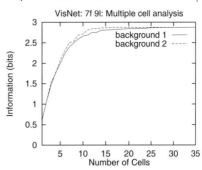

Fig. 4.50 Numerical results for experiment 2, with the 7 faces presented on a blank background during training and a cluttered background during testing. On the left are single cell information measures, and on the right are multiple cell information measures.

background. The cluttered background was intended to be like the background against which an object might be viewed in a natural scene. If a background is used in an experiment described here, the same background is always used, and it is always in the same position, with stimuli moved to different positions on it. The 9 stimulus locations are arranged in a square grid across the background, where the grid spacings are 32 pixels horizontally or vertically. Before images were presented to VisNet's input layer they were pre-processed by the standard set of input filters which accord with the general tuning profiles of simple cells in V1 (Hawken and Parker 1987); full details are given in Rolls and Milward (2000). To train the network a sequence of images is presented to VisNet's retina that corresponds to a single stimulus occurring in a randomized sequence of the 9 locations across a background. At each presentation the activation of individual neurons is calculated, then their firing rates are calculated, and then the synaptic weights are updated. After a stimulus has been presented in all the training locations, a new stimulus is chosen at random and the process repeated. The presentation of all the stimuli across all locations constitutes 1 epoch of training. In this manner the network is trained one layer at a time starting with layer 1 and finishing with layer 4. In the investigations described in this subsection, the numbers of training epochs for layers 1–4 were 50, 100, 100 and 75 respectively.

In this experiment (see Stringer and Rolls (2000), experiment 2), VisNet was trained with the 7 face stimuli presented on a blank background, but tested with the faces presented on each of the 2 cluttered backgrounds. Figure 4.50 shows results for experiment 2, with single and multiple cell information measures on the left and right respectively. It can be seen that a number of cells have reached the maximum possible single cell information measure of 2.8 bits ($\log_2$ of the number of stimuli) for this test case, and that the multiple cell information measures also reach the 2.8 bits indicating perfect performance. Compared to performance when shown against a blank background, there was very little deterioration in performance when testing with the faces presented on either of the two cluttered backgrounds. This is an interesting result to compare with many artificial vision systems that would need to carry out computationally intensive serial searching and template matching procedures in order to achieve such results. In contrast, the VisNet neural network architecture is able to perform such recognition relatively quickly through a simple feedforward computation. Further results from this experiment are presented in Fig. 4.51 where we show the response profiles of a 4th layer neuron to the 7 faces presented on cluttered background 1 during testing. It can be seen that this neuron achieves excellent invariant responses to the 7 faces even with the faces presented on a cluttered background. The response profiles are independent of location but differentiate between the faces in that the responses are maximal for only one of the faces and

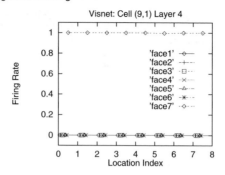

Fig. 4.51 Response profiles of a top layer neuron to the 7 faces from experiment 2 of Stringer and Rolls (2000), with the faces presented against cluttered background 1 during testing.

minimal for all other faces.

This is an interesting and important result, for it shows that after learning, special mechanisms for segmentation and for attention are not needed in order for neurons already tuned by previous learning to the stimuli to be activated correctly in the output layer. Although the experiments described here tested for position invariance, we predict and would expect that the same results would be demonstrable for size and view invariant representations of objects.

In experiments 3 and 4 of Stringer and Rolls (2000), VisNet was trained with the 7 face stimuli presented on either one of the 2 cluttered backgrounds, but tested with the faces presented on a blank background. Results for this experiment showed poor performance. The results of experiments 3 and 4 suggest that in order for a cell to *learn* invariant responses to different transforms of a stimulus when it is presented during training in a cluttered background, some form of segmentation is required in order to separate the figure (i.e. the stimulus or object) from the background. This segmentation might be performed using evidence in the visual scene about different depths, motions, colours, etc. of the object from its background. In the visual system, this might mean combining evidence represented in different cortical areas, and might be performed by cross-connections between cortical areas to enable such evidence to help separate the representations of objects from their backgrounds in the form-representing cortical areas.

Another mechanism that helps the operation of architectures such as VisNet and the primate visual system to learn about new objects in cluttered scenes is that the receptive fields of inferior temporal cortex neurons become much smaller when objects are seen against natural backgrounds (Sections 4.5.9.1 and 4.5.9). This will help greatly to learn about new objects that are being fixated, by reducing responsiveness to other features elsewhere in the scene.

Another mechanism that might help the learning of new objects in a natural scene is attention. An attentional mechanism might highlight the current stimulus being attended to and suppress the effects of background noise, providing a training representation of the object more like that which would be produced when it is presented against a blank background. The mechanisms that could implement such attentional processes are described in Chapter 6. If such attentional mechanisms do contribute to the development of view invariance, then it follows that cells in the temporal cortex may only develop transform invariant responses to objects to which attention is directed.

Part of the reason for the poor performance in experiments 3 and 4 was probably that the stimuli were always presented against the same fixed background (for technical reasons), and thus the neurons learned about the background rather than the stimuli. Part of the difficulty that hierarchical multilayer competitive networks have with learning in cluttered environments may

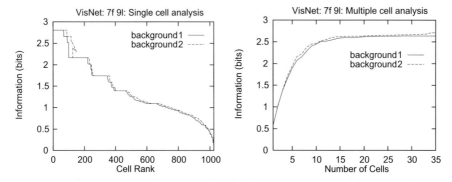

Fig. 4.52 Numerical results for experiment 5 of Stringer and Rolls (2000). In this experiment VisNet is first exposed to a completely random sequence of faces in different positions against a blank background during which layers 1–3 are allowed to learn. This builds general feature detecting neurons in the lower layers that are tuned to the face stimuli, but cannot develop view invariance since there is no temporal structure to the order in which different views of different faces occur. Then layer 4 is trained in the usual way with the 7 faces presented against a cluttered background, where the images are now presented such that different views of the same face occur close together in time. On the left are single cell information measures, and on the right are multiple cell information measures.

more generally be that without explicit segmentation of the stimulus from its background, at least some of the features that should be formed to encode the stimuli are not formed properly, because the neurons learn to respond to combinations of inputs which come partly from the stimulus, and partly from the background. To investigate this, Stringer and Rolls (2000) performed experiment 5 in which layers 1–3 were pretrained with stimuli to ensure that good feature combination neurons for stimuli were available, and then allowed learning in only layer 4 when stimuli were presented in the cluttered backgrounds. Layer 4 was then trained in the usual way with the 7 faces presented against a cluttered background. The results for this experiment are shown in Fig. 4.52, with single and multiple cell information measures on the left and right respectively. It was found that prior random exposure to the face stimuli led to much improved performance. Indeed, it can be seen that a number of cells have reached the maximum possible single cell information measure of 2.8 bits for this test case, although the multiple cell information measures do not quite reach the 2.8 bits that would indicate perfect performance for the complete face set.

These results demonstrate that the problem of developing position invariant neurons to stimuli occurring against cluttered backgrounds may be ameliorated by the prior existence of stimulus-tuned feature-detecting neurons in the early layers of the visual system, and that these feature-detecting neurons may be set up through previous exposure to the relevant class of objects. When tested in cluttered environments, the background clutter may of course activate some other neurons in the output layer, but at least the neurons that have learned to respond to the trained stimuli are activated. The result of this activity is sufficient for the activity in the output layer to be useful, in the sense that it can be read off correctly by a pattern associator connected to the output layer. Indeed, Stringer and Rolls (2000) tested this by connecting a pattern associator to layer 4 of VisNet. The pattern associator had seven neurons, one for each face, and 1,024 inputs, one from each neuron in layer 4 of VisNet. The pattern associator learned when trained with a simple associative Hebb rule (equation 4.12 on page 316) to activate the correct output neuron whenever one of the faces was shown in any position in the uncluttered environment. This ability was shown to be dependent on invariant neurons for each stimulus in the output layer of VisNet, for the pattern associator could not be taught the task if VisNet had not been previously trained with a trace learning rule to produce invariant representations. Then it was shown that exactly the correct neuron was activated when any of the faces was shown in any position with the cluttered background. This read-off by a pattern associator is exactly what we hypothesize takes place in the brain, in that the inferior temporal visual cortex (where neurons with invariant responses are found) projects to structures such as the orbitofrontal cortex and amygdala, where associations between the invariant visual representations and stimuli such as taste and touch are learned (Rolls and Treves 1998, Rolls 1999a, Rolls 2005) (see Chapter 3). Thus testing whether the output of an architecture such as VisNet can be used effectively by a pattern associator is a very biologically relevant way to evaluate the performance of this class of architecture.

4.5.6.2 Learning invariant representations of an object with multiple objects in the scene and with cluttered backgrounds

The results of the experiments just described suggest that in order for a neuron to *learn* invariant responses to different transforms of a stimulus when it is presented during training in a cluttered background, some form of segmentation is required in order to separate the figure (i.e. the stimulus or object) from the background. This segmentation might be performed using evidence in the visual scene about different depths, motions, colours, etc. of the object from its background. In the visual system, this might mean combining evidence represented in different cortical areas, and might be performed by cross-connections between cortical areas to enable such evidence to help separate the representations of objects from their backgrounds in the form-representing cortical areas.

A second way in which training a feature hierarchy network in a cluttered natural scene may be facilitated follows from the finding that the receptive fields of inferior temporal cortex neurons shrink from in the order of 70 degrees in diameter when only one object is present in a blank scene to much smaller values of as little as 5–10 degrees close to the fovea in complex natural scenes (Rolls, Aggelopoulos and Zheng 2003a). The proposed mechanism for this is that if there is an object at the fovea, this object, because of the high cortical magnification factor at the fovea, dominates the activity of neurons in the inferior temporal cortex by competitive interactions (Trappenberg, Rolls and Stringer 2002, Deco and Rolls 2004) (see Section 4.5.9). This allows primarily the object at the fovea to be represented in the inferior temporal cortex, and, it is proposed, for learning to be about this object, and not about the other objects in a whole scene.

Third, top-down spatial attention (Deco and Rolls 2004, Deco and Rolls 2005a) (see Chapter 6) could bias the competition towards a region of visual space where the object to be learned is located.

Fourth, if object 1 is presented during training with different objects present on different trials, then the competitive networks that are part of VisNet will learn to represent each object separately, because the features that are part of each object will be much more strongly associated together, than are those features with the other features present in the different objects seen on some trials during training (Stringer and Rolls 2007b, Stringer, Rolls and Tromans 2007b). It is a natural property of competitive networks that input features that co-occur very frequently together are allocated output neurons to represent the pattern as a result of the learning. Input features that do not co-occur frequently, may not have output neurons allocated to them. This principle may help feature hierarchy systems to learn representations of individual objects, even when other objects with some of the same features are present in the visual scene, but with different other objects on different trials. With this fundamental and interesting property of competitive networks, it has now become possible for VisNet to self-organize invariant representations of individual objects, even though each object is always presented during training with at least one other object present in the scene (Stringer and Rolls 2007b, Stringer, Rolls and Tromans 2007b).

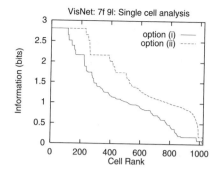
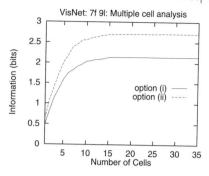

Fig. 4.53 Effects of partial occlusion of a stimulus: numerical results for experiment 6 of Stringer and Rolls, 2000, with the 7 faces presented on a blank background during both training and testing. Training was performed with the whole face. However, during testing there are two options: either (i) the top half of all the faces are occluded, or (ii) the bottom half of all the faces are occluded. On the left are single cell information measures, and on the right are multiple cell information measures.

4.5.6.3 VisNet simulations with partially occluded stimuli

In this section we examine the recognition of partially occluded stimuli. Many artificial vision systems that perform object recognition typically search for specific markers in stimuli, and hence their performance may become fragile if key parts of a stimulus are occluded. However, in contrast we demonstrate that the model of invariance learning in the brain discussed here can continue to offer robust performance with this kind of problem, and that the model is able to correctly identify stimuli with considerable flexibility about what part of a stimulus is visible.

In these simulations (Stringer and Rolls 2000), training and testing was performed with a blank background to avoid confounding the two separate problems of occlusion and background clutter. In object recognition tasks, artificial vision systems may typically rely on being able to locate a small number of key markers on a stimulus in order to be able to identify it. This approach can become fragile when a number of these markers become obscured. In contrast, biological vision systems may generalize or complete from a partial input as a result of the use of distributed representations in neural networks, and this could lead to greater robustness in situations of partial occlusion.

In this experiment (6 of Stringer and Rolls (2000)), the network was first trained with the 7 face stimuli without occlusion, but during testing there were two options: either (i) the top halves of all the faces were occluded, or (ii) the bottom halves of all the faces were occluded. Since VisNet was tested with either the top or bottom half of the stimuli no stimulus features were common to the two test options. This ensures that if performance is good with both options, the performance cannot be based on the use of a single feature to identify a stimulus. Results for this experiment are shown in Fig. 4.53, with single and multiple cell information measures on the left and right respectively. When compared with the performance without occlusion (Stringer and Rolls 2000), Fig. 4.53 shows that there is only a modest drop in performance in the single cell information measures when the stimuli are partially occluded.

For both options (i) and (ii), even with partially occluded stimuli, a number of cells continue to respond maximally to one preferred stimulus in all locations, while responding minimally to all other stimuli. However, comparing results from options (i) and (ii) shows that the network performance is better when the bottom half of the faces is occluded. This is consistent with psychological results showing that face recognition is performed more easily when the top halves of faces are visible rather than the bottom halves (see Bruce (1988)). The top half of a face will generally contain salient features, e.g. eyes and hair, that are particularly

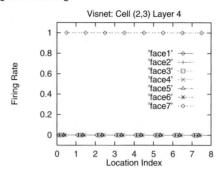

Fig. 4.54 Effects of partial occlusion of a stimulus. Response profiles of a top layer neuron to the 7 faces from experiment 6 of Stringer and Rolls (2000), with the bottom half of all the faces occluded during testing.

helpful for recognition of the individual, and it is interesting that these simulations appear to further demonstrate this point. Furthermore, the multiple cell information measures confirm that performance is better with the upper half of the face visible (option (ii)) than the lower half (option (i)). When the top halves of the faces are occluded the multiple cell information measure asymptotes to a suboptimal value reflecting the difficulty of discriminating between these more difficult images. Further results from experiment 6 are presented in Fig. 4.54 where we show the response profiles of a 4th layer neuron to the 7 faces, with the bottom half of all the faces occluded during testing. It can be seen that this neuron continues to respond invariantly to the 7 faces, responding maximally to one of the faces but minimally for all other faces.

Thus this model of the ventral visual system offers robust performance with this kind of problem, and the model is able to correctly identify stimuli with considerable flexibility about what part of a stimulus is visible, because it is effectively using distributed representations and associative processing.

4.5.7   Learning 3D transforms

In this section we describe investigations of Stringer and Rolls (2002) which show that trace learning can in the VisNet architecture solve the problem of in-depth rotation invariant object recognition by developing representations of the transforms which features undergo when they are on the surfaces of 3D objects. Moreover, it is shown that having learned how features on 3D objects transform as the object is rotated in depth, the network can correctly recognize novel 3D variations within a generic view of an object which is composed of previously learned feature combinations.

Rolls' hypothesis of how object recognition could be implemented in the brain postulates that trace rule learning helps invariant representations to form in two ways (Rolls 1992a, Rolls 1994a, Rolls 1995b, Rolls 2000a). The first process enables associations to be learned between different generic 3D views of an object where there are different qualitative shape descriptors. One example of this would be the front and back views of an object, which might have very different shape descriptors. Another example is provided by considering how the shape descriptors typical of 3D shapes, such as Y vertices, arrow vertices, cusps, and ellipse shapes, alter when most 3D objects are rotated in 3 dimensions. At some point in the 3D rotation, there is a catastrophic rearrangement of the shape descriptors as a new generic view can be seen (Koenderink 1990). An example of a catastrophic change to a new generic view is when a cup being viewed from slightly below is rotated so that one can see inside the cup from slightly above. The bottom surface disappears, the top surface of the cup changes from a cusp to an ellipse, and the inside of the cup with a whole set of new features comes into view. The second process is that within a generic view, as the object is rotated in depth, there will be no catastrophic changes in the qualitative 3D shape descriptors, but instead the quantitative values of the shape descriptors alter. For example, while the cup is being rotated within a generic view seen from somewhat below, the curvature of the cusp forming the top boundary will alter, but the qualitative shape descriptor will remain a cusp. Trace learning could help with both processes. That is, trace learning could help to associate together qualitatively different sets of shape descriptors that occur close together in time, and describe for example the generically different views of a cup. Trace learning could also help with the second process, and learn to associate together the different quantitative values of shape descriptors that typically occur when objects are rotated within a generic view.

We note that there is evidence that some neurons in the inferior temporal cortex may show the two types of 3D invariance. First, Booth and Rolls (1998) showed that some inferior temporal cortex neurons can respond to different generic views of familiar 3D objects. Second, some neurons do generalize across quantitative changes in the values of 3D shape descriptors while faces (Hasselmo, Rolls, Baylis and Nalwa 1989b) and objects (Tanaka 1996, Logothetis, Pauls and Poggio 1995) are rotated within generic views. Indeed, Logothetis, Pauls and Poggio (1995) showed that a few inferior temporal cortex neurons can generalize to novel (untrained) values of the quantitative shape descriptors typical of within-generic view object rotation.

In addition to the qualitative shape descriptor changes that occur catastrophically between different generic views of an object, and the quantitative changes of 3D shape descriptors that occur within a generic view, there is a third type of transform that must be learned for correct invariant recognition of 3D objects as they rotate in depth. This third type of transform is that which occurs to the surface features on a 3D object as it transforms in depth. The main aim here is to consider mechanisms that could enable neurons to learn this third type of transform, that is how to generalize correctly over the changes in the surface markings on 3D objects that are typically encountered as 3D objects rotate within a generic view. Examples of the types of perspective transforms investigated are shown in Fig. 4.55. Surface markings on the sphere that consist of combinations of three features in different spatial arrangements undergo characteristic transforms as the sphere is rotated from 0 degrees towards –60 degrees and +60 degrees. We investigated whether the class of architecture exemplified by VisNet, and the trace learning rule, can learn about the transforms that surface features of 3D objects typically undergo during 3D rotation in such a way that the network generalizes across the change of the quantitative values of the surface features produced by the rotation, and yet still discriminates between the different objects (in this case spheres). In the cases being considered, each object is identified by surface markings that consist of a different spatial arrangement of the same three features (a horizontal, vertical, and diagonal line, which become arcs on the surface of the object).

We note that it has been suggested that the finding that neurons may offer some degree of 3D rotation invariance after training with a single view (or limited set of views) represents a challenge for existing trace learning models, because these models assume that an initial exposure is required during learning to every transformation of the object to be recognized (Riesenhuber and Poggio 1998). Stringer and Rolls (2002) showed as described here that this is not the case, and that such models can generalize to novel within-generic views of an object provided that the characteristic changes that the features show as objects are rotated have been learned previously for the sets of features when they are present in different objects.

Elliffe, Rolls and Stringer (2002) demonstrated for a 2D system how the existence of translation invariant representations of low order feature combinations in the early layers of the visual system could allow correct stimulus identification in the output layer even when the

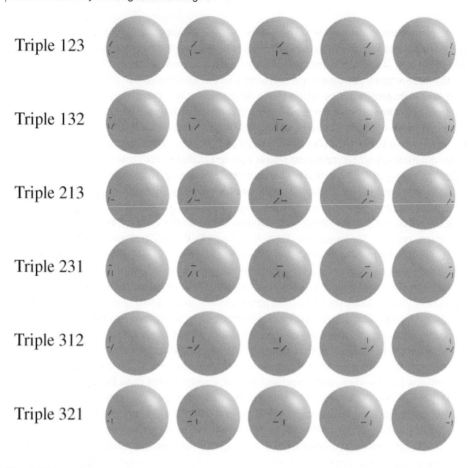

Triple 123					
Triple 132					
Triple 213					
Triple 231					
Triple 312					
Triple 321					

Fig. 4.55 Learning 3D perspectival transforms of features. Representations of the 6 visual stimuli with 3 surface features (triples) presented to VisNet during the simulations described in Section 4.5.7. Each stimulus is a sphere that is uniquely identified by a unique combination of three surface features (a vertical, diagonal and horizontal arc), which occur in 3 relative positions A, B, and C. Each row shows one of the stimuli rotated through the 5 different rotational views in which the stimulus is presented to VisNet. From left to right the rotational views shown are: (i) −60 degrees, (ii) −30 degrees, (iii) 0 degrees (central position), (iv) +30 degrees, and (v) +60 degrees. (After Stringer and Rolls 2002.)

stimulus was presented in a novel location where the stimulus had not previously occurred during learning. The proposal was that the low-order spatial feature combination neurons in the early stages contain sufficient spatial information so that a particular combination of those low-order feature combination neurons specifies a unique object, even if the relative positions of the low-order feature combination neurons are not known because these neurons are somewhat translation invariant (see Section 4.5.5.5). Stringer and Rolls (2002) extended this analysis to feature combinations on 3D objects, and indeed in their simulations described in this section therefore used surface markings for the 3D objects that consisted of triples of features.

The images used for training and testing VisNet were specially constructed for the purpose of demonstrating how the trace learning paradigm might be further developed to give rise to neurons that are able to respond invariantly to novel within-generic view perspectives of an object, obtained by rotations in-depth up to 30 degrees from any perspectives encountered during learning. The stimuli take the form of the surface feature combinations of 3-dimensional rotating spheres, with each image presented to VisNet's retina being a 2-dimensional projection of the surface features of one of the spheres. Each stimulus is uniquely identified by two or three surface features, where the surface features are (1) vertical, (2) diagonal, and (3) horizontal arcs, and where each feature may be centred at three different spatial positions, designated A, B, and C, as shown in Fig. 4.55. The stimuli are thus defined in terms of what features are present and their precise spatial arrangement with respect to each other. We refer to the two and three feature stimuli as 'pairs' and 'triples', respectively. Individual stimuli are denoted by three numbers which refer to the individual features present in positions A, B and C, respectively. For example, a stimulus with positions A and C containing a vertical and diagonal bar, respectively, would be referred to as stimulus 102, where the 0 denotes no feature present in position B. In total there are 18 pairs (120, 130, 210, 230, 310, 320, 012, 013, 021, 023, 031, 032, 102, 103, 201, 203, 301, 302) and 6 triples (123, 132, 213, 231, 312, 321).

To train the network each stimulus was presented to VisNet in a randomized sequence of five orientations with respect to VisNet's input retina, where the different orientations are obtained from successive in-depth rotations of the stimulus through 30 degrees. That is, each stimulus was presented to VisNet's retina from the following rotational views: (i) $-60°$, (ii) $-30°$, (iii) $0°$ (central position with surface features facing directly towards VisNet's retina), (iv) $30°$, (v) $60°$. Figure 4.55 shows representations of the 6 visual stimuli with 3 surface features (triples) presented to VisNet during the simulations. (For the actual simulations described here, the surface features and their deformations were what VisNet was trained and tested with, and the remaining blank surface of each sphere was set to the same greyscale as the background.) Each row shows one of the stimuli rotated through the 5 different rotational views in which the stimulus is presented to VisNet. At each presentation the activation of individual neurons is calculated, then the neuronal firing rates are calculated, and then the synaptic weights are updated. Each time a stimulus has been presented in all the training orientations, a new stimulus is chosen at random and the process repeated. The presentation of all the stimuli through all 5 orientations constitutes 1 epoch of training. In this manner the network was trained one layer at a time starting with layer 1 and finishing with layer 4. In the investigations described here, the numbers of training epochs for layers 1–4 were 50, 100, 100 and 75, respectively.

In experiment 1, VisNet was trained in two stages. In the first stage, the 18 feature pairs were used as input stimuli, with each stimulus being presented to VisNet's retina in sequences of five orientations as described above. However, during this stage, learning was only allowed to take place in layers 1 and 2. This led to the formation of neurons which responded to the feature pairs with some rotation invariance in layer 2. In the second stage, we used the 6 feature triples as stimuli, with learning only allowed in layers 3 and 4. However, during this second training stage, the triples were only presented to VisNet's input retina in the first 4 orientations (i)–(iv). After the two stages of training were completed, Stringer and Rolls (2002) examined whether the output layer of VisNet had formed top layer neurons that responded invariantly to the 6 triples when presented in all 5 orientations, not just the 4 in which the triples had been presented during training. To provide baseline results for comparison, the results from experiment 1 were compared with results from experiment 2 which involved no training in layers 1,2 and 3,4, with the synaptic weights left unchanged from their initial random values.

In Fig. 4.56 numerical results are given for the experiments described. On the left are the single cell information measures for all top (4th) layer neurons ranked in order of their invariance to the triples, while on the right are multiple cell information measures. To help to interpret these results we can compute the maximum single cell information measure according to

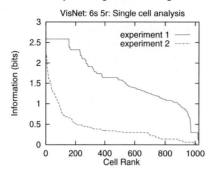
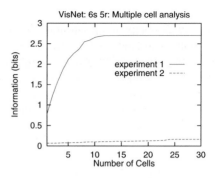

Fig. 4.56 Learning 3D perspectival transforms of features. Numerical results for experiments 1 and 2: on the left are single cell information measures, and on the right are multiple cell information measures.

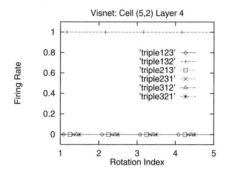

Fig. 4.57 Learning 3D perspectival transforms of features. Numerical results for experiment 1: response profiles of a top layer neuron to the 6 triples in all 5 orientations.

$$\text{Maximum single cell information} = \log_2(\text{Number of triples}), \qquad (4.39)$$

where the number of triples is 6. This gives a maximum single cell information measure of 2.6 bits for these test cases. The information results from the experiment demonstrate that even with the triples presented to the network in only four of the five orientations during training, layer 4 is indeed capable of developing rotation invariant neurons that can discriminate effectively between the 6 different feature triples in all 5 orientations, that is with correct recognition from all five perspectives. In addition, the multiple cell information for the experiment reaches the maximal level of 2.6 bits, indicating that the network as a whole is capable of perfect discrimination between the 6 triples in any of the 5 orientations. These results may be compared with the very poor baseline performance from the control experiment, where no learning was allowed before testing. Further results from experiment 1 are presented in Fig. 4.57 where we show the response profiles of a top layer neuron to the 6 triples. It can be seen that this neuron has achieved excellent invariant responses to the 6 triples: the response profiles are independent of orientation, but differentiate between triples in that the responses are maximal for triple 132 and minimal for all other triples. In particular, the cell responses are maximal for triple 132 presented in all 5 of the orientations.

Stringer and Rolls (2002) also performed a control experiment to show that the network really had learned invariant representations specific to the kinds of 3D deformations undergone by the surface features as the objects rotated in-depth. In the control experiment the network was trained on 'spheres' with non-deformed surface features; and then as predicted the network failed to operate correctly when it was tested with objects with the features present in the transformed way that they appear on the surface of a real 3D object.

Stringer and Rolls (2002) were thus able to show how trace learning can form neurons that can respond invariantly to novel rotational within-generic view perspectives of an object, obtained by within-generic view 3D rotations up to 30 degrees from any view encountered during learning. They were able to show in addition that this could occur for a novel view of an object which was not an interpolation from previously shown views. This was possible given that the low order feature combination sets from which an object was composed had been learned about in early layers of VisNet previously. The within-generic view transform invariant object recognition described was achieved through the development of true 3-dimensional representations of objects based on 3-dimensional features and feature combinations, which, unlike 2-dimensional feature combinations, are invariant under moderate in-depth rotations of the object. Thus, in a sense, these rotation invariant representations encode a form of 3-dimensional knowledge with which to interpret the visual input from the real world, that is able provide a basis for robust rotation invariant object recognition with novel perspectives. The particular finding in the work described here was that VisNet can learn how the surface features on 3D objects transform as the object is rotated in depth, and can use knowledge of the characteristics of the transforms to perform 3D object recognition. The knowledge embodied in the network is knowledge of the 3D properties of objects, and in this sense assists the recognition of 3D objects seen from different views.

The process investigated by Stringer and Rolls (2002) will only allow invariant object recognition over moderate 3D object rotations, since rotating an object through a large angle may lead to a catastrophic change in the appearance of the object that requires the new qualitative 3D shape descriptors to be associated with those of the former view. In that case, invariant object recognition must rely on the first process referred to at the start of this Section (4.5.7) in order to associate together the different generic views of an object to produce view invariant object identification. For that process, association of a few cardinal or generic views is likely to be sufficient (Koenderink 1990). The process described in this section of learning how surface features transform is likely to make a major contribution to the within-generic view transform invariance of object identification and recognition.

4.5.8 Capacity of the architecture, and incorporation of a trace rule into a recurrent architecture with object attractors

One issue that has not been considered extensively so far is the capacity of hierarchical feedforward networks of the type exemplified by VisNet that are used for invariant object recognition. One approach to this issue is to note that VisNet operates in the general mode of a competitive network, and that the number of different stimuli that can be categorized by a competitive network is in the order of the number of neurons in the output layer, as described in Section B.4. Given that the successive layers of the real visual system (V1, V2, V4, posterior inferior temporal cortex, anterior inferior temporal cortex) are of the same order of magnitude[21], VisNet is designed to work with the same number of neurons in each successive layer. The hypothesis is that because of redundancies in the visual world, each layer of the system by its convergence and competitive categorization can capture sufficient of the statistics of the visual input at each stage to enable correct specification of the properties of the world that specify objects. For example, V1 does not compute all possible combinations of a few lateral geniculate inputs, but instead represents linear series of geniculate inputs to form edge-like and bar-like feature analyzers, which are the dominant arrangement of pixels

---

[21] Of course the details are worth understanding further. V1 is for example somewhat larger than earlier layers, but on the other hand serves the dorsal as well as the ventral stream of visual cortical processing.

found at the small scale in natural visual scenes. Thus the properties of the visual world at this stage can be captured by a small proportion of the total number of combinations that would be needed if the visual world were random. Similarly, at a later stage of processing, just a subset of all possible combinations of line or edge analyzers would be needed, partly because some combinations are much more frequent in the visual world, and partly because the coding because of convergence means that what is represented is for a larger area of visual space (that is, the receptive fields of the neurons are larger), which also leads to economy and limits what otherwise would be a combinatorial need for feature analyzers at later layers. The hypothesis thus is that the effects of redundancies in the input space of stimuli that result from the statistical properties of natural images (Field 1987), together with the convergent architecture with competitive learning at each stage, produces a system that can perform invariant object recognition for large numbers of objects. Large in this case could be within one or two orders of magnitude of the number of neurons in any one layer of the network (or cortical area in the brain). The extent to which this can be realized can be explored with simulations of the type implemented in VisNet, in which the network can be trained with natural images which therefore reflect fully the natural statistics of the stimuli presented to the real brain.

We should note that a rich variety of information in perceptual space may be represented by subtle differences in the distributed representation provided by the output of the visual system. At the same time, the actual number of different patterns that may be stored in for example a pattern associator connected to the output of the visual system is limited by the number of input connections per neuron from the output neurons of the visual system (see Section B.2). One essential function performed by the ventral visual system is to provide an invariant representation which can be read by a pattern associator in such a way that if the pattern associator learns about one view of the object, then the visual system allows generalization to another view of the same object, because the same output neurons are activated by the different view. In the sense that any view can and must activate the same output neurons of the visual system (the input to the associative network), then we can say the invariance is made explicit in the representation. Making some properties of an input representation explicit in an output representation has a major function of enabling associative networks that use visual inputs in for example recognition, episodic memory, emotion and motivation to generalize correctly, that is invariantly with respect to image transforms that are all consistent with the same object in the world (Rolls and Treves 1998).

Another approach to the issue of the capacity of networks that use trace-learning to associate together different instances (e.g. views) of the same object is to reformulate the issue in the context of autoassociation (attractor) networks, where analytic approaches to the storage capacity of the network are well developed (see Section B.3, Amit (1989), and Rolls and Treves (1998)). This approach to the storage capacity of networks that associate together different instantiations of an object to form invariant representations has been developed by Parga and Rolls (1998) and Elliffe, Rolls, Parga and Renart (2000), and is described next.

In this approach, the storage capacity of a *recurrent* network which performs for example view invariant recognition of objects by associating together different views of the same object which tend to occur close together in time, was studied (Parga and Rolls 1998, Elliffe, Rolls, Parga and Renart 2000). The architecture with which the invariance is computed is a little different to that described earlier. In the model of Rolls ((1992a), (1994a), (1995b), Wallis and Rolls (1997), Rolls and Milward (2000), and Rolls and Stringer (2006)), the postsynaptic memory trace enabled different afferents from the preceding stage to modify onto the same postsynaptic neuron (see Fig. 4.58). In that model there were no recurrent connections between the neurons, although such connections were one way in which it was postulated the memory trace might be implemented, by simply keeping the representation of one view or aspect active until the next view appeared. Then an association would occur between representations that

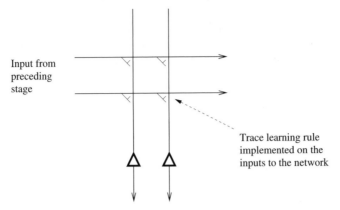

Fig. 4.58 The learning scheme implemented in VisNet. A trace learning rule is implemented in the feed-forward inputs to a competitive network.

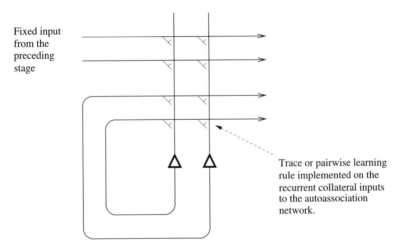

Fig. 4.59 The learning scheme considered by Parga and Rolls (1998) and Elliffe, Rolls, Parga and Renart (2000). There are inputs to the network from the preceding stage via unmodifiable synapses, and a trace or pairwise associative learning rule is implemented in the recurrent collateral synapses of an autoassociative memory to associate together the different exemplars (e.g. views) of the same object.

were active close together in time (within e.g. 100–300 ms).

In the model developed by Parga and Rolls (1998) and Elliffe, Rolls, Parga and Renart (2000), there is a set of inputs with fixed synaptic weights to a network. The network itself is a recurrent network, with a trace rule incorporated in the recurrent collaterals (see Fig. 4.59). When different views of the same object are presented close together in time, the recurrent collaterals learn using the trace rule that the different views are of the same object. After learning, presentation of any of the views will cause the network to settle into an attractor that represents all the views of the object, that is which is a view invariant representation of an object[22].

We envisage a set of neuronal operations which set up a synaptic weight matrix in the

---

[22] In this Section, the different exemplars of an object which need to be associated together are called views, for simplicity, but could at earlier stages of the hierarchy represent for example similar feature combinations (derived from the same object) in different positions in space.

	O_1v_1	O_1v_2	O_1v_3	O_1v_4	O_1v_5	O_2v_1	O_2v_2	O_2v_3	O_2v_4	O_2v_5	$\cdots$
O_1v_1	1	1	1	1	1						
O_1v_2	1	1	1	1	1						
O_1v_3	1	1	1	1	1						
O_1v_4	1	1	1	1	1						
O_1v_5	1	1	1	1	1						
O_2v_1						1	1	1	1	1	
O_2v_2						1	1	1	1	1	
O_2v_3						1	1	1	1	1	
O_2v_4						1	1	1	1	1	
O_2v_5						1	1	1	1	1	

Fig. 4.60 A schematic illustration of the first type of associations contributing to the synaptic matrix considered by Parga and Rolls (1998). Object 1 (O_1) has five views labelled v_1 to v_5, etc. The matrix is formed by associating the pattern presented in the columns with itself, that is with the same pattern presented as rows.

recurrent collaterals by associating together because of their closeness in time the different views of the same object.

In more detail, Parga and Rolls (1998) considered two main approaches. First, one could store in a synaptic weight matrix the s views of an object. This consists of equally associating all the views to each other, including the association of each view with itself. Choosing in Fig. 4.60 an example such that objects are defined in terms of five different views, this might produce (if each view produced firing of one neuron at a rate of 1) a block of 5×5 pairs of views contributing to the synaptic efficacies each with value 1. Object 2 might produce another block of synapses of value 1 further along the diagonal, and symmetric about it. Each object or memory could then be thought of as a single attractor with a distributed representation involving five elements (each element representing a different view). Then the capacity of the system in terms of the number P_o of objects that can be stored is just the number of separate attractors which can be stored in the network. For random fully distributed patterns this is as shown numerically by Hopfield (1982)

$$P_o = 0.14\, C \tag{4.40}$$

where there are C inputs per neuron (and $N = C$ neurons if the network is fully connected). Now the synaptic matrix envisaged here does not consist of random fully distributed binary elements, but instead we will assume has a sparseness $a = s/N$, where s is the number of views stored for each object, from any of which the whole representation of the object must be recognized. In this case, one can show (Gardner 1988, Tsodyks and Feigel'man 1988, Treves and Rolls 1991) that the number of objects that can be stored and correctly retrieved is

$$P_o = \frac{k\, C}{a\, \ln(1/a)} \tag{4.41}$$

where C is the number of synapses on each neuron devoted to the recurrent collaterals from other neurons in the network, and k is a factor that depends weakly on the detailed structure of the rate distribution, on the connectivity pattern, etc., but is approximately in the order of 0.2–0.3. A problem with this proposal is that as the number of views of each object increases to a large number (e.g. >20), the network will fail to retrieve correctly the internal representation

	O_1v_1	O_1v_2	O_1v_3	O_1v_4	O_1v_5	O_2v_1	O_2v_2	O_2v_3	O_2v_4	O_2v_5	. . .
O_1v_1	1	b	b	b	b						
O_1v_2	b	1	b	b	b						
O_1v_3	b	b	1	b	b						
O_1v_4	b	b	b	1	b						
O_1v_5	b	b	b	b	1						
O_2v_1						1	b	b	b	b	
O_2v_2						b	1	b	b	b	
O_2v_3						b	b	1	b	b	
O_2v_4						b	b	b	1	b	
O_2v_5						b	b	b	b	1	

Fig. 4.61 A schematic illustration of the second and main type of associations contributing to the synaptic matrix considered by Parga and Rolls (1998) and Elliffe, Rolls, Parga and Renart (2000). Object 1 (O_1) has five views labelled v_1 to v_5, etc. The association of any one view with itself has strength 1, and of any one with another view of the same object has strength b.

of the object starting from any one view (which is only a fraction $1/s$ of the length of the stored pattern that represents an object).

The second approach, taken by Parga and Rolls (1998) and Elliffe, Rolls, Parga and Renart (2000), is to consider the operation of the network when the associations between pairs of views can be described by a matrix that has the general form shown in Fig. 4.61. Such an association matrix might be produced by different views of an object appearing after a given view with equal probability, and synaptic modification occurring of the view with itself (giving rise to the diagonal term), and of any one view with that which immediately follows it. The same weight matrix might be produced not only by pairwise association of successive views because the association rule allows for associations over the short time scale of e.g. 100–200 ms, but might also be produced if the synaptic trace had an exponentially decaying form over several hundred milliseconds, allowing associations with decaying strength between views separated by one or more intervening views. The existence of a regime, for values of the coupling parameter between pairs of views in a finite interval, such that the presentation of any of the views of one object leads to the same attractor regardless of the particular view chosen as a cue, is one of the issues treated by Parga and Rolls (1998) and Elliffe, Rolls, Parga and Renart (2000). A related problem also dealt with was the capacity of this type of synaptic matrix: how many objects can be stored and retrieved correctly in a view invariant way? Parga and Rolls (1998) and Elliffe, Rolls, Parga and Renart (2000) showed that the number grows linearly with the number of recurrent collateral connections received by each neuron. Some of the groundwork for this approach was laid by the work of Amit and collaborators (Griniasty, Tsodyks and Amit 1993, Amit 1989).

A variant of the second approach is to consider that the remaining entries in the matrix shown in Fig. 4.61 all have a small value. This would be produced by the fact that sometimes a view of one object would be followed by a view of a different object, when for example a large saccade was made, with no explicit resetting of the trace. On average, any one object would follow another rarely, and so the case is considered when all the remaining associations between pairs of views have a low value.

Parga and Rolls (1998) and Elliffe, Rolls, Parga and Renart (2000) were able to show that invariant object recognition is feasible in attractor neural networks in the way described. The system is able to store and retrieve in a view invariant way an extensive number of objects, each defined by a finite set of views. What is implied by extensive is that the number of objects is proportional to the size of the network. The crucial factor that defines this size is the number of connections per neuron. In the case of the fully connected networks considered in this section, the size is thus proportional to the number of neurons. To be particular, the number of objects that can be stored is 0.081 $N/5$, when there are five views of each object. The number of objects is 0.073 $N/11$, when there are eleven views of each object. This is an interesting result in network terms, in that s views each represented by an independent random set of active neurons can, in the network described, be present in the same 'object' attraction basin. It is also an interesting result in neurophysiological terms, in that the number of objects that can be represented in this network scales linearly with the number of recurrent connections per neuron. That is, the number of objects P_o that can be stored is approximately

$$P_o = \frac{k\,C}{s} \tag{4.42}$$

where C is the number of synapses on each neuron devoted to the recurrent collaterals from other neurons in the network, s is the number of views of each object, and k is a factor that is in the region of 0.07–0.09 (Parga and Rolls 1998).

Although the explicit numerical calculation was done for a rather small number of views for each object (up to 11), the basic result, that the network can support this kind of 'object' phase, is expected to hold for any number of views (the only requirement being that it does not increase with the number of neurons). This is of course enough: once an object is defined by a set of views, when the network is presented with a somewhat different stimulus or a noisy version of one of them it will still be in the attraction basin of the object attractor.

Parga and Rolls (1998) thus showed that multiple (e.g. 'view') patterns could be within the basin of attraction of a shared (e.g. 'object') representation, and that the capacity of the system was proportional to the number of synapses per neuron divided by the number of views of each object.

Elliffe, Rolls, Parga and Renart (2000) extended the analysis of Parga and Rolls (1998) by showing that correct retrieval could occur where retrieval 'view' cues were distorted; where there was some association between the views of different objects; and where there was only partial and indeed asymmetric connectivity provided by the associatively modified recurrent collateral connections in the network. The simulations also extended the analysis by showing that the system can work well with sparse patterns, and indeed that the use of sparse patterns increases (as expected) the number of objects that can be stored in the network.

Taken together, the work described by Parga and Rolls (1998) and Elliffe, Rolls, Parga and Renart (2000) introduced the idea that the trace rule used to build invariant representations could be implemented in the recurrent collaterals of a neural network (as well as or as an alternative to its incorporation in the forward connections from one layer to another incorporated in VisNet), and provided a precise analysis of the capacity of the network if it operated in this way. In the brain, it is likely that the recurrent collateral connections between cortical pyramidal cells in visual cortical areas do contribute to building invariant representations, in that if they are associatively modifiable, as seems likely, and because there is continuing firing for typically 100–300 ms after a stimulus has been shown, associations between different exemplars of the same object that occur together close in time would almost necessarily become built into the recurrent synaptic connections between pyramidal cells.

Invariant representation of faces in the context of attractor neural networks has also been discussed by Bartlett and Sejnowski (1997) in terms of a model where different views of faces are presented in a fixed sequence (Griniasty, Tsodyks and Amit 1993). This is not however the general situation; normally any pair of views can be seen consecutively and they will become associated. The model described by Parga and Rolls (1998) treats this more general situation.

We wish to note the different nature of the invariant object recognition problem studied here, and the paired associate learning task studied by Miyashita and Chang (1988), Miyashita (1988), and Sakai and Miyashita (1991). In the invariant object recognition case no particular learning protocol is required to produce an activity of the inferior temporal cortex cells responsible for invariant object recognition that is maintained for 300 ms. The learning can occur rapidly, and the learning occurs between stimuli (e.g. different views) which occur with no intervening delay. In the paired associate task, which had the aim of providing a model of semantic memory, the monkeys must learn to associate together two stimuli that are separated in time (by a number of seconds), and this type of learning can take weeks to train. During the delay period the sustained activity is rather low in the experiments, and thus the representation of the first stimulus that remains is weak, and can only poorly be associated with the second stimulus. However, formally the learning mechanism could be treated in the same way as that used by Parga and Rolls (1998) for invariant object recognition. The experimental difference is just that in the paired associate task used by Miyashita et al., it is the weak memory of the first stimulus that is associated with the second stimulus. In contrast, in the invariance learning, it would be the firing activity being produced by the first stimulus (not the weak memory of the first stimulus) that can be associated together. It is possible that the perirhinal cortex makes a useful contribution to invariant object recognition by providing a short-term memory that helps successive views of the same objects to become associated together (Buckley, Booth, Rolls and Gaffan 2001).

The mechanisms described here using an attractor network with a trace associative learning rule would apply most naturally when a small number of representations need to be associated together to represent an object. One example is associating together what is seen when an object is viewed from different perspectives. Another example is scale, with respect to which neurons early in the visual system tolerate scale changes of approximately 1.5 octaves, so that the whole scale range could be covered by associating together a limited number of such representations (see Chapter 5 of Rolls and Deco (2002) and Fig. 4.2). The mechanism would not be so suitable when a large number of different instances would need to be associated together to form an invariant representation of objects, as might be needed for translation invariance. For the latter, the standard model of VisNet with the associative trace learning rule implemented in the feedforward connections (or trained by continuous spatial transformation learning as described in Section 4.5.11) would be more appropriate. However, both types of mechanism, with the trace rule in the feedforward or in recurrent collateral synapses, could contribute (separately or together) to achieve invariant representations. Part of the interest of the attractor approach described in this section is that it allows analytic investigation.

Another approach to training invariance is the purely associative mechanism continuous spatial transformation learning, described in Section 4.5.11. With this training procedure, the capacity is increased with respect to the number of training locations, with for example 169 training locations producing translation invariant representations for two face stimuli (Perry, Rolls and Stringer 2007). It will be of interest in future research to investigate how the VisNet architecture, whether trained with a trace or purely associative rule, scales up with respect to capacity as the number of neurons in the system increases. More distributed representations in the output layer, which may be facilitated by encouraging the system to form a self-organising map, by including short range excitation as well as longer range inhibition between the neurons (see Section 4.5.1), may also help to increase the capacity.

Fig. 4.62 The visual search task. The monkey had to search for and touch an object (in this case a banana) when shown in a complex natural scene, or when shown on a plain background. In each case a second object is present (a bottle) which the monkey must not touch. The stimuli are shown to scale. The screen subtended 70 deg × 55 deg. (After Rolls, Aggelopoulos and Zheng 2003.)

4.5.9 Vision in natural scenes – effects of background versus attention

Object-based attention refers to attention to an object. For example, in a visual search task the object might be specified as what should be searched for, and its location must be found. In spatial attention, a particular location in a scene is pre-cued, and the object at that location may need to be identified. Here we consider some of the neurophysiology of object selection and attention in the context of a feature hierarchy approach to invariant object recognition. The computational mechanisms of attention, including top-down biased competition, are described in Chapter 6.

4.5.9.1 Neurophysiology of object selection in the inferior temporal visual cortex

Much of the neurophysiology, psychophysics, and modelling of attention has been with a small number, typically two, of objects in an otherwise blank scene. In this Section, I consider how attention operates in complex natural scenes, and in particular describe how the inferior temporal visual cortex operates to enable the selection of an object in a complex natural scene (see also Rolls and Deco (2006)). The inferior temporal visual cortex contains distributed and invariant representations of objects and faces (Rolls 2000a, Rolls and Deco 2002, Booth and Rolls 1998, Rolls, Treves and Tovee 1997b, Rolls and Tovee 1995b, Tovee, Rolls and Azzopardi 1994, Hasselmo, Rolls and Baylis 1989a, Rolls and Baylis 1986, Rolls 2007i, Rolls 2007j, Rolls 2007f).

To investigate how attention operates in complex natural scenes, and how information is passed from the inferior temporal cortex (IT) to other brain regions to enable stimuli to be selected from natural scenes for action, Rolls, Aggelopoulos and Zheng (2003a) analyzed the responses of inferior temporal cortex neurons to stimuli presented in complex natural backgrounds. The monkey had to search for two objects on a screen, and a touch of one object was rewarded with juice, and of another object was punished with saline (see Fig. 4.4 for a schematic illustration and Fig. 4.62 for a version of the display with examples of the stimuli shown to scale). Neuronal responses to the effective stimuli for the neurons were compared when the objects were presented in the natural scene or on a plain background. It

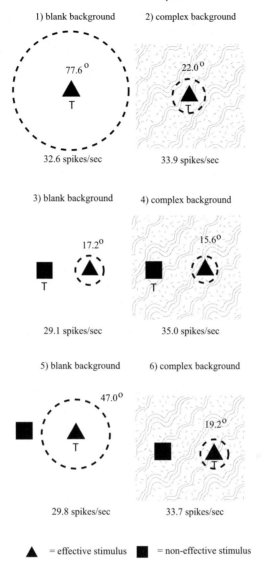

Fig. 4.63 Summary of the receptive field sizes of inferior temporal cortex neurons to a 5 degree effective stimulus presented in either a blank background (blank screen) or in a natural scene (complex background). The stimulus that was a target for action in the different experimental conditions is marked by **T**. When the target stimulus was touched, a reward was obtained. The mean receptive field diameter of the population of neurons analyzed, and the mean firing rate in spikes/s, is shown. The stimuli subtended 5 deg × 3.5 deg at the retina, and occurred on each trial in a random position in the 70 deg × 55 deg screen. The dashed circle is proportional to the receptive field size. Top row: responses with one visual stimulus in a blank (left) or complex (right) background. Middle row: responses with two stimuli, when the effective stimulus was not the target of the visual search. Bottom row: responses with two stimuli, when the effective stimulus was the target of the visual search. (After Rolls, Aggelopoulos, and Zheng 2003.)

was found that the overall response of the neuron to objects was hardly reduced when they were presented in natural scenes, and the selectivity of the neurons remained. However, the main finding was that the magnitudes of the responses of the neurons typically became much less in the real scene the further the monkey fixated in the scene away from the object (see

Fig. 4.5). A small receptive field size has also been found in inferior temporal cortex neurons when monkeys have been trained to discriminate closely spaced small visual stimuli (DiCarlo and Maunsell 2003).

It is proposed that this reduced translation invariance in natural scenes helps an unambiguous representation of an object which may be the target for action to be passed to the brain regions that receive from the primate inferior temporal visual cortex. It helps with the binding problem, by reducing in natural scenes the effective receptive field of at least some inferior temporal cortex neurons to approximately the size of an object in the scene.

It is also found that in natural scenes, the effect of object-based attention on the response properties of inferior temporal cortex neurons is relatively small, as illustrated in Fig. 4.63 (Rolls, Aggelopoulos and Zheng 2003a).

4.5.9.2   Attention in natural scenes – a computational account

The results summarized in Fig. 4.63 for 5 degree stimuli show that the receptive fields were large (77.6 degrees) with a single stimulus in a blank background (top left), and were greatly reduced in size (to 22.0 degrees) when presented in a complex natural scene (top right). The results also show that there was little difference in receptive field size or firing rate in the complex background when the effective stimulus was selected for action (bottom right, 19.2 degrees), and when it was not (middle right, 15.6 degrees) (Rolls, Aggelopoulos and Zheng 2003a). (For comparison, the effects of attention against a blank background were much larger, with the receptive field increasing from 17.2 degrees to 47.0 degrees as a result of object-based attention, as shown in Fig. 4.63, left middle and bottom.)

Trappenberg, Rolls and Stringer (2002) have suggested what underlying mechanisms could account for these findings, and simulated a model to test the ideas. The model utilizes an attractor network representing the inferior temporal visual cortex (implemented by the recurrent connections between inferior temporal cortex neurons), and a neural input layer with several retinotopically organized modules representing the visual scene in an earlier visual cortical area such as V4 (see Fig. 4.64). The attractor network aspect of the model produces the property that the receptive fields of IT neurons can be large in blank scenes by enabling a weak input in the periphery of the visual field to act as a retrieval cue for the object attractor. On the other hand, when the object is shown in a complex background, the object closest to the fovea tends to act as the retrieval cue for the attractor, because the fovea is given increased weight in activating the IT module because the magnitude of the input activity from objects at the fovea is greatest due to the higher magnification factor of the fovea incorporated into the model. This results in smaller receptive fields of IT neurons in complex scenes, because the object tends to need to be close to the fovea to trigger the attractor into the state representing that object. (In other words, if the object is far from the fovea, then it will not trigger neurons in IT which represent it, because neurons in IT are preferentially being activated by another object at the fovea.) This may be described as an attractor model in which the competition for which attractor state is retrieved is weighted towards objects at the fovea.

Attentional top-down object-based inputs can bias the competition implemented in this attractor model, but have relatively minor effects (in for example increasing receptive field size) when they are applied in a complex natural scene, as then as usual the stronger forward inputs dominate the states reached. In this network, the recurrent collateral connections may be thought of as implementing constraints between the different inputs present, to help arrive at firing in the network which best meets the constraints. In this scenario, the preferential weighting of objects close to the fovea because of the increased magnification factor at the fovea is a useful principle in enabling the system to provide useful output. The attentional object biasing effect is much more marked in a blank scene, or a scene with only two objects

Object bias

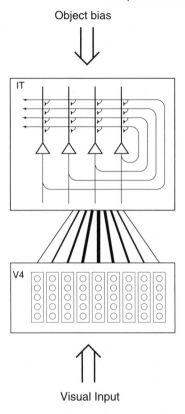

Visual Input

Fig. 4.64 The architecture of the inferior temporal cortex (IT) model of Trappenberg, Rolls and Stringer (2002) operating as an attractor network with inputs from the fovea given preferential weighting by the greater magnification factor of the fovea. The model also has a top-down object-selective bias input. The model was used to analyze how object vision and recognition operate in complex natural scenes.

present at similar distances from the fovea, which are conditions in which attentional effects have frequently been examined. The results of the investigation (Trappenberg, Rolls and Stringer 2002) thus suggest that top-down attention may be a much more limited phenomenon in complex, natural, scenes than in reduced displays with one or two objects present. The results also suggest that the alternative principle, of providing strong weight to whatever is close to the fovea, is an important principle governing the operation of the inferior temporal visual cortex, and in general of the output of the visual system in natural environments. This principle of operation is very important in interfacing the visual system to action systems, because the effective stimulus in making inferior temporal cortex neurons fire is in natural scenes usually on or close to the fovea. This means that the spatial coordinates of where the object is in the scene do not have to be represented in the inferior temporal visual cortex, nor passed from it to the action selection system, as the latter can assume that the object making IT neurons fire is close to the fovea in natural scenes.

There may of course be in addition a mechanism for object selection that takes into account the locus of covert attention when actions are made to locations not being looked at. However, the simulations described in this section suggest that in any case covert attention is likely to be a much less significant influence on visual processing in natural scenes than in reduced scenes with one or two objects present.

Given these points, one might question why inferior temporal cortex neurons can have such large receptive fields, which show translation invariance. At least part of the answer to this may be that inferior temporal cortex neurons must have the capability to be large if they are to deal with large objects. A V1 neuron, with its small receptive field, simply could not receive input from all the features necessary to define an object. On the other hand, inferior temporal cortex neurons may be able to adjust their size to approximately the size of objects, using in part the interactive effects described in Chapter 6, and need the capability for translation invariance because the actual relative positions of the features of an object could be at different relative positions in the scene. For example, a car can be recognized whichever way it is viewed, so that the parts (such as the bonnet or hood) must be identifiable as parts wherever they happen to be in the image, though of course the parts themselves also have to be in the correct relative positions, as allowed for by the hierarchical feature analysis architecture described in this chapter.

Some details of the simulations follow. Each independent module within 'V4' in Fig. 4.64 represents a small part of the visual field and receives input from earlier visual areas represented by an input vector for each possible location which is unique for each object. Each module was 6 degrees in width, matching the size of the objects presented to the network. For the simulations Trappenberg, Rolls and Stringer (2002) chose binary random input vectors representing objects with $N^{V4}a^{V4}$ components set to ones and the remaining $N^{V4}(1 - a^{V4})$ components set to zeros. N^{V4} is the number of nodes in each module and a^{V4} is the sparseness of the representation which was set to be $a^{V4} = 0.2$ in the simulations.

The structure labelled 'IT' represents areas of visual association cortex such as the inferior temporal visual cortex and cortex in the anterior part of the superior temporal sulcus in which neurons provide distributed representations of faces and objects (Booth and Rolls 1998, Rolls 2000a). Nodes in this structure are governed by leaky integrator dynamics (similar to those used in the mean field approach described in Section B.8.1) with time constant τ

$$\tau \frac{dh_i^{IT}(t)}{dt} = -h_i^{IT}(t) + \sum_j (w_{ij}^{IT} - c^{IT}) y_j^{IT}(t) + \sum_k w_{ik}^{IT-V4} y_k^{V4}(t) + k^{IT\_BIAS} I_i^{OBJ}. \quad (4.43)$$

The firing rate y_i^{IT} of the ith node is determined by a sigmoidal function from the activation h_i^{IT} as follows

$$y_i^{IT}(t) = \frac{1}{1 + \exp\left[-2\beta(h_i^{IT}(t) - \alpha)\right]}, \quad (4.44)$$

where the parameters $\beta = 1$ and $\alpha = 1$ represent the gain and the bias, respectively.

The recognition functionality of this structure is modelled as an attractor neural network (ANN) with trained memories indexed by μ representing particular objects. The memories are formed through Hebbian learning on sparse patterns,

$$w_{ij}^{IT} = k^{IT} \sum_\mu (\xi_i^\mu - a^{IT})(\xi_j^\mu - a^{IT}), \quad (4.45)$$

where k^{IT} (set to 1 in the simulations) is a normalization constant that depends on the learning rate, $a^{IT} = 0.2$ is the sparseness of the training pattern in IT, and ξ_i^μ are the components of the pattern used to train the network. The constant c^{IT} in equation 4.43 represents the strength of the activity-dependent global inhibition simulating the effects of inhibitory interneurons. The external 'top-down' input vector I^{OBJ} produces object-selective inputs, which are used as the attentional drive when a visual search task is simulated. The strength of this object bias is modulated by the value of k^{IT_BIAS} in equation (4.43).

The weights $w_{ij}^{\mathrm{IT}-\mathrm{V4}}$ between the V4 nodes and IT nodes were trained by Hebbian learning of the form

$$w_{ij}^{\mathrm{IT}-\mathrm{V4}} = k^{\mathrm{IT}-\mathrm{V4}}(k) \sum_{\mu} (\xi_i^{\mu} - a^{\mathrm{V4}})(\xi_j^{\mu} - a^{\mathrm{IT}}). \tag{4.46}$$

to produce object representations in IT based on inputs in V4. The normalizing modulation factor $k^{\mathrm{IT}-\mathrm{V4}}(k)$ allows the gain of inputs to be modulated as a function of their distance from the fovea, and depends on the module k to which the presynaptic node belongs. The model supports translation invariant object recognition of a single object in the visual field if the normalization factor is the same for each module and the model is trained with the objects placed at every possible location in the visual field. The translation invariance of the weight vectors between each 'V4' module and the IT nodes is however explicitly modulated in the model by the module-dependent modulation factor $k^{\mathrm{IT}-\mathrm{V4}}(k)$ as indicated in Fig. 4.64 by the width of the lines connecting V4 with IT. The strength of the foveal V4 module is strongest, and the strength decreases for modules representing increasing eccentricity. The form of this modulation factor was derived from the parameterization of the cortical magnification factors given by Dow, Snyder, Vautin and Bauer (1981)[23].

To study the ability of the model to recognize trained objects at various locations relative to the fovea the system was trained on a set of objects. The network was then tested with distorted versions of the objects, and the 'correlation' between the target object and the final state of the attractor network was taken as a measure of the performance. The correlation was estimated from the normalized dot product between the target object vector that was used during training the IT network, and the state of the IT network after a fixed amount of time sufficient for the network to settle into a stable state. The objects were always presented on backgrounds with some noise (introduced by flipping 2% of the bits in the scene which were not the test stimulus) in order to utilize the properties of the attractor network, and because the input to IT will inevitably be noisy under normal conditions of operation.

In the first simulation only one object was present in the visual scene in a plain (blank) background at different eccentricities from the fovea. As shown in Fig. 4.65a by the line labelled 'blank background', the receptive fields of the neurons were very large. The value of the object bias $k^{\mathrm{IT\_BIAS}}$ was set to 0 in these simulations. Good object retrieval (indicated by large correlations) was found even when the object was far from the fovea, indicating large IT receptive fields with a blank background. The reason that any drop is seen in performance as a function of eccentricity is because flipping 2% of the bits outside the object introduces some noise into the recall process. This demonstrates that the attractor dynamics can support translation invariant object recognition even though the translation invariant weight vectors between V4 and IT are explicitly modulated by the modulation factor $k^{\mathrm{IT}-\mathrm{V4}}$ derived from the cortical magnification factor.

In a second simulation individual objects were placed at all possible locations in a natural and cluttered visual scene. The resulting correlations between the target pattern and the asymptotic IT state are shown in Fig. 4.65a with the line labelled 'natural background'. Many objects in the visual scene are now competing for recognition by the attractor network, and the objects around the foveal position are enhanced through the modulation factor derived from the cortical magnification factor. This results in a much smaller size of the receptive field of IT neurons when measured with objects in natural backgrounds.

In addition to this major effect of the background on the size of the receptive field, which parallels and may account for the physiological findings outlined above and in Section 4.5.9.1,

---

[23]This parameterization is based on V1 data. However, it was shown that similar forms of the magnification factor hold also in V4 (Gattass, Sousa and Covey 1985). Similar results to the ones presented here can also be achieved with different forms of the modulation factor such as a shifted Gaussian.

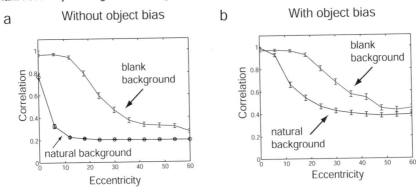

Fig. 4.65 Correlations as measured by the normalized dot product between the object vector used to train IT and the state of the IT network after settling into a stable state with a single object in the visual scene (blank background) or with other trained objects at all possible locations in the visual scene (natural background). There is no object bias included in the results shown in graph a, whereas an object bias is included in the results shown in b with k^{IT_BIAS}=0.7 in the experiments with a natural background and k^{IT_BIAS}=0.1 in the experiments with a blank background. (After Trappenberg, Rolls and Stringer 2002.)

there is also a dependence of the size of the receptive fields on the level of object bias provided to the IT network. Examples are shown in Fig. 4.65b where an object bias was used. The object bias biases the IT network towards the expected object with a strength determined by the value of k^{IT_BIAS}, and has the effect of increasing the size of the receptive fields in both blank and natural backgrounds (see Fig. 4.65b compared to a). This models the effect found neurophysiologically (Rolls, Aggelopoulos and Zheng 2003a)[24].

Some of the conclusions are as follows (Trappenberg, Rolls and Stringer 2002). When single objects are shown in a scene with a blank background, the attractor network helps neurons to respond to an object with large eccentricities of this object relative to the fovea of the agent. When the object is presented in a natural scene, other neurons in the inferior temporal cortex become activated by the other effective stimuli present in the visual field, and these forward inputs decrease the response of the network to the target stimulus by a competitive process. The results found fit well with the neurophysiological data, in that IT operates with almost complete translation invariance when there is only one object in the scene, and reduces the receptive field size of its neurons when the object is presented in a cluttered environment. The model described here provides an explanation of the responses of real IT neurons in natural scenes.

In natural scenes, the model is able to account for the neurophysiological data that the IT neuronal responses are larger when the object is close to the fovea, by virtue of fact that objects close to the fovea are weighted by the cortical magnification factor related modulation k^{IT-V4}.

The model accounts for the larger receptive field sizes from the fovea of IT neurons in natural backgrounds if the target is the object being selected compared to when it is not selected (Rolls, Aggelopoulos and Zheng 2003a). The model accounts for this by an effect of top-down bias which simply biases the neurons towards particular objects compensating for their decreasing inputs produced by the decreasing magnification factor modulation with increasing distance from the fovea. Such object-based attention signals could originate in the

---

[24] k^{IT_BIAS} was set to 0.7 in the experiments with a natural background and to 0.1 with a blank background, reflecting the fact that more attention may be needed to find objects in natural cluttered environments because of the noise present than in blank backgrounds. Equivalently, a given level of attention may have a smaller effect in a natural scene than in a blank background, as found neurophysiologically (Rolls, Aggelopoulos and Zheng 2003a).

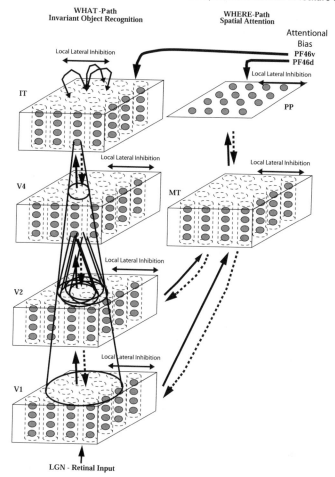

Fig. 4.66 Cortical architecture for hierarchical and attention-based visual perception after Deco and Rolls (2004). The system is essentially composed of five modules structured such that they resemble the two known main visual paths of the mammalian visual cortex. Information from the retino-geniculo-striate pathway enters the visual cortex through area V1 in the occipital lobe and proceeds into two processing streams. The occipital-temporal stream leads ventrally through V2–V4 and IT (inferior temporal visual cortex), and is mainly concerned with object recognition. The occipito-parietal stream leads dorsally into PP (posterior parietal complex), and is responsible for maintaining a spatial map of an object's location. The solid lines with arrows between levels show the forward connections, and the dashed lines the top-down backprojections. Short-term memory systems in the prefrontal cortex (PF46) apply top-down attentional bias to the object or spatial processing streams. (After Deco and Rolls 2004.)

prefrontal cortex and could provide the object bias for the inferior temporal visual cortex (Renart, Parga and Rolls 2000) (see Chapter 6).

Important properties of the architecture for obtaining the results just described are the high magnification factor at the fovea and the competition between the effects of different inputs, implemented in the above simulation by the competition inherent in an attractor network.

We have also been able to obtain similar results in a hierarchical feedforward network where each layer operates as a competitive network (Deco and Rolls 2004). This network thus captures many of the properties of our hierarchical model of invariant object recognition (Rolls 1992a, Wallis and Rolls 1997, Rolls and Milward 2000, Stringer and Rolls 2000, Rolls and Stringer 2001a, Elliffe, Rolls and Stringer 2002, Stringer and Rolls 2002, Rolls and Deco 2002, Stringer, Perry, Rolls and Proske 2006, Rolls and Stringer 2007, Rolls and Stringer 2006), but incorporates in addition a foveal magnification factor and top-down projections with a dorsal visual stream so that attentional effects can be studied, as shown in Fig. 4.66.

Deco and Rolls (2004) trained the network shown in Fig. 4.66 with two objects, and used the trace learning rule (Wallis and Rolls 1997, Rolls and Milward 2000) in order to achieve translation invariance. In a first experiment we placed only one object on the retina at different distances from the fovea (i.e. different eccentricities relative to the fovea). This corresponds to the blank background condition. In a second experiment, we also placed the object at different eccentricities relative to the fovea, but on a cluttered natural background. Larger receptive fields were found with the blank as compared to the cluttered natural background.

Deco and Rolls (2004) also studied the influence of object-based attentional top-down bias on the effective size of the receptive field of an inferior temporal cortex neuron for the case of an object in a blank or a cluttered background. To do this, they repeated the two simulations but now considered a non-zero top-down bias coming from prefrontal area 46v and impinging on the inferior temporal cortex neuron specific for the object tested. When no attentional object bias was introduced, a shrinkage of the receptive field size was observed in the complex vs the blank background. When attentional object bias was introduced, the shrinkage of the receptive field due to the complex background was somewhat reduced. This is consistent with the neurophysiological results (Rolls, Aggelopoulos and Zheng 2003a). In the framework of the model (Deco and Rolls 2004), the reduction of the shrinkage of the receptive field is due to the biasing of the competition in the inferior temporal cortex layer in favour of the specific IT neuron tested, so that it shows more translation invariance (i.e. a slightly larger receptive field). The increase of the receptive field size of an IT neuron, although small, produced by the external top-down attentional bias offers a mechanism for facilitation of the search for specific objects in complex natural scenes (see further Chapter 6).

We note that it is possible that a 'spotlight of attention' (Desimone and Duncan 1995) can be moved covertly away from the fovea as described in Chapter 6. However, at least during normal visual search tasks in natural scenes, the neurons are sensitive to the object at which the monkey is looking, that is primarily to the object that is on the fovea, as shown by Rolls, Aggelopoulos and Zheng (2003a) and Aggelopoulos and Rolls (2005), and described in Sections 4.5.9.1 and 4.5.10.

4.5.10 The representation of multiple objects in a scene

When objects have distributed representations, there is a problem of how multiple objects (whether the same or different) can be represented in a scene, because the distributed representations overlap, and it may not be possible to determine whether one has an amalgam of several objects, or a new object (Mozer 1991), or multiple instances of the same object, let alone the relative spatial positions of the objects in a scene. Yet humans can determine the relative spatial locations of objects in a scene even in short presentation times without eye movements (Biederman 1972) (and this has been held to involve some spotlight of attention). Aggelopoulos and Rolls (2005) analyzed this issue by recording from single inferior temporal cortex neurons with five objects simultaneously present in the receptive field. They found that although all the neurons responded to their effective stimulus when it was at the fovea, some could also respond to their effective stimulus when it was in some but not other parafoveal positions 10 degrees from the fovea. An example of such a neuron is shown in Fig. 4.67. The asymmetry is much more evident in a scene with 5 images present (Fig. 4.67A) than when

A　　　　　　　　　　**B**

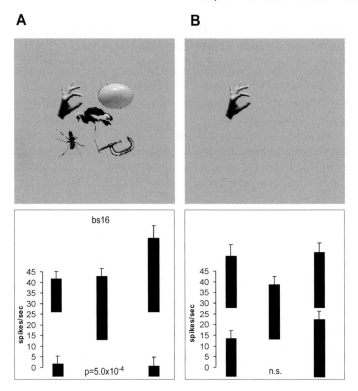

Fig. 4.67 (A). The responses (firing rate with the spontaneous rate subtracted, means ± sem) of an inferior temporal cortex neuron when tested with 5 stimuli simultaneously present in the close (10 deg) configuration with the parafoveal stimuli located 10 degrees from the fovea. (B). The responses of the same neuron when only the effective stimulus was presented in each position. The firing rate for each position is that when the effective stimulus (in this case the hand) for the neuron was in that position. The p value is that from the ANOVA calculated over the four parafoveal positions. (After Aggelopoulos and Rolls 2005.)

only one image is shown on an otherwise blank screen (Fig. 4.67B). Competition between different stimuli in the receptive field thus reveals the asymmetry in the receptive field of inferior temporal visual cortex neurons.

The asymmetry provides a way of encoding the position of multiple objects in a scene. Depending on which asymmetric neurons are firing, the population of neurons provides information to the next processing stage not only about which image is present at or close to the fovea, but where it is with respect to the fovea. This information is provided by neurons that have firing rates that reflect the relevant information, and stimulus-dependent synchrony is not necessary. Top-down attentional biasing input could thus, by biasing the appropriate neurons, facilitate bottom-up information about objects without any need to alter the time relations between the firing of different neurons. The exact position of the object with respect to the fovea, and effectively thus its spatial position relative to other objects in the scene, would then be made evident by the subset of asymmetric neurons firing.

This is thus the solution that these experiments indicate is used for the representation of multiple objects in a scene, an issue that has previously been difficult to account for in neural systems with distributed representations (Mozer 1991) and for which 'attention' has been a proposed solution. The learning of invariant representations of objects when multiple objects are present in a scene is considered in Section 4.5.6.2.

4.5.11 Learning invariant representations using spatial continuity: Continuous Spatial Transformation learning

The temporal continuity typical of objects has been used in an associative learning rule with a short-term memory trace to help build invariant object representations in the networks described previously in this chapter. Stringer, Perry, Rolls and Proske (2006) showed that spatial continuity can also provide a basis for helping a system to self-organize invariant representations. They introduced a new learning paradigm 'continuous spatial transformation (CT) learning' which operates by mapping spatially similar input patterns to the same postsynaptic neurons in a competitive learning system. As the inputs move through the space of possible continuous transforms (e.g. translation, rotation, etc.), the active synapses are modified onto the set of postsynaptic neurons. Because other transforms of the same stimulus overlap with previously learned exemplars, a common set of postsynaptic neurons is activated by the new transforms, and learning of the new active inputs onto the same postsynaptic neurons is facilitated.

The concept is illustrated in Fig. 4.68. During the presentation of a visual image at one position on the retina that activates neurons in layer 1, a small winning set of neurons in layer 2 will modify (through associative learning) their afferent connections from layer 1 to respond well to that image in that location. When the same image appears later at nearby locations, so that there is spatial continuity, the same neurons in layer 2 will be activated because some of the active afferents are the same as when the image was in the first position. The key point is that if these afferent connections have been strengthened sufficiently while the image is in the first location, then these connections will be able to continue to activate the same neurons in layer 2 when the image appears in overlapping nearby locations. Thus the same neurons in the output layer have learned to respond to inputs that have similar vector elements in common.

As can be seen in Fig. 4.68, the process can be continued for subsequent shifts, provided that a sufficient proportion of input cells stay active between individual shifts. This whole process is repeated throughout the network, both horizontally as the image moves on the retina, and hierarchically up through the network. Over a series of stages, transform invariant (e.g. location invariant) representations of images are successfully learned, allowing the network to perform invariant object recognition. A similar CT learning process may operate for other kinds of transformation, such as change in view or size.

Stringer, Perry, Rolls and Proske (2006) demonstrated that VisNet can be trained with continuous spatial transformation learning to form view invariant representations. They showed that CT learning requires the training transforms to be relatively close together spatially so that spatial continuity is present in the training set; and that the order of stimulus presentation is not crucial, with even interleaving with other objects possible during training, because it is spatial continuity rather the temporal continuity that drives the self-organizing learning with the purely associative synaptic modification rule.

Perry, Rolls and Stringer (2006) extended these simulations with VisNet of view invariant learning using CT to more complex 3D objects, and using the same training images in human psychophysical investigations, showed that view invariant object learning can occur when spatial but not temporal continuity applies in a training condition in which the images of different objects were interleaved. However, they also found that the human view invariance learning was better if sequential presentation of the images of an object was used, indicating that temporal continuity is an important factor in human invariance learning.

Perry, Rolls and Stringer (2007) extended the use of continuous spatial transformation learning to translation invariance. They showed that translation invariant representations can be learned by continuous spatial transformation learning; that the transforms must be close for this to occur; that the temporal order of presentation of each transformed image during

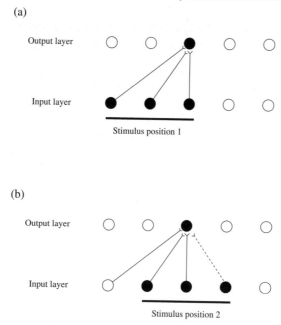

Fig. 4.68 An illustration of how continuous spatial transformation (CT) learning would function in a network with a single layer of forward synaptic connections between an input layer of neurons and an output layer. Initially the forward synaptic weights are set to random values. The top part (a) shows the initial presentation of a stimulus to the network in position 1. Activation from the (shaded) active input cells is transmitted through the initially random forward connections to stimulate the cells in the output layer. The shaded cell in the output layer wins the competition in that layer. The weights from the active input cells to the active output neuron are then strengthened using an associative learning rule. The bottom part (b) shows what happens after the stimulus is shifted by a small amount to a new partially overlapping position 2. As some of the active input cells are the same as those that were active when the stimulus was presented in position 1, the same output cell is driven by these previously strengthened afferents to win the competition again. The rightmost shaded input cell activated by the stimulus in position 2, which was inactive when the stimulus was in position 1, now has its connection to the active output cell strengthened (denoted by the dashed line). Thus the same neuron in the output layer has learned to respond to the two input patterns that have similar vector elements in common. As can be seen, the process can be continued for subsequent shifts, provided that a sufficient proportion of input cells stay active between individual shifts. (After Stringer, Rolls, Perry and Proske 2006.)

training is not crucial for learning to occur; that relatively large numbers of transforms can be learned; and that such continuous spatial transformation learning can be usefully combined with temporal trace training.

4.5.12 Lighting invariance

Object recognition should occur correctly even despite variations of lighting. In an investigation of this, Rolls and Stringer (2006) trained VisNet on a set of 3D objects generated with OpenGL in which the viewing angle and lighting source could be independently varied (see Fig. 4.69). After training with the trace rule on all the 180 views (separated by 1 deg, and rotated about the vertical axis in Fig. 4.69) of each of the four objects under the left lighting condition, we tested whether the network would recognize the objects correctly when they were shown again, but with the source of the lighting moved to the right so that the objects appeared different (see Fig. 4.69). Figure 4.70 shows that the single and multiple cell inform-

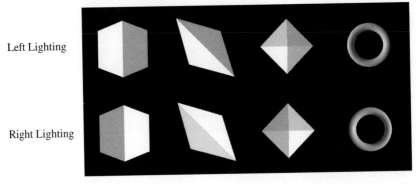

Left Lighting

Right Lighting

Fig. 4.69 Lighting invariance. VisNet was trained on a set of 3D objects (cube, tetrahedron, octahedron and torus) generated with OpenGL in which for training the objects had left lighting, and for testing the objects had right lighting. Just one view of each object is shown in the Figure, but for training and testing 180 views of each object separated by 1 deg were used. (After Rolls and Stringer 2006.)

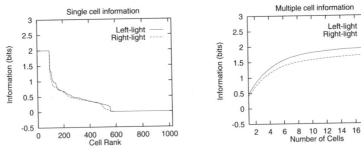

Fig. 4.70 Lighting invariance. The performance of the network after training with 180 views of each object lit from the left, when tested with the lighting again from the left (Left-light), and when tested with the lighting from the right (Right-light). The single cell information measure shows that many single neurons in layer 4 had the maximum amount of information about the objects, 2 bits, which indicates that they responded to all 180 views of one of the objects, and none of the 180 views of the other objects. The multiple cell information shows that the cells were sufficiently different in the objects to which they responded invariantly that all of the objects were perfectly represented when tested with the training images, and very well represented (with nearly 2 bits of information) when tested in the untrained lighting condition. (After Rolls and Stringer 2006.)

ation measures for the set of objects tested with the light source in the same position as during training (Left-light), and that the measures were almost as good with testing with the light source moved to the right position (Right-light). Thus lighting invariant object recognition was demonstrated (Rolls and Stringer 2006).

Some insight into the good performance with a change of lighting is that some neurons in the inferior temporal visual cortex respond to the outlines of 3D objects (Vogels and Biederman 2002), and these outlines will be relatively consistent across lighting variations. Although the features about the object represented in VisNet will include more than the representations of the outlines, the network may because it uses distributed representations of each object generalize correctly provided that some of the features are similar to those present during training. Under very difficult lighting conditions, it is likely that the performance of the network could be improved by including variations in the lighting during training, so that the trace rule could help to build representations that are explicitly invariant with respect to lighting.

4.5.13   Invariant global motion in the dorsal visual system

A key issue in understanding the cortical mechanisms that underlie motion perception is how we perceive the motion of objects such as a rotating wheel invariantly with respect to position on the retina, and size. For example, we perceive the wheel shown in Fig. 4.71a rotating clockwise independently of its position on the retina. This occurs even though the local motion for the wheels in the different positions may be opposite. How could this invariance of the visual motion perception of objects arise in the visual system? Invariant motion representations are known to be developed in the cortical dorsal visual system. Motion-sensitive neurons in V1 have small receptive fields (in the range 1–2 deg at the fovea), and can therefore not detect global motion, and this is part of the aperture problem (Wurtz and Kandel 2000b). Neurons in MT, which receives inputs from V1 and V2 (see Fig. 1.10), have larger receptive fields (e.g. 5 degrees at the fovea), and are able to respond to planar global motion, such as a field of small dots in which the majority (in practice as few as 55%) move in one direction, or to the overall direction of a moving plaid, the orthogonal grating components of which have motion at 45 degrees to the overall motion (Movshon, Adelson, Gizzi and Newsome 1985, Newsome, Britten and Movshon 1989). Further on in the dorsal visual system, some neurons in macaque visual area MST (but not MT) respond to rotating flow fields or looming with considerable translation invariance (Graziano, Andersen and Snowden 1994, Geesaman and Andersen 1996). In the cortex in the anterior part of the superior temporal sulcus, which is a convergence zone for inputs from the ventral and dorsal visual systems, some neurons respond to object-based motion, for example to a head rotating clockwise but not anticlockwise, independently of whether the head is upright or inverted which reverses the optic flow across the retina (Hasselmo, Rolls, Baylis and Nalwa 1989b).

In a unifying hypothesis with the design of the ventral cortical visual system, Rolls and Stringer (2007) proposed that the dorsal visual system uses a hierarchical feedforward network architecture (V1, V2, MT, MSTd, parietal cortex) with training of the connections with a short-term memory trace associative synaptic modification rule to capture what is invariant at each stage. The principle is illustrated in Fig. 4.71a. Simulations showed that the proposal is computationally feasible, in that invariant representations of the motion flow fields produced by objects self-organize in the later layers of the architecture (see examples in Fig. 4.71b–e). The model produces invariant representations of the motion flow fields produced by global in-plane motion of an object, in-plane rotational motion, looming vs receding of the object. The model also produces invariant representations of object-based rotation about a principal axis, of the type illustrated in Fig. 4.9 on page 272. Thus it is proposed that the dorsal and ventral visual systems may share some unifying computational principles (Rolls and Stringer 2007). Indeed, the simulations of Rolls and Stringer (2007) used a standard version of VisNet, with the exception that instead of using oriented bar receptive fields as the input to the first layer, local motion flow fields provided the inputs.

4.6   Further approaches to invariant object recognition

A related approach to invariant object recognition is described by Riesenhuber and Poggio (1999b), and builds on the hypothesis that not just shift invariance (as implemented in the Neocognitron of Fukushima (1980)), but also other invariances such as scale, rotation and even view, could be built into a feature hierarchy system, as suggested by Rolls (1992a) and incorporated into VisNet (Wallis, Rolls and Foldiak 1993, Wallis and Rolls 1997, Rolls and Milward 2000, Rolls and Stringer 2007) (see also Perrett and Oram (1993)). The approach of Riesenhuber and Poggio (1999b) (see also Riesenhuber and Poggio (1999a), Riesenhuber and Poggio (2000) and Serre, Wold, Bileschi, Riesenhuber and Poggio (2007)) is a feature

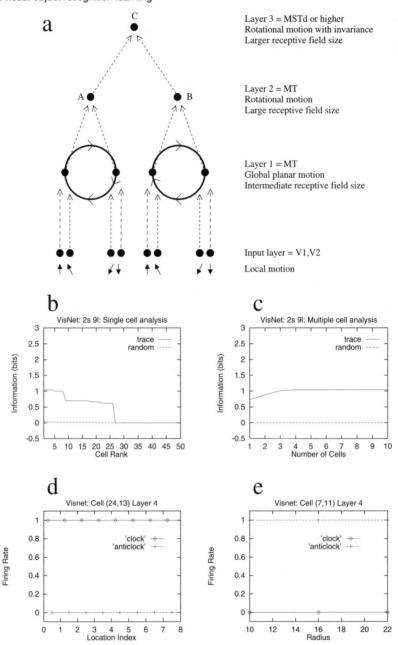

Fig. 4.71 (a) Two rotating wheels at different locations rotating in opposite directions. The local flow field is ambiguous. Clockwise or counterclockwise rotation can only be diagnosed by a global flow computation, and it is shown how the network is expected to solve the problem to produce position invariant global motion-sensitive neurons. One rotating wheel is presented at any one time, but the need is to develop a representation of the fact that in the case shown the rotating flow field is always clockwise, independently of the location of the flow field. (b–d) Translation invariance, with training on 9 locations. (b) Single cell information measures showing that some layer 4 neurons have perfect performance of 1 bit (clockwise vs anticlockwise) after training with the trace rule, but not with random initial synaptic weights in the untrained control condition. (c) The multiple cell information measure shows that small groups of neurons have perfect performance. (d) Position invariance illustrated for a single cell from layer 4, which responded only to the clockwise rotation, and for every one of the 9 positions. (e) Size invariance illustrated for a single cell from layer 4, which after training with three different radii of rotating wheel, responded only to anticlockwise rotation, independently of the size of the rotating wheels. (After Rolls and Stringer 2007.)

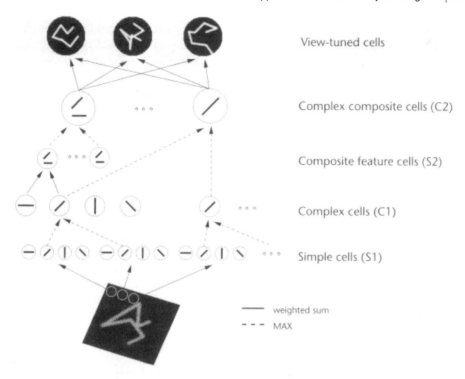

View-tuned cells

Complex composite cells (C2)

Composite feature cells (S2)

Complex cells (C1)

Simple cells (S1)

———— weighted sum

– – – MAX

Fig. 4.72 Sketch of Riesenhuber and Poggio's (1999a,b) model of invariant object recognition. The model includes layers of 'S' cells which perform template matching (solid lines), and 'C' cells (solid lines) which pool information by a non-linear MAX function to achieve invariance (see text). (After Riesenhuber and Poggio 1999a, b.)

hierarchy approach that uses alternate 'simple cell' and 'complex cell' layers in a way analogous to Fukushima (1980) (see Fig. 4.72). The function of each S cell layer is to build more complicated features from the inputs, and works by template matching. The function of each 'C' cell layer is to provide some translation invariance over the features discovered in the preceding simple cell layer (as in Fukushima (1980)), and operates by performing a MAX function on the inputs. The non-linear MAX function makes a complex cell respond only to whatever is the highest activity input being received, and is part of the process by which invariance is achieved according to this proposal. This C layer process involves 'implicitly scanning over afferents of the same type differing in the parameter of the transformation to which responses should be invariant (for instance, feature size for scale invariance), and then selecting the best-matching afferent' (Riesenhuber and Poggio 1999b). Brain mechanisms by which this computation could be set up are not part of the scheme, and the model is not fully self-organizing, so does not yet provide a biologically plausible model of invariant object recognition. However, the fact that the model sets out to achieve some of the processes specified by Rolls (1992a) (see Section 4.4) and implemented in VisNet (see Section 4.5) does represent useful convergent thinking towards how invariant object recognition may be implemented in the brain. Similarly, the approach of training a five-layer network with a more artificial gradient ascent approach with a goal function that does however include forming relatively time invariant representations and decorrelating the responses of neurons within each layer (Wyss, Konig and Verschure 2006) (both processes that have their counterpart in VisNet), also reflects convergent thinking.

Further evidence consistent with the approach developed in the investigations of VisNet described in this chapter comes from psychophysical studies. Wallis and Bülthoff (1999) and Perry, Rolls and Stringer (2006) describe psychophysical evidence for learning of view invariant representations by experience, in that the learning can be shown in special circumstances to be affected by the temporal sequence in which different views of objects are seen.

Another approach to the implementation of invariant representations in the brain is the use of neurons with Sigma-Pi synapses. Sigma-Pi synapses, described in Section A.2.3, effectively allow one input to a synapse to be multiplied or gated by a second input to the synapse. The multiplying input might gate the appropriate set of the other inputs to a synapse to produce the shift or scale change required. For example, the x^c input in equation A.14 could be a signal that varies with the shift required to compute translation invariance, effectively mapping the appropriate set of x_j inputs through to the output neurons depending on the shift required (Mel, Ruderman and Archie 1998, Mel and Fiser 2000, Olshausen, Anderson and Van Essen 1993, Olshausen, Anderson and Van Essen 1995). Local operations on a dendrite could be involved in such a process (Mel, Ruderman and Archie 1998). The explicit neural implementation of the gating mechanism seems implausible, given the need to multiply and thus remap large parts of the retinal input depending on shift and scale modifying connections to a particular set of output neurons. Moreover, the explicit control signal to set the multiplication required in V1 has not been identified. Moreover, if this was the solution used by the brain, the whole problem of shift and scale invariance could in principle be solved in one layer of the system, rather than with the multiple hierarchically organized set of layers actually used in the brain, as shown schematically in Fig. 4.2. The multiple layers actually used in the brain are much more consistent with the type of scheme incorporated in VisNet. Moreover, if a multiplying system of the type hypothesized by Mel, Ruderman and Archie (1998), Olshausen, Anderson and Van Essen (1993) and Olshausen, Anderson and Van Essen (1995) was implemented in a multilayer hierarchy with the shift and scale change emerging gradually, then the multiplying control signal would need to be supplied to every stage of the hierarchy. A further problem with such approaches is how the system is trained in the first place.

4.7 Visuo-spatial scratchpad memory, and change blindness

Given the fact that the responses of inferior temporal cortex neurons are quite locked to the stimulus being viewed, it is unlikely that IT provides the representation of the visual world that we think we see, with objects at their correct places in a visual scene. In fact, we do not really see the whole visual scene, as most of it is a memory reflecting what was seen when the eyes were last looking at a particular part of the scene. The evidence for this statement comes from change blindness experiments, which show that humans rather remarkably do not notice if, while they are moving their eyes and cannot respond to changes in the visual scene, a part of the scene changes (O'Regan, Rensink and Clark 1999, Rensink 2000). A famous example is that in which a baby was removed from the mother's arms during the subject's eye movement, and the subject failed to notice that the scene was any different. Similarly, unless we are fixating the location that is different in two alternated versions of a visual scene, we are remarkably insensitive to differences in the scene, such as a glass being present on a dining table in one but not another picture of a dining room. Given then that much of the apparent richness of our visual world is actually based on what was seen at previously fixated positions in the scene (with this being what the inferior temporal visual cortex represents), we may ask where this 'visuo-spatial' scratchpad (short-term memory) is located in the brain. One

Local attractor networks for a visuo–spatial scratchpad

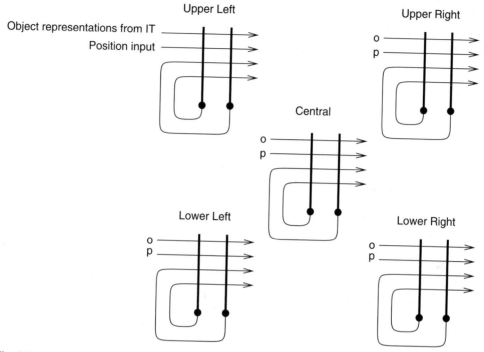

Fig. 4.73 A schematic model of a visuo-spatial scratchpad memory: multiple separate attractor networks could form associations between objects and their place in a scene, and maintain the activity of all the attractors active simultaneously. IT, inferior temporal visual cortex.

possibility is in the right parieto-occipital area, for patients with lesions in the parieto-occipital region have (dorsal) simultanagnosia, in which they can recognize objects, but cannot see more than one object at a time (Farah 2004). Alternatively, the network could be in the left inferior temporo-occipital regions, for patients with (ventral) simultanagnosia cannot recognize but can see multiple objects in a scene (Farah 2004).

The computational basis for this could be a number of separate, that is local, attractors each representing part of the space, and capable of being loaded by inputs from the inferior temporal visual cortex. According to this computational model, the particular attractor network in the visuo-spatial scratchpad memory would be addressed by information based on the position of the eyes, of covert attention, and probably the position of the head. While being so addressed, inputs to the scratch-pad from the inferior temporal cortex neurons would then provide information about the object at the fovea, together with some information about the location of objects in different parafoveal regions (see Section 4.5.10), and this would then enable object information to be associated by synaptic modification with the active neurons in the attractor network representing that location (see Fig. 4.73). Because there are separate spatially local attractors for each location, each of the attractors with its associated object information could be kept active simultaneously, to maintain for short periods information about the relative spatial position of multiple objects in a scene. The attractor for each spatial location would need to represent some information about the object present at that location (as otherwise a binding problem would arise between the multiple objects and the multiple locations), and this may be a reason why the object information in the visuo-spatial scratchpad is not detailed. The suggestion of different attractors for different regions of the scene is consistent with the architecture of the cerebral neocortex, in which the high density of connections including those of inhibitory interneurons is mainly local, within a range of 1–2 mm (see Section 1.10). (If the inhibitory connections were more widespread, so that the inhibition became more global within the visuo-spatial scratchpad memory, the system would be more like a continuous attractor network with multiple activity packets (Stringer, Rolls and Trappenberg 2004) (see Section B.5.4).)

It may only be when the inferior temporal visual cortex is representing objects at or close to the fovea in a complex scene that a great deal of information is present about an object, given the competitive processes described in this chapter combined with the large cortical magnification factor of the fovea. The perceptual system may be built in this way for the fundamental reasons described in this chapter (which enable a hierarchical competitive system to learn invariant representations that require feature binding), which account for why it cannot process a whole scene simultaneously. The visual system can, given the way in which it is built, thereby give an output in a form that is very useful for memory systems, but mainly about one or a few objects close to the fovea.

4.8 Different processes involved in different types of object identification

To conclude this chapter, it is proposed that there are (at least) three different types of process that could be involved in object identification. The first is the simple situation where different objects can be distinguished by different non-overlapping sets of features (see Section 4.3.1). An example might be a banana and an orange, where the list of features of the banana might include yellow, elongated, and smooth surface; and of the orange its orange colour, round shape, and dimpled surface. Such objects could be distinguished just on the basis of a list of the properties, which could be processed appropriately by a competitive network, pattern associator, etc. No special mechanism is needed for view invariance, because the list of properties is very similar from most viewing angles. Object recognition of this type may be common in animals, especially those with visual systems less developed than those of primates. However, this approach does not describe the shape and form of objects, and is insufficient to account for primate vision. Nevertheless, the features present in objects are valuable cues to object identity, and are naturally incorporated into the feature hierarchy approach.

A second type of process might involve the ability to generalize across a small range of views of an object, that is within a generic view, where cues of the first type cannot be used to solve the problem. An example might be generalization across a range of views of a cup when looking into the cup, from just above the near lip until the bottom inside of the cup comes into view. This type of process includes the learning of the transforms of the surface markings on 3D objects which occur when the object is rotated, as described in Section 4.5.7. Such generalization would work because the neurons are tuned as filters to accept a range of variation of the input within parameters such as relative size and orientation of the components of the features. Generalization of this type would not be expected to work when there is a catastrophic change in the features visible, as for example occurs when the cup is rotated so that one can suddenly no longer see inside it, and the outside bottom of the cup comes into view.

The third type of process is one that can deal with the sudden catastrophic change in the features visible when an object is rotated to a completely different view, as in the cup example just given (cf. Koenderink (1990)). Another example, quite extreme to illustrate the point, might be when a card with different images on its two sides is rotated so that one face and then the other is in view. This makes the point that this third type of process may involve arbitrary pairwise association learning, to learn which features and views are different aspects of the same object. Another example occurs when only some parts of an object are visible. For example, a red-handled screwdriver may be recognized either from its round red handle, or from its elongated silver-coloured blade.

The full view-invariant recognition of objects that occurs even when the objects share the same features, such as colour, texture, etc. is an especially computationally demanding task which the primate visual system is able to perform with its highly developed temporal lobe cortical visual areas. The neurophysiological evidence and the neuronal networks described in this chapter provide clear hypotheses about how the primate visual system may perform this task.

4.9   Conclusions

We have seen in this chapter that the feature hierarchy approach has a number of advantages in performing object recognition over other approaches (see Section 4.3), and that some of the key computational issues that arise in these architectures have solutions (see Sections 4.4 and 4.5). The neurophysiological and computational approach taken here focuses on a feature hierarchy model in which invariant representations can be built by self-organizing learning based on the statistics of the visual input.

The model can use temporal continuity in an associative synaptic learning rule with a short-term memory trace, and/or it can use spatial continuity in Continuous Spatial Transformation learning.

The model of visual processing in the ventral cortical stream can build representations of objects that are invariant with respect to translation, view, size, and lighting.

The model uses a feature combination neuron approach with the relative spatial positions of the objects specified in the feature combination neurons, and this provides a solution to the binding problem.

The model has been extended to provide an account of invariant representations in the dorsal visual system of the global motion produced by objects such as looming, rotation, and object-based movement.

The model has been extended to incorporate top-down feedback connections to model the control of attention by biased competition in for example spatial and object search tasks (see further Chapter 6).

The model has also been extended to account for how the visual system can select single objects in complex visual scenes, how multiple objects can be represented in a scene, and how invariant representations of single objects can be learned even when multiple objects are present in the scene.

It has also been suggested in a unifying proposal that adding a fifth layer to the model and training the system in spatial environments will enable hippocampus-like spatial view neurons or place cells to develop, depending on the size of the field of view (Section 2.3.5).

We have thus seen how many of the major computational issues that arise when formulating a theory of object recognition in the ventral visual system (such as feature binding, invariance learning, the recognition of objects when they are in cluttered natural scenes, the representation of multiple objects in a scene, and learning invariant representations of single objects when there are multiple objects in the scene), could be solved in the brain, with tests of the hypotheses performed by simulations that are consistent with complementary neuro-physiological results.

The approach described in this chapter is unifying in a number of ways. First, a set of simple organizational principles involving a hierarchy of cortical areas with convergence from stage to stage, and competitive learning using a modified associative learning rule with a short-term memory trace of preceding neuronal activity, provide a basis for understanding much processing in the ventral visual stream, from V1 to the inferior temporal visual cortex. Second, the same principles help to understand some of the processing in the dorsal visual stream by which invariant representations of the global motion of objects may be formed. Third, the same principles continued from the ventral visual stream onwards to the hippocampus help to show how spatial view and place representations may be built from the visual input. Fourth, in all these cases, the learning is possible because the system is able to extract invariant representations because it can utilize the spatio-temporal continuities and statistics in the world that help to define objects, moving objects, and spatial scenes. Fifth, a great simplification and economy in terms of brain design is that the computational principles need not be different in each of the cortical areas in these hierarchical systems, for some of the important properties of the processing in these systems to be performed.

In conclusion, we have seen in this chapter how a major form of memory, the invariant recognition of objects, involves not only the storage and retrieval of information, but also major computations to produce invariant representations. Once these invariant representations have been formed, they are used for many processes including not only recognition memory (see Section 2.2.6), but also associative learning of the rewarding and punishing properties of objects for emotion and motivation (see Chapter 3), the memory for the spatial locations of objects and rewards (see Chapter 2), the building of spatial representations based on visual input (Section 2.3.5), and as an input to short-term memory (Chapter 5), attention (Chapter 6), decision (Chapters 7 and 10), and action selection (Chapter 8) systems.

5 Short-term memory

5.1 Cortical short-term memory systems and attractor networks

There are a number of different short-term memory systems, each implemented in a different cortical area. The particular systems considered here each implement short-term memory by subpopulations of neurons that show maintained activity in a delay period, while a stimulus or event is being remembered. These memories may operate as autoassociative attractor networks, the operation of which is described in Section B.3. The actual autoassociation could be implemented by associatively modifiable synapses between connected pyramidal cells within an area, or by the forward and backward connections between adjacent cortical areas in a hierarchy.

One short-term memory system is in the dorso-lateral prefrontal cortex, area 46. This is involved in remembering the locations of spatial responses, in for example delayed spatial response tasks (Goldman-Rakic 1996, Fuster 2000). In such a task performed by a monkey, a light beside one of two response keys illuminates briefly, there is then a delay of several seconds, and then the monkey must touch the appropriate key in order to obtain a food reward. The monkey must not initiate the response until the end of the delay period, and must hold a central key continuously in the delay period. Lesions of the prefrontal cortex in the region of the principal sulcus impair the performance of this task if there is a delay, but not if there is no delay. Some neurons in this region fire in the delay period, while the response is being remembered (Fuster 1973, Fuster 1989, Goldman-Rakic 1996, Fuster 2000). Different neurons fire for the two different responses.

There is an analogous system in a more dorsal and posterior part of the prefrontal cortex involved in remembering the position in visual space to which an eye movement (a saccade) should be made (Funahashi, Bruce and Goldman-Rakic 1989, Goldman-Rakic 1996). In this case, the monkey may be asked to remember which of eight lights appeared, and after the delay to move his eyes to the light that was briefly illuminated. The short-term memory function is topographically organized, in that lesions in small parts of the system impair remembered eye movements only to that eye position. Moreover, neurons in the appropriate part of the topographic map respond to eye movements in one but not in other directions (see Fig. 5.1). Such a memory system could be easily implemented in such a topographically organized system by having local cortical connections between nearby pyramidal cells which implement an attractor network (Fig. 5.2). Then triggering activity in one part of the topographically organized system would lead to sustained activity in that part of the map, thus implementing a short-term or working memory for eye movements to that position in space.

Another short-term memory system is implemented in the inferior temporal visual cortex, especially more ventrally towards the perirhinal cortex (see Section 2.2.6). This memory is for whether a particular visual stimulus (such as a face) has been seen recently. This is implemented in two ways. One way is that some neurons respond more to a novel than to a familiar visual stimulus in such tasks, or in other cases respond to the familiar, selected, stimulus (Baylis and Rolls 1987, Miller and Desimone 1994) (see Section 2.2.6). The other way is that some neurons, especially more ventrally, continue to fire in the delay period of

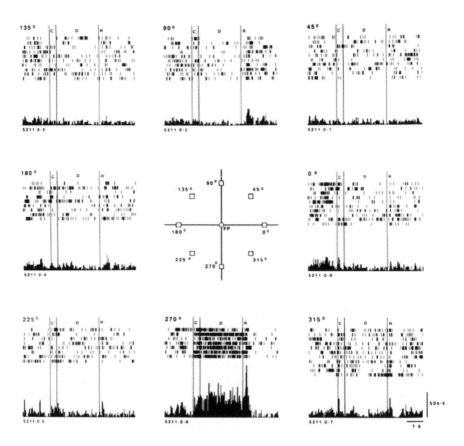

Fig. 5.1 The activity of a single neuron in the dorsolateral prefrontal cortical area involved in remembered saccades. Each row is a single trial, with each spike shown by a vertical line. A cue is shown in the cue (C) period, there is then a delay (D) period without the cue in which the cue position must be remembered, then there is a response (R) period. The monkey fixates the central fixation point (FP) during the cue and delay periods, and saccades to the position where the cue was shown, in one of the eight positions indicated, in the response period. The neuron increased its activity primarily for saccades to position 270°. The increase of activity was in the cue, delay, and response period while the response was made. The time calibration is 1 s. (Reproduced with permission from Funahashi, Bruce and Goldman-Rakic 1989.)

a delayed match to sample task (Fahy, Riches and Brown 1993, Miyashita 1993), and fire for several hundred milliseconds after a 16 ms visual stimulus has been presented (Rolls and Tovee 1994) (see Fig. C.17). These neurons can be considered to reflect the implementation of an attractor network between the pyramidal cells in this region (Amit 1995). A cortical syndrome that may reflect loss of such a short-term visual memory system is simultanagnosia, in which more than one visual stimulus cannot be remembered for more than a few seconds (Warrington and Weiskrantz 1973, Kolb and Whishaw 2003).

Continuing firing of neurons in short-term memory tasks in the delay period is also found in other cortical areas. For example, it is found in an object short-term memory task (delayed

Local autoassociation networks in the prefrontal cortex
for delayed spatial responses, eg. saccades

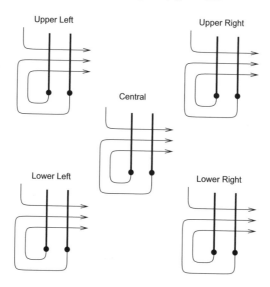

Fig. 5.2 A possible cortical model of a topographically organized set of attractor networks in the prefrontal cortex that could be used to remember the position to which saccades should be made. Excitatory local recurrent collateral Hebb-modifiable connections would enable a set of separate attractors to operate. The input that would trigger one of the attractors into continuing activity in a memory delay period would come from the parietal cortex, and topology of the inputs would result in separate attractors for remembering different positions in space. (For example inputs for the Upper Left of space would trigger an attractor that would remember the upper left of space.) Neurons in different parts of this cortical area would have activity related to remembering one part of space; and damage to a part of this cortical area concerned with one part of space would result in impairments in remembering targets to which to saccade for only one part of space.

match to sample described in Section 5.2) in the inferior frontal convexity cortex, in a region connected to the ventral temporal cortex (Fuster 1989, Wilson, O'Sclaidhe and Goldman-Rakic 1993). However, whether this network is distinct from the network in the dorsolateral prefrontal cortex involved in spatial short-term memory is not clear, as some neurons in these regions may be involved in both spatial and object short-term memory tasks (Rao, Rainer and Miller 1997). Heterogeneous populations of neurons, some with more spatial input, others with more object input, and top-down attentional modulation of the different subpopulations depending on the task, starts to provide an explanation for these findings (see Section 5.6 and Chapter 8).

Delay-related neuronal firing is also found in the parietal cortex when monkeys are remembering a target to which a saccade should be made (Andersen 1995); and in the motor cortex when a monkey is remembering a direction in which to reach with the arm (Georgopoulos 1995).

Another short-term memory system is human auditory–verbal short-term memory, which appears to be implemented in the left hemisphere at the junction of the temporal, parietal, and occipital lobes. Patients with damage to this system are described clinically as showing conduction aphasia, in that they cannot repeat a heard string of words (cannot conduct the input to the output) (Warrington and Weiskrantz 1973, Kolb and Whishaw 2003).

5.2 Prefrontal cortex short-term memory networks, and their relation to temporal and parietal perceptual networks

As described in Section 5.1, a common way that the brain uses to implement a short-term memory is to maintain the firing of neurons during a short memory period after the end of a stimulus (see Rolls and Treves (1998) and Fuster (2000)). In the inferior temporal cortex this firing may be maintained for a few hundred milliseconds even when the monkey is not performing a memory task (Rolls and Tovee 1994, Rolls, Tovee, Purcell, Stewart and Azzopardi 1994b, Rolls, Tovee and Panzeri 1999b, Desimone 1996) (see Fig. C.17). In more ventral temporal cortical areas such as the entorhinal cortex the firing may be maintained for longer periods in delayed match to sample tasks (Suzuki, Miller and Desimone 1997), and in the prefrontal cortex for even tens of seconds (Fuster 1997, Fuster 2000). In the dorsolateral and inferior convexity prefrontal cortex the firing of the neurons may be related to the memory of spatial responses or objects (Goldman-Rakic 1996, Wilson, O'Sclaidhe and Goldman-Rakic 1993) or both (Rao, Rainer and Miller 1997), and in the principal sulcus / arcuate sulcus region to the memory of places for eye movements (Funahashi, Bruce and Goldman-Rakic 1989) (see Figs. 1.9 and 1.11). The firing may be maintained by the operation of associatively modified recurrent collateral connections between nearby pyramidal cells producing attractor states in autoassociative networks (see Section B.3).

For the short-term memory to be maintained during periods in which new stimuli are to be perceived, there must be separate networks for the perceptual and short-term memory functions, and indeed two coupled networks, one in the inferior temporal visual cortex for perceptual functions, and another in the prefrontal cortex for maintaining the short-term memory during intervening stimuli, provide a precise model of the interaction of perceptual and short-term memory systems (Renart, Parga and Rolls 2000, Renart, Moreno, Rocha, Parga and Rolls 2001) (see Fig. 5.3). In particular, this model shows how a prefrontal cortex attractor (autoassociation) network could be triggered by a sample visual stimulus represented in the inferior temporal visual cortex in a delayed match to sample task, and could keep this attractor active during a memory interval in which intervening stimuli are shown. Then when the sample stimulus reappears in the task as a match stimulus, the inferior temporal cortex module shows a large response to the match stimulus, because it is activated both by the visual incoming match stimulus, and by the consistent backprojected memory of the sample stimulus still being represented in the prefrontal cortex memory module (see Fig. 5.3).

This computational model makes it clear that in order for ongoing perception to occur unhindered implemented by posterior cortex (parietal and temporal lobe) networks, there must be a separate set of modules that is capable of maintaining a representation over intervening stimuli. This is the fundamental understanding offered for the evolution and functions of the dorsolateral prefrontal cortex, and it is this ability to provide multiple separate short-term attractor memories that provides I suggest the basis for its functions in planning.

Renart, Parga and Rolls (2000) and Renart, Moreno, Rocha, Parga and Rolls (2001) performed analyses and simulations which showed that for working memory to be implemented in this way, the connections between the perceptual and the short-term memory modules (see Fig. 5.3) must be relatively weak. As a starting point, they used the neurophysiological data showing that in delayed match to sample tasks with intervening stimuli, the neuronal activity in the inferior temporal visual cortex (IT) is driven by each new incoming visual stimulus (Miller, Li and Desimone 1993b, Miller and Desimone 1994), whereas in the prefrontal cortex, neurons start to fire when the sample stimulus is shown, and continue the firing that represents the sample stimulus even when the potential match stimuli are being shown

Inferior temporal cortex (IT)　　　　　　　Prefrontal cortex (PF)

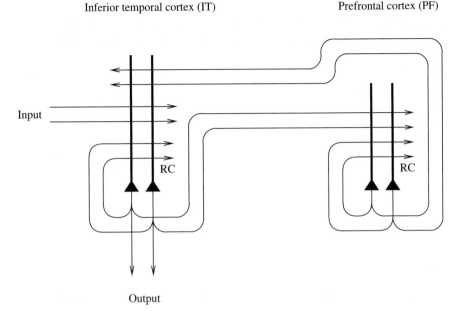

Output

Fig. 5.3 A short-term memory autoassociation network in the prefrontal cortex could hold active a working memory representation by maintaining its firing in an attractor state. The prefrontal module would be loaded with the to-be-remembered stimulus by the posterior module (in the temporal or parietal cortex) in which the incoming stimuli are represented. Backprojections from the prefrontal short-term memory module to the posterior module would enable the working memory to be unloaded, to for example influence on-going perception (see text). RC, recurrent collateral connections.

(Miller, Erickson and Desimone 1996). The architecture studied by Renart, Parga and Rolls (2000) was as shown in Fig. 5.3, with both the intramodular (recurrent collateral) and the intermodular (forward IT to PF, and backward PF to IT) connections trained on the set of patterns with an associative synaptic modification rule. A crucial parameter is the strength of the intermodular connections, g, which indicates the relative strength of the intermodular to the intramodular connections. (This parameter measures effectively the relative strengths of the currents injected into the neurons by the inter-modular relative to the intra-modular connections, and the importance of setting this parameter to relatively weak values for useful interactions between coupled attractor networks was highlighted by Renart, Parga and Rolls (1999b) and Renart, Parga and Rolls (1999a), as shown in Sections B.9 and 5.3.) The patterns themselves were sets of random numbers, and the simulation utilized a dynamical approach with neurons with continuous (hyperbolic tangent) activation functions (see Section 5.3) (Shiino and Fukai 1990, Kuhn 1990, Kuhn, Bos and van Hemmen 1991, Amit and Tsodyks 1991). The external current injected into IT by the incoming visual stimuli was sufficiently strong to trigger the IT module into a state representing the incoming stimulus. When the sample was shown, the initially silent PF module was triggered into activity by the weak ($g>0.002$) intermodular connections. The PF module remained firing to the sample stimulus even when IT was responding to potential match stimuli later in the trial, provided that g was less than 0.024, because then the intramodular recurrent connections could dominate the firing (see Fig. 5.4). If g was higher than this, then the PF module was pushed out of the attractor state produced by the sample stimulus. The IT module responded to each incoming potentially matching stimulus provided that g was not greater than approximately 0.024. Moreover, this value of g was sufficiently large that a larger response of the IT module was

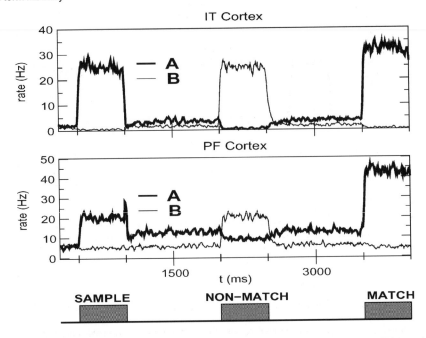

Fig. 5.4 Interaction between the prefrontal cortex (PF) and the inferior temporal cortex (IT) in a delayed match to sample task with intervening stimuli with the architecture illustrated in Fig. 5.3. Above: activity in the IT attractor module. Below: activity in the PF attractor module. The thick lines show the firing rates of the set of neurons with activity selective for the sample stimulus (which is also shown as the match stimulus, and is labelled **A**), and the thin lines the activity of the neurons with activity selective for the non-match stimulus, which is shown as an intervening stimulus between the sample and match stimulus and is labelled **B**. A trial is illustrated in which **A** is the sample (and match) stimulus. The prefrontal cortex module is pushed into an attractor state for the sample stimulus by the IT activity induced by the sample stimulus. Because of the weak coupling to the PF module from the IT module, the PF module remains in this sample-related attractor state during the delay periods, and even while the IT module is responding to the non-match stimulus. The PF module remains in its sample-related state even during the non-match stimulus because once a module is in an attractor state, it is relatively stable. When the sample stimulus reappears as the match stimulus, the PF module shows higher sample stimulus-related firing, because the incoming input from IT is now adding to the activity in the PF attractor network. This in turn also produces a match enhancement effect in the IT neurons with sample stimulus-related selectivity, because the backprojected activity from the PF module matches the incoming activity to the IT module. (After Renart, Parga and Rolls 2000; and Renart, Moreno, Rocha, Parga and Rolls 2001.)

found when the stimulus matched the sample stimulus (the match enhancement effect found neurophysiologically, and a mechanism by which the matching stimulus can be identified). This simple model thus shows that the operation of the prefrontal cortex in short-term memory tasks such as delayed match to sample with intervening stimuli, and its relation to posterior perceptual networks, can be understood by the interaction of two weakly coupled attractor networks, as shown in Figs. 5.3 and 5.4.

The same network can also be used to illustrate the interaction between the prefrontal cortex short-term memory system and the posterior (IT or PP) perceptual regions in visual search tasks, as illustrated in Fig. 5.5.

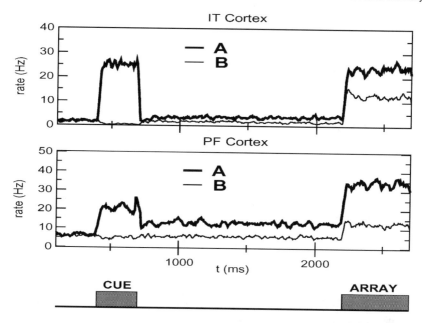

Fig. 5.5 Interaction between the prefrontal cortex (PF) and the inferior temporal cortex (IT) in a visual search task with the architecture illustrated in Fig. 5.3. Above: activity in the IT attractor module. Below: activity in the PF attractor module. The thick lines show the firing rates of the set of neurons with activity selective for search stimulus **A**, and the thin lines the activity of the neurons with activity selective for stimulus **B**. During the cue period either **A** or **B** is shown, to indicate to the monkey which stimulus to select when an array containing both **A** and **B** is shown after a delay period. The trial shown is for the case when **A** is the cue stimulus. When stimulus **A** is shown as a cue, then via the IT module, the PF module is pushed into an attractor state **A**, and the PF module remembers this state during the delay period. When the array **A** + **B** is shown later, there is more activity in the PF module for the neurons selective for **A**, because they have inputs both from the continuing attractor state held in the PF module and from the forward activity from the IT module which now contains both **A** and **B**. This PF firing to **A** in turn also produces greater firing of the population of IT neurons selective for **A** than in the IT neurons selective for **B**, because the IT neurons selective for **A** are receiving both **A**-related visual inputs, and **A**-related backprojected inputs from the PF module. (After Renart, Parga and Rolls 2000; and Renart, Moreno, Rocha, Parga and Rolls 2001.)

5.3   Computational details of the model of short-term memory

The model network of Renart, Parga and Rolls (2000) and Renart, Moreno, Rocha, Parga and Rolls (2001) consists of a large number of (excitatory) neurons arranged in two modules with the architecture shown in Fig. 5.3. Following Kuhn (1990) and Amit and Tsodyks (1991), each neuron is assumed to be a dynamical element which transforms an incoming afferent current into an output spike rate according to a given transduction function. A given afferent current I_{ai} to neuron i $(i = 1, \ldots, N)$ in module a $(a = \mathbf{IT}, \mathbf{PF})$ decays with a characteristic time constant τ but increases proportionally to the spike rates of the rest of the neurons in the network (from both inside and outside its module) connected to it, the contribution of each presynaptic neuron, e.g. neuron j from module b, and in proportion to the synaptic efficacy J_{ij}^{ab} between the two[25]. This can be expressed through the following equation

---

[25] On this occasion we vert to the theoretical physicists' usual notation for synaptic weights or couplings, J_{ij} instead of w_{ij}.

$$\frac{dI_{ai}(t)}{dt} = -\frac{I_{ai}(t)}{\tau} + \sum_{b,j} J_{ij}^{(a,b)} v_{bj} + h_{ai}^{(\text{ext})} . \tag{5.1}$$

An external current $h_{ai}^{(\text{ext})}$ from outside the network, representing the stimuli, can also be imposed on every neuron. Selective stimuli are modelled as proportional to the stored patterns, i.e. $h_{ai}^{\mu(\text{ext})} = h_a \eta_{ai}^{\mu}$, where h_a is the intensity of the external current to module a.

The transduction function of the neurons transforming currents into rates was chosen as a threshold hyperbolic tangent of gain G and threshold θ. Thus, when the current is very large the firing rates saturate to an arbitrary value of 1.

The synaptic efficacies between the neurons of each module and between the neurons in different modules are respectively

$$J_{ij}^{(a,a)} = \frac{J_0}{f(1-f)N_t} \sum_{\mu=1}^{P} (\eta_{ai}^{\mu} - f)(\eta_{aj}^{\mu} - f) \quad i \neq j \; ; \; a = \mathbf{IT}, \mathbf{PF} \tag{5.2}$$

$$J_{ij}^{(a,b)} = \frac{g}{f(1-f)N_t} \sum_{\mu=1}^{P} (\eta_{ai}^{\mu} - f)(\eta_{bj}^{\mu} - f) \quad \forall \; i,j \; ; \; a \neq b . \tag{5.3}$$

The intra-modular connections are such that a number P of sparse independent configurations of neural activity are dynamically stable, constituting the possible sustained activity states in each module. This is expressed by saying that each module has learned P binary patterns $\{\eta_{ai}^{\mu} = 0, 1, \; \mu = 1, \ldots, P\}$, each of them signalling which neurons are active in each of the sustained activity configurations. Each variable η_{ai}^{μ} is allowed to take the values 1 and 0 with probabilities f and $(1 - f)$ respectively, independently across neurons and across patterns. The inter-modular connections reflect the temporal associations between the sustained activity states of each module. In this way, every stored pattern μ in the IT module has an associated pattern in the PF module which is labelled by the same index. The normalization constant $N_t = N(J_0 + g)$ was chosen so that the sum of the magnitudes of the inter- and the intra-modular connections remains constant and equal to 1 while their relative values are varied. When this constraint is imposed the strength of the connections can be expressed in terms of a single independent parameter g measuring the relative intensity of the inter- vs the intra-modular connections (J_0 can be set equal to 1 everywhere).

Both modules implicitly include an inhibitory population of neurons receiving and sending signals to the excitatory neurons through uniform synapses. In this case the inhibitory population can be treated as a single inhibitory neuron with an activity dependent only on the mean activity of the excitatory population. We chose the transduction function of the inhibitory neuron to be linear with slope γ.

Since the number of neurons in a typical network one may be interested in is very large, e.g. $\sim 10^5 - 10^6$, the analytical treatment of the set of coupled differential equations (5.1) becomes untractable. On the other hand, when the number of neurons is large, a reliable description of the asymptotic solutions of these equations can be found using the techniques of statistical mechanics (Kuhn 1990). In this framework, instead of characterizing the states of the system by the state of every neuron, this characterization is performed in terms of *macroscopic* quantities called *order parameters* which measure and quantify some global properties of the network as a whole. The relevant order parameters appearing in the description of the system are the overlap of the state of each module with each of the stored patterns m_a^{μ} and the average activity of each module x_a, defined respectively as:

$$m_a^{\mu} = \frac{1}{\chi N} \ll \sum_i (\eta_{ai}^{\mu} - f) v_{ai} \gg_{\eta} \; ; \; x_a = \frac{1}{N} \ll \sum_i v_{ai} \gg_{\eta} , \tag{5.4}$$

where the symbol $\ll \ldots \gg_{\eta}$ stands for an average over the stored patterns.

Using the free energy per neuron of the system at zero temperature $\mathcal{F}$ (which is not written explicitly to reduce the technicalities to a minimum), Renart, Parga and Rolls (2000) and Renart, Moreno, Rocha, Parga and Rolls (2001) modelled the experiments by giving the order parameters the following dynamics:

$$\tau \frac{\partial m_a^\mu}{\partial t} = -\frac{\partial \mathcal{F}}{\partial m_a^\mu} \quad ; \quad \tau \frac{\partial x_a}{\partial t} = -\frac{\partial \mathcal{F}}{\partial x_a} \quad . \tag{5.5}$$

These dynamics ensure that the stationary solutions, corresponding to the values of the order parameters at the attractors, correspond also to minima of the free energy, and that, as the system evolves, the free energy is always minimized through its gradient. The time constant of the macroscopical dynamics was chosen to be equal to the time constant of the individual neurons, which reflects the assumption that neurons operate in parallel. Equations (5.5) were solved by a simple discretizing procedure (first order Runge–Kutta method). An appropriate value for the time interval corresponding to one computer iteration was found to be $\tau/10$ and the time constant was the value $\tau = 10$ ms.

Since not all neurons in the network receive the same inputs, not all of them behave in the same way, i.e. have the same firing rates. In fact, the neurons in each of the modules can be split into different subpopulations according to their state of activity in each of the stored patterns. The mean firing rate of the neurons in each subpopulation depends on the particular state realized by the network (characterized by the values of the order parameters). Associated with each pattern there are two large subpopulations denoted as foreground (all active neurons) and background (all inactive neurons) for that pattern. The overlap with a given pattern can be expressed as the difference between the mean firing rate of the neurons in its foreground and its background. The average was calculated over all other subpopulations to which each neuron in the foreground (background) belonged, where the probability of a given subpopulation is equal to the fraction of neurons in the module belonging to it (determined by the probability distribution of the stored patterns as given above). This partition of the neurons into subpopulations is appealing since, in neurophysiological experiments, cells are usually classified in terms of their response properties to a set of fixed stimuli, i.e. whether each stimulus is effective or ineffective in driving their response.

The modelling of the different experiments proceeded according to the macroscopic dynamics (5.5), where each stimulus was implemented as an extra current into free energy for a desired period of time.

Using this model, results of the type described in Section 5.2 were found (Renart, Parga and Rolls 2000, Renart, Moreno, Rocha, Parga and Rolls 2001). The paper by Renart, Moreno, Rocha, Parga and Rolls (2001) extended the earlier findings of Renart, Parga and Rolls (2000) to integrate-and-fire neurons, and it is results from the integrate-and-fire simulations that are shown in Figs. 5.4 and 5.5.

5.4 Computational necessity for a separate, prefrontal cortex, short-term memory system

This approach emphasizes that in order to provide a useful brain lesion test of prefrontal cortex short-term memory functions, the task set should require a short-term memory for stimuli over an interval in which other stimuli are being processed, because otherwise the posterior cortex perceptual modules could implement the short-term memory function by their own recurrent collateral connections. This approach also emphasizes that there are many at least partially independent modules for short-term memory functions in the prefrontal cortex (e.g.

several modules for delayed saccades; one or more for delayed spatial (body) responses in the dorsolateral prefrontal cortex; one or more for remembering visual stimuli in the more ventral prefrontal cortex; and at least one in the left prefrontal cortex used for remembering the words produced in a verbal fluency task – see Section 5.1; and Section 10.3 of Rolls and Treves (1998)).

This computational approach thus provides a clear understanding of why a separate (prefrontal) mechanism is needed for working memory functions, as elaborated in Section 5.2. It may also be commented that if a prefrontal cortex module is to control behaviour in a working memory task, then it must be capable of assuming some type of executive control. There may be no need to have a single central executive additional to the control that must be capable of being exerted by every short-term memory module. This is in contrast to what has traditionally been assumed for the prefrontal cortex (Shallice and Burgess 1996) (see also Section 10.5.3).

5.5 Synaptic modification is needed to set up but not to reuse short-term memory systems

To set up a new short-term memory attractor, synaptic modification is needed to form the new stable attractor. Once the attractor is set up, it may be used repeatedly when triggered by an appropriate cue to hold the short-term memory state active by continued neuronal firing even without any further synaptic modification (see Section B.3 and Kesner and Rolls (2001)). Thus manipulations that impair the long term potentiation of synapses (LTP) may impair the formation of new short-term memory states, but not the use of previously learned short-term memory states. Kesner and Rolls (2001) analyzed many studies of the effects of blockade of LTP in the hippocampus on spatial working memory tasks, and found evidence consistent with this prediction. Interestingly, it was found that if there was a large change in the delay interval over which the spatial information had to be remembered, then the task became susceptible, during the transition to the new delay interval, to the effects of blockade of LTP. The implication is that some new learning is required when the rat must learn the strategy of retaining information for longer periods when the retention interval is changed.

5.6 What, where, and object–place combination short-term memory in the prefrontal cortex

Given that inputs from the parietal cortex, involved in spatial computation, project more to the dorsolateral prefrontal cortex, for example to the cortex in the principal sulcus, and that inputs from the temporal lobe visual cortex, involved in computations about objects, project ventrolaterally to the prefrontal cortex (see Figs. 1.9, 1.11, and 1.10), it could be that the dorsolateral prefrontal cortex is especially involved in spatial short-term memory, and the inferior convexity prefrontal cortex more in object short-term memory (Goldman-Rakic 1996, Goldman-Rakic 1987, Fuster, Bauer and Jervey 1982). This organization-by-stimulus-domain hypothesis (Miller 2000) holds that spatial ('where') working memory is supported by the dorsolateral PFC in the neighborhood of the principal sulcus (Brodmann's area (BA) 46/9 in the middle frontal gyrus (MFG)); and object ('what') working memory is supported by the ventrolateral PFC on the lateral/inferior convexity (BA 45 in the inferior frontal gyrus (IFG)). Consistent with this, lesions of the cortex in the principal sulcus impair delayed spatial response memory, and lesions of the inferior convexity can impair delayed (object) matching to sample short-term memory (Goldman-Rakic 1996) (especially when there are intervening stimuli between the sample and the matching object, as described above). Further, Wilson, O'Sclaidhe and Goldman-Rakic (1993) found that neurons dorsolaterally in the prefrontal cortex were more likely to be related to spatial working memory, and in the inferior convexity to object working memory. Some fMRI studies in humans support this topographical organization (Leung, Gore and Goldman-Rakic 2002), and some do not (Postle and D'Esposito 2000, Postle and D'Esposito 1999). Rao, Rainer and Miller (1997) found in a task that had a spatial short-term memory component and an object short-term memory component that some prefrontal cortex neurons are involved in both, and thus questioned whether there is segregation of spatial and object short-term memory in the prefrontal cortex. Some segregation does seem likely, in that for example the neurons with activity related to delayed oculomotor saccades are in the frontal eye field (Funahashi, Bruce and Goldman-Rakic 1989) (see Fig. 5.1), and this area has not been implicated in object working memory.

Part of the conceptual resolution of the discussion about segregation of functions in the lateral prefrontal cortex is that sometimes combinations of objects and places must be held in short-term memory. For example, in one such task, a *conditional object–response (associative) task* with a delay, a monkey was shown one of two stimulus objects (O1 or O2), and after a delay had to make either a rightward or leftward oculomotor saccade response depending on which stimulus was shown. In another such task, a *delayed spatial response task*, the same stimuli were used, but the rule required was different, namely to respond after the delay towards the left or right location where the stimulus object had been shown (Asaad, Rainer and Miller 2000). The tasks could be run on some trial blocks with the mappings reversed. Thus the monkey had to remember in any trial block the particular object–place mapping that was required in the delay period. In this task, neurons were found that responded to combinations of the object and the spatial position (Asaad et al. 2000). This bringing together of the spatial and object components of the task is important in how the short-term memory task was solved, as described in Chapter 8. However, this makes the conceptual point that at least some mixing of the spatial and object representations in the lateral prefrontal cortex is needed in order for some short-term memory tasks to be solved, and thus total segregation of 'what' and 'where' processing in the lateral prefrontal cortex should not be expected.

Another factor in interpreting fMRI imaging studies of short-term memory is that differences of the timecourse of the activations from the lateral prefrontal cortex have been found in 'what' vs 'where' short-term memory components of a task (Postle and D'Esposito 2000). Deco, Rolls and Horwitz (2004) showed that differences in the fMRI BOLD signal from the dorsal as compared to the ventral prefrontal cortex in working memory tasks may reflect a higher level of inhibition in the dorsolateral prefrontal cortex. They demonstrated this by simulating a 'what' vs 'where' short-term memory task with integrate-and-fire neurons, and then integrated over the synaptic currents and convolved with the haemodynamic response function, as described in Section B.6.4, to predict the BOLD signal change. However, the fMRI data were most easily modelled by hypothesizing that the differences between these two prefrontal regions resulted from assigning a greater amount of inhibition to the dorsolateral portion of the prefrontal cortex. Both brain areas may show short-term memory maintenance capabilities related to their capacities to maintain stable attractors during delay periods, but the increased level of inhibition assumed in the dorsolateral PFC may be associated with the capacity of this brain region to support more complex functions. Higher inhibition in the dorsolateral prefrontal cortex might be useful for maintaining several separate short-term memory representations in nearby cortical modules (regions 1–3 mm across as defined by the spread of local high density recurrent collateral connections) and preventing the formation of a global attractor, which could be useful if several items must be held in memory for manipulation (Deco, Rolls and Horwitz 2004).

6 Attention, short-term memory, and biased competition

6.1 Introduction

Up to a few years ago, the investigation of attentional mechanisms was of interest mainly to psychophysicists and cognitive psychologists trying to understand the operating principles and computational constraints of visual perception. Especially over the last twenty years, visual search tasks have been widely used as a tool to explore the functional role and operating principles of attention in visual perception. The classical view of attention that has emerged from this research refers to two functionally distinct stages of visual processing. One stage, termed the pre-attentive stage, implies an unlimited-capacity system capable of processing the information contained in the entire visual field in parallel. The other stage is termed the attentive or focal stage, and is characterized by the serial processing of visual information corresponding to local spatial regions.

Recently, the combination of neuroscience and psychology in the study of visual perception is defining the cognitive neuroscience of attention. Cognitive neuroscience has started to explore more directly the neural mechanisms underlying visual attention in humans and primates. New observations from a number of cognitive neuroscience experiments led to an alternative account of attention termed the '**biased competition hypothesis**', which aims to explain the computational algorithms governing visual attention and their implementation in the brain's neural circuits and neural systems. According to this hypothesis, attentional selection operates in parallel by biasing an underlying competitive interaction between multiple stimuli in the visual field. Moreover, this hypothesis implies a theory of visual perception that is very distinct in nature from the classical purely feedforward analyses such as Marr's analysis of vision (Marr 1982), in that it is based in an essential way on a dynamical interaction and relaxation between feedforward and feedback processes. The massively feedforward and feedback connections that exist in the anatomy and physiology of the cortex (described in Section 1.11) implement the attentional mutual biasing interactions that result in a neurodynamical account of visual perception consistent with the seminal constructivist theories of Helmholtz (1867) and Gregory (1970).

In this chapter, the classical psychophysical view of selective visual attention is briefly described, then physiological findings that suggest an alternative neurodynamical view based on the biased competition hypothesis is developed. The operation of these biased competition processes is considered in a precise computational framework that enables multiple interacting brain systems with bottom-up and top-down effects to be analyzed.

We should note that one type of attentional process operates when salient features in a visual scene attract attention (Itti and Koch 2001). This visual processing is described as feedforward and bottom-up, in that it operates forward in the visual pathways from the visual input (see Fig. 6.10 in which the solid lines show the forward pathways). A second type of selective attentional process, with which we are concerned in this chapter, involves actively maintaining in short-term memory a location or object as the target of attention, and using this by top-down processes to influence earlier cortical processing. Some of the top-down or backprojection pathways in the visual system are shown in Fig. 6.10 on page 404 by the dashed lines.

6.2   The classical view: the spotlight metaphor and feature integration theory

Expansion of the cerebral cortex with its sensory and motor capabilities increases the problem of stimulus selection, i.e. the question as to what information it is relevant to react to. As we have seen for the visual system in Chapter 4, although there is a massively parallel character of the computations performed by the brain, it is important in natural scenes to limit the processing to one part of visual space at a time, to limit the binding problem, and simplify the interface to motor systems. Partly for these reasons, many animals employ a selection processing strategy for managing the enormous amount of information resulting from their interaction with the environment. This selection of relevant information is referred to as attention. The concept of attention implies that we can concentrate on certain portions of the sensory input, motor programs, memory contents, or internal representations to be processed preferentially, shifting the processing focus from one location to another or from one object to another in a serial fashion. This mechanism is commonly known by psychologists as selective or focal attention (Broadbent 1958, Kahneman 1973, Neisser 1967).

In the case of the visual system, only a small fraction of the information received reaches a level of processing that can be voluntarily reported or directly used to influence behaviour. The psychophysical work of Helmholtz (1867) provided the origin of a commonly employed metaphor for focal attention in terms of a spotlight (Treisman 1982, Crick 1984). This metaphor postulates the existence of a spotlight of attention that 'illuminates' a portion of the field of view where stimuli are processed in higher detail and brings them to a higher level of processing (Eriksen and Hoffmann 1973). In other words, information outside the spotlight is filtered out. Experimental maps of the attentional spotlight have been introduced by Sagi and Julesz (1986) by asking observers to detect the presence or absence of a peripheral probe dot while carrying out a concurrent letter discrimination task. Sperling and Weichselgartner (1995) demonstrated experimentally that the spotlight does not sweep continuously across the visual field, but rather fades in one place while increasing in strength in another. Pylyshyn and Storm (1988) have also shown that the focal selection performed by the spotlight does not necessarily involve contiguous parts of the visual field. Since Helmholtz, it has been clear that visual selective attention can diverge from the direction of gaze and that attention can be voluntarily focused on a peripheral part of the visual field, i.e. the spotlight can be moved about the scene with or without eye movements. This entails the distinction of shifts of attention into overt and covert shifts of attention (Helmholtz 1867, Pashler 1996). In the case of **overt attention**, eye movements (saccades) occur, whereas **covert attention** changes the focus selected without any movement of the eyes. It is largely covert attention with which we will be concerned in this chapter.

The Helmholtzian spotlight paradigm alludes to a serial processing mode responsible for the complete scanning of the visual display. A complementary aspect of visual attention originates from James (1890), who generalized Helmholtz's attentional theory by introducing the concept of dispersed attention. Dispersed attention is a parallel process that operates across the entire visual field. James (1890) proposed that focused and dispersed attention are extremes in the spectrum of attentional states. Based on these notions, Neisser (1967) formulated a view in which visual search is performed in two stages (Shaw and Shaw 1977, Shaw 1978). The first preattentive part comprises processes that are fast, parallel, and involuntary. The second attentive part comprises processes that are slower, serial, and voluntary.

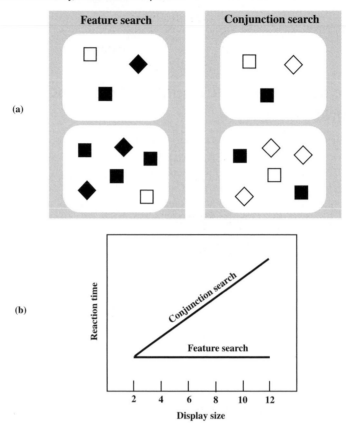

Fig. 6.1 Visual search experiments: feature and conjunction search. (a) Typical sample displays in visual feature and conjunction search tasks. The target (white square) 'pops out' in the case of feature search despite the variation in the number of distractors, whereas in the case of conjunction search the target is harder to find, especially when there are many distractors. (b) Feature search compared with conjunction search times. In feature searches, the subjects' reaction times do not increase as a function of the display size as they do in conjunction searches. (After Rolls and Deco 2002.)

An influential refinement of this latter approach is the *feature integration theory* of visual selective attention (Treisman and Gelade 1980). This concept explains numerous psychophysical experiments on visual search and offers an interpretation of the binding problem. The binding problem concerns the question of which mechanisms are involved in the fusion of features, such as colour, form and motion, that compose an object. The revised version of feature integration theory (Treisman 1988) is in many aspects different from the original theory by Treisman and Gelade (1980). In the feature integration theory, the first preattentive process runs in parallel across the complete visual field extracting single primitive features without integrating them. The second attentive stage corresponds to the serial specialized integration of information from a limited part of the field at any one time.

Evidence for these two stages of attentional visual processing comes from psychophysical experiments using visual search tasks where subjects examine a display containing randomly positioned items in order to detect an a priori defined target (see Fig. 6.1). All other items in the display which are different from the target serve the role of distractors. The number of items in the display is called the display size. The relevant variable typically measured is search time as a function of the display size.

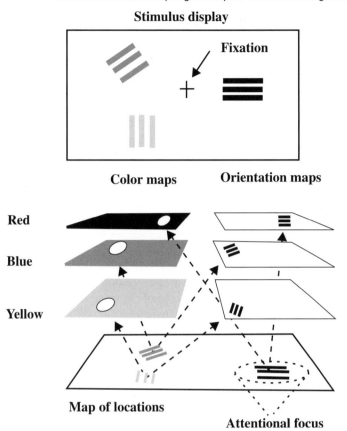

Fig. 6.2 Psychological model of feature integration for visual search experiments. The dimensions of colour and orientation are portrayed by a series of feature maps tuned to specific values. Stimuli activate neurons adjusted to their features on these maps. Attention is focused on a particular location and integrates the features at that location. (Adapted from Treisman 1988.)

Much work has been based on these two kinds of search paradigms: feature and conjunction search (Quinlan and Humphreys 1987, Wolfe, Cave and Franzel 1989, Treisman and Sato 1990). In a feature search task the target differs from the distractors in a single feature, e.g. only in its colour. In a conjunction search task the target is defined by a conjunction of features and each distractor shares at least one of those features with the target. So far, models based on the above two-stage processes have been able to distinguish feature from conjunction search on the basis of the observed slopes of the function relating search time to display size. The conjunction search experiments show that search time increases linearly with the display size, implying a serial process. On the other hand, search times in feature search can be independent of the display size. The latter result is consistent with the activation of only parallel processes, which generate 'pop out' of the target. Figure 6.2 gives a schematic account of such results. Feature integration theory achieves dynamic binding by selectively gating each of the separate feature maps so that only those features lying within the attentional spotlight are passed to higher level recognition systems.

The feature integration theory of Treisman has not been developed within a computational framework, but it involves clearly articulated processing stages: parallel coding of independent visual features, followed by serial coding of conjunctions (see Fig. 6.2). Feature integration theory essentially assumes the involvement of attention for visual conjunction search, based on an explicit serial scanning mechanism.

More recently, Nakayama and Silverman (1986) and Treisman (1988) have shown that there are some conjunction search tasks that can be accomplished in parallel. For example, Nakayama and Silverman (1986) showed that targets defined by colour and motion can be searched in parallel, and McLeod, Driver and Crisp (1988) showed that visual search for a conjunction of movement and form is parallel. On the other hand, targets defined by colour and orientation, or shape and orientation yielded large slopes in the reaction time versus display size graphs (Posner and Dehaene 1994). Further, conjunction search can yield reaction times that range continuously from roughly 0 ms per item, i.e. parallel, to 30–50 ms per item, contradicting the simple distinction between parallel and serial search. A modified theory (Duncan and Humphreys 1989) proposes that focal attention does not necessarily need to be constrained to spatial dimensions, but can also be involved in feature dimensions such as colour, motion, etc. as well. Thus, the objects possessing common features with the target may be prioritized for selection.

Some of the computational models of visual selective attention based on this classical view are described next, with more detail provided by Rolls and Deco (2002). These models postulate the existence of a **saliency or priority map** for registering the potentially interesting areas of the retinal input, and a gating mechanism for reducing the amount of incoming visual information, so that the limited computational resources of the brain can handle it.

The aim of a priority map is to represent topographically the relevance of the different parts of the visual field, in order to have an a posteriori mechanism for guiding the attentional focus onto salient regions of the retinal input. The focused region will be gated, so that only the information within it will be passed further, to the higher level, and will be processed. There are several implementations of priority maps. Koch and Ullman (1985) proposed to build such a map by bottom-up information (e.g. how different is a particular stimulus relative to its neighbourhood), which in combination with a winner-takes-all mechanism selects the currently most salient feature in the map and directs attention to its location via a gating strategy. Van de Laar, Heskes and Gielen (1997) generated a priority map in a task-dependent way in order to incorporate top-down information. They use this approach for handling visual search. The position on the priority map associated with the target of the search is maximized, i.e. the position is selected where all input features are equal or similar to the ones defining the target. Due to the fact that the target can change in each task, this approach defines a modifiable task-dependent priority map.

A more detailed account of visual search is the 'Guided Search Model' of Wolfe, Cave and Franzel (1989) (see also Wolfe (1994)). It is formulated in a computational framework and is used to explain psychophysical data. The basic idea is that a serial visual attention stage can be guided by a parallel feature-computation stage. The latter generates a priority map that is used for guiding the localized control of the focal attention mechanism in an explicit serial stage of processing. When saliency values along each dimension are summed to calculate the order of serial inspection, the target should be the first candidate. However, because of noise in the parallel processing stage, the target will not always be given the highest activation values. Consequently, some distractors will be inspected before conjunction targets, producing effects of display size and visual search. It is interesting to remark that in the 'Guided Search Model' the priority map is generated after the conjunction of the features, so that competition mechanisms are only involved at this high level.

It is important to remark that models utilizing the concept of priority maps are compatible with Treisman's feature integration theory. In fact, the routing of information lying within the attentional window during each attentional step offers a mechanism for the binding of the involved features. This is used to avoid the combinatorial explosion of computational resources that might be required if the brain utilized a hard-wired neural representation for each of the possible feature conjunctions that could occur in the visual world (though see Chapter 4 for a hypothesis about how this problem can be made tractable by representing only low-order combinations of features).

Other authors postulate as a binding and attentional mechanism the synchronous firing of neurons in order to change connection strengths (Crick 1984, Von der Malsburg and Bienenstock 1986, Crick and Koch 1990, Gray and Singer 1987, Gray and Singer 1989, Singer 1999). The synchronization specifies just a possible physical implementation of binding and is not directly associated with the computational description of attention. The temporal synchrony hypothesis of feature binding is considered in Sections 4.5.5.1 and C.3.7.

Further computational approaches related to the classical feature integration theory of attention are described by Rolls and Deco (2002).

6.3 The biased competition hypothesis in single neuron studies

The dichotomy between parallel and serial operations in visual search has been challenged by other alternative psychological models suggesting that all kinds of search task can be solved by a parallel competitive mechanism. Duncan (1980) and Duncan and Humphreys (1989) have proposed a scheme that integrates both attentional modes (i.e. parallel and serial) as an instantiation of a common principle. They explain both single feature and conjunction searches on the basis of the same operations involving, on the one hand, grouping between items in the field and, on the other hand, matching of those items or groups to a memory template of the target. This matching process supports items with features consistent with the template and inhibits those with different features. This would be the same for all the features comprising the stimuli: colour, shape, location, etc. This process of feature selection suggests that subjects utilize top-down information (from the template) independent of localization of the stimuli in space. The attentional theory of Duncan and Humphreys (1989) proposed that there is both parallel activation of a target template (from multiple items in the field) and competition between items (and between the template and non-matching items) so that, ultimately, only one object is selected. In particular, there is evidence suggesting that parallel competitive processes in the brain are responsible for human performance in visual selective attention tasks (Duncan, Humphreys and Ward 1997, Mozer and Sitton 1998, Phaf, Van der Heijden and Hudson 1990, Tsotsos 1990).

Duncan and Humphreys (1989) used the biased competition mechanism to explain serial visual search as a top-down template influencing the competitions between neurons coding for different object attributes in the early visual areas, leading to the selection of one object in the visual field. Subsequently, this biased competition mechanism has also been used in several models for explaining attentional effects in neural responses observed in the inferotemporal cortex (Usher and Niebur 1996), and in V2 and V4 (Reynolds, Chelazzi and Desimone 1999). Deco and Zihl (2001b) extended Usher and Niebur's model to simulate some psychophysical results of visual search experiments in humans. The hypothesis for this mechanism can be traced back to the 'adaptive resonance' model (Grossberg 1987) and the 'interactive activation' model (McClelland and Rumelhart 1981) in the neural network and connectionist literature.

A challenging question is therefore: Is the linearly increasing search time observed in some visual search tasks necessarily due to a serial mechanism? Or, could it also be explained by the dynamical time-consuming latency of a parallel process? In other words, are priority maps and spotlight mechanisms required? A second interesting question is to determine the characteristics of top-down aided competition in feature space. Clarification is needed of whether this competition is achieved independently in each feature dimension or whether it occurs after binding the feature dimensions of each item. In order to answer these fundamental questions about the nature of attentional operations in visual perception, the underlying neuronal and intermediate scale mechanisms have to be assessed using cognitive neuroscience techniques, including especially recordings of the activity of single neurons from the brain of behaving macaques, as well as functional brain imaging. In this section we review the electrophysiological facts that suggested the formulation of the biased competition hypothesis. The evidence on the biased competition hypothesis provided by functional brain imaging experiments will be described in Section 6.4. Sections 6.5–6.13 describe the computational mechanisms that are involved in the implementation of biased competition as a mechanism of attention.

6.3.1 Neurophysiology of attention

A number of neurophysiological experiments (Moran and Desimone 1985, Spitzer, Desimone and Moran 1988, Sato 1989, Motter 1993, Miller, Gochin and Gross 1993a, Chelazzi, Miller, Duncan and Desimone 1993, Motter 1994, Reynolds and Desimone 1999, Chelazzi 1998) have been performed suggesting biased competition neural mechanisms that are consistent with the theory of Duncan and Humphreys (1989) (i.e. with the role for a top-down memory target template in visual search).

The **biased competition hypothesis** of attention proposes that multiple stimuli in the visual field activate populations of neurons that engage in competitive interactions. Attending to a stimulus at a particular location or with a particular feature biases this competition in favour of neurons that respond to the feature or location of the attended stimulus. This attentional effect is produced by generating signals within areas outside the visual cortex that are then fed back to extrastriate areas, where they bias the competition such that when multiple stimuli appear in the visual field, the cells representing the attended stimulus 'win', thereby suppressing cells representing distracting stimuli (Duncan and Humphreys 1989, Desimone and Duncan 1995, Duncan 1996).

Single-cell recording studies in monkeys from extrastriate areas support the biased competition theory. Moran and Desimone (1985) showed that the firing activity of visually tuned neurons in the cortex was modulated if monkeys were instructed to attend to the location of the target stimulus. In these studies, Moran and Desimone first identified the V4 neuron's classic receptive field and then determined which stimulus was effective for exciting a response from the neuron (e.g. a vertical white bar) and which stimulus was ineffective (e.g. a horizontal black bar). In other words, the effective stimulus made the neuron fire whereas the ineffective stimulus did not (see Fig. 6.3). They presented these two stimuli simultaneously within the neuron's receptive field, which for V4 neurons may extend over several degrees of visual angle. The task required attending covertly to a cued spatial location. When spatial attention was directed to the effective stimulus, the pair elicited a strong response. On the other hand, when spatial attention was directed to the ineffective stimulus, the identical pair elicited a weak response, even though the effective stimulus was still in its original location (see Fig. 6.3).

Based on results of this type, the spatial attentional modulation could be described as a shrinkage of the classical receptive field around the attended location. Similar studies of Luck, Chelazzi, Hillyard and Desimone (1997) and Reynolds, Chelazzi and Desimone (1999) replicated this result in area V4, and showed similar attentional modulation effects in area V2 as well. Even in area V1 a weak attentional modulation has been described (McAdams and Maunsell 1999).

Maunsell (1995) and many others (Duhamel, Colby and Goldberg 1992, Colby, Duhamel

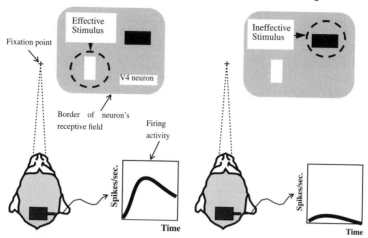

Fig. 6.3 Spatial attention and shrinking receptive fields in single-cell recordings of V4 neurons from the brain of a behaving monkey. The areas that are circled indicate the attended locations. When the monkey attended to effective sensory stimuli, the V4 neuron produced a good response, whereas a poor response was observed when the monkey attended to the ineffective sensory stimulus. The point fixated was the same in both conditions. (Adapted from Moran and Desimone 1985.)

and Goldberg 1993, Gnadt and Andersen 1988) have shown that the modification of neural activity by attentional and behavioural states of the animal is not only true for the extrastriate areas in the ventral stream, but is also true for the extrastriate areas of the dorsal stream as well. In particular, Maunsell (1995) demonstrated that the biased competitive interaction due to spatial and object attention exists not only for objects within the same receptive field, but also for objects in spatially distant receptive fields. This suggests that mechanisms exist to provide biased competition of a more global nature. Furthermore, Connor, Gallant, Preddie and Van Essen (1996) showed that the locus of spatial attention can modulate the structure of the receptive fields of V4 neurons. By asking the monkeys to discriminate subtle changes in features in particular points in visual space, they managed to shift the hot spot of the receptive field of nearby V4 neurons towards the spatial focus of attention.

One question then is whether there is a general mechanism, for example projections from the pulvinar as Olshausen, Anderson and Van Essen (1993) suggest, that modulates spatial attention and attentional gating in both the dorsal stream and the ventral stream. Alternatively, spatial attentional gating in the ventral stream could be modulated by the parietal cortex. In fMRI (functional magnetic resonance imaging) experiments that involve object discrimination, Corbetta and Shulman (1998) suggested that the dorsal fronto–parietal network is active concurrently with the ventral occipito–temporal regions. However, the time resolution of fMRI is insufficient to establish this, and single and multiple single neuron recording studies are the only way to address this, in that they operate at the speed of neural computation (which their firing implements), and in that they also provide evidence on what the computational elements, the neurons, are actually encoding in different areas. We note for example that the speed of the interactions between the dorsal and ventral visual streams is likely to take less than 100 ms, given the speed with which networks of real neurons in the brain interact, as described in Section B.6. Studies of this type, and experimental anatomical and disconnection studies, are needed to address the issue of the speed of interaction between the dorsal stream and the ventral stream, and whether this takes place through direct connections, or through their interaction with the early visual cortex, in order to implement these attentional processes.

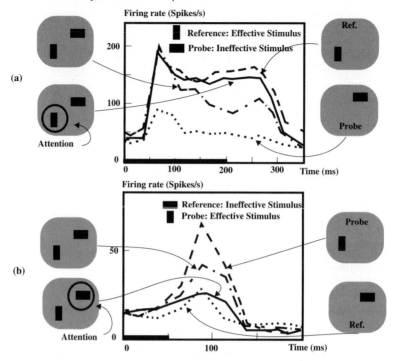

Fig. 6.4 Competitive interactions and attentional modulation of responses of single neurons in area V2. (a) Inhibitory suppression by the probe and attentional compensation. (b) Excitatory reinforcement by the probe and attentional compensation. The black horizontal bar at the bottom indicates stimulus duration. (Adapted from Reynolds, Chelazzi and Desimone 1999.)

6.3.2 The role of competition

In order to test at the neuronal level the biased competition hypothesis more directly, Reynolds, Chelazzi and Desimone (1999) performed single-cell recordings of V2 and V4 neurons in a behavioural paradigm that explicitly separated sensory processing mechanisms from attentional effects. They first examined the presence of competitive interactions in the absence of attentional effects by having the monkey attend to a location far outside the receptive field of the neuron that they were recording. They compared the firing activity response of the neuron when a single reference stimulus was within the receptive field, with the response when a probe stimulus was added to the field. When the probe was added to the field, the activity of the neuron was shifted toward the activity level that would have been evoked if the probe had appeared alone. This effect is shown in Fig. 6.4. When the reference was an effective stimulus (high response) and the probe was an ineffective stimulus (low response), the firing activity was suppressed after adding the probe (Fig. 6.4a). On the other hand, the response of the cell increased when an effective probe stimulus was added to an ineffective reference stimulus (Fig. 6.4b).

These results are explained in Section 6.7.1 by assuming that V2 and V1 neurons coding the different stimuli engage in competitive interactions, mediated for example through intermediary inhibitory neurons, as illustrated in Fig. 6.5.

The neurons in the extrastriate area receiving input from the competing neurons respond according to their input activity after the competition; that is, the response of a V4 neuron to two stimuli in its field is not the sum of its responses to both, but rather is a weighted average of the responses to each stimulus alone.

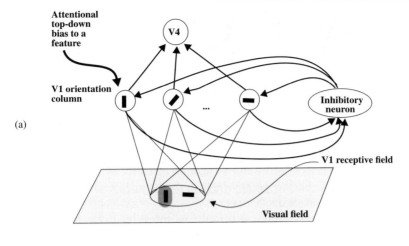

(a)

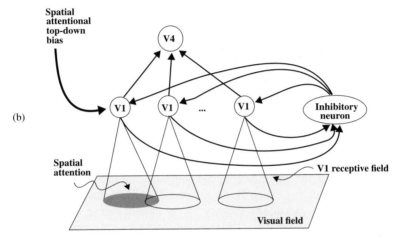

(b)

Fig. 6.5 Biased competition hypothesis at the neuronal level. (a) Attention to a particular top-down pre-specified feature. Intermediate inhibitory interneurons provide an inhibitory signal to V1 neurons in an orientation column (with receptive fields at the same spatial location) that are sensitive to an orientation different from the to-be-attended orientation. (b) Attention to a particular top-down prespecified spatial location. Inhibitory interneurons provide an inhibitory signal to V1 neurons with receptive fields corresponding to regions that are outside the to-be-attended location. In this schematic representation, we assume for simplicity direct connections from V1 to V4 neurons without intermediate V2 neurons. (After Rolls and Deco 2002.)

Attentional modulatory effects have been independently tested by repeating the same experiment, but now having the monkey attend to the reference stimulus within the receptive field of the recorded neuron. The effect of attention on the response of the V2 or V4 neuron was to almost compensate for the suppressive or excitatory effect of the probe (Reynolds, Chelazzi and Desimone 1999). That is, if the probe caused a suppression of the neuronal response to the reference when attention was outside the receptive field, then attending to the reference restored the neuron's activity to the level corresponding to the response of the neuron to the reference stimulus alone (Fig. 6.4a). Symmetrically, if the probe stimulus had increased the neuron's level of activity, attending to the reference stimulus compensated the response by shifting the activity to the level that had been recorded when the reference was presented alone (Fig. 6.4b). As is shown in Fig. 6.5, this attentional modulation can be understood by assuming that attention biases the competition between V1 neurons in favour of a specific location or feature.

6.3.3 Evidence for attentional bias

Direct physiological evidence for the existence of an attentional bias was provided by Luck, Chelazzi, Hillyard and Desimone (1997) and by Spitzer, Desimone and Moran (1988). Luck et al. (1997) discovered that attending to a location within the receptive field of a V2 or V4 neuron increased its spontaneous firing activity. They reported that in the absence of stimuli, the spontaneous firing activity of V2 and V4 neurons increased by 30–40% when the monkey attended to a location within the receptive field of the recorded neuron, compared with when attention was directed outside the field.

When a single stimulus is presented in the receptive field of a V4 neuron, Spitzer et al. (1988) observed an increase of the neuronal response to that stimulus when the monkey directed attention inside the receptive field, compared to when attention was directed outside the field.

6.3.4 Non-spatial attention

Additional evidence for the biased competition hypothesis as a mechanism for the selection of non-spatial attributes has been put forward by Chelazzi, Miller, Duncan and Desimone (1993). Chelazzi et al. (1993) measured the responses of inferior temporal cortex (IT) neurons in monkeys while the animals were looking at a display containing a target and a distractor. Figure 6.6 illustrates schematically the task design and results in the experiment of Chelazzi et al. (1993).

At the start of a trial, the macaque was cued with what was to be the target stimulus. After a delay period of 1.5 s, during which the display remained blank, the target and the distractor were simultaneously presented. The monkey had to initiate an eye movement towards the location of the target. Chelazzi et al. (1993) recorded activity in IT neurons using two kinds of stimuli: a highly effective stimulus for activating the IT neuron being recorded, and an ineffective stimulus, whose presence suppressed that neuron's response. In some trials, the effective stimulus was the target and the distractor was the ineffective stimulus, while in other trials the opposite arrangement held. In both conditions, the receptive field of each of the recorded neurons included both items (target and distractor). During the delay period, the neuron sensitive to the target showed a higher firing rate, presumably reflecting a top-down projection from a working memory system. After the delay period, the recordings of the average firing rates showed that the neuron sensitive to the target and the neuron sensitive to the distractor became active, but only the activity of the neuron sensitive to the target remained high (or even increased), while the activity of the neuron sensitive to the distractor decreased. These results clearly support the idea of two phases in the response of IT neurons. During the first phase, the activity of the neuron is enhanced due to the presence of the effective stimulus in the display, independently of the attentional state of the monkey, i.e. independently of whether the stimulus is the target. During the second phase, the response is maintained or increased only if the effective stimulus is the target, and the firing rate decreases if the stimulus is not a target. Thus, the activity of IT neurons depends on the internal attentional state of the monkey. Usher and Niebur (1996) formulated a detailed neural model that explains these data assuming parallel dynamic processing driven by a competition mechanism.

Further evidence on how object-based attention can facilitate neuronal activity in the inferior temporal visual cortex is found in an object search task (Rolls, Aggelopoulos and Zheng 2003a). The macaque is looking for one of two objects in a large (70 deg × 55 deg)

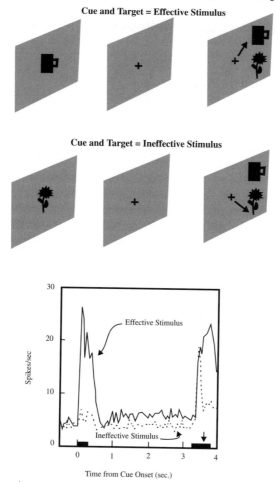

Fig. 6.6 Schematic illustration of the task design and results in the experiment of Chelazzi et al. (1993). Top: each trial starts with presentation of a cue stimulus at the fixation point, which the monkey has to retain in short-term memory. After a blank delay interval, an array appeared in random peripheral locations of the visual field. The animal was trained to make a saccadic eye movement to the stimulus array that matched the initial cue. Arrays of 1, 2, 3, and 5 stimuli were used. (The figure shows an array of 2 stimuli). Bottom: peristimulus time histograms of the firing rates of 20 recorded IT cells. On some trials, the cue and the target corresponded to the effective stimulus (e.g. the cup in the figure) of the cell, and in other trials to the ineffective stimulus (e.g. the flower in the figure). The black horizontal bar at the bottom left and right of the histograms indicates the cue and the array durations, respectively. The arrow indicates the average saccade latency. In both conditions the receptive field of each of the neurons included both items (target and distractor). See text for explanation. (Modified from Chelazzi et al. 1993.)

display. It is found that the receptive field of a neuron is much larger (on average 78 deg against a blank background) for the effective stimulus for the neuron when the stimulus is being searched for than when the stimulus is not being searched for and is just a distractor (when the receptive field size is 22 deg, see Section 4.5.9.1, and Fig. 4.63 on page 355). Thus top-down object-based attentional processes can increase the size of receptive fields in an object search task.

6.3.5 High-resolution buffer hypothesis

Attentional effects have also been observed in the early visual areas V1 and V2 under particular experimental conditions in which competing objects are present simultaneously in the visual field (Motter 1993, Roelfsema, Lamme and Spekreijse 1998, Ito and Gilbert 1999). The magnitude of such attention-related enhancement effects was about 15–25% of the response magnitude. However, Lee (1996) (see also Lee, Mumford, Romero and Lamme (1998)) have argued that the state-dependent modulation of the V1 responses is not simply an attentional gain-control mechanism, but reflects a more general role of V1 in visual processing. In particular, they proposed that V1 is a unique high-resolution buffer available to the cortex for calculations, that can be used by any computation, high or low level, that requires high-resolution image details and spatial precision. While the early response of the V1 neurons could be considered as these neurons operating as filters on the visual input (see Rolls and Deco (2002)), the late responses of V1 neurons might reflect the consequence of an elaborate interactive and concurrent computation involving the whole visual hierarchy via the feedfoward/feedback loops between the different cortical areas. This conjecture was triggered in part by the 'figure-highlighting' effect that Lamme (1995) observed in V1, i.e. that V1 neurons' activity was higher when their receptive fields were located inside the figure than when their receptive fields were in the background. In a series of experiments, Lee and his colleagues (Lee, Mumford, Romero and Lamme 1998, Lee, Yang, Romero and Mumford 2002a) showed that the figure-highlighting effect could be observed not only in texture figures, but also in luminance figures, in equi-luminance colour figures, and in figures defined by shape from shading. In particular, the recent research of Lee's group furnished two further important pieces of evidence in support of the high-resolution buffer hypothesis, and more generally, that perceptual computation is an emergent phenomenon that arises from the interactive and distributed computations between many cortical areas. First, they (Lee, Yang, Romero and Mumford 2002a) showed that the figure-highlighting effect in V1 due to shape from shading, a higher order visual construct, can be observed only after the stimulus has been made relevant to the monkeys' behaviour; and that the figure-highlighting effect is a top-down object-specific effect that depends on what the monkeys are looking for behaviourally. Second, they (Lee and Nguyen 2001) demonstrated that the illusory contours of Kanizsa squares could be observed in V1, but occurred 35 ms after V2 activation. This evidence, together with the curve-tracing experiment in V1 of Roelfsema, Lamme and Spekreijse (1998), supports the notion that higher order modulation effects in V1 are very spatially- and object-specific.

The basic premise of the high-resolution buffer hypothesis is that different cortical areas may interact through V1 in order to fulfil the specific computations required by the task. In Section 6.8, we will see that when the animal is searching for a specific object (visual search), or recognizing objects at a specific spatial location (object recognition), the early visual cortex, including V1, is actively involved in these processes, and serves as one of the sites of interaction between the dorsal and the ventral streams (Deco and Lee 2002, Deco and Lee 2004).

6.4 The biased competition hypothesis in functional brain imaging

In functional magnetic resonance imaging (fMRI) studies, additional evidence for similar mechanisms in human extrastriate cortex has been obtained (Kastner, De Weerd, Desimone and Ungerleider 1998, Kastner, Pinsk, De Weerd, Desimone and Ungerleider 1999). In line with the biased competition hypothesis, these studies have shown that multiple stimuli in the visual field interact in a mutually suppressive way when presented simultaneously, but not when presented sequentially, and that spatially directed attention to one stimulus location reduces the mutually suppressive effect. These studies also revealed increased activity in extrastriate cortex in the absence of visual stimulation, when subjects covertly directed attention to a peripheral location at which they expected the onset of visual stimuli. This increased activity in visual cortex was related to a top-down bias of neural signals, deriving from frontal and parietal areas, to favour the attended location. We will analyze these results in more detail in the next two subsections. Section 6.7.2 presents simulations of these fMRI experiments based on the particular computational theory and model of biased competition and attention described in Rolls and Deco (2002) and subsequent investigations described later in this chapter.

6.4.1   Neuroimaging of attention

Using fMRI in humans, Kastner, De Weerd, Desimone and Ungerleider (1998) in a first experiment tested for the presence of suppressive interactions between visual stimuli presented simultaneously within the visual field in the absence of directed attention. In a second experiment they considered the role of attentional modulation on these suppressive interactions. Figure 6.7 shows the design of the experiment. Complex images were presented in randomized order in four nearby locations within the right upper quadrant of the visual field under two different conditions: sequential (SEQ) and simultaneous (SIM). In the sequential condition, each stimulus appeared successively alone in one of the four locations, whereas in the simultaneous condition all four stimuli appeared at the same time in all four locations. Under the two conditions, the physical stimulation parameters integrated over time were identical. Suppressive interactions between stimuli can be demonstrated if the fMRI activity during the simultaneous condition is smaller than during the sequential presentations. In this case, the mutual suppression can be explained by means of competitive interactions between the simultaneously presented stimuli. In fact, they observed this effect in several visual areas. Figure 6.7 shows these suppressive effects in area V1, V2, V4, and TEO by the reduction of the fMRI signal in the unattended simultaneous condition (SIM blocks without shading) compared to the unattended sequential condition (SEQ blocks without shading). The difference in activation between sequential and simultaneous presentations increased from V1 to V4 and TEO (Fig. 6.7).

In a second experiment, Kastner et al. (1998) studied the influence of attention on the suppressive interactions between simultaneously presented stimuli. In this case, during each scan, four blocks of visual stimulation (SEQ-SIM-SIM-SEQ) were tested in an unattended and an attended condition. During the attended condition the subjects were instructed to covertly attend specifically to one of the four locations where the stimuli could appear. Consistent with the single-cell experiments reported in the previous section, Fig. 6.7 shows an attentional modulatory compensation of the otherwise suppressive interactions between stimuli. Spatially directed attention reduces these interactions by partially cancelling out their suppressive effects, as is shown in Fig. 6.7 (dark shading). A significantly greater compensatory influence of attention on the fMRI signal elicited by simultaneously presented stimuli, compared with that elicited by sequentially presented stimuli, can also be seen in Fig. 6.7.

6.4.2   Attentional effects in the absence of visual stimulation

In order to study in more detail the nature of the top-down signal that modulates the response to an attended versus an unattended stimulus in human visual cortical areas, Kastner, Pinsk, De Weerd, Desimone and Ungerleider (1999) extended their previous experiment and consid-

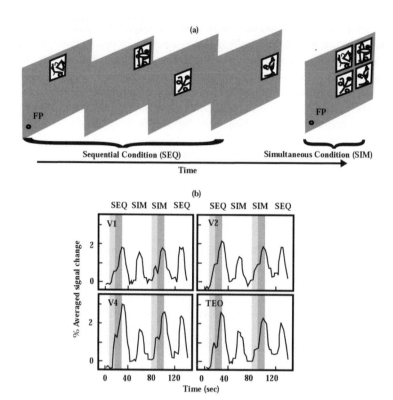

Fig. 6.7 fMRI signals in visual cortex averaged over all subjects. (a) Task. Subjects fixated a spot while stimuli appeared either asynchronously (left images, SEQ) or simultaneously (right images, SIM). The total amount of time each stimulus appeared was constant. Subjects either performed an attentionally demanding task at the fixation point or attended to one of the four stimuli. (b) fMRI signals. The light shading indicates the expectation period, the dark shading the attended presentations, and blocks without shading correspond to the unattended condition. (Adapted from Kastner et al. 1999.)

ered the influence and origin of top-down attentional bias in the absence of visual stimulation. This experiment relates to the increase in spontaneous firing activity demonstrated in monkey extrastriate cortex during attention when no stimulus is present, as described in Section 6.3.3.

They modified the previous experiment by including a new block in which the subject had to attend to a specific location in the absence of any stimuli. They implemented this block by marking the attended condition 10 s before the onset of the visual presentation (SIM or SEQ). They found increased activity related to attention in the absence of visual stimulation in extrastriate cortex when subjects covertly directed attention to a location where the onset of a visual stimulus was expected (light shading in Fig. 6.7).

Even more, during this expectation period they observed a strong signal increase in frontal and parietal areas, suggesting that the biasing attentional top-down signal to the extrastriate visual cortex could be derived from the fronto-parietal network.

In conclusion, these human neuroimaging experiments extend the validity of the biased competition hypothesis from the neuronal level to the intermediate level of cortical areas, and suggest candidate areas from where the biasing signal may originate.

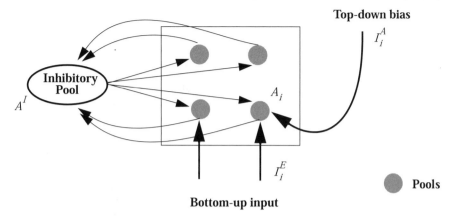

Fig. 6.8 Basic computational module for biased competition: a competitive network with external top-down bias. Excitatory pools (i.e. populations) of neurons with activity A_i for the ith pool are connected with a common inhibitory pool with activity A^I in order to implement a competition mechanism. I_i^E is the external bottom-up sensory input to the cells in pool i, and I_i^A attentional top-down bias, an external input coming from higher modules. The external top-down bias can shift the competition in favour of a specific pool or group of pools. This architecture is similar to that shown in Fig. B.18, but with competition between pools of similar neurons. (After Rolls and Deco 2002.)

6.5 A basic computational module for biased competition

We have seen in Fig. 6.5 how given forward (bottom-up) inputs to a network, competition between the principal (excitatory) neurons can be implemented by inhibitory neurons which receive from the principal neurons in the network and send back inhibitory connections to the principal neurons in the network. This competition can be biased by a top-down input to favour some of the populations of neurons, and this describes the biased competition hypothesis.

We can make the model of the biased competition hypothesis of attention more precise so that it can be investigated computationally by formulating it as shown in Fig. 6.8. Each population or pool of neurons is tuned to a different stimulus property, e.g. spatial location, or feature, or object. The more pools of the module that are active, the more active the common inhibitory pool will be and, consequently, the more feedback inhibition will affect the pools in the module, such that only the most excited group of pools will survive the competition. The external top-down bias can shift the competition in favour of a specific group of pools. Some non-linearity in the system, implemented for example by the fact that neurons have a threshold non-linearity below which they do not fire, can result in a small top-down bias having quite a large attentional effect, especially for relatively weak bottom-up inputs, as shown in a realistic spiking neuron simulation by Deco and Rolls (2005b) described in Section 6.9.

The architecture of Fig. 6.8 is that of a competitive network (described in Section B.4) but with top-down backprojections as illustrated in Fig. B.18. However, the network could equally well include associatively modifiable synapses in recurrent collateral connections between the excitatory (principal) neurons in the network, making the network into an autoassociation or attractor network capable of short-term memory, as described in Section B.3. The competition between the neurons in the attractor network is again implemented by the inhibitory feedback neurons.

The implementation of biased competition in a computational model can be at the mean-field level, in which the average firing rate of each population of neurons is specified. Equations to implement the dynamics of such a model are given in Section B.8.2 (see also Section 6.13). The advantages of this level of formulation are relative simplicity, and speed of computation.

The implementation can also be at the level of the spiking neuron by using an integrate-and-fire simulation (see Sections B.6 and 6.9). Rolls and Deco (2002) assume, with others (Tuckwell 1988, Brunel and Wang 2001, Amit and Brunel 1997, Del Giudice, Fusi and Mattia 2003), that a proper level of description at the microscopic level is captured by the spiking and synaptic dynamics of one-compartment, point-like models of neurons, such as *Integrate-and-Fire-Models*. The realistic dynamics allow the use of realistic biophysical constants (such as conductances, delays, etc.) in a thorough study of the realistic time scales and firing rates involved in the time course of the neural activity underlying cognitive processes, for comparison with experimental data. It is important for a *biologically plausible* model that the different time scales involved are properly described, because the dynamical system is sensitive to the underlying different spiking and synaptic time courses, and the non-linearities involved in these processes. For this reason, it is convenient to include a thorough description of the different time courses of the synaptic activity, by including fast and slow excitatory receptors (AMPA and NMDA) and GABA-inhibitory receptors. A second reason why this temporally realistic and detailed level of description of synaptic activity is required is the goal to perform realistic fMRI-simulations. These involve the realistic calculation of BOLD-signals (see Section B.6.4) that are intrinsically linked with the synaptic dynamics, as shown by Logothetis, Pauls, Augath, Trinath and Oeltermann (2001). A third reason is that one can consider the influence of neurotransmitters and pharmacological manipulations, e.g. the influence of dopamine on the NMDA and GABA receptor dynamics (Zheng, Zhang, Bunney and Shi 1999, Law-Tho, Hirsch and Crepel 1994), to study the effect on the global dynamics and on the related cortical functions (e.g. on working memory, Deco, Rolls and Horwitz (2004), and Deco and Rolls (2003)). A fourth reason for analysis at the level of spiking neurons is that the computational units of the brain are the neurons, in the sense that they transform a large set of inputs received from different neurons into an output spike train, that this is the single output signal of the neuron which is connected to other neurons, and that this is therefore the level at which the information is being transferred between the neurons, and thus at which the brain's representations and computations can be understood (Rolls and Treves 1998, Rolls and Deco 2002). The integrate-and-fire level also allows statistical effects related to the probability that spikes from different neurons will occur at different times to be investigated (which can be very important in decision-making as shown in Chapter 7), and allows single neuron recording studies to be simulated. Integrate-and-fire simulations are more difficult to set up, and are slow to run. Equations for such simulations are given in Sections 7.8 and B.6, and as applied to a biased competition model of attention by Deco and Rolls (2005b).

The computational investigations can be extended to systems with many interacting modules, as described in Section B.8.3. These could be arranged in a hierarchy, with repeated layers of bottom-up and top-down connections as illustrated in Fig. 6.10.

6.6 Neurodynamical architecture of a model of spatial and object-based attention

In order to analyze the principles of operation of attentional systems in the brain, Rolls and Deco (2002) described a cortical model of visual attention for object recognition and visual search based on the neurophysiological constraints described in Sections 6.3 and 6.4. The system is absolutely autonomous and each component of its functional behaviour is explicitly described in a complete mathematical framework. The model is described here, with further details available elsewhere (Deco 2001, Deco and Zihl 2001b, Rolls and Deco 2002, Deco

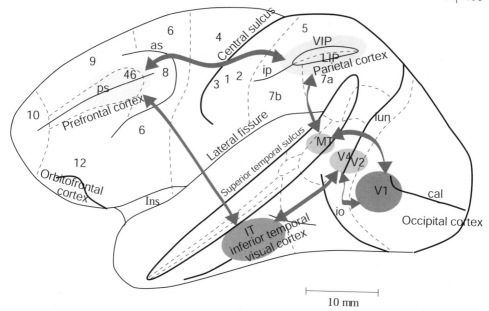

Fig. 6.9 Lateral view of the macaque brain showing some connections of the ventral and dorsal visual streams (V1, primary visual area; V2, V4, extrastriate visual areas; IT, inferior temporal visual cortex, PP, posterior parietal cortex) with the anterior brain areas (PFCv, ventrolateral prefrontal cortex; PFCd, dorsolateral prefrontal cortex). as, arcuate sulcus; cal, calcarine sulcus; Ins, insula; io, inferior occipital sulcus; ip, intraparietal sulcus; lun, lunate sulcus; ps, principal sulcus. (After Deco and Rolls 2005a.)

and Lee 2002, Corchs and Deco 2002, Heinke, Deco, Zihl and Humphreys 2002, Deco and Lee 2004, Deco and Rolls 2004, Deco and Rolls 2005a).

Top-down processes in attention are considered here, and how they interact with bottom-up processing, in a model of visual attentional processing that has multiple hierarchically organized modules in the architecture shown schematically in Figs. 6.9 and 6.10. The model shows how the dorsal (sometimes termed *where*) visual stream (reaching the posterior parietal cortex, PP) and the ventral (*what*) visual stream (via V4 to the inferior temporal cortex, IT) could interact through early visual cortical areas (such as V1 and V2) to account for many aspects of visual attention (Deco 2001, Deco and Zihl 2001b, Rolls and Deco 2002, Deco and Lee 2002, Corchs and Deco 2002, Heinke et al. 2002, Deco and Lee 2004, Deco and Rolls 2004). The source of the attentional bias in the model comes from short-term memory networks in for example the prefrontal cortex, as shown in Figs. 6.9 and 6.10.

The overall systems-level representation of the model simulated is shown in Fig. 6.11. The system is essentially composed of six modules structured such that they resemble the two known main visual paths of the mammalian visual cortex. Information from the retino-geniculo-striate pathway enters the visual cortex through area V1 in the occipital lobe and proceeds into two processing streams. The occipital-temporal stream leads ventrally through V2–V4 and IT (inferotemporal cortex), and the occipito-parietal stream leads dorsally into PP (posterior parietal complex). In this model system described by Rolls and Deco (2002), we chose to model with our ventral stream one particular aspect of the inferior temporal cortex function: translation invariant object recognition. (A fuller model of the processing that leads to invariant object representations is provided in Chapter 4.) We chose to model with our dorsal stream one particular aspect of parietal cortex function: encoding of visual space in retinotopic coordinates. This is obviously a great simplification of the complex hierarchical

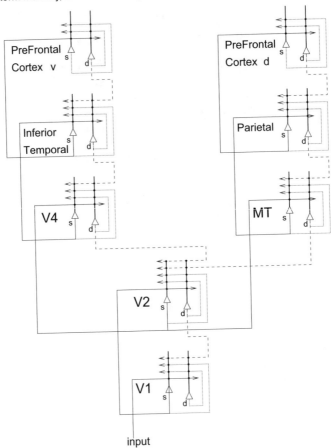

Fig. 6.10 The overall architecture of the model of object and spatial processing and attention, including the prefrontal cortical areas that provide the short-term memory required to hold the object or spatial target of attention active. Forward connections are indicated by solid lines; backprojections, which could implement top-down processing, by dashed lines; and recurrent connections within an area by dotted lines. The triangles represent pyramidal cell bodies, with the thick vertical line above them the dendritic trees. The cortical layers in which the cells are concentrated are indicated by s (superficial, layers 2 and 3) and d (deep, layers 5 and 6). The prefrontal cortical areas most strongly reciprocally connected to the inferior temporal cortex 'what' processing stream are labelled v to indicate that they are in the more ventral part of the lateral prefrontal cortex, area 46, close to the inferior convexity in macaques. The prefrontal cortical areas most strongly reciprocally connected to the parietal visual cortical 'where' processing stream are labelled d to indicate that they are in the more dorsal part of the lateral prefrontal cortex, area 46, in and close to the banks of the principal sulcus in macaques (see text).

architecture and functions of the primate visual system (Felleman and Van Essen 1991) (see Rolls and Deco (2002) Chapters 2–5 and 8), but the model is sufficient to test and demonstrate our fundamental proposals for how the object and spatial streams interact to implement visual attentional processes.

First, we give an overview of the entire architecture. The ventral stream consists of four modules as shown in Fig. 6.11: (1) a V1 module; (2) a V2–V4 module; (3) an IT module; and (4) a module v46 corresponding to the ventral part of area 46 of the prefrontal cortex that maintains a short-term memory of a recognized object or holds a representation of the target object in a visual search task. The V1 module contains $P \times P$ hypercolumns, covering

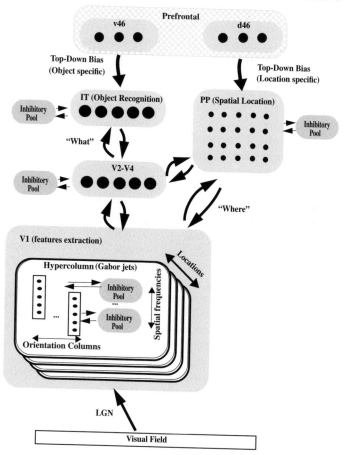

Fig. 6.11 The systems-level architecture of a model of the cortical mechanisms of visual attention. The system is essentially composed of six modules structured such that they resemble the two known main visual pathways of the primate visual cortex. Information from the retino-geniculo-striate pathway enters the visual cortex through area V1 in the occipital lobe and proceeds into two processing streams. The occipital-temporal stream leads ventrally through V2–V4 and IT (inferotemporal), and is mainly concerned with object recognition. The occipito-parietal stream leads dorsally into PP (posterior parietal complex) and is responsible for maintaining a spatial map of an object's location. (After Rolls and Deco 2002.)

an $N \times N$ pixel scene. Each hypercolumn contains L orientation columns of complex cells with K octave levels corresponding to different spatial frequencies. The complex cells are modelled by the power modulus of Gabor wavelets. There is one inhibitory pool interacting with complex cells of all orientations at each scale. This module sends spatial and feature information up to the dorsal stream and the ventral stream respectively. It also provides a high-resolution representation for the two streams to interact through recurrent feedback. This interaction between the streams may be important for several functions such as binding, and high-resolution visual analysis. Rolls and Deco (2002) first focused on the possible role of the interaction in mediating spatial and object attention in visual search and object recognition tasks. The V2–V4 module serves primarily to pool and channel the responses of V1 neurons to IT, to achieve a limited degree of translation invariance. It also implements a certain degree of localized competitive interaction between different targets. We use a topologically organized lattice to represent V2 or V4. Each node in this lattice has $L \times K$ cell assemblies as in a hypercolumn in V1. Each cell assembly, however, receives convergent input from the cell assemblies with the same tuning from a $M \times M$ hypercolumn neighbourhood in V1. The feedforward connections from V1 to the V4 module are modelled with convergent Gaussian weight functions, with symmetric recurrent connections. The IT module contains C pools, as the network is trained to search for or recognize C particular objects. Each of these cell assemblies is fully connected to each of the V4 pools. The connection weights from V4 to IT are trained by Hebbian learning rules in a learning phase.

The dorsal stream consists of three modules: (1) the V1 module; (2) a PP module; and (3) a module d46 corresponding to the dorsal part of area 46 of the prefrontal cortex that maintains a representation of a spatial location in a short-term spatial memory. This d46 module not only provides a short-term memory function, but can be used to generate an attentional bias for a spatial location. The PP module is responsible for mediating spatial attention modulation and for updating the spatial position of the attended object. A lattice of $N \times N$ nodes represents the topographical organization of module PP. Each node in the lattice corresponds to the spatial position of each pixel in the input image. Each of these assemblies monitors the activities from hypercolumns in V1–V2 via a Gaussian weighting function that connects topologically corresponding locations.

Prefrontal cortex area 46 (modules d46 and v46) is not explicitly simulated in the model described by Rolls and Deco (2002) and in more detail elsewhere (Deco 2001, Deco and Zihl 2001b, Rolls and Deco 2002, Deco and Lee 2002, Corchs and Deco 2002, Heinke et al. 2002, Deco and Lee 2004, Deco and Rolls 2004), but is part of the model. We assume that top-down feedback connections from these areas provide the external top-down bias that specifies the processing conditions of earlier modules. Concretely, the feedback connection from area v46 with the IT module specifies the target object in a visual search task; and the feedback connection from area d46 with the PP module generates the bias to a targeted spatial location in a recognition task at a fixed prespecified location.

The system operates in two different modes: the learning mode and the recognition mode. During the learning mode the synaptic connections between V4 and IT are trained by means of Hebbian learning during several presentations of a specific object at changing random positions in the visual field. This is the simple way in which translation invariant representations are produced in IT in this model. During the recognition mode there are two possibilities for running the system, illustrated in Fig. 6.12.

First, in **visual spatial search mode** (Fig. 6.12b), an object can be found in a scene by biasing the system with an external top-down (backprojection) component (from e.g. prefrontal area v46) to the IT module. This drives the competition in IT in favour of the pool associated with the specific object to be searched for. Then, the intermodular backprojection attentional modulation IT–V4–V1 will enhance the activity of the pools in V4 and V1 associated with the component features of the specific object to be searched for. This modulation will add to the visual input being received by V1, resulting in greater local activity where the features in the topologically organized visual input features match the backprojected features being facilitated. Finally, the enhanced firing in a particular part of V1 will lead to increased activity in the forward pathway from V1 to V2–V4 to PP, resulting in increased firing in the PP module in the location that corresponds to where the object being searched for is located. In this way, the architecture automatically finds the location of the object being searched for, and the location found is made explicit by which neurons in the spatially organized PP module are firing.

Second, in **visual object identification mode** (Fig. 6.12a), the PP module receives a top-down (backprojection) input (from e.g. prefrontal area d46) which specifies the location in which to identify an object. The spatially biased PP module then drives by its backprojections the competition in the V2–V4 module in favour of the pool associated with the specified

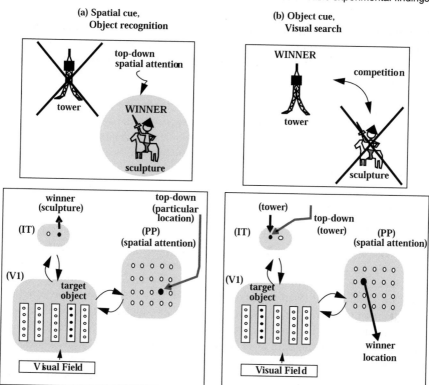

Fig. 6.12 Attentional modulation for finding an object (in visual object identification mode) at a specific spatial location using spatial bias to the PP module from for example a prefrontal module d46. See text for details. (b) Attentional modulation for finding a visual spatial location (in visual spatial search mode) when an object is specified by bias to the IT module from for example a prefrontal module v46. (After Rolls and Deco 2002; and Deco and Lee 2004.)

location. This biasing effect in V1 and V2–V4 will bias these modules to have a greater response for the specified location in space. The shape feature representations which happen to be present due to the visual input from the retina at that location in the V1 and V2–V4 modules will therefore be enhanced, and the enhanced firing of these shape features will by the feedforward pathway V1–V4–IT favour the IT object pool that contains the facilitated features, leading to recognition in IT of the object at the attentional location being specified in the PP module. The operation of these two attentional modes is shown schematically in Fig. 6.12.

A formal description of the model is provided in Sections 6.13 and B.8.3.

6.7 Simulations of basic experimental findings

According to the biased competition hypothesis multiple stimuli in the visual field activate populations of neurons that engage in competitive interactions. Moreover, attending to a stimulus at a particular location biases this competition in favour of neurons that respond to the location of the attended stimulus. Different experimental results seem to support these ideas. In particular, in Section 6.3 the results are described of Reynolds, Chelazzi and Desimone (1999) from single cell recording in V2 neurons in monkeys, which show inhibitory competitive effects and attentive biasing modulation at the neuronal level. In addition, in Section 6.4 the fMRI studies in humans were described of Kastner, Pinsk, De Weerd, Desimone and Ungerleider (1999), which are consistent with the idea of biased competition at the larger scale (i.e. mesoscopic) level in which the activation of more gross regions of the brain is measured.

In this section, we show that simulations based on the model introduced in Section 6.6, explain the results observed in both experiments. Consequently, the dynamical behaviour of the multimodular architecture described is Section 6.6 provides an account of attentional processes in vision that is consistent with the biased competition hypothesis at the (microscopic) level of neuronal firing and at the level of the activation of different large regions of cortex.

6.7.1 Simulations of single-cell experiments

In this Section, simulation results (Deco 2001, Deco and Zihl 2001b, Rolls and Deco 2002, Deco and Lee 2002, Corchs and Deco 2002, Heinke et al. 2002, Deco and Lee 2004) are described with the model outlined in Section 6.6 that correspond to the experiments by Reynolds, Chelazzi and Desimone (1999) on single cell recordings from V2 neurons in monkeys. We describe the dynamical behaviour of the model of the cortical architecture of visual attention by solving numerically the system of coupled differential equations in a computer simulation. For this experiment we included a module of V2 neurons. The input system processed an input image of 66×66 pixels ($N = 66$). The V1 hypercolumns covered the entire image uniformly. They were distributed in 33×33 locations ($P = 33$) and each hypercolumn was sensitive to two spatial frequencies and to eight different orientations (i.e. $K = 2$ and $L = 8$). The V2 module had 2×8 pools receiving convergent input from the pools of the same tuning from a 10×10 (i.e. $M = 10$) hypercolumn in the neighbourhood in V1. The feedforward connections from V1 to V2 are modelled with convergent Gaussian weight functions, with symmetric recurrent connections. We analyzed the firing activity of a single pool in the V2 module which was highly sensitive to a vertical bar presented in its receptive field (the effective stimulus) and poorly sensitive to a 75 degree oriented bar presented in its receptive field (ineffective stimulus). The size of the bars was 2×4 pixels. Following the experimental setup reviewed in Section 6.3, we plot in Figs. 6.13a and 6.13b the development of the firing activity of a V2 pool under four different conditions: (1) with a single reference stimulus within the receptive field; (2) with a single probe stimulus within the receptive field; (3) with a reference and a probe stimulus within the receptive field and without attention; and (4) with a reference and a probe stimulus within the receptive field and with attention directed to the spatial location of the reference stimulus. In our simulation, spatial attention was directed to the location of the reference stimulus by setting in module PP the top-down attentional bias coming from prefrontal area d46 equal to 0.05 if i and j corresponded to the location of the reference stimulus and zero elsewhere. In the unattended condition the external top-down bias was zero everywhere. The computational simulations of Fig. 6.13a and 6.13b should be compared with the experimental results shown in Fig. 6.4a and 6.4b, respectively. The same qualitative behaviour is observed in the model and the real neuronal data in all experimental conditions. The competitive interactions in the absence of attention are due to the intramodular competitive dynamics at the level of V1 (i.e. the suppressive and excitatory effect of the probe shown in Fig. 6.13a and 6.13b, respectively). The modulatory biasing corrections in the attended conditions are caused by the intermodular interactions between the V1 and PP pools, and between the PP pools and prefrontal top-down modulation.

We are also able to account for the findings of the experiments by Connor, Gallant, Preddie and Van Essen (1996), which showed that the locus of spatial attention can modulate the structure of the receptive fields of V4 neurons. By asking the monkeys to discriminate

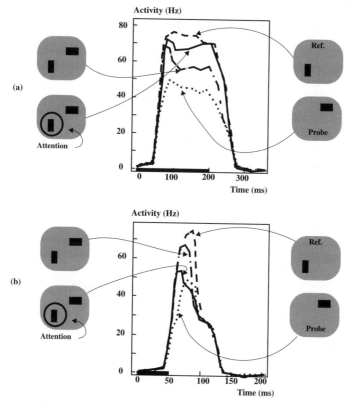

Fig. 6.13 Simulation of the experiment of Reynolds et al. (1999). (a) The stimulus was presented for 200 ms. When an optimal reference stimulus was presented alone, the cell's response (dashed line) was much stronger than its response (dotted line) when a suboptimal probe stimulus was presented alone in the receptive field. Simultaneous presentation of both the reference and the probe stimuli produced an intermediate response (dashed-dotted line), indicating that the probe was producing competitive suppression of the response to the reference stimulus. However, when spatial attention was directed toward the reference stimulus, the suppression due to the probe was largely eliminated: the neuronal response returned to the level when the reference was presented alone (continuous line). (b) The same manipulation as in (a) except that the stimulus was presented for only 50 ms. In this simulation, we used $I_o=0$, and slower dynamics, $\tau=15$ ms. (After Rolls and Deco 2002; see also Deco and Lee 2004.)

subtle changes in features in a particular point in visual space, they managed to shift the hot spot of the receptive field of V4 neurons in the neighbourhood of the location being fixated towards the spatial focus of attention. For these simulations, we used two cell pools in the V4 module. One pool received input from the vertically oriented cells in the V1 module. The other pool received input from the horizontally oriented cells in the V1 module. In our simulation, spatial attention was again specified by introducing a bias to the appropriate cell pool in the PP module. Figure 6.14 shows that the central 'hot spot' peak of the receptive field of V4 neurons was shifted spatially as different PP module pools received the top-down bias.

In conclusion, the dynamical evolution of the firing activity at the neuronal level of our model of the cortical architecture of visual attention (Deco 2001, Deco and Zihl 2001b, Rolls and Deco 2002, Deco and Lee 2002, Corchs and Deco 2002, Heinke et al. 2002, Deco and Lee 2004) is consistent with the single cell experiments of Reynolds, Chelazzi and Desimone (1999) and Connor, Gallant, Preddie and Van Essen (1996). This indicates that the particular computational model we propose, of how biased competition and interaction between the

Attentional Shifting of Receptive Field

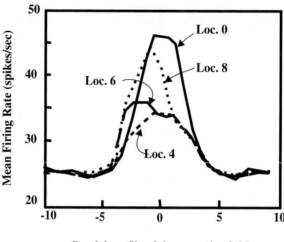

Spatial profile of the receptive field.

Fig. 6.14 Simulation of the experiment by Connor et al. (1993) showing that spatial attention can move the hot spot of the receptive field of a V4 neuron towards the location which is the focus of attention (if the receptive field is close to the focus of attention). The connection between the early V1 module and V4 was modelled with spatially local Gaussian weights centred at location 10, with standard deviation equal to 2.5. The V4 neuron had a more local spatial support than the ventral IT module's neuron in the other simulations in this series. Spatial attention allocated in the dorsal PP module pools corresponding to retinotopic locations 6 and 8 effectively shifted the peak of the receptive field of the V4 neuron to the left. Shift to the right can be produced by biasing locations 12 and 16 (not shown). Location 4 was far away from the centre of the receptive field. Allocating spatial attention to location 4 made the hot spot of the receptive field snap back to its centre position, but the responses of the V4 cell were markedly attenuated.

'what' and 'where' visual processing streams can be used to understand visual attention, is able to account for data at the neuronal level. This represents an advance beyond the biased competition hypothesis, in that it shows how object and spatial attention can be produced by dynamic interactions between the 'what' and 'where' streams, and in that as a computational model which has been simulated, the details of the model have been made fully explicit and have been defined quantitatively (see further Sections 6.13 and B.8.3).

6.7.2 Simulations of fMRI experiments

The dynamic evolution of activity at the cortical level, as shown for example by fMRI signals in experiments with humans, can be simulated in the framework of our model by integrating the pool of neuronal activity in a given area over space and time (Corchs and Deco 2002, Rolls and Deco 2002). The integration over space yields an average activity of the brain area considered at a given time. (The spatial resolution in most fMRI experiments is worse than 3 mm in any one dimension.) The integration over time is performed in order to simulate the relatively coarse temporal resolution of MRI experiments, which is in the order of a few seconds (see Section B.6.4). In this section, we simulate fMRI signals from V4 under the experimental conditions defined by Kastner, Pinsk, De Weerd, Desimone and Ungerleider (1999) (see Section 6.4). We used the same parameters as in the previous section with the only difference that the V1 hypercolumns included three levels of spatial resolution (i.e. $K=3$). The integrated activity over space at a given time t is given by

$$A^{V4}(t) = \sum_{k,p,q,l} A^{V4}_{kpql}(t) \ . \tag{6.1}$$

The temporal evolution is plotted at a coarse timescale of 2 s that emulates the temporal resolution of fMRI experiments. The integration over time in a time window of 2000 ms is given by

$$A^{V4}(T) = \sum_{t=T-2000}^{T} A^{V4}(t) \tag{6.2}$$

since the differential equations are solved iteratively at the millisecond scale. Following the experimental paradigm described in Section 6.4, we also use four complex images similar to the ones that Kastner, Pinsk, De Weerd, Desimone and Ungerleider (1999) used in their experiments. They were presented as input images in four nearby locations in the upper right quadrant. The stimuli were shown in the conditions described in Section 6.4. The images were shown in randomized order under two presentation conditions: sequential (SEQ) and simultaneous (SIM). In the SEQ condition, each stimulus was shown alone in one of the four locations for 250 ms. In the SIM condition, the stimuli appeared together in all four locations for the first 250 ms, followed by a blank period of 750 ms. This stimulation period of 1 s was repeated for each condition in blocks of 10 s interleaved with blank periods of 20 s (BLK). Two attentional conditions were simulated: (1) an unattended condition, during which no external top-down bias from prefrontal areas was present (i.e. $I_{ij}^{PP,A}$ is zero everywhere); and (2) an attended condition which started 10 s before the onset of visual presentation (the expectation period EXP) and continued during the subsequent 10 s block. The attended condition was implemented by setting $I_{ij}^{PP,A}$ equal to 0.07 for the locations associated with the lower left stimulus and zero elsewhere. Figure 6.15 shows the results of the computational simulations for a sequential stimulation block: BLK–EXP–SEQ(attended)–BLK–SIM–BLK–EXP–SIM(attended)–SEQ–BLK. These results should be compared with the experimental fMRI signal evolution shown in Fig. 6.6 for area V4.

As found in the experiments of Kastner et al. (1999), the simulations also showed that the fMRI signals were smaller during the SIM than during the SEQ presentations in the unattended conditions, because of the mutual suppression induced by competitively interacting stimuli. On the other hand, the average fMRI signals with attention increased more strongly for simultaneously presented stimuli than the corresponding ones for sequentially presented stimuli. Thus, the suppressive interactions were partially cancelled out by attention. Finally, during the expectation period activation increased in the absence of visual presentations, and further increased after the onset of visual stimuli.

In summary, these results demonstrate that the cortical attentional architecture described in Sections 6.6 and 6.13 shows and explains the typical dynamical competition and attention modulating effects found in attention experiments, even at the level of gross brain area activation as measured with fMRI (Corchs and Deco 2002).

6.8 The role of attention in object recognition and visual search

We now consider how the role of attention in object recognition and visual search can be understood with this quantitative approach. We concentrate on the macroscopic[26] level

---

[26]Physicists distinguish levels of analysis, and Rolls and Deco (2002) use microscopic to refer to the neuronal level, mesoscopic to refer to an intermediate level of activation of brain areas as shown for example by fMRI, and macroscopic to refer to the behaviour of the whole organism as measured for example in psychophysical experiments.

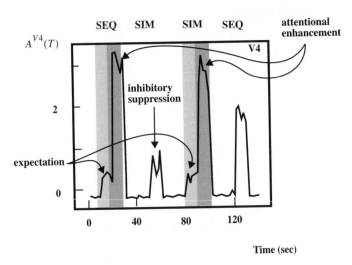

Fig. 6.15 Computer simulations of fMRI signals in module V4 based on the experiments of Kastner et al. (1999). Light shading indicates the expectation period, dark shading the attended presentations, and blocks without shading correspond to the unattended condition. See text and Section 6.4 for details. (After Corchs and Deco 2002; and Rolls and Deco 2002.)

of analysis, and consider the interplay between the microscopic neuronal dynamics and the macroscopic functional behaviour in object recognition and visual search. These two different functions of visual perception can be explained in a unifying fashion by our neurodynamical model of the visual cortical system (as described in Section 6.6).

A phenomenological description of these two perceptual functions is presented schematically in Fig. 6.16 in the context of a natural scene.

In the case of object recognition, a particular location in the natural scene is a priori specified with the aim of identification of the object which lies at that position. Therefore, object recognition asks for 'what' is at a predefined particular spatial location. In the naive framework of the spotlight metaphor, one can describe the role of attention in object recognition by imagining that the prespecification of the particular spatial location is realized by fixing an attentional window or spotlight at that position. The features inside the fixed attentional window should now be bounded and recognized. On the other hand, in visual search, a given target object (composed of a set of shape features) is a priori specified with the goal of finding out whether the target object is present in the scene and, if so, at which location. Consequently, visual search asks for 'where' a predefined set of shape features is located. A naive description of visual search in the framework of the spotlight paradigm considers that during visual search, attentional mechanisms shift a window through the entire scene in order to serially search for the target object at different positions. The neurodynamical system described in Section 6.6 was tested in these two modes of operation: **object recognition** in an attended spatial location (spatial attention); and **visual search** of a target object (object attention), as shown and described in Fig. 6.12 on page 407. The input image was the scene shown in Fig. 6.16. The objects to be identified and located were the sculpture, and the top of the tower as indicated in the image. In the following two subsections, we will describe the dynamics of object recognition and visual search under these two modes of attention.

The thrust of our computational neuroscience approach to attention, and the particular model we describe in Section 6.6, is that it shows how spatial and object attention mechanisms

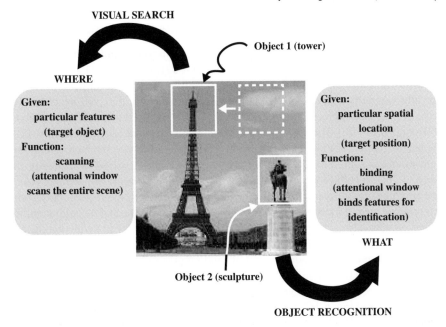

Fig. 6.16 The role of attentional mechanisms in object recognition and visual search in a natural scene. In the case of object recognition, a particular location in the natural scene is *a priori* specified with the aim of identification of the object which lies at that position. On the other hand, in visual search, a given target object (i.e. shape features) is *a priori* specified with the goal of finding out whether the target object is present in the scene and, if so, at which location. (After Rolls and Deco 2002; and Deco and Lee 2004.)

can be integrated and function as a unitary system in visual search and visual recognition tasks. The dynamical intra- and inter-modular interactions in our cortical model implement attentional top-down feedback mechanisms that embody a physiologically plausible system of active vision unifying in this way different perceptual functions. In our system, attention is a dynamical emergent property, rather than a separate mechanism operating independently of other perceptual and cognitive processes. The dynamical mechanisms that define our system work across the visual field in parallel, but due to the different latencies of settling due to the intra- and intermodular dynamics, actually exhibit temporal properties like those normally described as 'serial' or 'parallel' when used to describe visual search (see Section 6.10). (The whole system was described by Deco and Rolls (2004) and is illustrated in Fig. 4.66, and the simulation illustrated in Figs. 6.17 and 6.18 is a simplified simulation including only the IT–V1–PP modules performed by Deco and Lee (2004) just to show the main aspects of the dynamics.)

The model accounts for a number of the temporal properties of serial search tasks found psychophysically without either an explicit serial scanning process with an attentional spot-light, or a saliency map. The following two subsections 6.8.1 and 6.8.2 show how these properties arise. In doing this, the model offers new insight into how attention may actually work, and goes beyond the biased competition hypothesis not only by showing how the 'what' and 'where' visual processing streams interact, and how the system operates quantitatively, but also by providing a direct approach to the temporal properties of the system, leading to a new conceptualization of what was described previously as serial and parallel search.

6.8.1   Dynamics of spatial attention and object recognition

In the object recognition task, the system functioned in a **spatial attention mode** as shown in
Fig. 6.12a (see Deco and Lee (2002), Rolls and Deco (2002) and Deco and Lee (2004)). Spatial
attention was initiated by introducing a bias to a cell pool coding for a particular location,
and the aim was to perform object recognition for the object at the cued location. (This is
therefore also termed 'object identification mode'.) The input system processed a pixelized
66×66 image ($N = 66$). The V1 hypercolumns covered the entire image uniformly. They are
distributed in 33×33 locations ($P = 33$) and each hypercolumn was sensitive to three spatial
frequencies and to eight different orientations (i.e. $K = 3$ and $L = 8$). Consequently, the V1
module had 26,136 pools and three inhibitory pools. The IT module utilized had two pools
and one common inhibitory pool. Finally, the PP module contained 4,356 pools corresponding
to each possible spatial location, i.e. to each of the 66×66 pixels, and a common inhibitory
pool. Two objects (also shown in Fig. 6.16) were isolated in order to define two categories
to be associated with two different pools in the IT module. During the learning phase, these
two objects were presented randomly and at random positions in order to learn translation
invariant responses. The system required 1,000,000 different presentations for training the IT
pools. We used $\tau = \tau_P = 10$ ms and $T_r = 1$ ms.

When the image (Fig. 6.16) was presented, the spatial bias acting from the PP module as
a top-down effect on the V1 module facilitated V1 responses at the attended location. Any
features in the input image at that location produced larger responses in V1. This enhancement
of neural activity to some features in V1 effectively gated information in that area of the V1
module to the IT module for recognition (and in this way also performed a type of shift
invariance by using an attentional spatial modulation of early visual cortical processing).
When the spatially highlighted image patch contained features of one of the trained object
classes, the activity of the IT cell pools started to polarize in response to the features that were
part of one of the trained objects, resulting in only one cell pool surviving the competition.
The winner indicated the object class being recognized, identifying 'what was where', or
'what from where'. Thus object identification in IT was achieved by a spatial bias from PP
interacting with the image representation in V1.

The actual simulation results just outlined are shown in Fig. 6.17, which demonstrates
the neuronal activities in the three modules during object recognition in the spatial attention
mode[27]. The average population activity of the three modules at the sculpture location was
compared against the activity in all other locations when the spatial attention was allocated
to the sculpture location by the PP spatial input bias. Spatial attention allocated in the dorsal
stream PP module ultimately led to the dominance of the sculpture neurons' activity in
the ventral stream IT module. The bifurcation of the maximum activities in different pools
showed the propagation of the spatial attentional effect across the different modules. The
effect of attention, as indicated by the polarization of the responses, started at the dorsal
stream PP module, then propagated to the early stage V1 module, and then to the ventral
stream IT module. The relative time of onset of the attentional effect was not distinguishable
between the V1 module and the IT module because the attention-related computation in the V1
module and the IT module was concurrent and interactive. The polarization and stabilization
of neuronal pool activity in the IT module corresponded to recognition of the object in
the attended location. By moving the attentional spotlight to different spatial locations, the
system can gate information at different spatial locations to the IT module, realizing a form

---

[27] In the presentation of this and all subsequent simulations, we introduced a delay of 40 ms in the response
of the early module neurons relative to stimulus onset. This is because physiologically there is typically a 40 ms
delay between the presentation of the stimulus and the onset of V1 neurons' responses (Lee, Mumford, Romero and
Lamme 1998) (see Section B.6.6).

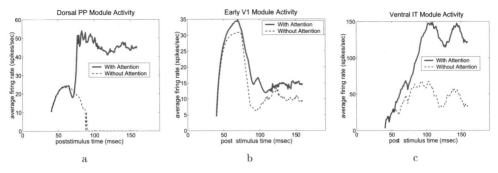

Fig. 6.17 Effect of spatial attention on neural activities in the three modules when performing object recognition. A top-down spatial attentional bias was introduced to the dorsal PP module pool that encodes the location of the sculpture in the scene (curves marked 'With Attention'), or there was no attentional input (curves marked 'Without Attention'). The responses of neuronal pools in the corresponding locations in the dorsal stream PP module and the V1 module, and the response of the neuronal pool encoding the sculpture in the ventral stream IT module were compared with and without spatial attention. (a) The evolution of the neuronal pool response at the dorsal stream PP module with and without the top-down spatial attentional bias. When the top-down bias was absent, the competition in the dorsal stream PP module was entirely determined by the bottom-up signals from V1. In this case, the sculpture shape did not provide the strongest input and was rapidly suppressed by the competitive interactions from the neuronal activities in the other locations in the scene. When there was a top-down spatial bias to the PP neuronal pool, the neuronal pool's activity rose rapidly and was maintained at a sustained level. (b) The increase in the activity of the neuronal pool in the dorsal stream PP module enhanced the activity at the corresponding retinotopic location in the early V1 module, particularly in the latter phase of the response, producing a highlighting effect. (c) The response of the ventral stream IT module neuron pool coding for the sculpture was substantially stronger when the spatial attention bias to the PP module was allocated to the location of the sculpture than when there was no spatial attention. The spatial highlighting gated the sculpture image to be analyzed and recognized by the ventral stream IT module neurons. Without spatial attention, the sculpture did not have bottom-up saliency to enable the domination of the sculpture neuron in the ventral stream IT module. (After Rolls and Deco 2002; and Deco and Lee 2004.)

of translation-invariant object recognition. Interestingly, a relatively small elevation in the V1 module was sufficient to bias the IT module cell pools to produce a large polarization in their responses.

It is important to emphasize that no explicit spotlight of attention is forced onto every module in the system in our model. Instead, given just a bias to one of the modules (in this case the spatial PP module), parallel and global dynamical evolution of the entire system converges to a state where a spotlight of attention in PP appears, and is explicitly used (even while it is emerging) to modulate the information processing channel for object recognition. Effectively spatial effects influence the function of the non-spatially organized IT ventral stream module through modulatory effects on information processing implemented through the topologically organized V1 module. An interesting aspect of our theory is that the process of object recognition can be influenced by spatial attention arising from a global dynamical continuing interaction between all the processing modules involved. Of course each local brain area has a defined functional role, but interesting global attention-related behaviour emerges from the constant cross-talk between the different modules in the ventral and dorsal visual paths, implemented partly through the early processing areas such as V1, using backprojections as well as forward connections.

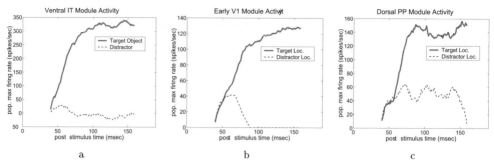

Fig. 6.18 Neuronal activities in the three modules during visual search in object attention mode. The maximum population activity of the neuronal pools corresponding to the identity or location of the sculpture in the scene in the three modules was compared against the maximum activity in pools coding any other locations or objects when the sculpture was the target object of attention. The effect of attention, i.e. differentiation of neuronal response between the target and distractor conditions, was observed to start at the ventral stream IT module, and then to propagate to the early V1 module and the dorsal stream PP module. (a) The neuronal activity of the top-down biased 'sculpture' neuronal pool in the ventral-stream module was compared against the maximum activity of all other object pools. The increase in the response of the sculpture pool relative to the response in all other pools was observed to rise rapidly as a result of the top-down object attentional bias applied to the IT module. (b) The maximum population activity at the sculpture location in the early V1 visual module was compared against the maximum activity of pools at all other locations in the scene. (c) The maximum activity of the pools coding in the dorsal stream PP module for the sculpture location was compared against the maximum activity of the pools encoding the other locations. (After Rolls and Deco 2002; and Deco and Lee 2004.)

6.8.2 Dynamics of object attention and visual search

In the visual search task, i.e. when the system was looking for a particular object in a visual scene, the system functioned in an **object attention mode** as shown in Fig. 6.12b (see Deco and Lee (2002), Rolls and Deco (2002) and Deco and Lee (2004)). Object attention was created by introducing a top-down bias to a particular cell pool in the IT module corresponding to a particular object class (as will be described in more detail below with Fig. 6.18). This ventral IT module pool backprojected the expected shape activity patterns over all spatial positions in the early V1 visual module through the top-down feedback connections. When the image (Fig. 6.16) containing the target object was presented, the hypercolumns in the early V1 visual module whose activities were closest to the top-down 'template' became more excited because of the interactive activation or resonance between the forward visual inputs and the backprojected activity from the IT module. Over time, these V1 hypercolumns with neuronal activities best matching the encoded object dominated over all the other hypercolumns, resulting in a spatially localized response peak in the early V1 visual module. Meanwhile, the dorsal PP module was not idle but actively participated by having all its pools engaged in the competitive process to narrow down the location of the target. The simultaneous competition in the spatial domain and in the object domain in the two extrastriate modules as mediated by their reciprocal connections with the early V1 module finally resulted in a localized peak of activation in the spatially mapped dorsal stream PP module, with a corresponding peak of activity for the object mapped in the ventral stream IT module, and corresponding activity in the early V1 module. This corresponds to finding the object's location in the image in a visual search task, or linking 'where is what', or computing 'where' from 'what'.

The actual simulation results just outlined are shown in Fig. 6.18, which compares the responses of the pools in the three modules corresponding to the location or identity of the attended object (the sculpture) to the responses at all other locations or identities. The evolution of the population maximum activity shows the polarization of responses that started in the ventral stream IT module, and then propagated to the other two modules. In this case, the attentional object bias was applied to the IT module, and this then propagated to the V1 module where features relevant to the object were biased on. This top-down bias interacted with features in the scene, resulting in larger activation of the features that were present in the object. However, because V1 is topologically mapped, the location of the features was contained in the V1 activations, and these then influenced the PP module to gradually settle at the location with extra activity in V1. Thus just providing object bias to the V1 module resulted in the spatial location of the object being made explicit in the PP module as a result of the interaction with the image representation provided for in V1.

It should be emphasized that because the V1 visual module interacted with both the PP and the IT modules simultaneously, the attentional effect observed in the later response of the neurons was not purely spatial or featural, but involved both components simultaneously. In the spatial attention mode, the PP module's bias initially highlighted the V1 module's response at a particular location, then the IT module got drawn into the process, and competition in the IT module, combined with the ongoing interaction via the reciprocal connections between the PP module and the IT module, produced the enhancement effect in the V1 module.

A similar situation also appeared in the object attention mode. An object attention effect of this magnitude has been observed in V4, but not in V1. We reduced the magnitude of the coupling between the early V1 module and the ventral IT module, and found that the system continues to perform well in the visual search task when the coupling strength is reduced from 1 to 0.4. With this coupling strength, the effect of object attention in V1 is more modest, and yet it can still produce a bias that leads to the emergence of a peak response at the dorsal stream PP module's spatial location map.

6.9 The neuronal and biophysical mechanisms of attention: linking computational and single-neuron data

The theoretical framework described in Section 6.6 and in detail by Rolls and Deco (2002) and Deco and Lee (2004) provides an account of a potential functional role for the backprojection connections in the visual cortex in visual attention. We now consider how closely this approach can account for the responses of single neurons in the system, and how well a detailed implementation of the model at the neuronal level can lead to the overall functional properties described above in Section 6.8. We then show that the same theoretical framework and model can also be directly related to psychophysical data on serial vs parallel processing (Section 6.10), and to neuropsychological data (Section 6.11). The framework and model operate in the same way to account for findings at all these levels of investigation, and in this sense provide a unifying framework.

Deco and Lee (2004) and Corchs and Deco (2002) (see Rolls and Deco (2002)) showed a long-latency enhancement effect on V1 units in the model under top-down attentional modulation (see Figs. 6.17 and 6.18) which is similar to the long-latency contextual modulation effects observed in early visual cortex (Lamme 1995, Zipser, Lamme and Schiller 1996, Lee et al. 1998, Roelfsema et al. 1998, Lee, Yang, Romero and Mumford 2002b). Interestingly, in our simulation, we found that the observed spatial or object attentional enhancement is stronger for weaker stimuli. This predicted result has been confirmed neurophysiologically by Reynolds, Pastemak and Desimone (2000). The mechanism for this may be that the top-down attentional influence can dominate the firing of the neurons relatively more as there are fewer feedforward forcing and shunting effects on the neurons. An extension of this model (Deco and Rolls 2004) can account for the reduced receptive fields of inferior temporal cortex neurons in natural scenes (Rolls, Aggelopoulos and Zheng 2003a), and makes predictions about how the receptive fields are affected by interactions of features within them, and by object-based attention (see Section 4.5.9.2 and Fig. 4.66 on page 361).

The model has also been extended to the level of spiking neurons which allows biophysical properties of the ion channels affected by synapses, and of the membrane dynamics, to be incorporated, and shows how the non-linear interactions between bottom-up effects (produced for example by altering stimulus contrast) and top-down attentional effects can account for new neurophysiological results in areas MT and V4 (Deco and Rolls 2005b). The model and simulations show that attention has its major modulatory effect at intermediate levels of bottom-up input, and that the effect of attention disappears at low and high levels of contrast of the competing stimulus. The model assumed no kind of multiplicative attentional effects on the gain of neuronal responses. Instead, in the model, both top-down attention and bottom-up input information (contrast) are implemented in the same way, via additive synaptic effects in the postsynaptic neurons. There is of course a non-linearity in the effective activation function of the integrate-and-fire neurons, and this is what we identify as the source of the apparently multiplicative effects (Martinez-Trujillo and Treue 2002) of top-down attentional biases on bottom-up inputs. The relevant part of the effective activation function of the neurons (the relation between the firing and the injected excitatory currents) is the threshold non-linearity, and the first steeply rising part of the activation function, where just above threshold the firing increases markedly with small increases in synaptic inputs (cf. Amit and Brunel (1997) and Brunel and Wang (2001)). Attention could therefore alternatively be interpreted as a phenomenon that results from purely additive synaptic effects, non-linear effects in the neurons, and cooperation–competition dynamics in the network, which together yield a variety of modulatory effects, including effects that appear (Martinez-Trujillo and Treue 2002) to be multiplicative. In addition, we were able to show that the non-linearity of the NMDA receptors may facilitate non-linear attentional effects, but is not necessary for them. This was shown by disabling the voltage-dependent non-linearity of the NMDA receptors in the simulations (Deco and Rolls 2005b).

More detail is now provided about the integrate-and-fire model of attention described by Deco and Rolls (2005b), as it shows how attentional processes can be understood at the neuronal and biophysical level. The design of the experiments and the different measures as implemented in our simulations are shown graphically in Fig. 6.19. Figure 6.19 shows the experimental design of Reynolds and Desimone (2003) and the architecture we used to simulate the results. They measured the neuronal response in V4, manipulating the contrast of the non-preferred stimulus and comparing the response to both stimuli when attention was allocated to the poor stimulus. They observed that the attentional suppressive effect of the competing non-preferred stimulus is higher when the contrast of that stimulus increases. In our simulations we measured neuronal responses from neurons in pool S1' in V4 to a preferred and a non-preferred stimulus simultaneously presented within the receptive field. We manipulated the contrast of the stimulus that was non-preferred for the neurons S1' (in the simulation by altering λ_{in} to S2). We analysed the effects of this manipulation for two conditions, namely without spatial attention, or with spatial attention on the non-preferred stimulus S2 implemented by adding an extra bias λ_{att} to S2.

Figure 6.20 (top) shows the results of our simulations for the design of Reynolds and Desimone (2003). We observed that the attentional suppressive effect implemented through λ_{att} on the responses of neurons S1' of the competing non-preferred stimulus is higher when the contrast of the non-preferred stimulus increases, as in the original neurophysiological experiments. The top figure shows the response of a V4 neuron to different log contrast levels

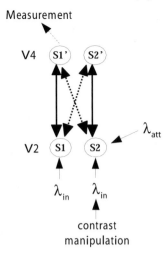

Fig. 6.19 Interaction between salience (contrast, a bottom-up influence) and attention (a top-down influence) in an integrate-and-fire model of biased competition. The architecture shows that used to model the neurophysiological experiment of Reynolds and Desimone (2003). In the model we measured neuronal responses from neurons in pool S1′ in V4 to a preferred and a non-preferred stimulus simultaneously presented within the receptive field. We manipulated the contrast of the stimulus that was non-preferred for the neurons S1′ (in the simulation by altering λ_{in} to S2). We analysed the effects of this manipulation for two conditions, namely without spatial attention or with spatial attention on the non-preferred stimulus S2 (implemented in these simulations by applying an extra bias λ_{att} to S2 from an external top-down source). We observed that the attentional suppressive effect implemented through λ_{att} on the responses of neurons S1′ of the competing non-preferred stimulus is higher when the contrast of the non-preferred stimulus increases, as in the original neurophysiological experiments. (After Deco and Rolls 2005b.)

(abscissa) in the no-attention condition (AO: attending outside the receptive field) and in the attention condition (AI: attending inside the receptive field). The top right part of Fig. 6.20 shows the difference between both conditions. As in the experimental observations the suppressive effect of the competing non-preferred stimulus is higher when the contrast of that stimulus increases, but at higher levels of salience (contrast), the top-down attentional effect disappears.

In order to study the relevance of NMDA synapses for the inter-area cortical dynamics of attention, we repeated the analysis shown in Fig. 6.20 (top), but with the voltage-dependent non-linearity removed from the NMDA receptors (in the feedforward, the feedback, and the recurrent collateral connections) by setting $[Mg^{2+}] = 0$ (which corresponds to removing the non-linear dependence of the NMDA synapses on the postsynaptic potential, see Deco and Rolls (2005b)). (We compensated for the effective change of synaptic strength by rerunning the mean field analysis to obtain the optimal parameters for the simulation, which was produced with $J_f = 1.6$ and $J_b = 0.42$, and then with these values, we reran the simulation.) The results are shown in Fig. 6.20 (middle), where it is clear that the same attentional effects can be found in exactly the same qualitative and even quantitative form as when the non-linear property of NMDA receptors is operating. The implication is that the non-linearity of the effective activation function (firing rate as a function of input current to a neuron) of the neurons (both the threshold and its steeply rising initial part) implicit in the integrate-and-fire model with AMPA and other receptors is sufficient to enable non-linear attentional interaction effects with bottom-up inputs to be produced. The non-linearity of the NMDA receptor may facilitate this process by its non-linearity, but is not necessary.

Deco and Rolls (2005b) further studied the relevance of the NMDA receptors by repeating

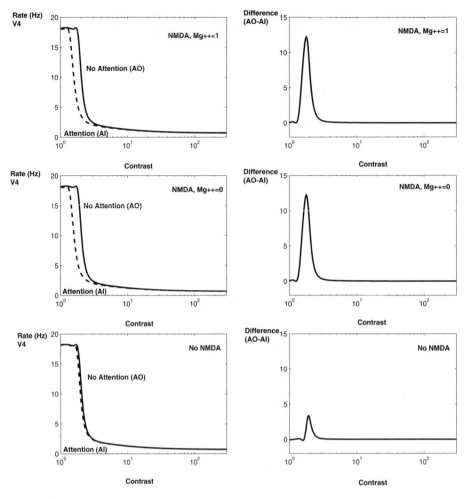

Fig. 6.20 (Top): results of our simulations for the effect of interaction between contrast and attention after the design of Reynolds and Desimone (2003). The left figure shows the response of V4 neurons to different log contrast levels (abscissa) in the no-attention condition (AO: attending outside the receptive field), and in the attention condition (AI: attending inside the receptive field) (see legend to Fig. 6.19). The right figure shows the difference between both conditions. As in the experimental observations the suppressive effect of the competing non-preferred stimulus is higher when the contrast of that stimulus increases, but at higher levels of salience (contrast) the attentional effect disappears. Middle: as top, but with the NMDA receptor non-linearity removed by setting $[Mg^{2+}] = 0$. Bottom: as top, but with the NMDA receptor time constants set to the same values as those of the AMPA receptors (see text). (After Deco and Rolls 2005b.)

the analysis in Fig. 6.20 (top), but with the time constants of the NMDA receptors set to be the same values as those of the AMPA receptors (and as in Fig. 6.20 (middle) with the NMDA voltage-dependent effects disabled by setting $[Mg^{2+}] = 0$. (We again compensated for the effective change of synaptic strength by rerunning the mean field analysis to obtain the optimal parameters for the simulation.) The results are shown in Fig. 6.20 (bottom), where it is shown that top-down attentional effects are now very greatly reduced. (That is, there is very little difference between the no-attention condition (AO: attending outside the receptive field), and the attention condition (AI: attending inside the receptive field).) This effect is not just because the NMDA receptor system with its long time constant may play a generic role in the operation of the integrate-and-fire system, by facilitating stability and helping to prevent oscillations, for a similar failure of attention to operate normally was also found with the mean field approach, in which the stability of the system is not an issue. Thus the long time constant of NMDA receptors does appear to be an important factor in enabling top-down attentional processes to modulate correctly the bottom-up effects to account for the effects of attention on neuronal activity. This is an interesting result which deserves further analysis. Deco and Rolls (2005b) did show that the mean field equation that effectively defines the non-linear transfer function of the neurons will be affected by the long time constant of the NMDA receptors.

These investigations thus show how attentional processes can be understood by the interactions between top-down and bottom-up influences on non-linear processes operating within neurons, and how these processes in turn impact the performance of large separate populations of interacting neurons.

6.10 Linking computational and psychophysical data: 'serial' vs 'parallel' processing

6.10.1 'Serial' vs 'parallel' search

In the visual search tasks we consider, subjects examine a display containing randomly positioned items in order to detect an *a priori* defined target (i.e. a target that the subject is paying attention to and must search for), and other items in the display which are different from the target serve the role of distractors. In a feature search task the target differs from the distractors in one single feature, e.g. only colour. In a conjunction search task the target is defined by a conjunction of features, and each distractor shares at least one of those features with the target. Conjunction search experiments show that search time increases linearly with the number of items in the display, which has been taken to imply a serial process, such as an attentional spotlight moving from item to item in the display (Treisman 1988). An example of a display with this 'serial' search is shown in Fig. 6.21b, in which an E is the target and Fs are the distractors. On the other hand, search times in a feature search can be independent of the number of items in the display, and this is described as a preattentive parallel search (Treisman 1988) (see further (Deco and Zihl 2001b, Rolls and Deco 2002, Deco and Lee 2004)). An example of a display with this 'parallel' search is shown in Fig. 6.21a, in which an E is the target and Xs are the distractors.

In more detail, the stimulus in Fig. 6.21a contains shapes E and X. Because the elementary features in E and X are distinct, i.e. their component lines have different orientations, E pops out from X, and its location can be rapidly localized independently of the number of distracting X shapes in the image. On the other hand, the stimulus in Fig. 6.21b contains E and F. Since both letters are composed of vertical and horizontal lines, there is no difference in elementary features to produce a preattentive pop-out, so they can be distinguished from each other only after their features are glued together by attention. It has been thought that because 'attention' is serial, the time required to localize the target in such an image increases linearly with the number of distractors in the image. The serial movement of the attentional spotlight has been thought to be governed by a *saliency map* or *priority map* for registering the potentially interesting areas in the retinal input and directing a *gating* mechanism for selecting information for further processing. Does the linear increase in search time observed in visual search tests necessarily imply a serial search process, a saliency map, or a gating mechanism? Could both

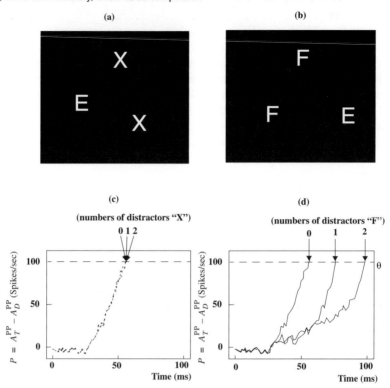

Fig. 6.21 (a) Parallel search example: an image that contains a target E in a field of X distractors. Since the elementary features in E and X are distinct, i.e. their component lines have different orientations, E pops out from X, and its location can be rapidly localized independently of the number of distracting X shapes in the image. This is called parallel search. (b) Serial search example: an image that contains a target E in a field of F distractors. Since both letters are composed of vertical and horizontal lines, there is no difference in the elementary features to produce a preattentive pop-out, so the E and F can be distinguished from each other only after their features are bound or glued by attention. The time required to locate the target in such an image increases linearly with the number of distractors in the image. This is called serial search and has been thought to involve the scanning of the scene with a covert attentional spotlight. (c – d) Simulation result of the network performing visual search on images (a) and (b) respectively. The difference (polarization) between the maximum activity in the neuronal pool corresponding to the target locations and the maximum activity of all other neuronal pools in the dorsal PP module is plotted as a function of time. (c) shows that the difference signal rose to a threshold, corresponding to localization of the object, at about the same time independently of the numbers of distractor items. (d) shows that the time for the polarization signal to rise to a threshold increased linearly with the number of distracting items, with an additional 25 ms required per item. (After Rolls and Deco 2002; and Deco and Lee 2004.)

the serial and the parallel search phenomena be explained by a single parallel neurodynamical process, without the extra serial control mechanism?

To investigate this issue, the stimuli shown in Fig. 6.21a and Fig. 6.21b were presented to the network described in Section 6.6, which had been trained to recognize X, E, and F in a translation invariant manner (Deco and Zihl 2001b, Rolls and Deco 2002). The aim was to find the location of the E in the display. The system received a top-down bias for the 'E' pool in the ventral IT module, and then was presented with stimuli containing E in a variable number of X shapes, or E in a variable number of F shapes. Let us use polarization, the difference between the maximal activity of the pools indicating the E location and that indicating the F location, i.e. $P = A_{\mathrm{T}}^{\mathrm{PP}} - A_{\mathrm{D}}^{\mathrm{PP}}$, as a measure to determine whether detection and localization

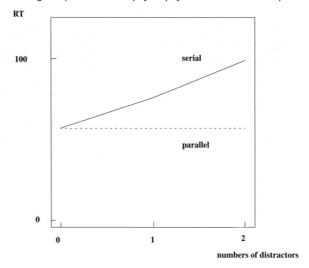

Fig. 6.22 Simulated reaction times (RT) for different types and numbers of distractors from the results shown in Fig. 6.21c and 6.21d for 'parallel' and 'serial' search examples. (After Rolls and Deco 2002; and Deco and Lee 2004 who show similar results for up 16 distractors.)

of the target had been achieved or not. We found that for the E in X case, the time required for the polarization to reach a certain threshold in the dorsal PP module was almost identical whether the number of X shapes was equal to 0, 1, or 2, as shown in Fig. 6.21c. On the other hand, when E and F were presented, the time required for polarization to reach threshold increased linearly with the number of distracting items. Although the system was running with the same parallel dynamics, it took an additional 25 ms for each additional distractor added to the stimulus as shown in Fig. 6.21d.

Figure 6.22 shows explicitly the simulated reaction times as a function of the number of distractors for both types of search. The system works across the visual field in parallel, but, due to the different dynamic latencies, resembles the two apparent different modes of visual attention, namely: serial focal search, and parallel search. In the case of serial search, the latency of the dynamics is longer indicating 'apparently' a serial component in the search, although the underlying mechanisms work in parallel. The typical linear increase in the search time with the display size is clearly obtained as the result of a slower convergence (latency) of the dynamics. In this case, the strong competition present in V1 and propagated to PP delays the convergence of the dynamics. The strong competition in the feature extraction module V1 is finally resolved by the feedback received from PP. In other words, stimulus similarity in the feature space is decided by competition mechanisms at the intra-modular level of V1 and at the inter-modular level of V1–PP.

The results of the simulations are consistent with psychophysical results (Quinlan and Humphreys 1987). Although the whole simulation is parallel, and involves no serial moving spotlight process, the search takes longer with more distractors because the constraints are then more difficult to satisfy, and the dynamics of the coupled set of networks takes longer to settle. (The constraints are more difficult to satisfy in the E vs F search task in that the features, which include oriented line elements, are more similar to each other in the E vs F case than in the E vs X case.) The linear increase in time observed in 'serial search' in the E–F case reflects simply the fact that when features are similar between objects, the similarity in the stimuli's representations in V1 will require more time for the competition to sort out the target against the distractors. This sorting out at the level of V1 requires a constant interaction with both the ventral stream IT and the dorsal stream PP pathways in the emergent process of the integration and combination of different features to form a shape.

This is an important result, for it provides direct computational evidence that some apparently serial cognitive tasks may in fact be performed by fully parallel processing neuronal networks with realistic dynamics. *It is proposed that for many computations that have been thought to be serial by the brain, the computation is in fact fully parallel, but as the constraints become more difficult, the dynamical system takes longer to settle into an attractor basin.* Further evidence comes from the analysis of feature conjunction search considered in Section 6.10.2. Another example of increasing reaction times due to longer settling into an attractor basin as a decision task becomes more difficult is provided in Chapter 7.

6.10.2 Visual conjunction search

Deco, Pollatos and Zihl (2002) extended the approach just described to deal with serial search when there are conjunctions of different numbers of features (see Rolls and Deco (2002)). An example of a conjunction search is a search for an object with a particular feature shape and colour, when the distractors are different combinations of the possible colours and shapes. A feature search is when the target differs from the distractor by a single feature dimension, e.g. shape.

The approaches to *visual conjunction search* are as follows (Rolls and Deco 2002). In the analysis of the visual perception of objects, we can usually decompose perceptual objects into general feature components that are not unique for a particular object. Put differently, the individuality of objects results from the specific composition of elementary features and their spatial relations rather than from the specificity of the component features (see Section 4.3). Therefore, the brain should be able to represent objects by representing each elementary feature component and binding together the feature components constituting a particular object to distinguish them from features of other objects. The problem of grouping together the single feature components constituting an individual object is the so-called binding problem (Treisman and Gelade 1980, Treisman 1988, Gray and Singer 1987, Gray and Singer 1989, Eckhorn, Bauer, Jordan, Brosch, Munk and Reitboeck 1988). In brief, the binding problem in perception deals with the question of how we specify what goes with what and where, in order to achieve the perception of a coherent integration of shape, colour, movement, and size in individual objects. Three main theories have been formulated for achieving such linking of features corresponding to individual objects. The first theory (see Section 4.3.5 and Barlow (1972)) assumes the existence of a convergence of connections from neurons which respond to different elementary feature dimensions onto higher-order neurons that react to a specific combination of features. The highest level corresponds to a grandmother neuron, which responds only when a specific object is presented. Perrett, Rolls and Caan (1982) and Tanaka (1996) have shown that some single neurons in area IT respond specifically to relatively complex combination of features. These neurons are sensitive to the spatial arrangement of the features in the objects, and thus the features must be bound together with the correct spatial relations (Rolls, Tovee, Purcell, Stewart and Azzopardi 1994b, Tanaka 1996). A potential problem of this approach is the combinatorial explosion of the number of grandmother neurons required for the specific selection of all possible objects (i.e. of all possible combinations of single features) (Barlow 1972). It is shown in Chapter 4 that a solution to this potential problem is to form neurons that encode only low-order combinations of features, to utilize a multilayer hierarchical network architecture, and to take advantage of the statistical regularities of natural images.

A second alternative theory assumes temporal encoding, and has been considered in Sections 4.5.5.1 and C.3.7.

The third theory suggests a possible mechanism for binding across dimensions through shared spatial locations (Treisman 1982, Treisman 1988). The idea is that one can code one object at a time, selected on the basis of its location at an early level where receptive fields are small. Spatial attentional mechanisms select that location by temporarily excluding stimuli from other spatial locations. All feature dimensions currently attended to are therefore bound. (A limitation of this approach is that it does not actually define the spatial relations between the parts, as the theory was developed to deal with for example binding colour and shape in a way which might be needed to distinguish a red triangle from a green square. In contrast, the theory developed in Chapter 4 does enable the spatial relations between features to be specified in the encoding scheme, as addressed specifically in Section 4.5.5.) In this Section (6.10.2) though, we consider how local spatial attentional mechanisms can help to ameliorate the binding problem. The argument is as follows. The mutual biasing attentional interaction between the posterior parietal module, and the different early level modules (V1, V2, V4, ...) coding independent feature dimensions, put 'what' and 'where' together. The neural activity that dynamically emerges in the posterior parietal cortex selects a spatial location that is effectively object-based, and links together (or selectively enhances) the corresponding elementary features (shape, colour, motion, etc.). This is achieved by modulating the neural activity in the respective feature maps, so that only neurons associated with the spatially attended location remain active, and by temporarily suppressing the response of the other neurons corresponding to objects at other locations. Consequently, only the attended features corresponding to one object will be further analyzed at the object perception level implemented by the inferotemporal module. We suggest that illusory conjunctions[28] arise when this attentional process is given insufficient time to settle dynamically to allow high activity to occur only in corresponding locations in for example separate feature and colour maps.

The architecture developed to understand conjunction search in the context of the model described in Section 6.6 extended that model by including for every location in the visual field different feature maps in the V1 module, for shape, colour, etc. as shown in Fig. 6.23 (Deco, Pollatos and Zihl 2002, Rolls and Deco 2002). The input retina is given as a matrix of visual items. The location of each item on the retina is specified by two indices ij, describing the position in row i and column j. Different feature maps in the primary visual cortex extract the local values of the features for an item at each position. Some of these maps are the shape-maps given by pools extracting Gabor feature components as described in Section 6.13.

In the model, selective attention results from *independent competition mechanisms operating within each feature dimension*. Let us assume that each visual item can be defined by M features. Each feature m can adopt $N(m)$ values, for example the feature 'colour' can have the values 'black' or 'white' (in this case $N(\text{colour}) = 2$). For each feature map m, there are $N(m)$ layers of neurons characterizing the presence of each feature value. A cell assembly consisting of a population (or pool) of fully connected excitatory neurons (pyramidal cells) is allocated to every location in each layer, in order to encode the presence of a specific feature value (e.g. colour 'white') at the corresponding position. This generates a sparsely distributed representation of the stimulus, in the sense that the activity of a population of neurons represents the presence of different features at a given position. The feature maps are topographically ordered, i.e. the receptive fields of the neurons belonging to cell assembly ij in one of these maps are limited to the location ij in the retinal input. We further assume that the cell assemblies in layers corresponding to one feature dimension are mutually inhibitory (e.g. at a given position the cell assembly coding the colour feature value 'white' inhibits the

---

[28] Illusory conjunctions are situations in which the binding of for example shape and colour occur incorrectly, e.g. when shape and colour may be misattributed between shapes with different colours.

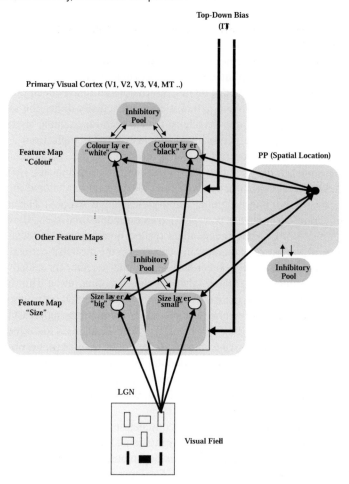

Fig. 6.23 Extended cortical architecture for visual attention and binding of multiple feature components (shape, colour, movement, ...). See text for details. (After Rolls and Deco 2002, and Deco, Pollatos and Zihl 2002.)

cell assembly coding 'black'). Let us denote by $A^{\mathrm{F}}_{pqmn}(t)$ the activity level of an excitatory pool at a location in the visual field, in the feature map m and layer (i.e. value) n.

The posterior parietal module is bidirectionally coupled with the different feature maps and serves to bind the different feature dimensions at each item location, in order to implement local conjunction detectors. The mutual coupling between a pool A^{F}_{pqmn} in the primary visual cortex and a posterior parietal pool A^{PP}_{ij} is defined, as before, by the Gaussian-like topographic connections given by equation 6.8.

We assume that the inferior temporal connections provide top-down information, consisting of the feature values for each feature dimension of the target item. This information is fed into the system by including an extra excitatory input to the corresponding feature layers. For example, if the target is defined as small, vertical, and black, then all the excitatory pools at every location in the layer coding 'small' in the feature map dimension 'size', in the layer coding 'vertical' in the feature map 'orientation', and in the layer coding 'black' in the feature map 'colour' receive an extra excitatory input from the inferior temporal (IT) module.

The neurodynamical equations that regulate the evolution of the extended cortical system are analogous to those in Section 6.13, and are given by Rolls and Deco (2002) and Deco, Pollatos and Zihl (2002).

The dynamical behaviour of the system can be described qualitatively as follows. The dynamics of the system, i.e. the temporal evolution of the activity level of each pool in the feature and posterior parietal maps, yields the formation of a focus of attention without explicitly assuming a spotlight, i.e. without the necessity of assuming a special serial scanning process. At each feature dimension the fixed point of the dynamics is given by a high activation of cell assemblies in the layers coding feature values which are shared by the target and sensitive to locations with items sharing this value. The remaining cell assemblies do not show any important activation. For example, if the target is 'black', in the colour map the activity in the 'white' layer will be suppressed, and the cell assemblies corresponding to 'black' items will be enhanced. This process implements a first competitive mechanism at the level of each feature dimension. The competitive mechanisms in each feature dimension are independent. In a given feature dimension, the pools coding different values (corresponding to different layers) compete at all locations with each other through the lateral inhibition given by the common inhibitory pool associated with the respective feature dimension. Only the pools receiving both excitatory inputs, i.e. the positive top-down input from the inferior temporal (IT) module, and the sensory input associated with the feature value at the corresponding location, will be able to win the competition. Therefore, if we are looking for 'black' objects, then the 'black' pools at locations corresponding to 'black' items will win the competition. *In the posterior parietal map, the populations corresponding to locations which are simultaneously activated to a maximum in all feature dimensions will be enhanced, suppressing the others.* In other words, the location that shows all feature dimensions corresponding to the top-down specification of the target is stimulated, and it will be further enhanced from top-down feedback when the target is at this location. This implements a second competitive mechanism at the level of conjunctive features. The latency of the dynamics, i.e. the speed of convergence, depends on all the competitive mechanisms. A way of analysing convergence is by monitoring the activity state just in the top posterior parietal map, because the state of this module reflects the total state of the dynamics of the system. Convergence depends therefore on the level of conflict within each feature dimension, i.e. on the properties of the distractors.

The whole system analyzes the information at all locations in parallel. Longer search times correspond to slower dynamical convergence at all levels of the parallel processing system without the need to assume a special serial scanning process.

The model was tested by simulating the visual search experiments of Quinlan and Humphreys (1987) involving feature and conjunction search. Let us assume that the items are defined by three feature dimensions ($M = 3$, e.g. size, orientation and colour), each having two values ($N(m) = 2$ for $m = 1, 2, 3$, e.g. size, big/small; orientation, horizontal/vertical; colour, white/black). Figure 6.24 shows examples for each kind of search. For each display size we repeat the experiment 100 times, each time with different randomly generated targets (i.e. different feature conjunctions), at random positions, and randomly generated distractors (depending on the target defined and the type of search task). To show the results, we plot the mean value T of the 100 simulated search times (in milliseconds[29]) as a function of the display size. The search times are defined by the number of simulation steps required for the system to converge.

The results obtained for different types of search are shown in Fig. 6.25. The slopes of the search time vs display size curves for all simulations are consistent with the existing experimental results (Quinlan and Humphreys 1987). In feature search (1,1, illustrated in Fig. 6.24a) the target is detected without any effects of display size on search time. Furthermore,

---

[29]We assume that one timestep update for the model is equivalent to 1 ms.

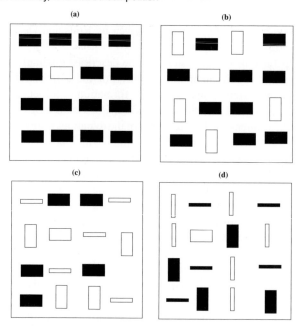

Fig. 6.24 Examples of visual search. The task is to locate the white wide horizontal bar in the display. (a) Feature search (1,1-search). (b) Standard conjunction search (2,1-search). (c) Triple conjunction search with the target differing from all distractors in one feature (3,1-search). (d) Triple conjunction search with the target differing from all distractors in two (3,2-search) features. (After Rolls and Deco 2002, and Deco, Pollatos and Zihl 2002.)

the standard conjunction search (2,1, illustrated in Fig. 6.24b), and triple conjunction search tasks generate reaction times that are a linear function of the display size. The slope of the function for the triple conjunction search task can be steeper or relatively flat, depending upon whether the target differs from the distractors in one (3,1) or two features (3,2), respectively (Deco, Pollatos and Zihl 2002, Rolls and Deco 2002).

The speed for the fully parallel network to settle is fast in the case of the feature search (1,1) because there is only one location, in the white feature map, that receives both top-down bias for the relevant feature values (white, horizontal, and wide in Fig. 6.24a) and bottom-up input from the visual stimulus with the same feature (white). No other feature map shows any polarization towards any particular location because there is no corresponding bottom-up and top-down input that is different for the other locations. Therefore, as only one location (in the white map) has any polarization towards a particular location, that location quickly wins the competition in the PP module. In contrast, in the conjunction searches, there are many locations in the feature maps where two or more bottom-up features from the visual display match features receiving top-down bias. Therefore the PP module, interacting with the feature maps, has to resolve the much more difficult task of selecting the single location where all three bottom-up features match the top-down biases, from many other locations where some feature inputs match in two or more of the feature maps the locations receiving top-down biases from the IT module. The PP module thus has to resolve which of all the conflicting locations across all of the feature maps has the maximal activation when conjoined across all the feature maps. Further, the number of locations in the feature maps that have distractors present with some of the relevant features in the target present increases with the number of distractors in the display, and thus the problem becomes harder with a larger set size, and the network takes longer to settle (see Rolls and Deco (2002) for a more detailed analysis of the settling time

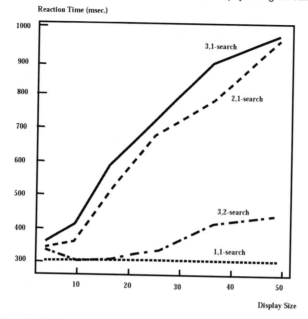

Fig. 6.25 Search times for feature search(1,1), standard conjunction search (2,1), and triple conjunction searches obtained utilizing the extended computational cortical model. (After Rolls and Deco 2002, and Deco, Pollatos and Zihl 2002.)

in the conjunction searches). It is part of the model that the different feature maps do not directly interact at the feature map level, but only through the interaction with the posterior parietal module. Thus the conjunction search involves reciprocal interactions between the feature maps and the PP module. Indeed, the model predicted different slopes for reaction time vs display size for different kinds of conjunction search (depending on the number of distinguishing feature dimensions between target and distractors, and the number of features by which each distractor differs from the target), and these predictions were consistent with psychophysical investigations (Deco, Pollatos and Zihl 2002, Rolls and Deco 2002).

The results of this neurodynamical model thus extend the ideas of Duncan and Humphreys (1989) who used the biased competition mechanism to conceptually explain serial visual search as involving a top-down process influencing the competition between neurons that code for different object attributes in the early visual areas, thus leading to the selection of one object in the visual field. In this section we have seen that our theory can be extended to account for visual conjunction search, with a fully parallel network producing effects that have previously been thought of as being serial (Deco, Pollatos and Zihl 2002, Rolls and Deco 2002).

6.11 Linking computational and neuropsychological data on attention

6.11.1 The neglect syndrome

In neurological patients, unilateral parietal cortex damage can lead to symptoms of the neglect syndrome, in which patients fail to notice objects or events in the hemispace opposite to their lesion site (Humphreys and Riddoch 1994, Vallar and Pernai 1986, Samuelsson, Jensen,

Ekholm, Naver and Blomstrand 1997, Halligan and Marshall 1994, Rafal and Robertson 1995). A significant characteristic of the neglect syndrome is extinction, the failure to perceive a stimulus contralateral to the lesion (contralesional) when a stimulus is simultaneously presented ipsilateral to the lesion (ipsilesional). In fact, extinction indicates that neglect is not caused by a visual sensory defect, but rather by a disorder in visually attending.

Unilateral visual neglect is far from being a unitary phenomenon. Humphreys and Heinke (1998) analyzed different forms of unilateral visual neglect experimentally and theoretically (see also Heinke and Humphreys (1999)). Some patients have deficits in reacting to stimuli presented on one side of space relative to their body (Halligan and Marshall 1994). Let us call this kind of syndrome space-based neglect. Others show a form of neglect that appears to be independent of the spatial location of the object in the visual field relative to the viewer's body (Tipper and Behrmann 1996, Behrmann and Moscovitch 1994, Arguin and Bub 1993, Driver and Halligan 1991, Young, Newcombe and Ellis 1991). For instance, several studies have found that patients may neglect the left side of an object (or perceptual group) whether or not it appears in the left or right hemifield with respect to the patient's body (Humphreys, Olson, Romani and Riddoch 1996, Walker 1995, Halligan and Marshall 1994, Arguin and Bub 1993, Driver, Baylis and Rafal 1992). This kind of visual disorder is called object-based neglect because only the left part of the object is neglected even when the object is rotated so that its left part fell in the right visual hemifield, or the object is translated to the right visual hemifield. In other words, in object-based neglect, parts (left or right) with respect to the object rather than with respect to egocentric space seem to be ignored.

6.11.2 A model of visual spatial neglect

The underlying causes leading to neglect are still not clear (Halligan and Marshall 1994, Rafal and Robertson 1995). A computational systems-level explanation of the neuropsychological findings on visual neglect would help us to better understand the mechanisms underlying the representation of visual space and the control of visual attention in space, and thus, the cognitive functioning of the brain, and disorders of this.

Theoretical models of visual neglect can usually be divided into approaches based on a representational or on an attentional account of the syndrome (Pouget and Driver 1999, Humphreys and Heinke 1998, Bisiach 1996, Driver, Baylis, Goodrich and Rafal 1994). A representational account interprets neglect as the result of impairment of one side of a particular spatial representation, whereas an attentional account considers neglect as a deficit in orienting visual attention to the affected hemispace. The attentional account is strongly favoured by two types of evidence: first, the asymmetrical effect of spatial cueing on neglect (Posner, Walker, Friedrich and Rafal 1984, Rafal and Robertson 1995) (see Section 6.11.3); and second the phenomenon of extinction in the framework of visual search (Eglin, Robertson and Knight 1989) (see Section 6.11.4). In both cases, the degree of impairment increases when the stimulus on the affected side has to compete with a second stimulus on the unaffected side, relative to the condition when only one stimulus is on the affected side. This kind of asymmetry is consistent with the idea that the stimulus in the neglected field attracts attention only in a weak way. In the next subsections, we explain both experimental results in the theoretical framework of our cortical model based on the biased competition hypothesis. Our account of visual neglect is based on different kinds of damage to the posterior parietal module, which is the module representing and controlling the spatial location of visual attention.

Before modelling visual neglect, let us briefly mention the different syndrome of hemi-anopia. Hemianopic patients do not perceive information coming from one hemifield. This kind of disorder can be accounted for by damage to the early visual sensory system, before or at the level of the primary visual cortex. In our model this can be simulated easily by cutting the input coming from the impaired hemifield, or by silencing in the primary module V1 the output of the neuronal pools whose receptive fields cover locations in the impaired hemifield (see Fig. 6.26a). This type of disruption causes the system to behave in the same way as a patient with hemianopia, i.e. the subject will not perceive information coming from one hemifield. Objects or parts of objects falling in the impaired hemifield will be ignored as if they did not exist. This kind of visual disorder is not a true neglect because only the low-level system is disrupted. In fact, patients with damage to the visual system at this level do not show visual neglect, but instead report not being able to see visual stimuli (though some residual visual processing is present perhaps because some visual information can bypass the primary visual cortex (Weiskrantz 1998)).

Let us now concentrate on visual neglect, with fuller accounts provided by Rolls and Deco (2002), Deco and Rolls (2002), Deco and Zihl (2001a), Heinke, Deco, Zihl and Humphreys (2002) and Deco and Zihl (2004). We consider in this section two kinds of neglect: first, space-based; and second, object-based. (The object-based neglect considered in the simulations described next is for the case when there is one object in the visual field, the left half of which is neglected independently of where the object is in the visual field. We discuss the case of two objects in the visual field below.) We show that space-based visual neglect can be explained by unilateral damage to the PP module of our cortical architecture (Deco and Zihl 2001a, Heinke, Deco, Zihl and Humphreys 2002, Rolls and Deco 2002, Deco and Zihl 2004). In outline, let us divide the neuronal pools in the PP module into two pools, for the left and right hemispheres (Fig. 6.26). The left (right) hemisphere is associated with the right (left) visual field. A group of neuronal pools in a given module can be impaired in an intrinsic way (Humphreys and Heinke 1998) by damaging only intrinsic inputs within the module. In mathematical terms, the intrinsic lesioning of a neuronal pool in the PP module is described by weighting the effects of the excitatory and inhibitory effects within a pool of neurons by a lesion factor L_{ij} as shown in equation 6.20. Values of L_{ij} equal to 1.0 leave the corresponding neuronal pools unaffected, whereas values of L_{ij} smaller than 1.0 damage the corresponding neuronal pools by reducing the influence of the intrinsic inputs. (The lattice of PP module neurons is addressed by ij.)

Although visual neglect can be present in the left or right hemispace, we refer in the following to left-sided visual neglect (produced by damage to the right parietal cortex), because this type is more frequently observed (Vallar and Pernai 1986). However, the model can also be applied to right-sided visual neglect.

Unilateral damage to the PP module in the right hemisphere as shown in Fig. 6.26b can produce left-sided **space-based visual hemi-neglect**, in which neglect is found when the object enters the left visual field. The unilateral damage was produced as shown by reducing the normal intra-pool interaction effects from 1.0 to 0.6 in the right parietal cortex, as shown in Fig. 6.26. In order to visualize the results of the damage, we plot the final state of the PP module after dynamical convergence. This provides a spatial map of locations where attention has settled. This topographically ordered final activation state of the PP module is shown overlaid on the input image, so that the attentional spatial map can be easily interpreted. We symbolize with a point (shown in grey or red) the pixels at locations that correspond to a PP neuronal pool that has an activity larger than a certain threshold $\vartheta = 0.08$. In this way, we can relate the attentional spatial map with the scan path of the overtly fixated locations during the perception of an object. Spatial locations in the PP module with high activity correspond to covertly spatially attended regions, and these potentially attract an overt visual fixation.

The left hemineglect produced by a right unilateral lesion in the model is shown in Fig. 6.27. Neglect of the entire left part of the visual field was indicated by disrupted processing of objects (Fig. 6.27a) or parts of an object (Fig. 6.27b) in the impaired left hemifield. If the object was completely in the intact right hemifield, the overt visual fixations are absolutely

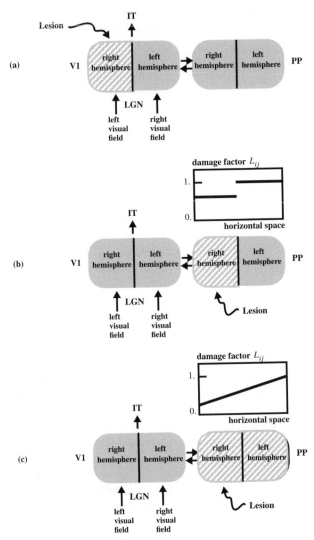

Fig. 6.26 Lesion patterns. (a) Hemianopia resulting from damage to the V1 module (primary visual cortex). (b) Left-sided space-based visual neglect resulting from unilateral damage to the PP (posterior parietal cortex) module in the right hemisphere. (c) Left-sided object-based visual neglect resulting from a gradient of damage to the PP module which is most severe on the far right. (After Deco and Zihl 2004; and Rolls and Deco 2002.)

normal (Fig. 6.27c) and consequently spatial attention is deployed on both sides of the object.

The explanation for left hemineglect is therefore that the neuronal pools corresponding to the right hemisphere are not able to achieve high activity due to the unilateral damage to them. This lack of high activity occurs in spite of the positive bias coming from pools in the right hemisphere of V1 that excite the respective pools in the right hemisphere PP module. The low activity level of the PP neuronal pools after the right unilateral lesion can be interpreted as neglect for all sensory information coming from the left visual hemifield.

Object-based visual neglect is produced in the computational model by graded damage that is most severe on the right, as shown in Fig. 6.26b. (The damage was graded from a

(a)   **(b)**   **(c)**

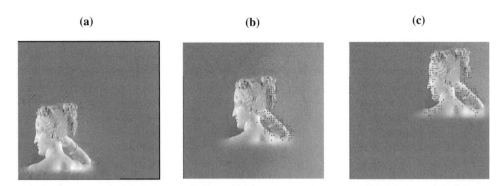

Fig. 6.27 Left-sided local space-based visual hemi-neglect for an object at different positions after unilateral damage to the PP module. The spots on the image show where activation in the parietal (PP) module is above a criterion after the network has settled. The results thus show that neurons in the PP module only reach the criterion when the object is in the right half of visual space. See text for details. (After Deco and Zihl 2004; and Rolls and Deco 2002.) (See colour plates Appendix E.)

(a)   **(b)**   **(c)**

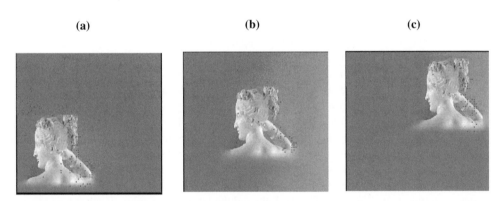

Fig. 6.28 Left-sided object-based visual neglect for an object at different translated positions after graded damage to the PP module. The damage increases gradually towards the right of the PP module. The spots on the image show where activation in the parietal (PP) module is above a criterion after the network has settled. The results thus show that neurons in the PP module only reach the criterion for the right half of the object, and do this independently of where the image is in visual space. See text for details. (After Deco and Zihl 2004; and Rolls and Deco 2002.) (See colour plates Appendix E.)

factor of 0.2 on the far right to 0.8 on the far left, as shown in Fig. 6.26b and specified in Rolls and Deco (2002).) Figure 6.28 shows the attentional spatial map obtained after graded impairment of the PP module. The left side of the object is neglected independently of where the object is in space. Translation of the object across the retina has no effect: the location of the neuronal pools in module PP with high activation is always restricted to the right part of the object with respect to the object frame. Although the absolute level of activity is lower when the object is in the left versus the right visual field, in both cases the left side of the object receives a weaker response than its right side, due to the horizontal activity gradient across the PP module. The intramodular inhibition between neuronal pools in PP drives the dynamical competition always in favour of the pools corresponding to the right side of the object, suppressing at the same time the activity of the pools associated with the left side of the object (see further Deco and Rolls (2002) and below). Hence, in this case the underlying biased competition causes an attentional spatial map that explains the covert fixation locations (Deco and Zihl 2004).

What happens in object-based neglect if there is more than one object in the visual field? In some patients an extraordinary effect is found in which the left half of each of a series of objects spread out horizontally in the visual field is not seen, or is 'neglected' (Marshall and Halligan 1993, Gilchrist, Humphreys and Riddoch 1996). Because this effect occurs separately for the left half of each object, it cannot be accounted for just by neglect of the left half of visual space. The impairment is called **object-based visual neglect**, because the neglect is with respect to each object, and to the visual field. In the simulation of the damage shown in Fig. 6.26c with the results shown in Fig. 6.28 the inhibition within the PP module was global, that is, the same inhibition was applied to all pools in the PP module (Deco and Zihl 2004, Rolls and Deco 2002). I conjectured that object-based neglect for the left half of each of a series of objects arranged horizontally could arise if lateral inhibition operating within a short range was used within modules that simulate the posterior parietal cortex (PP) and the primary visual cortex. Deco and Rolls (2002) tested this hypothesis, confirmed the prediction, and thus produced an explanation for object-based visual neglect with multiple objects in the visual field, as follows.

The results of four different experiments are shown in Fig. 6.29. In Fig. 6.29a the performance of the unlesioned model for the case of two objects (two flowers) is provided as the reference condition. The locations where in separate runs of the experiment the 'spotlight of attention' in the parietal module settled are shown as spots on the diagram. (Spots are placed on the diagram for spatial locations at which the activity of a PP neuronal pool was higher than a threshold. In the simulations described, the threshold was set at 0.0638. Each diagram shows the results of a single run of the simulation, and thus all neuronal pools that were above the threshold are shown in the diagram. The results on different simulation runs were very similar.) In the unlesioned condition shown in Fig. 6.29a the locations of the 'spotlight' were distributed onto the whole of both objects, indicating no neglect. In Fig. 6.29b a single object was presented in the right (more intact) part of visual space. The locations of the 'spotlight' were in the right half of the flower, and the left half of the object was neglected. Fig. 6.29c shows two objects well separated in the right and the left of the display. The left half of each object is neglected. The right hand part of the left object is 'seen', even though it is to the left of the right object. Thus the neglect is object-based, and not based on a neglect of the left half of egocentric space. This is the phenomenon of object neglect that is to be accounted for (Deco and Rolls 2002).

The deficit can be understood, with the help of the model, to arise because local spatial differentiation produced by the local lateral inhibition in the PP and V1 modules, superimposed on the linearly increasing deficit towards the left of visual space, results in some sparing of the right parts of each object wherever they are in the visual scene. The result of this combination of factors (for the stimulus conditions shown in Fig. 6.29c) is shown in Fig. 6.30. This shows the average firing rate of each of the neuronal pools at different horizontal positions in the PP module. The two regions of high firing correspond to the two flowers in Fig. 6.29c, and the short range lateral inhibition superimposed on the lesion effect which increases in severity towards the left of Fig. 6.30 produces a region of high firing at the right of each flower, and a region of lower firing at the left of each flower. With the threshold set where shown to reflect where there is strongest firing in the PP module, and thus where attention is preferentially located, spotlights of attention are located on the right side of each object, and the left half of each object is neglected (Deco and Rolls 2002).

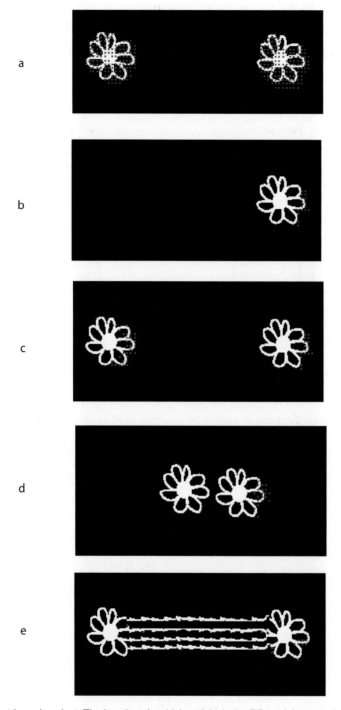

Fig. 6.29 Object-based neglect. The locations in which activity in the PP module exceeded the threshold after the network had settled with each stimulus are shown by spots. a. shows the operation of the unlesioned network, and b–e of the lesioned network (see text). (After Deco and Rolls 2002.) (See colour plates Appendix E.)

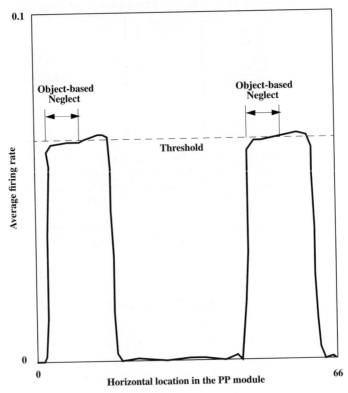

Fig. 6.30 The average firing rate of each of the neuronal pools at different horizontal positions in the posterior parietal (PP) module when the stimuli presented are as shown in Fig. 6.29c. The two regions of high firing correspond to the two flowers in Fig. 6.29c, and the short range lateral inhibition superimposed on the lesion effect which increases in severity towards the left of the Figure produces a region of high firing at the right of each flower, and a region of lower firing at the left of each flower. (After Deco and Rolls 2002.)

The model, and the resulting understanding, allow us to predict and explain a number of further phenomena that can arise with neglect (Marshall and Halligan 1993, Gilchrist, Humphreys and Riddoch 1996). One is shown in Fig. 6.29d, in which two objects are placed close together in the scene. In this case the left part of the right object, and the whole of the left object, are neglected. This can be understood to arise because the local spatial differentiation produced by the local lateral inhibition in the PP and V1 modules now operates to produce enhancement only on the right of the object complex, because of the lateral scale of the lateral inhibition relative to the separation of the objects.

Another phenomenon predicted and explained by the model is illustrated in Fig. 6.29e. If the two objects, though widely separated, are joined by lines, then only the right object is seen, but not the left (Gilchrist et al. 1996). This is again accounted for by the local lateral inhibition, which when convolved with the whole object, results in an enhanced positive edge only at the right of the combined object after superimposition on the lesion effect which increases linearly towards the left of the visual field, as described by Deco and Rolls (2002).

(a) Experiments

(b) Computer Simulations

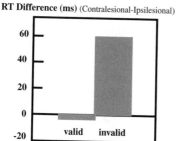

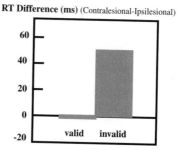

Fig. 6.31 Disengagement of attention: reaction times are longer for stimuli in the visual field contralateral to a parietal lesion only if attention has been drawn to the ipsilesional field (in the condition labelled 'invalid') (see text): (a) in patients with unilateral lesions of the parietal cortex (adapted from Rafal and Robertson 1997); (b) in simulation results with the attentional model. The plots depict the detection time difference between the contralesional and ipsilesional fields for the two cueing conditions, and the ipsilesional reaction time is the normal baseline. The effect is interpreted as a difficulty of disengaging attention from the ipsilesional (good) field towards the contralesional (impaired) field. (After Deco and Zihl 2004; and Rolls and Deco 2002.)

6.11.3 Disengagement of attention in neglect

A biased competition account of the underlying disturbances of attentional mechanisms that induce visual neglect is strongly supported by the asymmetrical effect of spatial cueing in neglect patients. In a typical spatial attention experiment using the precueing method, the subject is asked to respond, by pressing a key, to the appearance of a target at a peripheral location (Posner, Walker, Friedrich and Rafal 1984). The target is preceded by a precue that indicates to which visual hemifield the subject is to covertly attend. The cue is then followed by a target in either the correctly (valid cue) or the incorrectly (invalid cue) cued location.

This kind of experiment for measuring covert shifts of attention has been applied using simple reaction time paradigms in patients with unilateral lesions of the parietal cortex. Although under normal conditions these patients may neglect contralesional stimuli, they can often be instructed to attend to the neglected field. In fact, in the precueing paradigm, reaction times to valid cued targets in the hemifield contralateral to the lesion are almost normal in the sense that they are not much slower than those for targets that occur in the ipsilesional hemifield when that field was precued.

On the other hand, if the ipsilesional (good) field was precued, the patients were unusually slow to respond to the target when it unexpectedly appeared in the contralesional hemifield. In other words, patients are able to orient contralesionally to benefit from a valid cue, but they are impaired when attention is summoned by an invalid cue in the ipsilesional field and then the target occurs in the contralesional hemifield. This has been described as an inability to disengage attention (from the ipsilesional, good, hemifield). Figure 6.31a shows an example of this measured experimental asymmetry by plotting the detection time difference between the contralesional and ipsilesional fields for the two cueing conditions (Rafal and Robertson 1995).

These asymmetric reaction time patterns were described as extinction-like reaction time patterns to indicate their similarity to the clinical finding of extinction in these patients. The extinction-like asymmetric reaction time pattern has been found in several experimental studies (Posner, Walker, Friedrich and Rafal 1984, Posner, Walker, Friedrich and Rafal 1987, Baynes, Holtzman and Volpe 1986, Rafal and Robertson 1995). These studies demonstrate that the degree of asymmetry correlates with the severity of the clinical neglect (Morrow and

Ratcliff 1988).

In order to understand the underlying attentional dynamical mechanisms involved in these extinction-like phenomena, Deco and Zihl (2004) simulated the precueing experiments with the cortical architecture described in Section 6.6. Numerical experiments were performed by producing purely unilateral damage to the right hemisphere of the PP module as shown in Fig. 6.26b in order to simulate the behaviour of left neglect patients. The target was a letter 'E' that could appear centred in the left or right visual hemifield. During the first precueing period of 250 ms no stimulus was presented in the visual field, and the left or right hemifields were cued by applying an external attentional location-specific bias $I_{ij}^{PP,A} = 0.07$ to the neuronal pools in PP, corresponding to a 9×9 square centred in the right or left hemisphere, respectively. After 250 ms, the object to be recognized (the letter 'E') was presented as the stimulus in the left or right visual hemifield. Two pools in the IT module had been previously trained to learn the identity of the two stimuli 'E' and 'X', respectively. Four conditions were of interest: contralesional presentation of the stimulus preceded by a valid spatial cue (implemented by top-down bias to the part of the PP module for the right hemisphere) or by an invalid cue (top-down bias to the part of the PP module for the left hemisphere); and ipsilesional presentation of the stimulus preceded by a valid cue (implemented by top-down bias to the part of the PP module for the left hemisphere) or by an invalid cue (top-down bias to the part of the PP module for the right PP hemisphere). The reaction times were measured by detecting the time at which the IT pools reached a criterion of polarization in favour of the target, i.e. when the difference between the maximal activity of the IT pools corresponding to the target and non-targets $A_T^{IT} - A_D^{IT}$ was larger than a certain threshold ζ. (We chose $\zeta = 0.05$.) Figure 6.31b shows the numerical results. It is clear from the figure that the computational model reproduces the extinction-like asymmetric precueing effect very well (Deco and Zihl 2004).

Figure 6.32 shows the evolution of the underlying dynamics by plotting the maximum activities of the target assemblies and the distractor assemblies in the different modules IT, V1, and PP. The case of invalid precueing for the presentation of a contralesional and ipsilesional stimulus is shown. In the ipsilesional stimulus case, invalid precueing of the damaged right PP hemisphere polarized the PP activity in favour of the right hemisphere, but only very moderately, so that V1 was not even polarized at all (left versus right hemisphere). This was due to the fact that the pools in the PP module of the right hemisphere did not react to the cue as efficiently and quickly as usual because of the intrinsic damage. On the other hand, in the contralesional case, invalid precueing of the PP module in the left hemisphere polarized the PP activity strongly in favour of the left hemisphere. Consequently the activity in V1 was also strongly polarized in favour of the left hemisphere. Hence, after presentation of the stimulus in the contralesional visual field, the dynamics of the cortical system took much more time to invert the polarization in favour of the stimulus side in V1, and in the damaged and therefore slow right side of the PP module. Hence, in the contralesional stimulus case, the underlying biased intra- and inter-modular competition in V1 and PP explains the unusual delayed polarization of the IT pools that causes the asymmetric spatial precueing effect shown in Fig. 6.31 (Deco and Zihl 2004).

6.11.4 Extinction and visual search

Another kind of extinction-like effect observed in patients with unilateral neglect is found in visual search experiments. Eglin, Robertson and Knight (1989) studied the behaviour of patients with unilateral parietal lesions during a visual search task. When visual search arrays were presented to only the contralesional or ipsilesional hemifields, the patients did not perform differently in the two hemifields. However, when search arrays were presented to both hemifields simultaneously, the patients' reaction time for target detection differed

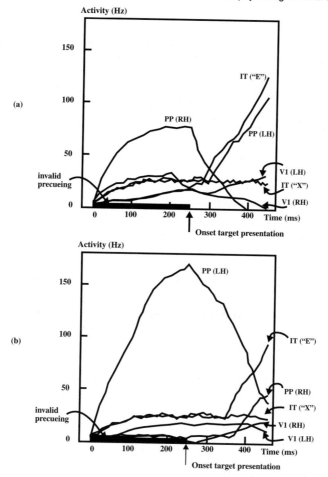

Fig. 6.32 Dynamical evolution of the computational model of attention with purely unilateral damage to the right PP module during the spatial precueing experiment. (a) Ipsilesional stimulus presentation and invalid precueing; (b) contralesional stimulus presentation and invalid precueing. The letter 'E' was the target and 'X' was the distractor. The activities to these stimuli, which appeared at time = 250 ms, are shown for the parietal (PP), V1, and inferior temporal (IT) modules. LH and RH denote the left and right hemisphere respectively. The black horizontal bars at the bottom indicate the precuing period. (After Rolls and Deco 2002; and Deco and Zihl 2004.)

between the two hemifields. The reaction time for target detection in the intact hemifield was not affected by the presence of distractor stimuli in the contralesional hemifield. In contrast, the reaction time for target detection in the contralesional hemifield was much slower when distractor stimuli were presented in the intact field. Thus, in both spatial cueing (Section 6.11.3) and visual search tasks, patients with unilateral lesions of the parietal lobe generally perform poorly at target detection on the contralesional side, and the performance declines even more for the contralesional side when stimuli are presented to the ipsilesional side, or when they are precued to expect a target to be in the ipsilesional hemifield.

Simulations with the model described in Section 6.6 with unilateral damage to the right hemisphere of the PP module as shown in Fig. 6.26b in order to simulate the behaviour of left neglect patients produced an explanation for these effects in patients (Deco and Zihl 2004, Rolls and Deco 2002). The results showed that target detection in the contralesional hemifield was strongly delayed by the presence of a distractor in the opposite hemifield. The results of the simulation are thus very similar to the performance observed by neglect patients in visual search tasks (Eglin, Robertson and Knight 1989).

In more detail, when the target is in the neglected contralesional hemifield, the activity of the PP neuronal pools corresponding to the location of the distractor in the opposite undamaged hemifield was very high, and therefore the attentional spatial competition between the target and distractor pools was delayed. This delay was augmented by the slowness of the intrinsically impaired PP pools being activated by the target. In contrast, when the target was in the undamaged ipsilesional hemifield, the activity of the PP neuronal pools corresponding to the location of the distractor in the neglected (contralesional) hemifield was much lower than in the TC2 condition. This was because of the slowness of the impaired neural pools in the right PP hemisphere receiving the input from the distractor. This effect facilitated the attentional spatial competition between the target and distractor pools. The rapidly increasing target activity in this condition supported even more the polarization in the PP module in favour of the target location.

In summary, the model accounts for the effects observed in search tasks in patients with unilateral parietal lesions as follows (Rolls and Deco 2002, Deco and Zihl 2004). Purely unilateral damage in the parietal (PP) module unbalances the dynamical competition, so that it is more difficult to 'disengage' spatial attention from stimuli in the undamaged ipsilesional hemifield. Effectively, the attractor state set up by the recurrent processing in the unlesioned parietal cortex once started, for example by a cue, is stable, and it is then difficult for the attractor in the lesioned parietal cortex to win the competition and gain attention even when a stimulus is presented to the lesioned parietal cortex. Part of the difficulty on the lesioned side is that because the recurrent intra-pool dynamics is impaired, it is more difficult than normal to stimulate the attractor on this side into high activity.

An important computational concept to help account for these neuropsychological phenomena is that once an attractor state has been started, it becomes quite stable, and a strong stimulus is needed to disengage or distract it from that stable state (see Sections B.3, 8.4 and 8.5). If a lesion impairs the ability of a pool to enter an attractor state, perhaps because the activity and recurrent collateral-mediated self-excitation of a population is decreased, then that pool or population of neurons becomes less stable, more distractible, and less able to distract an attractor state in the unlesioned network contralaterally.

More details of these simulations, and also predictions about the effects of top-down object-based attentional cueing applied to the IT module on spatial neglect, are described by Rolls and Deco (2002).

6.12 Conclusions

The model of attention described in this chapter (see also Rolls and Deco (2002)) represents an advance beyond the biased competition hypothesis, in that it shows how object and spatial attention can be produced by dynamic interactions between the 'what' and 'where' streams, and in that as a computational model that has been simulated, the details of the model have been made fully explicit and have been defined quantitatively. An interesting and important feature of the model is that the model does not use explicit multiplication as a computational method, but the modulation of attention (for example the effects of posterior parietal module (PP) activity on V1) appears to be like multiplication. This is an interesting contribution of the model, namely that multiplicative-like attentional gains are implemented without any explicit multiplicative operation (see Sections 6.9 and B.8.3).

In this chapter we considered the neuronal ('microscopic-level') neurodynamical mechanisms that underlie visual attention. We described a computational model of cortical systems based on the 'biased competition' hypothesis. The model consists of interconnected populations of cortical neurons distributed in different brain modules, which are related to the different areas of the dorsal or 'where' and ventral or 'what' processing pathways of the primate visual cortex. The 'where' pathway incorporates mutual connections between a feature extracting module (V1–V4), and a parietal module (PP) that consists of pools coding the locations of the stimuli. The 'what' path incorporates mutual connections between the feature extracting module (V1–V4) and an inferior temporal cortex module (IT) with pools of neurons coding for specific objects. External attentional top-down bias is defined as inputs coming from higher prefrontal cortex modules that hold what is to be paid attention to active in short-term memory. These short-term memory processes are not explicitly modelled in this chapter but are modelled in Chapter 5. Intermodular attentional biasing is modelled through the coupling between pools of different modules, which are explicitly modelled. Attention appears now as an emergent effect that supports the dynamical evolution to a state where the constraints given by the stimulus and the external bias are satisfied. Visual search and attention can be explained in this theoretical framework of a biased competitive neurodynamics. The top–down bias guides attention to concentrate at a given spatial location or on given features. The neural population dynamics are handled analytically in the framework of the mean-field approximation. Consequently, the whole process can be expressed as a system of coupled differential equations. The model has been extended to include the high resolution buffer hypothesis, and a 'microscopic' physical (i.e. neuron-level) implementation of the global precedence effect (see Rolls and Deco (2002)). We have also analyzed the attentional neurodynamics involved in visual search of hierarchical patterns, and also modelled a mechanism for feature binding that can account for conjunction visual search tasks (see Rolls and Deco (2002)).

The fundamental contributions of this model of attention (Rolls and Deco 2002, Deco and Lee 2004, Deco and Zihl 2004) are as follows:

1. Different functions involved in active visual perception have been integrated by a model based on the biased competition hypothesis. Attentional top-down bias guides the dynamics to concentrate at a given spatial location or on given (object) features. The model integrates, in a unifying form, the explanation of several existing types of experimental data obtained at different levels of investigation. At the microscopic neuronal level, we simulated single cell recordings, at the mesoscopic level of cortical areas we reproduced the results of fMRI (functional magnetic resonance imaging) studies, and at the macroscopic perceptual level we accounted for psychophysical performance. Specific predictions at different levels of investigation have also been made. These predictions inspired single cell, fMRI, and psychophysical experiments, that in part have been already performed and the results of which are consistent with the theory (see Rolls and Deco (2002)).

2. Attention is a dynamical emergent property in our system, rather than a separate mechanism operating independently of other perceptual and cognitive processes.

3. The computational perspective provides not only a concrete mathematical description of mechanisms involved in brain function, but also a model that allows complete simulation and prediction of neuropsychological experiments. Interference with the operation of some of the modules was used to predict impairment in visual information selection in patients suffering from brain injury. The resulting experiments support our understanding of the functional

of removing the D.C. component of the image (i.e. the mean value of the grey-scale intensity of the pixels). (The equivalent in the brain is the low-pass filtering performed by the retinal ganglion cells and lateral geniculate cells, as described in Chapter 2 of Rolls and Deco (2002). The visual representation in the LGN is essentially a contrast invariant pixel representation of the image, i.e. each neuron encodes the relative brightness value at one location in visual space referred to the mean value of the image brightness.) We denote this contrast invariant LGN representation by the $N \times N$ matrix Γ_{ij} defined by the equation

$$\Gamma_{ij} = \Gamma_{ij}^{\text{orig}} - \frac{1}{N^2} \sum_{i=1}^{N} \sum_{j=1}^{N} \Gamma_{ij}^{\text{orig}}. \tag{6.3}$$

Feedforward connections to a layer of V1 neurons perform the extraction of simple features such as bars at different locations, orientations, and sizes. Rolls and Deco (2002) argued (in Section 9.2.3) that realistic receptive fields for V1 neurons that extract these simple features can be represented by 2D-Gabor wavelets. Lee (1996) derived a family of discretized 2D-Gabor wavelets that satisfy the wavelet theory and the neurophysiological constraints for simple cells. They are given by an expression of the form

$$G_{kpql}(x, y) = a^{-k} \Psi_{\Theta_l} (a^{-k}(x - 2p) - a^{-k}(y - 2q)) \tag{6.4}$$

where
$$\Psi_{\Theta_l} = \Psi(x \cos(l\Theta_0) + y \sin(l\Theta_0), -x \sin(l\Theta_0) + y \cos(l\Theta_0)), \tag{6.5}$$

and the mother wavelet is given by

$$\Psi(x, y) = \frac{1}{\sqrt{2\pi}} e^{-\frac{1}{8}(4x^2 + y^2)} [e^{i\kappa x} - e^{-\frac{\kappa^2}{2}}]. \tag{6.6}$$

In the above equations $\Theta_0 = \pi/L$ denotes the step size of each angular rotation; l the index of rotation corresponding to the preferred orientation $\Theta_l = l\pi/L$; k denotes the octave; and the indices pq the position of the receptive field centre at $c_x = p(N/P)$ and $c_y = q(N/P)$. In this form, the receptive fields at all levels cover the spatial domain in the same way, i.e. by always overlapping the receptive fields in the same fashion. In the model we use $a = 2, b = 1$ and $\kappa = \pi$ corresponding to a spatial frequency bandwidth of one octave.

The neurons in the pools in **V1** have receptive fields performing a Gabor wavelet transform. Let us denote by I_{kpql}^{V1} the sensory input activity to a pool A_{kpql}^{V1} in V1 which is sensitive to a spatial frequency at octave k, to a preferred orientation defined by the rotation index l, and to stimuli at the centre location specified by the indices pq. The sensory input activity to a pool in V1 is therefore defined by the modulus of the convolution between the corresponding receptive fields and the image, i.e.

$$I_{kpql}^{V1} = \sqrt{\|\langle G_{kpql}, \Gamma \rangle\|^2} = \sqrt{\left\| \sum_{i=1}^{N} \sum_{j=1}^{N} G_{kpql}(i, j)\Gamma_{ij} \right\|^2} \tag{6.7}$$

and is normalized to a maximal saturation value of 0.025. Since in our numerical simulations the system needs only to learn a small number of objects (usually 2–4), we temporarily did not include the V2 and V4 module for simplicity in some of the simulations. We did however include an explicit module V2–V4 for the simulations corresponding to measures in brain areas V2 and V4 presented in Section 6.7.1. In the simulations where the V2–V4 module was not present, the V1 and IT cell assemblies were directly connected together, with full connectivity. In fact, the large receptive fields of V2 and V4 can be approximately taken into account by including them in V1 pools with receptive fields corresponding to several octaves of the 2D-Gabor transform wavelets (i.e. not only the typical narrow receptive fields of V1 but also larger receptive fields are included in the modelled V1). The reduced system connects all cell assemblies in V1 with all cell assemblies in IT. In contradistinction to the suggestion of Salinas and Abbott (1997), and to the mechanisms described in Chapter 4 for producing translation invariance, in this particular model translation invariance was implemented by an attentional intermodular biasing interaction between pools in modules V1–V4 and PP. For each V1–V4 neuron, the gain modulation observed decreases as the actual location where attention is focused moves away from the centre of the receptive field in a Gaussian-like way (Connor, Gallant, Preddie and Van Essen 1996). Consequently, the connections with the pools in the PP module are specified such that the modulation is Gaussian. Let us define in the PP module a pool A_{ij}^{PP} for each location ij in the visual field. The mutual (i.e. forward and back) connections between a pool A_{kpql}^{V1} in V1 (or V4) and a pool A_{ij}^{PP} in PP are therefore defined by

$$w_{pqij} = A \exp\left\{-\frac{(i-p)^2 + (j-q)^2}{2S^2}\right\} - B \tag{6.8}$$

These connections mean that the V1 pool A_{kpql}^{V1} will have maximal amplitude when spatial attention is located at $i = p$ and $j = q$ in the visual field, i.e. when the pool A_{ij}^{PP} in PP is maximally activated and provides an inhibitory contribution $-B$ at the locations not being attended to. In our simulations, we always used $S = 2$, $A = 1.5$ and $B = 0.1$. The V1–PP attentional modulation, in combination with the Hebbian learning that we will define later in this section, generate translation-invariant recognition pools in the module IT.

Let us now define the neurodynamical equations that regulate the temporal evolution of the whole system. (The dynamics correspond to those described in Section B.8.1.)

The activity level of the input current in the **V1 module** is given by

$$\tau\frac{\partial A_{kpql}^{V1}(t)}{\partial t} = -A_{kpql}^{V1} + \alpha F(A_{kpql}^{V1}(t)) - \beta F(A_k^{I,V1}(t)) + I_{kpql}^{V1}(t)$$
$$+I_{pq}^{V1-PP}(t) + I_{kpql}^{V1-IT}(t) + I_0 + \nu \tag{6.9}$$

where the attentional biasing coupling I_{pq}^{V1-PP} due to the intermodular 'where' connections with the pools in the parietal module PP is given by

$$I_{pq}^{V1-PP} = \sum_{i,j} W_{pqij} F(A_{ij}^{PP}(t)) \tag{6.10}$$

and the attentional biasing term I_{kpql}^{V1-IT} due to the intermodular 'what' connections with the pools in the temporal module IT is defined by

$$I_{kpql}^{V1-IT} = \sum_{c=1}^{C} w_{ckpql} F(A_c^{IT}(t)) \tag{6.11}$$

w_{ckpql} being the connection strength between the V1 pool A_{kpql}^{V1} and the IT pool A_c^{IT} corresponding to the coding of a specific object category c. We assume that the IT module has C pools corresponding to different object categories. For each spatial frequency level, a common inhibitory pool (designated with a superscript I) is defined. The current activity of these inhibitory pools obeys the following equations:

$$\tau_P \frac{\partial A_k^{I,V1}(t)}{\partial t} = -A_k^{I,V1}(t) + \gamma \sum_{p,q,l} F(A_{kpql}^{V1}(t)) - \delta F(A_k^{I,V1}(t)) \tag{6.12}$$

Similarly, the current activity of the excitatory pools in the **posterior parietal module PP** is given by

$$\tau \frac{\partial A_{ij}^{PP}(t)}{\partial t} = -A_{ij}^{PP} + \alpha F(A_{ij}^{PP}(t)) - \beta F(A^{I,PP}(t)) + I_{ij}^{PP-V1}(t)$$
$$+I_{ij}^{PP,A} + I_0 + \nu \tag{6.13}$$

where $I_{ij}^{PP,A}$ denotes an external attentional spatially specific top-down bias, the inter-modular attentional biasing I_{ij}^{PP-V1} through the connections with the pools in the module V1 is

$$I_{ij}^{PP-V1} = \sum_{k,p,q,l} W_{pqij} F(A_{kpql}^{V1}(t)) \tag{6.14}$$

and the activity current of the common PP inhibitory pool evolves according to

$$\tau_P \frac{\partial A^{I,PP}(t)}{\partial t} = -A^{I,PP}(t) + \gamma \sum_{i,j} F(A_{ij}^{PP}(t)) - \delta F(A^{I,PP}(t)) . \tag{6.15}$$

The dynamics of the **inferotemporal module IT** is given by

$$\tau \frac{\partial A_c^{IT}(t)}{\partial t} = -A_c^{IT} + \alpha F(A_c^{IT}(t)) - \beta F(A^{I,IT}(t)) + I_c^{IT-V1}(t)$$
$$+I_c^{IT,A} + I_0 + \nu \tag{6.16}$$

where $I_c^{IT,A}$ denotes an external attentional object-specific top-down bias, and the intermodular attentional biasing I_c^{IT-V1} between IT and V1 pools is

$$I_c^{IT-V1} = \sum_{k,p,q,l} w_{ckpql} F(A_{kpql}^{V1}(t)) \tag{6.17}$$

and the activity current of the common PP inhibitory pool evolves according to

$$\tau_P \frac{\partial A^{I,IT}(t)}{\partial t} = -A^{I,IT}(t) + \gamma \sum_c F(A_c^{IT}(t)) - \delta F(A^{I,IT}(t)) . \tag{6.18}$$

In our simulations, we use $\alpha = 0.95$, $\beta = 0.8$, $\gamma = 1$, $\delta = 0.1$, $I_0 = 0.025$, and the standard deviation of the additive noise ν, $\sigma_\nu = 0.02$. The values of the external bias $I_{ij}^{PP,A}$ and $I_c^{IT,A}$ are equal to 0.07 for the pools that eventually receive an external positive bias and otherwise are equal to zero. The choice of these parameters is uncritical and is based on biological parameters.

During a **learning phase** each object (or object category) is learned. This is done by training the connections between the modules V1 and IT by Hebbian learning. In order to achieve invariant translation the different objects are presented at random locations. The external attentional location-specific bias in PP $I_{ij}^{PP,A}$ is set so that only the pool ij corresponding to the spatial location of the object to be learned receives a positive bias. In this way the spatial attention defines the localization of the object to be learned. The external attentional object-specific bias in IT $I_c^{\text{IT,A}}$ is set similarly, so that only the pool c that will identify the object, receives a positive bias. We therefore define the identity of the object in a supervised way. After presentation of a given stimulus, i.e. a specific object at a specific location, and the corresponding external bias, the system evolves until convergence. After convergence, the V1–IT connections w_{ckpql} are trained through the following Hebbian rule

$$w_{ckpql} = w_{ckpql} + \eta F(A_c^{\text{IT}}(t))F(A_{kpql}^{\text{V1}}(t)) \tag{6.19}$$

(t) being large enough (i.e. after convergence) and η the learning coefficient. This procedure is repeated for all objects at all possible locations until the weights converge.

During the **recognition phase** there are two possibilities, namely to search for a specific object (visual search), or to identify an object at a given spatial location (object recognition), as shown in Fig. 6.12.

In the case of **visual search** the external attentional object-specific bias in IT $I_c^{\text{IT,A}}$ is set so that only the pool c corresponding to the category of the object to be searched for receives a positive bias, while the external attentional location-specific bias in PP $I_{ij}^{\text{PP,A}}$ is set equal to zero everywhere. The external attentional bias $I_c^{\text{IT,A}}$ drives the competition in the IT module so that the pool corresponding to the searched for object wins. The intermodular attentional modulation between IT and V1 biases the competition in V1 so that all features detected from the retinal inputs at different positions that are compatible with the specific object to be searched for will now win. Finally the intermodular attentional bias between V1 and PP drives the competition in V1 and in PP so that only the spatial location in PP and the associated V1 pools compatible with the presented stimulus and with the top-down specific category of the object to be searched for will remain active after convergence. At convergence, the final state in PP shows where the object has been found. In this form, the final activation state is neurodynamically driven by the stimulus, external top-down bias, and inter-modular bias, in an entirely parallel way. Attention is not a mechanism involved in the competition but just an emergent effect that supports the dynamical evolution to a state where all constraints are satisfied.

In the case of **object recognition**, the external attentional bias in PP $I_{ij}^{\text{PP,A}}$ is set so that only the pool associated with the spatial location where the object to be identified is receives a positive bias, i.e. a spatial region will be 'illuminated'. The other external bias $I_c^{\text{IT,A}}$ is zero everywhere. In this case, the dynamics evolves such that in PP only the pool associated with the top-down biased spatial location will win. This fact drives the competition in V1 such that only the pools corresponding to features of the stimulus at that location will win, biasing the dynamics in IT such that only the pool identifying the class of the features at that position will remain active, indicating the category of the object at that predefined spatial location.

To investigate the effects of damage to the system, the connections within a module can be reduced in strength. For example, neglect was simulated as described in Section 6.11 by damage to the parietal module as follows (Deco and Lee 2004). The intrinsic **lesioning** of a neuronal pool in the PP module is described by extending equation 6.13 to:

$$\tau\frac{\partial A_{ij}^{\text{PP}}(t)}{\partial t} = -A_{ij}^{\text{PP}} + L_{ij}\left\{\alpha F(A_{ij}^{\text{PP}}(t)) - \beta F(A^{\text{I,PP}}(t)) + I_0\right\} + I_{ij}^{\text{PP}-\text{V1}}(t)$$
$$+ I_{ij}^{\text{PP,A}} + \nu \tag{6.20}$$

where L_{ij} is a lesioning factor. Values of L_{ij} equal to 1.0 leave the corresponding neuronal pools unaffected, whereas values of L_{ij} smaller than 1.0 damage the corresponding neuronal pools by reducing the influence of the excitatory intrinsic inputs A_{ij}^{PP}, intrinsic inhibitory inputs $A^{\text{I,PP}}$, and external spontaneous inputs I_0.

Deco and Lee (2002) (see Rolls and Deco (2002)) used two performance measures of neural activities to characterize the temporal evolution of the units in different modules.

The first measure is the population average response of neuronal pools within a certain neighbourhood. This measure has often been used to describe data in neurophysiological experiments (Lee, Mumford, Romero and Lamme 1998).

The second measure is the population *maximum* activity of the neuronal pools associated with the target and with the distractors. To compute the maximum activity, for each point in time, we take the maximum response in any pool within a specified spatial neighbourhood at that time. More precisely, the maximum activity of pools within a spatial neighbourhood associated with the target T is defined by:

$$A_{\text{T}}^{\text{PP}} = \max(A_{ij}^{\text{PP}}) \text{ for } ij \text{ such that } \text{dist}(ij, xy) < 4$$

$$A_{\text{T}}^{\text{V1}} = \max(\sum_{k,l} A_{klpq}^{\text{V1}}) \text{ for } pq \text{ such that } \text{dist}(((N/P)p)((N/P)q), xy) < 4$$

$$A_{\text{T}}^{\text{IT}} = \max(A_{c}^{\text{IT}}) \text{ for } c \text{ corresponding to the target}$$

where xy denotes the location of the centre of the target, and ij and pq denote the spatial locations of the V1 module pools and the PP module pools in the same spatial coordinates. dist() is the Euclidean distance in the 2D map. The maximum distractor (D) activities are defined by:

$$A_{\text{D}}^{\text{PP}} = \max(A_{ij}^{\text{PP}}) \text{ for } ij \text{ such that } \text{dist}(ij, xy) \geq 4$$

$$A_{\text{D}}^{\text{V1}} = \max(\sum_{m,l} A_{mlpq}^{\text{V1}}) \text{ for } pq \text{ such that } \text{dist}(((N/P)p)((N/P)q), xy) \geq 4$$

$$A_{\text{D}}^{\text{IT}} = \max(A_{c}^{\text{IT}}) \text{ for } c \text{ corresponding to non-targets}$$

This measure is more sensitive for detecting and isolating the time point at which the neural activity becomes different under different conditions.

7 Probabilistic decision-making

7.1 Introduction

In this chapter, I show how an attractor network can model probabilistic decision-making. Attractor or autoassociation memory networks that can implement short-term memory are described in Section B.3. The attractor network is trained to have two (or more) attractor states, each one of which corresponds to one of the decisions. Each attractor set of neurons receives a biasing input which corresponds to the evidence in favour of that decision. When the network starts from a state of spontaneous firing, the biasing inputs encourage one of the attractors to gradually win the competition, but this process is influenced by the Poisson-like firing (spiking) of the neurons, so that which attractor wins is probabilistic. If the evidence in favour of the two decisions is equal, the network chooses each decision probabilistically on 50% of the trials. The model not only shows how probabilistic decision-making could be implemented in the brain, but also how the evidence can be accumulated over long periods of time because of the integrating action of the attractor short-term memory network; how this accounts for reaction times as a function of the magnitude of the difference between the evidence for the two decisions (difficult decisions take longer); and how Weber's Law appears to be implemented in the brain. Details of the model are provided by Deco and Rolls (2006) and in Sections 7.8–7.10.

The link between perception and action can be conceptualized by a chain of neural operations, which leads a stimulus to guide behaviour to make a decision in favour of a particular action or motor response. For example, when subjects discriminate two stimuli separated by a time interval, the chain of neural operations encompasses mechanisms from the encoding of sensory stimuli, the attentional filtering of relevant features, their maintenance in working memory, to the comparison leading to a motor response (Romo and Salinas 2001, Romo and Salinas 2003). The comparison step is a crucial operation in the decision-making process. A number of neurophysiological experiments on decision-making are providing information on the neural mechanisms underlying perceptual comparison, by analyzing the responses of neurons that correlate with the animal's behaviour (Werner and Mountcastle 1965, Talbot, Darian-Smith, Kornhuber and Mountcastle 1968, Salzman, Britten and Newsome 1990, Kim and Shadlen 1999, Gold and Shadlen 2000, Schall 2001, Hernandez, Zainos and Romo 2002, Romo, Hernandez, Zainos, Lemus and Brody 2002, Romo, Hernandez, Zainos and Salinas 2003, Romo, Hernandez and Zainos 2004, Smith and Ratcliff 2004, Sugrue, Corrado and Newsome 2005). An important finding is that cortical areas involved in generating motor responses also show activity reflecting a gradual accumulation of evidence for choosing one or another decision, such that the process of making a decision and action generation can not be differentiated (see for example, Gold and Shadlen (2000) and Romo, Hernandez and Zainos (2004)).

Complementary theoretical neuroscience models are approaching the problem by designing biologically realistic neural circuits that can perform the comparison of two signals (Wang 2002, Brody, Romo and Kepecs 2003b, Machens, Romo and Brody 2005). These models involve two populations of excitatory neurons, engaged in competitive interactions mediated by inhibition, and external sensory inputs that bias this competition in favor of one of the populations, producing a binary choice that develops gradually. Consistent with the neurophysiological findings, this neurodynamical picture integrates both the accumulation of perceptual evidence for the comparison, and motor choice in one unifying network. Even more, the models are able to account for the experimentally measured psychometric and neurometric curves, and reaction times.

The comparison of two stimuli for which is the more intense become more difficult as they become more similar. The "difference-threshold" is the amount of change needed for us to recognize that a change has occurred. Weber's Law (enunciated by Ernst Heinrich Weber 1795–1878) states that the ratio of the difference-threshold to the background intensity is a constant. Theoretical models on decision-making (Wang 2002, Brody et al. 2003b, Machens et al. 2005) have not investigated Weber's law, and therefore a thorough understanding of the neural substrate underlying the comparison process has been missing until recently (Deco and Rolls 2006).

In this chapter, the neurodynamical mechanisms engaged in the process of comparison in a decision-making paradigm is investigated, and these processes are related to the psychophysics, as described for example by Weber's Law. That is, the probabilistic behaviour of the neural responses responsible for detecting a just noticeable stimulus difference is part of what is described.

A good paradigm for studying the mechanisms of decision-making is the vibrotactile sequential discrimination task, because evidence on the neuronal basis is available. In the two-alternative, forced-choice task used, subjects must decide which of two mechanical vibrations applied sequentially to their fingertips has the higher frequency of vibration. Neuronal recording and behavioural analyses (Romo and Salinas 2003) have provided sufficient detail about the neuronal bases of these decisions for a quantitative model to be developed. In particular, single neuron recordings in the ventral premotor cortex (VPC) reveal neurons whose firing rate was dependent only on the difference between the two applied frequencies, the sign of that difference being the determining factor for correct task performance (Romo, Hernandez and Zainos 2004, de Lafuente and Romo 2005). Neuronal activity in other brain areas related to the performance of the task is summarized in Section 7.2. I consider other potential applications of this approach to decision-making in Section 7.7.

Deco and Rolls (2006) modelled the activity of these VPC neurons by means of a theoretical framework first proposed by Wang (2002), but investigated the role of finite-size fluctuations in the probabilistic behaviour of the decision-making neurodynamics, and especially the neural encoding of Weber's law. (The finite size fluctuations are the statistical effects caused by the chance firing of different numbers of spiking neurons in a short time period, which are significant in networks of less that infinite size, and which can influence the way in which a network operates or settles, as described further below.) The neurodynamical formulation is based on the principle of biased competition/cooperation that has been able to simulate and explain, in a unifying framework, attention, working memory, and reward processing in a variety of tasks and at different cognitive neuroscience experimental measurement levels (Rolls and Deco 2002, Deco and Lee 2002, Corchs and Deco 2002, Deco, Pollatos and Zihl 2002, Corchs and Deco 2004, Deco and Rolls 2002, Deco and Rolls 2003, Deco and Rolls 2004, Deco, Rolls and Horwitz 2004, Szabo, Almeida, Deco and Stetter 2004, Deco and Rolls 2005b, Deco and Rolls 2005a, Rolls and Deco 2006).

7.2   The neuronal data underlying the vibrotactile discrimination

The neuronal substrate of the ability to discriminate two sequential vibrotactile stimuli has been investigated by Romo and colleagues (Romo and Salinas 2001, Hernandez, Zainos and Romo 2002, Romo, Hernandez, Zainos, Lemus and Brody 2002, Romo, Hernandez, Zainos and Salinas 2003, Romo and Salinas 2003, Romo, Hernandez and Zainos 2004, de Lafuente and Romo 2005). They used a task where trained macaques (*Macaca mulatta*) must decide and report which of two mechanical vibrations applied sequentially to their fingertips has the higher frequency of vibration by pressing one of two pushbuttons. This decision-making paradigm requires therefore the following processes: (1) the perception of the first stimulus, a 500 ms long vibration at frequency f1; (2) the storing of a trace of the f1 stimulus in short-term memory during a delay of typically 3 s; (3) the perception of the second stimulus, a 500 ms long vibration at frequency f2; and (4) the comparison of the second stimulus f2 to the trace of f1, and choosing a motor act based on this comparison (f2-f1). The vibrotactile stimuli f1 and f2 utilized were in the range of frequencies called *flutter*, i.e. within approximately 5–50 Hz.

Deco and Rolls (2006) were particularly interested in modelling the responses of ventral premotor cortex (VPC) neurons (Romo, Hernandez and Zainos 2004). The activity of VPC neurons reflects the current and the remembered sensory stimuli, their comparison, and the motor response, i.e the entire cascade of decision-making processing linking the sensory evaluation to the motor response. Many VPC neurons encode f1 during both the stimulus presentation and the delay period. During the comparison period, the averaged firing rate of VPC neurons after a latency of a few hundred milliseconds reflects the result of the comparison, i.e. the sign of (f2-f1), and correlates with the behavioural response of the monkey. In particular, we are interested in VPC neurons which show the strongest response only during the comparison period and reflect the sign of the comparison f2-f1, i.e. these neurons are only activated during the presentation of f2, with some responding to the condition f1<f2, and others to the condition f1>f2. These neurons, which are shown in Fig. 2(G-H-I) of Romo, Hernandez and Zainos (2004), reflect the decision-making step of the comparison, and therefore we will model here their probabilistic dynamical behaviour as reported by the experimental work; and through the theoretical analyses we will relate their behaviour to Weber's law.

Earlier brain areas provide inputs useful to the VPC. In the primary somatosensory area S1 the average firing rates of neurons in S1 convey information about the vibrotactile frequency f1 or f2 during the stimulation period. (The neuronal responses stop reflecting information about the stimuli immediately after the end of the stimulus.) The firing rates increase monotonically with stimulus frequency (Romo and Salinas 2003). Neurons in the secondary somatosensory area S2 respond to f1 and show significant delay activity for a few hundred milliseconds after the end of the f1 stimulus (Romo et al. 2002). Some neurons have positive and others negative monotonic relationships between their firing rate and the vibrotactile stimulus frequency. During the initial part of f2 (ca. 200 ms) the firing rate reflects either f1 or f2; later, during the last 300 ms, the firing rate reflects the comparison (f2-f1), and therefore the result of the decision. Prefrontal cortex (PFC) neurons (Brody, Hernandez, Zainos and Romo 2003a) also have a positive or negative monotonic firing rate relationship with f1. Furthermore, PFC neurons convey information about f1 into the delay period, with some neurons carrying it only during the early part of the delay period (*early neurons*), others only during the late part of the delay period (*late neurons*), and others persistently throughout the entire delay period (*persistent neurons*). During the presentation of the second stimulus f2, PFC neurons also respond like S2 neurons. Some PFC neurons respond as a function of f2 during the initial part of the comparison period, whereas other neurons show a firing rate dependency only on f1 before and at the onset of the second stimulus. In the latter part of the comparison, the firing rate reflects the comparison f2-f1. Medial premotor cortex (MPC) neurons respond similarly to PFC neurons, i.e. MPC neurons respond during f1 itself, with either positive or negative monotonic firing rate relationships, during the late part of the delay period in an f1-dependent manner in the same way as the *late* PFC neurons, and during the comparison period reflecting the comparison f2-f1 (Hernandez et al. 2002).

In summary, in the sequential vibrotactile discrimination task, S1 is predominantly sensory and the primary motor cortex (M1) is predominantly motor. A number of other cortical areas have activity that reflects the encoding, short-term memory, and comparison functions involved, perhaps as a result of information exchange between these cortical areas: the differences between S2, MPC and VPC are reflected mainly in their different latencies. In a detection task, the activity of S1 neurons codes for the stimulus but not for the behavioural choice made, whereas neuronal activity in MPC correlates with behavioural choice and detection (de Lafuente and Romo 2005). Within this context, VPC (and MPC) neurons seem to reflect the core of the processing that links sensory information with action, and therefore they may represent the decision-making process itself, rather than the representation of the stimulus. Consequently VPC neurons are excellent candidates for encoding also the probabilistic behavioural response as expressed in Weber's law. Key questions are how VPC neurons (or neurons with similar activity in connected areas such as MPC) implement the decision-making process. What are the principles by which the probabilistic decisions are taken? How is the processing implemented by the neurons?

7.3 Theoretical framework: a probabilistic attractor network

The theoretical framework within which the new model was developed was utilized by Wang (2002), which is based on a neurodynamical model first introduced by Brunel and Wang (2001), and which has been recently extended and successfully applied to explain several experimental paradigms (Rolls and Deco 2002, Deco and Rolls 2002, Deco and Rolls 2003, Deco and Rolls 2004, Deco et al. 2004, Szabo et al. 2004, Deco and Rolls 2005b). In this framework, we model probabilistic decision-making by a single attractor network of interacting neurons organized into a discrete set of populations, as depicted in Fig. 7.1. Populations or pools of neurons are defined as groups of excitatory or inhibitory neurons sharing the same inputs and connectivities. The network contains N_E (excitatory) pyramidal cells and N_I inhibitory interneurons. In the simulations, we used $N_E = 800$ and $N_I = 200$, consistent with the neurophysiologically observed proportion of 80% pyramidal cells versus 20% interneurons (Abeles 1991, Rolls and Deco 2002). The neurons are fully connected (with synaptic strengths as specified below). The specific populations have specific functions in the task. In our minimal model, we assumed that the specific populations encode the categorical result of the comparison between the two sequentially applied vibrotactile stimulation, f1 and f2, i.e. the result that f1>f2 or the result that f1<f2. Each specific population of excitatory cells contains rN_E neurons (in our simulations $r = 0.1$). In addition there is one non-specific population, named "Non-specific", which groups all other excitatory neurons in the modelled brain area not involved in the present tasks, and one inhibitory population, named "Inhibitory", grouping the local inhibitory neurons in the modelled brain area. The latter population regulates the overall activity and implements competition in the network by spreading a global inhibition signal.

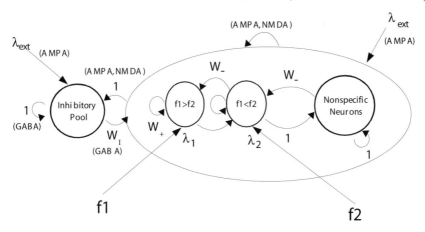

Fig. 7.1 The architecture of the neurodynamical model for a probabilistic decision-making network. The single attractor network has two populations or pools of neurons (f1>f2) and (f1<f2) which represent the decision states. One of these pools becomes active when a decision is made. If pool (f1>f2) is active, this corresponds to the decision that stimulus f1 is greater than stimulus f2. There is also a population of non-specific excitatory neurons, and a population of inhibitory neurons. Pool (f1>f2) is biased by λ_1 which reflects the strength of stimulus f1, and pool (f2>f1) is biased by λ_2 which reflects the strength of stimulus f2. (In the simulations performed f1 is the frequency of vibrotactile stimulus 1, f2 is the frequency of vibrotactile stimulus 2, and the stimuli must be compared to decide which is the higher frequency.) The integrate and fire network is subject to finite size noise, and therefore probabilistically settles into either an attractor with the population (f1>f2) active, or with the population (f1<f2) active, depending on the biasing inputs λ_1 and λ_2. The network is thus a biased competition model of decision-making. The weights connecting the different populations of neurons are shown as w_+, w_-, w_I, and 1, and the values found in the mean field analysis are given in the text. All neurons receive a small random Poisson set of input spikes λ_{ext} from other neurons in the system. The nonspecific excitatory neurons are connected to pool (f1>f2) as well as to pool (f1<f2). (After Deco and Rolls 2006.)

Because we were mainly interested in the non-stationary probabilistic behaviour of the network, the proper level of description at the microscopic level is captured by the spiking and synaptic dynamics of one-compartment *Integrate-and-Fire* (IF) neuron models (Deco and Rolls 2005a). An IF neuron integrates the afferent current generated by the incoming spikes, and fires when the depolarization of the cell membrane crosses a threshold (see Section B.6). At this level of detail the model allows the use of realistic biophysical time constants, latencies and conductances to model the synaptic current, which in turn allows a thorough study of the realistic time scales and firing involved in the time evolution of the neural activity. Consequently, the simulated neuronal dynamics, that putatively underlie cognitive processes, can be quantitatively compared with experimental data. For this reason, it is very useful to include a thorough description of the different time constants of the synaptic activity. The IF neurons are modelled as having three types of receptor mediating the synaptic currents flowing into them: AMPA, NMDA (both activated by glutamate), and GABA receptors. The excitatory recurrent post-synaptic currents (EPSCs) are considered to be mediated by AMPA (fast) and NMDA (slow) receptors; external EPSCs imposed onto the network from outside are modelled as being driven only by AMPA receptors. Inhibitory post-synaptic currents (IPSCs) to both excitatory and inhibitory neurons are mediated by GABA receptors. The details of the mathematical formulation are summarized in previous publications (Brunel and Wang 2001, Deco and Rolls 2005b), and are provided in Section 7.8.

We modified the conductance values for the synapses between pairs of neurons by synaptic connection weights, which can deviate from their default value 1. The structure and function of the network was achieved by differentially setting the weights within and between populations of neurons. The labelling of the weights is defined in Fig. 7.1. We assumed that the connections are already formed, by for example earlier self-organization mechanisms, as if they were established by Hebbian learning, i.e. the coupling will be strong if the pair of neurons have correlated activity (i.e. covarying firing rates), and weak if they are activated in an uncorrelated way. We assumed that the two decisions 'f1>f2' and 'f1<f2', corresponding to the two categories, are already encoded, in the sense that the monkey is already trained that pushing one or the other button, but not both, might produce a reward. As a consequence of this, neurons within a specific excitatory population are mutually coupled with a strong weight w_+, and each such population thus forms an attractor. Furthermore, the populations encoding these two decisions are likely to have anti-correlated activity in this behavioural context, resulting in weaker than average connections between the two different populations. Consequently, we choose a weaker value $w_- = 1 - r(w_+ - 1)/(1 - r)$, so that the overall recurrent excitatory synaptic drive in the spontaneous state remains constant as w_+ is varied (Brunel and Wang 2001). Neurons in the inhibitory population are mutually connected with an intermediate weight $w = 1$. They are also connected with all excitatory neurons in the same layer with the same intermediate weight, which for excitatory-to-inhibitory connections is $w = 1$, and for inhibitory-to-excitatory connections is denoted by a weight w_I. Neurons in a specific excitatory population are connected to neurons in the non-selective population in the same layer with a feedforward synaptic weight $w = 1$ and a feedback synaptic connection of weight w_-.

Each individual population is driven by two different kinds of input. First, all neurons in the model network receive spontaneous background activity from outside the module through $N_{ext} = 800$ external excitatory connections. Each connection carries a Poisson spike train at a spontaneous rate of 3 Hz, which is a typical spontaneous firing rate value observed in the cerebral cortex. This results in a background external input with a rate summed across all synapses of 2.4 kHz for each neuron. Second, the neurons in the two specific populations additionally receive external inputs encoding stimulus-specific information. They are assumed to originate from the somatosensory area S2 and from the PFC, encoding the frequency of both stimuli f1 (stored) and f2 (present) to be compared during the comparison period, i.e. when the second stimulus is applied. (Stimuli f1 and f2 influence λ_1 and λ_2 as shown in Fig. 7.1. The way in which the different S2 and PFC neurons described by Romo et al. (2004) are combined linearly to produce λ_1 and λ_2 is described by Deco and Rolls (2006).)

In summary, f1 is the frequency of vibrotactile stimulus 1, f2 is the frequency of vibrotactile stimulus 2, and the stimuli must be compared to decide which is the higher frequency. The single attractor network has two populations or pools of neurons (f1>f2) and (f1<f2) which represent the decision states (see Fig. 7.1). One of these pools becomes active when a decision is made. If pool (f1>f2) is active, this corresponds to the decision that stimulus f1 is greater than stimulus f2. Pool (f1>f2) is biased by λ_1 which reflects the frequency of stimulus f1, and pool (f2>f1) is biased by λ_2 which reflects the frequency of stimulus f2. The integrate and fire network is subject to finite size noise, and therefore probabilistically settles into an attractor either with the population (f1>f2) active, or with the population (f1<f2) active, depending on the biasing inputs λ_1 and λ_2. The network is thus a biased competition model of decision-making. All neurons receive a small random Poisson set of input spikes λ_{ext} from other neurons in the system.

7.4 Stationary multistability analysis: mean-field

A first requirement for using the network described above as a probabilistic decision-making neurodynamical framework is to tune its connectivity such that the network operates in a regime of multistability. This means that at least for the stationary conditions, i.e. for periods after the dynamical transients, different possible attractors are stable. The attractors of interest for our task correspond to high activation (high spiking rates) or low activation (low spiking rates) of the neurons in the specific populations (f1>f2) and (f1<f2). The activation of the specific population (f1>f2) and the simultaneous lack of activation of the specific population (f1<f2) corresponds to encoding associated with a motor response of the monkey reporting the categorical decision f1>f2. The opposite decision corresponds to the opposite attractor states in the two specific neuronal populations. Low activity in both specific populations (the "spontaneous state") corresponds to encoding that no decision has been made, i.e. the monkey does not answer or generates a random motor response. The same happens if both specific populations are activated (the "pair state"). Because the monkey responds in a probabilistic way depending on the different stimuli, the operating working point of the network should be such that both possible categorical decisions, i.e. both possible single states, and sometimes (depending on the stimuli) the pair and spontaneous states, are possible stable states.

The network's operating regimes just described can all occur if the synaptic connection weights are appropriate. To determine the correct weights a mean field analysis was used. Although a network of integrate-and-fire with randomness in the spikes being received is necessary to understand the dynamics of the network, and how these are related to probabilistic decision-making, this means that the spiking activities fluctuate from time-point to time-point and from trial to trial. Consequently, integrate-and-fire simulations are computationally expensive and their results probabilistic, which makes them rather unsuitable for systematic parameter explorations. To solve this problem, we simplified the dynamics via the *mean-field* approach at least for the stationary conditions, i.e. for periods after the dynamical transients, and then analyzed the bifurcation diagrams of the dynamics. The essence of the mean-field approximation is to simplify the integrate-and-fire equations by replacing after the diffusion approximation (Tuckwell 1988, Amit and Brunel 1997, Brunel and Wang 2001), the sums of the synaptic components by the average D.C. component and a fluctuation term. The stationary dynamics of each population can be described by the *population transfer function*, which provides the average population rate as a function of the average input current. The set of stationary, self-reproducing rates ν_i for the different populations i in the network can be found by solving a set of coupled self-consistency equations using the formulation derived by Brunel and Wang (2001) (see Section 7.9). The equations governing the activities in the mean-field approximation can hence be studied by standard methods of dynamical systems. The formulation departs from the equations describing the dynamics of one neuron to reach a stochastic analysis of the mean-first passage time of the membrane potentials, which results in a description of the population spiking rates as functions of the model parameters, in the limit of very large N. Obtaining a mean-field analysis of the stationary states that is consistent with the network when operating dynamically as an integrate-and-fire network is an important part of the approach used by Deco and Rolls (see Sections 7.9, B.7 and B.8).

To investigate how the stable states depend on the connection parameters w_+ and w_I, we solved the mean-field equations for particular values of these parameters starting at different initial conditions. For example, to investigate the stability of the state described by population (f1>f2) being in an active state and all other populations inactive, we initialize the system with that population at 10 Hz, all other excitatory populations (including the non-specific ones) at 3 Hz, and the inhibitory population at 9 Hz. If and only if, after solving the equations

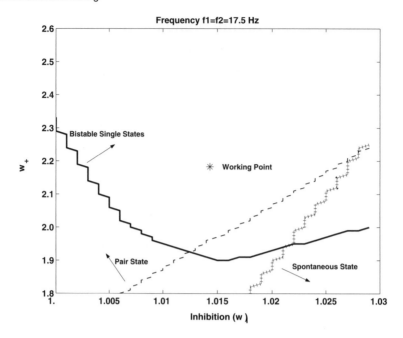

Fig. 7.2 Mean-field analysis to determine suitable values of the synaptic weights for the decision-making network. The bifurcation diagram is for the particular case where the behavioural decision-making is at chance due to f1 and f2 being equal. The diagram shows how the stable states of the average firing rate vary as a function of the synaptic strengths w_+ and w_I for the case: f1=f2=17.5 Hz corresponding to a low frequency of vibrotactile stimulation. The different regions where single states, a pair state, and a spontaneous firing rate state are stable are shown. In the following simulations we focus on the region of multistability (i.e. where either one or the other pool of neurons wins the competition), so that a probabilistic decision is possible, and therefore a convenient working point is one corresponding to a connectivity given by w_+=2.2 and w_I=1.015. (After Deco and Rolls 2006.)

numerically[30], the population (f1>f2) is still active (meaning that they have a firing rate $\geq$ 10 Hz) but no other excitatory population is active, we conclude that the state is stable. This procedure is then repeated for all other combinations of w_+ and w_I to find the region where the active population (f1>f2) is stable. The stable regions of the other states are found in the same way.

Figure 7.2 presents the bifurcation diagrams resulting from the mean-field analysis, for a particular case where the behavioural decision-making is hardest and is in fact purely random (i.e. at chance) due an equality between f1 and f2. Figure 7.2 shows how the stable states of average firing rate vary as a function of the strength of w_+ and w_I for the case: f1=f2=17.5 Hz corresponding to a low frequency of vibrotactile stimulation. In these cases, the specific populations (f1>f2) and (f1<f2) received an extra stimulation of λ_1 and λ_2, respectively, encoding the two vibrotactile stimuli to be compared. (The way in which these λ values were calculated simply reflects the neurons recorded in the VPC and connected areas, as described by Deco and Rolls (2006).) The different regions where single states, a pair state, and a spontaneous state are stable are shown. In the simulations, Deco and Rolls (2006) focused on a region of multistability, so that a probabilistic decision is possible, and therefore a convenient working point (see Fig. 7.2) is one corresponding to a connectivity given by $w_+ = 2.2$ and

---

[30] For all simulation periods studied, the mean-field equations were integrated using the Euler method with step size 0.1 and 4000 iterations, which always allowed for convergence.

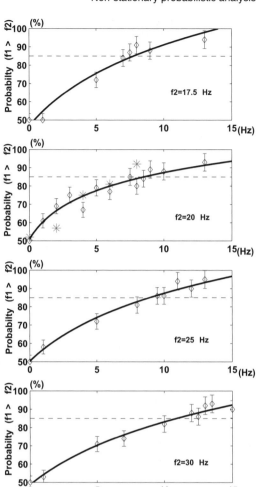

Fig. 7.3 Probability of correct discrimination (± sd) as a function of the difference between the two presented vibrotactile frequencies to be compared. In the simulations, we assume that f1>f2 by a Δ-value (labelled 'Delta frequency (f1-f2)'), i.e. f1=f2+Δ. The points correspond to the trial averaged spiking simulations. The line interpolates the points with a logarithmic function. The horizontal dashed line represents the threshold of correct classification for a performance of 85% correct discrimination. The second panel down includes actual neuronal data described by Romo and Salinas (2003) for the f2=20 Hz condition (indicated by *). (After Deco and Rolls 2006.)

$w_I = 1.015$.

Overall, Fig. 7.2 shows very large regions of stability, so that the network behaviour described here is very robust.

7.5 Non-stationary probabilistic analysis: spiking dynamics

A full characterization of the dynamics, and especially of its probabilistic behaviour, including the non-stationary regime of the system, can only be obtained through computer simulations of the spiking network model. Moreover, these simulations enable comparisons between the model in which spikes occur and neurophysiological data. The simulations of the spiking dynamics of the network were integrated numerically using the second order Runge–Kutta method with step size 0.05 ms. Each simulation was started by a period of 500 ms where no stimulus was presented, to allow the network to stabilize. The non-stationary evolution of spiking activity was averaged over 200 trials initialized with different random seeds. In all cases, Deco and Rolls (2006) aimed to model the behaviour of the VPC neurons as shown in Fig. 2(G-H-I) of Romo, Hernandez and Zainos (2004) which reflect the decision-making performed during the comparison period. Therefore, we studied the non-stationary probabilistic behaviour of the spiking network defined in Fig. 7.1, during this comparison period (during the presentation of f2), by stimulating the network simultaneously with f1 and f2. This was done by increasing the rate of the Poisson train to the neurons of both specific populations (f1>f2) and (f1<f2) by an extra value of λ_1 and λ_2, respectively, as these encode the two vibrotactile stimuli to be compared.

Figure 7.3 shows the probability of correct discrimination as a function of the difference between the two presented vibrotactile frequencies to be compared. We assume that f1>f2 by a Δ-value, i.e. f1=f2+Δ. (In Fig. 7.3 this value is called "Delta frequency (f1-f2)".) Each diamond-point in the Figure corresponds to the result calculated by averaging 200 trials of the full spiking simulations. The lines were calculated by fitting the points with a logarithmic function. A correct classification occurs when during the 500 ms comparison period, the network evolves to a 'single-state' attractor that shows a high level of spiking activity (larger than 10 Hz) for the population (f1>f2), and simultaneously a low level of spiking activity for the population (f1<f2) (at the level of the spontaneous activity). One can observe from the different panels corresponding to different base vibrotactile frequencies f2, that for reaching a threshold of correct classification of for example 85% (horizontal dashed line in Fig. 7.3), the difference between f1 and f2 must become larger as f2 increases. The second panel of Fig. 7.3 shows a good fit between the actual neuronal data described by Romo and Salinas (2003) for the f2=20 Hz condition (indicated by *), and the results obtained with the model. Figure 7.4 plots the critical discrimination Δ-value corresponding to an 85% correct performance level (the "difference-threshold") as a function of the base-frequency f2. The "difference-threshold" increases linearly as a function of the base-frequency. This corresponds to Weber's law for the vibrotactile discrimination task.

The analysis shown in Figs. 7.3 and 7.4 suggests that Weber's law, and consequently the ability to discriminate two stimuli, is encoded in the probability of performing a transition to the correct final attractor. To reinforce this hypothesis, Fig. 7.5 shows that Weber's law is not encoded in the firing rate of the VPC decision-making neurons that we modelled. We simulated again a situation corresponding to the cases where f1 is larger than f2 by a Δ-value, and therefore the network will perform correctly when the dynamics perform a transition to the final single attractor corresponding to high activity in the population (f1>f2) and low activity in the population (f1<f2). Figure 7.5 plots for three different frequencies f2, the rate of the (f1<f2) population (for the cases where this population correctly won the competition and the network has performed a transition to the proper attractor) as a function of the difference between the two vibrotactile frequencies to be compared. The plots show the results obtained with the spiking simulations (the diamond-points correspond to the average values over 200 trials, and the error bars to the standard deviation). The lines correspond to the mean-field

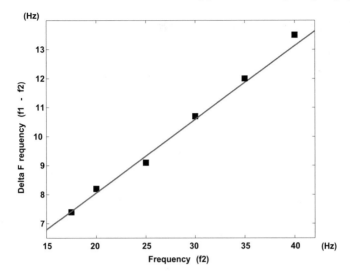

Fig. 7.4 Weber's law for the vibrotactile discrimination task. The critical discrimination Δ-value ('differ-ence-threshold') is shown corresponding to an 85% correct performance level as a function of the base frequency f2. The 'difference-threshold' increases linearly as a function of the base frequency. (After Deco and Rolls 2006.)

calculations. A good agreement between the spiking simulations and the consistent mean-field results is observed. The most interesting observation is the fact that the firing rate of the population (f1>f2) in the correct attractor, for different base frequencies f2 and for different differences between f1 and f2 (Δf), is practically constant, i.e. the firing rate of the population encoding the result of the comparison does not encode Weber's law.

Figure 7.6 shows a typical evolution of the network of VPC neurons during the comparison period for the specific case of having f1=30 Hz and f2=20 Hz. The top part of Fig. 7.6 plots the evolution of the spiking rate of the populations (f1>f2), (f1<f2), and the inhibitory population as a function of time. The utilized bin widths for the simulations were 20 ms. The transition shown corresponds to a correct trial, i.e. showing a transition to the correct final attractor encoding the result of the discrimination f1>f2. We observe that after 200 ms the populations (f1>f2) and (f1<f2) start to separate in such a way that the population (f1>f2) wins the competition and the network performs a transition to a single-state final attractor corresponding to a correct discrimination (i.e. high activity in the population (f1>f2) and low activity in the population (f1<f2)). The bottom part of Fig. 7.6 plots the corresponding rastergrams of 10 randomly selected neurons for each pool in the network. Each vertical line corresponds to the generation of a spike. The spatio-temporal spiking activity shows the transition to the correct final single-state attractor.

In Figure 2(G-H-I) of Romo et al. (2004), the authors analysed the response during f2 of VPC neurons performing the comparison as a function of both f1 and f2. Figure 7.7 shows the numerical results and analysis corresponding to those cases. Figure 7.7A plots a neuron of the population (f1<f2) during the comparison period of f1 and f2 vibrotactile stimulation. The labels on the left indicate f1, f2 pairs in terms of the vibrotactile frequencies. Each row of ticks is a trial, and each tick is a spike. All neurons were tested with 10 trials per stimulus pair, selecting only trials where the network performed correctly. The top 5 cases correspond to a situation where f1<f2 and therefore the population (f1<f2) is highly activated after 100–200 ms. The following 5 cases at the bottom correspond to a situation where f1>f2 and therefore the population (f1<f2) is not activated. (The population (f1>f2), not shown in Fig. 7.7, won

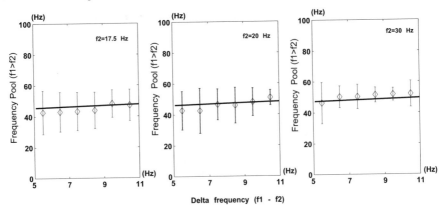

Fig. 7.5 Final stationary spiking rate of the (f1<f2) population (after transients) as a function of the difference between the two vibrotactile frequencies to be compared, for the cases where this population correctly won the competition and the network has performed a transition to the proper attractor. The plots show the results obtained with the spiking simulations (diamond-points correspond to the average values over 200 trials, and the error bars to the standard deviation). The lines correspond to the mean-field calculations. The rate of the population encoding the result of the comparison is independent of f2 and of the difference between f1 and f2. (After Deco and Rolls 2006.)

the competition in the 5 cases shown at the bottom of Fig. 7.7A, and therefore inhibited the (f1<f2) population in the correctly discriminated trials selected for this Figure.)

To analyse more quantitatively the dependence of the average firing rate of the VPC neurons encoding the comparisons as a function of f1 and f2, Romo et al. (2004) fitted and plotted the time evolution of the coefficients that directly measure the dependence on f1 and f2. Let us denote by $r(t)$ the trial averaged firing rate of the population (f1<f2) at time t. We determined the coefficients $a1(t), a2(t)$ and $a3(t)$ that fit the firing rate of the population (f1<f2) according to $r(t) = a1(t)f1 + a2(t)f2 + a3(t)$. We considered for all 10 f1,f2 pair combinations shown in Fig. 7.7A, 50 correct trials, using a bin width of 50 ms. Figure 7.7B plots the evolution of $a1(t)$ and $a2(t)$ during the comparison period. In this Figure, both coefficients evolve in an antisymmetrical fashion, indicating that the average firing rate $r(t)$ depends only on the difference between f1 and f2 (i.e. $a1(t) = -a2(t)$). Even more, in the range of vibrotactile flutter frequencies, the simulation and neurophysiological results show that the firing rate depends significantly only on the sign of the difference and not on the magnitudes of the vibrotactile frequency values.

Thus the present theoretical analysis suggests a specific neurophysiological prediction, that Weber's Law for frequency discrimination could be implemented not by the firing rate of a given population of neurons (which reflects just the sign of the difference between f1 and f2), but by the probability that that particular population will be activated, which is influenced by both the difference between f1 and f2 and by the absolute value of the frequency. This prediction could be tested by a trial-by-trial analysis of the neurophysiological data.

A second prediction is shown in Fig. 7.8. We calculated for a fixed f2=25 Hz and different f1>f2 (from 1 Hz to 13 Hz), the probability of correct or incorrect discrimination, and the corresponding reaction time. The reaction time was the time that the winning population ((f1>f2) for the correct cases, and (f1<f2) for the incorrect cases) took to cross a threshold of a firing rate of 20 Hz. (We considered the averaged reaction time over 200 trials.) Figure 7.8A plots the relation between the reaction time and the probability of correct classification. The larger the probability of correct classification, the faster is the decision-making, which is reasonable and consistent with the decision-making literature. Figure 7.8B plots the reaction

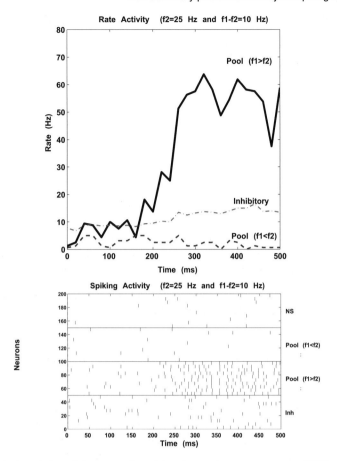

Fig. 7.6 Dynamical evolution of the network activity of ventral premotor cortex (VPC) neurons during the comparison period for the specific case of having f1=30 Hz and f2=20 Hz. The top part plots the evolution of the spiking rate of the populations (f1>f2), (f1<f2) and the inhibitory population as a function of time. The utilized bin widths for the simulations were 20 ms. The bottom part plots the corresponding rastergrams of 10 randomly selected neurons for each pool in the network. Each vertical line corresponds to the generation of a spike. The spatio-temporal spiking activity shows the transition to the correct final single-state attractor, i.e. a transition to the correct final attractor encoding the result of the discrimination (f1>f2). We observe that after 200 ms the populations (f1>f2) and (f1<f2) start to separate, in such a way that the population (f1>f2) wins the competition and the network performs a transition to a single-state final attractor corresponding to a correct discrimination (i.e. high activity in the population (f1>f2) and low activity in the population (f1<f2)). (After Deco and Rolls 2006.)

time of an incorrect decision, as a function of the probability of performing a misclassification. The behaviour is now the converse, in that a low probability of incorrect discrimination implies also shorter reaction times. This means that the reaction time of a correct or incorrect classification is similar, and therefore the dependence on the probability of a correct or incorrect classification is inverted.

The model also gives further insights into the mechanisms by which Weber's Law is implemented. We hypothesized that because $\Delta f/f$ is practically constant in the model, the difference of frequencies Δf required to push the single attractor network towards an attractor basin might increase with f because as f increases, shunting (divisive) inhibition produced by inhibitory feedback inputs (from the inhibitory interneurons) might act divisively on the

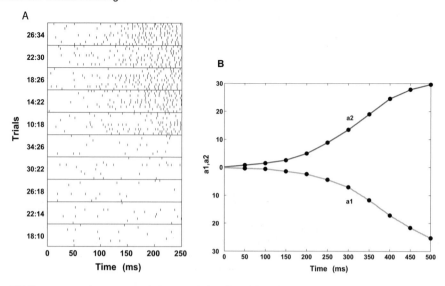

Fig. 7.7 Responses of a neuron of the population (f1<f2) during the comparison period of f1 and f2 stimulation. The simulations corresponds to the experimental cases measured and studied by Romo et al. (2004) (see Fig. 2G-H-I of that paper). The different stimulation cases labelled on the left indicate f1, f2 pairs of vibrotactile stimulation frequencies. (A) Rastergrams. Each row of ticks is a trial, and each tick is a spike. All neurons were tested with 10 trials for each stimulus pair, selecting only trials where the network performed correctly. (B) Evolution of fitting coefficients (see text) $a1(t)$ and $a2(t)$ during the comparison period. Both coefficients evolve in an antisymmetrical fashion, indicating that the average firing rate $r(t)$ is dependent only on the sign of the difference between f1 and f2 (i.e. $a1(t) = -a2(t)$), and not on the magnitude of the difference. (After Deco and Rolls 2006.)

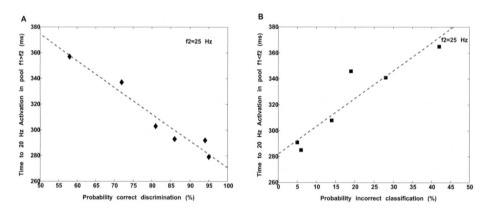

Fig. 7.8 Reaction time and probability dependence for a fixed f2=25 Hz and different f1>f2 (from 1 Hz to 13 Hz). The reaction time was the time that the winning population ((f1>f2) for the correct cases, and (f1<f2) for the incorrect cases) took to cross a threshold of 20 Hz. (The reaction time was averaged across 200 trials.) (A) Reaction time as a function of the probability of correct classification. The larger the probability the faster is the decision-making. (B) Reaction time of an incorrect decision, as a function of the probability of performing a misclassification. (After Deco and Rolls 2006.)

pyramidal cells in the attractor network to shunt the excitatory inputs f1 and f2. In more detail, as the base frequency f increases, more excitation will be provided to the network by the inputs λ_1 and λ_2, this will tend to increase the firing rates of the pyramidal cells which

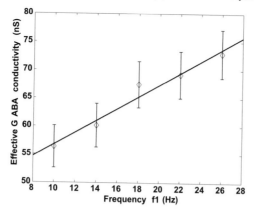

Fig. 7.9 The conductance in nS (mean ± sd) produced by the GABA inputs to the pyramidal cells as a function of the base frequency f1. The effective conductance produced through the GABA synapses (i.e. $I_{GABA}/(V - V_I)$) was averaged over the time window in which the stimuli were presented in one of the excitatory neuron pools, when the base frequency was f1, and f2-f1 was set to 8 Hz. (After Deco and Rolls 2006.)

will in turn provide a larger excitatory input to the inhibitory neurons. This will tend to make the inhibitory neurons fire faster, and their GABA synapses onto the pyramidal cells will be more active. Because these GABA synapses open chloride channels and act with a driving potential $V_I = -70$ mV which is relatively close to the membrane potential (which will be in the range $V_L = -70$ mV to $V_{thr} = -50$ mV), a large part of the GABA synaptic input to the pyramidal cells will tend to shunt, that is to act divisively upon, the excitatory inputs to the pyramidal cells from the vibrotactile biasing inputs λ_1 and λ_2. To compensate for this current shunting effect, f1 and f2 are likely to need to increase in proportion to the base frequency f in order to maintain the efficacy of their biasing effect. To assess this hypothesis, we measured the change in conductance produced by the GABA inputs as a function of the base frequency. Figure 7.9 shows that the conductance increases linearly with the base frequency (as does the firing rate of the GABA neurons, not illustrated). The shunting effect does appear therefore to be dividing the excitatory inputs to the pyramidal cells in the linear way as a function of f that we hypothesized.

Deco and Rolls (2006) therefore proposed that Weber's Law is implemented by shunting effects acting on pyramidal cells that are produced by inhibitory neuron inputs which increase linearly as the base frequency increases, so that the difference of frequencies Δf required to push the network reliably into one of its decision attractors must increase in proportion to the base frequency. We checked the excitatory inputs to the pyramidal cells (for which $V_E = 0$ mV), and found that their conductances were much smaller (in the order of 5 nS for the AMPA and 15 nS for the NMDA receptors) than those produced by the GABA receptors, so that it is the GABA-induced conductance changes that dominate, and that produce the shunting inhibition.

The results described above indicate that the probabilistic settling of the system is related to the finite size noise effects of the spiking dynamics of the individual neurons with their Poisson-like spike trains in a system of limited size. To investigate this further, we simulated networks with different numbers of neurons, N. The noise due to the finite size effects is expected to increase as the network becomes smaller, and indeed to be proportional to $1/\sqrt{N}$. We show in Fig. 7.10 the effects of altering N on the operation of the network, where $N = N_E + N_I$, and $N_E : N_I$, was held at 4:1 as in the simulations shown earlier. The simulations were for f1=30 Hz and f2=22 Hz. Figure 7.10 shows overall that when N is larger

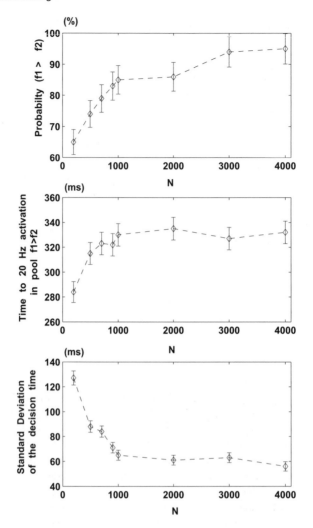

Fig. 7.10 The effects of altering N, the number of neurons in the network, on the operation of the decision-making network. The simulations were for f1=30 Hz and f2=22 Hz. The top panel shows the probability that the network will settle into the correct (f1>f2) attractor state. The mean $\pm$ the standard deviation is shown. The middle panel shows the time for a decision to be reached, that is for the system to reach a criterion of a firing rate of 20 Hz in the pool (f1>f2). The mean $\pm$ the standard deviation of the sampled mean is shown. The bottom panel shows the standard deviation of the reaction time. (After Deco and Rolls 2006.)

than approximately 1,000, the network shows the expected settling to the (f1 > f2) attractor state on a proportion of occasions that is in the range 85–93%, increasing only a little as the number of neurons reaches 4,000 (top panel). The settling remains probabilistic, as shown by the standard deviations in the probability that the (f1 > f2) attractor state will be reached (top panel). When N is less than approximately 1,000, the finite size noise effects become very marked, as shown by the fact that the network reaches the correct attractor state (f1>f2) much less frequently, and in that the time for a decision to be reached can be premature and fast, as the large fluctuations in the stochastic noise can cause the system to reach the criterion [in this case of a firing rate of 20 Hz in the pool (f1>f2)] too quickly.

The overall conclusion of the results shown in Fig. 7.10 is that the size of the network, N, does influence the probabilistic settling of the network to the decision state. None of these probabilistic attractor and decision-related settling effects would of course be found in a mean-field or purely rate simulation, without spiking activity. The size of N in the brain is likely to be greater than 1,000 (and probably in the neocortex in the range 4,000–12,000) (see Table 1.1). It will be of interest to investigate further this scaling as a function of the number of neurons in a population with a firing rate distribution that is close to what is found in the brain, namely close to exponential (Franco, Rolls, Aggelopoulos and Jerez 2007) (see Section C.3.1.2).

7.6 Properties of this model of decision-making

Key properties of this biased attractor model of decision-making are now considered.

The decisions are taken probabilistically because of the finite size noise due to spiking activity in the integrate-and-fire dynamical network, with the probability that a particular decision is made depending on the biasing inputs provided by the sensory stimuli f1 and f2. Deco and Rolls (2006) showed that the relevant parameters for the decision to be made to a criterion of a given percent correct about whether f1 is different from f2 by the network are found not to be the absolute value of f1 or f2, but the difference between them scaled by their absolute value. If the difference between the two stimuli at which they can be discriminated $\Delta f = f1\text{-}f2$, then it is found that Δf increases linearly as a function of the base frequency f2, which is Weber's Law. The results show that Weber's law does not depend on the final firing rates of neurons in the attractor, but instead reflects the nature of the probabilistic settling into a decision-related attractor, which depends on the statistical fluctuations in the network, the synaptic connectivity, and the difference between the bias input frequencies f1 and f2 scaled by the baseline input f2.

Weber's law is usually formulated as $\Delta f / (f_0 + f) = $ a constant, where f_0 allows the bottom part of the curve to asymptote at f_0. In vision, f_0 is sometimes referred to as "dark light". The result is that there is a part of the curve where Δf is linearly related to f, and the curve of Δf vs f need not go through the origin. This corresponds to the data shown in Fig. 7.4.

An analysis of the non-stationary evolution of the dynamics of the network model, performed by explicit full spiking simulations, shows that Weber's law is implemented in the probability of transition from the initial spontaneous firing state to one of the two possible attractor states. In this decision-making paradigm, the firing rates of neurons in the VPC encode the outcome of the comparison and therefore the decision and motor response, but not how strong the stimuli are, i.e. what Weber called "sensation" (as described for example in a detection task by de Lafuente and Romo (2005)). The probability of obtaining a specific decision, i.e. of detecting a just noticeable difference, is encoded in the stochastic dynamics of the network. More specifically, the origin of the fluctuations that will drive the transitions towards particular decisions depends on the connectivity between the different populations, on the size of the populations, and on the Poisson-like spike trains of the individual neurons in the system. In other words, the neural code for the outcome of the decision is reflected in the high rate of one of the populations of neurons, but whether the rate of a particular population becomes high is probabilistic. This means that an essential part of how the decision process is encoded is contained in the *synapses*, in the *finite size* of the network, and in the Poisson-like firing of individual neurons in the network.

The statistical fluctuations in the network are due to the finite size noise, which approximates to the square root of the (firing rate / number of neurons in the population) (see Mattia and Del Giudice (2002)), as shown in Fig. 7.10. This is the first time we know when the implementation of a psychophysical law is not the firing rate of the neurons, nor the spike timing, nor is single neuron based, but instead is based on the synaptic connectivity of the network and on statistical fluctuations due to the spiking activity in the network.

The way in which the system settles (i.e. the probability of reaching one attractor state vs the other from the initial spontaneous state, and the time it takes) depends on factors that include the distortion of the attractor landscapes produced by the biasing inputs λ_1 and λ_2 which will influence both the shapes and the depth of the attractor basins, and the finite size noise effects. Of particular importance in relation to Weber's law is likely to be that when λ_1 and λ_2 increase, the increased firing of the neurons in the two attractors results in more activity of the inhibitory feedback neurons, which then produce effectively divisive inhibition on the principal cells of the attractor network. This is reflected in the conductance change produced by the GABA inputs to the pyramidal cells shown in Fig. 7.9. The inhibitory feedback is mainly divisive because the GABA-activated channels operate primarily as a current shunt, and do not produce much hyperpolarization, given that V_I is relatively close to the membrane potential. After the division implemented by the feedback inhibition, the differential bias required to push the network reliably into one of the attractors must then be larger, and effectively the driving force ($\lambda_1 - \lambda_2$ or $\Delta\lambda$) must get larger in proportion to the inhibition. As the inhibition is proportional to λ, this produces the result that $\Delta\lambda/\lambda$ is approximately a constant. We thus propose that Weber's Law, $\Delta I/I$ is a constant, is implemented by shunting effects acting on pyramidal cells that are produced by inhibitory neuron inputs which increase linearly as the baseline input I increases, so that the difference of intensities ΔI required to push the network reliably into one of its attractors must increase in proportion to the base input I.

We emphasize that this account (Deco and Rolls 2006) of Weber's Law is intended to be a general account, and is not restricted to the particular data set or brain system against which the development of the model described here was validated.

Another interesting aspect of the model is that the recurrent connectivity, and the relatively long time constant of the NMDA receptors (Wang 2002), together enable the attractor network to accumulate evidence over a long time period of several hundred milliseconds. This is an important aspect of the functionality of attractor networks.

Although the model described here is effectively a single attractor network, we note that the network need not be localized to one brain region. Long-range connections between cortical areas enable networks in different brain areas to interact in the way needed to implement a single attractor network. The requirement is that the synapses between the neurons in any one pool be set up by Hebb-like associative synaptic modification, and this is likely to be a property of connectivity between areas as well as within areas (Rolls and Treves 1998, Rolls and Deco 2002). In this sense, the decision could be thought of as distributed across different brain areas. Consistent with this, Romo and colleagues have found neurons related to vibrotactile decisions not only in VPC, but in a number of connected brain areas including MPC, as described in Section 7.2. In order to achieve the desired probabilistic settling behaviour, the network we describe must not have very high inhibition, and, related to this, may sometimes not settle into one of its attractor states. In a forced choice task in which a decision must be reached on every trial, a possible solution is to have a second decision-making network, with parameters adjusted so that it will settle into one of its states (chosen at chance) even if a preceding network in the decision-making chain has not settled. This could be an additional reason for having a series of networks in different brain regions involved in the decision-making process.

The model described here is different in a number of ways from accumulator or counter models which may include a noise term and which undergo a random walk in real time, which is a diffusion process (Ratcliff, Zandt and McKoon 1999, Carpenter and Williams 1995) (see further Wang (2002) and Usher and McClelland (2001)). In accumulator models, a mechanism for computing the difference between the stimuli is not described, whereas in the current model this is achieved, and scaled by f, by the feedback inhibition included in the attractor network. Second, in the current model the decision corresponds to high firing rates in one of the attractors, and there is no arbitrary threshold that must be reached. Third, the noise in the current model is not arbitrary, but is accounted for by finite size noise effects of the spiking dynamics of the individual neurons with their Poisson-like spike trains in a system of limited size. Fourth, because the attractor network has recurrent connections, the way in which it settles into a final attractor state (and thus the decision process) can naturally take place over quite a long time, as information gradually and stochastically builds up due to the positive feedback in the recurrent network, the weights in the network, and the biasing inputs, as shown in Figs. 7.6 and 7.7.

The model of decision-making described here is also different to a model suggested by Sugrue, Corrado and Newsome (2005) in which it is suggested that the probabilistic relative value of each action directly dictates the instantaneous probability of choosing each action on the current trial. The present model shows how probabilistic decisions could be taken depending on the two biasing inputs (λ_1 and λ_2 in Fig. 7.1, which could be equal) to a biased competition attractor network subject to statistical fluctuations related to finite size noise in the dynamics of the integrate-and-fire network.

The current model of decision-making is part of a unified approach to attention, reward-reversal, and sequence learning, in which biasing inputs influence the operation of attractor networks that operate using biased competition (Rolls and Deco 2002, Deco and Rolls 2005a, Rolls 2005). The same approach is now seen to be useful in understanding decision-making and its relation to Weber's Law, and in understanding the details of the neuronal responses that are recorded during decision-making.

The model makes specific neurophysiological predictions. One, on reaction times in relation to $\Delta f / f$, is shown in Fig. 7.8. Another prediction is that the model shows that Weber's law for frequency discrimination could be implemented not by the firing rate of a given population of neurons (which reflects just the discrete decision taken), but by the probability that a particular population will be activated, which depends on $\Delta f / f$. This prediction could be tested by a trial-by-trial analysis of the neurophysiological data in which the firing of neurons at different base frequencies f and for different Δf is measured, to investigate whether the type of result shown in Fig. 7.3, and thereby in Fig. 7.4, which are derived from the model, are also found in the neuronal data from the experiments, and this would also usefully confirm that Weber's Law holds at the neuronal level in this particular vibrotactile task with a delay. In particular, although Romo, Hernandez and Zainos (2004) in their Fig. 5 show that choice probability and neuronal activity increases as a function of f2-f1, we predict that neurons should follow the functions shown in Figs. 7.3 and 7.4 for different values of Δf and f, and it would be of interest to test this prediction.

We note that Weber's law holds in most though not all discrimination situations, and to the extent that Weber's law does generally hold, the model described here provides a computational neuroscience-based account of how it arises. This is the first time we know when the implementation of a psychophysical law is not the firing rate of the neurons, nor the spike timing, nor is single neuron based, but instead is based on the synaptic connectivity of the network and on statistical fluctuations due to the spiking activity in the network.

In conclusion, we now have a model for how attractor networks could operate by biased competition to implement probabilistic decision-making. This type of model could operate in very many brain areas, as described in Section 7.7. This model of decision-making is part of the larger conceptual issue of how memory networks retrieve information. In this case the short-term memory property of the attractor network helps the network to integrate information over time to reach the decision. Although retrieval of information from attractor networks has been intensively studied using *inter alia* approaches from theoretical physics (see Section B.3, Amit (1989), and Rolls and Treves (1998)), the way in which the retrieval is probabilistic when an integrate-and-fire implementation with spiking neurons is considered has been less studied. The approaches of Brunel and Wang (2001) and Deco and Rolls (2006) do open up the issue of the probabilistic operation of memory networks with spiking dynamics.

We may raise the conceptually important issue of why the operation of what is effectively memory retrieval is probabilistic. Part of the answer is shown in Fig. 7.10, in which it is seen that even when a fully connected recurrent attractor network has 4,000 neurons, the operation of the network is still probabilistic. In this network of 4,000 neurons, there were 3,600 excitatory neurons and 360 neurons represented each pattern or decision (that is, the sparseness a was 0.1). The firing rates of the neurons corresponded to those found in VPC, with rates above 20 spikes/s considered to be a criterion for the attractor state being reached, and 40–50 spikes/s being typical when fully in the attractor state (see Fig. 7.5). Under these conditions, the probabilistic spiking of the excitatory (pyramidal) cells is what introduces noise into the network. (Deco and Rolls (2006) showed that it is this noise in the recurrent collateral firing, rather than external noise due to variability in the inputs, which makes the major contribution to the probabilistic behaviour of the network.) Thus, once the firing in the recurrent collaterals is spike implemented by integrate-and-fire neurons, the probabilistic behaviour seems inevitable, even up to quite large attractor network sizes.

We may then ask why the spiking activity of any neuron is probabilistic, and what the advantages are that this may confer. The answer I suggest is that the spiking activity is approximately Poisson-like (as if generated by a random process with a given mean rate), because the neurons are held close to their firing threshold, so that any incoming input can rapidly cause sufficient further depolarization to produce a spike. It is this ability to respond rapidly to an input, rather than having to charge up the cell membrane from the resting potential to the threshold, a slow process determined by the time constant of the neuron and influenced by that of the synapses, that enables neuronal networks in the brain, including attractor networks, to operate and retrieve information so rapidly (see Sections B.3.3.5 and B.6). The spike trains are essentially Poisson-like because the cell potential hovers noisily close to the threshold for firing, the noise being generated in part by the Poisson-like firing of the other neurons in the network.

The implication of these concepts is that the operation of networks in the brain is inherently noisy because of the Poisson-like timing of the spikes of the neurons, which itself is related to the mechanisms that enable neurons to respond rapidly to their inputs. However, the consequence of the Poisson-like firing is that, even with quite large attractor networks of thousands of neurons with hundreds of neurons representing each pattern or memory, the network inevitably settles probabilistically to a given attractor state. This results, *inter alia*, in decision-making being probabilistic. Factors that influence the probabilistic behaviour of the network include the strength of the inputs (with the difference in the inputs / the magnitude of the inputs as shown here being relevant to decision-making and Weber's Law); the depth and position of the basins of attraction, which if shallow or correlated with other basins will tend to slow the network; and, perhaps, the mean firing rates of the neurons during the decision-making itself, and the firing rate distribution (see below). In this context, the probabilistic behaviour of the network gives poorer and poorer and slower and slower performance as the difference between the inputs divided by the base frequency is decreased, as shown in Figs. 7.3 and 7.8.

7.7 Applications of this model of decision-making

This approach to how networks take decisions probably has implications throughout the brain. For example, the model is effectively a model of the dynamics of the recall of a memory in response to a recall cue. The way in which the attractor is reached depends on the strength of the recall cue, and inherent noise in the attractor network performing the recall because of the spiking activity in a finite size system. The recall will take longer if the recall cue is weak. Spontaneous stochastic effects may suddenly lead to the memory being recalled, and this may be related to the sudden recovery of a memory which one tried to remember some time previously.

This framework can also be extended very naturally to account for the probabilistic decision taken about for example which of several objects has been presented in a perceptual task. The model can also be extended to the case where one of a large number of possible decisions must be made. An example is a decision about which of a set of objects, perhaps with different similarity to each other, has been shown on each trial, and where the decisions are only probabilistically correct. When a decision is make between different numbers of alternatives, a classical result is Hick's Law, that the reaction time increases linearly with $\log_2$ of the number of alternatives from which a choice is being made. This has been interpreted as supporting a series of binary decisions each one taking a unit amount of time (Welford 1980). As the integrate-and-fire model we describe works completely in parallel, it will be very interesting to investigate whether Hick's Law is a property of the network. If so, this could be related to the fact that the activity of the inhibitory interneurons is likely to increase linearly with the number of alternatives between which a decision is being made (as each one adds additional bias to the system through a λ input), and that the GABA inhibitory interneurons implement a shunting, that is divisive, operation.

Another application is to changes in perception. Perceptions can change 'spontaneously' from one to another interpretation of the world, even when the visual input is constant, and a good example is the Necker cube, in which visual perception flips occasionally to make a different edge of the cube appear nearer to the observer. I hypothesize that this is due in part to adaptation effects in integrate-and-fire networks, and that the time of flipping depends on the average adaptation rate interacting with the statistical fluctuations in the network due to the Poisson-like spike firing that is a form of noise in the system. It will be possible to test this hypothesis in integrate-and-fire simulations. The same approach should provide a model of pattern and binocular rivalry, where one image is seen at a time even though two images are presented simultaneously. When these are images of objects or faces, the system that is especially important in the selection is the inferior temporal visual cortex (Blake and Logothetis 2002, Maier, Logothetis and Leopold 2005), for it is here that representations of whole objects are present, and the global interpretation of one object can compete with the global interpretation of another object. These simulation models are highly feasible, in that the effects of synaptic adaptation and neuronal adaptation in integrate-and-fire simulations have already been investigated (Deco and Rolls 2005d, Deco and Rolls 2005c).

Another potential application of this model of decision-making is to probabilistic decision tasks. In such tasks, the proportion of choices reflects, and indeed may be proportional to, the expected value of the different choices. This pattern of choices is known as the matching law (Sugrue, Corrado and Newsome 2005). An example of a probabilistic decision task in which the choices of the human participants in the probabilistic decision task clearly reflected the expected value of the choices (Rolls, McCabe and Redoute 2007b) is described in Section 3.10.2.3. A network of the type described in this chapter in which the biasing inputs λ_1 and λ_2 to the model are the expected values of the different choices will alter the proportion of the decisions it makes as a function of the relative expected values in a way similar to that shown in Fig. 7.3, and provides a model of this type of probabilistic reward-based decision-making.

Another application of this type of model is to taking decisions between the implicit and explicit systems in emotional decision-making (see Section 10.7 and Rolls (2005)), where again the two different systems could provide the biasing inputs λ_1 and λ_2 to the model.

To investigate the 'decision-related' switching of these systems, it may be important to use a firing rate distribution of the type found in the brain, in which few neurons have high rates, more neurons have intermediate rates, and many neurons have low rates (see Section C.3.1). It is important to model correctly the proportion of the current that is being passed through the NMDA receptors (which are voltage-dependent), as these receptors have a long time-constant, which will tend to smooth out short-term statistical fluctuations caused by the stochastic firing of the neurons (cf. Wang (1999)), and this will affect the statistics of the probabilistic switching of the network. This can only be done by modelling integrate-and-fire networks with the firing rates and the firing rate distributions found in a cortical area.

More generally, we can conceive of each cortical area as performing a local type of decision-making using attractor dynamics of the type described. Even memory recall is in effect the same local 'decision-making' process. The orbitofrontal cortex for example is involved in decisions about which visual stimulus is currently associated with reward, in for example a visual discrimination reversal task. Its computations are about stimuli, primary reinforcers, and secondary reinforcers (see Section 3.6). The dorsolateral prefrontal cortex takes an executive role in decision-making in a working memory task, in which information must be held available for in some cases intervening stimuli (see Section 5.1). The dorsal and posterior part of the dorsolateral prefrontal cortex may be involved in short-term memory-related decisions about where to move the eyes (see Section 5.1). The parietal cortex is involved in decision-making when the stimuli are for example optic flow patterns (Glimcher 2003). The hippocampus is involved in decision-making when the allocentric places of stimuli must be associated with rewards or objects (see Chapter 2). The somatosensory cortex and ventral premotor cortex are involved in decision-making when different vibrotactile frequencies must be compared (see Chapter 7). The cingulate cortex may be involved when action–outcome decisions must be taken (see Section 3.8). In each of these cases, local cortical processing that is related to the type of decision being made takes place, and all cortical areas are not involved in any one decision. The style of the decision-making-related computation in each cortical area appears to be of the form described in this chapter, in which the local recurrent collateral connections enable the decision-making process to accumulate evidence in time, falling gradually into an attractor that represents the decision made in the network. Because there is an attractor state into which the network falls, this can be described statistically as a non-linear diffusion process, the noise for the diffusion being the stochastical spiking of the neurons, and the driving force being the biasing inputs.

If decision-making in the cortex is largely local and typically specialized, it leaves open the question of how one stream for behavioural output is selected. This type of 'global decision-making' is considered in Sections 10.7 and 3.10.2.

7.8 The integrate-and-fire formulation used in the model of decision-making

Deco and Rolls (2006) used the mathematical formulation of integrate-and-fire (IF) neurons and synaptic currents described by Brunel and Wang (2001), but extended to multiple interact-ing networks. A brief summary of the framework that was used follows, with an introduction to integrate-and-fire simulations provided in Sections B.6 and B.6.3.

The dynamics of the sub-threshold membrane potential V of a neuron are given by the equation:

$$C_m \frac{dV(t)}{dt} = -g_m(V(t) - V_L) - I_{syn}(t), \tag{7.1}$$

where C_m is the membrane capacitance taken to be 0.5 nF for excitatory neurons and 0.2 nF for inhibitory neurons; g_m is the membrane leak conductance taken to be 25 nS for excitatory neurons and 20 nS for inhibitory neurons; V_L is the resting potential of -70 mV, and I_{syn} is the synaptic current. The firing threshold is taken to be $V_{thr} = -50$ mV, and the reset potential $V_{reset} = -55$ mV (see McCormick, Connors, Lighthall and Prince (1985)).

The synaptic current is given by a sum of glutamatergic, AMPA ($I_{AMPA,rec}$) and NMDA ($I_{NMDA,rec}$) mediated, currents from the excitatory recurrent collateral connection, one AMPA ($I_{AMPA,ext}$) mediated external excitatory current, and one inhibitory GABAergic current (I_{GABA}):

$$I_{syn}(t) = I_{AMPA,ext}(t) + I_{AMPA,rec}(t) + I_{NMDA,rec}(t) + I_{GABA}(t). \tag{7.2}$$

The synaptic currents are defined by:

$$I_{AMPA,ext}(t) = g_{AMPA,ext}(V(t) - V_E) \sum_{j=1}^{N_{ext}} s_j^{AMPA,ext}(t) \tag{7.3}$$

$$I_{AMPA,rec}(t) = g_{AMPA,rec}(V(t) - V_E) \sum_{j=1}^{N_E} w_j s_j^{AMPA,rec}(t) \tag{7.4}$$

$$I_{NMDA,rec}(t) = \frac{g_{NMDA}(V(t) - V_E)}{1 + [Mg^{++}]\exp(-0.062V(t))/3.57} \times \sum_{j=1}^{N_E} w_j s_j^{NMDA}(t) \tag{7.5}$$

$$I_{GABA}(t) = g_{GABA}(V(t) - V_I) \sum_{j=1}^{N_I} s_j^{GABA}(t) \tag{7.6}$$

where $V_E = 0$ mV, $V_I = -70$ mV, w_j are the synaptic weights, each receptor has its own fraction s_j of open channels, and its own synaptic conductance g. The NMDA synaptic current is dependent on the potential and controlled by the extracellular concentration of magnesium ($[Mg^{++}] = 1$ mM) (Jahr and Stevens 1990). The values for the synaptic conductances for excitatory neurons are $g_{AMPA,ext} = 2.08$ nS, $g_{AMPA,rec} = 0.104$ nS, $g_{NMDA} = 0.327$ nS and $g_{GABA} = 1.287$ nS; and for inhibitory neurons $g_{AMPA,ext} = 1.62$ nS, $g_{AMPA,rec} = 0.081$ nS, $g_{NMDA} = 0.258$ nS and $g_{GABA} = 1.002$ nS. These values are obtained from the ones used by Brunel and Wang (2001) by multiplication by a factor which corrects for the difference in the number of neurons used in our model and Brunel and Wang's model. In their work the conductances were calculated so that in an unstructured network the excitatory neurons have a spontaneous spiking rate of 3 Hz and the inhibitory neurons a spontaneous rate of 9 Hz.

The fractions of open channels are described by:

$$\frac{ds_j^{\text{AMPA,ext}}(t)}{dt} = -\frac{s_j^{\text{AMPA,ext}}(t)}{\tau_{\text{AMPA}}} + \sum_k \delta(t - t_j^k) \tag{7.7}$$

$$\frac{ds_j^{\text{AMPA,rec}}(t)}{dt} = -\frac{s_j^{\text{AMPA,rec}}(t)}{\tau_{\text{AMPA}}} + \sum_k \delta(t - t_j^k) \tag{7.8}$$

$$\frac{ds_j^{\text{NMDA}}(t)}{dt} = -\frac{s_j^{\text{NMDA}}(t)}{\tau_{\text{NMDA,decay}}} + \alpha x_j(t)(1 - s_j^{\text{NMDA}}(t)) \tag{7.9}$$

$$\frac{dx_j(t)}{dt} = -\frac{x_j(t)}{\tau_{\text{NMDA,rise}}} + \sum_k \delta(t - t_j^k) \tag{7.10}$$

$$\frac{ds_j^{\text{GABA}}(t)}{dt} = -\frac{s_j^{\text{GABA}}(t)}{\tau_{\text{GABA}}} + \sum_k \delta(t - t_j^k), \tag{7.11}$$

where the rise time constant for NMDA synapses is $\tau_{\text{NMDA,rise}} = 2$ ms (Spruston et al. 1995, Hestrin et al. 1990), the rise time constants for AMPA and GABA are neglected because they are smaller than 1 ms, and $\alpha = 0.5$ ms^{-1}. All synapses have a delay of 0.5 ms. The decay time constant for the AMPA synapses is $\tau_{\text{AMPA}} = 2$ ms (Spruston et al. 1995, Hestrin et al. 1990), for NMDA synapses is $\tau_{\text{NMDA,decay}} = 100$ ms (Spruston et al. 1995, Hestrin et al. 1990), and for GABA synapses $\tau_{\text{GABA}} = 10$ ms (Salin and Prince 1996, Xiang, Huguenard and Prince 1998). The sums over k represent a sum over spikes formulated as δ-peaks ($\delta(t)$) emitted by presynaptic neuron j at time t_j^k.

7.9 The mean-field approach used in the model of decision-making

The mean-field approximation used by Deco and Rolls (2006) was derived by Brunel and Wang (2001), assuming that the network of integrate-and-fire neurons is in a stationary state. In this formulation the potential of a neuron is calculated as:

$$\tau_x \frac{dV(t)}{dt} = -V(t) + \mu_x + \sigma_x \sqrt{\tau_x} \eta(t) \tag{7.12}$$

where $V(t)$ is the membrane potential, x labels the populations, τ_x is the effective membrane time constant, μ_x is the mean value the membrane potential would have in the absence of spiking and fluctuations, σ_x measures the magnitude of the fluctuations, and η is a Gaussian process with absolute exponentially decaying correlation function with time constant τ_{AMPA}. The quantities μ_x and σ_x^2 are given by:

$$\mu_x = \frac{(T_{\text{ext}}\nu_{\text{ext}} + T_{\text{AMPA}}n_x^{\text{AMPA}} + \rho_1 n_x^{\text{NMDA}})V_{\text{E}} + \rho_2 n_x^{\text{NMDA}}\langle V \rangle + T_{\text{I}}n_x^{\text{GABA}}V_{\text{I}} + V_{\text{L}}}{S_x} \tag{7.13}$$

$$\sigma_x^2 = \frac{g_{\text{AMPA,ext}}^2(\langle V \rangle - V_{\text{E}})^2 N_{\text{ext}}\nu_{\text{ext}}\tau_{\text{AMPA}}^2 \tau_x}{g_{\text{m}}^2 \tau_{\text{m}}^2}. \tag{7.14}$$

where ν_{ext} Hz is the external incoming spiking rate, ν_{I} is the spiking rate of the inhibitory population, $\tau_{\text{m}} = C_{\text{m}}/g_{\text{m}}$ with the values for the excitatory or inhibitory neurons depending on the population considered, and the other quantities are given by:

$$S_x = 1 + T_{\text{ext}}\nu_{\text{ext}} + T_{\text{AMPA}}n_x^{\text{AMPA}} + (\rho_1 + \rho_2)n_x^{\text{NMDA}} + T_{\text{I}}n_x^{\text{GABA}} \tag{7.15}$$

$$\tau_x = \frac{C_{\text{m}}}{g_{\text{m}}S_x} \tag{7.16}$$

$$n_x^{\text{AMPA}} = \sum_{j=1}^{p} r_j w_{jx}^{\text{AMPA}}\nu_j \tag{7.17}$$

$$n_x^{\text{NMDA}} = \sum_{j=1}^{p} r_j w_{jx}^{\text{NMDA}}\psi(\nu_j) \tag{7.18}$$

$$n_x^{\text{GABA}} = \sum_{j=1}^{p} r_j w_{jx}^{\text{GABA}}\nu_j \tag{7.19}$$

$$\psi(\nu) = \frac{\nu\tau_{\text{NMDA}}}{1 + \nu\tau_{\text{NMDA}}}\left(1 + \frac{1}{1 + \nu\tau_{\text{NMDA}}}\sum_{n=1}^{\infty}\frac{(-\alpha\tau_{\text{NMDA,rise}})^n T_n(\nu)}{(n+1)!}\right) \tag{7.20}$$

$$T_n(\nu) = \sum_{k=0}^{n}(-1)^k\binom{n}{k}\frac{\tau_{\text{NMDA,rise}}(1 + \nu\tau_{\text{NMDA}})}{\tau_{\text{NMDA,rise}}(1 + \nu\tau_{\text{NMDA}}) + k\tau_{\text{NMDA,decay}}} \tag{7.21}$$

$$\tau_{\text{NMDA}} = \alpha\tau_{\text{NMDA,rise}}\tau_{\text{NMDA,decay}} \tag{7.22}$$

$$T_{\text{ext}} = \frac{g_{\text{AMPA,ext}}\tau_{\text{AMPA}}}{g_{\text{m}}} \tag{7.23}$$

$$T_{\text{AMPA}} = \frac{g_{\text{AMPA,rec}}N_{\text{E}}\tau_{\text{AMPA}}}{g_{\text{m}}} \tag{7.24}$$

$$\rho_1 = \frac{g_{\text{NMDA}}N_{\text{E}}}{g_{\text{m}}J} \tag{7.25}$$

$$\rho_2 = \beta\frac{g_{\text{NMDA}}N_{\text{E}}(\langle V_x\rangle - V_{\text{E}})(J-1)}{g_{\text{m}}J^2} \tag{7.26}$$

$$J = 1 + \gamma\exp(-\beta\langle V_x\rangle) \tag{7.27}$$

$$T_{\text{I}} = \frac{g_{\text{GABA}}N_{\text{I}}\tau_{\text{GABA}}}{g_{\text{m}}} \tag{7.28}$$

$$\langle V_x\rangle = \mu_x - (V_{\text{thr}} - V_{\text{reset}})\nu_x\tau_x, \tag{7.29}$$

where p is the number of excitatory populations, r_x is the fraction of neurons in the excitatory x population, $w_{j,x}$ the weight of the connections from population x to population j, ν_x is the spiking rate of the x excitatory population, $\gamma = [\text{Mg}^{++}]/3.57$, $\beta = 0.062$ and the average membrane potential $\langle V_x\rangle$ has a value between -55 mV and -50 mV.

The spiking rate of a population as a function of the defined quantities is then given by:

$$\nu_x = \phi(\mu_x, \sigma_x), \tag{7.30}$$

where

$$\phi(\mu_x, \sigma_x) = \left(\tau_{\text{rp}} + \tau_x\int_{\beta(\mu_x,\sigma_x)}^{\alpha(\mu_x,\sigma_x)}du\sqrt{\pi}\exp(u^2)[1 + \text{erf}(u)]\right)^{-1} \tag{7.31}$$

$$\alpha(\mu_x, \sigma_x) = \frac{(V_{\text{thr}} - \mu_x)}{\sigma_x}\left(1 + 0.5\frac{\tau_{\text{AMPA}}}{\tau_x}\right) + 1.03\sqrt{\frac{\tau_{\text{AMPA}}}{\tau_x}} - 0.5\frac{\tau_{\text{AMPA}}}{\tau_x} \tag{7.32}$$

$$\beta(\mu_x, \sigma_x) = \frac{(V_{\text{reset}} - \mu_x)}{\sigma_x} \tag{7.33}$$

with erf(u) the error function and τ_{rp} the refractory period which is considered to be 2 ms for excitatory neurons and 1 ms for inhibitory neurons. To solve the equations defined by (7.30) for all xs we integrate numerically (7.29) and the differential equation below, which has fixed point solutions corresponding to equation 7.30:

$$\tau_x \frac{d\nu_x}{dt} = -\nu_x + \phi(\mu_x, \sigma_x).$$ (7.34)

7.10 The model parameters used in the simulations of decision-making

The fixed parameters of the model are shown in Table 7.1, and not only provide information about the values of the parameters used in the simulations, but also enable them to be compared to experimentally measured values.

Table 7.1 Parameters used in the integrate-and-fire simulations

N_E	800
N_I	200
r	0.1
w_+	2.2
w_I	1.015
N_{ext}	800
ν_{ext}	2.4 kHz
C_m (excitatory)	0.5 nF
C_m (inhibitory)	0.2 nF
g_m (excitatory)	25 nS
g_m (inhibitory)	20 nS
V_L	−70 mV
V_{thr}	−50 mV
V_{reset}	−55 mV
V_E	0 mV
V_I	−70 mV
$g_{AMPA,ext}$ (excitatory)	2.08 nS
$g_{AMPA,rec}$ (excitatory)	0.104 nS
g_{NMDA} (excitatory)	0.327 nS
g_{GABA} (excitatory)	1.25 nS
$g_{AMPA,ext}$ (inhibitory)	1.62 nS
$g_{AMPA,rec}$ (inhibitory)	0.081 nS
g_{NMDA} (inhibitory)	0.258 nS
g_{GABA} (inhibitory)	0.973 nS
$\tau_{NMDA,decay}$	100 ms
$\tau_{NMDA,rise}$	2 ms
τ_{AMPA}	2 ms
τ_{GABA}	10 ms
α	0.5 ms^{-1}

8 Action selection by biased attractor competition in the prefrontal cortex

8.1 Introduction

There is much evidence that the prefrontal cortex is involved in at least some types of working memory and related processes that depend on working memory such as planning (Goldman-Rakic 1996, Fuster 2000, Miller 2000). Working memory refers to an active system for maintaining and manipulating information in mind, held during a short period, usually of seconds, and is described in Chapter 5. In this chapter we consider how an attentional or rule attractor state held in a short-term memory in the prefrontal cortex can by top-down processing influence other networks by using biased competition to influence the mapping of sensory inputs to motor outputs, and can thus play an important role in action selection and decision-making (Deco and Rolls 2003).

Neurophysiological data obtained during an action selection task with a short-term memory component (Asaad, Rainer and Miller 2000) was used to build a theory of action selection and working memory with a firm neurophysiological foundation (Deco and Rolls 2003). Asaad et al. (2000) investigated the functions of the prefrontal cortex in working memory and action selection by analyzing neuronal activity when the monkey performed two different working memory tasks using the same stimuli and responses.

In a *conditional object–response (associative) task* with a delay, the monkey was shown one of two stimulus objects (O1 or O2), and after a delay had to make either a rightward or leftward oculomotor saccade response depending on which stimulus was shown.

In a *delayed spatial response task* the same stimuli were used, but the rule required was different, namely to respond after the delay towards the Left or Right location where the stimulus object had been shown (Asaad et al. 2000).

The main motivation for such studies was the fact that for real-world behaviour, the mapping between a stimulus and a response is typically more complicated than a one-to-one mapping. The same stimulus can lead to different behaviours depending on the situation, or the same behaviour may be elicited by different cueing stimuli. In the performance of these tasks populations (sometimes described as pools in the simulations) of neurons were found that responded in the delay period to the stimulus object or its position ('sensory pools'), to combinations of the response and the stimulus object or position ('intermediate pools'), and to the response required (left or right) ('premotor pools'). Moreover, the particular intermediate pool neurons that were active depended on the task, with neurons that responded to combinations of the stimulus object and response active when the mapping was from object to behavioural response, and neurons that responded to combinations of stimulus position and response when the mapping rule was from stimulus position to response (Asaad et al. 2000). In that different sets of intermediate population neurons are responsive depending on the task to be performed, PFC neurons provide a neural substrate for responding appropriately on the basis of an abstract rule or context. The model we developed showed how a short-term attractor network which held the current rule could bias the competition between the intermediate, combination-responsive, pools in such a way as to achieve the correct mapping

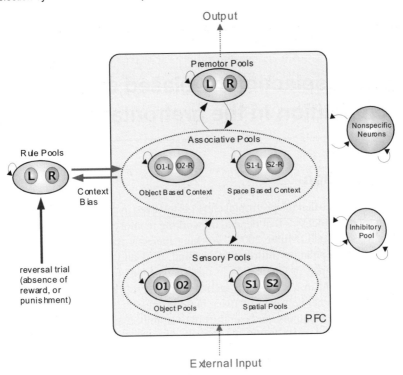

Fig. 8.1 Network architecture of the prefrontal cortex unified model of attention, working memory, and decision-making. There are sensory neuronal populations or pools for object type (O1 or O2) and spatial position (S1 or S2). These connect hierarchically (with stronger forward than backward connections) to the intermediate or 'associative' pools in which neurons may respond to combinations of the inputs received from the sensory pools for some types of mapping such as reversal, as described by Deco and Rolls (2003). For the simulation of the data of Asaad et al. (2000) these intermediate pools respond to O1–L, O2–R, S1–L, or S2–R. These intermediate pools receive an attentional bias, which in the case of this particular simulation biases either the O pools or the S pools. The intermediate pools are connected hierarchically to the premotor pools, which in this case code for a Left or Right response. Each of the pools is an attractor network in which there are stronger associatively modified synaptic weights between the neurons that represent the same state (e.g. object type for a sensory pool, or response for a premotor pool) than between neurons in the other pools or populations. However, all the neurons in the network are associatively connected by at least weak synaptic weights. The attractor properties, the competition implemented by the inhibitory interneurons, and the biasing inputs result in the same network implementing both short-term memory and biased competition, and the stronger feed forward than feedback connections between the sensory, intermediate, and premotor pools results in the hierarchical property by which sensory inputs can be mapped to motor outputs in a way that depends on the biasing contextual or rule input. (After Deco and Rolls 2003.)

from stimuli to responses. The bias from the rule pool acted selectively on either one set, or the other set, of intermediate neuron pools. That approach (Deco and Rolls 2003) is described in this chapter.

8.2 A hierarchical attractor model of action selection

Short-term memory attractor dynamics helps to understand the underlying mechanisms that implement this rule-dependent mapping from the stimulus object or the stimulus position to a delayed behavioural response. The attractor dynamics is used partly to provide the short-term memory to bridge the delay period. Deco and Rolls (2003) formulated a neurodynamical model that builds on the integrate-and-fire attractor network by introducing a hierarchically organized set of different attractor network pools in the lateral prefrontal cortex. The hierarchical structure is organized within the general framework of the biased competition model of attention (Chelazzi 1998, Rolls and Deco 2002). The hierarchical structure of the pools is to ensure that the mapping is from the sensory pools to the intermediate pools and then to the premotor pools, and is achieved by setting the synaptic weights to be stronger in the forward than in the reverse direction.

This concept of a set of attractor networks that are hierarchically organized in this way is an important concept, for they can be used both to map inputs to outputs, and to model top-down processes. It is formally somewhat similar to the interacting attractors used to solve short-term memory with intervening stimuli described in Chapter 5, and the interacting attractors used to describe attentional processing in Chapter 6.

The different populations or pools of neurons in the prefrontal cortical network are shown in Fig. 8.1. (In order to be able to analyze and constrain the problem, we adopted a minimalistic approach and assumed a minimal number of neuronal pools for coding two different objects and two positions. This simplification allows a detailed study of the dynamics, and is enough to capture the main aspects of the dynamics associated with the memory functions that we aimed to study.) There are four types of excitatory pool, namely: sensory, intermediate (or associative, in that they respond to combinations), premotor, and non-selective. The sensory pools encode information about the stimulus objects (O1 and O2), or the spatial locations of the stimuli (S1 and S2). The premotor pools encode the motor response (in our case the leftward (L) or rightward (R) oculomotor saccade). The intermediate (associative) pools are task-specific or rule-specific and perform the mapping between the sensory stimuli and the required motor response. The intermediate pools respond to combinations of the sensory stimuli and the response required, with one pool for each of the four possible stimulus–response combinations (O1–L, O2–R, S1–L and S2–R). The intermediate pools can be considered as being in two groups, one for the delayed object-response associative task (O1–L and O2–R), and the other for the delayed spatial response task (S1–L and S2–R). The intermediate pools receive an external biasing context or rule input (see Fig. 8.1) that reflects the current rule. The remaining excitatory neurons do not have specific sensory, response or biasing inputs, and are in a non-selective pool. All the inhibitory neurons are clustered into a common inhibitory pool, so that there is global competition throughout the network.

The parameters of the model (Deco and Rolls 2003) were set using a mean-field analysis of the type described in Sections 7.9, B.7 and B.8, as this analysis enables the dependencies of specific network behaviours on the network parameters to be assessed. In particular, we showed that the inter-pool connection strengths along the processing pathway cannot be equal, and a forward projection vs backprojection asymmetry is needed so that a response is computed by the network from the stimulus by virtue of the hierarchical organization produced by the connection strength asymmetry. The mean-field analysis showed the states that the system can reach, and enables further constraints to be identified to produce behaviour of the system that correlates best to the corresponding data, and also better theoretical descriptions for the dependencies of specific behaviours on the network parameters (see Loh, Szabo, Almeida, Stetter and Deco (2004)).

Figure 8.2 plots the rastergrams of randomly selected neurons for each pool in the network (5 neurons for each sensory, intermediate and premotor pool, 20 for the non-selective excitatory pool, and 10 for the inhibitory pool). After a pre-cue period of 500 ms a cue object (O1 or O2) is presented at a particular location (S1 or S2) during the cue period of 500 ms. (During this period the corresponding object sensory pool, O1 or O2, and spatial sensory pool, S1 or

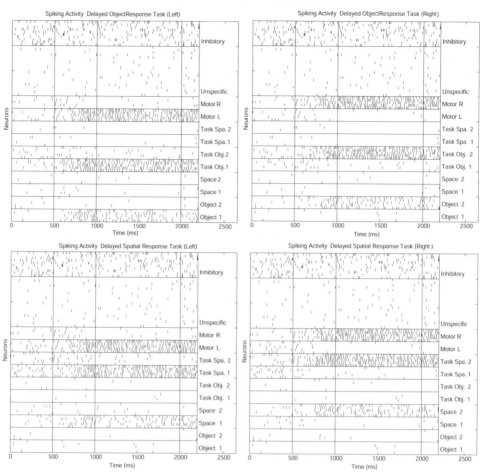

Fig. 8.2 Delayed Object–Response (upper) and Delayed Spatial–Response (lower) simulations. Rastergrams of randomly selected neurons for each pool in the PFC network (5 for each sensory, intermediate and premotor pool, 20 for the nonselective excitatory pool, and 10 for the inhibitory pool) and for all task conditions after the experimental paradigms of Asaad et al (2000). The spatio-temporal spiking activity shows that during the short-term memory delay period only the sensory cue, associated future oculomotor response, and intermediate neurons maintain persistent activity and build up the stable global attractor of the network. The underlying biased competition mechanisms are explicit. Pool names: Task Spa 2, intermediate pool responding in the delayed spatial response task to a combination of spatial location 2 and a Right motor response (S1–R); Task Obj 1, intermediate pool responding in the delayed object-response task to a combination of object 1 and a left motor response (O1–L, etc.); Space 1, sensory pool responding to the stimulus when it is in spatial position 1 (S1); Object 1, sensory pool responding to the stimulus when it is object 1 (O1). (After Deco and Rolls 2003.)

S2, receive external Poisson spikes with an increased rate ν_{ext} to $\nu_{ext} + \lambda_{input}$.) During the delay period of 1000 ms, the stimulus is removed. We assume that the monkey is performing correctly and therefore that he knows the context, i.e. which rule is active. The active rule is encoded by the external rule-specific input ($\nu_{ext} + \lambda_{rule}$) received by the group of intermediate pools that corresponds to the rule for the task being performed (object–response associative, *or* delayed spatial response). For the upper part of Fig. 8.2 the rule pools were biasing the intermediate (or associative) object-based pools (O1–L and O2–R), and thus it was which object was being presented (O1 or O2) that was mapped to the appropriate spatial response, L and R respectively. For the lower part of Fig. 8.2 the rule pools were biasing the intermediate (or associative) spatial-based pools (S1–L and S2–R), and thus it was the spatial position of the object being presented (S1 or S2) that was mapped to the appropriate spatial response, L and R respectively. The simulation shows that by biasing the intermediate pools of Fig. 8.1 which respond to combinations of inputs, the correct mapping from the sensory input to the motor output is produced. Thus a contextual state or rule can flexibly bias how the system responds to identical sensory inputs. In the simulations, the sensory pools S1 and O1 were simultaneously being activated (to represent object 1 being presented in spatial position 1), yet the network correctly mapped through the intermediate neurons because of the bias being applied to the correct motor response. Thus the system was able to switch from performing a delayed conditional object–place memory task to a delayed spatial response task, depending on the rule contextual bias being applied to the intermediate, combination, neurons.

An interesting property of the architecture is that the sensory neurons in pools for the irrelevant input sensory dimension (location for the object–response associative task, and object for the delayed spatial response task) are inhibited during the sensory cue period and are not sustained during the delay short-term memory period. This is despite the fact that external sensory inputs were being applied to both the spatial and the object sensory neurons, for example to O1 and S1, to represent the fact that on that trial object 1 was present and was in location S1. The reason for this is that there are backprojections in the system, so the intermediate neurons that are being biased by for example object have a top-down biasing effect on the O1 and O2 neurons, and given the global competition in the network implemented by the inhibitory neurons, the only sensory neurons that remain active on that trial are the O1 neurons. Thus only the relevant single pool attractors, given the rule context, that are suitable for the cue–response mapping survive the competition and are persistently maintained with high firing activity during the short-term memory delay period.

This suppression effect has been observed by Everling, Tinsley, Gaffan and Duncan (2002) by recording the activity of prefrontal neurons in monkeys carrying out a focused attention task. In their spatial cueing task, they observed strong filtering of the prefrontal cortex (PFC) response to unattended targets (which is similar to that observed in our simulations for irrelevant sensory dimensions). These attentional modulation effects (relative enhancement of neuronal response to an attended stimulus, and a relative suppression of the neuronal response to an unattended stimulus) are well known in posterior areas of the visual system, including the striate and prestriate cortex (Reynolds et al. 1999), parietal cortex (Bushnell, Goldberg and Robinson 1981), and inferotemporal cortex (Chelazzi 1998). The computational simulations (Rolls and Deco 2002, Deco and Rolls 2003) suggest that, in the PFC, filtering of ignored inputs may reach a level commensurate with the strong, global effects of selective attention in human behaviour, and that this selection in the prefrontal cortex is the basis of the attentional modulation found in more posterior sensory cortical areas, implemented through backprojections from the prefrontal cortex to the more posterior cortical areas (see Chapter 6). In other words, we see in the same set of networks in the prefrontal cortex both a kind of internal attentional mechanism that selects the relevant input dimensions for the present behavioural or task condition using competition implemented through the inhibitory neurons in an attractor network, and also a mechanism that maintains this information in short-term memory using the recurrent connections between the neurons in the attractor networks, and can in addition act as a top-down bias on temporal and parietal cortical areas. This neurodynamical architecture of the prefrontal cortex therefore unifies attentionally biased competition, and short-term memory mechanisms implemented by attractor networks with recurrent connections.

In another experiment, Asaad, Rainer and Miller (1998) aimed to explore the role of the prefrontal cortex in arbitrary stimulus–response learning, by studying the neural activity of lateral PFC neurons during performance of a *conditional visuomotor task*. The task required the monkeys to associate a foveally presented cue object (Object A or B), after a delay period, with a response consisting of a leftward or rightward saccadic eye movement. The cue period was 500 ms, and the short-term memory delay period separating the cue and response was 1,000 ms. They trained the monkeys under two different conditions, namely: (1) direct association; and (2) reverse association. The direct condition corresponded to the association of one object, for example A, with a leftward eye motor response, and the other object, for example B, with a rightward eye motor response. The reverse condition corresponded to the reversed association of cue and responses, i.e. object A was now associated with a rightward eye motor response, and object B with a leftward eye motor response. They found sensory neurons that responded to one or other of the objects, intermediate combination neurons that responded to object A and response L, and object B and response R (and one of this pair was active in the direct rule). There were also intermediate combination neurons that responded to object A and R, and others that responded to Object B and L during the reverse association. There were also L and R response neurons.

Deco and Rolls (2003) simulated the reversal of this conditional object-spatial response task using the architecture shown in Fig. 8.3. They found results analogous to those illustrated in Fig. 8.2, that is the external bias could select whether in this case the object to response mapping was direct or reversed. The spatio-temporal spiking activity showed that during the short-term memory delay period only the relevant sensory cue, associated future oculomotor response, and intermediate neurons maintain persistent activity, and build up a stable global attractor in the network. This model thus shows how a rule or context input can influence decision-making by biasing competition in a hierarchical network that thus implements a flexible mapping from input stimuli to motor outputs (Rolls and Deco 2002, Deco and Rolls 2003), and is able to perform stimulus-to-motor response reversal using top-down biased competition from a rule attractor module..

The model also shows how the same network can implement a short-term memory, and indeed how the competition required for the biased competition selection process can be implemented in an attractor network which itself requires inhibition implemented through the inhibitory neurons. The short-term memory of the system, evident by the continuing firing of the relevant neuronal sensory, intermediate combination, and motor pools in the delay period from 1,000 to 2,000 ms in Fig. 8.2, is implemented both by the recurrent associatively modified connections within each pool of neurons shown in Fig. 8.1, and by the associatively modified feedforward and feedback connections between the pools at the different levels of the hierarchy shown in Fig. 8.1.

It is an interesting property of the model that the system consists of sets of hierarchically but reciprocally connected attractor networks which together contribute to the short-term memory implemented in the system. We note that the types of neuron included in the model are the types recorded by Asaad, Rainer and Miller (2000) and Asaad, Rainer and Miller (1998) during the performance of the tasks, and that a combinatorial explosion of required neuron types may be avoided by the fact that neurons in the prefrontal cortex adapt their response properties to the task demands (Freedman, Riesenhuber, Poggio and Miller 2003).

8.3 Setting up the synaptic connectivity for the prefrontal cortex

Another issue is how the connectivity between the different populations of neurons in the prefrontal cortex or neuronal pools in the model is set up during the learning phase. One process, which works for many of the connections, is Hebbian associative learning. However,

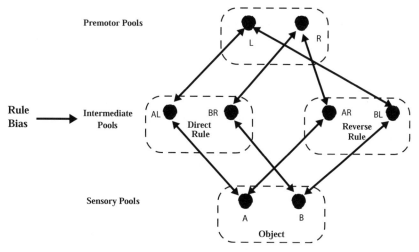

Fig. 8.3 Network architecture of the prefrontal cortex model of conditional object–spatial response reversal. The most relevant recurrent excitatory NMDA and AMPA synaptic connectivity in the prefrontal cortical architecture utilized for the numerical simulations of the experiment of Asaad et al (1998) on conditional object–response learning. All four possible sensory cue–response associations under both task conditions (direct and reversed) are included. In order to simplify the picture, only the connections with increased synaptic strength are shown and the inhibitory and non-selective pools and external influences are omitted. The architecture includes: two premotor pools of response neurons, one corresponding to leftward saccade responses (L) and the other corresponding to rightward saccade responses (R); two sensory pools of object selective neurons, one corresponding to the object A and the other corresponding to the object B; and four intermediate task-specific pools of associative neurons, one for each of the four possible stimulus–response associations. We group these intermediate pools into two groups, one corresponding to the direct condition, and the other corresponding to the reverse condition. The external rule bias acts on either the direct or the reversed pair of intermediate neuronal populations. (After Deco and Rolls 2003.)

even in the cases when the forward and backward connections are not identical (as in this model), the pattern of the synaptic weights required can still be set up during training by simple associative learning. All that is required even in these cases is some asymmetry in the strength of the forward and backward connections. This could be implemented by the forward and backward connections terminating on different parts of the dendrite, as occurs for connections between cortical areas (see Chapter 1, Rolls and Treves (1998), and Rolls and Deco (2002)). The implication of this would be that there would be a trend through prefrontal cortical areas, from those closer to the sensory input, through areas between the sensory and motor-related areas, to areas with response-related neuronal activity. With the connections through the networks in this direction, there would be stronger connections in the correct (forward) direction, because the forward connections are more likely to end on the main part of the dendrites of pyramidal cells, and the backprojections are more likely to end on the apical dendrites of cortical pyramidal cells (see Chapter 1 and Rolls and Treves (1998)). Such a trend, from prefrontal cortical areas that receive from posterior perceptual areas, through regions that are intermediate, through to regions closer to motor output, could in fact be one of the principles of prefrontal cortical connectivity, which would not be inconsistent with what is known about prefrontal connectivity. For example, the orbitofrontal cortex has mainly sensory inputs (with little response-related neuronal activity) (Rolls 1999a, Rolls 2005), and so does the ventrolateral prefrontal cortex (area 47/12). The dorsolateral prefrontal cortex is more of a mixed area, with neurons that respond to combinations of sensory inputs and responses, and where effects of biasing attentional signals are evident (Asaad et al. 2000, Asaad et al. 1998).

Finally the more dorsal and posterior prefrontal cortical areas may be more closely related to the responses being made, including oculomotor responses (Kandel et al. 2000).

Synaptic plasticity is dependent on the timing of the spikes in the pre-and post-synaptic neuron (Markram et al. 1997, Bi and Poo 2001, Senn et al. 2001, Dan and Poo 2004, Dan and Poo 2006), and a theoretical and computational analysis of these effects in the context of working memory formation in the prefrontal cortex has been performed by Fusi and colleagues (Fusi 2003, Fusi 2002, Fusi, Annunziato, Badoni, Salamon and Amit 2000, Fusi and Mattia 1999). They have shown how Hebbian dynamic learning can cope with both stability of the network states and stability of the learning process. They have shown that a spike-time based learning rule can result in a rate dependent long-term synaptic modification, and that a working memory prefrontal architecture similar to that described in this chapter (i.e. excitatory pools of neurons strongly connected within a pool, and weakly connected between other excitatory pools, and with a common inhibitory pool) can indeed be formed by this kind of spike-time based learning. Further, there is accumulating evidence (Sjöström, Turrigiano and Nelson 2001) that a more realistic description of the protocols for inducing LTP and LTD probably requires a combination of dependence on spike-timing – to take into account the effects of the backpropagating action potential – and dependence on the subthreshold depolarization of the post-synaptic neuron. However these spike timing-dependent synaptic modifications may be evident primarily at low firing rates rather than those that often occur in the brain (Sjöström, Turrigiano and Nelson 2001), and may not be especially reproducible in the cerebral neocortex.

However, this does not altogether answer the issue of how it is that prefrontal cortex neurons become tuned to the task that is being performed. For example, in the action selection tasks described and modelled above, some dorsolateral prefrontal cortex neurons become tuned to combinations of the object and the response to be made, and other neurons to combinations of the spatial position of the object and the response that must be made (Asaad et al. 2000, Asaad et al. 1998). More generally, neurons in the prefrontal cortex adapt their response properties to the task demands (Freedman et al. 2003, Miller, Nieder, Freedman and Wallis 2003, Everling, Tinsley, Gaffan and Duncan 2006), and this helps to avoid a combinatorial explosion of required neuron types. But how does this selection occur? I suggest that this is a self-organizing process of the following type.

Inputs reach the prefrontal cortex from many sensory and motor areas. For example there are major inputs to the more dorsolateral parts of the prefrontal cortex from the parietal cortex, and major inputs to the more inferior convexity parts of the prefrontal cortex from the temporal lobe visual and auditory cortical areas (see Figs. 1.8 – 1.11) (Jones and Powell 1970, Ungerleider 1995, Goldman-Rakic 1996, Fuster 1997, Pandya 1996, Petrides 2005). If we assume that each prefrontal cortex neuron receives probabilistically from these different input sources, then each prefrontal neuron will tend to be able to respond to a different combination of the inputs from these diverse sources. If there is some plasticity in these inputs, the prefrontal cortex will tend to act as a competitive self-organizing network, with neurons gradually by associative synaptic modification coming to respond better to the particular sets of inputs being received during particular tasks, and tending to respond differently to other neurons as part of the competitive process (see Section B.4). The competition would be realized through the inhibitory interneurons. The prefrontal neurons would also receive local recurrent excitatory connections from nearby (within a few mm) pyramidal cells, and these associatively modifiable connections would enable the network to operate as an autoassociation or attractor network to maintain neuronal activity in short-term memory periods, as described in Section B.3. While particular combinations of inputs were being received by neurons during the performance of a particular task, the neurons would continue to be in a situation in which competitive learning would maintain their selectivity for the combination of inputs to which they were responsive as a result of the low probability of connections, and the synaptic modifiability. These processes could keep the neurons ready for use in such short-term memory tasks for periods of hours or days. But if that task was no longer being performed on a regular basis (perhaps once a day or once a week), then by competitive processes (see Section B.4), other neurons would be recruited into activity to respond to the combinations of inputs happening to be active for the new task. The previously allocated neurons would then decrease their responsiveness, partly by associative long-term depression (LTD, see Sections 1.5 and B.4), and partly also by passive decay of synaptic strength (over perhaps days) unless a neuron is receiving strong presynaptic inputs, is winning the competition, and is thus undergoing further LTP as a consequence of performing the first task. Thus a property that would help the prefrontal cortex to operate as a short-term memory in almost any task is that if neurons are no longer being strongly activated by inputs and are winning the competition, then passive synaptic decay and associative LTD will allow these neurons to be reallocated to new combinations of inputs present in new tasks. In Section B.16 it is further suggested that memory reconsolidation might play a role in this, by reconsolidating memory representations that are being used, while allowing representations that are not being used to passively decay over, in the case of the prefrontal cortex, a period of perhaps days.

8.4 Pharmacological manipulation of the depth of basins of attraction: attentional, decision-making, and action selection deficits

This model (Deco and Rolls 2003) of decision-making with delays also has interesting implications for understanding disorders of attention and decision-making that follow frontal lobe damage or interference with dopamine systems.

The effect of neurotransmitters on short-term memory-related prefrontal neuronal activity has been studied intensively recently, because of its clinical relevance. Dysfunctions of dopamine receptors have been related to working memory deficits in schizophrenia (Okubo, Suhara, Suzuki, Kobayashi, Inoue, Terasaki, Someya, Sassa, Sudo, Matsushima, Ito, Tateno and Toru 1997b, Goldman-Rakic 1994, Goldman-Rakic 1999, Goldman-Rakic, Castner, Svensson, Siever and Williams 2004, Miyamoto, Duncan, Marx and Lieberman 2005, Egan and Weinberg 1997) (see Section 8.5). In addition, amphetamine administration increases dopamine levels and is correlated with improved working memory performance of schizophrenic patients (Daniel, Weinberger, Jones, Zigun, Coppola, Handel, Bigelow, Goldberg, Berman and Kleinman 1991). Experiments with behaving monkeys have found that delay neuronal activity has a bell-shaped curve in response to activation of dopamine receptors (Williams and Goldman-Rakic 1995). Brunel and Wang (2001) have explained this inverted U-shape dependence of persistent neuronal activity in delay periods of dopamine by considering a detailed model of the influence of dopamine D1 receptor activation on NMDA receptor-mediated EPSPs on pyramidal cells vs inhibitory interneurons in the PFC. In the prefrontal cortex dopamine acts through D1 receptors to increase NMDA receptor-activated excitatory currents in pyramidal cells (Zheng et al. 1999, Durstewitz and Seamans 2002, Seamans and Yang 2004), although higher concentrations of dopamine may act through D2 receptors to decrease NMDA receptor-activated excitatory currents (Zheng et al. 1999).

Following the dopamine D1 models utilized by Brunel and Wang (2001), Deco and Rolls (2003) extended the simulations of the experiments of Asaad et al. (2000) described in Section 8.2, by manipulating the level of dopamine in the PFC architecture. Deco and Rolls aimed to study the influence of dopamine levels not just in the context of short-term memory-related neuronal activity in the delay period, but also at the more global cognitive level. In particular, Deco and Rolls investigated by simulation how dopamine may influence context- or rule-dependent stimulus cue-to-response mapping in the delayed spatial response task.

Two different models of dopamine influence were simulated, following the approach specified by Brunel and Wang (2001) and the sources cited there and next. The first one consists of a simultaneous modulation of the NMDA and GABA conductances (g_{NMDA} and g_{GABA} (Deco and Rolls 2003)). We ran the simulations by scaling down both conductances by a factor of 0.6, which models the effect of increasing D2 receptor activation described by Zheng et al. (1999). The second model considers a differential dopamine D1 modulation of NMDA conductances in pyramidal cells and inhibitory interneurons following Muly, Szigeti and Goldman-Rakic (1998). In this second model which mimics the effect of decreasing D1 receptor activation, the NMDA conductances on pyramidal cells are multiplied by a factor $c_E(1 + 0.2/(1 + \exp((0.8 - D_1)/0.25))) = 0.91$ for $D_1 = 0.8$, and those on inhibitory interneurons are multiplied by $c_I(1 + 0.2/(1 + \exp((1.2 - D_1)/0.25))) = 0.97$ for $D_1 = 0.8$, where D_1 is the relative change of simulated D1 activation, and the constants c_E and c_I are chosen so that both factors are equal to 1 when $D_1 = 1$.

Both models, and a third model in which both types of modulation were present simultaneously, yielded the same qualitative effect. Figure 8.4 shows the results, for the first model of increased dopamine D2 receptor activation in which the NMDA-mediated excitatory conductances are decreased. A simulation is shown corresponding to the delayed spatial response task, and may be compared with the rastergram illustrated in Fig. 8.2 lower left panel. The effects found are not only a decrease of the delay-related short-term memory-related neuronal activity in all task conditions, but also an increase in the firing of the neurons that should not be firing in the particular task. (The neurons that should have a high firing rate in the delayed Left spatial response condition illustrated are the Space 1, Task Space 1, and Motor Left.) This decreased competition arises primarily because the NMDA receptor-activated conductances are decreased, so that the relevant neuronal pools do not enter into an attractor state reflected in high firing. Thus the difference between the neurons that should be firing in the task, and those that should not, is decreased. Consistent with this, in the rastergrams in Fig. 8.4, the level of activity of the spatial intermediate neurons and of both premotor neurons is comparable, meaning that the external sensory and context biasing were not able to drive the competition in the correct direction to produce a strong attractor. In fact, because both premotor neurons show similar activity, the monkey will not be able to decide which is the right response in that task and cue situation, and it is predicted will make more behavioural errors.

Thus Deco and Rolls (2003) showed that one effect of blockade of dopamine receptors, to limit the maximum current that can flow through NMDA receptor-activated ion channels (Chen, Greengard and Yan 2004, Seamans and Yang 2004), in the model of decision-making is to limit the rate of firing of the population of neurons that are in the current attractor, and this makes the attractor basin shallow. The implication of this is that attention can too easily be shifted if dopamine is low, so that the current attentional rule cannot be stably maintained, and so that the biasing effect of the attentional rule does not produce such strong biasing, leading also to incorrect mappings between stimuli and responses. This is consistent with previous work showing that in simpler, single attractor, networks, D1 agonists, which can increase NMDA and GABA receptor-mediated currents can increase the depth and width of basins of attraction (Durstewitz and Seamans 2002), which could affect working memory.

Part of the interest of the model studied by Deco and Rolls (2003) is that it is a hierarchical multilayer attractor network model of how attention can influence decision-making and action selection, and in this model the action selection was impaired by alterations of dopamine modelled by their effects in reducing NMDA receptor-mediated channel conductances.

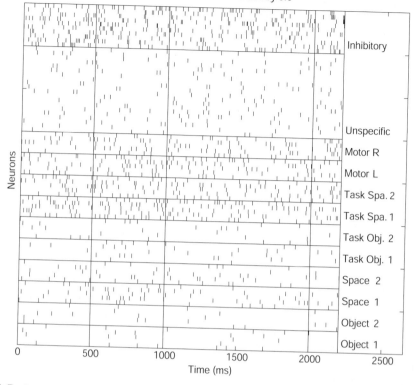

Spiking Activity Delayed Spatial Response Task (Left).
DA modulation of NMDA and GABA by 0.6

Fig. 8.4 Rastergrams of simulations of the delayed spatial response task after the experimental paradigm of Asaad et al. (2000), by manipulating the level of dopamine in our prefrontal cortex architecture. The dopamine effect consists of a simultaneous modulation of the NMDA and GABA conductances by a factor of 0.6. Note the similar level of activity for the intermediate spatial and both premotor pools for the dopamine condition. These would cause more oculomotor response errors. The spiking activity in the attractors is lower than that without any change in dopamine shown in the lower left panel of Fig. 8.2. (After Deco and Rolls 2003.)

8.5   Application to a neurodynamical systems hypothesis of schizophrenia

In the context of the effects of low NMDA receptor-mediated synaptic currents produced for example by D1 receptor blockade (Chen et al. 2004, Durstewitz and Seamans 2002, Seamans and Yang 2004), and the shallow basins of attraction produced by this manipulation in the model of decision-making (Deco and Rolls 2003) (see Section 8.4), it is of considerable interest that attention and decision-making (executive function) are impaired in patients with schizophrenia. It is suggested (Rolls 2005) that these impairments could be related to shallow basins of attraction in dorsolateral prefrontal cortex networks that implement the short-term memory required for attention, and the weakening of the biasing effect that this normally has on the neurons that map sensory inputs to motor outputs to implement executive function and attention. Consistent with this concept, NMDA receptor blockade by dissociative anesthetics (e.g. ketamine, and phencyclidine or 'angel dust') in normal subjects produces symptoms of schizophrenia including the cognitive symptoms such as distractibility and impaired executive function, and the negative symptoms such as the flattened affect or emotion (Goff and Coyle 2001, Coyle, Tsai and Goff 2003, Malhotra, Pinals, Weingartner, Sirocco, Missar, Pickar and Breier 1996, Newcomer, Farber, Jevtovic-Todorovic, Selke, Melson, Hershey, Craft and Olney 1999). (Consistent with the hypothesis of shallow basins of attraction, ketamine impairs performance at tasks that require short-term memory such as the Wisconsin card sorting task, delayed word recall, and verbal fluency.) Further, agents that indirectly enhance NMDA receptor function via the glycine modulatory site reduce the negative symptoms and variably improve functioning in schizophrenic subjects receiving typical antipsychotics (Goff and Coyle 2001). This is consistent with the theory that these agents deepen the basins of attraction by enhancing the effects of NMDA receptor activation. Further, clozapine (an atypical antipsychotic) is a partial agonist at the glycine modulatory site (Goff and Coyle 2001). While D1 dopamine receptor-mediated effects can increase NMDA receptor-mediated currents, D2 receptor-mediated effects can have the opposite effects (Goff and Coyle 2001, Seamans and Yang 2004), so that dopamine can exert a number of actions via effects on NMDA receptor-mediated currents. Thus the dopamine system may influence working memory systems via the dopaminergic effects on the activation of NMDA receptors by glutamate (Chen et al. 2004) and, in addition, alterations of NMDA receptor mediated functions by other agents also affect working memory. This convergent evidence helps to provide an understanding of some of the cognitive symptoms of and possible new treatments for schizophrenia.

Rolls (2005) extended these concepts to further help understanding of some of the symptoms of schizophrenia. He proposed that what appear to be the inconsistent negative symptoms of schizophrenia, the flattening of affect which may be related to orbitofrontal and anterior cingulate cortex dysfunction, can be understood within the same conceptual framework provided by the attractor network model. The hypothesis is that the flattening of affect in schizophrenia is due to the shallower basins of attraction in the orbitofrontal and anterior cingulate cortex, which correspond in terms of neuronal firing rates, to slower firing (Deco and Rolls 2003). Given that orbitofrontal cortex neurons represent emotional states, shallower basins of attraction would thus lead to less intense emotions. The same mechanism, reduction of the currents that can flow through NMDA receptor-activated synaptic channels, in fact by decreasing the firing rates of the neurons in the attractor, makes the short-term memory attractor states in the dorsolateral prefrontal cortex shallower and less stable, and in the orbitofrontal cortex corresponds to a reduction of affect.

Rolls (2005) also proposed that some of the positive symptoms of schizophrenia more related to temporal lobe function such as the hallucinations, delusions, paranoia, and loose (free, unconstrained and frequently bizarre) thought associations (Liddle 1987, Liddle, Barnes, Morris and Haque 1989, Baxter and Liddle 1998, Mueser and McGurk 2004) could result from shallower basins of attraction in those regions. A hypothesis proposed for the positive symptoms is that because the basins of attraction are shallow in the temporal lobe semantic memory networks, thoughts move too freely round the energy landscape, loosely from thought to weakly associated thought, leading to bizarre thoughts and associations, which may eventually over time be associated together in semantic memory to lead to false beliefs and delusions. Not only may the thoughts move from one to another too loosely and thus become bizarrely associated, due to the shallow basins of attraction, but in addition the thoughts themselves may be unstable and move into irrational states because the normal mutual constraints between coupled thoughts may operate too weakly (as each thought is itself weak due to the reduced firing rate), so that rational thoughts cannot sufficiently control and constrain bizarre thoughts and associations.

To develop these hypotheses described by Rolls (2005) about how alterations in the stability of attractor networks produced by transmitter- or receptor-activated conductance changes might contribute to the symptoms of schizophrenia, Loh, Rolls and Deco (2007a) and Loh, Rolls and Deco (2007b) simulated a single attractor network with integrate-and-fire neurons with spiking activity and thus statistical effects related to the spiking. An important concept is that these spiking-related statistical effects or fluctuations contribute to instability in the network, by providing the noise that causes the networks when they have shallow basins of attraction to jump between different attractor states, or to the spontaneous state. An attractor network was the architecture modelled as it is the generic class of network that could be related to schizophrenic symptoms as follows.

The cognitive or dysexecutive aspects of schizophrenia (which include distractibility, poor attention, and the dysexecutive syndrome (Liddle 1987, Green 1996, Mueser and McGurk 2004)) are hypothesized to be related to instabilities of activity states in attractor neural networks, due to the fact that the neurons are firing less fast, leading to shallower basins of attraction, and thus a difficulty in maintaining a stable short-term memory, normally the source of the bias in biased competition models of attention (Rolls and Deco 2002, Deco and Rolls 2005a) (see Chapter 6). (As described in Section B.3, the firing in an attractor network is maintained by the recurrent collateral connections with their associative synapses, and the higher the firing of the neurons, the more stable the attractor will be, and the more difficult it will be for external inputs to alter the neuronal firing dominated by the recurrent collateral connections to move the state away from the current attractor.) The shallower basins of attraction would result in distractibility, poor attention, and working memory difficulties. This is consistent with the hypothesis that at the core of the cognitive symptoms is a working memory deficit in which there is a difficulty in maintaining items in short-term memory (Goldman-Rakic 1994, Goldman-Rakic 1999).

The negative symptoms (a flattening of affect and a reduction in emotion and motivation (Liddle 1987, Mueser and McGurk 2004)) are hypothesized to be related to decreases in firing rates in the orbitofrontal cortex and/or anterior cingulate cortex (Rolls 2005), where neuronal firing rates, and activations in fMRI investigations, are correlated with reward value and pleasure (Rolls 2005, Rolls 2006c, Rolls 2007b), and by continuing due to attractor processes may help to implement ongoing mood states.

The positive symptoms of schizophrenia (which include bizarre (psychotic) trains of thoughts, hallucinations, and (paranoid) delusions (Liddle 1987, Mueser and McGurk 2004)) are hypothesized to be related to shallow basins of attraction in the temporal lobe semantic memory networks. This could result in thoughts moving too freely round the energy landscape, loosely from thought to weakly associated thought, leading to bizarre thoughts and associations.

With respect to the positive symptoms of schizophrenia, Loh, Rolls and Deco (2007a) and Loh, Rolls and Deco (2007b) proposed that attractor networks in the medial temporal lobes may be more likely to enter these unusual and bizarre states for a number of further reasons. The first is that statistical fluctuations due to the spiking activity of the different neurons in the network may lead the network to jump from the spontaneous level of activity to an attractor state, as well as between attractor states. These effects may become especially prominent at low firing rates. The second is that a reduction of GABA-activated inhibitory currents in schizophrenia might contribute to the networks being more likely to jump (given the statistical fluctuations) from a spontaneous firing state into an attractor, which could be linked to intrusive thoughts. The third is that because the NMDA receptor-mediated synaptic currents are reduced, resulting in a diminished contribution of the long time constants of the NMDA receptors which normally help to provide stability of attractor networks, the statistical fluctuations may be less smoothed in time, and may be more likely to lead the network to jump from the spontaneous level of activity to an attractor state, or between attractor states. This third factor is at present a hypothesis, and requires further quantitative testing in integrate-and-fire simulations.

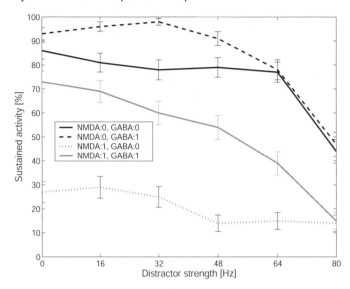

Fig. 8.5 Stability and distractibility as a function of the distractor strength and modulations of the synaptic efficacies. We assessed how often in 100 trials the average activity during the last second (2–3 s) stayed above 10 Hz in the S1 attractor. The modulation of the synapses NMDA:–1 and GABA:–1 corresponds to a reduction of 4.5% and 9%, respectively. The strength of the distractor stimulus applied to S2 is an increase in firing rate above the 2.4 kHz background activity which is distributed among 800 synapses per neuron. High distractibility corresponds to a low proportion of trials with sustained activity in the S1 attractor (which is what is plotted on the ordinate). The standard deviations were approximated with the binomial distribution. (After Loh, Rolls and Deco 2007a.)

For these reasons, Loh, Rolls and Deco (2007a) used an attractor network, with integrate-and-fire neurons with spiking activity and thus statistical effects related to the spiking, to investigate how transmitter and receptor changes implicated in schizophrenia affect the stability and firing rates of attractor networks, and could thus produce schizophreniform symptoms. As alterations in the efficacies of the NMDA and GABA channels have been identified in the pathology of schizophrenia (Coyle et al. 2003, Lewis, Hashimoto and Volk 2005), Loh, Rolls and Deco (2007a) investigated which alterations in the NMDA and GABA efficacies correspond to the dynamical systems hypothesis about the stability and distractability of attractor networks.

In the attractor network, there were 800 excitatory neurons, with 80 forming attractor S1 because of strong mutual synapses, another 80 forming attractor S2, and the remainder unallocated to an attractor. There were both AMPA and NMDA synapses between the neurons, and the general integrate-and-fire formulation specified in Section 7.8, and mean-field approach described in Section 7.9, were used. There were 200 inhibitory GABAergic neurons. In the simulations, typically a cue was applied to S1 for the first 500 ms to trigger it into an attractor state, and then the simulation was either left to run for 2,500 ms in a 'persistent condition' to measure whether the attractor was stable; or, in a 'distractor condition', at 1,000–1,500 ms S2 was applied to determine what strength S2 needed to be to distract the attractor from its S1 short-term memory state.

To investigate the computational basis of the *cognitive symptoms*, Loh, Rolls and Deco (2007a) computed the stability and distractibility of the attractor, short-term memory, network using persistent and distractor simulations. A distractor strength of 0 Hz corresponds to the persistent condition. Fig. 8.5 shows the stability and distractibility for reductions of NMDA and GABA currents. The reference state is (NMDA:0, GABA:0). In this state, pool S1 continued to maintain its attractor firing without any distractor (distractor strength = 0 Hz) throughout the delay period on almost 90 % of the trials. As the distractor stimulus strength was increased through the range 0–80 Hz, the network was less and less able to maintain the S1 attractor firing. In both conditions which reduce the NMDA current (labelled NMDA:-1), it is shown that the stability of the persistent state was reduced, and also the distractibility was increased, as shown by the fact that increasing distractor currents applied to S2 could move the attractor away from S1. The implication therefore is that a reduction of the NMDA currents could cause the cognitive symptoms of schizophrenia, by making short-term memory networks less stable and more distractible, thereby reducing the ability to maintain attention. Reducing only the GABA currents (NMDA:0, GABA:–1) had little effect on the stability or distractibility.

With respect to the cognitive symptoms, the attractor framework is very appropriate, as many of the cognitive symptoms of schizophrenia can be related to the type of short-term memory function implemented by the ongoing (i.e. persistent) firing of neurons in an attractor network that keeps the short-term memory active (Goldman-Rakic 1999). Such a short-term memory is implemented by continuing firing of neurons in for example the prefrontal cortex during working memory tasks in delay periods (Goldman-Rakic 1996, Miller and Cohen 2001), is required to provide the memory that holds the current object of attention active, and provides the source of the top-down bias to influence attention and action selection by biased competition in earlier cortical areas, as described in detail elsewhere (Rolls and Deco 2002, Deco and Rolls 2005a, Deco and Rolls 2005b, Deco and Rolls 2003) (see Chapter 6). The working memory could be implemented by associatively modifiable synapses between the recurrent collateral synapses of cortical pyramidal cells.

Consistent with this hypothesized role of a reduction in NMDA conductances being involved in schizophrenia, postmortem studies of schizophrenia have identified abnormalities in glutamate receptor density in regions such as the prefrontal cortex, thalamus and the temporal lobe, which are active during the performance of cognitive tasks (Meador-Woodruff and Healy 2000). Blockade of NMDA receptors by dissociative anesthetics such as ketamine reproduces in normal subjects schizophrenic symptoms including negative and cognitive impairments (Malhotra et al. 1996, Newcomer et al. 1999). In addition, agents that enhance NMDA receptor function improve the cognitive abilities of schizophrenic patients and also reduce the negative symptoms (Goff and Coyle 2001). Further, the hypofrontality in schizophrenia, that is less activation in frontal brain regions, during working memory tasks (Ingvar and Franzen 1974, Carter, Perlstein, Ganguli, Brar, Mintun and Cohen 1998), is in line with this hypothesis about the cognitive symptoms, since lower firing rates reflect shallow basins of attraction and thus less stability and more distractibility (Winterer, Musso, Beckmann, Mattay, Egan, Jones, Callicott, Coppola and Weinberger 2006, Loh, Rolls and Deco 2007a).

The *negative symptoms* such as the flattening of affect or reduced emotionality are envisaged to be related to a reduced firing rate of orbitofrontal cortex and/or anterior cingulate cortex (Rolls 2005), where neuronal firing rates and activations in fMRI investigations are correlated with reward value and pleasure (Rolls 2005, Rolls 2006c). We therefore assessed the changes of the firing rates caused by a reduction of the NMDA and GABA currents, and did this for both the spontaneous and persistent states. Since we are interested in the mean firing rate, we used a mean field formulation (Brunel and Wang 2001) which yields an approximation of the mean firing rates in the absence of statistical fluctuations caused by the spiking nature of the dynamics. Figure 8.6 shows the progression of mean firing rates when NMDA and GABA currents are reduced selectively (no modulation at Modulation=0). A reduction of

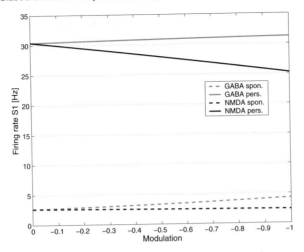

Fig. 8.6 Average firing rate computed with the mean-field technique for both the spontaneous (spon.), and persistent (pers., i.e. high firing rate attractor), states. The effects of reducing the NMDA and GABA synaptic efficacies are shown. A modulation of the synapses of NMDA:–1 and GABA:–1 corresponds to a reduction of 4.5% and 9% respectively of the efficacies. (After Loh, Rolls and Deco 2007a.)

the NMDA conductance reduces the firing rate produced by S1 in the persistent state (solid black line), whereas a reduction of the GABA conductance produces a slight increase in firing rate (solid grey line). Spiking simulations showed the same effects. Thus the negative symptoms could be accounted for by the same mechanism as the cognitive symptoms, namely a decrease in NMDA synaptic currents. With respect to the spontaneous firing rate (in the absence of any applied stimulus), there was little effect on the firing rates of a reduction in the NMDA currents, and a small increase produced by a reduction of the GABA efficacies, as shown in Figure 8.6.

These simulations thus support the hypothesis that because the basins of attraction are less deep in these orbitofrontal and anterior cingulate regions, due for example to reduced NMDA conductances, the neurons are firing more slowly, and thus the rewards and punishers that produce emotional states, and the ongoing emotional states, represented in these regions will be less intense. In particular, the simulations show that the same degree of reduction of NMDA conductances that makes attractor networks unstable as illustrated in Fig. 8.5 also decreases the firing rates as illustrated in Fig. 8.6. The emotional states represented in the orbitofrontal cortex and anterior cingulate cortex include states elicited by rewards, which produce positive emotional states, and states elicited by punishers, which include negative emotional states, and our hypothesis is that both would be reduced by the mechanism described (Rolls 2005, Rolls 2006c, Rolls 2007b) (see Chapter 3). Correspondingly, motivation would be reduced in the same way, in that motivation is a state in which we work to obtain goals (rewards) or avoid punishers, and the rewards and the punishers would be reduced in the way just described, as would the stability of motivational states to obtain particular rewards or avoid particular punishers (Rolls 2005).

The proposed mechanism that links the cognitive and negative symptoms of schizophrenia in an attractor framework is consistent with a close relation between the cognitive and negative symptoms. For example, as noted above, blockade of NMDA receptors by dissociative anesthetics such as ketamine produces in normal subjects schizophrenic symptoms including both negative and cognitive impairments (Malhotra et al. 1996, Newcomer et al. 1999); agents that enhance NMDA receptor function reduce the negative symptoms and improve the cognitive

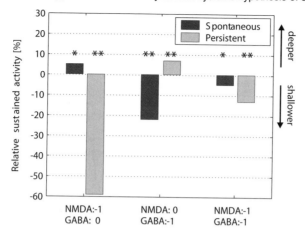

Fig. 8.7 Stability of the spontaneous and persistent state relative to the reference state (of NMDA:0 and GABA:0) for modulations of the synaptic efficacies. The stability was assessed by how often in 100 trials the average activity during the last second (2–3 s) stayed above 10 Hz. The value shows how often it stayed more in the respective state than in the reference state. A negative percentage means that the system was less stable than in the reference state. A modulation of the synapses shown as NMDA:−1 and GABA:−1 corresponds to a reduction of 4.5% and 9% respectively in their efficacies. We assessed with the Binomial distribution the statistical significance of the effects observed, with P<0.01 relative to the reference state marked by **, and P<0.02 by *. (After Loh, Rolls and Deco 2007a.)

abilities of schizophrenic patients (Goff and Coyle 2001); and the cognitive and negative symptoms occur early in the illness and may precede the positive symptoms.

With respect to the *positive symptoms* of schizophrenia, Loh, Rolls and Deco (2007a) proposed that both the spontaneous, and the persistent (attractor) states in neural networks in for example the temporal lobe are unstable, and statistical fluctuations can move thoughts loosely from thought to weakly associated thought, leading to bizarre thoughts and associations, which may eventually over time be associated together in semantic memory to lead to false beliefs and delusions. Loh, Rolls and Deco (2007a) therefore assessed how the stability of both spontaneous and persistent states changes when NMDA and GABA efficacies are modulated. Fig. 8.7 shows the stability of the spontaneous and persistent attractor relative to the unmodulated reference state (NMDA:0; GABA:0). A negative percentage means that the system was less stable than in the unmodulated state. A reduction of the NMDA conductances decreased the stability of the persistent state, and a reduction of the GABA currents destabilized the spontaneous state. A reduction of both NMDA and GABA produced a significant decrease in the stability of the persistent state, and a small decrease in the stability of the spontaneous state, as shown in Fig. 8.7. (The reduction of GABA conductances is responsible for the decreased stability of the spontaneous state, i.e. for the system jumping into an attractor from the spontaneous state. These changes together (a reduction of NMDA and GABA conductances) might produce wandering from one attractor state to another, which is what we proposed for the positive symptoms, and also jumps from the spontaneous to an attractor state, which might correspond to intrusive thoughts. In all cases, the jumps from one state to another are due to the statistical spike-related noise, which allows the system to jump over an energy barrier (Loh, Rolls and Deco 2007a, Loh, Rolls and Deco 2007b).

To investigate more directly the wandering between spontaneous and several different persistent attractor states, we simulated the condition with decreased NMDA and GABA conductances over a long time period in which no cue stimulus input was given. Fig. 8.8 shows

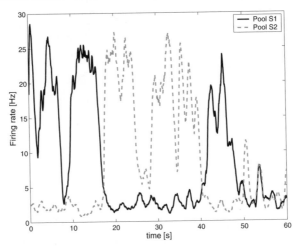

Fig. 8.8 Wandering between attractor states by virtue of statistical fluctuations caused by the randomness of the spiking activity. We simulated a single long trial (60 s) in the spontaneous test condition for the synaptic modification (NMDA:–1, GABA:–1). The two curves show the activity of the two selective pools over time smoothed with a 1 s sliding averaging window. The activity moves noisily between the attractor for the spontaneous state and the two persistent states S1 and S2. (After Loh, Rolls and Deco 2007a.)

the firing rates of the two selective pools S1 and S2. The high activity switches between the two attractors due to the influence of fluctuations, which corresponds to spontaneous wandering in a shallow energy landscape, i.e. thoughts move freely from one thought to another. I emphasize that any adaptation at the synaptic or neuronal level would facilitate this wandering from state to state (cf. Deco and Rolls (2005c) and Section 9.3), which depends also on the shallow basins of attraction and on the statistical spiking-related fluctuations. The adaptation would have the effect of gradually reducing the depth of the basin of attraction in which the neurons are currently active, facilitating a transition to another attractor basin.

The wandering from one thought to another loosely associated thought which is an aspect of the positive symptoms of schizophrenia may also be compared with the effects of S2 in moving the attractor away from S1 in the distractor condition, and this is shown in Fig. 8.5 to be a reduction in the NMDA synaptic efficacies. The positive symptoms may thus be accounted for in part by similar dynamical processes to those that might account for the cognitive symptoms, that is a reduction in the stability of the persistent states due to shallow basins of attraction, though for the positive symptoms the changes would be in networks probably in the temporal lobe involved in semantic and thought processing. Each thought would be insufficiently stable to resist being pulled to another loosely associated thought.

The integrate-and-fire simulations of Loh, Rolls and Deco (2007a) showed that two factors contribute to the instabilities observed in the attractor simulations when NMDA conductances are decreased. One is alteration in the depth of the basins of attraction, as described above. A second factor is that statistical fluctuations caused by chance bunching of spikes from different neurons will make the network more likely to jump over an energy barrier into another state. Both factors that contribute to the instability are taken into account in the integrate-and-fire spiking simulations with separate dynamical equations for the NMDA, AMPA and GABA synapses of Loh, Rolls and Deco (2007a).

Loh, Rolls and Deco (2007a) and Loh, Rolls and Deco (2007b) show how this statistical neurodynamical approach can be applied to a current concept of schizophrenia, that there is

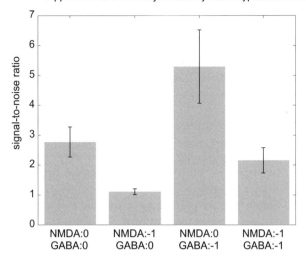

Fig. 8.9 Signal-to-noise ratio of the persistent state as a function of the modulations of the synaptic efficacies. We computed the mean and standard deviation of the averages of the firing rate in the last second of the simulation (2–3 s), as this reflects how stably a signal was maintained by the system. We conducted 1000 simulated trials. A modulation of the synapses shown as NMDA:-1 and GABA:-1 corresponds to a reduction of 4.5% and 9% respectively in their conductances. The signal-to-noise ratio is calculated by division of the mean firing rate by the standard deviation. The Figure shows the mean signal-to-noise ratio, and its standard deviation, for the different conditions. (After Loh, Rolls and Deco 2007a.)

an altered signal to noise ratio (Winterer and Weinberger 2004, Winterer et al. 2006). Figure 8.9 shows the signal-to-noise ratio of the persistent state simulations in which an initial stimulus should be maintained throughout the simulation. To be specific, we calculated the mean firing rate of the last second of the 3 s simulations and its variation across trials. We envision that this measure is related to imaging experiments such as Winterer et al. (2006) in which trial-to-trial variation is measured. We note that the signal-to-noise ratio measured in our model is related to both the level of noise in the spiking neural network and the depth of the basins of attraction of the dynamical system. We found that in both the cases in which NMDA was reduced (NMDA:-1, GABA:0; and NMDA:-1, GABA:-1), the signal-to-noise ratio was also reduced. This relates to recent experimental observations which show a decreased signal-to-noise ratio in schizophrenic patients (Winterer, Ziller, Dorn, Frick, Mulert, Wuebben, Herrmann and Coppola 2000, Winterer, Coppola, Goldberg, Egan, Jones, Sanchez and Weinberger 2004, Winterer et al. 2006). Loh, Rolls and Deco (2007a) and Loh, Rolls and Deco (2007b) thus related a decrease in the signal-to-noise ratio directly to modulations of receptor-activated synaptic conductances.

Dopamine has been linked to schizophrenia, and could influence the type of dynamical system described here. While D1 dopamine receptor-mediated effects can increase NMDA receptor-mediated currents, D2 receptor-mediated effects can have the opposite effects (Goff and Coyle 2001, Durstewitz and Seamans 2002, Seamans and Yang 2004). Our simulations (Loh, Rolls and Deco 2007a) suggest that an increase in the NMDA component could improve the cognitive and negative symptoms of schizophrenia. In this context, the D1 receptor has been shown to modulate the performance of working memory tasks (Sawaguchi and Goldman-Rakic 1991, Sawaguchi and Goldman-Rakic 1994, Goldman-Rakic 1999, Castner, Williams and Goldman-Rakic 2000). Imaging data also support the importance of the D1 receptor in schizophrenia (Okubo, Suhara, Sudo and Toru 1997a, Okubo, Suhara, Suzuki, Kobayashi, Inoue, Terasaki, Someya, Sassa, Sudo, Matsushima, Iyo, Tateno and Toru 1997c). We therefore suggest that an increased activation of D1 receptors might alleviate the cognitive and negative symptoms of schizophrenia (Goldman-Rakic et al. 2004, Miyamoto et al. 2005), by increasing NMDA receptor-mediated synaptic currents. Atypical neuroleptics might use this mechanism by increasing the presynaptic release of dopamine which in turn would increase the activation of the extrasynaptic D1 receptors (Castner et al. 2000, Moller 2005).

It is a possibility that dopamine influences the positive symptoms of schizophrenia in part in a different way. Dopamine receptor D2 antagonists are used to treat schizophrenia, mainly alleviating the positive symptoms whereas the cognitive and negative symptoms persist, especially for the typical neuroleptics (Mueser and McGurk 2004). One hypothesis raised by our simulations (Fig. 8.7) is that the positive symptoms are related in part to a decrease in GABA. In this context it is interesting that Seamans, Gorelova, Durstewitz and Yang (2001) found that the application of D2 antagonists prevented a decrease in eIPSC amplitude by dopamine. An implication is that if dopamine is too high (or effective) in schizophrenia, this would decrease inhibitory post-synaptic currents produced by GABA, leading to insufficient inhibition, and runaway instability from the spontaneous firing condition into an attractor. This instability would then be ameliorated by D2 antagonists.

There are related modelling approaches to schizophrenia and dopamine (Durstewitz, Kelc and Gunturkun 1999, Durstewitz, Seamans and Sejnowski 2000, Brunel and Wang 2001). However, these implement bottom-up approaches. They start from a detailed model of the effects of dopamine on neural and synaptic properties and analyse these effects at the neural network level. The approach taken by Rolls (2005) and Loh, Rolls and Deco (2007a) maps the symptoms of schizophrenia to effects in dynamical systems. In that framework, Loh, Rolls and Deco (2007a) and Loh, Rolls and Deco (2007b) considered which modulations at the synaptic level but operating in different brain regions could implement symptoms related to schizophrenia. These two approaches complement each other.

A particular contribution of the approach described here is that it provides a unified framework for considering the cognitive and negative symptoms of schizophrenia, and also for developing an understanding of the factors that could underlie the positive symptoms. An important part of the approach taken here is that statistical fluctuations caused by the probability of spiking of neurons influence the dynamics of the system, and that to understand the factors that influence the stability of such systems, it is important to treat formally the spiking dynamics, as was possible in integrate-and-fire simulations that allow not only the conductances of neurons at the synapses to be directly modelled, but also the effects of the spiking dynamics of the individual neurons on the global properties of a whole memory system to be modelled (Loh, Rolls and Deco 2007a).

Indeed, the approach taken here provides a way of linking changes and effects at the synaptic and receptor level to the global properties of a whole network involved in cognitive and memory functions. This bridging between levels is an important part of the approach taken in this book to how memory, attention, and decision-making are implemented in the brain, for it allows predictions to be made of how changes at one level of operation of the system (e.g. receptor-activated channel conductances) will influence the overall cognitive function through effects that become evident in large populations of interacting neurons.

8.6 Conclusions

In conclusion, the computational neuroscience approach, closely linked to neurophysiological and related evidence, provides a mathematical framework for studying the mechanisms involved in action selection as well as many other brain functions including short-term memory and attention. Analysis of networks of neurons each implemented at the integrate-and-fire neuronal level, and including non-linearities, enables many aspects of brain function, from the spiking activity of single neurons and the effects of pharmacological agents on synaptic currents, through fMRI and neuropsychological findings, to be integrated, and many aspects of cognitive function including visual cognition and attention to be modelled and understood. The theoretical approach described makes explicit predictions at all these levels which can be tested to develop and refine our understanding of the underlying processing, and its dynamics. The kind of analysis described in this chapter provides a fundamental approach for a deep understanding in neuroscience of how the brain performs complex tasks, including action selection, and of disorders in these functions.

9 Reward, decision, and action reversal using attractor dynamics

In this chapter we consider at the computational level how rapid reward reversal learning could be implemented in the brain. This is a very important process for rapidly updating which stimuli are currently treated as rewards and which are not, and is thus important in very much motivational, emotional, and social behaviour. The type of learning that is reversed is stimulus–stimulus, where the second stimulus is a reinforcer. I also consider (in Section 9.2) how mappings to actions can be rapidly reversed, where the mappings in this case are between stimuli and actions or responses. The ability to alter our behaviour rapidly in these ways is important in decision-making. I also consider in Section 9.3 how a short-term memory for the sequence of events can be formed using a similar attractor short-term memory approach with resetting of the attractor.

9.1 A neurophysiological and computational basis for stimulus–reinforcer association learning and reversal in the orbitofrontal cortex

The neurophysiological and lesion evidence described suggests that one function implemented by the orbitofrontal cortex is rapid stimulus–reinforcer association learning, and the correction of these associations when reinforcement contingencies in the environment change (see Section 3.6). To implement this, the orbitofrontal cortex has the necessary representation of primary reinforcers, such as taste and somatosensory inputs (see Section 3.4 and Chapter 5 of Rolls (2005)). It also receives information about objects, e.g. visual information, and can associate this very rapidly at the neuronal level with primary reinforcers such as taste, and reverse these associations. Another type of stimulus that can be conditioned in this way in the orbitofrontal cortex is olfactory, although here the learning is slower. It is likely that auditory stimuli can be associated with primary reinforcers in the orbitofrontal cortex, though there is less direct evidence of this yet.

The orbitofrontal cortex neurons that detect non-reward in a context-specific manner are likely to be used in behavioural extinction and reversal. Such non-reward neurons may help behaviour in situations in which stimulus–reinforcer associations must be disconnected, not only by helping to reset the reinforcer association of neurons in the orbitofrontal cortex, but also by sending a signal to the striatum which could be routed by the striatum to produce appropriate behaviours for non-reward (Rolls and Johnstone 1992, Williams, Rolls, Leonard and Stern 1993, Rolls 1994c, Rolls 1999a) (see Section 3.10.2 and Chapter 8 of Rolls (2005)). Indeed, the striatal route is one through which the orbitofrontal cortex may directly influence behaviour when the orbitofrontal cortex is decoding reinforcement contingencies in the environment, and is altering behaviour in response to altering reinforcement contingencies. Some of the evidence for this is that neurons with responses that reflect these orbitofrontal neuronal responses are found in the ventral part of the head of the caudate nucleus and the ventral striatum, which receive from the orbitofrontal cortex (Rolls, Thorpe and Maddison 1983b, Williams, Rolls,

Leonard and Stern 1993); and lesions of the ventral part of the head of the caudate nucleus impair visual discrimination reversal (Divac et al. 1967) (see further Section 3.10.2).

Decoding the reinforcement value of stimuli, which involves for previously neutral (e.g. visual) stimuli learning their association with a primary reinforcer, often rapidly, and which may involve not only rapid learning but also rapid relearning and alteration of responses when reinforcement contingencies change, is then a function proposed for the orbitofrontal cortex. This way of producing behavioural responses would be important in, for example, motivational and emotional behaviour. It would be important in motivational behaviour such as feeding and drinking by enabling primates to learn rapidly about the food reinforcement to be expected from visual stimuli (see Rolls (2005)). This is important, for primates frequently eat more than 100 varieties of food; vision by visual–taste association learning can be used to identify when foods are ripe; and during the course of a meal, the pleasantness of the sight of a food eaten in the meal decreases in a sensory-specific way (Rolls, Rolls and Rowe 1983a), a function that is probably implemented by the sensory-specific satiety-related responses of orbitofrontal visual neurons (Critchley and Rolls 1996a).

With regard to emotional behaviour, decoding and rapidly readjusting the reinforcement value of visual signals is likely to be crucial, for emotions can be described as responses elicited by reinforcing signals (Rolls 1986c, Rolls 1986a, Rolls 1990d, Rolls 1995d, Rolls 2005) (see Chapter 3). The ability to perform this learning very rapidly is probably very important in social situations in primates, in which reinforcing stimuli are continually being exchanged, and the reinforcement value of these must be continually updated (relearned), based on the actual reinforcers received and given. Although the operation of reinforcers such as taste, smell, and faces is best understood in terms of orbitofrontal cortex operation, there are tactile inputs that are likely to be concerned with reward evaluation (Rolls 2007d, McCabe, Rolls, Bilderbeck and McGlone 2007), and in humans the rewards processed in the orbitofrontal cortex include quite general rewards such as working for 'points' (Rolls, Hornak, Wade and McGrath 1994a) or for 'monetary' rewards (O'Doherty, Kringelbach, Rolls, Hornak and Andrews 2001a, Hornak, O'Doherty, Bramham, Rolls, Morris, Bullock and Polkey 2004).

Although the amygdala is concerned with some of the same functions as the orbitofrontal cortex, and receives similar inputs (see Figs. 3.3, 3.10 and 3.40), there is evidence that it may function less effectively in the very rapid learning and reversal of stimulus–reinforcer associations, as indicated by the greater difficulty in obtaining reversal from amygdala neurons (see, e.g., Rolls (2000d)), and by the greater effect of orbitofrontal lesions in leading to continuing behavioural responses to previously rewarded stimuli (see Sections 3.6.4 and 3.6.6). In primates the necessity for very rapid stimulus–reinforcement re-evaluation, and the development of powerful cortical learning systems, may result in the orbitofrontal cortex effectively taking over this aspect of amygdala functions (Rolls 1992b, Rolls 1999a, Rolls 2000d, Rolls 2005). In this section I consider the mechanism of rapid reversal learning that may be implemented in the orbitofrontal cortex by utilizing a working memory of which rule is currently active. The use of an attractor short-term memory to hold the current rule active may depend on the highly developed recurrent collateral set of synaptic connections present in the orbitofrontal cortex (and other cortical areas) but not the amygdala. This offers a more computational account of the different functions of the orbitofrontal cortex and amygdala in emotion than previous accounts (e.g. Pickens, Saddoris, Setlow, Gallagher, Holland and Schoenbaum (2003), and Holland and Gallagher (2004)).

We now consider how stimulus–reinforcer association learning and its reversal may be implemented in the orbitofrontal cortex. The suggested process for the initial association is illustrated in Fig. 3.6 on page 132. If the visual input (e.g. the sight of food) is present at the same time (or just before) the primary reinforcer (e.g. taste) is activating the postsynaptic neuron, then the set of synapses that are driven by the conditioned stimulus become strengthened by the associative process of long-term synaptic potentiation (LTP). The LTP occurs only if the post-synaptic neuron is strongly activated, because the NMDA receptors activated by the presynaptic release of the transmitter glutamate only become unblocked to allow Ca^{2+} entry when the postsynaptic neuron is sufficiently depolarized (see Appendix B, Rolls and Treves (1998) and Rolls and Deco (2002)). This pattern association learning can learn many associations between conditioned stimuli and primary reinforcers, in fact in the order of the number of synapses per neuron, which is in the order of 5,000–10,000 (see Appendix B, Rolls and Treves (1998) and Rolls and Deco (2002)). This type of learning also has many other desirable properties, including generalization to similar conditioned stimuli, and graceful degradation (fault tolerance) if the system sustains some damage (see Appendix B, Rolls and Treves (1998) and Rolls and Deco (2002)). This putative role of NMDA receptors could be tested by using NMDA-receptor blockers applied locally to individual neurons with visual responses in the orbitofrontal cortex during visual discrimination reversal, or by perfusion of the orbitofrontal cortex with an NMDA-receptor blocker to investigate whether this interferes with behavioural visual discrimination reversal.

A first approach to the reversal is as follows, and can be understood by referring to Fig. 3.6 on page 132 and Section 3.6.7. Consider a neuron with unconditioned responses to taste in the orbitofrontal cortex. When a particular visual stimulus, say a triangle, was associated with the taste of glucose, the active synaptic connections for this visual (conditioned) stimulus would have shown long-term synaptic potentiation on to the taste neuron, which would respond to the sight of the triangle. During reversal, the same visual stimulus, the triangle, would again activate the same synaptic afferents to the neuron, but that neuron would be inactive when the taste of saline was given. Active presynaptic inputs and a low level of postsynaptic activation is the condition for homosynaptic long-term synaptic depression (LTD, see Fig. 1.5 on page 9), which would then occur, resulting in a decline of the response of the neuron to the triangle. At the same time, visual presentation of a square would now be associated with the taste of glucose, which would activate the postsynaptic neuron, leading now to long-term potentiation of afferents on to that neuron made active by the sight of the square.

Although reversal might be implemented in the way just described by having long-term synaptic depression for synapses that represented the reward-associated stimulus before the reversal, and long-term potentiation of the new stimulus that after reversal is associated with reward, this would require one-trial LTP and one-trial homosynaptic LTD to account for one-trial stimulus–reward reversal (Thorpe, Rolls and Maddison 1983, Rolls, Critchley, Mason and Wakeman 1996b, Rolls 2000e). Moreover, the mechanism would not account for reversal learning set, the process by which during repeated reversal learning, performance gradually improves until reversal can occur in one trial. Even more, the mechanism would not account for the fact that after reversal learning set has been acquired, when the contingency is reversed, the animal makes a response to the current S+ expecting to get the reward, but instead obtains the punisher. On the very first subsequent trial on which the pre-reversal S– is shown, the animal will perform a response to it expecting now to get reward, *even though the post-reversal S+ has not since the reversal been associated with reward to produce LTP for the post-reversal S+*. (This is in fact illustrated in Fig. 3.28 on page 161.) To implement this very rapid stimulus–reinforcer association reversal, a different mechanism is therefore needed.

A model for how the very rapid, one-trial, reversal could be implemented has now been developed (Deco and Rolls 2005d). The model uses a short-term memory autoassociation attractor network with associatively modifiable synaptic connections (see Section B.3) to hold the neurons representing the current rule active (see Fig. 9.1). Rule one might correspond to 'stimulus 1 (e.g. a triangle) is associated with reward, and stimulus 2 (e.g. a square) is associated with punishment'. Rule 2 might correspond to the opposite contingency. A small,

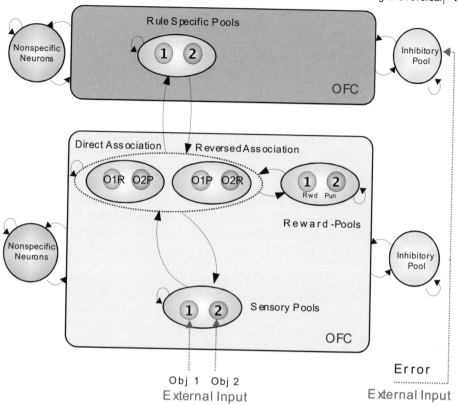

Fig. 9.1 Cortical architecture of the reward reversal model. There is a rule module (top) and a sensory – intermediate neuron – reward module (below). Neurons within each module are fully connected, and form attractor states. The sensory – intermediate neuron – reward module consists of three hierarchically organized levels of attractor network, with stronger synaptic connections in the forward than the backprojection direction. The intermediate level of the sensory – intermediate neuron – reward module contains neurons that respond to combinations of an object and its association with reward or punishment, e.g. object 1–reward (O1R, in the direct association set of pools), and object 1–punishment (O1P in the reversed association set of pools). The rule module acts as a biasing input to bias the competition between the object–reward combination neurons at the intermediate level of the sensory – intermediate neuron – reward module. The synaptic current flows into the cells are mediated by four different families of receptors. The recurrent excitatory postsynaptic currents are given by two different types of EPSP (excitatory post-synaptic potentials), respectively mediated by AMPA and NMDA receptors. These two glutamatergic excitatory synapses are on the pyramidal cells and interneurons. The external background is mediated by AMPA synapses on pyramidal cells and interneurons. Each neuron receives N_{ext} excitatory AMPA synaptic connections from outside the network. The visual input is also introduced by AMPA synapses on specific pyramidal cells. Inhibitory GABAergic synapses on pyramidal cells and interneurons yield corresponding IPSPs (inhibitory post-synaptic potentials). (See text for details). OFC, orbitofrontal cortex. (After Deco and Rolls 2005d.)

very biologically plausible, modification of the standard one-layer autoassociation network is that there is a small amount of adaptation in the recurrent collateral synapses that keep the neurons representing the current rule firing. Now consider the case when the neurons representing rule one are firing. How does the rule module reverse? The proposal is that when the non-reward or error neurons (described in Section 3.6.5.5) fire, this additional set of firing neurons destabilizes the rule attractor module, by for example producing extra firing of the inhibitory neurons in the orbitofrontal cortex, which in turn inhibit the excitatory neurons in the rule autoassociation network, thus quenching its attractor state. This error input to the rule attractor network is shown in Fig. 9.1. After neuronal firing in the network has stopped and the error signal, which may last for 10 s as illustrated in Fig. 3.28 on page 161, is no longer present, then firing gradually can build up again in the rule attractor network from the level of spontaneous activity. (This build-up may be assisted by non-specific inputs from other neurons in the area.) However, with the competitive processes operating within the rule attractor network between the populations of neurons representing rule 1 and those representing rule 2, and the fact that the neurons or synapses that are part of the rule 1 attractor are partly adapted, the neurons that win the competition and become active are those representing rule 2, and the rule attractor has reversed its state. *This provides a mechanism that implements a temporal memory of the previously activated pool. When the attractor state of the rule module is shut down by the inhibitory input, then the attractor state that subsequently emerges when firing starts again will be different from the state that has just been present, because of the synaptic adaptation in the synapses that supported the previous attractor state.* This process is illustrated in Fig. 9.2 (which is described more fully below), and takes one trial.

Reversal learning set takes a number of reversals to acquire because the correct attractors for the relevant rules, and their connections to other 'mapping' neurons, have to be learned. Once these have been learned, the reversal can be performed in one trial, is not based on new association learning, and requires no new synaptic modification for each reversal.

To achieve the correct 'mapping' from stimuli to their reinforcer association, and thus emotional state, the rule neurons bias the competition in a mapping module, illustrated in Fig. 9.1. The mapping module has sensory input neurons, intermediate 'conditional reward' neurons (of the type described in Section 3.6.5.4 and illustrated in Fig. 3.24 on page 157) which respond to combinations of stimuli and whether they are currently associated with reward (or for other neurons to a punisher), and output neurons that represent the reinforcement association of the stimulus currently being viewed. (In the case described there are four populations or pools of neurons at the intermediate level, two for the direct rewarding context: object 1–rewarding, object 2–punishing, and two for the reversal condition: object 1–punishing, object 2–rewarding). These intermediate pools or populations of neurons respond to combinations of the sensory stimuli and the expected reward, e.g. to object 1 and an expected reward (glucose obtained after licking), and are the conditional reward neurons described in Section 3.6.5.4 and illustrated in Fig. 3.24. The sensory – intermediate – reward module thus consists of three hierarchically organized levels of attractor network, with stronger synaptic connections in the forward direction from input to output than the backprojection direction. The rule module acts as a biasing input to bias the competition between the object–reward combination neurons at the intermediate level of the sensory – intermediate – reward module. This biasing is achieved because rule 1 has associatively strengthened connections to object 1–rewarding and object 2–punishing neurons. (The whole network could be set up by simple associative learning operating to strengthen connections made with low probability between different neurons that are conjunctively active during the task in the network – see Deco and Rolls (2005d).)

Thus when object 1, e.g. the triangle, is being presented and rule one for direct mapping is in the rule module and biasing the intermediate neurons of the sensory – intermediate – reward module, then the intermediate neurons that fire are the object 1–reward neurons (O1R in Fig. 9.1), and these in turn through associative connections activate the reward neurons (Rwd in Fig. 9.1) at the third, reward/punishment, level of the hierarchy. If on the other hand object 1, e.g. the triangle, is being presented and rule two for reversed mapping is in the rule module and biasing the intermediate neurons of the sensory – intermediate – reward module, then the intermediate neurons that fire are the object 1–punishment (O1P) neurons, and these in turn through associative connections activate the punishment neurons (Pun) at the third,

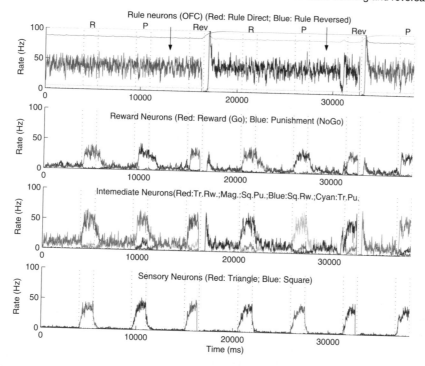

Fig. 9.2 Reward reversal model: temporal evolution of the averaged population activity for all neural pools (sensory, intermediate (stimulus–reward), and Reward/Punishment) in the stimulus – intermediate – reward module and the rule module, during the execution and the reversal of the Go/NoGo visual discrimination task with a pseudorandom trial sequence after Thorpe, Rolls and Maddison (1983) and Rolls, Critchley, Mason and Wakeman (1996). Bottom row: the sensory neuronal populations, one of which responds to Object 1, a triangle (red), and the other to Object 2, a square (blue). The intermediate conditional stimulus–reward and stimulus–punishment neurons respond to for example Object 1 (Tr) when it is associated with reward (Rw) (e.g. on trial 1, corresponding to O1R in Fig. 9.1), or to Object 2 (Sq) when it is associated with punishment (Pu) (e.g. on trial 2, O2P). The top row shows the firing rate activity in the rule module, with the thin line at the top of this graph showing the mean probability of release P_{rel} of transmitter from the synapses of each population of neurons. The arrows show when the contingencies reversed. R, Reward trial; P, Punishment Trial; Rev, Reversal trial, i.e. the first trial after the reward contingency was reversed when Reward was expected but Punishment was obtained. The intertrial interval was 4 s. The yellow line shows the average activity of the inhibitory neurons. (See text for further details.) (After Deco and Rolls 2005d.) (See colour plates Appendix E.)

reward/punishment, level of the hierarchy. This model can thus account for one-trial reversal learning, and provides an account for the presence of the conditional reward and conditional punishment neurons found by Thorpe, Rolls and Maddison (1983) and Rolls, Critchley, Mason and Wakeman (1996b) in the orbitofrontal cortex (Section 3.6.5.4).

Figure 9.2 shows the results of a simulation of the Go/NoGo visual discrimination task with one-trial reversal with a pseudorandom sequence of trials (Deco and Rolls 2005d). On each trial, either a triangle or a square was shown. In Fig. 9.2, on trial 1 the rule network was operating in the direct mapping state, the sensory pool responded to the triangle, the intermediate pool that was selected based on this sensory input and the direct rule bias was the triangle–reward pool, this pool led to activation of the Reward (or Go) pool, and a reward (R) was obtained. On trial 2 the sensory pool for the square responded, and this with the direct rule bias led to the intermediate square–Non-reward pool being selected, and this in turn led to Punishment neurons being active, leading to a NoGo response (i.e. no action). On trial 3 the sensory triangle pool was activated, leading because of the direct rule to activation of the intermediate triangle–reward pool, and Reward was decoded (leading to a Go response being made). However, because this was a reversal trial, punishment was obtained, leading to activation of the error input, which increased the inhibition in the rule module, and quenching of the rule module attractor. When the rule module attractor started up again, it started with the reverse rule neurons active, as they won the competition with the direct rule neurons, whose excitatory synapses had adapted during the previous few trials. On trial 4 the sensory–square input neurons were activated, and the intermediate neurons representing square–reward were activated (due to the biasing influence of the reversed rule input to these intermediate neurons), the Reward neurons in the third layer were activated (leading to a Go response), and reward was obtained. On trial 5 the sensory–triangle neurons activated the triangle–Non-reward intermediate neurons under the biasing influence of the reversed rule input, and Punishment was decoded by the third layer (resulting in a NoGo response). On trial 6, the sensory-square neurons were activated leading to activation of the intermediate square–reward neurons, and Reward (and a Go response) was produced. However, this was another reversal trial, non-reward or punishment activated the error inputs, and the rule neurons in the rule module were quenched, and started up again with the direct rule neurons active in the rule module, due to the synaptic depression of the synapses between the reversed rule neurons.

One implementation of the spike-frequency-adaptation mechanism that we used in the rule-module utilized short-term synaptic depression (Abbott and Nelson 2000), following the details provided by Dayan and Abbott (2001), page 185. In particular, the probability of release P_{rel} was decreased after each presynaptic spike by a factor $P_{rel} = P_{rel} \cdot f_D$ with $f_D = 0.994$. Between presynaptic action potentials the release probability P_{rel} is updated by

$$\tau_P \frac{dP_{rel}}{dt} = P_0 - P_{rel} \tag{9.1}$$

with $P_0 = 1$. The precise details of the adaptation mechanism are not crucial, and Deco and Rolls (2005d) also obtained good results with a spike frequency adaptation mechanism operating at the neuronal level and based on the inactivation of sodium channels after spike generation; and based on Ca^{++}-activated K^+ hyper-polarizing currents (Liu and Wang 2001).

It is an important part of the architecture that at the intermediate level of the sensory – intermediate – reward module one set of neurons fire if an object being presented is currently associated with reward, and a different set if the object being presented is currently associated with punishment. This representation means that these neurons can be used for different functions, such as the elicitation of emotional or autonomic responses, which can occur for example to particular stimuli associated with particular reinforcers (Rolls 2005). For example, particular emotions might arise if a particular cognitively processed input such as a particular person is associated with a particular type of reinforcer or reinforcement contingency.

It is also an interesting part of the architecture that associative synaptic modifiability (LTP, and LTD if present) is needed only to set up the functional architecture of the network while the reversal learning set is being acquired. However, once the correct synaptic connections have been set up to implement the architecture illustrated in Fig. 9.1, then no further synaptic modifiability is needed each time reversal occurs, as reversal is achieved just by the error signal quenching the current rule attractor, and the attractor for the other rule then starting up because its synapses are not adapted. This is an interesting prediction of the model. If tested by NMDA receptor blockers, which can block LTP, then it would be important to ensure that non-specific factors produced by the NMDA blockade such as less overall activity in the network, and the stabilizing effects of the long time constants of NMDA receptors, do not contribute to any result obtained. For this reason, use of a procedure for impairing synaptic modifiability other than NMDA receptor blockade would be useful in testing this prediction.

The network just described uses biased competition from a rule module to bias the mapping from sensory stimuli to the representation of a reward vs a punisher. An analogous rule network reversed in the same way by error signals quenching the current rule attractor can be used to reverse the mapping from stimuli via intermediate stimulus–response neurons to response neurons, and thus to switch the stimulus-to-motor response being mapped in a model of conditional response learning (Deco and Rolls 2003, Deco and Rolls 2005d) (see Section 9.2). While reward rule neurons have not been described yet for the orbitofrontal cortex, neurons that may correspond to stimulus–response rule neurons have been found in the dorsolateral prefrontal cortex (Wallis, Anderson and Miller 2001).

This model also provides a computational account of why the orbitofrontal cortex may play a more important role in rapid reversal learning than the amygdala. The account is based on the fact that a feature of cortical architecture is a highly developed set of local (within 1–2 mm) recurrent collateral excitatory associatively modifiable connections between pyramidal cells (Rolls and Deco 2002, Rolls and Treves 1998). These provide the basis for short-term memory attractor networks, and thus the basis for the rule attractor model which is at the heart of my suggestion for how rapid reversal learning is implemented (Deco and Rolls 2005d). In contrast, the amygdala is thought to have a much less well developed set of recurrent collateral excitatory connections, and thus may not be able to implement rapid reversal learning in the way described using competition biased by a rule module. Instead, the amygdala would need to rely on synaptic relearning as described in the first approach above, and this would be likely to be a slower process, and would certainly not lead to correct choice of the new S+ the first time it is presented after a punishment trial when the reversal contingency changes. Of course, in addition it is possible that the rapidity of LTP, and the efficacy of LTD, both of which would also facilitate rapid reversal, may be enhanced in the orbitofrontal cortex compared to the amygdala. Thus, the cortical neuronal reversal mechanism in the orbitofrontal cortex may be effectively a faster implementation in two ways than what is implemented in the amygdala. The cortical (in this case orbitofrontal cortex) mechanism may have evolved particularly to enable rapid updating by received reinforcers in social and other situations in primates. This hypothesis, that the orbitofrontal cortex, as a rapid learning mechanism, effectively provides an additional route for some of the functions performed by the amygdala, and is very important when this stimulus–reinforcer learning must be rapidly readjusted, has been developed elsewhere (Rolls 1990d, Rolls 1992b, Rolls 1996a, Rolls 1999a, Rolls 2000d, Rolls 2005).

Another feature of the rule attractor model of rapid reversal learning (Deco and Rolls 2005d) is that it does utilize a set of coupled attractor networks in the orbitofrontal cortex. Consistent with this, Hikosaka and Watanabe (2000) have shown that a short-term memory for reward, such as the flavour of a food, is represented by continuing firing in orbitofrontal cortex neurons in a reward delayed match-to-sample short-term memory task. This could be implemented by associatively modified synaptic connections between taste reward neurons (see Section 3.4) in the orbitofrontal cortex.

Although the mechanism has been described so far for visual-to-taste association learning, this is because neurophysiological experiments on this are most direct. It is likely, given the evidence from the effects of lesions, that taste is only one type of primary reinforcer about which such learning occurs in the orbitofrontal cortex, and is likely to be an example of a much more general type of stimulus–reinforcer learning system. Some of the evidence for this is that humans with orbitofrontal cortex damage are impaired at visual discrimination reversal when working for a reward that consists of points (Rolls, Hornak, Wade and McGrath 1994a) or money (Hornak, Bramham, Rolls, Morris, O'Doherty, Bullock and Polkey 2003) (see Section 3.6.6). Moreover, as described above, there is now evidence that the representation of the affective aspects of touch are represented in the human orbitofrontal cortex (Rolls, O'Doherty, Kringelbach, Francis, Bowtell and McGlone 2003d, Rolls 2007d, McCabe, Rolls, Bilderbeck and McGlone 2007), and learning about what stimuli are associated with this class of primary reinforcer is also likely to be an important aspect of the stimulus–reinforcer association learning performed by the orbitofrontal cortex, which is one way in which it contributes to decision-making.

9.2 Reversal of action selection

So far, we have considered the reversal of a stimulus–reinforcer association, which is a type of sensory–sensory association involved in emotional states and decision-making. However, other types of mapping can be reversed, and are also important in decision-making. One example is the mapping of stimuli to actions or behavioural responses. It is of interest to consider the reversal of this type of mapping, partly because it is important to contrast stimulus–response mapping from that involved in producing emotional states, and partly because the underlying neural substrates may be analogous, providing supporting evidence for the theory presented here of rapid reversals.

The experiment we consider will be the reversal of a *conditional object–visuomotor response task*, because there is evidence on the types of neuronal activity in the dorsolateral prefrontal cortex (PFC) during this task (Asaad, Rainer and Miller 1998), and neuronal data are important for providing a firm foundation for the computational model. The basic operation of the model (Deco and Rolls 2003) is described in Chapter 8. The task required the monkeys to make one response (e.g. a left oculomotor saccade) after a delay following the presentation of one object (e.g. A) at the fovea, and a different response (e.g. a right oculomotor saccade) after a delay following the presentation of another object (e.g. B) at the fovea. The cue period was 500 ms, and the short-term memory delay period separating the cue and response was 1,000 ms. Asaad et al. (1998) trained the monkeys under two different conditions, namely: (1) direct association; and (2) reverse association. The direct condition corresponded to the association of one object, for example A, with a leftward eye motor response, and the other object, for example B, with a rightward eye motor response. The reverse condition corresponded to the reversed association of cue and responses, i.e. object A was now associated with a rightward eye motor response, and object B with a leftward eye motor response. Although simulations of how the correct mappings could be achieved using the architecture shown in Fig. 8.1 are described by Deco and Rolls (2003) and described in Chapter 8, that work did not describe how the rule attractor itself was reversed when error signals were obtained.

Deco and Rolls (2005d) proposed that the same mechanism described above in Section 9.1 for reversing the rule module by an error signal is used in the action selection system. The proposal is that the error signal quenches the rule attractor shown in Fig. 8.1 by operating via inhibitory interneurons, and then the rule attractor starts up from the spontaneous firing state with the opposite attractor active, due to adaptation in the synapses or neurons of the previously active attractor.

Deco and Rolls (2005d) simulated this proposal using the architecture shown in Fig. 8.1. Figure 9.3A shows the simulation results corresponding to Fig. 5a in the paper of Asaad et al. (1998) (of which an example is shown in Fig. 9.3B). Fig. 9.3A plots the average firing activity of the two motor direction-selective response pools around the time of reversal at trial zero. The asterisks show the responses to the object that, having indicated a saccade in the neuron's preferred direction before the reversal, starts after the reversal at trial zero to indicate a saccade in the neuron's non-preferred direction. The squares show the opposite, namely the activity produced by the object that before reversal at trial 0 cued a saccade in the

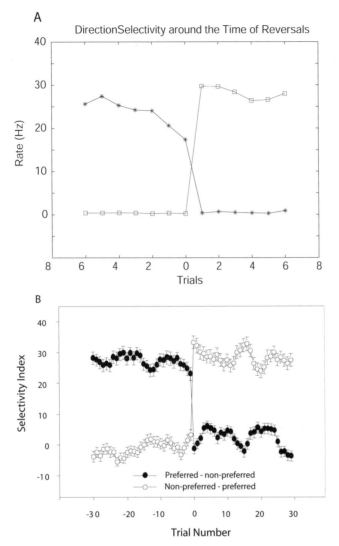

Fig. 9.3 Reversal of a conditional object–response task with a delay. Average firing activity of the two motor direction-selective pools around the time of reversal which occurred at trial zero. (A) Simulation results. The stars show the responses to the object that, having indicated a saccade in the neuron's preferred direction, begins at trial zero to indicate a saccade in the neuron's non-preferred direction. The squares show the opposite, namely the activity produced by the object that before reversal cued a saccade in the non-preferred direction, and after reversal required an eye movement in the neuron's preferred direction. After Deco and Rolls (2005d). (B) Neurophysiological results obtained in the experiment of Asaad et al. (1998) during reversal.

neuron's non-preferred direction, and after reversal required an eye movement in the preferred direction. The simulation results show the same rapid reversal context switching observed in the experiments, which corresponds dynamically with a change in the whole attractor structure due to the non-rewarding inhibitory signal provided at the time of reversal. This error signal resets the whole rule module to zero firing, and, because of the intrinsic temporal memory associated with the spike-frequency adaptation mechanism or short-term depression, when the rule module network starts up again, the opposite rule pool is active. This reverses the bias on the associative module, and the stimulus–response associations there are reversed.

Thus the dorsolateral prefrontal cortex may use hierarchical attractor networks with rule-based selection to implement flexible sensory-to-action mappings (as described in Chapter 8), and the rule attractor may be rapidly reversed, in one trial, as described in this chapter.

9.3 Sequence memory

The model can in principle be extended to more than one rule and, indeed, Deco and Rolls (2005c) described a network that can recall the order of a sequence of several items that are presented. The principle is that after a sequence of items has been presented to the attractor network with some habituation in the synapses or neurons, each time the network is quenched, the least recently presented item will be retrieved from the spontaneous firing, as its synapses or neurons are the least adapted.

The single attractor network implementation of a sequence memory described by Deco and Rolls (2005c) can store several items in a sequence without repeated training on any one sequence. The memory for the order in which the items were presented is not implemented by long-term associative synaptic modification such as long-term potentiation, but instead by short-term non-associative adaptation. The adaptation could be of the active neurons, or of the active synapses, as demonstrated. An advantage of the system is that the memory normally moves to the next item in the sequence when a trigger quenching signal is received, and so does not need to remember large numbers of associations at the neuronal timescale to bridge long delays, which is a disadvantage of some models of sequence memory referred to in Chapter 2 and Section B.3.3.10. Indeed, the adaptation must be partial, if the sequence is not to move on automatically, but is to be moved onto the next item in the sequence by an external signal, which quenches the current attractor. If the adaptation is more complete, then the item currently in the attractor will automatically become unstable, and the next least recently active attractor will then become active, without the need for an external signal producing inhibition to move the network onto the next item in a sequence. In automatic mode, the speed with which the system would move onto the next item need not be very fast, and is a function of how rapidly the adaptation occurs. The fact that the replay of the sequence can be slow is an advantage over some other ways that sequence memory might be implemented as referred to above.

The implementation of a sequence memory described here is now contrasted more formally with the more traditional method for storing a sequence of items in an attractor network, associating a time-delayed version of one item with the next item in the sequence (Kohonen 1977, Kohonen 1989, Hopfield 1982, Sompolinsky and Kanter 1986) (see Section B.3.3.10). For that implementation, the recurrent collateral connections of the attractor network implement a fixed time delay, and the delayed representation of the first item is associated with the next item. Because of the time delay, this is an asymmetric network, with in particular the connections between neurons that represent different items in a sequence not symmetric as in a standard autoassociative network (Kohonen 1977, Kohonen 1989, Hopfield 1982, Sompolinsky and Kanter 1986). A biological problem with this implementation of sequence memory is that the natural time delay in the recurrent collateral synapses is likely to be in the order of several milliseconds, so that when the sequence is recalled, the sequence will be recalled with a speed of several milliseconds between each item, or several hundred items per second, which is rather fast. In comparison, the network described here is more graceful in the way in which it recalls successive items in a sequence, in that either it can be triggered, with no precise timing necessary, by an external signal that resets the network into quiescence (and the next item is then recalled), or the sequence can be automatically recalled at a speed that depends on how fast or slowly the adaptation builds up, which could be over as long as many seconds.

Although the sequence of the items is not stored by associative long-term synaptic modification, each of the items must be trained into the attractor network by long-term associative synaptic modification. The items need not be learned before the sequence is first presented, for the associative synaptic modification could occur rapidly while each item in the sequence is being presented for the first time. The network can replay the sequence of items just presented, but it does not store the sequence itself as a fixed sequence in long-term memory. If the network operates using an external trigger to indicate when the next item should be recalled, this could be provided by something as simple as an excitatory non-specific input to a region. This will cause extra activation of the inhibitory interneurons, and essentially by competitive interactions implemented through the inhibitory neurons quench the attractor holding active the current item in the sequence. The magnitude of this reset signal need not be large, as shown by Deco and Rolls (2005c).

The type of sequence memory we describe is suitable for a short-term memory sequence mechanism. It would not incorporate and implement long-term frequently repeated fixed sequences of the type that might be involved in learning to play a piece of music and then playing the whole piece without the score. On the other hand, the sequence memory we describe would be suitable for a short-term scratchpad memory where only the most recent sequence would be remembered. In this respect it would be similar to the recency part of human auditory–verbal short-term or working memory, in which different sequences of the same items can be correctly used, and only the most recent sequence is remembered (Baddeley 1986). It is a remarkable property of the recency part of auditory–verbal short-term memory (and of the visuo-spatial scratchpad) that not just the items presented for memory, but the order in which the items were presented, is a generic property of this type of memory (Baddeley 1986). It is also a generic property of the type of sequence memory described here (Deco and Rolls 2005c). It is also a property of auditory–verbal short-term or working memory that its capacity is strictly limited, to seven plus or minus two items or 'chunks' (Miller 1956, Baddeley 1986). Because of the way in which the adaptation must be stronger while the sequence is being replayed for later than earlier items in a sequence, and because the attractor that emerges after quiescence will be subject to noise effects, the maximum number of items in a sequence that could be remembered by the network described here is also likely to be limited to a few items. Indeed, we would be surprised if the model described here could remember many more than seven items in a sequence. This limitation on the number of items in a sequence is in major contrast to the number of separate items that could be stored in the autoassociation network, which is in the order of the number of recurrent collateral synapses on each neuron if the representation is sparse (Rolls and Treves 1998) (see Section B.3). This would make the number of items in the network in the order of 5,000–10,000, from which a subset of perhaps seven plus or minus two could be used in any sequence. Further, we note that the temporal period over which any sequence is recalled will be limited by the time constant of the adaptation process.

Another property of the system described is that it would fail if an item in a sequence is repeated, e.g. 1-5-1-6, which would be recalled as 5-1-6. A solution to this potential problem is to use chunking (a strategy often used in human auditory–verbal short-term memory), by encoding the four-item sequence into, for example, 15-16.

More than one rule has also been simulated in a model of the Wisconsin task (Stemme, Deco, Busch and Schneider 2005).

9.4 Conclusions

In summary, computational neuroscience provides a mathematical framework for studying the mechanisms involved in brain function, such as visual attention (Chapter 6), working memory (Chapter 5), and the control of behaviour by reward mechanisms, as described in this chapter. Analysis of networks of neurons each implemented at the integrate-and-fire neuronal level, and including non-linearities, enables many aspects of brain function, from the spiking activity of single neurons and the effects of pharmacological agents on synaptic currents, through fMRI and neuropsychological findings, to be integrated, and many aspects of cognitive function including reward reversal learning, reversal of action selection, short-term memory, sequence memory, attention, and decision-making to be modelled and understood. The theoretical approach described makes explicit predictions at all these levels which can be tested to develop and refine our understanding of the underlying processing, and its dynamics. We believe that this kind of analysis is fundamental for a deep and unifying understanding in neuroscience of how the brain performs complex tasks, such as decision-making, and reversing behaviour.

10 Decision-making

I integrate some of the themes of this book by showing how there are different types of choice or decision that are made about rewards and punishers (see also Cardinal et al. (2002) and Berridge and Robinson (2003)), how emotion is related to these different types of decision (see Fig. 10.1), and how attractor short-term memory networks are involved in many decision-making processes. Attractor networks are involved for example by providing a top-down bias to influence attentional (Chapter 6), stimulus-to-action (Chapter 8) and stimulus-to-reward (Chapter 9) networks, by holding items in memory that are needed during delay periods (Chapters 5 and 8) or in planning (Section 10.5), and by being part of the mechanisms by which evidence is accumulated over time and then binary decisions are actually taken probabilistically depending on the evidence as the network falls into its basin of attraction (Chapter 7).

10.1 Selection of mainly autonomic responses, and their classical conditioning

Responses produced by primary rewards and punishers, such as salivation, a change of heart rate, or arousal, can become classically conditioned, and this is a form of stimulus–response learning (see Section 3.2.1 on page 116). These responses are important for fitness, and are being selected, but hardly merit the term 'decision'. Brain regions such as the amygdala, orbitofrontal cortex, and anterior cingulate cortex are involved in these responses.

10.2 Selection of approach or withdrawal, and their classical conditioning

Rewards and punishers also lead to approach or withdrawal, and these effects can be classically conditioned (see Section 3.2.1). This is an important way in which genes can influence the behaviour that is selected, and this might be thought of as a very simple, automated, 'decision'. However, there is little flexibility in the response that is selected, in that the behaviour is either approach (e.g. to a sweet taste), or withdrawal/rejection (e.g. to a bitter taste), and in this sense behaviour is being selected by the reinforcer, but the 'decision' is essentially an automated type of behaviour. This type of approach behaviour to rewards can be classically conditioned, resulting in conditioned 'incentive salience' or 'wanting' effects (Berridge and Robinson 1998, Berridge and Robinson 2003), and this learning is implemented via the amygdala and ventral striatum, is under the control of dopamine (Cardinal et al. 2002), and contributes to addiction (Robinson and Berridge 2003).

10.3   Selection of fixed stimulus–response habits

Stimulus–response connections can be reinforced by rewards or punishers to produce fixed habits (see Section 3.2.2 on page 118). Habits typically arise when behavioural responses are overlearned, and it is suggested that action–outcome learning sets up the correct stimulus–response conditions for a habit learning system to implement fixed responses to stimuli (Section 3.2.2). Once a habit has been learned, we may think of the behavioural selection as being a rather fixed type of 'decision'. The basal ganglia may be especially involved in habit learning (see Section 3.10.2), though they do receive inputs that may be important in this process from the amygdala and orbitofrontal cortex. Reinforcement learning (see Section B.15) using reward prediction errors implemented in dopamine neuron firing may or not be important in this habit learning (see Section 3.10.2).

10.4   Selection of arbitrary behaviours to obtain goals, action–outcome learning, and emotional learning

The real power of emotion, and rewards and punishers, occurs when goals for actions are specified by genes, and arbitrary actions can then be performed (instrumentally) to achieve the goals (see Chapter 3). The type of learning is action–outcome learning (see Sections 3.2.2, and 3.8). Motivated behaviour is made to obtain, terminate or avoid the goal, and when the reward or punisher is or is not obtained, terminated, or avoided, emotional states occur that may be further motivating. Stimulus–reinforcer association learning is also important in emotion, by allowing previously neutral stimuli to become associated with primary reinforcing stimuli, and thus to become goals for action (see Chapter 3). The rapid reversal of behaviour when the reinforcement contingencies change is also important, as described in Chapters 3 and 9.

Although in evolution Darwinian processes lead to gene-defined goals, it is also the case that in humans goals may be influenced by other processes, including cultural processes. Indeed, some goals are defined within a culture, for example writing a novel like one by Tolstoy vs one by Virginia Woolf. But it is argued that it is primary reinforcers specified by genes of the general type shown in Table 3.1 on page 114 that make us, for example, want to be recognized in society because of the advantages this can bring, to solve difficult problems, etc, and therefore to perform actions such as writing novels (see further Rolls (2005), Ridley (2003) Chapter 8, Ridley (1993a) pp. 310 ff, Laland and Brown (2002) pp. 271 ff, and Dawkins (1982)). Indeed, culture is influenced by human genetic propensities, and it follows that human cognitive, affective, and moral capacities are the product of a unique dynamic known as *gene–culture coevolution* (Gintis 2007, Bowles and Gintis 2005, Gintis 2003, Boyd, Gintis, Bowles and Richerson 2003).

We may also note that the theory that genes set many goals for action does not mean that our behaviour is determined by genes. Modern evolutionary theory has led to the understanding that many traits, particularly behavioural ones, may have some genetic basis but that does not mean that they will inevitably appear, because much depends on the environment (Dawkins 1995, Ridley 2003). Further, part of the power of my theory of emotion (Rolls 2005) is that in evolution genes specify rewards and punishers that are goals for action, but do not specify the actions themselves, which are flexible and can be learned.

The orbitofrontal cortex is important in representing the rewards and punishers, and in performing rapid stimulus–reinforcer association learning and reversal. This is the fundamental type of learning involved in producing learned emotional or affective states, and is stimulus–stimulus learning.

The orbitofrontal cortex is thus very important in emotion and affective states. The orbitofrontal cortex is not itself involved in action–outcome association learning, in that actions appear not to be represented in the orbitofrontal cortex (see Section 3.6). It is important for action–outcome learning though, in that it represents the affective outcomes. Brain regions such as the cingulate cortex may be involved in action–outcome association learning (see Section 3.8.2), and receive inputs about the outcomes, and predicted outcomes, from the orbitofrontal cortex.

Some of the primary reinforcers that may be the goals for action are included in Table 3.1 on page 114. We should note that reinforcers are really very diverse. Some genes specify reinforcers relevant to internal need states such as hunger and thirst. The genes must build receptors that are connected to central brain systems in for example the orbitofrontal cortex where the reward value relevant to the internal need state is represented, and where the internal need state (e.g. low plasma glucose concentration and an empty stomach) modulates the responses of the neurons so that they only respond to the taste of food when hunger is present (see Chapter 3 and Rolls (2005)). Other reinforcers are relevant to external stimuli without modulation by an internal need state, such as pain. Other reinforcers are relevant to social behaviour, promoting for example attraction, love, cooperation, generosity, reputation, and altruism (see Chapter 3, Section 10.6.4, Rolls (2005), and Adolphs (2003)). Other putative primary reinforcers are included in Table 3.1, and this list is not intended to be exhaustive.

A general rule is that rewards show a sensory-specific reduction of reward value over a period of typically several minutes, and this serves the function of allowing behaviour to switch to another reward, and thus helps to ensure that the range of rewards specified by genes are all selected in time, promoting reproductive fitness. In contrast, punishers do not show a sensory-specific reduction, as behaviour must be directed at these until the problem is removed (see Chapter 3 and Rolls (2005)).

10.5   The roles of the prefrontal cortex in decision-making and attention

The functions of the dorsolateral prefrontal cortex in short-term memory are considered in Section 5.2. There it is shown that for a short-term memory to be maintained during periods in which new stimuli are to be perceived, there must be separate networks for the perceptual and short-term memory functions, and indeed two coupled networks (with one in the inferior temporal visual cortex for perceptual functions, and another in the prefrontal cortex for maintaining the short-term memory during intervening stimuli) provide a precise model of the interaction of perceptual and short-term memory systems (Renart, Parga and Rolls 2000, Renart, Moreno, Rocha, Parga and Rolls 2001) (see Section 5.2 and Fig. 5.3 on page 379). In particular, this model shows how a prefrontal cortex attractor (autoassociation) network could be triggered by a sample visual stimulus represented in the inferior temporal visual cortex in a delayed match to sample task, and could keep this attractor active during a memory interval in which intervening stimuli are shown. Then when the sample stimulus reappears in the task as a match stimulus, the inferior temporal cortex module shows a large response to the match stimulus, because it is activated both by the visual incoming match stimulus, and by the consistent backprojected memory of the sample stimulus still being represented in the prefrontal cortex memory module (see Fig. 5.3).

This computational model makes it clear that in order for ongoing perception to occur unhindered in posterior cortex (parietal and temporal lobe) networks, there must be a separate set of modules that is capable of maintaining a representation over intervening stimuli. This is the fundamental understanding offered for the evolution and functions of the dorsolateral prefrontal cortex, and it is this ability to provide multiple separate short-term attractor memories that provides I suggest the basis for the functions of the dorsolateral prefrontal cortex in planning, probabilistic decision-making, and action selection (see Chapters 5–8).

This computational approach thus provides a clear understanding of why a separate (prefrontal) mechanism is needed for working memory functions. This understanding then provides a basis for understanding the contributions of the dorsolateral prefrontal cortex to attention and decision-making (Rolls and Deco 2002, Deco and Rolls 2003, Deco and Rolls 2005a, Deco and Rolls 2005b), as summarized next.

10.5.1 Prefrontal attentional influences on perceptual processing

Attention can control or influence decision-making. One way in which it does this is by a top-down influence of information held in a short-term memory in the prefrontal cortex on earlier perceptual modules in the temporal and parietal lobes. The general architecture is that illustrated in Fig. 5.3 on page 379 and shown in more detail in Fig. 6.9 on page 403. The information to which attention must be paid, for example spatial position in a scene, is loaded into the dorsolateral prefrontal cortex short-term memory, and this then biases competition between different representations in the parietal or temporal cortex (Desimone and Duncan 1995, Rolls and Deco 2002, Deco and Rolls 2004, Deco and Rolls 2005a) (see Chapter 6). This *biased competition* is understood at the detailed level of an integrate-and-fire neuronal network model in which the top-down bias can have highly non-linear effects on the competition between competing perceptual representations (Deco and Rolls 2005b, Deco and Rolls 2006).

10.5.2 Attentional influences on mapping from stimuli to responses

Another way in which attention can influence decision-making is by influencing the mapping from stimuli to responses. This is needed for example in tasks in which the rule is sometimes that one aspect of a stimulus, for example its spatial position, must be mapped to a particular spatial response, yet at other times the rule is that a different aspect of the stimulus, for example which object is being shown, must be mapped to a particular response. The prefrontal cortex contributes to this type of decision-making in two ways.

First it provides a short-term memory which holds active the current rule.

Second, if there is a delay between the stimulus and the response, short-term memory networks in the prefrontal cortex can bridge the delay. This type of rule-based mapping task has been studied using single neuron recording by Asaad, Rainer and Miller (1998) and Asaad, Rainer and Miller (2000), and neurons have been described that encode and hold active in the delay period the object and spatial properties of the stimuli, combinations of each of these stimulus properties with the response required, and the responses. Deco and Rolls (2003) have developed a model of this type of decision-making in which rule-encoding neurons in a short-term attractor network keep the current rule active, and this operates as in attentional networks to bias the competition at the level of the stimulus–response combination neurons, as described in Chapter 8. The formal architecture of the model is shown in Fig. 8.1 on page 476. This biased competition operates in such a way that when the correct combination neurons are biased, the mapping automatically occurs from the correct aspect of the stimulus (its spatial position or object identity) to the correct response after the delay period.

One interesting aspect of this model of how the prefrontal cortex implements this type of decision-making is that the network maps from stimuli to responses by having separate attractors for the stimuli, for the combinations of stimuli and responses, and for the responses. These attractor networks are hierarchically coupled by using asymmetrical feedforward vs feedback connections from stimulus neurons, through stimulus–response combination neurons, to response neurons, to perform the desired stimulus-to-motor response transform (Deco and Rolls 2003).

Another interesting aspect of this model of decision-making is that it can perform reversal, which it does by altering the rule module output to bias instead a different set of stimulus–response combination neurons that implement the reverse mapping (Deco and Rolls 2005d) (see Section 9.2). Another interesting aspect of the model is that it implements the short-term memory functions required because it consists of a set of attractor networks (described in Section B.3). The model is also very interesting for it shows how at the start of the delay period neurons can have firing that is part of a network that holds the stimulus representation active, but later in the delay period can have firing that reflects the behavioural response that will be made (see also Takeda and Funahashi (2002)). The network model of decision-making shows that individual neurons can change their activity from stimulus-related to response-related at different times in the delay period, and that this is an interesting property of hierarchically connected attractor networks. The model itself is described in detail by Deco and Rolls (2003), and is summarized in Chapter 8 (see also Deco and Rolls (2005a)). The model also provides a basis for understanding how, as the rewarded rules change in the Wisconsin card sorting task, the mapping can change from one stimulus dimension (e.g. the colour of the items on the cards) to another (e.g. the number of items on the cards), which is an example of an extradimensional shift which depends on the dorsolateral prefrontal cortex (Dias, Robbins and Roberts 1996, Stemme, Deco, Busch and Schneider 2005).

10.5.3 Executive control

If a prefrontal cortex module is to control behaviour in a working memory task, then it must be capable of assuming some type of executive control. There may be no need to have a single central executive that is additional to the control that must be capable of being exerted by short-term memory modules. This is in contrast to what has traditionally been assumed for the prefrontal cortex (Shallice and Burgess 1996). The concept of executive function in the prefrontal cortex may thus be implicit in its capability to function as a short-term memory that can control behaviour. Further, the role of the prefrontal cortex in executive function may be limited to situations in which a short-term or working memory functionality is required. For example, the execution of "free-will" tasks in which subjects make decisions about which finger to raise is impaired by damage to the prefrontal cortex, and causes activation of the prefrontal cortex (Frith, Friston, Liddle and Frackowiak 1991, Jahanshahi, Jenkins, Brown, Marsden, Passingham and Brooks 1995, Jahanshahi, Dinberger, Fuller and Frith 2000), yet is a task that places demands on a working memory for previous responses, as the subjects try to make different responses from trial to trial to demonstrate their "free will".

The impairment in verbal fluency tasks (in which a large number of different words must be produced with a given first letter) produced by left prefrontal cortex lesions (Baldo, Shimamura, Delis, Kramer and Kaplan 2001) may similarly be related to a difficulty in utilizing short-term memory to remember which words have already been produced, so that further words can be different.

It has also been argued that the prefrontal cortex may be especially involved in working memory in which items must be manipulated, for example in planning an optimal route or shopping expedition (Shallice 1982, Shallice and Burgess 1996, Petrides 1996). The rearrangement of items is essentially a syntactic function in which symbols must be flexibly related or linked to each other in particular ways (see Rolls (2005)), and this manipulation of syntactic relations may not itself be a function of the dorsolateral prefrontal cortex, damage to which does not impair syntactic and linguistic operations in general, which may depend more on specialized brain regions such as Broca's area (Kolb and Whishaw 2003, Caplan 1996). Thus the dorsolateral prefrontal cortex may provide the short-term memory capability which is required when several items must be held in short-term memory for manipulation by another processing region.

Overall, the implication of these concepts is that the off-line short-term memory functionality provided by the prefrontal cortex is fundamental to what it provides for brain computation, and that this functionality is useful in a number of tasks which are predicated on short-term memory such as attention, executive function (when short-term memory is required), planning, free-will, verbal fluency, and manipulation of items (which must be held in a short-term memory in order to be manipulated). All of these functions use the short-term memory functionality provided by the dorsolateral prefrontal cortex, but other parts of the computation may depend on other brain regions.

It may be noted that when decisions require not delay-related processing but instead reward and punishment evaluation, then it is the other part of the prefrontal cortex, the orbitofrontal cortex, that exerts executive control (see Section 10.4 and Chapter 3).

In the model of how evidence can be accumulated and decisions can be taken in an integrate-and-fire attractor network with probabilities that depend on the relative strengths of the evidence (see Chapter 7), the network parameters are set so that normally the network does fall into an attractor and reach a binary decision, even if this takes a long time. The network parameters can be set however so that the difference between the two (or more) competing inputs (scaled by their magnitude) must be greater than a threshold for the system to rise out of spontaneous firing into an attractor (Deco and Rolls 2006). Individual differences in this threshold could account for why some people take decisions quickly, and others more slowly, and could even be a contributor to impulsive behaviour.

10.5.4 Disorders of attention and decision-making

The model of decision-making with delays (Chapter 8 and Deco and Rolls (2003)) also has interesting implications for understanding disorders of attention and decision-making that follow frontal lobe damage or interference with dopamine systems, as described in Section 8.4. For example, Deco and Rolls (2003) simulated the effect of blockade of dopamine receptors, one effect of which is to limit the maximum current that can flow through NMDA receptor-activated ion channels (Chen et al. 2004, Seamans and Yang 2004). The effect of this in the model of decision-making is to limit the rate of firing of the population of neurons that are in the current attractor, and this makes the attractor basin shallow (Deco and Rolls 2003). The implication of this is that attention can too easily be shifted if dopamine is low, so that the current attentional rule can not be stably maintained, and so that the biasing effect of the attentional rule does not produce such strong biasing, leading also to incorrect mappings between stimuli and responses.

In the context of the effects of low NMDA receptor mediated currents produced for example by D1 receptor blockade (Chen et al. 2004) and the shallow basins of attraction in the model of decision-making produced by this manipulation (Deco and Rolls 2003), it is of considerable interest that attention and decision-making (executive function) are impaired in patients with schizophrenia, which could be related to shallow basins of attraction in dorsolateral prefrontal networks that implement the short-term memory required for attention, and the weakening of the biasing effect that this normally has on the neurons that map sensory inputs to motor outputs, as described in Section 8.4. This could account for some of the cognitive symptoms of schizophrenia (Section 8.5).

In a new hypothesis (Rolls 2005) described in Section 8.5, it is suggested that what appear to be the inconsistent negative symptoms of schizophrenia, the flattening of affect which may be related to orbitofrontal and anterior cingulate dysfunction, can be understood within the same conceptual framework provided by the attractor network model. The hypothesis is that the flattening of affect in schizophrenia is due to the shallower basins of attraction in the orbitofrontal cortex, which correspond in terms of neuronal firing rates, to slower firing (Deco and Rolls 2003). Given that orbitofrontal cortex neurons represent emotional states, shallower basins of attraction would thus lead to less intense emotions. This is thus a unifying theory of the cognitive and negative symptoms of schizophrenia, which accounts for both in terms of shallower basis of attraction related to less strong activation of glutamatergic neurons by for example reduced currents flowing through NMDA receptor-activated channels (see further Section 8.5, Loh, Rolls and Deco (2007a), and Loh, Rolls and Deco (2007b)).

10.6 Neuroeconomics, reward magnitude, expected value, and expected utility

Reward magnitude and punishment magnitude are represented in the orbitofrontal cortex, as shown by investigations in which reward and punisher magnitude has been parametrically varied (see Section 3.6). One type of evidence has been obtained with reward devaluation produced by sensory-specific satiety. Another has been with trial-by-trial variation of the monetary gain and loss, allowing correlation of activations of different parts of the orbitofrontal cortex with the magnitude of the gain or loss (O'Doherty, Kringelbach, Rolls, Hornak and Andrews 2001a, Rolls, McCabe and Redoute 2007b).

10.6.1 Expected utility ≈ expected value = probability multiplied by reward magnitude

However, the question arises of how a decision is influenced if the reward magnitude is high, but there is a small probability of obtaining the reward. Here we can adopt approaches used in reinforcement learning, and use the terms **reward value** (RV) or **reward magnitude** (RM) for the magnitude of the reward obtained on a trial, that is the **reward outcome**; and **expected value** (EV) as the probability of obtaining the reward multiplied by the Reward Magnitude (Glimcher 2003, Glimcher 2004, Kahneman and Tversky 1984, Sutton and Barto 1998, Dayan and Abbott 2001) (see also Sections B.15.2 and B.15.3). In an approach related to microeconomics, expected utility theory has provided a useful estimate of the desirability of actions, and indicates that, except for very high and very low probabilities and for decisions with framing issues, **expected utility**, indicated by choices, does approximately track expected value (Kahneman and Tversky 1979, Kahneman and Tversky 1984, Tversky and Kahneman 1986, Glimcher and Rustichini 2004, Gintis 2007). (If the probability of obtaining a reward is low, then we are less likely to choose it than when the probability is high.) However, deviations from this linear relation are important, and humans tend to overweigh the value of low probability gambles (and to be risk-seeking in this domain); and to underweigh the value of high probability gambles (and to be risk averse in this domain) (Tversky and Kahneman 1981, Paulus and Frank 2006). Activations in the anterior cingulate cortex appear to reflect individual differences in this weighting, for a lack of appropriate activation in the anterior cingulate cortex was linked to excessive risk-seeking in choices when there was a low probability of success, and excessive risk avoidance in choices when there was a high probability of success (Paulus and Frank 2006).

Dopamine neurons show increasing responses to conditioned stimuli predicting reward with increasing probability (Fiorillo, Tobler and Schultz 2003), and decrease their firing to predicted reward omission (Tobler et al. 2003). However, it also appears that at least some dopamine neurons have activity that is high when reward uncertainty is high (which occurs when reward probability is 0.5) (Fiorillo et al. 2003). As noted in Section 3.10.2.5, this dual coding (of reward prediction error, as described below, and of reward uncertainty) raises problems in how receiving neurons might use this multiplexed information.

Parietal cortex neurons with activity that precedes eye movements in for example area LIP show more activity if the expected value is high (Glimcher 2003, Glimcher 2004, Platt and Glimcher 1999, McCoy and Platt 2005). This modulation by expected value, as influenced by both probability and reward magnitude, of neurons studied in oculomotor tasks has now been found in a number of areas with oculomotor-related activity, including the cingulate cortex and the superior colliculus (McCoy and Platt 2005).

For both the dopamine and the parietal cortex neurons, it seems unlikely that the actual computation of probability multiplied by reward value is performed in those areas, as reward stimuli are not known to be encoded there.

It is therefore of interest to determine where in the brain representations of reward magnitude, known to be present in the orbitofrontal cortex (O'Doherty, Kringelbach, Rolls, Hornak and Andrews 2001a), become multiplied by reward probability to yield a signal that encodes expected value and even expected utility. In an fMRI investigation in which the reward value and expected value of monetary reward were altered by altering the probability of obtaining rewards for a particular choice, it was found that activations in the medial orbitofrontal cortex were correlated with Reward Magnitude and with Expected Value (Rolls, McCabe and Redoute 2007b). Moreover, it was found that expected utility, reflected in the choices made by the participants, approximately tracked the expected value, and in this sense expected utility was also reflected in activations in the medial orbitofrontal cortex (see Section 3.10.2.3).

10.6.2 Delay of reward, emotional choice, and rational choice

Another factor that can influence decisions for rewards is the delay before the reward is obtained. If the reward will not be available for a long time, then we discount the reward value. Most models assume an exponential decrease in the reward value as a function of the delay until the reward is obtained, as rational choice entails treating each moment of delay equally (Frederick, Loewenstein and O'Donoghue 2002, McClure, Laibson, Loewenstein and Cohen 2004). Impulsive preference changes may reflect a disproportionate valuation of rewards available in the immediate future (Ainslie 1992, Benabou and Pycia 2002, Rachlin 2000, Montague and Berns 2002, Metcalfe and Mischel 1999). It is possible that there are two systems that influence decisions in these circumstances.

One is a rational, logic-based, system requiring syntactic manipulation of symbols (see Section 10.7, Fig. 10.1, and Rolls (2005)) that can treat each moment of delay equally, and calculate choice based on an exponential decrease of reward value with increasing delay. This rational decision system might involve language or mathematical systems in the brain, and the ability to hold several items in a working memory while the trade-offs of different long-term courses of action are compared.

A different more emotion-based system that can operate implicitly might operate according to heuristics that have become built into the system during evolution which might value disproportionately immediate rewards compared to delayed rewards. This emotion-based system might involve the orbitofrontal cortex, which as we have seen (Section 3.6) represents different types of reward and punisher (e.g. monetary gain and loss), and lesions of which in humans lead to impairments in changing behaviour when rewards are received less often for particular choices (Hornak, O'Doherty, Bramham, Rolls, Morris, Bullock and Polkey 2004, Berlin, Rolls and Kischka 2004), to impulsive choices (Berlin, Rolls and Iversen 2005), and to impairments in gambling tasks (Bechara et al. 1994, Bechara et al. 1998). This suggested dissociation of decision systems is the same concept as that encompassed by the hypothesis of dual routes to action considered in Section 10.7, Fig. 10.1, and elsewhere (Rolls 1999a, Rolls 2003, Rolls 2004c, Rolls 2005, Rolls 2007a, Rolls 2007e). It is an interesting aspect of the impulsive decision-making of patients with orbitofrontal cortex damage that their perception of time is speeded up (Berlin, Rolls and Kischka 2004). This speeding up may contribute to why they take decisions relatively early, and in this sense act impulsively.

Consistent with the point being made about evolutionarily old emotion-based decision systems vs a recent rational system present in humans (see Section 10.7) is that humans trade off immediate costs/benefits against cost/benefits that are delayed by as much as decades, whereas non-human primates have not been observed to engage in unpreprogrammed delay of gratification involving more than a few minutes (Rachlin 1989, Kagel, Battalio and Green 1995)[31].

Moreover, individual differences in sensitivity to rewards and punishers could lead to personality differences with respect to impulsive behaviour, and indeed patients with Borderline Personality Disorder behave similarly with respect to their impulsive behaviour to patients with orbitofrontal cortex lesions (Berlin, Rolls and Kischka 2004, Berlin and Rolls 2004, Berlin, Rolls and Iversen 2005).

Consistent with dual emotional and rational bases for decisions in humans, a 'quasi-hyperbolic' time discounting function that splices together two discounting functions – an emotional one that distinguishes sharply between present and future, and a rational one that discounts exponentially and more shallowly – provides a good fit to experimental data including retirement saving, credit-card borrowing, and procrastination (Laibson 1997, Angeletos, Laibson, Repetto, Tobacman and Weinberg 2001, O'Donoghue and Rabin 1999). This dual mechanism process can be modelled formally by

$$r(t) = \beta\gamma^t r(0) \tag{10.1}$$

where $r(t)$ is the time discounted reward value at time t, and $r(0)$ is the reward value if received immediately at time $t = 0$ (McClure, Laibson, Loewenstein and Cohen 2004). β ($0 < \beta \le 1$) (or in fact its inverse) represents the uniform down-weighting of future compared to immediate rewards, and is the parameter that encompasses the effects of emotion on decision-making in this formulation. β is 1 at time zero, and is set to a value that scales a reward at any future time relative to the value at time 0. If $\beta = 0.8$, this indicates that relative to a reward of value r at time zero, the reward at any future time would have a value of 0.8. In this sense, it models the role of emotion in decision-making as down-valuing a reward at any future time compared to immediately by a uniform discounting factor β. The γ ($\gamma \le 1$) parameter is the discount rate in the standard exponential formula that treats a given delay equivalently independently of when it occurs (i.e. in any time interval, the value decreases by a fixed proportion of the value it has already reached), and encompasses the rational route to decision-making. In the model, it produces exponential decay of the value of a reward according to how long it is delayed. It is used in the model to capture the effects of long-term economic planning for the future.

McClure, Laibson, Loewenstein and Cohen (2004) performed an fMRI investigation in which smaller immediate rewards (today) could be chosen vs larger delayed rewards (given after delays of up to six weeks). (The monetary rewards were in the range \$5–\$40.) Brain areas that showed more activation for immediate vs delayed rewards (and reflected the β emotional

---

[31] Seasonal food storage is not an exception, in that it appears to be stereotyped and instinctive, and hence is unlike the generalizable nature of human planning (McClure, Laibson, Loewenstein and Cohen 2004).

parameter) included the medial orbitofrontal cortex, the medial prefrontal cortex/pregenual cingulate cortex, and the ventral striatum. Brain areas where activations reflected the decisions being made and the decision difficulty but which were not preferentially activated in relation to the immediate reward parameter β included the lateral prefrontal cortex (a brain region implicated in higher level cognitive functions including working memory and executive functions (Miller and Cohen 2001, Deco and Rolls 2003)), and a part of the parietal cortex implicated in numerical processing (Dehaene, Dehaene-Lambertz and Cohen 1998). (Activations in these prefrontal and parietal areas reflect the effects of the γ^t variable in equation 10.1.) Thus emotional decisions that emphasize the importance of immediate rewards may preferentially activate reward-related areas ('β areas') such as the medial orbitofrontal cortex, pregenual cingulate cortex, and the ventral striatum; whereas difficult decisions requiring cost–benefit analysis about the value of long-term rewards preferentially activate a more cognitive system ('γ areas') that may be involved in rational thought and multistep calculation.

10.6.3 Reward prediction error, temporal difference error, and choice

The expected value may alter from time to time, for example during a trial. For example, there is a reward prediction error when a reward is predicted but not obtained. Similarly, there is a reward prediction error when a reward is not expected but is obtained. The reward prediction error may be defined as the difference between the reward obtained and the reward predicted (see Sections B.15.2 and B.15.3). The firing of dopamine neurons may reflect these reward prediction errors (Schultz 1998, Schultz et al. 1997, Waelti et al. 2001, Schultz 2004, Schultz 2006) (but see Section 3.10.2.5, where problems such as the asymmetry of the error signals for positive vs negative error predictions are raised).

O'Doherty et al. (2004) related reward prediction error correlated activations of the ventral striatum to a 'critic' that learns to predict a future reward because these activations occurred even when no action was required in a Pavlovian conditioning task, and reward prediction error correlated activations of the dorsal striatum to an 'actor' because it showed stronger activation during instrumental learning than Pavlovian association[32].

The hypothesis that dopamine neuron firing provides a reward prediction error signal (Schultz 1998, Schultz et al. 1997, Waelti et al. 2001, Schultz 2004, Schultz 2006) appears to be inconsistent with the evidence that dopamine neuron firing and activations of parts of the striatum are also produced by aversive, novel, or intense/salient stimuli (Zink et al. 2003, Zink et al. 2004) (see Section 3.10.2.5). Indeed, Zink et al. (2004) argue, from an fMRI investigation in which caudate and nucleus accumbens activations were greater when responses were made to obtain money than when money was given passively, that the activity in these regions is not related to reward value or predictions, but instead to *saliency*, that is to an arousing event to which attentional and/or behavioural resources are redirected (see further Section 3.5).

Reward prediction error encoding is in contrast to that of many neurons in the head of the caudate nucleus, which fire in relation to predicted rewards, that is to expected reward value (Rolls, Thorpe and Maddison 1983b). They do this in that they start firing as soon as a cue such as a tone, or a light that precedes the tone, is given to indicate that a trial is starting, and continue to respond if a visual stimulus is shown indicating that a juice reward will be obtained, and stop responding if a different visual stimulus is shown indicating that aversive saline will be obtained (see Section 3.10.2.3 and Figs. 3.58, 3.59 and 3.60). Neurons that reflect negative reward prediction error (i.e. less reward is obtained than was expected) are found in the orbitofrontal cortex (see Section 3.6.5.5 and Thorpe, Rolls and Maddison (1983)).

---

[32] See Section B.15.3 for a description of the functions of a 'critic' and an 'actor' in reward prediction learning.

The reward prediction error approach to changes in expected value can be developed into a temporal difference learning approach, in which the temporal difference error depends on the difference in the reward value prediction at two successive time steps (see Section B.15.3 and Equation B.96). This temporal difference error is useful in some temporal difference reinforcement learning algorithms for producing learning that optimizes predictions, and thus how to learn optimal actions as events unfold in time, for example during a trial (see Section B.15.3). Temporal difference models have been applied to model the activity of dopamine neurons (Suri and Schultz 2001), and of fMRI activations related to the anticipation of reward (O'Doherty et al. 2003a).

Seymour et al. (2004) took the temporal difference approach in an fMRI analysis of a more complicated, second-order, pain conditioning task, with two successive visual cues to predict either low or high pain. The second cue was fully predictive of the strength of the subsequently experienced pain. The first cue only allowed a probabilistic prediction. Thus in a low proportion (18%) of the trials, the expectation evoked by the first cue was reversed by the second cue. The punisher value (pain) prediction thus alters on some trials after the second cue is delivered, generating a temporal difference prediction error. After many conditioning trials, the punisher prediction value becomes good on the 82% of trials where the first cue does predict the second cue, and during the learning the temporal difference error at the time the second cue is shown becomes low. However, on the 18% of trials where the first cue makes the incorrect prediction of the second cue, temporal difference prediction errors remain when the second cue is presented. The temporal difference error was correlated with activations in the ventral putamen (a part of the ventral striatum), the right insular cortex (probably providing a somatosensory representation of the left hand to which the pain was delivered), the right head of the caudate nucleus, and the substantia nigra (a region where dopamine neurons are located), suggesting that these areas are involved in learning expectations of pain. It should be noted that this was a conditioning procedure, and that although pain expectations were being learned, decisions were not being made by the subjects.

The temporal difference approach was taken in an fMRI study of a decision task by Rolls, McCabe and Redoute (2007b) described in Section 3.10.2.3. They showed in a probabilistic decision task in which the expected value was systematically varied that temporal difference (reward prediction) errors were reflected in activity in the ventral striatum (see Fig. 3.57 on page 229). However, the findings showed that care is needed in interpreting fMRI signals as related to temporal difference (reward prediction) errors, for the correlation with TD error was related to the fact that in the ventral striatum, the activations were related to the reward actually obtained on each trial, and changed at the point in each trial at which this information was made available to the participant (see Section 3.10.2.3). Thus the ventral striatal activation was related to decision-making in so far as its activation reflected the reward actually provided on a given trial (the reward magnitude or outcome).

The temporal difference approach to reinforcement learning described in Section B.15.3 has a weakness that although it can be used to predict internal signals during reinforcement learning in some tasks, it does not directly address learning with respect to actions that are not taken. Q-learning is an extension of TD learning which takes signals from actions not taken into account, for example information gained by observation of others (Montague, King-Casas and Cohen 2006).

10.6.4 Reciprocal altruism, strong reciprocity, generosity, and altruistic punishment

A concept used in economics is that humans take rational and self-interested decisions. However, in a number of games (and also in real-life situations), humans do not follow these principles exactly (Fehr and Rockenbach 2004, Montague, King-Casas and Cohen 2006).

One example is the 'prisoner's dilemma game' (PD). In the PD, two players simultaneously choose between cooperation and defection. If both decide to cooperate, they both earn a high outcome (e.g. 10); if both defect, they both receive a low outcome (e.g. 5); and, if one player cooperates and the other defects, the cooperator obtains a very low outcome (e.g. 1), whereas the defector receives a very high outcome (e.g. 15). Hence, it is always better for a player to defect for any given strategy of the opponent. The PD resembles a generic cooperation dilemma in which purely selfish behaviour leads to the defection of both players, even though mutual cooperation would maximize their joint payoff. Cooperation, however, is vulnerable to exploitation. The PD reflects the cooperation dilemma inherent in the provision of a public good, such as cooperative hunting or group defence, with only two individuals involved. More generally, a 'public good game' (PG) consists of an arbitrary number of players who are endowed with a certain number of tokens that they can either contribute to a project that is beneficial for the entire group (the public good) or keep for themselves. The dilemma arises from the fact that all group members profit equally from the public good, no matter whether they contributed or not, and that each player receives a lower individual profit from the tokens contributed to the public good than from the tokens kept. A purely selfish player refuses to contribute anything to the public good and free rides on the contributions of others. Considerable cooperation (contributions between 40 and 60 percent of the endowment) is typically observed in PGs with one-shot interactions (that is where the game is played once with a particular group of other players). However, cooperation is rarely stable if the game is played repeatedly, and deteriorates to low levels towards the end of the interaction period (Fehr and Rockenbach 2004).

Why is cooperation observed at all and what are the mechanisms that enable and sustain human cooperation in social dilemma situations, even in an environment with (a considerable number of) selfish subjects? *Strong reciprocity* appears to be crucial for the establishment of cooperation in groups with a share of selfish individuals. A person who is willing to reward fair behaviour and to punish unfair behaviour, even though this is often quite costly and provides no material benefit for the person, is called a 'strong reciprocator'. Strong reciprocity can occur in sequential dilemma situations, in which games are repeatedly played with the same set of players. In these situations, individual players use 'altruistic punishment' heavily, that is they punish at their own cost those who do not contribute to the public good. The effect is that a large increase in cooperation within the group is observed (Fehr and Rockenbach 2004). Perceived fairness can influence brain activations, and indeed in an fMRI investigation it was found that the effect of seeing a person in pain produced less activation in males' anterior insular / fronto-insular (i.e. agranular insular) cortex and anterior cingulate cortex if that person had acted unfairly (Singer, Seymour, O'Doherty, Stephan, Dolan and Frith 2006).

Another example is that when playing a monetary game with another human player, humans may provide information to the other player that will allow the other player to have a better chance of winning, even though to do this will cost the first player (Gneezy 2005, Gintis 2007). Why does this generosity occur? An explanation is that during evolution humans have developed heuristics for behaviour that, while not necessarily advantageous in every short-term situation, are in the long term useful strategies for promoting reciprocal altruism and hence reproductive fitness. In the case being considered, being seen to be willing to give something to another person can be taken as a sign that will enhance the reputation of the player as being honest and being willing to reciprocate, and of course being in a situation of reciprocal altruism can be more advantageous to each player in at least some situations than acting purely in terms of short-term interest. In this sense, the genes have produced a predisposition for a social behaviour which in the long run can increase (reproductive) fitness, but cannot prescribe for every detailed situation in which there might be a short-term cost. In the case of altruistic punishment, it has been shown that this strategy can survive in evolutionary models of social cooperation (Boyd, Gintis, Bowles and Richerson 2003, Bowles and Gintis 2004), and this suggests that there could be a genetic predisposition to this type of social behaviour too. Thus there is an account based in the genetically defined heuristics for the strong reciprocity found in some games even when the player knows that the goods will not be repaid, and the player even knows that there will be only a single game with each other player (Fehr and Fischbacher 2003, Fehr and Rockenbach 2004, Camerer and Fehr 2006). Interestingly, people play selfishly in this situation if they know that the opponent is a computer, emphasizing that the generous strategy is adopted in social situations, and is context-dependent.

In a similar way, being generous and 'forgiving' in tit-for-tat games can be helpful if both players have defected, for being generous occasionally may reinstate reciprocal positive play (altruism), which could be to the advantage of both players (Ridley 1996). Being (seen to be) honest can also be viewed as a useful (gene-based) strategy for promoting reciprocal altruism. Because in society it may be important in the long run to maintain one's reputation as a reciprocator, it may be important to be honest, generous, and forgiving, even though in the short term this may be disadvantageous. On the evolutionary timescale, it may promote (reproductive) fitness (of the relevant selfish genes) to be generous, forgiving, honest, and an altruistic punisher, because of the advantages reciprocal altruism brings. These heuristic ways of behaving may have evolved because of their long-term benefits, and this is an advance on traditional models in economics that have assumed that humans act selfishly and rationally to reach economic decisions. Of course, there are other advantages to being seen to be generous, including the status this provides partly because one can be seen as a potential provider of resources and protection (Ridley 1996, Rolls 2005). Some of these issues have been investigated in trust games (Montague et al. 2006, King-Casas, Tomlin, Anen, Camerere, Quartz and Montague 2005)[33]. In one such study (King-Casas et al. 2005), activations in the ventral part of the head of the caudate nucleus (which receives from the prefrontal cortex) were correlated with deviations from tit-for-tat reciprocity. In a similar brain region in the trustee, activations were also correlated with whether on the next move the trustee was going to increase or decrease the amount of money sent, thus reflecting the trustee's "intention to change the level of trust" (King-Casas et al. 2005). Thus activations in the brain do reflect how trust games are being played. Where in the brain the computations are being performed that result in the players' moves will be an interesting issue to unravel.

Framing issues (that is, how the task is described or framed (Kahneman and Tversky 1984)) are probably very important in the behaviours shown by individuals in these economic games. For example, if the instructions were to explicitly maximize the short term profit, then a rational selfish strategy would be likely to be adopted. Such a strategy might be more likely if a player was told that each opponent would be played only once; that the opponent was a computer; and/or if it was emphasized that the game had been set to evaluate quantitative economic reasoning, and logic. On the other hand, if the task instructions made it clear that there would be repeated games with another player, and that the choices made were being inspected by the experimenter, then this would tend to promote altruistic heuristics.

---

[33] In a trust game there is an exchange between two players and cooperation and defection can be parametrically encoded as the amount of money sent to one's partner. On each exchange, one player (the investor) is endowed with an amount of money. The investor can keep all the money or decide to invest some amount, which is tripled and sent to the other player (the trustee) who then decides what fraction to send back to the investor. The investor routinely does not keep all the money, but makes offers to the trustee that could be considered close to fair splits. This move is typically met with a reasonable (close to fair) return from the trustee. The initial offer from the investor entails some likelihood of a loss, and can be viewed as a cooperator signal. In repeated games between two players, reputations can be established.

Being informed that the other player was altruistic might also influence a player's strategy. (Reputations associated with church attendance might have a similar effect.)

Whether strategies are substitutable or complementary is also important in the behaviour that is selected. Self-regarding preferences and rationality may predict aggregate behaviour well when strategic substitutability applies. [Strategies are complements if agents have an incentive to match the strategies of other players. Strategies are substitutes if agents have an incentive to do the opposite of what the other players are doing. For example, if a firm can earn more profit by matching the prices chosen by other firms, then prices are strategic complements. If firms can earn more profit by choosing a low price when other firms choose high prices (and vice versa), then prices are strategic substitutes.] Other-regarding preferences may predict aggregate behaviour well when strategic complementarity applies (Camerer and Fehr 2006).

The biological bases of some of the predispositions for prosocial behaviour related to reciprocal altruism are starting to be investigated. It has been shown for example that the hormone oxytocin, implicated in attachment between mother and offspring and between partners (see Carter (1998), Insel and Young (2001), Winslow and Insel (2004) and Rolls (2005)), also increases trust in an economic game between humans (Kosfeld, Heinrichs, Zak, Fischbacher and Fehr 2005). In a bargaining game which is a probe for fairness, the ultimatum game (Montague et al. 2006), insula activation was produced by unfair offers (Sanfey, Rilling, Aronson, Nystrom and Cohen 2003), though such activation might just reflect autonomic activity associated with for example disgust (Nagai et al. 2004)[34]. Activation of the dorsolateral prefrontal cortex and anterior cingulate cortex was also produced by unfair offers. In a prisoner's dilemma game, cooperation with a human partner produced greater activation of the orbitofrontal cortex and related brain systems than did cooperation with a computer partner (Rilling, Gutman, Zeh, Pagnoni, Berns and Kilts 2002).

We have seen that there are evolutionary advantages to generosity, forgiveness, and altruistic punishment, and that these could be evolutionarily stable and hence lead to genetically inherited heuristics that influence behaviour (Ridley 1996, Ridley 1993b, Buss 1999, Boyd et al. 2003, Bowles and Gintis 2004, Rolls 2005). We may note that although the heuristics are universal (cross-cultural), the triggers are culturally defined. Indeed, the centrality of culture and complex social organization to the evolutionary success of Homo sapiens implies that individual fitness in humans will depend on the structure of cultural life. Since clearly culture is influenced by human genetic propensities, it follows that human cognitive, affective, and moral capacities are the product of a unique dynamic known as *gene–culture coevolution*. It is in part this coevolutionary process that has endowed us with preferences as predispositions that go beyond the self-regarding concerns emphasized in traditional economic and biological theory, and embrace such non-self-regarding values as a taste for cooperation, fairness, and retribution, the capacity to empathize, and the ability to value such constitutive behaviours as honesty, hard work, toleration of diversity, and loyalty to one's reference group (Gintis 2007, Bowles and Gintis 2005, Gintis 2003, Boyd et al. 2003).

However, while there probably are these predispositions, to varying extents in different individuals and even populations (because of genetic variation), this does not exclude at all

---

[34] In the one-round ultimatum game, a pair of players is given an endowment, say $100. The first player proposes a split of the money to the second player, who can respond by either accepting the proposal (take it) or rejecting it (leave it). If the proposal is rejected, neither player receives any money. A rational agent model predicts that proposers should offer as little as possible, and responders should accept whatever they are offered because something is better than nothing. However, responders routinely reject offers less than about 20% of the endowment, and, correspondingly, proposers routinely offer significant amounts. Thus humans routinely act with a sense of 'fairness' in the ultimatum game. While this is not in their short-term interest, it is a strategy or heuristic that may have evolved to promote reciprocation and in the long run mutual benefit for reciprocators.

the possibility that there may be rational reasons within a culture for cooperation, with these strategies operating on top of what is inherited. These predispositions to act altruistically may provide part of a foundation to which ethical principles are related (Ridley 1996). Ethical principles might *naturally* emphasize behaviours such as generosity, forgiveness, and even 'Honi soit qui mal y pense' (Evil be to him who evil thinks). Of course, ethical principles should not be subject to the naturalistic fallacy, that what is natural is right. However, ethical principles might fare best and gain most acceptance if what they promoted was not too inconsistent with inherited predispositions (Rolls 2005).

10.7 Dual routes to action: decisions and selection of actions by explicit rational thought

Rolls (2005) developed the view that there are two major types of route to action performed in relation to reward or punishment in humans. Examples of such actions include those associated with emotion and motivation.

The first ('implicit') route is via the brain systems that have been present in non-human primates such as monkeys, and to some extent in other mammals, for millions of years. These systems include the amygdala and, particularly well-developed in primates, the orbitofrontal cortex. These systems control behaviour in relation to previous associations of stimuli with reinforcement. The computation that controls the action thus involves assessment of the reinforcement-related value of a stimulus. This assessment may be based on a number of different factors:

One is the previous reinforcement history, which involves stimulus–reinforcer association learning using the amygdala, and its rapid updating especially in primates using the orbitofrontal cortex. This stimulus–reinforcer association learning may involve quite specific information about a stimulus, for example the energy associated with each type of food, by the process of conditioned appetite and satiety (Booth 1985).

A second is the current motivational state, for example whether hunger is present, whether other needs are satisfied, etc.

A third factor that affects the computed reward value of the stimulus is whether that reward has been received recently. If it has been received recently but in small quantity, this may increase the reward value of the stimulus. This is known as incentive motivation or the 'salted nut' phenomenon (Section 3.2.2.6). The adaptive value of such a process is that this positive feedback of reward value in the early stages of working for a particular reward tends to lock the organism on to behaviour being performed for that reward. This means that animals that are for example almost equally hungry and thirsty will show hysteresis in their choice of action, rather than continually switching from eating to drinking and back with each mouthful of water or food. This introduction of hysteresis into the reward evaluation system makes action selection a much more efficient process in a natural environment, for constantly switching between different types of behaviour would be very costly if all the different rewards were not available in the same place at the same time. (For example, walking half a mile between a site where water was available and a site where food was available after every mouthful would be very inefficient.) The amygdala is one structure that may be involved in this increase in the reward value of stimuli early on in a series of presentations, in that lesions of the amygdala (in rats) abolish the expression of this reward-incrementing process which is normally evident in the increasing rate of working for a food reward early on in a meal (Rolls and Rolls 1973, Rolls 2005).

A fourth factor is the computed absolute value of the reward or punishment expected or being obtained from a stimulus, e.g. the sweetness of the stimulus (set by evolution so that

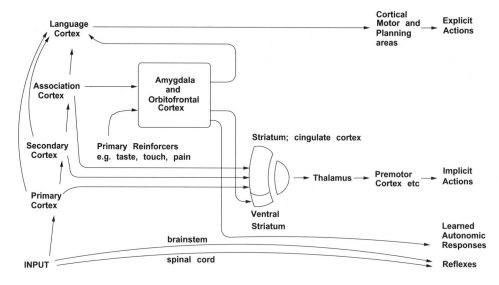

Fig. 10.1 Dual routes to the initiation of actions in response to rewarding and punishing stimuli. The inputs from different sensory systems to brain structures such as the orbitofrontal cortex and amygdala allow these brain structures to evaluate the reward- or punishment-related value of incoming stimuli, or of remembered stimuli. The different sensory inputs enable evaluations within the orbitofrontal cortex and amygdala based mainly on the primary (unlearned) reinforcement value for taste, touch, and olfactory stimuli, and on the secondary (learned) reinforcement value for visual and auditory stimuli. In the case of vision, the 'association cortex' that outputs representations of objects to the amygdala and orbitofrontal cortex is the inferior temporal visual cortex. One route for the outputs from these evaluative brain structures is via projections directly to structures such as the basal ganglia (including the striatum and ventral striatum) and cingulate cortex to enable implicit, direct behavioural responses based on the reward- or punishment-related evaluation of the stimuli to be made. The second route is via the language systems of the brain, which allow explicit (verbalizable) decisions involving multistep syntactic planning to be implemented.

sweet stimuli will tend to be rewarding, because they are generally associated with energy sources), or the pleasantness of touch (set by evolution to be pleasant according to the extent to which it brings animals of the opposite sex together, and depending on the investment in time that the partner is willing to put into making the touch pleasurable, a sign that indicates the commitment and value for the partner of the relationship, as in social grooming) (see Rolls (2005)).

After the reward value of the stimulus has been assessed in these ways, behaviour is then initiated based on approach towards or withdrawal from the stimulus. A critical aspect of the behaviour produced by this type of 'implicit' system is that it is aimed directly towards obtaining a sensed or expected reward, by virtue of connections to brain systems such as the basal ganglia that are concerned with the initiation of actions (see Fig. 10.1). The expectation may of course involve behaviour to obtain stimuli associated with reward, which might even be present in a fixed chain or sequence.

Now part of the way in which the behaviour is controlled with this first ('implicit') route is according to the reward value of the outcome. At the same time, the animal may only work for the reward if the cost is not too high. Indeed, in the field of behavioural ecology animals are often thought of as performing optimally on some cost–benefit curve (see, e.g., Krebs and Kacelnik (1991)). This does not at all mean that the animal thinks about the long-term rewards, and performs a cost–benefit analysis using a lot of thoughts about the costs, other rewards (short and long term) available and their costs, etc (see Section 10.6.2). Instead, it should be taken to mean that in evolution the system has evolved in such a way that the way in which the reward varies with the different energy densities or amounts of food and the delay before it is received can be used as part of the input to a mechanism that has also been built to track the costs of obtaining the food (e.g. energy loss in obtaining it, risk of predation, etc.), and to then select, given many such types of reward and the associated costs, the current behaviour that provides the most 'net reward'. Part of the value of having the computation expressed in this reward-minus-cost form is that there is then a suitable 'currency', or net reward value, to enable the animal to select the behaviour with currently the most net reward gain (or minimal aversive outcome).

Part of the evidence that this implicit route often controls emotional behaviour in humans is that humans with orbitofrontal cortex damage have impairments in selecting the correct action during visual discrimination reversal, yet can state explicitly what the correct action should be (Rolls, Hornak, Wade and McGrath 1994a, Rolls 1999b). The implication is that the intact orbitofrontal cortex is normally involved in making rapid emotion-related decisions, and that this emotion-related decision system is a separate system from the explicit system, which by serial reasoning can provide an alternative route to action. The explicit system may simply comment on the success or failure of actions that are initiated by the implicit system, and the explicit system may then be able to switch in to control mode to correct failures of the implicit system. Consistent evidence that an implicit system can control human behaviour is that in psychophysical and neurophysiological studies, it has been found that face stimuli presented for 16 ms and followed immediately by a mask are not consciously perceived, yet produce above chance identification (Rolls and Tovee 1994, Rolls, Tovee, Purcell, Stewart and Azzopardi 1994b, Rolls, Tovee and Panzeri 1999b, Rolls 2003, Rolls 2006b). In a similar backward masking paradigm, it was found that happy vs angry face expressions could influence how much beverage was wanted and consumed even when the faces were not consciously perceived (Winkielman and Berridge 2005, Winkielman and Berridge 2003). Thus unconscious emotion-related stimuli (in this case face expressions) can influence actions, and there is no need for processing to be conscious for actions to be initiated. Further, in blindsight, humans with damage to the primary visual cortex may not be subjectively aware of stimuli, yet may be able to guess what the stimulus was, or to perform reaching movements towards it (Weiskrantz 1998). Further, humans with striate cortex lesions may be influenced by emotional stimuli that are not perceived consciously (De Gelder, Vroomen, Pourtois and Weiskrantz 1999). Thus actions and emotions can be initiated without the necessity for the conscious route to be in control, and we should not infer that all actions require conscious processing (Rolls 2005).

The second ('explicit') route in (at least) humans involves a computation with many 'if ... then' statements, to implement a plan to obtain a reward. In this case, an immediately available reward may actually be deferred as part of the plan, which might involve working for a different more highly valued reward that was available only by long-term planning, if this was thought to be overall an optimal strategy in terms of resource usage (e.g. time). In this case, syntax is required, because the many symbols (e.g. names of people) that are part of the plan must be correctly linked or bound. Such linking might be of the form: 'if A does this, then B is likely to do this, and this will cause C to do this ...'. The requirement of syntax for this type of planning implies that an output to language systems in the brain is required for this type of planning (see Fig. 10.1). **Thus the explicit language system in humans may allow working for deferred rewards by enabling use of a one-off, individual, plan appropriate for each situation.** This explicit system may allow immediate rewards to be deferred, as part of a long-term plan. This ability to defer immediate rewards and plan syntactically in this way for the long term may be an important way in which the explicit system extends the capabilities of the implicit emotion systems that respond more directly to rewards and punishers, or to rewards and punishers with fixed expectancies such as can be learned by reinforcement learning (see Section B.15) (Rolls 2005).

Consistent with the point being made about evolutionarily old emotion-based decision systems vs a recent rational system present in humans (and perhaps other animals with syntactic processing) is that humans trade off immediate costs/benefits against cost/benefits that are delayed by as much as decades, whereas non-human primates have not been observed to engage in unpreprogrammed delay of gratification involving more than a few minutes (Rachlin 1989, Kagel, Battalio and Green 1995, McClure, Laibson, Loewenstein and Cohen 2004) (though this is a potentially interesting area for further investigation, see Section 10.6.2). Moreover, as described in Section 10.6.2, there appear to be different systems involved in these types of decision, with the orbitofrontal and pregenual cingulate cortices implicated in immediate emotion-related reward-based decision-making, and the lateral prefrontal cortex and parietal cortex implicated in long-term cost–benefit planning-related decision-making.

Another building block for such planning operations in the brain may be the type of short-term memory in which the prefrontal cortex is involved. This short-term memory may be, for example in non-human primates, of where in space a response has just been made. A development of this type of short-term response memory system in humans to enable multiple short-term memories to be held in place correctly, preferably with the temporal order of the different items in the short-term memory coded correctly, may be another building block for the multiple step 'if .... then' type of computation in order to form a multiple step plan. Such short-term memories are implemented in the (dorsolateral and inferior convexity) prefrontal cortex of non-human primates and humans (Goldman-Rakic 1996, Petrides 1996, Rolls and Deco 2002, Deco and Rolls 2003), and may be part of the reason why prefrontal cortex damage impairs planning and executive function (see Chapters 5 and 8, and Shallice and Burgess (1996)).

Of these two routes (see Fig. 10.1), it is the second that I have suggested elsewhere (Rolls 1999a, Rolls 2004c, Rolls 2005, Rolls 2007a, Rolls 2007e) is related to consciousness. The hypothesis is that consciousness is the state that arises by virtue of having the ability to think about one's own thoughts, which has the adaptive value of enabling one to correct long multistep syntactic plans. This latter system is thus the one in which explicit, declarative, processing occurs. Processing in this system is frequently associated with reason and rationality, in that many of the consequences of possible actions can be taken into account. The actual computation of how rewarding a particular stimulus or situation is, or will be, probably still depends on activity in the orbitofrontal cortex and amygdala, as the reward value of stimuli is computed and represented in these regions, and in that it is found that verbalized expressions of the reward (or punishment) value of stimuli are dampened by damage to these systems. (For example, damage to the orbitofrontal cortex renders painful input still identifiable as pain, but without the strong affective, 'unpleasant', reaction to it.)

This language system (or more formally, system with syntactic capabilities, see Rolls (2004c) and Rolls (2005)) that enables long-term planning may be contrasted with the first system in which behaviour is directed at obtaining the stimulus (including the remembered stimulus) which is currently most rewarding, as computed by brain structures that include the orbitofrontal cortex and amygdala. There are outputs from this system, perhaps those directed at the basal ganglia and cingulate cortex, which do not pass through the language system, and behaviour produced in this way is described as implicit, and verbal declarations cannot be made directly about the reasons for the choice made. When verbal declarations are made about decisions made in this first ('implicit') system, those verbal declarations may be confabulations, reasonable explanations or fabrications, of reasons why the choice was made. These reasonable explanations would be generated to be consistent with the sense of continuity and self that is a characteristic of reasoning in the language system (see further Rolls (2005)).

The question then arises of how decisions are made in animals such as humans that have both the implicit, direct reward-based, and the explicit, rational, planning systems (see Fig. 10.1). One particular situation in which the first, implicit, system may be especially important is when rapid reactions to stimuli with reward or punishment value must be made, for then the direct connections from structures such as the orbitofrontal cortex to the basal ganglia may allow rapid actions. Another is when there may be too many factors to be taken into account easily by the explicit, rational, planning, system: then the implicit system may be used to guide action.

In contrast, when the implicit system continually makes errors, it would then be beneficial for the organism to switch from automatic, direct, action based on obtaining what the orbitofrontal cortex system decodes as being the most positively reinforcing choice currently available, to the explicit conscious control system which can evaluate with its long-term planning algorithms what action should be performed next. Indeed, it would be adaptive for the explicit system to be regularly assessing performance by the more automatic system, and to switch itself in to control behaviour quite frequently, as otherwise the adaptive value of having the explicit system would be less than optimal.

Another factor that may influence the balance between control by the implicit and explicit systems is the presence of pharmacological agents such as alcohol, which may alter the balance towards control by the implicit system, may allow the implicit system to influence more the explanations made by the explicit system, and may within the explicit system alter the relative value it places on caution and restraint vs commitment to a risky action or plan.

How do we take a decision about whether to follow the implicit or the explicit route to action? One possibility is a cortical area in which the evidence can be accumulated and decisions can be taken in an integrate-and-fire attractor network with probabilities that depend on the relative strengths of the evidence, as described in Chapter 7. In this case, the evidence would be from the, possibly competing, implicit and explicit systems. Of course, top-down processing could bias the decision to take more account of one system than the other. Paying attention continuously to the rational explicit system would tend to bias decisions made according to the inputs to the decision network from that system, which would have increased activity because of the top-down bias. If this explicit system was working less effectively, or the inputs from the implicit system became stronger, then decisions might be biased more towards the implicit system. Some of the implications for ethical issues are discussed by Rolls (2005).

A second possibility, which could apply to all types of decision, is that the selection between all the different cortical processing streams might be taken in a structure that receives from all areas of the cortex, such as the basal ganglia, the first stage of which is shown as the striatum in Fig. 10.1. Some of these different cortical systems that have separate projections into the striatum are shown in Fig. 3.53 on page 222. A fundamental point here is that each cortical area contributes to decision-making for different types of decision, so there is not a single cortical decision-making system. The orbitofrontal cortex for example is involved in decisions about which visual stimulus is currently associated with reward, in for example a visual discrimination reversal task. Its computations are about stimuli, primary reinforcers and secondary reinforcers (see Section 3.6). The dorsolateral prefrontal cortex takes an executive role in decision-making in a working memory task, in which information must be held available for in some cases intervening stimuli (see Section 5.1). The dorsal and posterior part of the dorsolateral prefrontal cortex may be involved in short-term memory-related decisions about where to move the eyes (see Section 5.1). The parietal cortex is involved in decision-making when the stimuli are for example optic flow patterns (Glimcher 2003). The hippocampus is involved in decision-making when the allocentric places of stimuli must be associated with rewards or objects (see Chapter 2). The somatosensory cortex and ventral premotor cortex are involved in decision-making when different vibrotactile frequencies must be compared (see Chapter 7). The inferior temporal cortex may be involved in decision-making about which stimulus is seen (see Section 7.7 and Blake and Logothetis (2002)), and will be acted upon. The cingulate cortex may be involved when action–outcome decisions must be taken (see Section 3.8). In each of these cases, local cortical processing that is related to the type of decision being made takes place, and all cortical areas are not involved in any one decision.

The style of the decision-making related computation in each cortical area appears to be of the form described in Chapter 7, in which the local recurrent collateral connections that are a feature of cortical connectivity enable the decision-making process to accumulate evidence in time, falling gradually into an attractor which represents the decision made in the network. Because there is an attractor state into which the network falls, this can be described statistically as a non-linear diffusion process, the noise for the diffusion being the stochastical spiking of the neurons, as described in Chapter 7, and the driving force being the biasing inputs. The process is non-linear, in that once the system starts falling into an attractor basin, there is positive feedback from the recurrent collaterals, and the system falls into a stable state (see Fig. 7.6 on page 461).

The suggestion, according to this second possibility, is then that a second level of 'decision-making' takes place in the basal ganglia, which by competition between all the competing cortical inputs select one routing to behavioural output. The selection in this case appears to be by an evolutionarily old, primitive, and safe system that implements direct inhibition between the principal neurons of the network, which are GABA neurons in both the striatum and the globus pallidus, as described in Section 3.10.2 (page 221 ff.) and Fig. 3.62. It is assumed that these inhibitory connections are not associatively modifiable, so that these neurons do not form an attractor (or an anti-attractor)[35]. Without associatively modifiable connections between the principal neurons, the decision or selection process can be described as a linear diffusion, with the diffusion being driven by the biasing inputs, and the stochastic firing in the network implementing the diffusion. The basal ganglia would then according to this hypothesis select the strongest input to it from any cortical area (or combination of cortical areas, as described in Section 3.10.2).

The output of the basal ganglia could influence behaviour by two main methods, as described in Section 3.10.2. One is via connections to premotor or motor cortical areas or other motor systems (such as the nigro-collicular for eye movements). Forward associations of cortical inputs onto striatal neurons might allow for mapping into a motor response space as required for habit learning, for parts of the striatum do receive inputs from the motor cortex, and there are many movement-related neurons in the putamen and globus pallidus (see Section 3.10.2). The other main method would be by return connections to the neocortex via the thalamus, which could enable a processing stream selected in the basal ganglia to feed back to many cortical areas to influence their activity, and thus to contribute to the selection of a single output for behaviour. The single, or limited, output from the system as a whole is important, so that the motor system does not attempt to select many actions simultaneously. In this system, the threshold setting would be crucial, as with the threshold set too high there would be little behavioural output (which might correspond to Parkinson's disease), and if the threshold were too low, conflicting and inconsistent actions might be selected simultaneously.

---

[35] A network with direct inhibitory connections between its principal neurons could form an attractor, which would be defined by a population with strong mutual inhibitory synaptic weights, and a low firing rate when in the attractor. The learning rule required would be: For low presynaptic firing and low postsynaptic firing, increase the synaptic weight; or equivalently: For high presynaptic firing and high postsynaptic firing, decrease the synaptic weight (i.e. associative LTD).

The dopamine pathways to the striatum, and the return feedback connections to the dopamine neurons from the striatum, may play a role in this threshold setting (Section 3.10.2).

It is thus suggested that decision-making is inherently a two-stage process. First, there is local computation in a specialized cortical area that performs processing on its specialized inputs which involves settling into an attractor, taking the different constraints or biases into account to reach a local decision. This is inherently a non-linear diffusion process involving attractor dynamics. Of course this processing need not be restricted to only one cortical area, and forward and backward connections between connected areas may contribute to the attractor process, as described in Chapter 7. Indeed, when a decision is taken by a cortical area, the attractor into which it falls can be influenced by top-down biased competition from other areas, including for example a short-term memory system in for example the prefrontal cortex that holds active the current task or goal. Thus there is interaction between cortical areas in decision-making, perception, and memory recall, and this is part of the concept of the brain as a dynamical system described in this book. Second, there may be a more global competition to select one output stream for behaviour, and this may involve a linear diffusion process without inbuilt attractor short-term memory related dynamics, and may be implemented in a system such as the basal ganglia.

10.8 Apostasis

[36] Extraordinary progress has been made in the last 35 years in understanding how the brain might actually work. Thirty-five years ago, observations on how neurons respond in different brain areas during behaviour were only just starting, and there was very limited understanding of how any part of the brain might work or compute. Many of the observations appeared as interesting phenomena, but there was no conceptual framework in place for understanding how the neuronal responses might be generated, nor of how they were part of an overall computational framework. Through the developments that have taken place since then, some of them charted in this book, we now have at least plausible and testable working models that are consistent with a great deal of experimental data about how many different types of memory, perception, attention, and decision-making may be implemented in the brain. We have models, described in this book, and consistent with a great deal of neurophysiological data, of how perceptual systems build, by self-organizing learning and memory-related types of processing, representations of objects in the world in a form that is suitable as an input to memory systems, and how memory systems interact with perceptual systems. We have models of how short-term memory is implemented in the brain. We also, and quite closely related to these models, have detailed and testable models that make predictions about how attention works and is implemented in the brain. We also have testable models of long-term memory, including episodic memory and spatial memory, which again are based on and are consistent with what is being found to be implemented in the primate brain. In addition, we have an understanding, at the evolutionary and adaptive level, of emotion, and at the computational level of how different brain areas implement the information processing underlying emotion (see also Rolls (2005)). We also have models of how fundamental aspects of decision-making may be implemented as an inherent property of cortical attractor networks, which implement a non-linear diffusion process in falling into an attractor state (Chapter 7 and Section 10.7).

However, our understanding at the time of writing is developing to the stage where we can have not just a computational understanding of each of these systems separately, but also an understanding of how all these processes are linked and act together computationally. Even

---

[36] Apostasis – standing after.

more than this, we have shown how many aspects of brain function, such as the operation of short-term memory systems, of attention, the effects of emotional states on memory and perception, and even decision-making and action selection, can now start to be understood in terms of the reciprocal *interactions* of connected neuronal systems. Indeed, one of the implications of the research described in this book is that there are multiple memory systems in the brain (Rolls 2007g), each processing different types of information and using a range of computational implementations, and that interactions between these memory systems are important in understanding the operation of perception, memory, attention, and decision-making in the brain.

In the senses that there are a set of memory-related operations that are involved in all these types of processing, and that there are interactions between the systems involved, we now have a unifying approach to memory, attention, decision-making, and perception (including vision, taste and olfaction) in which computational neuroscience helps to provide a framework in which all the essential empirical findings from neuroscience can be linked into a coherent understanding.

This leads me to emphasize that the understanding of how the brain actually operates is crucially dependent on a knowledge of the responses of single neurons, the computing elements of the brain, for it is through the connected operations in networks of single neurons, each with their own individual response properties, that the interesting collective computational properties of the brain arise in neuronal networks.

In describing in this book at least part of this great development in understanding in the last 35 years of how a significant number of parts of the brain actually operate, and how they operate together, I wish to make the point that we are at an exciting and conceptually fascinating time in the history of brain research. We are starting to see how a number of parts of the brain *could* work. There is much now that can be done and needs to be done to develop our understanding of how the brain actually works. But the work described in this book does give an indication of some of the types of information processing that take place in the brain, and an indication of the way in which we are now entering the age in which our conceptual understanding of brain function can be based on our developing understanding of how the brain computes.

Understanding how the brain works normally is of course an important foundation for understanding its dysfunctions and its functioning when damaged. Some examples have been given in this book. I regard this as a very important long term aim of the type of work described in this book.

Through neural computation, understanding

Appendix 1 Introduction to linear algebra for neural networks

In this Appendix we review some simple elements of linear algebra relevant to understanding neural networks. This will provide a useful basis for a quantitative understanding of how neural networks operate (see Appendix B).

A.1 Vectors

A vector is an ordered set of numbers. An example of a vector is the set of numbers

$$\begin{bmatrix} 7 \\ 4 \end{bmatrix}$$

If we denote the jth element of this vector as w_j, then $w_1 = 7$, and $w_2 = 4$. We can denote the whole vector by $\mathbf{w}$. This notation is very economical. If the vector has 10,000 elements, then we can still refer to it in mathematical operations as $\mathbf{w}$. $\mathbf{w}$ might refer to the vector of 10,000 synaptic weights on the dendrites of a neuron. Another example of a vector is the set of firing rates of the axons that make synapses onto a dendrite, as shown in Fig. 1.2. The firing rate x of each axon forming the input vector can be indexed by j, and is denoted by x_j. The vector would be denoted by $\mathbf{x}$.

Certain mathematical operations can be performed with vectors. We start with the operation which is fundamental to simple models of neural networks, the inner product or dot product of two vectors.

A.1.1 The inner or dot product of two vectors

The operation of computing the activation h of a neuron from the firing rate on its input axons multiplied by the corresponding synaptic weight can be expressed as:

$$h = \sum_j x_j w_j \tag{A.1}$$

where $\sum_j$ indicates that the sum is over the C input axons to each neuron, indexed by j. Denoting the firing rate vector as $\mathbf{x}$ and the synaptic weight vector as $\mathbf{w}$, we can write

$$h = \mathbf{x} \cdot \mathbf{w} \qquad . \tag{A.2}$$

If the weight vector is

$$\mathbf{w} = \begin{bmatrix} 9 \\ 5 \\ 2 \end{bmatrix}$$

and the firing rate input vector is

$$\mathbf{x} = \begin{bmatrix} 3 \\ 6 \\ 7 \end{bmatrix}$$

then we can write

$$\mathbf{x} \cdot \mathbf{w} = (3 \cdot 9) + (6 \cdot 5) + (7 \cdot 2) = 71 \quad . \tag{A.3}$$

Thus in the inner or dot product, we multiply the corresponding terms, and then sum the result. As this is the simple mathematical operation that is used to compute the activation h in the most simplified abstraction of a neuron (see Chapter 1), we see that it is indeed the fundamental operation underlying many types of neural network. We will shortly see that some of the properties of neuronal networks can be understood in terms of the properties of the dot product. We next review a number of basic aspects of vectors and inner products between vectors.

There is a simple geometrical interpretation of vectors, at least in low-dimensional spaces. If we define, for example, x and y axes at right angles to each other in a two-dimensional space, then any two-component vector can be thought of as having a direction and length in that space that can be defined by the values of the two elements of the vector. If the first element is taken to correspond to x and the second to y, then the x axis lies in the direction [1,0] in the space, and the y axis in the direction [0,1], as shown in Fig. A.1. The line to point [1,1] in the space then lies at $45°$ to both axes, as shown in Fig. A.1.

A.1.2   The length of a vector

Consider taking the inner product of a vector

$$\mathbf{w} = \begin{bmatrix} 4 \\ 3 \end{bmatrix}$$

with itself. Then

$$\|\mathbf{w}\| = \sqrt{\mathbf{w} \cdot \mathbf{w}} = \sqrt{4^2 + 3^2} = 5. \tag{A.4}$$

This is the length of the vector. We can represent this operation in the two-dimensional graph shown in Fig. A.1. In this case, the coordinates where vector $\mathbf{w}$ ends in the space are [1,1]. The length of the vector (from [0,0] to [1,1] is obtained by Pythagoras' theorem. Pythagoras' theorem states that the length of the vector $\mathbf{w}$ is equal to the square root of the sum of the squares of the two sides. Thus we define the length of the vector $\mathbf{w}$ as

$$\|\mathbf{w}\| = \sqrt{\mathbf{w} \cdot \mathbf{w}} \tag{A.5}$$

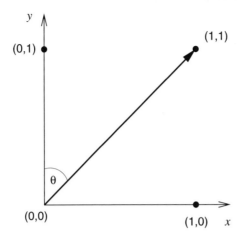

Fig. A.1 Illustration of a vector in a two-dimensional space. The basis for the space is made up of the x axis in the [1,0] direction, and the y axis in the [0,1] direction. (The first element of each vector is then the x value, and the second the y value. The values of x and y for different points, marked by a dot, in the space are shown. The origins of the axes are at point 0,0.) The [1,1] vector projects in the [1,1] (or 45°) direction to the point 1,1, with length 1.414.

In the [1,1] case, this value is $\sqrt{2} = 1.414$.

A.1.3 Normalizing the length of a vector

We can scale a vector in such a way that its length is equal to 1 by dividing it by its length. If we form the dot product of two normalized vectors, its maximum value will be 1, and its minimum value -1.

A.1.4 The angle between two vectors: the normalized dot product

The angle between two vectors $\mathbf{x}$ and $\mathbf{w}$ is defined in terms of the inner product as follows:

$$\cos \theta = \frac{\mathbf{x} \cdot \mathbf{w}}{\|\mathbf{x}\| \|\mathbf{w}\|} \tag{A.6}$$

For example, the angle between two vectors

$$\mathbf{x} = \begin{bmatrix} 0 \\ 1 \end{bmatrix} \quad \text{and} \quad \mathbf{w} = \begin{bmatrix} 1 \\ 1 \end{bmatrix}$$

where the length of vector $\mathbf{x}$ is $\sqrt{0.0 + 1.1} = 1$ and of vector $\mathbf{w}$ is $\sqrt{1.1 + 1.1} = \sqrt{2}$ is

$$\cos \theta = \frac{(0.1) + (1.1)}{1.\sqrt{2}} = 0.707. \tag{A.7}$$

Thus $\theta = \cos^{-1}(0.707) = 45°$.

We can give a simple geometrical interpretation of this as shown in Fig. A.1. However, equation A.6 is much easier to use in a high-dimensional space!

The dot product reflects the similarity between two vectors. Once the length of the vectors is fixed, the higher their dot product, the more similar are the two vectors. By normalizing the dot product, that is by dividing by the lengths of each vector as shown in equation A.6, we obtain a value that varies from -1 to $+1$. This normalized dot product is then just the cosine of the angle between the vectors, and is a very useful measure of the similarity between any two vectors, because it always lies in the range -1 to $+1$. It is closely related to the (Pearson product–moment) correlation coefficient between any two vectors, as we see if we write the equation in terms of its components

$$\cos \theta = \frac{\sum_j x_j w_j}{(\sum_j x_j^2)^{1/2} (\sum_j w_j^2)^{1/2}} \tag{A.8}$$

which is just the formula for the correlation coefficient between two sets of numbers with zero mean (or with the mean value removed by subtracting the mean of the components of each vector from each component of that vector).

Now consider two vectors that have a dot product of zero, that is where $\cos \theta = 0$ or the angle between the vectors is $90°$. Such vectors are described as orthogonal (literally at right angles) to each other. If our two orthogonal vectors were x and w, then the activation of the neuron, measured by the dot product of these two vectors, would be zero. If our two orthogonal vectors each had a mean of zero, their correlation would also be zero: the two vectors can then be described as unrelated or independent.

If, instead, the two vectors had zero angle between them, that is if $\cos \theta = 1$, then the dot product would be maximal (given the vectors' lengths), the normalized dot product would be 1, and the two vectors would be described as identical to each other apart from their length. Note that in this case their correlation would also be 1, even if the two vectors did not have zero mean components.

For intermediate similarities of the two vectors, the degree of similarity would be expressed by the relative magnitude of the dot product, or by the normalized dot product of the two vectors, which is just the cosine of the angle between them. These measures are closely related to the correlation between two vectors.

Thus we can think of the simple operation performed by neurons as measuring the similarity between their current input vector and their synaptic weight vector. Their activation, h, is this dot product. It is because of this simple operation that neurons can generalize to similar inputs; can still produce useful outputs if some of their inputs or synaptic weights are damaged or missing, that is they can show graceful degradation or fault tolerance; and can be thought of as learning to point their weight vectors towards input patterns, which is very useful in enabling neurons to categorize their inputs in competitive networks (see Section B.4).

A.1.5 The outer product of two vectors

Let us take a row vector having as components the firing rates of a set of output neurons in a pattern associator or competitive network, which we might denote as y, with components y_i and the index i running from 1 to the number N of output neurons. y is then a shorthand for writing down each component, e.g. [7,2,5,2,...], to indicate that the firing rate of neuron 1 is 7, etc. To avoid confusion, we continue in the following to denote the firing rate of input neuron j as x_j. Now recall (see Chapter 1 and Section B.2) how the synaptic weights are formed in a pattern associator using a Hebb rule as follows:

$$\delta w_{ij} = \alpha y_i x_j \tag{A.9}$$

where δw_{ij} is the change of the synaptic weight w_{ij} which results from the simultaneous (or conjunctive) presence of presynaptic firing x_j and postsynaptic firing or activation y_i, and α

is a learning rate constant which specifies how much the synapses alter on any one pairing. In a more compact vector notation, this expression would be

$$\delta \mathbf{w}_i = \alpha \mathbf{y}_i \mathbf{x}'$$ (A.10)

where the firing rates on the axons form a column vector with the values, for example, as follows[37]:

$$\mathbf{x}' = \begin{bmatrix} 2 \\ 0 \\ 3 \\ \cdots \end{bmatrix}$$

The weights are then updated by a change proportional (the α factor) to the following matrix (Table A.1):

Table A.1 Multiplication of a row vector [7 2 5 ....] by a column vector to form the external or tensor product, representing for example the changes to a matrix of synaptic weights $\mathbf{W}$

$$\begin{bmatrix} 7 & 2 & 5 & \cdots \end{bmatrix}$$

	7	2	5	.....
[2]	14	4	10	......
[0]	0	0	0	......
[3]	21	6	15	......
.....	.....	.....	.....	.....

This multiplication of the two vectors is called the outer, or tensor, product, and forms a matrix, in this case of (alterations to) synaptic weights. Thus we see that the operation of altering synaptic weights in a network can be thought of as forming a matrix of weight changes, which can then be used to alter the existing matrix of synaptic weights.

A.1.6 Linear and non-linear systems

The operations with which we have been concerned in this Appendix so far are linear operations. We should note that if two matrices operate linearly, we can form their product by matrix multiplication, and then replace the two matrices with the single matrix that is their product. We can thus effectively replace two synaptic matrices in a linear multilayer neural network with one synaptic matrix, the product of the two matrices. For this reason, multilayer neural networks if linear cannot achieve more than can be achieved in a single-layer linear network. It is only in non-linear networks that more can be achieved, in terms of mapping input vectors through the synaptic weight matrices, to produce particular mappings to output vectors. Much of the power of many networks in the brain comes from the fact that they are multilayer non-linear networks (in that the computing elements in each network, the neurons, have non-linear properties such as thresholds, and saturation at high levels of output). Because the matrix by matrix multiplication operations of linear algebra cannot be applied directly to

[37] The prime after the $\mathbf{x}$ is used here to remind us that this vector is a column vector, which can be thought of as a transformed row vector, and the prime indicates the transformed vector. We do not use the prime for most of this book in order to keep the notation uncluttered.

the operation of neural networks in the brain, we turn instead back to other aspects of linear algebra, which can help us to understand which classes of pattern can be successfully learned by different types of neural network.

A.1.7 Linear combinations of vectors, linear independence, and linear separability

We can multiply a vector by a scalar (a single value, e.g. 2) thus:

$$2 \cdot \begin{bmatrix} 4 \\ 1 \\ 3 \end{bmatrix} = \begin{bmatrix} 8 \\ 2 \\ 6 \end{bmatrix}$$

We can add two vectors thus:

$$\begin{bmatrix} 4 \\ 1 \\ 3 \end{bmatrix} + \begin{bmatrix} 2 \\ 7 \\ 2 \end{bmatrix} = \begin{bmatrix} 6 \\ 8 \\ 5 \end{bmatrix}$$

The sum of the two vectors is an example of a linear combination of vectors, which is in general a weighted sum of several vectors, component by component. Thus, the linear combination of vectors $\mathbf{v}_1$, $\mathbf{v}_2$, ... to form a vector $\mathbf{v}_s$ is expressed by the sum

$$\mathbf{v}_s = c_1 \mathbf{v}_1 + c_2 \mathbf{v}_2 + ... \tag{A.11}$$

where c_1 and c_2 are scalars.

By adding vectors in this way, we can produce any vector in the space spanned by a set of vectors as a linear combination of vectors in the set. If in a set of n vectors at least one can be written as a linear combination of the others, then the vectors are described as **linearly dependent**. If in a set of n vectors none can be written as a linear combination of the others, then the vectors are described as **linearly independent**. A linearly independent set of vectors has the properties that any vector in the space spanned by the set can be written in only one way as a linear combination of the set, and the space has dimension $d = n$. In contrast, a vector in a space spanned by a linearly dependent set can be written in an infinite number of equivalent ways, and the dimension d of the space is less than n.

Consider a set of linearly dependent vectors and the d-dimensional space they span. Two subsets of this set are described as **linearly separable** if the vectors of one subset (that is, their endpoints) can be separated from those of the other by a hyperplane, that is a subspace of dimension $d - 1$. *Subsets formed from a set of linearly independent vectors are always linearly separable.* For example, the four vectors:

$$\begin{bmatrix} 0 \\ 0 \end{bmatrix} \quad \begin{bmatrix} 0 \\ 1 \end{bmatrix} \quad \begin{bmatrix} 1 \\ 0 \end{bmatrix} \quad \begin{bmatrix} 1 \\ 1 \end{bmatrix}$$

are linearly dependent, because the fourth can be formed by a linear combination of the second and third (and also because the first, being the null vector, can be formed by multiplying any other vector by zero, a specific linear combination). In fact, $n = 4$ and $d = 2$. If we split this set into subset A including the first and fourth vector, and subset B including the second and third, the two subsets are not linearly separable, because there is no way to draw a line (which is the subspace of dimension $d - 1 = 1$) to separate the two subsets A and B. We will encounter this set of vectors in Appendix B, and this is the geometrical interpretation of why a one-layer, one-output neuron network cannot separate these patterns. Such a network (a simple perceptron) is equivalent to its (single) weight vector, and in turn the weight vector defines a set of parallel $d - 1$ dimensional hyperplanes. (Here $d = 2$, so a hyperplane is simply a line, any line perpendicular to the weight vector.) No line can be found that separates the first and fourth vector from the second and third, whatever the weight vector the line is perpendicular to, and hence no perceptron exists that performs the required classification (see Section A.2.1). To separate such patterns, a multilayer network with non-linear neurons is needed (see Appendix B).

Any set of linearly independent vectors comprise the basis of the space they span, and they are called basis vectors. All possible vectors in the space spanned by these vectors can be formed as linear combinations of these vectors. If the vectors of the basis are in addition mutually orthogonal, the basis is an orthogonal basis, and it is, further, an orthonormal basis if the vectors are chosen to be of unit length. Given any space of vectors with a preassigned meaning to each of their components (for example the space of patterns of activation, in which each component is the activation of a particular unit), the most natural, canonical choice for a basis is the set of vectors in which each vector has one component, in turn, with value 1, and all the others with value 0. For example, in the $d = 2$ space considered earlier, the natural choice is to take as basis vectors

$$\begin{bmatrix} 1 \\ 0 \end{bmatrix}$$

and

$$\begin{bmatrix} 0 \\ 1 \end{bmatrix}$$

from which all vectors in the space can be created. This can be seen from Fig. A.1. (A vector in the [−1,−1] direction would have the opposite direction of the vector shown in Fig. A.1.)

If we had three vectors that were all in the same plane in a three-dimensional (x, y, z) space, then the space they spanned would be less than three-dimensional. For example, the three vectors

$$\begin{bmatrix} 1 \\ 0 \\ 0 \end{bmatrix} \qquad \begin{bmatrix} 0 \\ 1 \\ 0 \end{bmatrix} \qquad \begin{bmatrix} -1 \\ -1 \\ 0 \end{bmatrix}$$

all lie in the same z plane, and span only a two-dimensional space. (All points in the space could be shown in the plane of the paper in Fig. A.1.)

A.2 Application to understanding simple neural networks

The operation of simple one-layer networks can be understood in terms of these concepts.

A.2.1 Capability and limitations of single-layer networks: linear separability and capacity

Single-layer perceptrons perform pattern classification, and can be trained by an associative (Hebb) learning rule or by an error-correction (delta) rule (see Appendix B). That is, each neuron classifies the input patterns it receives into classes determined by the teacher. Single-layer perceptrons are thus supervised networks, with a separate teacher for each output neuron. The classification is most clearly understood if the output neurons are binary, or are strongly non-linear, but the network will still try to obtain an optimal mapping with linear or near-linear output neurons.

When each neuron operates as a binary classifier, we can consider how many input patterns p can be classified by each neuron, and the classes of pattern that can be correctly classified. The result is that the maximum number of patterns that can be correctly classified by a neuron with C inputs is

$$p_{max} = 2C \tag{A.12}$$

when the inputs have random continuous-valued inputs, but the patterns must be linearly separable (see Hertz et al. (1991)). More generally, a network with a single binary unit can implement a classification between two subspaces of a space of possible input patterns provided that the p actual patterns given as examples of the correct classification are linearly separable.

The linear separability requirement can be made clear by considering a geometric interpretation of the logical AND problem, which is linearly separable, and the XOR (exclusive OR) problem, which is not linearly separable. The truth tables for the AND and XOR functions are shown in Table A.2 (there are two inputs, x_1 and x_2, and one output neuron):

Table A.2 Truth table for AND and XOR functions performed by a single output neuron with two inputs. 1 = active or firing; 0 = inactive.

Inputs		Output	
x_1	x_2	AND	XOR
0	0	0	0
1	0	0	1
0	1	0	1
1	1	1	0

For the AND function, we can plot the mapping required in a 2D graph as shown in Fig. A.2. A line can be drawn to separate the input coordinates for which 0 is required as the output from those for which 1 is required as the output. The problem is thus linearly separable. A neuron with two inputs can set its weights to values which draw this line through this space, and such a one-layer network can thus solve the AND function.

For the XOR function, we can plot the mapping required in a 2D graph as shown in Fig. A.3. No straight line can be drawn to separate the input coordinates for which 0 is required as the output from those for which 1 is required as the output. The problem is thus not linearly separable. For a one-layer network, no set of weights can be found that will perform the XOR, or any other non-linearly separable function.

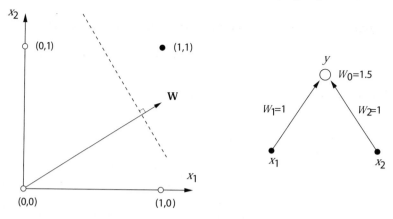

Fig. A.2 Left: the AND function shown in a 2D space. Input values for the two neurons are shown along the two axes of the space. The outputs required are plotted at the coordinates where the inputs intersect, and the values of the output required are shown as an open circle for 0, and a filled circle for 1. The AND function is linearly separable, in that a line can be drawn in the space which separates the coordinates for which 0 output is required from those from which a 1 output is required. **w** shows the direction of the weight vector. Right: a one-layer neural network can set its two weights w_1 and w_2 to values which allow the output neuron to be activated only if both inputs are present. In this diagram, w_0 is used to set a threshold for the neuron, and is connected to an input with value 1. The neuron thus fires only if the threshold of 1.5 is exceeded, which happens only if both inputs to the neuron are 1.

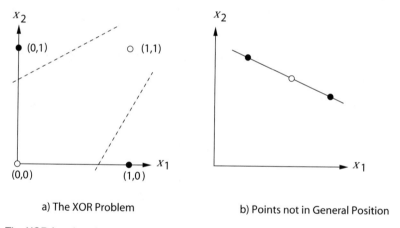

a) The XOR Problem   b) Points not in General Position

Fig. A.3 The XOR function shown in a 2D space. Input values for the two neurons are shown along the two axes of the space. The outputs required are plotted at the coordinates where the inputs intersect, and the values of the output required are shown as an open circle for 0, and a filled circle for 1. The XOR function is not linearly separable, in that a line cannot be drawn in the space to separate the coordinates for those from which a 0 output is required from those from which a 1 output is required. A one-layer neural network cannot set its two weights to values which allow the output neuron to be activated appropriately for the XOR function.

Although the inability of one-layer networks with binary neurons to solve non-linearly separable problems is a limitation, it is not in practice a major limitation on the processing that can be performed in a neural network for a number of reasons. First, if the inputs can take continuous values, then if the patterns are drawn from a random distribution, the one-layer network can map up to $2C$ of them. Second, as described for pattern associators, and for one-layer error-correcting perceptrons (see Appendix B), these networks could be preceded by an expansion recoding network such as a competitive network with more output than input neurons. This effectively provides a two-layer network for solving the problem, and multilayer networks are in general capable of solving arbitrary mapping problems. Ways in which such multilayer networks might be trained are discussed in Chapter 4 and Appendix B.

More generally, a binary output unit provides by its operation a hyperplane (the hyperplane orthogonal to its synaptic weight vector as shown in Fig. A.2) that divides the input space in two. The input space is of dimension C, if C is the number of input axons or connections. A one-layer network with a number n of binary output units is equivalent to n hyperplanes, that could potentially divide the input space into as many as 2^n regions, each corresponding to input patterns leading to a different output. However the number p of *arbitrary* examples of the correct classification (each example consisting of an input pattern and its required correct output) that the network may be able to implement is well below 2^n, and in fact depends on C not on n. This is because for p too large it will be impossible to position the n weight vectors such that all examples of input vectors for which the first output unit is required to be 'on' fall on one side of the hyperplane associated with the first weight vector, all those for which it is required to be 'off' fall on the other side, and simultaneously the same holds with respect to the second output unit (a different dichotomy), the third, and so on. The limit on p, which can be thought of also as the number of independent associations implemented by the network, when this is viewed as a heteroassociator (i.e. pattern associator) with binary outputs, can be calculated with the Gardner method (Gardner 1987, Gardner 1988) and depends on the statistics of the patterns. For input patterns that are also binary, random and with equal probability for each of the two states on every unit, the limit is $p_c = 2C$ (see further Appendix B, and Rolls and Treves (1998) Appendix A3).

A.2.2 Non-linear networks: neurons with non-linear activation functions

These concepts also help one to understand further the limitation of linear systems, and the power of non-linear systems. Consider the dot product operation by which the neuronal activation h is computed:

$$h = \sum_j x_j w_j. \tag{A.13}$$

If the output firing is just a linear function of the activation, any input pattern will produce a non-zero output unless it happens to be exactly orthogonal to the weight vector. For positive-only firing rates and synaptic weights, being orthogonal means taking non-zero values only on non-corresponding components. Since with distributed representations the non-zero components of different input firing vectors will in general be overlapping (i.e. some corresponding components in both firing rate vectors will be on, that is the vectors will overlap), this will result effectively in interference between any two different patterns that for example have to be associated to different outputs. Thus a basic limitation of linear networks is that they can perform pattern association perfectly only if the input patterns x are orthogonal; and for positive-only patterns that represent actual firing rates only if the different firing rate vectors are non-overlapping. Further, linear networks cannot of course perform any classification, just because they act linearly. (Classification implies producing output states that are clearly defined as being in one class, and not in other classes.) For example, in a linear network, if a pattern is presented that is intermediate between two patterns v_1 and v_2, such as $c_1 v_1 + c_2 v_2$, then the output pattern will be a linear combination of the outputs produced by v_1 and v_2 (e.g. $c_1 o_1 + c_2 o_2$), rather than being classified into o_1 or o_2. In contrast, with non-linear neurons, the patterns need not be orthogonal, only linearly separable, for a one-layer network to be able to correctly classify the patterns (provided that a sufficiently powerful learning rule is used – see Appendix B).

The networks just described, and most of those described in this book, are trained with a local learning rule, in which the pre- and post-synaptic terms needed to alter the synaptic weights are available locally in the synapses, in terms for example of the release of transmitter from the presynaptic terminal, and the depolarization of the postsynaptic neuron. This type of network is considered because this is a biologically plausible constraint (see Section B.13). It is much less biologically plausible to use an algorithm such as multilayer error backpropagation which calculates the correction to the value of a synapse that is needed taking into account the values of the errors of the neurons at later stages of the system and the strengths of all the synapses to these neurons (see Section B.12). This use of a local learning rule is a major difference of the networks described in this book, which is directed at neurally plausible computation, from connectionist networks, which typically assume non-local learning rules and which therefore operate very differently from real neural networks in the brain (see Section B.12 and McLeod, Plunkett and Rolls (1998)).

A.2.3 Non-linear networks: neurons with non-linear activations

Most of the networks described in this book calculate the activation h of each neuron as the linear product of the input firing weighted by the synaptic weight vector (see equation A.13). This corresponds in a real neuron to receiving currents from each of its synapses which sum to produce depolarization of the neuronal cell body and the spike initiation region which is located very close to the cell body. This is a reasonable reflection of what does happen in many neurons, especially those with large dendrites such as pyramidal cells (Koch 1999). This calculation of the activation h by a linear summation not only approximates to what happens in many real neurons, but is also a useful simplification which makes tractable the analysis of many classes of network that utilize such neurons. These analyses provide insight into the operation of networks of neurons, even if the linear summation assumption is not perfectly realized. Having computed the activation linearly, the neurons do of course for essentially all the networks described in this book, then utilize a non-linear activation function, which, as described above, provides the networks with much of their interesting computational power. Given that the activation functions of the neurons are non-linear, some non-linearity in the summation expressed in equation A.13 may in practice be lumped into the non-linearity in the activation function.

However, another class of neuron that is implemented in some networks in the brain utilizes non-linearity in the calculation of the activation h of the neuron, which reflects a local product of two inputs to a neuron. This could arise for example if one synapse makes a presynaptic contact with another synapse which in turn connects to the dendrite, or if two synapses are close together on a thin dendrite. In such situations, the current injected into the neuron could reflect the conjoint firing of the two classes of input (Koch 1999). The dendrite as a whole could then sum all such products into the cell body, leading to the description **Sigma-Pi**. This could be expressed by equation A.14

$$h = \sum_j \sum_k w_{jk} x_j x^c_k \qquad (A.14)$$

where x_j is the firing rate of input cell j, x^c_k is the firing rate of input cell k of class c, and w_{jk} is the connection strength. Such Sigma-Pi neurons were utilized in the model described in Section B.5.5 of how idiothetic inputs could update a continuous attractor network. Another possible application is to learning invariant representations in neural networks. For example, the x^c input in equation A.14 could be a signal that varies with the shift required to compute translation invariance, effectively mapping the appropriate set of x_j inputs through to the output neurons depending on the shift required (Mel, Ruderman and Archie 1998, Mel and Fiser 2000, Olshausen, Anderson and Van Essen 1993, Olshausen, Anderson and Van Essen 1995).

To train such a Sigma-Pi network requires that combinations of the two presynaptic inputs to a neuron be learned onto a neuron, using for example associativity with the post-synaptic term y, as exemplified in equation A.15

$$\delta w_{jk} = \alpha y x_j x^c{}_k. \tag{A.15}$$

This learning principle is exemplified in the model described in Section B.5.5 of how idiothetic inputs could update a continuous attractor network to perform path integration.

Sigma-Pi networks are clearly very powerful, but require rather specialized anatomical and biophysical arrangements (see Koch (1999)), and hence we do not use them unless they become very necessary in models of neural network operations in the brain. We have shown that in at least some applications such as path integration, it is possible to replace a Sigma-Pi network with a competitive network followed by a pattern association network (Stringer and Rolls 2006).

Appendix 2 Neural network models

B.1 Introduction

Formal models of neural networks are needed in order to provide a basis for understanding the processing and memory functions performed by real neuronal networks in the brain. The formal models included in this Appendix all describe fundamental types of network found in different brain regions, and the computations they perform. Each of the types of network described can be thought of as providing one of the fundamental building blocks that the brain uses. Often these building blocks are combined within a brain area to perform a particular computation.

The aim of this Appendix is to describe a set of fundamental networks used by the brain, including the parts of the brain involved in memory, attention, decision-making, and the building of perceptual representations. As each type of network is introduced, we will point briefly to parts of the brain in which each network is found. Understanding these models provides a basis for understanding the theories of how different types of memory functions are performed. The descriptions of these networks are kept relatively concise in this Appendix. More detailed descriptions of some of the quantitative aspects of storage in pattern associators and autoassociators are provided in the Appendices of Rolls and Treves (1998) *Neural Networks and Brain Function*. Another book that provides a clear and quantitative introduction to some of these networks is Hertz, Krogh and Palmer (1991) *Introduction to the Theory of Neural Computation*, and other useful sources include Dayan and Abbott (2001), Amit (1989) (for attractor networks), Koch (1999) (for a biophysical approach), Wilson (1999) (on spiking networks), Gerstner and Kistler (2002) (on spiking networks), and Rolls and Deco (2002).

Some of the background to the operation of the types of neuronal network described here, including a brief review of the evidence on neuronal structure and function, and on synaptic plasticity and the rules by which synaptic strength is modified, much based on studies with long-term potentiation, is provided in Chapter 1.

The network models on which we focus in this Appendix utilize a local learning rule, that is a rule for synaptic modification, in which the signals needed to alter the synaptic strength are present in the pre- and post-synaptic neurons. We focus on these networks because use of a local learning rule is biologically plausible. We discuss the issue of biological plausibility of the networks described, and show how they differ from less biologically plausible networks such as multilayer backpropagation of error networks, in Section B.13.

B.2 Pattern association memory

A fundamental operation of most nervous systems is to learn to associate a first stimulus with a second that occurs at about the same time, and to retrieve the second stimulus when the first is presented. The first stimulus might be the sight of food, and the second stimulus the taste of food. After the association has been learned, the sight of food would enable its taste to be retrieved. In classical conditioning, the taste of food might elicit an unconditioned response of

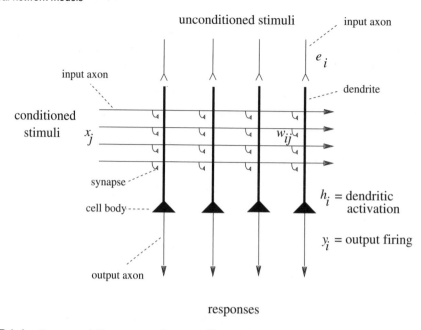

unconditioned stimuli

Fig. B.1 A pattern association memory. An unconditioned stimulus has activity or firing rate e_i for the ith neuron, and produces firing y_i of the ith neuron. An unconditioned stimulus may be treated as a vector, across the set of neurons indexed by i, of activity $\mathbf{e}$. The firing rate response can also be thought of as a vector of firing $\mathbf{y}$. The conditioned stimuli have activity or firing rate x_j for the jth axon, which can also be treated as a vector $\mathbf{x}$.

salivation, and if the sight of the food is paired with its taste, then the sight of that food would by learning come to produce salivation. Pattern associators are thus used where the outputs of the visual system interface to learning systems in the orbitofrontal cortex and amygdala that learn associations between the sight of objects and their taste or touch in stimulus–reinforcer association learning (see Chapter 3). Pattern association is also used throughout the cerebral (neo)cortical areas, as it is the architecture that describes the backprojection connections from one cortical area to the preceding cortical area (see Chapters 1, 2 and 6). Pattern association thus contributes to implementing top-down influences in attention, including the effects of attention from higher to lower cortical areas, and thus between the visual object and spatial processing streams (Rolls and Deco 2002) (see Chapter 6); the effects of mood on memory and visual information processing (see Section 3.11); the recall of visual memories; and the operation of short-term memory systems (see Chapter 5).

B.2.1 Architecture and operation

The essential elements necessary for pattern association, forming what could be called a prototypical pattern associator network, are shown in Fig. B.1. What we have called the second or unconditioned stimulus pattern is applied through unmodifiable synapses generating an input to each neuron, which, being external with respect to the synaptic matrix we focus on, we can call the external input e_i for the ith neuron. [We can also treat this as a vector, $\mathbf{e}$, as indicated in the legend to Fig. B.1. Vectors and simple operations performed with them are summarized in Appendix A. This unconditioned stimulus is dominant in producing or forcing the firing of the output neurons (y_i for the ith neuron, or the vector $\mathbf{y}$)]. At the same time, the first or conditioned stimulus pattern consisting of the set of firings on the horizontally running input axons in Fig. B.1 (x_j for the jth axon) (or equivalently the vector **x**) is applied through modifiable synapses w_{ij} to the dendrites of the output neurons. The synapses are modifiable in such a way that if there is presynaptic firing on an input axon x_j paired during learning with postsynaptic activity on neuron i, then the strength or weight w_{ij} between that axon and the dendrite increases. This simple learning rule is often called the Hebb rule, after Donald Hebb who in 1949 formulated the hypothesis that if the firing of one neuron was regularly associated with another, then the strength of the synapse or synapses between the neurons should increase[38]. After learning, presenting the pattern **x** on the input axons will activate the dendrite through the strengthened synapses. If the cue or conditioned stimulus pattern is the same as that learned, the postsynaptic neurons will be activated, even in the absence of the external or unconditioned input, as each of the firing axons produces through a strengthened synapse some activation of the postsynaptic element, the dendrite. The total activation h_i of each postsynaptic neuron i is then the sum of such individual activations. In this way, the 'correct' output neurons, that is those activated during learning, can end up being the ones most strongly activated, and the second or unconditioned stimulus can be effectively recalled. The recall is best when only strong activation of the postsynaptic neuron produces firing, that is if there is a threshold for firing, just like real neurons. The advantages of this are evident when many associations are stored in the memory, as will soon be shown.

Next we introduce a more precise description of the above by writing down explicit mathematical rules for the operation of the simple network model of Fig. B.1, which will help us to understand how pattern association memories in general operate. (In this description we introduce simple vector operations, and, for those who are not familiar with these, refer the reader to for example Appendix 1 of Rolls and Deco (2002).) We have denoted above a conditioned stimulus input pattern as **x**. Each of the axons has a firing rate, and if we count or index through the axons using the subscript j, the firing rate of the first axon is x_1, of the second x_2, of the jth x_j, etc. The whole set of axons forms a vector, which is just an ordered (1, 2, 3, etc.) set of elements. The firing rate of each axon x_j is one element of the firing rate vector **x**. Similarly, using i as the index, we can denote the firing rate of any output neuron as y_i, and the firing rate output vector as **y**. With this terminology, we can then identify any synapse onto neuron i from neuron j as w_{ij} (see Fig. B.1). In this book, the first index, i, always refers to the receiving neuron (and thus signifies a dendrite), while the second index, j, refers to the sending neuron (and thus signifies a conditioned stimulus input axon in Fig. B.1). We can now specify the learning and retrieval operations as follows:

B.2.1.1 Learning

The firing rate of every output neuron is forced to a value determined by the unconditioned (or external or forcing stimulus) input e_i. In our simple model this means that for any one neuron i,

$$y_i = \mathrm{f}(e_i) \tag{B.1}$$

which indicates that the firing rate is a function of the dendritic activation, taken in this case to reduce essentially to that resulting from the external forcing input (see Fig. B.1). The function f is called the activation function (see Fig. 1.3), and its precise form is irrelevant, at least during this learning phase. For example, the function at its simplest could be taken to be linear, so that the firing rate would be just proportional to the activation.

---

[38] In fact, the terms in which Hebb put the hypothesis were a little different from an association memory, in that he stated that if one neuron regularly comes to elicit firing in another, then the strength of the synapses should increase. He had in mind the building of what he called cell assemblies. In a pattern associator, the conditioned stimulus need not produce before learning any significant activation of the output neurons. The connection strengths must simply increase if there is associated pre- and postsynaptic firing when, in pattern association, most of the postsynaptic firing is being produced by a different input.

The Hebb rule can then be written as follows:

$$\delta w_{ij} = \alpha y_i x_j \tag{B.2}$$

where δw_{ij} is the change of the synaptic weight w_{ij} that results from the simultaneous (or conjunctive) presence of presynaptic firing x_j and postsynaptic firing or activation y_i, and α is a learning rate constant that specifies how much the synapses alter on any one pairing.

The Hebb rule is expressed in this multiplicative form to reflect the idea that both pre-synaptic and postsynaptic activity must be present for the synapses to increase in strength. The multiplicative form also reflects the idea that strong pre- and postsynaptic firing will produce a larger change of synaptic weight than smaller firing rates. It is also assumed for now that before any learning takes place, the synaptic strengths are small in relation to the changes that can be produced during Hebbian learning. We will see that this assumption can be relaxed later when a modified Hebb rule is introduced that can lead to a reduction in synaptic strength under some conditions.

B.2.1.2 Recall

When the conditioned stimulus is present on the input axons, the total activation h_i of a neuron i is the sum of all the activations produced through each strengthened synapse w_{ij} by each active neuron x_j. We can express this as

$$h_i = \sum_{j=1}^{C} x_j w_{ij} \tag{B.3}$$

where $\sum_{j=1}^{C}$ indicates that the sum is over the C input axons (or connections) indexed by j to each neuron.

The multiplicative form here indicates that activation should be produced by an axon only if it is firing, and only if it is connected to the dendrite by a strengthened synapse. It also indicates that the strength of the activation reflects how fast the axon x_j is firing, and how strong the synapse w_{ij} is. The sum of all such activations expresses the idea that summation (of synaptic currents in real neurons) occurs along the length of the dendrite, to produce activation at the cell body, where the activation h_i is converted into firing y_i. This conversion can be expressed as

$$y_i = f(h_i) \tag{B.4}$$

where the function f is again the activation function. The form of the function now becomes more important. Real neurons have thresholds, with firing occurring only if the activation is above the threshold. A threshold linear activation function is shown in Fig. 1.3b on page 6. This has been useful in formal analysis of the properties of neural networks. Neurons also have firing rates that become saturated at a maximum rate, and we could express this as the sigmoid activation function shown in Fig. 1.3c. Yet another simple activation function, used in some models of neural networks, is the binary threshold function (Fig. 1.3d), which indicates that if the activation is below threshold, there is no firing, and that if the activation is above threshold, the neuron fires maximally. Whatever the exact shape of the activation function, some non-linearity is an advantage, for it enables small activations produced by interfering memories to be minimized, and it can enable neurons to perform logical operations, such as to fire or respond only if two or more sets of inputs are present simultaneously.

B.2.2 A simple model

An example of these learning and recall operations is provided in a simple form as follows. The neurons will have simple firing rates, which can be 0 to represent no activity, and 1 to indicate high firing. They are thus binary neurons, which can assume one of two firing rates. If we have a pattern associator with six input axons and four output neurons, we could represent the network before learning, with the same layout as in Fig. B.1, as shown in Fig. B.2:

```
              U  C  S
              1  1  0  0
              ↓  ↓  ↓  ↓
      CS
      1 →     0  0  0  0
      0 →     0  0  0  0
      1 →     0  0  0  0
      0 →     0  0  0  0
      1 →     0  0  0  0
      0 →     0  0  0  0
```

Fig. B.2 Pattern association: before synaptic modification. The unconditioned stimulus (UCS) firing rates are shown as 1 if high and 0 if low as a row vector being applied to force firing of the four output neurons. The six conditioned stimulus (CS) firing rates are shown as a column vector being applied to the vertical dendrites of the output neurons which have initial synaptic weights of 0.

where $\mathbf{x}$ or the conditioned stimulus (CS) is 101010, and $\mathbf{y}$ or the firing produced by the unconditioned stimulus (UCS) is 1100. (The arrows indicate the flow of signals.) The synaptic weights are initially all 0.

After pairing the CS with the UCS during one learning trial, some of the synaptic weights will be incremented according to equation B.2, so that after learning this pair the synaptic weights will become as shown in Fig. B.3:

```
              U  C  S
              1  1  0  0
              ↓  ↓  ↓  ↓
      CS
      1 →     1  1  0  0
      0 →     0  0  0  0
      1 →     1  1  0  0
      0 →     0  0  0  0
      1 →     1  1  0  0
      0 →     0  0  0  0
```

Fig. B.3 Pattern association: after synaptic modification. The synapses where there is conjunctive pre- and post-synaptic activity have been strengthened to value 1.

We can represent what happens during recall, when, for example, we present the CS that has been learned, as shown in Fig. B.4:

```
CS
1 →    1  1  0  0
0 →    0  0  0  0
1 →    1  1  0  0
0 →    0  0  0  0
1 →    1  1  0  0
0 →    0  0  0  0
       ↓  ↓  ↓  ↓

       3  3  0  0 Activation hᵢ
       1  1  0  0 Firing yᵢ
```

Fig. B.4 Pattern association: recall. The activation h_i of each neuron i is converted with a threshold of 2 to the binary firing rate y_i (1 for high, and 0 for low).

The activation of the four output neurons is 3300, and if we set the threshold of each output neuron to 2, then the output firing is 1100 (where the binary firing rate is 0 if below threshold, and 1 if above). The pattern associator has thus achieved recall of the pattern 1100, which is correct.

We can now illustrate how a number of different associations can be stored in such a pattern associator, and retrieved correctly. Let us associate a new CS pattern 110001 with the UCS 0101 in the same pattern associator. The weights will become as shown next in Fig. B.5 after learning:

```
            U  C  S
            0  1  0  1
            ↓  ↓  ↓  ↓
   CS
   1 →      1  2  0  1
   1 →      0  1  0  1
   0 →      1  1  0  0
   0 →      0  0  0  0
   0 →      1  1  0  0
   1 →      0  1  0  1
```

Fig. B.5 Pattern association: synaptic weights after learning a second pattern association.

If we now present the second CS, the retrieval is as shown in Fig. B.6:

```
CS
1 →    1  2  0  1
1 →    0  1  0  1
0 →    1  1  0  0
0 →    0  0  0  0
0 →    1  1  0  0
1 →    0  1  0  1
       ↓  ↓  ↓  ↓

       1  4  0  3  Activation hᵢ
       0  1  0  1  Firing yᵢ
```

The Activation row reads $1\ 4\ 0\ 3$ Activation h_i and the Firing row reads $0\ 1\ 0\ 1$ Firing y_i.

Fig. B.6 Pattern association: recall with the second CS.

The binary output firings were again produced with the threshold set to 2. Recall is perfect.

This illustration shows the value of some threshold non-linearity in the activation function of the neurons. In this case, the activations did reflect some small cross-talk or interference from the previous pattern association of CS1 with UCS1, but this was removed by the threshold operation, to clean up the recall firing. The example also shows that when further associations are learned by a pattern associator trained with the Hebb rule, equation B.2, some synapses will reflect increments above a synaptic strength of 1. It is left as an exercise to the reader to verify that recall is still perfect to CS1, the vector 101010. (The activation vector **h** is 3401, and the output firing vector **y** with the same threshold of 2 is 1100, which is perfect recall.)

B.2.3 The vector interpretation

The way in which recall is produced, equation B.3, consists for each output neuron i of multiplying each input firing rate x_j by the corresponding synaptic weight w_{ij} and summing the products to obtain the activation h_i. Now we can consider the firing rates x_j where j varies from 1 to N', the number of axons, to be a vector. (A vector is simply an ordered set of numbers – see Appendix A.) Let us call this vector **x**. Similarly, on a neuron i, the synaptic weights can be treated as a vector, $\mathbf{w}_i$. (The subscript i here indicates that this is the weight vector on the ith neuron.) The operation we have just described to obtain the activation of an output neuron can now be seen to be a simple multiplication operation of two vectors to produce a single output value (called a scalar output). This is the inner product or dot product of two vectors, and can be written

$$h_i = \mathbf{x} \cdot \mathbf{w}_i. \tag{B.5}$$

The inner product of two vectors indicates how similar they are. If two vectors have corresponding elements the same, then the dot product will be maximal. If the two vectors are similar but not identical, then the dot product will be high. If the two vectors are completely different, the dot product will be 0, and the vectors are described as orthogonal. (The term orthogonal means at right angles, and arises from the geometric interpretation of vectors, which is summarized in Appendix A.) Thus the dot product provides a direct measure of how similar two vectors are.

It can now be seen that a fundamental operation many neurons perform is effectively to compute how similar an input pattern vector **x** is to their stored weight vector $\mathbf{w}_i$. The similarity measure they compute, the dot product, is a very good measure of similarity, and indeed, the standard (Pearson product–moment) correlation coefficient used in statistics is the same as a normalized dot product with the mean subtracted from each vector, as shown in Appendix A. (The normalization used in the correlation coefficient results in the coefficient varying always between $+1$ and -1, whereas the actual scalar value of a dot product clearly depends on the length of the vectors from which it is calculated.)

With these concepts, we can now see that during learning, a pattern associator adds to its weight vector a vector δw_i that has the same pattern as the input pattern x, if the postsynaptic neuron i is strongly activated. Indeed, we can express equation B.2 in vector form as

$$\delta w_i = \alpha y_i x. \tag{B.6}$$

We can now see that what is recalled by the neuron depends on the similarity of the recall cue vector x_r to the originally learned vector x. The fact that during recall the output of each neuron reflects the similarity (as measured by the dot product) of the input pattern x_r to each of the patterns used originally as x inputs (conditioned stimuli in Fig. B.1) provides a simple way to appreciate many of the interesting and biologically useful properties of pattern associators, as described next.

B.2.4 Properties

B.2.4.1 Generalization

During recall, pattern associators generalize, and produce appropriate outputs if a recall cue vector x_r is similar to a vector that has been learned already. This occurs because the recall operation involves computing the dot (inner) product of the input pattern vector x_r with the synaptic weight vector w_i, so that the firing produced, y_i, reflects the similarity of the current input to the previously learned input pattern x. (Generalization will occur to input cue or conditioned stimulus patterns x_r that are incomplete versions of an original conditioned stimulus x, although the term completion is usually applied to the autoassociation networks described in Section B.3.)

This is an extremely important property of pattern associators, for input stimuli during recall will rarely be absolutely identical to what has been learned previously, and automatic generalization to similar stimuli is extremely useful, and has great adaptive value in biological systems.

Generalization can be illustrated with the simple binary pattern associator considered above. (Those who have appreciated the vector description just given might wish to skip this illustration.) Instead of the second CS, pattern vector 110001, we will use the similar recall cue 110100, as shown in Fig. B.7:

```
CS
1 →    1  2  0  1
1 →    0  1  0  1
0 →    1  1  0  0
1 →    0  0  0  0
0 →    1  1  0  0
0 →    0  1  0  1
       ↓  ↓  ↓  ↓

       1  3  0  2  Activation hᵢ
       0  1  0  1  Firing yᵢ
```

$$1 \quad 3 \quad 0 \quad 2 \quad \text{Activation } h_i$$
$$0 \quad 1 \quad 0 \quad 1 \quad \text{Firing } y_i$$

Fig. B.7 Pattern association: generalization using an input vector similar to the second CS.

It is seen that the output firing rate vector, 0101, is exactly what should be recalled to CS2 (and not to CS1), so correct generalization has occurred. Although this is a small network trained with few examples, the same properties hold for large networks with large numbers of stored patterns, as described more quantitatively in Section B.2.7.1 on capacity below and in Appendix A3 of Rolls and Treves (1998).

B.2.4.2   Graceful degradation or fault tolerance

If the synaptic weight vector $\mathbf{w}_i$ (or the weight matrix, which we can call $\mathbf{W}$) has synapses missing (e.g. during development), or loses synapses, then the activation h_i or $\mathbf{h}$ is still reasonable, because h_i is the dot product (correlation) of $\mathbf{x}$ with $\mathbf{w}_i$. The result, especially after passing through the activation function, can frequently be perfect recall. The same property arises if for example one or some of the conditioned stimulus (CS) input axons are lost or damaged. This is a very important property of associative memories, and is not a property of conventional computer memories, which produce incorrect data if even only 1 storage location (for 1 bit or binary digit of data) of their memory is damaged or cannot be accessed. This property of graceful degradation is of great adaptive value for biological systems.

We can illustrate this with a simple example. If we damage two of the synapses in Fig. B.6 to produce the synaptic matrix shown in Fig. B.8 (where x indicates a damaged synapse which has no effect, but was previously 1), and now present the second CS, the retrieval is as follows:

```
CS
1 →    1  2  0  1
1 →    0  1  0  x
0 →    1  1  0  0
0 →    0  0  0  0
0 →    1  x  0  0
1 →    0  1  0  1
       ↓  ↓  ↓  ↓

       1  4  0  2  Activation hᵢ
       0  1  0  1  Firing yᵢ
```

$$1 \quad 4 \quad 0 \quad 2 \quad \text{Activation } h_i$$
$$0 \quad 1 \quad 0 \quad 1 \quad \text{Firing } y_i$$

Fig. B.8 Pattern association: graceful degradation when some synapses are damaged (x).

The binary output firings were again produced with the threshold set to 2. The recalled vector, 0101, is perfect. This illustration again shows the value of some threshold non-linearity in the activation function of the neurons. It is left as an exercise to the reader to verify that recall is still perfect to CS1, the vector 101010. (The output activation vector **h** is 3301, and the output firing vector **y** with the same threshold of 2 is 1100, which is perfect recall.)

B.2.4.3 The importance of distributed representations for pattern associators

A distributed representation is one in which the firing or activity of all the elements in the vector is used to encode a particular stimulus. For example, in a conditioned stimulus vector CS1 that has the value 101010, we need to know the state of all the elements to know which stimulus is being represented. Another stimulus, CS2, is represented by the vector 110001. We can represent many different events or stimuli with such overlapping sets of elements, and because in general any one element cannot be used to identify the stimulus, but instead the information about which stimulus is present is distributed over the population of elements or neurons, this is called a distributed representation (see Section 1.6). If, for binary neurons, half the neurons are in one state (e.g. 0), and the other half are in the other state (e.g. 1), then the representation is described as fully distributed. The CS representations above are thus fully distributed. If only a smaller proportion of the neurons is active to represent a stimulus, as in the vector 100001, then this is a sparse representation. For binary representations, we can quantify the sparseness by the proportion of neurons in the active (1) state.

In contrast, a local representation is one in which all the information that a particular stimulus or event has occurred is provided by the activity of one of the neurons, or elements in the vector. One stimulus might be represented by the vector 100000, another stimulus by the vector 010000, and a third stimulus by the vector 001000. The activity of neuron or element 1 would indicate that stimulus 1 was present, and of neuron 2, that stimulus 2 was present. The representation is local in that if a particular neuron is active, we know that the stimulus represented by that neuron is present. In neurophysiology, if such cells were present, they might be called 'grandmother cells' (cf. Barlow (1972), (1995)), in that one neuron might represent a stimulus in the environment as complex and specific as one's grandmother. Where the activity of a number of cells must be taken into account in order to represent a stimulus (such as an individual taste), then the representation is sometimes described as using ensemble encoding.

The properties just described for associative memories, generalization, and graceful degradation are only implemented if the representation of the CS or **x** vector is distributed. This occurs because the recall operation involves computing the dot (inner) product of the input pattern vector $\mathbf{x}_r$ with the synaptic weight vector $\mathbf{w}_i$. This allows the activation h_i to reflect the similarity of the current input pattern to a previously learned input pattern **x** only if several or many elements of the **x** and $\mathbf{x}_r$ vectors are in the active state to represent a pattern. If local encoding were used, e.g. 100000, then if the first element of the vector (which might be the firing of axon 1, i.e. x_1, or the strength of synapse $i1$, w_{i1}) is lost, the resulting vector is not similar to any other CS vector, and the activation is 0. In the case of local encoding, the important properties of associative memories, generalization and graceful degradation do not thus emerge. Graceful degradation and generalization are dependent on distributed representations, for then the dot product can reflect similarity even when some elements of the vectors involved are altered. If we think of the correlation between Y and X in a graph, then this correlation is affected only a little if a few X, Y pairs of data are lost (see Appendix A).

B.2.5 Prototype extraction, extraction of central tendency, and noise reduction

If a set of similar conditioned stimulus vectors $\mathbf{x}$ are paired with the same unconditioned stimulus e_i, the weight vector $\mathbf{w}_i$ becomes (or points towards) the sum (or with scaling, the average) of the set of similar vectors $\mathbf{x}$. This follows from the operation of the Hebb rule in equation B.2. When tested at recall, the output of the memory is then best to the average input pattern vector denoted $< \mathbf{x} >$. If the average is thought of as a prototype, then even though the prototype vector $< \mathbf{x} >$ itself may never have been seen, the best output of the neuron or network is to the prototype. This produces 'extraction of the prototype' or 'central tendency'. The same phenomenon is a feature of human memory performance (see McClelland and Rumelhart (1986) Chapter 17), and this simple process with distributed representations in a neural network accounts for the psychological phenomenon.

If the different exemplars of the vector $\mathbf{x}$ are thought of as noisy versions of the true input pattern vector $< \mathbf{x} >$ (with incorrect values for some of the elements), then the pattern associator has performed 'noise reduction', in that the output produced by any one of these vectors will represent the output produced by the true, noiseless, average vector $< \mathbf{x} >$.

B.2.6 Speed

Recall is very fast in a real neuronal network, because the conditioned stimulus input firings x_j ($j = 1, C$ axons) can be applied simultaneously to the synapses w_{ij}, and the activation h_i can be accumulated in one or two time constants of the dendrite (e.g. 10–20 ms). Whenever the threshold of the cell is exceeded, it fires. Thus, in effectively one step, which takes the brain no more than 10–20 ms, all the output neurons of the pattern associator can be firing with rates that reflect the input firing of every axon. This is very different from a conventional digital computer, in which computing h_i in equation B.3 would involve C multiplication and addition operations occurring one after another, or $2C$ time steps.

The brain performs parallel computation in at least two senses in even a pattern associator. One is that for a single neuron, the separate contributions of the firing rate x_j of each axon j multiplied by the synaptic weight w_{ij} are computed in parallel and added in the same timestep. The second is that this can be performed in parallel for all neurons $i = 1, N$ in the network, where there are N output neurons in the network. It is these types of parallel and time-continuous (see Section B.6) processing that enable these classes of neuronal network in the brain to operate so fast, in effectively so few steps.

Learning is also fast ('one-shot') in pattern associators, in that a single pairing of the conditioned stimulus $\mathbf{x}$ and the unconditioned stimulus (UCS) $\mathbf{e}$ which produces the unconditioned output firing $\mathbf{y}$ enables the association to be learned. There is no need to repeat the pairing in order to discover over many trials the appropriate mapping. This is extremely important for biological systems, in which a single co-occurrence of two events may lead to learning that could have life-saving consequences. (For example, the pairing of a visual stimulus with a potentially life-threatening aversive event may enable that event to be avoided in future.) Although repeated pairing with small variations of the vectors is used to obtain the useful properties of prototype extraction, extraction of central tendency, and noise reduction, the essential properties of generalization and graceful degradation are obtained with just one pairing. The actual time scales of the learning in the brain are indicated by studies of associative synaptic modification using long-term potentiation paradigms (LTP, see Section 1.5). Co-occurrence or near simultaneity of the CS and UCS is required for periods of as little as 100 ms, with expression of the synaptic modification being present within typically a few seconds.

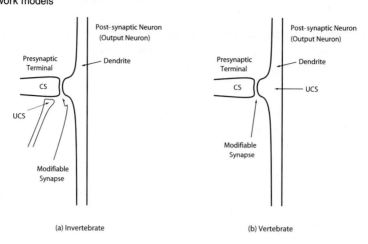

(a) Invertebrate   (b) Vertebrate

Fig. B.9 (b) In vertebrate pattern association learning, the unconditioned stimulus (UCS) may be made available at all the conditioned stimulus (CS) terminals onto the output neuron because the dendrite of the postsynaptic neuron is electrically short, so that the effect of the UCS spreads for long distances along the dendrite. (a) In contrast, in at least some invertebrate association learning systems, the unconditioned stimulus or teaching input makes a synapse onto the presynaptic terminal carrying the conditioned stimulus.

B.2.7 Local learning rule

The simplest learning rule used in pattern association neural networks, a version of the Hebb rule, is, as shown in equation B.2 above,

$$\delta w_{ij} = \alpha y_i x_j.$$

This is a local learning rule in that the information required to specify the change in synaptic weight is available locally at the synapse, as it is dependent only on the presynaptic firing rate x_j available at the synaptic terminal, and the postsynaptic activation or firing y_i available on the dendrite of the neuron receiving the synapse (see Fig. B.9b). This makes the learning rule biologically plausible, in that the information about how to change the synaptic weight does not have to be carried from a distant source, where it is computed, to every synapse. Such a non-local learning rule would not be biologically plausible, in that there are no appropriate connections known in most parts of the brain to bring in the synaptic training or teacher signal to every synapse.

Evidence that a learning rule with the general form of equation B.2 is implemented in at least some parts of the brain comes from studies of long-term potentiation, described in Section 1.5. Long-term potentiation (LTP) has the synaptic specificity defined by equation B.2, in that only synapses from active afferents, not those from inactive afferents, become strengthened. Synaptic specificity is important for a pattern associator, and most other types of neuronal network, to operate correctly. The number of independently modifiable synapses on each neuron is a primary factor in determining how many different memory patterns can be stored in associative memories (see Sections B.2.7.1 and B.3.3.7).

Another useful property of real neurons in relation to equation B.2 is that the postsynaptic term, y_i, is available on much of the dendrite of a cell, because the electrotonic length of the dendrite is short. In addition, active propagation of spiking activity from the cell body along the dendrite may help to provide a uniform postsynaptic term for the learning. Thus if a neuron is strongly activated with a high value for y_i, then any active synapse onto the cell will be capable of being modified. This enables the cell to learn an association between the pattern of activity on all its axons and its postsynaptic activation, which is stored as an addition to its weight vector $\mathbf{w}_i$. Then later on, at recall, the output can be produced as a vector dot product operation between the input pattern vector $\mathbf{x}$ and the weight vector $\mathbf{w}_i$, so that the output of the cell can reflect the correlation between the current input vector and what has previously been learned by the cell.

It is interesting that at least many invertebrate neuronal systems may operate very differently from those described here, as described by Rolls and Treves (1998) (see Fig. B.9a). If there were 5,000 conditioned stimulus inputs to a neuron, the implication is that every one would need to have a presynaptic terminal conveying the same UCS to each presynaptic terminal, which is hardly plausible. The implication is that at least some invertebrate neural systems operate very differently to those in vertebrates and, in such systems, the useful properties that arise from using distributed CS representations such as generalization would not arise in the same simple way as a property of the network.

B.2.7.1 Capacity

The question of the storage capacity of a pattern associator is considered in detail in Appendix A3 of Rolls and Treves (1998). It is pointed out there that, for this type of associative network, the number of memories that it can hold simultaneously in storage has to be analysed together with the retrieval quality of each output representation, and then only for a given quality of the representation provided in the input. This is in contrast to autoassociative nets (Section B.3), in which a critical number of stored memories exists (as a function of various parameters of the network), beyond which attempting to store additional memories results in it becoming impossible to retrieve essentially anything. With a pattern associator, instead, one will always retrieve something, but this something will be very small (in information or correlation terms) if too many associations are simultaneously in storage and/or if too little is provided as input.

The conjoint quality–capacity input analysis can be carried out, for any specific instance of a pattern associator, by using formal mathematical models and established analytical procedures (see e.g. Treves (1995), Rolls and Treves (1998), Treves (1990) and Rolls and Treves (1990)). This, however, has to be done case by case. It is anyway useful to develop some intuition for how a pattern associator operates, by considering what its capacity would be in certain well-defined simplified cases.

Linear associative neuronal networks These networks are made up of units with a linear activation function, which appears to make them unsuitable to represent real neurons with their positive-only firing rates. However, even purely linear units have been considered as provisionally relevant models of real neurons, by assuming that the latter operate sometimes in the linear regime of their transfer function. (This implies a high level of spontaneous activity, and may be closer to conditions observed early on in sensory systems rather than in areas more specifically involved in memory.) As usual, the connections are trained by a Hebb (or similar) associative learning rule. The capacity of these networks can be defined as the total number of associations that can be learned independently of each other, given that the linear nature of these systems prevents anything more than a linear transform of the inputs. This implies that if input pattern C can be written as the weighted sum of input patterns A and B, the output to C will be just the same weighted sum of the outputs to A and B. If there are N' input axons, then there can be only at most N' mutually independent input patterns (i.e. none able to be written as a weighted sum of the others), and therefore the capacity of linear networks, defined above, is just N', or equal to the number of inputs to each neuron. In general, a random set of less than N' vectors (the CS input pattern vectors) will tend to be mutually independent but not mutually orthogonal (at 90 deg to each other) (see Appendix A). If they are not orthogonal (the normal situation), then the dot product of them is not 0, and the output pattern activated by one of the input vectors will be partially activated by other input pattern vectors, in accordance with how similar they are (see equations B.5 and B.6). This amounts to interference, which is therefore the more serious the less orthogonal, on the whole, is the set of input vectors.

Since input patterns are made of elements with positive values, if a simple Hebbian learning rule like the one of equation B.2 is used (in which the input pattern enters directly with no subtraction term), the output resulting from the application of a stored input vector will be the sum of contributions from all other input vectors that have a non-zero dot product with it (see Appendix A), and interference will be disastrous. The only situation in which this would not occur is when different input patterns activate completely different input lines, but this is clearly an uninteresting circumstance for networks operating with distributed representations. A solution to this issue is to use a modified learning rule of the following form:

$$\delta w_{ij} = \alpha y_i (x_j - x) \tag{B.7}$$

where x is a constant, approximately equal to the average value of x_j. This learning rule includes (in proportion to y_i) increasing the synaptic weight if $(x_j - x) > 0$ (long-term potentiation), and decreasing the synaptic weight if $(x_j - x) < 0$ (heterosynaptic long-term depression). It is useful for x to be roughly the average activity of an input axon x_j across patterns, because then the dot product between the various patterns stored on the weights and the input vector will tend to cancel out with the subtractive term, except for the pattern equal to (or correlated with) the input vector itself. Then up to N' input vectors can still be learned by the network, with only minor interference (provided of course that they are mutually independent, as they will in general tend to be).

Table B.1 Effects of pre- and post-synaptic activity on synaptic modification

		Post-synaptic activation	
		0	high
	0	No change	Heterosynaptic LTD
Presynaptic firing			
	high	Homosynaptic LTD	LTP

This modified learning rule can also be described in terms of a contingency table (Table B.1) showing the synaptic strength modifications produced by different types of learning rule, where LTP indicates an increase in synaptic strength (called long-term potentiation in neurophysiology), and LTD indicates a decrease in synaptic strength (called long-term depression in neurophysiology). Heterosynaptic long-term depression is so-called because it is the decrease in synaptic strength that occurs to a synapse that is other than that through which the postsynaptic cell is being activated. This heterosynaptic long-term depression is the type of change of synaptic strength that is required (in addition to LTP) for effective subtraction of the average presynaptic firing rate, in order, as it were, to make the CS vectors appear more orthogonal to the pattern associator. The rule is sometimes called the Singer–Stent rule, after work by Singer (1987) and Stent (1973), and was discovered in the brain by Levy (Levy 1985, Levy and Desmond 1985) (see also Brown, Kairiss and Keenan (1990b)). Homosynaptic long-term depression is so-called because it is the decrease in synaptic strength that occurs to a synapse which is (the same as that which is) active. For it to occur, the postsynaptic neuron must simultaneously be inactive, or have only low activity. (This rule is sometimes called the BCM rule after the paper of Bienenstock, Cooper and Munro (1982); see Rolls and Deco (2002), Chapter 7).

Associative neuronal networks with non-linear neurons With non-linear neurons, that is with at least a threshold in the activation function so that the output firing y_i is 0 when the activation h_i is below the threshold, the capacity can be measured in terms of the number of different clusters of output pattern vectors that the network produces. This is because the non-linearities now present (one per output neuron) result in some clustering of the outputs produced by all possible (conditioned stimulus) input patterns $\mathbf{x}$. Input patterns that are similar to a stored input vector can produce, due to the non-linearities, output patterns even closer to the stored output; and vice versa, sufficiently dissimilar inputs can be assigned to different output clusters thereby increasing their mutual dissimilarity. As with the linear counterpart, in order to remove the correlation that would otherwise occur between the patterns because the elements can take only positive values, it is useful to use a modified Hebb rule of the form shown in equation B.7.

With fully distributed output patterns, the number p of associations that leads to different clusters is of order C, the number of input lines (axons) per output neuron (that is, of order N' for a fully connected network), as shown in Appendix A3 of Rolls and Treves (1998). If sparse patterns are used in the output, or alternatively if the learning rule includes a non-linear postsynaptic factor that is effectively equivalent to using sparse output patterns, the coefficient of proportionality between p and C can be much higher than one, that is, many more patterns can be stored than inputs onto each output neuron (see Appendix A3 of Rolls and Treves (1998)). Indeed, the number of different patterns or prototypes p that can be stored can be derived for example in the case of binary units (Gardner 1988) to be

$$p \approx C/[a_o log(1/a_o)] \tag{B.8}$$

where a_o is the sparseness of the output firing pattern $\mathbf{y}$ produced by the unconditioned stimulus. p can in this situation be much larger than C (see Appendix A3 of Rolls and Treves (1998), Rolls and Treves (1990) and Treves (1990)). This is an important result for encoding in pattern associators, for it means that provided that the activation functions are non-linear (which is the case with real neurons), there is a very great advantage to using sparse encoding, for then many more than C pattern associations can be stored. Sparse representations may well be present in brain regions involved in associative memory for this reason (see Appendix C).

The non-linearity inherent in the NMDA receptor-based Hebbian plasticity present in the brain may help to make the stored patterns more sparse than the input patterns, and this may be especially beneficial in increasing the storage capacity of associative networks in the brain by allowing participation in the storage of especially those relatively few neurons with high firing rates in the exponential firing rate distributions typical of neurons in sensory systems (see Appendix C).

B.2.7.2   Interference

Interference occurs in linear pattern associators if two vectors are not orthogonal, and is simply dependent on the angle between the originally learned vector and the recall cue or CS vector (see Appendix A), for the activation of the output neuron depends simply on the dot product of the recall vector and the synaptic weight vector (equation B.5). Also in non-linear pattern associators (the interesting case for all practical purposes), interference may occur if two CS patterns are not orthogonal, though the effect can be controlled with sparse encoding of the UCS patterns, effectively by setting high thresholds for the firing of output units. In

Input A	1	0	1
Input B	0	1	1
Required Output	1	1	0

Fig. B.10 A non-linearly separable mapping.

other words, the CS vectors need not be strictly orthogonal, but if they are too similar, some interference will still be likely to occur.

The fact that interference is a property of neural network pattern associator memories is of interest, for interference is a major property of human memory. Indeed, the fact that interference is a property of human memory and of neural network association memories is entirely consistent with the hypothesis that human memory is stored in associative memories of the type described here, or at least that network associative memories of the type described represent a useful exemplar of the class of parallel distributed storage network used in human memory.

It may also be suggested that one reason that interference is tolerated in biological memory is that it is associated with the ability to generalize between stimuli, which is an invaluable feature of biological network associative memories, in that it allows the memory to cope with stimuli that will almost never be identical on different occasions, and in that it allows useful analogies that have survival value to be made.

B.2.7.3 Expansion recoding

If patterns are too similar to be stored in associative memories, then one solution that the brain seems to use repeatedly is to expand the encoding to a form in which the different stimulus patterns are less correlated, that is, more orthogonal, before they are presented as CS stimuli to a pattern associator. The problem can be highlighted by a non-linearly separable mapping (which captures part of the eXclusive OR (XOR) problem), in which the mapping that is desired is as shown in Fig. B.10. The neuron has two inputs, A and B.

This is a mapping of patterns that is impossible for a one-layer network, because the patterns are not linearly separable[39]. A solution is to remap the two input lines A and B to three input lines 1–3, that is to use expansion recoding, as shown in Fig. B.11. This can be performed by a competitive network (see Section B.4). The synaptic weights on the dendrite of the output neuron could then learn the following values using a simple Hebb rule, equation B.2, and the problem could be solved as in Fig. B.12. The whole network would look like that shown in Fig. B.11.

Rolls and Treves (1998) show that competitive networks could help with this type of recoding, and could provide very useful preprocessing for a pattern associator in the brain. It is possible that the lateral nucleus of the amygdala performs this function, for it receives inputs from the temporal cortical visual areas, and may preprocess them before they become the inputs to associative networks at the next stage of amygdala processing (see Fig. 3.41). The granule cells of the cerebellum may operate similarly (see Rolls and Treves (1998)).

---

[39] See Appendix A. There is no set of synaptic weights in a one-layer net that could solve the problem shown in Fig. B.10. Two classes of patterns are not linearly separable if no hyperplane can be positioned in their N-dimensional space so as to separate them (see Appendix A). The XOR problem has the additional constraint that $A = 0, B = 0$ must be mapped to Output = 0.

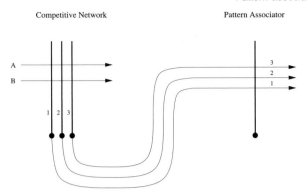

Fig. B.11 Expansion recoding. A competitive network followed by a pattern associator that can enable patterns that are not linearly separable to be learned correctly.

	Synaptic weight
Input 1 (A=1, B=0)	1
Input 2 (A=0, B=1)	1
Input 3 (A=1, B=1)	0

Fig. B.12 Synaptic weights on the dendrite of the output neuron in Fig. B.11.

B.2.8 Implications of different types of coding for storage in pattern associators

Throughout this section, we have made statements about how the properties of pattern associators – such as the number of patterns that can be stored, and whether generalization and graceful degradation occur – depend on the type of encoding of the patterns to be associated. (The types of encoding considered, local, sparse distributed, and fully distributed, are described above.) We draw together these points in Table B.2.

Table B.2 Coding in associative memories*

	Local	Sparse distributed	Fully distributed
Generalization, completion, graceful degradation	No	Yes	Yes
Number of patterns that can be stored	N (large)	of order $C/[a_o \log(1/a_o)]$ (can be larger)	of order C (usually smaller than N)
Amount of information in each pattern (values if binary)	Minimal ($\log(N)$ bits)	Intermediate ($N a_o \log(1/a_o)$ bits)	Large (N bits)

* N refers here to the number of output units, and C to the average number of inputs to each output unit. a_o is the sparseness of output patterns, or roughly the proportion of output units activated by a UCS pattern. Note: logs are to the base 2.

The amount of information that can be stored in each pattern in a pattern associator is considered in Appendix A3 of Rolls and Treves (1998).

In conclusion, the architecture and properties of pattern association networks make them very appropriate for stimulus–reinforcer association learning. Their high capacity enables them to learn the reinforcement associations for very large numbers of different stimuli.

B.3 Autoassociation or attractor memory

Autoassociative memories, or attractor neural networks, store memories, each one of which is represented by a pattern of neural activity. The memories are stored in the recurrent synaptic connections between the neurons of the network, for example in the recurrent collateral connections between cortical pyramidal cells. Autoassociative networks can then recall the appropriate memory from the network when provided with a fragment of one of the memories. This is called completion. Many different memories can be stored in the network and retrieved correctly. A feature of this type of memory is that it is content addressable; that is, the information in the memory can be accessed if just the contents of the memory (or a part of the contents of the memory) are used. This is in contrast to a conventional computer, in which the address of what is to be accessed must be supplied, and used to access the contents of the memory. Content addressability is an important simplifying feature of this type of memory, which makes it suitable for use in biological systems. The issue of content addressability will be amplified below.

An autoassociation memory can be used as a short-term memory, in which iterative processing round the recurrent collateral connection loop keeps a representation active by continuing neuronal firing. The short-term memory reflected in continuing neuronal firing for several hundred milliseconds after a visual stimulus is removed which is present in visual cortical areas such as the inferior temporal visual cortex (see Chapter 4) is probably implemented in this way. This short-term memory is one possible mechanism that contributes to the implementation of the trace memory learning rule which can help to implement invariant object recognition as described in Chapter 4. Autoassociation memories also appear to be used in a short-term memory role in the prefrontal cortex. In particular, the temporal visual cortical areas have connections to the ventrolateral prefrontal cortex which help to implement the short-term memory for visual stimuli (in for example delayed match to sample tasks, and visual search tasks, as described in Section 5.1). In an analogous way the parietal cortex has connections to the dorsolateral prefrontal cortex for the short-term memory of spatial responses (see Section 5.1). These short-term memories provide a mechanism that enables attention to be maintained through backprojections from prefrontal cortex areas to the temporal and parietal areas that send connections to the prefrontal cortex, as described in Chapter 6. Autoassociation networks implemented by the recurrent collateral synapses between cortical pyramidal cells also provide a mechanism for constraint satisfaction and also noise reduction whereby the firing of neighbouring neurons can be taken into account in enabling the network to settle into a state that reflects all the details of the inputs activating the population of connected neurons, as well as the effects of what has been set up during developmental plasticity as well as later experience. Attractor networks are also effectively implemented by virtue of the forward and backward connections between cortical areas (see Sections 1.11 and 5.1). An autoassociation network with rapid synaptic plasticity can learn each memory in one trial. Because of its 'one-shot' rapid learning, and ability to complete, this type of network is well suited for episodic memory storage, in which each past episode must be stored and recalled later from a fragment, and kept separate from other episodic memories (see Chapter 2).

B.3.1 Architecture and operation

The prototypical architecture of an autoassociation memory is shown in Fig. B.13. The external input e_i is applied to each neuron i by unmodifiable synapses. This produces firing y_i of each neuron, or a vector of firing on the output neurons $\mathbf{y}$. Each output neuron i is connected by a recurrent collateral connection to the other neurons in the network, via modifiable connection weights w_{ij}. This architecture effectively enables the output firing vector $\mathbf{y}$ to be associated

external input

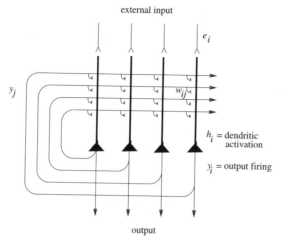

output

Fig. B.13 The architecture of an autoassociative neural network.

during learning with itself. Later on, during recall, presentation of part of the external input will force some of the output neurons to fire, but through the recurrent collateral axons and the modified synapses, other neurons in **y** can be brought into activity. This process can be repeated a number of times, and recall of a complete pattern may be perfect. Effectively, a pattern can be recalled or recognized because of associations formed between its parts. This of course requires distributed representations.

Next we introduce a more precise and detailed description of the above, and describe the properties of these networks. Ways to analyze formally the operation of these networks are introduced in Appendix A4 of Rolls and Treves (1998) and by Amit (1989).

B.3.1.1 Learning

The firing of every output neuron i is forced to a value y_i determined by the external input e_i. Then a Hebb-like associative local learning rule is applied to the recurrent synapses in the network:

$$\delta w_{ij} = \alpha y_i y_j. \tag{B.9}$$

It is notable that in a fully connected network, this will result in a symmetric matrix of synaptic weights, that is the strength of the connection from neuron 1 to neuron 2 will be the same as the strength of the connection from neuron 2 to neuron 1 (both implemented via recurrent collateral synapses).

It is a factor that is sometimes overlooked that there must be a mechanism for ensuring that during learning y_i does approximate e_i, and must not be influenced much by activity in the recurrent collateral connections, otherwise the new external pattern **e** will not be stored in the network, but instead something will be stored that is influenced by the previously stored memories. It is thought that in some parts of the brain, such as the hippocampus, there are processes that help the external connections to dominate the firing during learning (see Chapter 2, Treves and Rolls (1992) and Rolls and Treves (1998)).

B.3.1.2 Recall

During recall, the external input e_i is applied, and produces output firing, operating through the non-linear activation function described below. The firing is fed back by the recurrent collateral axons shown in Fig. B.13 to produce activation of each output neuron through the modified synapses on each output neuron. The activation h_i produced by the recurrent collateral effect on the ith neuron is, in the standard way, the sum of the activations produced in proportion to the firing rate of each axon y_j operating through each modified synapse w_{ij}, that is,

$$h_i = \sum_j y_j w_{ij} \qquad \text{(B.10)}$$

where $\sum_j$ indicates that the sum is over the C input axons to each neuron, indexed by j.

The output firing y_i is a function of the activation produced by the recurrent collateral effect (internal recall) and by the external input (e_i):

$$y_i = f(h_i + e_i) \qquad \text{(B.11)}$$

The activation function should be non-linear, and may be for example binary threshold, linear threshold, sigmoid, etc. (see Fig. 1.3). The threshold at which the activation function operates is set in part by the effect of the inhibitory neurons in the network (not shown in Fig. B.13). The connectivity is that the pyramidal cells have collateral axons that excite the inhibitory interneurons, which in turn connect back to the population of pyramidal cells to inhibit them by a mixture of shunting (divisive) and subtractive inhibition using GABA (gamma-amino-butyric acid) terminals, as described in Section B.6. There are many fewer inhibitory neurons than excitatory neurons (in the order of 5–10%, see Table 1.1) and of connections to and from inhibitory neurons (see Table 1.1), and partly for this reason the inhibitory neurons are considered to perform generic functions such as threshold setting, rather than to store patterns by modifying their synapses. Similar inhibitory processes are assumed for the other networks described in this Appendix. The non-linear activation function can minimize interference between the pattern being recalled and other patterns stored in the network, and can also be used to ensure that what is a positive feedback system remains stable. The network can be allowed to repeat this recurrent collateral loop a number of times. Each time the loop operates, the output firing becomes more like the originally stored pattern, and this progressive recall is usually complete within 5–15 iterations.

B.3.2 Introduction to the analysis of the operation of autoassociation networks

With complete connectivity in the synaptic matrix, and the use of a Hebb rule, the matrix of synaptic weights formed during learning is symmetric. The learning algorithm is fast, 'one-shot', in that a single presentation of an input pattern is all that is needed to store that pattern.

During recall, a part of one of the originally learned stimuli can be presented as an external input. The resulting firing is allowed to iterate repeatedly round the recurrent collateral system, gradually on each iteration recalling more and more of the originally learned pattern. Completion thus occurs. If a pattern is presented during recall that is similar but not identical to any of the previously learned patterns, then the network settles into a stable recall state in which the firing corresponds to that of the previously learned pattern. The network can thus generalize in its recall to the most similar previously learned pattern. The activation function of the neurons should be non-linear, since a purely linear system would not produce any categorization of the input patterns it receives, and therefore would not be able to effect anything more than a trivial (i.e. linear) form of completion and generalization.

Recall can be thought of in the following way, relating it to what occurs in pattern associators. The external input e is applied, produces firing y, which is applied as a recall cue on the recurrent collaterals as y^T. (The notation y^T signifies the transpose of y, which is implemented by the application of the firing of the neurons y back via the recurrent collateral axons as the next set of inputs to the neurons.) The activity on the recurrent collaterals is then multiplied by the synaptic weight vector stored during learning on each neuron to produce the new activation h_i which reflects the similarity between $\mathbf{y}^T$ and one of the stored patterns. Partial recall has thus occurred as a result of the recurrent collateral effect. The activations h_i after thresholding (which helps to remove interference from other memories stored in the network, or noise in the recall cue) result in firing y_i, or a vector of all neurons $\mathbf{y}$, which is already more like one of the stored patterns than, at the first iteration, the firing resulting from the recall cue alone, $\mathbf{y} = \mathbf{f}(\mathbf{e})$. This process is repeated a number of times to produce progressive recall of one of the stored patterns.

Autoassociation networks operate by effectively storing associations between the elements of a pattern. Each element of the pattern vector to be stored is simply the firing of a neuron. What is stored in an autoassociation memory is a set of pattern vectors. The network operates to recall one of the patterns from a fragment of it. Thus, although this network implements recall or recognition of a pattern, it does so by an association learning mechanism, in which associations between the different parts of each pattern are learned. These memories have sometimes been called autocorrelation memories (Kohonen 1977), because they learn correlations between the activity of neurons in the network, in the sense that each pattern learned is defined by a set of simultaneously active neurons. Effectively each pattern is associated by learning with itself. This learning is implemented by an associative (Hebb-like) learning rule.

The system formally resembles spin glass systems of magnets analyzed quantitatively in statistical mechanics. This has led to the analysis of (recurrent) autoassociative networks as dynamical systems made up of many interacting elements, in which the interactions are such as to produce a large variety of basins of attraction of the dynamics. Each basin of attraction corresponds to one of the originally learned patterns, and once the network is within a basin it keeps iterating until a recall state is reached that is the learned pattern itself or a pattern closely similar to it. (Interference effects may prevent an exact identity between the recall state and a learned pattern.) This type of system is contrasted with other, simpler, systems of magnets (e.g. ferromagnets), in which the interactions are such as to produce only a limited number of related basins, since the magnets tend to be, for example, all aligned with each other. The states reached within each basin of attraction are called attractor states, and the analogy between autoassociator neural networks and physical systems with multiple attractors was drawn by Hopfield (1982) in a very influential paper. He was able to show that the recall state can be thought of as the local minimum in an energy landscape, where the energy would be defined as

$$E = -\frac{1}{2} \sum_{i,j} w_{ij} (y_i - <y>)(y_j - <y>). \tag{B.12}$$

This equation can be understood in the following way. If two neurons are both firing above their mean rate (denoted by $<y>$), and are connected by a weight with a positive value, then the firing of these two neurons is consistent with each other, and they mutually support each other, so that they contribute to the system's tendency to remain stable. If across the whole network such mutual support is generally provided, then no further change will take place, and the system will indeed remain stable. If, on the other hand, either of our pair of neurons was not firing, or if the connecting weight had a negative value, the neurons would not support each other, and indeed the tendency would be for the neurons to try to alter ('flip' in the case of binary units) the state of the other. This would be repeated across the whole network until a situation in which most mutual support, and least 'frustration', was reached. What makes it possible to define an energy function and for these points to hold is that the matrix is symmetric (see Hopfield (1982), Hertz, Krogh and Palmer (1991), Amit (1989)).

Physicists have generally analyzed a system in which the input pattern is presented and then immediately removed, so that the network then 'falls' without further assistance (in what is referred to as the unclamped condition) towards the minimum of its basin of attraction. A more biologically realistic system is one in which the external input is left on contributing to the recall during the fall into the recall state. In this clamped condition, recall is usually faster, and more reliable, so that more memories may be usefully recalled from the network. The approach using methods developed in theoretical physics has led to rapid advances in the understanding of autoassociative networks, and its basic elements are described in Appendix A4 of Rolls and Treves (1998), and by Hertz, Krogh and Palmer (1991) and Amit (1989).

B.3.3 Properties

The internal recall in autoassociation networks involves multiplication of the firing vector of neuronal activity by the vector of synaptic weights on each neuron. This inner product vector multiplication allows the similarity of the firing vector to previously stored firing vectors to be provided by the output (as effectively a correlation), if the patterns learned are distributed. As a result of this type of 'correlation computation' performed if the patterns are distributed, many important properties of these networks arise, including pattern completion (because part of a pattern is correlated with the whole pattern), and graceful degradation (because a damaged synaptic weight vector is still correlated with the original synaptic weight vector). Some of these properties are described next.

B.3.3.1 Completion

Perhaps the most important and useful property of these memories is that they complete an incomplete input vector, allowing recall of a whole memory from a small fraction of it. The memory recalled in response to a fragment is that stored in the memory that is closest in pattern similarity (as measured by the dot product, or correlation). Because the recall is iterative and progressive, the recall can be perfect.

This property and the associative property of pattern associator neural networks are very similar to the properties of human memory. This property may be used when we recall a part of a recent memory of a past episode from a part of that episode. The way in which this could be implemented in the hippocampus is described in Chapter 2.

B.3.3.2 Generalization

The network generalizes in that an input vector similar to one of the stored vectors will lead to recall of the originally stored vector, provided that distributed encoding is used. The principle by which this occurs is similar to that described for a pattern associator.

B.3.3.3 Graceful degradation or fault tolerance

If the synaptic weight vector $\mathbf{w}_i$ on each neuron (or the weight matrix) has synapses missing (e.g. during development), or loses synapses (e.g. with brain damage or ageing), then the activation h_i (or vector of activations $\mathbf{h}$) is still reasonable, because h_i is the dot product (correlation) of $\mathbf{y}^{\mathrm{T}}$ with $\mathbf{w}_i$. The same argument applies if whole input axons are lost. If an output neuron is lost, then the network cannot itself compensate for this, but the next network in the brain is likely to be able to generalize or complete if its input vector has some elements missing, as would be the case if some output neurons of the autoassociation network were damaged.

B.3.3.4 Prototype extraction, extraction of central tendency, and noise reduction

These arise when a set of similar input pattern vectors $\{e\}$ (which induce firing of the output neurons $\{y\}$) are learned by the network. The weight vectors $\mathbf{w}_i$ (or strictly $\mathbf{w}_i^T$) become (or point towards) the average $\{< \mathbf{y} >\}$ of that set of similar vectors. This produces 'extraction of the prototype' or 'extraction of the central tendency', and 'noise reduction'. This process can result in better recognition or recall of the prototype than of any of the exemplars, even though the prototype may never itself have been presented. The general principle by which the effect occurs is similar to that by which it occurs in pattern associators. It of course only occurs if each pattern uses a distributed representation.

Related to outputs of the visual system to long-term memory systems (see Chapter 2), there has been intense debate about whether when human memories are stored, a prototype of what is to be remembered is stored, or whether all the instances or the exemplars are each stored separately so that they can be individually recalled (McClelland and Rumelhart (1986), Chapter 17, p. 172). Evidence favouring the prototype view is that if a number of different examples of an object are shown, then humans may report more confidently that they have seen the prototype before than any of the different exemplars, even though the prototype has never been shown (Posner and Keele 1968, Rosch 1975). Evidence favouring the view that exemplars are stored is that in categorization and perceptual identification tasks the responses made are often sensitive to the congruity between particular training stimuli and particular test stimuli (Brooks 1978, Medin and Schaffer 1978, Jacoby 1983a, Jacoby 1983b, Whittlesea 1983). It is of great interest that both types of phenomena can arise naturally out of distributed information storage in a neuronal network such as an autoassociator. This can be illustrated by the storage in an autoassociation memory of sets of stimuli that are all somewhat different examples of the same pattern. These can be generated, for example, by randomly altering each of the input vectors from the input stimulus. After many such randomly altered exemplars have been learned by the network, recall can be tested, and it is found that the network responds best to the original (prototype) input vector, with which it has never been presented. The reason for this is that the autocorrelation components that build up in the synaptic matrix with repeated presentations of the exemplars represent the average correlation between the different elements of the vector, and this is highest for the prototype. This effect also gives the storage some noise immunity, in that variations in the input that are random noise average out, while the signal that is constant builds up with repeated learning.

B.3.3.5 Speed

The recall operation is fast on each neuron on a single iteration, because the pattern $\mathbf{y}^T$ on the axons can be applied simultaneously to the synapses $\mathbf{w}_i$, and the activation h_i can be accumulated in one or two time constants of the dendrite (e.g. 10–20 ms). If a simple implementation of an autoassociation net such as that described by Hopfield (1982) is simulated on a computer, then 5–15 iterations are typically necessary for completion of an incomplete input cue $\mathbf{e}$. This might be taken to correspond to 50–200 ms in the brain, rather too slow for any one local network in the brain to function. However, it has been shown that if the neurons are treated not as McCulloch–Pitts neurons which are simply 'updated' at each iteration, or cycle of timesteps (and assume the active state if the threshold is exceeded), but instead are analyzed and modelled as 'integrate-and-fire' neurons in real continuous time, then the network can effectively 'relax' into its recall state very rapidly, in one or two time constants of the synapses (see Section B.6 and Treves (1993), Battaglia and Treves (1998a) and Appendix A5 of Rolls and Treves (1998)). This corresponds to perhaps 20 ms in the brain.

One factor in this rapid dynamics of autoassociative networks with brain-like 'integrate-and-fire' membrane and synaptic properties is that with some spontaneous activity, some of the neurons in the network are close to threshold already before the recall cue is applied, and hence some of the neurons are very quickly pushed by the recall cue into firing, so that information starts to be exchanged very rapidly (within 1–2 ms of brain time) through the modified synapses by the neurons in the network. The progressive exchange of information starting early on within what would otherwise be thought of as an iteration period (of perhaps 20 ms, corresponding to a neuronal firing rate of 50 spikes/s) is the mechanism accounting for rapid recall in an autoassociative neuronal network made biologically realistic in this way. Further analysis of the fast dynamics of these networks if they are implemented in a biologically plausible way with 'integrate-and-fire' neurons is provided in Section B.6, in Appendix A5 of Rolls and Treves (1998), and by Treves (1993). *The general approach applies to other networks with recurrent connections, not just autoassociators, and the fact that such networks can operate much faster than it would seem from simple models that follow discrete time dynamics is probably a major factor in enabling these networks to provide some of the building blocks of brain function.*

Learning is fast, 'one-shot', in that a single presentation of an input pattern **e** (producing **y**) enables the association between the activation of the dendrites (the post-synaptic term h_i) and the firing of the recurrent collateral axons $\mathbf{y}^T$, to be learned. Repeated presentation with small variations of a pattern vector is used to obtain the properties of prototype extraction, extraction of central tendency, and noise reduction, because these arise from the averaging process produced by storing very similar patterns in the network.

B.3.3.6 Local learning rule

The simplest learning used in autoassociation neural networks, a version of the Hebb rule, is (as in equation B.9)

$$\delta w_{ij} = \alpha y_i y_j.$$

The rule is a local learning rule in that the information required to specify the change in synaptic weight is available locally at the synapse, as it is dependent only on the presynaptic firing rate y_j available at the synaptic terminal, and the postsynaptic activation or firing y_i available on the dendrite of the neuron receiving the synapse. This makes the learning rule biologically plausible, in that the information about how to change the synaptic weight does not have to be carried to every synapse from a distant source where it is computed. As with pattern associators, since firing rates are positive quantities, a potentially interfering correlation is induced between different pattern vectors. This can be removed by subtracting the mean of the presynaptic activity from each presynaptic term, using a type of long-term depression. This can be specified as

$$\delta w_{ij} = \alpha y_i (y_j - z) \tag{B.13}$$

where α is a learning rate constant. This learning rule includes (in proportion to y_i) increasing the synaptic weight if $(y_j - z) > 0$ (long-term potentiation), and decreasing the synaptic weight if $(y_j - z) < 0$ (heterosynaptic long-term depression). This procedure works optimally if z is the average activity $< y_j >$ of an axon across patterns.

Evidence that a learning rule with the general form of equation B.9 is implemented in at least some parts of the brain comes from studies of long-term potentiation, described in Section 1.5. One of the important potential functions of heterosynaptic long-term depression is its ability to allow in effect the average of the presynaptic activity to be subtracted from the presynaptic firing rate (see Appendix A3 of Rolls and Treves (1998), and Rolls and Treves (1990)).

Autoassociation networks can be trained with the error-correction or delta learning rule described in Section B.11. Although a delta rule is less biologically plausible than a Hebb-like rule, a delta rule can help to store separately patterns that are very similar (see McClelland and Rumelhart (1988), Hertz, Krogh and Palmer (1991)).

B.3.3.7 Capacity

One measure of storage capacity is to consider how many orthogonal patterns could be stored, as with pattern associators. If the patterns are orthogonal, there will be no interference between them, and the maximum number p of patterns that can be stored will be the same as the number N of output neurons in a fully connected network. Although in practice the patterns that have to be stored will hardly be orthogonal, this is not a purely academic speculation, since it was shown how one can construct a synaptic matrix that effectively orthogonalizes any set of (linearly independent) patterns (Kohonen 1977, Kohonen 1989, Personnaz, Guyon and Dreyfus 1985, Kanter and Sompolinsky 1987). However, this matrix cannot be learned with a local, one-shot learning rule, and therefore its interest for autoassociators in the brain is limited. The more general case of random non-orthogonal patterns, and of Hebbian learning rules, is considered next.

With non-linear neurons used in the network, the capacity can be measured in terms of the number of input patterns $\mathbf{y}$ (produced by the external input $\mathbf{e}$, see Fig. B.13) that can be stored in the network and recalled later whenever the network settles within each stored pattern's basin of attraction. The first quantitative analysis of storage capacity (Amit, Gutfreund and Sompolinsky 1987) considered a fully connected Hopfield (1982) autoassociator model, in which units are binary elements with an equal probability of being 'on' or 'off' in each pattern, and the number C of inputs per unit is the same as the number N of output units. (Actually it is equal to $N - 1$, since a unit is taken not to connect to itself.) Learning is taken to occur by clamping the desired patterns on the network and using a modified Hebb rule, in which the mean of the presynaptic and postsynaptic firings is subtracted from the firing on any one learning trial (this amounts to a covariance learning rule, and is described more fully in Appendix A4 of Rolls and Treves (1998)). With such fully distributed random patterns, the number of patterns that can be learned is (for C large) $p \approx 0.14C = 0.14N$, hence well below what could be achieved with orthogonal patterns or with an 'orthogonalizing' synaptic matrix. Many variations of this 'standard' autoassociator model have been analyzed subsequently.

Treves and Rolls (1991) have extended this analysis to autoassociation networks that are much more biologically relevant in the following ways. First, some or many connections between the recurrent collaterals and the dendrites are missing (this is referred to as diluted connectivity, and results in a non-symmetric synaptic connection matrix in which w_{ij} does not equal w_{ji}, one of the original assumptions made in order to introduce the energy formalism in the Hopfield model). Second, the neurons need not be restricted to binary threshold neurons, but can have a threshold linear activation function (see Fig. 1.3). This enables the neurons to assume real continuously variable firing rates, which are what is found in the brain (Rolls and Tovee 1995b, Treves, Panzeri, Rolls, Booth and Wakeman 1999). Third, the representation need not be fully distributed (with half the neurons 'on', and half 'off'), but instead can have a small proportion of the neurons firing above the spontaneous rate, which is what is found in parts of the brain such as the hippocampus that are involved in memory (see Treves and Rolls (1994), and Chapter 6 of Rolls and Treves (1998)). Such a representation is defined as being sparse, and the sparseness a of the representation can be measured, by extending the binary notion of the proportion of neurons that are firing, as

$$a = \frac{(\sum\limits_{i=1}^{N} y_i/N)^2}{\sum\limits_{i=1}^{N} y_i^2/N} \tag{B.14}$$

where y_i is the firing rate of the ith neuron in the set of N neurons. Treves and Rolls (1991) have shown that such a network does operate efficiently as an autoassociative network, and can store (and recall correctly) a number of different patterns p as follows

$$p \approx \frac{C^{\mathrm{RC}}}{a \ln(\frac{1}{a})} k \tag{B.15}$$

where C^{RC} is the number of synapses on the dendrites of each neuron devoted to the recurrent collaterals from other neurons in the network, and k is a factor that depends weakly on the detailed structure of the rate distribution, on the connectivity pattern, etc., but is roughly in the order of 0.2–0.3.

The main factors that determine the maximum number of memories that can be stored in an autoassociative network are thus the number of connections on each neuron devoted to the recurrent collaterals, and the sparseness of the representation. For example, for $C^{\mathrm{RC}} = 12,000$ and $a = 0.02$, p is calculated to be approximately $36,000$. This storage capacity can be realized, with little interference between patterns, if the learning rule includes some form of heterosynaptic long-term depression that counterbalances the effects of associative long-term potentiation (Treves and Rolls (1991); see Appendix A4 of Rolls and Treves (1998)). It should be noted that the number of neurons N (which is greater than C^{RC}, the number of recurrent collateral inputs received by any neuron in the network from the other neurons in the network) is not a parameter that influences the number of different memories that can be stored in the network. The implication of this is that increasing the number of neurons (without increasing the number of connections per neuron) does not increase the number of different patterns that can be stored (see Rolls and Treves (1998) Appendix A4), although it may enable simpler encoding of the firing patterns, for example more orthogonal encoding, to be used. This latter point may account in part for why there are generally in the brain more neurons in a recurrent network than there are connections per neuron (see e.g. Chapter 2).

The non-linearity inherent in the NMDA receptor-based Hebbian plasticity present in the brain may help to make the stored patterns more sparse than the input patterns, and this may be especially beneficial in increasing the storage capacity of associative networks in the brain by allowing participation in the storage of especially those relatively few neurons with high firing rates in the exponential firing rate distributions typical of neurons in sensory systems (see Sections B.4.9.3 and C.3.1).

B.3.3.8 Context

The environmental context in which learning occurs can be a very important factor that affects retrieval in humans and other animals. Placing the subject back into the same context in which the original learning occurred can greatly facilitate retrieval.

Context effects arise naturally in association networks if some of the activity in the network reflects the context in which the learning occurs. Retrieval is then better when that context is present, for the activity contributed by the context becomes part of the retrieval cue for the memory, increasing the correlation of the current state with what was stored. (A strategy for retrieval arises simply from this property. The strategy is to keep trying to recall as many fragments of the original memory situation, including the context, as possible, as this will provide a better cue for complete retrieval of the memory than just a single fragment.)

The effects that mood has on memory including visual memory retrieval may be accounted for by backprojections from brain regions such as the amygdala and orbitofrontal cortex in which the current mood, providing a context, is represented, to brain regions involved in memory such as the perirhinal cortex, and in visual representations such as the inferior temporal visual cortex (see Rolls and Stringer (2001b) and Section 3.11). The very well-known effects of context in the human memory literature could arise in the simple way just described. An implication of the explanation is that context effects will be especially important at late stages of memory or information processing systems in the brain, for there information from a wide range of modalities will be mixed, and some of that information could reflect the context in which the learning takes place. One part of the brain where such effects may be strong is the hippocampus, which is implicated in the memory of recent episodes, and which receives inputs derived from most of the cortical information processing streams, including those involved in space (see Chapter 2).

B.3.3.9 Mixture states

If an autoassociation memory is trained on pattern vectors $\mathbf{A}$, $\mathbf{B}$, and $\mathbf{A} + \mathbf{B}$ (i.e. $\mathbf{A}$ and $\mathbf{B}$ are both included in the joint vector $\mathbf{A} + \mathbf{B}$; that is if the vectors are not linearly independent), then the autoassociation memory will have difficulty in learning and recalling these three memories as separate, because completion from either $\mathbf{A}$ or $\mathbf{B}$ to $\mathbf{A} + \mathbf{B}$ tends to occur during recall. (The ability to separate such patterns is referred to as configurational learning in the animal learning literature, see e.g. Sutherland and Rudy (1991).) This problem can be minimized by re-representing $\mathbf{A}$, $\mathbf{B}$, and $\mathbf{A} + \mathbf{B}$ in such a way that they are different vectors before they are presented to the autoassociation memory. This can be performed by recoding the input vectors to minimize overlap using, for example, a competitive network, and possibly involving expansion recoding, as described for pattern associators (see Section B.2, Fig. B.11). It is suggested that this is a function of the dentate granule cells in the hippocampus, which precede the CA3 recurrent collateral network (Treves and Rolls 1992, Treves and Rolls 1994) (see Chapter 2).

B.3.3.10 Memory for sequences

One of the first extensions of the standard autoassociator paradigm that has been explored in the literature is the capability to store and retrieve not just individual patterns, but whole sequences of patterns. Hopfield, in the same 1982 paper, suggested that this could be achieved by adding to the standard connection weights, which associate a pattern with itself, a new, asymmetric component, which associates a pattern with the next one in the sequence. In practice this scheme does not work very well, unless the new component is made to operate on a slower time scale than the purely autoassociative component (Kleinfeld 1986, Sompolinsky and Kanter 1986). With two different time scales, the autoassociative component can stabilize a pattern for a while, before the heteroassociative component moves the network, as it were, into the next pattern. The heteroassociative retrieval cue for the next pattern in the sequence is just the previous pattern in the sequence. A particular type of 'slower' operation occurs if the asymmetric component acts after a delay τ. In this case, the network sweeps through the sequence, staying for a time of order τ in each pattern.

One can see how the necessary ingredient for the storage of sequences is only a minor departure from purely Hebbian learning: in fact, the (symmetric) autoassociative component of the weights can be taken to reflect the Hebbian learning of strictly simultaneous conjunctions of pre- and post-synaptic activity, whereas the (asymmetric) heteroassociative component can be implemented by Hebbian learning of each conjunction of postsynaptic activity with presynaptic activity shifted a time τ in the past. Both components can then be seen as resulting from a generalized Hebbian rule, which increases the weight whenever postsynaptic activity is paired with presynaptic activity occurring within a given time range, which may extend from a few hundred milliseconds in the past up to include strictly simultaneous activity. This is similar to a trace rule (see Chapter 4), which itself matches very well the observed conditions for induction of long-term potentiation, and appears entirely plausible. The learning rule necessary for learning sequences, though, is more complex than a simple trace rule in that the time-shifted conjunctions of activity that are encoded in the weights must in retrieval produce activations that are time-shifted as well (otherwise one falls back into the Hopfield (1982) proposal, which does not quite work). The synaptic weights should therefore keep separate 'traces' of what was simultaneous and what was time-shifted during the original experience, and this is not very plausible.

Levy and colleagues (Levy, Wu and Baxter 1995, Wu, Baxter and Levy 1996) have investigated these issues further, and the temporal asymmetry that may be present in LTP (see Section 1.5) has been suggested as a mechanism that might provide some of the temporal properties that are necessary for the brain to store and recall sequences (Minai and Levy 1993, Abbott and Blum 1996, Markram, Pikus, Gupta and Tsodyks 1998, Abbott and Nelson 2000). A problem with this suggestion is that, given that the temporal dynamics of attractor networks are inherently very fast when the networks have continuous dynamics (see Section B.6), and that the temporal asymmetry in LTP may be in the order of only milliseconds to a few tens of milliseconds (see Section 1.5), the recall of the sequences would be very fast, perhaps 10–20 ms per step of the sequence, with every step of a 10-step sequence effectively retrieved and gone in a quick-fire session of 100–200 ms.

Another way in which a delay could be inserted in a recurrent collateral path in the brain is by inserting another cortical area in the recurrent path. This could fit in with the cortico-cortical backprojection connections described in Section 1.11, which would introduce some conduction delay (see Panzeri, Rolls, Battaglia and Lavis (2001)).

B.3.4 Use of autoassociation networks in the brain

Because of its 'one-shot' rapid learning, and ability to complete, this type of network is well suited for episodic memory storage, in which each episode must be stored and recalled later from a fragment, and kept separate from other episodic memories. It does not take a long time (the 'many epochs' of backpropagation networks) to train this network, because it does not have to 'discover the structure' of a problem. Instead, it stores information in the form in which it is presented to the memory, without altering the representation. An autoassociation network may be used for this function in the CA3 region of the hippocampus (see Chapter 2, and Rolls and Treves (1998) Chapter 6).

An autoassociation memory can also be used as a short-term memory, in which iterative processing round the recurrent collateral loop keeps a representation active until another input cue is received. This may be used to implement many types of short-term memory in the brain (see Section 5.1). For example, it may be used in the perirhinal cortex and adjacent temporal lobe cortex to implement short-term visual object memory (Miyashita and Chang 1988, Amit 1995); in the dorsolateral prefrontal cortex to implement a short-term memory for spatial responses (Goldman-Rakic 1996); and in the prefrontal cortex to implement a short-term memory for where eye movements should be made in space (see Chapter 5). Such an autoassociation memory in the temporal lobe visual cortical areas may be used to implement the firing that continues for often 300 ms after a very brief (16 ms) presentation of a visual stimulus (Rolls and Tovee 1994) (see e.g. Fig. C.17), and may be one way in which a short memory trace is implemented to facilitate invariant learning about visual stimuli (see Chapter 4). In all these cases, the short-term memory may be implemented by the recurrent excitatory collaterals that connect nearby pyramidal cells in the cerebral cortex. The connectivity in this system, that is the probability that a neuron synapses on a nearby neuron, may be in the region of 10% (Braitenberg and Schuz 1991, Abeles 1991).

The recurrent connections between nearby neocortical pyramidal cells may also be important in defining the response properties of cortical cells, which may be triggered by external inputs (from for example the thalamus or a preceding cortical area), but may be considerably dependent on the synaptic connections received from nearby cortical pyramidal cells.

The cortico-cortical backprojection connectivity described in Chapters 1 and 2 can be interpreted as a system that allows the forward-projecting neurons in one cortical area to be linked autoassociatively with the backprojecting neurons in the next cortical area (see Section 1.11 and Chapter 2). This would be implemented by associative synaptic modification in for example the backprojections. This particular architecture may be especially important in constraint satisfaction (as well as recall), that is it may allow the networks in the two cortical areas to settle into a mutually consistent state. This would effectively enable information in higher cortical areas, which would include information from more divergent sources, to influence the response properties of neurons in earlier cortical processing stages. This is an important function in cortical information processing of interacting associative networks.

B.4   Competitive networks, including self-organizing maps

B.4.1   Function

Competitive neural networks learn to categorize input pattern vectors. Each category of inputs activates a different output neuron (or set of output neurons – see below). The categories formed are based on similarities between the input vectors. Similar, that is correlated, input vectors activate the same output neuron. In that the learning is based on similarities in the input space, and there is no external teacher that forces classification, this is an unsupervised network. The term categorization is used to refer to the process of placing vectors into categories based on their similarity. The term classification is used to refer to the process of placing outputs in particular classes as instructed or taught by a teacher. Examples of classifiers are pattern associators, one-layer delta-rule perceptrons, and multilayer perceptrons taught by error backpropagation (see Sections B.2, B.3, B.11 and B.12). In supervised networks there is usually a teacher for each output neuron.

The categorization produced by competitive nets is of great potential importance in perceptual systems including the whole of the visual cortical processing hierarchies, as described in Chapter 4. Each category formed reflects a set or cluster of active inputs x_j which occur together. This cluster of coactive inputs can be thought of as a feature, and the competitive network can be described as building feature analyzers, where a feature can now be defined as a correlated set of inputs. During learning, a competitive network gradually discovers these features in the input space, and the process of finding these features without a teacher is referred to as self-organization.

Another important use of competitive networks is to remove redundancy from the input space, by allocating output neurons to reflect a set of inputs that co-occur.

Another important aspect of competitive networks is that they separate patterns that are somewhat correlated in the input space, to produce outputs for the different patterns that are less correlated with each other, and may indeed easily be made orthogonal to each other. This has been referred to as orthogonalization.

Another important function of competitive networks is that partly by removing redundancy from the input information space, they can produce sparse output vectors, without losing information. We may refer to this as sparsification.

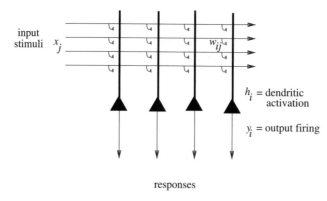

Fig. B.14 The architecture of a competitive network.

B.4.2 Architecture and algorithm

B.4.2.1 Architecture

The basic architecture of a competitive network is shown in Fig. B.14. It is a one-layer network with a set of inputs that make modifiable excitatory synapses w_{ij} with the output neurons. The output cells compete with each other (for example by mutual inhibition) in such a way that the most strongly activated neuron or neurons win the competition, and are left firing strongly. The synaptic weights, w_{ij}, are initialized to random values before learning starts. If some of the synapses are missing, that is if there is randomly diluted connectivity, that is not a problem for such networks, and can even help them (see below).

In the brain, the inputs arrive through axons, which make synapses with the dendrites of the output or principal cells of the network. The principal cells are typically pyramidal cells in the cerebral cortex. In the brain, the principal cells are typically excitatory, and mutual inhibition between them is implemented by inhibitory interneurons, which receive excitatory inputs from the principal cells. The inhibitory interneurons then send their axons to make synapses with the pyramidal cells, typically using GABA (gamma-aminobutyric acid) as the inhibitory transmitter.

B.4.2.2 Algorithm

1. Apply an input vector **x** and calculate the activation h_i of each neuron

$$h_i = \sum_j x_j w_{ij} \qquad (B.16)$$

where the sum is over the C input axons, indexed by j. (It is useful to normalize the length of each input vector **x**. In the brain, a scaling effect is likely to be achieved both by feedforward inhibition, and by feedback inhibition among the set of input cells (in a preceding network) that give rise to the axons conveying **x**.)

The output firing y_i^1 is a function of the activation of the neuron

$$y_i^1 = \text{f}(h_i). \qquad (B.17)$$

The function f can be linear, sigmoid, monotonically increasing, etc. (see Fig. 1.3).

2. Allow competitive interaction between the output neurons by a mechanism such as lateral or mutual inhibition (possibly with self-excitation), to produce a contrast-enhanced version of the firing rate vector

$$y_i = \text{g}(y_i^1). \qquad (B.18)$$

Function g is typically a non-linear operation, and in its most extreme form may be a winner-take-all function, in which after the competition one neuron may be 'on', and the others 'off'. Algorithms that produce softer competition without a single winner to produce a distributed representation are described in Section B.4.9.4 below.

3. Apply an associative Hebb-like learning rule

$$\delta w_{ij} = \alpha y_i x_j.$$
(B.19)

4. Normalize the length of the synaptic weight vector on each dendrite to prevent the same few neurons always winning the competition:

$$\sum_j (w_{ij})^2 = 1.$$
(B.20)

(A less efficient alternative is to scale the sum of the weights to a constant, e.g. 1.0.)

5. Repeat steps 1–4 for each different input stimulus **x**, in random sequence, a number of times.

B.4.3 Properties

B.4.3.1 Feature discovery by self-organization

Each neuron in a competitive network becomes activated by a set of consistently coactive, that is correlated, input axons, and gradually learns to respond to that cluster of coactive inputs. We can think of competitive networks as discovering features in the input space, where features can now be defined by a set of consistently coactive inputs. Competitive networks thus show how feature analyzers can be built, with no external teacher. The feature analyzers respond to correlations in the input space, and the learning occurs by self-organization in the competitive network. Competitive networks are therefore well suited to the analysis of sensory inputs. Ways in which they may form fundamental building blocks of sensory systems are described in Chapter 4.

The operation of competitive networks can be visualized with the help of Fig. B.15. The input patterns are represented as dots on the surface of a sphere. (The patterns are on the surface of a sphere because they are normalized to the same length.) The directions of the weight vectors of the three neurons are represented by '×'s. The effect of learning is to move the weight vector of each of the neurons to point towards the centre of one of the clusters of inputs. If the neurons are winner-take-all, the result of the learning is that although there are correlations between the input stimuli, the outputs of the three neurons are orthogonal. In this sense, orthogonalization is performed. At the same time, given that each of the patterns within a cluster produces the same output, the correlations between the patterns within a cluster become higher. In a winner-take-all network, the within-pattern correlation becomes 1, and the patterns within a cluster have been placed within the same category.

B.4.3.2 Removal of redundancy

In that competitive networks recode sets of correlated inputs to one or a few output neurons, then redundancy in the input representation is removed. Identifying and removing redundancy in sensory inputs is an important part of processing in sensory systems (cf. Barlow (1989)), in part because a compressed representation is more manageable as an output of sensory systems. The reason for this is that neurons in the receiving systems, for example pattern associators in the orbitofrontal cortex or autoassociation networks in the hippocampus, can then operate with the limited numbers of inputs that each neuron can receive. For example,

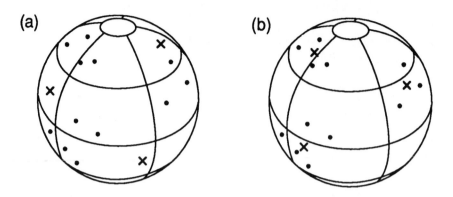

Fig. B.15 Competitive learning. The dots represent the directions of the input vectors, and the '×'s the weights for each of three output neurons. (a) Before learning. (b) After learning. (After Rumelhart and Zipser 1986.)

although the information that a particular face is being viewed is present in the 10^6 fibres in the optic nerve, the information is unusable by associative networks in this form, and is compressed through the visual system until the information about which of many hundreds of faces is present can be represented by less than 100 neurons in the temporal cortical visual areas (Rolls, Treves and Tovee 1997b, Abbott, Rolls and Tovee 1996). (Redundancy can be defined as the difference between the maximum information content of the input data stream (or channel capacity) and its actual content; see Appendix C.)

The recoding of input pattern vectors into a more compressed representation that can be conveyed by a much reduced number of output neurons of a competitive network is referred to in engineering as vector quantization. With a winner-take-all competitive network, each output neuron points to or stands for one of or a cluster of the input vectors, and it is more efficient to transmit the states of the few output neurons than the states of all the input elements. (It is more efficient in the sense that the information transmission rate required, that is the capacity of the channel, can be much smaller.) Vector quantization is of course possible when the input representation contains redundancy.

B.4.3.3 Orthogonalization and categorization

Figure B.15 shows visually how competitive networks reduce the correlation between different clusters of patterns, by allocating them to different output neurons. This is described as orthogonalization. It is a process that is very usefully applied to signals before they are used as inputs to associative networks (pattern associators and autoassociators) trained with Hebbian rules (see Sections B.2 and B.3), because it reduces the interference between patterns stored in these memories. The opposite effect in competitive networks, of bringing closer together very similar input patterns, is referred to as categorization.

These two processes are also illustrated in Fig. B.16, which shows that in a competitive network, very similar input patterns (with correlations higher in this case than approximately 0.8) produce more similar outputs (close to 1.0), whereas the correlations between pairs of input patterns that are smaller than approximately 0.7 become much smaller in the output representation. (This simulation used soft competition between neurons with graded firing rates.)

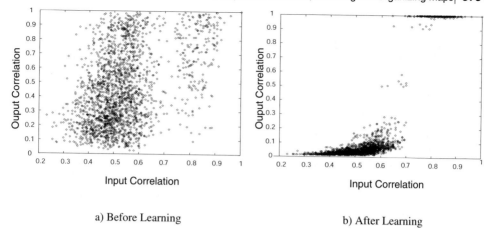

a) Before Learning   b) After Learning

Fig. B.16 Orthogonalization and categorization in a competitive network: (a) before learning; (b) after learning. The correlations between pairs of output vectors (abscissa) are plotted against the correlations of the corresponding pairs of input vectors that generated the output pair, for all possible pairs in the input set. The competitive net learned for 16 cycles. One cycle consisted of presenting the complete input set of stimuli in a renewing random sequence. The correlation measure shown is the cosine of the angle between two vectors (i.e. the normalized dot product). The network used had 64 input axons to each of 8 output neurons. The net was trained with 64 stimuli, made from 8 initial random binary vectors with each bit having a probability of 0.5 of being 1, from each of which 8 noisy exemplars were made by randomly altering 10 % of the 64 elements. Soft competition was used between the output neurons. (A normalized exponential activation function described in Section B.4.9.4 was used to implement the soft competition.) The sparseness a of the input patterns thus averaged 0.5; and the sparseness a of the output firing vector after learning was close to 0.17 (i.e. after learning, primarily one neuron was active for each input pattern; before learning, the average sparseness of the output patterns produced by each of the inputs was 0.39).

B.4.3.4 Sparsification

Competitive networks can produce more sparse representations than those that they receive, depending on the degree of competition. With the greatest competition, winner-take-all, only one output neuron remains active, and the representation is at its most sparse. This effect can be understood further using Figs. B.15 and B.16. This sparsification is useful to apply to representations before input patterns are applied to associative networks, because sparse representations allow many different pattern associations or memories to be stored in these networks (see Sections B.2 and B.3).

B.4.3.5 Capacity

In a competitive net with N output neurons and a simple winner-take-all rule for the competition, it is possible to learn up to N output categories, in that each output neuron may be allocated a category. When the competition acts in a less rudimentary way, the number of categories that can be learned becomes a complex function of various factors, including the number of modifiable connections per cell and the degree of dilution, or incompleteness, of the connections. Such a function has not yet been described analytically in general, but an upper bound on it can be deduced for the particular case in which the learning is fast, and can be achieved effectively in one shot, or one presentation of each pattern. In that case, the number of categories that can be learned (by the self-organizing process) will at most be equal to the number of associations that can be formed by the corresponding pattern associators, a process that occurs with the additional help of the driving inputs, which effectively determine the categorization in the pattern associator.

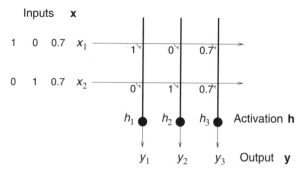

Fig. B.17 Separation of linearly dependent patterns by a competitive network. The network was trained on patterns 10, 01, and 11, applied on the inputs x_1 and x_2. After learning, the network allocated output neuron 1 to pattern 10, neuron 2 to pattern 01, and neuron 3 to pattern 11. The weights in the network produced during the learning are shown. Each input pattern was normalized to unit length, and thus for pattern 11, x_1=0.7 and x_2=0.7, as shown. Because the weight vectors were also normalized to unit length, w_{31}=0.7 and w_{32}=0.7.

Separate constraints on the capacity result if the output vectors are required to be strictly orthogonal. Then, if the output firing rates can assume only positive values, the maximum number p of categories arises, obviously, in the case when only one output neuron is firing for any stimulus, so that up to N categories are formed. If ensemble encoding of output neurons is used (soft competition), again under the orthogonality requirement, then the number of output categories that can be learned will be reduced according to the degree of ensemble encoding. The p categories in the ensemble-encoded case reflect the fact that the between-cluster correlations in the output space are lower than those in the input space. The advantages of ensemble encoding are that dendrites are more evenly allocated to patterns (see Section B.4.9.5), and that correlations between different input stimuli can be reflected in correlations between the corresponding output vectors, so that later networks in the system can generalize usefully. This latter property is of crucial importance, and is utilized for example when an input pattern is presented that has not been learned by the network. The relative similarity of the input pattern to previously learned patterns is indicated by the relative activation of the members of an ensemble of output neurons. This makes the number of different representations that can be reflected in the output of competitive networks with ensemble encoding much higher than with winner-take-all representations, even though with soft competition all these representations cannot strictly be learned.

B.4.3.6   Separation of non-linearly separable patterns

A competitive network can not only separate (e.g. by activating different output neurons) pattern vectors that overlap in almost all elements, but can also help with the separation of vectors that are not linearly separable. An example is that three patterns **A**, **B**, and **A+B** will lead to three different output neurons being activated (see Fig. B.17). For this to occur, the length of the synaptic weight vectors must be normalized (to for example unit length), so that they lie on the surface of a sphere or hypersphere (see Fig. B.15). (If the weight vectors of each neuron are scaled to the same sum, then the weight vectors do not lie on the surface of a hypersphere, and the ability of the network to separate patterns is reduced.)

The property of pattern separation makes a competitive network placed before an autoassociator network very valuable, for it enables the autoassociator to store the three patterns separately, and to recall **A+B** separately from **A** and **B**. This is referred to as the configuration learning problem in animal learning theory (Sutherland and Rudy 1991). Placing a competitive network before a pattern associator will enable a linearly inseparable problem to be solved. For example, three different output neurons of a two-input competitive network could respond to the patterns 01, 10, and 11, and a pattern associator can learn different outputs for neurons 1–3, which are orthogonal to each other (see Fig. B.11). This is an example of expansion recoding (cf. Marr (1969), who used a different algorithm to obtain the expansion). The sparsification that can be produced by the competitive network can also be advantageous in preparing patterns for presentation to a pattern associator or autoassociator, because the sparsification can increase the number of memories that can be associated or stored.

B.4.3.7 Stability

These networks are generally stable if the input statistics are stable. If the input statistics keep varying, then the competitive network will keep following the input statistics. If this is a problem, then a critical period in which the input statistics are learned, followed by stabilization, may be useful. This appears to be a solution used in developing sensory systems, which have critical periods beyond which further changes become more difficult. An alternative approach taken by Carpenter and Grossberg in their 'Adaptive Resonance Theory' (Carpenter 1997) is to allow the network to learn only if it does not already have categorizers for a pattern (see Hertz, Krogh and Palmer (1991), p. 228).

Diluted connectivity can help stability, by making neurons tend to find inputs to categorize in only certain parts of the input space, and then making it difficult for the neuron to wander randomly throughout the space later.

B.4.3.8 Frequency of presentation

If some stimuli are presented more frequently than others, then there will be a tendency for the weight vectors to move more rapidly towards frequently presented stimuli, and more neurons may become allocated to the frequently presented stimuli. If winner-take-all competition is used, the result is that the neurons will tend to become allocated during the learning process to the more frequently presented patterns. If soft competition is used, the tendency of neurons to move from patterns that are infrequently or never presented can be reduced by making the competition fairly strong, so that only a few neurons show any learning when each pattern is presented. Provided that the competition is moderately strong (see Section B.4.9.4), the result is that more neurons are allocated to frequently presented patterns, but one or some neurons are allocated to infrequently presented patterns. These points can all be easily demonstrated in simulations.

In an interesting development, it has been shown that if objects consisting of groups of features are presented during training always with another object present, then separate representations of each object can be formed provided that each object is presented many times, but on each occasion is paired with a different object (Stringer and Rolls 2007b, Stringer, Rolls and Tromans 2007b). This is related to the fact that in this scenario the frequency of co-occurrence of features within the same object is greater than that of features between different objects (see Section 4.5.6.2).

B.4.3.9 Comparison to principal component analysis (PCA) and cluster analysis

Although competitive networks find clusters of features in the input space, they do not perform hierarchical cluster analysis as typically performed in statistics. In hierarchical cluster analysis, input vectors are joined starting with the most correlated pair, and the level of the joining of vectors is indicated. Competitive nets produce different outputs (i.e. activate different output neurons) for each cluster of vectors (i.e. perform vector quantization), but do not compute the level in the hierarchy, unless the network is redesigned (see Hertz, Krogh and Palmer (1991)).

The feature discovery can also be compared to principal component analysis (PCA). (In PCA, the first principal component of a multidimensional space points in the direction of the vector that accounts for most of the variance, and subsequent principal components account for successively less of the variance, and are mutually orthogonal.) In competitive learning with a winner-take-all algorithm, the outputs are mutually orthogonal, but are not in an ordered series according to the amount of variance accounted for, unless the training algorithm is modified. The modification amounts to allowing each of the neurons in a winner-take-all network to learn one at a time, in sequence. The first neuron learns the first principal component. (Neurons trained with a modified Hebb rule learn to maximize the variance of their outputs – see Hertz, Krogh and Palmer (1991).) The second neuron is then allowed to learn, and because its output is orthogonal to the first, it learns the second principal component. This process is repeated. Details are given by Hertz, Krogh and Palmer (1991), but as this is not a biologically plausible process, it is not considered in detail here. We note that simple competitive learning is very helpful biologically, because it can separate patterns, but that a full ordered set of principal components as computed by PCA would probably not be very useful in biologically plausible networks. Our point here is that biological neuronal networks may operate well if the variance in the input representation is distributed across many input neurons, whereas principal component analysis would tend to result in most of the variance being allocated to a few neurons, and the variance being unevenly distributed across the neurons.

B.4.4 Utility of competitive networks in information processing by the brain

B.4.4.1 Feature analysis and preprocessing

Neurons that respond to correlated combinations of their inputs can be described as feature analyzers. Neurons that act as feature analyzers perform useful preprocessing in many sensory systems (see e.g. Chapter 8 of Rolls and Treves (1998)). The power of competitive networks in multistage hierarchical processing to build combinations of what is found at earlier stages, and thus effectively to build higher-order representations, is also described in Chapter 4 of this book. An interesting recent development is that competitive networks can learn about individual objects even when multiple objects are presented simultaneously, provided that each object is presented several times more frequently than it is paired with any other individual object (Stringer and Rolls 2007b) (see Section 4.5.6.2). This property arises because learning in competitive networks is primarily about forming representations of objects defined by a high correlation of coactive features in the input space (Stringer and Rolls 2007b).

B.4.4.2 Removal of redundancy

The removal of redundancy by competition is thought to be a key aspect of how sensory systems, including the ventral cortical visual system, operate. Competitive networks can also be thought of as performing dimension reduction, in that a set of correlated inputs may be responded to as one category or dimension by a competitive network. The concept of redundancy removal can be linked to the point that individual neurons trained with a modified Hebb rule point their weight vector in the direction of the vector that accounts for most of the variance in the input, that is (acting individually) they find the first principal component of the input space (see Section B.4.3.9 and Hertz, Krogh and Palmer (1991)). Although networks with anti-Hebbian synapses between the principal cells (in which the anti-Hebbian learning forces neurons with initially correlated activity to effectively inhibit each other) (Földiák 1991), and networks that perform Independent Component Analysis (Bell and Sejnowski 1995), could in principle remove redundancy more effectively, it is not clear that they are implemented biologically. In contrast, competitive networks are more biologically plausible, and illustrate redundancy reduction. The more general use of an unsupervised competitive preprocessor is discussed below (see Fig. B.24).

B.4.4.3 Orthogonalization

The orthogonalization performed by competitive networks is very useful for preparing signals for presentation to pattern associators and autoassociators, for this re-representation decreases interference between the patterns stored in such networks. Indeed, this can be essential if patterns are overlapping and not linearly independent, e.g. 01, 10, and 11. If three such binary patterns were presented to an autoassociative network, it would not form separate representations of them, because either of the patterns 01 or 10 would result by completion in recall of the 11 pattern. A competitive network allows a separate neuron to be allocated to each of the three patterns, and this set of orthogonal representations can be learned by associative networks (see Fig. B.17).

B.4.4.4 Sparsification

The sparsification performed by competitive networks is very useful for preparing signals for presentation to pattern associators and autoassociators, for this re-representation increases the number of patterns that can be associated or stored in such networks (see Sections B.2 and B.3).

B.4.4.5 Brain systems in which competitive networks may be used for orthogonalization and sparsification

One system is the hippocampus, in which the dentate granule cells are believed to operate as a competitive network in order to prepare signals for presentation to the CA3 autoassociative network (see Chapter 2). In this case, the operation is enhanced by expansion recoding, in that (in the rat) there are approximately three times as many dentate granule cells as there are cells in the preceding stage, the entorhinal cortex. This expansion recoding will itself tend to reduce correlations between patterns (cf. Marr (1970), and Marr (1969)).

Also in the hippocampus, the CA1 neurons are thought to act as a competitive network that recodes the separate representations of each of the parts of an episode that must be separately represented in CA3, into a form more suitable for the recall using pattern association performed by the backprojections from the hippocampus to the cerebral cortex (see Chapter 2 and Rolls and Treves (1998) Chapter 6).

The granule cells of the cerebellum may perform a similar function, but in this case the principle may be that each of the very large number of granule cells receives a very small random subset of inputs, so that the outputs of the granule cells are decorrelated with respect to the inputs (Marr (1969); see Rolls and Treves (1998) Chapter 9).

B.4.5 Guidance of competitive learning

Although competitive networks are primarily unsupervised networks, it is possible to influence the categories found by supplying a second input, as follows (Rolls 1989a). Consider a competitive network as shown in Fig. B.18 with the normal set of inputs **A** to be categorized, and with an additional set of inputs **B** from a different source. Both sets of inputs work in the normal way for a competitive network, with random initial weights, competition between the output neurons, and a Hebb-like synaptic modification rule that normalizes the lengths of the synaptic weight vectors onto each neuron. The idea then is to use the **B** inputs to influence the categories formed by the **A** input vectors. The influence of the **B** vectors works best if

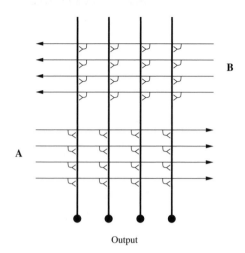

Output

Fig. B.18 Competitive net receiving a normal set of inputs **A**, but also another set of inputs **B** that can be used to influence the categories formed in response to **A** inputs.

they are orthogonal to each other. Consider any two **A** vectors. If they occur together with the same **B** vector, then the categories produced by the **A** vectors will be more similar than they would be without the influence of the **B** vectors. The categories will be pulled closer together if soft competition is used, or will be more likely to activate the same neuron if winner-take-all competition is used. Conversely, if any two **A** vectors are paired with two different, preferably orthogonal, **B** vectors, then the categories formed by the **A** vectors will be drawn further apart than they would be without the **B** vectors. The differences in categorization remain present after the learning when just the **A** inputs are used.

   This guiding function of one of the inputs is one way in which the consequences of sensory stimuli could be fed back to a sensory system to influence the categories formed when the **A** inputs are presented. This could be one function of backprojections in the cerebral cortex (Rolls 1989c, Rolls 1989a). In this case, the **A** inputs of Fig. B.18 would be the forward inputs from a preceding cortical area, and the **B** inputs backprojecting axons from the next cortical area, or from a structure such as the amygdala or hippocampus. If two **A** vectors were both associated with positive reinforcement that was fed back as the same **B** vector from another part of the brain, then the two **A** vectors would be brought closer together in the representational space provided by the output of the neurons. If one of the **A** vectors was associated with positive reinforcement, and the other with negative reinforcement, then the output representations of the two **A** vectors would be further apart. This is one way in which external signals could influence in a mild way the categories formed in sensory systems. Another is that if any **B** vector only occurred for important sensory **A** inputs (as shown by the immediate consequences of receiving those sensory inputs), then the **A** inputs would simply be more likely to have any representation formed than otherwise, due to strong activation of neurons only when combined **A** and **B** inputs are present.

   A similar architecture could be used to provide mild guidance for one sensory system (e.g. olfaction) by another (e.g. taste), as shown in Fig. B.19. (Another example of where this architecture could be used is convergence in the visual system at the next cortical stage of processing, with guiding feedback to influence the categories formed in the different regions of the preceding cortical area, as illustrated in Section 1.11.) The idea is that the taste inputs would be more orthogonal to each other than the olfactory inputs, and that the taste inputs would influence the categories formed in the olfactory input categorizer in layer 1, by feedback

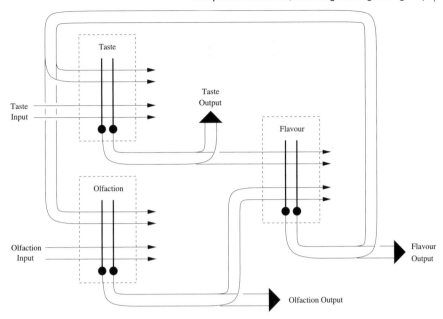

Fig. B.19 A two-layer set of competitive nets in which feedback from layer 2 can influence the categories formed in layer 1. Layer 2 could be a higher cortical visual area with convergence from earlier cortical visual areas (see Chapter 4). In the example, taste and olfactory inputs are received by separate competitive nets in layer 1, and converge into a single competitive net in layer 2. The categories formed in layer 2 (which may be described as representing 'flavour') may be dominated by the relatively orthogonal set of a few tastes that are received by the net. When these layer 2 categories are fed back to layer 1, they may produce in layer 1 categories in, for example, the olfactory network that reflect to some extent the flavour categories of layer 2, and are different from the categories that would otherwise be formed to a large set of rather correlated olfactory inputs. A similar principle may operate in any multilayer hierarchical cortical processing system, such as the ventral visual system, in that the categories that can be formed only at later stages of processing may help earlier stages to form categories relevant to what can be identified at later stages.

from a convergent net in layer 2. The difference from the previous architecture is that we now have a two-layer net, with unimodal or separate networks in layer 1, each feeding forward to a single competitive network in layer 2. The categories formed in layer 2 reflect the co-occurrence of a particular taste with particular odours (which together form flavour in layer 2). Layer 2 then provides feedback connections to both the networks in layer 1. It can be shown in such a network that the categories formed in, for example, the olfactory net in layer 1 are influenced by the tastes with which the odours are paired. The feedback signal is built only in layer 2, after there has been convergence between the different modalities. This architecture captures some of the properties of sensory systems, in which there are unimodal processing cortical areas followed by multimodal cortical areas. The multimodal cortical areas can build representations that represent the unimodal inputs that tend to co-occur, and the higher level representations may in turn, by the highly developed cortico-cortical backprojections, be able to influence sensory categorization in earlier cortical processing areas (Rolls 1989a). Another such example might be the effect by which the phonemes heard are influenced by the visual inputs produced by seeing mouth movements (cf. McGurk and MacDonald (1976)). This could be implemented by auditory inputs coming together in the cortex in the superior temporal sulcus onto neurons activated by the sight of the lips moving (recorded during experiments of Baylis, Rolls and Leonard (1987), and Hasselmo, Rolls, Baylis and Nalwa (1989b)), using

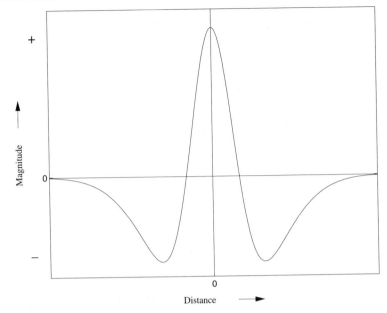

Fig. B.20 Mexican hat lateral spatial interaction profile.

Hebbian learning with co-active inputs. Backprojections from such multimodal areas to the early auditory cortical areas could then influence the responses of auditory cortex neurons to auditory inputs (see Section B.9 and cf. Calvert, Bullmore, Brammer, Campbell, Williams, McGuire, Woodruff, Iversen and David (1997)).

A similar principle may operate in any multilayer hierarchical cortical processing system, such as the ventral visual system, in that the categories that can be formed only at later stages of processing may help earlier stages to form categories relevant to what can be identified at the later stages as a result of the operation of backprojections (Rolls 1989a). The idea that the statistical correlation between the inputs received by neighbouring processing streams can be used to guide unsupervised learning within each stream has also been developed by Becker and Hinton (1992) and others (see Phillips, Kay and Smyth (1995)). The networks considered by these authors self-organize under the influence of collateral connections, such as may be implemented by cortico-cortical connections between parallel processing systems in the brain. They use learning rules that, although somewhat complex, are still local in nature, and tend to optimize specific objective functions. The locality of the learning rule, and the simulations performed so far, raise some hope that, once the operation of these types of networks is better understood, they might achieve similar computational capabilities to backpropagation networks (see Section B.12) while retaining biological plausibility.

B.4.6 Topographic map formation

A simple modification to the competitive networks described so far enables them to develop topological maps. In such maps, the closeness in the map reflects the similarity (correlation) between the features in the inputs. The modification that allows such maps to self-organize is to add short-range excitation and long-range inhibition between the neurons. The function to be implemented has a spatial profile that is described as having a Mexican hat shape (see Fig. B.20). The effect of this connectivity between neurons, which need not be modifiable, is to encourage neurons that are close together to respond to similar features in the input

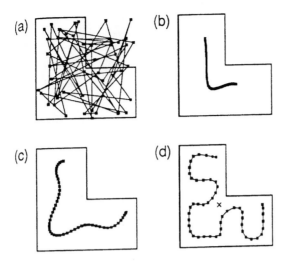

Fig. B.21 Kohonen feature mapping from a two-dimensional L-shaped region to a linear array of 50 units. Each unit has 2 inputs. The input patterns are the X,Y coordinates of points within the L-shape shown. In the diagrams, each point shows the position of a weight vector. Lines connect adjacent units in the 1 D (linear) array of 50 neurons. The weights were initialized to random values within the unit square (a). During feature mapping training, the weights evolved through stages (b) and (c) to (d). By stage (d) the weights have formed so that the positions in the original input space are mapped to a 1 D vector in which adjacent points in the input space activate neighbouring units in the linear array of output units. (Reproduced with permission from Hertz, Krogh and Palmer 1991, Fig. 9.13.)

space, and to encourage neurons that are far apart to respond to different features in the input space. When these response tendencies are present during learning, the feature analyzers that are built by modifying the synapses from the input onto the activated neurons tend to be similar if they are close together, and different if far apart. This is illustrated in Figs. B.21 and B.22. Feature maps built in this way were described by von der Malsburg (1973) and Willshaw and von der Malsburg (1976). It should be noted that the learning rule needed is simply the modified Hebb rule described above for competitive networks, and is thus local and biologically plausible. (For computational convenience, the algorithm that Kohonen (Kohonen 1982, Kohonen 1989, Kohonen 1995) has mainly used does not use Mexican hat connectivity between the neurons, but instead arranges that when the weights to a winning neuron are updated, so to a smaller extent are those of its neighbours – see further Hertz, Krogh and Palmer (1991).)

A very common characteristic of connectivity in the brain, found for example throughout the neocortex, consists of short-range excitatory connections between neurons, with inhibition mediated via inhibitory interneurons. The density of the excitatory connectivity even falls gradually as a function of distance from a neuron, extending typically a distance in the order of 1 mm from the neuron (Braitenberg and Schuz 1991), contributing to a spatial function quite like that of a Mexican hat. (Longer-range inhibitory influences would form the negative part of the spatial response profile.) This supports the idea that topological maps, though in some cases probably seeded by chemoaffinity, could develop in the brain with the assistance of the processes just described. It is noted that some cortico-cortical connections even within an area may be longer, skipping past some intermediate neurons, and then making connections after some distance with a further group of neurons. Such longer-range connections are found

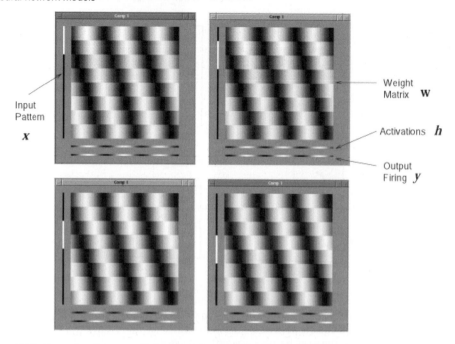

Fig. B.22 Example of a one-dimensional topological map that self-organized from inputs in a low-dimensional space. The network has 64 neurons (vertical elements in the diagram) and 64 inputs per neuron (horizontal elements in the diagram). The four different diagrams represent the net tested with different input patterns. The input patterns x are displayed at the left of each diagram, with white representing firing and black not firing for each of the 64 inputs. The central square of each diagram represents the synaptic weights of the neurons, with white representing a strong weight. The row vector below each weight matrix represents the activations of the 64 output neurons, and the bottom row vector the output firing y. The network was trained with a set of 8 binary input patterns, each of which overlapped in 8 of its 16 'on' elements with the next pattern. The diagram shows that as one moves through correlations in the input space (top left to top right to bottom left to bottom right), so the output neurons activated move steadily across the output array of neurons. Closely correlated inputs are represented close together in the output array of neurons. The way in which this occurs can be seen by inspection of the weight matrix. The network architecture was the same as for a competitive net, except that the activations were converted linearly into output firings, and then each neuron excited its neighbours and inhibited neurons further away. This lateral inhibition was implemented for the simulation by a spatial filter operating on the output firings with the following filter weights (cf. Fig. B.20): 5, 5, 5, 5, 5, 5, 5, 5, 5, 10, 10, 10, 10, 10, 10, 10, 10, 5, 5, 5, 5, 5, 5, 5, 5 which operated on the 64-element firing rate vector.

for example between different columns with similar orientation selectivity in the primary visual cortex. The longer range connections may play a part in stabilizing maps, and again in the exchange of information between neurons performing related computations, in this case about features with the same orientations.

If a low-dimensional space, for example the orientation sensitivity of cortical neurons in the primary visual cortex (which is essentially one-dimensional, the dimension being angle), is mapped to a two-dimensional space such as the surface of the cortex, then the resulting map can have long spatial runs where the value along the dimension (in this case orientation tuning) alters gradually, and continuously. Such self-organization can account for many aspects of the mapping of orientation tuning, and of ocular dominance columns, in V1 (Miller 1994, Harris, Ermentrout and Small 1997). If a high-dimensional information space is mapped to the two-dimensional cortex, then there will be only short runs of groups of neurons with similar feature responsiveness, and then the map must fracture, with a different type of feature mapped for a short distance after the discontinuity. This is exactly what Rolls suggests is the type of topology found in the anterior inferior temporal visual cortex, with the individual groupings representing what can be self-organized by competitive networks combined with a trace rule as described in Section 4.5. Here, visual stimuli are not represented with reference to their position on the retina, because here the neurons are relatively translation invariant. Instead, when recording here, small clumps of neurons with similar responses may be encountered close together, and then one moves into a group of neurons with quite different feature selectivity (personal observations). This topology will arise naturally, given the anatomical connectivity of the cortex with its short-range excitatory connections, because there are very many different objects in the world and different types of features that describe objects, with no special continuity between the different combinations of features possible.

Rolls' hypothesis contrasts with the view of Tanaka (1996), who has claimed that the inferior temporal cortex provides an alphabet of visual features arranged in discrete modules. The type of mapping found in higher cortical visual areas as proposed by Rolls implies that topological self-organization is an important way in which maps in the brain are formed, for it seems most unlikely that the locations in the map of different types of object seen in an environment could be specified genetically (Rolls and Stringer 2000). Consistent with this, Tsao, Freiwald, Tootell and Livingstone (2006) described with macaque fMRI 'anterior face patches' at A15 to A22. A15 might correspond to where we have analysed face-selective neurons (it might translate to 3 mm posterior to our sphenoid reference, see Section 4.2), and at this level there are separate regions specialized for face identity in areas TEa and TEm on the ventral lip of the superior temporal sulcus and the adjacent gyrus, and for face expression and movement in the cortex deep in the superior temporal sulcus (Hasselmo, Rolls and Baylis 1989a, Baylis, Rolls and Leonard 1987, Rolls 2007i). The 'middle face patch' of Tsao, Freiwald, Tootell and Livingstone (2006) was at A6, which is probably part of the posterior inferior temporal cortex, and, again consistent with self-organizing map principles, has a high concentration of face-selective neurons within the patch.

The biological utility of developing such topology-preserving feature maps may be that if the computation requires neurons with similar types of response to exchange information more than neurons involved in different computations (which is more than reasonable), then the total length of the connections between the neurons is minimized if the neurons that need to exchange information are close together (cf. Cowey (1979), Durbin and Mitchison (1990)). Examples of this include the separation of colour constancy processing in V4 from global motion processing in MT as follows (see Chapter 3 of Rolls and Deco (2002)). In V4, to compute colour constancy, an estimate of the illuminating wavelengths can be obtained by summing the outputs of the pyramidal cells in the inhibitory interneurons over several degrees of visual space, and subtracting this from the excitatory central ON colour-tuned region of the receptive field by (subtractive) feedback inhibition. This enables the cells to discount the illuminating wavelength, and thus compute colour constancy. For this computation, no inputs from motion-selective cells (which in the dorsal stream are colour insensitive) are needed. In MT, to compute global motion (e.g. the motion produced by the average flow of local motion elements, exemplified for example by falling snow), the computation can be performed by averaging in the larger (several degrees) receptive fields of MT the local motion inputs received by neurons in earlier cortical areas (V1 and V2) with small receptive fields (see Chapter 3 of Rolls and Deco (2002) and Rolls and Stringer (2007)). For this computation, no input from colour cells is useful. Having separate areas (V4 and MT) for these different computations minimizes the wiring lengths, for having intermingled colour and motion cells in a single cortical area would increase the average connection length between the neurons that need to be connected for the computations being performed. Minimizing the total connection length between neurons in the brain is very important in order to keep the size of the brain relatively small.

Placing close to each other neurons that need to exchange information, or that need to receive information from the same source, or that need to project towards the same destination, may also help to minimize the complexity of the rules required to specify cortical (and indeed brain) connectivity (Rolls and Stringer 2000). For example, in the case of V4 and MT, the connectivity rules can be simpler (e.g. connect to neurons in the vicinity, rather than look for colour-, or motion-marked cells, and connect only to the cells with the correct genetically specified label specifying that the cell is either part of motion or of colour processing). Further, the V4 and MT example shows that how the neurons are connected can be specified quite simply, but of course it needs to be specified to be different for different computations. Specifying a general rule for the classes of neurons in a given area also provides a useful simplification to the genetic rules needed to specify the functional architecture of a given cortical area (Rolls and Stringer 2000). In our V4 and MT example, the genetic rules would need to specify the rules separately for different populations of inhibitory interneurons if the computations performed by V4 and MT were performed with intermixed neurons in a single brain area. Together, these two principles, of minimization of wiring length, and allowing simple genetic specification of wiring rules, may underlie the separation of cortical visual information processing into different (e.g. ventral and dorsal) processing streams. The same two principles operating within each brain processing stream may underlie (taken together with the need for hierarchical processing to enable the computations to be biologically plausible in terms of the number of connections per neuron, and the need for local learning rules, see Section B.13) much of the overall architecture of visual cortical processing, and of information processing and its modular architecture throughout the cortex more generally.

The rules of information exchange just described could also tend to produce more gross topography in cortical regions. For example, neurons that respond to animate objects may have certain visual feature requirements in common, and may need to exchange information about these features. Other neurons that respond to inanimate objects might have somewhat different visual feature requirements for their inputs, and might need to exchange information strongly. (For example, selection of whether an object is a chisel or a screwdriver may require competition by mutual (lateral) inhibition to produce the contrast enhancement necessary to result in unambiguous neuronal responses.) The rules just described would account for neurons with responsiveness to inanimate and animate objects tending to be grouped in separate parts of a cortical map or representation, and thus separately susceptible to brain damage (see e.g. Farah (1990), Farah (2000)).

B.4.7 Invariance learning by competitive networks

In conventional competitive learning, the weight vector of a neuron can be thought of as moving towards the centre of a cluster of similar overlapping input stimuli (Rumelhart and Zipser 1985, Hertz, Krogh and Palmer 1991, Rolls and Treves 1998, Rolls and Deco 2002, Perry, Rolls and Stringer 2007). The weight vector points towards the centre of the set of stimuli in the category. The different training stimuli that are placed into the same category (i.e. activate the same neuron) are typically overlapping in that the pattern vectors are correlated with each other. Figure B.23a illustrates this.

For the formation of invariant representations, there are multiple occurrences of the object at different positions in the space. The object at each position represents a different transform (whether in position, size, view etc.) of the object. The different transforms may be uncorrelated with each other, as would be the case for example with an object translated so far in the space that there would be no active afferents in common between the two transforms.

(a) 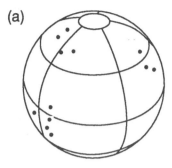   (b)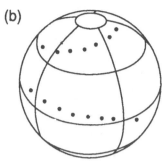

Fig. B.23 (a) Conventional competitive learning. A cluster of overlapping input patterns is categorized as being similar, and this is implemented by a weight vector of an output neuron pointing towards the centre of the cluster. Three clusters are shown, and each cluster might after training have a weight vector pointing towards it. (b) Invariant representation learning. The different transforms of an object may span an elongated region of the space, and the transforms at the far ends of the space may have no overlap (correlation), yet the network must learn to categorize them as similar. The different transforms of two different objects are represented.

Yet we need these two orthogonal patterns to be mapped to the same output. It may be a very elongated part of the input space that has to be mapped to the same output in invariance learning. These concepts are illustrated in Fig. B.23b.

Objects in the world have temporal and spatial continuity. That is, the statistics of the world are such that we tend to look at one object for some time, during which it may be transforming continuously from one view to another. The temporal continuity property is used in trace rule invariance training, in which a short-term memory in the associative learning rule normally used to train competitive networks is used to help build representations that reflect the continuity in time that characterizes the different transforms of each object, as described in Chapter 4. The transforms of an object also show spatial continuity, and this can also be used in invariance training in what is termed continuous spatial transform learning, described in Section 4.5.11.

In conventional competitive learning the overall weight vector points to the prototypical representation of the object. The only sense in which after normal competitive training (without translations etc) the network generalizes is with respect to the dot product similarity of any input vector compared to the central vector from the training set that the network learns. Continuous spatial transformation learning works by providing a set of training vectors that overlap, and between them cover the whole space over which an invariant transform of the object must be learned. Indeed, it is important for continuous spatial transformation learning that the different exemplars of an object are sufficiently close that the similarity of adjacent training exemplars is sufficient to ensure that the same postsynaptic neuron learns to bridge the continuous space spanned by the whole set of training exemplars of a given object (Stringer, Perry, Rolls and Proske 2006, Perry, Rolls and Stringer 2006, Perry, Rolls and Stringer 2007). This will enable the postsynaptic neuron to span a very elongated space of the different transforms of an object, as described in Section 4.5.11.

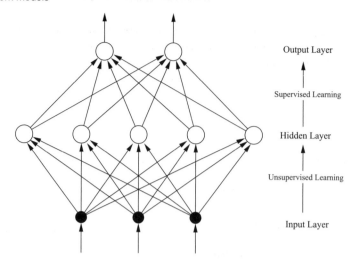

Fig. B.24 A hybrid network, in which for example unsupervised learning rapidly builds relatively orthogonal representations based on input differences, and this is followed by a one-layer supervised network (taught for example by the delta rule) that learns to classify the inputs based on the categorizations formed in the hidden/intermediate layer.

B.4.8 Radial Basis Function networks

As noted above, a competitive network can act as a useful preprocessor for other networks. In the neural examples above, competitive networks were useful preprocessors for associative networks. Competitive networks are also used as preprocessors in artificial neural networks, for example in hybrid two-layer networks such as that illustrated in Fig. B.24. The competitive network is advantageous in this hybrid scheme, because as an unsupervised network, it can relatively quickly (with a few presentations of each stimulus) discover the main features in the input space, and code for them. This leaves the second layer of the network to act as a supervised network (taught for example by the delta rule, see Section B.11), which learns to map the features found by the first layer into the output required. This learning scheme is very much faster than that of a (two-layer) backpropagation network, which learns very slowly because it takes it a long time to perform the credit assignment to build useful feature analyzers in layer one (the hidden layer) (see Section B.12).

The general scheme shown in Fig. B.24 is used in radial basis function (RBF) neural networks. The main difference from what has been described is that in an RBF network, the hidden neurons do not use a winner-take-all function (as in some competitive networks), but instead use a normalized activation function in which the measure of distance from a weight vector of the neural input is (instead of the dot product $\mathbf{x} \cdot \mathbf{w}_i$ used for most of the networks described in this book), a Gaussian measure of distance:

$$y_i = \frac{\exp[-(\mathbf{x} - \mathbf{w}_i)^2 / 2\sigma_i^2]}{\sum_k \exp[-(\mathbf{x} - \mathbf{w}_k)^2 / 2\sigma_k^2]}. \tag{B.21}$$

The effect is that the response y_i of neuron i is a maximum if the input stimulus vector $\mathbf{x}$ is centred at $\mathbf{w}_i$, the weight vector of neuron i (this is the upper term in equation B.21). The magnitude is normalized by dividing by the sum of the activations of all the k neurons in the network. If the input vector $\mathbf{x}$ is not at the centre of the receptive field of the neuron, then the response is decreased according to how far the input vector is from the weight vector $\mathbf{w}_i$ of the neuron, with the weighting decreasing as a Gaussian function with a standard deviation of σ. The idea is like that implemented with soft competition, in that the relative response of different neurons provides an indication of where the input pattern is in relation to the weight vectors of the different neurons. The rapidity with which the response falls off in a Gaussian radial basis function neuron is set by σ_i, which is adjusted so that for any given input pattern vector, a number of RBF neurons are activated. The positions in which the RBF neurons are located (i.e. the directions of their weight vectors, $\mathbf{w}$) are determined usually by unsupervised learning, e.g. the vector quantization that is produced by the normal competitive learning algorithm. The first layer of an RBF network is not different in principle from a network with soft competition, and it is not clear how biologically a Gaussian activation function would be implemented, so the treatment is not developed further here (see Hertz, Krogh and Palmer (1991), Poggio and Girosi (1990a), and Poggio and Girosi (1990b) for further details).

B.4.9 Further details of the algorithms used in competitive networks

B.4.9.1 Normalization of the inputs

Normalization is useful because in step 1 of the training algorithm described in Section B.4.2.2, the neuronal activations, formed by the inner product of the pattern and the normalized weight vector on each neuron, are scaled in such a way that they have a maximum value of 1.0. This helps different input patterns to be equally effective in the learning process. A way in which this normalization could be achieved by a layer of input neurons is given by Grossberg (1976a). In the brain, a number of factors may contribute to normalization of the inputs. One factor is that a set of input axons to a neuron will come from another network in which the firing is controlled by inhibitory feedback, and if the numbers of axons involved is large (hundreds or thousands), then the inputs will be in a reasonable range. Second, there is increasing evidence that the different classes of input to a neuron may activate different types of inhibitory interneuron (e.g. Buhl, Halasy and Somogyi (1994)), which terminate on separate parts of the dendrite, usually close to the site of termination of the corresponding excitatory afferents. This may allow separate feedforward inhibition for the different classes of input. In addition, the feedback inhibitory interneurons also have characteristic termination sites, often on or close to the cell body, where they may be particularly effective in controlling firing of the neuron by shunting (divisive) inhibition, rather than by scaling a class of input (see Section B.6).

B.4.9.2 Normalization of the length of the synaptic weight vector on each dendrite

This is necessary to ensure that one or a few neurons do not always win the competition. (If the weights on one neuron were increased by simple Hebbian learning, and there was no normalization of the weights on the neuron, then it would tend to respond strongly in the future to patterns with some overlap with patterns to which that neuron has previously learned, and gradually that neuron would capture a large number of patterns.) A biologically plausible way to achieve this weight adjustment is to use a modified Hebb rule:

$$\delta w_{ij} = \alpha y_i (x_j - w_{ij}) \tag{B.22}$$

where α is a constant, and x_j and w_{ij} are in appropriate units. In vector notation,

$$\delta \mathbf{w}_i = \alpha y_i (\mathbf{x} - \mathbf{w}_i) \tag{B.23}$$

where $\mathbf{w}_i$ is the synaptic weight vector on neuron i. This implements a Hebb rule that increases synaptic strength according to conjunctive pre- and post-synaptic activity, and also allows the strength of each synapse to decrease in proportion to the firing rate of the postsynaptic neuron (as well as in proportion to the existing synaptic strength). This results in a decrease in synaptic strength for synapses from weakly active presynaptic neurons onto strongly active postsynaptic neurons. Such a modification in synaptic strength is termed heterosynaptic long-term depression in the neurophysiological literature, referring to the fact that the synapses that weaken are other than those that activate the neuron.

This is an important computational use of heterosynaptic long-term depression (LTD). In that the amount of decrease of the synaptic strength depends on how strong the synapse is already, the rule is compatible with what is frequently reported in studies of LTD (see Section 1.5). This rule can maintain the sums of the synaptic weights on each dendrite to be very similar without any need for explicit normalization of the synaptic strengths, and is useful in competitive nets. This rule was used by Willshaw and von der Malsburg (1976). As is made clear with the vector notation above, the modified Hebb rule moves the direction of the weight vector $\mathbf{w}_i$ towards the current input pattern vector $\mathbf{x}$ in proportion to the difference between these two vectors and the firing rate y_i of neuron i.

If explicit weight (vector length) normalization is needed, the appropriate form of the modified Hebb rule is:

$$\delta w_{ij} = \alpha y_i (x_j - y_i w_{ij}). \tag{B.24}$$

This rule, formulated by Oja (1982), makes weight decay proportional to y_i^2, normalizes the synaptic weight vector (see Hertz, Krogh and Palmer (1991)), is still a local learning rule, and is known as the Oja rule.

B.4.9.3 Non-linearity in the learning rule

Non-linearity in the learning rule can assist competition (Rolls 1989b, Rolls 1996c). For example, in the brain, long-term potentiation typically occurs only when strong activation of a neuron has produced sufficient depolarization for the voltage-dependent NMDA receptors to become unblocked, allowing Ca^{2+} to enter the cell (see Section 1.5). This means that synaptic modification occurs only on neurons that are strongly activated, effectively assisting competition to select few winners. The learning rule can be written:

$$\delta w_{ij} = \alpha m_i x_j \tag{B.25}$$

where m_i is a (e.g. threshold) non-linear function of the post-synaptic firing y_i which mimics the operation of the NMDA receptors in learning. (It is noted that in associative networks the same process may result in the stored pattern being more sparse than the input pattern, and that this may be beneficial, especially given the exponential firing rate distribution of neurons, in helping to maximize the number of patterns stored in associative networks (see Sections B.2, B.3, and C.3.1).

B.4.9.4 Competition

In a simulation of a competitive network, a single winner can be selected by searching for the neuron with the maximum activation. If graded competition is required, this can be achieved by an activation function that increases greater than linearly. In some of the networks we have simulated (Rolls 1989b, Rolls 1989a, Wallis and Rolls 1997), raising the activation to a fixed power, typically in the range 2–5, and then rescaling the outputs to a fixed maximum (e.g. 1) is simple to implement. In a real neuronal network, winner-take-all competition can be implemented using mutual (lateral) inhibition between the neurons with non-linear activation functions, and self-excitation of each neuron (see e.g. Grossberg (1976a), Grossberg (1988), Hertz, Krogh and Palmer (1991)).

Another method to implement soft competition in simulations is to use the normalized exponential or 'softmax' activation function for the neurons (Bridle (1990); see Bishop (1995)):

$$y = \exp(h)/\sum_i \exp(h_i) \;. \tag{B.26}$$

This function specifies that the firing rate of each neuron is an exponential function of the activation, scaled by the whole vector of activations h_i, $i = 1, N$. The exponential function (in increasing supralinearly) implements soft competition, in that after the competition the faster firing neurons are firing relatively much faster than the slower firing neurons. In fact, the strength of the competition can be adjusted by using a 'temperature' T greater than 0 as follows:

$$y = \exp(h/T)/\sum_i \exp(h_i/T). \tag{B.27}$$

Very low temperatures increase the competition, until with $T \to 0$, the competition becomes 'winner-take-all'. At high temperatures, the competition becomes very soft. (When using the function in simulations, it may be advisable to prescale the firing rates to for example the range 0–1, both to prevent machine overflow, and to set the temperature to operate on a constant range of firing rates, as increasing the range of the inputs has an effect similar to decreasing T.)

The softmax function has the property that activations in the range $-\infty$ to $+\infty$ are mapped into the range 0 to 1.0, and the sum of the firing rates is 1.0. This facilitates interpretation of the firing rates under certain conditions as probabilities, for example that the competitive network firing rate of each neuron reflects the probability that the input vector is within the category or cluster signified by that output neuron (see Bishop (1995)).

B.4.9.5 Soft competition

The use of graded (continuous valued) output neurons in a competitive network, and soft competition rather than winner-take-all competition, has the value that the competitive net generalizes more continuously to an input vector that lies between input vectors that it has learned. Also, with soft competition, neurons with only a small amount of activation by any of the patterns being used will nevertheless learn a little, and move gradually towards the patterns that are being presented. The result is that with soft competition, the output neurons all tend to become allocated to one of the input patterns or one of the clusters of input patterns.

B.4.9.6 Untrained neurons

In competitive networks, especially with winner-take-all or finely tuned neurons, it is possible that some neurons remain unallocated to patterns. This may be useful, in case patterns in the unused part of the space occur in future. Alternatively, unallocated neurons can be made to move towards the parts of the space where patterns are occurring by allowing such losers in the competition to learn a little. Another mechanism is to subtract a bias term μ_i from y_i, and to use a 'conscience' mechanism that raises μ_i if a neuron wins frequently, and lowers μ_i if it wins infrequently (Grossberg 1976b, Bienenstock, Cooper and Munro 1982, De Sieno 1988).

B.4.9.7 Large competitive nets: further aspects

If a large neuronal network is considered, with the number of synapses on each neuron in the region of 10,000, as occurs on large pyramidal cells in some parts of the brain, then there is a potential disadvantage in using neurons with synaptic weights that can take on only positive values. This difficulty arises in the following way. Consider a set of positive normalized input firing rates and synaptic weight vectors (in which each element of the vector can take on any value between 0.0 and 1.0). Such vectors of random values will on average be more highly aligned with the direction of the central vector $(1,1,1,...,1)$ than with any other vector. An example can be given for the particular case of vectors evenly distributed on the positive 'quadrant' of a high-dimensional hypersphere: the average overlap (i.e. normalized dot product) between two binary random vectors with half the elements on and thus a sparseness of 0.5 (e.g. a random pattern vector and a random dendritic weight vector) will be approximately 0.5, while the average overlap between a random vector and the central vector will be approximately 0.707. A consequence of this will be that if a neuron begins to learn towards several input pattern vectors it will get drawn towards the average of these input patterns which will be closer to the 1,1,1,...,1 direction than to any one of the patterns. As a dendritic weight vector moves towards the central vector, it will become more closely aligned with more and more input patterns so that it is more rapidly drawn towards the central vector. The end result is that in large nets of this type, many of the dendritic weight vectors will point towards the central vector. This effect is not seen so much in small systems, since the fluctuations in the magnitude of the overlaps are sufficiently large that in most cases a dendritic weight vector will have an input pattern very close to it and thus will not learn towards the centre. In large systems, the fluctuations in the overlaps between random vectors become smaller by a factor of $\frac{1}{\sqrt{N}}$ so that the dendrites will not be particularly close to any of the input patterns.

One solution to this problem is to allow the elements of the synaptic weight vectors to take negative as well as positive values. This could be implemented in the brain by feedforward inhibition. A set of vectors taken with random values will then have a reduced mean correlation between any pair, and the competitive net will be able to categorize them effectively. A system with synaptic weights that can be negative as well as positive is not physiologically plausible, but we can instead imagine a system with weights lying on a hypersphere in the positive quadrant of space but with additional inhibition that results in the cumulative effects of some input lines being effectively negative. This can be achieved in a network by using positive input vectors, positive synaptic weight vectors, and thresholding the output neurons at their mean activation. A large competitive network of this general nature does categorize well, and has been described more fully elsewhere (Bennett 1990). In a large network with inhibitory feedback neurons, and principal cells with thresholds, the network could achieve at least in part an approximation to this type of thresholding useful in large competitive networks.

A second way in which nets with positive-only values of the elements could operate is by making the input vectors sparse and initializing the weight vectors to be sparse, or to have a reduced contact probability. (A measure a of neuronal population sparseness is defined (as before) in equation B.28:

$$a = \frac{(\sum\limits_{i=1}^{N} y_i/N)^2}{\sum\limits_{i=1}^{N} y_i^2/N} \tag{B.28}$$

where y_i is the firing rate of the ith neuron in the set of N neurons.) For relatively small net sizes simulated ($N = 100$) with patterns with a sparseness a of, for example, 0.1 or 0.2, learning onto the average vector can be avoided. However, as the net size increases, the sparseness required does become very low. In large nets, a greatly reduced contact probability between neurons (many synapses kept identically zero) would prevent learning of the average vector, thus allowing categorization to occur. Reduced contact probability will, however, prevent complete alignment of synapses with patterns, so that the performance of the network will be affected.

B.5 Continuous attractor networks

B.5.1 Introduction

Single-cell recording studies have shown that some neurons represent the current position along a continuous physical dimension or space even when no inputs are available, for example in darkness (see Chapter 2). Examples include neurons that represent the positions of the eyes (i.e. eye direction with respect to the head), the place where the animal is looking in space, head direction, and the place where the animal is located. In particular, examples of such classes of cells include head direction cells in rats (Ranck 1985, Taube, Muller and Ranck 1990a, Taube, Goodridge, Golob, Dudchenko and Stackman 1996, Muller, Ranck and Taube 1996) and primates (Robertson, Rolls, Georges-François and Panzeri 1999), which respond maximally when the animal's head is facing in a particular preferred direction; place cells in rats (O'Keefe and Dostrovsky 1971, McNaughton, Barnes and O'Keefe 1983, O'Keefe 1984, Muller, Kubie, Bostock, Taube and Quirk 1991, Markus, Qin, Leonard, Skaggs, McNaughton and Barnes 1995) that fire maximally when the animal is in a particular location; and spatial view cells in primates that respond when the monkey is looking towards a particular location in space (Rolls, Robertson and Georges-François 1997a, Georges-François, Rolls and Robertson 1999, Robertson, Rolls and Georges-François 1998). In the parietal cortex there are many spatial representations, in several different coordinate frames (see Chapter 4 of Rolls and Deco (2002) and Andersen, Batista, Snyder, Buneo and Cohen (2000)), and they have some capability to remain active during memory periods when the stimulus is no longer present. Even more than this, the dorsolateral prefrontal cortex networks to which the parietal networks project have the capability to maintain spatial representations active for many seconds or minutes during short-term memory tasks, when the stimulus is no longer present (see Section 5.1). In this section, we describe how such networks representing continuous physical space could operate. The locations of such spatial networks in the brain are the parietal areas, the prefrontal areas that implement short-term spatial memory and receive from the parietal cortex (see Section 5.1), and the hippocampal system which combines information about objects from the inferior temporal visual cortex with spatial information (see Chapter 2).

A class of network that can maintain the firing of its neurons to represent any location along a continuous physical dimension such as spatial position, head direction, etc. is a 'Continuous Attractor' neural network (CANN). It uses excitatory recurrent collateral connections between the neurons to reflect the distance between the neurons in the state space of the animal (e.g. head direction space). These networks can maintain the bubble of neural activity constant for long periods wherever it is started to represent the current state (head direction, position, etc) of the animal, and are likely to be involved in many aspects of spatial processing and memory, including spatial vision. Global inhibition is used to keep the number of neurons in a bubble or packet of actively firing neurons relatively constant, and to help to ensure that there is only one activity packet. Continuous attractor networks can be thought of as very similar to autoassociation or discrete attractor networks (described in Section B.3), and have the same architecture, as illustrated in Fig. B.25. The main difference is that the patterns stored in a CANN are continuous patterns, with each neuron having broadly tuned firing which decreases with for example a Gaussian function as the distance from the optimal firing location of the cell is varied, and with different neurons having tuning that overlaps throughout the space. Such tuning is illustrated in Fig. 2.16. For comparison, the autoassociation networks described in Section B.3 have discrete (separate) patterns (each pattern implemented by the firing of a particular subset of the neurons), with no continuous distribution of the patterns throughout the space (see Fig. 2.16). A consequent difference is that the CANN can maintain its firing at any location in the trained continuous space, whereas a discrete attractor or autoassociation

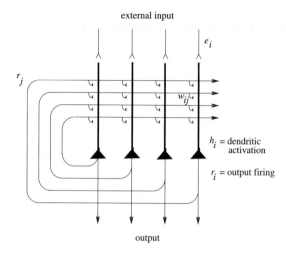

external input

e_i

r_j

w_{ij}

h_i = dendritic activation

r_i = output firing

output

Fig. B.25 The architecture of a continuous attractor neural network (CANN).

network moves its population of active neurons towards one of the previously learned attractor states, and thus implements the recall of a particular previously learned pattern from an incomplete or noisy (distorted) version of one of the previously learned patterns. The energy landscape of a discrete attractor network (see equation B.12) has separate energy minima, each one of which corresponds to a learned pattern, whereas the energy landscape of a continuous attractor network is flat, so that the activity packet remains stable with continuous firing wherever it is started in the state space. (The state space refers to the set of possible spatial states of the animal in its environment, e.g. the set of possible head directions.)

In Section B.5.2, we first describe the operation and properties of continuous attractor networks, which have been studied by for example Amari (1977), Zhang (1996), and Taylor (1999), and then, following Stringer, Trappenberg, Rolls and De Araujo (2002b), address four key issues about the biological application of continuous attractor network models.

One key issue in such continuous attractor neural networks is how the synaptic strengths between the neurons in the continuous attractor network could be learned in biological systems (Section B.5.3).

A second key issue in such continuous attractor neural networks is how the bubble of neuronal firing representing one location in the continuous state space should be updated based on non-visual cues to represent a new location in state space (Section B.5.5). This is essentially the problem of path integration: how a system that represents a memory of where the agent is in physical space could be updated based on idiothetic (self-motion) cues such as vestibular cues (which might represent a head velocity signal), or proprioceptive cues (which might update a representation of place based on movements being made in the space, during for example walking in the dark).

A third key issue is how stability in the bubble of activity representing the current location can be maintained without much drift in darkness, when it is operating as a memory system (Section B.5.6).

A fourth key issue is considered in Section B.5.8 in which we describe networks that store both continuous patterns and discrete patterns (see Fig. 2.16), which can be used to store for example the location in (continuous, physical) space where an object (a discrete item) is present.

B.5.2   The generic model of a continuous attractor network

The generic model of a continuous attractor is as follows. (The model is described in the context of head direction cells, which represent the head direction of rats (Taube et al. 1996, Muller et al. 1996) and macaques (Robertson, Rolls, Georges-François and Panzeri 1999), and can be reset by visual inputs after gradual drift in darkness.) The model is a recurrent attractor network with global inhibition. It is different from a Hopfield attractor network primarily in that there are no discrete attractors formed by associative learning of discrete patterns. Instead there is a set of neurons that are connected to each other by synaptic weights w_{ij} that are a simple function, for example Gaussian, of the distance between the states of the agent in the physical world (e.g. head directions) represented by the neurons. Neurons that represent similar states (locations in the state space) of the agent in the physical world have strong synaptic connections, which can be set up by an associative learning rule, as described in Section B.5.3. The network updates its firing rates by the following 'leaky-integrator' dynamical equations. The continuously changing activation h_i^{HD} of each head direction cell i is governed by the equation

$$\tau \frac{dh_i^{\mathrm{HD}}(t)}{dt} = -h_i^{\mathrm{HD}}(t) + \frac{\phi_0}{C^{\mathrm{HD}}} \sum_j (w_{ij} - w^{\mathrm{inh}}) r_j^{\mathrm{HD}}(t) + I_i^V, \qquad (\text{B.29})$$

where r_j^{HD} is the firing rate of head direction cell j, w_{ij} is the excitatory (positive) synaptic weight from head direction cell j to cell i, w^{inh} is a global constant describing the effect of inhibitory interneurons, and τ is the time constant of the system[40]. The term $-h_i^{\mathrm{HD}}(t)$ indicates the amount by which the activation decays (in the leaky integrator neuron) at time t. (The network is updated in a typical simulation at much smaller timesteps than the time constant of the system, τ.) The next term in equation B.29 is the input from other neurons in the network r_j^{HD} weighted by the recurrent collateral synaptic connections w_{ij} (scaled by a constant ϕ_0 and C^{HD} which is the number of synaptic connections received by each head direction cell from other head direction cells in the continuous attractor). The term I_i^V represents a visual input to head direction cell i. Each term I_i^V is set to have a Gaussian response profile in most continuous attractor networks, and this sets the firing of the cells in the continuous attractor to have Gaussian response profiles as a function of where the agent is located in the state space (see e.g. Fig. 2.16 on page 65), but the Gaussian assumption is not crucial. (It is known that the firing rates of head direction cells in both rats (Taube, Goodridge, Golob, Dudchenko and Stackman 1996, Muller, Ranck and Taube 1996) and macaques (Robertson, Rolls, Georges-François and Panzeri 1999) is approximately Gaussian.) When the agent is operating without visual input, in memory mode, then the term I_i^V is set to zero. The firing rate r_i^{HD} of cell i is determined from the activation h_i^{HD} and the sigmoid function

$$r_i^{\mathrm{HD}}(t) = \frac{1}{1 + e^{-2\beta(h_i^{\mathrm{HD}}(t) - \alpha)}}, \qquad (\text{B.30})$$

where α and β are the sigmoid threshold and slope, respectively.

B.5.3   Learning the synaptic strengths between the neurons that implement a continuous attractor network

So far we have said that the neurons in the continuous attractor network are connected to each other by synaptic weights w_{ij} that are a simple function, for example Gaussian, of the

---

[40]Note that for this section, we use r rather than y to refer to the firing rates of the neurons in the network, remembering that, because this is a recurrently connected network (see Fig. B.13), the output from a neuron y_i might be the input x_j to another neuron.

distance between the states of the agent in the physical world (e.g. head directions, spatial views etc) represented by the neurons. In many simulations, the weights are set by formula to have weights with these appropriate Gaussian values. However, Stringer, Trappenberg, Rolls and De Araujo (2002b) showed how the appropriate weights could be set up by learning. They started with the fact that since the neurons have broad tuning that may be Gaussian in shape, nearby neurons in the state space will have overlapping spatial fields, and will thus be co-active to a degree that depends on the distance between them. They postulated that therefore the synaptic weights could be set up by associative learning based on the co-activity of the neurons produced by external stimuli as the animal moved in the state space. For example, head direction cells are forced to fire during learning by visual cues in the environment that produce Gaussian firing as a function of head direction from an optimal head direction for each cell. The learning rule is simply that the weights w_{ij} from head direction cell j with firing rate r_j^{HD} to head direction cell i with firing rate r_i^{HD} are updated according to an associative (Hebb) rule

$$\delta w_{ij} = k r_i^{\mathrm{HD}} \, r_j^{\mathrm{HD}} \qquad (\mathrm{B.31})$$

where δw_{ij} is the change of synaptic weight and k is the learning rate constant. During the learning phase, the firing rate r_i^{HD} of each head direction cell i might be the following Gaussian function of the displacement of the head from the optimal firing direction of the cell

$$r_i^{\mathrm{HD}} = e^{-s_{\mathrm{HD}}^2 / 2\sigma_{\mathrm{HD}}^2}, \qquad (\mathrm{B.32})$$

where s_{HD} is the difference between the actual head direction x (in degrees) of the agent and the optimal head direction x_i for head direction cell i, and σ_{HD} is the standard deviation.

Stringer, Trappenberg, Rolls and De Araujo (2002b) showed that after training at all head directions, the synaptic connections develop strengths that are an almost Gaussian function of the distance between the cells in head direction space, as shown in Fig. B.26 (left). Interestingly if a non-linearity is introduced into the learning rule that mimics the properties of NMDA receptors by allowing the synapses to modify only after strong postsynaptic firing is present, then the synaptic strengths are still close to a Gaussian function of the distance between the connected cells in head direction space (see Fig. B.26, left). They showed that after training, the continuous attractor network can support stable activity packets in the absence of visual inputs (see Fig. B.26, right) provided that global inhibition is used to prevent all the neurons becoming activated. (The exact stability conditions for such networks have been analyzed by Amari (1977)). Thus Stringer, Trappenberg, Rolls and De Araujo (2002b) demonstrated biologically plausible mechanisms for training the synaptic weights in a continuous attractor using a biologically plausible local learning rule.

Stringer, Trappenberg, Rolls and De Araujo (2002b) went on to show that if there was a short term memory trace built into the operation of the learning rule, then this could help to produce smooth weights in the continuous attractor if only incomplete training was available, that is if the weights were trained at only a few locations. The same rule can take advantage in training the synaptic weights of the temporal probability distributions of firing when they happen to reflect spatial proximity. For example, for head direction cells the agent will necessarily move through similar head directions before reaching quite different head directions, and so the temporal proximity with which the cells fire can be used to set up the appropriate synaptic weights. This new proposal for training continuous attractor networks can also help to produce broadly tuned spatial cells even if the driving (e.g. visual) input (I_i^V in equation B.29) during training produces rather narrowly tuned neuronal responses. The learning rule with such temporal properties is a memory trace learning rule that strengthens synaptic connections between neurons, based on the temporal probability distribution of the firing. There are many versions of such rules (Rolls and Milward 2000, Rolls

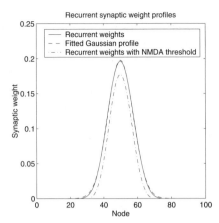

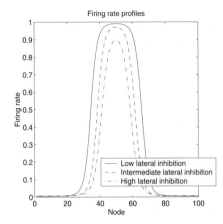

Fig. B.26 Training the weights in a continuous attractor network with an associative rule (equation B.31). Left: the trained recurrent synaptic weights from head direction cell 50 to the other head direction cells in the network arranged in head direction space (solid curve). The dashed line shows a Gaussian curve fitted to the weights shown in the solid curve. The dash-dot curve shows the recurrent synaptic weights trained with rule equation (B.31), but with a non-linearity introduced that mimics the properties of NMDA receptors by allowing the synapses to modify only after strong postsynaptic firing is present. Right: the stable firing rate profiles forming an activity packet in the continuous attractor network during the testing phase when the training (visual) inputs are no longer present. The firing rates are shown after the network has been initially stimulated by visual input to initialize an activity packet, and then allowed to settle to a stable activity profile without visual input. The three graphs show the firing rates for low, intermediate and high values of the lateral inhibition parameter w^{inh}. For both left and right plots, the 100 head direction cells are arranged according to where they fire maximally in the head direction space of the agent when visual cues are available. (After Stringer, Trappenberg, Rolls and de Araujo 2002.)

and Stringer 2001a), which are described more fully in Chapter 4, but a simple one that works adequately is

$$\delta w_{ij} = k \bar{r}_i^{\mathrm{HD}} \bar{r}_j^{\mathrm{HD}} \tag{B.33}$$

where δw_{ij} is the change of synaptic weight, and $\bar{r}^{\mathrm{HD}}$ is a local temporal average or trace value of the firing rate of a head direction cell given by

$$\bar{r}^{\mathrm{HD}}(t + \delta t) = (1 - \eta) r^{\mathrm{HD}}(t + \delta t) + \eta \bar{r}^{\mathrm{HD}}(t) \tag{B.34}$$

where η is a parameter set in the interval [0,1] which determines the contribution of the current firing and the previous trace. For $\eta = 0$ the trace rule (B.33) becomes the standard Hebb rule (B.31), while for $\eta > 0$ learning rule (B.33) operates to associate together patterns of activity that occur close together in time. The rule might allow temporal associations to influence the synaptic weights that are learned over times in the order of 1 s. The memory trace required for operation of this rule might be no more complicated than the continuing firing that is an inherent property of attractor networks, but it could also be implemented by a number of biophysical mechanisms, discussed in Chapter 4. Finally, we note that some long-term depression (LTD) in the learning rule could help to maintain the weights of different neurons equally potent (see Section B.4.9.2 and equation B.22), and could compensate for irregularity during training in which the agent might be trained much more in some than other locations in the space (see Stringer, Trappenberg, Rolls and De Araujo (2002b)).

B.5.4 The capacity of a continuous attractor network: multiple charts and packets

The capacity of a continuous attractor network can be approached on the following bases. First, as there are no discrete attractor states, but instead a continuous physical space is being represented, some concept of spatial resolution must be brought to bear, that is the number of different positions in the space that can be represented. Second, the number of connections per neuron in the continuous attractor will directly influence the number of different spatial positions (locations in the state space) that can be represented. Third, the sparseness of the representation can be thought of as influencing the number of different spatial locations (in the continuous state space) that can be represented, in a way analogous to that described for discrete attractor networks in equation B.14 (Battaglia and Treves 1998b). That is, if the tuning of the neurons is very broad, then fewer locations in the state space may be represented. Fourth, and very interestingly, if representations of different continuous state spaces, for example maps or charts of different environments, are stored in the same network, there may be little cost of adding extra maps or charts. The reason for this is that the large part of the interference between the different memories stored in such a network arises from the correlations between the different positions in any one map, which are typically relatively high because quite broad tuning of individual cells is common. In contrast, there are in general low correlations between the representations of places in different maps or charts, and therefore many different maps can be simultaneously stored in a continuous attractor network (Battaglia and Treves 1998b).

For a similar reason, it is even possible to have the activity packets that operate in different spaces simultaneously active in a single continuous attractor network of neurons, and to move independently of each other in their respective spaces or charts (Stringer, Rolls and Trappenberg 2004).

B.5.5 Continuous attractor models: path integration

So far, we have considered how spatial representations could be stored in continuous attractor networks, and how the activity can be maintained at any location in the state space in a form of short-term memory when the external (e.g. visual) input is removed. However, many networks with spatial representations in the brain can be updated by internal, self-motion (i.e. idiothetic), cues even when there is no external (e.g. visual) input. Examples are head direction cells in the presubiculum of rats and macaques, place cells in the rat hippocampus, and spatial view cells in the primate hippocampus (see Chapter 2). The major question arises about how such idiothetic inputs could drive the activity packet in a continuous attractor network and, in particular, how such a system could be set up biologically by self-organizing learning.

One approach to simulating the movement of an activity packet produced by idiothetic cues (which is a form of path integration whereby the current location is calculated from recent movements) is to employ a look-up table that stores (taking head direction cells as an example), for every possible head direction and head rotational velocity input generated by the vestibular system, the corresponding new head direction (Samsonovich and McNaughton 1997). Another approach involves modulating the strengths of the recurrent synaptic weights in the continuous attractor on one but not the other side of a currently represented position, so that the stable position of the packet of activity, which requires symmetric connections in different directions from each node, is lost, and the packet moves in the direction of the temporarily increased weights, although no possible biological implementation was proposed of how the appropriate dynamic synaptic weight changes might be achieved (Zhang 1996). Another mechanism (for head direction cells) (Skaggs, Knierim, Kudrimoti and McNaughton 1995) relies on

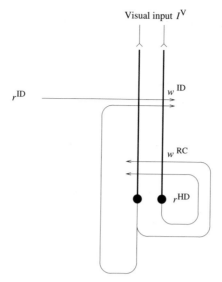

Fig. B.27 General network architecture for a one-dimensional continuous attractor model of head direction cells which can be updated by idiothetic inputs produced by head rotation cell firing r^{ID}. The head direction cell firing is r^{HD}, the continuous attractor synaptic weights are w^{RC}, the idiothetic synaptic weights are w^{ID}, and the external visual input is I^{V}.

a set of cells, termed (head) rotation cells, which are co-activated by head direction cells and vestibular cells and drive the activity of the attractor network by anatomically distinct connections for clockwise and counter-clockwise rotation cells, in what is effectively a look-up table. However, no proposal was made about how this could be achieved by a biologically plausible learning process, and this has been the case until recently for most approaches to path integration in continuous attractor networks, which rely heavily on rather artificial pre-set synaptic connectivities.

Stringer, Trappenberg, Rolls and De Araujo (2002b) introduced a proposal with more biological plausibility about how the synaptic connections from idiothetic inputs to a continuous attractor network can be learned by a self-organizing learning process. The essence of the hypothesis is described with Fig. B.27. The continuous attractor synaptic weights w^{RC} are set up under the influence of the external visual inputs I^{V} as described in Section B.5.3. At the same time, the idiothetic synaptic weights w^{ID} (in which the ID refers to the fact that they are in this case produced by idiothetic inputs, produced by cells that fire to represent the velocity of clockwise and anticlockwise head rotation), are set up by associating the change of head direction cell firing that has just occurred (detected by a trace memory mechanism described below) with the current firing of the head rotation cells r^{ID}. For example, when the trace memory mechanism incorporated into the idiothetic synapses w^{ID} detects that the head direction cell firing is at a given location (indicated by the firing r^{HD}) and is moving clockwise (produced by the altering visual inputs I^{V}), and there is simultaneous clockwise head rotation cell firing, the synapses w^{ID} learn the association, so that when that rotation cell firing occurs later without visual input, it takes the current head direction firing in the continuous attractor into account, and moves the location of the head direction attractor in the appropriate direction.

For the learning to operate, the idiothetic synapses onto head direction cell i with firing r_i^{HD} need two inputs: the memory traced term from other head direction cells $\bar{r}_j^{\mathrm{HD}}$ (given by equation B.34), and the head rotation cell input with firing r_k^{ID}; and the learning rule can be written

$$\delta w_{ijk}^{\text{ID}} = \tilde{k} \, r_i^{\text{HD}} \, \bar{r}_j^{\text{HD}} \, r_k^{\text{ID}}, \tag{B.35}$$

where $\tilde{k}$ is the learning rate associated with this type of synaptic connection. The head rotation cell firing (r_k^{ID}) could be as simple as one set of cells that fire for clockwise head rotation (for which k might be 1), and a second set of cells that fire for anticlockwise head rotation (for which k might be 2).

After learning, the firing of the head direction cells would be updated in the dark (when $I_i^V = 0$) by idiothetic head rotation cell firing r_k^{ID} as follows

$$\tau \frac{\mathrm{d} h_i^{\text{HD}}(t)}{\mathrm{d}t} = -h_i^{\text{HD}}(t) + \frac{\phi_0}{C^{\text{HD}}} \sum_j (w_{ij} - w^{inh}) r_j^{\text{HD}}(t) + I_i^V$$

$$+ \phi_1 \Big(\frac{1}{C^{\text{HD} \times \text{ID}}} \sum_{j,k} w_{ijk}^{\text{ID}} r_j^{\text{HD}} r_k^{\text{ID}} \Big). \tag{B.36}$$

Equation B.36 is similar to equation B.29, except for the last term, which introduces the effects of the idiothetic synaptic weights w_{ijk}^{ID}, which effectively specify that the current firing of head direction cell i, r_i^{HD}, must be updated by the previously learned combination of the particular head rotation now occurring indicated by r_k^{ID}, and the current head direction indicated by the firings of the other head direction cells r_j^{HD} indexed through j[41]. This makes it clear that the idiothetic synapses operate using combinations of inputs, in this case of two inputs. Neurons that sum the effects of such local products are termed Sigma-Pi neurons (see Section A.2.3). Although such synapses are more complicated than the two-term synapses used throughout the rest of this book, such three-term synapses appear to be useful to solve the computational problem of updating representations based on idiothetic inputs in the way described. Synapses that operate according to Sigma-Pi rules might be implemented in the brain by a number of mechanisms described by Koch (1999) (Section 21.1.1), Jonas and Kaczmarek (1999), and Stringer, Trappenberg, Rolls and De Araujo (2002b), including having two inputs close together on a thin dendrite, so that local synaptic interactions would be emphasized.

Simulations demonstrating the operation of this self-organizing learning to produce movement of the location being represented in a continuous attractor network were described by Stringer, Trappenberg, Rolls and De Araujo (2002b), and one example of the operation is shown in Fig. B.28. They also showed that, after training with just one value of the head rotation cell firing, the network showed the desirable property of moving the head direction being represented in the continuous attractor by an amount that was proportional to the value of the head rotation cell firing. Stringer, Trappenberg, Rolls and De Araujo (2002b) also describe a related model of the idiothetic cell update of the location represented in a continuous attractor, in which the rotation cell firing directly modulates in a multiplicative way the strength of the recurrent connections in the continuous attractor in such a way that clockwise rotation cells modulate the strength of the synaptic connections in the clockwise direction in the continuous attractor, and vice versa.

It should be emphasized that although the cells are organized in Fig. B.28 according to the spatial position being represented, there is no need for cells in continuous attractors that represent nearby locations in the state space to be close together, as the distance in the state space between any two neurons is represented by the strength of the connection between them,

---

[41] The term $\phi_1 / C^{\text{HD} \times \text{ID}}$ is a scaling factor that reflects the number $C^{\text{HD} \times \text{ID}}$ of inputs to these synapses, and enables the overall magnitude of the idiothetic input to each head direction cell to remain approximately the same as the number of idiothetic connections received by each head direction cell is varied.

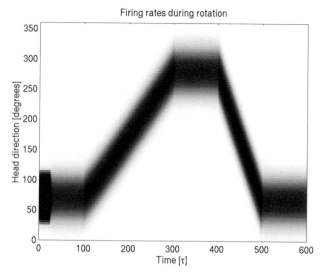

Fig. B.28 Idiothetic update of the location represented in a continuous attractor network. The firing rate of the cells with optima at different head directions (organized according to head direction on the ordinate) is shown by the blackness of the plot, as a function of time. The activity packet was initialized to a head direction of 75 degrees, and the packet was allowed to settle without visual input. For timestep=0 to 100 there was no rotation cell input, and the activity packet in the continuous attractor remained stable at 75 degrees. For timestep=100 to 300 the clockwise rotation cells were active with a firing rate of 0.15 to represent a moderate angular velocity, and the activity packet moved clockwise. For timestep=300 to 400 there was no rotation cell firing, and the activity packet immediately stopped, and remained still. For timestep=400 to 500 the anti-clockwise rotation cells had a high firing rate of 0.3 to represent a high velocity, and the activity packet moved anticlockwise with a greater velocity. For timestep=500 to 600 there was no rotation cell firing, and the activity packet immediately stopped.

not by where the neurons are physically located. This enables continuous attractor networks to represent spaces with arbitrary topologies, as the topology is represented in the connection strengths (Stringer, Trappenberg, Rolls and De Araujo 2002b, Stringer, Rolls, Trappenberg and De Araujo 2002a, Stringer, Rolls and Trappenberg 2005, Stringer and Rolls 2002). Indeed, it is this that enables many different charts each with its own topology to be represented in a single continuous attractor network (Battaglia and Treves 1998b).

In the network described so far, self-organization occurs, but one set of synapses is Sigma-Pi. We have gone on to show that the Sigma-Pi synapses are not necessary, and can be replaced by a competitive network that learns to respond to combinations of the spatial position and the idiothetic velocity, as illustrated in Fig. B.29 (Stringer and Rolls 2006).

B.5.6 Stabilization of the activity packet within the continuous attractor network when the agent is stationary

With irregular learning conditions (in which identical training with high precision of every node cannot be guaranteed), the recurrent synaptic weights between nodes in the continuous attractor will not be of the perfectly regular and symmetric form normally required in a continuous attractor neural network. This can lead to drift of the activity packet within the continuous attractor network of e.g. head direction cells when no visual cues are present, even when the agent is not moving. This drift is a common property of the short-term memories of spatial position implemented in the brain, which emphasizes the computational problems

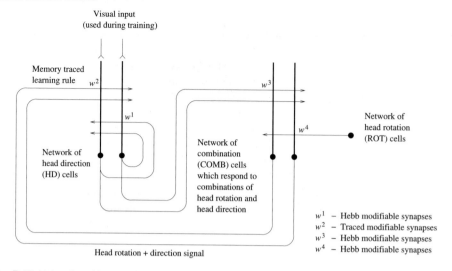

Fig. B.29 Network architecture for a two-layer self-organizing neural network model of the head direction system. The network architecture contains a layer of head direction (HD) cells representing the head direction of the agent, a layer of combination (COMB) cells representing a combination of head direction and rotational velocity, and a layer of rotation (ROT) cells which become active when the agent rotates. There are four types of synaptic connection in the network, which operate as follows. The w_{ij}^1 synapses are Hebb-modifiable recurrent connections between head direction cells. These connections help to support stable packets of activity within this continuous attractor layer of head direction cells in the absence of visual input. The combination cells receive inputs from the head direction cells through the Hebb-modifiable w_{ij}^3 synapses, and inputs from the rotation cells through the Hebb-modifiable w_{ij}^4 synapses. These synaptic inputs encourage combination cells by competitive learning to respond to particular combinations of head direction and rotational velocity. In particular, the combination cells only become significantly active when the agent is rotating. The head direction cells receive inputs from the combination cells through the w_{ij}^2 synapses. The $w_{i,j}^2$ synapses are trained using a 'trace' learning rule, which incorporates a temporal trace of recent combination cell activity. This rule introduces an asymmetry into the w_{ij}^2 weights, which plays an important role in shifting the activity packet through the layer of head direction cells during path integration in the dark. (After Stringer and Rolls 2006.)

that can arise in continuous attractor networks if the weights between nodes are not balanced in different directions in the space being represented. An approach to stabilizing the activity packet when it should not be drifting in real nervous systems, which does help to minimize the drift that can occur, is now described.

The activity packet may be stabilized within a continuous attractor network, when the agent is stationary and the network is operating in memory mode without an external stabilizing input, by enhancing the firing of those cells that are already firing. In biological systems this might be achieved through mechanisms for short-term synaptic enhancement (Koch 1999). Another way is to take advantage of the non-linearity of the activation function of neurons with NMDA receptors, which only contribute to neuronal firing once the neuron is sufficiently depolarized (Wang 1999). The effect is to enhance the firing of neurons that are already reasonably well activated. The effect has been utilized in a model of a network with recurrent excitatory synapses that can maintain active an arbitrary set of neurons that are initially sufficiently strongly activated by an external stimulus (see Lisman, Fellous and Wang (1998), and, for a discussion on whether these networks could be used to implement short-term memories, see Kesner and Rolls (2001)).

We have incorporated this non-linearity into a model of a head direction continuous attractor network by adjusting the sigmoid threshold α_i (see equation B.30) for each head direction cell i as follows (Stringer, Trappenberg, Rolls and De Araujo 2002b). If the head direction cell firing rate r_i^{HD} is lower than a threshold value, γ, then the sigmoid threshold α_i is set to a relatively high value α^{high}. Otherwise, if the head direction cell firing rate r_i^{HD} is greater than or equal to the threshold value, γ, then the sigmoid threshold α_i is set to a relatively low value α^{low}. It was shown that this procedure has the effect of enhancing the current position of the activity packet within the continuous attractor network, and so prevents the activity packet drifting erratically due to the noise in the recurrent synaptic weights produced for example by irregular learning. An advantage of using the non-linearity in the activation function of a neuron (produced for example by the operation of NMDA receptors) is that this tends to enable packets of activity to be kept active without drift even when the packet is not in one of the energy minima that can result from irregular learning (or from diluted connectivity in the continuous attractor as described below). Thus use of this non-linearity increases the number of locations in the continuous physical state space at which a stable activity packet can be maintained (Stringer, Trappenberg, Rolls and De Araujo 2002b).

The same process might help to stabilize the activity packet against drift caused by the probabilistic spiking of neurons in the network (cf. Chapter 7).

B.5.7 Continuous attractor networks in two or more dimensions

Some types of spatial representation used by the brain are of spaces that exist in two or more dimensions. Examples are the two- (or three-) dimensional space representing where one is looking at in a spatial scene. Another is the two- (or three-) dimensional space representing where one is located. It is possible to extend continuous attractor networks to operate in higher dimensional spaces than the one-dimensional spaces considered so far (Taylor 1999, Stringer, Rolls, Trappenberg and De Araujo 2002a). Indeed, it is also possible to extend the analyses of how idiothetic inputs could be used to update two-dimensional state spaces, such as the locations represented by place cells in rats (Stringer, Rolls, Trappenberg and De Araujo 2002a) and the location at which one is looking represented by primate spatial view cells (Stringer, Rolls and Trappenberg 2005, Stringer and Rolls 2002). Interestingly, the number of terms in the synapses implementing idiothetic update do not need to increase beyond three (as in Sigma-Pi synapses) even when higher dimensional state spaces are being considered (Stringer, Rolls, Trappenberg and De Araujo 2002a). Also interestingly, a continuous attractor network can in fact represent the properties of very high dimensional spaces, because the properties of the spaces are captured by the connections between the neurons of the continuous attractor, and these connections are of course, as in the world of discrete attractor networks, capable of representing high dimensional spaces (Stringer, Rolls, Trappenberg and De Araujo 2002a). With these approaches, continuous attractor networks have been developed of the two-dimensional representation of rat hippocampal place cells with idiothetic update by movements in the environment (Stringer, Rolls, Trappenberg and De Araujo 2002a), and of primate hippocampal spatial view cells with idiothetic update by eye and head movements (Stringer, Rolls and Trappenberg 2005, Rolls and Stringer 2005, Stringer and Rolls 2002). Continuous attractor models with some similar properties have also been applied to understanding motor control, for example the generation of a continuous movement in space (Stringer and Rolls 2007a, Stringer, Rolls and Taylor 2007a).

B.5.8 Mixed continuous and discrete attractor networks

It has now been shown that attractor networks can store both continuous patterns and discrete patterns, and can thus be used to store for example the location in (continuous, physical) space where an object (a discrete item) is present (see Fig. 2.16 and Rolls, Stringer and Trappenberg (2002)). In this network, when events are stored that have both discrete (object) and continuous (spatial) aspects, then the whole place can be retrieved later by the object, and the object can be retrieved by using the place as a retrieval cue. Such networks are likely to be present in parts of the brain that receive and combine inputs both from systems that contain representations of continuous (physical) space, and from brain systems that contain representations of discrete objects, such as the inferior temporal visual cortex. One such brain system is the hippocampus, which appears to combine and store such representations in a mixed attractor network in the CA3 region, which thus is able to implement episodic memories which typically have a spatial component, for example where an item such as a key is located (see Chapter 2). This network thus shows that in brain regions where the spatial and object processing streams are brought together, then a single network can represent and learn associations between both types of input. Indeed, in brain regions such as the hippocampal system, it is essential that the spatial and object processing streams are brought together in a single network, for it is only when both types of information are in the same network that spatial information can be retrieved from object information, and vice versa, which is a fundamental property of episodic memory (see Chapter 2). It may also be the case that in the prefrontal cortex, attractor networks can store both spatial and discrete (e.g. object-based) types of information in short-term memory (see Section 5.1).

B.6 Network dynamics: the integrate-and-fire approach

The concept that attractor (autoassociation) networks can operate very rapidly if implemented with neurons that operate dynamically in continuous time was introduced in Section B.3.3.5. The result described was that the principal factor affecting the speed of retrieval is the time constant of the synapses between the neurons that form the attractor ((Treves 1993, Rolls and Treves 1998, Battaglia and Treves 1998a, Panzeri, Rolls, Battaglia and Lavis 2001). This was shown analytically by Treves (1993), and described by Rolls and Treves (1998) Appendix 5. We now describe in more detail the approaches that produce these results, and the actual results found on the speed of processing.

The networks described so far in this chapter, and analyzed in Appendices 3 and 4 of Rolls and Treves (1998), were described in terms of the steady-state activation of networks of neuron-like units. Those may be referred to as 'static' properties, in the sense that they do not involve the time dimension. In order to address 'dynamical' questions, the time dimension has to be reintroduced into the formal models used, and the adequacy of the models themselves has to be reconsidered in view of the specific properties to be discussed.

Consider for example a real network whose operation has been described by an autoassociative formal model that acquires, with learning, a given attractor structure. How does the state of the network approach, in real time during a retrieval operation, one of those attractors? How long does it take? How does the amount of information that can be read off the network's activity evolve with time? Also, which of the potential steady states is indeed a stable state that can be reached asymptotically by the net? How is the stability of different states modulated by external agents? These are examples of dynamical properties, which to be studied require the use of models endowed with some dynamics.

B.6.1 From discrete to continuous time

Already at the level of simple models in which each unit is described by an input–output relation, one may introduce equally simple 'dynamical' rules, in order both to fully specify the model, and to simulate it on computers. These rules are generally formulated in terms of 'updatings': time is considered to be discrete, a succession of time steps, and at each time step the output of one or more of the units is set, or updated, to the value corresponding to its input variable. The input variable may reflect the outputs of other units in the net as updated at the previous time step or, if delays are considered, the outputs as they were at a prescribed number of time steps in the past. If all units in the net are updated together, the dynamics is referred to as parallel; if instead only one unit is updated at each time step, the dynamics is sequential. (One main difference between the Hopfield (1982) model of an autoassociator and a similar model considered earlier by Little (1974) is that the latter was based on parallel rather than sequential dynamics.) Many intermediate possibilities obviously exist, involving the updating of groups of units at a time. The order in which sequential updatings are performed may for instance be chosen at random at the beginning and then left the same in successive cycles across all units in the net; or it may be chosen anew at each cycle; yet a third alternative is to select at each time step a unit, at random, with the possibility that a particular unit may be selected several times before some of the other ones are ever updated. The updating may also be made probabilistic, with the output being set to its new value only with a certain probability, and otherwise remaining at the current value.

Variants of these dynamical rules have been used for decades in the analysis and computer simulation of physical systems in statistical mechanics (and field theory). They can reproduce in simple but effective ways the stochastic nature of transitions among discrete quantum states, and they have been subsequently considered appropriate also in the simulation of neural network models in which units have outputs that take discrete values, implying that a change from one value to another can only occur in a sudden jump. To some extent, different rules are equivalent, in that they lead, in the evolution of the activity of the net along successive steps and cycles, to the same set of possible steady states. For example, it is easy to realize that when no delays are introduced, states that are stable under parallel updating are also stable under sequential updating. The reverse is not necessarily true, but on the other hand states that are stable when updating one unit at a time are stable irrespective of the updating order. Therefore, static properties, which can be deduced from an analysis of stable states, are to some extent robust against differences in the details of the dynamics assigned to the model. (This is a reason for using these dynamical rules in the study of the thermodynamics of physical systems.) Such rules, however, bear no relation to the actual dynamical processes by which the activity of real neurons evolves in time, and are therefore inadequate for the discussion of dynamical issues in neural networks.

A first step towards realism in the dynamics is the substitution of discrete time with continuous time. This somewhat parallels the substitution of the discrete output variables of the most rudimentary models with continuous variables representing firing rates. Although continuous output variables may evolve also in discrete time, and as far as static properties are concerned differences are minimal, with the move from discrete to continuous outputs the main raison d'etre for a dynamics in terms of sudden updatings ceases to exist, since continuous variables can change continuously in continuous time. A paradox arises immediately, however, if a continuous time dynamics is assigned to firing rates. The paradox is that firing rates, although in principle continuous if computed with a generic time-kernel, tend to vary in jumps as new spikes – essentially discrete events – come to be included in the kernel. To avoid this paradox, a continuous time dynamics can be assigned, instead, to instantaneous continuous variables such as membrane potentials. Hopfield (1984), among others, has introduced a model of an autoassociator in which the output variables represent membrane potentials and evolve continuously in time, and has suggested that under certain conditions the stable states attainable by such a network are essentially the same as for a network of binary units evolving in discrete time. If neurons in the central nervous system communicated with each other via the transmission of graded membrane potentials, as they do in some peripheral and invertebrate neural systems, this model could be an excellent starting point. The fact that, centrally, transmission is primarily via the emission of discrete spikes makes a model based on membrane potentials as output variables inadequate to correctly represent spiking dynamics.

B.6.2 Continuous dynamics with discontinuities

In principle, a solution would be to keep the membrane potential as the basic dynamical variable, evolving in continuous time, and to use as the output variable the spike emission times, as determined by the rapid variation in membrane potential corresponding to each spike. A point-like neuron can generate spikes by altering the membrane potential V according to continuous equations of the Hodgkin–Huxley type:

$$C\frac{dV}{dt} = g_0(V_{\text{rest}} - V) + g_{\text{Na}}mh^3(V_{\text{Na}} - V) + g_{\text{K}}n^4(V_{\text{K}} - V) + I \tag{B.37}$$

$$\tau_m\frac{dm}{dt} = m_\infty(V) - m \tag{B.38}$$

$$\tau_h\frac{dh}{dt} = h_\infty(V) - h \tag{B.39}$$

$$\tau_n\frac{dn}{dt} = n_\infty(V) - n. \tag{B.40}$$

The changes in the membrane potential, driven by the input current I, interact with the opening and closing of intrinsic conductances (here a sodium conductance, whose channels are gated by the 'particles' m and h, and a potassium conductance, whose channels are gated by n; Hodgkin and Huxley (1952)). These equations provide an effective description, phenomenological but broadly based on physical principles, of the conductance changes underlying action potentials, and they are treated in any standard neurobiology text.

From the point of view of formal models of neural networks, this level of description is too complicated to be the basis for an analytic understanding of the operation of networks, and it must be simplified. The most widely used simplification is the so-called integrate-and-fire model (see for example MacGregor (1987) and Brunel and Wang (2001)), which is legitimized by the observation that (sodium) action potentials are typically brief and self-similar events. If, in particular, the only relevant variable associated with the spike is its time of emission (at the soma, or axon hillock), which essentially coincides with the time the potential V reaches a certain threshold level V_{thr}, then the conductance changes underlying the rest of the spike can be omitted from the description, and substituted with the ad hoc prescription that (i) a spike is emitted, with its effect on receiving units and on the unit itself; and (ii) after a brief time corresponding to the duration of the spike plus a refractory period, the membrane potential is reset and resumes its integration of the input current I. After a spike the membrane potential is taken to be reset to a value V_{reset}. This type of simplified dynamics of the membrane potentials is thus in continuous time with added discontinuities: continuous in between spikes, with discontinuities occurring at different times for each neuron in a population, every time a neuron emits a spike.

A leaky integrate-and-fire neuron can be modelled as follows. The model describes the depolarization of the membrane potential V (which typically is dynamically changing as a result of the synaptic effects described below between approximately –70 and –50 mV) until threshold V_{thr} (typically –50 mV) is reached when a spike is emitted and the potential is reset to V_{reset} (typically –55 mV). The membrane time constant τ_{m} is set by the membrane capacitance C_{m} and the membrane leakage conductance g_{m} where $\tau_{\text{m}} = C_{\text{m}}/g_{\text{m}}$. V_{L} denotes

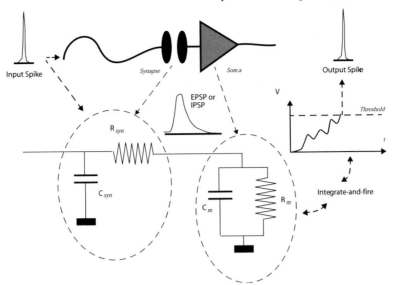

Fig. B.30 Integrate-and-fire neuron. The basic circuit of an integrate-and-fire model consists of the neuron's membrane capacitance C_m in parallel with the membrane's resistance R_m (the reciprocal of the membrane conductance g_m) driven by a synaptic current with a conductance and time constant determined by the synaptic resistance R_{syn} (the reciprocal of the synaptic conductance g_j) and capacitance C_{syn} shown in the Figure. These effects produce excitatory or inhibitory post-synaptic potentials, EPSPs or IPSPs. These potentials are integrated by the cell, and if a threshold V_{thr} is reached a δ-pulse (spike) is fired and transmitted to other neurons, and the membrane potential is reset. (After Deco and Rolls 2003.)

the resting potential of the cell, typically –70 mV. Changes in the membrane potential are defined by the following equation

$$C_m \frac{dV(t)}{dt} = g_m\left(V_L - V(t)\right) + \sum_j g_j\left(V_{AMPA} - V(t)\right) + \sum_j g_j\left(V_{GABA} - V(t)\right). \quad \text{(B.41)}$$

The first term on the right of the equation describes how the membrane potential decays back towards the resting potential of the cell depending on how far the cell potential V is from the resting potential V_L, and the membrane leak conductance g_m. The second term on the right represents the excitatory synaptic current that could be injected through AMPA receptors. This is a sum over all AMPA synapses indexed by j on the cell. At each synapse, the current is driven into the cell by the difference between the membrane potential V and the reversal potential V_{AMPA} of the channels opened by AMPA receptors, weighted by the synaptic conductance g_j. This synaptic conductance changes dynamically as a function of the time since a spike reached the synapse, as shown below. Due to their reversal potential V_{AMPA} of typically 0 mV, these currents will tend to depolarize the cell, that is to move the membrane potential towards the firing threshold. The third term on the right represents the inhibitory synaptic current that could be injected through GABA receptors. Due to their reversal potential V_{GABA} of typically –70 mV, these currents will tend to hyperpolarize the cell, that is to move the membrane potential away from the firing threshold. There may be other types of receptor on a cell, for example NMDA receptors, and these operate analogously though with interesting differences, as described in Section B.6.3.

The opening of each synaptic conductance g_j is driven by the arrival of spikes at the presynaptic terminal j, and its closing can often be described as a simple exponential process. A simplified equation for the dynamics of $g_j(t)$ is then

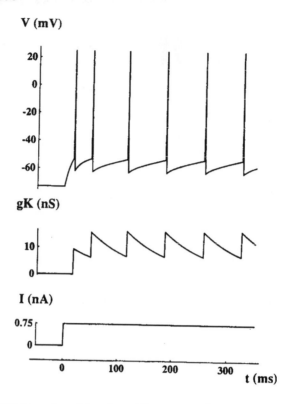

Fig. B.31 Model behaviour of an integrate-and-fire neuron: the membrane potential and adaptation-producing potassium conductance in response to a step of injected current. The spikes were added to the graph by hand, as they do not emerge from the simplified voltage equation. (From Treves 1993.)

$$\frac{dg_j(t)}{dt} = -\frac{g_j(t)}{\tau} + \Delta g_j \sum_l \delta(t - \Delta t - t_l). \tag{B.42}$$

According to the above equation, each synaptic conductance opens instantaneously by a fixed amount Δg_j a time Δt after the emission of the presynaptic spike at t_l. Δt summarizes delays (axonal, synaptic, and dendritic), and each opening superimposes linearly, without saturating, on previous openings. The value of τ in this equation will be different for AMPA receptors (typically 2–10 ms), NMDA receptors (typically 100 ms), and GABA receptors (typically 10 ms).

In order to model the phenomenon of adaptation in the firing rate, prominent especially with pyramidal cells, it is possible to include a time-varying intrinsic (potassium-like) conductance in the cell membrane (Brown, Gähwiler, Griffith and Halliwell 1990a) (shown as g_K in equations B.43 and B.44). This can be done by specifying that this conductance, which if open tends to shunt the membrane and thus to prevent firing, opens by a fixed amount with the potential excursion associated with each spike, and then relaxes exponentially to its closed state. In this manner sustained firing driven by a constant input current occurs at lower rates after the first few spikes, in a way similar, if the relevant parameters are set appropriately, to the behaviour observed in vitro of many pyramidal cells (for example, Lanthorn, Storn and Andersen (1984), Mason and Larkman (1990)).

The equations for the dynamics of each neuron with adaptation are then

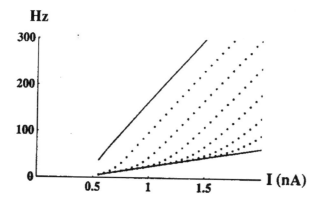

Fig. B.32 Current-to-frequency transduction in a pyramidal cell modelled as an integrate-and-fire neuron. The top solid curve is the firing frequency in the absence of adaptation, $\Delta g_K = 0$. The dotted curves are the instantaneous frequencies computed as the inverse of the ith interspike interval (top to bottom, $i = 1, ..., 6$). The bottom solid curve is the adapted firing curve ($i \to \infty$). With or without adaptation, the input–output transform is close to threshold–linear. (From Treves 1993.)

$$C_m \frac{dV(t)}{dt} = g_m\left(V_L - V(t)\right) + \sum_j g_j\left(V_{AMPA} - V(t)\right) + \sum_j g_j\left(V_{GABA} - V(t)\right) + g_K(t)\left(V_K - V(t)\right)$$

$$(B.43)$$

and

$$\frac{dg_K(t)}{dt} = -\frac{g_K(t)}{\tau_K} + \sum_k \Delta g_K \delta(t - t_k) \qquad (B.44)$$

supplemented by the prescription that when at time $t = t_{k+1}$ the potential reaches the level V_{thr}, a spike is emitted, and hence included also in the sum of equation B.44, and the potential resumes its evolution according to equation B.43 from the reset level V_{reset}. The resulting behaviour is exemplified in Fig. B.31, while Fig. B.32 shows the input–output transform (current to frequency transduction) operated by an integrate-and-fire unit of this type with firing rate adaptation. One should compare this with the transduction operated by real cells, as exemplified for example in Fig. 1.4.

It should be noted that synaptic conductance dynamics is not always included in integrate-and-fire models: sometimes it is substituted with current dynamics, which essentially amounts to neglecting non-linearities due to the appearance of the membrane potential in the driving force for synaptic action (see for example, Amit and Tsodyks (1991), Gerstner (1995)); and sometimes it is simplified altogether by assuming that the membrane potential undergoes small sudden jumps when it receives instantaneous pulses of synaptic current (see the review in Gerstner (1995)). The latter simplification is quite drastic and changes the character of the dynamics markedly; whereas the former can be a reasonable simplification in some circumstances, but it produces serious distortions in the description of inhibitory $GABA_A$ currents, which, having an equilibrium (Cl^-) synaptic potential close to the operating range of the membrane potential, are quite sensitive to the instantaneous value of the membrane potential itself.

B.6.3 An integrate-and-fire implementation

In this subsection the mathematical equations that describe the spiking activity and synapse dynamics in some of the integrate-and-fire simulations performed by Deco and Rolls (Deco and Rolls 2003, Deco, Rolls and Horwitz 2004, Deco and Rolls 2005d, Deco and Rolls 2005c, Deco and Rolls 2005b, Deco and Rolls 2006) are set out, in order to show in more detail how an integrate-and-fire simulation is implemented. The simulation is that of Deco, Rolls and Horwitz (2004), and follows in general the formulation described by Brunel and Wang (2001).

Each neuron is described by an integrate-and-fire model. The subthreshold membrane potential $V(t)$ of each neuron evolves according to the following equation:

$$C_m \frac{dV(t)}{dt} = -g_m(V(t) - V_L) - I_{syn}(t) \tag{B.45}$$

where $I_{syn}(t)$ is the total synaptic current flow into the cell, V_L is the resting potential, C_m is the membrane capacitance, and g_m is the membrane conductance. When the membrane potential $V(t)$ reaches the threshold V_{thr} a spike is generated, and the membrane potential is reset to V_{reset}. The neuron is unable to spike during the first τ_{ref} which is the absolute refractory period.

The total synaptic current is given by the sum of glutamatergic excitatory components (NMDA and AMPA) and inhibitory components (GABA). The external excitatory contributions (ext) from outside the network are produced through AMPA receptors ($I_{AMPA,ext}$), while the excitatory recurrent synapses (rec) within the network act through AMPA and NMDA receptors ($I_{AMPA,rec}$ and $I_{NMDA,rec}$). The total synaptic current is therefore given by:

$$I_{syn}(t) = I_{AMPA,ext}(t) + I_{AMPA,rec}(t) + I_{NMDA,rec}(t) + I_{GABA}(t) \tag{B.46}$$

where

$$I_{AMPA,ext}(t) = g_{AMPA,ext}(V(t) - V_E) \sum_{j=1}^{N_{ext}} s_j^{AMPA,ext}(t) \tag{B.47}$$

$$I_{AMPA,rec}(t) = g_{AMPA,rec}(V(t) - V_E) \sum_{j=1}^{N_E} w_j s_j^{AMPA,rec}(t) \tag{B.48}$$

$$I_{NMDA,rec}(t) = \frac{g_{NMDA,rec}(V(t) - V_E)}{(1 + [Mg^{++}] \exp(-0.062V(t))/3.57)} \sum_{j=1}^{N_E} w_j s_j^{NMDA,rec}(t) \tag{B.49}$$

$$I_{GABA}(t) = g_{GABA}(V(t) - V_I) \sum_{j=1}^{N_I} s_j^{GABA}(t) \tag{B.50}$$

In the preceding equations the reversal potential of the excitatory synaptic currents $V_E = 0$ mV and of the inhibitory synaptic currents $V_I = -70$ mV. The different form for the NMDA receptor-activated channels implements the voltage-dependence of NMDA receptors. This voltage-dependency, and the long time constant of the NMDA receptors, are important in the effects produced through NMDA receptors (Brunel and Wang 2001, Wang 1999). The synaptic strengths w_j are specified in the papers by Deco and Rolls (Deco and Rolls 2003, Deco, Rolls and Horwitz 2004, Deco and Rolls 2005d, Deco and Rolls 2005c, Deco and Rolls 2005b, Deco and Rolls 2006), and depend on the architecture being simulated. The fractions of open channels s are given by:

$$\frac{ds_j^{\text{AMPA,ext}}(t)}{dt} = -\frac{s_j^{\text{AMPA,ext}}(t)}{\tau_{\text{AMPA}}} + \sum_k \delta(t - t_j^k) \qquad \text{(B.51)}$$

$$\frac{ds_j^{\text{AMPA,rec}}(t)}{dt} = -\frac{s_j^{\text{AMPA,rec}}(t)}{\tau_{\text{AMPA}}} + \sum_k \delta(t - t_j^k) \qquad \text{(B.52)}$$

$$\frac{ds_j^{\text{NMDA,rec}}(t)}{dt} = -\frac{s_j^{\text{NMDA,rec}}(t)}{\tau_{\text{NMDA,decay}}} + \alpha x_j(t)(1 - s_j^{\text{NMDA,rec}}(t)) \qquad \text{(B.53)}$$

$$\frac{dx_j(t)}{dt} = -\frac{x_j(t)}{\tau_{\text{NMDA,rise}}} + \sum_k \delta(t - t_j^k) \qquad \text{(B.54)}$$

$$\frac{ds_j^{\text{GABA}}(t)}{dt} = -\frac{s_j^{\text{GABA}}(t)}{\tau_{\text{GABA}}} + \sum_k \delta(t - t_j^k) \qquad \text{(B.55)}$$

where the sums over k represent a sum over spikes emitted by presynaptic neuron j at time t_j^k. The value of $\alpha = 0.5$ ms^{-1}.

Typical values of the conductances for pyramidal neurons are: $g_{\text{AMPA,ext}}$=2.08, $g_{\text{AMPA,rec}}$=0.052, $g_{\text{NMDA,rec}}$=0.164, and g_{GABA}=0.67 nS; and for interneurons: $g_{\text{AMPA,ext}}$=1.62, $g_{\text{AMPA,rec}}$=0.0405, $g_{\text{NMDA,rec}}$=0.129 and g_{GABA}=0.49 nS.

Further details of an integrate-and-fire simulation performed to analyse decision-making (Deco and Rolls 2006) are given in Section 7.8, and a full list of the values of the parameters used is given in Section 7.10.

B.6.4 Simulation of fMRI signals: hemodynamic convolution of synaptic activity

The links between neural and synaptic activity, and fMRI measurements, are still not fully understood. The fMRI signal is unfortunately strongly filtered and perturbed by the hemodynamic delay inherent in the blood oxygen level-dependent (BOLD) contrast mechanism (Buxton and Frank 1997). The fMRI signal is only a secondary consequence of neuronal activity, and yields therefore a blurred distortion of the temporal development of the underlying brain processes. Regionally, increased oxidative metabolism causes a transient decrease in oxyhemoglobin and increase in deoxyhemoglobin, as well as an increase in CO_2 and NO. This provokes over several seconds a local dilatation and increased blood flow in the affected regions that leads by overcompensation to a relative decrease in the concentration of deoxyhemoglobin in the venules draining the activated region, and the alteration of deoxyhemoglobin, which is paramagnetic, can be detected by changes in $T2$ or $T2^*$ in the MRI signal as a result of the decreased susceptibility and thus decreased local inhomogeneity which increases the MR intensity value (Glover 1999, Buxton and Frank 1997, Buxton, Wong and Frank 1998).

The functional magnetic resonance neuroimaging (fMRI) BOLD (blood oxygen level-dependent) signal is likely to reflect the total synaptic activity in an area (as ions need to be pumped back across the cell membrane) rather than the spiking neuronal activity (Logothetis et al. 2001), and is spatially and temporally filtered. The filtering reflects the inherent spatial resolution with which the blood flow changes, as well as the resolution of the scanner, and filtering which may be applied for statistical purposes, and the slow temporal response of the

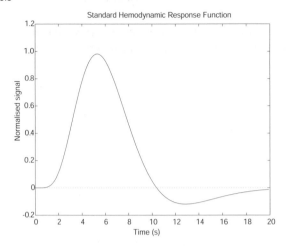

Fig. B.33 The standard hemodynamic response function $h(t)$ (see text).

blood flow changes (Glover 1999, Buxton and Frank 1997, Buxton et al. 1998). Glover (1999) demonstrated that a good fitting of the hemodynamical response $h(t)$ can be achieved by the following analytic function:

$$h(t) = c_1 t^{n_1} e^{-\frac{t}{t_1}} - a_2 c_2 t^{n_2} e^{-\frac{t}{t_2}}$$

$$c_i = \max(t^{n_i} e^{-\frac{t}{t_i}})$$

where t is the time, and c_1, c_2, a_2, n_1, and n_2 are parameters that are adjusted to fit the experimentally measured hemodynamical response. Figure B.33 plots the hemodynamic standard response $h(t)$ for a biologically realistic set of parameters (see Deco, Rolls and Horwitz (2004)).

The temporal evolution of fMRI signals can be simulated from an integrate-and-fire population of neurons by convolving the total synaptic activity in the simulated population of neurons with the standard hemodynamic response formulation of Glover (1999) presented above (Deco, Rolls and Horwitz 2004, Horwitz and Tagamets 1999). The rationale for this is that the major metabolic expenditure in neural activity is the energy required to pump back against the electrochemical gradient the ions that have entered neurons as a result of the ion channels opened by synaptic activity, and that mechanisms have evolved to increase local neuronal blood flow in order to help this increased metabolic demand to be met. (In fact, the increased blood flow overcompensates, and the blood oxygenation level-dependent (BOLD) signal by reflecting the consequent alteration of deoxyhaemoglobin which is paramagnetic reflects this.) The total synaptic current (I_{syn}) is given by the sum of the absolute values of the glutamatergic excitatory components (implemented through NMDA and AMPA receptors) and inhibitory components (GABA) (Tagamets and Horwitz 1998, Horwitz, Tagamets and McIntosh 1999, Rolls and Deco 2002, Deco et al. 2004). In our integrate-and-fire simulations the external excitatory contributions are produced through AMPA receptors ($I_{\text{AMPA,ext}}$), while the excitatory recurrent synaptic currents are produced through AMPA and NMDA receptors ($I_{\text{AMPA,rec}}$ and $I_{\text{NMDA,rec}}$). The GABA inhibitory currents are denoted by I_{GABA}. Consequently, the simulated fMRI signal activity S_{fMRI} is calculated by the following convolution equation:

$$S_{\text{fMRI}}(t) = \int_0^\infty h(t - t') I_{\text{syn}}(t') \, dt'.$$

It is noted here that it could be useful to weight the corresponding currents by the electro-chemical gradients against which each ion that passes through the different channels must be pumped back.

Deco, Rolls and Horwitz (2004) applied this approach to predicting fMRI BOLD signals based on activity simulated at the integrate-and-fire level of neuronal activity in the dorsolateral prefrontal cortex. They showed that differences in the fMRI BOLD signal from the dorsal as compared to the ventral prefrontal cortex in working memory tasks may reflect a higher level of inhibition in the dorsolateral prefrontal cortex, as described in Section 5.6. In their simulation the convolution was calculated numerically by sampling the total synaptic activity every 0.1 s and introducing a cut-off at a delay of 25 s. The parameters utilized for the hemodynamic standard response $h(t)$ were taken from the paper of Glover (1999), and were: $n_1 = 6.0$, $t_1 = 0.9$s, $n_2 = 12.0$, $t_2 = 0.9$s, and $a_2 = 0.2$.

B.6.5 The speed of processing of one-layer attractor networks with integrate-and-fire neurons

Given that the analytic approach to the rapidity of the dynamics of attractor networks with integrate-and-fire dynamics (Treves 1993, Rolls and Treves 1998) applies mainly when the state is close to the attractor basin, it is of interest to check the performance of such networks by simulation when the completion of partial patterns that may be towards the edge of the attractor basin can be tested. Simmen, Rolls and Treves (1996a) and Treves, Rolls and Simmen (1997) made a start with this, and showed that retrieval could indeed be fast, within 1–2 time constants of the synapses. However, they found that they could not load the systems they simulated with many patterns, and the firing rates during the retrieval process tended to be unstable. The cause of this turned out to be that the inhibition they used to maintain the activity level during retrieval was subtractive, and it turns out that divisive (shunting) inhibition is much more effective in such networks, as described by Rolls and Treves (1998) in Appendix 5. Divisive inhibition is likely to be organized by inhibitory inputs that synapse close to the cell body (where the reversal potential is close to that of the channels opened by GABA receptors), in contrast to synapses on dendrites, where the different potentials result in opening of the same channels producing hyperpolarization (that is an effectively subtractive influence with respect to the depolarizing currents induced by excitatory (glutamate-releasing) terminals). Battaglia and Treves (1998a) therefore went on to study networks with neurons where the inhibitory neurons could be made to be divisive by having them synapse close to the cell body in neurons modelled with multiple (ten) dendritic compartments. The excitatory inputs terminated on the compartments more distant from the cell body in the model. They found that with this divisive inhibition, the neuronal firing during retrieval was kept under much better control, and the number of patterns that could be successfully stored and retrieved was much higher. Some details of their simulation follow.

Battaglia and Treves (1998a) simulated a network of 800 excitatory and 200 inhibitory cells in its retrieval of one of a number of memory patterns stored in the synaptic weights representing the excitatory-to-excitatory recurrent connections. The memory patterns were assigned at random, drawing the value of each unit in each of the patterns from a binary distribution with sparseness 0.1, that is a probability of 1 in 10 for the unit to be active in the pattern. No baseline excitatory weight was included, but the modifiable weights were instead constrained to remain positive (by clipping at zero synaptic modifications that would make a synaptic weight negative), and a simple exponential decay of the weight with successive modifications was also applied, to prevent runaway synaptic modifications within a rudimentary model of forgetting. Both excitation on inhibitory units and inhibition were mediated by non-modifiable uniform synaptic weights, with values chosen so as to satisfy stability conditions of the type shown in equations A5.13 of Rolls and Treves (1998). Both inhibitory and excitatory neurons were of the general integrate-and-fire type, but excitatory units had in addition an extended dendritic cable, and they received excitatory inputs only at the more distal end of the cable, and inhibitory inputs spread along the cable. In this way, inhibitory inputs reached the soma of excitatory cells with variable delays, and in any case earlier than synchronous excitatory inputs, and at the same time they could shunt the excitatory inputs, resulting in a largely multiplicative form of inhibition (Abbott 1991). The uniform connectivity was not complete, but rather each type of unit could contact units of the other type with a probability of 0.5, and the same was true for inhibitory-to-inhibitory connections.

After 100 (simulated) ms of activity evoked by external inputs uncorrelated with any of the stored patterns, a cue was provided that consisted of the external input becoming correlated with one of the patterns, at various levels of correlation, for 300 ms. After that, external inputs were removed, but when retrieval operated successfully the activity of the units remained strongly correlated with the memory pattern, or even reached a higher level of correlation if a rather corrupted cue had been used, so that, if during the 300 ms the network had stabilized into a state rather distant from the memory pattern, it got much closer to it once the cue was removed. All correlations were quantified using information measures (see Appendix C)), in terms of mutual information between the firing rate pattern across units and the particular memory pattern being retrieved, or in terms of mutual information between the firing rate of one unit and the set of patterns, or, finally, in terms of mutual information between the decoded firing rates of a subpopulation of 10 excitatory cells and the set of memory patterns. The same algorithms were used to extract information measures as were used for example by Rolls, Treves, Tovee and Panzeri (1997d) with real neuronal data from inferior temporal cortex neurons. The firing rates were measured over sliding windows of 30 ms, after checking that shorter windows produced noisier measures. The effect of using a relatively long window, 30 ms, for measuring rates is an apparent linear early rise in information values with time. Nevertheless, in the real system the activity of these cells is 'read' by other cells receiving inputs from them, and that in turn have their own membrane capacitance-determined characteristic time for integrating input activity, a time broadly in the order of 30 ms. Using such a time window for integrating firing rates did not therefore artificially slow down the read-out process.

It was shown that the time course of different information measures did not depend significantly on the firing rates prevailing during the retrieval state, nor on the resistance–capacitance-determined membrane time constants of the units. Figure B.34 shows that the rise in information after providing the cue at time = 100 ms followed a roughly exponential approach to its steady-state value, which continued until the steady state switched to a new value when the retrieval cue was removed at time = 400 ms. The time constant of the approach to the first steady state was a linear function, as shown in Fig. B.34, of the time constant for excitatory conductances, as predicted by the analysis. (The proportionality factor in the Figure is 2.5, or a collective time constant 2.5 times longer than the synaptic time constant.) The approach to the second steady-state value was more rapid, and the early apparent linear rise prevented the detection of a consistent exponential mode. Therefore, it appears that the cue leads to the basin of attraction of the correct retrieval state by activating transient modes, whose time constant is set by that of excitatory conductances; once the network is in the correct basin, its subsequent reaching the 'very bottom' of the basin after the removal of the cue is not accompanied by any prominent transient mode (see further Battaglia and Treves (1998a)).

Overall, these simulations confirm that recurrent networks, in which excitation is mediated mainly by fast (AMPA, see Section 1.5) channels, can reach asynchronous steady firing states very rapidly, over a few tens of milliseconds, and the rapid approach to steady state is reflected

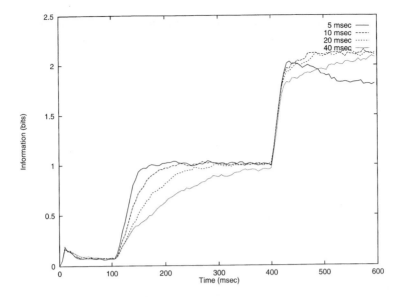

Fig. B.34 Time course of the transinformation about which memory pattern had been selected, as decoded from the firing rates of 10 randomly selected excitatory units. Excitatory conductances closed exponentially with time constants of 5, 10, 20 and 40 ms (curves from top to bottom). A cue of correlation 0.2 with the memory pattern was presented from 100 to 400 ms, uncorrelated external inputs with the same mean strength and sparseness as the cue were applied at earlier times, and no external inputs were applied at later times. (After Battaglia and Treves 1998b.)

in the relatively rapid rise of information quantities that measure the speed of the operation in functional terms.

An analysis based on integrate-and-fire model units thus indicates that recurrent dynamics can be so fast as to be practically indistinguishable from purely feedforward dynamics, in contradiction to what simple intuitive arguments would suggest. This makes it hazardous to draw conclusions on the underlying circuitry on the basis of the experimentally observed speed with which selective neuronal responses arise, as attempted by Thorpe and Imbert (1989). The results also show that networks that implement feedback processing can settle into a global retrieval state very rapidly, and that rapid processing is not just a feature of feedforward networks.

We return to the intuitive understanding of this rapid processing. The way in which networks with continuous dynamics (such as networks made of real neurons in the brain, and networks modelled with integrate-and-fire neurons) can be conceptualized as settling so fast into their attractor states is that spontaneous activity in the network ensures that some neurons are close to their firing threshold when the retrieval cue is presented, so that the firing of these neurons is influenced within 1–2 ms by the retrieval cue. These neurons then influence other neurons within milliseconds (given the point that some other neurons will be close to threshold) through the modified recurrent collateral synapses that store the information. In this way, the neurons in networks with continuous dynamics can influence each other within a fraction of the synaptic time constant, and retrieval can be very rapid.

B.6.6 The speed of processing of a four-layer hierarchical network with integrate-and-fire attractor dynamics in each layer

Given that the visual system has a whole series of cortical areas organized predominantly hierarchically (e.g. V1 to V2 to V4 to inferior temporal cortex), the issue arises of whether the rapid information processing that can be performed for object recognition is predominantly feedforward, or whether there is sufficient time for feedback processing within each cortical area implemented by the local recurrent collaterals to contribute to the visual information processing being performed. Some of the constraints are as follows.

An analysis of response latencies indicates that there is sufficient time for only 10–20 ms per processing stage in the visual system. In the primate cortical ventral visual system the response latency difference between neurons in layer 4Cβ of V1 and inferior temporal cortical cells is approximately 60 ms (Bullier and Nowak 1995, Nowak and Bullier 1997, Schmolesky, Wang, Hanes, Thompson, Leutgeb, Schall and Leventhal 1998). For example, the latency of the responses of neurons in V1 is approximately 30–40 ms (Celebrini, Thorpe, Trotter and Imbert 1993), and in the temporal cortex visual areas approximately 80–110 ms (Baylis, Rolls and Leonard 1987, Sugase, Yamane, Ueno and Kawano 1999). Given that there are 4–6 stages of processing in the ventral visual system from V1 to the anterior inferior temporal cortex, the difference in latencies between each ventral cortical stage is on this basis approximately 10 ms (Rolls 1992a, Oram and Perrett 1994). Information theoretic analyses of the responses of single visual cortical cells in primates reveal that much of the information that can be extracted from neuronal spike trains is often found to be present in periods as short as 20–30 ms (Tovee, Rolls, Treves and Bellis 1993, Tovee and Rolls 1995, Heller, Hertz, Kjaer and Richmond 1995, Rolls, Tovee and Panzeri 1999b). Backward masking experiments indicate that each cortical area needs to fire for only 20–30 ms to pass information to the next stage (Rolls and Tovee 1994, Rolls, Tovee, Purcell, Stewart and Azzopardi 1994b, Kovacs, Vogels and Orban 1995, Rolls, Tovee and Panzeri 1999b, Rolls 2003) (see Section C.3.4). Rapid serial visual presentation of image sequences shows that cells in the temporal visual cortex are still face selective when faces are presented at the rate of 14 ms/image (Keysers, Xiao, Foldiak and Perrett 2001). Finally, event-related potential studies in humans provide strong evidence that the visual system is able to complete some analyses of complex scenes in less than 150 ms (Thorpe, Fize and Marlot 1996).

To investigate whether feedback processing within each layer could contribute to information processing in such a multilayer system in times as short as 10–20 ms per layer, Panzeri, Rolls, Battaglia and Lavis (2001) simulated a four-layer network with attractor networks in each layer. The network architecture is shown schematically in Fig. B.35. All the neurons realized integrate-and-fire dynamics, and indeed the individual layers and neurons were implemented very similarly to the implementation used by Battaglia and Treves (1998a). In particular, the current flowing from each compartment of the multicompartment neurons to the external medium was expressed as:

$$I(t) = g_{\text{leak}}(V(t) - V^0) + \sum_j g_j(t)(V(t) - V_j), \tag{B.56}$$

where g_{leak} is a constant passive leakage conductance, V^0 the membrane resting potential, $g_j(t)$ the value of the jth synapse conductance at time t, and V_j the reversal potential of the jth synapse. $V(t)$ is the potential in the compartment at time t. The most important parameter in the simulation, the AMPA inactivation time constant, was set to 10 ms. The recurrent collateral (RC) integration time constant of the membrane of excitatory cells was 20 ms long for the simulations presented. The synaptic conductances decayed exponentially in time, obeying the equation

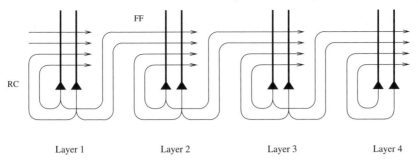

Layer 1   Layer 2   Layer 3   Layer 4

Fig. B.35 The structure of the excitatory connections in the network. There are feedforward (FF) connections between each layer and the next, and excitatory recurrent collaterals (RC) in each layer. Inhibitory connections are also present within each layer, but they are not shown in this Figure. (After Panzeri, Rolls, Battaglia and Lavis 2001.)

$$\frac{\mathrm{d}g_j}{\mathrm{d}t} = -\frac{g_j}{\tau_j} + \Delta g_j \sum_k \delta(t - \Delta t - t_k^j), \tag{B.57}$$

where τ_j is the synaptic decay time constant, Δt is a delay term summarizing axonal and synaptic delays, and Δg_j is the amount that the conductance is increased when the presynaptic unit fires a spike. Δg_j thus represents the (unidirectional) coupling strength between the pre-synaptic and the post-synaptic cell. t_k^j is the time at which the pre-synaptic unit fires its kth spike.

An example of the rapid information processing of the system is shown in Fig. B.36, obtained under conditions in which the local recurrent collaterals can contribute to correct performance because the feedforward (FF) inputs from the previous stage are noisy. (The noise implemented in these simulations was some imperfection in the FF signals produced by some alterations to the FF synaptic weights.) Figure B.36 shows that, when the FF carry an incomplete signal, some information is still transmitted successfully in the 'No RC' condition (in which the recurrent collateral connections in each layer are switched off), and with a relatively short latency. However, the noise term in the FF synaptic strengths makes the retrieval fail more and more layer by layer. When in contrast the recurrent collaterals (RC) are present and operating after Hebbian training, the amount of information retrieved is now much higher, because the RC are able to correct a good part of the erroneous information injected into the neurons by the noisy FF synapses. In Layer 4, 66 ms after cue injection in Layer 1, the information in the Hebbian RC case is 0.2 bits higher than that provided by the FF connections in the 'No RC' condition. This shows that the RC are able to retrieve information in Layer 4 that is not available by any other purely FF mechanism after only roughly 50–55 ms from the time when Layer 1 responds. (This corresponds to 17–18 ms per layer.)

A direct comparison of the latency differences in layers 1–4 of the integrate-and-fire network simulated by Panzeri, Rolls, Battaglia and Lavis (2001) is shown in Fig. B.37. The results are shown for the Hebbian condition illustrated in Fig. B.36, and separate curves are shown for each of the layers 1–4. The Figure shows that, with the time constant of the synapses set to 10 ms, the network can operate with full utilization of and benefit from recurrent processing within each layer in a time which enables the signal to propagate through the 4-layer system with a time course of approximately 17 ms per layer.

The overall results of Panzeri, Rolls, Battaglia and Lavis (2001) were as follows. Through the implementation of continuous dynamics, latency differences were found in information retrieval of only 5 ms per layer when local excitation was absent and processing was purely feedforward. However, information latency differences increased significantly when non-associative local excitation (simulating spontaneous firing or unrelated inputs present in the

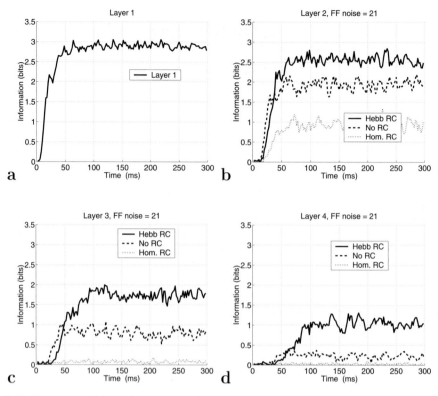

Fig. B.36 The speed of information processing in a 4-layer network with integrate-and-fire neurons. The information time course of the average information carried by the responses of a population of 30 excitatory neurons in each layer. In the simulations considered here, there is noise in the feedforward (FF) synapses. Layer 1 was tested in just one condition. Layers 2–4 are tested in three different conditions: No RC (in which the recurrent collateral synaptic effects do not operate), Hebbian RC (in which the recurrent collaterals have been trained by as associative rule and can help pattern retrieval in each layer), and a control condition named Homogeneous RC (in which the recurrent collaterals could inject current into the neurons, but no useful information was provided by them because they were all set to the same strength). (After Panzeri, Rolls, Battaglia and Lavis 2001.)

brain) was included. It was also found that local recurrent excitation through associatively modified synapses can contribute significantly to processing in as little as 15 ms per layer, including the feedforward and local feedback processing. Moreover, and in contrast to purely feed-forward processing, the contribution of local recurrent feedback was useful and approximately this rapid even when retrieval was made difficult by noise. These findings provide evidence that cortical information processing can be very fast even when local recurrent circuits are critically involved. The time cost of this recurrent processing is minimal when compared with a feedforward system with spontaneous firing or unrelated inputs already present, and the performance is better than that of a purely feedforward system when noise is present.

It is concluded that local feedback loops within each cortical area can contribute to fast visual processing and cognition.

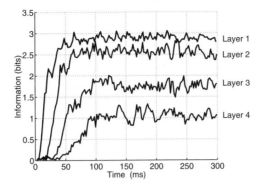

Fig. B.37 The speed of information processing in a 4-layer network with integrate-and-fire neurons. The information time course of the average information carried by the responses of a population of 30 excitatory neurons in each layer. The results are shown for the Hebbian condition illustrated in Fig. B.36, and separate curves are shown for each of the layers 1–4. The Figure shows that, with the time constant of the synapses set to 10 ms, the network can operate with full utilization of and benefit from recurrent processing within each layer in a time in the order of 17 ms per layer. (After Panzeri, Rolls, Battaglia and Lavis 2001.)

B.6.7 Spike response model

In this section, we describe another mathematical model that models the activity of single spiking neurons. This model captures the principal effects of real neurons in a realistic way and is simple enough to permit analytical calculations (Gerstner, Ritz and Van Hemmen 1993). In contrast to some integrate-and-fire models (Tuckwell 1988), which are essentially given by differential equations, the spike-response model is based on response kernels that describe the integrated effect of spike reception or emission on the membrane potential. In this model, spikes are generated by a threshold process (i.e. the firing time t' is given by the condition that the membrane potential reaches the firing threshold θ; that is, $h(t') = \theta$). Figure B.38 (bottom) shows schematically the spike-generating mechanism.

The membrane potential is given by the integration of the input signal weighted by a kernel defined by the equations

$$h(t') = h^{\text{refr}}(t') + h^{\text{syn}}(t') \tag{B.58}$$

$$h^{\text{refr}}(t') = \int_0^\infty \eta^{\text{refr}}(z)\delta(t' - z - t'_{\text{last}})dz \tag{B.59}$$

$$h^{\text{syn}}(t') = \sum_j J_j \int_0^\infty \Lambda(z', t' - t'_{\text{last}})s(t' - z')dz' . \tag{B.60}$$

The kernel $\eta^{\text{refr}}(z)$ is the refractory function. If we consider only absolute refractoriness, $\eta^{\text{refr}}(z)$ is given by:

$$\eta^{\text{refr}}(z) = \begin{cases} -\infty & \text{for } 0 < z \leq \tau^{\text{refr}} \\ 0 & \text{for } z \geq \tau^{\text{refr}} \end{cases} \tag{B.61}$$

where τ^{refr} is the absolute refractory time. The time t'_{last} corresponds to the last postsynaptic spike (i.e. the most recent firing of the particular neuron). The second response function is the synaptic kernel $\Lambda(z', t' - t'_{\text{last}})$. It describes the effect of an incoming spike on the membrane potential at the soma of the postsynaptic neuron, and it eventually includes also the dependence on the state of the receiving neuron through the difference $t' - t'_{\text{last}}$ (i.e. through the time that has passed since the last postsynaptic spike). The input spike train yields

$s(t' - z') = \sum_i \delta(t' - z' - t_{ij})$, t_{ij} being the ith spike at presynaptic input j. In order to simplify the discussion and without losing generality, let us consider only a single synaptic input, and therefore we can remove the subindex j. In addition, we assume that the synaptic strength J is positive (i.e. excitatory). Integrating equations B.59 and B.60, we obtain

$$h(t') = \eta^{\text{refr}}(t' - t'_{\text{last}}) + J \sum_i \Lambda(t' - t_i, t' - t'_{\text{last}}) \tag{B.62}$$

Synaptic kernels are of the form

$$\Lambda(t' - t_i, t' - t'_{\text{last}}) = \text{H}(t' - t_i)\text{H}(t_i - t'_{\text{last}})\Psi(t' - t_i) \tag{B.63}$$

where $\text{H}(s)$ is the step (or Heaviside) function which vanishes for $s \leq 0$ and takes a value of 1 for $s > 0$. After firing, the membrane potential is reset according to the renewal hypothesis.

This spike-response model is not used in the models described in this book, but is presented to show alternative approaches to modelling the dynamics of network activity.

B.7 Network dynamics: introduction to the mean-field approach

Units whose potential and conductances follow the integrate-and-fire equations in Section B.6 can be assembled together in a model network of any composition and architecture. It is convenient to imagine that units are grouped into classes, such that the parameters quantifying the electrophysiological properties of the units are uniform, or nearly uniform, within each class, while the parameters assigned to synaptic connections are uniform or nearly uniform for all connections from a given presynaptic class to another given postsynaptic class. The parameters that have to be set in a model at this level of description are quite numerous, as listed in Tables B.3 and B.4.

In the limit in which the parameters are constant within each class or pair of classes, a mean-field treatment can be applied to analyze a model network, by summing equations that describe the dynamics of individual units to obtain a more limited number of equations that describe the dynamical behaviour of groups of units (Frolov and Medvedev 1986). The treatment is exact in the further limit in which very many units belong to each class, and is an approximation if each class includes just a few units. Suppose that N_C is the number of classes defined. Summing equations B.43 and B.44 across units of the same class results in N_C functional equations describing the evolution in time of the fraction of cells of a particular class that at a given instant have a given membrane potential. In other words, from a treatment in which the evolution of the variables associated with each unit is followed separately, one moves to a treatment based on density functions, in which the common behaviour of units of the same class is followed together, keeping track solely of the portion of units at any given value of the membrane potential. Summing equation B.42 across connections with the same class of origin and destination results in $N_C \times N_C$ equations describing the dynamics of the overall summed conductance opened on the membrane of a cell of a particular class by all the cells of another given class. A more explicit derivation of mean-field equations is given by Treves (1993) and in Section B.8.

The system of mean-field equations can have many types of asymptotic solutions for long times, including chaotic, periodic, and stationary ones. The stationary solutions are stationary in the sense of the mean fields, but in fact correspond to the units of each class firing tonically at a certain rate. They are of particular interest as the dynamical equivalent of the steady

Table B.3 Cellular parameters (chosen according to the class of each unit)

V_{rest}	Resting potential
V_{thr}	Threshold potential
V_{ahp}	Reset potential
V_{K}	Potassium conductance equilibrium potential
C	Membrane capacitance
τ_{K}	Potassium conductance time constant
g_0	Leak conductance
Δg_{K}	Extra potassium conductance following a spike
Δt	Overall transmission delay

Table B.4 Synaptic parameters (chosen according to the classes of presynaptic and postsynaptic units)

V_α	Synapse equilibrium potential
τ_α	Synaptic conductance time constant
Δg_α	Conductance opened by one presynaptic spike
Δt_α	Delay of the connection

states analyzed by using non-dynamical model networks. In fact, since the neuronal current-to-frequency transfer function resulting from the dynamical equations is rather similar to a threshold linear function (see Fig. B.32), and since each synaptic conductance is constant in time, the stationary solutions are essentially the same as the states described using model networks made up of threshold linear, non-dynamical units. Thus the dynamical formulation reduces to the simpler formulation in terms of steady-state rates when applied to asymptotic stationary solutions; but, among simple rate models, it is equivalent only to those that allow description of the continuous nature of neuronal output, and not to those, for example based on binary units, that do not reproduce this fundamental aspect. The advantages of the dynamical formulation are that (i) it enables one to describe the character and prevalence of other types of asymptotic solutions, and (ii) it enables one to understand how the network reaches, in time, the asymptotic behaviour.

The development of this mean-field approach, and the foundations for its application to models of cortical visual processing and attention, are described in Section B.8.

B.8   Mean-field based neurodynamics

A model of brain functions requires the choice of an appropriate theoretical framework, which permits the investigation and simulation of large-scale biologically realistic neural networks. Starting from the mathematical models of biologically realistic single neurons (i.e. spiking neurons), one can derive models that describe the joint activity of pools of equivalent neurons. This kind of neurodynamical model at the neuronal assembly level is motivated by the experimental observation that cortical neurons of the same type that are near to each other tend to receive similar inputs. As described in the previous section, it is convenient in this simplified approach to neural dynamics to consider all neurons of the same type in a small cortical volume as a computational unit of a neural network. This computational unit is called a neuronal pool or assembly. The mathematical description of the dynamical evolution of neuronal pool activity in multimodular networks, associated with different cortical areas, establishes the roots of the dynamical approach that are used in Chapters 6 and 7, and in Rolls and Deco (2002)

Chapters 9–11. In this Section (B.8), we introduce the mathematical fundamentals utilized for a neurodynamical description of pool activity (see also Section 7.9). Beginning at the microscopic level and using single spiking neurons to form the pools of a network, we derive the mathematical formulation of the neurodynamics of cell assemblies. Further, we introduce the basic architecture of neuronal pool networks that fulfil the basic mechanisms consistent with the biased competition hypothesis. Each of these networks corresponds to cortical areas that also communicate with each other. We describe therefore the dynamical interaction between different modules or networks, which will be the basis for the implementation of attentional top-down bias.

B.8.1   Population activity

We now introduce thoroughly the concept of a neuronal pool and the differential equations representing the neurodynamics of pool activity.

Starting from individual spiking neurons one can derive a differential equation that describes the dynamical evolution of the averaged activity of a pool of extensively many equivalent neurons. Several areas of the brain contain groups of neurons that are organized in populations of units with (somewhat) similar properties (though in practice the neurons convey independent information, as described in Appendix C). These groups for mean-field modelling purposes are usually called pools of neurons and are constituted by a large and similar population of identical spiking neurons that receive similar external inputs and are mutually coupled by synapses of similar strength. Assemblies of motor neurons (Kandel, Schwartz and Jessel 2000) and the columnar organization in the visual and somatosensory cortex (Hubel and Wiesel 1962, Mountcastle 1957) are examples of these pools. Each single cell in a pool can be described by a spiking model, e.g. the spike response model presented in Section B.6.7. Due to the fact that for large-scale cortical modelling, neuronal pools form a relevant computational unit, we adopt a population code. We take the activity level of each pool of neurons as the relevant dependent variable rather than the spiking activity of individual neurons. We therefore derive a dynamical model for the mean activity of a neural population. In a population of M neurons, the mean activity $A(t)$ is determined by the proportion of active neurons by counting the number of spikes $n_{\text{spikes}}(t, t + \Delta t)$ in a small time interval Δt and dividing by M and by Δt (Gerstner 2000), i.e. formally

$$A(t) = \lim_{\Delta t \to 0} \frac{n_{\text{spikes}}(t, t + \Delta t)}{M \Delta t}. \tag{B.64}$$

As indicated by Gerstner (2000), and as depicted in Fig. B.38, the concept of pool activity is quite different from the definition of the average firing rate of a single neuron. Contrary to the concept of temporal averaging over many spikes of a single cell, which requires that the input is slowly varying compared with the size of the temporal averaging window, a coding scheme based on pool activity allows rapid adaptation to real-world situations with quickly changing inputs. It is possible to derive dynamical equations for pool activity levels by utilizing the mean-field approximation (Wilson and Cowan 1972, Abbott 1991, Amit and Tsodyks 1991). The mean-field approximation consists of replacing the temporally averaged discharge rate of a cell with an equivalent momentary activity of a neural population (ensemble average) that corresponds to the assumption of ergodicity. According to this approximation, we categorize each cell assembly by means of its activity $A(t)$. A pool of excitatory neurons without external input can be described by the dynamics of the pool activity given by

$$\tau \frac{\partial A(t)}{\partial t} = -A(t) + q\text{F}(A(t)) \tag{B.65}$$

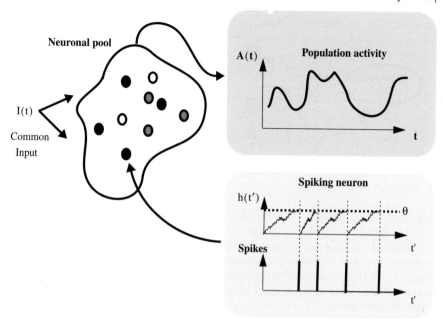

Fig. B.38 Population averaged rate of a neuronal pool of spiking neurons (top) and the action potential generating mechanism of single neurons (bottom). In a neuronal pool, the mean activity $A(t)$ is determined by the proportion of active neurons by counting the number of spikes in a small time interval Δt and dividing by the number of neurons in the pool and by Δt. Spikes are generated by a threshold process. The firing time t' is given by the condition that the membrane potential $h(t')$ reaches the firing threshold θ. The membrane potential $h(t')$ is given by the integration of the input signal weighted by a given kernel (see text for details). (After Rolls and Deco 2002.)

where the first term on the right hand side is a decay term and the second term takes into account the excitatory stimulation between the neurons in the pool. In the previous equation, the non-linearity

$$F(x) = \frac{1}{T_r - \tau \log(1 - \frac{1}{\tau x})} \tag{B.66}$$

is the response function (transforming current into discharge rate) for a spiking neuron with deterministic input, membrane time constant τ, and absolute refractory time T_r. Equation B.65 was derived by Gerstner (2000) assuming adiabatic conditions. Gerstner (2000) has shown that the population activity in a homogeneous population of neurons can be described by an integral equation. A systematic reduction of the integral equation to a single differential equation of the form B.65 always supposes that the activity changes only slowly compared with the typical interval length. In other words, the mean-field approach described in the above equations and utilized in parts of Chapters 4, 6, 7 and 8 generates a dynamics that neglects fast, transient behaviour. This means that we are assuming that rapid oscillations (and synchronization) do not play a computational role at least for the brain functions that we will consider. Rapid oscillations of neural activity could have a relevant functional role, namely of dynamical cooperation between pools in the same or different brain areas. It is well known in the theory of dynamical systems that the synchronization of oscillators is a cooperative phenomenon. Cooperative mechanisms might complement the competitive mechanisms on which our computational cortical model is based.

An example of the application of the mean field approach, in a model of decision-making (Deco and Rolls 2006), is provided in Section 7.9.

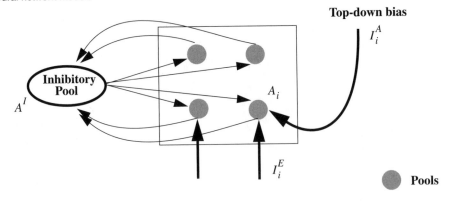

Fig. B.39 Basic computational module for biased competition: a competitive network with external top-down bias. Excitatory pools with activity A_i for the ith pool are connected with a common inhibitory pool with activity A^I in order to implement a competition mechanism. I_i^E is the external sensory input to the cells in pool i, and I_i^A attentional top-down bias, an external input coming from higher modules. The external top-down bias can shift the competition in favour of a specific pool or group of pools. This architecture is similar to that shown in Fig. B.18, but with competition between pools of similar neurons. (After Rolls and Deco 2002.)

B.8.2 A basic computational module based on biased competition

We are interested in the neurodynamics of modules composed of several pools that implement a competitive mechanism[42]. This can be achieved by connecting the pools of a given module with a common inhibitory pool, as is schematically shown in Fig. B.39.

In this way, the more pools of the module that are active, the more active the common inhibitory pool will be, and consequently, the more feedback inhibition will affect the pools in the module, such that only the most excited group of pools will survive the competition. On the other hand, external top-down bias could shift the competition in favour of a specific group of pools. This basic computational module implements therefore the biased competition hypothesis described in Chapter 6. Let us assume that there are m pools in a given module. The system of differential equations describing the dynamics of such a module is given by two differential equations, both of the type of equation B.65. The first differential equation describes the dynamics of the activity level of the excitatory pools (pyramidal neurons) and is mathematically expressed by

$$\tau \frac{\partial A_i(t)}{\partial t} = -A_i(t) + aF(A_i(t)) - bF(A^I(t)) +$$
$$I_0 + I_i^E(t) + I_i^A(t) + \nu \quad ; \qquad \text{for } i = 1, ..., m \qquad \text{(B.67)}$$

and the second one describes the dynamics of the activity level of the common inhibitory pool for each feature dimension (stellate neurons)

$$\tau_p \frac{\partial A^I(t)}{\partial t} = -A^I(t) + c \sum_{i=1}^{m} F(A_i(t)) - dF(A^I(t)) \qquad \text{(B.68)}$$

where $A_i(t)$ is the activity for pool i, $A^I(t)$ is the activity in the inhibitory pool, I_0 is a diffuse spontaneous background input, $I^E(t)$ is the external sensory input to the cells in pool i, and ν is additive Gaussian noise. The attentional top-down bias $I_i^A(t)$ is defined as an external input coming from higher modules that is not explicitly modelled.

---

[42]These neurodynamics are used in Chapter 6.

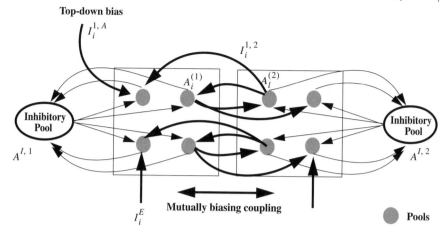

Top-down bias

Fig. B.40 Two competitive networks mutually biased through intermodular connections. The activity $A_i^{(1)}$ of the ith excitatory pool in module 1 (on the left) and of the lth excitatory pool in module 2 (on the right) are connected by the mutually biasing coupling $I_i^{1,2}$. The architecture could implement top-down feedback originating from the interaction between brain areas that are explicitly modelled in the system. (Module 2 might be the higher module.) The external top-down bias $I_i^{1,A}$ corresponds to the coupling to pool i of module 1 from brain area A that is not explicitly modelled in the system. (After Rolls and Deco 2002.)

A qualitative description of the main fixed point attractors of the system of differential equations B.67 and B.68 was provided by Usher and Niebur (1996). Basically, we will be interested in the fixed points corresponding to zero activity and larger activation. The parameters will therefore be fixed such that the dynamics evolves to these attractors.

B.8.3 Multimodular neurodynamical architectures

In order to model complex psychophysically and neuropsychologically relevant brain functions such as visual search or object recognition (see e.g. Chapter 6), we must take into account the computational role of individual brain areas and their mutual interaction. The macroscopic phenomenological behaviour will therefore be the result of the mutual interaction of several computational modules.

The dynamical coupling of different basic modules in a multimodular architecture can be described, in our neurodynamical framework, by allowing mutual interaction between pools belonging to different modules. Figure B.40 shows this idea schematically. The system of differential equations describing the global dynamics of such a multimodular system is given by a set of equations of the type of equation B.65.

The excitatory pools belonging to a module obey the following equations:

$$\tau \frac{\partial A_i^{(j)}(t)}{\partial t} = -A_i^{(j)}(t) + aF(A_i^{(j)}(t)) - bF(A^{I,j}(t)) +$$

$$I_i^{j,k} + I_0 + I_i^E(t) + I_i^A(t) + \nu \qquad \text{for } i = 1, ..., m \qquad \text{(B.69)}$$

and the corresponding inhibitory pools evolve according to

$$\tau_p \frac{\partial A^{I,j}(t)}{\partial t} = -A^{I,j}(t) + c \sum_{i=1}^{m} F(A_i^{(j)}(t)) - dF(A^{I,j}(t)). \qquad \text{(B.70)}$$

The mutual coupling $I_i^{j,k}$ between module (j) and (k) is given by

$$I_i^{j,k} = \sum_l W_{il} F(I_l^{(k)}(t))$$

(B.71)

where W_{il} is the synaptic coupling strength between the pool i of module (j) and pool l of module (k). This mutual coupling term can be interpreted as a top-down bias originating from the interaction between brain areas that is explicitly modelled in our system. On the other hand, the external top-down bias I_i^A corresponds to the coupling with brain areas A that are not explicitly modelled in our system.

Additionally, it is interesting to note that the top-down bias in this kind of architecture modulates the response of the pool activity in a multiplicative manner. Responses of neurons in parietal area 7a are modulated by combined eye and head movement, exhibiting a multiplicative gain modulation that modifies the amplitude of the neural responses to retinal input but does not change the preferred retinal location of a cell, nor in general the width of the receptive field (Brotchie, Andersen, Snyder and Goodman 1995). It has also been suggested that multiplicative gain modulation might play a role in translation invariant object representation (Salinas and Abbott 1997). We will use this multiplicative effect for formulating an architecture for attentional gain modulation, which can contribute to correct translation invariant object recognition in ways to be described in Chapter 6.

We show now that multiplicative-like responses can arise from the top-down biased mutual interaction between pools. Another alternative architecture that can also perform product operations on additive synaptic inputs was proposed by Salinas and Abbott (1996). Our basic architecture for showing this multiplicative effect is presented schematically in Fig. B.41a.

Two pools are mutually connected via fixed weights. The first pool or unit receives a bottom-up visual input I_1^V, modelled by the response of a vertically oriented complex cell. The second pool receives a top-down attentional bias $I_2^A = B$. The two pools are mutually coupled with unity weight. The equations describing the activities of the two pools are given by:

$$\tau \frac{\partial A_1(t)}{\partial t} = -A_1(t) + \alpha F(A_1(t)) + I_o + I_1^V + \nu$$

(B.72)

$$\tau \frac{\partial A_2(t)}{\partial t} = -A_2(t) + \alpha F(A_2(t)) + I_o + I_2^A + \nu$$

(B.73)

where A_1 and A_2 are the activities of pool 1 and pool 2 respectively, $\alpha = 0.95$ is the coefficient of recurrent self-excitation of the pool, ν is the noise input to the pool drawn from a normal distribution $N(\mu = 0, \sigma = 0.02)$, and $I_o = 0.025$ is a direct current biasing input to the pool.

Simulation of the above dynamical equations produces the results shown in Fig. B.41b. The orientation tuning curve of unit (or pool) 1 was modulated by a top-down bias B introduced to unit (pool) 2. The gain modulation was transmitted through the coupling from pool 2 to pool 1 after a few steps of evolution of the dynamical equations. Without the feedback from unit 2, unit 1 exhibits the orientation tuning curve shown as $(B = 0)$. As B increased, the increase in pool 1's response to the vertical bar was significantly greater than the increase in its response to the horizontal bar. Therefore, the attentional gain modulation produced in pool 1 through the mutual coupling was not a simple additive effect, but had a strong multiplicative component. The net effect was that the width of the orientation tuning curve of the cell was roughly preserved under attentional modulation. This was due to the non-linearity in the activation function.

This finding is basically consistent with the effect of attention on the orientation tuning curves of neurons in V4 (McAdams and Maunsell 1999).

Summarizing, the neurodynamics of the competitive mechanisms between neuronal pools, and their mutual gain modulation, are the two main ingredients used for proposing a cortical

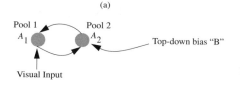

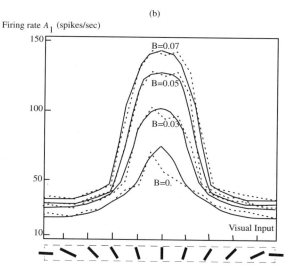

Fig. B.41 (a) The basic building block of the top-down attentional system utilizes non-specific competition between pools within the same module and specific mutual facilitation between pools in different modules. Excitatory neuronal pools within the same module compete with each other through one or more inhibitory neuronal pool(s) I_I with activity A^{I_I}. Excitatory pool 1 (with activity A_1) receives a bottom-up (visual) input I_1^V, and excitatory pool 2 receives a top-down ('attentional') bias input I_2^A. Excitatory neuronal pools in the two different modules can excite each other via mutually biased coupling. (b) The effect of altering the bias input B to pool 2 on the responses or activity of pool 1 to its orientation-tuned visual input (see text). (After Rolls and Deco 2002.)

architecture that models attention and different kinds of object search in a visual scene (see Chapter 6 and Section 6.13, and Rolls and Deco (2002) Chapters 9–11).

B.9 Interacting attractor networks

It is prototypical of the cerebral neocortical areas that there are recurrent collateral connections between the neurons within an area or module, and forward connections to the next cortical area in the hierarchy, which in turn sends backprojections (see Section 1.11). This architecture, made explicit in Fig. 5.3, immediately suggests, given that the recurrent connections within a module, and the forward and backward connections, are likely to be associatively modifiable, that the operation incorporates at least to some extent, interactions between coupled attractor (autoassociation) networks. For these reasons, it is important to analyze the rules that govern the interactions between coupled attractor networks. This has been done using the formal type of model described in Section 5.3.

One boundary condition is when the coupling between the networks is so weak that there is effectively no interaction. This holds when the coupling parameter g between the networks is less than approximately 0.002, where the coupling parameter indicates the relative strength

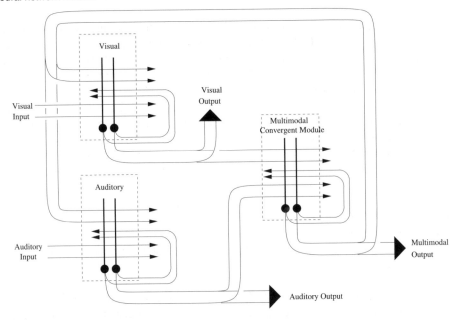

Fig. B.42 A two-layer set of attractor nets in which feedback from layer 2 can influence the states reached in layer 1. Layer 2 could be a higher cortical visual area with convergence from earlier cortical visual areas (see Chapter 4). Layer 2 could also be a multimodal area receiving inputs from unimodal visual and auditory cortical areas, as labelled. Each of the 3 modules has recurrent collateral synapses that are trained by an associative synaptic learning rule, and also inter-modular synaptic connections in the forward and backward direction that are also associatively trained. Attractors are formed within modules, the different modules interact, and attractors are also formed by the forward and backward inter-modular connections. The higher area may not only affect the states reached during attractor settling in the input layers, but may also, as a result of this, influence the representations that are learned in earlier cortical areas. A similar principle may operate in any multilayer hierarchical cortical processing system, such as the ventral visual system, in that the categories that can be formed only at later stages of processing may help earlier stages to form categories relevant to what can be diagnosed at later stages.

of the inter-modular to the intra-modular connections, and measures effectively the relative strengths of the currents injected into the neurons by the inter-modular relative to the intra-modular (recurrent collateral) connections (Renart, Parga and Rolls 1999b). At the other extreme, if the coupling parameter is strong, all the networks will operate as a single attractor network, together able to represent only one state (Renart, Parga and Rolls 1999b). This critical value of the coupling parameter (at least for reciprocally connected networks with symmetric synaptic strengths) is relatively low, in the region of 0.024 (Renart, Parga and Rolls 1999b). This is one reason why cortico-cortical backprojections are predicted to be quantitatively relatively weak, and for this reason it is suggested end on the apical parts of the dendrites of cortical pyramidal cells (see Section 1.11). In the strongly coupled regime when the system of networks operates as a single attractor, the total storage capacity (the number of patterns that can be stored and correctly retrieved) of all the networks will be set just by the number of synaptic connections onto any single neuron received from other neurons in the network, a number in the order of a few thousand (see Section B.3). This is one reason why connected cortical networks are thought not to act in the strongly coupled regime, because the total number of memories that could be represented in the whole of the cerebral cortex would be so small, in the order of a few thousand, depending on the sparseness of the patterns (see equation B.15) (O'Kane and Treves 1992).

Between these boundary conditions, that is in the region where the inter-modular coupling parameter g is in the range 0.002–0.024, it has been shown that interesting interactions can occur (Renart, Parga and Rolls 1999b, Renart, Parga and Rolls 1999a). In a bimodular architecture, with forward and backward connections between the modules, the capacity of one module can be increased, and an attractor is more likely to be found under noisy conditions, if there is a consistent pattern in the coupled attractor. By consistent we mean a pattern that during training was linked associatively by the forward and backward connections, with the pattern being retrieved in the first module. This provides a quantitative model for understanding some of the effects that backprojections can produce by supporting particular states in earlier cortical areas (Renart, Parga and Rolls 1999b). The total storage capacity of the two networks is however, in line with O'Kane and Treves (1992), not a great deal greater than the storage capacity of one of the modules alone. Thus the help provided by the attractors in falling into a mutually compatible global retrieval state (in e.g. the scenario of a hierarchical system) is where the utility of such coupled attractor networks must lie. Another interesting application of such weakly coupled attractor networks is in coupled perceptual and short-term memory systems in the brain, described in Section 5.1 and Chapter 6.

In a trimodular attractor architecture shown in Fig. B.42 (which is similar to the architecture of the multilayer competitive net illustrated in Fig. B.19 but has recurrent collateral connections within each module), further interesting interactions occur that account for effects such as the McGurk effect, in which what is seen affects what is heard (Renart, Parga and Rolls 1999a). The effect was originally demonstrated with the perception of auditory syllables, which were influenced by what is seen (McGurk and MacDonald 1976). The trimodular architecture (studied using similar methods to those used by Renart, Parga and Rolls (1999b) and frequently utilizing scenarios in which first a stimulus was presented to a module, then removed during a memory delay period in which stimuli were applied to other modules) showed a phase with $g < 0.005$ in which the modules operated in an isolated way. With g in the range 0.005–0.012, an 'independent' regime existed in which each module could be in a separate state to the others, but in which interactions between the modules occurred, which could assist or hinder retrieval in a module depending on whether the states in the other modules were consistent or inconsistent. It is in this 'independent' regime that a module can be in a continuing attractor that can provide other modules with a persistent external modulatory input that is helpful for tasks such as making comparisons between stimuli processed sequentially (as in delayed match-to-sample tasks and visual search tasks) (see Section 5.1). In this regime, if the modules are initially quiescent, then application of a stimulus to one input module propagates to the central module, and from it to the non-stimulated input module as well (see Fig. B.42). When g grows beyond 0.012, the picture changes and the independence between the modules is lost. The delay activity states found in this region (of the phase space) *always* involve the three modules in attractors correlated with consistent features associated in the synaptic connections. Also, since g is now larger, changes in the properties of the external stimuli have more impact on the delay activity states. The general trend seen in this phase under the change of stimulus after a previous consistent attractor has been reached is that, first, if the second stimulus is not effective enough (it is weak or brief), it is unable to move any of the modules from their current delay activity states. If the stimulus is made more effective, then as soon as it is able to change the state of the stimulated input module, the internal and non-stimulated input modules follow, and the whole network moves into the new consistent attractor selected by the second stimulus. In this case, the interaction between the modules is so large that it does not allow contradictory local delay activity states to coexist, and the network is described as being in a 'locked' state.

The conclusion is that the most interesting scenario for coupled attractor networks is when they are weakly coupled (in the trimodular architecture $0.005 < g < 0.012$), for then interactions occur whereby how well one module responds to its own inputs can be influenced by the states of the other modules, but it can retain partly independent representations. This emphasizes the importance of weak interactions between coupled modules in the brain (Renart, Parga and Rolls 1999b, Renart, Parga and Rolls 1999a, Renart, Parga and Rolls 2000).

These generally useful interactions between coupled attractor networks can be useful in implementing top-down constraint satisfaction (see Section 1.11) and short-term memory (see Section 5.1). One type of constraint satisfaction in which they are also probably important is cross-modal constraint satisfaction, which occurs for example when the sight of the lips moving assists the hearing of syllables. If the experimenter mismatches the visual and auditory inputs, then auditory misperception can occur, as in the McGurk effect. In such experiments (McGurk and MacDonald 1976) the subject receives one stimulus through the auditory pathway (e.g. the syllables *ga-ga*) and a *different* stimulus through the visual pathway (e.g. the lips of a person performing the movements corresponding to the syllables *ba-ba* on a video monitor). These stimuli are such that their acoustic waveforms as well as the lip motions needed to pronounce them are rather different. One can then assume that although they share the same vowel 'a', the internal representation of the syllables is dominated by the consonant, so that the representations of the syllables *ga-ga* and *ba-ba* are not correlated either in the primary visual cortical areas or in the primary auditory ones. At the end of the experiment, the subject is asked to repeat what he heard. When this procedure is repeated with many subjects, it is found that roughly 50% of them claim to have heard either the auditory stimulus (*ga-ga*), or the visual one (*ba-ba*). The rest of the subjects report to have heard neither the auditory nor the visual stimuli, but actually a combination of the two (e.g. *gabga*) or even something else including phonemes not presented auditorially or visually (e.g. *gagla*).

Renart, Parga and Rolls (1999a) were able to show that the McGurk effect can be accounted for by the operation of coupled attractor networks of the form shown in Fig. B.42. One input module is for the auditory input, the second is for the visual input, and both converge into a higher area which represents the syllable formed on the evidence of combination of the two inputs. There are backprojections from the convergent module back to the input modules. Persistent (continuing) inputs were applied to both the inputs, and during associative training of all the weights the visual and auditory inputs corresponded to the same syllable. When tested with inconsistent visual and auditory inputs, it was found for g between ~ 0.10 and ~ 0.11, the convergent module can either remain in a symmetric state in which it represents a mixture of the two inputs, or choose between one of the inputs, with either situation being stable. For lower g the convergent module always settles into a state corresponding to the input in one of the input modules. It is the random fluctuations produced during the convergence to the attractor that determine the pattern selected by the convergent module. When the convergent module becomes correlated with *one* of its stored patterns, the signal back-projected to the input module stimulated with the feature associated with that pattern becomes stronger and the overlap in this module is increased. Thus, with low values of the inter-module coupling parameter g, situations are found in which sometimes the input to one module dominates, and sometimes the input to the other module dominates what is represented in the convergent module, and sometimes mixture states are stable in the convergent module. This model can thus account for the influences that visual inputs can have on what is heard, in for example the McGurk effect.

The interactions between coupled attractor networks can lead to the following effects. Facilitation can occur in a module if its external input is matched by an input from another module, whereas suppression in a module of its response to an external input can occur if the two inputs mismatch. This type of interaction can be used in imaging studies to identify brain regions where different signals interact with each other. One example is to locate brain regions where multimodal inputs converge. If the inputs in two sensory modalities are consistent based on previous experience, then facilitation will occur, whereas if they are inconsistent, suppression of the activity in a module can occur. This is one of the effects described in the bimodular and trimodular architectures investigated by Renart, Parga and Rolls (1999b), Renart, Parga and Rolls (1999a) and Rolls and Stringer (2001b), and found in architectures such as that illustrated in Fig. B.42.

If a multimodular architecture is trained with each of many patterns (which might be visual stimuli) in one module associated with one of a few patterns (which might be mood states) in a connected module, then interesting effects due to this asymmetry are found, as described in Section 3.11 and by Rolls and Stringer (2001b).

An interesting issue that arises is how rapidly a system of interacting attractor networks such as that illustrated in Fig. B.42 settles into a stable state. Is it sufficiently rapid for the interacting attractor effects described to contribute to cortical information processing? It is likely that the settling of the whole system is quite rapid, if it is implemented (as it is in the brain) with synapses and neurons that operate with continuous dynamics, where the time constant of the synapses dominates the retrieval speed, and is in the order of 15 ms for each module, as described in Section B.6 and by Panzeri, Rolls, Battaglia and Lavis (2001). In that Section, it is shown that a multimodular attractor network architecture can process information in approximately 15 ms per module (assuming an inactivation time constant for the synapses of 10 ms), and similarly fast settling may be expected of a system of the type shown in Fig. B.42.

B.10 Sequence memory implemented by adaptation in an attractor network

Sequence memory can be implemented by using synaptic adaptation to effectively encode the order of the items in a sequence, as described in Section 9.3 (Deco and Rolls 2005c). Whenever the attractor system is quenched into inactivity, the next member of the sequence emerges out of the spontaneous activity, because the least recently activated member of the sequence has the least synaptic or neuronal adaptation. This mechanism could be implemented in recurrent networks such as the hippocampal CA3 or the prefrontal cortex.

B.11 Perceptrons and one-layer error correction networks

The networks described in the next two Sections (B.11 and B.12) are capable of mapping a set of inputs to a set of required outputs using correction when errors are made. Although some of the networks are very powerful in the types of mapping they can perform, the power is obtained at the cost of learning algorithms that do not use local learning rules. A local learning rule specifies that synaptic strengths should be altered on the basis of information available locally at the synapse, for example the activity of the presynaptic and the post-synaptic neurons. Because the networks described here do not use local learning rules, their biological plausibility remains at present uncertain. One of the aims of future research must be to determine whether comparably difficult problems to those solved by the networks described in Sections B.11 and B.12 can be solved by biologically plausible neuronal networks.

We now describe one-layer networks taught by an error correction algorithm. The term *perceptron* refers strictly to networks with binary threshold activation functions. The outputs might take the values only 1 or 0 for example. The term perceptron arose from networks designed originally to solve perceptual problems (Rosenblatt 1961, Minsky and Papert 1969), and these networks are referred to briefly below. If the output neurons have continuous-valued

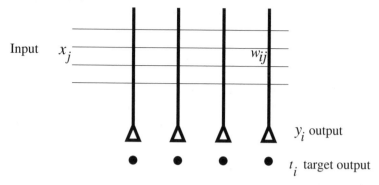

Fig. B.43 One-layer perceptron.

firing rates, then a more general error-correcting rule called the delta rule is used, and is introduced in this Section (B.11). For such networks, the activation function may be linear, or it may be non-linear but monotonically increasing, without a sharp threshold, as in the sigmoid activation function (see Fig. 1.3).

B.11.1 Architecture and general description

The one-layer error-correcting network has a set of inputs that it is desired to map or classify into a set of outputs (see Fig. B.43). During learning, an input pattern is selected, and produces output firing by activating the output neurons through modifiable synapses, which then fire as a function of their typically non-linear activation function. The output of each neuron is then compared with a target output for that neuron given that input pattern, an error between the actual output and the desired output is determined, and the synaptic weights on that neuron are then adjusted to minimize the error. This process is then repeated for all patterns until the average error across patterns has reached a minimum. A one-layer error-correcting network can thus produce output firing for each pattern in a way that has similarities to a pattern associator. It can perform more powerful mappings than a pattern associator, but requires an error to be computed for each neuron, and for that error to affect the synaptic strength in a way that is not altogether local. A more detailed description follows.

These one-layer networks have a target for each output neuron (for each input pattern). They are thus an example of a supervised network. With the one-layer networks taught with the delta rule or perceptron learning rule described next, there is a separate teacher for each output neuron, as shown in Fig. B.43.

B.11.2 Generic algorithm for a one-layer error correction network)

For each input pattern and desired target output:

1. Apply an input pattern to produce input firing $\mathbf{x}$, and obtain the activation of each neuron in the standard way by computing the dot product of the input pattern and the synaptic weight vector. The synaptic weight vector can be initially zero, or have random values.

$$h_i = \sum_j x_j w_{ij} \tag{B.74}$$

where $\sum_j$ indicates that the sum is over the C input axons (or connections) indexed by j to each neuron.

2. Apply an activation function to produce the output firing y_i:

$$y_i = f(h_i) . \qquad (B.75)$$

This activation function f may be sigmoid, linear, binary threshold, linear threshold, etc. If the activation function is non-linear, this helps to classify the inputs into distinct output patterns, but a linear activation function may be used if an optimal linear mapping is desired (see Adaline and Madaline, below).

3. Calculate the difference for each cell i between the target output t_i and the actual output y_i produced by the input, which is the error Δ_i

$$\Delta_i = t_i - y_i. \qquad (B.76)$$

4. Apply the following learning rule, which corrects the (continuously variable) weights according to the error and the input firing x_j

$$\delta w_{ij} = k(t_i - y_i)x_j \qquad (B.77)$$

where k is a constant that determines the learning rate. This is often called the delta rule, the Widrow–Hoff rule, or the LMS (least mean squares) rule (see below).

5. Repeat steps 1–4 for all input pattern – output target pairs until the root mean square error becomes zero or reaches a minimum.

In general, networks taught by the delta rule may have linear, binary threshold, or non-linear but monotonically increasing (e.g. sigmoid) activation functions, and may be taught with binary or continuous input patterns (see Rolls and Treves (1998), Chapter 5). The properties of these variations are made clear next.

B.11.3 Capability and limitations of single-layer error-correcting networks

Perceptrons perform pattern classification. That is, each neuron classifies the input patterns it receives into classes determined by the teacher. This is thus an example of a supervised network, with a separate teacher for each output neuron. The classification is most clearly understood if the output neurons are binary, or are strongly non-linear, but the network will still try to obtain an optimal mapping with linear or near-linear output neurons.

When each neuron operates as a binary classifier, we can consider how many input patterns p can be classified by each neuron, and the classes of pattern that can be correctly classified. The result is that the maximum number of patterns that can be correctly classified by a neuron with C inputs is

$$p_{max} = 2C \qquad (B.78)$$

when the inputs have random continuous-valued inputs, but the patterns must be linearly separable (see Section A.2.1, and Hertz, Krogh and Palmer (1991)). For a one-layer network, no set of weights can be found that will perform the XOR (exclusive OR), or any other non-linearly separable function (see Appendix A).

Although the inability of one-layer networks with binary neurons to solve non-linearly separable problems is a limitation, it is not in practice a major limitation on the processing that can be performed in a neural network for a number of reasons. First, if the inputs can take continuous values, then if the patterns are drawn from a random distribution, the one-layer network can map up to $2C$ of them. Second, as described for pattern associators, the perceptron could be preceded by an expansion recoding network such as a competitive network with more output than input neurons. This effectively provides a two-layer network for solving the problem, and multilayer networks are in general capable of solving arbitrary mapping problems. Ways in which such multilayer networks might be trained are discussed later in this Appendix.

We now return to the issue of the capacity of one-layer perceptrons, that is, how many patterns p can be correctly mapped to correct binary outputs if the input patterns are linearly separable.

B.11.3.1 Output neurons with continuous values, and random patterns

Before treating this case, we note that if the inputs are orthogonal, then just as in the pattern associator, C patterns can be correctly classified, where there are C inputs, x_j, $(j = 1, C)$, per neuron. The argument is the same as for a pattern associator.

We consider next the capacity of a one-layer error-correcting network that learns patterns drawn from a random distribution. For neurons with continuous output values, whether the activation function is linear or not, the capacity (for fully distributed inputs) is set by the criterion that the set of input patterns must be linearly independent (see Hertz, Krogh and Palmer (1991)). (Three patterns are linearly independent if any one cannot be formed by addition (with scaling allowed) of the other two patterns – see Appendix A.) Given that there can be a maximum of C linearly independent patterns in a C-dimensional space (see Appendix A), the capacity of the perceptron with such patterns is C patterns. If we choose p random patterns with continuous values, then they will be linearly independent for $p \leq C$ (except for cases with very low probability when the randomly chosen values may not produce linearly independent patterns). (With random continuous values for the input patterns, it is very unlikely that the addition of any two, with scaling allowed, will produce a third pattern in the set.) Thus with continuous valued input patterns,

$$p_{\text{max}} = C. \tag{B.79}$$

If the inputs are not linearly independent, networks trained with the delta rule produce a least mean squares (LMS) error (optimal) solution (see below).

B.11.3.2 Output neurons with binary threshold activation functions

Let us consider here strictly defined perceptrons, that is, networks with (binary) threshold output neurons, and taught by the perceptron learning procedure.

Capacity with fully distributed output patterns

The condition here for correct classification is that described in Appendix A for the AND and XOR functions, that the patterns must be linearly separable. If we consider random continuous-valued inputs, then the capacity is

$$p_{\text{max}} = 2C \tag{B.80}$$

(see Cover (1965), Hertz, Krogh and Palmer (1991); this capacity is the case with C large, and the number of output neurons small). The interesting point to note here is that, even with fully distributed inputs, a perceptron is capable of learning more (fully distributed) patterns than there are inputs per neuron. This formula is in general valid for large C, but happens to hold also for the AND function illustrated in Appendix A.2.1.

Sparse encoding of the patterns

If the output patterns **y** are sparse (but still distributed), then just as with the pattern associator, it is possible to map many more than C patterns to correct outputs. Indeed, the number of different patterns or prototypes p that can be stored is

$$p \approx C/a \qquad (B.81)$$

where a is the sparseness of the target pattern **t**. p can in this situation be much larger than C (cf. Rolls and Treves (1990), and Rolls and Treves (1998) Appendix A3).

Perceptron convergence theorem

It can be proved that such networks will learn the desired mapping in a finite number of steps (Block 1962, Minsky and Papert 1969, Hertz, Krogh and Palmer 1991). (This of course depends on there being such a mapping, the condition for this being that the input patterns are linearly separable.) This is important, for it shows that single-layer networks can be proved to be capable of solving certain classes of problem.

As a matter of history, Minsky and Papert (1969) went on to emphasize the point that no one-layer network can correctly classify non-linearly separable patterns. Although it was clear that multilayer networks can solve such mapping problems, Minsky and Papert were pessimistic that an algorithm for training such a multilayer network would be found. Their emphasis that neural networks might not be able to solve general problems in computation, such as computing the XOR, which is a non-linearly separable mapping, resulted in a decline in research activity in neural networks. In retrospect, this was unfortunate, for humans are rather poor at solving parity problems such as the XOR (Thorpe, O'Regan and Pouget 1989), yet can perform many other useful neural network operations very quickly. Algorithms for training multilayer perceptrons were gradually discovered by a number of different investigators, and became widely known after the publication of the algorithm described by Rumelhart, Hinton and Williams (1986b), and Rumelhart, Hinton and Williams (1986a). Even before this, interest in neural network pattern associators, autoassociators and competitive networks was developing (see Hinton and Anderson (1981), Kohonen (1977), Kohonen (1988)), but the acceptance of the algorithm for training multilayer perceptrons led to a great rise in interest in neural networks, partly for use in connectionist models of cognitive function (McClelland and Rumelhart 1986, McLeod, Plunkett and Rolls 1998), and partly for use in applications (see Bishop (1995)).

In that perceptrons can correctly classify patterns provided only that they are linearly separable, but pattern associators are more restricted, perceptrons are more powerful learning devices than Hebbian pattern associators.

B.11.3.3 Gradient descent for neurons with continuous-valued outputs

We now consider networks trained by the delta (error correction) rule B.77, and having continuous-valued outputs. The activation function may be linear or non-linear, but provided that it is differentiable (in practice, does not include a sharp threshold), the network can be thought of as gradually decreasing the error on every learning trial, that is as performing some type of gradient descent down a continuous error function. The concept of gradient descent arises from defining an error ϵ for a neuron as

$$\epsilon = \sum_{\mu}(t^{\mu} - y^{\mu})^2 \qquad (B.82)$$

where μ indexes the patterns learned by the neuron. The error function for a neuron in the direction of a particular weight would have the form shown in Fig. B.44. The delta rule can

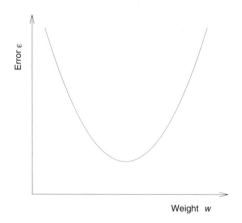

Fig. B.44 The error function ϵ for a neuron in the direction of a particular weight w.

be conceptualized as performing gradient descent of this error function, in that for the jth synaptic weight on the neuron

$$\delta w_j = -k\partial\epsilon/\partial w_j \qquad (B.83)$$

where $\partial\epsilon/\partial w_j$ is just the slope of the error curve in the direction of w_j in Fig. B.44. This will decrease the weight if the slope is positive and increase the weight if the slope is negative. Given equation B.76, and recalling that $h = \sum_j x_j w_j$, equation B.44 becomes

$$\delta w_j = -k\partial/\partial w_j \sum_\mu [(t^\mu - \mathrm{f}(h^\mu))^2] \qquad (B.84)$$

$$= 2k \sum_\mu [(t^\mu - y^\mu)]\mathrm{f}'(h)x_j$$

where $\mathrm{f}'(h)$ is the derivative of the activation function. Provided that the activation function is monotonically increasing, its derivative will be positive, and the sign of the weight change will only depend on the mean sign of the error. Equation B.85 thus shows one way in which, from a gradient descent conceptualization, equation B.77 can be derived.

With linear output neurons, this gradient descent is proved to reach the correct mapping (see Hertz, Krogh and Palmer (1991)). (As with all single-layer networks with continuous-valued output neurons, a perfect solution is only found if the input patterns are linearly independent. If they are not, an optimal mapping is achieved, in which the sum of the squares of the errors is a minimum.) With non-linear output neurons (for example with a sigmoid activation function), the error surface may have local minima, and is not guaranteed to reach the optimal solution, although typically a near-optimal solution is achieved. Part of the power of this gradient descent conceptualization is that it can be applied to multilayer networks with neurons with non-linear but differentiable activation functions, for example with sigmoid activation functions (see Hertz, Krogh and Palmer (1991)).

B.11.4 Properties

The properties of single-layer networks trained with a delta rule (and of perceptrons) are similar to those of pattern associators trained with a Hebbian rule in many respects (see Section B.2). In particular, the properties of generalization and graceful degradation are similar, provided that (for both types of network) distributed representations are used. The main differences are in the types of pattern that can be separated correctly, the learning speed (in that delta-rule networks can take advantage of many training trials to learn to separate patterns that could not be learned by Hebbian pattern associators), and in that the delta-rule network needs an error term to be supplied for each neuron, whereas an error term does not have to be supplied for a pattern associator, just an unconditioned or forcing stimulus. Given these overall similarities and differences, the properties of one-layer delta-rule networks are considered here briefly.

B.11.4.1 Generalization

During recall, delta-rule one-layer networks with non-linear output neurons produce appropriate outputs if a recall cue vector x_r is similar to a vector that has been learned already. This occurs because the recall operation involves computing the dot (inner) product of the input pattern vector x_r with the synaptic weight vector w_i, so that the firing produced, y_i, reflects the similarity of the current input to the previously learned input pattern x. Distributed representations are needed for this property. If two patterns that a delta-rule network has learned to separate are very similar, then the weights of the network will have been adjusted to force the different outputs to occur correctly. At the same time, this will mean that the way in which the network generalizes in the space between these two vectors will be very sharply defined. (Small changes in the input vector will force it to be classified one way or the other.)

B.11.4.2 Graceful degradation or fault tolerance

One-layer delta-rule networks show graceful degradation provided that the input patterns x are distributed.

B.11.4.3 Prototype extraction, extraction of central tendency, and noise reduction

These occur as for pattern autoassociators.

B.11.4.4 Speed

Recall is very fast in a one-layer pattern associator or perceptron, because it is a feedforward network (with no recurrent or lateral connections). Recall is also fast if the neuron has cell-like properties, because the stimulus input firings x_j ($j = 1, C$ axons) can be applied simultaneously to the synapses w_{ij}, and the activation h_i can be accumulated in one or two time constants of the synapses and dendrite (e.g. 10–20 ms) (see Section B.6.6). Whenever the threshold of the cell is exceeded, it fires. Thus, in effectively one time step, which takes the brain no more than 10–20 ms, all the output neurons of the delta-rule network can be firing with rates that reflect the input firing of every axon.

Learning is as fast ('one-shot') in perceptrons as in pattern associators if the input patterns are orthogonal. If the patterns are not orthogonal, so that the error correction rule has to work in order to separate patterns, then the network may take many trials to achieve the best solution (which will be perfect under the conditions described above).

B.11.4.5 Non-local learning rule

The learning rule is not truly local, as it is in pattern associators, autoassociators, and competitive networks, in that with one-layer delta-rule networks, the information required to change each synaptic weight is not available in the presynaptic terminal (reflecting the presynaptic rate) and the postsynaptic activation. Instead, an error for the neuron must be computed, possibly by another neuron, and then this error must be conveyed back to the postsynaptic neuron to provide the postsynaptic error term, which together with the presynaptic rate determines how much the synapse should change, as in equation B.77,

$$\delta w_{ij} = k(t_i - y_i)x_j$$

where $(t_i - y_i)$ is the error.

A rather special architecture would be required if the brain were to utilize delta-rule error-correcting learning. One such architecture might require each output neuron to be supplied with its own error signal by another neuron. The possibility (Albus 1971) that this is implemented in one part of the brain, the cerebellum, is described in Rolls and Treves (1998) Chapter 9. Another functional architecture would require each neuron to compute its own error by subtracting its current activation by its x inputs from another set of afferents providing the target activation for that neuron. A neurophysiological architecture and mechanism for this is not currently known.

B.11.4.6 Interference

Interference is less of a property of single-layer delta rule networks than of pattern autoassociators and autoassociators, in that delta rule networks can learn to separate patterns even when they are highly correlated. However, if patterns are not linearly independent, then the delta rule will learn a least mean squares solution, and interference can be said to occur.

B.11.4.7 Expansion recoding

As with pattern associators and autoassociators, expansion recoding can separate input patterns into a form that makes them learnable, or that makes learning more rapid with only a few trials needed, by delta rule networks. It has been suggested that this is the role of the granule cells in the cerebellum, which provide for expansion recoding by 1,000:1 of the mossy fibre inputs before they are presented by the parallel fibres to the cerebellar Purkinje cells (Marr 1969, Albus 1971, Rolls and Treves 1998).

B.11.4.8 Utility of single-layer error-correcting networks in information processing by the brain

In the cerebellum, each output cell, a Purkinje cell, has its own climbing fibre, that distributes from its inferior olive cell its terminals throughout the dendritic tree of the Purkinje cell. It is this climbing fibre that controls whether learning of the x inputs supplied by the parallel fibres onto the Purkinje cell occurs, and it has been suggested that the function of this architecture is for the climbing fibre to bring the error term to every part of the postsynaptic neuron (see Rolls and Treves (1998) Chapter 9). This rather special arrangement with each output cell apparently having its own teacher is probably unique in the brain, and shows the lengths to which the brain might need to go to implement a teacher for each output neuron. The requirement for error-correction learning is to have the neuron forced during a learning phase into a state that reflects its error while presynaptic afferents are still active, and rather special arrangements are needed for this.

B.12 Multilayer perceptrons: backpropagation of error networks

B.12.1 Introduction

So far, we have considered how error can be used to train a one-layer network using a delta rule. Minsky and Papert (1969) emphasized the fact that one-layer networks cannot solve certain classes of input–output mapping problems (as described above). It was clear then that these restrictions would not apply to the problems that can be solved by feedforward multilayer networks, if they could be trained. A multilayer feedforward network has two or more connected layers, in which connections allow activity to be projected forward from one layer to the next, and in which there are no lateral connections within a layer. Such a multilayer network has an output layer (which can be trained with a standard delta rule using an error provided for each output neuron), and one or more hidden layers, in which the neurons do not receive separate error signals from an external teacher. (Because they do not provide the outputs of the network directly, and do not directly receive their own teaching error signal, these layers are described as hidden.) To solve an arbitrary mapping problem (in which the inputs are not linearly separable), a multilayer network could have a set of hidden neurons that would remap the inputs in such a way that the output layer can be provided with a linearly separable problem to solve using training of its weights with the delta rule. The problem was: how could the synaptic weights into the hidden neurons be trained in such a way that they would provide an appropriate representation? Minsky and Papert (1969) were pessimistic that such a solution would be found and, partly because of this, interest in computations in neural networks declined for many years. Although some work in neural networks continued in the following years (e.g. (Marr 1969, Marr 1970, Marr 1971, Willshaw and Longuet-Higgins 1969, Willshaw 1981, Malsburg 1973, Grossberg 1976a, Grossberg 1976b, Arbib 1964, Amari 1982, Amari, Yoshida and Kanatani 1977)), widespread interest in neural networks was revived by the type of approach to associative memory and its relation to human memory taken by the work described in the volume edited by Hinton and Anderson (1981), and by Kohonen (Kohonen 1977, Kohonen 1989). Soon after this, a solution to training a multilayer perceptron using backpropagation of error became widely known (Rumelhart, Hinton and Williams 1986b, Rumelhart, Hinton and Williams 1986a) (although earlier solutions had been found), and very great interest in neural networks and also in neural network approaches to cognitive processing (connectionism) developed (Rumelhart and McClelland 1986, McClelland and Rumelhart 1986, McLeod, Plunkett and Rolls 1998).

B.12.2 Architecture and algorithm

An introduction to the way in which a multilayer network can be trained by backpropagation of error is described next. Then we consider whether such a training algorithm is biologically plausible. A more formal account of the training algorithm for multilayer perceptrons (sometimes abbreviated MLP) is given by Rumelhart, Hinton and Williams (1986b), Rumelhart, Hinton and Williams (1986a), and Hertz, Krogh and Palmer (1991).

Consider the two-layer network shown in Fig. B.45. Inputs to the hidden neurons in layer A feed forward activity to the output neurons in layer B. The neurons in the network have a sigmoid activation function. One reason for such an activation function is that it is non-linear, and non-linearity is needed to enable multilayer networks to solve difficult (non-linearly separable) problems. (If the neurons were linear, the multilayer network would be equivalent to a one-layer network, which cannot solve such problems.) Neurons B1 and B2 of the output layer, B, are each trained using a delta rule and an error computed for each output neuron from the target output for that neuron when a given input pattern is being applied to the network. Consider now the error that needs to be used to train neuron A1 by a delta rule. This error clearly influences the error of neuron B1 in a way that depends on the magnitude of the synaptic weight from neuron A1 to B1; and on the error of neuron B2 in a way that depends on the magnitude of the synaptic weight from neuron A1 to B2. In other words, the error for neuron A1 depends on:

the weight from A1 to B1 (w_{11}) · error of neuron B1
+ the weight from A1 to B2 (w_{21}) · error of neuron B2.

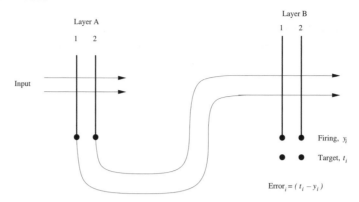

Fig. B.45 A two-layer perceptron. Inputs are applied to layer A through modifiable synapses. The outputs from layer A are applied through modifiable synapses to layer B. Layer B can be trained using a delta rule to produce firing y_i which will approach the target t_i. It is more difficult to modify the weights in layer A, because appropriate error signals must be backpropagated from layer B.

In this way, the error calculation can be propagated backwards through the network to any neuron in any hidden layer, so that each neuron in the hidden layer can be trained, once its error is computed, by a delta rule (which uses the computed error for the neuron and the presynaptic firing at the synapse to correct each synaptic weight). For this to work, the way in which each neuron is activated and sends a signal forward must be continuous (not binary), so that the extent to which there is an error in, for example, neuron B1 can be related back in a graded way to provide a continuously variable correction signal to previous stages. This is one of the requirements for enabling the network to descend a continuous error surface. The activation function must be non-linear (e.g. sigmoid) for the network to learn more than could be learned by a single-layer network. (Remember that a multilayer linear network can always be made equivalent to a single-layer linear network, and that there are some problems that cannot be solved by single-layer networks.) For the way in which the error of each output neuron should be taken into account to be specified in the error correction rule, the position at which the output neuron is operating on its activation function must also be taken into account. For this, the slope of the activation function is needed, and because the slope is needed, the activation function must be differentiable. Although we indicated use of a sigmoid activation function, other activation functions that are non-linear and monotonically increasing (and differentiable) can be used. (For further details, see Rumelhart, Hinton and Williams (1986b), Rumelhart, Hinton and Williams (1986a), and Hertz, Krogh and Palmer (1991)).

B.12.3 Properties of multilayer networks trained by error backpropagation

B.12.3.1 Arbitrary mappings

Arbitrary mappings of non-linearly separable patterns can be achieved. For example, such networks can solve the XOR problem, and parity problems in general of which XOR is a special case. (The parity problem is to determine whether the sum of the (binary) bits in a vector is odd or even.) Multilayer feedforward backpropagation of error networks are not guaranteed to converge to the best solution, and may become stuck in local minima in the error surface. However, they generally perform very well.

B.12.3.2 Fast operation

The network operates as a feedforward network, without any recurrent or feedback processing. Thus (once it has learned) the network operates very quickly, with a time proportional to the number of layers.

B.12.3.3 Learning speed

The learning speed can be very slow, taking many thousands of trials. The network learns to gradually approximate the correct input–output mapping required, but the learning is slow because of the credit assignment problem for neurons in the hidden layers. The credit assignment problem refers to the issue of how much to correct the weights of each neuron in the hidden layer. As the example above shows, the error for a hidden neuron could influence the errors of many neurons in the output layers, and the error of each output neuron reflects the error from many hidden neurons. It is thus difficult to assign credit (or blame) on any single trial to any particular hidden neuron, so an error must be estimated, and the net run until the weights of the crucial hidden neurons have become altered sufficiently to allow good performance of the network. Another factor that can slow learning is that if a neuron operates close to a horizontal part of its activation function, then the output of the neuron will depend rather little on its activation, and correspondingly the error computed to backpropagate will depend rather little on the activation of that neuron, so learning will be slow.

More general approaches to this issue suggest that the number of training trials for such a network will (with a suitable training set) be of the same order of magnitude as the number of synapses in the network (see Cortes, Jaeckel, Solla, Vapnik and Denker (1996)).

B.12.3.4 Number of hidden neurons and generalization

Backpropagation networks are generally intended to discover regular mappings between the input and output, that is mappings in which generalization will occur usefully. If there were one hidden neuron for every combination of inputs that had to be mapped to an output, then this would constitute a look-up table, and no generalization between similar inputs (or inputs not yet received) would occur. The best way to ensure that a backpropagation network learns the structure of the problem space is to set the number of neurons in the hidden layers close to the minimum that will allow the mapping to be implemented. This forces the network not to operate as a look-up table. A problem is that there is no general rule about how many hidden neurons are appropriate, given that this depends on the types of mappings required. In practice, these networks are sometimes trained with different numbers of hidden neurons, until the minimum number required to perform the required mapping has been approximated.

B.13 Biologically plausible networks

Given that the error for a hidden neuron in an error backpropagation network is calculated by propagating backwards information based on the errors of all the output neurons to which a hidden neuron is connected, and all the relevant synaptic weights, and the activations of the output neurons to define the part of the activation function on which they are operating, it is implausible to suppose that the correct information to provide the appropriate error for each hidden neuron is propagated backwards between real neurons. A hidden neuron would have to 'know', or receive information about, the errors of all the neurons to which it is connected, and its synaptic weights to them, and their current activations. If there were more than one hidden layer, this would be even more difficult.

To expand on the difficulties: first, there would have to be a mechanism in the brain for providing an appropriate error signal to each output neuron in the network. With the possible exception of the cerebellum, an architecture where a separate error signal could be provided for each output neurons is difficult to identify in the brain. Second, any retrograde passing of messages across multiple-layer forward-transmitting pathways in the brain that could be used for backpropagation seems highly implausible, not only because of the difficulty of getting the correct signal to be backpropagated, but also because retrograde signals passed by axonal transport in a multilayer net would take days to arrive, long after the end of any feedback given in the environment indicating a particular error. Third, as noted in Section 1.11, the backprojection pathways that are present in the cortex seem suited to perform recall, and this would make it difficult for them also to have the correct strength to carry the correct error signal.

A problem with the backpropagation of error approach in a biological context is thus that in order to achieve their competence, backpropagation networks use what is almost certainly a learning rule that is much more powerful than those that could be implemented biologically, and achieve their excellent performance by performing the mapping though a minimal number of hidden neurons. In contrast, real neuronal networks in the brain probably use much less powerful learning rules, in which errors are not propagated backwards, and at the same time have very large numbers of hidden neurons, without the bottleneck that helps to provide backpropagation networks with their good performance. A consequence of these differences between backpropagation and biologically plausible networks may be that the way in which biological networks solve difficult problems may be rather different from the way in which backpropagation networks find mappings. Thus the solutions found by connectionist systems may not always be excellent guides to how biologically plausible networks may perform on similar problems. Part of the challenge for future work is to discover how more biologically plausible networks than backpropagation networks can solve comparably hard problems, and then to examine the properties of these networks, as a perhaps more accurate guide to brain computation.

As stated above, it is a major challenge for brain research to discover whether there are algorithms that will solve comparably difficult problems to backpropagation, but with a local learning rule. Such algorithms may be expected to require many more hidden neurons than backpropagation networks, in that the brain does not appear to use information bottlenecks to help it solve difficult problems. The issue here is that much of the power of backpropagation algorithms arises because there is a minimal number of hidden neurons to perform the required mapping using a final one-layer delta-rule network. Useful generalization arises in such networks because with a minimal number of hidden neurons, the net sets the representation they provide to enable appropriate generalization. The danger with more hidden neurons is that the network becomes a look-up table, with one hidden neuron for every required output, and generalization when the inputs vary becomes poor. The challenge is to find a more biologically plausible type of network that operates with large numbers of neurons, and yet that still provides useful generalization. An example of such an approach is described in Chapter 4.

B.14 Contrastive Hebbian learning: the Boltzmann machine

In a move towards a learning rule that is more local than in backpropagation networks, yet that can solve similar mapping problems in a multilayer architecture, we describe briefly contrastive Hebbian learning. The multilayer architecture has forward connections through the network to the output layer, and a set of matching backprojections from the output layer through each of the hidden layers to the input layer. The forward connection strength between any pair of neurons has the same value as the backward connection strength between the same two neurons, resulting in a symmetric set of forward and backward connection strengths. An input pattern is applied to the multilayer network, and an output is computed using normal feedforward activation processing with neurons with a sigmoid (non-linear and monotonically increasing) activation function. The output firing then via the backprojections is used to create firing of the input neurons. This process is repeated until the firing rates settle down, in an iterative way (which is similar to the settling of the autoassociative nets described in Section B.3). After settling, the correlations between any two neurons are remembered, for this type of unclamped operation, in which the output neurons fire at the rates that the process just described produces. The correlations reflect the normal presynaptic and postsynaptic terms used in the Hebb rule, e.g. $(x_j y_i)^{uc}$, where 'uc' refers to the unclamped condition, and as usual x_j is the firing rate of the input neuron, and y_i is the activity of the receiving neuron. The output neurons are then clamped to their target values, and the iterative process just described is repeated, to produce for every pair of synapses in the network $(x_j y_i)^c$, where the c refers now to the clamped condition. An error correction term for each synapse is then computed from the difference between the remembered correlation of the unclamped and the clamped conditions, to produce a synaptic weight correction term as follows:

$$\delta w_{ij} = k[(x_j y_i)^c - (x_j y_i)^{uc}], \tag{B.85}$$

where k is a learning rate constant. This process is then repeated for each input pattern to output pattern to be learned. The whole process is then repeated many times with all patterns until the output neurons fire similarly in the clamped and unclamped conditions, that is until the errors have become small. Further details are provided by Hinton and Sejnowski (1986). The version described above is the mean field (or deterministic) Boltzmann machine (Peterson and Anderson 1987, Hinton 1989). More traditionally, a Boltzmann machine updates one randomly chosen neuron at a time, and each neuron fires with a probability that depends on its activation (Ackley, Hinton and Sejnowski 1985, Hinton and Sejnowski 1986). The latter version makes fewer theoretical assumptions, while the former may operate an order of magnitude faster (Hertz, Krogh and Palmer 1991).

In terms of biological plausibility, it certainly is the case that there are backprojections between adjacent cortical areas (see Chapter 1). Indeed, there are as many backprojections between adjacent cortical areas as there are forward projections. The backward projections seem to be more diffuse than the forward projections, in that they connect to a wider region of the preceding cortical area than the region that sends the forward projections. If the backward and the forward synapses in such an architecture were Hebb-modifiable, then there is a possibility that the backward connections would be symmetric with the forward connections. Indeed, such a connection scheme would be useful to implement top-down recall, as summarized in Chapter 2 and described by Rolls and Treves (1998) in their Chapter 6. What seems less biologically plausible is that after an unclamped phase of operation, the correlations between all pairs of neurons would be remembered, there would then be a clamped phase of operation with each output neuron clamped to the required rate for that particular input pattern, and then the synapses would be corrected by an error correction rule that would require a comparison of the correlations between the neuronal firing of every pair of neurons in the unclamped and clamped conditions.

Although this algorithm has the disadvantages that it is not very biologically plausible, and does not operate as well as standard backpropagation, it has been made use of by O'Reilly and Munakata (2000) in approaches to connectionist modelling in cognitive neuroscience.

B.15   Reinforcement learning

In supervised networks, an error signal is provided for each output neuron in the network, and whenever an input to the network is provided, the error signals specify the magnitude and direction of the error in the output produced by each neuron. These error signals are then used to correct the synaptic weights in the network in such a way that the output errors for each input pattern to be learned gradually diminish over trials (see Sections B.11 and B.12). These networks have an architecture that might be similar to that of the pattern associator shown in Fig. B.1, except that instead of an unconditioned stimulus, there is an error correction signal provided for each output neuron. Such a network trained by an error correcting (or delta) rule is known as a one-layer perceptron. The architecture is not very plausible for most brain regions, in that it is not clear how an individual error signal could be computed for each of thousands of neurons in a network, and fed into each neuron as its error signal and then used in a delta rule synaptic correction (see Section B.11).

The architecture can be generalized to a multilayer feedforward architecture with many layers between the input and output (Rumelhart, Hinton and Williams 1986a), but the learning is very non-local and rather biologically implausible (see Section B.12), in that an error term (magnitude and direction) for each neuron in the network must be computed from the errors and synaptic weights of all subsequent neurons in the network that any neuron influences, usually on a trial-by-trial basis, by a process known as error backpropagation. Thus although computationally powerful, an issue with perceptrons and multilayer perceptrons that makes them generally biologically implausible for many brain regions is that a separate error signal must be supplied for each output neuron, and that with multilayer perceptrons, computed error backpropagation must occur.

When operating in an environment, usually a simple binary or scalar signal representing success or failure of the whole network or organism is received. This is usually action-dependent feedback that provides a single evaluative measure of the success or failure. Evaluative feedback tells the learner whether or not, and possibly by how much, its behaviour has improved; or it provides a measure of the 'goodness' of the behaviour. Evaluative feedback does not directly tell the learner what it should have done, and although it may provide an index of the degree (i.e. magnitude) of success, it does not include directional information telling the learner how to change its behaviour towards a target, as does error-correction learning (see Barto (1995)). Partly for this reason, there has been some interest in networks that can be taught with such a single reinforcement signal. In this Section (B.15), approaches to such networks are described. It is noted that such networks are classified as reinforcement networks in which there is a single teacher, and that these networks attempt to perform an optimal mapping between an input vector and an output neuron or set of neurons. They thus solve the same class of problems as single layer and multilayer perceptrons. They should be distinguished from pattern-association networks in the brain, which might learn associations between previously neutral stimuli and primary reinforcers such as taste (signals which might be interpreted appropriately by a subsequent part of the brain), but do not attempt to produce arbitrary mappings between an input and an output, using a single reinforcement signal.

A class of problems to which such reinforcement networks might be applied are motor-control problems. It was to such a problem that Barto and Sutton (Barto 1985, Sutton and Barto 1981) applied a reinforcement learning algorithm, the associative reward–penalty algorithm described next. The algorithm can in principle be applied to multilayer networks, and the learning is relatively slow. The algorithm is summarized in Section B.15.1 and by Hertz, Krogh and Palmer (1991). More recent developments in reinforcement learning (Sections B.15.2 and B.15.3) are described by Sutton and Barto (1998) and reviewed by Dayan and Abbott (2001).

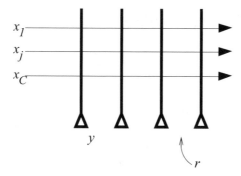

Fig. B.46 A network trained by a single reinforcement input r. The inputs to each neuron are $x_j, j = 1, C$; and y is the output of one of the output neurons.

B.15.1 Associative reward–penalty algorithm of Barto and Sutton

The terminology of Barto and Sutton is followed here (see Barto (1985)).

B.15.1.1 Architecture

The architecture, shown in Fig. B.46, uses a single reinforcement signal, r, = +1 for reward, and –1 for penalty. The inputs x_j take real (continuous) values. The output of a neuron, y, is binary, +1 or –1. The weights on the output neuron are designated w_j.

B.15.1.2 Operation

1. An input vector is applied to the network, and produces activation, h, in the normal way as follows:

$$h = \sum_{j=1}^{C} x_j w_j \tag{B.86}$$

where $\sum_{j=1}^{C}$ indicates that the sum is over the C input axons (or connections) indexed by j to each neuron.

2. The output y is calculated from the activation with a noise term η included. The principle of the network is that if the added noise on a particular trial helps performance, then whatever change it leads to should be incorporated into the synaptic weights, in such a way that the next time that input occurs, the performance is improved.

$$y = \begin{cases} +1 & \text{if } h + \eta \geq 0, \\ -1 & \text{else.} \end{cases} \tag{B.87}$$

where η = the noise added on each trial.

3. Learning rule. The weights are changed as follows:

$$\delta w_j = \begin{cases} \rho(y - E[y|h])x_j & \text{if } r = +1, \\ \rho\lambda(-y - E[y|h])x_j & \text{if } r = -1. \end{cases} \tag{B.88}$$

ρ and λ are learning-rate constants. (They are set so that the learning rate is higher when positive reinforcement is received than when negative reinforcement is received.) $E[y|h]$ is the expectation of y given h (usually a sigmoidal function of h with the range ± 1). $E[y|h]$ is a (continuously varying) indication of how the neuron usually responds to the current input pattern, i.e. if the actual output y is larger than normally expected, by computing $h = \sum w_j x_j$, because of the noise term, and the reinforcement is +1, increase the weight from x_j; and vice versa. The expectation could be the prediction generated before the noise term is incorporated.

This network combines an associative capacity with its properties of generalization and graceful degradation, with a single 'critic' or error signal for the whole network (Barto 1985). [The term $y - \mathrm{E}[y|h]$ in Equation B.88 can be thought of as an error for the output of the neuron: it is the difference between what occurred, and what was expected to occur. The synaptic weight is adjusted according to the sign and magnitude of the error of the postsynaptic firing, multiplied by the presynaptic firing, and depending on the reinforcement r received. The rule is similar to a Hebb synaptic modification rule (Equation B.2), except that the postsynaptic term is an error instead of the postsynaptic firing rate, and the learning is modulated by the reinforcement.] The network can solve difficult problems (such as balancing a pole by moving a trolley that supports the pole from side to side, as the pole starts to topple). Although described for single-layer networks, the algorithm can be applied to multilayer networks. The learning rate is very slow, for there is a single reinforcement signal on each trial for the whole network, not a separate error signal for each neuron in the network as is the case in a perceptron trained with an error rule (see Section B.11).

This associative reward–penalty reinforcement-learning algorithm is certainly a move towards biological relevance, in that learning with a single reinforcer can be achieved. That single reinforcer might be broadcast throughout the system by a general projection system. It is not clear yet how a biological system might store the expected output $\mathrm{E}[y|h]$ for comparison with the actual output when noise has been added, and might take into account the sign and magnitude of this difference. Nevertheless, this is an interesting algorithm, which is related to the temporal difference reinforcement learning algorithm described in Section B.15.3.

B.15.2 Reward prediction error or delta rule learning, and classical conditioning

In classical or Pavlovian associative learning, a number of different types of association may be learned (see Section 3.2.1). This type of associative learning may be performed by networks with the general architecture and properties of pattern associators (see Section B.2 and Fig. B.1). However, the time course of the acquisition and extinction of these associations can be expressed concisely by a modified type of learning rule in which an error correction term is used (introduced in Section B.15.1), rather than the postsynaptic firing y itself as in Equation B.2. Use of this modified, error correction, type of learning also enables some of the properties of classical conditioning to be explained (see Dayan and Abbott (2001) for review), and this type of learning is therefore described briefly here. The rule is known in learning theory as the Rescorla–Wagner rule, after Rescorla and Wagner (1972).

The Rescorla–Wagner rule is a version of error correction or delta-rule learning (see Section B.11), and is based on a simple linear prediction of the expected reward value, denoted by v, associated with a stimulus representation x ($x = 1$ if the stimulus is present, and $x = 0$ if the stimulus is absent). The **expected reward value** v is expressed as the input stimulus variable x multiplied by a weight w

$$v = wx. \tag{B.89}$$

The **reward prediction error** is the difference between the expected reward value v and the actual **reward outcome** r obtained, i.e.

$$\Delta = r - v \tag{B.90}$$

where Δ is the reward prediction error. The value of the weight w is learned by a rule designed to minimize the expected squared error $< (r - v)^2 >$ between the actual reward outcome r and the predicted reward value v. The angle brackets indicate an average over the presentations of the stimulus and reward. The delta rule will perform the required type of learning:

$$\delta w = k(r - v)x \tag{B.91}$$

where δw is the change of synaptic weight, k is a constant that determines the learning rate, and the term $(r - v)$ is the reward prediction error Δ (equivalent to the error in the postsynaptic firing, rather than the postsynaptic firing y itself as in Equation B.2). Application of this rule during conditioning with the stimulus x presented on every trial results in the weight w approaching the asymptotic limit $w = r$ exponentially over trials as the error Δ becomes zero. In extinction, when $r = 0$, the weight (and thus the output of the system) exponentially decays to $w = 0$. This rule thus helps to capture the time course over trials of the acquisition and extinction of conditioning. The rule also helps to account for a number of properties of classical conditioning, including blocking, inhibitory conditioning, and overshadowing (see Dayan and Abbott (2001)).

How this functionality is implemented in the brain is not yet clear. We consider one suggestion (Schultz et al. 1995b, Schultz 2004, Schultz 2006) after we introduce a further sophistication of reinforcement learning which allows the time course of events within a trial to be taken into account.

B.15.3 Temporal Difference (TD) learning

An important advance in the area of reinforcement learning was the introduction of algorithms that allow for learning to occur when the reinforcement is delayed or received over a number of time steps, and which allow effects within a trial to be taken into account (Sutton and Barto 1998, Sutton and Barto 1990). A solution to these problems is the addition of an adaptive critic that learns through a time difference (TD) algorithm how to predict the future value of the reinforcer. The time difference algorithm takes into account not only the current reinforcement just received, but also a temporally weighted average of errors in predicting future reinforcements. The temporal difference error is the error by which any two temporally adjacent error predictions are inconsistent (see Barto (1995)). The output of the critic is used as an effective reinforcer instead of the instantaneous reinforcement being received (see Sutton and Barto (1998), Sutton and Barto (1990), and Barto (1995)). This is a solution to the temporal credit assignment problem, and enables future rewards to be predicted. Summaries are provided by Doya (1999), Schultz, Dayan and Montague (1997), and Dayan and Abbott (2001).

In reinforcement learning, a learning agent takes an *action* $\mathbf{u}(t)$ in response to the *state* $\mathbf{x}(t)$ of the environment, which results in the change of the state

$$\mathbf{x}(t + 1) = F(\mathbf{x}(t), \mathbf{u}(t)), \tag{B.92}$$

and the delivery of the reinforcement signal, or *reward*

$$r(t + 1) = R(\mathbf{x}(t), \mathbf{u}(t)). \tag{B.93}$$

In the above equations, $\mathbf{x}$ is a vector representation of inputs x_j, and equation B.92 indicates that the next state $\mathbf{x}(t + 1)$ at time $(t + 1)$ is a function F of the state at the previous time step of the inputs and actions at that time step in a closed system. In equation B.93 the reward at the next time step is determined by a reward function R which uses the current sensory inputs and action taken. The time t may refer to time within a trial.

The goal is to find a *policy* function G which maps sensory inputs **x** to actions

$$\mathbf{u}(t) = G(\mathbf{x}(t)) \tag{B.94}$$

which maximizes the cumulative sum of the rewards based on the sensory inputs.

The current action $\mathbf{u}(t)$ affects all future states and accordingly all future rewards. The maximization is realized by the use of the *value function* V of the states to predict, given the sensory inputs **x**, the cumulative sum (possibly discounted as a function of time) of all future rewards $V(\mathbf{x})$ (possibly within a learning trial) as follows:

$$V(\mathbf{x}) = E[r(t+1) + \gamma r(t+2) + \gamma^2 r(t+3) + ...] \tag{B.95}$$

where $r(t)$ is the reward at time t, and $E[\cdot]$ denotes the expected value of the sum of future rewards up to the end of the trial. $0 \leq \gamma \leq 1$ is a discount factor that makes rewards that arrive sooner more important than rewards that arrive later, according to an exponential decay function. (If $\gamma = 1$ there is no discounting.) It is assumed that the presentation of future cues and rewards depends only on the current sensory cues and not the past sensory cues. The right-hand side of equation B.95 is evaluated for the dynamics in equations B.92–B.94 with the initial condition $\mathbf{x}(t) = \mathbf{x}$. The two basic ingredients in reinforcement learning are the estimation (which we term $\hat{V}$) of the value function V, and then the improvement of the policy or action **u** using the value function (Sutton and Barto 1998).

The basic algorithm for learning the value function is to minimize the *temporal difference* (TD) *error* $\Delta(t)$ for time t within a trial, and this is computed by a 'critic' for the estimated value predictions $\hat{V}(\mathbf{x}(t))$ at successive time steps as

$$\Delta(t) = [r(t) + \gamma \hat{V}(\mathbf{x}(t))] - \hat{V}(\mathbf{x}(t-1)) \tag{B.96}$$

where $\hat{V}(\mathbf{x}(t)) - \hat{V}(\mathbf{x}(t-1))$ is the difference in the reward value prediction at two successive time steps, giving rise to the terminology temporal difference learning. If we introduce the term $\hat{v}$ as the estimate of the cumulated reward by the end of the trial, we can define it as a function $\hat{V}$ of the current sensory input $\mathbf{x}(t)$, i.e. $\hat{v} = \hat{V}(\mathbf{x})$, and we can also write equation B.96 as

$$\Delta(t) = r(t) + \gamma \hat{v}(t) - \hat{v}(t-1) \tag{B.97}$$

which draws out the fact that it is differences at successive timesteps in the reward value predictions $\hat{v}$ that are used to calculate Δ.

$\Delta(t)$ is used to improve the estimates $\hat{v}(t)$ by the 'critic', and can also be used (by an 'actor') to learn appropriate actions.

For example, when the value function is represented (in the critic) as

$$\hat{V}(\mathbf{x}(t)) = \sum_{j=1}^{n} w_j^C x_j(t) \tag{B.98}$$

the learning algorithm for the (value) weight w_j^C in the critic is given by

$$\delta w_j^C = k_c \Delta(t) x_j(t-1) \tag{B.99}$$

where δw_j^C is the change of synaptic weight, k_c is a constant that determines the learning rate for the sensory input x_j, and $\Delta(t)$ is the Temporal Difference error at time t. Under certain conditions this learning rule will cause the estimate $\hat{v}$ to converge to the true value (Dayan and Sejnowski 1994).

A simple way of improving the policy of the actor is to take a stochastic action

$$u_i(t) = g(\sum_{j=1}^{n} w_{ij}^A x_j(t) + \mu_i(t)), \qquad (B.100)$$

where g() is a scalar version of the policy function G, w_{ij}^A is a weight in the actor, and $\mu_i(t)$ is a noise term. The TD error $\Delta(t)$ as defined in equation B.96 then signals the unexpected delivery of the reward $r(t)$ or the increase in the state value $\hat{V}(\mathbf{x}(t))$ above expectation, possibly due to the previous choice of action $u_i(t-1)$. The learning algorithm for the action weight w_{ij}^A in the actor is given by

$$\delta w_{ij}^A = k_a \Delta(t)(u_i(t-1) - < u_i >)x_j(t-1), \qquad (B.101)$$

where $< u_i >$ is the average level of the action output, and k_a is a learning rate constant in the actor.

Thus, the TD error $\Delta(t)$, which signals the error in the reward prediction at time t, works as the main teaching signal in both learning the value function (implemented in the critic), and the selection of actions (implemented in the actor). The usefulness of a separate critic is that it enables the TD error to be calculated based on the difference in reward value predictions at two successive time steps as shown in equation B.96.

The algorithm has been applied to modelling the time course of classical conditioning (Sutton and Barto 1990). The algorithm effectively allows the future reinforcement predicted from past history to influence the responses made, and in this sense allows behaviour to be guided not just by immediate reinforcement, but also by 'anticipated' reinforcements. Different types of temporal difference learning are described by Sutton and Barto (1998). An application is to the analysis of decisions when future rewards are discounted with respect to immediate rewards (Dayan and Abbott 2001, Tanaka, Doya, Okada, Ueda, Okamoto and Yamawaki 2004). Another application is to the learning of sequences of actions to take within a trial (Suri and Schultz 1998).

The possibility that dopamine neuron firing may provide an error signal useful in training neuronal systems to predict reward has been discussed in Section 3.10.2.5. It has been proposed that the firing of the dopamine neurons can be thought of as an error signal about reward prediction, in that the firing occurs in a task when a reward is given, but then moves forward in time within a trial to the time when a stimulus is presented that can be used to predict when the taste reward will be obtained (Schultz et al. 1995b) (see Fig. 3.63). The argument is that there is no prediction error when the taste reward is obtained if it has been signalled by a preceding conditioned stimulus, and that is why the dopamine midbrain neurons do not respond at the time of taste reward delivery, but instead, at least during training, to the onset of the conditioned stimulus (Waelti, Dickinson and Schultz 2001). If a different conditioned stimulus is shown that normally predicts that no taste reward will be given, there is no firing of the dopamine neurons to the onset of that conditioned stimulus.

This hypothesis has been built into models of learning in which the error signal is used to train synaptic connections in dopamine pathway recipient regions (such as presumably the striatum and orbitofrontal cortex) (Houk, Adams and Barto 1995, Schultz 2004, Schultz, Dayan and Montague 1997, Waelti, Dickinson and Schultz 2001, Dayan and Abbott 2001). Some difficulties with the hypothesis are discussed in Section 3.10.2.5 on page 243. The difficulties include the fact that dopamine is released in large quantities by aversive stimuli (see Section 3.10.2.5); that error computations for differences between the expected reward and the actual reward received on a trial are computed in the primate orbitofrontal cortex, where expected reward, actual reward, and error neurons are all found, and lesions of which impair the ability to use changes in reward contingencies to reverse behaviour (see Section 3.6.5.5); that the tonic, sustained, firing of the dopamine neurons in the delay period of a task with probabilistic rewards may reflect reward uncertainty, and not the expected reward, nor the magnitude of the prediction error (see Section 3.10.2.5 and Shizgal and Arvanitogiannis (2003)); and that reinforcement learning is suited to setting up connections that might be required in fixed tasks such as motor habit or sequence learning, for reinforcement learning algorithms seek to set weights correctly in an 'actor', but are not suited to tasks where rules must be altered flexibly, as in rapid one-trial reversal, for which a very different type of mechanism is described in Chapter 9.

The temporal difference approach to reinforcement learning has a weakness that although it can be used to predict internal signals during reinforcement learning in some tasks, it does not directly address learning with respect to actions that are not taken. Q-learning can be considered as an extension of TD learning which adds additional terms to take into account signals from actions that are not taken, for example information gained by observation of others (Montague, King-Casas and Cohen 2006).

Overall, reinforcement learning algorithms are certainly a move towards biological relevance, in that learning with a single reinforcer can be achieved in systems that might learn motor habits or fixed sequences. Whether a single prediction error is broadcast throughout a neural system by a general projection system, such as the dopamine pathways in the brain, which distribute to large parts of the striatum and the prefrontal cortex, remains to be clearly established (see further Chapters 3 and 10).

B.16 Forgetting in associative neural networks and in the brain, and memory reconsolidation

Forgetting is an important feature of associative neural networks and the brain, and is important in their successful operation. There are a number of different mechanisms for forgetting, and a number of different reasons why forgetting is important in particular classes of network.

Consider attractor, that is autoassociation, networks, which are used for short-term memory, episodic memory, etc. These networks have a critical storage capacity, as described in Section B.3, and if this is exceeded, most of the memories in the network become unretrievable. It is therefore crucial to have a mechanism for forgetting in these networks.

One mechanism is decay of synaptic strength. The simple forgetting mechanism is just an exponential decay of the synaptic value back to its baseline, which may be exponential in time or in the number of learning changes incurred (Nadal, Toulouse, Changeux and Dehaene 1986). This form of forgetting does not require keeping track of each individual change and preserves linear superposition, that is each memory is added linearly to previous memories, as provided for by equation B.9 on page 561. In calculating the storage capacity of pattern associators and of autoassociators, the inclusion or exclusion of simple exponential decay does not change significantly the calculation of capacity, and only results in a different prefactor (one 2.7 times the other) for the maximum number of associations that can be stored. Therefore a forgetting mechanism as simple as exponential decay is normally omitted, and one has just to remember that its inclusion would reduce the critical capacity obtained to roughly 0.37 of that without the decay. This type of memory has been called a palimpsest.

Another form of forgetting, which is potentially interesting in terms of biological plausibility, is implemented by setting limits to the range allowed for each synaptic strength or weight (Parisi 1986). As a particular synapse hits the upper or lower limit on its range, it is taken to be unable to further modify in the direction that would take it beyond the limit. Only after modifications in the opposite direction have taken it away from the limit does the synapse regain its full plasticity. A forgetting scenario of this sort requires a slightly more complicated formal analysis (since it violates linear superposition of different memories), but it effectively results in a progressive, exponential degradation of older memories similar to that produced by straight exponential decay of synaptic weights.

A combined forgetting rule that may be particularly attractive in the context of modelling synapses between pyramidal cells is implemented by setting a lower limit, that is, zero, on the excitatory weight (just requiring that the associated conductance be a non-negative quantity!), and allowing exponential decay of the value of the weight with time. Again, this type of combined forgetting rule places demands on the analytical techniques that have to be used to calculate the storage capacity, but leads to functionally similar effects (Rolls and Treves 1998).

Two conditions under which synaptic strengths may decrease are described in Fig. 1.6. Heterosynaptic long-term depression, which can occur for inactive presynaptic terminals on active postsynaptic neurons, can be useful computationally in the following ways. First, it is a useful way to subtract the effect of the mean presynaptic firing rate of each neuron in a pattern associator, which removes the effect of the mean firing rate in increasing the correlation between different input patterns used in the network, as is made evident in equation B.7. This orthogonalizing effect helps to maximize the storage capacity of pattern associators. The same situation applies to autoassociation (attractor) networks (see equation B.13). This decrease of firing rate for inactive inputs may of course result in some loss of memories previously stored in these association networks, if a particular synapse had been strengthened as part of a previous memory. Homosynaptic long-term depression might contribute to a similar function.

Heterosynaptic long-term depression (LTD) is also useful in competitive networks, for it provides a way for the synaptic weight vectors of different neurons to be kept of approximately equal length, and this is important to ensure that the different categories of input patterns find different output neurons to activate. In the case of competitive networks, the appropriate effect is achieved if the subtractive term in the presynaptic component depends on the existing strength of the synapse, as shown in equation B.22. The fact that in studies of LTD it is sometimes remarked that LTD is easier to demonstrate after LTP has been induced lends support to the likelihood that LTD of the form indicated in equation B.22 that depends on the existing synaptic strength is implemented in the brain. Because of the computational significance of LTD that depends on the existing strength of synapses for competitive networks, it would be useful to see further experimental exploration of this.

Forgetting in attractor networks takes two forms that can be clearly distinguished. One is that the current attractor state implemented by the continuing firing of one set of neurons in the network is labile, and may be interrupted by a strong new input which forces the network into a new attractor state, or may be interrupted by quenching effects through non-specific effects implemented through for example inhibitory neurons (Chapter 9). Both these effects could be facilitated by synaptic or neuronal adaptation, as described in Chapter 9.

The second form of forgetting in attractor networks is of the strengthened synaptic connections that specify each of the different attractor memories in the network. If the network is to be used for large numbers of different short-term memories, then these synaptic weights must decay or be overwritten by LTD as described above. This is likely to be required for short-term memory networks in the prefrontal cortex which must adapt themselves to be capable of storing the particular stimuli and actions that may be required in particular tasks (see e.g. Chapter 8), in short-term memory networks that implement the visuo-spatial scratchpad, etc. We may note that because short-term memory networks have these two different aspects, once an attractor set of synaptic connections has been imprinted in a network by synaptic modification, then no further synaptic modification is necessary to use that network repeatedly for holding the neurons in one of the stored attractors active to implement the short-term memory in a delay period (Kesner and Rolls 2001).

Forgetting may be less important in semantic networks. (Semantic networks store structured information with appropriate associative links and hierarchical structure, for example a family tree, or one's geographical knowledge (McClelland and Rumelhart 1986).) We may note that because any one associative memory network has a memory capacity that is related to the number of associative synapses onto each neuron from other neurons in the network, semantic memory is likely to involve connections between modules in the cortex, where each module might be defined by a 1–3 mm region of cortex with high local connectivity between the neurons. For this type of memory, forgetting is not so much the requirement as incorporating new semantic knowledge, that is making new appropriate links, and perhaps weakening existing links. In this scenario, the fact that when a memory is retrieved, as would occur when a sematic memory is being updated or extended, then it may need to be reconsolidated, suggests a possible useful function for memory reconsolidation (see below), as it could facilitate the restructuring of a semantic memory. In contrast, such restructuring would not be a very useful property of an episodic memory, in which each episode must be clearly distinguished from others.

Reconsolidation refers to a process in which after a memory has been stored, it may be weakened or lost if recall is performed during the presence of a protein synthesis inhibitor (Debiec, LeDoux and Nader 2002, Debiec, Doyere, Nader and LeDoux 2006). The implication that has been drawn is that whenever a memory is recalled, some reconsolidation process requiring protein synthesis may be needed.

One possible function of reconsolidation is that it may allow some restructuring of a memory, as described above, though this might be useful more in semantic than episodic memory systems.

A second possible computational function is that reconsolidation might be useful as a mechanism to ensure that whenever a memory is retrieved, additional LTP (long-term potentiation of synaptic strength) is not added to the existing LTP. This could be achieved if during the recall process the memory strength is reset to a low value from which it is then strengthened. Indeed, a potential problem with memory systems is what separates storage from recall, in that whenever recall occurs, pre- and post-synaptic activity is present at the relevant synapses for the memory, and thus one might expect another round of synaptic strengthening to occur. Reconsolidation, by effectively resetting the baseline of synaptic strength during recall, might then provide for the restrengthened synapses not to be stronger than they were before the memory recall. A relevant point here is that in associative memories, the amount of information stored and retrieved from any one synapse is quite low, in the order of 0.2–0.3 bits for autoassociators (Rolls and Treves 1998, Treves and Rolls 1991) and a little higher for pattern associators (Rolls and Treves 1998), so that in any case having synaptic strengths that could be repeatedly strengthened by superposition of different memories with distributed representations and with precision maintained at each strengthening would not appear to be a necessary property of the synapses in such memory systems. Under these circumstances, allowing during recall a weakening of a memory, and then its reconsolidation from a relatively fixed baseline might not lead to loss of useful information, and might be a possible solution to continually strengthening synapses every time a memory is recalled.

A third possible computational function of reconsolidation is that it could enable the selective retention of 'useful' memories (or in fact memories being used), and the forgetting of memories not being used, as follows. Consider a memory system in which there is slow exponential decay of synaptic strength with time, a not altogether unlikely scenario given the properties of a biological system. In this situation memories will gradually be lost, perhaps with a different time course in different memory systems, which might be in the order of days, weeks, months or years. In this scenario, if a piece of information was actually recalled because an environmental situation occurred in which for example there was a retrieval cue for a memory, then that memory (i.e. the synaptic strengths) would by reconsolidation be strengthened back to near its initial value. That memory would then be strong and available for future use, compared to other memories not recalled that would be passively decaying. The passive decay of memories not being recalled and reset by reconsolidation would be useful in cleaning out the memory stores so that any critical capacity was not reached, and at the same time in minimizing interference (due to generalization to similar patterns) between memories in store. An example might be the number of one's hotel room, which while it is being repeatedly recalled for use while in that hotel and thus restored, would then decay passively and gradually be lost when it was not longer being actively recalled and hence reconsolidated. One could propose that in some memory systems the passive decay might be relatively rapid, occurring within hours or days. An example might be the dorsolateral prefrontal cortex, where depending on the requirements of the short-term memory or planning tasks being performed, synapses might by reconsolidation keep representations used in attractor networks available while a given task was being performed. However, when that task was no longer being performed, passive synaptic decay would mean that neurons allocated to that task would gradually decline, and instead new attractor landscapes (i.e. memories) could be set up for new tasks or planning, without interference from representations that were previously being used. There is some evidence at the phenomenological level that neuronal representations are made and kept relevant to whatever task is being performed (Miller et al. 2003, Everling et al. 2006), and I have just proposed a possible mechanism for this implemented by reconsolidation.

Memories stored early in life may be stored better, and later recalled better, than those stored later in life. There are a number of possible reasons for this. One is that the transmitters that generally facilitate synaptic modification, such as acetylcholine and noradrenaline (see Sections 3.10.5 and 3.10.6), may become depleted with ageing.

Another mechanism, not necessarily independent, is that new synaptic modification, as assessed by long-term potentiation (LTP), appears to be less long-lasting with ageing (Burke and Barnes 2006). Another mechanism may be that storing memories in a flat energy landscape (i.e. without much prior synaptic modification) may help these memories to stand out from those added later. While this would not be a natural property of the type of autoassociation palimpsest memory described above, it could be a property of the way in which an episodic memory stored in the hippocampus may be retrieved into the neocortex where it can be incorporated into a semantic memory (see Chapter 2), the relevant example of which in this case would be an autobiographical memory.

In semantic memories, it could be that the first stored links tend to provide the framework around which other information is structured.

Another factor in the apparent strength of early memories may be that some may be stored with an affective component, and this may not only make the memory strong by activation of the cholinergic and related systems described in Section 3.10.5, but may also mean that part at least of the memory is stored in different brain structures such as the amygdala which may have relatively more persistent and less flexible or reversible memories than other memory systems.

Another factor in the importance and stability of synaptic modification early in life arises in perceptual systems, in which it is important to allow neurons to become tuned to the statistics of for example the visual environment, but once feature analyzers have been formed, stability of the feature analyzers in early cortical processing layers may be important so that later stages in the hierarchy can perform reliable object recognition which achieves stability only if the input filters to the system do not keep changing (see Chapter 4). This could be the importance of a critical period for learning early on in perceptual development.

Sleep has been proposed as a state in which useful forgetting or consolidation of memories could occur. One suggestion was that if deep basins of attraction formed in a memory network, then this could impair performance, as the memories in the basins would tend to be recalled whatever the retrieval cue. If noise, present in the disorganized patterns of neural firing during sleep, caused these memories to be recalled, this would indicate that they were 'parasitic', and the suggestion was that associative synaptic weakening (LTD) of synapses of neurons with high firing during sleep would tend to decrease the depth of those basins of attraction, and improve the performance of the memory (Crick and Mitchison 1995). At least at the formal level of neural networks, the suggestion does have some merit as a possible way to 'clean up' associative networks, even if it is not a process implemented in the brain. Although the idea of some role of sleep in memory remains active, this remains to be fully established (Walker and Stickgold 2006).

The idea that sleep could be a time when memories are unloaded from the hippocampus to be consolidated in long term, possibly semantic, memories during sleep (Marr 1971) (allowing hippocampal episodic memories to then be overwritten by new episodic memories) continues to be explored. It has been shown for example that after hippocampal spatial representations have been altered by experience during the day, these changes are reflected in neuronal activity in the neocortex during sleep (Wilson and McNaughton 1994, Wilson 2002). The type of experience might involve repeated locomotion between two places, and the place fields of rat hippocampal neurons for those places may become associated with each other because of coactivity of the neurons representing the frequently visited places. The altered co-firing of the hippocampal neurons for those places may then be reflected in neocortical representations of those places. This could then result in altered representations in the neocortex, if LTP occurs during sleep in the neocortex. Of course, any change in neocortical neuronal activity might just reflect the altered representations in the hippocampus, which would be expected to influence the neocortical representations via hippocampo-neocortical backprojections, even without any neocortical learning (see Chapter 2).

In conclusion, we have seen in this Section that forgetting has important functions in the brain, and is a necessary property of many different types of memory system if they are to continue to function efficiently and to allow new learning in the same networks in the brain.

B.17 Brain computation compared to computation on a digital computer

To highlight some of the principles of brain computation by for example the cortex described in this Appendix and throughout this book, it is interesting to compare the principles of computation by the brain with those of a digital computer.

An item of data is retrieved from the memory of a digital computer by providing the address of the data in memory, and then the data can be manipulated (moved, compared, added to the data at another address in the computer etc.) using typically a 32 bit or 64 bit binary word of data. Pointers to memory locations are thus used extensively. In contrast, in the cortex, the data are used as the access key (in for example a pattern associator), and the neurons with synaptic weights that match the data respond. Memory in the brain is thus *content-addressable*. In one time constant of the synapses/cell membranes the brain has thus found the correct output. In contrast, on a digital computer a serial search is required, in which the data at every address must be retrieved and compared in turn to the test data to discover if there is a match.

Cortical computation including that performed by associative memories and competitive networks operates by vector similarity – the dot product of the input and of the synaptic weight vector are compared, and the neurons with the highest dot product will be most activated. Even if an exact match is not found, some output is likely to result. In contrast, in a digital computer, logic operations (such as AND, OR, XOR) and exact mathematical operations (such as addition, subtraction, multiplication, and division) are computed. (There is no bit-wise similarity between the binary representations of 7 (0111) and 8 (1000).) The similarity computations performed by the brain may be very useful, in enabling similarities to be seen and parallels to be drawn, and this may be an interesting aspect of human creativity, realized for example in Finnegans's Wake by James Joyce. However, the lateral thinking must be controlled, to prevent bizarre similarities being found, and this is argued to be related to the symptoms of schizophrenia in Section 8.5.

Because exact computations are performed in a digital computer, there is no in-built fault tolerance or graceful degradation. If one bit of a memory has a fault, the whole memory chip must be discarded. In contrast, the brain is naturally fault tolerant, because it uses vector similarity (between its input firing rate vector and synaptic weight vectors) in its calculations, and linked to this, distributed representations. This makes the brain robust developmentally with respect to 'missing synapses', and robust with respect to losing some synapses or neurons later (see e.g. Section B.2).

To enable the vector similarity comparison to have high capacity (for example memory capacity) the 'word length' in the brain is typically long, with between 10,000 and 50,000 synapses onto every neuron being common in cortical areas. (Remember that the leading term in the factor that determines the storage capacity of an associative memory is the number of synapses per neuron – see Sections B.2 and B.3.) In contrast, the word length in typical digital computers at 32 or 64 bits is much shorter, though with the binary and exact encoding used this allows great precision in a digital computer.

To comment further on the encoding: in the cortex, the code must not be too compact, so that it can be read by neuronally plausible dot product decoding, as shown in Appendix C. In contrast, the binary encoding used in a digital computer is optimally efficient, with one bit stored and retrievable for each binary memory location.

The precision of the components in a digital computer is that every modifiable memory location must store one bit accurately. In contrast, it is of interest that synapses in the brain need not work with exact precision, with for example typically less that one bit per synapse being usable in associative memories (Treves and Rolls 1991, Rolls and Treves 1998). The precision of the encoding of information in the firing rate of a neuron is likely to be a few bits – perhaps 3 – as judged by the standard deviation and firing rate range of individual cortical neurons.

This brings us to the speed of computation. In the brain, considerable information can be read in 20 ms from the firing rate of an individual neuron (e.g. 0.2 bits, see e.g. Fig. C.15), leading to estimates of 10–30 bits/s for primate temporal cortex visual cells (Rolls, Treves and Tovee 1997b), and 2–3 bits/s for rat hippocampal cells (Skaggs, McNaughton, Gothard and Markus 1993) (see Section C.3.4). Though this is very slow compared to a digital computer, the brain does have the advantage that a single neuron receives spikes from thousands of individual neurons, and computes its output from all of these inputs within a period of approximately 10–20 ms (determined largely by the time constant of the synapses), as described in this Appendix. Moreover, each neuron, up to at least the order of tens of neurons, conveys independent information, as described in Appendix C.

Computation in a conventional digital computer is inherently serial, with a single central processing unit that must fetch the data from a memory address, manipulate the word of data, and store it again at a memory address. In contrast, brain computation is parallel in at least three senses. First, an individual neuron in performing a dot product between its input firing rate vector and its synaptic weight vector does operate in an analog way to sum all the injected currents through the thousands of synapses to calculate the activation h_i, and fire if a threshold is reached, in a time in the order of the synaptic time constant. To implement this on a digital computer would take $2C$ operations (C multiply operations, and C add operations, where C is the number of synapses per neuron – see equation B.3). Second, each neuron in a single network (e.g. a small region of the cortex with of the order of hundreds of thousands of neurons) does this dot product computation in parallel, followed by interaction through the GABA inhibitory neurons, which again is fast. (It is in the order of the time constant of the synapses involved, operates in continuous time, and does not have to wait at all until the dot product operation of the pyramidal cells has been completed by all neurons given the spontaneous neuronal activity which allows some neurons to be influenced rapidly.) This interaction sets the threshold in associative and competitive networks, and helps to set the sparseness of the representation of the population of neurons. Third, different brain areas operate in parallel. An example is that the ventral visual stream computes object representations, while simultaneously the dorsal visual streams computes (inter alia) the types of global motion described in Section 4.5.13. Another example is that within a hierarchical system in the brain, every stage operates simultaneously, as a pipeline processor, with a good example being V1–V2–V4–IT, which can all operate simultaneously as the data are pipelined through.

We could refer to the computation that takes place in different modules, that is in networks that are relatively separate in terms of the number of connections between modules relative to those within modules, such as those in the dorsal and ventral visual streams, as being parallel computation. Within a single module or network, such as the CA3 region of the hippocampus, or inferior temporal visual cortex, we could refer to the computation as being *parallel distributed computation*, in that the closely connected neurons in the network all contribute to the result of the computation. For example, with distributed representations in an attractor network, all the neurons interact with each other directly and through the inhibitory interneurons to retrieve and then maintain a stable pattern in short term memory (Section B.3). In a competitive network involved in pattern categorization, all the neurons interact through the inhibitory interneurons to result in an active population of neurons that represents the best match between the input stimulus and what has been learned previously by the network, with neurons with a poor match being inhibited by neurons with a good match (Section B.4). In a more complicated scenario with closely connected interacting modules, such as the prefrontal cortex and the inferior temporal cortex during top-down attention tasks and more generally forward and backward connections between adjacent cortical areas, we might also use the term parallel distributed computation, as the bottom-up and top-down interactions may be important in how the whole dynamical system of interconnected networks settles (see examples in Chapters 5, 6 and 8 and Section B.9).

Digital computers do not have noise to contend with as part of the computation, as they use binary logic levels, and perform exact computation. In contrast, brain computation is inherently noisy, and this gives it a non-exact, probabilistic, character. One of the sources of noise in the brain is the spiking activity of each neuron. Each neuron must transmit information by spikes, for an all-or-none spike carried along an axon ensures that the signal arrives faithfully, and is not subject to the uncertain cable transmission line losses of analog potentials. But once a neuron needs to spike, then it turns out to be important to have spontaneous activity, so that neurons do not all have to charge up from a hyperpolarized baseline whenever a new input is received. The fact that neurons are kept near threshold, with therefore some spontaneous spiking, in inherent to the rapid operation of for example autoassociative retrieval, as described in Section B.3.3.5. But keeping the neurons close to threshold, and the spiking activity received from other neurons, results in spontaneous spike trains that are approximately Poisson, that is randomly timed. The result of the interaction of all these randomly timed inputs is that in a network of finite size there will be statistical fluctuations, which influence which memory is recalled, which decision is taken, etc. as described in Chapter 7. Thus brain computation is inherently noisy and probabilistic.

Digital computers can perform arbitrary syntactical operations on operands, because they use different pointers to point to the address of each of the different operands required (corresponding even for example to the subject, the verb, and the object of a sentence). In contrast, as data are not accessed in the brain by pointers that can point anywhere, but instead just have neurons firing to represent a data item, a real problem arises in specifying which neurons firing represent for example the subject, the verb, and the object, and distributed representations potentially make this even more difficult. The brain thus inherently finds syntactical operations difficult. We do not know how the brain implements the syntax required for language. But we do know that the firing of neurons conveys 'meaning' based on spatial location in the brain. For example, a neuron firing in V1 indicates that a bar or edge matching the filter characteristic of the neuron is present at a particular location in space. Another neuron in V1 encodes another feature at another position in space. A neuron in the inferior temporal visual cortex indicates (with other neurons helping to form a distributed representation) that a particular object or face is present in the visual scene. Perhaps the implementation of the syntax required for language that is implemented in the brain also utilizes the spatial location of the network in the cortex to help specify what syntactical role the representation should perform. This is a suggestion I make, as it is one way that the brain could deal with the implementation of the syntax required for language.

The physical architecture (what is connected to what) of a digital computer is fixed. In contrast, the connectivity of the brain alters as a result of experience and learning, and indeed it is alterations in the strength of the synapses (which implement the connectivity) that underlies learning and memory. Indeed, self-organization in for example competitive networks has a strong influence on how the brain is matched to the statistics of the incoming signals, and of the architecture that develops. In a digital computer, every connection must be specified. In contrast, in the brain there are far too few genes (of order 30,000) for the synaptic connections in the brain (of order 10^{15}, given approximately 10^{11} neurons each with in the order of 10^4 synapses) for the genes to specify every connection[43]. The genes must therefore specify some much more general rules, such as that each CA3 neuron should make approximately 12,000 synapses with other CA3 neurons, and receive approximately 48 synapses from dentate granule cells (see Chapter 2). The actual connections made would then be made randomly within these constraints, and then strengthened or lost as a result of self-organization based on for example conjunctive pre- and post-synaptic activity. Some of the rules that may be specified genetically have been suggested on the basis of a comparison of the architecture of different brain areas (Rolls and Stringer 2000). Moreover, it has been shown that if these rules are selected by a genetic algorithm based on the fitness of the network that self-organizes and learns based on these rules, then architectures are built that solve different computational problems in one-layer networks, including pattern association learning, autoassociation memory, and competitive learning (Rolls and Stringer 2000). The architecture of the brain is thus interestingly adaptive, but guided in the long term by genetic selection of the building rules.

---

[43] For comparison, a computer with 1 Gb of memory has approximately 10^{10} modifiable locations, and if it had a 100 Gb disk that would have approximately 10^{12} modifiable locations.

The learning rules that are implemented in the brain that are most widely accepted are associative, as exemplified by LTP and LTD. This, and the vector similarity operations implemented by neurons, set the stage for processes such as pattern association, autoassociation, and competitive learning to occur naturally, but not for logical operations such as XOR and NAND or arithmetic operations. Of course, the non-linearity inherent in the firing threshold of neurons is important in many of the properties of associative memories and competitive learning, as described in this Appendix, and indeed are how some of the non-linearities that can be seen with attention can arise (Deco and Rolls 2005b).

Because the brain has populations of neurons that are simultaneously active (operating in parallel), but are interconnected, many properties arise naturally in dynamical neural systems, including the interactions that give rise to top-down attention (Chapter 6), the effects of mood on memory (Section 3.11) etc. Because simultaneous activity of different computational nodes does not occur in digital computers, these dynamical systems properties that arise from interacting subsystems do not occur naturally, though they can be simulated.

The cortex has recurrent excitatory connections within a cortical area, and reciprocal, forward and feedback, connections between adjacent cortical areas in the hierarchy. The excitatory connections enable cortical activity to be maintained over short periods, making short-term memory an inherent property of the cortex, and also autoassociative long-term memory with completion from a partial cue (given associative synaptic modifiability in these connections). Completion is a difficult and serial process to identify a possible correct partial match on a digital computer. The short-term memory property of the cortex is part of what makes the cortex a dynamical interacting system, with for example what is in short-term memory in for example the prefrontal cortex acting to influence memory recall, perception, and even what decision is taken, in other networks, by top-down biased competition (see Chapters 5–10). There is a price that the brain pays for this positive feedback inherent in its recurrent cortical circuitry, which is that this circuitry is inherently unstable, and requires strong control by inhibitory interneurons to minimize the risk of epilepsy.

Finally, we can note that many brain systems are organized hierarchically. A major reason for this is that this enables the connectivity to be kept within the limits of which neurons appear capable (up to 50,000 synapses per neuron), yet for global computation (such as the presence of a particular object anywhere in the visual field) to be achieved, as exemplified by VisNet (see Fig. 4.2). Another important reason is that this simplifies the learning that is required at each stage and enables it to be a local operation, in contrast to backpropagation of error networks where similar problems could in principle be solved in a two-layer network (with one hidden layer), but would require training with a non-local learning rule (see Section B.12) as well as potentially neurons with very large numbers of connections.

Appendix 3 Information theory, and neuronal encoding

In order to understand the operation of memory and perceptual systems in the brain, it is necessary to know how information is encoded by neurons and populations of neurons.

We have seen that one parameter that influences the number of memories that can be stored in an associative memory is the sparseness of the representation, and it is therefore important to be able to quantify the sparseness of the representations.

We have also seen that the properties of an associative memory system depend on whether the representation is distributed or local (grandmother cell like), and it is important to be able to assess this quantitatively for neuronal representations.

It is also necessary to know how the information is encoded in order to understand how memory systems operate. Is the information that must be stored and retrieved present in the firing rates (the number of spikes in a fixed time), or is it present in synchronized firing of subsets of neurons? This has implications for how each stage of processing would need to operate. If the information is present in the firing rates, how much information is available from the spiking activity in a short period, of for example 20 or 50 ms? For each stage of cortical processing to operate quickly (in for example 20 ms), it is necessary for each stage to be able to read the code being provided by the previous cortical area within this order of time. Thus understanding the neural code is fundamental to understanding how each stage of processing works in the brain, and for understanding the speed of processing at each stage.

To treat all these questions quantitatively, we need quantitative ways of measuring sparseness, and also ways of measuring the information available from the spiking activity of single neurons and populations of neurons, and these are the topics addressed in this Appendix, together with some of the main results obtained, which provide answers to these questions.

Because single neurons are the computing elements of the brain and send the results of their processing by spiking activity to other neurons, we can understand brain processing by understanding what is encoded by the neuronal firing at each stage of the brain (e.g. each cortical area), and determining how what is encoded changes from stage to stage. Each neuron responds differently to a set of stimuli (with each neuron tuned differently to the members of the set of stimuli), and it is this that allows different stimuli to be represented. We can only address the richness of the representation therefore by understanding the differences in the responses of different neurons, and the impact that this has on the amount of information that is encoded. These issues can only be adequately and directly addressed at the level of the activity of single neurons and of populations of single neurons, and understanding at this neuronal level (rather than at the level of thousands or millions of neurons as revealed by functional neuroimaging) is essential for understanding brain computation.

Information theory provides the means for quantifying how much neurons communicate to other neurons, and thus provides a quantitative approach to fundamental questions about information processing in the brain. To investigate what in neuronal activity carries information, one must compare the amounts of information carried by different codes, that is different descriptions of the same activity, to provide the answer. To investigate the speed of information transmission, one must define and measure information rates from neuronal responses. To investigate to what extent the information provided by different cells is redundant or instead independent, again one must measure amounts of information in order to provide quantitative evidence. To compare the information carried by the number of spikes, by the timing of the spikes within the response of a single neuron, and by the relative time of firing of different neurons reflecting for example stimulus-dependent neuronal synchronization, information theory again provides a quantitative and well-founded basis for the necessary comparisons. To compare the information carried by a single neuron or a group of neurons with that reflected in the behaviour of the human or animal, one must again use information theory, as it provides a single measure which can be applied to the measurement of the performance of all these different cases. In all these situations, there is no quantitative and well-founded alternative to information theory.

This Appendix briefly introduces the fundamental elements of information theory in Section C.1. A more complete treatment can be found in many books on the subject (e.g. Abramson (1963), Hamming (1990), and Cover and Thomas (1991)), including also Rieke, Warland, de Ruyter van Steveninck and Bialek (1996) which is specifically about information transmitted by neuronal firing. Section C.2 discusses the extraction of information measures from neuronal activity, in particular in experiments with mammals, in which the central issue is how to obtain accurate measures in conditions of limited sampling, that is where the numbers of trials of neuronal data that can be obtained are usually limited by the available recording time. Section C.3 summarizes some of the main results obtained so far on neuronal encoding. The essential terminology is summarized in a Glossary at the end of this Appendix in Section C.4. The approach taken in this Appendix is based on and updated from that provided by Rolls and Treves (1998).

C.1 Information theory and its use in the analysis of formal models

Although information theory was a surprisingly late starter as a mathematical discipline, having being developed and formalized by C. Shannon (1948), the intuitive notion of information is immediate to us. It is also very easy to understand why we use logarithms in order to quantify this intuitive notion, of how much we know about something, and why the resulting quantity is always defined in relative rather than absolute terms. An introduction to information theory is provided next, with a more formal summary given in Section C.1.3.

C.1.1 The information conveyed by definite statements

Suppose somebody, who did not know, is told that Reading is a town west of London. How much information is he given? Well, that depends. He may have known it was a town in England, but not whether it was east or west of London; in which case the new information amounts to the fact that of two *a priori* (i.e. initial) possibilities (E or W), one holds (W). It is also possible to interpret the statement in the more precise sense, that Reading is west of London, rather than east, north or south, i.e. one out of four possibilities; or else, west rather that north-west, north, etc. Clearly, the larger the number k of *a priori* possibilities, the more one is actually told, and a measure of information must take this into account. Moreover, we would like independent pieces of information to just add together. For example, our person may also be told that Cambridge is, out of l possible directions, north of London. Provided nothing was known on the mutual location of Reading and Cambridge, there are now overall $k \times l$ *a priori* (initial) possibilities, only one of which remains *a posteriori* (after receiving the information). Given that the number of possibilities for independent events are multiplicative, but that we would like the measure of information to be additive, we use logarithms when we measure information, as logarithms have this property. We thus define the amount I of information gained when we are informed in which of k possible locations Reading is located as

$$I(k) = \log_2 k. \tag{C.1}$$

Then when we combine independent information, for example producing $k \times l$ possibilities from independent events with k and l possibilities respectively, we obtain

$$I(k \times l) = \log_2(k \times l) = \log_2 k + \log_2 l = I(k) + I(l). \tag{C.2}$$

Thus in our example, the information about Cambridge adds up to that about Reading. We choose to take logarithms in base 2 as a mere convention, so that the answer to a yes/no question provides one unit, or bit, of information. Here it is just for the sake of clarity that we used different symbols for the number of possible directions with respect to which Reading and Cambridge are localized; if both locations are specified for example in terms of E, SE, S, SW, W, NW, N, NE, then obviously $k = l = 8$, $I(k) = I(l) = 3$ bits, and $I(k \times l) = 6$ bits. An important point to note is that the *resolution* with which the direction is specified determines the amount of information provided, and that in this example, as in many situations arising when analysing neuronal codings, the resolution could be made progressively finer, with a corresponding increase in information proportional to the log of the number of possibilities.

C.1.2   The information conveyed by probabilistic statements

The situation becomes slightly less trivial, and closer to what happens among neurons, if information is conveyed in less certain terms. Suppose for example that our friend is told, instead, that Reading has odds of 9 to 1 to be west, rather than east, of London (considering now just two *a priori* possibilities). He is certainly given some information, albeit less than in the previous case. We might put it this way: out of 18 equiprobable *a priori* possibilities (9 west + 9 east), 8 (east) are eliminated, and 10 remain, yielding

$$I = \log_2(18/10) = \log_2(9/5) \tag{C.3}$$

as the amount of information given. It is simpler to write this in terms of probabilities

$$I = \log_2 P^{\text{posterior}}(W)/P^{\text{prior}}(W) = \log_2(9/10)/(1/2) = \log_2(9/5). \tag{C.4}$$

This is of course equivalent to saying that the amount of information given by an uncertain statement is equal to the amount given by the absolute statement

$$I = -\log_2 P^{\text{prior}}(W) \tag{C.5}$$

minus the amount of uncertainty remaining after the statement, $I = -\log_2 P^{\text{posterior}}(W)$. A successive clarification that Reading is indeed west of London carries

$$I' = \log_2((1)/(9/10)) \tag{C.6}$$

bits of information, because 9 out of 10 are now the *a priori* odds, while *a posteriori* there is certainty, $P^{\text{posterior}}(W) = 1$. In total we would seem to have

$$I^{\text{TOTAL}} = I + I' = \log_2(9/5) + \log_2(10/9) = 1 \text{ bit} \tag{C.7}$$

as if the whole information had been provided at one time. This is strange, given that the two pieces of information are clearly not independent, and only independent information should be additive. In fact, we have cheated a little. Before the clarification, there was still one residual possibility (out of 10) that the answer was 'east', and this must be taken into account by writing

$$I = \mathrm{P^{posterior}}(\mathrm{W}) \log_2 \frac{\mathrm{P^{posterior}}(\mathrm{W})}{\mathrm{P^{prior}}(\mathrm{W})} + \qquad \text{(C.8)}$$

$$\mathrm{P^{posterior}}(\mathrm{E}) \log_2 \frac{\mathrm{P^{posterior}}(\mathrm{E}}{\mathrm{P^{prior}}(\mathrm{E})}$$

as the information contained in the first message. This little detour should serve to emphasize two aspects that are easy to forget when reasoning intuitively about information, and that in this example cancel each other. In general, when uncertainty remains, that is there is more than one possible *a posteriori* state, one has to average information values for each state with the corresponding *a posteriori* probability measure. In the specific example, the sum $I + I'$ totals slightly *more* than 1 bit, and the amount in excess is precisely the information 'wasted' by providing *correlated* messages.

C.1.3   Information sources, information channels, and information measures

In summary, the expression quantifying the information provided by a definite statement that event s, which had an *a priori* probability $P(s)$, has occurred is

$$I(s) = \log_2(1/P(s)) = -\log_2 P(s), \qquad \text{(C.9)}$$

whereas if the statement is probabilistic, that is several *a posteriori* probabilities remain non-zero, the correct expression involves summing over all possibilities with the corresponding probabilities:

$$I = \sum_s \left[\mathrm{P^{posterior}}(s) \log_2 \frac{\mathrm{P^{posterior}}(s)}{\mathrm{P^{prior}}(s)} \right]. \qquad \text{(C.10)}$$

When considering a discrete set of mutually exclusive events, it is convenient to use the metaphor of a set of *symbols* comprising an *alphabet* S. The occurrence of each event is then referred to as the emission of the corresponding symbol by an information *source*. The *entropy* of the source, H, is the average amount of information per source symbol, where the average is taken across the alphabet, with the corresponding probabilities

$$H(S) = -\sum_{s \in S} P(s) \log_2 P(s). \qquad \text{(C.11)}$$

An information *channel* receives symbols s from an alphabet S and emits symbols s' from alphabet S'. If the *joint* probability of the channel receiving s and emitting s' is given by the product

$$P(s, s') = P(s)P(s') \qquad \text{(C.12)}$$

for any pair s, s', then the input and output symbols are *independent* of each other, and the channel transmits zero information. Instead of joint probabilities, this can be expressed with conditional probabilities: the conditional probability of s' given s is written $P(s'|s)$, and if the two variables are independent, it is just equal to the unconditional probability $P(s')$. In general, and in particular if the channel does transmit information, the variables are not independent, and one can express their joint probability in two ways in terms of conditional probabilities

$$P(s, s') = P(s'|s)P(s) = P(s|s')P(s'), \tag{C.13}$$

from which it is clear that

$$P(s'|s) = P(s|s')\frac{P(s')}{P(s)}, \tag{C.14}$$

which is called Bayes' theorem (although when expressed as here in terms of probabilities it is strictly speaking an identity rather than a theorem). The information transmitted by the channel conditional to its having emitted symbol s' (or specific transinformation, $I(s')$) is given by equation C.10, once the unconditional probability $P(s)$ is inserted as the prior, and the conditional probability $P(s|s')$ as the posterior:

$$I(s') = \sum_s P(s|s') \log_2 \frac{P(s|s')}{P(s)}. \tag{C.15}$$

Symmetrically, one can define the transinformation conditional to the channel having received symbol s

$$I(s) = \sum_{s'} P(s'|s) \log_2 \frac{P(s'|s)}{P(s')}. \tag{C.16}$$

Finally, the average transinformation, or **mutual information**, can be expressed in fully symmetrical form

$$I = \sum_s P(s) \sum_{s'} P(s'|s) \log_2 \frac{P(s'|s)}{P(s')} \tag{C.17}$$

$$= \sum_{s,s'} P(s, s') \log_2 \frac{P(s, s')}{P(s)P(s')}.$$

The **mutual information** can also be expressed as the entropy of the source using alphabet S minus the *equivocation* of S with respect to the new alphabet S' used by the channel, written

$$I = H(S) - H(S|S') \equiv H(S) - \sum_{s'} P(s')H(S|s'). \tag{C.18}$$

A channel is characterized, once the alphabets are given, by the set of conditional probabilities for the output symbols, $P(s'|s)$, whereas the unconditional probabilities of the input symbols $P(s)$ depend of course on the source from which the channel receives. Then, the *capacity* of the channel can be defined as the maximal mutual information across all possible sets of input probabilities $P(s)$. Thus, the information transmitted by a channel can range from zero to the lower of two independent upper bounds: the entropy of the source, and the capacity of the channel.

C.1.4 The information carried by a neuronal response and its averages

Considering the processing of information in the brain, we are often interested in the amount of information the response r of a neuron, or of a population of neurons, carries about an event happening in the outside world, for example a stimulus s shown to the animal. Once the inputs and outputs are conceived of as sets of symbols from two alphabets, the neuron(s) may be regarded as an information channel. We may denote with $P(s)$ the *a priori* probability that the particular stimulus s out of a given set was shown, while the conditional probability $P(s|r)$ is the *a posteriori* probability, that is updated by the knowledge of the response r. The response-specific transinformation

$$I(r) = \sum_s P(s|r) \log_2 \frac{P(s|r)}{P(s)} \tag{C.19}$$

takes the extreme values of $I(r) = -\log_2 P(s(r))$ if r unequivocally determines $s(r)$ (that is, $P(s|r)$ equals 1 for that one stimulus and 0 for all others);
and $I(r) = \sum_s P(s) \log_2(P(s)/P(s)) = 0$ if there is no relation between s and r, that is they are independent, so that the response tells us nothing new about the stimulus and thus $P(s|r) = P(s)$.

This is the information conveyed by each particular response. One is usually interested in further averaging this quantity over all possible responses r,

$$< I >= \sum_r P(r) \left[\sum_s P(s|r) \log_2 \frac{P(s|r)}{P(s)} \right]. \tag{C.20}$$

The angular brackets <> are used here to emphasize the averaging operation, in this case over responses. Denoting with $P(s, r)$ the *joint probability* of the pair of events s and r, and using Bayes' theorem, this reduces to the symmetric form (equation C.18) for the **mutual information** $I(S, R)$

$$< I >= \sum_{s,r} P(s,r) \log_2 \frac{P(s,r)}{P(s)P(r)} \tag{C.21}$$

which emphasizes that responses tell us about stimuli just as much as stimuli tell us about responses. This is, of course, a general feature, independent of the two variables being in this instance stimuli and neuronal responses. In fact, what is of interest, besides the mutual information of equations C.20 and C.21, is often the information specifically conveyed about each stimulus,

$$I(s) = \sum_r P(r|s) \log_2 \frac{P(r|s)}{P(r)} \tag{C.22}$$

which is a direct quantification of the variability in the responses elicited by that stimulus, compared to the overall variability. Since $P(r)$ is the probability distribution of responses averaged across stimuli, it is again evident that the stimulus-specific information measure of equation C.22 depends not only on the stimulus s, but also on all other stimuli used. Likewise, the mutual information measure, despite being of an average nature, is dependent on what set of stimuli has been used in the average. This emphasizes again the relative nature of all information measures. More specifically, it underscores the relevance of using, while measuring the information conveyed by a given neuronal population, stimuli that are either representative of real-life stimulus statistics, or of particular interest for the properties of the population being examined[44].

---

[44]The quantity $I(s, R)$, which is what is shown in equation C.22 and where R draws attention to the fact that this quantity is calculated across the full set of responses R, has also been called the stimulus-specific surprise, see DeWeese and Meister (1999). Its average across stimuli is the mutual information $I(S, R)$.

C.1.4.1 A numerical example

To make these notions clearer, we can consider a specific example in which the response of a neuron to the presentation of, say, one of four visual stimuli (A, B, C, D) is recorded for 10 ms, during which the neuron emits either 0, 1, or 2 spikes, but no more. Imagine that the neuron tends to respond more vigorously to visual stimulus B, less to C, even less to A, and never to D, as described by the table of conditional probabilities $P(r|s)$ shown in Table C.1. Then, if different visual stimuli are presented with equal probability,

Table C.1 The conditional probabilities $P(r|s)$ that different neuronal responses (r=0, 1, or 2 spikes) will be produced by each of four stimuli (A–D).

	r=0	r=1	r=2
s=A	0.6	0.4	0.0
s=B	0.0	0.2	0.8
s=C	0.4	0.5	0.1
s=D	1.0	0.0	0.0

the table of joint probabilities $P(s,r)$ will be as shown in Table C.2. From these two tables

Table C.2 Joint probabilities $P(s,r)$ that different neuronal responses (r=0, 1, or 2 spikes) will be produced by each of four equiprobable stimuli (A–D).

	r=0	r=1	r=2
s=A	0.15	0.1	0.0
s=B	0.0	0.05	0.2
s=C	0.1	0.125	0.025
s=D	0.25	0.0	0.0

one can compute various information measures by directly applying the definitions above. Since visual stimuli are presented with equal probability, $P(s) = 1/4$, the entropy of the stimulus set, which corresponds to the maximum amount of information any transmission channel, no matter how efficient, could convey on the identity of the stimuli, is $H_s = -\sum_s [P(s) \log_2 P(s)] = -4[(1/4)\log_2(1/4)] = \log_2 4 = 2$ bits. There is a more stringent upper bound on the mutual information that this cell's responses convey on the stimuli, however, and this second bound is the channel capacity T of the cell. Calculating this quantity involves maximizing the mutual information across prior visual stimulus probabilities, and it is a bit complicated to do, in general. In our particular case the maximum information is obtained when only stimuli B and D are presented, each with probability 0.5. The resulting capacity is $T = 1$ bit. We can easily calculate, in general, the entropy of the responses. This is not an upper bound characterizing the source, like the entropy of the stimuli, nor an upper bound characterizing the channel, like the capacity, but simply a bound on the mutual information for this specific combination of source (with its related visual stimulus probabilities) and channel (with its conditional probabilities). Since only three response levels are possible within the short recording window, and they occur with uneven probability, their entropy is considerably lower than H_s, at $H_r = -\sum_r P(r) \log_2 P(r) = -P(0)\log_2 P(0) - P(1)\log_2 P(1) - P(2)\log_2 P(2) = -0.5\log_2 0.5 - 0.275\log_2 0.275 - 0.225\log_2 0.225 = 1.496$ bits. The actual average information I that the responses transmit about the stimuli, which is a measure of the correlation in the variability of stimuli and responses, does not exceed the absolute variability of either stimuli (as quantified by the first bound) or responses (as quantified by the last bound), nor the capacity of the channel. An explicit calculation using the joint probabilities of the second table in expression C.21 yields $I = 0.733$ bits. This is of course only the average value, averaged both across stimuli and across responses.

The information conveyed by a particular response can be larger. For example, when the cell emits two spikes it indicates with a relatively large probability stimulus B, and this is reflected in the fact that it then transmits, according to expression C.19, $I(r = 2) = 1.497$ bits, more than double the average value.

Similarly, the amount of information conveyed about each individual visual stimulus varies with the stimulus, depending on the extent to which it tends to elicit a differential response. Thus, expression C.22 yields that only $I(s = C) = 0.185$ bits are conveyed on average about stimulus C, which tends to elicit responses with similar statistics to the average statistics across stimuli, and are therefore not easily interpretable. On the other hand, exactly 1 bit of information is conveyed about stimulus D, since this stimulus never elicits any response, and when the neuron emits no spike there is a probability of $1/2$ that the stimulus was stimulus D.

C.1.5   The information conveyed by continuous variables

A general feature, relevant also to the case of neuronal information, is that if, among a *continuum* of *a priori* possibilities, only one, or a discrete number, remains *a posteriori*, the information is strictly infinite. This would be the case if one were told, for example, that Reading is exactly $10'$ west, $1'$ north of London. The *a priori* probability of precisely this set of coordinates among the continuum of possible ones is zero, and then the information diverges to infinity. The problem is only theoretical, because in fact, with continuous distributions, there are always one or several factors that limit the resolution in the *a posteriori* knowledge, rendering the information finite. Moreover, when considering the mutual information in the conjoint probability of occurrence of two sets, e.g. stimuli and responses, it suffices that at least one of the sets is discrete to make matters easy, that is, finite. Nevertheless, the identification and appropriate consideration of these resolution-limiting factors in practical cases may require careful analysis.

C.1.5.1   Example: the information retrieved from an autoassociative memory

One example is the evaluation of the information that can be retrieved from an autoassociative memory. Such a memory stores a number of firing patterns, each one of which can be considered, as in Appendix B, as a vector $\mathbf{r}^\mu$ with components the firing rates $\{r_i^\mu\}$, where the subscript i indexes the neuron (and the superscript μ indexes the pattern). In retrieving pattern μ, the network in fact produces a distinct firing pattern, denoted for example simply as $\mathbf{r}$. The quality of retrieval, or the similarity between $\mathbf{r}^\mu$ and $\mathbf{r}$, can be measured by the average mutual information

$$< I(\mathbf{r}^\mu, \mathbf{r}) > = \sum_{\mathbf{r}^\mu, \mathbf{r}} P(\mathbf{r}^\mu, \mathbf{r}) \log_2 \frac{P(\mathbf{r}^\mu, \mathbf{r})}{P(\mathbf{r}^\mu)P(\mathbf{r})} \tag{C.23}$$

$$\approx \sum_i \sum_{r_i^\mu, r_i} P(r_i^\mu, r_i) \log_2 \frac{P(r_i^\mu, r_i)}{P(r_i^\mu)P(r_i)}.$$

In this formula the 'approximately equal' sign $\approx$ marks a simplification that is not necessarily a reasonable approximation. If the simplification is valid, it means that in order to extract an information measure, one need not compare whole vectors (the entire firing patterns) with each other, and may instead compare the firing rates of individual cells at storage and retrieval, and sum the resulting single-cell information values. The validity of the simplification is a matter that will be discussed later and that has to be verified, in the end, experimentally, but for the purposes of the present discussion we can focus on the single-cell terms. If either

r_i or r_i^μ has a continuous distribution of values, as it will if it represents not the number of spikes emitted in a fixed window, but more generally the firing rate of neuron i computed by convolving the firing train with a smoothing kernel, then one has to deal with probability densities, which we denote as $p(r)dr$, rather than the usual probabilities $P(r)$. Substituting $p(r)dr$ for $P(r)$ and $p(r^\mu, r)drdr^\mu$ for $P(r^\mu, r)$, one can write for each single-cell contribution (omitting the cell index i)

$$< I(r^\mu, r) >_i = \int dr^\mu dr \; p(r^\mu, r) \log_2 \frac{p(r^\mu, r)}{p(r^\mu)p(r)} \qquad (C.24)$$

and we see that the differentials $dr^\mu dr$ cancel out between numerator and denominator inside the logarithm, rendering the quantity well defined and finite. If, however, r^μ were to *exactly* determine r, one would have

$$p(r^\mu, r)dr^\mu dr = p(r^\mu)\delta(r - r(r^\mu))dr^\mu dr = p(r^\mu)dr^\mu \qquad (C.25)$$

and, by losing one differential on the way, the mutual information would become infinite. It is therefore important to consider what prevents r^μ from fully determining r in the case at hand – in other words, to consider the sources of noise in the system. In an autoassociative memory storing an extensive number of patterns (see Appendix A4 of Rolls and Treves (1998)), one source of noise always present is the interference effect due to the concurrent storage of all other patterns. Even neglecting other sources of noise, this produces a finite resolution width ρ, which allows one to write an expression of the type $p(r|r^\mu)dr = \exp -(r - r(r^\mu))^2/2\rho^2 dr$ which ensures that the information is finite as long as the resolution ρ is larger than zero.

One further point that should be noted, in connection with estimating the information retrievable from an autoassociative memory, is that the mutual information between the current distribution of firing rates and that of the stored pattern does not coincide with the information *gain* provided by the memory device. Even when firing rates, or spike counts, are all that matter in terms of information carriers, as in the networks considered in this book, one more term should be taken into account in evaluating the information gain. This term, to be subtracted, is the information contained in the external input that elicits the retrieval. This may vary a lot from the retrieval of one particular memory to the next, but of course an efficient memory device is one that is able, when needed, to retrieve much more information than it requires to be present in the inputs, that is, a device that produces a large information gain.

Finally, one should appreciate the conceptual difference between the information a firing pattern carries about another one (that is, about the pattern stored), as considered above, and two different notions: (a) the information produced by the network in selecting the correct memory pattern and (b) the information a firing pattern carries about something in the outside world. Quantity (a), the information intrinsic to selecting the memory pattern, is ill defined when analysing a real system, but is a well-defined and particularly simple notion when considering a formal model. If p patterns are stored with equal strength, and the selection is errorless, this amounts to $\log_2 p$ bits of information, a quantity often, but not always, small compared with the information in the pattern itself. Quantity (b), the information conveyed about some outside correlate, is not defined when considering a formal model that does not include an explicit account of what the firing of each cell represents, but is well defined and measurable from the recorded activity of real cells. It is the quantity considered in the numerical example with the four visual stimuli, and it can be generalized to the information carried by the activity of several cells in a network, and specialized to the case that the network operates as an associative memory. One may note, in this case, that the capacity to retrieve memories with high fidelity, or high information content, is only useful to the extent that the representation to be retrieved carries that amount of information about something relevant – or, in other words, that it is pointless to store and retrieve with great care largely meaningless messages. This type of argument has been used to discuss the role of the mossy fibres in the operation of the CA3 network in the hippocampus (Treves and Rolls 1992, Rolls and Treves 1998).

C.2 Estimating the information carried by neuronal responses

C.2.1 The limited sampling problem

We now discuss in more detail the application of these general notions to the information transmitted by neurons. Suppose, to be concrete, that an animal has been presented with stimuli drawn from a discrete set, and that the responses of a set of C cells have been recorded following the presentation of each stimulus. We may choose any quantity or set of quantities to characterize the responses; for example let us assume that we consider the firing rate of each cell, r_i, calculated by convolving the spike response with an appropriate smoothing kernel. The response space is then C times the continuous set of all positive real numbers, $(\mathbf{R}/2)^C$. We want to evaluate the average information carried by such responses about which stimulus was shown. In principle, it is straightforward to apply the above formulas, e.g. in the form

$$< I(s, \mathbf{r}) > = \sum_s \mathrm{P}(s) \int \Pi_i dr_i \, p(\mathbf{r}|s) \log_2 \frac{p(\mathbf{r}|s)}{p(\mathbf{r})} \tag{C.26}$$

where it is important to note that $p(\mathbf{r})$ and $p(\mathbf{r}|s)$ are now probability densities defined over the high-dimensional vector space of multi-cell responses. The product sign Π signifies that this whole vector space has to be integrated over, along all its dimensions. $p(\mathbf{r})$ can be calculated as $\sum_s p(\mathbf{r}|s)\mathrm{P}(s)$, and therefore, in principle, all one has to do is to estimate, from the data, the conditional probability densities $p(\mathbf{r}|s)$ – the distributions of responses following each stimulus. In practice, however, in contrast to what happens with formal models, in which there is usually no problem in calculating the exact probability densities, real data come in limited amounts, and thus sample only sparsely the vast response space. This limits the accuracy with which, from the experimental *frequency* of each possible response, we can estimate its *probability*, in turn seriously impairing our ability to estimate $< I >$ correctly. We refer to this as the limited sampling problem. This is a purely technical problem that arises, typically when recording from mammals, because of external constraints on the duration or number of repetitions of a given set of stimulus conditions. With computer simulation experiments, and also with recordings from, for example, insects, sufficient data can usually be obtained that straightforward estimates of information are accurate enough (Strong, Koberle, de Ruyter van Steveninck and Bialek 1998, Golomb, Kleinfeld, Reid, Shapley and Shraiman 1994). The problem is, however, so serious in connection with recordings from monkeys and rats in which limited numbers of trials are usually available for neuronal data, that it is worthwhile to discuss it, in order to appreciate the scope and limits of applying information theory to neuronal processing.

In particular, if the responses are continuous quantities, the probability of observing exactly the same response twice is infinitesimal. In the absence of further manipulation, this would imply that each stimulus generates its own set of unique responses, therefore any response that has actually occurred could be associated unequivocally with one stimulus, and the mutual information would always equal the entropy of the stimulus set. This absurdity shows that in order to estimate probability densities from experimental frequencies, one has to resort to some *regularizing* manipulation, such as smoothing the point-like response values by convolution with suitable kernels, or binning them into a finite number of discrete bins.

C.2.1.1 Smoothing or binning neuronal response data

The issue is how to estimate the underlying probability distributions of neuronal responses to a set of stimuli from only a limited number of trials of data (e.g. 10–30) for each stimulus. Several strategies are possible. One is to discretize the response space into bins, and estimate the probability density as the histogram of the fraction of trials falling into each bin. If the bins are too narrow, almost every response is in a different bin, and the estimated information will be overestimated. Even if the bin width is increased to match the standard deviation of each underlying distribution, the information may still be overestimated. Alternatively, one may try to 'smooth' the data by convolving each response with a Gaussian with a width set to the standard deviation measured for each stimulus. Setting the standard deviation to this value may actually lead to an underestimation of the amount of information available, due to oversmoothing. Another possibility is to make a bold assumption as to what the general shape of the underlying densities should be, for example a Gaussian. This may produce closer estimates. Methods for regularizing the data are discussed further by Rolls and Treves (1998) in their Appendix A2, where a numerical example is given.

C.2.1.2 The effects of limited sampling

The crux of the problem is that, whatever procedure one adopts, limited sampling tends to produce distortions in the estimated probability densities. The resulting mutual information estimates are intrinsically biased. The bias, or average error of the estimate, is upward if the raw data have not been regularized much, and is downward if the regularization procedure chosen has been heavier. The bias can be, if the available trials are few, much larger than the true information values themselves. This is intuitive, as fluctuations due to the finite number of trials available would tend, on average, to either produce or emphasize differences among the distributions corresponding to different stimuli, differences that are preserved if the regularization is 'light', and that are interpreted in the calculation as carrying genuine information. This is illustrated with a quantitative example by Rolls and Treves (1998) in their Appendix A2.

Choosing the right amount of regularization, or the best regularizing procedure, is not possible *a priori*. Hertz, Kjaer, Eskander and Richmond (1992) have proposed the interesting procedure of using an artificial neural network to regularize the raw responses. The network can be trained on part of the data using backpropagation, and then used on the remaining part to produce what is in effect a clever data-driven regularization of the responses. This procedure is, however, rather computer intensive and not very safe, as shown by some self-evident inconsistency in the results (Heller, Hertz, Kjaer and Richmond 1995). Obviously, the best way to deal with the limited sampling problem is to try and use as many trials as possible. The improvement is slow, however, and generating as many trials as would be required for a reasonably unbiased estimate is often, in practice, impossible.

C.2.2 Correction procedures for limited sampling

The above point, that data drawn from a single distribution, when artificially paired, at random, to different stimulus labels, results in 'spurious' amounts of apparent information, suggests a simple way of checking the reliability of estimates produced from real data (Optican, Gawne, Richmond and Joseph 1991). One can disregard the true stimulus associated with each response, and generate a randomly reshuffled pairing of stimuli and responses, which should therefore, being not linked by any underlying relationship, carry no mutual information about each other. Calculating, with some procedure of choice, the spurious information obtained in this way, and comparing with the information value estimated with the same procedure for the real pairing, one can get a feeling for how far the procedure goes into eliminating the apparent information due to limited sampling. Although this spurious information, I_s, is only indicative of the amount of bias affecting the original estimate, a simple heuristic trick (called 'bootstrap'[45]) is to subtract the spurious from the original value, to obtain a somewhat 'corrected' estimate. This procedure can result in quite accurate estimates (see Rolls and Treves (1998), Tovee, Rolls, Treves and Bellis (1993))[46].

A different correction procedure (called 'jack-knife') is based on the assumption that the bias is proportional to $1/N$, where N is the number of responses (data points) used in the estimation. One computes, beside the original estimate $< I_N >$, N auxiliary estimates $< I_{N-1} >_k$, by taking out from the data set response k, where k runs across the data set from 1 to N. The corrected estimate

$$< I > = N < I_N > -(1/N) \sum_k (N-1) < I_{N-1} >_k \qquad \text{(C.27)}$$

is free from bias (to leading order in $1/N$), if the proportionality factor is more or less the same in the original and auxiliary estimates. This procedure is very time-consuming, and it suffers from the same imprecision of any algorithm that tries to determine a quantity as the result of the subtraction of two large and nearly equal terms; in this case the terms have been made large on purpose, by multiplying them by N and $N - 1$.

A more fundamental approach (Miller 1955) is to derive an analytical expression for the bias (or, more precisely, for its leading terms in an expansion in $1/N$, the inverse of the sample size). This allows the estimation of the bias from the data itself, and its subsequent subtraction, as discussed in Treves and Panzeri (1995) and Panzeri and Treves (1996). Such a procedure produces satisfactory results, thereby lowering the size of the sample required for a given accuracy in the estimate by about an order of magnitude (Golomb, Hertz, Panzeri, Treves and Richmond 1997). However, it does not, in itself, make possible measures of the information contained in very complex responses with few trials. As a rule of thumb, the number of trials per stimulus required for a reasonable estimate of information, once the subtractive correction is applied, is of the order of the effectively independent (and utilized) bins in which the response space can be partitioned (Panzeri and Treves 1996). This correction procedure is the one that we use standardly (Rolls, Treves, Tovee and Panzeri 1997d, Rolls, Critchley and Treves 1996a, Rolls, Treves, Robertson, Georges-François and Panzeri 1998, Booth and Rolls 1998, Rolls, Tovee and Panzeri 1999b, Rolls, Franco, Aggelopoulos and Jerez 2006b).

C.2.3 The information from multiple cells: decoding procedures

The bias of information measures grows with the dimensionality of the response space, and for all practical purposes the limit on the number of dimensions that can lead to reasonably accurate direct measures, even when applying a correction procedure, is quite low, two to three. This implies, in particular, that it is not possible to apply equation C.26 to extract the information content in the responses of several cells (more than two to three) recorded

---

[45] In technical usage bootstrap procedures utilize random pairings of responses with stimuli with replacement, while shuffling procedures utilize random pairings of responses with stimuli without replacement.

[46] Subtracting the 'square' of the spurious fraction of information estimated by this bootstrap procedure as used by Optican, Gawne, Richmond and Joseph (1991) is unfounded and does not work correctly (see Rolls and Treves (1998) and Tovee, Rolls, Treves and Bellis (1993)).

simultaneously. One way to address the problem is then to apply some strong form of regularization to the multiple cell responses. Smoothing has already been mentioned as a form of regularization that can be tuned from very soft to very strong, and that preserves the structure of the response space. Binning is another form, which changes the nature of the responses from continuous to discrete, but otherwise preserves their general structure, and which can also be tuned from soft to strong. Other forms of regularization involve much more radical transformations, or changes of variables.

Of particular interest for information estimates is a change of variables that transforms the response space into the stimulus set, by applying an algorithm that derives a predicted stimulus from the response vector, i.e. the firing rates of all the cells, on each trial. Applying such an algorithm is called decoding. Of course, the predicted stimulus is not necessarily the same as the actual one. Therefore the term decoding should not be taken to imply that the algorithm works successfully, each time identifying the actual stimulus. The predicted stimulus is simply a function of the response, as determined by the algorithm considered. Just as with any regularizing transform, it is possible to compute the mutual information between actual stimuli s and predicted stimuli s', instead of the original one between stimuli s and responses r. Since information about (real) stimuli can only be lost and not be created by the transform, the information measured in this way is bound to be lower in value than the real information in the responses. If the decoding algorithm is efficient, it manages to preserve nearly all the information contained in the raw responses, while if it is poor, it loses a large portion of it. If the responses themselves provided all the information about stimuli, and the decoding is optimal, then predicted stimuli coincide with the actual stimuli, and the information extracted equals the entropy of the stimulus set.

The procedure for extracting information values after applying a decoding algorithm is indicated in Fig. C.1 (in which s? is s'). The underlying idea indicated in Fig. C.1 is that if we know the average firing rate of each cell in a population to each stimulus, then on any single trial we can guess (or decode) the stimulus that was present by taking into account the responses of all the cells. The decoded stimulus is s', and the actual stimulus that was shown is s. What we wish to know is how the percentage correct, or better still the information, based on the evidence from any single trial about which stimulus was shown, increases as the number of cells in the population sampled increases. We can expect that the more cells there are in the sample, the more accurate the estimate of the stimulus is likely to be. If the encoding was local, the number of stimuli encoded by a population of neurons would be expected to rise approximately linearly with the number of neurons in the population. In contrast, with distributed encoding, provided that the neuronal responses are sufficiently independent, and are sufficiently reliable (not too noisy), information from the ensemble would be expected to rise linearly with the number of cells in the ensemble, and (as information is a log measure) the number of stimuli encodable by the population of neurons might be expected to rise exponentially as the number of neurons in the sample of the population was increased.

Table C.3 Decoding. s' is the decoded stimulus, i.e. that predicted from the neuronal responses r.

$$
\begin{array}{ccccc}
s & \Rightarrow & r & \rightarrow & s' \\
& I(s,r) & & & \\
\hline
& & I(s,s') & &
\end{array}
$$

The procedure is schematized in Table C.3 where the double arrow indicates the transformation from stimuli to responses operated by the nervous system, while the single arrow indicates the further transformation operated by the decoding procedure. $I(s, s')$ is the mutual information between the actual stimuli s and the stimuli s' that are predicted to have been

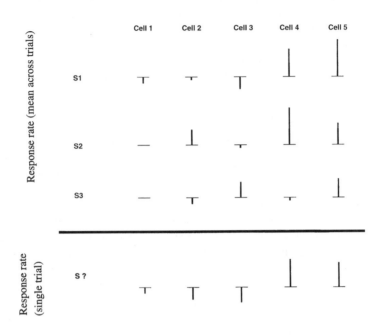

Fig. C.1 This diagram shows the average response for each of several cells (Cell 1, etc.) to each of several stimuli (S1, etc.). The change of firing rate from the spontaneous rate is indicated by the vertical line above or below the horizontal line, which represents the spontaneous rate. We can imagine guessing or predicting from such a table the predicted stimulus S? (i.e. s') that was present on any one trial.

shown based on the decoded responses.

A slightly more complex variant of this procedure is a decoding step that extracts from the response on each trial not a single predicted stimulus, but rather probabilities that each of the possible stimuli was the actual one. The joint probabilities of actual and posited stimuli can be averaged across trials, and information computed from the resulting probability matrix $(S \times S)$. Computing information in this way takes into account the relative uncertainty in assigning a predicted stimulus to each trial, an uncertainty that is instead not considered by the previous procedure based solely on the identification of the maximally likely stimulus (Treves 1997). *Maximum likelihood* information values I_{ml} based on a single stimulus tend therefore to be higher than *probability* information values I_p based on the whole set of stimuli, although in very specific situations the reverse could also be true.

The same correction procedures for limited sampling can be applied to information values computed after a decoding step. Values obtained from maximum likelihood decoding, I_{ml}, suffer from limited sampling more than those obtained from probability decoding, I_p, since each trial contributes a whole 'brick' of weight $1/N$ (N being the total number of trials), whereas with probabilities each brick is shared among several slots of the $(S \times S)$ probability matrix. The neural network procedure devised by Hertz, Kjaer, Eskander and Richmond

(1992) can in fact be thought of as a decoding procedure based on probabilities, which deals with limited sampling not by applying a correction but rather by strongly regularizing the original responses.

When decoding is used, the rule of thumb becomes that the minimal number of trials per stimulus required for accurate information measures is roughly equal to the size of the stimulus set, if the subtractive correction is applied (Panzeri and Treves 1996). This correction procedure is applied as standard in our multiple cell information analyses that use decoding (Rolls, Treves and Tovee 1997b, Booth and Rolls 1998, Rolls, Treves, Robertson, Georges-François and Panzeri 1998, Franco, Rolls, Aggelopoulos and Treves 2004, Aggelopoulos, Franco and Rolls 2005, Rolls, Franco, Aggelopoulos and Jerez 2006b).

C.2.3.1 Decoding algorithms

Any transformation from the response space to the stimulus set could be used in decoding, but of particular interest are the transformations that either approach optimality, so as to minimize information loss and hence the effect of decoding, or else are implementable by mechanisms that *could* conceivably be operating in the real system, so as to extract information values that could be extracted by the system itself.

The optimal transformation is in theory well-defined: one should estimate from the data the conditional probabilities $P(r|s)$, and use Bayes' rule to convert them into the conditional probabilities $P(s'|r)$. Having these for any value of r, one could use them to estimate I_p, and, after selecting for each particular real response the stimulus with the highest conditional probability, to estimate I_{ml}. To avoid biasing the estimation of conditional probabilities, the responses used in estimating $P(r|s)$ should not include the particular response for which $P(s'|r)$ is going to be derived (jack-knife cross-validation). In practice, however, the estimation of $P(r|s)$ in usable form involves the fitting of some simple function to the responses. This need for fitting, together with the approximations implied in the estimation of the various quantities, prevents us from defining the really optimal decoding, and leaves us with various algorithms, depending essentially on the fitting function used, which are hopefully close to optimal in some conditions. We have experimented extensively with two such algorithms, that both approximate Bayesian decoding (Rolls, Treves and Tovee 1997b). Both these algorithms fit the response vectors produced over several trials by the cells being recorded to a product of conditional probabilities for the response of each cell given the stimulus. In one case, the single cell conditional probability is assumed to be Gaussian (truncated at zero); in the other it is assumed to be Poisson (with an additional weight at zero). Details of these algorithms are given by Rolls, Treves and Tovee (1997b).

Biologically plausible decoding algorithms are those that limit the algebraic operations used to types that could be easily implemented by neurons, e.g. dot product summations, thresholding and other single-cell non-linearities, and competition and contrast enhancement among the outputs of nearby cells. There is then no need for ever fitting functions or other sophisticated approximations, but of course the degree of arbitrariness in selecting a particular algorithm remains substantial, and a comparison among different choices based on which yields the higher information values may favour one choice in a given situation and another choice with a different data set.

To summarize, the key idea in decoding, in our context of estimating information values, is that it allows substitution of a possibly very high-dimensional response space (which is difficult to sample and regularize) with a reduced object much easier to handle, that is with a discrete set equivalent to the stimulus set. The mutual information between the new set and the stimulus set is then easier to estimate even with limited data, and if the assumptions about population coding, underlying the particular decoding algorithm used, are justified, the value obtained approximates the original target, the mutual information between stimuli and responses. For each response recorded, one can use all the responses except for that one to generate estimates of the average response vectors (the average response for each neuron in the population) to each stimulus. Then one considers how well the selected response vector matches the average response vectors, and uses the degree of matching to estimate, for all stimuli, the probability that they were the actual stimuli. The form of the matching embodies the general notions about population encoding, for example the 'degree of matching' might be simply the dot product between the current vector and the average vector ($\mathbf{r}^{\text{av}}$), suitably normalized over all average vectors to generate probabilities

$$P(s'|\mathbf{r}(s)) = \frac{\mathbf{r}(s) \cdot \mathbf{r}^{\text{av}}(s')}{\sum_{s''} \mathbf{r}(s) \cdot \mathbf{r}^{\text{av}}(s'')} \tag{C.28}$$

where s'' is a dummy variable. (This is called dot product decoding in Fig. 4.15.) One ends up, then, with a table of conjoint probabilities $P(s, s')$, and another table obtained by selecting for each trial the most likely (or predicted) single stimulus s^{P}, $P(s, s^{\text{P}})$. Both s' and s^{P} stand for all possible stimuli, and hence belong to the same set S. These can be used to estimate mutual information values based on probability decoding (I_{p}) and on maximum likelihood decoding (I_{ml}):

$$< I_{\text{p}} > = \sum_{s \in S} \sum_{s' \in S} P(s, s') \log_2 \frac{P(s, s')}{P(s)P(s')} \tag{C.29}$$

and

$$< I_{\text{ml}} > = \sum_{s \in S} \sum_{s^{\text{P}} \in S} P(s, s^{\text{P}}) \log_2 \frac{P(s, s^{\text{P}})}{P(s)P(s^{\text{P}})} . \tag{C.30}$$

Examples of the use of these procedures are available (Rolls, Treves and Tovee 1997b, Booth and Rolls 1998, Rolls, Treves, Robertson, Georges-François and Panzeri 1998, Rolls, Aggelopoulos, Franco and Treves 2004, Franco, Rolls, Aggelopoulos and Treves 2004, Rolls, Franco, Aggelopoulos and Jerez 2006b), and some of the results obtained are described in Section C.3.

C.2.4 Information in the correlations between the spikes of different cells: a decoding approach

Simultaneously recorded neurons sometimes shows cross-correlations in their firing, that is the firing of one is systematically related to the firing of the other cell. One example of this is neuronal response synchronization. The cross-correlation, to be defined below, shows the time difference between the cells at which the systematic relation appears. A significant peak or trough in the cross-correlation function could reveal a synaptic connection from one cell to the other, or a common input to each of the cells, or any of a considerable number of other possibilities. If the synchronization occurred for only some of the stimuli, then the presence of the significant cross-correlation for only those stimuli could provide additional evidence separate from any information in the firing rate of the neurons about which stimulus had been shown. Information theory in principle provides a way of quantitatively assessing the relative contributions from these two types of encoding, by expressing what can be learned from each type of encoding in the same units, bits of information.

Figure C.2 illustrates how synchronization occurring only for some of the stimuli could be used to encode information about which stimulus was presented. In the Figure the spike trains of three neurons are shown after the presentation of two different stimuli on one trial. As shown by the cross-correlogram in the lower part of the figure, the responses of cell 1

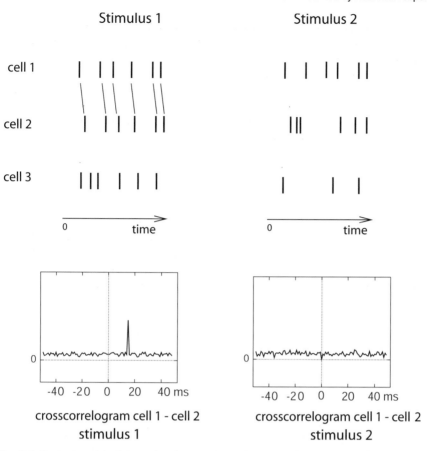

Fig. C.2 Illustration of the information that could be carried by spike trains. The responses of three cells to two different stimuli are shown on one trial. Cell 3 reflects which stimulus was shown in the number of spikes produced, and this can be measured as spike count or rate information. Cells 1 and 2 have no spike count or rate information, because the number of spikes is not different for the two stimuli. Cells 1 and 2 do show some synchronization, reflected in the cross-correlogram, that is stimulus dependent, as the synchronization is present only when stimulus 1 is shown. The contribution of this effect is measured as the stimulus-dependent synchronization information.

and cell 2 are synchronized when stimulus 1 is presented, as whenever a spike from cell 1 is emitted, another spike from cell 2 is emitted after a short time lag. In contrast, when stimulus 2 is presented, synchronization effects do not appear. Thus, based on a measure of the synchrony between the responses of cells 1 and 2, it is possible to obtain some information about what stimulus has been presented. The contribution of this effect is measured as the stimulus-dependent synchronization information. Cells 1 and 2 have no information about what stimulus was presented from the number of spikes, as the same number is found for both stimuli. Cell 3 carries information in the spike count in the time window (which is also called the firing rate) about what stimulus was presented. (Cell 3 emits 6 spikes for stimulus 1 and 3 spikes for stimulus 2.)

The example shown in Fig. C.2 is for the neuronal responses on a single trial. Given that the neuronal responses are variable from trial to trial, we need a method to quantify the information that is gained from a single trial of spike data in the context of the measured variability in the responses of all of the cells, including how the cells' responses covary in a way which may be partly stimulus-dependent, and may include synchronization effects. The direct approach is to apply the Shannon mutual information measure (Shannon 1948, Cover and Thomas 1991)

$$I(s, \mathbf{r}) = \sum_{s \in S} \sum_{\mathbf{r}} P(s, \mathbf{r}) \log_2 \frac{P(s, \mathbf{r})}{P(s)P(\mathbf{r})}, \tag{C.31}$$

where $P(s, \mathbf{r})$ is a probability table embodying a relationship between the variable s (here, the stimulus) and $\mathbf{r}$ (a vector where each element is the firing rate of one neuron).

However, because the probability table of the relation between the neuronal responses and the stimuli, $P(s, \mathbf{r})$, is so large (given that there may be many stimuli, and that the response space which has to include spike timing is very large), in practice it is difficult to obtain a sufficient number of trials for every stimulus to generate the probability table accurately, at least with data from mammals in which the experiment cannot usually be continued for many hours of recording from a whole population of cells. To circumvent this undersampling problem, Rolls, Treves and Tovee (1997b) developed a decoding procedure (described in Section C.2.3), in which an estimate (or guess) of which stimulus (called s') was shown on a given trial is made from a comparison of the neuronal responses on that trial with the responses made to the whole set of stimuli on other trials. One then obtains a conjoint probability table $P(s, s')$, and then the mutual information based on probability estimation (PE) decoding (I_p) between the estimated stimuli s' and the actual stimuli s that were shown can be measured:

$$< I_p > = \sum_{s \in S} \sum_{s' \in S} P(s, s') \log_2 \frac{P(s, s')}{P(s)P(s')} \tag{C.32}$$

$$= \sum_{s \in S} P(s) \sum_{s' \in S} P(s'|s) \log_2 \frac{P(s'|s)}{P(s')}. \tag{C.33}$$

These measurements are in the low dimensional space of the number of stimuli, and therefore the number of trials of data needed for each stimulus is of the order of the number of stimuli, which is feasible in experiments. In practice, it is found that for accurate information estimates with the decoding approach, the number of trials for each stimulus should be at least twice the number of stimuli (Franco, Rolls, Aggelopoulos and Treves 2004).

The nature of the decoding procedure is illustrated in Fig. C.3. The left part of the diagram shows the average firing rate (or equivalently spike count) responses of each of 3 cells (labelled as Rate Cell 1,2,3) to a set of 3 stimuli. The last row (labelled Response single trial) shows the data that might be obtained from a single trial and from which the stimulus that was shown (St. ?) must be estimated or decoded, using the average values across trials shown in the top part of the table, and the probability distribution of these values. The decoding step essentially compares the vector of responses on trial St.? with the average response vectors obtained previously to each stimulus. This decoding can be as simple as measuring the correlation, or dot (inner) product, between the test trial vector of responses and the response vectors to each of the stimuli. This procedure is very neuronally plausible, in that the dot product between an input vector of neuronal activity and the synaptic response vector on a single neuron (which might represent the average incoming activity previously to that stimulus) is the simplest operation that it is conceived that neurons might perform (Rolls and Treves 1998, Rolls and Deco 2002). Other decoding procedures include a Bayesian procedure based on a Gaussian or Poisson assumption of the spike count distributions as described in detail by Rolls, Treves and Tovee (1997b). The Gaussian one is what we have used (Franco, Rolls, Aggelopoulos and Treves 2004, Aggelopoulos, Franco and Rolls 2005), and it is described below.

The new step taken by Franco, Rolls, Aggelopoulos and Treves (2004) is to introduce into the Table Data(s, r) shown in the upper part of Fig. C.3 new columns, shown on the

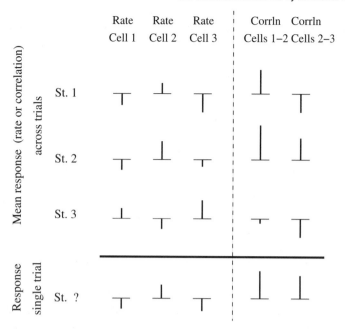

Fig. C.3 The left part of the diagram shows the average firing rate (or equivalently spike count) responses of each of 3 cells (labelled as Rate Cell 1,2,3) to a set of 3 stimuli. The right two columns show a measure of the cross-correlation (averaged across trials) for some pairs of cells (labelled as Corrln Cells 1–2 and 2–3). The last row (labelled Response single trial) shows the data that might be obtained from a single trial and from which the stimulus that was shown (St. ? or s') must be estimated or decoded, using the average values across trials shown in the top part of the table. From the responses on the single trial, the most probable decoded stimulus is stimulus 2, based on the values of both the rates and the cross-correlations. (After Franco, Rolls, Aggelopoulos and Treves 2004.)

right of the diagram, containing a measure of the cross-correlation (averaged across trials in the upper part of the table) for some pairs of cells (labelled as Corrln Cells 1–2 and 2–3). The decoding procedure can then take account of any cross-correlations between pairs of cells, and thus measure any contributions to the information from the population of cells that arise from cross-correlations between the neuronal responses. If these cross-correlations are stimulus-dependent, then their positive contribution to the information encoded can be measured. This is the new concept for information measurement from neuronal populations introduced by Franco, Rolls, Aggelopoulos and Treves (2004). We describe next how the cross-correlation information can be introduced into the Table, and then how the information analysis algorithm can be used to measure the contribution of different factors in the neuronal responses to the information that the population encodes.

To test different hypotheses, the decoding can be based on all the columns of the Table (to provide the total information available from both the firing rates and the stimulus-dependent synchronization), on only the columns with the firing rates (to provide the information available from the firing rates), and only on the columns with the cross-correlation values (to provide the information available from the stimulus-dependent cross-correlations). Any information from stimulus-dependent cross-correlations will not necessarily be orthogonal to the rate information, and the procedures allow this to be checked by comparing the total information to that from the sum of the two components. If cross-correlations are present but are not stimulus-dependent, these will not contribute to the information available about which stimulus was shown.

The measure of the synchronization introduced into the Table Data(s, r) on each trial is, for example, the value of the Pearson cross-correlation coefficient calculated for that trial at the appropriate lag for cell pairs that have significant cross-correlations (Franco, Rolls, Aggelopoulos and Treves 2004). This value of this Pearson cross-correlation coefficient for a single trial can be calculated from pairs of spike trains on a single trial by forming for each cell a vector of 0s and 1s, the 1s representing the time of occurrence of spikes with a temporal resolution of 1 ms. Resulting values within the range -1 to 1 are shifted to obtain positive values. An advantage of basing the measure of synchronization on the Pearson cross-correlation coefficient is that it measures the amount of synchronization between a pair of neurons independently of the firing rate of the neurons. The lag at which the cross-correlation measure was computed for every single trial, and whether there was a significant cross-correlation between neuron pairs, can be identified from the location of the peak in the cross-correlogram taken across all trials. The cross-correlogram is calculated by, for every spike that occurred in one neuron, incrementing the bins of a histogram that correspond to the lag times of each of the spikes that occur for the other neuron. The raw cross-correlogram is corrected by subtracting the "shift predictor" cross-correlogram (which is produced by random re-pairings of the trials), to produce the corrected cross-correlogram.

Further details of the decoding procedures are as follows (see Rolls, Treves and Tovee (1997b) and Franco, Rolls, Aggelopoulos and Treves (2004)). The full probability table estimator (PE) algorithm uses a Bayesian approach to extract $P(s'|\mathbf{r})$ for every single trial from an estimate of the probability $P(\mathbf{r}|s')$ of a stimulus–response pair made from all the other trials (as shown in Bayes' rule shown in equation C.34) in a cross-validation procedure described by Rolls et al. (1997b).

$$P(s'|\mathbf{r}) = \frac{P(\mathbf{r}|s')P(s')}{P(\mathbf{r})}. \tag{C.34}$$

where $P(\mathbf{r})$ (the probability of the vector containing the firing rate of each neuron, where each element of the vector is the firing rate of one neuron) is obtained as:

$$P(\mathbf{r}) = \sum_{s'} P(\mathbf{r}|s')P(s'). \tag{C.35}$$

This requires knowledge of the response probabilities $P(\mathbf{r}|s')$ which can be estimated for this purpose from $P(\mathbf{r}, s')$, which is equal to $P(s') \prod_c P(r_c|s')$, where r_c is the firing rate of cell c. We note that $P(r_c|s')$ is derived from the responses of cell c from all of the trials except for the current trial for which the probability estimate is being made. The probabilities $P(r_c|s')$ are fitted with a Gaussian (or Poisson) distribution whose amplitude at r_c gives $P(r_c|s')$. By summing over different test trial responses to the same stimulus s, we can extract the probability that by presenting stimulus s the neuronal response is interpreted as having been elicited by stimulus s',

$$P(s'|s) = \sum_{\mathbf{r} \in \text{test}} P(s'|\mathbf{r})P(\mathbf{r}|s). \tag{C.36}$$

After the decoding procedure, the estimated relative probabilities (normalized to 1) were averaged over all 'test' trials for all stimuli, to generate a (Regularized) table $P^R{}_N(s, s')$ describing the relative probability of each pair of actual stimulus s and posited stimulus s' (computed with N trials). From this probability table the mutual information measure (I_p) was calculated as described above in equation C.33.

We also generate a second (Frequency) table $P^F{}_N(s, s^P)$ from the fraction of times an actual stimulus s elicited a response that led to a predicted (single most likely) stimulus s^P.

From this probability Table the mutual information measure based on maximum likelihood decoding (I_{ml}) was calculated with equation C.37:

$$< I_{ml} > = \sum_{s \in S} \sum_{s^P \in S} P(s, s^P) \log_2 \frac{P(s, s^P)}{P(s)P(s^P)} .$$
(C.37)

A detailed comparison of maximum likelihood and probability decoding is provided by Rolls, Treves and Tovee (1997b), but we note here that probability estimate decoding is more regularized (see below) and therefore may be safer to use when investigating the effect on the information of the number of cells. For this reason, the results described by Franco, Rolls, Aggelopoulos and Treves (2004) were obtained with probability estimation (PE) decoding. The maximum likelihood decoding does give an immediate measure of the percentage correct.

Another approach to decoding is the dot product (DP) algorithm which computes the normalized dot products between the current firing vector **r** on a "test" (i.e. the current) trial and each of the mean firing rate response vectors in the "training" trials for each stimulus s' in the cross-validation procedure. (The normalized dot product is the dot or inner product of two vectors divided by the product of the length of each vector. The length of each vector is the square root of the sum of the squares.) Thus, what is computed are the cosines of the angles of the test vector of cell rates with, in turn for each stimulus, the mean response vector to that stimulus. The highest dot product indicates the most likely stimulus that was presented, and this is taken as the predicted stimulus s^P for the probability table $P(s, s^P)$. (It can also be used to provide percentage correct measures.)

We note that any decoding procedure can be used in conjunction with information estimates both from the full probability table (to produce I_p), and from the most likely estimated stimulus for each trial (to produce I_{ml}).

Because the probability tables from which the information is calculated may be unregularized with a small number of trials, a bias correction procedure to correct for the undersampling is applied, as described in detail by Rolls, Treves and Tovee (1997b) and Panzeri and Treves (1996). In practice, the bias correction that is needed with information estimates using the decoding procedures described by Franco, Rolls, Aggelopoulos and Treves (2004) and by Rolls et al. (1997b) is small, typically less than 10% of the uncorrected estimate of the information, provided that the number of trials for each stimulus is in the order of twice the number of stimuli. We also note that the distortion in the information estimate from the full probability table needs less bias correction than that from the predicted stimulus table (i.e. maximum likelihood) method, as the former is more regularized because every trial makes some contribution through much of the probability table (see Rolls et al. (1997b)). We further note that the bias correction term becomes very small when more than 10 cells are included in the analysis (Rolls et al. 1997b).

Examples of the use of these procedures are available (Franco, Rolls, Aggelopoulos and Treves 2004, Aggelopoulos, Franco and Rolls 2005), and some of the results obtained are described in Section C.3.

C.2.5 Information in the correlations between the spikes of different cells: a second derivative approach

Another information theory-based approach to stimulus-dependent cross-correlation information has been developed as follows by Panzeri, Schultz, Treves and Rolls (1999a) and Rolls, Franco, Aggelopoulos and Reece (2003b). A problem that must be overcome is the fact that with many simultaneously recorded neurons, each emitting perhaps many spikes at different times, the dimensionality of the response space becomes very large, the information tends to be overestimated, and even bias corrections cannot save the situation. The approach described in this Section (C.2.5) limits the problem by taking short time epochs for the information analysis, in which low numbers of spikes, in practice typically 0, 1, or 2, spikes are likely to occur from each neuron.

In a sufficiently short time window, at most two spikes are emitted from a population of neurons. Taking advantage of this, the response probabilities can be calculated in terms of pairwise correlations. These response probabilities are inserted into the Shannon information formula C.38 to obtain expressions quantifying the impact of the pairwise correlations on the information $I(t)$ transmitted in a short time t by groups of spiking neurons:

$$I(t) = \sum_{s \in S} \sum_{\mathbf{r}} P(s, \mathbf{r}) \log_2 \frac{P(s, \mathbf{r})}{P(s)P(\mathbf{r})} \tag{C.38}$$

where $\mathbf{r}$ is the firing rate response vector comprised by the number of spikes emitted by each of the cells in the population in the short time t, and $P(s, \mathbf{r})$ refers to the joint probability distribution of stimuli with their respective neuronal response vectors.

The information depends upon the following two types of correlation:

C.2.5.1 The correlations in the neuronal response variability from the average to each stimulus (sometimes called "noise" correlations) γ:

$\gamma_{ij}(s)$ (for $i \neq j$) is the fraction of coincidences above (or below) that expected from uncorrelated responses, relative to the number of coincidences in the uncorrelated case (which is $\bar{n}_i(s)\bar{n}_j(s)$, the bar denoting the average across trials belonging to stimulus s, where $n_i(s)$ is the number of spikes emitted by cell i to stimulus s on a given trial)

$$\gamma_{ij}(s) = \frac{\overline{n_i(s)n_j(s)}}{(\bar{n}_i(s)\bar{n}_j(s))} - 1, \tag{C.39}$$

and is named the 'scaled cross-correlation density'. It can vary from -1 to ∞; negative $\gamma_{ij}(s)$'s indicate anticorrelation, whereas positive $\gamma_{ij}(s)$'s indicate correlation[47]. $\gamma_{ij}(s)$ can be thought of as the amount of trial by trial concurrent firing of the cells i and j, compared to that expected in the uncorrelated case. $\gamma_{ij}(s)$ (for $i \neq j$) is the 'scaled cross-correlation density' (Aertsen, Gerstein, Habib and Palm 1989, Panzeri, Schultz, Treves and Rolls 1999a), and is sometimes called the "noise" correlation (Gawne and Richmond 1993, Shadlen and Newsome 1994, Shadlen and Newsome 1998).

C.2.5.2 The correlations in the mean responses of the neurons across the set of stimuli (sometimes called "signal" correlations) ν:

---

[47] $\gamma_{ij}(s)$ is an alternative, which produces a more compact information analysis, to the neuronal cross-correlation based on the Pearson correlation coefficient $\rho_{ij}(s)$ (equation C.40), which normalizes the number of coincidences above independence to the standard deviation of the number of coincidences expected if the cells were independent. The normalization used by the Pearson correlation coefficient has the advantage that it quantifies the strength of correlations between neurons in a rate-independent way. For the information analysis, it is more convenient to use the scaled correlation density $\gamma_{ij}(s)$ than the Pearson correlation coefficient, because of the compactness of the resulting formulation, and because of its scaling properties for small t. $\gamma_{ij}(s)$ remains finite as $t \to 0$, thus by using this measure we can keep the t expansion of the information explicit. Keeping the time-dependence of the resulting information components explicit greatly increases the amount of insight obtained from the series expansion. In contrast, the Pearson noise-correlation measure applied to short timescales approaches zero at short time windows:

$$\rho_{ij}(s) \equiv \frac{\overline{n_i(s)n_j(s)} - \bar{n}_i(s)\bar{n}_j(s)}{\sigma_{n_i(s)}\sigma_{n_j(s)}} \simeq t\,\gamma_{ij}(s)\,\sqrt{\bar{r}_i(s)\bar{r}_j(s)}, \tag{C.40}$$

where $\sigma_{n_i(s)}$ is the standard deviation of the count of spikes emitted by cell i in response to stimulus s.

$$\nu_{ij} = \frac{< \overline{n}_i(s)\overline{n}_j(s) >_s}{< \overline{n}_i(s) >_s < \overline{n}_j(s) >_s} - 1 = \frac{< \overline{r}_i(s)\overline{r}_j(s) >_s}{< \overline{r}_i(s) >_s < \overline{r}_j(s) >_s} - 1 \quad \text{(C.41)}$$

where $\overline{r}_i(s)$ is the mean rate of response of cell i (among C cells in total) to stimulus s over all the trials in which that stimulus was present. ν_{ij} can be thought of as the degree of similarity in the mean response profiles (averaged across trials) of the cells i and j to different stimuli. ν_{ij} is sometimes called the "signal" correlation (Gawne and Richmond 1993, Shadlen and Newsome 1994, Shadlen and Newsome 1998).

C.2.5.3 Information in the cross-correlations in short time periods

In the short timescale limit, the first (I_t) and second (I_{tt}) information derivatives describe the information $I(t)$ available in the short time t

$$I(t) = t \, I_t + \frac{t^2}{2} \, I_{tt} \; . \quad \text{(C.42)}$$

(The zeroth order, time-independent term is zero, as no information can be transmitted by the neurons in a time window of zero length. Higher order terms are also excluded as they become negligible.)

The instantaneous information rate I_t is[48]

$$I_t = \sum_{i=1}^{C} \left\langle \overline{r}_i(s) \log_2 \frac{\overline{r}_i(s)}{\langle \overline{r}_i(s') \rangle_{s'}} \right\rangle_s \; . \quad \text{(C.43)}$$

This formula shows that this information rate (the first time derivative) should not be linked to a high signal to noise ratio, but only reflects the extent to which the mean responses of each cell are distributed across stimuli. It does not reflect anything of the variability of those responses, that is of their noisiness, nor anything of the correlations among the mean responses of different cells.

The effect of (pairwise) correlations between the cells begins to be expressed in the second time derivative of the information. The expression for the instantaneous information 'acceleration' I_{tt} (the second time derivative of the information) breaks up into three terms:

$$\begin{aligned}
I_{tt} = &\frac{1}{\ln 2} \sum_{i=1}^{C} \sum_{j=1}^{C} \langle \overline{r}_i(s) \rangle_s \langle \overline{r}_j(s) \rangle_s \left[\nu_{ij} + (1 + \nu_{ij}) \ln\left(\frac{1}{1 + \nu_{ij}}\right) \right] \\
&+ \sum_{i=1}^{C} \sum_{j=1}^{C} \left[\langle \overline{r}_i(s)\overline{r}_j(s)\gamma_{ij}(s) \rangle_s \right] \log_2\left(\frac{1}{1 + \nu_{ij}}\right) \\
&+ \sum_{i=1}^{C} \sum_{j=1}^{C} \left\langle \overline{r}_i(s)\overline{r}_j(s)(1 + \gamma_{ij}(s)) \log_2 \left[\frac{(1 + \gamma_{ij}(s)) \langle \overline{r}_i(s')\overline{r}_j(s') \rangle_{s'}}{\langle \overline{r}_i(s')\overline{r}_j(s')(1 + \gamma_{ij}(s')) \rangle_{s'}} \right] \right\rangle_s .
\end{aligned} \quad \text{(C.44)}$$

The first of these terms is all that survives if there is no noise correlation at all. Thus the *rate component* of the information is given by the sum of I_t (which is always greater than or equal to zero) and of the first term of I_{tt} (which is instead always less than or equal to zero).

The second term is non-zero if there is some correlation in the variance to a given stimulus, even if it is independent of which stimulus is present; this term thus represents the contribution of *stimulus-independent noise correlation* to the information.

---

[48]Note that s' is used in equations C.43 and C.44 just as a dummy variable to stand for s, as there are two summations performed over s.

The third component of I_{tt} represents the contribution of *stimulus-modulated noise correlation*, as it becomes non-zero only for stimulus-dependent noise correlations. These last two terms of I_{tt} together are referred to as the correlational components of the information.

The application of this approach to measuring the information in the relative time of firing of simultaneously recorded cells, together with further details of the method, are described by Panzeri, Treves, Schultz and Rolls (1999b), Rolls, Franco, Aggelopoulos and Reece (2003b), and Rolls, Aggelopoulos, Franco and Treves (2004), and in Section C.3.7.

C.3   Neuronal encoding: results obtained from applying information-theoretic analyses

How is information encoded in cortical areas such as the inferior temporal visual cortex? Can we read the code being used by the cortex? What are the advantages of the encoding scheme used for the neuronal network computations being performed in different areas of the cortex? These are some of the key issues considered in this Section (C.3). Because information is exchanged between the computing elements of the cortex (the neurons) by their spiking activity, which is conveyed by their axon to synapses onto other neurons, the appropriate level of analysis is how single neurons, and populations of single neurons, encode information in their firing. More global measures that reflect the averaged activity of large numbers of neurons (for example, PET (positron emission tomography) and fMRI (functional magnetic resonance imaging), EEG (electroencephalographic recording), and ERPs (event-related potentials)) cannot reveal how the information is represented, or how the computation is being performed.

Although information theory provides the natural mathematical framework for analysing the performance of neuronal systems, its applications in neuroscience have been for many years rather sparse and episodic (e.g. MacKay and McCulloch (1952); Eckhorn and Popel (1974); Eckhorn and Popel (1975); Eckhorn, Grusser, Kroller, Pellnitz and Popel (1976)). One reason for this limited application of information theory has been the great effort that was apparently required, due essentially to the limited sampling problem, in order to obtain accurate results. Another reason has been the hesitation in analysing as a single complex 'black-box' large neuronal systems all the way from some external, easily controllable inputs, up to neuronal activity in some central cortical area of interest, for example including all visual stations from the periphery to the end of the ventral visual stream in the temporal lobe. In fact, two important bodies of work, that have greatly helped revive interest in applications of the theory in recent years, both sidestep these two problems. The problem with analyzing a huge black-box is avoided by considering systems at the sensory periphery; the limited sampling problem is avoided either by working with insects, in which sampling can be extensive (Bialek, Rieke, de Ruyter van Steveninck and Warland 1991, de Ruyter van Steveninck and Laughlin 1996, Rieke, Warland, de Ruyter van Steveninck and Bialek 1996), or by utilizing a formal model instead of real data (Atick and Redlich 1990, Atick 1992). Both approaches have provided insightful quantitative analyses that are in the process of being extended to more central mammalian systems (see e.g. Atick, Griffin and Relich (1996)).

In the treatment provided here, we focus on applications to the mammalian brain, using examples from a whole series of investigations on information representation in visual cortical areas, the original papers on which refer to related publications.

C.3.1   The sparseness of the distributed encoding used by the brain

Some of the types of representation that might be found at the neuronal level are summarized next (cf. Section 1.6). A **local representation** is one in which all the information that a particular stimulus or event occurred is provided by the activity of one of the neurons. This is sometimes called a grandmother cell representation, because in a famous example, a single neuron might be active only if one's grandmother was being seen (see Barlow (1995)). A **fully distributed representation** is one in which all the information that a particular stimulus or event occurred is provided by the activity of the full set of neurons. If the neurons are binary (for example, either active or not), the most distributed encoding is when half the neurons are active for any one stimulus or event. A **sparse distributed representation** is a distributed representation in which a small proportion of the neurons is active at any one time.

C.3.1.1   Single neuron sparseness a^s

Equation C.45 defines a measure of the single neuron sparseness, a^s:

$$a^s = \frac{(\sum_{s=1}^{S} y_s/S)^2}{(\sum_{s=1}^{S} y_s^2)/S} \tag{C.45}$$

where y_s is the mean firing rate of the neuron to stimulus s in the set of S stimuli (Rolls and Treves 1998). For a binary representation, a^s is 0.5 for a fully distributed representation, and $1/S$ if a neuron responds to one of a set of S stimuli. Another measure of sparseness is the kurtosis of the distribution, which is the fourth moment of the distribution. It reflects the length of the tail of the distribution. (An actual distribution of the firing rates of a neuron to a set of 65 stimuli is shown in Fig. C.4. The sparseness a^s for this neuron was 0.69 (see Rolls, Treves, Tovee and Panzeri (1997d).)

It is important to understand and quantify the sparseness of representations in the brain, because many of the useful properties of neuronal networks such as generalization and completion only occur if the representations are not local (see Appendix B), and because the value of the sparseness is an important factor in how many memories can be stored in such neural networks. Relatively sparse representations (low values of a^s) might be expected in memory systems as this will increase the number of different memories that can be stored and retrieved. Less sparse representations might be expected in sensory systems, as this could allow more information to be represented (see Table B.2).

Barlow (1972) proposed a single neuron doctrine for perceptual psychology. He proposed that sensory systems are organized to achieve as complete a representation as possible with the minimum number of active neurons. He suggested that at progressively higher levels of sensory processing, fewer and fewer cells are active, and that each represents a more and more specific happening in the sensory environment. He suggested that 1,000 active neurons (which he called cardinal cells) might represent the whole of a visual scene. An important principle involved in forming such a representation was the reduction of redundancy. The implication of Barlow's (1972) approach was that when an object is being recognized, there are, towards the end of the visual system, a small number of neurons (the cardinal cells) that are so specifically tuned that the activity of these neurons encodes the information that one particular object is being seen. (He thought that an active neuron conveys something of the order of complexity of a word.) The encoding of information in such a system is described as local, in that knowing the activity of just one neuron provides evidence that a particular stimulus (or, more exactly, a given 'trigger feature') is present. Barlow (1972) eschewed 'combinatorial rules of usage of nerve cells', and believed that the subtlety and sensitivity of perception results from the mechanisms determining when a single cell becomes active. In contrast, with distributed or ensemble encoding, the activity of several or many neurons must be known in order to identify which stimulus is present, that is, to read the code. It is the relative firing of the different neurons in the ensemble that provides the information about which object is present.

At the time Barlow (1972) wrote, there was little actual evidence on the activity of neurons in the higher parts of the visual and other sensory systems. There is now considerable evidence, which is now described.

First, it has been shown that the representation of which particular object (face) is present is actually rather distributed. Baylis, Rolls and Leonard (1985) showed this with the responses of temporal cortical neurons that typically responded to several members of a set of five faces, with each neuron having a different profile of responses to each face (see examples in Fig. 4.14 on page 278). It would be difficult for most of these single cells to tell which of even five faces, let alone which of hundreds of faces, had been seen. (At the same time, the neurons discriminated between the faces reliably, as shown by the values of d', taken, in the case of the neurons, to be the number of standard deviations of the neuronal responses that separated the response to the best face in the set from that to the least effective face in the set. The values of d' were typically in the range 1–3.)

Second, the distributed nature of the representation can be further understood by the finding that the firing rate probability distribution of single neurons, when a wide range of natural visual stimuli are being viewed, is approximately exponential, with rather few stimuli producing high firing rates, and increasingly large numbers of stimuli producing lower and lower firing rates, as illustrated in Fig. C.5a (Rolls and Tovee 1995b, Baddeley, Abbott, Booth, Sengpiel, Freeman, Wakeman and Rolls 1997, Treves, Panzeri, Rolls, Booth and Wakeman 1999, Franco, Rolls, Aggelopoulos and Jerez 2007).

For example, the responses of a set of temporal cortical neurons to 23 faces and 42 non-face natural images were measured, and a distributed representation was found (Rolls and Tovee 1995b). The tuning was typically graded, with a range of different firing rates to the set of faces, and very little response to the non-face stimuli (see example in Fig. C.4). The spontaneous firing rate of the neuron in Fig. C.4 was 20 spikes/s, and the histogram bars indicate the change of firing rate from the spontaneous value produced by each stimulus. Stimuli that are faces are marked F, or P if they are in profile. B refers to images of scenes that included either a small face within the scene, sometimes as part of an image that included a whole person, or other body parts, such as hands (H) or legs. The non-face stimuli are unlabelled. The neuron responded best to three of the faces (profile views), had some response to some of the other faces, and had little or no response, and sometimes had a small decrease of firing rate below the spontaneous firing rate, to the non-face stimuli. The sparseness value a^s for this cell across all 68 stimuli was 0.69, and the response sparseness a^s_r (based on the evoked responses minus the spontaneous firing of the neuron) was 0.19. It was found that the sparseness of the representation of the 68 stimuli by each neuron had an average across all neurons of 0.65 (Rolls and Tovee 1995b). This indicates a rather distributed representation. (If neurons had a continuum of firing rates equally distributed between zero and maximum rate, a^s would be 0.75, while if the probability of each response decreased linearly, to reach zero at the maximum rate, a^s would be 0.67). If the spontaneous firing rate was subtracted from the firing rate of the neuron to each stimulus, so that the changes of firing rate, that is the active responses of the neurons, were used in the sparseness calculation, then the 'response sparseness' a^s_r had a lower value, with a mean of 0.33 for the population of neurons, or 0.60 if calculated over the set of faces rather than over all the face and non-face stimuli. Thus the representation was rather distributed. (It is, of course, important to remember the relative nature of sparseness measures, which (like the information measures to be discussed below)

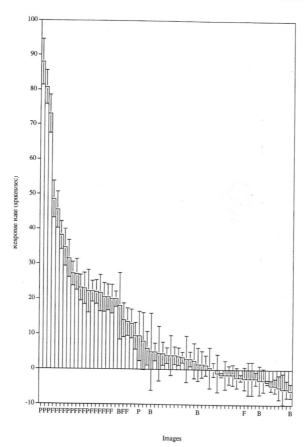

Images

Fig. C.4 Firing rate distribution of a single neuron in the temporal visual cortex to a set of 23 face (F) and 45 non-face images of natural scenes. The firing rate to each of the 68 stimuli is shown. The neuron does not respond to just one of the 68 stimuli. Instead, it responds to a small proportion of stimuli with high rates, to more stimuli with intermediate rates, and to many stimuli with almost no change of firing. This is typical of the distributed representations found in temporal cortical visual areas. (After Rolls and Tovee 1995b.)

depend strongly on the stimulus set used.) Thus we can reject a cardinal cell representation. As shown below, the readout of information from these cells is actually much better in any case than would be obtained from a local representation, and this makes it unlikely that there is a further population of neurons with very specific tuning that use local encoding.

These data provide a clear answer to whether these neurons are grandmother cells: they are not, in the sense that each neuron has a graded set of responses to the different members of a set of stimuli, with the prototypical distribution similar to that of the neuron illustrated in Fig. C.4. On the other hand, each neuron does respond very much more to some stimuli than to many others, and in this sense is tuned to some stimuli.

Figure C.5 shows data of the type shown in Fig. C.4 as firing rate probability density functions, that is as the probability that the neuron will be firing with particular rates. These data were from inferior temporal cortex neurons, and show when tested with a set of 20 face and non-face stimuli how fast the neuron will be firing in a period 100–300 ms after the visual stimulus appears (Franco, Rolls, Aggelopoulos and Jerez 2007). Figure C.5a shows an example of a neuron where the data fit an exponential firing rate probability distribution, with

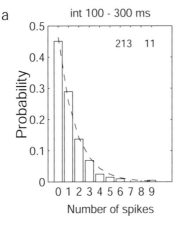 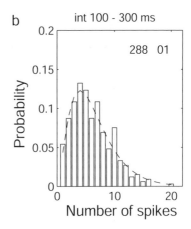

Fig. C.5 Firing rate probability distributions for two neurons in the inferior temporal visual cortex tested with a set of 20 face and non-face stimuli. (a) A neuron with a good fit to an exponential probability distribution (dashed line). (b) A neuron that did not fit an exponential firing rate distribution (but which could be fitted by a gamma distribution, dashed line). The firing rates were measured in an interval 100–300 ms after the onset of the visual stimuli, and similar distributions are obtained in other intervals. (After Franco, Rolls, Aggelopoulos and Jerez 2007.)

many occasions on which the neuron was firing with a very low firing rate, and decreasingly few occasions on which it fired at higher rates. This shows that the neuron can have high firing rates, but only to a few stimuli. Figure C.5b shows an example of a neuron where the data do not fit an exponential firing rate probability distribution, with insufficiently few very low rates. Of the 41 responsive neurons in this data set, 15 had a good fit to an exponential firing rate probability distribution; the other 26 neurons did not fit an exponential but did fit a gamma distribution in the way illustrated in Fig. C.5b. For the neurons with an exponential distribution, the mean firing rate across the stimulus set was 5.7 spikes/s, and for the neurons with a gamma distribution was 21.1 spikes/s ($t=4.5$, $df=25$, $p< 0.001$). It may be that neurons with high mean rates to a stimulus set tend to have few low rates ever, and this accounts for their poor fit to an exponential firing rate probability distribution, which fits when there are many low firing rate values in the distribution as in Fig. C.5a.

The large set of 68 stimuli used by Rolls and Tovee (1995b) was chosen to produce an approximation to a set of stimuli that might be found to natural stimuli in a natural environment, and thus to provide evidence about the firing rate distribution of neurons to natural stimuli. Another approach to the same fundamental question was taken by Baddeley, Abbott, Booth, Sengpiel, Freeman, Wakeman, and Rolls (1997) who measured the firing rates over short periods of individual inferior temporal cortex neurons while monkeys watched continuous videos of natural scenes. They found that the firing rates of the neurons were again approximately exponentially distributed (see Fig. C.6), providing further evidence that this type of representation is characteristic of inferior temporal cortex (and indeed also V1) neurons.

The actual distribution of the firing rates to a wide set of natural stimuli is of interest, because it has a rather stereotypical shape, typically following a graded unimodal distribution with a long tail extending to high rates (see for example Figs. C.5a and C.6). The mode of the distribution is close to the spontaneous firing rate, and sometimes it is at zero firing. If the number of spikes recorded in a fixed time window is taken to be constrained by a fixed maximum rate, one can try to interpret the distribution observed in terms of optimal inform-ation transmission (Shannon 1948), by making the additional assumption that the coding

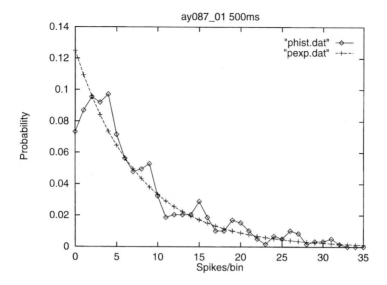

Fig. C.6 The probability of different firing rates measured in short (e.g. 100 ms or 500 ms) time windows of a temporal cortex neuron calculated over a 5 min period in which the macaque watched a video showing natural scenes, including faces. An exponential fit (+) to the data (diamonds) is shown. (After Baddeley, Abbott, Booth, Sengpiel, Freeman, Wakeman and Rolls 1997.)

is noiseless. An exponential distribution, which maximizes entropy (and hence information transmission for noiseless codes) is the most efficient in terms of energy consumption if its mean takes an optimal value that is a decreasing function of the relative metabolic cost of emitting a spike (Levy and Baxter 1996). This argument would favour sparser coding schemes the more energy expensive neuronal firing is (relative to rest). Although the tail of actual firing rate distributions is often approximately exponential (see for example Figs. C.5a and C.6; Baddeley, Abbott, Booth, Sengpiel, Freeman, Wakeman and Rolls (1997); Rolls, Treves, Tovee and Panzeri (1997d); and Franco, Rolls, Aggelopoulos and Jerez (2007)), the maximum entropy argument cannot apply as such, because noise is present and the noise level varies as a function of the rate, which makes entropy maximization different from information maximization. Moreover, a mode at low but non-zero rate, which is often observed (see e.g. Fig. C.5b), is inconsistent with the energy efficiency hypothesis.

A simpler explanation for the characteristic firing rate distribution arises by appreciating that the value of the activation of a neuron across stimuli, reflecting a multitude of contributing factors, will typically have a Gaussian distribution; and by considering a physiological input–output transform (i.e. activation function), and realistic noise levels. In fact, an input–output transform that is supralinear in a range above threshold results from a fundamentally linear transform and fluctuations in the activation, and produces a variance in the output rate, across repeated trials, that increases with the rate itself, consistent with common observations. At the same time, such a supralinear transform tends to convert the Gaussian tail of the activation distribution into an approximately exponential tail, without implying a fully exponential distribution with the mode at zero. Such basic assumptions yield excellent fits with observed distributions (Treves, Panzeri, Rolls, Booth and Wakeman 1999), which often differ from exponential in that there are too few very low rates observed, and too many low rates (Rolls, Treves, Tovee and Panzeri 1997d, Franco, Rolls, Aggelopoulos and Jerez 2007).

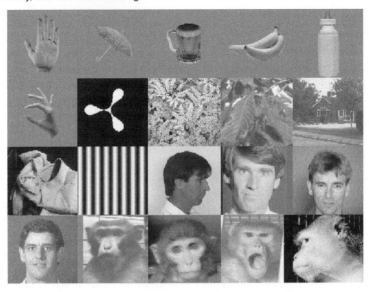

Fig. C.7 The set of 20 stimuli used to investigate the tuning of inferior temporal cortex neurons by Franco, Rolls, Aggelopoulos and Jerez 2007. These objects and faces are typical of those encoded in the ways described here by inferior temporal cortex neurons. The code can be read off simply from the firing rates of the neurons about which object or face was shown, and many of the neurons have invariant responses.

This peak at low but non-zero rates may be related to the low firing rate spontaneous activity that is typical of many cortical neurons. Keeping the neurons close to threshold in this way may maximize the speed with which a network can respond to new inputs (because time is not required to bring the neurons from a strongly hyperpolarized state up to threshold). The advantage of having low spontaneous firing rates may be a further reason why a curve such as an exponential cannot sometimes be exactly fitted to the experimental data.

A conclusion of this analysis was that the firing rate distribution may arise from the threshold non-linearity of neurons combined with short-term variability in the responses of neurons (Treves, Panzeri, Rolls, Booth and Wakeman 1999).

However, given that the firing rate distribution for some neurons is approximately exponential, some properties of this type of representation are worth elucidation. The sparseness of such an exponential distribution of firing rates is 0.5. This has interesting implications, for to the extent that the firing rates are exponentially distributed, this fixes an important parameter of cortical neuronal encoding to be close to 0.5. Indeed, only one parameter specifies the shape of the exponential distribution, and the fact that the exponential distribution is at least a close approximation to the firing rate distribution of some real cortical neurons implies that the sparseness of the cortical representation of stimuli is kept under precise control. The utility of this may be to ensure that any neuron receiving from this representation can perform a dot product operation between its inputs and its synaptic weights that produces similarly distributed outputs; and that the information being represented by a population of cortical neurons is kept high. It is interesting to realize that the representation that is stored in an associative network (see Appendix B) may be more sparse than the 0.5 value for an exponential firing rate distribution, because the non-linearity of learning introduced by the voltage dependence of the NMDA receptors (see Appendix B) effectively means that synaptic modification in, for example, an autoassociative network will occur only for the neurons with relatively high firing rates, i.e. for those that are strongly depolarized.

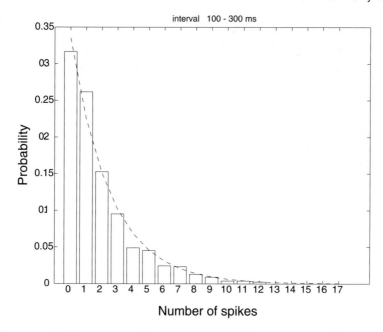

Fig. C.8 An exponential firing rate probability distribution obtained by pooling the firing rates of a population of 41 inferior temporal cortex neurons tested to a set of 20 face and non-face stimuli. The firing rate probability distribution for the 100–300 ms interval following stimulus onset was formed by adding the spike counts from all 41 neurons, and across all stimuli. The fit to the exponential distribution (dashed line) was high. (After Franco, Rolls, Aggelopoulos and Jerez 2007.)

The single neuron selectivity reflects response distributions of individual neurons across time to different stimuli. As we have seen, part of the interest of measuring the firing rate probability distributions of individual neurons is that one form of the probability distribution, the exponential, maximizes the entropy of the neuronal responses for a given mean firing rate, which could be used to maximize information transmission consistent with keeping the firing rate on average low, in order to minimize metabolic expenditure (Levy and Baxter 1996, Baddeley, Abbott, Booth, Sengpiel, Freeman, Wakeman and Rolls 1997). Franco, Rolls, Aggelopoulos and Jerez (2007) showed that while the firing rates of some single inferior temporal cortex neurons (tested in a visual fixation task to a set of 20 face and non-face stimuli illustrated in Fig. C.7) do fit an exponential distribution, and others with higher spontaneous firing rates do not, as described above, it turns out that there is a very close fit to an exponential distribution of firing rates if all spikes from all the neurons are considered together. This interesting result is shown in Fig. C.8.

One implication of the result shown in Fig. C.8 is that a neuron with inputs from the inferior temporal visual cortex will receive an exponential distribution of firing rates on its afferents, and this is therefore the type of input that needs to be considered in theoretical models of neuronal network function in the brain (see Appendix B). The second implication is that at the level of single neurons, an exponential probability density function is consistent with minimizing energy utilization, and maximizing information transmission, for a given mean firing rate (Levy and Baxter 1996, Baddeley, Abbott, Booth, Sengpiel, Freeman, Wakeman and Rolls 1997).

C.3.1.2 Population sparseness a^p

If instead we consider the responses of a population of neurons taken at any one time (to one stimulus), we might also expect a sparse graded distribution, with few neurons firing fast to a particular stimulus. It is important to measure the population sparseness, for this is a key parameter that influences the number of different stimuli that can be stored and retrieved in networks such as those found in the cortex with recurrent collateral connections between the excitatory neurons, which can form autoassociation or attractor networks if the synapses are associatively modifiable (Hopfield 1982, Treves and Rolls 1991, Rolls and Treves 1998, Rolls and Deco 2002) (see Appendix B). Further, in physics, if one can predict the distribution of the responses of the system at any one time (the population level) from the distribution of the responses of a component of the system across time, the system is described as ergodic, and a necessary condition for this is that the components are uncorrelated (Lehky, Sejnowski and Desimone 2005). Considering this in neuronal terms, the average sparseness of a population of neurons over multiple stimulus inputs must equal the average selectivity to the stimuli of the single neurons within the population provided that the responses of the neurons are uncorrelated (Földiák 2003).

The sparseness a^p of the population code may be quantified (for any one stimulus) as

$$a^p = \frac{(\sum\limits_{n=1}^{N} y_n/N)^2}{(\sum\limits_{n=1}^{N} y_n^2)/N} \tag{C.46}$$

where y_n is the mean firing rate of neuron n in the set of N neurons.

This measure, a^p, of the sparseness of the representation of a stimulus by a population of neurons has a number of advantages. One is that it is the same measure of sparseness that has proved to be useful and tractable in formal analyses of the capacity of associative neural networks and the interference between stimuli that use an approach derived from theoretical physics (Rolls and Treves 1990, Treves 1990, Treves and Rolls 1991, Rolls and Treves 1998) (see Appendix B). We note that high values of a^p indicate broad tuning of the population, and that low values of a^p indicate sparse population encoding.

Franco, Rolls, Aggelopoulos and Jerez (2007) measured the population sparseness of a set of 29 inferior temporal cortex neurons to a set of 20 stimuli that included faces and objects (see Fig. C.7). Figure C.9a shows, for any one stimulus picked at random, the normalized firing rates of the population of neurons. The rates are ranked with the neuron with the highest rate on the left. For different stimuli, the shape of this distribution is on average the same, though with the neurons in a different order. (The rates of each neuron were normalized to a mean of 10 spikes/s before this graph was made, so that the neurons can be combined in the same graph, and so that the population sparseness has a defined value, as described by Franco, Rolls, Aggelopoulos and Jerez (2007).) The population sparseness a^p of this normalized (i.e. scaled) set of firing rates is 0.77.

Figure C.9b shows the probability distribution of the normalized firing rates of the population of (29) neurons to any stimulus from the set. This was calculated by taking the probability distribution of the data shown in Fig. C.9a. This distribution is not exponential because of the normalization of the firing rates of each neuron, but becomes exponential as shown in Fig. C.8 without the normalization step.

A very interesting finding of Franco, Rolls, Aggelopoulos and Jerez (2007) was that when the single cell sparseness a^s and the population sparseness a^p were measured from the same set of neurons in the same experiment, the values were very close, in this case 0.77. (This

a

b

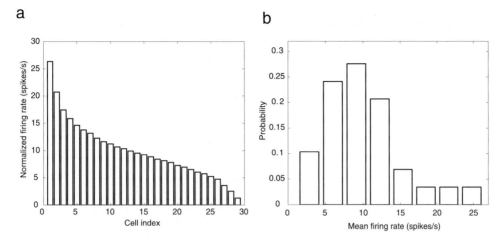

Fig. C.9 Population sparseness. (a) The firing rates of a population of inferior temporal cortex neurons to any one stimulus from a set of 20 face and non-face stimuli. The rates of each neuron were normalized to the same average value of 10 spikes/s, then for each stimulus, the cell firing rates were placed in rank order, and then the mean firing rates of the first ranked cell, second ranked cell, etc. were taken. The graph thus shows how, for any one stimulus picked at random, the expected normalized firing rates of the population of neurons. (b) The population normalized firing rate probability distributions for any one stimulus. This was computed effectively by taking the probability density function of the data shown in (a). (After Franco, Rolls, Aggelopoulos and Jerez 2007.)

was found for a range of measurement intervals after stimulus onset, and also for a larger population of 41 neurons.)

The single cell sparseness a^s and the population sparseness a^p can take the same value if the response profiles of the neurons are uncorrelated, that is each neuron is independently tuned to the set of stimuli (Lehky et al. 2005). Franco, Rolls, Aggelopoulos and Jerez (2007) tested whether the response profiles of the neurons to the set of stimuli were uncorrelated in two ways. In a first test, they found that the mean (Pearson) correlation between the response profiles computed over the 406 neuron pairs was low, 0.049 ± 0.013 (sem). In a second test, they computed how the multiple cell information available from these neurons about which stimulus was shown increased as the number of neurons in the sample was increased, and showed that the information increased approximately linearly with the number of neurons in the ensemble. The implication is that the neurons convey independent (non-redundant) information, and this would be expected to occur if the response profiles of the neurons to the stimuli are uncorrelated.

We now consider the concept of ergodicity. The single neuron selectivity, a^s, reflects response distributions of individual neurons across time and therefore stimuli in the world (and has sometimes been termed "lifetime sparseness"). The population sparseness a^p reflects response distributions across all neurons in a population measured simultaneously (to for example one stimulus). The similarity of the average values of a^s and a^p (both 0.77 for inferior temporal cortex neurons (Franco, Rolls, Aggelopoulos and Jerez 2007)) indicates, we believe for the first time experimentally, that the representation (at least in the inferior temporal cortex) is ergodic. The representation is ergodic in the sense of statistical physics, where the average of a single component (in this context a single neuron) across time is compared with the average of an ensemble of components at one time (cf. Masuda and Aihara (2003) and Lehky et al. (2005)). This is described further next.

In comparing the neuronal selectivities a^s and population sparsenesses a^p, we formed a table in which the columns represent different neurons, and the stimuli different rows (Földiák 2003). We are interested in the probability distribution functions (and not just their summary values a^s, and a^p), of the columns (which represent the individual neuron selectivities) and the rows (which represent the population tuning to any one stimulus). We could call the system strongly ergodic (cf. Lehky et al. (2005)) if the selectivity (probability density or distribution function) of each individual neuron is the same as the average population sparseness (probability density function). (Each neuron would be tuned to different stimuli, but have the same shape of the probability density function.) We have seen that this is not the case, in that the firing rate probability distribution functions of different neurons are different, with some fitting an exponential function, and some a gamma function (see Fig. C.5). We can call the system weakly ergodic if individual neurons have different selectivities (i.e. different response probability density functions), but the average selectivity (measured in our case by $<a^s>$) is the same as the average population sparseness (measured by $<a^p>$), where $<\tilde{a}>$ indicates the ensemble average. We have seen that for inferior temporal cortex neurons are the neuron selectivity probability density functions are different (see Fig. C.5), but that their average $<a^s>$ is the same as the average (across stimuli) $<a^p>$ of the population sparseness, 0.77, and thus conclude that the representation in the inferior temporal visual cortex of objects and faces is weakly ergodic (Franco, Rolls, Aggelopoulos and Jerez 2007).

We note that weak ergodicity necessarily occurs if $<a^s>$ and $<a^p>$ are the same and the neurons are uncorrelated, that is each neuron is independently tuned to the set of stimuli (Lehky et al. 2005). The fact that both hold for the inferior temporal cortex neurons studied by Franco, Rolls, Aggelopoulos and Jerez (2007) thus indicates that their responses are uncorrelated, and this is potentially an important conclusion about the encoding of stimuli by these neurons. This conclusion is confirmed by the linear increase in the information with the number of neurons which is the case not only for this set of neurons (Franco, Rolls, Aggelopoulos and Jerez 2007), but also in other data sets for the inferior temporal visual cortex (Rolls, Treves and Tovee 1997b, Booth and Rolls 1998). Both types of evidence thus indicate that the encoding provided by at least small subsets (up to e.g. 20 neurons) of inferior temporal cortex neurons is approximately independent (non-redundant), which is an important principle of cortical encoding.

C.3.1.3   Comparisons of sparseness between areas: the hippocampus, insula, orbitofrontal cortex, and amygdala

In the study of Franco, Rolls, Aggelopoulos and Jerez (2007) on inferior temporal visual cortex neurons, the selectivity of individual cells for the set of stimuli, or single cell sparseness a^s, had a mean value of 0.77. This is close to a previously measured estimate, 0.65, which was obtained with a larger stimulus set of 68 stimuli (Rolls and Tovee 1995b). Thus the single neuron probability density functions in these areas do not produce very sparse representations. Therefore the goal of the computations in the inferior temporal visual cortex may not be to produce sparse representations (as has been proposed for V1 (Field 1994, Olshausen and Field 1997, Vinje and Gallant 2000, Olshausen and Field 2004)). Instead one of the goals of the computations in the inferior temporal visual cortex may be to compute invariant representations of objects and faces (Rolls 2000a, Rolls and Deco 2002, Rolls 2007i, Rolls and Stringer 2006) (see Chapter 4), and to produce not very sparse distributed representations in order to maximize the information represented (see Table B.2 on page 559). In this context, it is very interesting that the representations of different stimuli provided by a population of inferior temporal cortex neurons are decorrelated, as shown by the finding that the mean (Pearson) correlation between the response profiles to a set of 20 stimuli computed over 406 neuron pairs was low, 0.049 ± 0.013 (sem) (Franco, Rolls, Aggelopoulos and Jerez 2007). The implication is that decorrelation is being achieved in the inferior temporal visual cortex, but not by forming a sparse code. It will be interesting to investigate the mechanisms for this.

In contrast, the representation in some memory systems may be more sparse. For example, in the hippocampus in which spatial view cells are found in macaques, further analysis of data described by Rolls, Treves, Robertson, Georges-François and Panzeri (1998) shows that for the representation of 64 locations around the walls of the room, the mean single cell sparseness $<a^s>$ was 0.34 ± 0.13 (sd), and the mean population sparseness a^p was 0.33 ± 0.11. The more sparse representation is consistent with the view that the hippocampus is involved in storing memories, and that for this, more sparse representations than in perceptual areas are relevant. These sparseness values are for spatial view neurons, but it is possible that when neurons respond to combinations of spatial view and object (Rolls, Xiang and Franco 2005c), or of spatial view and reward (Rolls and Xiang 2005), the representations are more sparse. It is of interest that the mean firing rate of these spatial view neurons across all spatial views was 1.77 spikes/s (Rolls, Treves, Robertson, Georges-François and Panzeri 1998). (The mean spontaneous firing rate of the neurons was 0.1 spikes/s, and the average across neurons of the firing rate for the most effective spatial view was 13.2 spikes/s.) It is also notable that weak ergodicity is implied for this brain region too (given the similar values of $<a^s>$ and $<a^p>$), and the underlying basis for this is that the response profiles of the different hippocampal neurons to the spatial views are uncorrelated. Further support for these conclusions is that the information about spatial view increases linearly with the number of hippocampal spatial view neurons (Rolls, Treves, Robertson, Georges-François and Panzeri 1998), again providing evidence that the response profiles of the different neurons are uncorrelated.

Further evidence is now available on ergodicity in three further brain areas, the macaque insular primary taste cortex, the orbitofrontal cortex, and the amygdala. In all these brain areas sets of neurons were tested with an identical set of 24 oral taste, temperature, and texture stimuli. (The stimuli were: Taste - 0.1 M NaCl (salt), 1 M glucose (sweet), 0.01 M HCl (sour), 0.001 M quinine HCl (bitter), 0.1 M monosodium glutamate (umami), and water; Temperature - 10°C, 37°C and 42°C; flavour - blackcurrant juice; viscosity - carboxymethyl-cellulose 10 cPoise, 100 cPoise, 1000 cPoise and 10000 cPoise; fatty / oily - single cream, vegetable oil, mineral oil, silicone oil (100 cPoise), coconut oil, and safflower oil; fatty acids - linoleic acid and lauric acid; capsaicin; and gritty texture.) Further analysis of data described by Verhagen, Kadohisa and Rolls (2004) showed that in the primary taste cortex the mean value of a^s across 58 neurons was 0.745 and of a^p (normalized) was 0.708. Further analysis of data described by Rolls, Verhagen and Kadohisa (2003e), Verhagen, Rolls and Kadohisa (2003), Kadohisa, Rolls and Verhagen (2004) and Kadohisa, Rolls and Verhagen (2005a) showed that in the orbitofrontal cortex the mean value of a^s across 30 neurons was 0.625 and of a^p was 0.611. Further analysis of data described by Kadohisa, Rolls and Verhagen (2005b) showed that in the amygdala the mean value of a^s across 38 neurons was 0.811 and of a^p was 0.813. Thus in all these cases, the mean value of a^s is close to that of a^p, and weak ergodicity is implied. The values of a^s and a^p are also relatively high, implying the importance of representing large amounts of information in these brain areas about this set of stimuli by using a very distributed code, and also perhaps about the stimulus set, some members of which may be rather similar to each other.

C.3.2 The information from single neurons

Examples of the responses of single neurons (in this case in the inferior temporal visual cortex) to sets of objects and/or faces (of the type illustrated in Fig. C.7) are shown in Figs. 4.13, 4.14 and C.4. We now consider how much information these types of neuronal response convey about the set of stimuli S, and about each stimulus s in the set. The mutual information $I(S, R)$ that the set of responses R encode about the set of stimuli S is calculated with equation C.21

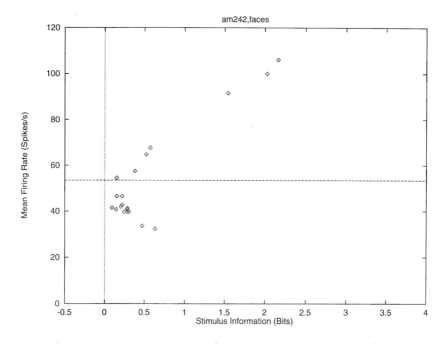

Fig. C.10 The stimulus-specific information $I(s, R)$ available in the response of the same single neuron as in Fig. C.4 about each of the stimuli in the set of 20 face stimuli (abscissa), with the firing rate of the neuron to the corresponding stimulus plotted as a function of this on the ordinate. The horizontal line shows the mean firing rate across all stimuli. (From Rolls, Treves, Tovee and Panzeri 1997.)

and corrected for the limited sampling using the analytic bias correction procedure described by Panzeri and Treves (1996) as described in detail by Rolls, Treves, Tovee and Panzeri (1997d). The information $I(s, R)$ about each single stimulus s in the set S, termed the stimulus-specific information (Rolls, Treves, Tovee and Panzeri 1997d) or stimulus-specific surprise (DeWeese and Meister 1999), obtained from the set of the responses R of the single neuron is calculated with equation C.22 and corrected for the limited sampling using the analytic bias correction procedure described by Panzeri and Treves (1996) as described in detail by Rolls, Treves, Tovee and Panzeri (1997d). (The average of $I(s, R)$ across stimuli is the mutual information $I(S, R)$.)

Figure C.10 shows the stimulus-specific information $I(s, R)$ available in the neuronal response about each of 20 face stimuli calculated for the neuron (am242) whose firing rate response profile to the set of 65 stimuli is shown in Fig. C.4. Unless otherwise stated, the information measures given are for the information available on a single trial from the firing rate of the neuron in a 500 ms period starting 100 ms after the onset of the stimuli. It is shown in Fig. C.10 that 2.2, 2.0, and 1.5 bits of information were present about the three face stimuli to which the neuron had the highest firing rate responses. The neuron conveyed some but smaller amounts of information about the remaining face stimuli. The average information $I(S, R)$ about this set (S) of 20 faces for this neuron was 0.55 bits. The average firing rate of this neuron to these 20 face stimuli was 54 spikes/s. It is clear from Fig. C.10 that little information was available from the responses of the neuron to a particular face stimulus if that response was close to the average response of the neuron across all stimuli. At the same time, it is clear from Fig. C.10 that information was present depending on how far the firing

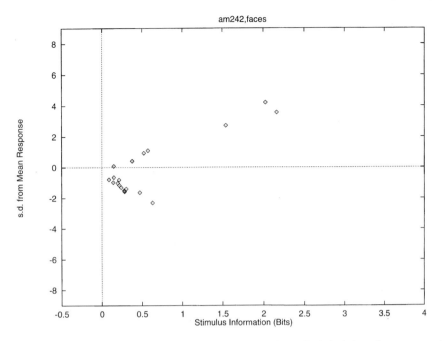

Fig. C.11 The relation for a single cell between the number of standard deviations the response to a stimulus was from the average response to all stimuli (see text, z score) plotted as a function of $I(s, R)$, the information available about the corresponding stimulus, s. (From Rolls, Treves, Tovee and Panzeri 1997, Fig. 2c.)

rate to a particular stimulus was from the average response of the neuron to the stimuli. Of particular interest, it is evident that information is present from the neuronal response about which face was shown if that neuronal response was below the average response, as well as when the response was greater than the average response.

One intuitive way to understand the data shown in Fig. C.10 is to appreciate that low probability firing rate responses, whether they are greater than or less than the mean response rate, convey much information about which stimulus was seen. This is of course close to the definition of information. Given that the firing rates of neurons are always positive, and follow an asymmetric distribution about their mean, it is clear that deviations above the mean have a different probability to occur than deviations by the same amount below the mean. One may attempt to capture the relative likelihood of different firing rates above and below the mean by computing a z score obtained by dividing the difference between the mean response to each stimulus and the overall mean response by the standard deviation of the response to that stimulus. The greater the number of standard deviations (i.e. the greater the z score) from the mean response value, the greater the information might be expected to be. We therefore show in Fig. C.11 the relation between the z score and $I(s, R)$. (The z score was calculated by obtaining the mean and standard deviation of the response of a neuron to a particular stimulus s, and dividing the difference of this response from the mean response to all stimuli by the calculated standard deviation for that stimulus.) This results in a C-shaped curve in Figs. C.10 and C.11, with more information being provided by the cell the further its response to a stimulus is in spikes per second or in z scores either above or below the mean response to all stimuli (which was 54 spikes/s). The specific C-shape is discussed further in Section C.3.4.

The information $I(s, R)$ about each stimulus in the set of 65 stimuli is shown in Fig. C.12 for the same neuron, am242. The 23 face stimuli in the set are indicated by a diamond, and the

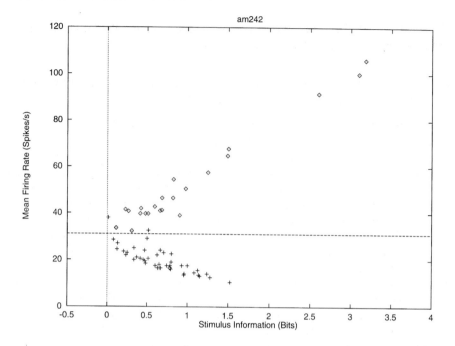

Fig. C.12 The information $I(s, R)$ available in the response of the same neuron about each of the stimuli in the set of 23 face and 42 non-face stimuli (abscissa), with the firing rate of the neuron to the corresponding stimulus plotted as a function of this on the ordinate. The 23 face stimuli in the set are indicated by a diamond, and the 42 non-face stimuli by a cross. The horizontal line shows the mean firing rate across all stimuli. (After Rolls, Treves, Tovee and Panzeri 1997.)

42 non-face stimuli by a cross. Using this much larger and more varied stimulus set, which is more representative of stimuli in the real world, a C-shaped function again describes the relation between the information conveyed by the cell about a stimulus and its firing rate to that stimulus. In particular, this neuron reflected information about most, but not all, of the faces in the set, that is those faces that produced a higher firing rate than the overall mean firing rate to all the 65 stimuli, which was 31 spikes/s. In addition, it conveyed information about the majority of the 42 non-face stimuli by responding at a rate below the overall mean response of the neuron to the 65 stimuli. This analysis usefully makes the point that the information available in the neuronal responses about which stimulus was shown is relative to (dependent upon) the nature and range of stimuli in the test set of stimuli.

The evidence makes it clear that a single cortical visual neuron tuned to faces conveys information not just about one face, but about a whole set of faces, with the information conveyed on a single trial related to the difference in the firing rate response to a particular stimulus compared to the average response to all stimuli.

The analyses just described for neurons with visual responses are general, in that they apply in a very similar way to olfactory neurons recorded in the macaque orbitofrontal cortex (Rolls, Critchley and Treves 1996a).

The neurons in this sample reflected in their firing rates for the post-stimulus period 100 to 600 ms on average 0.36 bits of mutual information about which of 20 face stimuli was presented (Rolls, Treves, Tovee and Panzeri 1997d). Similar values have been found in other experiments (Tovee, Rolls, Treves and Bellis 1993, Tovee and Rolls 1995, Rolls, Tovee and Panzeri 1999b, Rolls, Franco, Aggelopoulos and Jerez 2006b). The information in short temporal epochs of the neuronal responses is described in Section C.3.4.

C.3.3 The information from single neurons: temporal codes versus rate codes within the spike train of a single neuron

In the third of a series of papers that analyze the response of single neurons in the primate inferior temporal cortex to a set of static visual stimuli, Optican and Richmond (1987) applied information theory in a particularly direct and useful way. To ascertain the relevance of stimulus-locked temporal modulations in the firing of those neurons, they compared the amount of information about the stimuli that could be extracted from just the firing rate, computed over a relatively long interval of 384 ms, with the amount of information that could be extracted from a more complete description of the firing, that included temporal modulation. To derive this latter description (the temporal code within the spike train of a single neuron) they applied principal component analysis (PCA) to the temporal response vectors recorded for each neuron on each trial. The PCA helped to reduce the dimensionality of the neuronal response measurements. A temporal response vector was defined as a vector with as components the firing rates in each of 64 successive 6 ms time bins. The (64×64) covariance matrix was calculated across all trials of a particular neuron, and diagonalized. The first few eigenvectors of the matrix, those with the largest eigenvalues, are the principal components of the response, and the weights of each response vector on these four to five components can be used as a reduced description of the response, which still preserves, unlike the single value giving the mean firing rate along the entire interval, the main features of the temporal modulation within the interval. Thus a four- to five-dimensional temporal code could be contrasted with a one-dimensional rate code, and the comparison made quantitative by measuring the respective values for the mutual information with the stimuli.

Although the initial claim (Optican, Gawne, Richmond and Joseph 1991, Eskandar, Richmond and Optican 1992), that the temporal code carried nearly three times as much information as the rate code, was later found to be an artefact of limited sampling, and more recent analyses tend to minimize the additional information in the temporal description (Tovee, Rolls, Treves and Bellis 1993, Heller, Hertz, Kjaer and Richmond 1995), this type of application has immediately appeared straightforward and important, and it has led to many developments. By concentrating on the code expressed in the output rather than on the characterization of the neuronal channel itself, this approach is not affected much by the potential complexities of the preceding black box. Limited sampling, on the other hand, is a problem, particularly because it affects much more codes with a larger number of components, for example the four to five components of the PCA temporal description, than the one-dimensional firing rate code. This is made evident in the paper by Heller, Hertz, Kjaer and Richmond (1995), in which the comparison is extended to several more detailed temporal descriptions, including a binary vector description in which the presence or not of a spike in each 1 ms bin of the response constitutes a component of a 320-dimensional vector. Obviously, this binary vector must contain at least all the information present in the reduced descriptions, whereas in the results of Heller, Hertz, Kjaer and Richmond (1995), despite the use of a sophisticated neural network procedure to control limited sampling biases, the binary vector appears to be the code that carries the least information of all. In practice, with the data samples available in the experiments that have been done, and even when using analytic procedures to control limited sampling (Panzeri and Treves 1996), reliable comparison can be made only with up to two- to three-dimensional codes.

Tovee, Rolls, Treves and Bellis (1993) and Tovee and Rolls (1995) obtained further evidence that little information was encoded in the temporal aspects of firing within the spike train of a single neuron in the inferior temporal cortex by taking short epochs of the firing of neurons, lasting 20 ms or 50 ms, in which the opportunity for temporal encoding would be limited (because there were few spikes in these short time intervals). They found that a considerable proportion (30%) of the information available in a long time period of 400 ms utilizing temporal encoding within the spike train was available in time periods as short as 20 ms when only the number of spikes was taken into account.

Overall, the main result of these analyses applied to the responses to static stimuli in the temporal visual cortex of primates is that not much more information (perhaps only up to 10% more) can be extracted from temporal codes than from the firing rate measured over a judiciously chosen interval (Tovee, Rolls, Treves and Bellis 1993, Heller, Hertz, Kjaer and Richmond 1995). Indeed, it turns out that even this small amount of 'temporal information' is related primarily to the onset latency of the neuronal responses to different stimuli, rather than to anything more subtle (Tovee, Rolls, Treves and Bellis 1993). Consistent with this point, in earlier visual areas the additional 'temporally encoded' fraction of information can be larger, due especially to the increased relevance, earlier on, of precisely locked transient responses (Kjaer, Hertz and Richmond 1994, Golomb, Kleinfeld, Reid, Shapley and Shraiman 1994, Heller, Hertz, Kjaer and Richmond 1995). This is because if the responses to some stimuli are more transient and to others more sustained, this will result in more information if the temporal modulation of the response of the neuron is taken into account. However, the relevance of more substantial temporal codes for static visual stimuli remains to be demonstrated. For non-static visual stimuli and for other cortical systems, similar analyses have largely yet to be carried out, although clearly one expects to find much more prominent temporal effects e.g. in the auditory system (Nelken, Prut, Vaadia and Abeles 1994, deCharms and Merzenich 1996), for reasons similar to those just annunciated.

C.3.4 The information from single neurons: the speed of information transfer

It is intuitive that if short periods of firing of single cells are considered, there is less time for temporal modulation effects. The information conveyed about stimuli by the firing rate and that conveyed by more detailed temporal codes become similar in value. When the firing periods analyzed become shorter than roughly the mean interspike interval, even the statistics of firing rate values on individual trials cease to be relevant, and the information content of the firing depends solely on the mean firing rates across all trials with each stimulus. This is expressed mathematically by considering the amount of information provided as a function of the length t of the time window over which firing is analyzed, and taking the limit for $t \to 0$ (Skaggs, McNaughton, Gothard and Markus 1993, Panzeri, Biella, Rolls, Skaggs and Treves 1996). To first order in t, only two responses can occur in a short window of length t: either the emission of an action potential, with probability tr_s, where r_s is the mean firing rate calculated over many trials using the same window and stimulus; or no action potential, with probability $1 - tr_s$. Inserting these conditional probabilities into equation C.22, taking the limit and dividing by t, one obtains for the derivative of the stimulus-specific transinformation

$$dI(s)/dt = r_s \log_2(r_s/ <r>) + (<r> -r_s)/\ln 2, \qquad (C.47)$$

where $<r>$ is the grand mean rate across stimuli. This formula thus gives the rate, in bits/s, at which information about a stimulus begins to accumulate when the firing of a cell is recorded. Such an information rate depends only on the mean firing rate to that stimulus and on the grand mean rate across stimuli. As a function of r_s, it follows the U-shaped curve in Fig. C.13. The curve is universal, in the sense that it applies irrespective of the detailed firing statistics

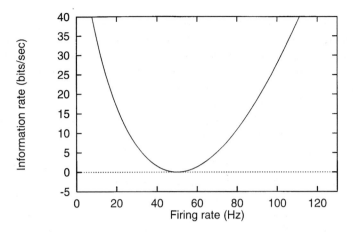

Fig. C.13 Time derivative of the stimulus-specific information as a function of firing rate, for a cell firing at a grand mean rate of 50 Hz. For different grand mean rates, the graph would simply be rescaled.

of the cell, and it expresses the fact that the emission or not of a spike in a short window conveys information in as much as the mean response to a given stimulus is above or below the overall mean rate. No information is conveyed about those stimuli the mean response to which is the same as the overall mean. In practice, although the curve describes only the universal behaviour of the initial slope of the specific information as a function of time, it approximates well the full stimulus-specific information $I(s, R)$ computed even over rather long periods (Rolls, Critchley and Treves 1996a, Rolls, Treves, Tovee and Panzeri 1997d).

Averaging equation C.47 across stimuli one obtains the time derivative of the mutual information. Further dividing by the overall mean rate yields the adimensional quantity

$$\chi = \sum_s P(s)(r_s/ <r>) \log_2(r_s/ <r>) \tag{C.48}$$

which measures, in bits, the mutual information per spike provided by the cell (Bialek, Rieke, de Ruyter van Steveninck and Warland 1991, Skaggs, McNaughton, Gothard and Markus 1993). One can prove that this quantity can range from 0 to $\log_2(1/a)$

$$0 < \chi < \log_2(1/a), \tag{C.49}$$

where a is the single neuron sparseness a^s defined in Section C.3.1.1. For mean rates r_s distributed in a nearly binary fashion, χ is close to its upper limit $\log_2(1/a)$, whereas for mean rates that are nearly uniform, or at least unimodally distributed, χ is relatively close to zero (Panzeri, Biella, Rolls, Skaggs and Treves 1996). In practice, whenever a large number of more or less 'ecological' stimuli are considered, mean rates are not distributed in arbitrary ways, but rather tend to follow stereotyped distributions (which for some neurons approximate an exponential distribution of firing rates – see Section C.3.1 (Treves, Panzeri, Rolls, Booth and Wakeman 1999, Baddeley, Abbott, Booth, Sengpiel, Freeman, Wakeman and Rolls 1997, Rolls and Treves 1998, Rolls and Deco 2002, Franco, Rolls, Aggelopoulos and Jerez 2007)), and as a consequence χ and a (or, equivalently, its logarithm) tend to covary (rather than to be independent variables (Skaggs and McNaughton 1992)). Therefore, measuring sparseness is in practice nearly equivalent to measuring information per spike, and the rate of rise in mutual information, $\chi <r>$, is largely determined by the sparseness a and the overall mean firing rate $<r>$.

The important point to note about the single-cell information rate $\chi < r >$ is that, to the extent that different cells express non-redundant codes, as discussed below, the instantaneous *information flow* across a population of C cells can be taken to be simply $C\chi < r >$, and this quantity can easily be measured directly without major limited sampling biases, or else inferred indirectly through measurements of the sparseness a. Values for the information rate $\chi < r >$ that have been published range from 2–3 bits/s for rat hippocampal cells (Skaggs, McNaughton, Gothard and Markus 1993), to 10–30 bits/s for primate temporal cortex visual cells (Rolls, Treves and Tovee 1997b), and could be compared with analogous measurements in the sensory systems of frogs and crickets, in the 100–300 bits/s range (Rieke, D. and Bialek 1993).

If the first time-derivative of the mutual information measures information flow, successive derivatives characterize, at the single-cell level, different firing modes. This is because whereas the first derivative is universal and depends only on the mean firing rates to each stimulus, the next derivatives depend also on the variability of the firing rate around its mean value, across trials, and take different forms in different firing regimes. Thus they can serve as a measure of discrimination among firing regimes with limited variability, for which, for example, the second derivative is large and positive, and firing regimes with large variability, for which the second derivative is large and negative. Poisson firing, in which in every short period of time there is a fixed probability of emitting a spike irrespective of previous firing, is an example of large variability, and the second derivative of the mutual information can be calculated to be

$$d^2 I/dt^2 = [\ln a + (1 - a)] < r >^2 /(a \ln 2), \tag{C.50}$$

where a is the single neuron sparseness a^s defined in Section C.3.1.1. This quantity is always negative. Strictly periodic firing is an example of zero variability, and in fact the second time-derivative of the mutual information becomes infinitely large in this case (although actual information values measured in a short time interval remain of course finite even for exactly periodic firing, because there is still some variability, ± 1, in the number of spikes recorded in the interval). Measures of mutual information from short intervals of firing of temporal cortex visual cells have revealed a degree of variability intermediate between that of periodic and of Poisson regimes (Rolls, Treves, Tovee and Panzeri 1997d). Similar measures can also be used to contrast the effect of the graded nature of neuronal responses, once they are analyzed over a finite period of time, with the information content that would characterize neuronal activity if it reduced to a binary variable (Panzeri, Biella, Rolls, Skaggs and Treves 1996). A binary variable with the same degree of variability would convey information at the same instantaneous rate (the first derivative being universal), but in for example 20–30% reduced amounts when analyzed over times of the order of the interspike interval or longer.

Utilizing these approaches, Tovee, Rolls, Treves and Bellis (1993) and Tovee and Rolls (1995) measured the information available in short epochs of the firing of single neurons, and found that a considerable proportion of the information available in a long time period of 400 ms was available in time periods as short as 20 ms and 50 ms. For example, in periods of 20 ms, 30% of the information present in 400 ms using temporal encoding with the first three principal components was available. Moreover, the exact time when the epoch was taken was not crucial, with the main effect being that rather more information was available if information was measured near the start of the spike train, when the firing rate of the neuron tended to be highest (see Figs. C.14 and C.15). The conclusion was that much information was available when temporal encoding could not be used easily, that is in very short time epochs of 20 or 50 ms.

It is also useful to note from Figs. C.14, C.15 and 4.13 the typical time course of the responses of many temporal cortex visual neurons in the awake behaving primate. Although

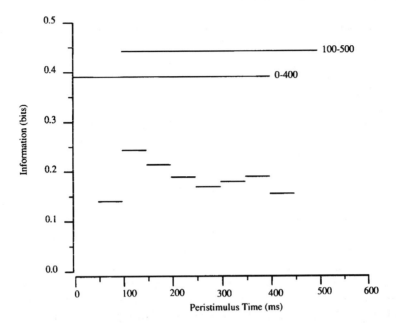

Fig. C.14 The average information I(S,R) available in short temporal epochs (50 ms as compared to 400 ms) of the spike trains of single inferior temporal cortex neurons about which face had been shown. (From Tovee and Rolls 1995.)

the firing rate and availability of information is highest in the first 50–100 ms of the neuronal response, the firing is overall well sustained in the 500 ms stimulus presentation period. Cortical neurons in the primate temporal lobe visual system, in the taste cortex (Rolls, Yaxley and Sienkiewicz 1990), and in the olfactory cortex (Rolls, Critchley and Treves 1996a), do not in general have rapidly adapting neuronal responses to sensory stimuli. This may be important for associative learning: the outputs of these sensory systems can be maintained for sufficiently long while the stimuli are present for synaptic modification to occur. Although rapid synaptic adaptation within a spike train is seen in some experiments in brain slices (Markram and Tsodyks 1996, Abbott, Varela, Sen and Nelson 1997), it is not a very marked effect in at least some brain systems in vivo, when they operate in normal physiological conditions with normal levels of acetylcholine, etc.

To pursue this issue of the speed of processing and information availability even further, Rolls, Tovee, Purcell, Stewart and Azzopardi (1994b) and Rolls and Tovee (1994) limited the period for which visual cortical neurons could respond by using backward masking. In this paradigm, a short (16 ms) presentation of the test stimulus (a face) was followed after a delay of 0, 20, 40, 60, etc. ms by a masking stimulus (which was a high contrast set of letters) (see Fig. C.16). They showed that the mask did actually interrupt the neuronal response, and that at the shortest interval between the stimulus and the mask (a delay of 0 ms, or a 'Stimulus Onset Asynchrony' of 20 ms), the neurons in the temporal cortical areas fired for approximately 30 ms (see Fig. C.17). Under these conditions, the subjects could identify which of five faces had been shown much better than chance. Interestingly, under these conditions, when the inferior temporal cortex neurons were firing for 30 ms, the subjects felt that they were guessing, and conscious perception was minimal (Rolls, Tovee, Purcell, Stewart and Azzopardi 1994b), the neurons conveyed on average 0.10 bits of information (Rolls, Tovee and Panzeri 1999b). With a stimulus onset asynchrony of 40 ms, when the inferior temporal cortex neurons were

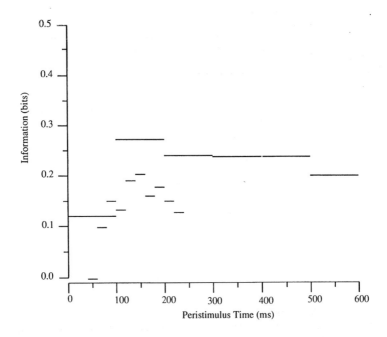

Fig. C.15 The average information I(S,R) available in short temporal epochs (20 ms and 100 ms) of the spike trains of single inferior temporal cortex neurons about which face had been shown. (From Tovee and Rolls 1995.)

firing for 50 ms, not only did the subjects' performance improve, but the stimuli were now perceived clearly, consciously, and the neurons conveyed on average 0.16 bits of information. This has contributed to the view that consciousness has a higher threshold of activity *in a given pathway*, in this case a pathway for face analysis, than does unconscious processing and performance using the same pathway (Rolls 2003, Rolls 2006b).

The issue of how rapidly information can be read from neurons is crucial and funda-mental to understanding how rapidly memory systems in the brain could operate in terms of reading the code from the input neurons to initiate retrieval, whether in a pattern associator of autoassociation network (see Appendix B). This is also a crucial issue for understanding how any stage of cortical processing operates, given that each stage includes associative or competitive network processes that require the code to be read before it can pass useful output to the next stage of processing (see Chapter 4; Rolls and Deco (2002); and Panzeri, Rolls, Battaglia and Lavis (2001)). For this reason, we have performed further analyses of the speed of availability of information from neuronal firing, and the neuronal code. A rapid readout of information from any one stage of for example visual processing is important, for the ventral visual system is organized as a hierarchy of cortical areas, and the neuronal response latencies are approximately 100 ms in the inferior temporal visual cortex, and 40–50 ms in the primary visual cortex, allowing only approximately 50–60 ms of processing time for V1–V2–V4–inferior temporal cortex (Baylis, Rolls and Leonard 1987, Nowak and Bullier 1997, Rolls and Deco 2002). There is much evidence that the time required for each stage of processing is relatively short. For example, in addition to the evidence already presented, visual stimuli presented in succession approximately 15 ms apart can be separately identified (Keysers and Perrett 2002); and the reaction time for identifying visual stimuli is relatively short and requires

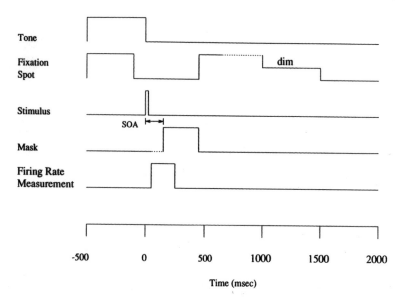

Fig. C.16 Backward masking paradigm. The visual stimulus appeared at time 0 for 16 ms. The time between the start of the visual stimulus and the masking image is the Stimulus Onset Asynchrony (SOA). A visual fixation task was being performed to ensure correct fixation of the stimulus. In the fixation task, the fixation spot appeared in the middle of the screen at time −500 ms, was switched off 100 ms before the test stimulus was shown, and was switched on again at the end of the mask stimulus. Then when the fixation spot dimmed after a random time, fruit juice could be obtained by licking. No eye movements could be performed after the onset of the fixation spot. (After Rolls and Tovee 1994.)

a relatively short cortical processing time (Rolls 2003, Bacon-Mace, Mace, Fabre-Thorpe and Thorpe 2005).

In this context, Delorme and Thorpe (2001) have suggested that just one spike from each neuron is sufficient, and indeed it has been suggested that the order of the first spike in different neurons may be part of the code (Delorme and Thorpe 2001, Thorpe, Delorme and Van Rullen 2001, VanRullen, Guyonneau and Thorpe 2005). (Implicit in the spike order hypothesis is that the first spike is particularly important, for it would be difficult to measure the order for anything other than the first spike.) An alternative view is that the number of spikes in a fixed time window over which a postsynaptic neuron could integrate information is more realistic, and this time might be in the order of 20 ms for a single receiving neuron, or much longer if the receiving neurons are connected by recurrent collateral associative synapses and so can integrate information over time (Deco and Rolls 2006, Rolls and Deco 2002, Panzeri, Rolls, Battaglia and Lavis 2001). Although the number of spikes in a short time window of e.g. 20 ms is likely to be 0, 1, or 2, the information available may be more than that from the first spike alone, and Rolls, Franco, Aggelopoulos and Jerez (2006b) examined this by measuring neuronal activity in the inferior temporal visual cortex, and then applying quantitative information theoretic methods to measure the information transmitted by single spikes, and within short time windows.

The cumulative single cell information about which of the twenty stimuli (Fig. C.7) was shown from all spikes and from the first spike starting at 100 ms after stimulus onset is shown in Fig. C.18. A period of 100 ms is just longer than the shortest response latency of the neurons from which recordings were made, so starting the measure at this time provides the best chance for the single spike measurement to catch a spike that is related to the stimulus. The means

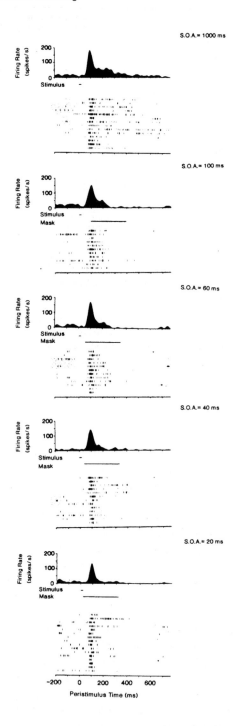

Fig. C.17 Firing of a temporal cortex cell to a 20 ms presentation of a face stimulus when the face was followed with different stimulus onset asynchronies (SOAs) by a masking visual stimulus. At an SOA of 20 ms, when the mask immediately followed the face, the neuron fired for only approximately 30 ms, yet identification above change (by 'guessing') of the face at this SOA by human observers was possible. (After Rolls and Tovee 1994; and Rolls, Tovee, Purcell et al. 1994.)

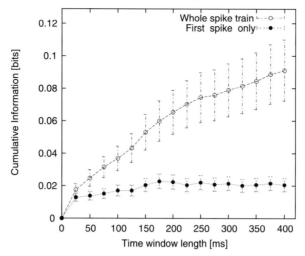

Fig. C.18 Speed of information availability in the inferior temporal visual cortex. Cumulative single cell information from all spikes and from the first spike with the analysis starting at 100 ms after stimulus onset. The mean and sem over 21 neurons are shown. (After Rolls, Franco, Aggelopoulos and Jerez 2006b.)

and standard errors across the 21 different neurons are shown. The cumulated information from the total number of spikes is larger than that from the first spike, and this is evident and significant within 50 ms of the start of the time epoch. In calculating the information from the first spike, just the first spike in the analysis window starting in this case at 100 ms after stimulus onset was used.

Because any one neuron receiving information from the population being analyzed has multiple inputs, we show in Fig. C.19 the cumulative information that would be available from multiple cells (21) about which of the 20 stimuli was shown, taking both the first spike after the time of stimulus onset (0 ms), and the total number of spikes after 0 ms from each neuron. The cumulative information even from multiple cells is much greater when all the spikes rather than just the first spike are used.

An attractor network might be able to integrate the information arriving over a long time period of several hundred milliseconds (see Chapter 7), and might produce the advantage shown in Fig. C.19 for the whole spike train compared to the first spike only. However a single layer pattern association network might only be able to integrate the information over the time constants of its synapses and cell membrane, which might be in the order of 15–30 ms (Panzeri, Rolls, Battaglia and Lavis 2001, Rolls and Deco 2002) (see Section B.2). In a hierarchical processing system such as the visual cortical areas, there may only be a short time during which each stage may decode the information from the preceding stage, and then pass on information sufficient to support recognition to the next stage (Rolls and Deco 2002) (see Chapter 4). We therefore analyzed the information that would be available in short epochs from multiple inputs to a neuron, and show the multiple cell information for the population of 21 neurons in Fig. C.20 (for 20 ms and 50 epochs). We see in this case that the first spike information, because it is being made available from many different neurons (in this case 21 selective neurons discriminating between the stimuli each with p<0.001 in an ANOVA), fares better relative to the information from all the spikes in these short epochs, but is still less than the information from all the spikes (particularly in the 50 ms epoch). In particular, for the epoch starting 100 ms after stimulus onset in Fig. C.21 the information in the 20 ms epoch is 0.37 bits, and from the first spike is 0.24 bits. Correspondingly, for a 50 ms epoch, the values in the epoch starting at 100 ms post stimulus were 0.66 bits for the 50 ms epoch, and 0.40

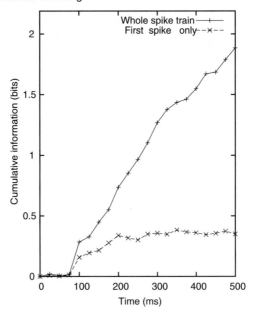

Fig. C.19 Speed of information availability in the inferior temporal visual cortex. Cumulative multiple cell information from all spikes and first spike starting at the time of stimulus onset (0 ms) for the population of 21 neurons about the set of 20 stimuli. (After Rolls, Franco, Aggelopoulos and Jerez 2006b.)

bits for the first spike. Thus with a population of neurons, having just one spike from each can allow considerable information to be read if only a limited period (of e.g. 20 or 50 ms) is available for the readout, though even in these cases, more information was available if all the spikes in the short window are considered (Fig. C.20).

To show how the information increases with the number of neurons in the ensemble in these short epochs, we show in Fig. C.21 the information from different numbers of neurons for a 20 ms epoch starting at time = 100 ms with respect to stimulus onset, for both the first spike condition and the condition with all the spikes in the 20 ms window. The linear increase in the information in both cases indicates that the neurons provide independent information, which could be because there is no redundancy or synergy, or because these cancel (Rolls, Franco, Aggelopoulos and Reece 2003b, Rolls, Franco, Aggelopoulos and Reece 2003b). It is also clear from Fig. C.21 that even with the population of neurons, and with just a short time epoch of 20 ms, more information is available from the population if all the spikes in 20 ms are considered, and not just the first spike. The 20 ms epoch analyzed for Fig. C.21 is for the post-stimulus time period of 100–120 ms.

To assess whether there is information that is specifically related to the order in which the spikes arrive from the different neurons, Rolls, Franco, Aggelopoulos and Jerez (2006b) computed for every trial the order across the different simultaneously recorded neurons in which the first spike arrived to each stimulus, and used this in the information theoretic analysis. The control condition was to randomly allocate the order values for each trial between the neurons that had any spikes on that trial, thus shuffling or scrambling the order of the spike arrival times in the time window. In both cases, just the first spike in the time window was used in the information analysis. (In both the order and the shuffled control conditions, on some trials some neurons had no spikes, and this itself, in comparison with the fact that some neurons had spiked on that trial, provided some information about which stimulus had been shown. However, by explicitly shuffling in the control condition the order

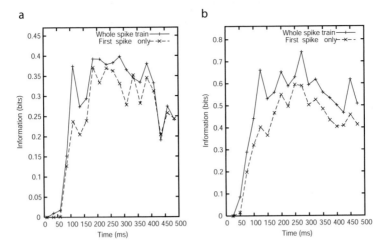

Fig. C.20 Speed of information availability in the inferior temporal visual cortex. (a) Multiple cell information from all spikes and 1 spike in 20 ms time windows taken at different post-stimulus times starting at time 0. (b) Multiple cell information from all spikes and 1 spike in 50 ms time windows taken at different post-stimulus times starting at time 0. (After Rolls, Franco, Aggelopoulos and Jerez 2006b.)

of the spikes for the neurons that had spiked on that trial, comparison of the control with the unshuffled order condition provides a clear measure of whether the order of spike arrival from the different neurons itself carries useful information about which stimulus was shown.) The data set was 36 cells with significantly different (p<0.05) responses to the stimulus set where it was possible to record simultaneously from groups of 3 and 4 cells (so that the order on each trial could be measured) in 11 experiments. Taking a 75 ms time window starting 100 ms after stimulus onset, the information with the order of arrival times of the spikes was 0.142 ± 0.02 bits, and in the control (shuffled order) condition was 0.138 ± 0.02 bits (mean across the 11 experiments $\pm$ sem). Thus the information increase by taking into account the order of spike arrival times relative to the control condition was only (0.142 - 0.138) = 0.004 bits per experiment (which was not significant). For comparison, the information calculated for the first spike using the same dot product decoding as described above was 0.136 ± 0.03 bits per experiment. Analogous results were obtained for different time windows. Thus taking the spike order into account compared to a control condition in which the spike order was scrambled made essentially no difference to the amount of information that was available from the populations of neurons about which stimulus was shown.

The results show that although considerable information is present in the first spike, more information is available under the more biologically realistic assumption that neurons integrate spikes over a short time window (depending on their time constants) of for example 20 ms. The results shown in Fig. C.21 are of considerable interest, for they show that even when one increases the number of neurons in the population, the information available from the number of spikes in a 20 ms time window is larger than the information available from just the first spike. Thus although intuitively one might think that one can compensate by taking a population of neurons rather than just a single neuron when using just the first spike instead of the number of spikes available in a fixed time window, this compensation by increasing neuron numbers is insufficient to make the first spike code as efficient as taking the number of spikes.

Further, in this first empirical test of the hypothesis that there is information that is specifically related to the order in which the spikes arrive from the different neurons, which has

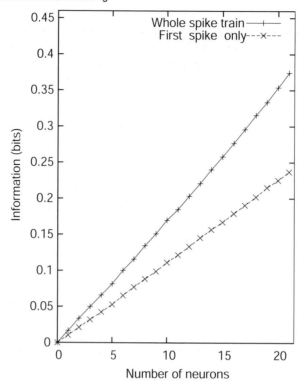

Fig. C.21 Speed of information availability in the inferior temporal visual cortex. Multiple cell information from all spikes and 1 spike in a 20 ms time window starting at 100 ms after stimulus onset as a function of the number of neurons in the ensemble. (After Rolls, Franco, Aggelopoulos and Jerez 2006b.)

been proposed by Thorpe et al (Delorme and Thorpe 2001, Thorpe, Delorme and Van Rullen 2001, VanRullen, Guyonneau and Thorpe 2005), we found that in the inferior temporal visual cortex there was no significant evidence that the order of the spike arrival times from different simultaneously recorded neurons is important. Indeed, the evidence found in the experiments was that the number of spikes in the time window is the important property that is related to the amount of information encoded by the spike trains of simultaneously recorded neurons. The fact that there was also more information in the number of spikes in a fixed time window than from the first spike only is also evidence that is not consistent with the spike order hypothesis, for the order between neurons can only be easily read from the first spike, and just using information from the first spike would discard extra information available from further spikes even in short time windows.

The encoding of information that uses the number of spikes in a short time window that is supported by the analyses described by Rolls, Franco, Aggelopoulos and Jerez (2006b) deserves further elaboration. It could be thought of as a rate code, in that the number of spikes in a short time window is relevant, but is not a rate code in the rather artificial sense considered by Thorpe et al. (Delorme and Thorpe 2001, Thorpe et al. 2001, VanRullen et al. 2005) in which a rate is estimated from the interspike interval. This is not just artificial, but also begs the question of how, once the rate is calculated from the interspike interval, this decoded rate is passed on to the receiving neurons, or how, if the receiving neurons calculate the interspike interval at every synapse, they utilize it. In contrast, the spike count code in a short time window that is considered here is very biologically plausible, in that each spike would inject current into the post-synaptic neuron, and the neuron would integrate all such currents in a dendrite over a time period set by the synaptic and membrane time constants, which will result in an integration time constant in the order of 15–20 ms. Explicit models of exactly this dynamical processing at the integrate-and-fire neuronal level have been described to define precisely these operations (Deco and Rolls 2003, Deco and Rolls 2005d, Deco, Rolls and Horwitz 2004, Deco and Rolls 2005b, Rolls and Deco 2002). Even though the number of spikes in a short time window of e.g. 20 ms is likely to be 0, 1, or 2, it can be 3 or more for effective stimuli (Rolls, Franco, Aggelopoulos and Jerez 2006b), and this is more efficient than using the first spike.

To add some detail here, a neuron receiving information from a population of inferior temporal cortex neurons of the type described here would have a membrane potential that varied continuously in time reflecting with a time constant in the order of 15–20 ms (resulting from a time constant of order 10 ms for AMPA synapses, 100 ms for NMDA synapses, and 20 ms for the cell membrane) a dot (inner) product over all synapses of each spike count and the synaptic strength. This continuously time varying membrane potential would lead to spikes whenever the results of this integration process produced a depolarization that exceeded the firing threshold. The result is that the spike train of the neuron would reflect continuously with a time constant in the order of 15–20 ms the likelihood that the input spikes it was receiving matched its set of synaptic weights. The spike train would thus indicate in continuous time how closely the stimulus or input matched its most effective stimulus (for a dot product is essentially a correlation). In this sense, no particular starting time is needed for the analysis, and in this respect it is a much better component of a dynamical system than is a decoding that utilizes an order in which the order of the spike arrival times is important and a start time for the analysis must be assumed.

I note that an autoassociation or attractor network implemented by recurrent collateral connections between the neurons can, using its short-term memory, integrate its inputs over much longer periods, for example over 500 ms in a model of how decisions are made (Deco and Rolls 2006) (see Chapter 7), and thus if there is time, the extra information available in more than the first spike or even the first few spikes that is evident in Figs. C.18 and C.19 could be used by the brain.

The conclusions from the single cell information analyses are thus that most of the information is encoded in the spike count; that large parts of this information are available in short temporal epochs of e.g. 20 ms or 50 ms; and that any additional information which appears to be temporally encoded is related to the latency of the neuronal response, and reflects sudden changes in the visual stimuli. Therefore a neuron in the next cortical area would obtain considerable information within 20–50 ms by measuring the firing rate of a single neuron. Moreover, if it took a short sample of the firing rate of many neurons in the preceding area, then very much information is made available in a short time, as shown above and in Section C.3.5.

C.3.5   The information from multiple cells: independent information versus redundancy across cells

The rate at which a single cell provides information translates into an instantaneous information flow across a population (with a simple multiplication by the number of cells) only to the extent that different cells provide different (independent) information. To verify whether this condition holds, one cannot extend to multiple cells the simplified formula for the first time-derivative, because it is made simple precisely by the assumption of independence between spikes, and one cannot even measure directly the full information provided by multiple (more than two to three) cells, because of the limited sampling problem discussed above.

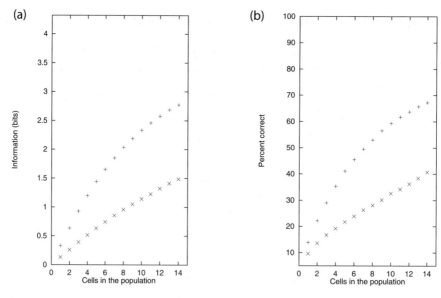

Fig. C.22 (a) The information available about which of 20 faces had been seen that is available from the responses measured by the firing rates in a time period of 500 ms (+) or a shorter time period of 50 ms (x) of different numbers of temporal cortex cells. (b) The corresponding percentage correct from different numbers of cells. (From Rolls, Treves and Tovee 1997b.)

Therefore one has to analyze the degree of independence (or conversely of redundancy) either directly among pairs – at most triplets – of cells, or indirectly by using decoding procedures to transform population responses. Obviously, the results of the analysis will vary a great deal with the particular neural system considered and the particular set of stimuli, or in general of neuronal correlates, used. For many systems, before undertaking to quantify the analysis in terms of information measures, it takes only a simple qualitative description of the responses to realize that there is a lot of redundancy and very little diversity in the responses. For example, if one selects pain-responsive cells in the somatosensory system and uses painful electrical stimulation of different intensities, most of the recorded cells are likely to convey pretty much the same information, signalling the intensity of the stimulation with the intensity of their single-cell response. Therefore, an analysis of redundancy makes sense only for a neuronal system that functions to represent, and enable discriminations between, a large variety of stimuli, and only when using a set of stimuli representative, in some sense, of that large variety.

Rolls, Treves and Tovee (1997b) measured the information available from a population of inferior temporal cortex neurons using the decoding method described in Section C.2.3, and found that the information increased approximately linearly, as shown in Fig. 4.15 on page 279, and in Fig. C.22 for a 50 ms interval as well as for a 500 ms measuring period. (It is shown below that the increase is limited only by the information ceiling of 4.32 bits necessary to encode the 20 stimuli. If it were not for this approach to the ceiling, the increase would be approximately linear (Rolls, Treves and Tovee 1997b).) To the extent that the information increases linearly with the number of neurons, the neurons convey independent information, and there is no redundancy, at least with numbers of neurons in this range. Although these and some of the other results described in this Appendix are for face-selective neurons in the inferior temporal visual cortex, similar results were obtained for neurons responding to objects in the inferior temporal visual cortex (Booth and Rolls 1998), and for neurons responding to spatial view in the hippocampus (Rolls, Treves, Robertson, Georges-François and Panzeri 1998).

Although those neurons were not simultaneously recorded, a similar approximately linear increase in the information from *simultaneously* recorded cells as the number of neurons in the sample increased also occurs (Rolls, Franco, Aggelopoulos and Reece 2003b, Rolls, Aggelopoulos, Franco and Treves 2004, Franco, Rolls, Aggelopoulos and Treves 2004, Aggelopoulos, Franco and Rolls 2005, Rolls, Franco, Aggelopoulos and Jerez 2006b). These findings imply little redundancy, and that the number of stimuli that can be encoded increases approximately exponentially with the number of neurons in the population, as illustrated in Figs. 4.16 and C.22.

The issue of redundancy is considered in more detail now. Redundancy can be defined with reference to a multiple channel of capacity $T(C)$ which can be decomposed into C separate channels of capacities $T_i, i = 1, ..., C$:

$$R = 1 - T(C)/\sum_i T_i \tag{C.51}$$

so that when the C channels are multiplexed with maximal efficiency, $T(C) = \sum_i T_i$ and $R = 0$. What is measured more easily, in practice, is the redundancy defined with reference to a specific source (the set of stimuli with their probabilities). Then in terms of mutual information

$$R' = 1 - I(C)/\sum_i I_i. \tag{C.52}$$

Gawne and Richmond (1993) measured the redundancy R' among pairs of nearby primate inferior temporal cortex visual neurons, in their response to a set of 32 Walsh patterns. They found values with a mean $< R' > = 0.1$ (and a mean single-cell transinformation of 0.23 bits). Since to discriminate 32 different patterns takes 5 bits of information, in principle one would need at least 22 cells each providing 0.23 bits of strictly orthogonal information to represent the full entropy of the stimulus set. Gawne and Richmond reasoned, however, that, because of the overlap, y, in the information they provided, more cells would be needed than if the redundancy had been zero. They constructed a simple model based on the notion that the overlap, y, in the information provided by any two cells in the population always corresponds to the average redundancy measured for nearby pairs. A redundancy $R' = 0.1$ corresponds to an overlap $y = 0.2$ in the information provided by the two neurons, since, counting the overlapping information only once, two cells would yield 1.8 times the amount transmitted by one cell alone. If a fraction of $1 - y = 0.8$ of the information provided by a cell is novel with respect to that provided by another cell, a fraction $(1 - y)^2$ of the information provided by a third cell will be novel with respect to what was known from the first pair, and so on, yielding an estimate of $I(C) = I(1) \sum_{i=0}^{C-1} (1 - y)^i$ for the total information conveyed by C cells. However such a sum saturates, in the limit of an infinite number of cells, at the level $I(\infty) = I(1)/y$, implying in their case that even with very many cells, no more than $0.23/0.2 = 1.15$ bits could be read off their activity, or less than a quarter of what was available as entropy in the stimulus set! Gawne and Richmond (1993) concluded, therefore, that the average overlap among non-nearby cells must be considerably lower than that measured for cells close to each other.

The model above is simple and attractive, but experimental verification of the actual scaling of redundancy with the number of cells entails collecting the responses of several cells interspersed in a population of interest. Gochin, Colombo, Dorfman, Gerstein and Gross (1994) recorded from up to 58 cells in the primate temporal visual cortex, using sets of two to five visual stimuli, and applied decoding procedures to measure the information content in the population response. The recordings were not simultaneous, but comparison with simultaneous recordings from a smaller number of cells indicated that the effect of recording the individual responses on separate trials was minor. The results were expressed in terms of the *novelty* N in the information provided by C cells, which being defined as the ratio of such information to C times the average single-cell information, can be expressed as

$$N = 1 - R' \tag{C.53}$$

and is thus the complement of the redundancy. An analysis of two different data sets, which included three information measures per data set, indicated a behaviour $N(C) \approx 1/\sqrt{C}$, reminiscent of the improvement in the overall noise-to-signal ratio characterizing C independent processes contributing to the same signal. The analysis neglected however to consider limited sampling effects, and more seriously it neglected to consider saturation effects due to the information content approaching its ceiling, given by the entropy of the stimulus set. Since this ceiling was quite low, for 5 stimuli at $\log_2 5 = 2.32$ bits, relative to the mutual information values measured from the population (an average of 0.26 bits, or 1/9 of the ceiling, was provided by single cells), it is conceivable that the novelty would have taken much larger values if larger stimulus sets had been used.

A simple formula describing the approach to the ceiling, and thus the saturation of information values as they come close to the entropy of the stimulus set, can be derived from a natural extension of the Gawne and Richmond (1993) model. In this extension, the information provided by single cells, measured as a fraction of the ceiling, is taken to coincide with the average overlap among pairs of randomly selected, not necessarily nearby, cells from the population. The actual value measured by Gawne and Richmond would have been, again, $1/22 = 0.045$, below the overlap among nearby cells, $y = 0.2$. The assumption that y, measured across any pair of cells, would have been as low as the fraction of information provided by single cells is equivalent to conceiving of single cells as 'covering' a random portion y of information space, and thus of randomly selected pairs of cells as overlapping in a fraction $(y)^2$ of that space, and so on, as postulated by the Gawne and Richmond (1993) model, for higher numbers of cells. The approach to the ceiling is then described by the formula

$$I(C) \approx H\{1 - \exp[C\ln(1 - y)]\} \tag{C.54}$$

that is, a simple exponential saturation to the ceiling. This simple law indeed describes remarkably well the trend in the data analyzed by Rolls, Treves and Tovee (1997b). Although the model has no reason to be exact, and therefore its agreement with the data should not be expected to be accurate, the crucial point it embodies is that deviations from a purely linear increase in information with the number of cells analyzed are due solely to the ceiling effect. Aside from the ceiling, due to the sampling of an information space of finite entropy, the information contents of different cells' responses are independent of each other. Thus, in the model, the observed redundancy (or indeed the overlap) is purely a consequence of the finite size of the stimulus set. If the population were probed with larger and larger sets of stimuli, or more precisely with sets of increasing entropy, and the amount of information conveyed by single cells were to remain approximately the same, then the fraction of space 'covered' by each cell, again y, would get smaller and smaller, tending to eliminate redundancy for very large stimulus entropies (and a fixed number of cells). The actual data were obtained with limited numbers of stimuli, and therefore cannot probe directly the conditions in which redundancy might reduce to zero. The data are consistent, however, with the hypothesis embodied in the simple model, as shown also by the near exponential approach to lower ceilings found for information values calculated with reduced subsets of the original set of stimuli (Rolls, Treves and Tovee 1997b).

The implication of this set of analyses, some performed towards the end of the ventral visual stream of the monkey, is that the representation of at least some classes of objects in those areas is achieved with minimal redundancy by cells that are allocated each to analyse a different aspect of the visual stimulus. This minimal redundancy is what would be expected of a self-organizing system in which different cells acquired their response selectivities through a random process, with or without local competition among nearby cells (see Section B.4). At the same time, such low redundancy could also very well result in a system that is organized under some strong teaching input, so that the emerging picture is compatible with a simple random process, but could be produced in other ways. The finding that, at least with small numbers of neurons, redundancy may be effectively minimized, is consistent not only with the concept of efficient encoding, but also with the general idea that one of the functions of the early visual system is to progressively minimize redundancy in the representation of visual stimuli (Attneave 1954, Barlow 1961). However, the ventral visual system does much more than produce a non-redundant representation of an image, for it transforms the representation from an image to an invariant representation of objects, as described in Chapter 4. Moreover, what is shown in this section is that the information about objects can be read off from just the spike count of a population of neurons, using decoding as simple as the simplest that could be performed by a receiving neuron, dot product decoding. In this sense, the information about objects is made explicit in the firing rate of the neurons in the inferior temporal cortex, in that it can be read off in this way.

We consider in Section C.3.7 whether there is more to it than this. Does the synchronization of neurons (and it would have to be stimulus-dependent synchronization) add significantly to the information that could be encoded by the number of spikes, as has been suggested by some?

Before this, we consider why encoding by a population of neurons is more powerful than the encoding than is possible by single neurons, adding to previous arguments that a distributed representation is much more computationally useful than a local representation, by allowing properties such as generalization, completion, and graceful degradation in associative neuronal networks (see Appendix B).

C.3.6 Should one neuron be as discriminative as the whole organism, in object encoding systems?

In the analysis of random dot motion with a given level of correlation among the moving dots, single neurons in area MT in the dorsal visual system of the primate can be approximately as sensitive or discriminative as the psychophysical performance of the whole animal (Zohary, Shadlen and Newsome 1994). The arguments and evidence presented here (e.g. in Section C.3.5) suggest that this is not the case for the ventral visual system, concerned with object identification. Why should there be this difference?

Rolls and Treves (1998) suggest that the dimensionality of what is being computed may account for the difference. In the case of visual motion (at least in the study referred to), the problem was effectively one-dimensional, in that the direction of motion of the stimulus along a line in 2D space was extracted from the activity of the neurons. In this low-dimensional stimulus space, the neurons may each perform one of a few similar computations on a particular (local) portion of 2D space, with the side effect that, by averaging over a larger receptive field than in V1, one can extract a signal of a more global nature. Indeed, in the case of more global motion, it is the average of the neuronal activity that can be computed by the larger receptive fields of MT neurons that specifies the average or global direction of motion.

In contrast, in the higher dimensional space of objects, in which there are very many different objects to represent as being different from each other, and in a system that is not concerned with location in visual space but on the contrary tends to be relatively invariant with respect to location, the goal of the representation is to reflect the many aspects of the input information in a way that enables many different objects to be represented, in what is effectively a very high dimensional space. This is achieved by allocating cells, each with an intrinsically limited discriminative power, to sample as thoroughly as possible the many dimensions of the space. Thus the system is geared to use efficiently the parallel computations of all its neurons precisely for tasks such as that of face discrimination, which was used as an experimental probe. Moreover, object representation must be kept higher dimensional, in that it may have to be decoded by dot product decoders in associative memories, in which the input patterns must be in a space that is as high-dimensional as possible (i.e. the activity on different input axons should not be too highly correlated). In this situation, each neuron should act somewhat independently of its neighbours, so that each provides its own separate contribution that adds together with that of the other neurons (in a linear manner, see above and Figs. 4.15, C.22 and 4.16) to provide *in toto* sufficient information to specify which out of perhaps several thousand visual stimuli was seen. The computation involves in this case not an average of neuronal activity (which would be useful for e.g. head direction (Robertson, Rolls, Georges-François and Panzeri 1999)), but instead comparing the dot product of the activity of the population of neurons with a previously learned vector, stored in, for example, associative memories as the weight vector on a receiving neuron or neurons.

Zohary, Shadlen and Newsome (1994) put forward another argument which suggested to them that the brain could hardly benefit from taking into account the activity of more than a very limited number of neurons. The argument was based on their measurement of a small (0.12) correlation between the activity of simultaneously recorded neurons in area MT. They suggested that there would because of this be decreasing signal-to-noise ratio advantages as more neurons were included in the population, and that this would limit the number of neurons that it would be useful to decode to approximately 100. However, a measure of correlations in the activity of different neurons depends entirely on the way the space of neuronal activity is sampled, that is on the task chosen to probe the system. Among face cells in the temporal cortex, for example, much higher correlations would be observed when the task is a simple two-way discrimination between a face and a non-face, than when the task involves finer identification of several different faces. (It is also entirely possible that some face cells could be found that perform as well in a given particular face / non-face discrimination as the whole animal.) Moreover, their argument depends on the type of decoding of the activity of the population that is envisaged (see further Robertson, Rolls, Georges-François and Panzeri (1999)). It implies that the average of the neuronal activity must be estimated accurately. If a set of neurons uses dot product decoding, and then the activity of the decoding population is scaled or normalized by some negative feedback through inhibitory interneurons, then the effect of such correlated firing in the sending population is reduced, for the decoding effectively measures the relative firing of the different neurons in the population to be decoded. This is equivalent to measuring the angle between the current vector formed by the population of neurons firing, and a previously learned vector, stored in synaptic weights. Thus, with for example this biologically plausible decoding, it is not clear whether the correlation Zohary, Shadlen and Newsome (1994) describe would place a severe limit on the ability of the brain to utilize the information available in a population of neurons.

The main conclusion from this and the preceding Section is that the information available from a set or ensemble of temporal cortex visual neurons increases approximately linearly as more neurons are added to the sample. This is powerful evidence that distributed encoding is used by the brain; and the code can be read just by knowing the firing rates in a short time of the population of neurons. The fact that the code can be read off from the firing rates, and by a principle as simple and neuron-like as dot product decoding, provides strong support for the general approach taken in this book to brain function.

It is possible that more information would be available in the relative time of occurrence of the spikes, either within the spike train of a single neuron, or between the spike trains of different neurons, and it is to this that we now turn.

C.3.7 The information from multiple cells: the effects of cross-correlations between cells

Using the second derivative methods described in Section C.2.5 (see Rolls, Franco, Aggelopoulos and Reece (2003b)), the information available from the number of spikes vs that from the cross-correlations between simultaneously recorded cells has been analyzed for a population of neurons in the inferior temporal visual cortex (Rolls, Aggelopoulos, Franco and Treves 2004). The stimuli were a set of 20 objects, faces, and scenes presented while the monkey performed a visual discrimination task. If synchronization was being used to bind the parts of each object into the correct spatial relationship to other parts, this might be expected to be revealed by stimulus-dependent cross-correlations in the firing of simultaneously recorded groups of 2–4 cells using multiple single-neuron microelectrodes.

A typical result from the information analysis described in Section C.2.5 on a set of three simultaneously recorded cells from this experiment is shown in Fig. C.23. This shows that most of the information available in a 100 ms time period was available in the rates, and that there was little contribution to the information from stimulus-dependent ('noise') correlations (which would have shown as positive values if for example there was stimulus-dependent synchronization of the neuronal responses); or from stimulus-independent 'noise' correlation effects, which might if present have reflected common input to the different neurons so that their responses tended to be correlated independently of which stimulus was shown.

The results for the 20 experiments with groups of 2–4 simultaneously recorded inferior temporal cortex neurons are shown in Table C.4. (The total information is the total from equations C.43 and C.44 in a 100 ms time window, and is not expected to be the sum of the contributions shown in Table C.4 because only the information from the cross terms (for $i \neq j$) is shown in the table for the contributions related to the stimulus-dependent contributions and the stimulus-independent contributions arising from the 'noise' correlations.) The results show that the greatest contribution to the information is that from the rates, that is from the numbers of spikes from each neuron in the time window of 100 ms. The average value of -0.05 for the cross term of the stimulus independent 'noise' correlation-related contribution is consistent with on average a small amount of common input to neurons in the inferior temporal visual cortex. A positive value for the cross term of the stimulus-dependent 'noise' correlation related contribution would be consistent with on average a small amount of stimulus-dependent synchronization, but the actual value found, 0.04 bits, is so small that for 17 of the 20 experiments it is less than that which can arise by chance statistical fluctuations of the time of arrival of the spikes, as shown by MonteCarlo control rearrangements of the same data. Thus on average there was no significant contribution to the information from stimulus-dependent synchronization effects (Rolls, Aggelopoulos, Franco and Treves 2004).

Thus, this data set provides evidence for considerable information available from the number of spikes that each cell produces to different stimuli, and evidence for little impact of common input, or of synchronization, on the amount of information provided by sets of *simultaneously recorded* inferior temporal cortex neurons. Further supporting data for the inferior temporal visual cortex are provided by Rolls, Franco, Aggelopoulos and Reece (2003b). In that parts as well as whole objects are represented in the inferior temporal cortex (Perrett,

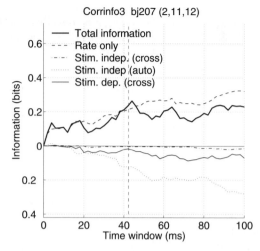

Corrinfo3 bj207 (2,11,12)

Fig. C.23 A typical result from the information analysis described in Section C.2.5 on a set of 3 simultane-ously recorded inferior temporal cortex neurons in an experiment in which 20 complex stimuli effective for IT neurons (objects, faces and scenes) were shown. The graphs show the contributions to the information from the different terms in equations C.43 and C.44 on page 681, as a function of the length of the time window, which started 100 ms after stimulus onset, which is when IT neurons start to respond. The rate information is the sum of the term in equation C.43 and the first term of equation C.44. The contribution of the stimulus-independent noise correlation to the information is the second term of equation C.44, and is separated into components arising from the correlations between cells (the cross component, for $i \neq j$) and from the autocorrelation within a cell (the auto component, for $i = j$). This term is non-zero if there is some correlation in the variance to a given stimulus, even if it is independent of which stimulus is present. The contribution of the stimulus-dependent noise correlation to the information is the third term of equation C.44, and only the cross term is shown (for $i \neq j$), as this is the term of interest. (After Rolls, Aggelopoulos, Franco and Treves 2004.)

Table C.4 The average contributions (in bits) of different components of equations C.43 and C.44 to the information available in a 100 ms time window from 13 sets of simultaneously recorded inferior temporal cortex neurons when shown 20 stimuli effective for the cells.

rate	0.26
stimulus–dependent "noise" correlation-related, cross term	0.04
stimulus–independent "noise" correlation-related, cross term	-0.05
total information	0.31

Rolls and Caan 1982), and in that the parts must be bound together in the correct spatial con-figuration for the inferior temporal cortex neurons to respond (Rolls, Tovee, Purcell, Stewart and Azzopardi 1994b), we might have expected temporal synchrony, if used to implement feature binding, to have been evident in these experiments.

We have also explored neuronal encoding under natural scene conditions in a task in which top-down attention must be used, a visual search task. We applied the decoding information theoretic method of Section C.2.4 to the responses of neurons in the inferior temporal visual cortex recorded under conditions in which feature binding is likely to be needed, that is when the monkey had to choose to touch one of two simultaneously presented objects, with the stimuli presented in a complex natural background (Aggelopoulos, Franco and Rolls 2005). The investigation is thus directly relevant to whether stimulus-dependent synchrony contributes to encoding under natural conditions, and when an attentional task was being

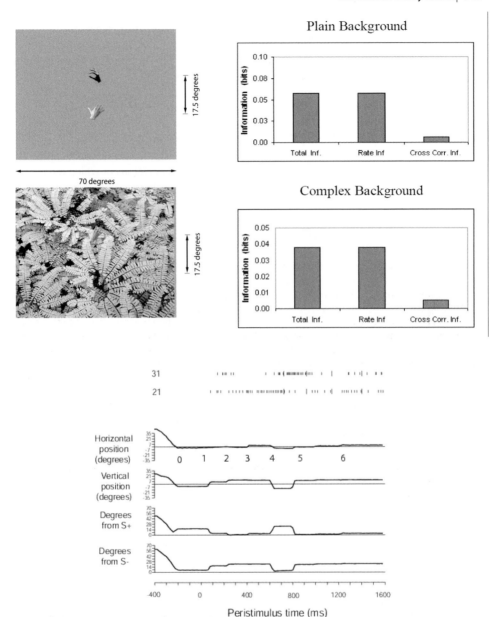

Fig. C.24 Left: the objects against the plain background, and in a natural scene. Right: the information available from the firing rates (Rate Inf) or from stimulus-dependent synchrony (Cross-Corr Inf) from populations of simultaneously recorded inferior temporal cortex neurons about which stimulus had been presented in a complex natural scene. The total information (Total Inf) is that available from both the rate and the stimulus-dependent synchrony, which do not necessarily contribute independently. Bottom: eye position recordings and spiking activity from two neurons on a single trial of the task. (Neuron 31 tended to fire more when the macaque looked at one of the stimuli, S–, and neuron 21 tended to fire more when the macaque looked at the other stimulus, S+. Both stimuli were within the receptive field of the neuron.) (After Aggelopoulos, Franco and Rolls 2005.)

performed. In the attentional task, the monkey had to find one of two objects and to touch it to obtain reward. This is thus an object-based attentional visual search task, where the top-down bias is for the object that has to be found in the scene (Aggelopoulos, Franco and Rolls 2005). The objects could be presented against a complex natural scene background. Neurons in the inferior temporal visual cortex respond in some cases to object features or parts, and in other cases to whole objects provided that the parts are in the correct spatial configuration (Perrett, Rolls and Caan 1982, Desimone, Albright, Gross and Bruce 1984, Rolls, Tovee, Purcell, Stewart and Azzopardi 1994b, Tanaka 1996), and so it is very appropriate to measure whether stimulus-dependent synchrony contributes to information encoding in the inferior temporal visual cortex when two objects are present in the visual field, and when they must be segmented from the background in a natural visual scene, which are the conditions in which it has been postulated that stimulus-dependent synchrony would be useful (Singer 1999, Singer 2000).

Aggelopoulos, Franco and Rolls (2005) found that between 99% and 94% of the information was present in the firing rates of inferior temporal cortex neurons, and less that 5% in any stimulus-dependent synchrony that was present, as illustrated in Fig. C.24. The implication of these results is that any stimulus-dependent synchrony that is present is not quantitatively important as measured by information theoretic analyses under natural scene conditions. This has been found for the inferior temporal visual cortex, a brain region where features are put together to form representations of objects (Rolls and Deco 2002), where attention has strong effects, at least in scenes with blank backgrounds (Rolls, Aggelopoulos and Zheng 2003a), and in an object-based attentional search task.

The finding as assessed by information theoretic methods of the importance of firing rates and not stimulus-dependent synchrony is consistent with previous information theoretic approaches (Rolls, Franco, Aggelopoulos and Reece 2003b, Rolls, Aggelopoulos, Franco and Treves 2004, Franco, Rolls, Aggelopoulos and Treves 2004). It would of course also be of interest to test the same hypothesis in earlier visual areas, such as V4, with quantitative, information theoretic, techniques. In connection with rate codes, it should be noted that the findings indicate that the number of spikes that arrive in a given time is what is important for very useful amounts of information to be made available from a population of neurons; and that this time can be very short, as little as 20–50 ms (Tovee and Rolls 1995, Rolls and Tovee 1994, Rolls, Tovee and Panzeri 1999b, Rolls and Deco 2002, Rolls, Tovee, Purcell, Stewart and Azzopardi 1994b, Rolls 2003, Rolls, Franco, Aggelopoulos and Jerez 2006b). Further, it was shown that there was little redundancy (less than 6%) between the information provided by the spike counts of the simultaneously recorded neurons, making spike counts an efficient population code with a high encoding capacity.

The findings (Aggelopoulos, Franco and Rolls 2005) are consistent with the hypothesis that feature binding is implemented by neurons that respond to features in the correct relative spatial locations (Rolls and Deco 2002, Elliffe, Rolls and Stringer 2002), and not by temporal synchrony and attention (Malsburg 1990, Singer, Gray, Engel, Konig, Artola and Brocher 1990, Abeles 1991, Hummel and Biederman 1992, Singer and Gray 1995, Singer 1999, Singer 2000). In any case, the computational point made in Section 4.5.5.1 is that even if stimulus-dependent synchrony was useful for grouping, it would not without much extra machinery be useful for binding the relative spatial positions of features within an object, or for that matter of the positions of objects in a scene which appears to be encoded in a different way (Aggelopoulos and Rolls 2005) (see Section 4.5.10).

So far, we know of no analyses that have shown with information theoretic methods that considerable amounts of information are available about the stimulus from the stimulus-dependent correlations between the responses of neurons in the primate ventral visual system. The use of such methods is needed to test quantitatively the hypothesis that stimulus-dependent synchronization contributes substantially to the encoding of information by neurons.

C.3.8   Conclusions on cortical neuronal encoding

The conclusions emerging from this set of information theoretic analyses, many in cortical areas towards the end of the ventral visual stream of the monkey, and others in the hippocampus for spatial view cells (Rolls, Treves, Robertson, Georges-François and Panzeri 1998), in the presubiculum for head direction cells (Robertson, Rolls, Georges-François and Panzeri 1999), and in the orbitofrontal cortex for olfactory cells (Rolls, Critchley and Treves 1996a) for which subsequent analyses have shown a linear increase in information with the number of cells in the population, are as follows.

The representation of at least some classes of objects in those areas is achieved with minimal redundancy by cells that are allocated each to analyze a different aspect of the visual stimulus (Abbott, Rolls and Tovee 1996, Rolls, Treves and Tovee 1997b) (as shown in Sections C.3.5 and C.3.7). This minimal redundancy is what would be expected of a self-organizing system in which different cells acquired their response selectivities through processes that include some randomness in the initial connectivity, and local competition among nearby cells (see Appendix B). Towards the end of the ventral visual stream redundancy may thus be effectively minimized, a finding consistent with the general idea that one of the functions of the early visual system is indeed that of progressively minimizing redundancy in the representation of visual stimuli (Attneave 1954, Barlow 1961). Indeed, the evidence described in Sections C.3.5, C.3.7 and C.3.4 shows that the exponential rise in the number of stimuli that can be decoded when the firing rates of different numbers of neurons are analyzed indicates that the encoding of information using firing rates (in practice the number of spikes emitted by each of a large population of neurons in a short time period) is a very powerful coding scheme used by the cerebral cortex, and that the information carried by different neurons is close to independent provided that the number of stimuli being considered is sufficiently large.

Quantitatively, the encoding of information using firing rates (in practice the number of spikes emitted by each of a large population of neurons in a short time period) is likely to be far more important than temporal encoding, in terms of the number of stimuli that can be encoded. Moreover, the information available from an ensemble of cortical neurons when only the firing rates are read, that is with no temporal encoding within or between neurons, is made available very rapidly (see Figs. C.14 and C.15 and Section C.3.4). Further, the neuronal responses in most ventral or 'what' processing streams of behaving monkeys show sustained firing rate differences to different stimuli (see for example Fig. 4.13 for visual representations, for the olfactory pathways Rolls, Critchley and Treves (1996a), for spatial view cells in the hippocampus Rolls, Treves, Robertson, Georges-François and Panzeri (1998), and for head direction cells in the presubiculum Robertson, Rolls, Georges-François and Panzeri (1999)), so that it may not usually be necessary to invoke temporal encoding for the information about the stimulus. Further, as indicated in Section C.3.7, information theoretic approaches have enabled the information that is available from the firing rate and from the relative time of firing (synchronization) of inferior temporal cortex neurons to be directly compared with the same metric, and most of the information appears to be encoded in the numbers of spikes emitted by a population of cells in a short time period, rather than by the temporal synchronization of the responses of different neurons when certain stimuli appear (see Section C.3.7 and Aggelopoulos, Franco and Rolls (2005)).

Information theoretic approaches have also enabled different types of readout or decoding that could be performed by the brain of the information available in the responses of cell populations to be compared (Rolls, Treves and Tovee 1997b, Robertson, Rolls, Georges-François and Panzeri 1999). It has been shown for example that the multiple cell representation of information used by the brain in the inferior temporal visual cortex (Rolls, Treves and Tovee 1997b, Aggelopoulos, Franco and Rolls 2005), olfactory cortex (Rolls, Critchley and

Treves 1996a), hippocampus (Rolls, Treves, Robertson, Georges-François and Panzeri 1998), and presubiculum (Robertson, Rolls, Georges-François and Panzeri 1999) can be read fairly efficiently by the neuronally plausible dot product decoding, and that the representation has all the desirable properties of generalization and graceful degradation, as well as exponential coding capacity (see Sections C.3.5 and C.3.7).

Information theoretic approaches have also enabled the information available about different aspects of stimuli to be directly compared. For example, it has been shown that inferior temporal cortex neurons make explicit much more information about what stimulus has been shown rather than where the stimulus is in the visual field (Tovee, Rolls and Azzopardi 1994), and this is part of the evidence that inferior temporal cortex neurons provide translation invariant representations. In a similar way, information theoretic analysis has provided clear evidence that view invariant representations of objects and faces are present in the inferior temporal visual cortex, in that for example much information is available about what object has been shown from any single trial on which any view of any object is presented (Booth and Rolls 1998).

Information theory has also helped to elucidate the way in which the inferior temporal visual cortex provides a representation of objects and faces, in which information about which object or face is shown is made explicit in the firing of the neurons in such a way that the information can be read off very simply by memory systems such as the orbitofrontal cortex, amygdala, and perirhinal cortex / hippocampal systems. The information can be read off using dot product decoding, that is by using a synaptically weighted sum of inputs from inferior temporal cortex neurons (see further Section 2.2.6 and Chapter 4). Moreover, information theory has helped to show that for many neurons considerable invariance in the representations of objects and faces are shown by inferior temporal cortex neurons (e.g. Booth and Rolls (1998)). Examples of some of the types of objects and faces that are encoded in this way are shown in Fig. C.7. Information theory has also helped to show that inferior temporal cortex neurons maintain their object selectivity even when the objects are presented in complex natural backgrounds (Aggelopoulos, Franco and Rolls 2005) (see further Chapter 4 and Section 2.2.6).

Information theory has also enabled the information available in neuronal representations to be compared with that available to the whole animal in its behaviour (Zohary, Shadlen and Newsome 1994) (but see Section C.3.6).

Finally, information theory also provides a metric for directly comparing the information available from neurons in the brain (see Chapter 4 and this Appendix) with that available from single neurons and populations of neurons in simulations of visual information processing (see Chapter 4).

In summary, the evidence from the application of information theoretic and related approaches to how information is encoded in the visual, hippocampal, and olfactory cortical systems described during behaviour leads to the following working hypotheses:

1. Much information is available about the stimulus presented in the number of spikes emitted by single neurons in a fixed time period, the firing rate.

2. Much of this firing rate information is available in short periods, with a considerable proportion available in as little as 20 ms. This rapid availability of information enables the next stage of processing to read the information quickly, and thus for multistage processing to operate rapidly. This time is the order of time over which a receiving neuron might be able to utilize the information, given its synaptic and membrane time constants. In this time, a sending neuron is most likely to emit 0, 1, or 2 spikes.

3. This rapid availability of information is confirmed by population analyses, which indicate that across a population on neurons, much information is available in short time periods.

4. More information is available using this rate code in a short period (of e.g. 20 ms) than from just the first spike.

5. Little information is available by time variations within the spike train of individual neurons for static visual stimuli (in periods of several hundred milliseconds), apart from a small amount of information from the onset latency of the neuronal response. A static stimulus encompasses what might be seen in a single visual fixation, what might be tasted with a stimulus in the mouth, what might be smelled in a single breath, etc. For a time-varying stimulus, clearly the firing rate will vary as a function of time.

6. Across a population of neurons, the firing rate information provided by each neuron tends to be independent; that is, the information increases approximately linearly with the number of neurons. This applies of course only when there is a large amount of information to be encoded, that is with a large number of stimuli. The outcome is that the number of stimuli that can be encoded rises exponentially in the number of neurons in the ensemble. (For a small stimulus set, the information saturates gradually as the amount of information available from the neuronal population approaches that required to code for the stimulus set.) This applies up to the number of neurons tested and the stimulus set sizes used, but as the number of neurons becomes very large, this is likely to hold less well. An implication of the independence is that the response profiles to a set of stimuli of different neurons are uncorrelated.

7. The information in the firing rate across a population of neurons can be read moderately efficiently by a decoding procedure as simple as a dot product. This is the simplest type of processing that might be performed by a neuron, as it involves taking a dot product of the incoming firing rates with the receiving synaptic weights to obtain the activation (e.g. depolarization) of the neuron. This type of information encoding ensures that the simple emergent properties of associative neuronal networks such as generalization, completion, and graceful degradation (see Appendix B) can be realized very naturally and simply.

8. There is little additional information to the great deal available in the firing rates from any stimulus-dependent cross-correlations or synchronization that may be present. Stimulus-dependent synchronization might in any case only be useful for grouping different neuronal populations, and would not easily provide a solution to the binding problem in vision. Instead, the binding problem in vision may be solved by the presence of neurons that respond to combinations of features in a given spatial position with respect to each other.

9. There is little information available in the order of the spike arrival times of different neurons for different stimuli that is separate or additional to that provided by a rate code. The presence of spontaneous activity in cortical neurons facilitates rapid neuronal responses, because some neurons are close to threshold at any given time, but this also would make a spike order code difficult to implement.

10. Analysis of the responses of single neurons to measure the sparseness of the representation indicates that the representation is distributed, and not grandmother cell like (or local). Moreover, the nature of the distributed representation, that it can be read by dot product decoding, allows simple emergent properties of associative neuronal networks such as generalization, completion, and graceful degradation (see Appendix B) to be realized very naturally and

simply.

11. The representation is not very sparse in the perceptual systems studied (as shown for example by the values of the single cell sparseness a^s), and this may allow much information to be represented. At the same time, the responses of different neurons to a set of stimuli are decorrelated, in the sense that the correlations between the response profiles of different neurons to a set of stimuli are low. Consistent with this, the neurons convey independent information, at least up to reasonable numbers of neurons. The representation may be more sparse in memory systems such as the hippocampus, and this may help to maximize the number of memories that can be stored in associative networks.

12. The nature of the distributed representation can be understood further by the firing rate probability distribution, which has a long tail with low probabilities of high firing rates. The firing rate probability distributions for some neurons fit an exponential distribution, and for others there are too few very low rates for a good fit to the exponential distribution. An implication of an exponential distribution is that this maximizes the entropy of the neuronal responses for a given mean firing rate under some conditions. It is of interest that in the inferior temporal visual cortex, the firing rate probability distribution is very close to exponential if a large number of neurons are included without scaling of the firing rates of each neuron. An implication is that a receiving neuron would see an exponential firing rate probability distribution.

13. The population sparseness a^p, that is the sparseness of the firing of a population of neurons to a given stimulus (or at one time), is the important measure for setting the capacity of associative neuronal networks. In populations of neurons studied in the inferior temporal cortex, hippocampus, and orbitofrontal cortex, it takes the same value as the single cell sparseness a^s, and this is a situation of weak ergodicity that occurs if the response profiles of the different neurons to a set of stimuli are uncorrelated.

Understanding the neuronal code, the subject of this Appendix, is fundamental for understanding how memory and related perceptual systems in the brain operate, as follows:

Understanding the neuronal code helps to clarify what neuronal operations would be useful in memory and in fact in most mammalian brain systems (e.g. dot product decoding, that is taking a sum in a short time of the incoming firing rates weighted by the synaptic weights).

It clarifies how rapidly memory and perceptual systems in the brain could operate, in terms of how long it takes a receiving neuron to read the code.

It helps to confirm how the properties of those memory systems in terms of generalization, completion, and graceful degradation occur, in that the representation is in the correct form for these properties to be realized.

Understanding the neuronal code also provides evidence essential for understanding the storage capacity of memory systems, and the representational capacity of perceptual systems.

Understanding the neuronal code is also important for interpreting functional neuroimaging, for it shows that functional imaging that reflects incoming firing rates and thus currents injected into neurons, and probably not stimulus-dependent synchronization, is likely to lead to useful interpretations of the underlying neuronal activity and processing. Of course, functional neuroimaging cannot address the details of the representation of information in the brain in the way that is essential for understanding how neuronal networks in the brain could operate, for this level of understanding (in terms of all the properties and working hypotheses described above) comes only from an understanding of how single neurons and populations of neurons encode information.

C.4 Information theory terms – a short glossary

1. The **amount of information**, or **surprise**, in the occurrence of an event (or symbol) s_i of probability $P(s_i)$ is

$$I(s_i) = \log_2 1/P(s_i) = -\log_2 P(s_i). \tag{C.55}$$

(The measure is in bits if logs to the base 2 are used.) This is also the amount of **uncertainty** removed by the occurrence of the event.

2. The average amount of information per source symbol over the whole alphabet (S) of symbols s_i is the **entropy**,

$$H(S) = -\sum_i P(s_i) \log_2 P(s_i) \tag{C.56}$$

(or *a priori* entropy).

3. The probability of the pair of symbols s and s' is denoted $P(s, s')$, and is $P(s)P(s')$ only when the two symbols are **independent**.

4. Bayes theorem (given the output s', what was the input s ?) states that

$$P(s|s') = \frac{P(s'|s)P(s)}{P(s')} \tag{C.57}$$

where $P(s'|s)$ is the **forward** conditional probability (given the input s, what will be the output s' ?), and $P(s|s')$ is the **backward** (or posterior) conditional probability (given the output s', what was the input s ?). The prior probability is $P(s)$.

5. **Mutual information**. Prior to reception of s', the probability of the input symbol s was $P(s)$. This is the *a priori* probability of s. After reception of s', the probability that the input symbol was s becomes $P(s|s')$, the conditional probability that s was sent given that s' was received. This is the *a posteriori* probability of s. The difference between the *a priori* and *a posteriori* uncertainties measures the gain of information due to the reception of s'. Once averaged across the values of both symbols s and s', this is the **mutual information**, or **transinformation**

$$I(S, S') = \sum_{s,s'} P(s, s')\{\log_2[1/P(s)] - \log_2[1/P(s|s')]\} \tag{C.58}$$

$$= \sum_{s,s'} P(s, s') \log_2[P(s|s')/P(s)].$$

Alternatively,

$$I(S, S') = H(S) - H(S|S'). \tag{C.59}$$

$H(S|S')$ is sometimes called the **equivocation** (of S with respect to S').

Appendix 4 Glossary

Instrumental reinforcers are stimuli that, if their occurrence, termination, or omission is made contingent upon the making of an action, alter the probability of the future emission of that action (Gray 1975, Mackintosh 1983, Dickinson 1980, Lieberman 2000) (see Section 3.2). Rewards and punishers are instrumental reinforcing stimuli. The notion of an action here is that an arbitrary action, e.g. turning right vs turning left, will be performed in order to obtain the reward or avoid the punisher, so that there is no pre-wired connection between the response and the reinforcer. Some stimuli are **primary (unlearned) reinforcers** (e.g., the taste of food if the animal is hungry, or pain); while others may become reinforcing by learning, because of their association with such primary reinforcers, thereby becoming '**secondary reinforcers**'. This type of learning may thus be called '**stimulus–reinforcer association learning**', and occurs via a stimulus–stimulus associative learning process.

A **positive reinforcer** (such as food) increases the probability of emission of a response on which it is contingent, the process is termed **positive reinforcement**, and the outcome is a **reward** (such as food).

A **negative reinforcer** (such as a painful stimulus) increases the probability of emission of a response that causes the negative reinforcer to be omitted (as in **active avoidance**) or terminated (as in **escape**), and the procedure is termed **negative reinforcement**.

Punishment refers to procedures in which the probability of an action is decreased. Punishment thus describes procedures in which an action decreases in probability if it is followed by a painful stimulus, as in **passive avoidance**. Punishment can also be used to refer to a procedure involving the omission or termination of a reward ('**extinction**' and '**time out**' respectively), both of which decrease the probability of responses (Gray 1975, Mackintosh 1983, Dickinson 1980, Lieberman 2000).

A **punisher** when delivered acts instrumentally to decrease the probability of responses on which it is contingent, or when not delivered (escaped from or avoided) acts as a negative reinforcer in that it then increases the probability of the action on which its non-delivery is contingent. Note that my definition of a punisher, which is similar to that of an aversive stimulus, is of a stimulus or event that can either decrease the probability of actions on which it is contingent, or increase the probability of actions on which its non-delivery is contingent. The term **punishment** is restricted to situations where the probability of an action is being decreased.

Emotions are states elicited by reinforcers, where the states have the set of functions described in Chapter 3 and by Rolls (2005). My argument is that an affectively positive or 'appetitive' stimulus (which produces a state of pleasure) acts operationally as a **reward**, which when delivered acts instrumentally as a positive reinforcer, or when not delivered (omitted or terminated) acts to decrease the probability of responses on which it is contingent. Conversely

I argue that an affectively negative or aversive stimulus (which produces an unpleasant state) acts operationally as a **punisher**, which when delivered acts instrumentally to decrease the probability of responses on which it is contingent, or when not delivered (escaped from or avoided) acts as a negative reinforcer in that it then increases the probability of the action on which its non-delivery is contingent[49].

Classical conditioning or **Pavlovian conditioning**. When a **conditioned stimulus (CS)** (such as a tone) is paired with a primary reinforcer or **unconditioned stimulus (US)** (such as a painful stimulus), then there are opportunities for a number of types of association to be formed. Some of these involve 'classical conditioning' or 'Pavlovian conditioning', in which no action is performed that affects the contingency between the conditioned stimulus and the unconditioned stimulus. Typically an **unconditioned response (UR)**, for example an alteration of heart rate, is produced by the US, and will come to be elicited by the CS as a **conditioned response (CR)**. These responses are typically autonomic (such as the heart beating faster), or endocrine (for example the release of adrenaline (epinephrine in American usage) by the adrenal gland). In addition, the organism may learn to perform an instrumental response with the skeletal muscles in order to alter the probability that the primary reinforcer will be obtained. In our example, the experimenter might alter the contingencies so that when the tone sounded, if the organism performed a response such as pressing a lever, then the painful stimulus could be avoided. In the instrumental learning situation there are still opportunities for many classically conditioned responses, including emotional states such as fear, to occur. The associative processes involved in classical conditioning, and the influences that these processes may have on instrumental performance, are described in Section 3.2.

Motivated behaviour occurs when an animal will perform an instrumental (i.e. arbitrary operant) response to obtain a reward or to escape from or avoid a punisher. If this criterion of an arbitrary operant response is not met, and only a fixed response can be performed, then the term **drive** can be used to describe the state of the animal when it will work to obtain or escape from the stimulus.

Homeostasis is the regulation of the internal milieu. The controls of food and water intake described by Rolls (2005) are examples of behaviours that maintain homeostasis.

Fitness is the reproductive potential of genes. Through the process of natural selection and reproduction, fit genes are selected for the next generation.

Long-term potentiation (LTP) is the increase in synaptic strength that can occur during learning. It is typically associative, depending on conjunctive presynaptic activity and postsynaptic depolarization.

Long-term depression (LTD) is the decrease in synaptic strength that can occur during learning. It is typically associative, occurring when the presynaptic activity is low and the postsynaptic depolarization is high (heterosynaptic long-term depression); or when the presynaptic activity is high and the postsynaptic activity is only moderate (homosynaptic long-term depression) (see Fig. 1.5).

---

[49] My definition of a punisher, which is similar to that of an aversive stimulus, is given above.

References

Abbott, L. F. (1991). Realistic synaptic inputs for model neural networks, *Network* **2**: 245–258.

Abbott, L. F. and Blum, K. I. (1996). Functional significance of long-term potentiation for sequence learning and prediction, *Cerebral Cortex* **6**: 406–416.

Abbott, L. F. and Nelson, S. B. (2000). Synaptic plasticity: taming the beast, *Nature Neuroscience* **3**: 1178–1183.

Abbott, L. F., Rolls, E. T. and Tovee, M. J. (1996). Representational capacity of face coding in monkeys, *Cerebral Cortex* **6**: 498–505.

Abbott, L. F., Varela, J. A., Sen, K. and Nelson, S. B. (1997). Synaptic depression and cortical gain control, *Science* **275**: 220–224.

Abeles, M. (1991). *Corticonics: Neural Circuits of the Cerebral Cortex*, Cambridge University Press, Cambridge.

Abramson, N. (1963). *Information Theory and Coding*, McGraw-Hill, New York.

Ackley, D. H., Hinton, G. E. and Sejnowski, T. J. (1985). A learning algorithm for Boltzmann machines, *Cognitive Science* **9**: 147–169.

Adams, C. D. (1982). Variations in the sensitivity of instrumental responding to reinforcer devaluation, *Quarterly Journal of Experimental Psychology B* **34**: 77–98.

Adams, C. D. and Dickinson, A. (1981). Instrumental responding following reinforcer devaluation, *Quarterly Journal of Experimental Psychology B* **33**: 109–121.

Adams, J. E. (1976). Naloxone reversal of analgesia produced by brain stimulation in the human, *Pain* **2**: 161–166.

Adolphs, R. (2003). Cognitive neuroscience of human social behavior, *Nature Reviews Neuroscience* **4**: 165–178.

Adolphs, R., Tranel, D., Damasio, H. and Damasio, A. R. (1994). Impaired recognition of emotion in facial expressions following bilateral damage to the human amygdala, *Nature* **372**: 669–672.

Adolphs, R., Tranel, D., Damasio, H. and Damasio, A. R. (1995). Fear and the human amygdala, *Journal of Neuroscience* **15**: 5879–5891.

Adolphs, R., Tranel, D., Hamann, S., Young, A. W., Calder, A. J., Phelps, E. A., Anderson, A., Lee, G. P. and Damasio, A. R. (1999). Recognition of facial emotion in nine individuals with bilateral amygdala damage, *Neuropsychologia* **37**: 1111–1117.

Adolphs, R., Tranel, D. and Baron-Cohen, S. (2002). Amygdala damage impairs recognition of social emotions from facial expressions, *Journal of Cognitive Neuroscience* **14**: 1–11.

Adolphs, R., Gosselin, F., Buchanan, T. W., Tranel, D., Schyns, P. and Damasio, A. R. (2005). A mechanism for impaired fear recognition after amygdala damage, *Nature* **433**: 68–72.

Aertsen, A. M. H. J., Gerstein, G. L., Habib, M. K. and Palm, G. (1989). Dynamics of neuronal firing correlation: modulation of 'effective connectivity', *Journal of Neurophysiology* **61**: 900–917.

Aggelopoulos, N. C. and Rolls, E. T. (2005). Natural scene perception: inferior temporal cortex neurons encode the positions of different objects in the scene, *European Journal of Neuroscience* **22**: 2903–2916.

Aggelopoulos, N. C., Franco, L. and Rolls, E. T. (2005). Object perception in natural scenes: encoding by inferior temporal cortex simultaneously recorded neurons, *Journal of Neurophysiology* **93**: 1342–1357.

Aggleton, J. P. (1992). The functional effects of amygdala lesions in humans, a comparison with findings from monkeys, *in* J. P. Aggleton (ed.), *The Amygdala*, Wiley-Liss, New York, chapter 19, pp. 485–503.

Aggleton, J. P. and Passingham, R. E. (1981). Syndrome produced by lesions of the amygdala in monkeys (Macaca mulatta), *Journal of Comparative and Physiological Psychology* **95**: 961–977.

Aggleton, J. P. (ed.) (2000). *The Amygdala, A Functional Analysis*, 2nd edn, Oxford University Press, Oxford.

Aggleton, J. P., Burton, M. J. and Passingham, R. E. (1980). Cortical and subcortical afferents to the amygdala in the rhesus monkey (Macaca mulatta), *Brain Research* **190**: 347–368.

Aigner, T. G., Mitchell, S. J., Aggleton, J. P., DeLong, M. R., Struble, R. G., Price, D. L., Wenk, G. L., Pettigrew, K. D. and Mishkin, M. (1991). Transient impairment of recognition memory following ibotenic acid lesions of the basal forebrain in macaques, *Experimental Brain Research* **86**: 18–26.

Ainslie, G. (1992). *Picoeconomics*, Cambridge University Press, Cambridge.

Akil, H., Mayer, D. J. and Liebeskind, J. C. (1976). Antagonism of stimulation-produced analgesia by naloxone, a narcotic antagonist, *Science* **191**: 961–962.

Albus, J. S. (1971). A theory of cerebellar function, *Mathematical Biosciences* **10**: 25–61.

Alexander, G. E., Crutcher, M. D. and DeLong, M. R. (1990). Basal ganglia thalamo-cortical circuits: parallel substrates for motor, oculomotor, 'prefrontal' and 'limbic' functions, *Progress in Brain Research* **85**: 119–146.

Alvarez, P. and Squire, L. R. (1994). Memory consolidation and the medial temporal lobe: a simple network model, *Proceedings of the National Academy of Sciences USA* **91**: 7041–7045.

Amaral, D. G. (1986). Amygdalohippocampal and amygdalocortical projections in the primate brain, *in* R. Schwarcz and Y. Ben-Ari (eds), *Excitatory Amino Acids and Epilepsy*, Plenum Press, New York, pp. 3–18.

Amaral, D. G. (1987). Memory: anatomical organization of candidate brain regions, *in* F. Plum and V. Mountcastle (eds), *Higher Functions of the Brain. Handbook of Physiology, Part I*, American Physiological Society, Washington, DC, pp. 211–294.

Amaral, D. G. (1993). Emerging principles of intrinsic hippocampal organization, *Current Opinion in Neurobiology* **3**: 225–229.

Amaral, D. G. (2003). The amygdala, social behavior, and danger detection, *Annals of the New York Academy of Sciences* **1000**: 337–347.

Amaral, D. G. and Price, J. L. (1984). Amygdalo-cortical projections in the monkey (Macaca fascicularis), *Journal of Comparative Neurology* **230**: 465–496.

Amaral, D. G. and Witter, M. P. (1989). The three-dimensional organization of the hippocampal formation: a review of anatomical data, *Neuroscience* **31**: 571–591.

Amaral, D. G. and Witter, M. P. (1995). The hippocampal formation, *in* G. Paxinos (ed.), *The Rat Nervous System*, Academic Press, San Diego, pp. 443–493.

Amaral, D. G., Ishizuka, N. and Claiborne, B. (1990). Neurons, numbers and the hippocampal network, *Progress in Brain Research* **83**: 1–11.

Amaral, D. G., Price, J. L., Pitkanen, A. and Carmichael, S. T. (1992). Anatomical organization of the primate amygdaloid complex, *in* J. P. Aggleton (ed.), *The Amygdala*, Wiley-Liss, New York, chapter 1, pp. 1–66.

Amaral, D. G., Bauman, M. D., Capitanio, J. P., Lavenex, P., Mason, W. A., Mauldin-Jourdain, M. L. and Mendoza, S. P. (2003). The amygdala: is it an essential component of the neural network for social cognition?, *Neuropsychologia* **41**: 517–522.

Amari, S. (1977). Dynamics of pattern formation in lateral-inhibition type neural fields, *Biological Cybernetics* **27**: 77–87.

Amari, S. (1982). Competitive and cooperative aspects in dynamics of neural excitation and self-organization, *in* S. Amari and M. A. Arbib (eds), *Competition and Cooperation in Neural Nets*, Springer, Berlin, chapter 1, pp. 1–28.

Amari, S., Yoshida, K. and Kanatani, K.-I. (1977). A mathematical foundation for statistical neurodynamics, *SIAM Journal of Applied Mathematics* **33**: 95–126.

Amiez, C., Joseph, J. P. and Procyk, E. (2006). Reward encoding in the monkey anterior cingulate cortex, *Cerebral Cortex* **16**: 1040–1055.

Amit, D. J. (1989). *Modelling Brain Function*, Cambridge University Press, New York.

Amit, D. J. (1995). The Hebbian paradigm reintegrated: local reverberations as internal representations, *Behavioral and Brain Sciences* **18**: 617–657.

Amit, D. J. and Brunel, N. (1997). Model of global spontaneous activity and local structured activity during delay periods in the cerebral cortex, *Cerebral Cortex* **7**: 237–252.

Amit, D. J. and Tsodyks, M. V. (1991). Quantitative study of attractor neural network retrieving at low spike rates. I. Substrate – spikes, rates and neuronal gain, *Network* **2**: 259–273.

Amit, D. J., Gutfreund, H. and Sompolinsky, H. (1987). Statistical mechanics of neural networks near saturation, *Annals of Physics (New York)* **173**: 30–67.

Andersen, P., Dingledine, R., Gjerstad, L., Langmoen, I. A. and Laursen, A. M. (1980). Two different responses of hippocampal pyramidal cells to application of gamma-aminobutyric acid, *Journal of Physiology* **307**: 279–296.

Andersen, R. A. (1995). Coordinate transformations and motor planning in the posterior parietal cortex, *in* M. S. Gazzaniga (ed.), *The Cognitive Neurosciences*, MIT Press, Cambridge, MA, chapter 33, pp. 519–532.

Andersen, R. A., Batista, A. P., Snyder, L. H., Buneo, C. A. and Cohen, Y. E. (2000). Programming to look and reach in the posterior parietal cortex, *in* M. Gazzaniga (ed.), *The New Cognitive Neurosciences*, 2 edn, MIT Press, Cambridge, MA, chapter 36, pp. 515–524.

Anderson, A. K. and Phelps, E. A. (2001). Lesions of the human amygdala impair enhanced perception of emotionally salient events, *Nature* **17**: 305–309.

Anderson, A. K., Christoff, K., Stappen, I., Panitz, D., Ghahremani, D. G., Glover, G., Gabrieli, J. D. and Sobel, N. (2003). Dissociated neural representations of intensity and valence in human olfaction, *Nature Neuroscience* **6**: 196–202.

Anderson, M. E. (1978). Discharge patterns of basal ganglia neurons during active maintenance of postural stability and adjustment to chair tilt, *Brain Research* **143**: 325–338.

Anderson, S. W., Bechara, A., Damasio, H., Tranel, D. and Damasio, A. R. (1999). Impairment of social and moral behaviour related to early damage in human prefrontal cortex, *Nature Neuroscience* **2**: 1032–1037.

Angeletos, G.-M., Laibson, D., Repetto, A., Tobacman, J. and Weinberg, S. (2001). The hyperbolic buffer stock model: calibration, simulation, and empirical evaluation, *Journal of Economic Perspectives* **15**: 47–68.

Arbib, M. A. (1964). *Brains, Machines, and Mathematics*, McGraw-Hill, New York (2nd Edn 1987 Springer).

Arguin, M. and Bub, D. N. (1993). Evidence for an independent stimulus-centered reference frame from a case of visual hemineglect, *Cortex* **29**: 349–357.

Aron, A. R., Fletcher, P. C., Bullmore, E. T., Sahakian, B. J. and Robbins, T. W. (2003). Stop-signal inhibition disrupted by damage to inferior frontal gyrus in humans, *Nature Neuroscience* **6**: 115–116.

Artola, A. and Singer, W. (1993). Long term depression: related mechanisms in cerebellum, neocortex and hippocampus, *in* M. Baudry, R. F. Thompson and J. L. Davis (eds), *Synaptic Plasticity: Molecular, Cellular and Functional Aspects*, MIT Press, Cambridge, MA, chapter 7, pp. 129–146.

Asaad, W. F., Rainer, G. and Miller, E. K. (1998). Neural activity in the primate prefrontal cortex during associative learning, *Neuron* **21**: 1399–1407.

Asaad, W. F., Rainer, G. and Miller, E. K. (2000). Task-specific neural activity in the primate prefrontal cortex, *Journal of Neurophysiology* **84**: 451–459.

Atick, J. J. (1992). Could information theory provide an ecological theory of sensory processing?, *Network* **3**: 213–251.

Atick, J. J. and Redlich, A. N. (1990). Towards a theory of early visual processing, *Neural Computation* **2**: 308–320.

Atick, J. J., Griffin, P. A. and Relich, A. N. (1996). The vocabulary of shape: principal shapes for probing perception and neural response, *Network* **7**: 1–5.

Attneave, F. (1954). Some informational aspects of visual perception, *Psychological Review* **61**: 183–193.

Bacon-Mace, N., Mace, M. J., Fabre-Thorpe, M. and Thorpe, S. J. (2005). The time course of visual processing: backward masking and natural scene categorisation, *Vision Research* **45**: 1459–1469.

Baddeley, A. (1986). *Working Memory*, Oxford University Press, New York.

Baddeley, R. J., Abbott, L. F., Booth, M. J. A., Sengpiel, F., Freeman, T., Wakeman, E. A. and Rolls, E. T. (1997). Responses of neurons in primary and inferior temporal visual cortices to natural scenes, *Proceedings of the Royal Society B* **264**: 1775–1783.

Baldo, J. V., Shimamura, A. P., Delis, D. C., Kramer, J. and Kaplan, E. (2001). Verbal and design fluency in patients with frontal lobe lesions, *Journal of the International Neuropsychological Society* **7**: 586–596.

Ballard, D. H. (1990). Animate vision uses object-centred reference frames, *in* R. Eckmiller (ed.), *Advanced Neural Computers*, North-Holland, Amsterdam, pp. 229–236.

Ballard, D. H. (1993). Subsymbolic modelling of hand-eye co-ordination, *in* D. E. Broadbent (ed.), *The Simulation of Human Intelligence*, Blackwell, Oxford, chapter 3, pp. 71–102.

Balleine, B. W. (1992). Instrumental performance following a shift in primary motivation depends upon incentive learning, *Journal of Experimental Psychology* **18**: 236–250.

Balleine, B. W. (1994). Asymmetrical interactions between thirst and hunger in Pavlovian–instrumental transfer, *Quarterly Journal of Experimental Psychology B* **47**: 211–231.

Balleine, B. W. and Dickinson, A. (1991). Instrumental performance following reinforcer devaluation depends upon incentive learning, *Quarterly Journal of Experimental Psychology B* **43**: 279–296.

Balleine, B. W. and Dickinson, A. (1998). The role of incentive learning in instrumental outcome revaluation by sensory-specific satiety, *Animal Learning and Behavior* **26**: 46–59.

Banks, W. P. (1978). Encoding and processing of symbolic information in comparative judgements, *in* G. H. Bower (ed.), *The Psychology of Learning and Motivation: Advances in Theory and Research*, Academic Press, pp. 101–159.

Barbas, H. (1988). Anatomic organization of basoventral and mediodorsal visual recipient prefrontal regions in the rhesus monkey, *Journal of Comparative Neurology* **276**: 313–342.

Barbas, H. (1993). Organization of cortical afferent input to the orbitofrontal area in the rhesus monkey, *Neuroscience* **56**: 841–864.

Barbas, H. (1995). Anatomic basis of cognitive–emotional interactions in the primate prefrontal cortex, *Neuroscience and Biobehavioral Reviews* **19**: 499–510.

Barbas, H. and Pandya, D. N. (1989). Architecture and intrinsic connections of the prefrontal cortex in the rhesus monkey, *Journal of Comparative Neurology* **286**: 353–375.

Barlow, H. (1995). The neuron doctrine in perception, *in* M. S. Gazzaniga (ed.), *The Cognitive Neurosciences*, MIT Press, Cambridge, MA, chapter 26, pp. 415–435.

Barlow, H. B. (1961). Possible principles underlying the transformation of sensory messages, *in* W. Rosenblith (ed.), *Sensory Communication*, MIT Press, Cambridge, MA.

Barlow, H. B. (1972). Single units and sensation: a neuron doctrine for perceptual psychology, *Perception* **1**: 371–394.

Barlow, H. B. (1985). Cerebral cortex as model builder, *in* D. Rose and V. G. Dobson (eds), *Models of the Visual Cortex*, Wiley, Chichester, pp. 37–46.

Barlow, H. B. (1989). Unsupervised learning, *Neural Computation* **1**: 295–311.

Barlow, H. B., Kaushal, T. P. and Mitchison, G. J. (1989). Finding minimum entropy codes, *Neural Computation* **1**: 412–423.

Baron-Cohen, S., Wheelwright, S. and Joliffe, T. (1997). Is there a 'language of the eyes'? Evidence from normal adults, and adults with autism or Asperger syndrome, *Visual Cognition* **4**: 311–331.

Baron-Cohen, S., Ring, H. A., Bullmore, E. T., Wheelwright, S., Ashwin, C. and Williams, S. C. R. (2000). The amygdala theory of autism, *Neuroscience and Biobehavioral Reviews* **24**: 355–364.

Bartlett, M. S. and Sejnowski, T. J. (1997). Viewpoint invariant face recognition using independent component analysis and attractor networks, *in* M. Mozer, M. Jordan and T. Petsche (eds), *Advances in Neural Information Processing Systems 9*, MIT Press, Cambridge, MA, pp. 817–823.

Barto, A. G. (1985). Learning by statistical cooperation of self-interested neuron-like computing elements, *COINS*

Tech. Rep., University of Massachusetts, Department of Computer and Information Science, Amherst **85-11**: 1–.

Barto, A. G. (1995). Adaptive critics and the basal ganglia, *in* J. C. Houk, J. L. Davis and D. G. Beiser (eds), *Models of Information Processing in the Basal Ganglia*, MIT Press, Cambridge, MA, chapter 11, pp. 215–232.

Bassett, J. and Taube, J. S. (2005). Head direction signal generation: ascending and descending information streams, *in* S. I. Wiener and J. S. Taube (eds), *Head Direction Cells and the Neural Mechanisms of Spatial Orientation*, MIT Press, Cambridge, MA, chapter 5, pp. 83–109.

Battaglia, F. and Treves, A. (1998a). Stable and rapid recurrent processing in realistic autoassociative memories, *Neural Computation* **10**: 431–450.

Battaglia, F. P. and Treves, A. (1998b). Attractor neural networks storing multiple space representations: a model for hippocampal place fields, *Physical Review E* **58**: 7738–7753.

Bauman, M. D., Lavenex, P., Mason, W. A., Capitanio, J. P. and Amaral, D. G. (2004). The development of social behaviour following neonatal amygdala lesions in rhesus monkeys, *Journal of Cognitive Neuroscience* **16**: 1388–1411.

Baxter, M. G. and Murray, E. A. (2000). Reinterpreting the behavioural effects of amygdala lesions in non-human primates, *in* J. P. Aggleton (ed.), *The Amygdala: a Functional Analysis*, 2nd edn, Oxford University Press, Oxford, chapter 16, pp. 545–568.

Baxter, M. G. and Murray, E. A. (2001a). Effects of hippocampal lesions on delayed nonmatching-to-sample in monkeys: a reply to Zola and Squire, *Hippocampus* **11**: 201–203.

Baxter, M. G. and Murray, E. A. (2001b). Opposite relationship of hippocampal and rhinal cortex damage to delayed nonmatching-to-sample deficits in monkeys, *Hippocampus* **11**: 61–71.

Baxter, M. G. and Murray, E. A. (2002). The amygdala and reward, *Nature Reviews Neuroscience* **3**: 563–573.

Baxter, R. D. and Liddle, P. F. (1998). Neuropsychological deficits associated with schizophrenic syndromes, *Schizophrenia Research* **30**: 239–249.

Bayer, H. M. and Glimcher, P. W. (2005). Midbrain dopamine neurons encode a quantitative reward prediction error signal, *Neuron* **47**: 129–141.

Baylis, G. C. and Rolls, E. T. (1987). Responses of neurons in the inferior temporal cortex in short term and serial recognition memory tasks, *Experimental Brain Research* **65**: 614–622.

Baylis, G. C., Rolls, E. T. and Leonard, C. M. (1985). Selectivity between faces in the responses of a population of neurons in the cortex in the superior temporal sulcus of the monkey, *Brain Research* **342**: 91–102.

Baylis, G. C., Rolls, E. T. and Leonard, C. M. (1987). Functional subdivisions of temporal lobe neocortex, *Journal of Neuroscience* **7**: 330–342.

Baylis, L. L. and Gaffan, D. (1991). Amygdalectomy and ventromedial prefrontal ablation produce similar deficits in food choice and in simple object discrimination learning for an unseen reward, *Experimental Brain Research* **86**: 617–622.

Baylis, L. L. and Rolls, E. T. (1991). Responses of neurons in the primate taste cortex to glutamate, *Physiology and Behavior* **49**: 973–979.

Baylis, L. L., Rolls, E. T. and Baylis, G. C. (1994). Afferent connections of the orbitofrontal cortex taste area of the primate, *Neuroscience* **64**: 801–812.

Baynes, K., Holtzman, H. and Volpe, V. (1986). Components of visual attention: alterations in response pattern to visual stimuli following parietal lobe infarction, *Brain* **109**: 99–144.

Bear, M. F. and Singer, W. (1986). Modulation of visual cortical plasticity by acetylcholine and noradrenaline, *Nature* **320**: 172–176.

Bechara, A., Damasio, A. R., Damasio, H. and Anderson, S. W. (1994). Insensitivity to future consequences following damage to human prefrontal cortex, *Cognition* **50**: 7–15.

Bechara, A., Tranel, D., Damasio, H. and Damasio, A. R. (1996). Failure to respond autonomically to anticipated future outcomes following damage to prefrontal cortex, *Cerebral Cortex* **6**: 215–225.

Bechara, A., Damasio, H., Tranel, D. and Damasio, A. R. (1997). Deciding advantageously before knowing the advantageous strategy, *Science* **275**: 1293–1295.

Bechara, A., Damasio, H., Tranel, D. and Anderson, S. W. (1998). Dissociation of working memory from decision making within the human prefrontal cortex, *Journal of Neuroscience* **18**: 428–437.

Bechara, A., Damasio, H., Damasio, A. R. and Lee, G. P. (1999). Different contributions of the human amygdala and ventromedial prefrontal cortex to decision making, *Journal of Neurosience* **19**: 5473–5481.

Bechara, A., Damasio, H., Tranel, D. and Damasio, A. R. (2005). The Iowa Gambling Task and the somatic marker hypothesis: some questions and answers, *Trends in Cognitive Sciences* **9**: 159–162.

Becker, S. and Hinton, G. E. (1992). Self-organizing neural network that discovers surfaces in random-dot stereograms, *Nature* **355**: 161–163.

Behrmann, M. and Moscovitch, M. (1994). Object-centered neglect in patients with unilateral neglect: effects of left-right coordinates of objects, *Journal of Cognitive Neuroscience* **6**: 151–155.

Bell, A. J. and Sejnowski, T. J. (1995). An information-maximation approach to blind separation and blind deconvolution, *Neural Computation* **7**: 1129–1159.

Beluzzi, J. D., Grant, N., Garsky, V., Sarantakis, D., Wise, C. D. and Stein, L. (1976). Analgesia induced in vivo by central administration of enkephalin in rat, *Nature* **260**: 625–626.

Benabou, R. and Pycia, M. (2002). Dynamic inconsistency and self-control: a planner–doer interpretation, *Economics Letters* **77**: 419–424.

Bennett, A. (1990). Large competitive networks, *Network* **1**: 449–462.

Berlin, H. and Rolls, E. T. (2004). Time perception, impulsivity, emotionality, and personality in self-harming borderline personality disorder patients, *Journal of Personality Disorders* **18**: 358–378.

Berlin, H., Rolls, E. T. and Kischka, U. (2004). Impulsivity, time perception, emotion, and reinforcement sensitivity in patients with orbitofrontal cortex lesions, *Brain* **127**: 1108–1126.

Berlin, H., Rolls, E. T. and Iversen, S. D. (2005). Borderline Personality Disorder, impulsivity, and the orbitofrontal cortex, *American Journal of Psychiatry* **58**: 234–245.

Berridge, K. C. and Robinson, T. E. (1998). What is the role of dopamine in reward: hedonic impact, reward learning, or incentive salience?, *Brain Research Reviews* **28**: 309–369.

Berridge, K. C. and Robinson, T. E. (2003). Parsing reward, *Trends in Neurosciences* **26**: 507–513.

Bertino, M., Beauchamp, G. K. and Engelman, K. (1991). Naltrexone, an opioid blocker, alters taste perception and nutrient intake in humans, *American Journal of Physiology* **261**: 59–63.

Bi, G.-Q. and Poo, M.-M. (1998). Activity-induced synaptic modifications in hippocampal culture, dependence on spike timing, synaptic strength and cell type, *Journal of Neuroscience* **18**: 10464–10472.

Bi, G.-Q. and Poo, M.-M. (2001). Synaptic modification by correlated activity: Hebb's postulate revisited, *Annual Review of Neuroscience* **24**: 139–166.

Bialek, W., Rieke, F., de Ruyter van Steveninck, R. R. and Warland, D. (1991). Reading a neural code, *Science* **252**: 1854–1857.

Biederman, I. (1972). Perceiving real-world scenes, *Science* **177**: 77–80.

Biederman, I. (1987). Recognition-by-components: A theory of human image understanding, *Psychological Review* **94**(2): 115–147.

Bienenstock, E. L., Cooper, L. N. and Munro, P. W. (1982). Theory for the development of neuron selectivity: orientation specificity and binocular interaction in visual cortex, *Journal of Neuroscience* **2**: 32–48.

Bierer, L. M., Haroutunian, V., Gabriel, S., Knott, P. J., Carlin, L. S., Purohit, D. P., Perl, D. P., Schmeidler, J., Kanof, P. and Davis, K. L. (1995). Neurochemical correlates of dementia severity in Alzheimer's disease: relative importance of the cholinergic deficits, *Journal of Neurochemistry* **64**: 749–760.

Binford, T. O. (1981). Inferring surfaces from images, *Artificial Intelligence* **17**: 205–244.

Bishop, C. M. (1995). *Neural Networks for Pattern Recognition*, Clarendon Press, Oxford.

Bisiach, E. (1996). Unilateral neglect and the structure of space representation, *Current Directions in Psychological Science* **5**: 62–65.

Blair, H. T., Schafe, G. E., Bauer, E. P., Rodrigues, S. M. and LeDoux, J. E. (2001). Synaptic plasticity in the lateral amygdala: a cellular hypothesis of fear conditioning, *Learning and Memory* **8**: 229–242.

Blair, H. T., Tinkelman, A., Moita, M. A. P. and LeDoux, J. E. (2003). Associative plasticity in neurons of the lateral amygdala during auditory fear conditioning, *Annals of the New York Academy of Sciences* **985**: 485–487.

Blair, R. J., Morris, J. S., Frith, C. D., Perrett, D. I. and Dolan, R. J. (1999). Dissociable neural responses to facial expressions of sadness and anger, *Brain* **122**: 883–893.

Blair, R. J. R. (2003). Facial expressions, their communicatory functions and neuro-cognitive substrates, *Philosophical Transactions of the Royal Society of London B* **358**: 561–572.

Blake, R. and Logothetis, N. K. (2002). Visual competition, *Nature Reviews Neuroscience* **3**: 13–21.

Blaney, P. H. (1986). Affect and memory: a review, *Psychological Bulletin* **99**: 229–246.

Bliss, T. V. P. and Collingridge, G. L. (1993). A synaptic model of memory: long-term potentiation in the hippocampus, *Nature* **361**: 31–39.

Block, H. D. (1962). The perceptron: a model for brain functioning, *Reviews of Modern Physics* **34**: 123–135.

Blood, A. J. and Zatorre, R. J. (2001). Intensely pleasureable responses to music correlate with activity of brain regions implicated in reward and emotion, *Proceedings of the National Academy of Sciences USA* **98**: 11818–11823.

Blood, A. J., Zatorre, R. J., Bermudez, P. and Evans, A. C. (1999). Emotional responses to pleasant and unpleasant music correlate with activity in paralimbic brain regions, *Nature Neuroscience* **2**: 382–387.

Bloomfield, S. (1974). Arithmetical operations performed by nerve cells, *Brain Research* **69**: 115–124.

Bolles, R. C. and Cain, R. A. (1982). Recognizing and locating partially visible objects: The local-feature-focus method, *International Journal of Robotics Research* **1**: 57–82.

Booth, D. A. (1985). Food-conditioned eating preferences and aversions with interoceptive elements: learned appetites and satieties, *Annals of the New York Academy of Sciences* **443**: 22–37.

Booth, M. C. A. and Rolls, E. T. (1998). View-invariant representations of familiar objects by neurons in the inferior temporal visual cortex, *Cerebral Cortex* **8**: 510–523.

Borsini, F. and Rolls, E. T. (1984). Role of noradrenaline and serotonin in the basolateral region of the amygdala in food preferences and learned taste aversions in the rat, *Physiology and Behavior* **33**: 37–43.

Boussaoud, D., Desimone, R. and Ungerleider, L. G. (1991). Visual topography of area TEO in the macaque, *Journal of Computational Neurology* **306**: 554–575.

Bowles, S. and Gintis, H. (2004). The evolution of strong reciprocity: cooperation in heterogeneous populations, *Theoretical Population Biology* **65**: 17–28.

Bowles, S. and Gintis, H. (2005). Prosocial emotions, *in* L. E. Blume and S. N. Durlauf (eds), *The Economy as an Evolving Complex System III*, Santa Fe Institute, Santa Fe, NM.

Boyd, R., Gintis, H., Bowles, S. and Richerson, P. J. (2003). The evolution of altruistic punishment, *Proceedings of the National Academy of Sciences USA* **100**: 3531–3535.

Brady, M., Ponce, J., Yuille, A. and Asada, H. (1985). Describing surfaces, *A. I. Memo 882, The Artificial Intelligence* **17**: 285–349.

Braitenberg, V. and Schuz, A. (1991). *Anatomy of the Cortex*, Springer-Verlag, Berlin.

Brebner, K., Childress, A. R. and Roberts, D. C. (2002). A potential role for GABA (B) agonists in the treatment of psychostimulant addiction, *Alcohol and Alcoholism* **37**: 478–484.

Bremner, J. D., Vythilingam, M., Vermetten, E., Nazeer, A., Adil, J., Khan, S., Staib, L. H. and Charney, D. S. (2002). Reduced volume of orbitofrontal cortex in major depression, *Biological Psychiatry* **51**: 273–279.

Bridle, J. S. (1990). Probabilistic interpretation of feedforward classification network outputs, with relationships to statistical pattern recognition, *in* F. Fogelman-Soulie and J. Herault (eds), *Neurocomputing: Algorithms, Architectures and Applications*, Springer-Verlag, New York, pp. 227–236.

Broadbent, D. E. (1958). *Perception and Communication*, Pergamon, Oxford.

Brody, C. D., Hernandez, A., Zainos, A. and Romo, R. (2003a). Timing and neural encoding of somatosensory parametric working memory in macaque prefrontal cortex, *Cerebral Cortex* **13**: 1196–1207.

Brody, C. D., Romo, R. and Kepecs, A. (2003b). Basic mechanisms for graded persistent activity: discrete attractors, continuous attractors, and dynamic representations, *Current Opinion in Neurobiology* **13**: 204–211.

Brooks, L. R. (1978). Nonanalytic concept formation and memory for instances, *in* E. Rosch and B. B. Lloyd (eds), *Cognition and Categorization*, Erlbaum, Hillsdale, NJ.

Brotchie, P., Andersen, R., Snyder, L. and Goodman, S. (1995). Head position signals used by parietal neurons to encode locations of visual stimuli, *Nature London* **375**: 232–235.

Brothers, L. and Ring, B. (1993). Mesial temporal neurons in the macaque monkey with responses selective for aspects of social stimuli, *Behavioural Brain Research* **57**: 53–61.

Brown, D. A., Gähwiler, B. H., Griffith, W. H. and Halliwell, J. V. (1990a). Membrane currents in hippocampal neurons, *Progress in Brain Research* **83**: 141–160.

Brown, M. and Xiang, J. (1998). Recognition memory: neuronal substrates of the judgement of prior occurrence, *Progress in Neurobiology* **55**: 149–189.

Brown, T. H. and Zador, A. (1990). The hippocampus, *in* G. Shepherd (ed.), *The Synaptic Organization of the Brain*, Oxford University Press, New York, pp. 346–388.

Brown, T. H., Kairiss, E. W. and Keenan, C. L. (1990b). Hebbian synapses: biophysical mechanisms and algorithms, *Annual Review of Neuroscience* **13**: 475–511.

Brown, T. H., Ganong, A. H., Kairiss, E. W., Keenan, C. L. and Kelso, S. R. (eds) (1989). *Long-term Potentiation in Two Synaptic Systems of the Hippocampal Brain Slice*, Academic Press, San Diego.

Brown, V. J., Desimone, R. and Mishkin, M. (1995). Responses of cells in the tail of the caudate nucleus during visual discrimination learning, *Journal of Neurophysiology* **74**: 1083–1094.

Bruce, V. (1988). *Recognising Faces*, Erlbaum, Hillsdale, NJ.

Brun, V. H., Otnass, M. K., Molden, S., Steffenach, H. A., Witter, M. P., Moser, M. B. and Moser, E. I. (2002). Place cells and place recognition maintained by direct entorhinal–hippocampal circuitry, *Science* **296**: 2243–2246.

Brunel, N. and Wang, X. J. (2001). Effects of neuromodulation in a cortical network model of object working memory dominated by recurrent inhibition, *Journal of Computational Neuroscience* **11**: 63–85.

Buckley, M. J. and Gaffan, D. (2000). The hippocampus, perirhinal cortex, and memory in the monkey, *in* J. J. Bolhuis (ed.), *Brain, Perception, and Memory: Advances in Cognitive Neuroscience*, Oxford University Press, Oxford, pp. 279–298.

Buckley, M. J. and Gaffan, D. (2006). Perirhinal contributions to object perception, *Trends in Cognitive Sciences* **10**: 100–107.

Buckley, M. J., Booth, M. C. A., Rolls, E. T. and Gaffan, D. (2001). Selective perceptual impairments following perirhinal cortex ablation, *Journal of Neuroscience* **21**: 9824–9836.

Buhl, E. H., Halasy, K. and Somogyi, P. (1994). Diverse sources of hippocampal unitary inhibitory postsynaptic potentials and the number of synaptic release sites, *Nature* **368**: 823–828.

Buhmann, J., Lange, J., von der Malsburg, C., Vorbrüggen, J. C. and Würtz, R. P. (1991). Object recognition in the dynamic link architecture: Parallel implementation of a transputer network, *in* B. Kosko (ed.), *Neural Networks for Signal Processing*, Prentice Hall, Englewood Cliffs, NJ, pp. 121–159.

Bullier, J. and Nowak, L. (1995). Parallel versus serial processing: new vistas on the distributed organization of the visual system, *Current Opinion in Neurobiology* **5**: 497–503.

Bunsey, M. and Eichenbaum, H. (1996). Conservation of hippocampal memory function in rats and humans, *Nature* **379**: 255–257.

Burgess, N., Recce, M. and O'Keefe, J. (1994). A model of hippocampal function, *Neural Networks* **7**: 1065–1081.

Burgess, N., Jackson, A., Hartley, T. and O'Keefe, J. (2000). Predictions derived from modelling the hippocampal role in navigation, *Biological Cybernetics* **83**: 301–312.

Burgess, N., Maguire, E. A. and O'Keefe, J. (2002). The human hippocampus and spatial and episodic memory,

Neuron **35**: 625–641.

Burke, S. N. and Barnes, C. A. (2006). Neural plasticity in the ageing brain, *Nature Reviews Neuroscience* **7**: 30–40.

Burton, M. J., Rolls, E. T. and Mora, F. (1976). Effects of hunger on the responses of neurones in the lateral hypothalamus to the sight and taste of food, *Experimental Neurology* **51**: 668–677.

Burwell, R. D., Witter, M. P. and Amaral, D. G. (1995). Perirhinal and postrhinal cortices of the rat: a review of the neuroanatomical literature and comparison with findings from the monkey brain, *Hippocampus* **5**: 390–408.

Bush, G., Luu, P. and Posner, M. I. (2000). Cognitive and emotional influences in anterior cingulate cortex, *Trends in Cognitive Sciences* **4**: 215–222.

Bush, G., Vogt, B. A., Holmes, J., Dales, A. M., Greve, D., Jenike, M. A. and Rosen, B. R. (2002). Dorsal anterior cingulate cortex: a role in reward-based decision making, *Proceedings of the National Academy of Sciences USA* **99**: 523–528.

Bushnell, C., Goldberg, M. and Robinson, D. (1981). Behavioral enhancement of visual responses in monkey cerebral cortex. I. Modulation in posterior parietal cortex related to selective visual attention, *Journal of Neurophysiology* **46**: 755–772.

Buss, D. M. (1999). *Evolutionary Psychology: The New Science of the Mind*, Allyn and Bacon, Boston, MA.

Bussey, T. J. and Everitt, B. J. (1997). Dissociable effects of cingulate and medial frontal cortex lesions on stimulus–reward learning using a novel Pavlovian autoshaping procedure for the rat: implications for the neurobiology of emotion, *Behavioral Neuroscience* **111**: 908–919.

Bussey, T. J. and Saksida, L. M. (2005). Object memory and perception in the medial temporal lobe: an alternative approach, *Current Opinion in Neurobiology* **15**: 730–737.

Bussey, T. J., Muir, J. L., Everitt, B. J. and Robbins, T. W. (1997). Triple dissociation of anterior cingulate, posterior cingulate, and medial frontal cortices on visual discrimination tasks using a touchscreen testing procedure for the rat, *Behavioral Neuroscience* **111**: 920–936.

Bussey, T. J., Saksida, L. M. and Murray, E. A. (2002). Perirhinal cortex resolves feature ambiguity in complex visual discriminations, *European Journal of Neuroscience* **15**: 365–374.

Bussey, T. J., Saksida, L. M. and Murray, E. A. (2003). Impairments in visual discrimination after perirhinal cortex lesions: testing "declarative" versus "perceptual-mnemonic" views of perirhinal cortex function, *European Journal of Neuroscience* **17**: 649–660.

Bussey, T. J., Saksida, L. M. and Murray, E. A. (2005). The perceptual-mnemonic / feature conjunction model of perirhinal cortex function, *Quarterly Journal of Experimental Psychology* **58B**: 269–282.

Butter, C. M. (1969). Perseveration in extinction and in discrimination reversal tasks following selective prefrontal ablations in Macaca mulatta, *Physiology and Behavior* **4**: 163–171.

Butter, C. M. and Snyder, D. R. (1972). Alterations in aversive and aggressive behaviors following orbitofrontal lesions in rhesus monkeys, *Acta Neurobiologica Experimentalis* **32**: 525–565.

Butter, C. M., McDonald, J. A. and Snyder, D. R. (1969). Orality, preference behavior, and reinforcement value of non-food objects in monkeys with orbital frontal lesions, *Science* **164**: 1306–1307.

Butter, C. M., Snyder, D. R. and McDonald, J. A. (1970). Effects of orbitofrontal lesions on aversive and aggressive behaviors in rhesus monkeys, *Journal of Comparative Physiology and Psychology* **72**: 132–144.

Buxton, R. B. and Frank, L. R. (1997). A model for the coupling between cerebral blood flow and oxygen metabolism during neural stimulation, *Journal of Cerebral Blood Flow and Metabolism* **17**: 64–72.

Buxton, R. B., Wong, E. C. and Frank, L. R. (1998). Dynamics of blood flow and oxygenation changes during brain activation: the balloon model, *Magnetic Resonance in Medicine* **39**: 855–864.

Caan, W., Perrett, D. I. and Rolls, E. T. (1984). Responses of striatal neurons in the behaving monkey. 2. Visual processing in the caudal neostriatum, *Brain Research* **290**: 53–65.

Cador, M., Robbins, T. W. and Everitt, B. J. (1989). Involvement of the amygdala in stimulus–reward associations: interaction with the ventral striatum, *Neuroscience* **30**: 77–86.

Cahusac, P. M. B., Miyashita, Y. and Rolls, E. T. (1989). Responses of hippocampal formation neurons in the monkey related to delayed spatial response and object-place memory tasks, *Behavioural Brain Research* **33**: 229–240.

Cahusac, P. M. B., Rolls, E. T., Miyashita, Y. and Niki, H. (1993). Modification of the responses of hippocampal neurons in the monkey during the learning of a conditional spatial response task, *Hippocampus* **3**: 29–42.

Calder, A. J., Young, A. W., Rowland, D., Perrett, D. I., Hodges, J. R. and Etcoff, N. L. (1996). Facial emotion recognition after bilateral amygdala damage: differentially severe impairment of fear, *Cognitive Neuropsycology* **13**: 699–745.

Calder, A. J., Keane, J., Manes, F., Antoun, N. and Young, A. W. (2000). Impaired recognition and experience of disgust following brain injury, *Nature Neuroscience* **3**: 1077–1078.

Calder, A. J., Keane, J., Lawrence, A. D. and Manes, F. (2004). Impaired recognition of anger following damage to the ventral striatum, *Brain* **127**: 1958–1969.

Calvert, G. A., Bullmore, E. T., Brammer, M. J., Campbell, R., Williams, S. C. R., McGuire, P. K., Woodruff, P. W. R., Iversen, S. D. and David, A. S. (1997). Activation of auditory cortex during silent lip-reading, *Science* **276**: 593–596.

Camerer, C. F. and Fehr, E. (2006). When does "economic man" dominate social behavior?, *Science* **311**: 47–52.

Canli, T., Zhao, Z., Desmond, J. E., Kang, E., Gross, J. and Gabrieli, J. D. (2001). An fMRI study of personality influences on brain reactivity to emotional stimuli, *Behavioral Neuroscience* **115**: 33–42.

Canli, T., Sivers, H., Whitfield, S. L., Gotlib, I. H. and Gabrieli, J. D. (2002). Amygdala response to happy faces as a function of extraversion, *Science* **296**: 2191.

Caplan, D. (1996). *Language: Structure, Processing and Disorders*, MIT Press, Cambridge, MA.

Cardinal, N. and Everitt, B. J. (2004). Neural and psychological mechanisms underlying appetitive learning: links to drug addiction, *Current Opinion in Neurobiology* **14**: 156–162.

Cardinal, N., Pennicott, D. R., Sugathapala, C. L., Robbins, T. W. and Everitt, B. J. (2001). Impulsive choice induced in rats by lesions of the nucleus accumbens core, *Science* **292**: 2499–2501.

Cardinal, N., Parkinson, J. A., Hall, J. and Everitt, B. J. (2002). Emotion and motivation: the role of the amygdala, ventral striatum, and prefrontal cortex, *Neuroscience and Biobehavioral Reviews* **26**: 321–352.

Carmichael, S. T. and Price, J. L. (1994). Architectonic subdivision of the orbital and medial prefrontal cortex in the macaque monkey, *Journal of Comparative Neurology* **346**: 366–402.

Carmichael, S. T. and Price, J. L. (1995a). Limbic connections of the orbital and medial prefrontal cortex in macaque monkeys, *Journal of Comparative Neurology* **363**: 615–641.

Carmichael, S. T. and Price, J. L. (1995b). Sensory and premotor connections of the orbital and medial prefrontal cortex of macaque monkeys, *Journal of Comparative Neurology* **363**: 642–664.

Carmichael, S. T. and Price, J. L. (1995c). Sensory and premotor connections of the orbital and medial prefrontal cortex of macaque monkeys, *Journal of Comparative Neurology* **363**: 642–664.

Carmichael, S. T., Clugnet, M.-C. and Price, J. L. (1994). Central olfactory connections in the macaque monkey, *Journal of Comparative Neurology* **346**: 403–434.

Carpenter, G. A. (1997). Distributed learning, recognition and prediction by ART and ARTMAP neural networks, *Neural Networks* **10**(8): 1473–1494.

Carpenter, R. H. S. and Williams, M. (1995). Neural computation of log likelihood in control of saccadic eye movements, *Nature* **377**: 59–62.

Carter, C. S., Perlstein, W., Ganguli, R., Brar, J., Mintun, M. and Cohen, J. D. (1998). Functional hypofrontality and working memory dysfunction in schizophrenia, *American Journal of Psychiatry* **155**: 1285–1287.

Carter, S. C. (1998). Neuroendocrine perpectives on social attachment and love, *Psychoneuroendocrinology* **23**: 779–818.

Cassaday, H. J. and Rawlins, J. N. (1997). The hippocampus, objects, and their contexts, *Behavioral Neuroscience* **111**: 1228–1244.

Castner, S. A., Williams, G. V. and Goldman-Rakic, P. S. (2000). Reversal of antipsychotic-induced working memory deficits by short-term dopamine D1 receptor stimulation, *Science* **287**: 2020–2022.

Celebrini, S., Thorpe, S., Trotter, Y. and Imbert, M. (1993). Dynamics of orientation coding in area V1 of the awake primate, *Visual Neuroscience* **10**: 811–825.

Cerella, J. (1986). Pigeons and perceptrons, *Pattern Recognition* **19**: 431–438.

Chakravarty, I. (1979). A generalized line and junction labeling scheme with applications to scene analysis, *IEEE Transactions PAMI* pp. 202–205.

Chelazzi, L. (1998). Serial attention mechanisms in visual search: a critical look at the evidence, *Psychological Research* **62**: 195–219.

Chelazzi, L., Miller, E., Duncan, J. and Desimone, R. (1993). A neural basis for visual search in inferior temporal cortex, *Nature (London)* **363**: 345–347.

Chen, G., Greengard, P. and Yan, Z. (2004). Potentiation of NMDA receptor currents by dopamine D1 receptors in prefrontal cortex, *Proceedings of the National Academy of Sciences USA* **101**: 2596–2600.

Chiavaras, M. M. and Petrides, M. (2001). Three-dimensional probabilistic atlas of the human orbitofrontal sulci in standardised stereotaxic space, *Neuroimage* **13**: 479–496.

Chiba, A. A., Johnson, D. L. and Kesner, R. P. (1992). The effects of lesions of the dorsal hippocampus or the ventral hippocampus on performance of a spatial location order recognition task, *Society for Neuroscience Abstracts* **18**: 1422.

Chiba, A. A., Kesner, R. P. and Reynolds, A. M. (1994). Memory for spatial location as a function of temporal lag in rats: role of hippocampus and medial prefrontal cortex, *Behavioral and Neural Biology* **61**: 123–131.

Childress, A. R., Mozley, P. D., McElgin, W., Fitzgerald, J., Reivich, M. and O'Brien, C. P. (1999). Limbic activation during cue-induced cocaine craving, *American Journal of Psychiatry* **156**: 11–18.

Cho, Y. H. and Kesner, R. P. (1995). Relational object association learning in rats with hippocampal lesions, *Behavioural Brain Research* **67**: 91–98.

Christie, B. R. (1996). Long-term depression in the hippocampus, *Hippocampus* **6**: 1–2.

Clark, D. A. and Beck, A. T. (1999). *Scientific Foundations of Cognitive Theory and Therapy of Depression*, Wiley, New York.

Clark, L., Cools, R. and Robbins, T. W. (2004). The neuropsychology of ventral prefrontal cortex: decision-making and reversal learning, *Brain and Cognition* **55**: 41–53.

Coghill, R. C., Talbot, J. D., Evans, A. C., Meyer, E., Gjedde, A., Bushnell, M. C. and Duncan, G. H. (1994). Distributed processing of pain and vibration in the human brain, *Journal of Neuroscience* **14**: 4095–4108.

Colby, C. L., Duhamel, J. R. and Goldberg, M. E. (1993). Ventral intraparietal area of the macaque - anatomic location and visual response properties, *Journal of Neurophysiology* **69**: 902–914.

Collingridge, G. L. and Bliss, T. V. P. (1987). NMDA receptors: their role in long-term potentiation, *Trends in Neurosciences* **10**: 288–293.

Colwill, R. M. and Rescorla, R. A. (1985). Postconditioning devaluation of a reinforcer affects instrumental responding, *Journal of Experimental Psychology* **11**: 120–132.

Colwill, R. M. and Rescorla, R. A. (1988). Associations between the discriminative stimulus and the reinforcer in instrumental learning, *Journal of Experimental Psychology* **14**: 155–164.

Colwill, R. M. and Rescorla, R. A. (1990). Evidence for the hierarchical structure of instrumental learning, *Animal Learning and Behaviour* **18**: 71–82.

Connor, C. E., Gallant, J. L., Preddie, D. and Van Essen, D. (1996). Responses in area V4 depend on the spatial relationship between stimulus and attention, *Journal of Neurophysiology* **75**: 1306–1308.

Cooper, J. R., Bloom, F. E. and Roth, R. H. (2003). *The Biochemical Basis of Neuropharmacology*, 8th edn, Oxford University Press, Oxford.

Corbetta, M. and Shulman, G. (1998). Human cortical mechanisms of visual attention during orienting and search, *Philosophical Transactions of the Royal Society of London* **353**: 1353–1362.

Corchs, S. and Deco, G. (2002). Large-scale neural model for visual attention: integration of experimental single cell and fMRI data, *Cerebral Cortex* **12**: 339–348.

Corchs, S. and Deco, G. (2004). Feature-based attention in human visual cortex: simulation of fMRI data, *Neuroimage* **21**: 36–45.

Cortes, C., Jaeckel, L. D., Solla, S. A., Vapnik, V. and Denker, J. S. (1996). Learning curves: asymptotic values and rates of convergence, *Neural Information Processing Systems* **6**: 327–334.

Corwin, R. L. and Buda-Levin, A. (2004). Behavioral models of binge-type eating, *Physiology and Behavior* **82**: 123–130.

Cover, T. M. (1965). Geometrical and statistical properties of systems of linear inequalities with applications in pattern recognition, *IEEE Transactions on Electronic Computers* **14**: 326–334.

Cover, T. M. and Thomas, J. A. (1991). *Elements of Information Theory*, Wiley, New York.

Cowell, R. A., Bussey, T. J. and Saksida, L. M. (2006). Why does brain damage impair memory? a connectionist model of object recognition memory in perirhinal cortex, *Journal of Neuroscience* **26**: 12186–12197.

Cowey, A. (1979). Cortical maps and visual perception, *Quarterly Journal of Experimental Psychology* **31**: 1–17.

Coyle, J. T., Tsai, G. and Goff, D. (2003). Converging evidence of NMDA receptor hypofunction in the pathophysiology of schizophrenia, *Annals of the New York Academy of Sciences* **1003**: 318–327.

Craig, A. D., Chen, K., Bandy, D. and Reiman, E. M. (2000). Thermosensory activation of insular cortex, *Nature Neuroscience* **3**: 184–190.

Crane, J. and Milner, B. (2005). What went where? Impaired object-location learning in patients with right hippocampal lesions, *Hippocampus* **15**: 216–231.

Crick, F. H. C. (1984). Function of the thalamic reticular complex: the searchlight hypothesis, *Proceedings of the National Academy of Sciences USA* **81**: 4586–4590.

Crick, F. H. C. and Koch, C. (1990). Towards a neurobiological theory of consciousness, *Seminars in the Neurosciences* **2**: 263–275.

Crick, F. H. C. and Mitchison, G. (1995). REM sleep and neural nets, *Behavioural Brain Research* **69**: 147–155.

Critchley, H. D. and Rolls, E. T. (1996a). Hunger and satiety modify the responses of olfactory and visual neurons in the primate orbitofrontal cortex, *Journal of Neurophysiology* **75**: 1673–1686.

Critchley, H. D. and Rolls, E. T. (1996b). Olfactory neuronal responses in the primate orbitofrontal cortex: analysis in an olfactory discrimination task, *Journal of Neurophysiology* **75**: 1659–1672.

Critchley, H. D. and Rolls, E. T. (1996c). Responses of primate taste cortex neurons to the astringent tastant tannic acid, *Chemical Senses* **21**: 135–145.

Cromwell, H. C. and Schultz, W. (2003). Effects of expectations for different reward magntitudes on neuronal activity in primate striatum, *Journal of Neurophysiology* **89**: 2823–2838.

Crutcher, M. D. and DeLong, M. R. (1984a). Single cell studies of the primate putamen. I. Functional organisation, *Experimental Brain Research* **53**: 233–243.

Crutcher, M. D. and DeLong, M. R. (1984b). Single cell studies of the primate putamen. II. Relations to direction of movements and pattern of muscular activity, *Experimental Brain Research* **53**: 244–258.

Damasio, A. R. (1994). *Descartes' Error: Emotion, Reason, and the Human Brain*, Grosset/Putnam, New York.

Damasio, H., Grabowski, T., Frank, R., Galaburda, A. M. and Damasio, A. R. (1994). The return of Phineas Gage: clues about the brain from the skull of a famous patient, *Science* **264**: 1102–1105.

Dan, Y. and Poo, M.-M. (2004). Spike-timing dependent plasticity of neural circuits, *Neuron* **44**: 23–30.

Dan, Y. and Poo, M.-M. (2006). Spike-timing dependent plasticity: from synapse to perception, *Physiological Reviews* **86**: 1033–1048.

Dane, C. and Bajcsy, R. (1982). An object-centred three-dimensional model builder, *Proceedings of the 6th International Conference on Pattern Recognition*, pp. 348–350.

Daniel, D., Weinberger, D., Jones, D., Zigun, J., Coppola, R., Handel, S., Bigelow, L., Goldberg, T., Berman, K. and Kleinman, J. (1991). The effect of amphetamine on regional cerebral blood flow during cognitive activation in schizophrenia, *Journal of Neuroscience* **11**: 1907–1917.

Davidson, R. J. (1992). Anterior cerebral asymmetry and the nature of emotion, *Brain and Cognition* **6**: 245–268.

Davidson, R. J. (2003). Affective neuroscience and psychophysiology: toward a synthesis, *Psychophysiology* **40**: 655–665.

Davidson, R. J., Ekman, P., Saron, C., Senulis, J. and Friesen, W. V. (1990). Approach/withdrawal and cerebral asymmetry, *Journal of Personality and Social Research* **58**: 330–341.

Davis, M. (1992). The role of the amygdala in conditioned fear, *in* J. P. Aggleton (ed.), *The Amygdala*, Wiley-Liss, New York, chapter 9, pp. 255–306.

Davis, M. (1994). The role of the amygdala in emotional learning, *International Review of Neurobiology* **36**: 225–266.

Davis, M. (2000). The role of the amygdala in conditioned and unconditioned fear and anxiety, *in* J. P. Aggleton (ed.), *The Amygdala: a Functional Analysis*, 2nd edn, Oxford University Press, Oxford, chapter 6, pp. 213–287.

Davis, M., Campeau, S., Kim, M. and Falls, W. A. (1995). Neural systems and emotion: the amygdala's role in fear and anxiety, *in* J. L. McGaugh, N. M. Weinberger and G. Lynch (eds), *Brain and Memory: Modulation and Mediation of Neuroplasticity*, Oxford University Press, New York, pp. 3–40.

Dawkins, M. S. (1995). *Unravelling Animal Behaviour*, 2nd edn, Longman, Harlow.

Dawkins, R. (1982). *The Extended Phenotype*, Freeman, Oxford.

Day, M., Langston, R. and Morris, R. G. (2003). Glutamate-receptor-mediated encoding and retrieval of paired-associate learning, *Nature* **424**: 205–209.

Dayan, P. and Abbott, L. F. (2001). *Theoretical Neuroscience*, MIT Press, Cambridge, MA.

Dayan, P. and Sejnowski, T. J. (1994). TD(λ) converges with probability 1, *Machine Learning* **14**: 295–301.

De Araujo, I. E. T. and Rolls, E. T. (2004). Representation in the human brain of food texture and oral fat, *Journal of Neuroscience* **24**: 3086–3093.

De Araujo, I. E. T., Rolls, E. T. and Stringer, S. M. (2001). A view model which accounts for the response properties of hippocampal primate spatial view cells and rat place cells, *Hippocampus* **11**: 699–706.

De Araujo, I. E. T., Kringelbach, M. L., Rolls, E. T. and Hobden, P. (2003a). Representation of umami taste in the human brain, *Journal of Neurophysiology* **90**: 313–319.

De Araujo, I. E. T., Kringelbach, M. L., Rolls, E. T. and McGlone, F. (2003b). Human cortical responses to water in the mouth, and the effects of thirst, *Journal of Neurophysiology* **90**: 1865–1876.

De Araujo, I. E. T., Rolls, E. T., Kringelbach, M. L., McGlone, F. and Phillips, N. (2003c). Taste-olfactory convergence, and the representation of the pleasantness of flavour in the human brain, *European Journal of Neuroscience* **18**: 2059–2068.

De Araujo, I. E. T., Rolls, E. T., Velazco, M. I., Margot, C. and Cayeux, I. (2005). Cognitive modulation of olfactory processing, *Neuron* **46**: 671–679.

De Gelder, B., Vroomen, J., Pourtois, G. and Weiskrantz, L. (1999). Non-conscious recognition of affect in the absence of striate cortex, *NeuroReport* **10**: 3759–3763.

de Lafuente, V. and Romo, R. (2005). Neuronal correlates of subjective sensory experience, *Nature Neuroscience* **12**: 1698–1703.

de Ruyter van Steveninck, R. R. and Laughlin, S. B. (1996). The rates of information transfer at graded-potential synapses, *Nature* **379**: 642–645.

De Sieno, D. (1988). Adding a conscience to competitive learning, *IEEE International Conference on Neural Networks (San Diego 1988)*, Vol. 1, IEEE, New York, pp. 117–124.

Deadwyler, S., Hayashizaki, S., Cheer, J. and Hampson, R. E. (2004). Reward, memory and substance abuse: functional neuronal circuits in the nucleus accumbens, *Neuroscience and Biobehavioral Reviews* **27**: 703–711.

DeAngelis, G. C., Cumming, B. G. and Newsome, W. T. (2000). A new role for cortical area MT: the perception of stereoscopic depth, *in* M. Gazzaniga (ed.), *The New Cognitive Neurosciences, Second Edition*, MIT Press, Cambridge, MA, chapter 21, pp. 305–314.

Debiec, J., LeDoux, J. E. and Nader, K. (2002). Cellular and systems reconsolidation in the hippocampus, *Neuron* **36**: 527–538.

Debiec, J., Doyere, V., Nader, K. and LeDoux, J. E. (2006). Directly reactivated, but not indirectly reactivated, memories undergo reconsolidation in the amygdala, *Proceedings of the National Academy of Sciences USA* **103**: 3428–3433.

deCharms, R. C. and Merzenich, M. M. (1996). Primary cortical representation of sounds by the coordination of action-potential timing, *Nature* **381**: 610–613.

Deco, G. (2001). Biased competition mechanisms for visual attention, *in* S. Wermter, J. Austin and D. Willshaw (eds), *Emergent Neural Computational Architectures Based on Neuroscience*, Springer, Heidelberg, pp. 114–126.

Deco, G. and Lee, T. S. (2002). A unified model of spatial and object attention based on inter-cortical biased competition, *Neurocomputing* **44–46**: 775–781.

Deco, G. and Lee, T. S. (2004). The role of early visual cortex in visual integration: a neural model of recurrent interaction, *European Journal of Neuroscience* **20**: 1089–1100.

Deco, G. and Rolls, E. T. (2002). Object-based visual neglect: a computational hypothesis, *European Journal of Neuroscience* **16**: 1994–2000.

Deco, G. and Rolls, E. T. (2003). Attention and working memory: a dynamical model of neuronal activity in the prefrontal cortex, *European Journal of Neuroscience* **18**: 2374–2390.

Deco, G. and Rolls, E. T. (2004). A neurodynamical cortical model of visual attention and invariant object recognition, *Vision Research* **44**: 621–644.

Deco, G. and Rolls, E. T. (2005a). Attention, short term memory, and action selection: a unifying theory, *Progress in Neurobiology* **76**: 236–256.

Deco, G. and Rolls, E. T. (2005b). Neurodynamics of biased competition and cooperation for attention: a model with spiking neurons, *Journal of Neurophysiology* **94**: 295–313.

Deco, G. and Rolls, E. T. (2005c). Sequential memory: a putative neural and synaptic dynamical mechanism, *Journal of Cognitive Neuroscience* **17**: 294–307.

Deco, G. and Rolls, E. T. (2005d). Synaptic and spiking dynamics underlying reward reversal in the orbitofrontal cortex, *Cerebral Cortex* **15**: 15–30.

Deco, G. and Rolls, E. T. (2006). A neurophysiological model of decision-making and Weber's law, *European Journal of Neuroscience* **24**: 901–916.

Deco, G. and Zihl, J. (2001a). A neurodynamical model of visual attention: Feedback enhancement of spatial resolution in a hierarchical system, *Journal of Computational Neuroscience* **10**: 231–253.

Deco, G. and Zihl, J. (2001b). Top-down selective visual attention: a neurodynamical approach, *Visual Cognition* **8**: 119–140.

Deco, G. and Zihl, J. (2004). A biased competition based neurodynamical model of visual neglect, *Medical Engineering and Physics* **26**: 733–743.

Deco, G., Pollatos, O. and Zihl, J. (2002). The time course of selective visual attention: theory and experiments, *Vision Research* **42**: 2925–2945.

Deco, G., Rolls, E. T. and Horwitz, B. (2004). 'What' and 'where' in visual working memory: a computational neurodynamical perspective for integrating fMRI and single-neuron data, *Journal of Cognitive Neuroscience* **16**: 683–701.

DeCoteau, W. E. and Kesner, R. P. (2000). A double dissociation between the rat hippocampus and medial caudoputamen in processing two forms of knowledge, *Behavioral Neuroscience* **114**: 1096–1108.

Dehaene, S., Dehaene-Lambertz, G. and Cohen, L. (1998). Abstract representations of numbers in the animal and human brain, *Trends in Neurosciences* **21**: 355–361.

Del Giudice, P., Fusi, S. and Mattia, M. (2003). Modeling the formation of working memory with networks of integrate-and-fire neurons connected by plastic synapses, *Journal of Physiology (Paris)* **97**: 659–681.

Delatour, B. and Witter, M. P. (2002). Projections from the parahippocampal region to the prefrontal cortex in the rat: evidence of multiple pathways, *European Journal of Neuroscience* **15**: 1400–1407.

Delgado, M. R., Nystrom, L. E., Fissell, C., Noll, D. C. and Fiez, J. A. (2000). Tracking the human hemodynamic responses to reward and punishment in the striatum, *Journal of Neurophysiology* **84**: 3072–3077.

DeLong, M. R., Georgopoulos, A. P., Crutcher, M. D., Mitchell, S. J., Richardson, R. T. and Alexander, G. E. (1984). Functional organization of the basal ganglia: Contributions of single-cell recording studies, *Functions of the Basal Ganglia. CIBA Foundation Symposium*, Pitman, London, pp. 64–78.

Delorme, A. and Thorpe, S. J. (2001). Face identification using one spike per neuron: resistance to image degradations, *Neural Networks* **14**: 795–803.

Derbyshire, S. W. G., Vogt, B. A. and Jones, A. K. P. (1998). Pain and Stroop interference tasks activate separate processing modules in anterior cingulate cortex, *Experimental Brain Research* **118**: 52–60.

Desimone, R. (1996). Neural mechanisms for visual memory and their role in attention, *Proceedings of the National Academy of Sciences USA* **93**: 13494–13499.

Desimone, R. and Duncan, J. (1995). Neural mechanisms of selective visual attention, *Annual Review of Neuroscience* **18**: 193–222.

Desimone, R., Albright, T. D., Gross, C. G. and Bruce, C. (1984). Stimulus-selctive responses of inferior temporal neurons in the macaque, *Journal of Neuroscience* **4**: 2051–2062.

Devinsky, O., Morrell, M. J. and Vogt, B. A. (1995). Contributions of anterior cingulate cortex to behaviour, *Brain* **118**: 279–306.

DeWeese, M. R. and Meister, M. (1999). How to measure the information gained from one symbol, *Network* **10**: 325–340.

Diamond, M. E., Huang, W. and Ebner, F. F. (1994). Laminar comparison of somatosensory cortical plasticity, *Science* **265**: 1885–1888.

Dias, R., Robbins, T. W. and Roberts, A. C. (1996). Dissociation in prefrontal cortex of affective and attentional shifts, *Nature* **380**: 69–72.

DiCarlo, J. J. and Maunsell, J. H. R. (2003). Anterior inferotemporal neurons of monkeys engaged in object recognition can be highly sensitive to object retinal position, *Journal of Neurophysiology* **89**: 3264–3278.

DiChiara, G., Acquas, E. and Carboni, E. (1992). Drug motivation and abuse: a neurobiological perspective, *Annals of the New York Academy of Sciences* **654**: 207–219.

Dickinson, A. (1980). *Contemporary Animal Learning Theory*, Cambridge University Press, Cambridge.

Dickinson, A. (1985). Actions and habits – the development of behavioural autonomy, *Philosophical Transactions of the Royal Society of London B* **308**: 67–78.

Dickinson, A. (1986). Re-examination of the role of the instrumental contingency in the sodium-appetitive irrelevant incentive effect, *Quarterly Journal of Experimental Psychology B* **38**: 161–172.

Dickinson, A. (1994). Instrumental conditioning, *in* N. J. Mackintosh (ed.), *Animal Learning and Cognition*, Academic Press, San Diego, pp. 45–80.

Dickinson, A. and Balleine, B. (1994). Motivational control of goal-directed action, *Animal Learning and Behaviour* **22**: 1–18.

Dickinson, A. and Dawson, G. R. (1987a). Pavlovian processes in the motivational control of instrumental performance, *Quarterly Journal of Experimental Psychology B* **39**: 201–213.

Dickinson, A. and Dawson, G. R. (1987b). The role of the instrumental contigency in the motivational control of performance, *Quarterly Journal of Experimental Psychology B* **39**: 77–93.

Dickinson, A. and Dearing, M. F. (1979). Appetitive-aversive interactions and inhibitory processes, *in* A. Dickinson and R. A. Boakes (eds), *Mechanisms of Learning and Motivation*, Erlbaums, Hillsdale, NJ, pp. 203–231.

Dickinson, A., Nicholas, D. J. and Adams, C. D. (1983). The effects of the instrumental training contingency on susceptibility to reinforcer devaluation, *Quarterly Journal of Experimental Psychology B* **35**: 35–51.

Dickinson, A., Balleine, B., Watt, A., Gonzalez, F. and Boakes, R. A. (1995). Motivational control after extended instrumental training, *Animal Learning and Behaviour* **23**: 197–206.

Divac, I. (1975). Magnocellular nuclei of the basal forebrain project to neocortex, brain stem, and olfactory bulb. Review of some functional correlates, *Brain Research* **93**: 385–398.

Divac, I. and Oberg, R. G. E. (1979). Current conceptions of neostriatal functions, *in* I. Divac and R. G. E. Oberg (eds), *The Neostriatum*, Pergamon, New York, pp. 215–230.

Divac, I., Rosvold, H. E. and Szwarcbart, M. K. (1967). Behavioral effects of selective ablation of the caudate nucleus, *Journal of Comparative and Physiological Psychology* **63**: 184–190.

Dolan, R. J. (1997). Mood disorders and abnormal cingulate cortex, *Trends in Cognitive Sciences* **1**: 283–284.

Dolan, R. J. (1999). On the neurology of morals, *Nature Neuroscience* **15**: 5999–6013.

Dolan, R. J., Bench, C. J., Brown, R. G., Scott, L. C., Friston, K. J. and Frackowiak, C. S. (1992). Regional cerebral blood flow abnormalities in depressed patients with cognitive impairment, *Journal of Neurology, Neurosurgery, and Psychiatry* **55**: 768–773.

Dolan, R. J., Fletcher, P., Morris, J., Kapur, N., Deakin, J. F. W. and Frith, C. D. (1996). Neural activation during covert processing of positive emotional facial expressions, *Neuroimage* **4**: 194–200.

Dolan, R. J., Fink, G. R., Rolls, E. T., Booth, M., Holmes, A., Frackowiak, R. S. J. and Friston, K. J. (1997). How the brain learns to see objects and faces in an impoverished context, *Nature* **389**: 596–599.

Douglas, R. J. and Martin, K. A. C. (1990). Neocortex, *in* G. M. Shepherd (ed.), *The Synaptic Organization of the Brain*, 3rd edn, Oxford University Press, Oxford, chapter 12, pp. 389–438.

Douglas, R. J., Mahowald, M. A. and Martin, K. A. C. (1996). Microarchitecture of cortical columns, *in* A. Aertsen and V. Braitenberg (eds), *Brain Theory: Biological Basis and Computational Theory of Vision*, Elsevier, Amsterdam.

Douglas, R. J., Markram, H. and Martin, K. A. C. (2004). Neocortex, *in* G. M. Shepherd (ed.), *The Synaptic Organization of the Brain*, 5th edn, Oxford University Press, Oxford, chapter 12, pp. 499–558.

Dow, B. W., Snyder, A. Z., Vautin, R. G. and Bauer, R. (1981). Magnification factor and receptive field size in foveal striate cortex of the monkey, *Experimental Brain Research* **44**: 213–218.

Doya, K. (1999). What are the computations of the cerebellum, the basal ganglia and the cerebral cortex?, *Neural Networks* **12**: 961–974.

Drevets, W. C. and Raichle, M. E. (1992). Neuroanatomical circuits in depression: implications for treatment mechanisms, *Psychopharmacology Bulletin* **28**: 261–274.

Drevets, W. C., Price, J. L., Simpson, J. R. J., Todd, R. D., Reich, T., Vannier, M. and Raichle, M. (1997). Subgenual prefrontal cortex abnormalities in mood disorders, *Nature* **386**: 824–847.

Driver, J. and Halligan, P. (1991). Can visual neglect operate in object-centred co-ordinates? An affirmative single-case study, *Cognitive Neuropsychology* **8**: 475–496.

Driver, J., Baylis, G. and Rafal, R. (1992). Preserved figure-ground segregation and symmetry perception in visual neglect, *Nature* **360**: 73–75.

Driver, J., Baylis, G., Goodrich, S. and Rafal, R. (1994). Axis-based neglect of visual shapes, *Neuropsychologia* **32**: 1353–1365.

Dudchenko, P. A., Wood, E. R. and Eichenbaum, H. (2000). Neurotoxic hippocampal lesions have no effect on odor span and little effect on odor recognition memory but produce significant impairments on spatial span, recognition, and alternation, *Journal of Neuroscience* **20**: 2964–2977.

Duhamel, J. R., Colby, C. L. and Goldberg, M. E. (1992). The updating of the representation of visual space in parietal cortex by intended eye movements, *Science* **255**: 90–92.

Dulac, C. and Torello, A. T. (2003). Molecular detection of pheromone signals in mammals: from genes to behaviour, *Nature Reviews Neuroscience* **4**: 551–562.

Dunbar, R. (1996). *Grooming, Gossip, and the Evolution of Language*, Faber and Faber, London.

Duncan, J. (1980). The locus of interference in the perception of simultaneous stimuli, *Psychological Review* **87**: 272–300.

Duncan, J. (1996). Cooperating brain systems in selective perception and action, *in* T. Inui and J. L. McClelland (eds), *Attention and Performance XVI*, MIT Press, Cambridge, MA, pp. 549–578.

Duncan, J. and Humphreys, G. (1989). Visual search and stimulus similarity, *Psychological Review* **96**: 433–458.

Duncan, J., Humphreys, G. and Ward, R. (1997). Competitive brain activity in visual attention, *Current Opinion in Neurobiology* **7**: 255–261.

Dunn, L. T. and Everitt, B. J. (1988). Double dissociations of the effects of amygdala and insular cortex lesions on conditioned taste aversion, passive avoidance, and neophobia in the rat using the excitotoxin ibotenic acid, *Behavioral Neuroscience* **102**: 3–23.

Dunnett, S. B. and Iversen, S. D. (1982a). Neurotoxic lesions of ventrolateral but not anteromedial neostriatum impair differential reinforcement of low rates (DRL) performance, *Behavioural Brain Research* **6**: 213–226.

Dunnett, S. B. and Iversen, S. D. (1982b). Sensorimotor impairments following localised kainic acid and 6-hydroxydopamine lesions of the neostriatum, *Brain Research* **248**: 121–127.

Durbin, R. and Mitchison, G. (1990). A dimension reduction framework for understanding cortical maps, *Nature* **343**: 644–647.

Durstewitz, D. and Seamans, J. K. (2002). The computational role of dopamine D1 receptors in working memory, *Neural Networks* **15**: 561–572.

Durstewitz, D., Kelc, M. and Gunturkun, O. (1999). A neurocomputational theory of the dopaminergic modulation of working memory functions, *Journal of Neuroscience* **19**: 2807–2822.

Durstewitz, D., Seamans, J. K. and Sejnowski, T. J. (2000). Dopamine-mediated stabilization of delay-period activity in a network model of prefrontal cortex, *Journal of Neurophysiology* **83**: 1733–1750.

Easton, A. and Gaffan, D. (2000). Amygdala and the memory of reward: the importance of fibres of passage from the basal forebrain, *in* J. P. Aggleton (ed.), *The Amygdala: a Functional Analysis*, 2nd edn, Oxford University Press, Oxford, chapter 17, pp. 569–586.

Easton, A., Ridley, R. M., Baker, H. F. and Gaffan, D. (2002). Unilateral lesions of the cholinergic basal forebrain and fornix in one hemisphere and inferior temporal cortex in the opposite hemisphere produce severe learning impairments in rhesus monkeys, *Cerebral Cortex* **12**: 729–736.

Eccles, J. C. (1984). The cerebral neocortex: a theory of its operation, *in* E. G. Jones and A. Peters (eds), *Cerebral Cortex: Functional Properties of Cortical Cells*, Vol. 2, Plenum, New York, chapter 1, pp. 1–36.

Eckhorn, R. and Popel, B. (1974). Rigorous and extended application of information theory to the afferent visual system of the cat. I. Basic concepts, *Kybernetik* **16**: 191–200.

Eckhorn, R. and Popel, B. (1975). Rigorous and extended application of information theory to the afferent visual system of the cat. II. Experimental results, *Kybernetik* **17**: 7–17.

Eckhorn, R., Grusser, O. J., Kroller, J., Pellnitz, K. and Popel, B. (1976). Efficiency of different neural codes: information transfer calculations for three different neuronal systems, *Biological Cybernetics* **22**: 49–60.

Eckhorn, R., Bauer, R., Jordan, W., Brosch, M., Munk, M. and Reitboeck, H. (1988). Coherent oscillations: A mechanism of feature linking in the visual cortex?, *Biological Cybernetics* **60**: 121–128.

Edelman, S. (1999). *Representation and Recognition in Vision*, MIT Press, Cambridge, MA.

Egan, M. and Weinberg, D. (1997). Neurobiology of schizophrenia, *Current Opinion in Neurobiology* **7**: 701–707.

Eglin, M., Robertson, L. and Knight, R. (1989). Visual search performance in the neglect syndrome, *Journal of Cognitive Neuroscience* **1**: 372–385.

Eichenbaum, H. (1997). Declarative memory: insights from cognitive neurobiology, *Annual Review of Psychology* **48**: 547–572.

Eichenbaum, H. and Cohen, N. J. (2001). *From Conditioning to Conscious Recollection: Memory Systems of the Brain*, Oxford University Press, New York.

Eichenbaum, H., Otto, T. and Cohen, N. J. (1992). The hippocampus - what does it do?, *Behavioural and Neural Biology* **57**: 2–36.

Eisenberger, N. I. and Lieberman, M. D. (2004). Why rejection hurts: a common neural alarm system for physical and social pain, *Trends in Cognitive Neuroscience* **8**: 294–300.

Ekstrom, A. D., Kahana, M. J., Caplan, J. B., Fields, T. A., Isham, E. A., Newman, E. L. and Fried, I. (2003). Cellular networks underlying human spatial navigation, *Nature* **425**: 184–188.

Elithorn, A., Piercy, M. F. and Crosskey, M. A. (1955). Prefrontal leucotomy and the anticipation of pain, *Journal of Neurology, Neurosurgery and Psychiatry* **18**: 34–43.

Elliffe, M. C. M., Rolls, E. T., Parga, N. and Renart, A. (2000). A recurrent model of transformation invariance by association, *Neural Networks* **13**: 225–237.

Elliffe, M. C. M., Rolls, E. T. and Stringer, S. M. (2002). Invariant recognition of feature combinations in the visual system, *Biological Cybernetics* **86**: 59–71.

Engel, A. K., Konig, P., Kreiter, A. K., Schillen, T. B. and Singer, W. (1992). Temporal coding in the visual system: new vistas on integration in the nervous system, *Trends in Neurosciences* **15**: 218–226.

Epstein, R. and Kanwisher, N. (1998). A cortical representation of the local visual environment, *Nature* **392**: 598–601.

Eriksen, C. W. and Hoffmann, J. (1973). The extent of processing of noise elements during selective encoding from visual displays, *Perception and Psychophysics* **14**: 155–160.

Erreger, K., Chen, P. E., Wyllie, D. J. and Traynelis, S. F. (2004). Glutamate receptor gating, *Critical Reviews in*

Neurobiology **16**: 187–224.

Eskandar, E. N., Richmond, B. J. and Optican, L. M. (1992). Role of inferior temporal neurons in visual memory. I. Temporal encoding of information about visual images, recalled images, and behavioural context, *Journal of Neurophysiology* **68**: 1277–1295.

Eslinger, P. and Damasio, A. (1985). Severe disturbance of higher cognition after bilateral frontal lobe ablation: patient EVR, *Neurology* **35**: 1731–1741.

Estes, W. K. (1948). Discriminative conditioning II Effects of Pavlovian conditioned stimulus upon a subsequently established operant response, *Journal of Experimental Psychology* **38**: 173–177.

Estes, W. K. (1986). Memory for temporal information, *in* J. A. Michon and J. L. Jackson (eds), *Time, Mind and Behavior*, Springer-Verlag, New York, pp. 151–168.

Etcoff, N. L. (1989). Asymmetries in recognition of emotion, *in* F. Boller and F. Grafman (eds), *Handbook of Psychology*, Vol. 3, Elsevier, Amsterdam, pp. 363–382.

Evarts, E. V. and Wise, S. P. (1984). Basal ganglia outputs and motor control, *Functions of the Basal Ganglia. CIBA Foundation Symposium*, Vol. 107, Pitman, London, pp. 83–96.

Everitt, B. (1997). Craving cocaine cues: cognitive neuroscience meets drug addiction research, *Trends in Cognitive Sciences* **1**: 1–2.

Everitt, B. J. and Robbins, T. W. (1992). Amygdala-ventral striatal interactions and reward-related processes, *in* J. P. Aggleton (ed.), *The Amygdala*, Wiley, Chichester, chapter 15, pp. 401–429.

Everitt, B. J., Cador, M. and Robbins, T. W. (1989). Interactions between the amygdala and ventral striatum in stimulus–reward association: studies using a second order schedule of sexual reinforcement, *Neuroscience* **30**: 63–75.

Everitt, B. J., Morris, K. A., O'Brien, A. and Robbins, T. W. (1991). The basolateral amygdala-ventral striatal system and conditioned place preference: further evidence of limbic-striatal interactions underlying reward-related processes, *Neuroscience* **42**: 1–18.

Everitt, B. J., Cardinal, R. N., Hall, J., Parkinson, J. A. and Robbins, T. W. (2000). Differential involvement of amygdala subsystems in appetitive conditioning and drug addiction, *in* J. P. Aggleton (ed.), *The Amygdala: a Functional Analysis*, 2nd edn, Oxford University Press, Oxford, chapter 10, pp. 353–390.

Everitt, B. J., Cardinal, R. N., Parkinson, J. A. and Robbins, T. W. (2003). Appetitive behaviour: impact of amygdala-dependent mechanisms of emotional learning, *Annals of the New York Academy of Sciences* **985**: 233–250.

Everling, S., Tinsley, C., Gaffan, D. and Duncan, J. (2002). Filtering of neural signals by focused attention in the monkey prefrontal cortex, *Nature Neuroscience* **5**: 671–676.

Everling, S., Tinsley, C. J., Gaffan, D. and Duncan, J. (2006). Selective representation of task-relevant objects and locations in the monkey prefrontal cortex, *European Journal of Neuroscience* **23**: 2197–2214.

Fahy, F. L., Riches, I. P. and Brown, M. W. (1993). Neuronal activity related to visual recognition memory and the encoding of recency and familiarity information in the primate anterior and medial inferior temporal and rhinal cortex, *Experimental Brain Research* **96**: 457–492.

Farah, M. J. (1990). *Visual Agnosia*, MIT Press, Cambridge, MA.

Farah, M. J. (2000). *The Cognitive Neuroscience of Vision*, Blackwell, Oxford.

Farah, M. J. (2004). *Visual Agnosia*, 2nd edn, MIT Press, Cambridge, MA.

Farah, M. J., Meyer, M. M. and McMullen, P. A. (1996). The living/nonliving dissociation is not an artifact: giving an *a priori* implausible hypothesis a strong test, *Cognitive Neuropsychology* **13**: 137–154.

Farrow, T. F., Zheng, Y., Wilkinson, I. D., Spence, S. A., Deakin, J. F., Tarrier, N., Griffiths, P. D. and Woodruff, P. W. (2001). Investigating the functional anatomy of empathy and forgiveness, *NeuroReport* **12**: 2433–2438.

Faugeras (1993). *The Representation, Recognition and Location of 3-D Objects*, MIT Press, Cambridge, MA.

Faugeras, O. D. and Hebert, M. (1986). The representation, recognition and location of 3-D objects, *International Journal of Robotics Research* **5**: 27–52.

Fazeli, M. S. and Collingridge, G. L. (eds) (1996). *Cortical Plasticity: LTP and LTD*, Bios, Oxford.

Fehr, E. and Fischbacher, U. (2003). The nature of human altruism, *Nature* **425**: 785–791.

Fehr, E. and Rockenbach, B. (2004). Human altruism: economic, neural, and evolutionary perspectives, *Current Opinion in Neurobiology* **14**: 784–790.

Feigenbaum, J. D. and Rolls, E. T. (1991). Allocentric and egocentric spatial information processing in the hippocampal formation of the behaving primate, *Psychobiology* **19**: 21–40.

Feldman, J. A. (1985). Four frames suffice: a provisional model of vision and space, *Behavioural Brain Sciences* **8**: 265–289.

Felleman, D. J. and Van Essen, D. C. (1991). Distributed hierarchical processing in the primate cerebral cortex, *Cerebral Cortex* **1**: 1–47.

Fellows, L. K. and Farah, M. J. (2003). Ventromedial frontal cortex mediates affective shifting in humans: evidence from a reversal learning paradigm, *Brain* **126**: 1830–1837.

Fellows, L. K. and Farah, M. J. (2005). Different underlying impairments in decision-making after ventromedial and dorsolateral frontal lobe damage in humans, *Cerebral Cortex* **15**: 58–63.

Ferbinteanu, J., Holsinger, R. M. and McDonald, R. J. (1999). Lesions of the medial or lateral perforant path have different effects on hippocampal contributions to place learning and on fear conditioning to context, *Behavioral*

Brain Research **101**: 65–84.

Fibiger, H. C., LePiane, F. G., Jakubovic, A. and Phillips, A. G. (1987). The role of dopamine in intracranial self-stimulation of the ventral tegmental area, *Journal of Neuroscience* **7**: 3888–3896.

Field, D. J. (1987). Relations between the statistics of natural images and the response properties of cortical cells, *Journal of the Optical Society of America, A* **4**: 2379–2394.

Field, D. J. (1994). What is the goal of sensory coding?, *Neural Computation* **6**: 559–601.

Finkel, L. H. and Edelman, G. M. (1987). Population rules for synapses in networks, *in* G. M. Edelman, W. E. Gall and W. M. Cowan (eds), *Synaptic Function*, John Wiley & Sons, New York, pp. 711–757.

Fiorillo, C. D., Tobler, P. N. and Schultz, W. (2003). Discrete coding of reward probability and uncertainty by dopamine neurons, *Science* **299**: 1898–1902.

Florian, C. and Roullet, P. (2004). Hippocampal CA3-region is crucial for acquisition and memory consolidation in Morris water maze task in mice, *Behavioral Brain Research* **154**: 365–374.

Földiák, P. (1991). Learning invariance from transformation sequences, *Neural Computation* **3**: 193–199.

Földiák, P. (1992). Models of sensory coding, *Technical Report CUED/F–INFENG/TR 91*, University of Cambridge, Department of Engineering.

Földiák, P. (2003). Sparse coding in the primate cortex, *in* M. A. Arbib (ed.), *Handbook of Brain Theory and Neural Networks*, 2nd edn, MIT Press, Cambridge, MA, pp. 1064–1608.

Fortin, N. J., Agster, K. L. and Eichenbaum, H. B. (2002). Critical role of the hippocampus in memory for sequences of events, *Nature Neuroscience* **5**: 458–462.

Foster, T. C., Castro, C. A. and McNaughton, B. L. (1989). Spatial selectivity of rat hippocampal neurons: dependence on preparedness for movement, *Science* **244**: 1580–1582.

Francis, S., Rolls, E. T., Bowtell, R., McGlone, F., O'Doherty, J., Browning, A., Clare, S. and Smith, E. (1999). The representation of pleasant touch in the brain and its relationship with taste and olfactory areas, *NeuroReport* **10**: 453–459.

Franco, L., Rolls, E. T., Aggelopoulos, N. C. and Treves, A. (2004). The use of decoding to analyze the contribution to the information of the correlations between the firing of simultaneously recorded neurons, *Experimental Brain Research* **155**: 370–384.

Franco, L., Rolls, E. T., Aggelopoulos, N. C. and Jerez, J. M. (2007). Neuronal selectivity, population sparseness, and ergodicity in the inferior temporal visual cortex, *Biological Cybernetics* **DOI 10.1007/s00422-007-0149-1**: 1–14.

Frederick, S., Loewenstein, T. and O'Donoghue (2002). Time discounting and time preference: a critical review, *Journal of Economic Literature* **40**: 351–401.

Freedman, D. J., Riesenhuber, M., Poggio, T. and Miller, E. K. (2003). A comparison of primate prefrontal and inferior temporal cortices during visual categorisation, *Journal of Neuroscience* **23**: 5235–5246.

Freeman, W. J. and Watts, J. W. (1950). *Psychosurgery in the Treatment of Mental Disorders and Intractable Pain*, 2nd edn, Thomas, Springfield, IL.

Frégnac, Y. (1996). Dynamics of cortical connectivity in visual cortical networks: an overview, *Journal of Physiology, Paris* **90**: 113–139.

Frey, S. and Petrides, M. (2002). Orbitofrontal cortex and memory formation, *Neuron* **36**: 171–176.

Frey, S., Kostopoulos, P. and Petrides, M. (2000). Orbitofrontal involvement in the processing of unpleasant auditory information, *European Journal of Neuroscience* **12**: 3709–3712.

Fried, I., MacDonald, K. A. and Wilson, C. (1997). Single neuron activity in human hippocampus and amygdala during recognition of faces and objects, *Neuron* **18**: 753–765.

Friedman, D. P., Murray, E. A., O'Neill, J. B. and Mishkin, M. (1986). Cortical connections of the somatosensory fields of the lateral sulcus of macaques: evidence for a corticolimbic pathway for touch, *Journal of Comparative Neurology* **252**: 323–347.

Frith, C. D., Friston, K., Liddle, P. F. and Frackowiak, R. S. (1991). Willed action and the prefrontal cortex in man: a study with PET, *Proceedings of the Royal Society of London B* **244**: 241–246.

Frith, U. (2001). Mind blindness and the brain in autism, *Neuron* **32**: 969–979.

Frolov, A. A. and Medvedev, A. V. (1986). Substantiation of the "point approximation" for describing the total electrical activity of the brain with use of a simulation model, *Biophysics* **31**: 332–337.

Fukushima, K. (1975). Cognitron: a self-organizing neural network, *Biological Cybernetics* **20**: 121–136.

Fukushima, K. (1980). Neocognitron: a self-organizing neural network model for a mechanism of pattern recognition unaffected by shift in position, *Biological Cybernetics* **36**: 193–202.

Fukushima, K. (1988). Neocognitron: A hierarchical neural network model capable of visual pattern recognition unaffected by shift in position, *Neural Networks* **1**: 119–130.

Fukushima, K. (1989). Analysis of the process of visual pattern recognition by the neocognitron, *Neural Networks* **2**: 413–420.

Fukushima, K. (1991). Neural networks for visual pattern recognition, *IEEE Transactions E* **74**: 179–190.

Fukushima, K. and Miyake, S. (1982). Neocognitron: A new algorithm for pattern recognition tolerant of deformations and shifts in position, *Pattern Recognition* **15**(6): 455–469.

Fulton, J. F. (1951). *Frontal Lobotomy and Affective Behavior. A Neurophysiological Analysis*, W. W. Norton, New

York.

Funahashi, S., Bruce, C. and Goldman-Rakic, P. (1989). Mnemonic coding of visual space in monkey dorsolateral prefrontal cortex, *Journal of Neurophysiology* **61**: 331–349.

Fusi, S. (2002). Hebbian spike-driven synaptic plasticity for learning patterns of mean firing rates, *Biological Cybernetics* **87**: 459–470.

Fusi, S. (2003). Spike-driven synaptic plasticity for learning correlated patterns of mean firing rates, *Reviews in the Neurosciences* **14**: 73–84.

Fusi, S. and Mattia, M. (1999). Collective behavior of networks with linear (VLSI) integrate and fire neuron, *Neural Computation* **11**: 633–652.

Fusi, S., Annunziato, M., Badoni, D., Salamon, A. and Amit, D. J. (2000). Spike-driven synaptic plasticity: theory, simulation, VLSI implementation, *Neural Computation* **12**: 2227–2258.

Fuster, J. M. (1973). Unit activity in prefrontal cortex during delayed-response performance: neuronal correlates of transient memory, *Journal of Neurophysiology* **36**: 61–78.

Fuster, J. M. (1989). *The Prefrontal Cortex*, 2nd edn, Raven Press, New York.

Fuster, J. M. (1997). *The Prefrontal Cortex*, 3rd edn, Lippincott-Raven, Philadelphia.

Fuster, J. M. (2000). *Memory Systems in the Brain*, Raven Press, New York.

Fuster, J. M. and Jervey, J. P. (1982). Neuronal firing in the inferotemporal cortex of the monkey in a visual memory task, *Journal of Neuroscience* **2**: 361–375.

Fuster, J. M., Bauer, R. H. and Jervey, J. P. (1982). Cellular discharge in the dorsolateral prefrontal cortex of the monkey in cognitive tasks, *Experimental Neurology* **77**: 679–694.

Fyhn, M., Molden, S., Witter, M. P., Moser, E. I. and Moser, M.-B. (2004). Spatial representation in the entorhinal cortex, *Science* **2004**: 1258–1264.

Gabbott, P. L., Warner, T. A., Jays, P. R. and Bacon, S. J. (2003). Areal and synaptic interconnectivity of prelimbic (area 32), infralimbic (area 25) and insular cortices in the rat, *Brain Research* **993**: 59–71.

Gaffan, D. (1992). Amygdala and the memory of reward, *in* J. P. Aggleton (ed.), *The Amygdala*, Wiley-Liss, New York, chapter 18, pp. 471–483.

Gaffan, D. (1993). Additive effects of forgetting and fornix transection in the temporal gradient of retrograde amnesia, *Neuropsychologia* **31**: 1055–1066.

Gaffan, D. (1994). Scene-specific memory for objects: a model of episodic memory impairment in monkeys with fornix transection, *Journal of Cognitive Neuroscience* **6**: 305–320.

Gaffan, D. and Harrison, S. (1987). Amygdalectomy and disconnection in visual learning for auditory secondary reinforcement by monkeys, *Journal of Neuroscience* **7**: 2285–2292.

Gaffan, D. and Harrison, S. (1989a). A comparison of the effects of fornix section and sulcus principalis ablation upon spatial learning by monkeys, *Behavioural Brain Research* **31**: 207–220.

Gaffan, D. and Harrison, S. (1989b). Place memory and scene memory: effects of fornix transection in the monkey, *Experimental Brain Research* **74**: 202–212.

Gaffan, D. and Saunders, R. C. (1985). Running recognition of configural stimuli by fornix transected monkeys, *Quarterly Journal of Experimental Psychology* **37B**: 61–71.

Gaffan, D., Saunders, R. C., Gaffan, E. A., Harrison, S., Shields, C. and Owen, M. J. (1984). Effects of fornix section upon associative memory in monkeys: role of the hippocampus in learned action, *Quarterly Journal of Experimental Psychology* **36B**: 173–221.

Gaffan, D., Gaffan, E. A. and Harrison, S. (1989). Visual-visual associative learning and reward-associative learning in monkeys; the role of the amygdala, *Journal of Neuroscience* **9**: 558–564.

Gaffan, E. A., Gaffan, D. and Harrison, S. (1988). Disconnection of the amygdala from visual association cortex impairs visual reward-association learning in monkeys, *Journal of Neuroscience* **8**: 3144–3150.

Gallagher, M. (2000). The amygdala and associative learning, *in* J. P. Aggleton (ed.), *The Amygdala: a Functional Analysis*, 2nd edn, Oxford University Press, Oxford, chapter 6, pp. 213–287.

Gallagher, M. and Holland, P. C. (1992). Understanding the function of the central nucleus: is simple conditioning enough?, *in* J. P. Aggleton (ed.), *The Amygdala: Neurobiological Aspects of Emotion, Memory, and Mental Dysfunction*, Wiley-Liss, New York, pp. 307–321.

Gallagher, M. and Holland, P. C. (1994). The amygdala complex: multiple roles in associative learning and attention, *Proceedings of the National Academy of Sciences USA* **91**: 11771–11776.

Gallant, J. L., Connor, C. E. and Van-Essen, D. C. (1998). Neural activity in areas V1, V2 and V4 during free viewing of natural scenes compared to controlled viewing, *NeuroReport* **9**: 85–90.

Garcia, J. (1989). Food for Tolman: cognition and cathexis in context, *in* T. Archer and L.-G. Nilsson (eds), *Aversion, Avoidance and Anxiety*, Erlbaum, Hillsdale, NJ, pp. 45–85.

Gardner, E. (1987). Maximum storage capacity in neural networks, *Europhysics Letters* **4**: 481–485.

Gardner, E. (1988). The space of interactions in neural network models, *Journal of Physics A* **21**: 257–270.

Gardner-Medwin, A. R. (1976). The recall of events through the learning of associations between their parts, *Proceedings of the Royal Society of London, Series B* **194**: 375–402.

Gattass, R., Sousa, A. P. B. and Covey, E. (1985). Cortical visual areas of the macaque: possible substrates for pattern recognition mechanisms, *Experimental Brain Research, Supplement 11*.

Gawin, F. H. (1991). Cocaine addiction: psychology and neurophysiology, *Science* **251**: 1580–1586.

Gawne, T. J. and Richmond, B. J. (1993). How independent are the messages carried by adjacent inferior temporal cortical neurons?, *Journal of Neuroscience* **13**: 2758–2771.

Gaykema, R. P., van der Kuil, J., Hersh, L. B. and Luiten, P. G. (1991). Patterns of direct projections from the hippocampus to the medial septum-diagonal band complex: anterograde tracing with phaseolus vulgaris leucoagglutinin combined with immunohistochemistry of choline acetyltransferase, *Neuroscience* **43**: 349–360.

Gazzaniga, M. S. (1988). Brain modularity: towards a philosophy of conscious experience, *in* A. J. Marcel and E. Bisiach (eds), *Consciousness in Contemporary Science*, Oxford University Press, Oxford, chapter 10, pp. 218–238.

Geesaman, B. J. and Andersen, R. A. (1996). The analysis of complex motion patterns by form/cue invariant MSTd neurons, *Journal of Neuroscience* **16**: 4716–4732.

Gemba, H., Sasaki, K. and Brooks, V. B. (1986). Error potentials in limbic cortex (anterior cingulate area 24) of monkeys during motor learning, *Neuroscience Letters* **8**: 223–227.

George, M. S., Ketter, T. A., Parekh, P. I., Herscovitch, P. and Post, R. M. (1996). Gender differences in regional cerebral blood flow during transient self-induced sadness or happiness, *Biological Psychiatry* **40**: 859–871.

Georges-François, P., Rolls, E. T. and Robertson, R. G. (1999). Spatial view cells in the primate hippocampus: allocentric view not head direction or eye position or place, *Cerebral Cortex* **9**: 197–212.

Georgopoulos, A. P. (1995). Motor cortex and cognitive processing, *in* M. S. Gazzaniga (ed.), *The Cognitive Neurosciences*, MIT Press, Cambridge, MA, chapter 32, pp. 507–517.

Gerstner, W. (1995). Time structure of the activity in neural network models, *Physical Review E* **51**: 738–758.

Gerstner, W. (2000). Population dynamics of spiking neurons: fast transients, asynchronous states, and locking, *Neural Computation* **12**: 43–89.

Gerstner, W. and Kistler, W. (2002). *Spiking Neuron Models: Single Neurons, Populations and Plasticity*, Cambridge University Press, Cambridge.

Gerstner, W., Ritz, R. and Van Hemmen, L. (1993). A biologically motivated and analytically solvable model of collective oscillations in the cortex, *Biological Cybernetics* **68**: 363–374.

Gerstner, W., Kreiter, A. K., Markram, H. and Herz, A. V. (1997). Neural codes: firing rates and beyond, *Proceedings of the National Academy of Sciences USA* **94**: 12740–12741.

Gewirtz, J. C. and Davis, M. (1998). Application of Pavlovian higher-order conditioning to the analysis of the neural substrates of fear conditioning, *Neuropharmacology* **37**: 453–459.

Gibson, J. J. (1950). *The Perception of the Visual World*, Houghton Mifflin, Boston.

Gibson, J. J. (1979). *The Ecological Approach to Visual Perception*, Houghton Mifflin, Boston.

Gilbert, P. E. and Kesner, R. P. (2002). The amygdala but not the hippocampus is involved in pattern separation based on reward value, *Neurobiology of Learning and Memory* **77**: 338–353.

Gilbert, P. E. and Kesner, R. P. (2003). Localization of function within the dorsal hippocampus: the role of the CA3 subregion in paired-associate learning, *Behavioral Neuroscience* **117**: 1385–1394.

Gilbert, P. E. and Kesner, R. P. (2006). The role of dorsal CA3 hippocampal subregion in spatial working memory and pattern separation, *Behavioural Brain Research* **169**: 142–149.

Gilbert, P. E., Kesner, R. P. and DeCoteau, W. E. (1998). Memory for spatial location: role of the hippocampus in mediating spatial pattern separation, *Journal of Neuroscience* **18**: 804–810.

Gilbert, P. E., Kesner, R. P. and Lee, I. (2001). Dissociating hippocampal subregions: double dissociation between dentate gyrus and CA1, *Hippocampus* **11**: 626–636.

Gilchrist, I., Humphreys, G. W. and Riddoch, M. J. (1996). Grouping and extinction: evidence for low-level modulation of selection, *Cognitive Neuropsychology* **13**: 1223–1256.

Gintis, H. (2003). The hitchhiker's guide to altruism: genes, culture, and the internalization of norms, *Journal of Theoretical Biology* **220**: 407–418.

Gintis, H. (2007). Towards a unified behavioral science, *Behavioral and Brain Sciences, in press*.

Glimcher, P. (2003). The neurobiology of visual-saccadic decision making, *Annual Reviews of Neuroscience* **26**: 133–179.

Glimcher, P. (2004). *Decisions, Uncertainty, and the Brain*, MIT Press, Cambridge, MA.

Glimcher, P. and Rustichini, A. (2004). Neuroeconomics: the consilience of brain and decision, *Science* **306**: 447–452.

Glover, G. H. (1999). Deconvolution of impulse response in event-related BOLD fMRI, *Neuroimage* **9**: 416–429.

Gnadt, J. W. and Andersen, R. A. (1988). Monkey related motor planning activity in posterior parietal cortex of macaque, *Experimental Brain Research* **70**: 216–220.

Gneezy, U. (2005). Deception: the role of consequences, *American Economic Review* **95**: 384–394.

Gochin, P. M., Colombo, M., Dorfman, G. A., Gerstein, G. L. and Gross, C. G. (1994). Neural ensemble encoding in inferior temporal cortex, *Journal of Neurophysiology* **71**: 2325–2337.

Goff, D. C. and Coyle, J. T. (2001). The emerging role of glutamate in the pathophysiology and treatment of schizophrenia, *American Journal of Psychiatry* **158**: 1367–1377.

Gold, A. E. and Kesner, R. P. (2005). The role of the ca3 subregion of the dorsal hippocampus in spatial pattern completion in the rat, *Hippocampus* **15**: 808–814.

Gold, J. I. and Shadlen, M. N. (2000). Representation of a perceptual decision in developing oculomotor commands,

Nature **404**: 390–394.

Goldberg, M. E. (2000). The control of gaze, *in* E. R. Kandel, J. H. Schwartz and T. M. Jessell (eds), *Principles of Neural Science*, 4th edn, McGraw-Hill, New York, chapter 39, pp. 782–800.

Goldman, P. S. and Nauta, W. J. H. (1977). An intricately patterned prefronto-caudate projection in the rhesus monkey, *Journal of Comparative Neurology* **171**: 369–386.

Goldman-Rakic, P. (1994). Working memory dysfunction in schizophrenia, *Journal of Neuropsychology and Clinical Neuroscience* **6**: 348–357.

Goldman-Rakic, P. S. (1987). Circuitry of primate prefrontal cortex and regulation of behavior by representational memory, *Handbook of Physiology, Section 1, The Nervous System*, Vol. V. Higher Functions of the Brain, Part 1, American Physiological Society, Bethesda, MD, pp. 373–417.

Goldman-Rakic, P. S. (1996). The prefrontal landscape: implications of functional architecture for understanding human mentation and the central executive, *Philosophical Transactions of the Royal Society B* **351**: 1445–1453.

Goldman-Rakic, P. S. (1999). The physiological approach: functional architecture of working memory and disordered cognition in schizophrenia, *Biological Psychiatry* **46**: 650–661.

Goldman-Rakic, P. S., Castner, S. A., Svensson, T. H., Siever, L. J. and Williams, G. V. (2004). Targeting the dopamine D1 receptor in schizophrenia: insights for cognitive dysfunction, *Psychopharmacology (Berlin)* **174**: 3–16.

Goleman, D. (1995). *Emotional Intelligence*, Bantam, New York.

Golomb, D., Kleinfeld, D., Reid, R. C., Shapley, R. M. and Shraiman, B. (1994). On temporal codes and the spatiotemporal response of neurons in the lateral geniculate nucleus, *Journal of Neurophysiology* **72**: 2990–3003.

Golomb, D., Hertz, J. A., Panzeri, S., Treves, A. and Richmond, B. J. (1997). How well can we estimate the information carried in neuronal responses from limited samples?, *Neural Computation* **9**: 649–665.

Goodglass, H. and Kaplan, E. (1979). Assessment of cognitive deficit in brain-injured patient, *in* M. S. Gazzaniga (ed.), *Handbook of Behavioural Neurobiology*, Vol. 2, Neuropsychology, Plenum, New York, pp. 3–22.

Goodrich-Hunsaker, N. J., Hunsaker, M. R. and Kesner, R. P. (2005). Effects of hippocampus sub-regional lesions for metric and topological spatial information processing, *Society for Neuroscience Abstracts*.

Grabenhorst, F., Rolls, E. T. and Bilderbeck, A. (2008). How cognition modulates affective responses to taste and flavor.

Gray, C. M. and Singer, W. (1987). Stimulus-specific neuronal oscillations in the cat visual cortex: a cortical functional unit, *Society of Neuroscience Abstracts* **13**: 403.

Gray, C. M. and Singer, W. (1989). Stimulus-specific neuronal oscillations in orientation columns of cat visual cortex, *Proceedings of National Academy of Sciences USA* **86**: 1698–1702.

Gray, J. A. (1970). The psychophysiological basis of introversion-extraversion, *Behaviour Research and Therapy* **8**: 249–266.

Gray, J. A. (1975). *Elements of a Two-Process Theory of Learning*, Academic Press, London.

Gray, J. A., Young, A. M. J. and Joseph, M. H. (1997). Dopamine's role, *Science* **278**: 1548–1549.

Gray, T. S., Piechowski, R. A., Yracheta, J. M., Rittenhouse, P. A., Betha, C. L. and Van der Kar, L. D. (1993). Ibotenic acid lesions in the bed nucleus of the stria terminalis attenuate conditioned stress-induced increases in prolactin, ACTH and corticosterone, *Neuroendocrinology* **57**: 517–524.

Graybiel, A. M. and Kimura, M. (1995). Adaptive neural networks in the basal ganglia, *in* J. C. Houk, J. L. Davis and D. G. Beiser (eds), *Models of Information Processing in the Basal Ganglia*, MIT Press, Cambridge, MA, chapter 5, pp. 103–116.

Graziano, M. S. A., Andersen, R. A. and Snowden, R. J. (1994). Tuning of MST neurons to spiral motions, *Journal of Neuroscience* **14**: 54–67.

Green, M. F. (1996). What are the functional consequences of neurocognitive deficits in schizophrenia?, *American Journal of Psychiatry* **153**: 321–330.

Gregory, R. L. (1970). *The Intelligent Eye*, McGraw-Hill, New York.

Grill, H. J. and Norgren, R. (1978). Chronically decerebrate rats demonstrate satiation but not bait shyness, *Science* **201**: 267–269.

Grill-Spector, K. and Malach, R. (2004). The human visual cortex, *Annual Review of Neuroscience* **27**: 649–677.

Grill-Spector, K., Sayres, R. and Ress, D. (2006). High-resolution imaging reveals highly selective nonface clusters in the fusiform face area, *Nature Neuroscience* **9**: 1177–1185.

Grimson, W. E. L. (1990). *Object Recognition by Computer*, MIT Press, Cambridge, MA.

Griniasty, M., Tsodyks, M. V. and Amit, D. J. (1993). Conversion of temporal correlations between stimuli to spatial correlations between attractors, *Neural Computation* **35**: 1–17.

Gross, C. G., Bender, D. B. and Gerstein, G. L. (1979). Activity of inferior temporal neurons in behaving monkeys, *Neuropsychologia* **17**: 215–229.

Gross, C. G., Desimone, R., Albright, T. D. and Schwartz, E. L. (1985). Inferior temporal cortex and pattern recognition, *Experimental Brain Research* **Suppl. 11**: 179–201.

Grossberg, S. (1976a). Adaptive pattern classification and universal recoding i: parallel development and coding of neural feature detectors, *Biological Cybernetics* **23**: 121–134.

Grossberg, S. (1976b). Adaptive pattern classification and universal recoding ii: feedback, expectation, olfaction, illusions, *Biological Cybernetics* **23**: 1187–202.

Grossberg, S. (1987). Competitive learning: from interactive activation to adaptive resonance, *Cognitive Science* **11**: 23–63.

Grossberg, S. (1988). Non-linear neural networks: principles, mechanisms, and architectures, *Neural Networks* **1**: 17–61.

Groves, P. M. (1983). A theory of the functional organization of the neostriatum and the neostriatal control of voluntary movement, *Brain Research Reviews* **5**: 109–132.

Groves, P. M., Garcia-Munoz, M., Linder, J. C., Manley, M. S., Martone, M. E. and Young, S. J. (1995). Elements of the intrinsic organization and information processing in the neostriatum, *in* J. C. Houk, J. L. Davis and D. G. Beiser (eds), *Models of Information Processing in the Basal Ganglia*, MIT Press, Cambridge, MA, chapter 4, pp. 51–96.

Grueninger, W. E., Kimble, D. P., Grueninger, J. and Levine, S. (1965). GSR and corticosteroid response in monkeys with frontal ablations, *Neuropsychologia* **3**: 205–216.

Grusser, O.-J. and Landis, T. (1991). *Visual Agnosias*, MacMillan, London.

Guest, S., Grabenhorst, F., Essick, G., Chen, Y., Young, M., McGlone, F., de Araujo, I. and Rolls, E. T. (2007). Human cortical representation of oral temperature.

Gulyas, A. I., Miles, R., Hajos, N. and Freund, T. F. (1993). Precision and variability in postsynaptic target selection of inhibitory cells in the hippocampal ca3 region, *European Journal of Neuroscience* **5**: 1729–1751.

Gurney, K., Prescott, T. J. and Redgrave, P. (2001a). A computational model of action selection in the basal ganglia I: A new functional anatomy, *Biological Cybernetics* **84**: 401–410.

Gurney, K., Prescott, T. J. and Redgrave, P. (2001b). A computational model of action selection in the basal ganglia II: Analysis and simulation of behaviour, *Biological Cybernetics* **84**: 411–423.

Gutig, R. and Sompolinsky, H. (2006). The tempotron: a neuron that learns spike timing-based decisions, *Nature Neuroscience* **9**: 420–428.

Hadland, K. A., Rushworth, M. F. S., Gaffan, D. and Passingham, R. E. (2003). The effect of cingulate lesions on social behaviour and emotion, *Neuropsychologia* **41**: 919–931.

Hafting, T., Fyhn, M., Molden, S., Moser, M. B. and Moser, E. I. (2005). Microstructure of a spatial map in the entorhinal cortex, *Nature* **436**: 801–806.

Halgren, E. (1992). Emotional neurophysiology of the amygdala within the context of human cognition, *in* J. P. Aggleton (ed.), *The Amygdala*, Wiley-Liss, New York, chapter 7, pp. 191–228.

Halligan, P. and Marshall, J. (1994). *Spatial Neglect: Position Papers on the Theory and Practice*, Lawrence Erlbaum, Hillsdale, NJ.

Hamming, R. W. (1990). *Coding and Information Theory*, 2nd edn, Prentice-Hall, Englewood Cliffs, New Jersey.

Hampson, R. E., Hedberg, T. and Deadwyler, S. A. (2000). Differential information processing by hippocampal and subicular neurons, *Annals of the New York Academy of Sciences* **911**: 151–165.

Hampton, A. N., Bossaerts, P. and O'Doherty, J. P. (2006). The role of the ventromedial prefrontal cortex in abstract state-based inference during decision making in humans, *Journal of Neuroscience* **26**: 8360–8367.

Hampton, R. R. (2005). Monkey perirhinal cortex is critical for visual memory, but not for visual perception: reexamination of the behavioural evidence from monkeys, *Quarterly Journal of Experimental Psychology* **58B**: 283–299.

Handelmann, G. E. and Olton, D. S. (1981). Spatial memory following damage to hippocampal ca3 pyramidal cells with kainic acid: impairment and recovery with preoperative training, *Brain Research* **217**: 41–58.

Hannesson, D. K., Howland, G. J. and Phillips, A. G. (2004). Interaction between perirhinal and medial prefrontal cortex is required for temporal order but not recognition memory for objects in rats, *Journal of Neuroscience* **24**: 4596–4604.

Hargreaves, E. L., Rao, G., Lee, I. and Knierim, J. J. (2005). Major dissociation between medial and lateral entorhinal input to dorsal hippocampus, *Science* **308**: 1792–1794.

Harlow, J. M. (1848). Passage of an iron rod though the head, *Boston Medical and Surgical Journal* **39**: 389–393.

Harris, A. E., Ermentrout, G. B. and Small, S. L. (1997). A model of ocular dominance column development by competition for trophic factor, *Proceedings of the National Academy of Sciences USA* **94**: 9944–9949.

Hasselmo, M. E. and Bower, J. M. (1993). Acetylcholine and memory, *Trends in Neurosciences* **16**: 218–222.

Hasselmo, M. E. and Eichenbaum, H. B. (2005). Hippocampal mechanisms for the context-dependent retrieval of episodes, *Neural Networks* **18**: 1172–1190.

Hasselmo, M. E., Rolls, E. T. and Baylis, G. C. (1989a). The role of expression and identity in the face-selective responses of neurons in the temporal visual cortex of the monkey, *Behavioural Brain Research* **32**: 203–218.

Hasselmo, M. E., Rolls, E. T., Baylis, G. C. and Nalwa, V. (1989b). Object-centered encoding by face-selective neurons in the cortex in the superior temporal sulcus of the monkey, *Experimental Brain Research* **75**: 417–429.

Hasselmo, M. E., Schnell, E. and Barkai, E. (1995). Learning and recall at excitatory recurrent synapses and cholinergic modulation in hippocampal region CA3, *Journal of Neuroscience* **15**: 5249–5262.

Hatfield, T., Han, J. S., Conley, M., Gallagher, M. and Holland, P. (1996). Neurotoxic lesions of basolateral, but not central, amygdala interfere with Pavlovian second-order conditioning and reinforcer devaluation effects, *Journal of Neuroscience* **16**: 5256–5265.

Hawken, M. J. and Parker, A. J. (1987). Spatial properties of the monkey striate cortex, *Proceedings of the Royal Society, London B* **231**: 251–288.

Haxby, J. V. (2006). Fine structure in representations of faces and objects, *Nature Neuroscience* **9**: 1084–1086.

Haxby, J. V., Hoffman, E. A. and Gobbini, M. I. (2002). Human neural systems for face recognition and social communication, *Biological Psychiatry* **51**: 59–67.

Hebb, D. O. (1949). *The Organization of Behavior: a Neuropsychological Theory*, Wiley, New York.

Hebert, M. A., Ardid, D., Henrie, J. A., Tamashiro, K., Blanchard, D. C. and Blanchard, R. J. (1999). Amygdala lesions produce analgesia in a novel, ethologically relevant acute pain test, *Physiology and Behavior* **67**: 99–105.

Hegde, J. and Van Essen, D. C. (2000). Selectivity for complex shapes in primate visual area V2, *Journal of Neuroscience* **20**: RC61.

Heimer, L., Switzer, R. D. and Van Hoesen, G. W. (1982). Ventral striatum and ventral pallidum. Components of the motor system?, *Trends in Neurosciences* **5**: 83–87.

Heinke, D. and Humphreys, G. (1999). Modelling emergent attentional properties, *in* D. Heinke, G. Humphreys and A. Olson (eds), *Connectionist Models in Cognitive Neuroscience - The 5th Neural Computation and Psychology Workshop*, Springer, Berlin, pp. 240–251.

Heinke, D., Deco, G., Zihl, J. and Humphreys, G. (2002). A computational neuroscience account of visual neglect, *Neurocomputing* **44–46**: 811–816.

Heller, J., Hertz, J. A., Kjaer, T. W. and Richmond, B. J. (1995). Information flow and temporal coding in primate pattern vision, *Journal of Computational Neuroscience* **2**: 175–193.

Helmholtz, H. v. (1867). *Handbuch der physiologischen Optik*, Voss, Leipzig.

Hernandez, A., Zainos, A. and Romo, R. (2002). Temporal evolution of a decision-making process in medial premotor cortex, *Neuron* **33**: 959–972.

Herrnstein, R. J. (1984). Objects, categories, and discriminative stimuli, *in* H. L. Roitblat, T. G. Bever and H. S. Terrace (eds), *Animal Cognition*, Lawrence Erlbaum and Associates, Hillsdale, NJ.

Hertz, J. A., Krogh, A. and Palmer, R. G. (1991). *Introduction to the Theory of Neural Computation*, Addison-Wesley, Wokingham, UK.

Hertz, J. A., Kjaer, T. W., Eskander, E. N. and Richmond, B. J. (1992). Measuring natural neural processing with artificial neural networks, *International Journal of Neural Systems* **3 (Suppl.)**: 91–103.

Herz, R. S. and von Clef, J. (2001). The influence of verbal labeling on the perception of odors: evidence for olfactory illusions?, *Perception* **30**: 381–391.

Hestrin, S., Sah, P. and Nicoll, R. (1990). Mechanisms generating the time course of dual component excitatory synaptic currents recorded in hippocampal slices, *Neuron* **5**: 247–253.

Hikosaka, K. and Watanabe, M. (2000). Delay activity of orbital and lateral prefrontal neurons of the monkey varying with different rewards, *Cerebral Cortex* **10**: 263–271.

Hinton, G. E. (1989). Deterministic Boltzmann learning performs steepest descent in weight-space, *Neural Computation* **1**: 143–150.

Hinton, G. E. and Anderson, J. A. (1981). *Parallel Models of Associative Memory*, Erlbaum, Hillsdale, NJ.

Hinton, G. E. and Ghahramani, Z. (1997). Generative models for discovering sparse distributed representations, *Philosophical Transactions of the Royal Society of London, B* **352**: 1177–1190.

Hinton, G. E. and Sejnowski, T. J. (1986). Learning and relearning in Boltzmann machines, *in* D. Rumelhart and J. L. McClelland (eds), *Parallel Distributed Processing*, Vol. 1, MIT Press, Cambridge, MA, chapter 7, pp. 282–317.

Hinton, G. E., Dayan, P., Frey, B. J. and Neal, R. M. (1995). The "wake-sleep" algorithm for unsupervised neural networks, *Science* **268**: 1158–1161.

Hodgkin, A. L. and Huxley, A. F. (1952). A quantitative description of membrane current and its application to conduction and excitation in nerve, *Journal of Physiology* **117**: 500–544.

Hoebel, B. G., Rada, P., Mark, G. P., Parada, M., Puig de Parada, M., Pothos, E. and Hernandez, L. (1996). Hypothalamic control of accumbens dopamine: a system for feeding reinforcement, *in* G. Bray and D. Ryan (eds), *Molecular and Genetic Aspects of Obesity*, Vol. 5, Louisiana State University Press, Baton Rouge, LA, pp. 263–280.

Hoffman, E. A. and Haxby, J. V. (2000). Distinct representations of eye gaze and identity in the distributed neural system for face perception, *Nature Neuroscience* **3**: 80–84.

Hoge, J. and Kesner, R. P. (2006). Effects of subregional lesions of the hippocampus on temporal order for objects, *Society for Neuroscience Abstracts*.

Holland, P. C. and Gallagher, M. (1999). Amygdala circuitry in attentional and representational processes, *Trends in Cognitive Sciences* **3**: 65–73.

Holland, P. C. and Gallagher, M. (2003). Double disosociation of the effects of lesions of basolateral and central amygdala on conditioned stimulus-potentiated feeding and Pavlovian-instrumental transfer, *European Journal of Neuroscience* **17**: 1680–1694.

Holland, P. C. and Gallagher, M. (2004). Amygdala-frontal interactions and reward expectancy, *Current Opinion in Neurobiology* **14**: 148–155.

Holland, P. C. and Straub, J. J. (1979). Differential effects of two ways of devaluing the unconditioned stimulus after pavlovian appetitive conditioning, *Journal of Experimental Psychology* **5**: 65–78.

Holman, J. G. and Mackintosh, N. J. (1981). The control of appetitive instrumental responding does not depend on classical conditioning to the discriminative stimulus, *Quarterly Journal of Experimental Psychology B* **33**: 21–31.

Hölscher, C. and Rolls, E. T. (2002). Perirhinal cortex neuronal activity is actively related to working memory in the macaque, *Neural Plasticity* **9**: 41–51.

Hölscher, C., Jacob, W. and Mallot, H. A. (2003a). Reward modulates neuronal activity in the hippocampus of the rat, *Behavioural Brain Research* **142**: 181–191.

Hölscher, C., Rolls, E. T. and Xiang, J. Z. (2003b). Perirhinal cortex neuronal activity related to long term familiarity memory in the macaque, *European Journal of Neuroscience* **18**: 2037–2046.

Hopfield, J. J. (1982). Neural networks and physical systems with emergent collective computational abilities, *Proceedings of the National Academy of Sciences USA* **79**: 2554–2558.

Hopfield, J. J. (1984). Neurons with graded response have collective computational properties like those of two-state neurons, *Proceedings of the National Academy of Sciences USA* **81**: 3088–3092.

Hornak, J., Rolls, E. T. and Wade, D. (1996). Face and voice expression identification in patients with emotional and behavioural changes following ventral frontal lobe damage, *Neuropsychologia* **34**: 247–261.

Hornak, J., Bramham, J., Rolls, E. T., Morris, R. G., O'Doherty, J., Bullock, P. R. and Polkey, C. E. (2003). Changes in emotion after circumscribed surgical lesions of the orbitofrontal and cingulate cortices, *Brain* **126**: 1691–1712.

Hornak, J., O'Doherty, J., Bramham, J., Rolls, E., Morris, R., Bullock, P. and Polkey, C. (2004). Reward-related reversal learning after surgical excisions in orbitofrontal and dorsolateral prefrontal cortex in humans, *Journal of Cognitive Neuroscience* **16**: 463–478.

Hornykiewicz, O. (1973). Dopamine in the basal ganglia: its role and therapeutic implications including the use of L-Dopa, *British Medical Bulletin* **29**: 172–178.

Horvitz, J. C. (2000). Mesolimbocortical and nigrostriatal dopamine responses to salient non-reward events, *Neuroscience* **96**: 651–656.

Horwitz, B. and Tagamets, M.-A. (1999). Predicting human functional maps with neural net modeling, *Human Brain Mapping* **8**: 137–142.

Horwitz, B., Tagamets, M.-A. and McIntosh, A. R. (1999). Neural modeling, functional brain imaging, and cognition, *Trends in Cognitive Sciences* **3**: 85–122.

Houk, J. C., Adams, J. L. and Barto, A. C. (1995). A model of how the basal ganglia generates and uses neural signals that predict reinforcement, *in* J. C. Houk, J. L. Davies and D. G. Beiser (eds), *Models of Information Processing in the Basal Ganglia*, MIT Press, Cambridge, MA, chapter 13, pp. 249–270.

Hubel, D. H. and Wiesel, T. N. (1962). Receptive fields, binocular interaction, and functional architecture in the cat's visual cortex, *Journal of Physiology* **160**: 106–154.

Hubel, D. H. and Wiesel, T. N. (1968). Receptive fields and functional architecture of monkey striate cortex, *Journal of Physiology, London* **195**: 215–243.

Huerta, P. T., Sun, L. D., Wilson, M. A. and Tonegawa, S. (2000). Formation of temporal memory requires nmda receptors within CA1 pyramidal neurons, *Neuron* **25**: 473–480.

Hughes, J. (1975). Isolation of an endogenous compound from the brain with pharmacological properties similar to morphine, *Brain Research* **88**: 293–308.

Hughes, J., Smith, T. W., Kosterlitz, H. W., Fothergill, L. A., Morgan, B. A. and Morris, H. R. (1975). Identification of two related pentapeptides from the brain with potent opiate antagonist activity, *Nature* **258**: 577–579.

Hummel, J. E. and Biederman, I. (1992). Dynamic binding in a neural network for shape recognition, *Psychological Review* **99**: 480–517.

Humphreys, G. and Heinke, D. (1998). Spatial representation and selection in the brain: Neuropsychological and computational constraints, *Visual Cognition* **5**: 9–47.

Humphreys, G. and Riddoch, J. (1994). Attention to within-object and between-object spatial representations: Multiple sites for visual selection, *Cognitive Neuropsychology* **11**: 207–241.

Humphreys, G., Olson, A., Romani, C. and Riddoch, J. (1996). Competitive mechanisms of selection by space and object: A neuropsychological approach, *in* A. Kramer, M. Coles and G. Logan (eds), *Converging Operations in the Study of Visual Selective Attention*, American Psychological Association, Washington, DC, pp. 365–393.

Hunt, S. P. and Mantyh, P. W. (2001). The molecular dynamics of pain control, *Nature Reviews Neuroscience* **2**: 83–91.

Huston, J. P. and Borbely, A. A. (1973). Operant conditioning in forebrain ablated rats by use of rewarding hypothalamic stimulation, *Brain Research* **50**: 467–472.

Huttenlocher, D. P. and Ullman, S. (1990). Recognizing solid objects by alignment with an image, *International Journal of Computer Vision* **5**: 195–212.

Ingvar, D. H. and Franzen, G. (1974). Abnormalities of cerebral blood flow distribution in patients with chronic schizophrenia, *Acta Psychiatrica Scandinavica* **50**: 425–462.

Insausti, R., Amaral, D. G. and Cowan, W. M. (1987). The entorhinal cortex of the monkey. II. Cortical afferents, *Journal of Comparative Neurology* **264**: 356–395.

Insel, T. R. and Young, I. J. (2001). The neurobiology of attachment, *Nature Reviews Neuroscience* **2**: 129–136.

Ishai, A., Ungerleider, L. G., Martin, A., Schouten, J. L. and Haxby, J. V. (1999). Distributed representation of objects in the human ventral visual pathway, *Proceedings of the National Academy of Sciences USA* **96**: 9379–9384.

Ishai, A., Ungerleider, L. G., Martin, A. and Haxby, J. V. (2000). The representation of objects in the human occipital and temporal cortex, *Journal of Cognitive Neuroscience* **12**: 35–51.

Ishizuka, N., Weber, J. and Amaral, D. G. (1990). Organization of intrahippocampal projections originating from CA3 pyramidal cells in the rat, *Journal of Comparative Neurology* **295**: 580–623.

Ito, M. (1984). *The Cerebellum and Neural Control*, Raven Press, New York.

Ito, M. (1989). Long-term depression, *Annual Review of Neuroscience* **12**: 85–102.

Ito, M. (1993a). Cerebellar mechanisms of long-term depression, *in* M. Baudry, R. F. Thompson and J. L. Davis (eds), *Synaptic Plasticity: Molecular, Cellular and Functional Aspects*, MIT Press, Cambridge, MA, chapter 6, pp. 117–128.

Ito, M. (1993b). Synaptic plasticity in the cerebellar cortex and its role in motor learning, *Canadian Journal of Neurological Science* **Suppl. 3**: S70–S74.

Ito, M. and Gilbert, C. D. (1999). Attention modulates contextual influences in the primary visual cortex of alert monkeys, *Neuron* **22**: 593–604.

Ito, M. and Komatsu, H. (2004). Representation of angles embedded within contour stimuli in area V2 of macaque monkeys, *Journal of Neuroscience* **24**: 3313–3324.

Ito, S., Stuphorn, V., Brown, J. W. and Schall, J. D. (2003). Performance monitoring by the anterior cingulate cortex during saccade countermanding, *Science* **320**: 120–122.

Itti, L. and Koch, C. (2001). Computational modelling of visual attention, *Nature Reviews Neuroscience* **2**: 194–203.

Iversen, S. D. (1979). Behaviour after neostriatal lesions in animals, *in* I. Divac (ed.), *The Neostriatum*, Pergamon, Oxford, pp. 195–210.

Iversen, S. D. (1984). Behavioural effects of manipulation of basal ganglia neurotransmitters, *Functions of the Basal Ganglia. CIBA Foundation Symposium*, Vol. 107, Pitman, London, pp. 183–195.

Iversen, S. D. and Mishkin, M. (1970). Perseverative interference in monkey following selective lesions of the inferior prefrontal convexity, *Experimental Brain Research* **11**: 376–386.

Jacob, S., McClintock, M. K., Zelano, B. and Ober, C. (2002). Paternally inherited HLA alleles are associated with women's choice of male odour, *Nature Genetics* **30**: 175–179.

Jacobsen, C. F. (1936). The functions of the frontal association areas in monkeys, *Comparative Psychology Monographs* **13**: 1–60.

Jacoby, L. L. (1983a). Perceptual enhancement: persistent effects of an experience, *Journal of Experimental Psychology: Learning, Memory, and Cognition* **9**: 21–38.

Jacoby, L. L. (1983b). Remembering the data: analyzing interaction processes in reading, *Journal of Verbal Learning and Verbal Behavior* **22**: 485–508.

Jahanshahi, M., Jenkins, I. H., Brown, R. G., Marsden, C. D., Passingham, R. E. and Brooks, D. J. (1995). Self-initiated versus externally triggered movements. I: an investigation using measurement of regional cerebral blood flow with PET and movement-related potentials in normal and Parkinson's disease subjects, *Brain* **118**: 913–933.

Jahanshahi, M., Dinberger, G., Fuller, R. and Frith, C. D. (2000). The role of the dorsolateral prefrontal cortex in random number generation: a study with positron emission tomography, *Neuroimage* **12**: 713–725.

Jahr, C. and Stevens, C. (1990). Voltage dependence of NMDA-activated macroscopic conductances predicted by single-channel kinetics, *Journal of Neuroscience* **10**: 3178–3182.

Jakab, R. L. and Leranth, C. (1995). Septum, *in* G. Paxinos (ed.), *The Rat Nervous System*, Academic Press, San Diego.

James, W. (1890). *The Principles of Psychology*, Henry Holt, New York.

Janssen, P., Vogels, R. and Orban, G. A. (1999). Macaque inferior temporal neurons are selective for disparity-defined three-dimensional shapes, *Proceedings of the National Academy of Sciences* **96**: 8217–8222.

Janssen, P., Vogels, R. and Orban, G. A. (2000). Selectivity for 3D shape that reveals distinct areas within macaque inferior temporal cortex, *Science* **288**: 2054–2056.

Janssen, P., Vogels, R., Liu, Y. and Orban, G. A. (2003). At least at the level of inferior temporal cortex, the stereo correspondence problem is solved, *Neuron* **37**: 693–701.

Jarrard, L. E. (1993). On the role of the hippocampus in learning and memory in the rat, *Behavioral and Neural Biology* **60**: 9–26.

Jarrard, L. E. and Davidson, T. L. (1990). Acquisition of concurrent conditional discriminations in rats with ibotenate lesions of hippocampus and subiculum, *Psychobiology* **18**: 68–73.

Jarvis, C. D. and Mishkin, M. (1977). Responses of cells in the inferior temporal cortex of monkeys during visual discrimination reversals, *Society for Neuroscience Abstracts* **3**: 1794.

Jay, T. M. and Witter, M. P. (1991). Distribution of hippocampal CA1 and subicular efferents in the prefrontal cortex of the rat studied by means of anterograde transport of Phaseolus vulgaris–leucoagglutinin, *Journal of Comparative Neurology* **313**: 574–586.

Jeffery, K. J. and Hayman, R. (2004). Plasticity of the hippocampal place cell representation, *Reviews in the Neurosciences* **15**: 309–331.

Jeffery, K. J., Anderson, M. I., Hayman, R. and Chakraborty, S. (2004). A proposed architecture for the neural representation of spatial context, *Neuroscience and Biobehavioral Reviews* **28**: 201–218.

Jensen, O. and Lisman, J. E. (1996). Theta/gamma networks with slow NMDA channels learn sequences and encode episodic memory: role of NMDA channels in recall, *Learning and Memory* **3**: 264–278.

Jensen, O. and Lisman, J. E. (2005). Hippocampal sequence-encoding driven by a cortical multi-item working memory buffer, *Trends in the Neurosciences* **28**: 67–72.

Jensen, O., Idiart, M. A. and Lisman, J. E. (1996). Physiologically realistic formation of autoassociative memory in networks with theta/gamma oscillations: role of fast NMDA channels, *Learning and Memory* **3**: 243–256.

Jerman, T., Kesner, R. P. and Hunsaker, M. R. (2006). Disconnection analysis of CA3 and DG in mediating encoding but not retrieval in a spatial maze learning task, *Learning and Memory* **13**: 458–464.

Johnson, T. N., Rosvold, H. E. and Mishkin, M. (1968). Projections from behaviorally defined sectors of the prefrontal cortex to the basal ganglia, septum and diencephalon of the monkey, *Experimental Neurology* **21**: 20–34.

Johnston, D. and Amaral, D. (2004). Hippocampus, *in* G. M. Shepherd (ed.), *The Synaptic Organization of the Brain*, 5th edn, Oxford University Press, Oxford, chapter 11, pp. 455–498.

Johnstone, S. and Rolls, E. T. (1990). Delay, discriminatory, and modality specific neurons in striatum and pallidum during short-term memory tasks, *Brain Research* **522**: 147–151.

Jonas, E. A. and Kaczmarek, L. K. (1999). The inside story: subcellular mechanisms of neuromodulation, *in* P. S. Katz (ed.), *Beyond Neurotransmission*, Oxford University Press, New York, chapter 3, pp. 83–120.

Jones, B. and Mishkin, M. (1972). Limbic lesions and the problem of stimulus–reinforcement associations, *Experimental Neurology* **36**: 362–377.

Jones, E. G. and Peters, A. (eds) (1984). *Cerebral Cortex, Functional Properties of Cortical Cells*, Vol. 2, Plenum, New York.

Jones, E. G. and Powell, T. P. S. (1970). An anatomical study of converging sensory pathways within the cerebral cortex of the monkey, *Brain* **93**: 793–820.

Jones-Gotman, M. and Zatorre, R. J. (1988). Olfactory identification in patients with focal cerebral excision, *Neuropsychologia* **26**: 387–400.

Jouandet, M. and Gazzaniga, M. S. (1979). The frontal lobes, *in* M. S. Gazzaniga (ed.), *Handbook of Behavioural Neurobiology*, Vol. 2, Neuropsychology, Plenum, New York, pp. 25–59.

Julius, D. and Basbaum, A. L. (2001). Molecular mechansims of nociception, *Nature* **413**: 203–210.

Jung, M. W. and McNaughton, B. L. (1993). Spatial selectivity of unit activity in the hippocampal granular layer, *Hippocampus* **3**: 165–182.

Jurgens, U. (2002). Neural pathways underlying vocal control, *Neuroscience and Biobehavioral Reviews* **26**: 235–258.

Kadohisa, M., Rolls, E. T. and Verhagen, J. V. (2004). Orbitofrontal cortex neuronal representation of temperature and capsaicin in the mouth, *Neuroscience* **127**: 207–221.

Kadohisa, M., Rolls, E. T. and Verhagen, J. V. (2005a). Neuronal representations of stimuli in the mouth: the primate insular taste cortex, orbitofrontal cortex, and amygdala, *Chemical Senses* **30**: 401–419.

Kadohisa, M., Rolls, E. T. and Verhagen, J. V. (2005b). The primate amygdala: neuronal representations of the viscosity, fat texture, grittiness and taste of foods, *Neuroscience* **132**: 33–48.

Kagan, J. (1966). Reflection-impulsivity: the generality of dynamics of conceptual tempo, *Journal of Abnormal Psychology* **1**: 917–924.

Kagel, J. H., Battalio, R. C. and Green, L. (1995). *Economic Choice Theory: An Experimental Analysis of Animal Behaviour*, Cambridge University Press, Cambridge.

Kahneman, D. (1973). *Attention and Effort*, Prentice-Hall, Englewood Cliffs, NJ.

Kahneman, D. and Tversky, A. (1979). Prospect theory: An analysis of decision under risk, *Econometrica* **47**: 263–292.

Kahneman, D. and Tversky, A. (1984). Choices, values, and frames, *American Psychologist* **4**: 341–350.

Kandel, E. R. (2000). Cellular mechanisms of learning and the biological basis of individuality, *in* E. R. Kandel, J. H. Schwartz and T. H. Jessell (eds), *Principles of Neural Science*, 4th edn, McGraw-Hill, New York, chapter 63, pp. 1247–1279.

Kandel, E. R., Schwartz, J. H. and Jessel, T. H. (2000). *Principles of Neural Science*, 4th edn, McGraw-Hill, New York.

Kanter, I. and Sompolinsky, H. (1987). Associative recall of memories without errors, *Physical Review A* **35**: 380–392.

Kanwisher, N., McDermott, J. and Chun, M. M. (1997). The fusiform face area: a module in human extrastriate cortex specialized for face perception, *Journal of Neuroscience* **17**: 4301–4311.

Kapp, B. S., Whalen, P. J., Supple, W. F. and Pascoe, J. P. (1992). Amygdaloid contributions to conditioned arousal and sensory information processing, *in* J. P. Aggleton (ed.), *The Amygdala*, Wiley-Liss, New York, chapter 8, pp. 229–245.

Kastner, S., De Weerd, P., Desimone, R. and Ungerleider, L. (1998). Mechanisms of directed attention in the human extrastriate cortex as revealed by functional MRI, *Science* **282**: 108–111.

Kastner, S., Pinsk, M., De Weerd, P., Desimone, R. and Ungerleider, L. (1999). Increased activity in human visual cortex during directed attention in the absence of visual stimulation, *Neuron* **22**: 751–761.

Kelley, A. E. (1999). Neural integrative activities of nucleus accumbens subregions in relation to learning and motivation, *Psychobiology* **27**: 198–213.

Kelley, A. E. (2004). Ventral striatal control of appetitive motivation: role in ingestive behaviour and reward-related learning, *Neuroscience and Biobehavioral Reviews* **27**: 765–776.

Kelly, R. M. and Strick, P. L. (2004). Macro-architecture of basal ganglia loops with the cerebral cortex: use of rabies virus to reveal multisynaptic circuits, *Progress in Brain Research* **143**: 449–459.

Kemp, J. M. and Powell, T. P. S. (1970). The cortico-striate projections in the monkey, *Brain* **93**: 525–546.

Kesner, R. P. (1998). Neural mediation of memory for time: role of hippocampus and medial prefrontal cortex, *Psychological Bulletin Reviews* **5**: 585–596.

Kesner, R. P. (2007). Ventral but not dorsal CA1 disrupts temporal pattern separation of odors, *in preparation*.

Kesner, R. P. and Gilbert, P. E. (2006). The role of the medial caudate nucleus, but not the hippocampus, in a delayed-matching-to sample task for motor response, *European Journal of Neuroscience* **23**: 1888–1894.

Kesner, R. P. and Rolls, E. T. (2001). Role of long term synaptic modification in short term memory, *Hippocampus* **11**: 240–250.

Kesner, R. P., Gilbert, P. E. and Barua, L. A. (2002). The role of the hippocampus in memory for the temporal order of a sequence of odors, *Behavioral Neuroscience* **116**: 286–290.

Kesner, R. P., Lee, I. and Gilbert, P. (2004). A behavioral assessment of hippocampal function based on a subregional analysis, *Reviews in the Neurosciences* **15**: 333–351.

Kesner, R. P., Hunsaker, M. R. and Gilbert, P. E. (2005). The role of CA1 in the acquisition of an object-trace-odor paired associate task, *Behavioral Neuroscience* **119**: 781–786.

Keysers, C. and Perrett, D. I. (2002). Visual masking and RSVP reveal neural competition, *Trends in Cognitive Sciences* **6**: 120–125.

Keysers, C. and Perrett, D. I. (2004). Demystifying social cognition: a Hebbian perspective, *Trends in Cognitive Sciences* **8**: 501–507.

Keysers, C., Xiao, D., Foldiak, P. and Perrett, D. (2001). The speed of sight, *Journal of Cognitive Neuroscience* **13**: 90–101.

Kievit, J. and Kuypers, H. G. J. M. (1975). Subcortical afferents to the frontal lobe in the rhesus monkey studied by means of retrograde horseradish peroxidase transport, *Brain Research* **85**: 261–266.

Killcross, S. and Coutureau, E. (2003). Coordination of actions and habits in the medial prefrontal cortex of rats, *Cerebral Cortex* **13**: 400–408.

Killcross, S., Robbins, T. W. and Everitt, B. J. (1997). Different types of fear-conditioned behaviour mediated by separate nuclei within amygdala, *Nature* **388**: 377–380.

Kim, J. N. and Shadlen, M. N. (1999). Neural correlates of a decision in the dorsolateral prefrontal cortex of the macaque, *Nature Neuroscience* **2**: 176–185.

King-Casas, B., Tomlin, D., Anen, C., Camerere, C. F., Quartz, S. R. and Montague, P. R. (2005). Getting to know you: reputation and trust in a two-person economic exchange, *Science* **308**: 78–83.

Kirkwood, A., Dudek, S. M., Gold, J. T., Aizenman, C. D. and Bear, M. F. (1993). Common forms of synaptic plasticity in the hippocampus and neocortex "in vitro", *Science* **260**: 1518–1521.

Kjaer, T. W., Hertz, J. A. and Richmond, B. J. (1994). Decoding cortical neuronal signals: networks models, information estimation and spatial tuning, *Journal of Computational Neuroscience* **1**: 109–139.

Kleinfeld, D. (1986). Sequential state generation by model neural networks, *Proceedings of the National Academy of Sciences of the USA* **83**: 9469–9473.

Kling, A. and Steklis, H. D. (1976). A neural substrate for affiliative behavior in nonhuman primates, *Brain, Behavior, and Evolution* **13**: 216–238.

Kling, A. S. and Brothers, L. A. (1992). The amygdala and social behavior, *in* J. P. Aggleton (ed.), *The Amygdala*, Wiley-Liss, New York, chapter 13, pp. 353–377.

Kluver, H. and Bucy, P. C. (1939). Preliminary analysis of functions of the temporal lobe in monkeys, *Archives of Neurology and Psychiatry* **42**: 979–1000.

Knutson, B., Adams, C. M., Fong, G. W. and Hommer, D. (2001). Anticipation of increasing monetary reward selectively recruits nucleus accumbens, *Journal of Neuroscience* **21**: 1–5.

Koch, C. (1999). *Biophysics of Computation*, Oxford University Press, Oxford.

Koch, C. and Ullman, S. (1985). Shifts in selective visual attention: Towards the underlying neural circuitry, *Human Neurobiology* **4**: 219–227.

Koenderink, J. J. (1990). *Solid Shape*, MIT Press, Cambridge, MA.

Koenderink, J. J. and Van Doorn, A. J. (1979). The internal representation of solid shape with respect to vision, *Biological Cybernetics* **32**: 211–217.

Koenderink, J. J. and van Doorn, A. J. (1991). Affine structure from motion, *Journal of the Optical Society of America, A* **8**: 377–385.

Kohonen, T. (1977). *Associative Memory: A System Theoretical Approach*, Springer, New York.

Kohonen, T. (1982). Clustering, taxonomy, and topological maps of patterns, *in* M. Lang (ed.), *Proceedings of the Sixth International Conference on Pattern Recognition*, IEEE Computer Society Press, Silver Spring, MD, pp. 114–125.

Kohonen, T. (1988). *Self-Organization and Associative Memory*, 2nd edn, Springer-Verlag, New York.

Kohonen, T. (1989). *Self-Organization and Associative Memory*, 3rd (1984, 1st edn; 1988, 2nd edn) edn, Springer-Verlag, Berlin.

Kohonen, T. (1995). *Self-Organizing Maps*, Springer-Verlag, Berlin.

Kolb, B. and Whishaw, I. Q. (2003). *Fundamentals of Human Neuropsychology*, 5th edn, Worth, New York.

Konorski, J. (1967). *Integrative Activity of the Brain: An Interdisciplinary Approach*, University of Chicago Press, Chicago.

Koob, G. F. (1992). Dopamine, addiction and reward, *Seminars in the Neurosciences* **4**: 139–148.

Koob, G. F. (1996). Hedonic valence, dopamine and motivation, *Molecular Psychiatry* **1**: 186–189.

Koob, G. F. and Le Moal, M. (1997). Drug abuse: hedonic homeostatic dysregulation, *Science* **278**: 52–58.

Kosfeld, M., Heinrichs, M., Zak, P. J., Fischbacher, U. and Fehr, E. (2005). Oxytocin increases trust in humans, *Nature* **435**: 673–676.

Koski, L. and Paus, T. (2000). Functional connectivity of anterior cingulate cortex within human frontal lobe: a brain mapping meta-analysis, *Experimental Brain Research* **133**: 55–65.

Kosslyn, S. M. (1994). *Image and Brain: The Resolution of the Imagery Debate*, MIT Press, Cambridge, Mass.

Kovacs, G., Vogels, R. and Orban, G. A. (1995). Cortical correlate of pattern backward masking, *Proceedings of the National Academy of Sciences USA* **92**: 5587–5591.

Kowalska, D. M., Bachevalier, J. and Mishkin, M. (1991). The role of the inferior prefrontal convexity in performance of delayed nonmatching-to-sample, *Neuropsychologia* **29**: 583–600.

Krebs, J. R. and Kacelnik, A. (1991). Decision making, *in* J. R. Krebs and N. B. Davies (eds), *Behavioural Ecology*, 3rd edn, Blackwell, Oxford, chapter 4, pp. 105–136.

Kreiman, G., Koch, C. and Freid, I. (2000). Category-specific visual responses of single neurons in the human temporal lobe, *Nature Neuroscience* **3**: 946–953.

Krettek, J. E. and Price, J. L. (1974). A direct input from the amygdala to the thalamus and the cerebral cortex, *Brain Research* **67**: 169–174.

Krettek, J. E. and Price, J. L. (1977). The cortical projections of the mediodorsal nucleus and adjacent thalamic nuclei in the rat, *Journal of Comparative Neurology* **171**: 157–192.

Krieman, G., Koch, C. and Fried, I. (2000). Category-specific visual responses of single neurons in the human medial temporal lobe, *Nature Neuroscience* **3**: 946–953.

Kringelbach, M. L. and Rolls, E. T. (2003). Neural correlates of rapid reversal learning in a simple model of human social interaction, *Neuroimage* **20**: 1371–1383.

Kringelbach, M. L. and Rolls, E. T. (2004). The functional neuroanatomy of the human orbitofrontal cortex: evidence from neuroimaging and neuropsychology, *Progress in Neurobiology* **72**: 341–372.

Kringelbach, M. L., O'Doherty, J., Rolls, E. T. and Andrews, C. (2003). Activation of the human orbitofrontal cortex to a liquid food stimulus is correlated with its subjective pleasantness, *Cerebral Cortex* **13**: 1064–1071.

Krolak-Salmon, P., Henaff, M. A., Isnard, J., Tallon-Baudry, C., Guenot, M., Vighetto, A., Bertrand, O. and Mauguiere, F. (2003). An attention modulated response to disgust in human ventral anterior insula, *Annals of Neurology* **53**: 446–453.

Kuhar, M. J., Pert, C. B. and Snyder, S. H. (1973). Regional distribution of opiate receptor binding in monkey and human brain, *Nature* **245**: 447–450.

Kuhn, R. (1990). Statistical mechanics of neural networks near saturation, *in* L. Garrido (ed.), *Statistical Mechanics of Neural Networks*, Springer-Verlag, Berlin.

Kuhn, R., Bos, S. and van Hemmen, J. L. (1991). Statistical mechanics for networks of graded response neurons, *Physical Review A* **243**: 2084–2087.

LaBar, K. S., Gitelman, D. R., Parrish, T. B., Kim, Y.-H., Nobre, A. C. and Mesulam, M.-M. (2001). Hunger selectively modulates corticolimbic activation to food stimuli in humans, *Behavioral Neuroscience* **115**: 493–500.

Laibson, D. (1997). Golden eggs and hyperbolic discounting, *Quarterly Journal of Economics* **112**: 443–477.

Laland, K. N. and Brown, G. R. (2002). *Sense and Nonsense. Evolutionary Perspectives on Human Behaviour*, Oxford University Press, Oxford.

Lamme, V. A. F. (1995). The neurophysiology of figure-ground segregation in primary visual cortex., *Journal of Neuroscience* **15**: 1605–1615.

Land, M. F. (1999). Motion and vision: why animals move their eyes, *Journal of Comparative Physiology A* **185**: 341–352.

Land, M. F. and Collett, T. S. (1997). A survey of active vision in invertebrates, *in* M. V. Srinivasan and S. Venkatesh (eds), *From Living Eyes to Seeing Machines*, Oxford University Press, Oxford.

Lane, R. D., Fink, G. R., Chau, P. M. L. and Dolan, R. J. (1997a). Neural activation during selective attention to subjective emotional responses, *Neuroreport* **8**: 3969–3972.

Lane, R. D., Reiman, E. M., Ahern, G. L., Schwartz, G. E. and Davidson, R. J. (1997b). Neuroanatomical correlates of happiness, sadness, and disgust, *American Journal of Psychiatry* **154**: 926–933.

Lane, R. D., Reiman, E. M., Bradley, M. M., Lang, P. J., Ahern, G. L., Davidson, R. J. and Schwartz, G. E. (1997c). Neuroanatomical correlates of pleasant and unpleasant emotion, *Neuropsychologia* **35**: 1437–1444.

Lane, R. D., Reiman, E., Axelrod, B., Yun, L.-S., Holmes, A. H. and Schwartz, G. (1998). Neural correlates of levels of emotional awareness. Evidence of an interaction between emotion and attention in the anterior cingulate cortex, *Journal of Cognitive Neuroscience* **10**: 525–535.

Lanthorn, T., Storn, J. and Andersen, P. (1984). Current-to-frequency transduction in CA1 hippocampal pyramidal cells: slow prepotentials dominate the primary range firing, *Experimental Brain Research* **53**: 431–443.

Lassalle, J. M., Bataille, T. and Halley, H. (2000). Reversible inactivation of the hippocampal mossy fiber synapses in mice impairs spatial learning, but neither consolidation nor memory retrieval, in the Morris navigation task, *Neurobiology of Learning and Memory* **73**: 243–257.

Lavenex, P. and Amaral, D. G. (2000). Hippocampal-neocortical interaction: a hierarchy of associativity, *Hippocampus* **10**: 420–430.

Lavenex, P., Suzuki, W. A. and Amaral, D. G. (2004). Perirhinal and parahippocampal cortices of the macaque monkey: Intrinsic projections and interconnections, *Journal of Comparative Neurology* **472**: 371–394.

Law-Tho, D., Hirsch, J. and Crepel, F. (1994). Dopamine modulation of synaptic transmission in rat prefrontal cortex: An in vitro electrophysiological study, *Neuroscience Research* **21**: 151–160.

Lawrence, A. D., Calder, A. J., McGowan, S. W. and Grasby, P. M. (2002). Selective disruption of the recogntion of facial expressions of anger, *NeuroReport* **13**: 881–884.

LeDoux, J. E. (1987). Emotion, *in* F. Plum and V. B. Mountcastle (eds), *Handbook of Physiology: The Nervous System*, Vol. 5, Higher cortical functions of the brain, American Physiological Society, Bethesda MD, pp. 419–459.

LeDoux, J. E. (1992). Emotion and the amygdala, *in* J. P. Aggleton (ed.), *The Amygdala*, Wiley-Liss, New York, chapter 12, pp. 339–351.

LeDoux, J. E. (1994). Emotion, memory and the brain, *Scientific American* **220 (June)**: 50–57.

LeDoux, J. E. (1995). Emotion: clues from the brain, *Annual Review of Psychology* **46**: 209–235.

LeDoux, J. E. (1996). *The Emotional Brain*, Simon and Schuster, New York.

LeDoux, J. E. (2000). The amygdala and emotion: a view through fear, *in* J. P. Aggleton (ed.), *The Amygdala: a Functional Analysis*, Oxford University Press, Oxford, chapter 7, pp. 289–310.

LeDoux, J. E., Iwata, J., Cicchetti, P. and Reis, D. J. (1988). Different projections of the central amygdaloid nucleus mediate autonomic and behavioral correlates of conditioned fear, *Journal of Neuroscience* **8**: 2517–2529.

Lee, I. and Kesner, R. P. (2002). Differential contribution of NMDA receptors in hippocampal subregions to spatial working memory, *Nature Neuroscience* **5**: 162–168.

Lee, I. and Kesner, R. P. (2003a). Differential roles of dorsal hippocampal subregions in spatial working memory with short versus intermediate delay, *Behavioral Neuroscience* **117**: 1044–1053.

Lee, I. and Kesner, R. P. (2003b). Time-dependent relationship between the dorsal hippocampus and the prefrontal cortex in spatial memory, *Journal of Neurosciennce* **23**: 1517–1523.

Lee, I. and Kesner, R. P. (2004a). Differential contributions of dorsal hippocampal subregions to memory acquisition and retrieval in contextual fear-conditioning, *Hippocampus* **14**: 301–310.

Lee, I. and Kesner, R. P. (2004b). Encoding versus retrieval of spatial memory: double dissociation between the dentate gyrus and the perforant path inputs into CA3 in the dorsal hippocampus, *Hippocampus* **14**: 66–76.

Lee, I., Rao, G. and Knierim, J. J. (2004). A double dissociation between hippocampal subfields: differential time course of CA3 and CA1 place cells for processing changed environments, *Neuron* **42**: 803–815.

Lee, I., Jerman, T. S. and Kesner, R. P. (2005). Disruption of delayed memory for a sequence of spatial locations following CA1 or CA3 lesions of the dorsal hippocampus, *Neurobiology of Learning and Memory* **84**: 138–147.

Lee, T. and Nguyen, M. (2001). Dynamics of subjective contour formation in the early visual cortex, *Proceedings of the National Academy of Science* **98**: 1907–1911.

Lee, T. S. (1996). Image representation using 2D Gabor wavelets, *IEEE Transactions on Pattern Analysis and Machine Intelligence* **18,10**: 959–971.

Lee, T. S., Mumford, D., Romero, R. D. and Lamme, V. A. F. (1998). The role of primary visual cortex in higher level vision, *Vision Research* **38**: 2429–2454.

Lee, T. S., Yang, C. F., Romero, R. D. and Mumford, D. (2002a). Neural activity in early visual cortex reflects behavioral experience and higher-order perceptual saliency, *Nature Neuroscience* **5**: 589–597.

Lee, T. S., Yang, C. Y., Romero, R. D. and Mumford, D. (2002b). Neural activity in early visual cortex reflects behavioral experience and higher order perceptual saliency, *Nature Neuroscience* **5**: 589–597.

Lehky, S. R., Sejnowski, T. J. and Desimone, R. (2005). Selectivity and sparseness in the responses of striate complex cells, *Vision Research* **45**: 57–73.

Leonard, C. M., Rolls, E. T., Wilson, F. A. W. and Baylis, G. C. (1985). Neurons in the amygdala of the monkey with responses selective for faces, *Behavioural Brain Research* **15**: 159–176.

Lester, R. A. and Jahr, C. E. (1995). NMDA channel behavior depends on agonist affinity, *Journal of Neuroscience* **12**: 635–643.

Lester, R. A., Clements, J. D., Westbrook, G. L. and Jahr, C. E. (1990). Channel kinetics determine the time course of NMDA receptor-mediated synaptic currents, *Nature* **346**: 565–567.

Leung, H., Gore, J. and Goldman-Rakic, P. (2002). Sustained mnemonic response in the human middle frontal gyrus during on-line storage of spatial memoranda, *Journal of Cognitive Neuroscience* **14**: 659–671.

Leutgeb, S., Leutgeb, J. K., Treves, A., Moser, M. B. and Moser, E. I. (2004). Distinct ensemble codes in hippocampal areas CA3 and CA1, *Science* **305**: 1295–1298.

Leutgeb, S., Leutgeb, J. K., Treves, A., Meyer, R., Barnes, C. A., McNaughton, B. L., Moser, M.-B. and Moser,

E. I. (2005). Progressive transformation of hippocampal neuronal representations in "morphed" environments, *Neuron* **48**: 345–358.

Levine, A. S. and Billington, C. J. (2004). Opioids as agents of reward-related feeding: a consideration of the evidence, *Physiology and Behaviour* **82**: 57–61.

Levitt, J. B., Lund, J. S. and Yoshioka, T. (1996). Anatomical substrates for early stages in cortical processing of visual information in the macaque monkey, *Behavioural Brain Research* **76**: 5–19.

Levy, W. B. (1985). Associative changes in the synapse: LTP in the hippocampus, *in* W. B. Levy, J. A. Anderson and S. Lehmkuhle (eds), *Synaptic Modification, Neuron Selectivity, and Nervous System Organization*, Erlbaum, Hillsdale, NJ, chapter 1, pp. 5–33.

Levy, W. B. (1989). A computational approach to hippocampal function, *in* R. D. Hawkins and G. H. Bower (eds), *Computational Models of Learning in Simple Neural Systems*, Academic Press, San Diego, pp. 243–305.

Levy, W. B. (1996). A sequence predicting ca3 is a flexible associator that learns and uses context to solve hippocampal-like tasks, *Hippocampus* **6**: 579–590.

Levy, W. B. and Baxter, R. A. (1996). Energy efficient neural codes, *Neural Computation* **8**: 531–543.

Levy, W. B. and Desmond, N. L. (1985). The rules of elemental synaptic plasticity, *in* W. B. Levy, J. A. Anderson and S. Lehmkuhle (eds), *Synaptic Modification, Neuron Selectivity, and Nervous System Organization*, Erlbaum, Hillsdale, NJ, chapter 6, pp. 105–121.

Levy, W. B., Colbert, C. M. and Desmond, N. L. (1990). Elemental adaptive processes of neurons and synapses: a statistical/computational perspective, *in* M. Gluck and D. Rumelhart (eds), *Neuroscience and Connectionist Theory*, Erlbaum, Hillsdale, NJ, chapter 5, pp. 187–235.

Levy, W. B., Wu, X. and Baxter, R. A. (1995). Unification of hippocampal function via computational/encoding considerations, *International Journal of Neural Systems* **6, Suppl.**: 71–80.

Lewis, D. A., Hashimoto, T. and Volk, D. W. (2005). Cortical inhibitory neurons and schizophrenia, *Nature Reviews Neuroscience* **6**: 312–324.

Li, H., Matsumoto, K. and Watanabe, H. (1999). Different effects of unilateral and bilateral hippocampal lesions in rats on the performance of radial maze and odor-paired associate tasks, *Brain Research Bulletin* **48**: 113–119.

Liddle, P. F. (1987). The symptoms of chronic schizophrenia: a re-examination of the positive-negative dichotomy, *British Journal of Psychiatry* **151**: 145–151.

Liddle, P. F., Barnes, T. R., Morris, D. and Haque, S. (1989). Three syndromes in chronic schizophrenia, *British Journal of Psychiatry* **7**: 119–122.

Lieberman, D. A. (ed.) (2000). *Learning*, Wadsworth, Belmont, CA.

Liebeskind, J. C. and Paul, L. A. (1977). Psychological and physiological mechanisms of pain, *Annual Review of Psychology* **88**: 41–60.

Liebeskind, J. C., Giesler, G. J. and Urca, G. (1985). Evidence pertaining to an endogenous mechanism of pain inhibition in the central nervous system, *in* Y. Zotterman (ed.), *Sensory Functions of the Skin*, Pergamon, Oxford.

Liebman, J. M. and Cooper, S. J. (eds) (1989). *Neuropharmacological Basis of Reward*, Oxford University Press, Oxford.

Lisman, J. E. and Idiart, M. A. (1995). Storage of 7 ± 2 short-term memories in oscillatory subcycles, *Science* **267**: 1512–1515.

Lisman, J. E. and Idiart, M. A. (1999). Relating hippocampal circuitry to function: recall of memory sequences by reciprocal dentate-CA3 interactions, *Neuron* **22**: 233–242.

Lisman, J. E., Fellous, J. M. and Wang, X. J. (1998). A role for NMDA-receptor channels in working memory, *Nature Neuroscience* **1**: 273–275.

Lisman, J. E., Talamini, L. M. and Raffone, A. (2005). Recall of memory sequences by interaction of the dentate and CA3: a revised model of the phase precession, *Neural Networks* **18**: 1191–1201.

Little, W. A. (1974). The existence of persistent states in the brain, *Mathematical Bioscience* **19**: 101–120.

Liu, Y. and Wang, X.-J. (2001). Spike-frequency adaptation of a generalized leaky integrate-and-fire model neuron, *Journal of Computational Neuroscience* **10**: 25–45.

Logothetis, N. K. and Sheinberg, D. L. (1996). Visual object recognition, *Annual Review of Neuroscience* **19**: 577–621.

Logothetis, N. K., Pauls, J., Bulthoff, H. H. and Poggio, T. (1994). View-dependent object recognition by monkeys, *Current Biology* **4**: 401–414.

Logothetis, N. K., Pauls, J. and Poggio, T. (1995). Shape representation in the inferior temporal cortex of monkeys, *Current Biology* **5**: 552–563.

Logothetis, N. K., Pauls, J., Augath, M., Trinath, T. and Oeltermann, A. (2001). Neurophysiological investigation of the basis of the fMRI signal, *Nature* **412**: 150–157.

Loh, M., Szabo, M., Almeida, R., Stetter, M. and Deco, G. (2004). Computational neuroscience for cognitive brain functions, *in* W. Dubitzky and F. Azuaje (eds), *Artificial Intelligence: Methods and Tools for Systems Biology*, Vol. Computational Biology Series Volume 5, Kluwer, Reihe.

Loh, M., Rolls, E. T. and Deco, G. (2007a). A dynamical systems hypothesis of schizophrenia.

Loh, M., Rolls, E. T. and Deco, G. (2007b). Statistical fluctuations in attractor networks related to schizophrenia,

Pharmacopsychiatry **Supplement SX**: in press.

Lovibond, P. F. (1983). Facilitation of instrumental behaviour by Pavlovian appetitive conditioned stimulus, *Journal of Experimental Psychology* **9**: 225–247.

Lowe, D. (1985). *Perceptual Organization and Visual Recognition*, Kluwer, Boston.

Luck, S. J., Chelazzi, L., Hillyard, S. A. and Desimone, R. (1997). Neural mechanisms of spatial selective attention in areas V1, V2, and V4 of macaque visual cortex, *Journal of Neurophysiology* **77**: 24–42.

Lund, J. S. (1984). Spiny stellate neurons, *in* A. Peters and E. Jones (eds), *Cerebral Cortex, Vol. 1, Cellular Components of the Cerebral Cortex*, Plenum, New York, chapter 7, pp. 255–308.

Lynch, M. A. (2004). Long-term potentiation and memory, *Physiological Reviews* **84**: 87–136.

Lyness, W. H., Friedle, N. M. and Moore, K. E. (1980). Destruction of dopaminergic nerve terminals in nucleus accumbens: effect of D-amphetamine self-administration, *Pharmacology, Biochemistry, and Behavior* **11**: 553–556.

Maaswinkel, H., Jarrard, L. E. and Whishaw, I. Q. (1999). Hippocampectomized rats are impaired in homing by path integration, *Hippocampus* **9**: 553–561.

MacGregor, R. J. (1987). *Neural and Brain Modelling*, Academic Press, San Diego.

Machens, C. K., Romo, R. and Brody, C. D. (2005). Flexible control of mutual inhibition: a neural model of two-interval discrimination, *Science* **307**: 1121–1124.

MacKay, D. M. and McCulloch, W. S. (1952). The limiting information capacity of a neuronal link, *Bulletin of Mathematical Biophysics* **14**: 127–135.

Mackintosh, N. J. (1983). *Conditioning and Associative Learning*, Oxford University Press, Oxford.

Madsen, J. and Kesner, R. P. (1995). The temporal-distance effect in subjects with dementia of the Alzheimer type, *Alzheimer's Disease and Associated Disorders* **9**: 94–100.

Maier, A., Logothetis, N. K. and Leopold, D. A. (2005). Global competition dictates local suppression in pattern rivalry, *Journal of Vision* **5**: 668–677.

Malhotra, A. K., Pinals, D. A., Weingartner, H., Sirocco, K., Missar, C. D., Pickar, D. and Breier, A. (1996). NMDA receptor function and human cognition: the effects of ketamine in healthy volunteers, *Neuropsychopharmacology* **14**: 301–307.

Malkova, L. and Mishkin, M. (2003). One-trial memory for object-place associations after separate lesions of hippocampus and posterior parahippocampal region in the monkey, *Journal of Neuroscience* **23**: 1956–1965.

Malkova, L., Gaffan, D. and Murray, E. A. (1997). Excitotoxic lesions of the amygdala fail to produce impairment in visual learning for auditory secondary reinforcement but interfere with reinforcer devaluation effects in rhesus monkeys, *Journal of Neuroscience* **17**: 6011–6120.

Malkova, L., Bachevalier, J., Mishkin, M. and Saunders, R. C. (2001). Neurotoxic lesions of perirhinal cortex impair visual recognition memory in rhesus monkeys, *Neuroreport* **12**: 1913–1917.

Malsburg, C. v. d. (1973). Self-organization of orientation-sensitive columns in the striate cortex, *Kybernetik* **14**: 85–100.

Malsburg, C. v. d. (1990). A neural architecture for the representation of scenes, *in* J. L. McGaugh, N. M. Weinburger and G. Lynch (eds), *Brain Organization and Memory: Cells, Systems and Circuits*, Oxford University Press, Oxford, chapter 18, pp. 356–372.

Markram, H. and Siegel, M. (1992). The inositol 1,4,5-triphosphate pathway mediates cholinergic potentiation of rat hippocampal neuronal responses to NMDA, *Journal of Physiology* **447**: 513–533.

Markram, H. and Tsodyks, M. (1996). Redistribution of synaptic efficacy between neocortical pyramidal neurons, *Nature* **382**: 807–810.

Markram, H., Lübke, J., Frotscher, M. and Sakmann, B. (1997). Regulation of synaptic efficacy by coincidence of postsynaptic APs and EPSPs, *Science* **275**: 213–215.

Markram, H., Pikus, D., Gupta, A. and Tsodyks, M. (1998). Information processing with frequency-dependent synaptic connections, *Neuropharmacology* **37**: 489–500.

Markus, E. J., Qin, Y. L., Leonard, B., Skaggs, W., McNaughton, B. L. and Barnes, C. A. (1995). Interactions between location and task affect the spatial and directional firing of hippocampal neurons, *Journal of Neuroscience* **15**: 7079–7094.

Marr, D. (1969). A theory of cerebellar cortex, *Journal of Physiology* **202**: 437–470.

Marr, D. (1970). A theory for cerebral cortex, *Proceedings of The Royal Society of London, Series B* **176**: 161–234.

Marr, D. (1971). Simple memory: a theory for archicortex, *Philosophical Transactions of The Royal Society of London, Series B* **262**: 23–81.

Marr, D. (1982). *Vision*, Freeman, San Francisco.

Marr, D. and Nishihara, H. K. (1978). Representation and recognition of the spatial organization of three dimensional structure, *Proceedings of the Royal Society of London B* **200**: 269–294.

Marshall, J. (1951). Sensory disturbances in cortical wounds with special reference to pain, *Journal of Neurology, Neurosurgery and Psychiatry* **14**: 187–204.

Marshall, J. and Halligan, P. (1993). Visuo-spatial neglect: a new copying test to assess perceptual parsing, *Journal of Neurology* **240**: 37–40.

Marshall, J. F., Richardson, J. S. and Teitelbaum, P. (1974). Nigrostriatal bundle damage and the lateral hypothalamic syndrome, *Journal of Comparative and Physiological Psychology* **87**: 808–830.

Marshuetz, C. (2005). Order information in working memory: an integrative review of evidence from brain and behavior, *Psychological Bulletin* **131**: 323–339.

Martin, K. A. C. (1984). Neuronal circuits in cat striate cortex, *in* E. Jones and A. Peters (eds), *Cerebral Cortex, Vol. 2, Functional Properties of Cortical Cells*, Plenum, New York, chapter 9, pp. 241–284.

Martin, S. J., Grimwood, P. D. and Morris, R. G. (2000). Synaptic plasticity and memory: an evaluation of the hypothesis, *Annual Review of Neuroscience* **23**: 649–711.

Martinez, C. O., Do, V. H., Martinez, J. L. J. and Derrick, B. E. (2002). Associative long-term potentiation (LTP) among extrinsic afferents of the hippocampal CA3 region in vivo, *Brain Research* **940**: 86–94.

Martinez-Trujillo, J. and Treue, S. (2002). Attentional modulation strength in cortical area MT depends on stimulus contrast, *Neuron* **35**: 365–370.

Mason, A. and Larkman, A. (1990). Correlations between morphology and electrophysiology of pyramidal neurones in slices of rat visual cortex. I. Electrophysiology, *Journal of Neuroscience* **10**: 1415–1428.

Masuda, N. and Aihara, K. (2003). Ergodicity of spike trains: when does trial averaging make sense?, *Neural Computation* **15**: 1341–1372.

Matsumoto, K., Suzuki, W. and Tanaka, K. (2001). Neuronal correlates of goal-based motor selection in the prefrontal cortex, *Science* **301**: 229–232.

Matsumura, N., Nishijo, H., Tamura, R., Eifuku, S., Endo, S. and Ono, T. (1999). Spatial- and task-dependent neuronal responses during real and virtual translocation in the monkey hippocampal formation, *Journal of Neuroscience* **19**: 2318–2393.

Matthews, G. and Gilliland, K. (1999). The personality theories of H.J.Eysenck and J.A.Gray: a comparative review, *Personality and Individual Differences* **26**: 583–626.

Mattia, M. and Del Giudice, P. (2002). Population dynamics of interacting spiking neurons, *Physical Review E* **66**: 051917.

Maunsell, J. H. R. (1995). The brain's visual world: representation of visual targets in cerebral cortex, *Science* **270**: 764–769.

Mayberg, H. S. (1997). Limbic-cortical dysregulation: a proposed model of depression, *Journal of Neuropsychiatry* **9**: 471–481.

Mayberg, H. S. (2003). Positron emission tomography imaging in depression: a neural systems perspective, *Neuroimaging Clinics of North America* **13**: 805–815.

Mayberg, H. S., Brannan, S. K., Mahurin, R. K., Jerabek, P. A., Brickman, J. S., Tekell, J. L., Silva, J. A., McGinnis, S., Glass, T. G., Martin, C. C. and Fox, P. T. (1997). Cingulate function in depression: a potential predictor of treatment response, *NeuroReport* **8**: 1057–1061.

Mayberg, H. S., Liotti, M., Brannan, S. K., McGinnis, S., Mahurin, R. K., Jerabek, P. A., Silva, J. A., Tekell, J. L., Martin, C. C., Lancaster, J. L. and Fox, P. T. (1999). Reciprocal limbic-cortical function and negative mood: converging PET findings in depression and normal sadness, *American Journal of Psychiatry* **156**: 675–682.

Mayberg, H. S., Lozano, A. M., Voon, V., McNeely, H. E., Seminowicz, D., Hamani, C., Schwalb, J. M. and Kennedy, S. H. (2005). Deep brain stimulation for treatment-resistant depression, *Neuron* **45**: 651–660.

McAdams, C. and Maunsell, J. H. R. (1999). Effects of attention on orientation-tuning functions of single neurons in macaque cortical area v4, *Journal of Neuroscience* **19**: 431–441.

McCabe, C. and Rolls, E. T. (2007). Umami as a delicious flavor formed by convergence of taste and olfactory pathways in the human brain, *European Journal of Neuroscience* **25**: 1855–1864.

McCabe, C., Rolls, E. T., Bilderbeck, A. and McGlone, F. (2007). Cognitive influences on the affective representation of touch and the sight of touch in the human brain.

McClelland, J. L. and Rumelhart, D. E. (1981). An interactive activation model of context effects in letter perception. Part I: an account of basic findings, *Psychological Review* **88**: 375–407.

McClelland, J. L. and Rumelhart, D. E. (1986). A distributed model of human learning and memory, *in* J. L. McClelland and D. E. Rumelhart (eds), *Parallel Distributed Processing*, Vol. 2, MIT Press, Cambridge, MA, chapter 17, pp. 170–215.

McClelland, J. L. and Rumelhart, D. E. (1988). *Explorations in Parallel Distributed Processing*, MIT Press, Cambridge, MA.

McClelland, J. L., McNaughton, B. L. and O'Reilly, R. C. (1995). Why there are complementary learning systems in the hippocampus and neocortex: insights from the successes and failures of connectionist models of learning and memory, *Psychological Review* **102**: 419–457.

McClure, S. M., Berns, G. S. and Montague, P. R. (2003). Temporal prediction errors in a passive learning task activate human striatum, *Neuron* **38**: 339–346.

McClure, S. M., Laibson, D. I., Loewenstein, G. and Cohen, J. D. (2004). Separate neural systems value immediate and delayed monetary rewards, *Science* **306**: 503–507.

McCormick, D., Connors, B., Lighthall, J. and Prince, D. (1985). Comparative electrophysiology of pyramidal and sparsely spiny stellate neurons in the neocortex, *Journal of Neurophysiology* **54**: 782–806.

McCoy, A. N. and Platt, M. L. (2005). Expectations and outcomes: decision-making in the primate brain, *Journal of Comparative Physiology A* **191**: 201–211.

McDonald, A. J. (1992). Cell types and intrinsic connections to the amygdala, *in* J. P. Aggleton (ed.), *The Amygdala*, Wiley-Liss, New York, chapter 2, pp. 67–96.

McEchron, M. D., Tseng, W. and Disterhoft, J. F. (2003). Single neurons in CA1 hippocampus encode trace interval duration during trace heart rate (fear) conditioning in rabbit, *Journal of Neuroscience* **23**: 1535–1547.

McGaugh, J. L. (2000). Memory - a century of consolidation, *Science* **287**: 248–251.

McGinty, D. and Szymusiak, R. (1988). Neuronal unit activity patterns in behaving animals: brainstem and limbic system, *Annual Review of Psychology* **39**: 135–168.

McGurk, H. and MacDonald, J. (1976). Hearing lips and seeing voices, *Nature* **264**: 746–748.

McLeod, P., Driver, J. and Crisp, J. (1988). Visual search for a conjunction of movement and form is parallel, *Nature* **332**: 154–155.

McLeod, P., Plunkett, K. and Rolls, E. T. (1998). *Introduction to Connectionist Modelling of Cognitive Processes*, Oxford University Press, Oxford.

McNaughton, B. L. (1991). Associative pattern completion in hippocampal circuits: new evidence and new questions, *Brain Research Reviews* **16**: 193–220.

McNaughton, B. L. and Morris, R. G. M. (1987). Hippocampal synaptic enhancement and information storage within a distributed memory system, *Trends in Neuroscience* **10**: 408–415.

McNaughton, B. L. and Nadel, L. (1990). Hebb-Marr networks and the neurobiological representation of action in space, *in* M. A. Gluck and D. E. Rumelhart (eds), *Neuroscience and Connectionist Theory*, Erlbaum, Hillsdale, NJ, pp. 1–64.

McNaughton, B. L., Barnes, C. A. and O'Keefe, J. (1983). The contributions of position, direction, and velocity to single unit activity in the hippocampus of freely-moving rats, *Experimental Brain Research* **52**: 41–49.

McNaughton, B. L., Barnes, C. A., Meltzer, J. and Sutherland, R. J. (1989). Hippocampal granule cells are necessary for normal spatial learning but not for spatially selective pyramidal cell discharge, *Experimental Brain Research* **76**: 485–496.

McNaughton, B. L., Chen, L. L. and Markus, E. J. (1991). "Dead reckoning", landmark learning, and the sense of direction: a neurophysiological and computational hypothesis, *Journal of Cognitive Neuroscience* **3**: 190–202.

McNaughton, B. L., Battaglia, F. P., Jensen, O., Moser, E. I. and Moser, M.-B. (2006). Path integration and the neural basis of the hippocampal map, *Nature Reviews Neuroscience* **7**: 663–676.

Meador-Woodruff, J. H. and Healy, D. J. (2000). Glutamate receptor expression in schizophrenic brain, *Brain Research: Brain Research Reviews* **31**: 288–294.

Medin, D. L. and Schaffer, M. M. (1978). Context theory of classification learning, *Psychological Review* **85**: 207–238.

Mel, B. W. (1997). SEEMORE: Combining color, shape, and texture histogramming in a neurally-inspired approach to visual object recognition, *Neural Computation* **9**: 777–804.

Mel, B. W. and Fiser, J. (2000). Minimizing binding errors using learned conjunctive features, *Neural Computation* **12**: 731–762.

Mel, B. W., Ruderman, D. L. and Archie, K. A. (1998). Translation-invariant orientation tuning in visual "complex" cells could derive from intradendritic computations, *Journal of Neuroscience* **18**(11): 4325–4334.

Melzack, R. and Wall, P. D. (1996). *The Challenge of Pain*, Penguin, Harmondsworth, UK.

Meredith, M. (2001). Human vomeronasal organ function: a critical review of best and worst cases, *Chemical Senses* **26**: 433–445.

Mesulam, M.-M. (1990). Human brain cholinergic pathways, *Progress in Brain Research* **84**: 231–241.

Mesulam, M.-M. and Mufson, E. J. (1982a). Insula of the Old World monkey. I: Architectonics in the insulo-orbito-temporal component of the paralimbic brain, *Journal of Comparative Neurology* **212**: 1–22.

Mesulam, M.-M. and Mufson, E. J. (1982b). Insula of the Old World monkey. III. Efferent cortical output and comments on function, *Journal of Comparative Neurology* **212**: 38–52.

Metcalfe, J. and Mischel, W. (1999). A hot/cool-system analysis of delay of gratification: dynamics of willpower, *Psychological Review* **106**: 3–19.

Meunier, M., Bachevalier, J. and Mishkin, M. (1997). Effects of orbital frontal and anterior cingulate lesions on object and spatial memory in rhesus monkeys, *Neuropsychologia* **35**: 999–1015.

Middleton, F. A. and Strick, P. L. (1996a). New concepts about the organization of the basal ganglia., *in* J. A. Obeso (ed.), *Advances in Neurology: The Basal Ganglia and the Surgical Treatment for Parkinson's Disease*, Raven, New York.

Middleton, F. A. and Strick, P. L. (1996b). The temporal lobe is a target of output from the basal ganglia, *Proceedings of the National Academy of Sciences of the USA* **93**: 8683–8687.

Middleton, F. A. and Strick, P. L. (2000). Basal ganglia output and cognition: evidence from anatomical, behavioral, and clinical studies, *Brain and Cognition* **42**: 183–200.

Mikami, A., Nakamura, K. and Kubota, K. (1994). Neuronal responses to photographs in the superior temporal sulcus of the rhesus monkey, *Behavioural Brain Research* **60**: 1–13.

Miller, E. K. and Cohen, J. D. (2001). An integrative theory of prefrontal cortex function, *Annual Review of Neuroscience* **24**: 167–202.

Miller, E. K. and Desimone, R. (1994). Parallel neuronal mechanisms for short-term memory, *Science* **263**: 520–522.

Miller, E. K., Gochin, P. M. and Gross, C. G. (1993a). Suppression of visual responses of neurons in inferior temporal cortex of the awake macaque by addition of a second stimulus, *Brain Research* **616**: 25–29.

Miller, E. K., Li, L. and Desimone, R. (1993b). Activity of neurons in anterior inferior temporal cortex during a short-term memory task, *Journal of Neuroscience* **13**: 1460–1478.

Miller, E. K., Erickson, C. and Desimone, R. (1996). Neural mechanisms of visual working memory in prefrontal cortex of the macaque, *Journal of Neuroscience* **16**: 5154–5167.

Miller, E. K., Nieder, A., Freedman, D. J. and Wallis, J. D. (2003). Neural correlates of categories and concepts, *Current Opinion in Neurobiology* **13**: 198–203.

Miller, G. A. (1955). Note on the bias of information estimates, *Information Theory in Psychology; Problems and Methods II-B* pp. 95–100.

Miller, G. A. (1956). The magic number seven, plus or minus two: some limits on our capacity for the processing of information, *Psychological Review* **63**: 81–93.

Miller, G. F. (2000). *The Mating Mind*, Heinemann, London.

Miller, K. D. (1994). Models of activity-dependent neural development, *Progress in Brain Research* **102**: 303–308.

Millhouse, O. E. (1986). The intercalated cells of the amygdala, *Journal of Comparative Neurology* **247**: 246–271.

Millhouse, O. E. and DeOlmos, J. (1983). Neuronal configuration in lateral and basolateral amygdala, *Neuroscience* **10**: 1269–1300.

Milner, B. (1963). Effects of different brain lesions on card sorting, *Archives of Neurology* **9**: 90–100.

Milner, B. (1982). Some cognitive effects of frontal-lobe lesions in man, *Philosophical Transactions of the Royal Society B* **298**: 211–226.

Milner, P. (1974). A model for visual shape recognition, *Psychological Review* **81**: 521–535.

Minai, A. A. and Levy, W. B. (1993). Sequence learning in a single trial, *International Neural Network Society World Congress of Neural Networks* **2**: 505–508.

Minsky, M. L. and Papert, S. A. (1969). *Perceptrons*, expanded 1988 edn, MIT Press, Cambridge, MA.

Mirenowicz, J. and Schultz, W. (1996). Preferential activation of midbrain dopamine neurons by appetitive rather than aversive stimuli, *Nature* **279**: 449–451.

Mishkin, M. and Aggleton, J. (1981). Multiple functional contributions of the amygdala in the monkey, *in* Y. Ben-Ari (ed.), *The Amygdaloid Complex*, Elsevier, Amsterdam, pp. 409–420.

Mishkin, M. and Manning, F. J. (1978). Non-spatial memory after selective prefrontal lesions in monkeys, *Brain Research* **143**: 313–324.

Miyamoto, S., Duncan, G. E., Marx, C. E. and Lieberman, J. A. (2005). Treatments for schizophrenia: a critical review of pharmacology and mechanisms of action of antipsychotic drugs, *Molecular Psychiatry* **10**: 79–104.

Miyashita, Y. (1988). Neuronal correlate of visual associative long-term memory in the primate temporal cortex, *Nature* **335**: 817–820.

Miyashita, Y. (1993). Inferior temporal cortex: where visual perception meets memory, *Annual Review of Neuroscience* **16**: 245–263.

Miyashita, Y. and Chang, H. S. (1988). Neuronal correlate of pictorial short-term memory in the primate temporal cortex, *Nature* **331**: 68–70.

Miyashita, Y., Rolls, E. T., Cahusac, P. M. B., Niki, H. and Feigenbaum, J. D. (1989). Activity of hippocampal neurons in the monkey related to a conditional spatial response task, *Journal of Neurophysiology* **61**: 669–678.

Miyashita, Y., Okuno, H., Tokuyama, W., Ihara, T. and Nakajima, K. (1996). Feedback signal from medial temporal lobe mediates visual associative mnemonic codes of inferotemporal neurons, *Cognitive Brain Research* **5**: 81–86.

Miyashita, Y., Kameyama, M., Hasegawa, I. and Fukushima, T. (1998). Consolidation of visual associative long-term memory in the temporal cortex of primates, *Neurobiology of Learning and Memory* **1**: 197–211.

Mizumori, S. J., Ragozzino, K. E., Cooper, B. G. and Leutgeb, S. (1999). Hippocampal representational organization and spatial context, *Hippocampus* **9**: 444–451.

Moller, H. J. (2005). Antipsychotic and antidepressive effects of second generation antipsychotics: two different pharmacological mechanisms?, *European Archives of Psychiatry and Clinical Neuroscience* **255**: 190–201.

Monaghan, D. T. and Cotman, C. W. (1985). Distribution of N-methyl-D-aspartate-sensitive L-[3H]glutamate-binding sites in the rat brain, *Journal of Neuroscience* **5**: 2909–2919.

Moniz, E. (1936). *Tentatives Opératoires dans le Traitment de Certaines Psychoses*, Masson, Paris.

Montague, P. R. and Berns, G. S. (2002). Neural economics and the biological substrates of valuation, *Neuron* **36**: 265–284.

Montague, P. R., Gally, J. A. and Edelman, G. M. (1991). Spatial signalling in the development and function of neural connections, *Cerebral Cortex* **1**: 199–220.

Montague, P. R., King-Casas, B. and Cohen, J. D. (2006). Imaging valuation models in human choice, *Annual Review of Neuroscience* **29**: 417–448.

Moore, D. B., Lee, P., Paiva, M., Walker, D. W. and Heaton, M. B. (1998). Effects of neonatal ethanol exposure on cholinergic neurons of the rat medial septum, *Alcohol* **15**: 219–226.

Mora, F., Sanguinetti, A. M., Rolls, E. T. and Shaw, S. G. (1975). Differential effects on self-stimulation and motor behaviour produced by microintracranial injections of a dopamine-receptor blocking agent, *Neuroscience*

Letters **1**: 179–184.

Mora, F., Rolls, E. T. and Burton, M. J. (1976a). Modulation during learning of the responses of neurones in the lateral hypothalamus to the sight of food, *Experimental Neurology* **53**: 508–519.

Mora, F., Rolls, E. T., Burton, M. J. and Shaw, S. G. (1976b). Effects of dopamine-receptor blockade on self-stimulation in the monkey, *Pharmacology, Biochemistry and Behavior* **4**: 211–216.

Mora, F., Mogenson, G. J. and Rolls, E. T. (1977). Activity of neurones in the region of the substantia nigra during feeding, *Brain Research* **133**: 267–276.

Mora, F., Avrith, D. B., Phillips, A. G. and Rolls, E. T. (1979). Effects of satiety on self-stimulation of the orbitofrontal cortex in the monkey, *Neuroscience Letters* **13**: 141–145.

Mora, F., Avrith, D. B. and Rolls, E. T. (1980). An electrophysiological and behavioural study of self-stimulation in the orbitofrontal cortex of the rhesus monkey, *Brain Research Bulletin* **5**: 111–115.

Moran, J. and Desimone, R. (1985). Selective attention gates visual processing in the extrastriate cortex, *Science* **229**: 782–784.

Morecraft, R. J., Geula, C. and Mesulam, M.-M. (1992). Cytoarchitecture and neural afferents of orbitofrontal cortex in the brain of the monkey, *Journal of Comparative Neurology* **323**: 341–358.

Morris, J. S., Fritch, C. D., Perrett, D. I., Rowland, D., Young, A. W., Calder, A. J. and Dolan, R. J. (1996a). A differential neural response in the human amygdala to fearful and happy face expressions, *Nature* **383**: 812–815.

Morris, J. S., Frith, C. D., Perrett, D. I., Rowland, D., Young, A. W., Calder, A. J. and Dolan, R. J. (1996b). A differential neural response in the human amygdala to fearful and happy facial expressions, *Nature* **383**: 812–815.

Morris, J. S., De Gelder, B., Weiskrantz, L. and Dolan, R. J. (2001). Differential extrageniculostriate and amygdala responses to presentation of emotional faces in a cortically blind field, *Brain* **124**: 1241–1252.

Morris, R. G. (2003). Long-term potentiation and memory, *Philosophical Transactions of the Royal Society of London B* **358**: 643–647.

Morris, R. G., Moser, E. I., Riedel, G., Martin, S. J., Sandin, J., Day, M. and O'Carroll, C. (2003). Elements of a neurobiological theory of the hippocampus: the role of activity-dependent synaptic plasticity in memory, *Philosophical Transactions of the Royal Society of London B* **358**: 773–786.

Morris, R. G. M. (1989). Does synaptic plasticity play a role in information storage in the vertebrate brain?, *in* R. G. M. Morris (ed.), *Parallel Distributed Processing: Implications for Psychology and Neurobiology*, Oxford University Press, Oxford, chapter 11, pp. 248–285.

Morrot, G., Brochet, F. and Dubourdieu, D. (2001). The color of odors, *Brain and Language* **79**: 309–320.

Morrow, L. and Ratcliff, G. (1988). The disengagement of covert attention and the neglect syndrome, *Psychobiology* **16**: 261–269.

Moscovitch, M., Rosenbaum, R. S., Gilboa, A., Addis, D. R., Westmacott, R., Grady, C., McAndrews, M. P., Levine, B., Black, S., Winocur, G. and Nadel, L. (2005). Functional neuroanatomy of remote episodic, semantic and spatial memory: a unified account based on multiple trace theory, *Journal of Anatomy* **207**: 35–66.

Moser, E. I. (2004). Hippocampal place cells demand attention, *Neuron* **42**: 183–185.

Moser, M. B. and Moser, E. I. (1998). Functional differentiation in the hippocampus, *Hippocampus* **8**: 608–619.

Motter, B. (1994). Neural correlates of attentive selection for colours or luminance in extrastriate area V4, *Journal of Neuroscience* **14**: 2178–2189.

Motter, B. C. (1993). Focal attention produces spatially selective processing in visual cortical areas V1, V2, and V4 in the presence of competing stimuli, *Journal of Neurophysiology* **70**: 909–919.

Mountcastle, V. B. (1957). Modality and topographic properties of single neurons of cat's somatosensory cortex, *Journal of Neurophysiology* **20**: 408–434.

Mountcastle, V. B. (1984). Central nervous mechanisms in mechanoreceptive sensibility, *in* I. Darian-Smith (ed.), *Handbook of Physiology, Section 1: The Nervous System, Vol III, Sensory Processes, Part 2*, American Physiological Society, Bethesda, MD, pp. 789–878.

Movshon, J. A., Adelson, E. H., Gizzi, M. S. and Newsome, W. T. (1985). The analysis of moving visual patterns, *in* C. Chagas, R. Gattass and C. G. Gross (eds), *Pattern Recognition Mechanisms*, Springer-Verlag, New York, pp. 117–151.

Moyer, J. R. J., Deyo, R. A. and Disterhoft, J. F. (1990). Hippocampectomy disrupts trace eye-blink conditioning in rabbits, *Behavioral Neuroscience* **104**: 243–252.

Mozer, M. C. (1991). *The Perception of Multiple Objects: A Connectionist Approach*, MIT Press, Cambridge, MA.

Mozer, M. C. and Sitton, M. (1998). Computational modeling of spatial attention, *in* H. Pashler (ed.), *Attention*, UCL Press, London, pp. 341–393.

Mueser, K. T. and McGurk, S. R. (2004). Schizophrenia, *Lancet* **363**: 2063–2072.

Muir, J. L., Everitt, B. J. and Robbins, T. W. (1994). AMPA-induced excitotoxic lesions of the basal forebrain: a significant role for the cortical cholinergic system in attentional function, *Journal of Neuroscience* **14**: 2313–2326.

Muller, R. U., Kubie, J. L., Bostock, E. M., Taube, J. S. and Quirk, G. J. (1991). Spatial firing correlates of neurons in the hippocampal formation of freely moving rats, *in* J. Paillard (ed.), *Brain and Space*, Oxford University Press, Oxford, pp. 296–333.

Muller, R. U., Ranck, J. B. and Taube, J. S. (1996). Head direction cells: properties and functional significance, *Current Opinion in Neurobiology* **6**: 196–206.

Muly, E., Szigeti, K. and Goldman-Rakic, P. (1998). D1 receptor in interneurons of macaque prefrontal cortex: Distribution and subcellular localization, *Journal of Neuroscience* **18**: 10553–10565.

Mundy, J. and Zisserman, A. (1992). Introduction – towards a new framework for vision, *in* J. Mundy and A. Zisserman (eds), *Geometric Invariance in Computer Vision*, MIT Press, Cambridge, MA, pp. 1–39.

Murray, E. A., Gaffan, D. and Mishkin, M. (1993). Neural substrates of visual stimulus–stimulus association in rhesus monkeys, *Journal of Neuroscience* **13**: 4549–4561.

Murray, E. A., Gaffan, E. A. and Flint, R. W. (1996). Anterior rhinal cortex and amygdala: dissociation of their contributions to memory and food preference in rhesus monkeys, *Behavioral Neuroscience* **110**: 30–42.

Murray, E. A., Baxter, M. G. and Gaffan, D. (1998). Monkeys with rhinal cortex damage or neurotoxic hippocampal lesions are impaired on spatial scene learning and object reversals, *Behavioral Neuroscience* **112**: 1291–1303.

Naber, P. A., Lopes da Silva, F. H. and Witter, M. P. (2001). Reciprocal connections between the entorhinal cortex and hippocampal fields CA1 and the subiculum are in register with the projections from CA1 to the subiculum, *Hippocampus* **11**: 99–104.

Nadal, J. P., Toulouse, G., Changeux, J. P. and Dehaene, S. (1986). Networks of formal neurons and memory palimpsests, *Europhysics Letters* **1**: 535–542.

Nagai, Y., Critchley, H. D., Featherstone, E., Trimble, M. R. and Dolan, R. J. (2004). Activity in ventromedial prefrontal cortex covaries with sympathetic skin conductance level: a physiological account of a "default mode" of brain function, *Neuroimage* **22**: 243–251.

Nakahara, H., Amari, S. and Hikosaka, O. (2002). Self-organisation in the basal ganglia with modulation of reinforcement signals, *Neural Computation* **14**: 819–844.

Nakamura, K., Kawashima, R., Ito, K., Sugiura, M., Kato, T., Nakamura, A., Hatano, K., Nagumo, S., Kubota, K., Fukuda, H. and Kojima, S. (1999). Activation of the right inferior frontal cortex during assessment of facial emotion, *Journal of Neurophysiology* **82**: 1610–1614.

Nakayama, K. and Silverman, G. H. (1986). Serial and parallel processing of visual feature conjunctions, *Nature* **320**: 264–265.

Nakazawa, K., Quirk, M. C., Chitwood, R. A., Watanabe, M., Yeckel, M. F., Sun, L. D., Kato, A., Carr, C. A., Johnston, D., Wilson, M. A. and Tonegawa, S. (2002). Requirement for hippocampal CA3 NMDA receptors in associative memory recall, *Science* **297**: 211–218.

Nakazawa, K., Sun, L. D., Quirk, M. C., Rondi-Reig, L., Wilson, M. A. and Tonegawa, S. (2003). Hippocampal CA3 NMDA receptors are crucial for memory acquisition of one-time experience, *Neuron* **38**: 305–315.

Nanry, K. P., Mundy, W. R. and Tilson, H. A. (1989). Colchicine-induced alterations of reference memory in rats: role of spatial versus non-spatial task components, *Behavioral Brain Research* **35**: 45–53.

Nauta, W. J. H. (1964). Some efferent connections of the prefrontal cortex in the monkey, *in* J. M. Warren and K. Akert (eds), *The Frontal Granular Cortex and Behavior*, McGraw Hill, New York, pp. 397–407.

Nauta, W. J. H. (1972). Neural associations of the frontal cortex, *Acta Neurobiologica Experimentalis* **32**: 125–140.

Nauta, W. J. H. and Domesick, V. B. (1978). Crossroads of limbic and striatal circuitry: hypothalamonigral connections, *in* K. E. Livingston and O. Hornykiewicz (eds), *Limbic Mechanisms*, Plenum, New York, pp. 75–93.

Neisser, U. (1967). *Cognitive Psychology*, Appleton-Century-Crofts, New York.

Nelken, I., Prut, Y., Vaadia, E. and Abeles, M. (1994). Population responses to multifrequency sounds in the cat auditory cortex: one- and two-parameter families of sounds, *Hearing Research* **72**: 206–222.

Newcomer, J. W., Farber, N. B., Jevtovic-Todorovic, V., Selke, G., Melson, A. K., Hershey, T., Craft, S. and Olney, J. W. (1999). Ketamine-induced NMDA receptor hypofunction as a model of memory impairment and psychosis, *Neuropsychopharmacology* **20**: 106–118.

Newsome, W. T., Britten, K. H. and Movshon, J. A. (1989). Neuronal correlates of a perceptual decision, *Nature* **341**: 52–54.

Nicholls, M. E. R., Ellis, B. E., Clement, J. G. and Yoshino, M. (2004). Detecting hemifacial asymmetries in emotional expression with three-dimensional computerised image analysis, *Proceedings of the Royal Society of London B* **271**: 663–668.

Nicoll, R. A. and Malenka, R. C. (1995). Contrasting properties of two forms of long-term potentiation in the hippocampus, *Nature* **377**: 115–118.

Niki, H. and Watanabe, M. (1979). Prefrontal and cingulate unit activity during timing behavior in the monkey, *Brain Research* **171**: 213–224.

Nishijo, H., Ono, T. and Nishino, H. (1988). Single neuron responses in amygdala of alert monkey during complex sensory stimulation with affective significance, *Journal of Neuroscience* **8**: 3570–3583.

Niv, Y., Duff, M. O. and Dayan, P. (2005). Dopamine, uncertainty, and TD learning, *Behavioral and Brain Functions* **1**: 6.

Nowak, L. and Bullier, J. (1997). The timing of information transfer in the visual system, *in* K. Rockland, J. Kaas and A. Peters (eds), *Cerebral Cortex: Extrastriate Cortex in Primate*, Plenum, New York, p. 870.

Oberg, R. G. E. and Divac, I. (1979). "Cognitive" functions of the striatum, *in* I. Divac and R. G. E. Oberg (eds), *The Neostriatum*, Pergamon, New York, pp. 291–314.

O'Brien, C. P., Childress, A. R., Ehrman, R. and Robbins, S. J. (1998). Conditioning factors in drug abuse: can they explain compulsion?, *Journal of Psychopharmacology* **12**: 15–22.

O'Doherty, J., Rolls, E. T., Francis, S., Bowtell, R., McGlone, F., Kobal, G., Renner, B. and Ahne, G. (2000). Sensory-specific satiety related olfactory activation of the human orbitofrontal cortex, *NeuroReport* **11**: 893–897.

O'Doherty, J., Kringelbach, M. L., Rolls, E. T., Hornak, J. and Andrews, C. (2001a). Abstract reward and punishment representations in the human orbitofrontal cortex, *Nature Neuroscience* **4**: 95–102.

O'Doherty, J., Rolls, E. T., Francis, S., Bowtell, R. and McGlone, F. (2001b). The representation of pleasant and aversive taste in the human brain, *Journal of Neurophysiology* **85**: 1315–1321.

O'Doherty, J., Deichmann, R., Critchley, H. D. and Dolan, R. J. (2002). Neural response during anticipation of a primary taste reward, *Neuron* **33**: 815–826.

O'Doherty, J., Dayan, P., Friston, K. J., Critchley, H. D. and Dolan, R. J. (2003a). Temporal difference models and reward-related learning in the human brain, *Neuron* **38**: 329–337.

O'Doherty, J., Winston, J., Critchley, H. D., Perrett, D. I., Burt, D. M. and Dolan, R. J. (2003b). Beauty in a smile: the role of the medial orbitofrontal cortex in facial attractiveness, *Neuropsychologia* **41**: 147–155.

O'Doherty, J., Dayan, P., Schultz, J., Deichmann, R., Friston, K. and Dolan, R. J. (2004). Dissociable roles of ventral and dorsal striatum in instrumental conditioning, *Science* **304**: 452–454.

O'Donoghue, T. and Rabin, M. (1999). Doing it now or later, *American Economic Review* **89**: 103–124.

Oja, E. (1982). A simplified neuron model as a principal component analyzer, *Journal of Mathematical Biology* **15**: 267–273.

O'Kane, D. and Treves, A. (1992). Why the simplest notion of neocortex as an autoassociative memory would not work, *Network* **3**: 379–384.

O'Keefe, J. (1984). Spatial memory within and without the hippocampal system, *in* W. Seifert (ed.), *Neurobiology of the Hippocampus*, Academic Press, London, pp. 375–403.

O'Keefe, J. (1990). A computational theory of the hippocampal cognitive map, *Progress in Brain Research* **83**: 301–312.

O'Keefe, J. and Dostrovsky, J. (1971). The hippocampus as a spatial map: preliminary evidence from unit activity in the freely moving rat, *Brain Research* **34**: 171–175.

O'Keefe, J. and Nadel, L. (1978). *The Hippocampus as a Cognitive Map*, Clarendon Press, Oxford.

Okubo, Y., Suhara, T., Sudo, Y. and Toru, M. (1997a). Possible role of dopamine D1 receptors in schizophrenia, *Molecular Psychiatry* **2**: 291–292.

Okubo, Y., Suhara, T., Suzuki, K., Kobayashi, K., Inoue, O., Terasaki, O., Someya, Y., Sassa, T., Sudo, Y., Matsushima, E., Ito, M., Tateno, Y. and Toru, M. (1997b). Decreased prefrontal dopamine D1 receptors in schizophrenia revealed by PET, *Nature* **385**: 634–636.

Okubo, Y., Suhara, T., Suzuki, K., Kobayashi, K., Inoue, O., Terasaki, O., Someya, Y., Sassa, T., Sudo, Y., Matsushima, E., Iyo, M., Tateno, Y. and Toru, M. (1997c). Decreased prefrontal dopamine D1 receptors in schizophrenia revealed by PET, *Nature* **385**: 634–636.

Olausson, H., Lamarre, Y., Backlund, H., Morin, C., Wallin, B. G., Starck, G., Ekholm, S., Strigo, I., Worsley, K., Vallbo, A. B. and Bushnell, M. C. (2002). Unmyelinated tactile afferents signal touch and project to insular cortex, *Nature Neuroscience* **5**: 900–904.

Olshausen, B. A. and Field, D. J. (1997). Sparse coding with an incomplete basis set: a strategy employed by V1, *Vision Research* **37**: 3311–3325.

Olshausen, B. A. and Field, D. J. (2004). Sparse coding of sensory inputs, *Current Opinion in Neurobiology* **14**: 481–487.

Olshausen, B. A., Anderson, C. H. and Van Essen, D. C. (1993). A neurobiological model of visual attention and invariant pattern recognition based on dynamic routing of information, *Journal of Neuroscience* **13**: 4700–4719.

Olshausen, B. A., Anderson, C. H. and Van Essen, D. C. (1995). A multiscale dynamic routing circuit for forming size- and position-invariant object representations, *Journal of Computational Neuroscience* **2**: 45–62.

O'Mara, S. M., Rolls, E. T., Berthoz, A. and Kesner, R. P. (1994). Neurons responding to whole-body motion in the primate hippocampus, *Journal of Neuroscience* **14**: 6511–6523.

Ongur, D. and Price, J. L. (2000). The organisation of networks within the orbital and medial prefrontal cortex of rats, monkeys and humans, *Cerebral Cortex* **10**: 206–219.

Ongur, D., Drevets, W. C. and Price, J. L. (1998). Glial reduction in the subgenual prefrontal cortex in mood disorders, *Proceedings of the National Academy of Sciences USA* **95**: 13290–13295.

Ongur, D., Ferry, A. T. and Price, J. L. (2003). Architectonic subdivision of the human orbital and medial prefrontal cortex, *Journal of Comparative Neurology* **460**: 425–449.

Ono, T. and Nishijo, H. (1992). Neurophysiological basis of the Kluver–Bucy syndrome: responses of monkey amygdaloid neurons to biologically significant objects, *in* J. P. Aggleton (ed.), *The Amygdala*, Wiley-Liss, New York, chapter 6, pp. 167–190.

Ono, T., Nishino, H., Sasaki, K., Fukuda, M. and Muramoto, K. (1980). Role of the lateral hypothalamus and amygdala in feeding behavior, *Brain Research Bulletin* **5, Suppl.**: 143–149.

Ono, T., Nakamura, K., Nishijo, H. and Eifuku, S. (1993). Monkey hippocampal neurons related to spatial and nonspatial functions, *Journal of Neurophysiology* **70**: 1516–1529.

Optican, L. M. and Richmond, B. J. (1987). Temporal encoding of two-dimensional patterns by single units in primate inferior temporal cortex: III. Information theoretic analysis, *Journal of Neurophysiology* **57**: 162–178.

Optican, L. M., Gawne, T. J., Richmond, B. J. and Joseph, P. J. (1991). Unbiased measures of transmitted information and channel capacity from multivariate neuronal data, *Biological Cybernetics* **65**: 305–310.

Oram, M. W. and Perrett, D. I. (1994). Modeling visual recognition from neurophysiological constraints, *Neural Networks* **7**: 945–972.

O'Regan, J. K., Rensink, R. A. and Clark, J. J. (1999). Change-blindness as a result of 'mudsplashes', *Nature* **398**: 1736–1753.

O'Reilly, J. and Munakata, Y. (2000). *Computational Explorations in Cognitive Neuroscience*, MIT Press, Cambridge, MA.

O'Reilly, R. C. and Rudy, J. W. (2001). Conjunctive representations in learning and memory: principles of cortical and hippocampal function, *Psychological Review* **108**: 311–345.

Otto, T. and Eichenbaum, H. (1992). Neuronal activity in the hippocampus during delayed non-match to sample performance in rats: evidence for hippocampal processing in recognition memory, *Hippocampus* **2**: 323–334.

Padoa-Schioppa, C. and Assad, J. A. (2006). Neurons in the orbitofrontal cortex encode economic value, *Nature* **441**: 223–226.

Pager, J. (1974). A selective modulation of the olfactory bulb electrical activity in relation to the learning of palatability in hungry and satiated rats, *Physiology and Behavior* **12**: 189–196.

Pager, J., Giachetti, I., Holley, A. and LeMagnen, J. (1972). A selective control of olfactory bulb electrical activity in relation to food deprivation and satiety in rats, *Physiology and Behavior* **9**: 573–580.

Pandya, D. N. (1996). Comparison of prefrontal architecture and connections, *Philosophical Transactions of the Royal Society B* **351**: 1423–1432.

Panzeri, S. and Treves, A. (1996). Analytical estimates of limited sampling biases in different information measures, *Network* **7**: 87–107.

Panzeri, S., Biella, G., Rolls, E. T., Skaggs, W. E. and Treves, A. (1996). Speed, noise, information and the graded nature of neuronal responses, *Network* **7**: 365–370.

Panzeri, S., Schultz, S. R., Treves, A. and Rolls, E. T. (1999a). Correlations and the encoding of information in the nervous system, *Proceedings of the Royal Society B* **266**: 1001–1012.

Panzeri, S., Treves, A., Schultz, S. and Rolls, E. T. (1999b). On decoding the responses of a population of neurons from short time epochs, *Neural Computation* **11**: 1553–1577.

Panzeri, S., Rolls, E. T., Battaglia, F. and Lavis, R. (2001). Speed of feedforward and recurrent processing in multilayer networks of integrate-and-fire neurons, *Network: Computation in Neural Systems* **12**: 423–440.

Pare, D., Quirk, G. J. and LeDoux, J. E. (2004). New vistas on amygala networks in conditioned fear, *Journal of Neurophysiology* **92**: 1–9.

Parga, N. and Rolls, E. T. (1998). Transform invariant recognition by association in a recurrent network, *Neural Computation* **10**: 1507–1525.

Parisi, G. (1986). A memory which forgets, *Journal of Physics A* **19**: L617–L619.

Parker, A. J. (2007). Binocular depth perception and the cerebral cortex, *Nature Reviews Neuroscience* **8**: 379–391.

Parker, A. J., Cumming, B. G. and Dodd, J. V. (2000). Binocular neurons and the perception of depth, *in* M. Gazzaniga (ed.), *The New Cognitive Neurosciences, Second Edition*, MIT Press, Cambridge, MA, chapter 18, pp. 263–277.

Parkinson, J. K., Murray, E. A. and Mishkin, M. (1988). A selective mnemonic role for the hippocampus in monkeys: memory for the location of objects, *Journal of Neuroscience* **8**: 4059–4167.

Pashler, H. (1996). *The Psychology of Attention*, MIT Press, Cambridge, MA.

Passingham, R. (1975). Delayed matching after selective prefrontal lesions in monkeys (Macaca mulatta), *Brain Research* **92**: 89–102.

Paton, J. J., Belova, M. A., Morrison, S. E. and Salzman, C. D. (2006). The primate amygdala represents the positive and negative value of visual stimuli during learning, *Nature* **439**: 865–870.

Patton, J. H., Stanford, M. S. and Barratt, E. S. (1995). Factor structure of the Barratt impulsiveness scale, *Journal of Clinical Psychology* **51**: 768–774.

Paulus, M. P. and Frank, L. R. (2006). Anterior cingulate activity modulates nonlinear decision weight function of uncertain prospects, *Neuroimage* **30**: 668–677.

Peng, H. C., Sha, L. F., Gan, Q. and Wei, Y. (1998). Energy function for learning invariance in multilayer perceptron, *Electronics Letters* **34**(3): 292–294.

Percheron, G., Yelnik, J. and François, C. (1984a). The primate striato-pallido-nigral system: an integrative system for cortical information, *in* J. S. McKenzie, R. E. Kemm and L. N. Wilcox (eds), *The Basal Ganglia: Structure and Function*, Plenum, New York, pp. 87–105.

Percheron, G., Yelnik, J. and François, C. (1984b). A Golgi analysis of the primate globus pallidus. III. Spatial organization of the striato-pallidal complex, *Journal of Comparative Neurology* **227**: 214–227.

Percheron, G., Yelnik, J., François, C., Fenelon, G. and Talbi, B. (1994). Informational neurology of the basal ganglia related system, *Revue Neurologique (Paris)* **150**: 614–626.

Perl, E. R. and Kruger, L. (1996). Nociception and pain: evolution of concepts and observations, *in* L. Kruger (ed.), *Pain and Touch*, Academic Press, San Diego, chapter 4, pp. 180–211.

Perrett, D. I. and Oram, M. W. (1993). Neurophysiology of shape processing, *Image and Vision Computing* **11**: 317–333.

Perrett, D. I. and Rolls, E. T. (1983). Neural mechanisms underlying the visual analysis of faces, *in* J.-P. Ewert, R. R. Capranica and D. J. Ingle (eds), *Advances in Vertebrate Neuroethology*, Plenum Press, New York, pp. 543–566.

Perrett, D. I., Rolls, E. T. and Caan, W. (1982). Visual neurons responsive to faces in the monkey temporal cortex, *Experimental Brain Research* **47**: 329–342.

Perrett, D. I., Smith, P. A. J., Mistlin, A. J., Chitty, A. J., Head, A. S., Potter, D. D., Broennimann, R., Milner, A. D. and Jeeves, M. A. (1985a). Visual analysis of body movements by neurons in the temporal cortex of the macaque monkey: a preliminary report, *Behavioural Brain Research* **16**: 153–170.

Perrett, D. I., Smith, P. A. J., Potter, D. D., Mistlin, A. J., Head, A. S., Milner, D. and Jeeves, M. A. (1985b). Visual cells in temporal cortex sensitive to face view and gaze direction, *Proceedings of the Royal Society of London, Series B* **223**: 293–317.

Perry, G., Rolls, E. T. and Stringer, S. M. (2006). Spatial vs temporal continuity in view invariant visual object recognition learning, *Vision Research* **46**: 3994–4006.

Perry, G., Rolls, E. T. and Stringer, S. M. (2007). Continuous transformation learning of translation invariant representations, *Neural Computation*.

Personnaz, L., Guyon, I. and Dreyfus, G. (1985). Information storage and retrieval in spin-glass-like neural networks, *Journal de Physique Lettres (Paris)* **46**: 359–365.

Peters, A. (1984a). Bipolar cells, *in* A. Peters and E. G. Jones (eds), *Cerebral Cortex, Vol. 1, Cellular Components of the Cerebral Cortex*, Plenum, New York, chapter 11, pp. 381–407.

Peters, A. (1984b). Chandelier cells, *in* A. Peters and E. G. Jones (eds), *Cerebral Cortex, Vol. 1, Cellular Components of the Cerebral Cortex*, Plenum, New York, chapter 10, pp. 361–380.

Peters, A. and Jones, E. G. (eds) (1984). *Cerebral Cortex, Vol. 1, Cellular Components of the Cerebral Cortex*, Plenum, New York.

Peters, A. and Regidor, J. (1981). A reassessment of the forms of nonpyramidal neurons in area 17 of the cat visual cortex, *Journal of Comparative Neurology* **203**: 685–716.

Peters, A. and Saint Marie, R. L. (1984). Smooth and sparsely spinous nonpyramidal cells forming local axonal plexuses, *in* A. Peters and E. G. Jones (eds), *Cerebral Cortex, Vol. 1, Cellular Components of the Cerebral Cortex*, New York, Plenum, chapter 13, pp. 419–445.

Peterson, C. and Anderson, J. R. (1987). A mean field theory learning algorithm for neural networks, *Complex Systems* **1**: 995–1015.

Petri, H. L. and Mishkin, M. (1994). Behaviorism, cognitivism, and the neuropsychology of memory, *American Scientist* **82**: 30–37.

Petrides, M. (1985). Deficits on conditional associative-learning tasks after frontal- and temporal-lobe lesions in man, *Neuropsychologia* **23**: 601–614.

Petrides, M. (1996). Specialized systems for the processing of mnemonic information within the primate frontal cortex, *Philosophical Transactions of the Royal Society of London B* **351**: 1455–1462.

Petrides, M. (2005). Lateral prefrontal cortex: architectonic and functional organization, *Philosophical Transactions of the Royal Society of London, B* **360**: 781–795.

Petrides, M. and Pandya, D. N. (1988). Association fiber pathways to the frontal cortex from the superior temporal region in the rhesus monkey, *Journal of Comparative Neurology* **273**: 52–66.

Petrides, M. and Pandya, D. N. (1994). Comparative architectonic analysis of the human and macaque frontal cortex, *in* J. Grafman and F. Boller (eds), *Handbook of Neuropsychology*, Vol. 9, Elsevier, Amsterdam, pp. 17–58.

Petrovich, P., Petersson, K. M., Ghatan, P. H., Ston-Elander, S. and Ingvar, M. (2000). Pain-related cerebral activation is altered by a distracting cognitive task, *Pain* **85**: 19–30.

Phaf, H., Van der Heijden, A. and Hudson, P. (1990). A connectionist model for attention in visual selection tasks, *Cognitive Psychology* **22**: 273–341.

Phelps, E. (2004). Human emotion and memory: interactions of the amygdala and hippocampal complex, *Current Opinion in Neurobiology* **14**: 198–202.

Phelps, E., O'Connor, K. J., Gatenby, J. C., Gore, J. C., Grillon, C. and Davis, M. (2001). Activation of the left amygdala to a cognitive representation of fear, *Nature Neuroscience* **4**: 437–441.

Phillips, A. G. and Fibiger, H. C. (1989). Neuroanatomical bases of intracranial self-stimulation: untying the Gordian knot, *in* J. M. Liebman and S. J. Cooper (eds), *The Neuropharmacological Basis of Reward*, Oxford University Press, Oxford, pp. 66–105.

Phillips, A. G. and Fibiger, H. C. (1990). Role of reward and enhancement of conditioned reward in persistence of responding for cocaine, *Behavioral Pharmacology* **1**: 269–282.

Phillips, A. G., Mora, F. and Rolls, E. T. (1981). Intra-cerebral self-administration of amphetamine by rhesus monkeys, *Neuroscience Letters* **24**: 81–86.

Phillips, M. L. (2004). Facial processing deficits and social dysfunction: how are they related?, *Brain* **127**: 1691–1692.

Phillips, M. L., Young, A. W., Scott, S. K., Calder, A. J., Andrew, C., Giampetro, V., Williams, S. C. R., Bullmore, E. T., Brammer, M. and Gray, J. A. (1998). Neural responses to facial and vocal expressions of fear and disgust, *Proceedings of the Royal Society of London B* **265**: 1809–1817.

Phillips, M. L., Drevets, W. C., Rauch, S. L. and Lane, R. (2003). Neurobiology of emotion perception II: Implications for major psychiatric disorders, *Biological Psychiatry* **54**: 515–528.

Phillips, M. L., Williams, L. M., Heining, M., Herba, C. M., Russell, T., Andrew, C., Bullmore, E. T., Brammer, M. J., Williams, S. C., Morgan, M., Young, A. W. and Gray, J. A. (2004). Differential neural responses to overt and covert presentations of facial expressions of fear and disgust, *Neuroimage* **21**: 1484–1496.

Phillips, R. R., Malamut, B. L., Bachevalier, J. and Mishkin, M. (1988). Dissociation of the effects of inferior temporal and limbic lesions on object discrimination learning with 24-h intertrial intervals, *Behavioural Brain Research* **27**: 99–107.

Phillips, W. A., Kay, J. and Smyth, D. (1995). The discovery of structure by multi-stream networks of local processors with contextual guidance, *Network* **6**: 225–246.

Pickens, C. L., Saddoris, M. P., Setlow, B., Gallagher, M., Holland, P. C. and Schoenbaum, G. (2003). Different roles for orbitofrontal cortex and basolateral amygdala in a reinforcer devaluation task, *Journal of Neuroscience* **23**: 11078–11084.

Pitkanen, A. (2000). Connectivitiy of the rat amygdaloid complex, *in* J. P. Aggleton (ed.), *The Amygdala: a Functional Analysis*, Oxford University Press, Oxford, chapter 2, pp. 31–116.

Pitkanen, A., Kelly, J. L. and Amaral, D. G. (2002). Projections from the lateral, basal, and accessory basal nuclei of the amygdala to the entorhinal cortex in the macaque monkey, *Hippocampus* **12**: 186–205.

Platt, M. L. and Glimcher, P. W. (1999). Neural correlates of decision variables in parietal cortex, *Nature* **400**: 233–238.

Poggio, T. and Edelman, S. (1990). A network that learns to recognize three-dimensional objects, *Nature* **343**: 263–266.

Poggio, T. and Girosi, F. (1990a). Networks for approximation and learning, *Proceedings of the IEEE* **78**: 1481–1497.

Poggio, T. and Girosi, F. (1990b). Regularization algorithms for learning that are equivalent to multilayer networks, *Science* **247**: 978–982.

Posner, M. and Dehaene, S. (1994). Attentional networks, *Trends in Neurosciences* **17**: 75–79.

Posner, M., Walker, J., Friedrich, F. and Rafal, B. (1984). Effects of parietal injury on covert orienting of attention, *Journal of Neuroscience* **4**: 1863–1874.

Posner, M., Walker, J., Friedrich, F. and Rafal, R. (1987). How do the parietal lobes direct covert attention?, *Neuropsychologia* **25**: 135–146.

Posner, M. I. and Keele, S. W. (1968). On the genesis of abstract ideas, *Journal of Experimental Psychology* **77**: 353–363.

Postle, B. R. and D'Esposito, M. (1999). "What" – then – "Where" in visual working memory: An event-related fMRI study, *Journal of Cognitive Neuroscience* **11**: 585–597.

Postle, B. R. and D'Esposito, M. (2000). Evaluating models of the topographical organization of working memory function in frontal cortex with event-related fMRI, *Psychobiology* **28**: 132–145.

Poucet, B. (1989). Object exploration, habituation, and response to a spatial change in rats following septal or medial frontal cortical damage, *Behavioral Neuroscience* **103**: 1009–1016.

Pouget, A. and Driver, J. (1999). Visual neglect, *in* R. Wilson and F. Keil (eds), *MIT Encyclopedia of Cognitive Sciences*, MIT Press, Cambridge, MA, pp. 869–871.

Powell, T. P. S. (1981). Certain aspects of the intrinsic organisation of the cerebral cortex, *in* O. Pompeiano and C. Ajmone Marsan (eds), *Brain Mechanisms and Perceptual Awareness*, Raven Press, New York, pp. 1–19.

Preuss, T. M. and Goldman-Rakic, P. S. (1989). Connections of the ventral granular frontal cortex of macaques with perisylvian premotor and somatosensory areas: anatomical evidence for somatic representation in primate frontal association cortex, *Journal of Comparative Neurology* **282**: 293–316.

Price, J. L., Carmichael, S. T., Carnes, K. M., Clugnet, M.-C. and Kuroda, M. (1991). Olfactory input to the prefrontal cortex, *in* J. L. Davis and H. Eichenbaum (eds), *Olfaction: A Model System for Computational Neuroscience*, MIT Press, Cambridge, MA, pp. 101–120.

Pritchard, T. C., Hamilton, R. B., Morse, J. R. and Norgren, R. (1986). Projections of thalamic gustatory and lingual areas in the monkey, *Journal of Comparative Neurology* **244**: 213–228.

Pylyshyn, Z. W. and Storm, R. W. (1988). Tracking multiple independent targets: Evidence for a parallel tracking mechanism, *Spatial Vision* **3**: 1–19.

Quinlan, P. T. and Humphreys, G. W. (1987). Visual search for targets defined by combinations of color, shape, and size: An examination of the task constraints on feature and conjunction searches, *Perception and Psychophysics* **41**: 455–472.

Quirk, G. J., Armony, J. L., Repa, J. C., Li, X.-F. and LeDoux, J. E. (1996). Emotional memory: a search for sites of plasticity, *Cold Spring Harbor Symposia on Quantitative Biology* **61**: 247–257.

Quiroga, R. Q., Reddy, L., Kreiman, G., Koch, C. and Fried, I. (2005). Invariant visual representation by single neurons in the human brain, *Nature* **453**: 1102–1107.

Rachlin, H. (1989). *Judgement, Decision, and Choice: A Cognitive/Behavioural Synthesis*, Freeman, New York.

Rachlin, H. (2000). *The Science of Self-Control*, Harvard Univeristy Press, Cambridge, MA.

Rafal, R. and Robertson, L. (1995). The neurology of visual attention, *in* M. S. Gazzaniga (ed.), *The Cognitive Neurosciences*, MIT Press, Cambridge, MA, pp. 625–648.

Rahman, S., Sahakian, B. J., Hodges, J. R., Rogers, R. D. and Robbins, T. W. (1997). Brainstem innervation of prefrontal and anterior cingulate cortex in the rhesus monkey revealed by retrograde transport of HRP, *Brain* **122**: 1469–1493.

Rainville, P., Duncan, G. H., Price, D. D., Carrier, B. and Bushnell, M. C. (1997). Pain affect encoded in human anterior cingulate but not somatosensory cortex, *Science* **277**: 968–971.

Rajkowska, G. (2000). Postmortem studies in mood disorders indicate altered numbers of neurons and glial cells, *Biological Psychiatry* **48**: 766–777.

Ranck, Jr., J. B. (1985). Head direction cells in the deep cell layer of dorsolateral presubiculum in freely moving rats, *in* G. Buzsáki and C. H. Vanderwolf (eds), *Electrical Activity of the Archicortex*, Akadémiai Kiadó, Budapest.

Rao, S. C., Rainer, G. and Miller, E. K. (1997). Integration of what and where in the primate prefrontal cortex, *Science* **276**: 821–824.

Ratcliff, R., Zandt, T. V. and McKoon, G. (1999). Connectionist and diffusion models of reaction time, *Psychological Reviews* **106**: 261–300.

Rawlins, J. N. P. (1985). Associations across time: the hippocampus as a temporary memory store, *Behavioral Brain Science* **8**: 479–496.

Redgrave, P., Prescott, T. J. and Gurney, K. (1999). Is the short-latency dopamine response too short to signal reward error?, *Trends in Neuroscience* **22**: 146–151.

Renart, A., Parga, N. and Rolls, E. T. (1999a). Associative memory properties of multiple cortical modules, *Network* **10**: 237–255.

Renart, A., Parga, N. and Rolls, E. T. (1999b). Backprojections in the cerebral cortex: implications for memory storage, *Neural Computation* **11**: 1349–1388.

Renart, A., Parga, N. and Rolls, E. T. (2000). A recurrent model of the interaction between the prefrontal cortex and inferior temporal cortex in delay memory tasks, *in* S. Solla, T. Leen and K.-R. Mueller (eds), *Advances in Neural Information Processing Systems*, Vol. 12, MIT Press, Cambridge Mass, pp. 171–177.

Renart, A., Moreno, R., Rocha, J., Parga, N. and Rolls, E. T. (2001). A model of the IT-PF network in object working memory which includes balanced persistent activity and tuned inhibition, *Neurocomputing* **38–40**: 1525–1531.

Rensink, R. A. (2000). Seeing, sensing, and scrutinizing, *Vision Research* **40**: 1469–1487.

Rescorla, R. A. (1990a). Evidence for an association between the discriminative stimulus and the response–outcome association in instrumental learning, *Journal of Experimental Psychology* **16**: 326–334.

Rescorla, R. A. (1990b). The role of information about the response–outcome relation in instrumental discrimination learning, *Journal of Experimental Psychology* **16**: 262–270.

Rescorla, R. A. and Solomon, R. L. (1967). Two-process learning theory: relationships between Pavlovian conditioning and instrumental learning, *Psychology Reviews* **74**: 151–182.

Rescorla, R. A. and Wagner, A. R. (1972). A theory of Pavlovian conditioning: the effectiveness of reinforcement and non-reinforcement, *Classical Conditioning II: Current Research and Theory*, Appleton-Century-Crofts, New York, pp. 64–69.

Reynolds, J. and Desimone, R. (1999). The role of neural mechanisms of attention in solving the binding problem, *Neuron* **24**: 19–29.

Reynolds, J. and Desimone, R. (2003). Interacting roles of attention and visual saliency in V4, *Neuron* **37**: 853–863.

Reynolds, J. H., Chelazzi, L. and Desimone, R. (1999). Competitive mechanisms subserve attention in macaque areas V2 and V4, *Journal of Neuroscience* **19**: 1736–1753.

Reynolds, J. H., Pastemak, T. and Desimone, R. (2000). Attention increases sensitivity of v4 neurons, *Neuron* **26**: 703–714.

Reynolds, J. N. and Wickens, J. R. (2002). Dopamine-dependent plasticity of corticostriatal synapses, *Neural Networks* **15**: 507–521.

Rhodes, P. (1992). The open time of the NMDA channel facilitates the self-organisation of invariant object responses in cortex, *Society for Neuroscience Abstracts* **18**: 740.

Ridley, M. (1993a). *Evolution*, Blackwell, Oxford.

Ridley, M. (1993b). *The Red Queen: Sex and the Evolution of Human Nature*, Penguin, London.

Ridley, M. (1996). *The Origins of Virtue*, Viking, London.

Ridley, M. (2003). *Nature via Nurture*, Harper, London.

Ridley, R. M., Hester, N. S. and Ettlinger, G. (1977). Stimulus- and response-dependent units from the occipital and temporal lobes of the unanaesthetized monkey performing learnt visual tasks, *Experimental Brain Research* **27**: 539–552.

Rieke, F., D., W. and Bialek, W. (1993). Coding efficiency and information rates in sensory neurons, *Europhysics Letters* **22**: 151–156.

Rieke, F., Warland, D., de Ruyter van Steveninck, R. R. and Bialek, W. (1996). *Spikes: Exploring the Neural Code*, MIT Press, Cambridge, MA.

Riesenhuber, M. and Poggio, T. (1998). Just one view: Invariances in inferotemporal cell tuning, *in* M. I. Jordan, M. J. Kearns and S. A. Solla (eds), *Advances in Neural Information Processing Systems*, Vol. 10, MIT Press, Cambridge, MA, pp. 215–221.

Riesenhuber, M. and Poggio, T. (1999a). Are cortical models really bound by the "binding problem"?, *Neuron*

24: 87–93.

Riesenhuber, M. and Poggio, T. (1999b). Hierarchical models of object recognition in cortex, *Nature Neuroscience* **2**: 1019–1025.

Riesenhuber, M. and Poggio, T. (2000). Models of object recognition, *Nature Neuroscience Supplement* **3**: 1199–1204.

Rilling, J. K., Gutman, D. A., Zeh, T. R., Pagnoni, G., Berns, G. S. and Kilts, C. D. (2002). A neural basis for social cooperation, *Neuron* **24**: 395–405.

Risold, P. Y. and Swanson, L. W. (1997). Connections of the rat lateral septal complex, *Brain Research Reviews* **24**: 115–195.

Rizzolatti, G. and Craighero, L. (2004). The mirror-neuron system, *Annual Review of Neuroscience* **27**: 169–192.

Robbins, T. W., Cador, M., Taylor, J. R. and Everitt, B. J. (1989). Limbic-striatal interactions in reward-related processes, *Neuroscience and Biobehavioral Reviews* **13**: 155–162.

Roberts, D. C. S., Koob, G. F., Klonoff, P. and Fibiger, H. C. (1980). Extinction and recovery of cocaine self-administration following 6-hydroxydopamine lesions of the nucleus accumbens, *Pharmacology, Biochemistry and Behavior* **12**: 781–787.

Robertson, R. G., Rolls, E. T. and Georges-François, P. (1998). Spatial view cells in the primate hippocampus: Effects of removal of view details, *Journal of Neurophysiology* **79**: 1145–1156.

Robertson, R. G., Rolls, E. T., Georges-François, P. and Panzeri, S. (1999). Head direction cells in the primate pre-subiculum, *Hippocampus* **9**: 206–219.

Robinson, T. E. and Berridge, K. C. (1993). The neural basis of drug craving: an incentive-sensitization theory of addiction, *Brain Research Reviews, Neuroscience and Biobehavioral Reviews* **18**: 247–291.

Robinson, T. E. and Berridge, K. C. (2003). Addiction, *Annual Review of Psychology* **54**: 25–53.

Roelfsema, P. R., Lamme, V. A. and Spekreijse, H. (1998). Object-based attention in the primary visual cortex of the macaque monkey, *Nature* **395**: 376–381.

Rogan, M. T., Staubli, U. V. and LeDoux, J. E. (1997). Fear conditioning induces associative long-term potentiation in the amygdala, *Nature* **390**: 604–607.

Rogers, J. L., Hunsaker, M. R. and Kesner, R. P. (2006). Effects of ventral and dorsal CA1 subregional lesions on trace fear conditioning, *Neurobiology of Learning and Memory* **86**: 72–81.

Roland, P. E. and Friberg, L. (1985). Localization of cortical areas activated by thinking, *Journal of Neurophysiology* **53**: 1219–1243.

Rolls, B. J., Rolls, E. T., Rowe, E. A. and Sweeney, K. (1981a). Sensory specific satiety in man, *Physiology and Behavior* **27**: 137–142.

Rolls, B. J., Rowe, E. A., Rolls, E. T., Kingston, B., Megson, A. and Gunary, R. (1981b). Variety in a meal enhances food intake in man, *Physiology and Behavior* **26**: 215–221.

Rolls, E. T. (1975). *The Brain and Reward*, Pergamon Press, Oxford.

Rolls, E. T. (1981a). Central nervous mechanisms related to feeding and appetite, *British Medical Bulletin* **37**: 131–134.

Rolls, E. T. (1981b). Processing beyond the inferior temporal visual cortex related to feeding, learning, and striatal function, *in* Y. Katsuki, R. Norgren and M. Sato (eds), *Brain Mechanisms of Sensation*, Wiley, New York, chapter 16, pp. 241–269.

Rolls, E. T. (1981c). Responses of amygdaloid neurons in the primate, *in* Y. Ben-Ari (ed.), *The Amygdaloid Complex*, Elsevier, Amsterdam, pp. 383–393.

Rolls, E. T. (1982). Neuronal mechanisms underlying the formation and disconnection of associations between visual stimuli and reinforcement in primates, *in* C. Woody (ed.), *Conditioning: Representation of Involved Neural Functions*, Plenum, New York, pp. 363–373.

Rolls, E. T. (1984a). Activity of neurons in different regions of the striatum of the monkey, *in* J. McKenzie, R. Kemm and L. Wilcox (eds), *The Basal Ganglia: Structure and Function*, Plenum, New York, pp. 467–493.

Rolls, E. T. (1984b). Neurons in the cortex of the temporal lobe and in the amygdala of the monkey with responses selective for faces, *Human Neurobiology* **3**: 209–222.

Rolls, E. T. (1986a). Neural systems involved in emotion in primates, *in* R. Plutchik and H. Kellerman (eds), *Emotion: Theory, Research, and Experience*, Vol. 3: Biological Foundations of Emotion, Academic Press, New York, chapter 5, pp. 125–143.

Rolls, E. T. (1986b). Neuronal activity related to the control of feeding, *in* R. Ritter, S. Ritter and C. Barnes (eds), *Feeding Behavior: Neural and Humoral Controls*, Academic Press, New York, chapter 6, pp. 163–190.

Rolls, E. T. (1986c). A theory of emotion, and its application to understanding the neural basis of emotion, *in* Y. Oomura (ed.), *Emotions. Neural and Chemical Control*, Japan Scientific Societies Press; and Karger, Tokyo; and Basel, pp. 325–344.

Rolls, E. T. (1987). Information representation, processing and storage in the brain: analysis at the single neuron level, *in* J.-P. Changeux and M. Konishi (eds), *The Neural and Molecular Bases of Learning*, Wiley, Chichester, pp. 503–540.

Rolls, E. T. (1989a). Functions of neuronal networks in the hippocampus and cerebral cortex in memory, *in* R. Cotterill (ed.), *Models of Brain Function*, Cambridge University Press, Cambridge, pp. 15–33.

Rolls, E. T. (1989b). Functions of neuronal networks in the hippocampus and neocortex in memory, *in* J. Byrne and W. Berry (eds), *Neural Models of Plasticity: Experimental and Theoretical Approaches*, Academic Press, San Diego, chapter 13, pp. 240–265.

Rolls, E. T. (1989c). Information processing and basal ganglia function, *in* C. Kennard and M. Swash (eds), *Hierarchies in Neurology*, Springer-Verlag, London, chapter 15, pp. 123–142.

Rolls, E. T. (1989d). Information processing in the taste system of primates, *Journal of Experimental Biology* **146**: 141–164.

Rolls, E. T. (1989e). Parallel distributed processing in the brain: implications of the functional architecture of neuronal networks in the hippocampus, *in* R. G. M. Morris (ed.), *Parallel Distributed Processing: Implications for Psychology and Neurobiology*, Oxford University Press, Oxford, chapter 12, pp. 286–308.

Rolls, E. T. (1989f). The representation and storage of information in neuronal networks in the primate cerebral cortex and hippocampus, *in* R. Durbin, C. Miall and G. Mitchison (eds), *The Computing Neuron*, Addison-Wesley, Wokingham, England, chapter 8, pp. 125–159.

Rolls, E. T. (1990a). Functions of neuronal networks in the hippocampus and of backprojections in the cerebral cortex in memory, *in* J. McGaugh, N. Weinberger and G. Lynch (eds), *Brain Organization and Memory: Cells, Systems and Circuits*, Oxford University Press, New York, chapter 9, pp. 184–210.

Rolls, E. T. (1990b). Functions of the primate hippocampus in spatial processing and memory, *in* D. S. Olton and R. P. Kesner (eds), *Neurobiology of Comparative Cognition*, L. Erlbaum, Hillsdale, NJ, chapter 12, pp. 339–362.

Rolls, E. T. (1990c). Theoretical and neurophysiological analysis of the functions of the primate hippocampus in memory, *Cold Spring Harbor Symposia in Quantitative Biology* **55**: 995–1006.

Rolls, E. T. (1990d). A theory of emotion, and its application to understanding the neural basis of emotion, *Cognition and Emotion* **4**: 161–190.

Rolls, E. T. (1992a). Neurophysiological mechanisms underlying face processing within and beyond the temporal cortical visual areas, *Philosophical Transactions of the Royal Society* **335**: 11–21.

Rolls, E. T. (1992b). Neurophysiology and functions of the primate amygdala, *in* J. P. Aggleton (ed.), *The Amygdala*, Wiley-Liss, New York, chapter 5, pp. 143–165.

Rolls, E. T. (1992c). The processing of face information in the primate temporal lobe, *in* V. Bruce and M. Burton (eds), *Processing Images of Faces*, Ablex, Norwood, NJ, chapter 3. 41–68.

Rolls, E. T. (1993). The neural control of feeding in primates, *in* D. Booth (ed.), *Neurophysiology of Ingestion*, Pergamon, Oxford, chapter 9, pp. 137–169.

Rolls, E. T. (1994a). Brain mechanisms for invariant visual recognition and learning, *Behavioural Processes* **33**: 113–138.

Rolls, E. T. (1994b). Neurophysiological and neuronal network analysis of how the primate hippocampus functions in memory, *in* J. Delacour (ed.), *The Memory System of the Brain*, World Scientific, London, pp. 713–744.

Rolls, E. T. (1994c). Neurophysiology and cognitive functions of the striatum, *Revue Neurologique (Paris)* **150**: 648–660.

Rolls, E. T. (1995a). Central taste anatomy and neurophysiology, *in* R. Doty (ed.), *Handbook of Olfaction and Gustation*, Dekker, New York, chapter 24, pp. 549–573.

Rolls, E. T. (1995b). Learning mechanisms in the temporal lobe visual cortex, *Behavioural Brain Research* **66**: 177–185.

Rolls, E. T. (1995c). A model of the operation of the hippocampus and entorhinal cortex in memory, *International Journal of Neural Systems* **6, Supplement**: 51–70.

Rolls, E. T. (1995d). A theory of emotion and consciousness, and its application to understanding the neural basis of emotion, *in* M. S. Gazzaniga (ed.), *The Cognitive Neurosciences*, MIT Press, Cambridge, MA, chapter 72, pp. 1091–1106.

Rolls, E. T. (1996a). The orbitofrontal cortex, *Philosophical Transactions of the Royal Society B* **351**: 1433–1444.

Rolls, E. T. (1996b). Roles of long term potentiation and long term depression in neuronal network operations in the brain, *in* M. S. Fazeli and G. L. Collingridge (eds), *Cortical Plasticity: LTP and LTD*, Bios, Oxford, chapter 11, pp. 223–250.

Rolls, E. T. (1996c). A theory of hippocampal function in memory, *Hippocampus* **6**: 601–620.

Rolls, E. T. (1997a). Consciousness in neural networks?, *Neural Networks* **10**: 1227–1240.

Rolls, E. T. (1997b). Neural processing underlying food selection, *in* H. Macbeth (ed.), *Food Preferences and Intake: Continuity and Change*, Berghahn, Oxford, chapter 4, pp. 39–53.

Rolls, E. T. (1997c). A neurophysiological and computational approach to the functions of the temporal lobe cortical visual areas in invariant object recognition, *in* M. Jenkin and L. Harris (eds), *Computational and Psychophysical Mechanisms of Visual Coding*, Cambridge University Press, Cambridge, chapter 9, pp. 184–220.

Rolls, E. T. (1997d). Taste and olfactory processing in the brain and its relation to the control of eating, *Critical Reviews in Neurobiology* **11**: 263–287.

Rolls, E. T. (1999a). *The Brain and Emotion*, Oxford University Press, Oxford.

Rolls, E. T. (1999b). The functions of the orbitofrontal cortex, *Neurocase* **5**: 301–312.

Rolls, E. T. (1999c). Spatial view cells and the representation of place in the primate hippocampus, *Hippocampus* **9**: 467–480.

Rolls, E. T. (2000a). Functions of the primate temporal lobe cortical visual areas in invariant visual object and face recognition, *Neuron* **27**: 205–218.

Rolls, E. T. (2000b). Hippocampo-cortical and cortico-cortical backprojections, *Hippocampus* **10**: 380–388.

Rolls, E. T. (2000c). Memory systems in the brain, *Annual Review of Psychology* **51**: 599–630.

Rolls, E. T. (2000d). Neurophysiology and functions of the primate amygdala, and the neural basis of emotion, *in* J. P. Aggleton (ed.), *The Amygdala: Second Edition. A Functional Analysis*, Oxford University Press, Oxford, chapter 13, pp. 447–478.

Rolls, E. T. (2000e). The orbitofrontal cortex and reward, *Cerebral Cortex* **10**: 284–294.

Rolls, E. T. (2000f). Précis of The Brain and Emotion, *Behavioral and Brain Sciences* **23**: 177–233.

Rolls, E. T. (2001a). The representation of umami taste in the human and macaque cortex, *Sensory Neuron* **3**: 227–242.

Rolls, E. T. (2001b). The rules of formation of the olfactory representations found in the orbitofrontal cortex olfactory areas in primates, *Chemical Senses* **26**: 595–604.

Rolls, E. T. (2003). Consciousness absent and present: a neurophysiological exploration, *Progress in Brain Research* **144**: 95–106.

Rolls, E. T. (2004a). Convergence of sensory systems in the orbitofrontal cortex in primates and brain design for emotion, *The Anatomical Record Part A* **281**: 1212–1225.

Rolls, E. T. (2004b). The functions of the orbitofrontal cortex, *Brain and Cognition* **55**: 11–29.

Rolls, E. T. (2004c). A higher order syntactic thought (HOST) theory of consciousness, *in* R. J. Gennaro (ed.), *Higher Order Theories of Consciousness*, John Benjamins, Amsterdam, chapter 7, pp. 137–172.

Rolls, E. T. (2004d). The operation of memory systems in the brain, *in* J. Feng (ed.), *Computational Neuroscience: A Comprehensive Approach*, CRC Press (UK), London, chapter 16, pp. 491–534.

Rolls, E. T. (2004e). Taste, olfactory, texture and temperature multimodal representations in the brain, and their relevance to the control of appetite, *Primatologie* **6**: 5–32.

Rolls, E. T. (2005). *Emotion Explained*, Oxford University Press, Oxford.

Rolls, E. T. (2006a). Brain mechanisms underlying flavour and appetite, *Philosophical Transactions of the Royal Society B* **361**: 1123–1136.

Rolls, E. T. (2006b). Consciousness absent and present: a neurophysiological exploration of masking, *in* H. Ogmen and B. G. Breitmeyer (eds), *The First Half Second*, MIT Press, Cambridge, MA, chapter 6, pp. 89–108.

Rolls, E. T. (2006c). The neurophysiology and functions of the orbitofrontal cortex, *in* D. H. Zald and S. L. Rauch (eds), *The Orbitofrontal Cortex*, Oxford University Press, Oxford, chapter 5, pp. 95–124.

Rolls, E. T. (2007a). The affective neuroscience of consciousness: higher order syntactic thoughts, dual routes to emotion and action, and consciousness, *in* P. D. Zelazo, M. Moscovitch and E. Thompson (eds), *Cambridge Handbook of Consciousness*, Cambridge University Press, New York, chapter 29, pp. 831–859.

Rolls, E. T. (2007b). The anterior and midcingulate cortices and reward, *in* B. Vogt (ed.), *Cingulate Neurobiology and Disease*, Vol. 1, Infrastructure, Diagnosis and Treatment, Oxford University Press, Oxford, chapter 8.

Rolls, E. T. (2007c). The central representation of flavor, *in* G. Shepherd, S. Firestein and D. V. Smith (eds), *Handbook of the Senses, Vol 2, Olfaction and Taste*, Academic Press, New York.

Rolls, E. T. (2007d). The cognitive and affective processing of touch in the brain, *Neuroscience and Biobehavioral Reviews, in press*.

Rolls, E. T. (2007e). Emotion, higher order syntactic thoughts, and consciousness, *in* L. Weiskrantz and M. Davies (eds), *Frontiers of Consciousness*, Oxford University Press, Oxford.

Rolls, E. T. (2007f). Invariant representations of objects in natural scenes in the temporal cortex visual areas, *in* S. Funahashi (ed.), *Representation and the Brain*, Springer-Verlag, Berlin, chapter 3, pp. 47–102.

Rolls, E. T. (2007g). Memory systems: multiple systems in the brain and their interactions, *in* H. L. Roediger, Y. Dudai and S. M. Fitzpatrick (eds), *Science of Memory: Concepts*, Oxford University Press, New York, chapter 59, pp. 345–351.

Rolls, E. T. (2007h). A neuro-biological approach to emotional intelligence, *in* G. Matthews, M. Zeidner and R. Roberts (eds), *The Science of Emotional Intelligence: Knowns and Unknowns*, Oxford University Press, Oxford, chapter 3, pp. 72–100.

Rolls, E. T. (2007i). The representation of information about faces in the temporal and frontal lobes of primates including humans, *Neuropsychologia* **45**: 124–143.

Rolls, E. T. (2007j). Sensory processing in the brain related to the control of food intake, *Proceedings of the Nutrition Society* **66**: 96–112.

Rolls, E. T. (2007k). Understanding the mechanisms of food intake and obesity, *Obesity Reviews* **8**: 67–72.

Rolls, E. T. (2008a). Face processing in different brain areas, and critical band masking, *Journal of Neuropsychology, in press*.

Rolls, E. T. (2008b). The primate hippocampus and episodic memory, *in* E. Dere, J. P. Huston and A. Easton (eds), *Episodic Memory Research*, Elsevier, Amsterdam.

Rolls, E. T. and Baylis, G. C. (1986). Size and contrast have only small effects on the responses to faces of neurons in the cortex of the superior temporal sulcus of the monkey, *Experimental Brain Research* **65**: 38–48.

Rolls, E. T. and Baylis, L. L. (1994). Gustatory, olfactory and visual convergence within the primate orbitofrontal cortex, *Journal of Neuroscience* **14**: 5437–5452.

Rolls, E. T. and Critchley, H. D. (2007). The representation of olfactory information by populations of neurons in the primate orbitofrontal cortex, *in preparation*.

Rolls, E. T. and Deco, G. (2002). *Computational Neuroscience of Vision*, Oxford University Press, Oxford.

Rolls, E. T. and Deco, G. (2006). Attention in natural scenes: neurophysiological and computational bases, *Neural Networks* **19**: 1383–1394.

Rolls, E. T. and Johnstone, S. (1992). Neurophysiological analysis of striatal function, *in* G. Vallar, S. Cappa and C. Wallesch (eds), *Neuropsychological Disorders Associated with Subcortical Lesions*, Oxford University Press, Oxford, chapter 3, pp. 61–97.

Rolls, E. T. and Kesner, R. P. (2006). A theory of hippocampal function, and tests of the theory, *Progress in Neurobiology* **79**: 1–48.

Rolls, E. T. and McCabe, C. (2007). Enhanced affective brain representations of chocolate in cravers vs non-cravers, *European Journal of Neuroscience*.

Rolls, E. T. and Milward, T. (2000). A model of invariant object recognition in the visual system: learning rules, activation functions, lateral inhibition, and information-based performance measures, *Neural Computation* **12**: 2547–2572.

Rolls, E. T. and O'Mara, S. (1993). Neurophysiological and theoretical analysis of how the hippocampus functions in memory, *in* T. Ono, L. Squire, M. Raichle, D. Perrett and M. Fukuda (eds), *Brain Mechanisms of Perception and Memory: From Neuron to Behavior*, Oxford University Press, New York, chapter 17, pp. 276–300.

Rolls, E. T. and O'Mara, S. M. (1995). View-responsive neurons in the primate hippocampal complex, *Hippocampus* **5**: 409–424.

Rolls, E. T. and Rolls, B. J. (1973). Altered food preferences after lesions in the basolateral region of the amygdala in the rat, *Journal of Comparative and Physiological Psychology* **83**: 248–259.

Rolls, E. T. and Scott, T. R. (2003). Central taste anatomy and neurophysiology, *in* R. Doty (ed.), *Handbook of Olfaction and Gustation*, 2nd edn, Dekker, New York, chapter 33, pp. 679–705.

Rolls, E. T. and Stringer, S. M. (2000). On the design of neural networks in the brain by genetic evolution, *Progress in Neurobiology* **61**: 557–579.

Rolls, E. T. and Stringer, S. M. (2001a). Invariant object recognition in the visual system with error correction and temporal difference learning, *Network: Computation in Neural Systems* **12**: 111–129.

Rolls, E. T. and Stringer, S. M. (2001b). A model of the interaction between mood and memory, *Network: Computation in Neural Systems* **12**: 89–109.

Rolls, E. T. and Stringer, S. M. (2005). Spatial view cells in the hippocampus, and their idiothetic update based on place and head direction, *Neural Networks* **18**: 1229–1241.

Rolls, E. T. and Stringer, S. M. (2006). Invariant visual object recognition: a model, with lighting invariance, *Journal of Physiology – Paris* **100**: 43–62.

Rolls, E. T. and Stringer, S. M. (2007). Invariant global motion recognition in the dorsal visual system: a unifying theory, *Neural Computation* **19**: 139–169.

Rolls, E. T. and Tovee, M. J. (1994). Processing speed in the cerebral cortex and the neurophysiology of visual masking, *Proceedings of the Royal Society, B* **257**: 9–15.

Rolls, E. T. and Tovee, M. J. (1995a). The responses of single neurons in the temporal visual cortical areas of the macaque when more than one stimulus is present in the visual field, *Experimental Brain Research* **103**: 409–420.

Rolls, E. T. and Tovee, M. J. (1995b). Sparseness of the neuronal representation of stimuli in the primate temporal visual cortex, *Journal of Neurophysiology* **73**: 713–726.

Rolls, E. T. and Treves, A. (1990). The relative advantages of sparse versus distributed encoding for associative neuronal networks in the brain, *Network* **1**: 407–421.

Rolls, E. T. and Treves, A. (1998). *Neural Networks and Brain Function*, Oxford University Press, Oxford.

Rolls, E. T. and Williams, G. V. (1987a). Neuronal activity in the ventral striatum of the primate, *in* M. B. Carpenter and A. Jayamaran (eds), *The Basal Ganglia II – Structure and Function – Current Concepts*, Plenum, New York, pp. 349–356.

Rolls, E. T. and Williams, G. V. (1987b). Sensory and movement-related neuronal activity in different regions of the primate striatum, *in* J. S. Schneider and T. I. Lidsky (eds), *Basal Ganglia and Behavior: Sensory Aspects and Motor Functioning*, Hans Huber, Bern, pp. 37–59.

Rolls, E. T. and Xiang, J.-Z. (2005). Reward–spatial view representations and learning in the primate hippocampus, *Journal of Neuroscience* **25**: 6167–6174.

Rolls, E. T. and Xiang, J.-Z. (2006). Spatial view cells in the primate hippocampus, and memory recall, *Reviews in the Neurosciences* **17**: 175–200.

Rolls, E. T., Kelly, P. H. and Shaw, S. G. (1974a). Noradrenaline, dopamine and brain-stimulation reward, *Pharmacology, Biochemistry and Behavior* **2**: 735–740.

Rolls, E. T., Rolls, B. J., Kelly, P. H., Shaw, S. G. and Dale, R. (1974b). The relative attenuation of self-stimulation, eating and drinking produced by dopamine-receptor blockade, *Psychopharmacologia (Berlin)* **38**: 219–310.

Rolls, E. T., Burton, M. J. and Mora, F. (1976). Hypothalamic neuronal responses associated with the sight of food, *Brain Research* **111**: 53–66.

Rolls, E. T., Judge, S. J. and Sanghera, M. (1977). Activity of neurones in the inferotemporal cortex of the alert monkey, *Brain Research* **130**: 229–238.

Rolls, E. T., Sanghera, M. K. and Roper-Hall, A. (1979a). The latency of activation of neurons in the lateral hypothalamus and substantia innominata during feeding in the monkey, *Brain Research* **164**: 121–135.

Rolls, E. T., Thorpe, S. J., Maddison, S., Roper-Hall, A., Puerto, A. and Perrett, D. (1979b). Activity of neurones in the neostriatum and related structures in the alert animal, *in* I. Divac and R. Oberg (eds), *The Neostriatum*, Pergamon Press, Oxford, pp. 163–182.

Rolls, E. T., Burton, M. J. and Mora, F. (1980). Neurophysiological analysis of brain-stimulation reward in the monkey, *Brain Research* **194**: 339–357.

Rolls, E. T., Perrett, D. I., Caan, A. W. and Wilson, F. A. W. (1982). Neuronal responses related to visual recognition, *Brain* **105**: 611–646.

Rolls, E. T., Rolls, B. J. and Rowe, E. A. (1983a). Sensory-specific and motivation-specific satiety for the sight and taste of food and water in man, *Physiology and Behavior* **30**: 185–192.

Rolls, E. T., Thorpe, S. J. and Maddison, S. P. (1983b). Responses of striatal neurons in the behaving monkey. 1. Head of the caudate nucleus, *Behavioural Brain Research* **7**: 179–210.

Rolls, E. T., Thorpe, S. J., Boytim, M., Szabo, I. and Perrett, D. I. (1984). Responses of striatal neurons in the behaving monkey. 3. Effects of iontophoretically applied dopamine on normal responsiveness, *Neuroscience* **12**: 1201–1212.

Rolls, E. T., Baylis, G. C. and Leonard, C. M. (1985). Role of low and high spatial frequencies in the face-selective responses of neurons in the cortex in the superior temporal sulcus, *Vision Research* **25**: 1021–1035.

Rolls, E. T., Murzi, E., Yaxley, S., Thorpe, S. J. and Simpson, S. J. (1986). Sensory-specific satiety: food-specific reduction in responsiveness of ventral forebrain neurons after feeding in the monkey, *Brain Research* **368**: 79–86.

Rolls, E. T., Baylis, G. C. and Hasselmo, M. E. (1987). The responses of neurons in the cortex in the superior temporal sulcus of the monkey to band-pass spatial frequency filtered faces, *Vision Research* **27**: 311–326.

Rolls, E. T., Scott, T. R., Sienkiewicz, Z. J. and Yaxley, S. (1988). The responsiveness of neurones in the frontal opercular gustatory cortex of the macaque monkey is independent of hunger, *Journal of Physiology* **397**: 1–12.

Rolls, E. T., Baylis, G. C., Hasselmo, M. and Nalwa, V. (1989a). The representation of information in the temporal lobe visual cortical areas of macaque monkeys, *in* J. Kulikowski, C. Dickinson and I. Murray (eds), *Seeing Contour and Colour*, Pergamon, Oxford.

Rolls, E. T., Miyashita, Y., Cahusac, P. M. B., Kesner, R. P., Niki, H., Feigenbaum, J. and Bach, L. (1989b). Hippocampal neurons in the monkey with activity related to the place in which a stimulus is shown, *Journal of Neuroscience* **9**: 1835–1845.

Rolls, E. T., Sienkiewicz, Z. J. and Yaxley, S. (1989c). Hunger modulates the responses to gustatory stimuli of single neurons in the caudolateral orbitofrontal cortex of the macaque monkey, *European Journal of Neuroscience* **1**: 53–60.

Rolls, E. T., Yaxley, S. and Sienkiewicz, Z. J. (1990). Gustatory responses of single neurons in the orbitofrontal cortex of the macaque monkey, *Journal of Neurophysiology* **64**: 1055–1066.

Rolls, E. T., Cahusac, P. M. B., Feigenbaum, J. D. and Miyashita, Y. (1993). Responses of single neurons in the hippocampus of the macaque related to recognition memory, *Experimental Brain Research* **93**: 299–306.

Rolls, E. T., Hornak, J., Wade, D. and McGrath, J. (1994a). Emotion-related learning in patients with social and emotional changes associated with frontal lobe damage, *Journal of Neurology, Neurosurgery and Psychiatry* **57**: 1518–1524.

Rolls, E. T., Tovee, M. J., Purcell, D. G., Stewart, A. L. and Azzopardi, P. (1994b). The responses of neurons in the temporal cortex of primates, and face identification and detection, *Experimental Brain Research* **101**: 474–484.

Rolls, E. T., Critchley, H. D. and Treves, A. (1996a). The representation of olfactory information in the primate orbitofrontal cortex, *Journal of Neurophysiology* **75**: 1982–1996.

Rolls, E. T., Critchley, H. D., Mason, R. and Wakeman, E. A. (1996b). Orbitofrontal cortex neurons: role in olfactory and visual association learning, *Journal of Neurophysiology* **75**: 1970–1981.

Rolls, E. T., Critchley, H., Wakeman, E. A. and Mason, R. (1996c). Responses of neurons in the primate taste cortex to the glutamate ion and to inosine 5′-monophosphate, *Physiology and Behavior* **59**: 991–1000.

Rolls, E. T., Robertson, R. G. and Georges-François, P. (1997a). Spatial view cells in the primate hippocampus, *European Journal of Neuroscience* **9**: 1789–1794.

Rolls, E. T., Treves, A. and Tovee, M. J. (1997b). The representational capacity of the distributed encoding of information provided by populations of neurons in the primate temporal visual cortex, *Experimental Brain Research* **114**: 149–162.

Rolls, E. T., Treves, A., Foster, D. and Perez-Vicente, C. (1997c). Simulation studies of the CA3 hippocampal subfield modelled as an attractor neural network, *Neural Networks* **10**: 1559–1569.

Rolls, E. T., Treves, A., Tovee, M. and Panzeri, S. (1997d). Information in the neuronal representation of individual stimuli in the primate temporal visual cortex, *Journal of Computational Neuroscience* **4**: 309–333.

Rolls, E. T., Treves, A., Robertson, R. G., Georges-François, P. and Panzeri, S. (1998). Information about spatial view in an ensemble of primate hippocampal cells, *Journal of Neurophysiology* **79**: 1797–1813.

Rolls, E. T., Critchley, H. D., Browning, A. S., Hernadi, A. and Lenard, L. (1999a). Responses to the sensory properties of fat of neurons in the primate orbitofrontal cortex, *Journal of Neuroscience* **19**: 1532–1540.

Rolls, E. T., Tovee, M. J. and Panzeri, S. (1999b). The neurophysiology of backward visual masking: information analysis, *Journal of Cognitive Neuroscience* **11**: 335–346.

Rolls, E. T., Stringer, S. M. and Trappenberg, T. P. (2002). A unified model of spatial and episodic memory, *Proceedings of The Royal Society B* **269**: 1087–1093.

Rolls, E. T., Aggelopoulos, N. C. and Zheng, F. (2003a). The receptive fields of inferior temporal cortex neurons in natural scenes, *Journal of Neuroscience* **23**: 339–348.

Rolls, E. T., Franco, L., Aggelopoulos, N. C. and Reece, S. (2003b). An information theoretic approach to the contributions of the firing rates and the correlations between the firing of neurons, *Journal of Neurophysiology* **89**: 2810–2822.

Rolls, E. T., Kringelbach, M. L. and De Araujo, I. E. T. (2003c). Different representations of pleasant and unpleasant odors in the human brain, *European Journal of Neuroscience* **18**: 695–703.

Rolls, E. T., O'Doherty, J., Kringelbach, M. L., Francis, S., Bowtell, R. and McGlone, F. (2003d). Representations of pleasant and painful touch in the human orbitofrontal and cingulate cortices, *Cerebral Cortex* **13**: 308–317.

Rolls, E. T., Verhagen, J. V. and Kadohisa, M. (2003e). Representations of the texture of food in the primate orbitofrontal cortex: neurons responding to viscosity, grittiness, and capsaicin, *Journal of Neurophysiology* **90**: 3711–3724.

Rolls, E. T., Aggelopoulos, N. C., Franco, L. and Treves, A. (2004). Information encoding in the inferior temporal visual cortex: contributions of the firing rates and the correlations between the firing of neurons, *Biological Cybernetics* **90**: 19–32.

Rolls, E. T., Browning, A. S., Inoue, K. and Hernadi, S. (2005a). Novel visual stimuli activate a population of neurons in the primate orbitofrontal cortex, *Neurobiology of Learning and Memory* **84**: 111–123.

Rolls, E. T., Franco, L. and Stringer, S. M. (2005b). The perirhinal cortex and long-term familiarity memory, *Quarterly Journal of Experimental Psychology B* **58**: 234–245.

Rolls, E. T., Xiang, J.-Z. and Franco, L. (2005c). Object, space and object-space representations in the primate hippocampus, *Journal of Neurophysiology* **94**: 833–844.

Rolls, E. T., Critchley, H. D., Browning, A. S. and Inoue, K. (2006a). Face-selective and auditory neurons in the primate orbitofrontal cortex, *Experimental Brain Research* **170**: 7487.

Rolls, E. T., Franco, L., Aggelopoulos, N. C. and Jerez, J. M. (2006b). Information in the first spike, the order of spikes, and the number of spikes provided by neurons in the inferior temporal visual cortex, *Vision Research* **46**: 4193–4205.

Rolls, E. T., Stringer, S. M. and Elliot, T. (2006c). Entorhinal cortex grid cells can map to hippocampal place cells by competitive learning, *Network: Computation in Neural Systems* **17**: 447–465.

Rolls, E. T., Critchley, H., Verhagen, J. V. and Kadohisa, M. (2007a). The representation of information about taste in the primate orbitofrontal cortex, *in preparation*.

Rolls, E. T., McCabe, C. and Redoute, J. (2007b). Expected value, reward outcome, and temporal difference error representations in a probabilistic decision task, *Cerebral Cortex, in press*.

Rolls, E. T., Verhagen, J. V., Gabbott, P. and Kadohisa, M. (2007c). Taste and oral texture representations in the primate medial orbitofrontal and pregenual cingulate cortices.

Romo, R. and Salinas, E. (2001). Touch and go: decision-making mechanisms in somatosensation, *Annual Review of Neuroscience* **24**: 107–137.

Romo, R. and Salinas, E. (2003). Flutter discrimination: neural codes, perception, memory and decision making, *Nature Reviews Neuroscience* **4**: 203–218.

Romo, R., Hernandez, A., Zainos, A., Lemus, L. and Brody, C. D. (2002). Neural correlates of decision-making in secondary somatosensory cortex, *Nature Neuroscience* **5**: 1217–1225.

Romo, R., Hernandez, A., Zainos, A. and Salinas, E. (2003). Correlated neuronal discharges that increase coding efficiency during perceptual discrimination, *Neuron* **38**: 649–657.

Romo, R., Hernandez, A. and Zainos, A. (2004). Neuronal correlates of a perceptual decision in ventral premotor cortex, *Neuron* **41**: 165–173.

Rosch, E. (1975). Cognitive representations of semantic categories, *Journal of Experimental Psychology: General* **104**: 192–233.

Rosenblatt, F. (1961). *Principles of Neurodynamics: Perceptrons and the Theory of Brain Mechanisms*, Spartan, Washington, DC.

Rosenkilde, C. E. (1979). Functional heterogeneity of the prefrontal cortex in the monkey: a review, *Behavioral and Neural Biology* **25**: 301–345.

Rosenkilde, C. E., Bauer, R. H. and Fuster, J. M. (1981). Single unit activity in ventral prefrontal cortex in behaving monkeys, *Brain Research* **209**: 375–394.

Rosenthal, D. M. (1993). Thinking that one thinks, *in* M. Davies and G. W. Humphreys (eds), *Consciousness*, Blackwell, Oxford, chapter 10, pp. 197–223.

Rosenthal, D. M. (2004). Varieties of higher order theory, *in* R. J. Gennaro (ed.), *Higher Order Theories of Consciousness*, John Benjamins, Amsterdam, pp. 17–44.

Rosenthal, D. M. (2005). *Consciousness and Mind*, Oxford University Press, Oxford.

Royet, J. P., Zald, D., Versace, R., Costes, N., Lavenne, F., Koenig, O., Gervais, R., Routtenberg, A., Gardner, E. I. and Huang, Y. H. (2000). Emotional responses to pleasant and unpleasant olfactory, visual, and auditory stimuli: a positron emission tomography study, *Journal of Neuroscience* **20**: 7752–7759.

Rudebeck, P. H., Walton, M. E., Smyth, A. N., Bannerman, D. M. and Rushworth, M. F. S. (2006). Separate neural pathways process different decision costs, *Nature Neuroscience* **9**: 1161–1168.

Rumelhart, D. E. and McClelland, J. L. (1986). *Parallel Distributed Processing*, Vol. 1: Foundations, MIT Press, Cambridge, MA.

Rumelhart, D. E. and Zipser, D. (1985). Feature discovery by competitive learning, *Cognitive Science* **9**: 75–112.

Rumelhart, D. E., Hinton, G. E. and Williams, R. J. (1986a). Learning internal representations by error propagation, *in* D. E. Rumelhart, J. L. McClelland and the PDP Research Group (eds), *Parallel Distributed Processing: Explorations in the Microstructure of Cognition*, Vol. 1, MIT Press, Cambridge, MA, chapter 8, pp. 318–362.

Rumelhart, D. E., Hinton, G. E. and Williams, R. J. (1986b). Learning representations by back-propagating errors, *Nature* **323**: 533–536.

Rupniak, N. M. J. and Gaffan, D. (1987). Monkey hippocampus and learning about spatially directed movements, *Journal of Neuroscience* **7**: 2331–2337.

Rushworth, M. F. S., Hadland, K. A., Paus, T. and Sipila, P. K. (2002). Role of the human medial frontal cortex in task-switching: a combined fMRI and TMS study, *Journal of Neurophysiology* **87**: 2577–2592.

Rushworth, M. F. S., Hadland, K. A., Gaffan, D. and Passingham, R. E. (2003). The effect of cingulate cortex lesions on task switching and working memory, *Journal of Cognitive Neuroscience* **15**: 338–353.

Rushworth, M. F. S., Walton, M. E., Kennerley, S. W. and Bannerman, D. M. (2004). Action sets and decisions in the medial frontal cortex, *Trends in Cognitive Sciences* **8**: 410–417.

Russchen, F. T., Amaral, D. G. and Price, J. L. (1985). The afferent connections of the substantia innominata in the monkey, Macaca fascicularis, *Journal of Comparative Neurology* **242**: 1–27.

Rylander, G. (1948). Personality analysis before and after frontal lobotomy, *Association for Research into Nervous and Mental Disorders* **27** (**The Frontal Lobes**): 691–705.

Sagi, D. and Julesz, B. (1986). Enhanced detection in the aperture of focal attention during simple shape discrimination tasks, *Nature* **321**: 693–695.

Saint-Cyr, J. A., Ungerleider, L. G. and Desimone, R. (1990). Organization of visual cortical inputs to the striatum and subsequent outputs to the pallido-nigral complex in the monkey, *Journal of Comparative Neurology* **298**: 129–156.

Sakai, K. and Miyashita, Y. (1991). Neural organisation for the long-term memory of paired associates, *Nature* **354**(6349): 152–155.

Salin, P. and Prince, D. (1996). Spontaneous GABA-A receptor mediated inhibitory currents in adult rat somatosensory cortex, *Journal of Neurophysiology* **75**: 1573–1588.

Salinas, E. and Abbott, L. F. (1996). A model of multiplicative neural responses in parietal cortex, *Proceedings of the National Academy of Sciences USA* **93**: 11956–11961.

Salinas, E. and Abbott, L. F. (1997). Invariant visual responses from attentional gain fields, *Journal of Neurophysiology* **77**: 3267–3272.

Salzman, C. D., Britten, K. H. and Newsome, W. T. (1990). Cortical microstimulation influences perceptual judgements of motion direction, *Nature* **346**: 174–177.

Samsonovich, A. and McNaughton, B. (1997). Path integration and cognitive mapping in a continuous attractor neural network model, *Journal of Neuroscience* **17**: 5900–5920.

Samuelsson, H., Jensen, C., Ekholm, S., Naver, H. and Blomstrand, C. (1997). Anatomical and neurobiological correlates of acute and chronic visuo-spatial neglect following right hemispheres stroke, *Cortex* **33**: 271–285.

Sanfey, A. G., Rilling, J. K., Aronson, J. A., Nystrom, L. E. and Cohen, J. D. (2003). The neural basis of economic decision-making in the ultimatum game, *Science* **300**: 1755–1758.

Sanghera, M. K., Rolls, E. T. and Roper-Hall, A. (1979). Visual responses of neurons in the dorsolateral amygdala of the alert monkey, *Experimental Neurology* **63**: 610–626.

Saper, C. B., Loewy, A. D., Swanson, L. W. and Cowan, W. M. (1976). Direct hypothalamo-autonomic connections, *Brain Research* **117**: 305–312.

Saper, C. B., Swanson, L. W. and Cowan, W. M. (1979). An autoradiographic study of the efferent connections of the lateral hypothalamic area in the rat, *Journal of Comparative Neurology* **183**: 689–706.

Sargolini, F., Fyhn, M., Hafting, T., McNaughton, B. L., Witter, M. P., Moser, M. B. and Moser, E. I. (2006). Conjunctive representation of position, direction, and velocity in entorhinal cortex, *Science* **312**: 758–762.

Sato, T. (1989). Interactions of visual stimuli in the receptive fields of inferior temporal neurons in macaque, *Experimental Brain Research* **77**: 23–30.

Sato, T., Kawamura, T. and Iwai, E. (1980). Responsiveness of inferotemporal single units to visual pattern stimuli in monkeys performing discrimination, *Experimental Brain Research* **38**: 313–319.

Save, E., Guazzelli, A. and Poucet, B. (2001). Dissociation of the effects of bilateral lesions of the dorsal hippocampus and parietal cortex on path integration in the rat, *Behavioral Neuroscience* **115**: 1212–1223.

Sawaguchi, T. and Goldman-Rakic, P. S. (1991). D1 dopamine receptors in prefrontal cortex: Involvement in working memory, *Science* **251**: 947–950.

Sawaguchi, T. and Goldman-Rakic, P. S. (1994). The role of D1-dopamine receptor in working memory: local injections of dopamine antagonists into the prefrontal cortex of rhesus monkeys performing an oculomotor delayed-response task, *Journal of Neurophysiology* **71**: 515–528.

Schacter, G. B., Yang, C. R., Innis, N. K. and Mogenson, G. J. (1989). The role of the hippocampal–nucleus accumbens pathway in radial-arm maze performance, *Brain Research* **494**: 339–349.

Schall, J. D. (2001). Neural basis of deciding, choosing and acting, *Nature Reviews Neuroscience* **2**: 33–42.

Schmolesky, M., Wang, Y., Hanes, D., Thompson, K., Leutgeb, S., Schall, J. and Leventhal, A. (1998). Signal timing across the macaque visual system, *Journal of Neurophysiology* **79**: 3272–3277.

Schoenbaum, G. and Eichenbaum, H. (1995). Information encoding in the rodent prefrontal cortex. I. Single-neuron activity in orbitofrontal cortex compared with that in pyriform cortex, *Journal of Neurophysiology* **74**: 733–750.

Schoenbaum, G., Roesch, M. R. and Stalnaker, T. A. (2006). Orbitofrontal cortex, decision-making and drug addiction, *Trends in Neurosciences* **29**: 116–124.

Schultz, S. and Rolls, E. T. (1999). Analysis of information transmission in the schaffer collaterals, *Hippocampus* **9**: 582–598.

Schultz, W. (1998). Predictive reward signal of dopamine neurons, *Journal of Neurophysiology* **80**: 1–27.

Schultz, W. (2004). Neural coding of basic reward terms of animal learning theory, game theory, microeconomics and behavioural ecology, *Current Opinion in Neurobiology* **14**: 139–147.

Schultz, W. (2006). Behavioral theories and the neurophysiology of reward, *Annual Review of Psychology* **57**: 87–115.

Schultz, W., Apicella, P., Scarnati, E. and Ljungberg, T. (1992). Neuronal activity in the ventral striatum related to the expectation of reward, *Journal of Neuroscience* **12**: 4595–4610.

Schultz, W., Apicella, P., Romo, R. and Scarnati, E. (1995a). Context-dependent activity in primate striatum reflecting past and future behavioral events, *in* J. C. Houk, J. L. Davis and D. G. Beiser (eds), *Models of Information Processing in the Basal Ganglia*, MIT Press, Cambridge, MA, chapter 2, pp. 11–27.

Schultz, W., Romo, R., Ljunberg, T., Mirenowicz, J., Hollerman, J. R. and Dickinson, A. (1995b). Reward-related signals carried by dopamine neurons, *in* J. C. Houk, J. L. Davis and D. G. Beiser (eds), *Models of Information Processing in the Basal Ganglia*, MIT Press, Cambridge, MA, chapter 12, pp. 233–248.

Schultz, W., Dayan, P. and Montague, P. R. (1997). A neural substrate of prediction and reward, *Science* **275**: 1593–1599.

Schultz, W., Tremblay, L. and Hollerman, J. R. (2003). Changes in behavior-related neuronal activity in the striatum during learning, *Trends in Neurosciences* **26**: 312–328.

Schwaber, J. S., Kapp, B. S., Higgins, G. A. and Rapp, P. R. (1982). Amygdaloid and basal forebrain direct connections with the nucleus of the solitary tract and the dorsal motor nucleus, *Journal of Neuroscience* **2**: 1424–1438.

Scott, S. K., Young, A. W., Calder, A. J., Hellawell, D. J., Aggleton, J. P. and Johnson, M. (1997). Impaired auditory recognition of fear and anger following bilateral amygdala lesions, *Nature* **385**: 254–257.

Scott, T. R., Yaxley, S., Sienkiewicz, Z. J. and Rolls, E. T. (1986). Gustatory responses in the frontal opercular cortex of the alert cynomolgus monkey, *Journal of Neurophysiology* **56**: 876–890.

Scott, T. R., Karadi, Z., Oomura, Y., Nishino, H., Plata-Salaman, C. R., Lenard, L., Giza, B. K. and Aou, S. (1993). Gustatory neural coding in the amygdala of the alert monkey, *Journal of Neurophysiology* **69**: 1810–1820.

Scott, T. R., Yan, J. and Rolls, E. T. (1995). Brain mechanisms of satiety and taste in macaques, *Neurobiology* **3**: 281–292.

Seamans, J. K. and Yang, C. R. (2004). The principal features and mechanisms of dopamine modulation in the prefrontal cortex, *Progress in Neurobiology* **74**: 1–58.

Seamans, J. K., Gorelova, N., Durstewitz, D. and Yang, C. R. (2001). Bidirectional dopamine modulation of GABAergic inhibition in prefrontal cortical pyramidal neurons, *Journal of Neuroscience* **21**: 3628–3638.

Seigel, M. and Auerbach, J. M. (1996). Neuromodulators of synaptic strength, *in* M. S. Fazeli and G. L. Collingridge (eds), *Cortical Plasticity*, Bios, Oxford, chapter 7, pp. 137–148.

Seleman, L. D. and Goldman-Rakic, P. S. (1985). Longitudinal topography and interdigitation of corticostriatal projections in the rhesus monkey, *Journal of Neuroscience* **5**: 776–794.

Selfridge, O. G. (1959). Pandemonium: A paradigm for learning, *The Mechanization of Thought Processes*, H. M. Stationery Office, London.

Seltzer, B. and Pandya, D. N. (1978). Afferent cortical connections and architectonics of the superior temporal sulcus and surrounding cortex in the rhesus monkey, *Brain Research* **149**: 1–24.

Seltzer, B. and Pandya, D. N. (1989). Frontal lobe connections of the superior temporal sulcus in the rhesus monkey, *Journal of Comparative Neurology* **281**: 97–113.

Sem-Jacobsen, C. W. (1968). *Depth-Electrographic Stimulation of the Human Brain and Behavior: From Fourteen Years of Studies and Treatment of Parkinson's Disease and Mental Disorders with Implanted Electrodes*, C. C. Thomas, Springfield, IL.

Sem-Jacobsen, C. W. (1976). Electrical stimulation and self-stimulation in man with chronic implanted electrodes. Interpretation and pitfalls of results, *in* A. Wauquier and E. T. Rolls (eds), *Brain-Stimulation Reward*, North-Holland, Amsterdam, pp. 505–520.

Senn, W., Markram, H. and Tsodyks, M. (2001). An algorithm for modifying neurotransmitter release probability based on pre- and postsynaptic spike timing, *Neural Computation* **13**: 35–67.

Serre, T., Wold, L., Bileschi, S., Riesenhuber, M. and Poggio, T. (2007). Robust object recognition with cortex-like mechanisms, *IEEE Transactions on Pattern Analysis and Machine Intelligence* **3**: 411–426.

Setlow, B., Gallagher, M. and Holland, P. C. (2002). The basolateral complex of the amygdala is necessary for acquisition but not expression of CS motivational value in appetitive Pavlovian second-order conditioning, *European Journal of Neuroscience* **15**: 1841–1853.

Seymour, B., O'Doherty, J., Dayan, P., Koltzenburg, M., Jones, A. K., Dolan, R. J., Friston, K. J. and Frackowiak, R. S. (2004). Temporal difference models describe higher-order learning in humans, *Nature* **429**: 664–667.

Shadlen, M. and Movshon, J. (1999). Synchrony unbound: A critical evaluation of the temporal binding hypothesis, *Neuron* **24**: 67–77.

Shadlen, M. and Newsome, W. (1994). Is there a signal in the noise?, *Current Opinion in Neurobiology* **5**: 248–250.

Shadlen, M. and Newsome, W. (1998). The variable discharge of cortical neurons: implications for connectivity, computation and coding, *Journal of Neuroscience* **18**: 3870–3896.

Shallice, T. (1982). Specific impairments of planning, *Philosophical Transactions of the Royal Society of London B* **298**: 199–209.

Shallice, T. and Burgess, P. (1996). The domain of supervisory processes and temporal organization of behaviour, *Philosophical Transactions of the Royal Society B,* **351**: 1405–1411.

Shannon, C. E. (1948). A mathematical theory of communication, *AT&T Bell Laboratories Technical Journal* **27**: 379–423.

Sharp, P. E. (1996). Multiple spatial–behavioral correlates for cells in the rat postsubiculum: multiple regression analysis and comparison to other hippocampal areas, *Cerebral Cortex* **6**: 238–259.

Sharp, P. E. (ed.) (2002). *The Neural Basis of Navigation: Evidence From Single Cell Recording*, Kluwer, Boston.

Shashua, A. (1995). Algebraic functions for recognition, *IEEE Transactions on Pattern Analysis and Machine Intelligence* **17**: 779–789.

Shaw, M. (1978). A capacity allocation of cognitive resources to spatial locations, *Journal of Experimental Psychology: Human Perception and Performance* **4**: 586–598.

Shaw, M. and Shaw, P. (1977). Optimal allocation of cognitive resources to spatial locations, *Journal of Experimental Psychology: Human Perception and Performance* **3**: 201–211.

Shepherd, G. M. (2004). *The Synaptic Organisation of the Brain*, 5th edn, Oxford University Press, Oxford.

Shevelev, I. A., Novikova, R. V., Lazareva, N. A., Tikhomirov, A. S. and Sharaev, G. A. (1995). Sensitivity to cross-like figures in cat striate neurons, *Neuroscience* **69**: 51–57.

Shidara, M. and Richmond, B. J. (2002). Anterior cingulate: single neuronal signals related to degreee of reward expectancy, *Science* **296**: 1709–1711.

Shiino, M. and Fukai, T. (1990). Replica-symmetric theory of the nonlinear analogue neural networks, *Journal of Physics A: Math. Gen.* **23**: L1009–L1017.

Shima, K. and Tanji, J. (1998). Role for cingulate motor area cells in voluntary movement selection based on reward, *Science* **13**: 1335–1338.

Shizgal, P. and Arvanitogiannis, A. (2003). Gambling on dopamine, *Science* **299**: 1856–1858.

Sillito, A. M. (1984). Functional considerations of the operation of GABAergic inhibitory processes in the visual cortex, *in* E. G. Jones and A. Peters (eds), *Cerebral Cortex, Vol. 2, Functional Properties of Cortical Cells*, Plenum, New York, chapter 4, pp. 91–117.

Sillito, A. M., Grieve, K. L., Jones, H. E., Cudeiro, J. and Davis, J. (1995). Visual cortical mechanisms detecting focal orientation discontinuities, *Nature* **378**: 492–496.

Simmen, M. W., Rolls, E. T. and Treves, A. (1996a). On the dynamics of a network of spiking neurons, *in* F. Eekman and J. Bower (eds), *Computations and Neuronal Systems: Proceedings of CNS95*, Kluwer, Boston.

Simmen, M. W., Treves, A. and Rolls, E. T. (1996b). Pattern retrieval in threshold-linear associative nets, *Network* **7**: 109–122.

Singer, T., Seymour, B., O'Doherty, J. P., Stephan, K. E., Dolan, R. J. and Frith, C. D. (2006). Empathic neural responses are modulated by the perceived fairness of others, *Nature* **439**: 466–469.

Singer, W. (1987). Activity-dependent self-organization of synaptic connections as a substrate for learning, *in* J.-P. Changeux and M. Konishi (eds), *The Neural and Molecular Bases of Learning*, Wiley, Chichester, pp. 301–335.

Singer, W. (1995). Development and plasticity of cortical processing architectures, *Science* **270**: 758–764.

Singer, W. (1999). Neuronal synchrony: A versatile code for the definition of relations?, *Neuron* **24**: 49–65.

Singer, W. (2000). Response synchronisation: A universal coding strategy for the definition of relations, *in* M. Gazzaniga (ed.), *The New Cognitive Neurosciences*, 2nd edn, MIT Press, Cambridge, MA, chapter 23, pp. 325–338.

Singer, W. and Gray, C. M. (1995). Visual feature integration and the temporal correlation hypothesis, *Annual Review of Neuroscience* **18**: 555–586.

Singer, W., Gray, C., Engel, A., Konig, P., Artola, A. and Brocher, S. (1990). Formation of cortical cell assemblies, *Cold Spring Harbor Symposium on Quantitative Biology* **55**: 939–952.

Sjöström, P. J., Turrigiano, G. G. and Nelson, S. B. (2001). Rate, timing, and cooperativity jointly determine cortical synaptic plasticity, *Neuron* **32**: 1149–1164.

Skaggs, W. E. and McNaughton, B. L. (1992). Quantification of what it is that hippocampal cell firing encodes, *Society for Neuroscience Abstracts* **18**: 1216.

Skaggs, W. E., McNaughton, B. L., Gothard, K. and Markus, E. (1993). An information theoretic approach to deciphering the hippocampal code, *in* S. Hanson, J. D. Cowan and C. L. Giles (eds), *Advances in Neural Information Processing Systems*, Vol. 5, Morgan Kaufmann, San Mateo, CA, pp. 1030–1037.

Skaggs, W. E., Knierim, J. J., Kudrimoti, H. S. and McNaughton, B. L. (1995). A model of the neural basis of the rat's sense of direction, *in* G. Tesauro, D. S. Touretzky and T. K. Leen (eds), *Advances in Neural Information Processing Systems*, Vol. 7, MIT Press, Cambridge, MA, pp. 173–180.

Sloper, J. J. and Powell, T. P. S. (1979a). An experimental electron microscopic study of afferent connections to the primate motor and somatic sensory cortices, *Philosophical Transactions of the Royal Society of London, Series B* **285**: 199–226.

Sloper, J. J. and Powell, T. P. S. (1979b). A study of the axon initial segment and proximal axon of neurons in the primate motor and somatic sensory cortices, *Philosophical Transactions of the Royal Society of London, Series B* **285**: 173–197.

Small, D. M., Zald, D. H., Jones-Gotman, M., Zatorre, R. J., Petrides, M. and Evans, A. C. (1999). Human cortical gustatory areas: a review of functional neuroimaging data, *NeuroReport* **8**: 3913–3917.

Smith, M. L. and Milner, B. (1981). The role of the right hippocampus in the recall of spatial location, *Neuropsychologia* **19**: 781–793.

Smith, P. L. and Ratcliff, R. (2004). Psychology and neurobiology of simple decisions, *Trends in Neurosciences* **27**: 161–168.

Somogyi, P. and Cowey, A. C. (1984). Double bouquet cells, *in* A. Peters and E. G. Jones (eds), *Cerebral Cortex, Vol. 1, Cellular Components of the Cerebral Cortex*, Plenum, New York, chapter 9, pp. 337–360.

Somogyi, P., Kisvarday, Z. F., Martin, K. A. C. and Whitteridge, D. (1983). Synaptic connections of morphologically identified and physiologically characterized large basket cells in the striate cortex of the cat, *Neuroscience* **10**: 261–294.

Sompolinsky, H. and Kanter, I. (1986). Temporal association in asymmetric neural networks, *Physical Review Letters* **57**: 2861–2864.

Sperling, G. and Weichselgartner, J. (1995). Episodic theory of the dynamics of spatial attention, *Psychological Review* **102**: 503–532.

Spiegler, B. J. and Mishkin, M. (1981). Evidence for the sequential participation of inferior temporal cortex and amygdala in the acquisition of stimulus–reward associations, *Behavioural Brain Research* **3**: 303–317.

Spiridon, M., Fischl, B. and Kanwisher, N. (2006). Location and spatial profile of category-specific regions in human extrastriate cortex, *Human Brain Mapping* **27**: 77–89.

Spitzer, H., Desimone, R. and Moran, J. (1988). Increased attention enhances both behavioral and neuronal performance, *Science* **240**: 338–340.

Spruston, N., Jonas, P. and Sakmann, B. (1995). Dendritic glutamate receptor channel in rat hippocampal CA3 and CA1 pyramidal neurons, *Journal of Physiology* **482**: 325–352.

Squire, L. R. (1992). Memory and the hippocampus: A synthesis from findings with rats, monkeys and humans, *Psychological Review* **99**: 195–231.

Stankiewicz, B. and Hummel, J. (1994). Metricat: A representation for basic and subordinate-level classification, *in* G. W. Cottrell (ed.), *Proceedings of the 18th Annual Conference of the Cognitive Science Society*, Erlbaum, San Diego, pp. 254–259.

Starkstein, S. E. and Robinson, R. G. (1991). The role of the frontal lobe in affective disorder following stroke, *in* H. M. Eisenberg (ed.), *Frontal Lobe Function and Dysfunction*, Oxford University Press, New York, pp. 288–303.

Stefanacci, L., Suzuki, W. A. and Amaral, D. G. (1996). Organization of connections between the amygdaloid complex and the perirhinal and parahippocampal cortices in macaque monkeys, *Journal of Comparative Neurology* **375**: 552–582.

Steiner, J. E., Glaser, D., Hawilo, M. E. and Berridge, K. C. (2001). Comparative expression of hedonic impact: affective reactions to taste by human infants and other primates, *Neuroscience and Biobehavioral Reviews* **25**: 53–74.

Stemme, A., Deco, G., Busch, A. and Schneider, W. X. (2005). Neurons and the synaptic basis of the fMRI signal associated with cognitive flexibility, *Neuroimage* **26**: 454–470.

Stent, G. S. (1973). A psychological mechanism for Hebb's postulate of learning, *Proceedings of the National Academy of Sciences USA* **70**: 997–1001.

Stern, C. E. and Passingham, R. E. (1995). The nucleus accumbens in monkeys (Macaca fascicularis): III. Reversal learning, *Experimental Brain Research* **106**: 239–247.

Stern, C. E. and Passingham, R. E. (1996). The nucleus accumbens in monkeys (Macaca fascicularis): II. Emotion and motivation, *Behavioural Brain Research* **75**: 179–193.

Stone, V. E., Baron-Cohen, S., Calder, A., Keane, J. and Young, A. (2003). Acquired theory of mind impairments in individuals with bilateral amygdala lesions, *Neuropsychologia* **41**: 209–220.

Storm-Mathiesen, J., Zimmer, J. and Ottersen, O. P. (1990). Understanding the brain through the hippocampus, *Progress in Brain Research* **83**: 1–.

Strauss, E. and Moscowitsch, M. (1981). Perception of facial expressions, *Brain and Language* **13**: 308–332.

Strick, P. L., Dum, R. P. and Picard, N. (1995). Macro-organization of the circuits connecting the basal ganglia with the cortical motor areas, *in* J. C. Houk, J. L. Davis and D. G. Beiser (eds), *Models of Information Processing in the Basal Ganglia*, MIT Press, Cambridge, MA, chapter 6, pp. 117–130.

Stringer, S. M. and Rolls, E. T. (2000). Position invariant recognition in the visual system with cluttered environments, *Neural Networks* **13**: 305–315.

Stringer, S. M. and Rolls, E. T. (2002). Invariant object recognition in the visual system with novel views of 3D objects, *Neural Computation* **14**: 2585–2596.

Stringer, S. M. and Rolls, E. T. (2006). Self-organizing path integration using a linked continuous attractor and competitive network: path integration of head direction, *Network: Computation in Neural Systems* **17**: 419–445.

Stringer, S. M. and Rolls, E. T. (2007a). Hierarchical dynamical models of motor function, *Neurocomputing* **70**: 975–990.

Stringer, S. M. and Rolls, E. T. (2007b). Learning transform invariant object recognition in the visual system with multiple stimuli present during training, *Neural Networks, in press.*

Stringer, S. M., Rolls, E. T., Trappenberg, T. P. and De Araujo, I. E. T. (2002a). Self-organizing continuous attractor networks and path integration: Two-dimensional models of place cells, *Network: Computation in Neural Systems* **13**: 429–446.

Stringer, S. M., Trappenberg, T. P., Rolls, E. T. and De Araujo, I. E. T. (2002b). Self-organizing continuous attractor networks and path integration: One-dimensional models of head direction cells, *Network: Computation in Neural Systems* **13**: 217–242.

Stringer, S. M., Rolls, E. T. and Trappenberg, T. P. (2004). Self-organising continuous attractor networks with multiple activity packets, and the representation of space, *Neural Networks* **17**: 5–27.

Stringer, S. M., Rolls, E. T. and Trappenberg, T. P. (2005). Self-organizing continuous attractor network models of hippocampal spatial view cells, *Neurobiology of Learning and Memory* **83**: 79–92.

Stringer, S. M., Perry, G., Rolls, E. T. and Proske, J. H. (2006). Learning invariant object recognition in the visual system with continuous transformations, *Biological Cybernetics* **94**: 128–142.

Stringer, S. M., Rolls, E. T. and Taylor, P. (2007a). Learning movement sequences with a delayed reward signal in a hierarchical model of motor function, *Neural Networks* **29**: 172–181.

Stringer, S. M., Rolls, E. T. and Tromans, J. M. (2007b). Invariant object recognition with trace learning and multiple stimuli present during training.

Strong, S. P., Koberle, R., de Ruyter van Steveninck, R. R. and Bialek, W. (1998). Entropy and information in neural spike trains, *Physical Review Letters* **80**: 197–200.

Sugase, Y., Yamane, S., Ueno, S. and Kawano, K. (1999). Global and fine information coded by single neurons in the temporal visual cortex, *Nature* **400**: 869–873.

Sugrue, L. P., Corrado, G. S. and Newsome, W. T. (2005). Choosing the greater of two goods: neural currencies for valuation and decision making, *Nature Reviews Neuroscience* **6**: 363–375.

Suri, R. E. and Schultz, W. (1998). Learning of sequential movements by neural network model with dopamine-like reinforcement signal, *Experimental Brain Research* **121**: 350–354.

Suri, R. E. and Schultz, W. (2001). Temporal difference model reproduces anticipatory neural activity, *Neural Computation* **13**: 841–862.

Sutherland, N. S. (1968). Outline of a theory of visual pattern recognition in animal and man, *Proceedings of the Royal Society, B* **171**: 297–317.

Sutherland, R. J. and Rudy, J. W. (1991). Exceptions to the rule of space, *Hippocampus* **1**: 250–252.

Sutherland, R. J., Whishaw, I. Q. and Kolb, B. (1983). A behavioural analysis of spatial localization following electrolytic, kainate- or colchicine-induced damage to the hippocampal formation in the rat, *Behavioral Brain Research* **7**: 133–153.

Sutton, R. S. (1988). Learning to predict by the methods of temporal differences, *Machine Learning* **3**: 9–44.

Sutton, R. S. and Barto, A. G. (1981). Towards a modern theory of adaptive networks: expectation and prediction, *Psychological Review* **88**: 135–170.

Sutton, R. S. and Barto, A. G. (1990). Time-derivative models of Pavlovian reinforcement, *in* M. Gabriel and J. Moore (eds), *Learning and Computational Neuroscience*, MIT Press, Cambridge, MA, pp. 497–537.

Sutton, R. S. and Barto, A. G. (1998). *Reinforcement Learning*, MIT Press, Cambridge, MA.

Suzuki, W. A. and Amaral, D. G. (1994a). Perirhinal and parahippocampal cortices of the macaque monkey – cortical afferents, *Journal of Comparative Neurology* **350**: 497–533.

Suzuki, W. A. and Amaral, D. G. (1994b). Topographic organization of the reciprocal connections between the monkey entorhinal cortex and the perirhinal and parahippocampal cortices, *Journal of Neuroscience* **14**: 1856–1877.

Suzuki, W. A., Miller, E. K. and Desimone, R. (1997). Object and place memory in the macaque entorhinal cortex, *Journal of Neurophysiology* **78**: 1062–1081.

Swanson, L. W. and Cowan, W. M. (1977). An autoradiographic study of the organization of the efferent connections of the hippocampal formation in the rat, *Journal of Comparative Neurology* **172**: 49–84.

Szabo, M., Almeida, R., Deco, G. and Stetter, M. (2004). Cooperation and biased competition model can explain attentional filtering in the prefrontal cortex, *European Journal of Neuroscience* **19**: 1969–1977.

Szentagothai, J. (1978). The neuron network model of the cerebral cortex: a functional interpretation, *Proceedings of the Royal Society of London, Series B* **201**: 219–248.

Tabuchi, E., Mulder, A. B. and Wiener, S. I. (2003). Reward value invariant place responses and reward site associated activity in hippocampal neurons of behaving rats, *Hippocampus* **13**: 117–132.

Tagamets, M. and Horwitz, B. (1998). Integrating electrophysical and anatomical experimental data to create a large-scale model that simulates a delayed match-to-sample human brain study, *Cerebral Cortex* **8**: 310–320.

Taira, K. and Rolls, E. T. (1996). Receiving grooming as a reinforcer for the monkey, *Physiology and Behavior* **59**: 1189–1192.

Takagi, S. F. (1991). Olfactory frontal cortex and multiple olfactory processing in primates, *in* A. Peters and E. G. Jones (eds), *Cerebral Cortex*, Vol. 9, Plenum Press, New York, pp. 133–152.

Takeda, K. and Funahashi, S. (2002). Prefrontal task-related activity representing visual cue location or saccade direction in spatial working memory tasks, *Journal of Neurophysiology* **87**: 567–588.

Talbot, W. H., Darian-Smith, I., Kornhuber, H. H. and Mountcastle, V. B. (1968). The sense of flutter vibration: comparison of the human capacity with response patterns of mechanoreceptive afferents from the monkey hand, *Journal of Neurophysiology* **31**: 301–334.

Tanaka, K. (1993). Neuronal mechanisms of object recognition, *Science* **262**: 685–688.

Tanaka, K. (1996). Inferotemporal cortex and object vision, *Annual Review of Neuroscience* **19**: 109–139.

Tanaka, K., Saito, C., Fukada, Y. and Moriya, M. (1990). Integration of form, texture, and color information in the inferotemporal cortex of the macaque, *in* E. Iwai and M. Mishkin (eds), *Vision, Memory and the Temporal Lobe*, Elsevier, New York, chapter 10, pp. 101–109.

Tanaka, K., Saito, H., Fukada, Y. and Moriya, M. (1991). Coding visual images of objects in the inferotemporal cortex of the macaque monkey, *Journal of Neurophysiology* **66**: 170–189.

Tanaka, S. C., Doya, K., Okada, G., Ueda, K., Okamoto, Y. and Yamawaki, S. (2004). Prediction of immediate and future rewards differentially recruits cortico-basal ganglia loops, *Nature Neuroscience* **7**: 887–893.

Tanila, H. (1999). Hippocampal place cells can develop distinct representations of two visually identical environments, *Hippocampus* **9**: 235–246.

Taube, J. S., Muller, R. U. and Ranck, Jr., J. B. (1990a). Head-direction cells recorded from the postsubiculum in freely moving rats. I. Description and quantitative analysis, *Journal of Neuroscience* **10**: 420–435.

Taube, J. S., Muller, R. U. and Ranck, Jr., J. B. (1990b). Head-direction cells recorded from the postsubiculum in freely moving rats. II. Effects of environmental manipulations, *Journal of Neuroscience* **10**: 436–447.

Taube, J. S., Goodridge, J. P., Golob, E. G., Dudchenko, P. A. and Stackman, R. W. (1996). Processing the head direction signal: a review and commentary, *Brain Research Bulletin* **40**: 477–486.

Taylor, J. G. (1999). Neural 'bubble' dynamics in two dimensions: foundations, *Biological Cybernetics* **80**: 393–409.

Thomson, A. M. and Deuchars, J. (1994). Temporal and spatial properties of local circuits in neocortex, *Trends in Neurosciences* **17**: 119–126.

Thorpe, S. J. and Imbert, M. (1989). Biological constraints on connectionist models, *in* R. Pfeifer, Z. Schreter and F. Fogelman-Soulie (eds), *Connectionism in Perspective*, Elsevier, Amsterdam, pp. 63–92.

Thorpe, S. J., Rolls, E. T. and Maddison, S. (1983). Neuronal activity in the orbitofrontal cortex of the behaving monkey, *Experimental Brain Research* **49**: 93–115.

Thorpe, S. J., O'Regan, J. K. and Pouget, A. (1989). Humans fail on XOR pattern classification problems, *in* L. Personnaz and G. Dreyfus (eds), *Neural Networks: From Models to Applications*, I.D.S.E.T., Paris, pp. 12–25.

Thorpe, S. J., Fize, D. and Marlot, C. (1996). Speed of processing in the human visual system, *Nature* **381**: 520–522.

Thorpe, S. J., Delorme, A. and Van Rullen, R. (2001). Spike-based strategies for rapid processing, *Neural Networks* **14**: 715–725.

Tiffany, S. T. and Drobes, D. J. (1990). Imagery and smoking urges: the manipulation of affective content, *Addiction and Behaviour* **15**: 531–539.

Tinbergen, N. (1951). *The Study of Instinct*, Oxford University Press, Oxford.

Tinbergen, N. (1963). On aims and methods of ethology, *Zeitschrift fur Tierpsychologie* **20**: 410–433.

Tipper, S. P. and Behrmann, M. (1996). Object-centered not scene-based visual neglect, *Journal of Experimental Psychology, Human Perception and Performance* **22**: 1261–1278.

Tobler, P. N., Dickinson, A. and Schultz, W. (2003). Coding of predicted reward omission by dopamine neurons in a conditioned inhibition paradigm, *Journal of Neuroscience* **23**: 10402–10410.

Torrey, E. F., Webster, M., Knable, M., Johnson, N. and Yolken, R. H. (2000). Stanley Foundation Brain Collection and Neuropathology Consortium, *Schizophrenia Research* **44**: 151–155.

Tou, J. T. and Gonzalez, A. G. (1974). *Pattern Recognition Principles*, Addison-Wesley, Reading, MA.

Tovee, M. J. and Rolls, E. T. (1995). Information encoding in short firing rate epochs by single neurons in the primate temporal visual cortex, *Visual Cognition* **2**: 35–58.

Tovee, M. J., Rolls, E. T., Treves, A. and Bellis, R. P. (1993). Information encoding and the responses of single neurons in the primate temporal visual cortex, *Journal of Neurophysiology* **70**: 640–654.

Tovee, M. J., Rolls, E. T. and Azzopardi, P. (1994). Translation invariance and the responses of neurons in the temporal visual cortical areas of primates, *Journal of Neurophysiology* **72**: 1049–1060.

Tovee, M. J., Rolls, E. T. and Ramachandran, V. S. (1996). Rapid visual learning in neurones of the primate temporal visual cortex, *NeuroReport* **7**: 2757–2760.

Trappenberg, T. P., Rolls, E. T. and Stringer, S. M. (2002). Effective size of receptive fields of inferior temporal visual cortex neurons in natural scenes, *in* T. G. Dietterich, S. Becker and Z. Gharamani (eds), *Advances in Neural Information Processing Systems*, Vol. 14, MIT Press, Cambridge, MA, pp. 293–300.

Treisman, A. (1982). Perceptual grouping and attention in visual search for features and for objects, *Journal of Experimental Psychology: Human Perception and Performance* **8**: 194–214.

Treisman, A. (1988). Features and objects: The fourteenth Barlett memorial lecture, *The Quarterly Journal of Experimental Psychology* **40A**: 201–237.

Treisman, A. and Gelade, G. (1980). A feature-integration theory of attention, *Cognitive Psychology* **12**: 97–136.

Treisman, A. and Sato, S. (1990). Conjunction search revisited, *Journal of Experimental Psychology: Human Perception and Performance,* **16**: 459–478.

Tremblay, L. and Schultz, W. (1998). Modifications of reward expectation-related neuronal activity during learning in primate striatum, *Journal of Neurophysiology* **80**: 964–977.

Tremblay, L. and Schultz, W. (1999). Relative reward preference in primate orbitofrontal cortex, *Nature* **398**: 704–708.

Tremblay, L. and Schultz, W. (2000). Modifications of reward expectation-related neuronal activity during learning in primate orbitofrontal cortex, *Journal of Neurophysiology* **83**: 1877–1885.

Treves, A. (1990). Graded-response neurons and information encodings in autoassociative memories, *Physical Review A* **42**: 2418–2430.

Treves, A. (1991). Dilution and sparse encoding in threshold-linear nets, *Journal of Physics A* **23**: 1–9.

Treves, A. (1993). Mean-field analysis of neuronal spike dynamics, *Network* **4**: 259–284.

Treves, A. (1995). Quantitative estimate of the information relayed by the Schaffer collaterals, *Journal of Computational Neuroscience* **2**: 259–272.

Treves, A. (1997). On the perceptual structure of face space, *Biosystems* **40**: 189–196.

Treves, A. and Panzeri, S. (1995). The upward bias in measures of information derived from limited data samples, *Neural Computation* **7**: 399–407.

Treves, A. and Rolls, E. T. (1991). What determines the capacity of autoassociative memories in the brain?, *Network* **2**: 371–397.

Treves, A. and Rolls, E. T. (1992). Computational constraints suggest the need for two distinct input systems to the hippocampal CA3 network, *Hippocampus* **2**: 189–199.

Treves, A. and Rolls, E. T. (1994). A computational analysis of the role of the hippocampus in memory, *Hippocampus* **4**: 374–391.

Treves, A., Rolls, E. T. and Simmen, M. (1997). Time for retrieval in recurrent associative memories, *Physica D* **107**: 392–400.

Treves, A., Panzeri, S., Rolls, E. T., Booth, M. and Wakeman, E. A. (1999). Firing rate distributions and efficiency of information transmission of inferior temporal cortex neurons to natural visual stimuli, *Neural Computation* **11**: 611–641.

Tsao, D. Y., Freiwald, W. A., Tootell, R. B. and Livingstone, M. S. (2006). A cortical region consisting entirely of face-selective cells, *Science* **311**: 617–618.

Tsodyks, M. V. and Feigel'man, M. V. (1988). The enhanced storage capacity in neural networks with low activity level, *Europhysics Letters* **6**: 101–105.

Tsotsos, J. (1990). Analyzing vision at the complexity level, *Behavioral and Brain Sciences* **13**: 423–469.

Tuckwell, H. (1988). *Introduction to Theoretical Neurobiology*, Cambridge University Press, Cambridge.

Turner, B. H. (1981). The cortical sequence and terminal distribution of sensory related afferents to the amygdaloid complex of the rat and monkey, *in* Y. Ben-Ari (ed.), *The Amygdaloid Complex*, Elsevier, Amsterdam, pp. 51–62.

Tversky, A. and Kahneman, D. (1981). The framing of decisions and the psychology of choice, *Science* **211**: 453–458.

Tversky, A. and Kahneman, D. (1986). Rational choice and the framing of decisions, *Journal of Business* **59**: 251–278.

Ullman, S. (1996). *High-Level Vision. Object Recognition and Visual Cognition*, Bradford/MIT Press, Cambridge, MA.

Ullsperger, M. and von Cramon, D. Y. (2001). Subprocesses of performance monitoring: a dissociation of error processing and response competition revealed by event-related fMRI and ERPs, *Neuroimage* **14**: 1387–1401.

Ungerleider, L. G. (1995). Functional brain imaging studies of cortical mechanisms for memory, *Science* **270**: 769–775.

Ungerleider, L. G. and Haxby, J. V. (1994). 'What' and 'Where' in the human brain, *Current Opinion in Neurobiology* **4**: 157–165.

Ungerleider, L. G. and Mishkin, M. (1982). Two cortical visual systems, *in* D. Ingle, M. A. Goodale and R. J. W. Mansfield (eds), *Analysis of Visual Behaviour*, MIT Press, Cambridge, MA.

Usher, M. and McClelland, J. (2001). On the time course of perceptual choice: the leaky competing accumulator model, *Psychological Reviews* **108**: 550–592.

Usher, M. and Niebur, E. (1996). Modelling the temporal dynamics of IT neurons in visual search: A mechanism for top-down selective attention, *Journal of Cognitive Neuroscience* **8**: 311–327.

Valenstein, E. S. (1974). *Brain Control. A Critical Examination of Brain Stimulation and Psychosurgery*, Wiley,

New York.

Vallar, G. and Pernai, D. (1986). The anatomy of unilateral neglect after right-hemisphere stroke lesions. a clinical/CT-scan correlation study in man, *Neuropsychologia* **24**: 609–622.

Van de Laar, P., Heskes, T. and Gielen, S. (1997). Task-dependent learning of attention, *Neural Networks* **10**: 981–992.

Van der Kooy, D., Koda, L. Y., McGinty, J. F., Gerfen, C. R. and Bloom, F. E. (1984). The organization of projections from the cortex, amygdala, and hypothalamus to the nucleus of the solitary tract in rat, *Journal of Comparative Neurology* **224**: 1–24.

Van Essen, D., Anderson, C. H. and Felleman, D. J. (1992). Information processing in the primate visual system: an integrated systems perspective, *Science* **255**: 419–423.

van Haeften, T., Baks-te Bulte, L., Goede, P. H., Wouterlood, F. G. and Witter, M. P. (2003). Morphological and numerical analysis of synaptic interactions between neurons in deep and superficial layers of the entorhinal cortex of the rat, *Hippocampus* **13**: 943–952.

Van Hoesen, G. W. (1981). The differential distribution, diversity and sprouting of cortical projections to the amygdala in the rhesus monkey, *in* Y. Ben-Ari (ed.), *The Amygdaloid Complex*, Elsevier, Amsterdam, pp. 77–90.

Van Hoesen, G. W. (1982). The parahippocampal gyrus. New observations regarding its cortical connections in the monkey, *Trends in Neurosciences* **5**: 345–350.

Van Hoesen, G. W., Yeterian, E. H. and Lavizzo-Mourey, R. (1981). Widespread corticostriate projections from temporal cortex of the rhesus monkey, *Journal of Comparative Neurology* **199**: 205–219.

Van Hoesen, G. W., Morecraft, R. J. and Vogt, B. A. (1993). Connections of the monkey cingulate cortex, *in* B. A. Vogt and M. Gabriel (eds), *The Neurobiology of the Cingulate Cortex and Limbic Thalamus: A Comprehensive Handbook*, Birkhauser, Boston, pp. 249–284.

van Veen, V., Cohen, J. D., Botvinick, M. M., Stenger, A. V. and Carter, C. S. (2001). Anterior cingulate cortex, conflict monitoring, and levels of processing, *Neuroimage* **14**: 1302–1308.

Vann, S. D. and Aggleton, J. P. (2004). The mammillary bodies: two memory systems in one?, *Nature Reviews Neuroscience* **5**: 35–44.

VanRullen, R., Guyonneau, R. and Thorpe, S. J. (2005). Spike times make sense, *Trends in Neuroscience* **28**: 1–4.

Vazdarjanova, A. and Guzowski, J. F. (2004). Differences in hippocampal neuronal population responses to modifications of an environmental context: Evidence for distinct, yet complementary, functions of CA3 and CA1 ensembles, *Journal of Neuroscience* **24**: 6489–6496.

Verhagen, J. V., Rolls, E. and Kadohisa, M. (2003). Neurons in the primate orbitofrontal cortex respond to fat texture independently of viscosity, *Journal of Neurophysiology* **90**: 1514–1525.

Verhagen, J. V., Kadohisa, M. and Rolls, E. T. (2004). The primate insular taste cortex: neuronal representations of the viscosity, fat texture, grittiness, and the taste of foods in the mouth, *Journal of Neurophysiology* **92**: 1685–1699.

Vinje, W. E. and Gallant, J. L. (2000). Sparse coding and decorrelation in primary visual cortex during natural vision, *Science* **287**: 1273–1276.

Voellm, B. A., De Araujo, I. E. T., Cowen, P. J., Rolls, E. T., Kringelbach, M. L., Smith, K. A., Jezzard, P., Heal, R. J. and Matthews, P. M. (2004). Methamphetamine activates reward circuitry in drug naive human subjects, *Neuropsychopharmacology* **29**: 1715–1722.

Vogels, R. and Biederman, I. (2002). Effects of illumination intensity and direction on object coding in macaque inferior temporal cortex, *Cerebral Cortex* **12**: 756–766.

Vogt, B. A. and Pandya, D. N. (1987). Cingulate cortex of the rhesus monkey: II. Cortical afferents, *Journal of Comparative Neurology* **262**: 271–289.

Vogt, B. A. and Sikes, R. W. (2000). The medial pain system, cingulate cortex, and parallel processing of nociceptive information, *Progress in Brain Research* **122**: 223–235.

Vogt, B. A., Pandya, D. N. and Rosene, D. L. (1987). Cingulate cortex of the rhesus monkey: I. Cytoarchitecture and thalamic afferents, *Journal of Comparative Neurology* **262**: 256–270.

Vogt, B. A., Derbyshire, S. and Jones, A. K. P. (1996). Pain processing in four regions of human cingulate cortex localized with co-registered PET and MR imaging, *European Journal of Neuroscience* **8**: 1461–1473.

Vogt, B. A., Berger, G. R. and Derbyshire, S. W. G. (2003). Structural and functional dichotomy of human midcingulate cortex, *European Journal of Neuroscience* **18**: 3134–3144.

Vogt, B. (ed.) (2007). *Cingulate Neurobiology and Disease*, Oxford University Press, Oxford.

Von der Malsburg, C. and Bienenstock, E. (1986). Statistical coding and short-term synaptic plasticity: a scheme for knowledge representation in the brain, *in* E. Bienenstock, F. Fogelman-Soulie and G. Weisbach (eds), *Disordered Systems and Biological Organization, NATO ASI Series*, Vol. F20, Springer, Berlin, pp. 247–272.

Waelti, P., Dickinson, A. and Schultz, W. (2001). Dopamine responses comply with basic assumptions of formal learning theory, *Nature* **412**: 43–48.

Walker, M. P. and Stickgold, R. (2006). Sleep, memory, and plasticity, *Annual Review of Psychology* **57**: 139–166.

Walker, R. (1995). Spatial and object-based neglect, *Neurocase* **1**: 371–383.

Wallace, D. G. and Whishaw, I. Q. (2003). NMDA lesions of Ammon's horn and the dentate gyrus disrupt the direct and temporally paced homing displayed by rats exploring a novel environment: evidence for a role of the hippocampus in dead reckoning, *European Journal of Neuroscience* **18**: 513–523.

Wallenstein, G. V. and Hasselmo, M. E. (1997). GABAergic modulation of hippocampal population activity: sequence learning, place field development, and the phase precession effect, *Journal of Neurophysiology* **78**: 393–408.

Wallis, G. and Baddeley, R. (1997). Optimal unsupervised learning in invariant object recognition, *Neural Computation* **9**: 883–894.

Wallis, G. and Bülthoff, H. (1999). Learning to recognize objects, *Trends in Cognitive Sciences* **3**: 22–31.

Wallis, G. and Rolls, E. T. (1997). Invariant face and object recognition in the visual system, *Progress in Neurobiology* **51**: 167–194.

Wallis, G., Rolls, E. T. and Foldiak, P. (1993). Learning invariant responses to the natural transformations of objects, *International Joint Conference on Neural Networks* **2**: 1087–1090.

Wallis, J. D. and Miller, E. K. (2003). Neuronal activity in primate dorsolateral and orbital prefrontal cortex during performance of a reward preference task, *European Journal of Neuroscience* **18**: 2069–2081.

Wallis, J., Anderson, K. and Miller, E. (2001). Single neurons in prefrontal cortex encode abstract rules, *Nature* **411**: 953–956.

Walton, M. E., Bannerman, D. M. and Rushworth, M. F. S. (2002). The role of rat medial frontal cortex in effort-based decision making, *Journal of Neuroscience* **22**: 10996–11003.

Walton, M. E., Bannerman, D. M., Alterescu, K. and Rushworth, M. F. S. (2003). Functional specialization within medial frontal cortex of the anterior cingulate for evaluating effort-related decisions, *Journal of Neuroscience* **23**: 6475–6479.

Wang, X. J. (1999). Synaptic basis of cortical persistent activity: the importance of NMDA receptors to working memory, *Journal of Neuroscience* **19**: 9587–9603.

Wang, X. J. (2002). Probabilistic decision making by slow reverberation in cortical circuits, *Neuron* **36**: 955–968.

Warrington, E. K. and Weiskrantz, L. (1973). An analysis of short-term and long-term memory defects in man, *in* J. A. Deutsch (ed.), *The Physiological Basis of Memory*, Academic Press, New York, chapter 10, pp. 365–395.

Warthen, M. W. and Kesner, R. P. (2007). CA3 involvement in one-trial short-term memory for cued recall object-place associations, *In preparation*.

Wasserman, E., Kirkpatrick-Steger, A. and Biederman, I. (1998). Effects of geon deletion, scrambling, and movement on picture identification in pigeons, *Journal of Experimental Psychology – Animal Behavior Processes* **24**: 34–46.

Watanabe, K., Lauwereyns, J. and Hikosaka, O. (2003). Neural correlates of rewarded and unrewarded eye movements in the primate caudate nucleus, *Journal of Neuroscience* **23**: 10052–10057.

Watanabe, S., Lea, S. E. G. and Dittrich, W. H. (1993). What can we learn from experiments on pigeon discrimination?, *in* H. P. Zeigler and H.-J. Bischof (eds), *Vision, Brain, and Behavior in Birds*, MIT Press, Cambridge, MA, pp. 351–376.

Weiskrantz, L. (1956). Behavioral changes associated with ablation of the amygdaloid complex in monkeys, *Journal of Comparative and Physiological Psychology* **49**: 381–391.

Weiskrantz, L. (1998). *Blindsight*, 2nd edn, Oxford University Press, Oxford.

Weiss, C., Bouwmeester, H., Power, J. M. and Disterhoft, J. F. (1999). Hippocampal lesions prevent trace eyeblink conditioning in the freely moving rat, *Behavioural Brain Research* **99**: 123–132.

Weiss, F. and Koob, G. F. (2001). Drug addiction: functional neurotoxicity of the brain reward systems, *Neurotoxicity Research* **3**: 145–156.

Welford, A. T. (ed.) (1980). *Reaction Times*, Academic Press, London.

Werner, G. and Mountcastle, V. B. (1965). Neural activity in mechanoreceptive cutaneous afferents: stimulus-response relations, Weber functions, and information transmission, *Journal of Neurophysiology* **28**: 359–397.

West, R. A. and Larson, C. R. (1995). Neurons of the anterior mesial cortex related to faciovocal activity in the awake monkey, *Journal of Neurophysiology* **74**: 1856–1869.

Whishaw, I. Q., Hines, D. J. and Wallace, D. G. (2001). Dead reckoning (path integration) requires the hippocampal formation: evidence from spontaneous exploration and spatial learning tasks in light (allothetic) and dark (idiothetic) tests, *Behavioral Brain Research* **127**: 49–69.

Whitehouse, P., Price, D., Struble, R., Clarke, A., Coyle, J. and Delong, M. (1982). Alzheimer's disease in senile dementia: loss of neurones in the basal forebrain, *Science* **215**: 1237–1239.

Whitelaw, R. B., Markou, A., Robbins, T. W. and Everitt, B. J. (1996). Excitotoxic lesions of the basolateral amygdala impair the acquisition of cocaine-seeking behaviour under a second-order schedule of reinforcement, *Psychopharmacology* **127**: 213–224.

Whittlesea, B. W. A. (1983). *Representation and Generalization of Concepts: the Abstractive and Episodic Perspectives Evaluated*, Unpublished doctoral dissertation, MacMaster University.

Widrow, B. and Hoff, M. E. (1960). Adaptive switching circuits, *1960 IRE WESCON Convention Record, Part 4 (Reprinted in Anderson and Rosenfeld, 1988)*, IRE, New York, pp. 96–104.

Widrow, B. and Stearns, S. D. (1985). *Adaptive Signal Processing*, Prentice-Hall, Englewood Cliffs, NJ.

Wiener, S. I. and Taube, J. (eds) (2005). *Head Direction Cells and the Neural Mechanisms Underlying Directional Orientation*, MIT Press, Cambridge, MA.

Williams, G. and Goldman-Rakic, P. (1995). Modulation of memory fields by dopamine D1 receptors in the prefrontal cortex, *Nature* **376**: 572–575.

Williams, G. V., Rolls, E. T., Leonard, C. M. and Stern, C. (1993). Neuronal responses in the ventral striatum of the behaving macaque, *Behavioural Brain Research* **55**: 243–252.

Williams, Z. M., Bush, G., Rauch, S. L., Cosgrove, G. R. and Eskandar, E. N. (2004). Human anterior cingulate neurons and the integration of monetary reward with motor responses, *Nature Neuroscience* **7**: 1370–1375.

Wills, T. J., Lever, C., Cacucci, F., Burgess, N. and O'Keefe, J. (2005). Attractor dynamics in the hippocampal representation of the local environment, *Science* **308**: 873–876.

Willshaw, D. J. (1981). Holography, associative memory, and inductive generalization, *in* G. E. Hinton and J. A. Anderson (eds), *Parallel Models of Associative Memory*, Erlbaum, Hillsdale, NJ, chapter 3, pp. 83–104.

Willshaw, D. J. and Buckingham, J. T. (1990). An assessment of Marr's theory of the hippocampus as a temporary memory store, *Philosophical Transactions of The Royal Society of London, Series B* **329**: 205–215.

Willshaw, D. J. and Longuet-Higgins, H. C. (1969). The holophone – recent developments, *in* D. Mitchie (ed.), *Machine Intelligence*, Vol. 4, Edinburgh University Press, Edinburgh.

Willshaw, D. J. and von der Malsburg, C. (1976). How patterned neural connections can be set up by self-organization, *Proceedings of The Royal Society of London, Series B* **194**: 431–445.

Wilson, C. J. (1995). The contribution of cortical neurons to the firing pattern of striatal spiny neurons, *in* J. C. Houk, J. L. Davis and D. G. Beiser (eds), *Models of Information Processing in the Basal Ganglia*, MIT Press, Cambridge, MA, chapter 3, pp. 29–50.

Wilson, F. A. W. and Rolls, E. T. (1990a). Learning and memory are reflected in the responses of reinforcement-related neurons in the primate basal forebrain, *Journal of Neuroscience* **10**: 1254–1267.

Wilson, F. A. W. and Rolls, E. T. (1990b). Neuronal responses related to reinforcement in the primate basal forebrain, *Brain Research* **509**: 213–231.

Wilson, F. A. W. and Rolls, E. T. (1990c). Neuronal responses related to the novelty and familiarity of visual stimuli in the substantia innominata, diagonal band of broca and periventricular region of the primate, *Experimental Brain Research* **80**: 104–120.

Wilson, F. A. W. and Rolls, E. T. (1993). The effects of stimulus novelty and familiarity on neuronal activity in the amygdala of monkeys performing recognition memory tasks, *Experimental Brain Research* **93**: 367–382.

Wilson, F. A. W. and Rolls, E. T. (2005). The primate amygdala and reinforcement: a dissociation between rule-based and associatively-mediated memory revealed in amygdala neuronal activity, *Neuroscience* **133**: 1061–1072.

Wilson, F. A. W., Riches, I. P. and Brown, M. W. (1990). Hippocampus and medial temporal cortex: neuronal responses related to behavioural responses during the performance of memory tasks by primates, *Behavioral Brain Research* **40**: 7–28.

Wilson, F. A. W., O'Sclaidhe, S. P. and Goldman-Rakic, P. S. (1993). Dissociation of object and spatial processing domains in primate prefrontal cortex, *Science* **260**: 1955–1958.

Wilson, H. and Cowan, J. (1972). Excitatory and inhibitory interactions in localised populations of model neurons, *Biophysics Journal* **12**: 1–24.

Wilson, H. R. (1999). *Spikes, Decisions and Actions: Dynamical Foundations of Neuroscience*, Oxford University Press, Oxford.

Wilson, M. A. (2002). Hippocampal memory formation, plasticity, and the role of sleep, *Neurobiology of Learning and Memory* **78**: 565–569.

Wilson, M. A. and McNaughton, B. L. (1994). Reactivation of hippocampal ensemble memories during sleep, *Science* **265**: 603–604.

Winkielman, P. and Berridge, K. C. (2003). What is an unconscious emotion?, *Cognition and Emotion* **17**: 181–211.

Winkielman, P. and Berridge, K. C. (2005). Unconscious affective reactions to masked happy versus angry faces influence consumption behavior and judgments of value, *Personality amd Social Psychology Bulletin* **31**: 111–135.

Winslow, J. T. and Insel, T. R. (2004). Neuroendrocrine basis of social recognition, *Current Opinion in Neurobiology* **14**: 248–253.

Winston, P. H. (1975). Learning structural descriptions from examples, *in* P. H. Winston (ed.), *The Psychology of Computer Vision*, McGraw-Hill, New York.

Winterer, G. and Weinberger, D. R. (2004). Genes, dopamine and cortical signal-to-noise ratio in schizophrenia, *Trends in Neurosciences* **27**: 683–690.

Winterer, G., Ziller, M., Dorn, H., Frick, K., Mulert, C., Wuebben, Y., Herrmann, W. M. and Coppola, R. (2000). Schizophrenia: reduced signal-to-noise ratio and impaired phase-locking during information processing, *Clinical Neurophysiology* **111**: 837–849.

Winterer, G., Coppola, R., Goldberg, T. E., Egan, M. F., Jones, D. W., Sanchez, C. E. and Weinberger, D. R. (2004). Prefrontal broadband noise, working memory, and genetic risk for schizophrenia, *American Journal of Psychiatry* **161**: 490–500.

Winterer, G., Musso, F., Beckmann, C., Mattay, V., Egan, M. F., Jones, D. W., Callicott, J. H., Coppola, R. and Weinberger, D. R. (2006). Instability of prefrontal signal processing in schizophrenia, *American Journal of Psychiatry* **163**: 1960–1968.

Wirth, S., Yanike, M., Frank, L. M., Smith, A. C., Brown, E. N. and Suzuki, W. A. (2003). Single neurons in the monkeys hippocampus and learning of new associations, *Science* **300**: 1578–1581.

Witter, M. P. (1993). Organization of the entorhinal–hippocampal system: a review of current anatomical data,

Hippocampus **3**: 33–44.

Witter, M. P., Groenewegen, H. J., Lopes da Silva, F. H. and Lohman, A. H. M. (1989a). Functional organization of the extrinsic and intrinsic circuitry of the parahippocampal region, *Progress in Neurobiology* **33**: 161–254.

Witter, M. P., Van Hoesen, G. W. and Amaral, D. G. (1989b). Topographical organisation of the entorhinal projection to the dentate gyrus of the monkey, *Journal of Neuroscience* **9**: 216–228.

Witter, M. P., Naber, P. A., van Haeften, T., Machielsen, W. C., Rombouts, S. A., Barkhof, F., Scheltens, P. and Lopes da Silva, F. H. (2000a). Cortico-hippocampal communication by way of parallel parahippocampal-subicular pathways, *Hippocampus* **10**: 398–410.

Witter, M. P., Wouterlood, F. G., Naber, P. A. and Van Haeften, T. (2000b). Anatomical organization of the parahippocampal-hippocampal network, *Annals of the New York Academcy of Sciences* **911**: 1–24.

Wolfe, J. M. (1994). Guided search 2.0: A revised model of visual search, *Psychonomic Bulletin and Review* **1**: 202–238.

Wolfe, J. M., Cave, K. R. and Franzel, S. L. (1989). Guided search: An alternative to the feature integration model for visual search, *Journal of Experimental Psychology: Human Perception and Performance* **15**: 419–433.

Wood, E. R., Agster, K. M. and Eichenbaum, H. (2004). One-trial odor–reward association: a form of event memory not dependent on hippocampal function, *Behavioral Neuroscience* **118**: 526–539.

Wu, X., Baxter, R. A. and Levy, W. B. (1996). Context codes and the effect of noisy learning on a simplified hippocampal CA3 model, *Biological Cybernetics* **74**: 159–165.

Wurtz, R. H. and Kandel, E. R. (2000a). Central visual pathways, *in* E. R. Kandel, J. H. Schwartz and T. M. Jessell (eds), *Principles of Neural Science*, 4th edn, McGraw-Hill, New York, chapter 27, pp. 543–547.

Wurtz, R. H. and Kandel, E. R. (2000b). Perception of motion depth and form, *in* E. R. Kandel, J. H. Schwartz and T. M. Jessell (eds), *Principles of Neural Science*, 4th edn, McGraw-Hill, New York, chapter 28, pp. 548–571.

Wyss, R., Konig, P. and Verschure, P. F. (2006). A model of the ventral visual system based on temporal stability and local memory, *PLoS Biology* **4**: e120.

Xavier, G. F., Oliveira-Filho, F. J. and Santos, A. M. (1999). Dentate gyrus-selective colchicine lesion and disruption of performance in spatial tasks: difficulties in "place strategy" because of a lack of flexibility in the use of environmental cues?, *Hippocampus* **9**: 668–681.

Xiang, J. Z. and Brown, M. W. (1998). Differential neuronal encoding of novelty, familiarity and recency in regions of the anterior temporal lobe, *Neuropharmacology* **37**: 657–676.

Xiang, J. Z. and Brown, M. W. (2004). Neuronal responses related to long-term recognition memory processes in prefrontal cortex, *Neuron* **42**: 817–829.

Xiang, Z., Huguenard, J. and Prince, D. (1998). GABA-A receptor mediated currents in interneurons and pyramidal cells of rat visual cortex, *Journal of Physiology* **506**: 715–730.

Yamane, S., Kaji, S. and Kawano, K. (1988). What facial features activate face neurons in the inferotemporal cortex of the monkey?, *Experimental Brain Research* **73**: 209–214.

Yan, J. and Scott, T. R. (1996). The effect of satiety on responses of gustatory neurons in the amygdala of alert cynomolgus macaques, *Brain Research* **740**: 193–200.

Yaxley, S., Rolls, E. T., Sienkiewicz, Z. J. and Scott, T. R. (1985). Satiety does not affect gustatory activity in the nucleus of the solitary tract of the alert monkey, *Brain Research* **347**: 85–93.

Yaxley, S., Rolls, E. T. and Sienkiewicz, Z. J. (1988). The responsiveness of neurones in the insular gustatory cortex of the macaque monkey is independent of hunger, *Physiology and Behavior* **42**: 223–229.

Yaxley, S., Rolls, E. T. and Sienkiewicz, Z. J. (1990). Gustatory responses of single neurons in the insula of the macaque monkey, *Journal of Neurophysiology* **63**: 689–700.

Yin, H. H., Knowlton, B. J. and Balleine, B. W. (2004). Lesions of dorsolateral striatum preserve outcome expectancy but disrupt habit formation in instrumental learning, *European Journal of Neuroscience* **19**: 181–189.

Yoganarasimha, D., Yu, X. and Knierim, J. J. (2006). Head direction cell representations maintain internal coherence during conflicting proximal and distal cue rotations: comparison with hippocampal place cells, *Journal of Neuroscience* **26**: 622–631.

Yokel, R. A. and Wise, R. A. (1975). Increased lever pressing for amphetamine after pimozide in rats: implications for a dopamine theory of reinforcement, *Science* **187**: 547–549.

Young, A., Newcombe, F. and Ellis, A. (1991). Different impairments contribute to neglect dyslexia, *Cognitive Neuropsychology* **8**: 177–191.

Young, A. W., Aggleton, J. P., Hellawell, D. J., Johnson, M., Broks, P. and Hanley, J. R. (1995). Face processing impairments after amygdalotomy, *Brain* **118**: 15–24.

Young, A. W., Hellawell, D. J., Van de Wal, C. and Johnson, M. (1996). Facial expression processing after amygdalotomy, *Neuropsychologia* **34**: 31–39.

Zald, D. H. and Rauch, S. L. (eds) (2006). *The Orbitofrontal Cortex*, Oxford University Press, Oxford.

Zatorre, R. J. and Jones-Gotman, M. (1991). Human olfactory discrimination after unilateral frontal or temporal lobectomy, *Brain* **114**: 71–84.

Zatorre, R. J., Jones-Gotman, M., Evans, A. C. and Meyer, E. (1992). Functional localization of human olfactory cortex, *Nature* **360**: 339–340.

Zatorre, R. J., Jones-Gotman, M. and Rouby, C. (2000). Neural mechanisms involved in odor pleasantness and intensity judgments, *NeuroReport* **11**: 2711–2716.

Zhang, K. (1996). Representation of spatial orientation by the intrinsic dynamics of the head-direction cell ensemble: A theory, *Journal of Neuroscience* **16**: 2112–2126.

Zhang, M., Gosnell, B. A. and Kelley, A. E. (1998). Intake of high-fat food is selectively enhanced by mu opioid receptor stimulation within the nucleus accumbens, *Journal of Pharmacology and Experimental Therapeutics* **285**: 908–914.

Zheng, P., Zhang, X.-X., Bunney, B. S. and Shi, W.-X. (1999). Opposite modulation of cortical N-methyl-D-aspartate receptor-mediated responses by low and high concentrations of dopamine, *Neuroscience* **91**: 527–535.

Zink, C. F., Pagnoni, G., Martin, M. E., Dhamala, M. and Berns, G. S. (2003). Human striatal responses to salient nonrewarding stimuli, *Journal of Neuroscience* **23**: 8092–8097.

Zink, C. F., Pagnoni, G., Martin-Skurski, M. E., Chappelow, J. C. and Berns, G. S. (2004). Human striatal responses to monetary reward depend on saliency, *Neuron* **42**: 509–517.

Zipser, K., Lamme, V. and Schiller, P. (1996). Contextual modulation in primary visual cortex, *Journal of Neuroscience* **16**: 7376–7389.

Zohary, E., Shadlen, M. N. and Newsome, W. T. (1994). Correlated neuronal discharge rate and its implications for psychophysical performance, *Nature* **370**: 140–143.

Zola-Morgan, S., Squire, L. R., Amaral, D. G. and Suzuki, W. A. (1989). Lesions of perirhinal and parahippocampal cortex that spare the amygdala and hippocampal formation produce severe memory impairment, *Journal of Neuroscience* **9**: 4355–4370.

Zola-Morgan, S., Squire, L. R. and Ramus, S. J. (1994). Severity of memory impairment in monkeys as a function of locus and extent of damage within the medial temporal lobe memory system, *Hippocampus* **4**: 483–494.

Zucker, S. W., Dobbins, A. and Iverson, L. (1989). Two stages of curve detection suggest two styles of visual computation, *Neural Computation* **1**: 68–81.

Index

Appendix 5 Colour Plates

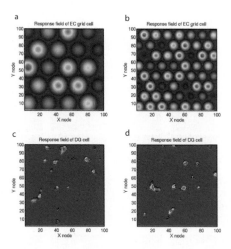

Fig. 2.19. Simulation of competitive learning in the dentate gyrus to produce place cells from the entorhinal cortex grid cell inputs. (a and b) Firing rate profiles of two entorhinal cortex (EC) grid cells with frequencies of 4 and 7 cycles. (c and d) Firing rate profiles of two dentate gyrus (DG) cells with no training. (After Rolls, Stringer and Elliot 2006.)

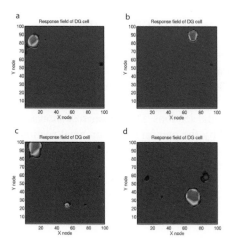

Fig. 2.20. Simulation of competitive learning in the dentate gyrus to produce place cells from the entorhinal cortex grid cell inputs. (a and b) Firing rate profiles of two DG cells after training with the Hebb rule. (c and d) Firing rate profiles of two DG cells after training with the trace rule with $\eta=0.8$. (After Rolls, Stringer and Elliot 2006.)

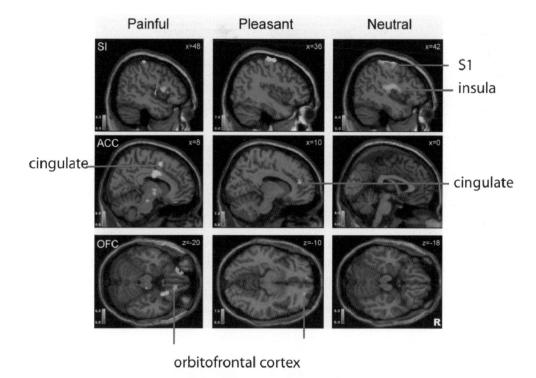

Fig. 3.5. Brain activation to painful, pleasant, and neutral touch of the human brain. The top row shows strongest activation of the somatosensory cortex S1/insula by the neutral touch, on sagittal sections (parallel to the midline). The middle row shows activation of the most anterior part of the anterior cingulate cortex by the pleasant touch, and of a more posterior part by the painful touch, on sagittal sections. The bottom row shows activation of the orbitofrontal cortex by the pleasant and by the painful touch, on axial sections (in the horizontal plane). The activations were thresholded at p<0.0001 to show the extent of the activations. (After Rolls, O'Doherty et al., 2003d.)

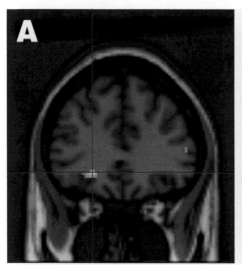 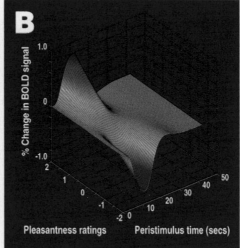

3.14. Areas of the human orbitofrontal cortex with activations correlating with pleasantness ratings for food in the mouth. (A) Coronal section through the region of the orbitofrontal cortex from the random effects group analysis showing the peak in the left orbitofrontal cortex (Talairach co-ordinates X,Y,Z= –22,34,–8, z-score=4.06), in which the BOLD signal in the voxels shown in yellow was significantly correlated with the subjects' subjective pleasantness ratings of the foods throughout an experiment in which the subjects were hungry and found the food pleasant, and were then fed to satiety with the food, after which the pleasantness of the food decreased to neutral or slightly unpleasant. The design was a sensory-specific satiety design, and the pleasantness of the food not eaten in the meal, and the BOLD activation in the orbitofrontal cortex, were not altered by eating the other food to satiety. The two foods were tomato juice and chocolate milk. (B) Plot of the magnitude of the fitted haemodynamic response from a representative single subject against the subjective pleasantness ratings (on a scale from –2 to +2) and peristimulus time in seconds. (After Kringelbach, O'Doherty, Rolls and Andrews 2003.)

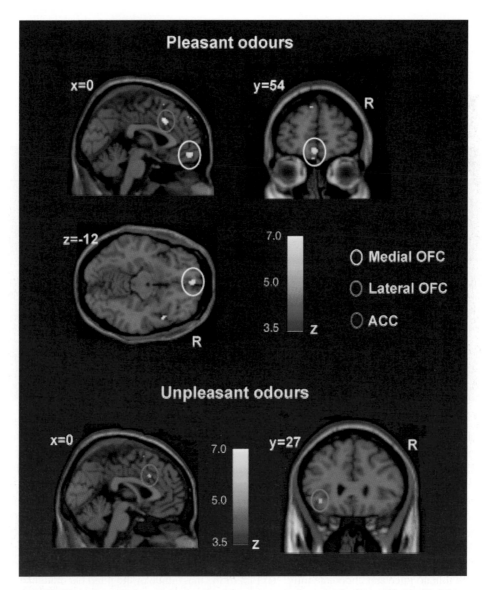

Fig. 3.17 The representation of pleasant and unpleasant odours in the human brain. Top: group conjunction results for the 3 pleasant odours. Sagittal, horizontal and coronal views are shown at the levels indicated, all including the same activation in the medial orbitofrontal cortex, OFC (X,Y,Z = 0,54,–12; z=5.23). Also shown is activation for the 3 pleasant odours in the anterior cingulate cortex, ACC (X,Y,Z= 2,20,32; z=5.44). These activations were significant at p<0.05 fully corrected for multiple comparisons. Bottom: Group conjunction results for the 3 unpleasant odours. The sagittal view (left) shows an activated region of the anterior cingulate cortex (X,Y,Z= 0,18,36; z=4.42, p<0.05, S.V.C.). The coronal view (right) shows an activated region of the lateral orbitofrontal cortex (–36,27,–8; z=4.23, p<0.05 S.V.C.). All the activations were thresholded at p<0.00001 to show the extent of the activations. (After Rolls, Kringelbach and De Araujo 2003c.)

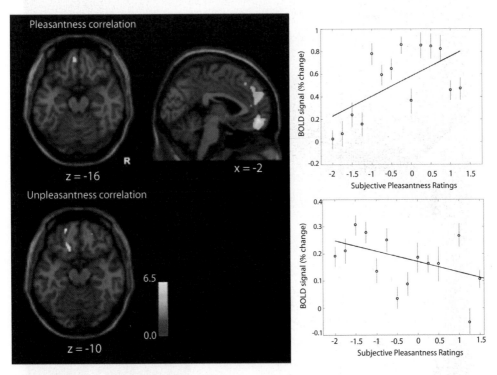

Fig. 3.18 The representation of pleasant and unpleasant odours in the human brain. Random effects group correlation analysis of the BOLD signal with the subjective pleasantness ratings. On the top left is shown the region of the medio-rostral orbitofrontal (peak at [–2,52,–10]; z=4.28) correlating positively with pleasantness ratings, as well as the region of the anterior cingulate cortex in the top middle. On the far top-right of the figure is shown the relation between the subjective pleasantness ratings and the BOLD signal from this cluster (in the medial orbitofrontal cortex at Y=52), together with the regression line. The means and sem across subjects are shown. At the bottom of the figure is shown the regions of left more lateral orbitofrontal cortex (peaks at [–20,54,–14]; z=4.26 and [–16,28,–18]; z=4.08) correlating negatively with pleasantness ratings. On the far bottom-right of the figure is shown the relation between the subjective pleasantness ratings and the BOLD signal from the first cluster (in the lateral orbitofrontal cortex at Y=54), together with the regression line. The means and sem across subjects are shown. The activations were thresholded at p<0.0001 for extent. (After Rolls, Kringelbach and De Araujo 2003c.)

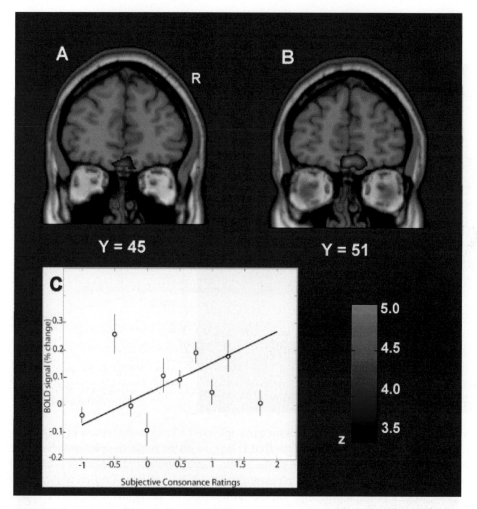

Fig. 3.21 Flavour formation in the human brain, shown by cross-modal olfactory–taste convergence. Brain areas where activations were correlated with the subjective ratings for stimulus (taste–odour) consonance and pleasantness. (A) A second-level, random effects analysis based on individual contrasts (the consonance ratings being the only effect of interest) revealed a significant activation in a medial part of the anterior orbitofrontal cortex. (B) Random effects analysis based on the pleasantness ratings showed a significant cluster of activation located in a (nearby) medial part of the anterior orbitofrontal cortex. The images were thresholded at $p<0.0001$ for illustration. (C) The relation between the BOLD signal from the cluster of voxels in the medial orbitofrontal cortex shown in (A) and the subjective consonance ratings. The analyses shown included all the stimuli included in this investigation. The means and standard errors of the mean across subjects are shown, together with the regression line, for which $r=0.52$. (After DeAraujo, Rolls, Kringelbach, McGlone and Phillips 2003c.)

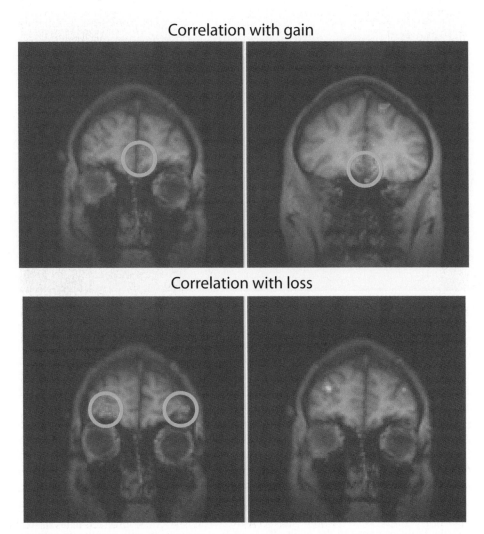

Fig. 3.25 Correlation of brain activations with the amount of money won (upper) or lost (lower) in a visual discrimination reversal task with probabilistic monetary reward and loss. Voxels in the OFC and other regions whose activity increases relative to the increasing magnitude of Reward or of Punishment obtained. Voxels in an area of left medial OFC (Talairach coordinates [X,Y,Z]: [–6,34,–28]) correlated positively with Reward, and voxels in an area of right lateral OFC (Talairach co-ordinates [X,Y,Z]: [28,60,–6]) correlated positively with Punishment. (After O'Doherty, Kringelbach, Rolls, Hornak and Andrews 2001a.)

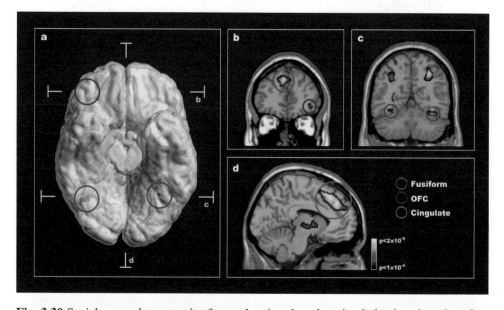

Fig. 3.30 Social reversal: composite figure showing that changing behaviour based on face expression is correlated with increased brain activity in the human orbitofrontal cortex. (a) The figure is based on two different group statistical contrasts from the neuroimaging data which are superimposed on a ventral view of the human brain with the cerebellum removed, and with indication of the location of the two coronal slices (b, c) and the transverse slice (d). The red activations in the orbitofrontal cortex (denoted OFC, maximal activation: z=4.94: 42,42,–8; and z=5.51; X,Y,Z=–46,30,–8) shown on the rendered brain arise from a comparison of reversal events with stable acquisition events, while the blue activations in the fusiform gyrus (denoted Fusiform, maximal activation: z>8, 36,–60,–20; and z=7.80, –30,–56,–16) arise from the main effects of face expression. (b) The coronal slice through the frontal part of the brain shows the cluster in the right orbitofrontal cortex across all nine subjects when comparing reversal events with stable acquisition events. Significant activity was also seen in an extended area of the anterior cingulate/paracingulate cortex (denoted Cingulate, maximal activation: z=6.88, –8,22,52; green circle). (c) The coronal slice through the posterior part of the brain shows the brain response to the main effects of face expression with significant activation in the fusiform gyrus and the cortex in the intraparietal sulcus (maximal activation: z>8, 32,–60,46; and z>8, –32,–60,44). (d) The transverse slice shows the extent of the activation in the anterior cingulate/paracingulate cortex when comparing reversal events with stable acquisition events. Group statistical results are superimposed on a ventral view of the human brain with the cerebellum removed, and on coronal and transverse slices of the same template brain (activations are thresholded at p=0.0001 for purposes of illustration to show their extent). (After Kringelbach and Rolls 2003.)

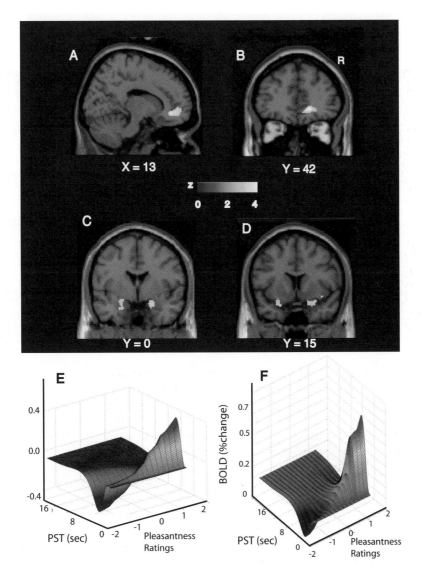

Fig. 3.33 Cognition and emotion. Group (random) effects analysis showing the brain regions where the BOLD signal was correlated with pleasantness ratings given to the test odour. The pleasantness ratings were being modulated by the word labels. (A) Activations in the rostral anterior cingulate cortex, in the region adjoining the medial OFC, shown in a sagittal slice. (B) The same activation shown coronally. (C) Bilateral activations in the amygdala. (D) These activations extended anteriorly to the primary olfactory cortex. The image was thresholded at p<0.0001 uncorrected in order to show the extent of the activation. (E) Parametric plots of the data averaged across all subjects showing that the percentage BOLD change (fitted) correlates with the pleasantness ratings in the region shown in A and B. The parametric plots were very similar for the primary olfactory region shown in D. PST, post-stimulus time (s). (F) Parametric plots for the amygdala region shown in C. (After DeAraujo, Rolls, Velazco, Margot and Cayeux 2005.)

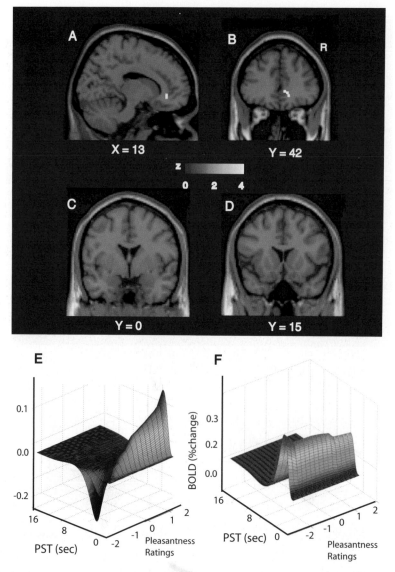

Fig. 3.34 Cognition and emotion. Group (random) effects analysis showing the brain regions where the BOLD signal was correlated with pleasantness ratings given to the clean air. The pleasantness ratings were being modulated by the word labels. (A) Activations in the rostral anterior cingulate cortex, in the region adjoining the medial OFC, shown in a sagittal slice. (B) The same activation shown coronally. No significant correlations were found with clean air in the amygdala (C) or primary olfactory cortex (D). The image was thresholded at $p<0.0001$ uncorrected in order to show the extent of the activation. (E) Parametric plots of the data averaged across all subjects showing that the percentage BOLD change (fitted) correlates with the pleasantness ratings in the region shown in A and B. PST, post-stimulus time (s). (F) Parametric plots showing activation related to stimulus presentation but not related to the pleasantness ratings for the amygdala region shown in C. (After DeAraujo, Rolls, Velazco, Margot and Cayeux 2005.)

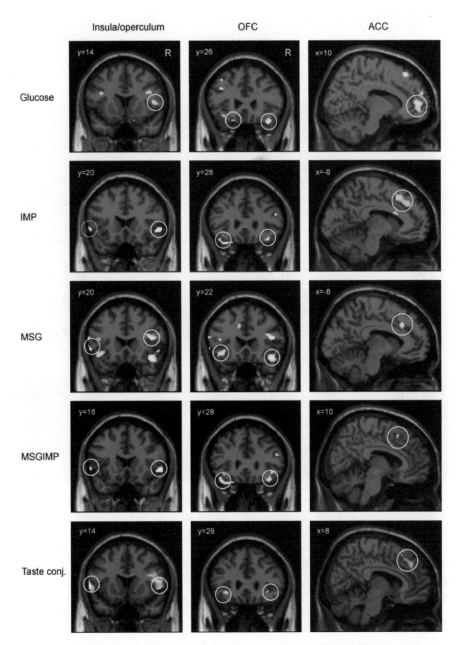

Fig. 3.50 Activation of the human primary taste cortex in the insula/frontal operculum; the orbitofrontal cortex (OFC); and the anterior cingulate cortex (ACC) by taste. The stimuli used included glucose, two umami taste stimuli (monosodium glutamate (MSG) and inosine monophosphate (IMP)), and a mixture of the two umami stimuli. Taste conj. refers to a conjunction analysis over all the taste stimuli. The taste of glucose activated the pregenual cingulate cortex, and the other tastes produced activation further back in the cingulate cortex (right column). (After DeAraujo, Kringelbach, Rolls and Hobden 2003.)

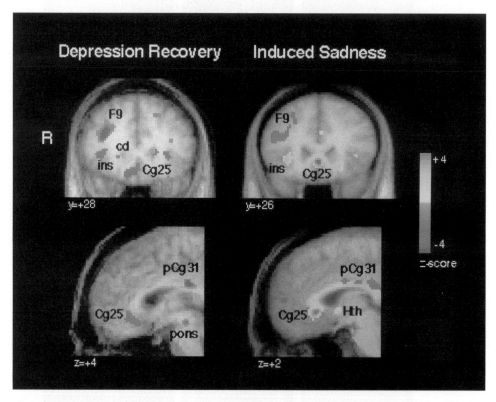

Fig. 3.52 Changes in the subgenual cingulate area (Cg25) associated with the recovery from depression (left), and with the induction of a mood state of sadness (right). Left images: z-score maps demonstrating changes in regional glucose metabolism (fluorodeoxyglucose PET) in depressed patients following 6 weeks of treatment with the antidepressant fluoxetine. Upper, coronal view; lower, sagittal view). Green indicates that the change is a decrease, and red or yellow an increase (see calibration bar on far right). Right images: changes in regional cerebral blood flow (oxygen-15 water PET) in healthy volunteers 10 min after induction of acute sadness. The recovery from depression and the induction of sadness produce opposite changes in Cg25. Reciprocal changes were seen in a dorsal part of the prefrontal cortex, labelled F9. F, frontal; cd, caudate nucleus; ins, anterior insula; Cg25, subgenual cingulate; Hth, hypothalamus; pCG31, posterior cingulate; R, right. (After Mayberg et al. 1999.)

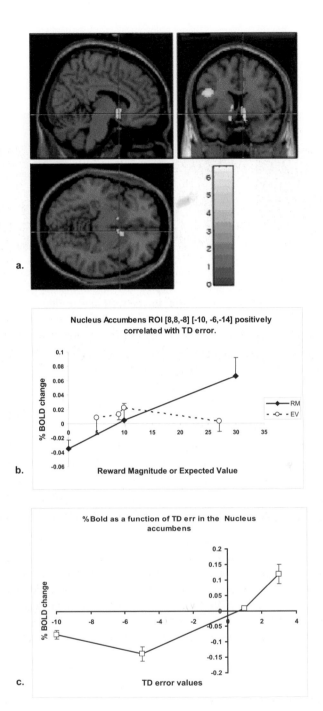

Fig. 3.57 Temporal Difference (TD) error signal in the ventral striatum in a probabilistic monetary decision-making task. (a) A positive correlation between the BOLD signal and the Temporal Difference error was found in the ventral striatum at MNI coordinates [8 8 -8] (p<0.048 fully corrected) and [-10 6 -14] (p<0.01 svc). (b) The percent change in the BOLD signal for the three Reward Magnitudes (RMs of 30 pence, 10 pence, or 0 pence) for the regions of interest defined by the correlation analysis. The means and standard errors are shown. The percent change in the BOLD signal for the four Expected Values (EVs of 27 pence, 10 pence, 9 pence, and 5 pence) for the same region of interest are also shown. (c) The percent change in the BOLD signal as a function of the TD error in the nucleus accumbens (means ± sem). (After Rolls, McCabe and Redoute 2007.)

(a) (b) (c)

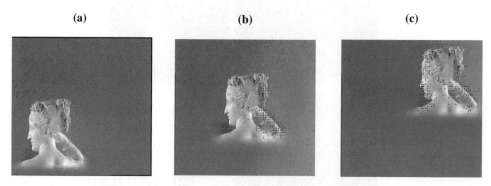

Fig. 6.27. Left-sided local space-based visual hemi-neglect for an object at different positions after unilateral damage to the PP module. The spots on the image show where activation in the parietal (PP) module is above a criterion after the network has settled. The results thus show that neurons in the PP module only reach the criterion when the object is in the right half of visual space. See text for details. (After Deco and Zihl 2004; and Rolls and Deco 2002.)

(a) (b) (c)

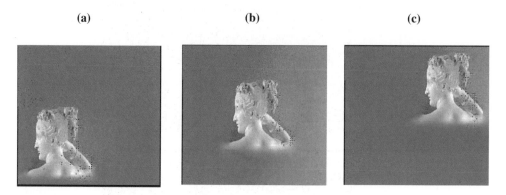

Fig. 6.28. Left-sided object-based visual hemi-neglect for an object at different translated positions after graded damage to the PP module. The damage increases gradually towards the right of the PP module. The spots on the image show where activation in the parietal (PP) module is above a criterion after the network has settled. The results thus show that neurons in the PP module only reach the criterion for the right half of the object, and do this independently of where the image is in visual space. See text for details. (After Deco and Zihl 2004; and Rolls and Deco 2002.)

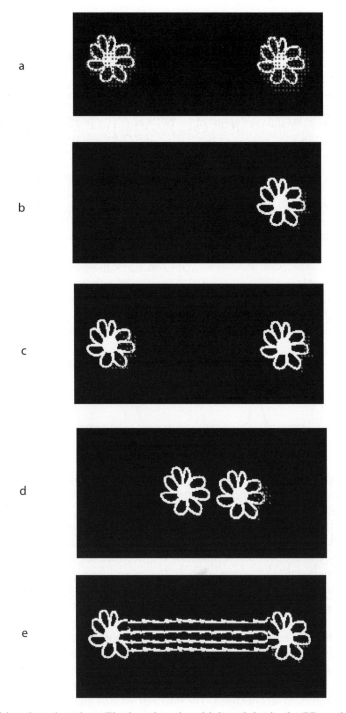

Fig. 6.29. Object-based neglect. The locations in which activity in the PP module exceeded the threshold after the network had settled with each stimulus are shown by spots. a. shows the operation of the unlesioned network, and b–e of the lesioned network (see text). (After Deco and Rolls 2002.)

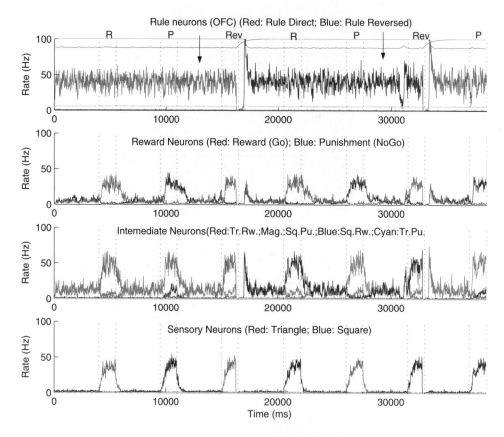

Fig. 9.2 Reward reversal model: temporal evolution of the averaged population activity for all neural pools (sensory, intermediate (stimulus–reward), and Reward/Punishment) in the stimulus – intermediate – reward module and the rule module, during the execution and the reversal of the Go/NoGo visual discrimination task with a pseudorandom trial sequence after Thorpe, Rolls and Maddison (1983) and Rolls, Critchley, Mason and Wakeman (1996). Bottom row: the sensory neuronal populations, one of which responds to Object 1, a triangle (red), and the other to Object 2, a square (blue). The intermediate conditional stimulus–reward and stimulus-punishment neurons respond to for example Object 1 (Tr) when it is associated with reward (Rw) (e.g. on trial 1, corresponding to O1R in Fig. 9.1), or to Object 2 (Sq) when it is associated with punishment (Pu) (e.g. on trial 2, O2P). The top row shows the firing rate activity in the rule module, with the thin line at the top of this graph showing the mean probability of release P_{rel} of transmitter from the synapses of each population of neurons. The arrows show when the contingencies reversed. R: Reward trial; P: Punishment Trial; Rev: Reversal trial, i.e. the first trial after the reward contingency was reversed when Reward was expected but Punishment was obtained. The intertrial interval was 4 s. The yellow line shows the average activity of the inhibitory neurons. (See text for further details.) (After Deco and Rolls 2005d.)